- Don't give people subsidies and tax breaks to produce harmful goods and unnecessarily waste resources; either eliminate all resource subsidies or reward only producers who reduce resource waste, pollution, and environmental degradation (principle of economic and ecological wisdom).
- We cannot have a healthy economy in a sick environment (economics-as-if-the-earth-mattered principle).

Politics

- Human population growth ultimately makes democracy and individualism impossible (principle of freedom erosion).
- Anticipating and preventing problems is cheaper and more effective than reacting to and trying to cure them; an ounce of prevention is worth a pound of cure (prevention or input control principle).
- Every crisis is an opportunity for change (bad-news-can-be-good-news principle).
- Think globally, act locally (principle of change).
- Don't ever call yourself a conservative unless what you want to conserve is the earth (principle of true conservatism).

Worldview and Ethics

- We are part of nature (principle of oneness).
- We are a valuable species, but we are not superior to other species; all living beings, human and nonhuman, have the same inherent worth (principle of humility).
- Every living thing has a right to live, or at least struggle to live, simply because it exists; this right is not dependent on its actual or potential use to us (respect-for-nature principle).
- Our role is to understand and work with the rest of nature, not conquer it (principle of cooperation).
- The best things in life aren't things (principle of love, caring, and joy).
- Something is right when it tends to maintain the earth's life-support systems for us and other species and wrong when it tends otherwise; the bottom line is that the earth is the bottom line (principle of sustainability and ecocentrism).
- It is wrong for humans to cause the premature extinction of any wild species and the elimination and degradation of their habitats (preservation of wildlife and biodiversity principle).
- It is wrong to treat people and other living things primarily as factors of production, whose value is expressed only in economic terms (economics-is-not-everything principle).
- We have a right to protect ourselves against harmful and dangerous organisms but only when we cannot avoid being exposed to such organisms or safely escape from the situation; in protecting ourselves we should do the least possible harm to such organisms (principle of self-defense).

- We have a right to kill other organisms to provide enough food for our survival and good health and to meet other basic survival and health needs, but we do not have such rights to meet nonbasic or frivolous wants (principle of survival).
- When we alter nature to meet what we consider to be basic or nonbasic needs, we should choose the method that does the least possible harm to other living things; in minimizing harm it is in general worse to harm a species than an individual organism, and still worse to harm a biotic community (principle of minimum wrong).
- We must leave the earth in as good a shape as we found it, if not better (rights-of-the-unborn principle).
- All people must be held responsible for their own pollution and environmental degradation (responsibility-of-the-born principle).
- People are entitled to a fair share of the world's resources as long as they are assuming their responsibility for sustaining the earth (principle of equity).
- No individual, corporation, or nation has a right to an ever-increasing share of the earth's finite resources; don't let need slide into greed (principle of enoughness).
- In protecting and sustaining nature, go further than the law requires (ethics-often-exceeds-legality principle).
- To prevent excessive deaths of people and other species, people must prevent excessive births (birth-control-is-better-than-death-control principle).
- Everything we are and have or will have ultimately comes from the sun and the earth; the earth can get along without us, but we can't get along without the earth; an exhausted earth is an exhausted economy (respect-your-roots or earth-first principle).
- Don't do anything that depletes the earth's physical, chemical, and biological capital that supports all life and human economic activities; the earth deficit is the ultimate deficit (balanced-earth budget principle).
- Love thy species and other species today and in the future as thyself (principle of species love and protection).
- To love, cherish, and understand the earth and yourself, take time to experience and sense the air, water, soil, plants, animals, bacteria, and other parts of the earth directly; learning about the earth indirectly from books, TV images, and ideas is not enough (direct-experience-is-the-best-teacher principle).
- Learn about and love your local environment and live gently within that place; walk lightly on the earth (love-your-neighborhood principle).

The Valdez Disaster

On March 24, 1989 the *Exxon Valdez* tanker went off course in Prince William Sound after leaving the port of Valdez, Alaska and hit submerged rocks on a reef. About 11 million gallons of crude oil—22% of its cargo—gushed from several gashes in the hull, creating the worst oil spill in U.S. waters and spoiling one of America's most beautiful and richest wildlife areas.

Blood tests after the accident indicated that the captain, who had a history of alcohol abuse known to Exxon officials, was drunk on duty. When the accident happened, he had retired to his cabin and had turned over the ship to an unqualified third mate. The rapidly spreading oil slick coated and killed thousands of sea birds and sea otters and untold numbers of fish, jeopardized the area's $100 million-a-year fishing industry, and covered hundreds of miles of shoreline with tarlike goo. Recovery is expected to take 5 to 10 years.

In the early 1970s, conservationists predicted that a large, damaging oil spill might occur in these icy, treacherous waters. But officials of Alyeska, a company formed by the oil companies extracting oil in Alaska, said that a large spill was "highly unlikely." They assured Congress that they would be at the scene of any accident within five hours and have enough equipment and trained people to clean up any spill.

However, when the Valdez spill occurred, Alyeska and Exxon officials did not have enough equipment and personnel and did too little, too late. Outraged citizens and some elected officials are now looking more closely at oil company proposals to drill for oil in Alaska's national Arctic Wildlife Refuge and in offshore areas along all U.S. coasts.

Resource Conservation and Management

Resource
Conservation
and Management

G. Tyler Miller, Jr.

Wadsworth Publishing Company
Belmont, California
A Division of Wadsworth, Inc.

Environmental Studies Editor: Jack Carey
Production Editor: Leland Moss
Managing Designer: Andrew H. Ogus
Print Buyer: Barbara Britton
Copy Editor: Noel Deeley
Art Editor: Donna Kalal
Editor Assistant: Sue Belmessieri
Compositor: Graphic Typesetting Service
Make-up Artist: Edie Williams
Photo Researcher: Stephen Forsling
Technical Illustrators: Darwin and Vally Hennings, John
and Judith Waller, Rachel Ciemma, Jeanne M.
Schreiber, Joan Carol, Susan Breitbard, Shirley Bortoli,
and Salinda Tyson
Cover photograph © 1989 David Muench

Printed in the United States of America   48

  2 3 4 5 6 7 8 9 10—94 93 92

Library of Congress Cataloging-in-Publication Data
  Resource conservation and management / G. Tyler Miller, Jr.
     p.   cm.
  Includes bibliographies and index.
  ISBN 0-534-01278-6
  1. Conservation of natural resources   2. Natural
resources—Management   I. Title
S936.M54 1989   89-5431
333.7'2—dc19   CIP

Preface:
To the Instructor

Goals This book is designed to be used in introductory courses on resource conservation and management ranging in length from one quarter to two semesters. My goals for the book are to:

- cover the diverse materials of an introductory course on resource conservation and management in an accurate, balanced, and interesting way without the use of mathematics or complex chemical and biological information

- help your students discover that dealing with resource issues is fun, interesting, and important to their lives

- allow you to use the material in a flexible manner to meet your needs, depending on course length and what you believe are the important topics

- show how resource and environmental problems are interrelated and must be understood and dealt with on a local, regional, national, and global basis

- give a realistic but hopeful view of how much has been done and what remains to be done in sustaining the earth

- indicate what students can do in their personal lives and lifestyles to help sustain rather than degrade the earth's life-support systems

- introduce students to key concepts and principles that govern how nature works and apply them to possible solutions to problems of resource conservation and management

This last goal is a key feature of this book. Most introductory textbooks in this field do not make effective use of basic principles and concepts to help students understand resource use and management issues. Thus, they give students no way to tie together and evaluate the massive amount of information in the field.

This book is one of a series of three textbooks designed for different introductory courses on environmental science and resource conservation. *Living in the Environment* (6th ed., Wadsworth, 1990, 650 pages) includes much less detailed discussions of forest resources, rangelands, wildlife, and freshwater and marine fisheries and fuller discussions of pollution, environmental health, and environmental economics, politics, and ethics. *Environmental Science: An Introduction* (2d ed., Wadsworth, 1988, 406 pages) is a brief version of *Living in the Environment* that omits detailed discussions of many topics.

Resource Conservation and Management (546 pages) is a new and different book. Its organizational pattern is different from the other two textbooks (see Brief Contents on p. xiii), including much broader and more detailed discussions of renewable living resources (Chapters 10 through 17) and less detailed discussions of ecological concepts, population, and pollution. For example, *Living in the Environment* and *Environmental Science* cover the topics of food, fishery, rangeland, forest, and wildlife resources in three chapters. In this book seven chapters are devoted to those topics.

Readability Students often complain that textbooks are difficult and boring. I have tried to overcome this problem by writing this book in a clear, interesting, and informal style. I relate the information in the book to the real world and to the student's own life. I keep sentences and paragraphs fairly short. I do not use a long word when a short one can express an idea just as well.

Flexibility Those of you using this book have courses that last for different lengths of time. I asked hundreds of you what should be covered and what should be omitted in this book and in what order topics should be covered. I got hundreds of different answers.

I had two choices. I could write a short textbook that omitted many topics and would not meet the needs of many instructors. Or I could write a larger book and design it to be flexible enough to be used in many different ways. That is the path I chose. I divided the book into four major parts:

- Resource Use and Conservation: History and Concepts (six chapters)

- Renewable Air, Water, and Soil Resources and Their Management (three chapters)
- Renewable Living Resources and Their Management (eight chapters)
- Mineral and Energy Resources and Their Management (three chapters)

After you have covered all or most of the principles in Part One (especially Chapters 1, 3, 4, 5, and 6), you can cover the rest of the book in almost any order. Parts Two, Three, and Four, chapters within these parts, and many sections within these chapters can be moved around or omitted to accommodate courses with different lengths and emphases.

Other Major Features   I used a number of methods to ensure the book's accuracy, thoroughness, breadth of viewpoint, and relevance:

- *Balanced discussions of opposing views* on major resource issues, especially in the 23 boxed Pro/Con discussions found throughout the book (see pp. 351, 357, 381, 401, 437, 506 for examples)
- Content based on an *extensive review of the professional literature* (from more than 10,000 research sources; key readings are listed at the end of each chapter)
- *Extensive manuscript review* by 41 experts and teachers (see list on p. xii) to help make the material accurate and up-to-date. Several experts reviewed each chapter in this text or related material in *Living in the Environment* and *Environmental Science*. Teachers of resource conservation courses or related courses reviewed most or all of the manuscript
- 7 *guest coauthors* (see page xi) for five of the chapters on renewable living resources (Chapters 12, 13, 15, 16, 17)) to improve accuracy
- 8 *Guest Essays* (see p. xi) to provide more information and expose the reader to various points of view
- 61 *Case Studies* to give in-depth information about key issues and to apply concepts (see pp. 34, 105, 158, 189, 193, 227, 281, 311, 352, 430, 444 for examples)
- 53 *Spotlights* to highlight important issues and to give further insights into resource problems (see pp. 125, 314, 375, 439, 475, 498, 514 for examples)
- 406 *diagrams and carefully selected photographs* to illustrate complex ideas in a simple manner and to show that topics in the book relate to the real world (see pp. 29, 96, 120, 124, 128, 184, 213, 221, 310, 369, 372, 392, 411, 486 for examples of diagrams)
- *Student preface* to introduce students to the book's purposes and major features (see pp. viii–x)

- *Summary of key ideas* inside the front cover

Learning Aids   To help students learn more effectively, I have included a number of aids:

- *General Questions and Issues:* Each chapter begins with several simply worded questions. They give the student an overview of the chapter and can also be used as review questions after the chapter is completed.
- *Key Terms:* When any new term is defined it is shown in **boldfaced type.**
- *Discussion Topics:* Each chapter has several discussion questions designed to encourage students to think about and apply what they have learned.
- *Glossary:* All key terms are defined in a glossary near the end of the book.

My Biases   Like you, I am biased about resource and environmental problems. I believe that they are urgent problems we must deal with. There are two major types of controversies in this field. Some are fundamental and based on quite different worldviews about how nature works and what our role in nature should be. I have a sustainable-earth worldview, as discussed and applied throughout this textbook. I try to live my life based on this view of the way I believe the world works (see Spotlight on p. 541). However, I also present an opposing worldview in this book and have a major proponent of that worldview defend this position (pp. 24–25).

The other types of controversy in this field occur between people with or without the same worldview who agree on a general goal but differ in how it should be achieved. Throughout the text, especially in Pro/Con boxed material, I give both sides of such controversies. Rather than prescribing solutions, I encourage students to think about these problems and to come to their own conclusions.

Help Me Improve This Book   I need your help in improving this book in future editions. Writing and publishing a textbook is an extremely complex process. Thus, any textbook is almost certain to contain some typographical and other errors. To minimize errors, I have had all or parts of the manuscript reviewed by a larger number of teachers and experts than any other textbook in this field. Nevertheless, some errors will probably slip through.

If you find any errors, please write them down and send them to me. Most errors can be corrected in subsequent printings of this edition, rather than waiting for a new edition.

I would also appreciate your telling me how to improve the book. We all have the same goal: finding the best way to teach students about this field. Helping me do this helps you and your students. I also hope you will encourage your students to evaluate the book and send me their suggestions for improvement.

Send any errors you find and your suggestions for improvement to Jack Carey, Science Editor, Wadsworth Publishing Company, 10 Davis Drive, Belmont, CA 94002. He will send them on to me. Time does not permit me to answer your letters, but be aware of how much I appreciate learning from you.

Supplementary Materials Dr. David Cotter at Georgia College has written an excellent instructor's manual for use with this text. It contains sample multiple-choice test questions with answers, suggested projects, field trips, experiments, and a list of topics suitable for term papers and reports for each chapter. Master sheets for making overhead transparencies of many key diagrams are also available from the publisher.

Acknowledgments I wish to thank the many students and teachers who responded so favorably to the first five editions of *Living in the Environment* and the two editions of *Environmental Science* and offered many helpful suggestions for improvement. These suggestions included the idea of publishing a book emphasizing resource conservation and management.

I am also deeply indebted to the 188 reviewers, who pointed out errors and suggested many important improvements, and to the writers who coauthored several chapters and wrote guest essays. I am especially thankful for the detailed and extremely helpful reviews of all versions of this manuscript by John H. Bounds, Department of Geography, Sam Houston State University, and John G. Hewston, College of Natural Resources, Humboldt State University. Any errors and deficiencies left are mine, not theirs.

Others have also made important contributions. They include production editor Leland Moss, copy editor Noel Deeley, art editor Donna Kalal, photo researcher Stephen Forsling, designer Andrew Ogus, and artists Darwin and Vally Hennings, John and Judith Waller, Rachel Ciemma, Jeanne M. Schreiber, Joan Carol, Susan Breitbard, Shirley Bortoli, and Salinda Tyson.

I also wish to thank Sue Belmessieri, editorial assistant, for coordinating reviews and somehow juggling several hundred tasks at the same time with competence and good humor. Above all I wish to thank Jack Carey, science editor at Wadsworth, for his encouragement, help, friendship, and superb reviewing system. It helps immensely to work with the best and most experienced editor in college textbook publishing.

G. Tyler Miller, Jr.

Preface:
To the Student

Why Study About Resource and Environmental Issues? The answer is because they are interesting, and they are involved in almost everything you do. When you decide what to buy, use, or eat, you are making decisions about what resources to use, and this resource use has impacts on the air, water, soil, other people, and other forms of life now and in the future. Fortunately, learning about major resource and environmental issues is not difficult.

This is not just another college course to be passed for credit. It is an introduction to how nature works, how the environment has been and is being used and abused, and what you can do to protect and improve it for yourself and other people, future generations, and other living things. I am convinced that nothing else deserves more of your energy, time, concern, and personal involvement.

I have presented opposing views on these complex and highly controversial life-and-death issues in a balanced way. My goal is not to tell you what to think but to provide you with concepts and information you can use to reach your own conclusions.

Emphasis on Concepts The purpose of education is not to stuff yourself full of facts. Instead it is to learn and understand a small number of basic concepts or principles that can be used to integrate numerous facts into meaningful patterns. About 98% of everything you hear or read is false, distorted, or irrelevant. The goal of education is to learn how to sift through mountains of information and ideas and find the 2% that is really useful and worth knowing.

Inside the front cover of this book you will find a list of key principles that summarizes what I have learned so far about how the world works and what my role in it should be. These ideas are not original. They are the result of over 40 years of reading books and articles, tens of thousands of conversations with others, letters from students like you, and direct observations of nature.

I use these principles to evaluate other ideas and to make decisions about what to buy or not buy and

how to live my life with increased joy. I am also constantly striving to improve this list by modifying or removing some ideas and adding new ones. I make no claims about whether these ideas are true. They are merely what I have found to be useful.

Facts by themselves are useless. Does this mean that you should stop learning facts? No. This book is filled with facts and numbers. Why? Because facts are stepping-stones to ideas. They help illuminate ideas, illustrate ideas from different vantage points, and show trends. Once you understand a key idea, you can flush most of the facts that led to it from your mind. Then you can use the idea to organize and understand the meaning of new facts, which may lead to still more new ideas. I deliberately keep very few facts in my mind. But I know where to find them when I need them.

Trying to discover the 2% of knowledge that is really worth knowing is an exciting and never-ending process. It's great fun. As you draw up your own list, please send me any ideas you have. We are all in this together and we need all the help we can get.

In Chapters 3 through 6 you will learn some key concepts. These concepts will help you understand and evaluate the resource and environmental problems and options for dealing with them discussed in the rest of this book.

How I Became Involved I feel you are entitled to know how I became involved in resource and environmental concerns and to what degree I try to put what I write about into practice in my own life and lifestyle. In 1966, when what we now know as the environmental movement began in the United States, I heard a scientist give a lecture on the problems of overpopulation and environmental abuse. Afterward I went to him and said, "If even a fraction of what you have said is true, I will feel ethically obligated to give up my present scientific research on the corrosion of metals and devote the rest of my life to these issues. Frankly, I don't want to believe a word you have said, and I'm going into the literature to try to prove what you have said is either untrue or grossly distorted."

After six months of study I was convinced of the seriousness of these problems. Since then I have been studying, teaching, and writing about them. I have also attempted to live my life in an ecologically sound way—with varying degrees of success—by treading as lightly as possible on the earth. Working toward this goal has involved making more compromises and trade-offs than I have liked. But I continue the effort (see p. 541 for a summary of my own progress in attempting to work with nature).

My Biases Just as you would expect an economics professor to be biased toward economics, I am biased about resource and environmental problems. I believe they are serious problems that we *must* solve.

Most of our actions are based on our *worldview*—how we think the world works and what we believe our role in the world or in nature should be. Some disagreements about environmental and resource issues are between people with quite different worldviews.

I have a *sustainable-earth worldview,* which I describe throughout this textbook and try to put into practice in my own lifestyle. However, I also present an opposing worldview in this book and have a proponent of this worldview defend this position (pp. 24–25).

You may have a mix of these two worldviews. Or you may have an entirely different worldview. Two things are important. One is to make sure that you know what your worldview is so you can understand why you think and act as you do. The other is to constantly evaluate your worldview and to be open to changing it. The main goal of learning should be to help you define and evaluate your worldview and to live your life in ways consistent with your worldview.

Other controversies in this field occur between people who agree on a general goal but differ over how it should be achieved. Throughout the text and especially in boxed Pro/Con material I give both sides of such controversies.

I could give you my opinion on these issues, but I have chosen not to. Why? Because I want to help you learn to analyze ideas and information and think for yourself.

Readability Students often complain that textbooks are difficult and boring. They are usually right, although some are unwilling to put in the time and hard work that reading and understanding always take.

I have tried to overcome this problem by writing this book in a clear, interesting, and informal style. I keep sentences and paragraphs fairly short. I do not use long words when short ones can express an idea just as well. My goal is to communicate with you, not confuse you.

I also relate the information in the book to the real world and to your own lifestyle, in the main text and in boxed Spotlights, Case Studies, and Pro/Con discussions of issues sprinkled throughout the book.

A Realistic but Hopeful Local, National, and Global Outlook We face many resource and environmental problems. But a problem is an opportunity for change. Pessimists who think we are doomed and optimists who blindly think everything will be all right regardless of what we do are dangerous people. These extreme positions are mind games that people use to avoid thinking about problems and becoming involved in bringing about change. This book is written for doers who care about the earth, not bench-sitters and toe-dippers who care only about themselves.

In this book I offer a realistic but hopeful view of the future. Much has been done since 1966, when many people first became aware of the resource and environmental problems we face today. But much more needs to be done to protect the earth, which keeps you and all other forms of life alive. This book suggests ways that you can help sustain—not degrade—the earth.

As you will learn, most environmental and resource problems and their possible solutions are interrelated. Treating them in isolation is a recipe for disaster. They must also be considered on a local, national, and global scale—as this book does.

How the Book Is Organized This book is divided into four major parts:

- Resource Use and Conservation: History and Concepts (six chapters)
- Renewable Air, Water, and Soil Resources and Their Management (three chapters)
- Renewable Living Resources and Their Management (eight chapters)
- Mineral and Energy Resources and Their Management (three chapters)

Look at the Brief Contents on p. xiii to see the topics covered in each part. Before studying each chapter, I also suggest that you look over its detailed contents given on pp. xiv–xxii. This gives you a road map of where you will be going.

This Book Is Flexible I have designed the book so that it can be used in courses of different lengths and emphases. This gives your teacher great flexibility in designing the course you are taking.

The material in Part One gives you the background, basic definitions, and concepts needed to understand the rest of the book. Once you have studied most or all of Part One, you can cover the other three parts in any order your instructor assigns. Chapters in these parts and many sections within chapters can be rearranged or omitted. So don't be concerned if your instructor skips around and omits material.

General Questions and Issues I have put a number of aids in this book to help you learn. Each chapter begins with a few general questions to give you an idea of what you will be learning in each chapter. After you finish a chapter, you can go back and try to answer these questions to review what you have learned.

You may be disappointed that each chapter does not have a summary. But after 25 years of teaching, I have found that chapter summaries do more harm than good. Some students read the summary without reading the chapter and get an incomplete understanding of the material. As a college student, you should be making your own summaries. This forces you to learn how to learn—the real goal of your education.

Vocabulary Each chapter will introduce new terms, whose meanings you need to know and understand. When a term is introduced and defined, it is printed in **boldface**. There is also a glossary of all key terms at the end of the book.

Visual Aids Learning requires verbal and visual inputs. I have developed a number of diagrams to illustrate concepts and complex ideas in a simple manner. I have also used a number of carefully selected photos to give you a better picture of how topics discussed in this book relate to the real world.

Discussion Topics Each chapter ends with a set of discussion questions designed to encourage you to think and to apply what you have learned to your personal lifestyle. They also ask you to take sides on controversial issues and to back up your conclusions and beliefs.

I have not provided questions that test your recall of facts. This important but mechanical task is left to you and your instructor. As a college student, you should know how to learn definitions and facts on your own. It is done the old-fashioned way—reading, marking key passages, making notes and summaries, and writing and studying flash cards.

Further Readings If you become especially interested in some of the topics in this book, you can get more information by reading other books and articles. A list of suggested readings is given at the end of each chapter. Also, Appendix 1 is a list of publications you can use to keep up to date on the material in this book.

Interact with the Book When I read something, I interact with it. I mark sentences and paragraphs with a highlighter or pen. I put an asterisk in the margin next to something I think is important and double asterisks next to something I think is really important. I write comments in the margins, such as *Beautiful, Confusing, Bull, Wrong,* and so on.

I fold down the top corner of pages with highlighted passages and the top and bottom corners of especially important pages. This way I can flip through a book and quickly review the key passages. I hope you will interact in such ways with this book. You will learn more and have more fun. I hope you will often disagree with what I have written and take the time to think about or write down why.

Save This Book After you finish this course, you may be tempted to discard this book or resell it to the bookstore. But learning is a lifelong process and you will have to deal with the vital issues discussed here for the rest of your life. Therefore, I hope you will keep this book in your personal library for future use. Or at least pass it on free to someone whom you want to learn about the earth.

Help Me Improve the Book I need your help in improving future editions. Writing and publishing a book is an incredibly complex process. That means that this or any other book is likely to have some typographical and factual errors. If you find what you believe to be an error, write it down and send it to me.

I would also appreciate learning what you like and dislike about the book. This information helps me make the book better. Some of the things you will read here were suggested by students like you.

Send any errors you find and any suggestions for improvement to Jack Carey, Biology Editor, Wadsworth Publishing Company, 10 Davis Drive, Belmont, CA 94002. He will send them on to me.

I won't be able to answer your letters, but be aware of how much I appreciate your help. Your input will help me, students who take this course in the future, and the earth.

And Now Relax and enjoy yourself as you learn more about the exciting and challenging issues we all face in sustaining the earth's life-support systems.

G. Tyler Miller, Jr.

Guest Co-Authors

Chapter 12 *Marine and Freshwater Fishery Resources*
Donald M. Baltz, Coastal Fisheries Institute, Louisiana State University
Peter B. Moyle, Department of Wildlife and Fisheries Biology, University of California, Davis

Chapter 15 *Management and Conservation of Forest Resources*
Carl H. Reidel, Environmental Program, University of Vermont

Chapter 16 *Depletion and Extinction of Wild Plants and Animals,* and
Chapter 17 *Wildlife Protection and Management*
Jack R. Nelson, Department of Forestry and Range Management, Washington State University
Jack Ward Thomas, Pacific Northwest Forest and Range Experiment Station, USDA–Forest Service

Authors of Guest Essays

Edward J. Kormondy, Chancellor and Professor of Biology, University of Hawaii–Hilo/West Oahu College (p. 115)
Amory B. Lovins, Energy policy consultant, Rocky Mountain Institute (p. 509)
Norman Myers, Consultant in environment and development (p. 386)
Philip R. Pryde, Department of Geography, San Diego State University (p. 214)

Julian L. Simon, Professor of Economics and Business Administration, University of Maryland (p. 24)
Robert Leo Smith, Professor of Wildlife Biology, Division of Forestry, West Virginia University (p. 452)
Gus Speth, President, World Resources Institute (p. 22)
Alvin M. Weinberg, Distinguished Fellow, Institute of Energy Analysis (p. 507)

Reviewers

Larry G. Allen, California State University at Northridge

Richard Behan, Northern Arizona University

Roger G. Bland, Central Michigan University

Keith L. Blidstein, Winthrop College

John H. Bounds, Sam Houston State University

Edward E. DeMartini

Jane Eheman, Shippensburg University

Kenneth O. Fulgham, Humboldt State University

Fred Gilbert, Washington State University

Harold Goetz, North Dakota State University

Ernest Gould

Paul K. Grogger, University of Colorado at Colorado Springs

William Hardenberg, Southern Illinois University

Neil A. Harriman, University of Wisconsin, Oshkosh

Grant A. Harris, Washington State University

John G. Hewston, Humboldt State University

Michael Horn, California State University at Fullerton

Hugo H. John, The University of Connecticut

Theodore W. Kury, State University College at Buffalo

Mark Lapping, Kansas State University

Thomas A. Leege, Idaho Department of Fish and Game

Robert D. Loring, De Pauw University

A. Steven Messenger, Northern Illinois University

Rolf Monteen, California Polytechnic State University

M. Duane Nellis, Kansas State University

Richard J. Pedersen, U.S. Forest Service

William A. Peirce, Case Western Reserve University

David E. Pulliam, U.S. Department of the Interior

G. L. Reynolds, University of Central Arkansas

Benjamin F. Richason III, St. Cloud State University

Ronald Robberecht, University of Idaho

Terry Roelofs, Humboldt State University

Steven T. Ross, University of Southern Mississippi

Robert E. Roth, Ohio State University

Michael P. Shields, Southern Illinois University

William Sloey, University of Wisconsin at Oshkosh

Jerry J. Smith, San Jose State University

Norman R. Stewart, University of Wisconsin at Milwaukee

Frank Studincka, University of Wisconsin at Platteville

Tom Tietenberg, Colby College

Robert R. Van Kirk, Humboldt State University

Nancy Lee Wilkinson, San Francisco State University

Fred T. Witzig, University of Minnesota at Duluth

Malcolm J. Zwolinski, University of Arizona

Contents in Brief

Detailed Contents

Resource Conservation and Management

PART ONE

Resource Use and Conservation: History and Concepts

USDA/Soil Conservation Service

It is only in the most recent, and brief, period of their tenure that human beings have developed in sufficient numbers, and acquired enough power, to become one of the most potentially dangerous organisms that the planet has ever hosted.

John McHale

The environmental crisis is an outward manifestation of a crisis of mind and spirit. There could be no greater misconception of its meaning than to believe it is concerned only with endangered wildlife, human-made ugliness, and pollution. These are part of it, but more importantly, the crisis is concerned with the kind of creatures we are and what we must become in order to survive.

Lynton K. Caldwell

CHAPTER 1

Population, Resources, Environmental Degradation, and Pollution: An Overview

General Questions and Issues

1. How rapidly is the human population increasing?
2. What are the major types of resources, and how can they be depleted or degraded?
3. What are the major types of pollution?
4. What are the relationships among human population size, resource use, technology, environmental degradation, and pollution?
5. What are the two major schools of thought about how to solve present and future resource and environmental problems?

We must stop mortgaging the future to the present. We must stop destroying the air we breathe, the water we drink, the food we eat, and the forests that inspire awe in our hearts. . . . We need to prevent pollution at the source, not try to clean it up later. . . . It's time to remember that conservation is the cheapest and least polluting form of energy. . . . We need to come together and choose a new direction. We need to transform our society into one in which people live in true harmony—harmony among nations, harmony among the races of humankind, and harmony with nature. . . . We will either reduce, reuse, recycle, and restore—or we will perish.

Rev. Jesse Jackson

W e are at a critical turning point. We have spent billions to send a handful of people to the moon, only to learn the importance of protecting the diversity of life on the beautiful blue planet that's our home. While technological optimists promise a life of abundance for everyone, conservationists and environmentalists warn that the earth's life-support systems are being strained and degraded.

We face a complex mix of interrelated problems. One is population growth. World population has more than doubled, from 2.5 billion in 1950 to 5.2 billion in 1988. If present trends continue, by 2100 the world's population will at least double to 10.4 billion and may reach 14 billion.

Another problem is the way we are using resources. The resources that keep us alive and support the world's economic output come from the sun and the earth's air, water, soil, plants, and animals. Although energy cannot be recycled, the earth recycles and reuses chemicals needed to sustain plant and animal life.

The earth is remarkably resilient. It can dilute, break down, and recycle many of the chemicals we add to the air, water, and soil as long as we don't overload these natural processes. It can replenish topsoil, water, air, forests, grasslands, and wildlife as long as we don't use these resources faster than they are renewed.

Think of the earth's resources as our savings account—our natural capital. As long as we live off the interest on this capital, we and other species can be sustained. But we are depleting this natural capital. We recycle and reuse little of what we extract from the earth and change into products. Instead we dump the chemicals produced by resource extraction and use into the air, water, and soil, hoping they won't build up to harmful levels. We also produce products that the earth's natural processes can't recycle for us.

The earth's 5.2 billion people live on only about 2% of the planet's land area. But these people grow crops, graze livestock, and remove forest and mineral resources from another 60% of the earth's land area. Most of the remaining land is desert, covered with ice, or too steep to be useful.

Think of the earth's life-support systems as a series of rubber bands that can be stretched and restretched a long way without breaking. Growing evidence indicates that we are stretching some of these rubber bands close to and in some cases beyond their breaking points.

Each year more of the world's forests, grasslands, and wetlands disappear, and deserts grow in size. Vital topsoil is washed or blown away from farmland (see photo of severe soil erosion in South Dakota on p. 1) and chokes rivers with sediment. Water is being withdrawn from underground deposits faster than it is replenished. The oil that runs cars and heats homes and is used to produce food and most of the products we use will probably be used up in your lifetime.

Toxic wastes produced by factories and homes are accumulating and poisoning soil and water resources. Pesticides used to grow food contaminate the groundwater that many of us drink and some of the food we eat.

As levels of carbon dioxide and several other gases we are adding to the atmosphere rise, the earth's lower atmosphere is expected to become warmer. Such a change in the earth's climate will disrupt our ability to grow food by making some areas much drier and other areas much wetter. Higher temperatures will also expand the oceans, which will flood low-lying coastal cities and cropland.

A thin layer of ozone gas in the upper atmosphere filters out and protects you and most other forms of life from the sun's harmful ultraviolet radiation. Chemicals called chlorofluorocarbons (CFCs), which we release into the lower atmosphere, are drifting into the upper atmosphere. There they are reacting with and depleting ozone gas faster than it is produced.

Burning coal, oil, and gasoline is increasing the amount of ozone, acids, and other pollutants in the atmosphere near the earth. These chemicals are killing trees, fish, and people. As forests and grasslands disappear, as soils erode, as deserts and cities expand, and as soils and lakes acidify, an increasing number of the earth's plant and animal species are disappearing forever.

Why are we fouling our own life-support systems? The answer is a combination of survival, greed, apathy, and ignorance about our ultimate dependence on the sun and earth for everything we have or will have. To survive, poor people cut trees and deplete soil faster than those resources can be renewed. More affluent people deplete and degrade the earth's resources to support short-term economic growth and throwaway lifestyles.

The bad news is that we are doing this. The good news is that we know how to sustain the earth for human beings and other species by conserving and managing the earth's resources. That is what this book is about.

1-1 HUMAN POPULATION GROWTH

The J-Shaped Curve of Human Population Growth
Plotting the estimated number of people on earth over time gives us a curve with the shape of the letter J (Figure 1-1). This increase in the size of the human population is an example of **exponential growth.** Such growth happens when some factor—such as population size—grows by a constant percentage of the

---

SPOTLIGHT The Nature of Exponential Growth

An example of *arithmetic growth* is 1, 2, 3, 4, 5, and so on. *Exponential growth* means that a quantity increases by doubling: 2, 4, 8, 16, 32, and so on. We can use a fable to understand exponential growth:

Once there were two kings who enjoyed playing chess with various prizes going to the winner. After one of their matches the winner asked for a new type of prize. He asked that the losing king place a grain of wheat on the first square of the chessboard, two on the second, four on the third, and so on. The number of wheat grains were to double each time until all sixty-four squares on the board were filled.

The losing king, who didn't understand the nature of exponential growth, was delighted to get off so easy; he agreed to the proposal. It was the biggest mistake he ever made.

The winning king wanted to start with one grain of wheat and double it 63 times. This amounts to one less than 2^{64} grains of wheat. This still doesn't seem like much. But it is more than 500 times all the wheat harvested in the world this year. It is probably larger than all the wheat that has ever been harvested on earth!

From this example we can understand some of the properties of exponential growth. It is deceptive because it starts off slowly. But a few doublings leads quickly to enormous numbers. Why? Because after the second doubling each additional doubling is more than the total of all preceding growth.

The time it takes in years for a doubling to take place depends on the annual percentage growth rate. Doubling time can be calculated by dividing the annual percentage growth rate into 70 (70/% growth = doubling time in years). This year the world's population grew by 1.7%. If this rate continues, the number of people on earth will double in 41 years (70/1.7 = 41 years).

---

whole during each unit of time. One of the greatest shortcomings of the human race is our failure to understand the implications of exponential growth (see Spotlight above).

For most of human history, people lived in small groups and survived by hunting wild game and gathering wild edible plants. During this period the earth's population grew exponentially at a slow average rate of only 0.002% a year. This slow, early phase of exponential growth is represented by the horizontal part of the curve plotted in Figure 1-1.

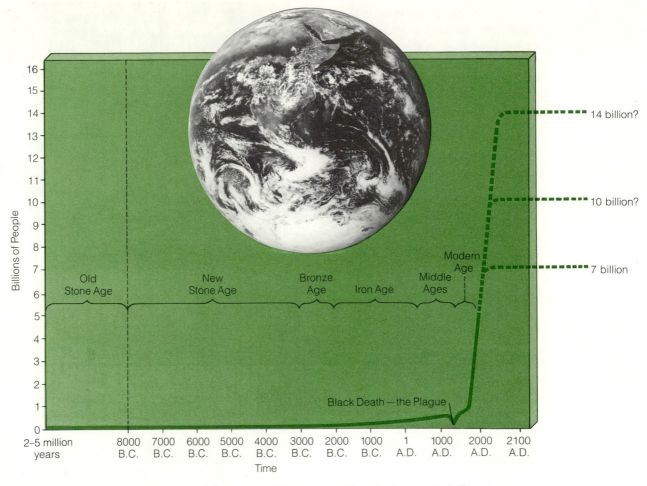

Figure 1-1 J-shaped curve of past exponential world population growth with projections to 2020. (Data from World Bank and United Nations)

Since then, the average annual exponential growth rate of the human population has increased. It reached an all-time high of 2.06% in 1970, before dropping somewhat to 1.7% today. Because of this large exponential increase, the curve of population growth has rounded the bend of the *J* and is heading almost straight up from the horizontal axis (Figure 1-1).

With this increase in the rate of exponential growth, it has taken less time to add each billion people. It took 2 to 5 million years to add the first billion people; 130 years to add the second billion; 30 years to add the third billion; 15 years to add the fourth billion; and only 12 years to add the fifth billion. With present growth rates, the sixth billion will be added during the 10-year period between 1987 and 1997, and the seventh billion 10 years later in 2007. This rapid increase in population size has had severe effects on other species, and on the air, water, and soil upon which we and other forms of life depend.

In 1988, the earth's population increased by 90 million. This amounted to an average increase of 1.7 million people a week, 247,000 a day, or 10,270 an hour. At this rate of exponential growth, it takes:

■ less than five days to replace people equal in number to the Americans killed in all U.S. wars

■ ten months to add 75 million people—the number killed in the bubonic plague epidemic of the fourteenth century, the world's greatest disaster

■ less than two years to add 165 million people—the number of soldiers killed in all wars fought during the past 200 years

These figures give you an idea of what it means to go around the bend of the *J* curve of exponential growth. This massive increase in population is happening when:

■ At least half the adults on this planet cannot read or write.

■ One out of six people is hungry or malnourished and does not have adequate housing (Figure 1-2).

■ One out of five lacks clean drinking water.

■ One out of three does not have adequate sewage disposal, health care, and fuel to keep warm and cook food.

UNICEF/Bernard Wolf

Figure 1-2 One-sixth of the people in the world don't have adequate housing. Lean-to sidewalk shelters like these are homes for many families in Dacca, Bangladesh.

Population Growth in the More Developed and Less Developed Countries The world's 175 countries can be divided into two groups based on the average annual per capita gross national product (GNP)—the average market value of all goods and services produced per year per person in each country (Figure 1-4).

The world's 33 **more developed countries (MDCs)** are highly industrialized and have a high average GNP per person. Most are in the temperate (or middle) latitudes and have generally favorable climates and fertile soils: Japan, the USSR, Australia, New Zealand, and all countries in Europe and North America. These MDCs' 1.2 billion people (23% of the world's population) use about 80% of the world's mineral and energy resources. If the present population in these countries continues to grow exponentially at 0.6% a year, their population will double in 117 years.

The 142 **less developed countries (LDCs)** have low to moderate industrialization and low to moderate average GNPs per person. Most are located in the tropical (or low) latitudes in Africa, Asia, and Latin America. Many of these countries have less favorable climates and less fertile soils than most MDCs.

The LDCs contain 4 billion people or 77% of the world's population. But they use only about 20% of the world's mineral and energy resources. Over 86% of the world's babies are born in the LDCs. But 98% of all infant and childhood deaths occur in these countries. (See Spotlight on p. 9.) If the population of these countries continues to grow exponentially at 2.1% a year, their populations will double in 33 years.

UN population experts forecast that unless we have a global nuclear war or widespread famine and disease, by 2100 the earth's population will be 10.4 billion—more than twice that in 1988. Most of this increase will take place in the LDCs (Figure 1-5).

Dividing the world into MDCs and LDCs can be misleading. Some MDCs are richer and more industrialized than others, and some LDCs are poorer than others. Poverty is also found in the richest countries. We get a more accurate picture by dividing the world's countries into groups based on their degree of industrialization and their average GNP per person (Figure 1-3).

Figure 1-3 Division of world's countries into categories based on their degree of industrial development and average GNP per person. (Data from Population Reference Bureau. Map based on a modified Goode's projection, copyright by the University of Chicago, Department of Geography, and used by their permission.)

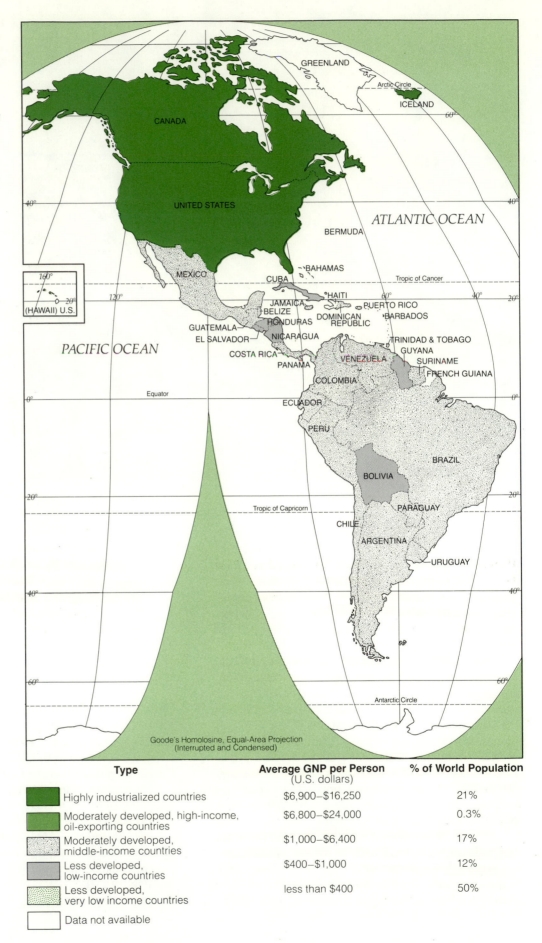

Goode's Homolosine, Equal-Area Projection
(Interrupted and Condensed)

Type	Average GNP per Person (U.S. dollars)	% of World Population
Highly industrialized countries	$6,900–$16,250	21%
Moderately developed, high-income, oil-exporting countries	$6,800–$24,000	0.3%
Moderately developed, middle-income countries	$1,000–$6,400	17%
Less developed, low-income countries	$400–$1,000	12%
Less developed, very low income countries	less than $400	50%
Data not available		

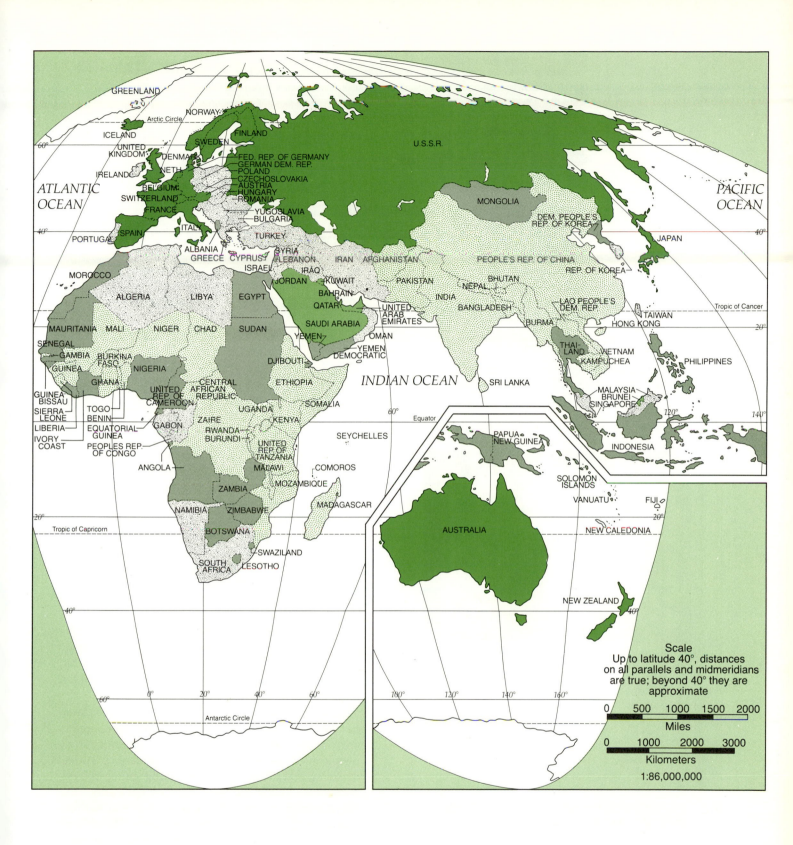

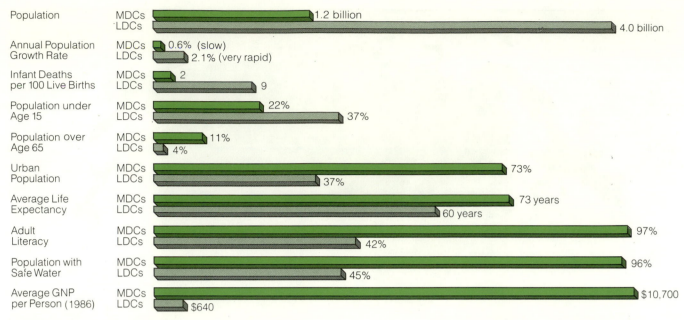

Population	MDCs	1.2 billion
	LDCs	4.0 billion
Annual Population Growth Rate	MDCs	0.6% (slow)
	LDCs	2.1% (very rapid)
Infant Deaths per 100 Live Births	MDCs	2
	LDCs	9
Population under Age 15	MDCs	22%
	LDCs	37%
Population over Age 65	MDCs	11%
	LDCs	4%
Urban Population	MDCs	73%
	LDCs	37%
Average Life Expectancy	MDCs	73 years
	LDCs	60 years
Adult Literacy	MDCs	97%
	LDCs	42%
Population with Safe Water	MDCs	96%
	LDCs	45%
Average GNP per Person (1986)	MDCs	$10,700
	LDCs	$640

Figure 1-4 Some characteristics of more developed countries (MDCs) and less developed countries (LDCs) in 1988. (Data from United Nations and Population Reference Bureau)

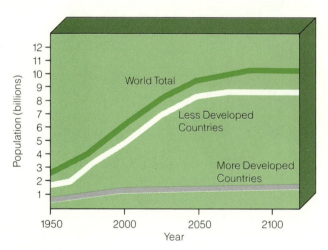

Figure 1-5 Past and projected population size for the more developed countries, less developed countries, and the world, 1950–2120. (Data from United Nations)

1-2 RESOURCES AND ENVIRONMENTAL DEGRADATION

What Is a Resource? A **resource** is anything we get from the physical environment to meet our needs and wants. Some resources are directly available for use. Examples are fresh air, fresh water in rivers and lakes, and naturally growing edible plants. But most resources, such as oil, iron, groundwater (water found

in underground deposits), fish, modern crops, and game animals, aren't directly available. They become resources only because of our ingenuity, economic systems, and cultural beliefs.

To be widely used, a resource must be available in a useful and acceptable form and at an affordable price. We have used science and technology to find, extract, process, and convert some of the earth's materials into resources and products that can be bought at reasonable prices. For example, groundwater found below the earth's surface wasn't a resource until we developed the technology for drilling a well and installing pumps to bring it to the surface. Petroleum was a mysterious fluid until we learned how to find it, extract it, and refine it into gasoline, home heating oil, road tar, and other products at affordable prices.

Cultural beliefs can also determine what is classified as a resource. For example, fried grasshoppers are a delicacy and a useful source of protein for some people in Africa. To most people in affluent countries, however, grasshoppers are a revolting source of food.

People differ in the resources they need and want. The resource needs of the poor are minimal but represent absolute needs, not merely wants. The affluent use much larger quantities of resources to satisfy a range of wants far beyond basic survival needs.

Take a few minutes to make a list of the resources you truly need. Then make another list of the resources that you use each day only because you want them. Then make a third list of resources you want and hope to use in the future.

We are feeding more people than ever before. Yet there are more hungry and poor people today than at any time during human history. One out of every five people on earth is desperately poor. These 1 billion people live mostly in 79 low-income and very low income countries (Figure 1-3).

They are too poor to buy or grow enough food and to buy the fuel they need for heating and cooking. At least 20 million and probably 40 million of these people die unnecessarily each year from preventable malnutrition (lack of enough protein and other nutrients needed for good health) and diseases. Half of those who die are children under age 5 (Figure 1-6). Most of these children die from diarrhea and measles, deadly diseases for people weakened by malnutrition.

During your lunch hour, at least 2,300 (probably 4,600) people died prematurely from hunger, malnutrition, and poverty-related diseases. When you eat lunch tomorrow, at least 55,000 (probably 110,000) more will have died. This death toll is the equivalent of 137 to 275 jumbo jet planes, each carrying 400 passengers, crashing every day with no survivors.

Yet this tragic news is rarely covered by the media. Why? Because it happens every day. Because it happens mostly in rural areas and urban slums in LDCs away from the glare of TV cameras and reporters. And because most people don't want to hear about it.

Life for the world's poor people is a harsh, daily struggle for survival. In typical rural villages or urban slums, groups of malnourished children sit around wood or dung (dried manure) fires eating breakfasts of bread and coffee. The air is filled with the stench of refuse and open sewers.

Children and women carry heavy jars or cans of water, often for long distances, from a muddy, microbe-infested river, canal, or village water faucet. Some people sleep on the street in the open, under makeshift canopies (Figure 1-2). Others sleep on dirt floors in crowded single-room shacks, often made from straw, cardboard, rusting metal, or drainage pipes.

Parents with seven to nine children are lucky to have an annual income of $300—an average of 82 cents a day. Some people in affluent countries consider poor people ignorant for having so many children. To most poor parents, however, having many children, especially boys, makes good sense. They know that three or four of their children will probably die of hunger or childhood diseases, such as diarrhea or measles, that rarely kill in affluent countries.

They must have many children so that two or three will survive to adulthood.

Poor parents need children to help grow food or to beg in the streets. A few surviving children are also a form of social security to help their parents survive in old age (typically in their forties). For people living near the edge of survival, having too many children may cause problems. But having too few children can contribute to premature death.

The bad news is that so many of the world's poor are dying every day. The good news is that most of these premature deaths could be prevented at little cost—if enough of us really cared.

F. Mattioli/

Figure 1-6 This Ethiopian child is one of the estimated 750 million people on earth who suffer malnutrition caused by a diet without enough protein and other nutrients needed for good health.

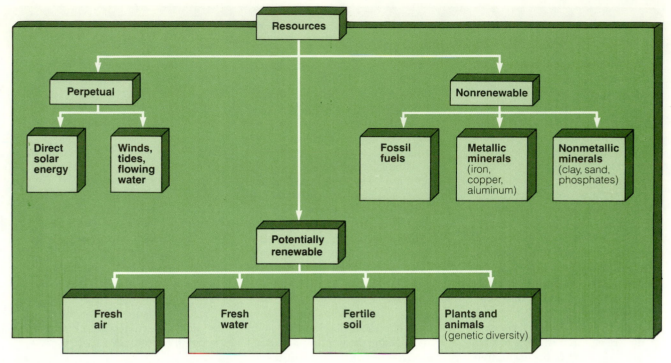

Figure 1-7 Major types of resources. This scheme, however, isn't fixed; potentially renewable resources can be converted to nonrenewable resources if used for a prolonged time faster than they are renewed by natural processes.

Types of Resources Resources can be classified as perpetual, nonrenewable, and renewable (Figure 1-7). A **perpetual resource,** such as solar energy, is virtually inexhaustible on a human time scale. **Nonrenewable, or exhaustible, resources** exist in a fixed amount (stock) in various places in the earth's crust. Examples are copper, aluminum, coal, and oil. They can be exhausted either because they are not replaced by natural processes (copper and aluminum) or because they are replaced more slowly than they are used (oil and coal). The world's supply of oil took millions of years to form. However, affordable supplies of oil will probably be gone by 2059, two hundred years after the first oil well was drilled in Titusville, Pennsylvania.

Some supplies of nonrenewable resources will always be left in the earth's crust. Instead of being physically exhausted, they become economically depleted when it's too expensive to extract and process what is left.

Typically, a nonrenewable resource such as copper or oil is considered **economically depleted** when 80% of its total estimated supply has been removed and used. At this point finding, extracting, and processing the rest usually costs more than it's worth. Why? Because what is left is too dilute (low-grade copper ore) or is found only in remote and difficult-to-tap deposits (deep oil wells in remote areas such as the Antarctic).

Some nonrenewable resources can be recycled or reused to extend supplies—copper, aluminum, iron, and glass, for example. **Recycling** involves collecting and remelting or reprocessing a resource. For example, aluminum beverage cans can be collected, melted, and converted into new beverage cans or other aluminum products. **Reuse** involves using a resource over and over in the same form. For example, refillable beverage bottles can be collected, washed, and refilled.

Other nonrenewable resources, such as fossil fuels (coal, oil, and natural gas), can't be recycled or reused. Once burned, these fuels lose their high-quality, useful energy forever (see Spotlight on p. 11).

Sometimes we can find a substitute or replacement for a nonrenewable resource that's scarce or too expensive. Some resource economists believe that we can use our ingenuity to find a substitute for any nonrenewable resource.

But substitution isn't always possible. Some materials have unique properties that can't easily be matched. In other cases, replacements may be inferior, too costly, or too scarce. Economic disruption can occur while a substitute for a widely used renewable resource is being found and phased into manufacturing processes.

A **potentially renewable resource** is one that can be depleted in the short run if used or polluted too rapidly but ultimately is replaced through natural processes. Examples are trees in forests, grasses in grasslands, wild animals, fresh surface water in lakes and rivers, most deposits of groundwater, fresh air, and fertile soil.

Classifying something as a renewable resource, however, doesn't mean that it can't be depleted and that it will always stay renewable. The highest rate at which a renewable resource can be used without decreasing its potential for renewal throughout the world or in a particular area is called its **sustained yield.**

If this yield is exceeded, the base supply of a renewable resource begins to shrink. If such unsustainable use continues, the resource can become nonrenewable on a human time scale or sometimes nonexistent—a process known as **environmental degradation** (see Spotlight on p. 12). The key to maintaining the supply of a nonrenewable resource is to keep its rate of use at or below its natural replacement rate (sustained yield).

Some resource experts define another type of resource: **aesthetic** or **amenity resources.** Examples are solitude, scenic beauty, and peaceful surroundings. As population levels rise and the need to "get away from it all" increases, aesthetic resources become more scarce and important.

Conserving Resources Resource conservation involves using, managing, and protecting resources so that they will be available on a sustainable basis for present and future generations. People who actively support this effort are called **conservationists.** Sometimes they are also known as **environmentalists,** although this term is more often used to describe those who are primarily concerned with preventing pollution of the air, water, and soil.

Most people are in favor of conserving resources.

But they often disagree over which resources are essential and how much of each resource should be conserved for future generations.

Some conservationists, known as **preservationists,** stress the need to limit human uses of important resources such as wilderness, estuaries (where freshwater rivers and the oceans meet), and wetlands (coastal and inland areas normally covered with water). Preservationists emphasize protection from development and human use, except for nondestructive recreation, education, and research.

Others, known as **scientific conservationists,** stress using the findings of science and technology to manage resources today in ways that don't damage them for future generations. They believe that publicly owned land resources such as national forests should be used for a mixture of human purposes including timbering, mining, recreation, grazing, hunting, construction, and water conservation. This guideline for resource management is known as the *principle of multiple use.* Scientific conservationists also believe that potentially renewable resources such as trees and wildlife should be managed so that they are not removed faster than they are replaced by natural processes. This guideline for use of renewable resources is known as the *principle of sustained yield.*

Still others, known as **sustainable-earth conservationists,** go further. They believe that nature exists for all the earth's living species, not just for us. They view humans as no more important than any other species. This life-centered approach sees human beings as part of nature—not apart from nature and not as conquerors of nature. To them conservation means:

Several types of environmental degradation can change potentially renewable resources into nonrenewable or permanently extinct resources:

- covering productive land with water, silt, concrete, asphalt, or buildings to such an extent that crop growth declines and places for wildlife to live (habitats) are lost
- cultivating land without proper soil management so that crop growth is reduced by soil erosion and depletion of plant nutrients
- irrigating cropland without sufficient drainage so that excessive buildup of water (waterlogging) or salts (salinization) in the soil decreases crop growth
- removing trees from large areas without adequate replanting (deforestation) so that wildlife habitats are destroyed and long-term timber growth is decreased
- depleting grass on land grazed by livestock (overgrazing) so that soil is eroded to the point where grasslands are converted into deserts (desertification)
- killing various forms (species) of wild plant and animal life through destruction of habitat, commercial hunting, pest control, and pollution to the point where these species no longer exist (extinction)

In many parts of the world sustained yields for potentially renewable resources are being exceeded —sometimes to an alarming degree. Table 1-1 summarizes the status of key resources that sustain life on earth. What do you think should be done?

- working with—not against—nature
- interfering with nonhuman species only to meet important needs
- not wasting resources
- seeing that resource use doesn't seriously degrade the earth's life-support systems for people and other species now and in the future

Types of Resource Scarcity The term **scarcity** means that there isn't an unlimited supply of some resource we need or want. Resource scarcity can be absolute or relative. Both types lead to a rapid rise in the price of raw materials, goods, and services, economic disruption, and an attempt to find and phase in substitute resources.

Absolute resource scarcity occurs when there aren't enough actual or affordable supplies of a resource left to meet present or future demand. A period of absolute resource scarcity begins when the demand for a resource exceeds the supply. It continues until the resource is economically depleted. For example, the world's affordable supplies of nonrenewable oil may be used up within your lifetime. The period of absolute and increasing scarcity and cost of oil may begin between 1995 and 2010.

Relative resource scarcity occurs when enough of a resource is still available to meet demand but its distribution is imbalanced. For example, between 1973 and 1979 the world had enough oil to meet demand. But not enough oil was produced and distributed to meet the needs and wants of the United States, Japan, and many western European countries. During this period of relative resource scarcity, the price of oil rose from $3 to $35 a barrel (see Case Study on p. 16). A shortage or catastrophic price rise for a resource because of either absolute or relative scarcity is known as a **resource crisis.**

Most energy analysts believe that the oil glut of the 1980s is only temporary. Some time between 1995 and 2010 they expect the world to enter a period of increasing absolute scarcity of oil. When this happens, experts project that OPEC countries will increase their share of the world's oil market from 27% in 1988 to 60% in the 1990s. OPEC will dominate world oil markets and raise prices even more than in the 1970s. The price of a barrel of oil is projected to rise to at least $32 and perhaps as high as $98.

The Department of Energy and most major oil companies project that by 1995 the United States could be dependent on imported oil for 60% of its oil consumption—much higher than in 1977 (Figure 1-8). This would drain the already debt-ridden United States of vast amounts of money, leading to severe inflation and widespread economic recession, perhaps even a major depression. It would also increase the chances of war as the world's MDCs compete for greater control over dwindling oil supplies to avoid economic collapse.

Since 1981 the United States has done little to prepare for such a possibility. In 1987 polls showed that less than 5% of the American public listed energy as an important national problem.

Will There Be Enough Resources? During the past 100 years and especially since 1950, affluent countries have gone around the bend on a J-shaped curve of increasing average consumption per person of renewable and nonrenewable resources. With only 23% of the world's population, the MDCs use 80% of the world's processed energy and mineral resources.

The United States has only 4.8% of the world's population. Yet it produces about 21% of all goods and services

Table 1-1 Health Report for Some of the Earth's Vital Resources

Topsoil on Cropland	Topsoil is eroding faster than it forms on about 35% of the world's cropland—amounting to a loss of about 26 billion tons of topsoil a year (see photo on p. 1). Crop productivity on one-third of the earth's irrigated cropland has been reduced by buildup of salt in topsoil. Waterlogging of topsoil has reduced crop productivity on at least one-tenth of the world's cropland.
Forest Cover	Almost half of the world's original expanse of tropical forests has been cleared. Each year 50,000 square miles of tropical forest are cleared and another 50,000 square miles are degraded. Within 50 years there may be little of these forests left. One-third of the people on earth cannot get enough fuelwood to meet their basic needs or are forced to meet their needs by cutting trees faster than they are being replenished. In MDCs 77 million acres of forest have been damaged by air pollution.
Desert Area	About 2 billion acres of once-productive land have become desert in the last 50 years. Each year almost 15 million acres of new desert are formed.
Grasslands	Millions of acres of grasslands have been overgrazed by livestock; some, especially in Africa and the Middle East, have been converted to desert. Almost two-thirds of the rangeland in the United States is in fair to poor condition.
Coastal and Inland Wetlands	Between 25% and 50% of the world's wetlands have been drained, built upon, or seriously polluted. Worldwide, millions of acres of wetlands are lost each year. The United States has lost half of its wetlands.
Oceans	Most of the wastes we dump into the air, water, and land eventually end up in the oceans. Oil slicks, floating plastic debris, polluted estuaries and beaches, contaminated fish and shellfish are visible signs that we are using the oceans as the world's largest trash dump.
Lakes	Thousands of lakes in eastern North America and in Scandinavia have become so acidic that they contain no fish; thousands of other lakes are dying; thousands of lakes are depleted of much of their oxygen because of inputs of various chemicals produced by human activities.
Drinking Water	In LDCs 61% of the people living in rural areas and 26% of urban dwellers do not have access to safe drinking water. Each year 5 million die from preventable waterborne diseases. In parts of China, India, Africa, and North America water is being withdrawn from underground deposits (aquifers) faster than it is being replenished by precipitation. In the United States one-fourth of the groundwater withdrawn each year is not replenished. Pesticides contaminate some groundwater deposits in 32 states. In MDCs hundreds of thousands of industrial and municipal landfills and settling ponds, over 2 million underground tanks for storing gasoline and other chemicals, and thousands of abandoned toxic waste dumps threaten groundwater supplies.
Climate	Emissions of carbon dioxide and other gases into the atmosphere from fossil fuel burning and other human activities may raise the average temperature of the earth's lower atmosphere several degrees between now and 2050. This would disrupt food production and flood low-lying coastal cities and croplands.
Atmosphere	Chlorofluorocarbons released into the lower atmosphere are drifting into the upper atmosphere and reacting with and gradually depleting ozone faster than it is being formed. This will let in more ultraviolet radiation from the sun. Skin cancer and eye cataracts will increase and our immune system defenses against many infectious diseases will be weakened. Levels of eye-burning smog, damaging ozone gas, and acid rain in the lower atmosphere will increase and yields of some important food crops will decrease.
Wildlife	Several thousand species of plants and animals become extinct each year mostly because of human activities; if deforestation (especially of tropical forests), desertification, and destruction of wetlands and coral reefs continue at present rates, at least 500,000 and perhaps 1 million species will become extinct over the next 20 years.

Data from Worldwatch Institute and World Resources Institute.

The relative scarcity of oil between 1973 and 1979 was caused by a mix of factors. One was rapid economic growth during the 1960s, stimulated by low oil prices. Another factor was the growing dependence of the United States and many other MDCs on imported oil.

A third factor was that between 1973 and 1979 the Organization of Petroleum Exporting Countries (OPEC)* was able to control the world's supply, distribution, and price of oil. About 57% of the world's proven oil reserves are in the OPEC countries, compared to only 4% in the United States. In 1973 OPEC produced 56% of the world's oil and supplied about 84% of all oil imported by other countries.

During 1973 the United States imported about 30% of its oil (Figure 1-8), with almost half coming from OPEC countries. Other MDCs, such as Japan and most western European countries, have little or no domestic oil supplies. They were and still are more dependent on imported oil than the United States.

*OPEC was formed in 1960 so that LDCs with much of the world's known and projected oil supplies could get a higher price for this resource and stretch remaining supplies by forcing the world to reduce oil use and waste. Today its 13 members are Algeria, Ecuador, Gabon, Indonesia, Iran, Iraq, Kuwait, Libya, Nigeria, Qatar, Saudi Arabia, United Arab Emirates, and Venezuela.

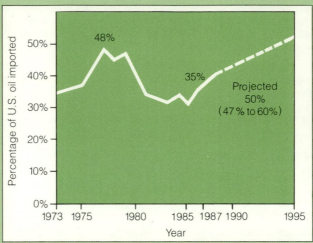

Figure 1-8 Percentage of U.S. oil imported between 1973 and 1988 with projections to 1995. (Data from U.S. Department of Energy and Spears and Associates, Tulsa, Oklahoma)

This dependence of most MDCs on OPEC countries for imported oil set the stage for the two phases of the relative oil scarcity crisis of the 1970s. First, in 1973 Arab members of OPEC reduced oil exports to Western industrial countries and banned all shipments of their oil to the United States because of its support of Israel in its 18-day war with Egypt and Syria.

This embargo lasted until March 1974 and caused a fivefold increase in the average world price of crude oil (Figure 1-9). The increase contributed to double-digit inflation in the United States and many other countries, high interest rates, soaring international debt, and a global economic recession. Americans, accustomed to cheap and plentiful fuel, waited for hours to buy gasoline and turned down thermostats in homes and offices.

Despite the sharp price increase, U.S. dependence on imported oil increased from 30% to 48% between 1973 and 1977 (Figure 1-8). OPEC imports increased from 48% to 67% during the same period. This increasing dependence was caused mostly by the government's failure to lift oil price controls that kept prices arti-

---

and uses about one-third of the world's processed nonrenewable energy and mineral resources. It also produces at least one-third of the world's pollution. For example, the average U.S. citizen consumes 50 times more steel, 56 times more energy, 170 times more synthetic rubber and newsprint, 250 times more motor fuel, and 300 times more plastic than the average citizen of India.

Since 1960 the gap between the rich and poor countries has been widening (Figure 1-10). There is increasing concern that depletion of nonrenewable resources and degradation of renewable resources by MDCs and LDCs may leave insufficient resources for many LDCs to become MDCs. Many analysts call for MDCs to waste fewer resources and to help LDCs become more self-sufficient and obtain a fairer share of the world's resources. These controversial issues are discussed throughout this book.

1-3 POLLUTION

What Is Pollution? Any change in air, water, soil, or food that can affect the health, survival, or activities of human beings in an unwanted way is called **pollution.** When pollution occurs, a resource is no longer fit for its intended use. Usually pollution is defined in terms of harmful effects on human life. But some expand the term to include harmful effects on other forms of life. Most pollutants are solid, liquid, or gaseous chemicals; they can also take the form of energy emissions (excessive heat, noise, or radiation).

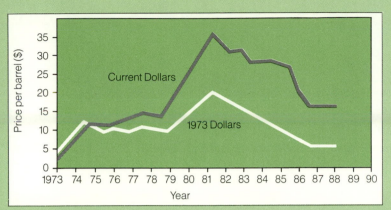

Figure 1-9 Average world crude oil prices between 1973 and 1988. (Data from Department of Energy and Department of Commerce)

ficially low and discouraged energy conservation.

The artificially low prices sent a false message to consumers and set the stage for the second phase of the oil distribution crisis. In 1979 available world oil supplies decreased when the revolution in Iran shut down most of that country's production. Gasoline waiting lines became even longer, and by 1981 the average world price of crude oil rose to about $35 a barrel.

A combination of energy conservation, substitution of other energy sources for oil, and increased oil production by non-OPEC countries led to a drop in world oil consumption between 1979 and 1986. The drop in demand and the inability of OPEC countries to reduce their oil production enough to sustain relative resource scarcity and high prices led to a glut of oil.

Because supply exceeded demand, the price of oil dropped from $35 to around $17 per barrel between 1981 and 1988. This meant that the inflation-adjusted price of crude oil in 1988 was about the same as in 1974 (Figure 1-9).

This oil glut has had good and bad effects for MDCs such as the United States and for LDCs heavily dependent on imported oil. It has stimulated economic growth and created new jobs (except in the oil industry), and it has reduced the rate of inflation.

At the same time, the price drop has had a number of undesirable effects:

■ a sharp decrease in the search for new oil in the United States and most other countries

■ economic chaos in many oil-producing countries, especially those with large international debts (such as Mexico), and in major oil-producing states (such as Texas, Oklahoma, and Louisiana)

■ loss of many jobs in oil and related industries

■ failure or near-failure of many U.S. banks with massive outstanding loans to oil companies and oil-producing LDCs such as Mexico

■ a decreased rate of improvement in energy efficiency and decreased development of energy alternatives to replace oil

■ increased dependence on imported oil from a low of 31% in 1985 to 41% in 1988 (Figure 1-8)

What do you think should be done?

A major problem is that people differ in what they consider an acceptable level of pollution. For example, visible and invisible chemicals spewed into the air and water by a factory might harm people and other forms of life living nearby and in downwind and downstream areas. The plant owners could reduce these effects to acceptable levels by installing expensive pollution control equipment. But these extra costs might force the owners to shut the plant down. Workers who would lose their jobs might feel that the risks from the polluted air and water are minor compared to losing their source of income.

The same level of pollution can also affect two people quite differently. Some forms of air pollution might be a slight nuisance to a healthy person but life-threatening to someone with emphysema. As philosopher Georg Hegel pointed out, the nature of tragedy is not the conflict between right and wrong but between right and right.

Sources and Types of Pollution Pollutants can enter the environment naturally (for example, volcanic eruptions) or through human activities (for example, burning coal). Most natural pollution is dispersed over a large area and is often diluted or broken down to harmless levels by natural processes.

In contrast, most serious pollution from human activities occurs in or near urban and industrial areas. There large amounts of pollutants are concentrated in small volumes of air, water, and soil. Some pollutants

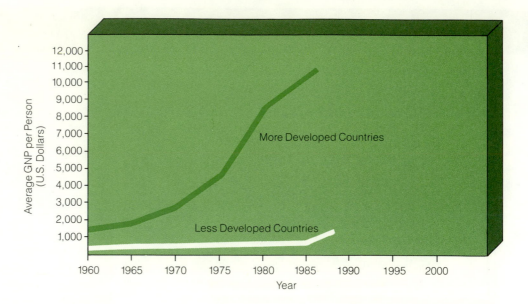

Figure 1-10 The gap in average GNP per person between the more developed and the less developed countries has been widening since 1960, raising fears in many LDCs that they might become never-developed countries. Adjusting for inflation, the average GNP per person in LDCs has decreased since 1960. (Data from United Nations)

contaminate the areas where they are produced. Others are carried by winds or flowing water to other areas.

Most potential pollutants added to the environment by natural processes and many of those we produce are broken down into harmless chemicals or acceptable levels by natural processes and recycled. In nature there are virtually no wastes. The waste products of one plant or animal are resources for others.

But human beings often overload the earth's dilution and degradation processes. We have learned how to put together some of the earth's raw materials in new ways. Thousands of synthetic chemicals and products have replaced natural products (Figure 1-11). Worldwide, about 70,000 different synthetic chemicals are in everyday use. About 1,000 new ones are added each year.

We know little about the potential harmful effects of 80% of these chemicals on people, other animals, and plants. Many of these synthetic chemicals and products, such as DDT, PCBs, and most plastics, are broken down slowly in the environment. Others, such as toxic compounds of mercury and lead, don't break down at all.

Effects of Pollution   Pollution can have a number of unwanted effects:

- *Nuisance and aesthetic insult:* unpleasant smells and tastes, reduced atmospheric visibility, and soiling of buildings and monuments

- *Property damage:* corrosion of metals, weathering or dissolution of building and monument materials, and soiling of clothes, buildings, and monuments

- *Damage to plant and nonhuman animal life:* decreased tree and crop production, harmful health effects on animals, and extinction

- *Damage to human health:* spread of infectious diseases, respiratory system irritation and diseases, genetic and reproductive harm, and cancers

- *Disruption of natural life-support systems at local, regional, and global levels:* climate change and decreased natural recycling of chemicals and energy inputs needed for good health and survival of people and other forms of life

Three factors determine how severe the effects of a pollutant will be. One is its *chemical nature*—how active and harmful it is to specific types of plants and animals. Another is its *concentration*—the amount per unit of volume of air, water, or soil. A third factor is its *persistence*—how long it stays in the air, water, or soil.

During its lifetime a particular plant or animal is typically exposed to many different types and concentrations of pollutants with different degrees of persistence. This explains why it's rarely possible to show that a particular pollutant caused a particular effect or the premature death of a specific plant or animal.

People who know little about the nature of science can be misled by statements such as "Science hasn't proven absolutely that smoking has killed anyone." Such a statement is true but meaningless. *Instead of establishing absolute truth or proof, science establishes only a certain degree of confidence in the validity of an idea.*

Usually such confidence is based on statistical evidence. For example, so far no one has been able to show what specific chemicals in cigarette smoke cause lung cancer in people. Yet smoking and lung cancer have been linked together by a massive amount of statistical evidence from more than 33,000 scientific studies of people and test animals.

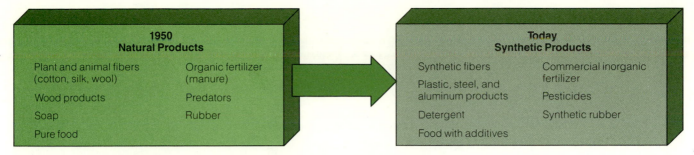

Figure 1-11 Some synthetic products that have been substituted for natural products in industrialized countries since 1945. Some of these synthetic products take a long time to break down in the environment.

Pollution Control We can control pollution in two ways: input control and output control. **Input pollution control** prevents potential pollutants from entering the environment or sharply reduces the amounts released. For example, sulfur impurities can be removed from coal before it's burned. This stops or sharply reduces emissions of the air pollutant sulfur dioxide. This chemical can damage plants and our respiratory systems. In the atmosphere some of it is converted to tiny droplets of sulfuric acid. When these acidic droplets fall to the earth's surface in precipitation, they can damage and weaken some types of trees. They can also kill fish and other forms of life in lakes.

Reducing unnecessary use and waste of matter and energy resources is another major way to reduce harmful inputs of chemicals and excessive heat into the environment. We can also recycle or reuse chemical outputs from human activities instead of discarding them. We can impose taxes, incentives, or other economic and political devices to make the resource inputs of a process so expensive that people will use these resources more efficiently. This decreases outputs of waste materials and makes recycling and reuse more profitable.

So far most attempts to control pollution have been based on treating rather than preventing the problem. **Output pollution control** approaches deal with wastes after they've entered the environment. The problem is that output approaches often remove a pollutant from one part of the environment and cause pollution in another part.

For example, air pollution control equipment in smokestacks can remove most of the sulfur dioxide, solid particles, and other chemicals produced by burning coal and other fossil fuels. But this leaves us with mountains of toxic ash or gooey liquids formed by removing the pollutants. What do we do with these chemicals? We could use our ingenuity to recycle or reuse most of them. But mostly we bury them and hope they won't contaminate underground water supplies used for drinking water.

1-4 RELATIONSHIPS AMONG POPULATION, RESOURCE USE, TECHNOLOGY, ENVIRONMENTAL DEGRADATION, AND POLLUTION

The Roots of Environmental Degradation and Pollution Who pollutes and degrades resources? You, me, everybody. Some of us pollute and degrade resources more than others, but we all do it.

We do it directly when we consume resources and indirectly when these resources are extracted and transformed to products we need or want. According to one model, the total environmental degradation and pollution—the environmental impact of population—depends on three factors: **(1)** the number of people, **(2)** the average number of units of resources each person uses, and **(3)** how these resources are used—the environmental degradation and pollution caused when each unit of resource is used (Figure 1-12).

Overpopulation occurs when the people in a country, a region, or the world use resources to such an extent that the resulting degradation or depletion of the resource base and pollution of the air, water, and soil are damaging their life-support systems. The data in Table 1-1 suggest that the planet is already overpopulated. Overpopulation can occur from growing numbers of people, growing affluence (resource consumption), or both.

Differences in the importance of these factors have been used to identify two types of overpopulation: people overpopulation and consumption overpopulation (Figure 1-13). **People overpopulation** exists where there are more people than the available supplies of food, water, and other important resources can support. It can also happen when the rate of population growth so exceeds the rate of economic growth that an increasing number of people are too poor to grow or buy enough food, fuel, and other resources.

In this type of overpopulation, population size and the resulting environmental degradation of potentially renewable soil, grasslands, forests, and wildlife tend to be the key factors determining total environ-

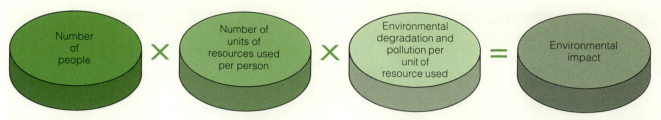

Figure 1-12 Simplified model of how three factors affect overall environmental degradation and pollution, or environmental impact.

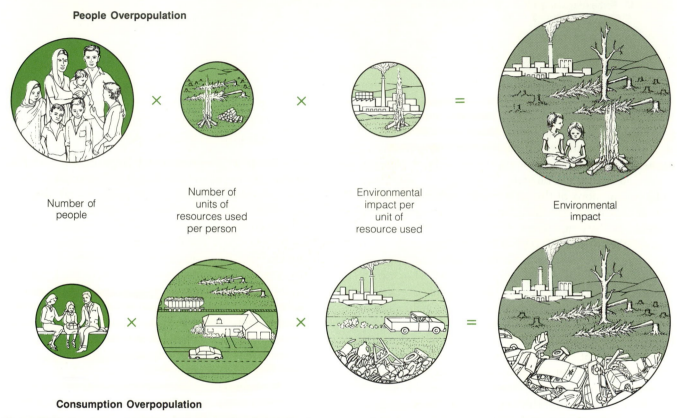

Figure 1-13 Two types of overpopulation based on the relative importance of the factors in the model shown in Figure 1-12. Circle size shows relative importance of each factor. People overpopulation is caused mostly by growing numbers of people. Consumption overpopulation is caused mostly by growing affluence (resource consumption).

mental impact (Figure 1-13). In the world's poorest LDCs, people overpopulation causes premature death for at least 12 million and perhaps 40 million people each year and bare survival for hundreds of millions more. Many analysts fear this plight will get worse unless population growth is brought under control and improved resource management is used to restore degraded renewable resources.

MDCs such as the United States, Great Britain, West Germany, the Soviet Union, and Japan, are said by some to have a second type of overpopulation, called **consumption overpopulation.** It exists when a small number of people use resources at such a high rate that significant pollution and environmental degradation occurs. With this type of overpopulation, high rates of resource use per person and the resulting high

levels of pollution per person tend to be the key factors determining overall environmental impact (Figure 1-13). The world's affluent people are the principal depleters of the earth's savings account of resources.

Other Factors The three-factor model shown in Figures 1-12 and 1-13, though useful, is too simple. The actual situation is a complex mix of interacting problems and factors shown in simplified form in Figure 1-14. For example, pollution and environmental degradation are increased not only by population size but also by *population distribution*—the number of people within an area.

The most severe air and water pollution problems usually happen when large numbers of people are concentrated in urban areas. However, spreading

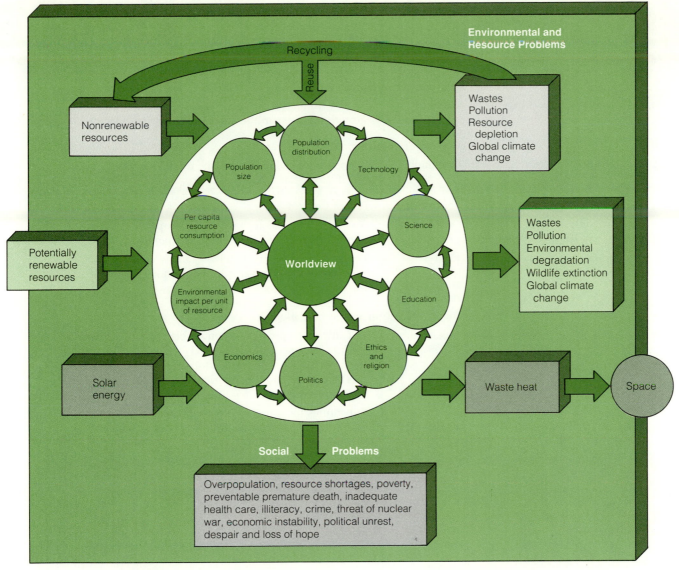

Figure 1-14 Environmental, resource, and social problems are caused by a complex, poorly understood mix of interacting factors, as illustrated by this simplified model. Only a few of the many possible interactions are shown. Understanding more about how these multiple factors interact is the key to dealing with these problems.

people out can have a harmful effect on potentially renewable soil, forest, grassland, aquatic, and recreational resources. *War* also has a disastrous environmental impact.

Some *scientific and technological developments* create new environmental problems or aggravate existing ones. For example, burning coal, oil, and natural gas to provide energy for heating, cooling, and transportation is the cause of most air pollution problems. Other forms of pollution are caused by increased use of science and technology to manufacture, use, and discard plastics, DDT, chlorofluorocarbons, radioactive wastes, and other materials that take a long time to break down in the environment.

But science and technology can also help solve environmental and resource problems. Substitutes have

been developed for many scarce resources. Light bulbs have replaced whale oil in lamps. This has helped protect the world's dwindling population of whales from extinction. Some forms of resource waste have also been reduced. For example, we now get more energy from burning a ton of coal than we did 100 years ago. Until the 1970s most detergents were not biodegradable. Today they are. Scientists and engineers have also developed output methods for controlling and cleaning up many forms of pollution. Our problem and challenge isn't to stop technological advancement but to use it to sustain rather than degrade the earth's life-support systems.

Economic, political, and ethical factors are also involved in causing and solving resource and environmental problems. We can manage our economic

Cornucopians	Neo-Malthusians
Role of Humans on Earth	
Conquer nature to promote increasing economic growth.	Work with nature to promote kinds of economic growth that sustain the earth's life-support systems.
Seriousness of Environmental Problems	
Exaggerated; can be cured by increased economic growth and technological innovations.	Serious now and could become more serious without a shift to sustainable forms of economic growth.
Population Growth and Control	
Should not be controlled; people are our most vital source for solving the world's problems.	Should be controlled to prevent disruption of local, regional, and global life-support systems.
People should be free to have as many children as they want.	People should be free to have as many children as they want only if this freedom does not infringe on the rights of others to survive.
Resource Depletion and Degradation	
We will not run out of potentially renewable resources because of better management or a switch to substitutes.	In many areas potentially renewable resources have already been seriously degraded (Table 1-1). There are no substitutes for the earth's topsoil, grasslands, forests, fisheries, and wildlife that keep us alive and support many of our economic activities.
We will not run out of nonrenewable resources because we can find more, mine less concentrated deposits, or find substitutes.	Substitutes for some nonrenewable resources may not be found or may take too long to phase in without causing economic hardship.
Increases in economic growth and technological innovation can reduce resource depletion, pollution, and environmental degradation to acceptable levels.	Because of high rates of resource use and unnecessary waste, MDCs are causing unacceptable regional and global resource depletion, pollution, and environmental degradation.
Energy Resources	
Emphasize use of nuclear power and nonrenewable oil, coal, and natural gas.	Emphasize use of energy conservation, perpetual solar, wind, and flowing water, and sustainable use of potentially renewable biomass (wood, crop wastes).

systems to control pollution, environmental degradation, and resource waste by making such practices unprofitable (in market economies) or illegal (in centrally controlled economies). Economic rewards can also be used to encourage development and use of appropriate or less harmful technology.

In democratic countries we can also use the political process to enact and enforce pollution control and land-use control laws. However, such economic and political action will happen only when enough citizens and leaders realize that to abuse the world's life-support systems for short-term economic gain and political power is both unwise and wrong.

1-5 WHAT SHOULD BE DONE? NEO-MALTHUSIANS VERSUS CORNUCOPIANS

Two Opposing Views There are conflicting views about what the role of people in the world should be, how serious the world's present and projected environmental and resource problems really are, and what should be done about them. **Neo-Malthusians** (called "gloom-and-doom pessimists" by their opponents) believe that if present trends continue, the world will become more crowded and more polluted, and many resources will be depleted or degraded. They also

Cornucopians	Neo-Malthusians

Resource Conservation

Reducing unnecessary resource waste, recycling, and reuse are desirable but not if this decreases economic growth for the present generation.	Reducing unnecessary resource waste is vital for sustaining the earth's life-support systems and long-term economic productivity. It stretches supplies of nonrenewable resources, sustains supplies of potentially renewable resources, and reduces the environmental impact of resource extraction and use.
We can find a substitute for any scarce resource, so resource conservation is not necesary unless it promotes economic growth.	Substitutes may not be found or may be inferior or too costly.

Wildlife

The earth's wild plant and animal species are here to serve our needs.	Premature extinction of any wild species by human activities is wrong. These potentially renewable resources should be used only on a sustainable basis to meet vital needs, not frivolous wants.

Pollution Control

Pollution control should not be increased at the expense of short-term economic growth, which can provide funds for pollution control.	Inadequate pollution control damages people and other forms of life and reduces long-term economic productivity.
Polluters should be given government subsidies and tax breaks to install pollution-control equipment.	Polluters should pay for reducing pollution to acceptable levels. Goods and services should include the costs of pollution control so that consumers will know the effects of what they buy and use. Using the "taxpayer pays" approach hides the harmful costs of using goods and services.
Emphasize output control to reduce pollution once it has entered the environment.	Emphasize input control to prevent pollution from entering the environment.
Burn, dump, or bury waste materials.	Think of waste materials as resources that should be recycled, reused, or converted to useful forms.

believe that this will lead to greater political and economic turmoil and increase the threat of nuclear and conventional wars as the rich get richer and the poor get poorer. Most neo-Malthusians are conservationists.

The term *neo-Malthusian* refers to an updated and expanded version of a hypothesis proposed in 1789 by Thomas Robert Malthus, an English clergyman and economist. He believed that human population growing exponentially will eventually outgrow food supplies and will be reduced in size by starvation, disease, and war.

Members of an opposing group are called **cornucopians** (or "unrealistic technological optimists" by their opponents). Most cornucopians are economists. They believe that if present trends continue, economic growth and technological advances will produce a less crowded, less polluted, and more resource-rich world. It will also be a world in which most people will be healthier, will live longer, and will have greater material wealth. The term *cornucopian* comes from *cornucopia*, the horn of plenty, a symbol of abundance. Major differences between these two schools of thought are summarized in the Pro/Con box above and are also discussed in the two Guest Essays ending this chapter.

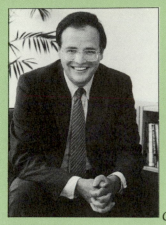

Gus Speth

Gus Speth has been president of the World Resources Institute since 1982. He served as head of the President's Council on Environmental Quality (CEQ) between 1979 and 1981, after serving as a member of the council from 1977 to 1979. Before his appointment to the CEQ, he was a staff attorney for the Natural Resources Defense Council, a public interest group he helped found in 1970.

Since 1970 many disturbing studies and reports have been issued by organizations concerned with conserving and sustaining the world's resources and economic systems. These reports have sounded a persistent warning: International efforts to stem the spread of human poverty, hunger, and misery aren't achieving their goals; the staggering growth of the human population, coupled with ever-increasing human demands, is beginning to cause permanent damage to the earth's resource base.

One such warning was issued in 1980 by the Council on Environmental Quality and the U.S. State Department. Called *The Global 2000 Report to the President*, it was the result of a three-year effort by more than a dozen agencies of the U.S. government to make long-term projections about various population, resource, and environmental concerns. Since then these projections have been updated in annual volumes of *World Resources* (published each year since 1986), issued jointly by the World Resources Institute

and the International Institute for Environment and Development.

Given the obvious limitations of such projections, the report can best be seen as a reconnaissance of the future. And the results of that reconnaissance and its later updates are disturbing.

The conclusions of these studies indicate the potential for deepening global problems between now and the end of this century and long after that if policies and practices around the world continue as they are today. The next century will begin a more crowded world, containing more than 6 billion human beings. It could be a world where growing numbers of people suffer hunger and privation; where losses of croplands, grasslands, and forests mount while human numbers and needs increase; where per capita supplies of fresh water, timber, and fish are diminished; where deterioration of the earth's air and water accelerates; and where plant and animal species vanish at unprecedented rates.

These findings confront the United States and the other countries of the world with one of the most difficult challenges facing our planet during the coming decades. Disturbing as these findings are, however, it is important to stress what the conclusions of these and other related reports represent: not predictions of what will happen, but projections of what could happen if we don't change our ways. I believe that as the people and governments of the world come to realize the full dimensions of the challenge before us, we will take the actions needed to meet it.

The first thing we must do is to get serious about the conservation of resources—renewable and nonrenewable alike. We can no longer take for granted the renewability of our renewable resources. We must realize that the natural systems—the air and water, the forests, the land—that yield food, shelter, and other necessities of life are susceptible to disruption, contamination, and destruction.

In some parts of the world, particularly in the less developed countries, the ability of biological systems to support human populations is being seriously damaged by human demands for grazing land, firewood, and building materials. Nor are these stresses confined to the less developed countries: In recent

Throwaway and Sustainable-Earth Worldviews The debate between cornucopians and neo-Malthusians has been going on for decades. But it's more than an intellectual debate between people who often use the same data and trends to reach quite different conclusions. Members of these opposing groups have sharply different views of how the world works and what our role in the world should be.

Cornucopians usually have a **throwaway worldview,** also known as a **frontier worldview.** They see

the earth as a place of unlimited resources, where any type of resource conservation that hampers short-term economic growth is unnecessary. If we pollute or deplete the resources in one area, they believe, we will find substitutes and control the pollution through technology. If resources become scarce or a substitute can't be found, they believe we can get materials from the moon and asteroids in the "new frontier" of space. This worldview is based on two beliefs: We are more important than any other species, and through sci-

years, the United States has been losing annually about 3 million acres of rural land—one-third of our prime agricultural land—due to the spread of housing developments, highways, shopping malls, and the like. We are also losing the equivalent, in terms of production capability, of about 3 million more acres a year because of soil degradation, erosion, and salt buildup in irrigated soil.

Achieving the necessary restraint in the use of renewable resources will call for new ways of thinking by the peoples and governments of the world. It will require the widespread adoption of a "conserver society" ethic. This approach to resources and environment, while attuned to the needs of each society, recognizes not only the importance of resources and environment to our own sustenance, well-being, and security, but also our obligation to pass this vital legacy along to future generations.

Fortunately, we are beginning to see signs that people in the United States and in other countries are becoming aware of the limits to our resources and the importance of conserving them. Energy problems, for example, are pointing the way to a future in which conservation is the password. As energy supplies go down and prices go up, we learn that conserving—getting more and more out of each barrel of oil or ton of coal—is the cheapest and safest approach.

Learning to conserve nonrenewable resources like oil and coal is the first step toward building a conserver society that values, nurtures, and protects all its resources. Such a society appreciates economy in design and avoidance of waste. It realizes the limits to low-cost resources and to the environment's carrying capacity. It insists that market prices reflect all costs, social and private, so that consumers are fully aware in the most direct way of the real costs of consumption.

But the conserver society ethic alone is not enough. It's unrealistic to expect people living at the margin of existence—people fighting desperately for their own survival—to think about the long-term survival of the planet. When people need to burn wood to keep from freezing, they will cut down trees.

For this reason, an equally important element in an effective strategy to deal with global resource problems must be the *sustainable development* of the less developed countries of the world. Development, far from being in conflict with resource conservation and environmental protection, is essential to achieving these goals. It is only through sound, sustainable economic development that real progress can be made in alleviating hunger and poverty and in erasing the conditions that contribute so dangerously to the destruction of our planet's carrying capacity.

Clearly the trends discussed in these reports, especially the growing disparity in income between the rich and poor peoples of the world, greatly heighten the chances for global instability—for exploitation of fears, resentments, and frustrations; for incitement to violence; for conflicts based on resources. The humanitarian reasons for acting generously to alleviate global poverty and injustice are compelling enough in themselves. But we must also recognize the extent to which poverty and resource problems can threaten the security of countries throughout the world.

These growing tensions can only be defused through a much greater emphasis on equity—on a fair sharing of the means to development and the products of growth, not only among nations but also within nations. It should be obvious that the interests of all countries of the world, more developed and less developed alike, are inextricably linked. In helping other countries become more self-sufficient, we help ourselves.

Guest Essay Discussion

1. What specific obligations, if any, do you feel we have to future generations?

2. How would you define *sustainable development* for the less developed countries of the world? If this goal is adopted, what effects might it have on your life and lifestyle?

3. Do you agree that the means to economic development and the products of economic growth must be shared more fairly not only among countries but also within countries? How would you bring about this greater emphasis on equity?

ence and technology we can conquer, control, and change nature to meet our present and future needs and wants.

In contrast, most neo-Malthusians have a **sustainable-earth worldview.*** They believe that the earth does

not have infinite resources and that ever-increasing production and consumption will put severe stress on the natural processes that renew and maintain the air, water, and soil and support the earth's variety of potentially renewable plant and animal life. They also believe that present and future resource and environmental problems are caused by our lack of understanding how nature works, our attempts to dominate nature, and our failure to recognize that we're part of—not apart from and superior to—nature.

---

*Others have used the terms *sustainable worldview* and *conserver worldview* to describe this idea. I add the word *earth* to make clear that it's all the earth's life-support systems and life, not just human beings and their societies, that must be sustained.

There Is No Environmental, Population, or Resource Crisis

Julian L. Simon

Julian L. Simon is professor of economics and business administration at the University of Maryland. He has effectively presented and defended the cornucopian position in many articles and books, including The Ultimate Resource *and* The Resourceful Earth *(see Further Readings).*

This book and most others discussing environmental and resource problems begin with the proposition that there is an environmental and resource crisis. If this means that the situation of humanity is worse now than in the past, then the idea of a crisis—and all that follows from it—is dead wrong. In almost every respect important to humanity, the trends have been improving, not deteriorating.

Our world now supports 5.2 billion people. In the 19th century the earth could sustain only 1 billion. And 10,000 years ago, only 1 million people could keep themselves alive. People are living more healthily than ever before, too.

One would expect lovers of humanity—people who hate war and worry about famine in Africa—to jump with joy at this extraordinary triumph of the human mind and human organization over the raw forces of nature. Instead, they lament that there are so many human beings, and wring their hands about the problems that more people inevitably bring.

The recent extraordinary decrease in the death rate—to my mind, the greatest miracle in history—accounts for the bumper crop of humanity. Recall that it took thousands of years to increase life expectancy at birth from the 20s to the 30s. Then in just the last 200 years, life expectancy in the advanced countries jumped from the mid-30s to the 70s. And starting well after World War II, life expectancy at birth in the poor countries, even the very poorest, has leaped upward (averaging 60 in 1988), because of progress in agriculture, sanitation, and medicine. Average life expectancy at birth in China, the world's most populous country, was 66 in 1988, an increase of 22 years

since the 1950s. Is this not an astounding triumph?

In the short run, another baby reduces income per person by causing output to be divided among more people. And as the British economist Thomas Malthus argued in 1798, more workers laboring with existing capital results in less output per worker. However, if resources are not fixed, then the Malthusian doctrine of diminishing resources, resurrected by today's neo-Malthusians, does not apply. Given some time to adjust to shortages with known methods and new inventions, free people create additional resources.

It is amazing but true that a resource shortage due to population or income growth usually leaves us better off than if the shortage had never arisen. If firewood had not become scarce in 17th century England, coal would not have been developed. If coal and whale oil shortages hadn't loomed, oil wells would not have been dug.

The prices of food, metals, and other raw materials have been declining by every measure since the beginning of the 19th century and as far back as we know. That is, raw materials have been getting less scarce instead of more scarce throughout history, defying the commonsense notion that if one begins with an inventory of a resource and uses some up, there will be less left. This is despite, and indirectly because of, increasing population.

All statistical studies show that population growth doesn't lead to slower economic growth, though this defies common sense. Nor is a high population density a drag on economic development. Statistical comparison across nations reveals that higher population density is associated with faster instead of slower growth. Drive around on Hong Kong's smooth-flowing highways for an hour or two. You will then realize that a large concentration of human beings in a small area does not make impossible comfortable existence and exciting economic expansion, if the system gives individuals the freedom to exercise their talents and pursue economic opportunities. The experience of densely populated Singapore makes clear that Hong Kong is not unique either.

In 1983 a blue-ribbon panel of scientists summarized their wisdom in *The Resourceful Earth.* Among the findings, besides those I have noted above, were:

- Many people are still hungry, but the food supply has been improving since at least World War II, as measured by grain prices, production per consumer, and the famine death rate.
- Land availability won't increasingly constrain world agriculture in coming decades.
- In the U.S., the trend is toward higher-quality cropland, suffering less from erosion than the past.

- The widely published report of increasingly rapid urbanization of U.S. farmland was based on faulty data.
- Trends in world forests are not worrying, though in some places deforestation is troubling.
- There is no statistical evidence for rapid loss of plant and animal wildlife species in the next two decades. An increased rate of extinction cannot be ruled out if tropical deforestation is severe, but no evidence about linkage has yet been demonstrated.
- Water does not pose a problem of physical scarcity or disappearance, although the world and U.S. situations do call for better institutional management through more rational systems of property rights.
- There is no persuasive reason to believe that the world oil price will rise in coming decades. The price may fall well below what it has been.
- Compared to coal, nuclear power is no more expensive and is probably much cheaper, under most circumstances. It is also much cheaper than oil.
- Nuclear power gives every evidence of costing fewer lives per unit of energy produced than does coal or oil.
- Solar energy sources (including wind and wave power) are too dilute to compete economically for much of humankind's energy needs, though for specialized uses and certain climates they can make a valuable contribution.
- Threats of air and water pollution have been vastly overblown. The air and water in the United States have been getting cleaner, rather than dirtier.

We don't say that all is well everywhere, and we don't predict that all will be rosy in the future. Children are hungry and sick; people live out lives of physical or intellectual poverty and lack of opportunity; war or some other pollution may do us in. *The Resourceful Earth* does show that for most relevant matters we've examined, total global and U.S. trends are improving instead of deteriorating.

Also, we do not say that a better future happens automatically or without effect. It will happen because men and women—sometimes as individuals, sometimes as enterprises working for profit, sometimes as voluntary non-profit-making groups, and sometimes as governmental agencies—will address problems with muscle and mind, and will probably overcome, as has been usual through history.

We are confident that the nature of the physical world permits continued improvement in humankind's economic lot in the long run, indefinitely. Of course, there are always newly arising local problems, shortages, and pollutions, due to climate or to increased population and income. Sometimes temporary large-scale problems arise. But the world's physical conditions and the resilience in a well-functioning economic and social system enable us to overcome such problems, and the solutions usually leave us better off than if the problem had never arisen; that is the great lesson to be learned from human history.

Guest Essay Discussion

1. Do you agree with the author's contention that there is no environmental, population, or resource crisis? Explain. After you've finished this course, come back and answer this question again to see if your views have changed.

2. In effect, the author of this essay and the one that preceded it have taken the same general trends, projected them into the future, and come to quite different conclusions. How can this happen? What criteria can we use to decide who's more likely to be correct?

3. In 1967, Herman Kahn (now deceased), a leading cornucopian and Julian Simon's coeditor for *The Resourceful Earth*, wrote a book using existing trends to project the future from 1967 to 2000. In his book Kahn said that pollution, environmental degradation, and population growth were not problems. Yet shortly after that, in the 1970s, they became major societal concerns. Environmentalists and conservationists contend that Kahn's attitude shows the tendency of cornucopians to ignore problems or declare them not serious, despite clear evidence to the contrary. Do you agree with this analysis? Explain.

Some neo-Malthusians have used the term *Spaceship Earth* to help people see the need to protect the earth's life-support systems. However, other neo-Malthusians have criticized this image. They believe that the spaceship analogy reinforces the idea that our role is to dominate and control nature. Thinking of the earth as a spaceship encourages us to view the earth merely as a machine that we can change and manage at will and to believe that we understand how nature works.

We must recognize that the earth's resource and environmental problems and their possible solutions are interconnected in complex ways that we're only beginning to understand and will never understand completely. We should be guided by the motto of philosopher and mathematician Alfred North Whitehead, "Seek simplicity and distrust it," and by writer and social critic H. L. Mencken, who warned, "For every problem there is a solution—simple, neat, and wrong."

What's the use of a house if you don't have a decent planet to put it on?

Henry David Thoreau

DISCUSSION TOPICS

1. Is the world overpopulated? Explain. Is the United States suffering from consumption overpopulation? Explain.

2. Do you favor instituting policies designed to reduce population growth and stabilize **(a)** the size of the world's population as soon as possible and **(b)** the size of the U.S. population as soon as possible? Explain.

3. Explain why you agree or disagree with the following proposition: High levels of resource use by the United States and other MDCs is beneficial. MDCs stimulate the economic growth of LDCs by buying their raw materials. High levels of resource use also stimulate economic growth in MDCs. This provides money for more financial aid to LDCs and for reducing pollution and environmental degradation.

4. Explain why you agree or disagree with the following proposition: The world will never run out of resources because technological innovations will produce substitutes or allow use of lower grades of scarce resources.

5. Do your own views more closely resemble those of a neo-Malthusian or a cornucopian? Does your lifestyle show that you're acting as a cornucopian or a neo-Malthusian? Compare your views with those of others in your class.

6. What are the major resource and environmental problems in **(a)** the city, town, or rural area where you live and **(b)** the state in which you live? Which of these problems affect you directly?

FURTHER READINGS

Brown, Lester R. , et al. Annual. *State of the World*. New York: W. W. Norton.

Council on Environmental Quality. *Annual Report*. Washington, D.C.: Government Printing Office.

Council on Environmental Quality and U.S. Department of State. 1980. *The Global 2000 Report to the President*, Vols. 1–3. Washington, D.C.: Government Printing Office.

Dahlberg, Kenneth A., et al. 1985. *Environment and the Global Arena*. Durham, N.C.: Duke University Press.

Durrell, Lee. 1986. *State of the Ark: An Atlas of Conservation in Action*. Garden City, N.Y.: Doubleday.

Ehrlich, Anne H., and Paul R. Ehrlich. 1987. *Earth*. New York: Franklin Watts.

Ehrlich, Paul R., and John P. Holdren, eds. 1988. *The Cassandra Conference: Resources and the Human Predicament*. Texas Station: Texas A&M University Press.

Goldsmith, Edward, and Nicholas Hildyard. 1988. *The Earth Report: The Essential Guide to Global Ecological Issues*. Los Angeles: Price Stern Sloan.

Hardin, Garrett. 1985. *Filters Against Folly*. East Rutherford, N.J.: Viking.

Myers, Norman, ed. 1984. *Gaia: An Atlas of Planet Management*. Garden City, N.Y.: Anchor Press/Doubleday.

Repetto, Robert. 1986. *World Enough and Time: Successful Strategies for Resource Management*. New Haven, Conn.: World Resources Institute.

Repetto, Robert. 1987. "Population, Resources, Environment: An Uncertain Future," *Population Bulletin*, vol. 42, no. 2, 1–44.

Schumacher, E. F. 1973. *Small Is Beautiful: Economics As If People Mattered*. New York: Harper & Row.

Simon, Julian L. 1981. *The Ultimate Resource*. Princeton, N.J.: Princeton University Press.

Simon, Julian L., and Herman Kahn, eds. 1984. *The Resourceful Earth*. New York: Basil Blackwell.

Watt, K. E. F. 1982. *Understanding the Environment*. Newton, Mass.: Allyn & Bacon.

World Resources Institute and International Institute for Environment and Development. Annual. *World Resources*. New York: Basic Books.

CHAPTER 2

Brief History of Resource Exploitation and Conservation

General Questions and Issues

1. How did early and advanced hunter-gatherer societies affect the environment, and what was their relationship to nature?

2. What major impacts have early agricultural societies and present-day nonindustrialized agricultural societies had on the environment, and what is their relationship to nature?

3. How do present-day industrialized societies affect the environment, and what is their relationship to nature?

4. What are the major phases in the history of resource exploitation, resource conservation, and environmental protection in the United States?

5. What major environmental protection and resource conservation problems do we face during the 1990s and beyond?

A continent ages quickly once we come.

Ernest Hemingway

T he earliest form of humans, known as *Homo habilis,* is believed to have lived in southern Africa about 1.7 to 2 million years ago. They probably survived mostly by scavenging meat from the bodies of dead animals and gathering and eating wild plants. They also learned to make simple tools and weapons and may have done some hunting for food.

They were followed by two other humanoid species, *Homo erectus* (about 1.5 million years ago) and *Homo sapiens* (about 200,000 years ago). Evidence indicates that these early humanoids were **hunter-gatherers** who got food by gathering edible wild plants and hunting wild game from the nearby environment.

Our species, *Homo sapiens sapiens,* has lived on earth for about 30,000 to 40,000 years. During most of this time we, like the human species that came before us, have been hunter-gatherers who developed more sophisticated tools and weapons.

About 10,000 years ago some people began breeding wild animals and cultivating wild plants. This marked the beginning of a cultural change from hunters and gatherers of wild plants and animals to farmers and herders of domesticated plants and animals. About 275 years ago some people began inventing various machines that led to a new cultural change known as the Industrial Revolution.

The J-shaped curves of exponentially increasing population, resource use, pollution, and environmental degradation are symptoms of these cultural changes from hunting-gathering to agricultural to industrial societies. To see where we might be headed and how we can influence our path, it is useful to learn about how we have used and abused the earth during these cultural changes.

2-1 HUNTING-AND-GATHERING SOCIETIES

Early Hunter-Gatherers Archaeological findings and anthropological studies indicate that most hunter-gatherers lived in small groups of rarely more than 50 people, who worked together to get enough food to survive. Men did the hunting (Figure 2-1). Most groups in tropical areas were probably dominated by women because they typically gathered 60% to 80% of the food and raised the children. In polar areas, where vegetation was scarce, men supplied most of the food by

Figure 2-1 Most people who have lived on earth have survived by hunting wild game and gathering wild plants. The hunter (left) has killed a guinea fowl. The women (right) are gathering plants for food in the northern Kalahari desert in southern Africa.

hunting and catching fish, thereby probably dominating most groups.

Sometimes a group became so large that its members could not find enough food within reasonable walking distances. Then the entire group moved to another area or split up and moved to different areas, sometimes only when food was scarce. Many of these widely scattered bands were nomadic. They moved with the seasons and migrations of game animals to get enough food and to minimize work effort.

These hunter-gatherers were experts in survival. Their knowledge of nature enabled them to predict the weather and find water even in the desert. They discovered a variety of plants and animals that could be eaten and used as medicines. By using stones to chip sticks, other stones, and animal bones, they made primitive weapons and tools for killing animals, catching fish, cutting plants, and scraping hides for clothing and shelter.

Although women typically gave birth to four or five children, usually only one or two children survived to adulthood. Infant deaths from infectious diseases and infanticide (killing the newborn) led to an average life expectancy of about 30 years. This helped keep population size in balance with food supplies.

Early hunter-gatherers exploited their environment for food and other resources—as do all forms of

life. But their numbers were small, most moved from place to place, and they used only their own muscle energy to modify the environment. Their environmental impact was small and localized.

Advanced Hunter-Gatherers Archaeological evidence indicates that hunter-gatherers gradually developed improved tools and hunting weapons. Examples are spears with sharp-edged stone points mounted on wooden shafts and later the bow and arrow (about 12,000 years ago). Some learned to work together to hunt herds of reindeer, woolly mammoths, European bison, and other big game. They used fire to flush game from thickets toward hunters lying in wait and to stampede herds of animals into traps or over cliffs. Some also learned to burn vegetation to promote the growth of food plants and plants favored by the animals they hunted.

Advanced hunter-gatherers had a greater impact on their environment than early hunter-gatherers, especially in using fire to convert forests into grasslands. But because of their small numbers, nomadic behavior, and dependence on their own muscle power to modify the environment, their environmental impact was still fairly small. Both early and advanced hunter-gatherers were examples of *people in nature,* who learned to survive by understanding nature.

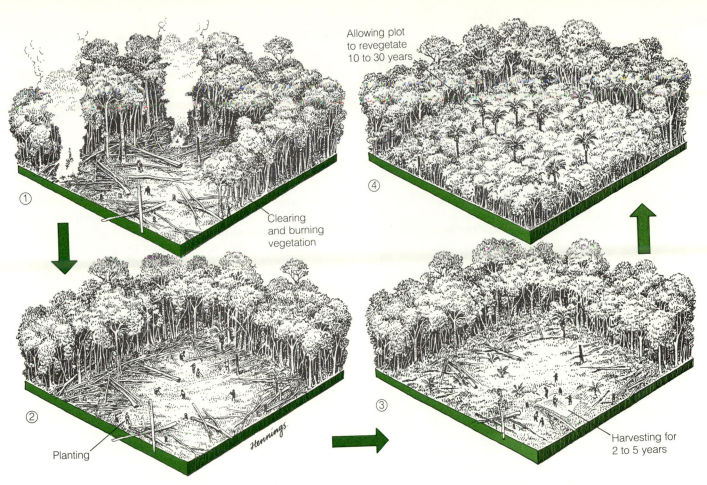

Figure 2-2 Probably the first technique used to grow crops was a combination of slash-and-burn and shifting cultivation in tropical forests. This method is a sustainable way to grow crops only if a small portion of the forest is cleared. Soil fertility will not be restored unless each abandoned plot is left unplanted for 20 to 30 years.

Labels in figure:
- Allowing plot to revegetate 10 to 30 years
- ① Clearing and burning vegetation
- ② Planting
- ③ Harvesting for 2 to 5 years
- ④
- Hennings.

2-2 AGRICULTURAL SOCIETIES

Domestication of Wild Animals and Plants One of the most significant changes in human history is believed to have begun about 10,000 years ago. Groups of people in several parts of the world began domesticating—herding, taming, and breeding—wild game for food, clothing, and carrying loads. They also began domesticating selected wild food plants, planting and growing them close to home instead of gathering them over a large area.

Archaeological evidence indicates that the first type of plant cultivation, which we now call *horticulture*, probably began in tropical forest areas. It is believed that people discovered they could grow yam, taro, arrowroot, and other wild food plants by digging holes with a stick (a primitive hoe) and placing roots or tubers of these plants in the holes.

To prepare for planting, they cleared small patches of forests by **slash-and-burn cultivation**—cutting down trees and other vegetation, leaving the cut vegetation on the ground to dry, and then burning it (Figure 2-2). The ashes that were left added plant nutrients to the nutrient-poor soils found in most tropical forest areas.

Roots and tubers were then planted in holes dug between tree stumps.

These early growers also used **shifting cultivation** as a part of this horticultural system (Figure 2-2). After a plot had been planted and harvested for two to five years, few crops could be grown. By then either the soil was depleted of nutrients or the patch had been invaded by a dense growth of vegetation from the surrounding forest. When yields dropped, the horticulturists shifted (moved) to a new area of forest. A new plot was then cleared to begin a new cycle of cutting, burning, planting, and harvesting for several years. The growers learned that each abandoned patch had to be left fallow (unplanted) for ten to thirty years before the soil was fertile enough to grow crops again.

These growers practiced **subsistence agriculture**, growing only enough food to feed their families. Their dependence on human muscle power and crude stone or stick tools meant that they could cultivate only small plots; thus, they had relatively little impact on their environment.

True *agriculture* (as opposed to horticulture) began about 7,000 years ago with the invention of the metal plow, pulled by domesticated animals and steered by

Archaeological evidence and historical records show that a number of agriculture-based urban societies in the Middle East, North Africa, and the Mediterranean area prospered economically between 3500 B.C. and 500 A.D. But they did so by degrading their land resource base so severely that they eventually helped bring about their own downfall.

As late as 7000 B.C., the sites of the great Sumerian and Babylonian civilizations (on land that now makes up much of Iran and Iraq) were covered with productive forests and grasslands. But with each generation, the elaborate network of irrigation canals that supported these civilizations became filled with more silt from deforestation, soil erosion, and overgrazing. More and more slaves and laborers were needed to keep the irrigation channels free of silt.

By 3000 B.C. much of this once-productive land had been converted into the barren desert that makes up much of Iran and Iraq today. A combination of environmental degradation, climate change, periodic drought, and series of invading armies eventually led to the downfall of the Babylonian civilization.

Severe environmental degradation also took place in other areas around the Mediterranean Sea and in Saharan Africa, where the remains of great cities are now buried in the sand. Some analysts argue that unless we learn from these past environmental lessons and use our knowledge and technology to work with rather than against nature, we will repeat these mistakes on a regional and global scale. What do you think?

Emergence of Agriculture-Based Urban Societies The gradual shift from hunting and gathering to farming had four major effects:

- Population began to increase because of a larger, more constant supply of food.

- People cleared increasingly larger areas of land and began to control and shape the surface of the earth to suit their needs.

- Urbanization—the formation of cities—began because a small number of farmers could produce enough food to feed their families plus a surplus that could be traded to other people. Many former farmers moved into permanent villages. Some villages gradually grew into towns and cities, which served as centers for trade, government, and religion.

- Specialized occupations and long-distance trade developed as former farmers in villages and towns learned crafts such as weaving, toolmaking, and pottery to produce handmade goods that could be exchanged for food.

About 5,500 years ago, this trade interdependence between rural farmers and urban dwellers led to the gradual development of a number of *agriculture-based urban societies* near early agricultural settlements. The trade in food and manufactured goods created wealth and the need for a managerial class to regulate the distribution of goods, services, and land.

As ownership of land and water rights became a valuable economic resource, conflict increased. Armies and their leaders rose to power and took over large areas of land. These rulers forced powerless people—slaves and landless peasants—to do the hard, disagreeable work of producing food and constructing irrigation systems, temples, and other projects. Male leaders dominated most of these societies.

the farmer. Animal-pulled plows greatly increased crop productivity. They allowed farmers to cultivate larger plots of land and to break up fertile grassland soils, which previously couldn't be cultivated because of their thick and widespread root systems.

In some arid (dry) regions early farmers further increased crop output by diverting nearby water into hand-dug ditches and canals to irrigate crops. With this animal- and irrigation-assisted agriculture, families usually grew enough food to survive. Sometimes they had enough food left over for sale or for storage to provide food when flooding, prolonged dry spells, insect infestation, or other natural disasters reduced crop productivity.

Male farmers typically produced more food than most male hunters. So the shift to agriculture marked the beginning of an increase in male domination.

Environmental Impact The rise of agriculture-based urban societies created a much greater environmental impact than that of hunting-and-gathering societies and early subsistence farmers. The growing populations of these emerging civilizations needed more food and more wood for fuel and buildings. To meet these needs, vast areas of forest were cut down and grasslands were plowed up. Such massive land clearing destroyed and degraded the habitats of many forms of plant and animal wildlife, causing or hastening their extinction.

Poor management of many of the cleared areas led to greatly increased deforestation and soil erosion. Overgrazing of grasslands by huge herds of sheep, goats, and cattle helped convert once-fertile land to desert. The topsoil that washed off these barren areas polluted streams, rivers, lakes, and irrigation canals, making them useless.

The concentration of large numbers of people and their wastes in cities helped spread infectious human diseases and parasites. The gradual degradation of the vital resource base of soil, water, forests, grazing land, and wildlife was a major factor in the downfall of many great civilizations (see Spotlight on p. 30).

The gradual spread of agriculture meant that most of the earth's population shifted from hunter-gatherers *in nature* to shepherds, farmers, and urban dwellers *against nature*. This change in how people viewed their relationship to nature is believed by many analysts to be the major cause of today's resource and environmental problems.

2-3 INDUSTRIAL SOCIETIES: THE INDUSTRIAL REVOLUTION

Early Industrial Societies The next major cultural change, the *Industrial Revolution*, began in England in the mid-1700s and spread to the United States in the 1800s. It involved a shift from small-scale production of goods by hand to large-scale production of goods by machines. Horse-drawn wagons, plows, grain reapers, and wind powered ships were replaced by fossil-fuel-powered locomotives, cars, trucks, tractors, grain reapers, and ships.

Within a few decades, these innovations changed agriculture-based urban societies in western Europe and North America into even more urbanized *early industrial societies*. These societies and the more advanced ones that followed were based on using human ingenuity to increase the average amount of energy used per person (Figure 2-3). Farm, manufacturing, and transportation machines fueled by coal and oil took over jobs once done by people and and draft animals. This led to greatly increased production, trade, and distribution of goods.

The growth in industries increased the flow of mineral raw materials, fuel, timber, and food into the cities that served as industrial centers. As a result, environmental degradation increased in nonurban areas supplying these resources. Industrialization also produced greater outputs of smoke, ash, garbage, and other wastes in urban areas.

Fossil-fuel-powered farm machines, commercial fertilizers, and new plant breeding techniques greatly increased the amount of crops that could be grown per acre of cultivated land. Greater agricultural productivity reduced the number of people needed to produce food and increased the number of former farmers migrating from rural to urban areas. Many found jobs in the growing number of mechanized factories. There they worked long hours for low pay in boring assembly line jobs. Most factories were noisy, dirty, and dangerous places to work.

Society	Kilocalories per Person per Day
Modern Industrial (United States)	230,000
Modern Industrial (other developed nations)	125,000
Early Industrial	60,000
Advanced Agricultural	20,000
Early Agricultural	12,000
Hunter-Gatherer	5,000
Primitive	2,000

Figure 2-3 Average direct and indirect daily energy use per person at various stages of human cultural development.

Advanced Industrial Societies After World War I (1914–18), more efficient machines and mass production techniques were developed, forming the basis of today's *advanced industrial societies* in the United States, Japan, and other MDCs. These societies are characterized by:

- greatly increased production and consumption of goods, stimulated by mass advertising to create artificial wants

- greatly increased dependence on nonrenewable resources such as oil, natural gas, coal, and various metals

- a shift from dependence on natural materials, which are degradable, to synthetic materials, many of which break down slowly in the environment (Figure 1-9, p. 15)

- a sharp rise in the amount of energy used per person for transportation, manufacturing, agriculture, lighting, heating, and cooling (Figure 2-3)

Advanced industrial societies benefit most people living in them. These benefits include:

- creation and mass production of many useful and economically affordable products

- significant increases in the average GNP per person (Figure 1-3, pp. 6–7)

- a sharp increase in average agricultural productivity per person because of advanced industrialized agriculture, in which a small number of farmers produce large amounts of food

- a sharp rise in average life expectancy from improvements in sanitation, hygiene, nutrition, medicine, and birth control

- a gradual decline in the rate of population growth because of improvements in health, birth control, education, average income, and old-age security

In some ways people in today's advanced industrial societies behave like their hunter-gatherer ancestors. Most women have one or two children that survive to adulthood. Most people don't grow their own food. Instead, they hunt and gather food in grocery stores or in fast-food and other restaurants. Our gatherer ancestors also ate "fast foods"—nuts, berries, fruits, greens, and roots that could be gathered and eaten immediately. But these early forms of fast food were much more nutritious than those people eat today. Like hunter-gatherers, many people in MDCs move from place to place during their lifetimes.

Environmental Impact   Along with their many benefits, advanced industrialized societies have intensified many existing resource and environmental problems and created new ones. These problems now threaten human well-being at the:

- *local level:* contamination of groundwater with toxic pollutants

- *regional level:* damage to forests and degradation of lakes caused by pollutants

- *global level:* possible climate change from the atmospheric buildup of carbon dioxide and other gases and depletion of the ozone layer

The combination of industrialized agriculture, increased mining, and urbanization has increased the degradation of potentially renewable topsoil, forests and grasslands, and wildlife populations (Table 1-1, p. 13)—the same problems that contributed to the downfall of earlier civilizations (see Spotlight on p. 30).

Industrialization has given people much greater control over nature and has decreased the number of people living close to the land. As a result, people, especially in MDCs and in urban areas, have intensified the view that their role is to conquer nature. Many analysts believe that as long as we have this worldview, we will continue to abuse the earth's life-support systems.

2-4   HISTORICAL OVERVIEW OF RESOURCE EXPLOITATION, RESOURCE CONSERVATION, AND ENVIRONMENTAL PROTECTION IN THE UNITED STATES

America's First Conservationists   When Europeans discovered North America in the fifteenth and sixteenth centuries, they found that it had a diverse network of families, clans, tribes, and nations of aborig-

University of Washington Libraries

Figure 2-4   Chief Sealth of the Duwamish tribe of the state of Washington. His 1855 letter to President Franklin Pierce criticized the country's white settlers for exploiting and degrading the earth's resources. (Special Collections Division University of Washington Libraries, Photo by: Sammis Negative No.: NA15/1)

inal people—called *Indians* by the Europeans and now often referred to as *Native Americans.*

Although there were exceptions, most Native Americans had cultures based on a deep respect for the land and its animals. This concern for wildlife was rooted in their religions and was based on the fact that they depended directly on wildlife for their tools, weapons, utensils, food, clothing, and shelter.

In 1855 Chief Sealth (Figure 2-4) of the Duwamish tribe of the state of Washington wrote a letter to President Franklin Pierce about the U.S. government's offer to buy the tribe's land, the heart of which is now occupied by Seattle. The following passage from this letter shows the respect that most early Native Americans had for wild animals:

If I decide to accept your offer, I will make one condition. The white man must treat the beasts of this land as his brothers. I am a savage and do not understand any other way. I have seen a thousand rotting buffaloes on the prairies left by the white man who shot them from a passing train. I am a savage and I do not understand how the smoking iron horse can be more important than the buffalo that we kill only to stay alive. What is man without the beasts? If all the beasts were gone, men would die from great loneliness of spirit for whatever happens to the beasts also happens to man. All things are connected.

Figure 2-5 Thousands of snowgeese in a National Wildlife Refuge near Albuquerque, New Mexico. When European settlers arrived in North America, such sights were common.

Figure 2-6 California redwood forest.

Frontier Expansion and Resource Exploitation

(1607–1900) When European colonists began settling in North America in 1607, they found a vast continent. It appeared to have abundant and inexhaustible supplies of timber, fertile soil, wildlife, water, minerals, and other resources for their own use and for export to Europe.

Seventy-pound turkeys roamed through the woods. Enormous flocks of geese (Figure 2-5), ducks, and passenger pigeons blotted out the sun. Streams overflowed with so many fish that horses could not cross. Lakes contained 12-foot sturgeon that could only be killed with axes.

Remarkably diverse forests seemed to stretch almost endlessly from the Atlantic coast to the Great Plains. Forests beyond the Great Plains were even more dramatic. Pine forests in the Rocky Mountains, the great Douglas-fir forests of the Pacific Northwest, and the monumental redwoods of California (Figure 2-6) were an inspiration for poets and artists and a symbol of the resource wealth of a nation.

American settlers responded to this seemingly inexhaustible abundance with the frontier view that most of the continent was a hostile wilderness to be conquered, opened up, cleared, and exploited as quickly as possible. This attitude led to enormous resource waste and little regard for future resource needs. This frontier mentality was summarized by Chief Sealth in his letter to President Pierce:

We know that the white man does not understand our ways. One portion of the land is the same to him as the next, for he is a stranger who comes in the night and takes from the land whatever he needs. The earth is not his brother but his enemy, and when he has conquered it, he moves on.

Initially, frontier expansion had relatively little effect on North America's vast populations of wild species, except near settlements. However, after almost 100 years of unrestricted hunting, the abundance of game such as deer had been sharply reduced in the eastern coastal areas. By 1700 all the original thirteen colonies except Georgia had established closed hunting seasons to protect deer. But most protective game laws were poorly enforced by local officials.

In 1870, California established the country's first wildlife refuge, the Lake Merritt Wildfowl Sanctuary (now in the city of Oakland). By 1880, game species in all states were protected by law, but most states didn't hire game wardens to enforce the laws, and the

When European explorers discovered North America in the late 1400s, various tribes of Native Americans depended heavily on bison for their survival. The meat was their staple diet. The skin was used for tepees, moccasins, and clothes. The gut made their bowstrings, and the horns their spoons. Even the dried feces, called "buffalo chips" by English-speaking settlers, were used for fuel.

In 1500, before European settlers came to North America, between 60 million and 125 million grass-eating American bison roamed the plains, prairies, and woodlands over most of the continent (Figure 2-7). Their numbers were so large that they were thought to be inexhaustible. By 1906, however, the once-massive range of the American bison was reduced to a tiny area, and the species was nearly driven to extinction, mostly because of overhunting and loss of habitat.

By the late 1600s some Plains Native American tribes had begun hunting bison using horses descended from those brought earlier by Spanish explorers. They hunted on foot and on horseback, armed only with lances and bows and arrows. Occasionally they drove bison over cliffs. This hunting hardly made a dent in the vast bison population.

As settlers moved west after the Civil War, the sustainable balance between Native Americans and the bison was upset. Plains Native Americans traded bison skins to settlers for steel knives and firearms and began killing bison in larger numbers.

But much more severe depletion of this resource was caused by other factors. First, as railroads spread westward in the late 1860s, railroad companies hired professional bison hunters to supply construction crews with meat. The well-known railroad bison hunter "Buffalo Bill" Cody killed an estimated 4,280 bison in only 18 months—surely a world record. Passengers also gunned down bison from train windows purely for the "joy" of killing, leaving the carcasses to rot.

As farmers settled the plains, they shot bison because the animals destroyed crops. Ranchers killed them because they competed with cattle and sheep for grass and knocked over fences, telegraph poles, and sod houses.

An army of commercial hunters shot millions of bison for their hides and for their tongues, which were considered a delicacy. Instead of being eaten, however, most of the meat was left to rot. "Bone pickers" then collected the bleached bones that whitened the prairies and shipped them east for use as fertilizer.

A final major factor in the near extinction of the bison occurred after the Civil War. The U.S. Army killed millions of bison to subdue Plains tribes of Native Americans and take over their lands by killing off their major source of food.

Between 1870 and 1875 at least 2.5 million bison were slaughtered each year.

By 1890 only one herd of about 1 million bison was left. Commercial hunters and skinners descended on this herd, and by 1892 only 85 bison were left. These were given refuge in Yellowstone National Park and protected by an 1893 law against the killing of wild animals in national parks.

In 1905 sixteen people formed the American Bison Society to protect and rebuild the captive population of the animal. In the early 1900s the federal government established the National Bison Range near Missoula, Montana. Since then, captive herds on this federal land and other herds mostly on privately owned land scattered throughout the West have been protected by law.

Today there are about 75,000 bison in the United States—one-fifth of them on the National Bison Range. Some captive bison are crossbred with cattle to produce hybrids, called beefalo. They have a tasty meat, grow faster and are easier to raise than cattle, and need no expensive grain feed.

Figure 2-7 Severe shrinkage of the range of the bison between 1500 and 1906, primarily as a result of overhunting and settlement.

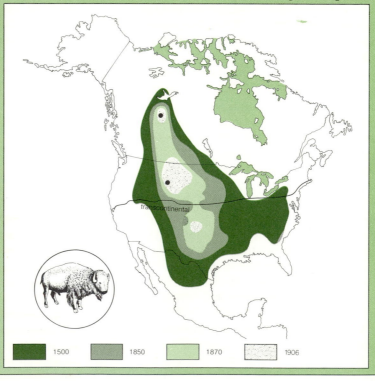

| 1500 | 1850 | 1870 | 1906 |

federal government had no authority to regulate the taking of wildlife by sport and commercial hunters.

After the Civil War ended in 1865, the government turned its attention to expanding the frontier westward. This meant taming Native American tribes and the American bison that were obstacles to settling the plains (see Case Study on p. 34). Commercial hunters slaughtered hundreds of thousands of wild ducks and geese in areas where they concentrated during the winter (Figure 2-5, p. 33). In the late 1800s hunters also killed large numbers of herons, snowy egrets (Figure 2-8), and other exotically plumed birds to supply feathers for women's fashions.

After the Civil War, cattle and sheep ranchers began a period of rapid expansion on western rangelands. Federal land-use policies encouraged the use of most public rangelands by any and all livestock operators at no charge. By 1900, after more than 50 years of continuous close grazing by cattle, sheep, and horses, much of this rangeland had been severely overgrazed.

Another key factor in resource exploitation and degradation was the transfer of vast areas of public land to private interests between 1850 and 1900. In 1850 about 80% of the total land area of the United States was government owned. Most of this land had been taken from Native American tribes and nations, whose people had lived on it for centuries. The government signed and then broke dozens of treaties giving various nations and tribes of Native Americans ownership of large tracts of land. In 1891 an old Sioux Indian summarized this behavior: "They made us many promises, more than I can remember, but they never kept but one; they promised to take our land and they took it."

During the mid-1800s several laws were passed to promote rapid transfer of vast holdings of public land into private ownership. The purpose of these laws was to encourage settlement and economic development of the continent and to give the country increased security from its enemies.

By 1900 more than half of the public land had been given away or sold at low cost to railroad, timber, and mining companies, land developers, states, schools, universities, and homesteaders. By artificially lowering the prices of resources, these land transfers encouraged widespread exploitation, waste, and degradation of much of the country's forests, grasslands, and minerals. Most of this land was obtained and exploited by speculators and large corporations.

Early Conservation Warnings (1832–70) Between 1832 and 1870, a number of people warned that America's forest, grassland, and wildlife resources were being depleted and degraded at an alarming rate. These early conservationists included George Catlin, Horace Greeley, Ralph Waldo Emerson, Frederick Law Olmsted, Charles W. Eliot, Henry David Thoreau, and

Cornell Laboratory of Ornithology/O.S. Pettingill

Figure 2-8 The snowy egret was hunted to near extinction in the late 1800s because its feathers were used to adorn women's hats. Since being protected, it is no longer threatened with extinction.

George Perkins Marsh (Figure 2-9). They proposed that part of the unspoiled wilderness owned by the government be protected from resource exploitation.

These warnings were largely ignored or vigorously opposed by many citizens and politicians. They believed that the country's forests and wildlife would last forever and that people had the right to do with private and public land as they pleased.

In 1864 George Perkins Marsh, a scientist and congressman from Vermont, published a book, *Man and Nature* (see Further Readings), that helped legislators and influential citizens see the need for resource conservation. Marsh questioned the idea that the country's resources were inexhaustible and showed how the rise and fall of past civilizations were linked to their use and misuse of their resource base. He also set forth basic resource conservation principles still used today.

Beginnings of the Federal Government's Role in Resource Conservation (1870–1916) In the late 1800s the American conservation movement emerged, as a number of citizens and government officials began realizing the extent of deforestation and wildlife depletion throughout the country. The federal role in

Figure 2-9 Some early American conservationists.

Henry David Thoreau
1817–1862

George P. Marsh
1801–1882

John Muir
1838–1914

Gifford Pinchot
1865–1946

Theodore Roosevelt
1858–1919

Aldo Leopold
1886–1948

forest and wildlife resource conservation began in 1872, when the government set aside over 2 million acres of forest mostly in northeastern Wyoming as Yellowstone National Park and banned all hunting in the area.

Congress protected this land mostly because it was viewed as essentially useless for resource exploitation. However, this action marked the beginning of the *first wave of resource conservation* in the United States.

The American Forestry Association was organized in 1875 to develop public support for protection of the country's existing forests and for reforestation. In 1885 New York became the first state to set up a state forest. It preserved a large tract in the Adirondacks with the condition that it "shall be kept forever as wild forest lands."

In 1890 the Census Bureau and historian Frederick J. Turner declared that the United States had been settled to the point that its *geographic frontier was closed.* This helped federal officials recognize the need to begin conserving resources on lands still under federal ownership.

In 1891 Congress passed the Forest Reserve Act.

It set aside Yellowstone Timberland Reserve as the first federal forest reserve. The act also authorized the president to set aside additional federal lands to ensure future availability of adequate timber and to protect water resources. This was a turning point in establishing the responsibility of the federal government for protecting public lands from resource exploitation.

Between 1891 and 1897, Presidents Benjamin Harrison and Grover Cleveland withdrew millions of acres of public land, located mostly in the West, from timber cutting. Powerful and wealthy political foes—especially Westerners accustomed to using these public lands as they pleased—called these actions undemocratic and un-American.

In 1892 California nature writer John Muir (Figure 2-9) founded the Sierra Club to help protect public lands from resource exploitation. Despite warnings by early conservationists, at the turn of the century American forests were still being cut down much faster than they were being replaced by natural regrowth and tree planting efforts (Figure 2-10).

The Lacey Act of 1900 made it illegal to transport live or dead wild animals, or their parts, across state

Figure 2-10 In 1900, Pacific Coast loggers were cutting gigantic trees such as this Douglas fir. Teams of horses, mules, or oxen dragged the logs from the forests.

Figure 2-11 The first national wildlife refuge was set up off the coast of Florida in 1903 to protect the brown pelican from extinction.

borders without a federal permit. Although this federal law reduced commercial hunting, it did not end the excessive slaughter of wildlife.

More effective protection of forests and wildlife didn't occur until Theodore Roosevelt, an ardent conservationist, became president. The period of his presidency, from 1901 to 1909, is regarded by many as the country's golden age of conservation.

Roosevelt's first step was to convince Congress to grant him executive powers to establish federal wildlife refuges. In 1903 he established the first federal refuge at Pelican Island off the east coast of Florida for preservation of the endangered brown pelican (Figure 2-11). Roosevelt also tripled the size of the forest reserves and transferred administration of them from the Department of the Interior, which had a reputation for lax enforcement, to the Department of Agriculture.

In 1905 a group of private citizens founded the National Audubon Society to protect wildlife. During the same year, Congress created the U.S. Forest Service to manage and protect the forest reserves. Roosevelt appointed Gifford Pinchot as its first chief (Figure 2-9). Pinchot pioneered efforts to manage potentially renewable forest resources scientifically according to the principles of sustained yield and multiple use.

In 1907, Congress, upset over Roosevelt's addition of vast tracts to the forest reserves, amended the Forest Reserve Act of 1891 to ban further withdrawals of public forests by the president. This amendment also changed the name of the reserves to *national forests*—implying that these lands should not be preserved from all types of development. On the day before the amendment became law, Roosevelt defiantly reserved another 16 million acres of national forests.

Early in this century conservationists disagreed over how the beautiful Hetch Hetchy Valley in what is now Yosemite National Park was to be used. This controversy split the American conservation movement into two schools of thought, the preservationists and the scientific conservationists.

Scientific conservationists, led by Gifford Pinchot, wanted to build a dam and flood the valley to provide a dependable supply of drinking water for San Francisco. Preservationists, led by John Muir, wanted to keep this beautiful spot from being flooded. After a long and highly publicized battle, the dam was built and the valley was flooded. The controversy between the two schools of thought continues today (see Spotlight on p. 38).

In 1912 Congress created the U.S. National Park System, and in 1916 it passed the National Park System Organic Act. This law declared that national parks are to be set aside to conserve and preserve scenery, wildlife, and natural and historic objects for the use, observation, health, and pleasure of people. The parks are to be maintained in a manner that leaves them unimpaired for future generations.

The same law established the National Park Service within the Department of the Interior to manage the system. By then the system had 16 national parks and 21 national monuments, most of them in the western states. The Park Service's first director, Stephen Mather, recruited a corps of professional park rangers to manage the parks.

During the Republican administrations of 1921–33, the government increased emphasis on using public resources to favor big business and promote economic growth. Indeed, while Herbert Hoover was president between 1929 and 1933, he proposed that the federal government return all remaining federal lands to the states or sell them to private interests. The economic depression of the 1930s, however, made the financial burden of owning such lands unattractive to state governments and private interests.

Expanding Federal Role in Wildlife and Public Land Management (1933–60)

The *second wave of national resource conservation* began in the early 1930s, as President Franklin D. Roosevelt attempted to get the country out of the Great Depression (1929–41). Conservation of resources benefited because financially strapped landowners were eager to sell vast tracts of land at low prices to the government.

To provide jobs for 2 million unemployed young men, Roosevelt established the Civilian Conservation Corps (CCC). The CCC planted trees, developed parks and recreation areas, restored silted waterways, provided flood control, controlled soil erosion, protected wildlife, and carried out other conservation projects.

SPOTLIGHT   Preservation Versus Scientific Conservation (1910–Present)

Past and present preservationists emphasize protecting large areas of public lands from mining, timbering, and other forms of development so they can be enjoyed by present generations and passed on unspoiled to future generations. Establishing protected parks, wilderness areas, and wildlife refuges helps save these potentially renewable public resources from being degraded by short-term—"quick buck"—economic development.

Preservationists were led by naturalist John Muir (Figure 2-9) and, after Muir's death in 1914, by forester Aldo Leopold (Figure 2-9). According to Leopold, the role of the human species should be that of a member and protector of nature—not its conqueror.

Another effective supporter of wilderness preservation was Robert Marshall, an officer in the U.S. Forest Service. In 1935 he and Leopold founded the Wilderness Society. Others who have led preservationist efforts in recent years include David Brower (former head of the Sierra Club and founder of Friends of the Earth), Ernest Swift, and Stewart L. Udall.

In contrast, scientific conservationists see public lands as resources to be used now to enhance economic growth and national strength. They must be protected from degradation by being managed efficiently and scientifically for sustained yield and multiple use. Early scientific conservationists were led by Theodore Roosevelt, Gifford Pinchot, John Wesley Powell, Charles Van Hise, and others.

According to Roosevelt and Pinchot, conservation experts would form an elite corps of resource managers in the federal bureaucracy. They would be protected from excessive political pressure and could design and implement management strategies based on scientific criteria. Pinchot angered Muir and other preservationists, who had been active allies in Roosevelt's conservation efforts, when he stated his principle of the wise use of resources:

The first great fact about conservation is that it stands for development. There has been a fundamental misconception that conservation means nothing but the husbanding of resources for future generations. There could be no more serious mistake. . . . The first principle of conservation is the use of the natural resources now existing on this continent for the benefit of the people who live here now.

Although they differed on how resources should be used, most early preservationists and scientific conservationists called for *equitable (fair) use of publicly owned resources.* Both schools felt that such resources belong to all the people and should be managed by the federal government for widespread and fair use by everyone. They were against letting public resources fall into the hands of a few for private profit.

The goal of equity has not been achieved. Since 1910 the rights to much of the forest and mineral resources on public lands and the water resources supplied by federally financed dam and irrigation projects in the West have gone to large, privately owned farms, ranching operations, mining companies, and timber companies. Often, the rights to resources on public lands have been sold to these influential private interests at below normal market prices.

During the Depression the federal government built and operated many large dams in the arid western states, such as Hoover Dam on the Colorado River. These projects stimulated the economy by providing jobs, irrigation water, flood control, and cheap electricity.

Several laws passed during the 1930s further extended federal authority over the protection of wildlife at the expense of local and state authority. One important law was the Federal Bird Hunting Stamp Act of 1934, which required waterfowl hunters to buy a special hunting permit, called a duck stamp, each year. Since 1934 the sale of these permits has brought in over $300 million for use in waterfowl research and the purchase of waterfowl refuge lands.

In 1933 the Soil Erosion Service under the Department of Agriculture was created. Its mission was to correct some of the massive erosion problems that ruined many of the farms of the Great Plains states. This erosion, brought about by prolonged drought and lack of soil conservation, contributed to the Great Depression. It forced large numbers of bankrupt farmers in the Midwest to migrate to eastern and western cities in search of nonexistent jobs, as described in John Steinbeck's novel *The Grapes of Wrath*. In 1935 the Soil Erosion Service was renamed the Soil Conservation Service, and Hugh H. Bennett became its first director.

The passage of the Taylor Grazing Act in 1934 marked the beginning of the regulation of grazing of domesticated livestock on public lands, especially in the West, which for many decades had been overgrazed by ranchers. This act placed 80 million acres of public land into grazing districts. Each was to be managed jointly by the Grazing Service, established within the Department of the Interior, and committees of local ranchers.

This law also required permits and fees for the use of federal grazing lands and placed limits on the number of animals that could be grazed. Nevertheless, most grazing permits went to the wealthier and more politically powerful western ranchers.

From the start, ranchers resented government interference with their long-established, unregulated use of public land. Since 1934 they have led repeated efforts to have these lands removed from government ownership and turned over to private ranching, mining, timber, and development interests.

In 1935 Paul B. Sears wrote *Deserts on the March*. In this book he warned that continuing abuse of western rangeland could convert much of it to desert, as earlier civilizations had learned the hard way. This warning was largely ignored.

Until passage of the Federal Land Policy and Management Act in 1976, western congressional delegations kept the Grazing Service (which in 1946 became the Bureau of Land Management, or BLM) poorly funded and staffed and without enforcement authority. This allowed many ranchers and mining and timber companies to continue abusing western public lands.

In 1937 the Federal Aid in Wildlife Restoration Act (also known as the Pittman-Robertson Act) levied a federal tax on all sales of guns and ammunition. These federal funds plus matching state funds have provided more than $2.1 billion for states to buy land for wildlife conservation (mostly for game species), to support wildlife research, and to reintroduce wildlife in depleted areas.

Between 1940 and 1960, there were few new developments in federal resource conservation policy because of preoccupation with World War II (1941–1945) and economic recovery after the war. However, postwar federal aid, including the G.I. bill, helped establish many new wildlife biology and wildlife management programs and departments at the country's expanding colleges and universities.

In 1948 the United States had its first major air pollution disaster, when pollutants from a steel mill, zinc smelter, and sulfuric acid plant stagnated over the town of Donora, Pennsylvania. About 6,000 of the town's 14,000 inhabitants fell ill, and 20 of them died from breathing the polluted air. The incident caused some people to question the sight of belching smokestacks as an acceptable nuisance and a sign of economic progress.

In 1948 William Voight warned about the dangers of rapid population growth and overpopulation in his book *The Road to Survival*. The same year, Fairfield Osborn wrote about the need to increase efforts to protect and conserve the country's natural resources during the period of rapid economic growth after World War II. Few people took either of these warnings seriously until the 1960s.

Rise of the Environmental Movement (1960–80) The *third wave of national resource conservation* began during the short administration of John F. Kennedy (1961–63). These efforts were expanded under the administration of Lyndon B. Johnson (1963–68).

In 1962 biologist Rachel Carson (Figure 2-12) published *Silent Spring* (see Further Readings). This book described the pollution of air, water, and wildlife from the widespread use of slowly degradable pesticides such as DDT. It helped broaden the concept of resource conservation to include the preservation of the *quality* of the air, water, and soil, which were under assault by a country experiencing rapid economic growth. The public's unprecedented response to Carson's book was the beginning of what is now known as the environmental movement in the United States.

Another important factor in this movement was the publication in 1963 of *The Quiet Crisis* (see Further

Figure 2-12 Biologist Rachel Carson (1907–1964) was a pioneer in increasing public awareness of pollution. She died without knowing that her efforts were a key in starting today's environmental movement.

Readings) by Stewart L. Udall, secretary of the interior under Kennedy. This book described past abuse of the country's resource base and called for renewed efforts to conserve resources. It repeated and brought up to date many of the concerns voiced by George P. Marsh in 1864, Paul B. Sears in 1935, and Fairfield Osborn in 1948 (see Further Readings).

In 1964 Congress passed the Wilderness Act. It authorizes the government to protect undeveloped tracts of public land as part of the National Wilderness System unless Congress later decides they are needed for the national good. Between 1965 and 1970, the emerging science of ecology received widespread media coverage. At the same time, the popular writings of biologists such as Paul Ehrlich, Barry Commoner, and Garrett Hardin helped the public become aware of the interlocking relationships between population growth, resource use, and pollution (Figure 1-12, p. 18).

During this period a number of events covered by the media increased public awareness of pollution:

- In 1963 high concentrations of air pollutants accumulated in the air above New York City, killing about 300 people and injuring thousands.

- In the mid-1960s foam caused by widespread use of nonbiodegradable substances in synthetic laundry and cleaning detergents began appearing on creeks and rivers (Figure 2-13).

- In 1969 the oil-polluted Cuyahoga River running through Cleveland, Ohio, caught fire. Two bridges were burned by the five-story-high flames (Figure 2-14).

- In 1969 oil leaking from an offshore well near Santa Barbara, California, coated beaches and wildlife with oil (Figure 2-15).

- By the late 1960s Lake Erie had become severely polluted. Large numbers of fish died, numbers of desirable species of commercial and game fish dropped sharply, and many bathing beaches had to be closed.

- During the late 1960s and early 1970s several well-known species of wildlife, such as the American bald eagle (Figure 2-16), the grizzly bear, the whooping crane, and the peregrine falcon, were threatened with extinction, mostly from pollution and loss of habitat.

Since 1965 the public has developed increased awareness of the ecological importance of forests, wetlands, estuaries, oceans, and other land and aquatic systems in maintaining clean air and water and in providing wildlife habitats. The new public awareness led to increased emphasis on resource preservation (rather than scientific conservation) in the form of wilderness, national parks, national forests, and wildlife refuges. This trend was bitterly opposed by lumber, mining, and ranching interests, who wanted to continue using public resources at low prices and with as few restrictions as possible.

On April 22, 1970, the first annual Earth Day took place in the United States. About 20 million people in more than 2,000 communities took to the streets to demand better environmental quality. Elected officials got the message. Between 1969 and 1980 Congress passed more than two dozen separate pieces of legislation to protect the air, water, land, and wildlife (see Appendix 2).

A presidential election was coming up in 1972, and Richard M. Nixon was hoping to be reelected. The massive and growing public support for better environmental quality spurred him into action. In 1972 he used his executive powers to create the Environmental Protection Agency (EPA) to manage the country's air, water, and solid waste pollution problems.

Congress empowered the EPA to set environmental standards for major air and water pollutants and to enforce most of the federal environmental laws. (Most resource conservation laws are enforced by the Bureau of Land Management, the Fish and Wildlife Service, and the Park Service in the Department of the Interior, and the Forest Service in the Department of Agriculture.)

The laws attempt to provide environmental protection and resource conservation by:

Figure 2-13 Foam on a creek caused by nondegradable components in synthetic laundry detergents in 1966.

Figure 2-14 The oil-polluted Cuyahoga River, which runs through Cleveland, Ohio caught fire in 1969.

Figure 2-15 Straw being used to soak up oil released by rupture of an oil well off the coast of Santa Barbara, California, in 1969.

Figure 2-16 During the late 1960s and early 1970s the number of American bald eagles in the lower 48 states declined, because of loss of habitat, illegal hunting, and reproductive failure caused by exposure to pesticides in its primary diet of fish. Federal protection has led to recovery in many areas.

- Setting pollution level standards or limiting emissions or effluents of various types of pollutants. Examples are the Federal Water Pollution Control Act of 1972 and the Clean Air Acts of 1965, 1970, and 1977.

- Screening new substances before they are widely used in order to determine their safety. An example is the Toxic Substances Control Act of 1976.

- Requiring that any project to be undertaken by a government agency be evaluated to project its environmental impact before it is started. An example is the National Environmental Policy Act of 1969.

- Setting aside or protecting various natural systems, resources, or species from harm. Examples are the Wilderness Act of 1964 and the Endangered Species Act of 1973.

- Encouraging resource conservation. Examples are the Resource Conservation and Recovery Act of 1976 and to some extent the National Energy Act of 1978.

The 1970s is sometimes called the environmental decade. But the roots of the important legislation passed during this period were developed in the 1960s.

Between 1965 and 1980 people learned that the country's *environmental frontier* was closed. Also during this period, the country's concern for protecting public land and wildlife resources was expanded to help protect our shared air and water resources. People began to realize that there is no infinite "away"—no place to get rid of the wastes produced by a heavily industrialized society whose economy runs on converting the earth's resources to wastes as fast as possible.

The 1973 OPEC oil embargo and the shutdown of oil production in Iran in 1979 led to oil shortages and sharp rises in the price of oil between 1973 and 1981 (see Case Study on pp. 16–17). This period of relative oil scarcity showed the need for effective conservation of energy resources—especially oil.

In 1977 President Jimmy Carter created the Department of Energy to help the country deal with shortages of oil. He, along with most conservationists, realized that the United States and other industrialized countries must develop a long-range energy strategy.

Most efforts to make the United States face up to the end of the cheap-oil era were undermined by Carter's political defeat and the temporary oil glut of the 1980s. These events sent a false message to many consumers and elected officials that energy conservation and a search for oil substitutes were no longer high priorities.

During his term Carter appointed a number of competent and experienced administrators to key posts in the EPA, the Department of the Interior, and the Department of Energy. He drew heavily on established environmental and conservation organizations for such appointees and for advice on environmental and resource policy. He also created the Superfund to clean up abandoned hazardous waste sites such as the Love Canal suburb in Niagara Falls, New York (see Case Study on p. 240).

Just before leaving office, Carter used the Antiquities Act of 1906 to increase public lands protected from development. He tripled the amount of land in the National Wilderness System, primarily by adding vast tracts of public land in Alaska. This also doubled the area under the administration of the National Park Service.

Many conservationists believe that in retrospect Carter will be recognized for his efforts to conserve and preserve the country's resources. He also attempted—against overwhelming political odds—to change the long-standing actions of government, industries, and individuals from resource exploitation and waste to resource conservation and protection.

Continuing Controversy and Some Retrenchment (the 1980s) The Federal Land Policy and Management Act of 1976 gave the Bureau of Land Management its first real authority to manage the public lands, mostly in the West, under its control. This angered western ranchers, farmers, miners, users of off-road motorized vehicles, and others, who had been doing pretty much as they pleased on these public lands.

In the late 1970s, western ranchers, who had been paying low fees for grazing rights that encouraged overgrazing, launched a political campaign known as the sagebrush rebellion. Its major goal, like that of earlier similar efforts, was to remove most western public lands from public ownership and turn them over to the states. Then they planned to persuade state legislatures to sell or lease the resource-rich lands at low prices to ranching, mining, timber, land development, and other private interests.

In 1981 Ronald Reagan, a self-declared sagebrush rebel, became president, having won the election by a large margin. He had campaigned as a champion of strong national defense, less federal government control, and reduced government spending to lower the national debt and help combat the economic recession that had followed the sharp rises in oil prices during the 1970s.

During his eight years in office, Reagan mounted a massive attack on the country's major conservation and environmental laws. He:

- Appointed people who came from industries or legal firms that opposed existing federal environmental, resource conservation, and land use legislation and policies to key positions in the Interior Department, BLM, and EPA. President Harry S Truman recognized the dangers of such appointments when he said, "You don't set foxes to watching the chickens just because they have a lot of experience in the hen house."

- Barred established environmental and conservation organizations and leaders from having input into such appointments and into the administration's environmental and resource policies.

- Made the enforcement of existing environmental and resource conservation laws difficult by encouraging drastic budget and staff cuts in enforcement agencies.

- Greatly increased energy and mineral development and cutting of timber by private enterprise on public lands. Often the government sold these public resources at giveaway prices to private corporations, shortchanging the citizens, who jointly own the resources. Such sales also lost revenues that could have been used to reduce the federal debt or to prevent cuts in environmental and resource conservation programs.

- Put ranchers rather than the BLM and the Forest Service back in charge of grazing policy on public lands.

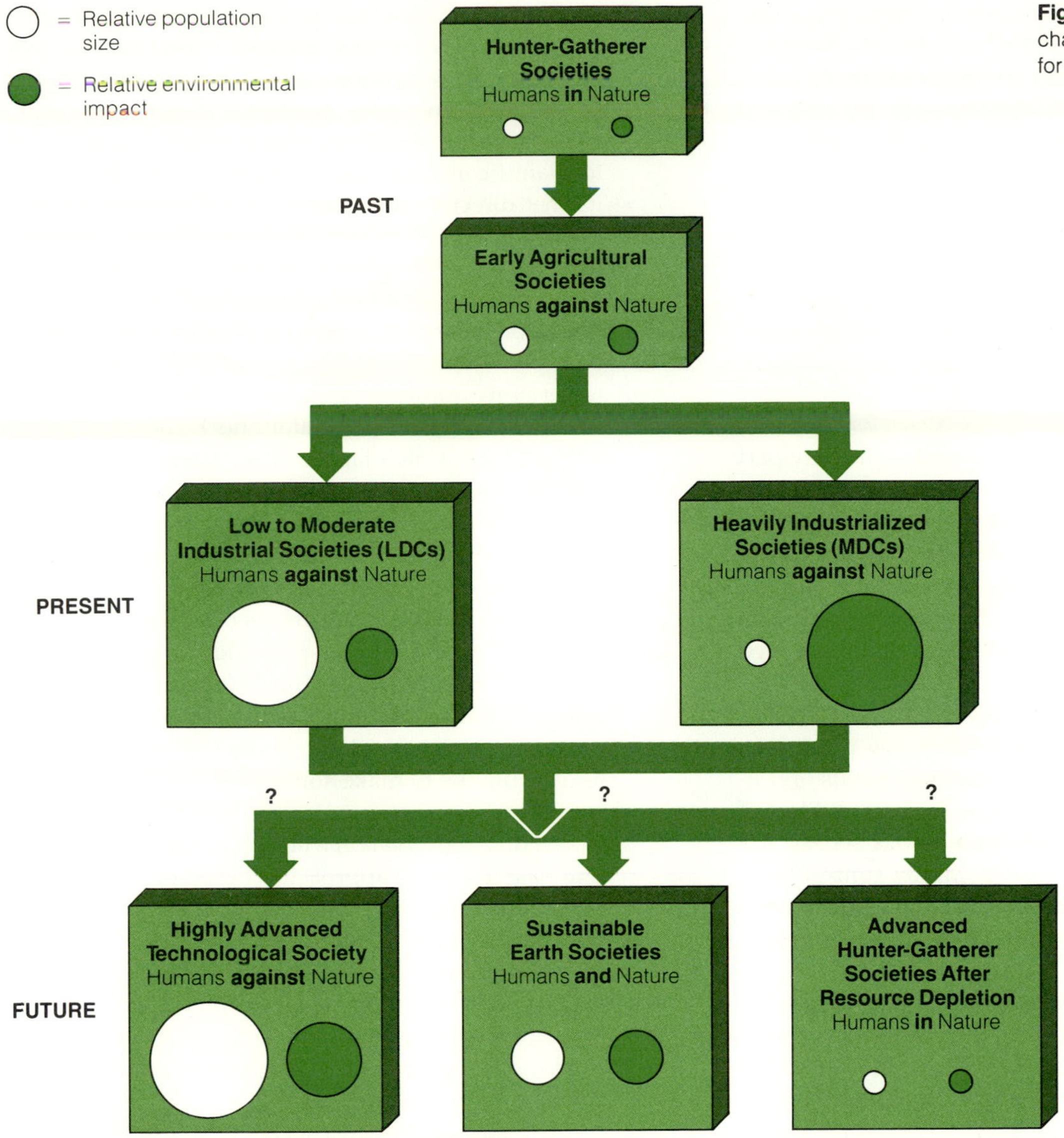

Figure 2-17 Past major cultural changes and some possibilities for the next cultural change.

Legend:
○ = Relative population size
● = Relative environmental impact

PAST

Hunter-Gatherer Societies
Humans **in** Nature

Early Agricultural Societies
Humans **against** Nature

PRESENT

Low to Moderate Industrial Societies (LDCs)
Humans **against** Nature

Heavily Industrialized Societies (MDCs)
Humans **against** Nature

FUTURE

Highly Advanced Technological Society
Humans **against** Nature

Sustainable Earth Societies
Humans **and** Nature

Advanced Hunter-Gatherer Societies After Resource Depletion
Humans **in** Nature

■ Increased the federal budget for nuclear power. This way of producing electricity is still not economically competitive with most other energy alternatives even though taxpayers have given the nuclear industry over $40 billion in subsidies.

■ Cut federal funding for energy conservation by 70% and lowered automobile gas mileage standards.

■ Eliminated tax incentives for encouraging residential solar energy and energy conservation.

■ Drastically cut funding for programs to provide energy conservation and fuel aid for the poor.

■ Reduced funding for research and development on perpetual and renewable energy resources by 85%.

Although Reagan was an immensely popular president, most of the public strongly opposed his environmental and resource policies. These policies were blunted by strong opposition from Congress, public outrage, and legal challenges by environmental and conservation organizations, whose membership soared in this period.

The net effect of the Reagan years was to slow down the momentum for environmental protection and resource conservation built up in the 1970s. Environmental and conservation organizations had to spend much of their time and money fighting off a vigorous attempt to move backwards.

2-5 SOME POSSIBLE FUTURES

The Next Cultural Change Some futurists project that over the next 50 to 75 years we will undergo another major cultural change, resulting in one of several possibilities (Figure 2-17):

- a series of *sustainable-earth societies* throughout the world, consisting of people working with nature to sustain the earth's life-support systems for humans and other species

- a series of *superindustrialized societies* based on major advances in technology that allow people even greater control over nature

- a small number of people in scattered bands trying to survive as *modern hunter-gatherers* in a world polluted and depleted of resources by global nuclear war or excessive industrialization and population growth without adequate resource conservation and environmental protection

An Agenda for the 1990s and Beyond The easy part of the drive to protect the environment and conserve resources is over. So far emphasis has been on protection of human health from damage by a few dozen conventional air and water pollutants. Most of these chemicals can be seen or smelled and are emitted by easily identifiable cars, factories, and other so-called *point sources*.

In the 1990s we need to get much more serious about protecting human health from the potentially harmful effects of trace amounts of thousands of hazardous chemicals in our air, water, and food. Most of these chemicals can't be detected by our senses and are rarely covered by present pollution control laws. Many are emitted into the environment from millions of widely dispersed, hard-to-identify, and hard-to-control *nonpoint sources*.

In the 1990s and beyond we are faced with a set of complex, less visible, widely dispersed, long-term environmental and resource problems. Many of these are global and regional problems such as global warming, ozone depletion, and acid deposition—the fallout of acidic air pollutants onto forests and lakes.

Reducing the degree of global warming will require sharply reducing emissions of carbon dioxide and other gases that can warm the earth's atmosphere. Slowing the depletion of the earth's ozone layer and the global warming requires banning all uses of chlorofluorocarbons (CFCs). Reducing destruction of forests and aquatic life in many lakes by acid deposition will require a sharp reduction in emissions of sulfur dioxide and nitrogen oxide by fossil fuel burning, power plants, industrial plants, and motor vehicles. These important policies will require international agreements and cooperation.

Dealing with these newly recognized long-term environmental threats will not be easy or cheap. It will require a shift in emphasis from output control of pollutants to input control—preventing potential pollutants from entering the environment. As Ben Franklin reminded us a long time ago, "An ounce of prevention is worth a pound of cure."

To get us unhooked from from our present addiction to oil, we will need to greatly increase recycling and reuse of nonrenewable mineral resources, conserve much more energy, and use a mix of perpetual and renewable energy resources. Individuals will have to change consumption habits and other lifestyle habits that directly and indirectly cause resource waste, pollution, and environmental degradation (see Spotlight on p. 45).

Measuring and evaluating short- and long-term risks from a large number of potential pollutants will be expensive and scientifically difficult. Considerable uncertainty and large gaps exist in the scientific data used to make environmental and resource-use decisions. There is also far too little monitoring of environmental conditions. We will have to greatly increase funding for environmental monitoring and for scientific research on environmental and resource problems.

But we don't have unlimited funds to protect the environment. Which hazardous chemicals should get priority attention? How far should we go in reducing the risks? How much of limited federal, state, corporate, and household funds should be used to achieve our goals? Such decisions involve much controversy and require us to make some trade-offs and personal sacrifices.

Wildlife conservation will have to place much greater emphasis on input approaches based on preservation of large natural areas throughout the world, in contrast to our present output approach of protecting a few endangered animal species in zoos and other expensive sanctuaries. An essential part of such a strategy is the urgent need to prevent, or at least slow down, the present rapid depletion of the world's remaining tropical forests.

We also need to increase efforts to restore degraded forests, grasslands, and wetlands. This will require increased funding for the emerging field of *restoration ecology*.

Because pollution, resource conservation, and population policies are largely developed independent of each other, solving a problem in one area can create problems in other areas. We urgently need to develop integrated environmental protection, resource conservation, and population regulation strategies based on recognizing that these problems are interrelated.

We will also have to step up efforts to make international, national, state, and local institutions more responsive to short- and long-term environmental and resource problems. Complaints about delays and excessive paperwork caused by federal environmental and resource conservation bureaucracies are legitimate. Federal bureaucrats often attempt to manage local and regional problems without understanding unique conditions and possible solutions.

Despite such problems, the federal government must still play an important role in undertaking and supporting research to determine environmental risks, establishing national standards and regulations, and intervening where states fail to take action. It is essential that current and future presidents rebuild the morale and expertise of the EPA and the Interior, Agriculture, and Energy departments. Presidents with vision can draw from the vast reservoir of support of the American public for environmental protection and resource conservation. A 1988 *New York Times*-CBS News poll showed that two-thirds of the public agree that "continuing environmental improvement must be made regardless of cost."

Presently states and localities assume most of the responsibility for issuing permits, inspecting and monitoring, enforcement, and other forms of management of environmental and conservation standards. This trend needs to be supported and accelerated by returning more federal tax revenues to the states. Such a shift is possible because most states now have strong and professional environmental protection and resource conservation agencies.

States in turn will have to encourage communities and citizens to develop public and private task forces and other organizations to diagnose local problems and find acceptable solutions. They will also have to educate citizens to support the changes in corporate

---

SPOTLIGHT **Everyone Wants Clean Air and Water, but . . .**

Everyone wants to breathe clean air and drink uncontaminated water. But how much are you willing to pay in taxes to protect the environment and conserve resources? What changes in your lifestyle would you really be willing to make?

These are crucial questions. Why? Because each of us must recognize the truth in Pogo's statement, "We have met the enemy, and it is us," and begin to change our lifestyles accordingly.

People want clean air and most want factories to be inspected and required by the government to install air and water pollution control equipment. Most also want companies that violate air and water pollution control laws to be fined and corporate executives jailed.

But how many people want the same types of laws and standards to apply to their own polluting activities? For example, recent measurements have shown that the air inside most of today's houses, offices, and stores—where people spend most of their time— is more polluted and hazardous than the outside air.

How many people want the nuisance and expense of annual inspections of their homes for indoor air pollution? How many favor being forced to install indoor

air pollution control systems? How many want to be told that they cannot use certain types of building materials and common household chemicals? How many favor laws requiring fireplaces, wood stoves, and oil furnaces to have air pollution controls?

How many people favor much stricter semiannual inspections of air pollution control equipment on their motor vehicles and tough fines for not keeping these systems in good working order. In the United States almost 60% of such equipment on cars and trucks has either been dismantled or is not working properly.

People want clean water. But how many city dwellers support the sharp increases in monthly sewage treatment bills this will require. How many rural dwellers support mandatory annual testing of their well water and septic tank systems? How many want to be told they have to install purification systems when their drinking water is found to be contaminated?

People know that the growing volume of trash is a major problem. But how many support laws that would require them to separate their trash into paper, bottles, cans for recycling, and food wastes for composting? How many insist that we pass laws banning throwa-

way bottles and cans and that we recycle and reuse our containers?

Everyone is against hazardous waste. Thousands of abandoned leaking hazardous-waste dumps, hundreds of thousands of underground storage tanks, and tens of thousands of unlined settling ponds and landfills can contaminate groundwater supplies providing 96% of the drinking water in U.S. rural areas and 20% in urban areas. But how many support the large increase in federal and state taxes needed to clean up these potential sources of pollution?

People also want proper management of radioactive nuclear waste and industrial hazardous waste produced in supplying the electricity, products, and services they use. But how many oppose locating a nuclear waste dump, a hazardous waste incinerator, a landfill, or a recycling plant anywhere near them? How many want to be told that they will be heavily fined if they put a partially filled container of paint thinner, pesticide, cleaning product, or other hazardous waste in their trash or pour it down their drain?

These are the questions and issues we must now face up to if we really care about the earth. How would you answer these questions?

and individual behavior and the increased expenditures needed to meet federal and state pollution standards and resource conservation goals.

In an era of budget deficits it will not be easy to implement much of the environmental and resource conservation agenda of the 1990s and beyond. But failure to insist that these problems be dealt with by local, state, and federal governments and by individual lifestyle changes will lead to long-term environmental and economic grief. We must learn that short-term economic greed eventually leads to long-term economic and environmental grief.

We found our house—the planet—with drinkable, potable water, with good soil to grow food, with clean air to breathe. We at least must leave it in as good a shape as we found it, if not better.

Rev. Jesse Jackson

DISCUSSION TOPICS

1. Those wishing to avoid dealing with environmental and resource problems sometimes argue: "People have always polluted and despoiled this planet, so why all the fuss over pollution and resource conservation? We've survived so far and for most people things have gotten better, not worse." Identify the core of truth in this position and then discuss its serious deficiencies.

2. Explain how in one sense the roots of our present environmental and resource problems and our increased alienation from nature began with the invention of agriculture about 10,000 years ago.

3. Do you think we would be better off if agriculture had never been discovered and we were still hunters and gatherers today? Explain.

4. Make a list of the major benefits and drawbacks of an advanced industrial society such as the United States. Do you feel that the benefits of such a society to its citizens outweigh its drawbacks? Explain. What are the alternatives?

5. Cornucopians believe that continued economic growth and technological innovation in today's industrial societies offer the best way to solve the environmental and resource problems we face. Neo-Malthusians believe that these problems can be effectively dealt with only by changing from a predominantly industrial society to a sustainable-earth society over the next 50 to 75 years. Which position do you support? Why?

6. Do you believe that a cultural change to a sustainable-earth society is possible in the United States over the next 50 to 75 years? What changes, if any, have you made and what changes do you plan to make in your lifestyle to help bring about such a change?

FURTHER READINGS

Borrelli, Peter, ed. 1988. *Crossroads: Environmental Priorities for the Future.* Covelo, Calif.: Island Press.

Carson, Rachel. 1962. *Silent Spring.* Boston: Houghton Mifflin.

Congressional Quarterly. 1983. *The Battle for Natural Resources.* Washington, D.C.: Congressional Quarterly, Inc.

Conservation Foundation. 1987. *State of the Environment: A View Toward the Nineties.* Washington, D.C.: Conservation Foundation.

Fox, Stephen. 1981. *John Muir and His Legacy: The American Conservation Movement.* Boston: Little, Brown.

Graham, Frank. 1971. *Man's Dominion: The Story of Conservation in America.* New York: M. Evans.

Hartzog, George B., Jr. 1988. *Battling for the National Parks.* Mt. Kisco, N.Y.: Moyer Bell.

Hays, Samuel P. 1987. *Beauty, Health, and Permanence: Environmental Politics in the United States 1955–1985.* New York: Cambridge University Press.

Hughes, J. Donald. 1975. *Ecology in Ancient Civilizations.* Albuquerque, N.M.: University of New Mexico Press.

Hyams, Edward. 1976. *Soils and Civilization.* New York: Harper & Row.

Leopold, Aldo. 1949. *A Sand County Almanac.* New York: Oxford University Press.

Maczak, Antoni, and William R. Parker, eds. 1978. *Natural Resources in European History.* Washington, D.C.: Resources for the Future.

Marsh, George Perkins. 1864. *Man and Nature.* New York: Scribners.

Osborn, Fairfield. 1948. *Our Plundered Planet.* Boston: Little, Brown.

Petulla, Joseph M. 1988. *American Environmental History,* 2nd ed. Columbus, Ohio: Merrill.

Repetto, Robert. 1986. *World Enough and Time.* New Haven, Conn.: Yale University Press.

Repetto, Robert, ed. 1986. *The Global Possible: Resources, Development, and the New Century.* New Haven, Conn.: Yale University Press.

Roe, Frank G. 1970. *The North American Buffalo.* Toronto: University of Toronto Press.

Sears, Paul B. 1980. *Deserts on the March.* Norman: University of Oklahoma Press.

Shanks, Bernard. 1984. *This Land Is Your Land.* San Francisco: Sierra Club Books.

Thibodeau, Francis R., and Herman H. Field, eds. 1984. *Sustaining Tomorrow: A Strategy for World Conservation and Development.* Hanover, N.H.: University Press of New England.

Udall, Stewart L. 1963. *The Quiet Crisis.* New York: Holt, Rinehart & Winston (1988 reprint and updating: Gibbs, Smith, Layton, Utah).

Vig, Norman J., and Michael J. Craft. 1984. *Environmental Policy in the 1980s.* Washington, D.C.: Congressional Quarterly Press.

Winner, Langdon. 1986. *The Whale and the Reactor: A Search for Limits in an Age of High Technology.* Chicago: University of Chicago Press.

Zaslowsky, Dyan, and Wilderness Society. 1986. *These American Lands.* New York: Henry Holt.

CHAPTER 3

Economics, Politics, and Ethics of Resource Use and Management

General Questions and Issues

1. What are the major types of economic goods and resources?

2. What types of economic systems are found throughout the world?

3. What is economic growth and how can it be redirected and managed to sustain the earth's life-support systems?

4. How do public and private political decisions affect resource use and environmental quality?

5. How can political and economic systems be used to regulate resource use and reduce environmental degradation and pollution?

6. What worldview is needed to achieve a sustainable-earth society?

As important as technology, politics, law, and ethics are to the pollution question, all such approaches are bound to have disappointing results, for they ignore the primary fact that pollution is primarily an economic problem, which must be understood in economic terms.

Larry E. Ruff

Life forces us to make trade-offs or choices to get as many of our needs and wants as possible and to have as much control over our lives as possible. We do this individually and in groups by making *economic and political decisions.*

The basic economic problem is that we cannot use the world's limited resources to produce enough material goods and services to satisfy everyone's unlimited wants. Therefore, individuals, businesses, and societies must make **economic decisions** about what goods and services to produce, how to produce them, how much to produce, and how to distribute them to people. **Economics** is the study of how individuals and groups make such decisions about how to meet their needs and wants. Because producing and using anything has some harmful impact on the environment, economic decisions also affect the quality of the environment.

Private politics is the process by which we try to gain power to satisfy our physical and emotional needs and wants within family, workplace, and other nongovernment groups. **Public politics** is the process by which individuals and groups try to influence or control the policies and actions of governments of the local, state, national, or international community.

Public politics plays a major role in regulating the world's economic systems and influencing economic decisions. Public political decisions can also help prevent the degradation of commonly owned or shared resources such as air, water, wildlife, and public land.

Individual and public economic and political decisions are built around our **worldview**—how we think the world works and what we think our role is—and our **ethics**—what we believe to be right or wrong behavior. In this chapter we will see how individual and group economic and political decisions and worldviews interact to affect resource use and environmental quality.

3-1 ECONOMIC GOODS AND RESOURCES

Economic Goods, Needs, and Wants An **economic good** is any material item or service that gives people satisfaction and whose present or ultimate supply is

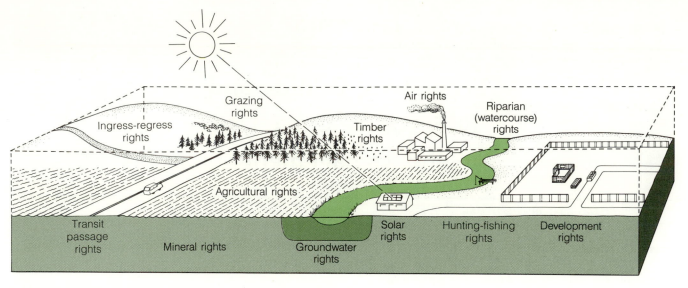

Figure 3-1 Types of legal rights associated with private land ownership.

limited. Some of these goods are *material items* like food, gasoline, cars, and TV sets. Others are *services*—intangible things such as medical care, education, defense, and cleaning. An **economy** is a system of production, distribution, and consumption of economic goods.

The types and amounts of certain economic goods—food, clothing, water, oxygen, shelter—that you must have to survive and to stay healthy are your **economic needs**. Anything beyond this is an **economic want**. What you believe you need and want is influenced by the customs and conventions of the society you live in and your level of affluence.

Private and Public Goods Any economic good that can be owned and enjoyed on a private, or exclusive, basis is a **private good.** Such goods can be produced and sold in units. Most things you buy in the marketplace are private goods.

On the other hand, **public goods** cannot be divided and sold in units, and can be enjoyed by anybody. National defense is an example. Once provided for any citizen by a given level of expenditure, it is available to all. Other examples are police forces, fire departments, courts of law, public parks, public education, clean air, clean water, beautiful scenery, flood control projects, and wild plants and animals.

However, the funds available to supply a public good may not meet the overall demand for the good. For example, there is often not enough money to provide the police protection, courts, parks, education and other public goods that the population needs. Then these public good behave like private goods. One more unit used by me means there is one less unit available to others.

Private producers have little incentive to provide public goods and will undersupply them. Thus, governments step in and use tax revenues to provide public goods or to pay others to supply these goods. With limited tax revenues the government can't satisfy all needs and wants for public goods.

Scarcity and Price All private economic goods are scarce. Otherwise they would cost us nothing. The **price** of a good usually reflects how scarce it is and how much it is valued by people.

But price is not always a good indicator of how scarce a good is. A producer of a good who has complete control over its supply—a **monopoly**—can reduce the supply to create artificial scarcity and raise its price. When a few large firms dominate the market for a good, they have an **oligopoly.** If these firms agree to set the price for the good they produce, they have the same effect as a monopoly. When countries that are the major suppliers of a good get together to regulate the supply and determine the price of a good such as oil, they form a **cartel.** OPEC is an example.

Governments can use tax dollars to encourage production or conservation of a good. They can do this by giving tax breaks, payments, and other *subsidies* to suppliers of a good. This reduces production costs, encourages suppliers to produce or conserve the good, and can lower the price consumers pay for the good. But this artificially low price reduces consumers' incentive to conserve this resource.

A government can also add taxes to the price of a good that is being overproduced or that is causing unacceptable environmental problems. This encourages consumers to conserve, extends the supply, and stimulates the search for a substitute.

Economic Resources The things used in an economy to produce material goods and services are called **economic resources** or **factors of production.** They are usually divided into three groups:

1. **Natural resources:** resources produced by the earth's natural processes. It includes the area of the earth's solid surface, nutrients and minerals in the soil and deeper layers of the earth's crust, wild and domesticated plants and animals, water, air, and nature's waste disposal and recycling services.

2. **Capital or intermediate goods:** manufactured items made from natural resources and used as inputs to produce and distribute economic goods and services bought by consumers. It includes tools, machinery, equipment, factory buildings, and transportation and distribution facilities.

3. **Labor:** the physical and mental talents of people. *Workers* sell their time and talents for *wages. Entrepreneurs* and *investors* assume the risk. *Managers* take responsibility for combining the natural resources, capital goods, and workers to produce an economic good. *Profit* is the reward entrepreneurs and investors get for taking the risks for supplying an economic good they believe people need or want. If they guess wrong, they lose the time and money they have invested and earn no profit.

Note two important characteristics of economic resources. First, using and combining them depends on the ability of people to discover ways to extract raw materials from the earth and convert them to economic goods. Second, virtually everything we have or will have comes ultimately from the sun and the earth.

Private, Common, and Public Property Resources

Any resource owned by individuals or groups of individuals is a **private property resource**. People tend to maintain and improve resources they own. If you own a house, you have a strong incentive to paint, repair, and improve it. These improvements help maintain or increase the economic value of the house.

There are several types of private ownership for a resource such as land (Figure 3-1). The most complete form of private ownership is the fee simple absolute. This gives the titleholder rights over the land and its resources "from the center of the earth to the heavens above."

A **common property resource** is one to which people have virtually free and unmanaged access. Most are potentially renewable resources. Examples are air, fish in parts of the ocean not under the control of a coastal country, wildlife in areas where there are no

---

SPOTLIGHT Tragedy of the Commons

Abuse and depletion of common property resources has been called the **tragedy of the commons.** This tragedy occurs because each user reasons, "If I don't use this resource, someone else will. Anyway, the little bit I use or the little bit of pollution I create is not enough to matter."

When the number of users is small and the supply is large, there is no problem. But eventually the cumulative effect of many people trying to maximize their use of a common property resource depletes or degrades the usable supply. Then no one can make a profit or otherwise benefit from the resource.

In terms of short-term profits, it makes sense for whalers to deplete a common property resource. Whales are not a highly profitable long-term investment because they reproduce too slowly. It costs a lot to maintain and replace whaling ships, buy fuel, pay crews, and market whale products over a long time. The most profitable approach for whalers is to harvest whales as quickly as possible until it costs too much to harvest the few that are left and invest the profits in another business.

The problem is that whales are more than just another unit of production. They are potentially renewable resources that have other public good values as part of the earth's biological diversity that are not included in the economic decisions of whalers.

---

controls on hunting and harvesting, the carbon dioxide content of the lower atmosphere, and the ozone content of the stratosphere.

Anyone has a right to use or abuse common property resources. Thus, they can easily be polluted or overharvested and converted from renewable to slowly renewable or nonrenewable resources (see Spotlight above).

Other resources, called **public property resources**, fall somewhere between private and common property resources. Such resources are owned jointly by all people of a country, state, or locality but are managed for them by the government. Examples are public lands such as national and state forests, wildlife refuges, parks, and areas protected from most uses except hiking and camping in the national wilderness preservation system.

3-2 ECONOMIC SYSTEMS

An **economic system** is a method that a group of people use to choose what goods and services to produce, how to produce them, how much to produce, and how to distribute them to people. There are four general ways to answer these basic economic questions: traditional, pure market, pure command, and mixed economic systems.

Traditional Economic System: Custom Decides In a **traditional economic system** people use past customs and traditions to answer the basic economic questions. Often these systems are **subsistence economies,** where families, tribes, or other groups produce only enough goods to meet their basic survival needs, with little or no surplus left over for sale or trade.

Traditional systems are found in tribal communities, which are rapidly disappearing. Decisions about what plants to gather, what crops to plant, what animals to hunt, who will do each of these tasks, and how food will be distributed are based on what the tribe has done in the past. Everyone's role is understood and fixed by custom. Upward economic mobility by individuals is discouraged and is rare. Technological changes and innovations that clash with tradition and threaten social order are also discouraged.

Societies with nontraditional economies also make decisions based on tradition. For example, male domination has been a tradition so far in almost all economies.

Pure Market Economic System: The Market Decides In a **pure market economic system,** also known as **pure capitalism,** all economic decisions are made in *markets,* where buyers (demanders) and sellers (suppliers) of economic goods freely interact without government or other interference.

Since people don't have the time, ability, or money to make all the things they need, suppliers specialize in producing particular goods. This gives the suppliers money to buy the specialized goods they need or want.

In its pure form this is a *produce-or-die distribution system.* Only those who receive wages and produce can afford to buy goods. Those who don't produce anything have no income and can't buy anything. They starve to death.

This system is based on private property, freedom of choice, and pure competition. All economic resources are owned by private individuals and private institutions, rather than by the government. All private persons or businesses are free to keep their earnings and the things they buy with their earnings. They can also use, sell, or give away what they own without any restrictions.

All buying and selling is based on **pure competition,** in which many small buyers and many small sellers act independently. No seller or buyer is large enough to control the supply, demand, or price of a good. Anyone is allowed to produce a product and attempt to sell it to others. But to participate, sellers and buyers must accept the going market price.

The major argument for the pure market system is that resources are distributed among those who can afford to buy them as cheaply as possible. A second argument for this system is that it emphasizes personal freedom. No one can tell you what you must buy or what you can and cannot have if you can afford the going market price.

Supply, Demand, and Market Equilibrium in the Pure Market System Economic decisions in the pure market system are governed by interactions of demand, supply, and price. **Market demand** is how much of an economic good consumers are willing and able to buy at different prices in a given time period.

Suppose that price is the only factor affecting the market demand for an economic good. Then, as its price rises, the quantity demanded falls. As its price falls, the quantity demanded increases. This inverse (opposite) relationship between price and market demand for an economic good is called the **law of demand.** Plotting this information on a graph gives a *demand curve* for an economic good such as gasoline over a period of time (Figure 3-2).

Market supply is how much of an economic good producers are willing and able to produce and sell at different prices in a given period of time. If price is the only factor affecting the market supply of an economic good, then as its price rises, suppliers will try to supply more. As its price falls, the quantity supplied will drop. This direct relationship between price and market supply for an economic good is called the **law of supply.** This information can be plotted as a *supply curve* for an economic good such as gasoline over a period of time (Figure 3-2).

In a pure market system buyers want to pay as little as possible for an economic good and sellers want to get as high a price as possible. **Market equilibrium** occurs when the quantity supplied equals the quantity demanded and the price is no higher than buyers are willing to pay and no lower than sellers are willing to accept. If price, supply, and demand are the only factors involved, the demand and supply curves for an economic good intersect at the *market equilibrium point* (Figure 3-2). This point gives the price buyers are willing to pay for an economic good and the amount suppliers are willing to supply at this price.

But things are not this simple. Factors other than price affect the supply of and demand for a good. These factors shift the original supply and demand curves to the right or the left, upsetting the market

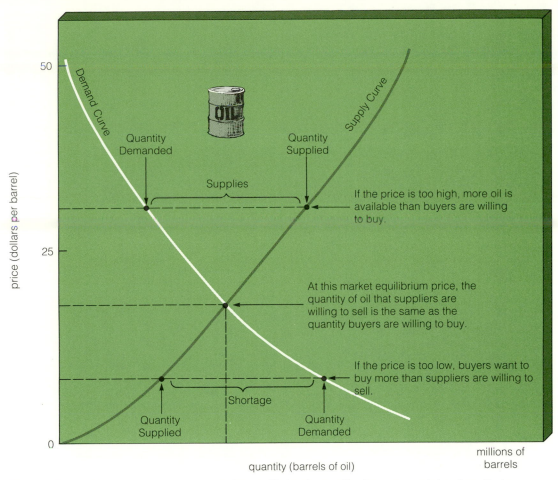

Figure 3-2 Monthly supply, demand, and market equilibrium for gasoline in a pure market system. If price, supply, and demand are the only factors involved, the market equilibrium point occurs where the demand and supply curves intersect.

equilibrium and establishing new equilibrium points.

Factors that increase demand shift the demand curve to the right (Figure 3-3), and those that decrease demand shift it to the left. Examples are changes in the number of buyers, in buyer taste, in average income, and in prices of related goods. The supply curve for an economic good like gasoline can be shifted to the right or left by changes in technology, in production costs, in taxes, in prices of related goods, and in the number of suppliers (Figure 3-4).

Usually, both curves shift (Figure 3-5). If buyers want to buy more gasoline than suppliers have available, the price rises. The high price brings bigger profits, encouraging suppliers to produce and sell more gasoline and perhaps attracting more suppliers. But this increase in suppliers may increase the supply so much that more is available than buyers want. Then the surplus supply pushes the price of gasoline back down.

Pure Command Economic System: The Government Decides In a **pure command economic system,** or **totally planned economy,** all economic decisions are made by the government. It determines what economic goods are produced, how they are produced, how much of each is produced, how much each will cost, and how they are distributed.

The pure command economy is based on the belief that government control is the most efficient way to produce, use, and distribute scarce resources. Socialism and its purer form, communism, are types of command economic systems.

Mixed Economic Systems: The Real World None of the world's countries have a pure market economy or a pure command economy. Instead they have **mixed economic systems** that fall somewhere between the pure market and pure command systems and have some elements of tradition (Figure 3-6).

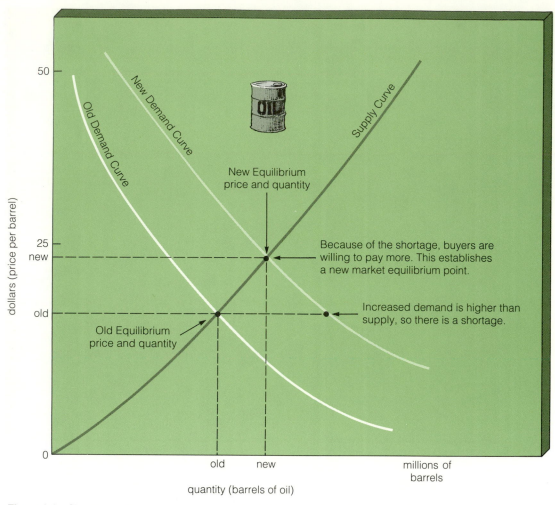

Figure 3-3 Short-term effects of an increase in demand for gasoline. Demand can increase because of more drivers, a switch to bigger cars with lower fuel efficiency, more spendable income for travel, or decreased use of mass transit. The original demand curve shown in Figure 3-2 shifts to the right. The increased demand creates a temporary shortage. Buyers are then willing to pay more. This establishes a new market equilibrium point. A similar situation occurs if the demand for gasoline decreases because of fewer drivers, a switch to more fuel-efficient cars, less spendable income for travel, or increased use of mass transit. In that case the original demand curve shifts to the left. Decreased demand creates a temporary surplus. Then competition stimulates sellers to charge less, until the price reaches a new market equilibrium point.

Why? Because pure markets are not able to provide all community needs. Government intervention is needed to:

- promote and maintain competitive markets by preventing formation of monopolies

- provide national security and other public goods

- promote fairness (equity) through the redistribution of income and wealth, especially to people unable to meet their basic needs

- ensure economic stability by preventing cycles of boom and depression that commonly occur in a pure market system

- help compensate owners for large-scale destruction of assets by floods, earthquakes, hurricanes, and other natural disasters

- prevent or reduce pollution

- manage public land resources

The Soviet Union, China, Cuba, and most eastern European countries have mixed economies that blend socialism and capitalism with emphasis on socialism (Figure 3-6). In these countries the central government owns most resources and makes most economic decisions.

However, they have recently introduced some elements of capitalism to give individuals more incentive to produce, to increase production efficiency, and to overcome bureaucratic inefficiency. For example, farmers in China are required to produce a certain amount of food for general distribution. But anything they produce beyond this quota can be kept for private use or sold for personal profit.

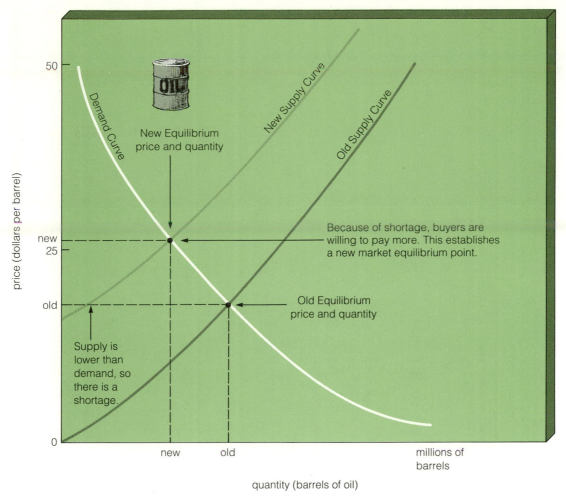

Figure 3-4 Short-term effects of a decrease in the supply of gasoline. A decrease can occur if the cost of finding, extracting, and refining oil increases or if existing oil deposits are economically depleted and not replaced by new discoveries. Also, if oil producers expect higher prices in the future, they may lower present production with the hope of making larger profits later. The original supply curve shown in Figure 3-2 shifts to the left. During the shortage buyers are willing to pay more for gasoline. Thus, the price reaches a higher market equilibrium point. A similar situation occurs if the supply increases. In that case the original supply curve shifts to the right, reflecting a temporary surplus. Then competition stimulates sellers to charge less, and the price moves down to a new market equilibrium point.

Some government regulation of an economy is needed. But too much can stifle innovation and competition, increase inefficiency, and waste money. Black (illegal) markets are also found in countries with strict government control. These are major reasons most command economic systems mix in some capitalism.

3-3 ECONOMIC GROWTH, PRODUCTIVITY, AND EXTERNAL COSTS

Gross National Product and Economic Growth The **gross national product (GNP)** is the market value in current dollars of all goods and services produced by an economy during a year. To get a better idea of how much economic output is actually growing or declining, economists use the **real GNP**: the gross national product minus *inflation*—any increase in the average price level of goods and services.

All market and centrally planned mixed economies in the world today seek to increase their economic growth. **Economic growth** is an increase in the real value of all goods and services produced by an economy. In other words, it is an increase in real GNP. Economic growth creates a larger economic pie. However, you and others care little about how much bigger the pie is if you are not getting a bigger slice.

To show how the average person's slice of the economic pie is changing, economists calculate the **average per capita real GNP**: the real GNP divided by the total population. If population expands faster than economic growth, the average per capita (per person)

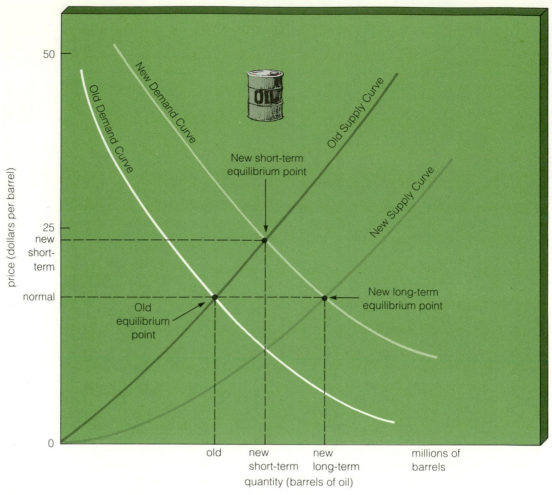

Figure 3-5 An increase in consumer demand for gasoline can eventually lead to an increase in supply. A short-term increase in demand creates a shortage and establishes a new, short-term market equilibrium point at a higher price. If enough oil is available, the higher price pulls more producers into the market and increases the supply. Competition between suppliers can then lead to a surplus. This pushes the price back down and establishes a new, long-term market equilibrium point. These are only a few of the many complex interactions of supply, demand, and market equilibrium in a pure market economy.

GNP falls. The pie has grown but the average slice per person has shrunk.

Between 1972 and 1988 the average per capita GNP in the United States has increased more than three-fold. But adjusted for inflation, the average real per capita GNP (in 1972 dollars) rose only slightly during this period. The average slice has stayed about the same.

GNP and the Quality of Life Most governments use real GNP and average per capita real GNP as measures of their society's well-being. But these indicators do not and were never intended to measure social welfare or quality of life. Instead, they measure the speed at which an economy is running.

Real GNP and real per capita GNP can give a general picture of the relative wealth of countries and in some cases the average living standards of their peo-

ple. But this picture is distorted. Why? One reason is that these indicators include the values of both beneficial and harmful goods and services.

For example, producing more cigarettes raises the real GNP. But it also causes more cancer and heart disease. Ironically, these diseases increase the real GNP still further by increasing health and insurance costs. But the real GNP figures tell us nothing about the deaths and decreased quality of life suffered by the disease victims. They also don't tell us how resources and income are distributed among the people in a country—how many people have a large slice and how many have only a few crumbs of the economic pie.

Indicators of Social Well-Being What we need are indicators that distinguish between good and bad economic goods and indicate who receives the "goods" and who receives the "bads." For example, if you get

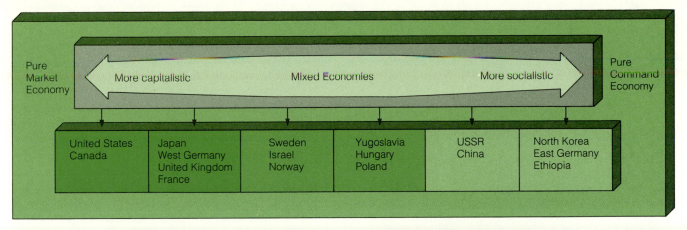

Figure 3-6 Countries throughout the world have mixed economic systems that fall somewhere between the extremes of a pure market system and a pure command system.

United States Canada	Japan West Germany United Kingdom France	Sweden Israel Norway	Yugoslavia Hungary Poland	USSR China	North Korea East Germany Ethiopia

sick from pollution, your medical bills are included in the GNP as a "good."

If GNP measures "goods" *and* "bads," why not subtract the "bads" to get an estimate of the annual change in social well-being? Economists William Nordhaus and James Tobin have developed an indicator called **net economic welfare (NEW)** to estimate the annual change in quality of life in a country.

Nordhaus and Tobin calculate the NEW by putting a price tag on pollution and other "negative" goods and services included in the GNP—those that do not improve the quality of life. The costs of these negative factors are then subtracted from the GNP to give the NEW. The values of household services—cleaning, cooking, repairs—that people do without pay are also added. These services contribute to life quality but do not show up in the GNP.

The NEW can then be divided by a country's population to estimate the **average per capita net economic welfare.** These indicators can then be adjusted for inflation. Applying this indicator to the United States shows that since 1940 the average real NEW per person has risen at about half the rate of the average real GNP per person.

The NEW was developed in 1972, but is still not widely used. One reason is that putting a price tag on the "bads" is not easy and is controversial. Another reason is that some politicians prefer using the real GNP per person because it can make people think they are better off than they are.

Social factors can also be used to evaluate average life quality in a country or part of a country. The Overseas Development Council has devised the *physical quality of life indicator (PQLI)*, based on three social indicators—average life expectancy, infant mortality, and literacy. But this indicator is also not widely used.

Economist Kenneth Boulding suggested indicators to measure progress toward a sustainable-earth society. One indicator would measure the value of goods and services based on sustainable use of perpetual and renewable resources and on increased recycling and reuse of nonrenewable resources. A second indicator would represent the value of goods and services based on the throwaway use of nonrenewable resources with little or no recycling or reuse. Progress toward a sustainable-earth society would be indicated by an increase in the first indicator over the value of the second indicator.

To some critics, it is inhumane and unethical for governments not to regularly use a combination of social indicators. Social indicators, like all indicators, are not perfect. But they are better than GNP, which is not designed to measure life and environmental quality. Without them we know too little about what is happening to people and the environment and what needs to be done. Social indicators also give us better ways to find out what works.

Productivity Growth: Doing More with Less There are several ways to increase economic growth. One is to produce more goods and services by using more of the factors of production (natural resources, capital, labor). This is the supply-side, or produce-more, approach.

A production increase can be brought about by an increase in population size—more people means more potential workers and consumers. It will also occur if there is an increase in average output and consumption of goods by each person. To conservationists this "growth-mania," based on the idea that all economic growth is good, is wasteful and harmful. It does not distinguish between the production of "bads" and "goods" (see Pro/Con on p. 56).

Another way to increase production is to increase productivity by finding more efficient ways to use the factors of production. **Productivity** is a measure of the

Should Economic Growth Be Unlimited or Redirected?

Proponents of unlimited economic growth argue that it is:

■ The best way to increase material abundance and raise average standards of living. If the pie keeps growing, there is a better chance that the size of each person's slice will also grow.

■ The best cure for poverty. As long as the economic pie is growing, more wealth can "trickle down" to the world's poor.

■ Needed to provide money for environmental protection. The best way to reduce pollution is to control pollution, not economic growth.

Most critics of unlimited economic growth are not against all economic growth. Instead, they believe growth should be redirected to produce things that reduce environmental pollution and degradation, that conserve resources, and that improve life quality. At the same time, we should move toward a stable world population through improved education, infant care, health, status of women, and family planning.

These critics counter some of the conventional arguments for unlimited economic growth as follows:

■ Directed—not unlimited—economic growth is the best way to raise average living standards and help the poor.

■ The "trickle down" idea may sound good on paper, but much too little trickles down. Despite decades of worldwide economic growth, the gap in average real GNP per person between the rich and the poor is growing (Figure 1-10, p. 16).

■ We need to maximize the average real per capita NEW, not the average real per capita GNP. Economists agree that GNP is not designed to measure changes in the quality of life. But so far they have not been successful in persuading most countries to use various available quality-of-life indicators. This is an area where economists and conservationists should join forces.

What do you think?

duction by making better use of what we have—doing more with what we have. This allows lower prices, more effective competition, higher profits, and a higher average standard of living.

Improving productivity without increasing consumption conserves more resources and helps protect the environment more than simply increasing production or output. Nevertheless, increasing productivity will not solve all our resource and environmental problems. We also need to emphasize increasing the production of goods and services that benefit the health and well-being of people and the earth.

New technology is one key to increasing economic productivity. For example, computer-run, robot production machines can work continuously under conditions that would be harmful to people. Such innovations require large investments in research and development and education. A high national savings rate is also needed to provide for investment to increase productivity.

Another key factor is a low interest rate on borrowed capital. Any country with a large national debt tends to have high interest rates. A large part of the government's tax income must be used to pay interest on the debt. This leaves less money for investment in productivity. Interest rates remain high to encourage domestic and foreign investors to keep lending the government money to make up the difference between what it takes in and spends each year.

The United States now spends only 1.6% of its GNP on non-military research and development, about half the percentage of most other industrialized countries. Between 1980 and 1988 government spending on civilian research and development adjusted for inflation fell by 24%. About 13% of the American work force is functionally illiterate, compared to only 0.5% in Japan, accounting in part for Japan's higher productivity. Since 1970 there has been a significant drop in the number of Americans pursuing careers in the science and technology needed to increase productivity.

The United States saves only 2% of its national income, compared to an average of 11% in other MDCs. Between 1981 and 1989 the United States went from being the world's largest lender of money to the world's largest borrower of money—25% of it from other countries. Since 1986 almost 25% of the annual federal budget has been used to pay interest on the national debt, compared to only 10% between 1950 and 1979. Many economists warn that the country is sitting on a $2.5 trillion debt bomb whose timer is steadily ticking away. Each day the United States falls $400 million deeper in debt.

Low national savings and a huge debt are major reasons why the real cost of capital investment funds in the United States in 1985 was 6%, compared to only 1.5% in Japan. This penalizes U.S. businesses that invest in long-term growth and productivity and

output of economic goods and services produced by the input of the factors of production (natural resources, capital goods, and labor).

Increasing productivity means getting more output from the same or less input of the factors of pro-

encourages Japanese businesses to do so. Thus, it is not surprising that annual productivity growth in the United States has dropped sharply since 1970, with a slight improvement in the mid-1980s.

Internal and External Costs   The price you pay for a car reflects the costs of building and operating the factory, raw materials, labor, marketing, shipping, and company and dealer profits. After you buy the car, you also have to pay for gasoline, maintenance, and repair. All these direct costs, paid for by the seller and buyer of an economic good, are called **internal costs.**

Making, distributing, and using any economic good also involve what economists call **externalities.** These are social benefits ("goods") and social costs ("bads") outside the market process. They are not included in the market price of an economic good or service. For example, if a car dealer builds an aesthetically pleasing sales building, this is an **external benefit** to other people at no cost to them.

On the other hand, when a factory emits pollutants into the environment, their harmful effects are an **external cost** passed on to society and in some cases future generations.

The external costs of our love affair with the automobile are many. Pollution from making cars and driving them and accidents caused by unsafe cars harm people and kill some of them unnecessarily. This means that car insurance, health insurance, and medical bills go up for everyone. Air pollution from cars also kills or weakens some types of trees, raising the price of lumber, paper, and this textbook.

Taxes may also go up. Why? Because the public may demand that the government spend a lot of money to regulate the land, air, and water pollution and degradation caused by producing and using cars and by mining and processing the raw materials used to make them.

Because these harmful costs are external and hence aren't included in the market price, you don't connect them with the car or type of car you are driving. But as a consumer and taxpayer, you pay these hidden costs sooner or later.

If you use a car, you can pass many other external costs on to society. You increase these costs when you throw trash out of a car, drive a car that gets poor gas mileage and thus adds more pollution per mile than a more efficient car, dismantle or don't maintain a car's air pollution control device, drive with a noisy muffler, don't keep your motor tuned, and wash your car when water is scarce. You don't pay directly for these harmful activities. But you and others pay indirectly in the form of higher taxes, higher health costs, higher health insurance, and higher cleaning bills.

Internalizing External Costs   As long as it pays to pollute, deplete, degrade, and waste, few people are

going to volunteer to change—to commit economic suicide. Suppose you own a company and believe that it is wrong to pollute the environment any more than can be handled by the earth's natural processes. If you voluntarily install expensive pollution controls and your competitors don't, your product will cost more. Your profits would decline and your firm would stagnate compared with competing firms. Sooner or later you'll probably go bankrupt and your employees will lose their jobs.

A general way to deal with the problem of external costs is for the government to force producers to include all or most of them in the initial price of all economic goods. Then the price of an economic good would be its **true cost:** its internal costs plus its short- and long-term external costs. This is what economists call *internalizing the external costs.*

Internalizing external costs requires government action. Why? Because few people are going to increase their cost of doing business unless their competitors have to do it. Government intervention since 1968 has helped internalize some of the external costs of pollution. For example, factories are now required to install equipment to reduce their emissions of certain pollutants they discharge into the air and water, and cars now must have air pollution control equipment. But this job is only partly done, and we keep discovering new external costs.

What would happen if we internalized enough of the external costs of pollution and waste to achieve more optimum levels of pollution and resource use? Economic growth would be redirected. We would increase the beneficial parts of the GNP, decrease the harmful parts, increase production of beneficial goods, and raise the NEW.

On the other hand, some things you like would not be available anymore because they would cost producers so much to make that few people could afford to buy them. You would pay more for most things because their market prices would be closer to their true costs. But everything would be "up front"— external costs would no longer be hidden. You would have the information you need to make informed economic decisions.

Moreover, real prices wouldn't always be higher. Some things could even get cheaper. Internalizing external costs stimulates producers to find ways to cut costs by increasing productivity. Doing so helps them compete with producers in countries where external costs are not internalized.

Internalizing external costs makes so much sense you might be wondering why it's not more widely done. One reason is that many producers of harmful and wasteful goods fear they would have to charge so much that they couldn't stay in business or would have to give up government subsidies that have helped hide the external costs.

Another problem is that it's not easy to put a price tag on all the harmful effects of making and using an economic good. People disagree on the values they attach to various costs and benefits. But making difficult choices about resource use is what economics and politics is all about. To see how to do this, we must have some understanding of how politics and government work and how they interact with economic systems and environmental ethics.

3-4 PUBLIC AND PRIVATE POLITICS

Reaction-to-Crisis Public Politics Public politics is concerned with the distribution of resources and benefits—who gets what, when, and how. Because there is always competition for scarce resources to satisfy unlimited wants, decision makers in democratic governments must deal with an array of conflicting groups. Each special-interest group is asking for resources or

---

SPOTLIGHT **The American Political System: Muddling Through**

The writers of the U.S. Constitution wanted to develop a political system strong enough to provide security and order and to protect liberty and property . They wanted to do this without giving too much power to the federal government.

Therefore, the Constitution established three power-sharing branches of the federal government—legislative, executive, and judicial (Figure 3-7). These branches are connected and controlled by a series of checks and balances to prevent one branch from gaining too much power. Once federal laws are passed, they are supposed to be implemented and enforced by various bureaucratic agencies in the executive

branch of the federal government (Figure 3-8) and by the Justice Department.

The government established by the Constitution was not designed for efficiency. Instead it was designed for consensus and accommodation to promote survival and adaptation through gradual change. By staying as close to the middle of the road as possible, the government attempts to steer its way through crises. Ralph Waldo Emerson once said, "Democracy is a raft which will never sink, but then your feet are always in the water."

Despite serious shortcomings in the U.S. political system, environmental and resource conservation laws and agencies have improved the quality of the environment and

prevented some forms of resource degradation, as discussed in Section 2-4. On a per capita basis, few other countries spend as much as the United States does to protect the environment.

Thus, the system is muddling through. Some analysts believe that the U.S. political-economic system is working reasonably well and no fundamental changes need to be made. "If it's not broken, don't fix it," they say. Others think the system must undergo changes that will improve its ability to deal with, anticipate, or prevent the growing number of regional, national, and global environmental and resource problems we face today. What do you think?

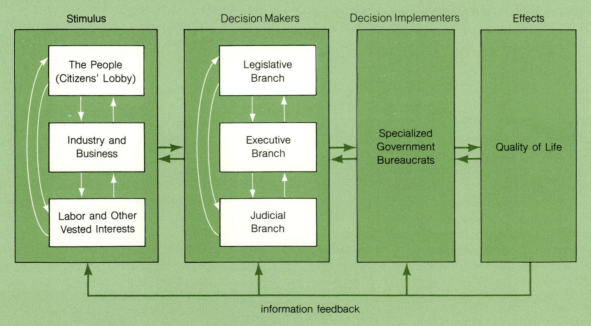

Figure 3-7 Crude model of the U.S. political system.

money or relief from taxes to help purchase or control more of certain resources. Interest groups that are highly organized and well funded usually have the most influence.

Environmental quality and resource conservation are only two of the problems decision-makers face. Others include an adequate national defense, a strong economy, a healthy and adequately fed population, interest on the national debt, and care for the elderly, sick, and poor.

Political systems are designed to bring about gradual or incremental change, not revolutionary change. Rapid change is difficult because of the distribution of power among different branches of government, conflicts among interest groups, conflicting information from experts, and lack of money (see Spotlight below).

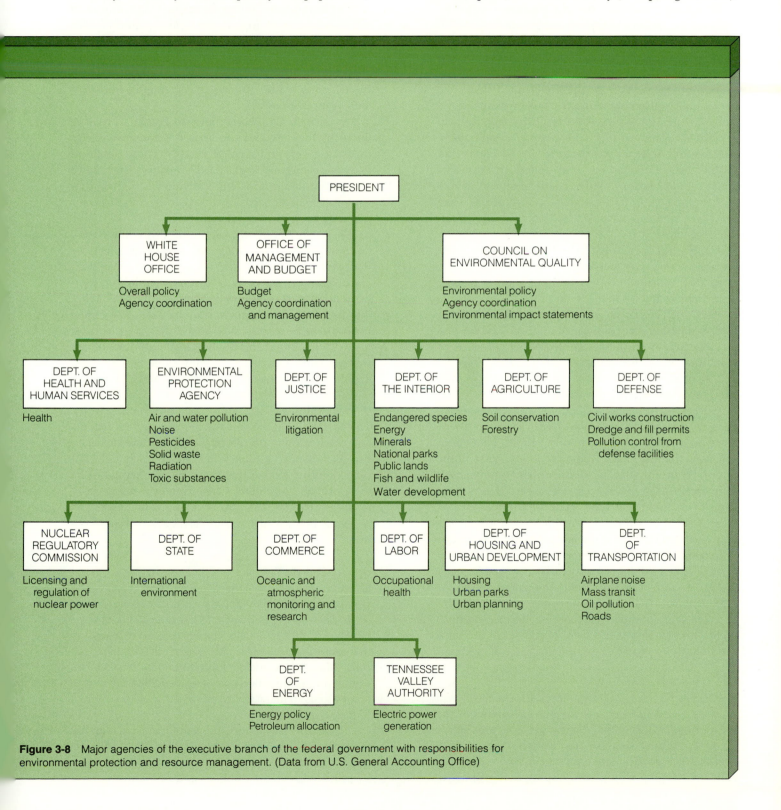

Figure 3-8 Major agencies of the executive branch of the federal government with responsibilities for environmental protection and resource management. (Data from U.S. General Accounting Office)

Because tax income is limited, developing and adopting a budget is the most important thing decision makers do. This involves answering two key questions: What resource use and distribution problems will be addressed? How much of limited tax income will be used to address each problem? Someone once said that the way to understand human history is to study budgets.

Politicians would like to solve problems with *win-win solutions*, where everyone comes out ahead. But most political decisions about resource distribution are *win-lose situations,* in which some people benefit and some are hurt.

For example, suppose the government bans the use of high-sulfur coal in electric power plants in the United States to reduce the harmful effects of acid deposition. This will benefit people, forests, and streams and lakes in the eastern United States and southeastern Canada. But coal miners in West Virginia, Illinois, Pennsylvania, and other states where high-sulfur coal is mined will be out of work. They and their families will suffer hardship from this political decision.

Politics has been called the *art of compromise*—finding ways to balance competing interests. Most politicians who remain in power become good at finding compromises and making trade-offs that give a little to each side. They play an important role in holding society together, preventing chaos and disorder, and making incremental changes. If people get some of what they want, they are less likely to rebel. They are also more likely to elect those who meet some of their needs and wants or promise to do so.

Successful politicians usually practice *pressure-and-crisis-politics.* To stay in power, they focus on short-term problems and favor highly visible, short-term solutions that may make some problems worse in the future. Politicians who call for the public to make short-term sacrifices in the interests of projected long-term gains often find it hard to win or hold office.

For example, suppose a presidential candidate ran on a platform calling for the federal tax on gasoline to be raised to the point where gasoline would cost about three dollars a gallon—an approach now used in many European countries. The candidate argues that this tax raise is necessary to encourage conservation of oil and gasoline and to enhance future economic, environmental, and military security. Would you vote for a candidate who promises to triple the price of gasoline?

Anticipatory Public Politics Emphasis on short-term rewards is natural because no one knows what the future holds. "Take what you can get now and worry about the future later," we say. But short-term, reaction-to-crisis politics is like putting a bunch of Band-Aids on a gaping wound and hoping they will hold.

For some things Band-Aids work. But in an interconnected world facing serious environmental and resource problems and potential nuclear annihilation, we need more than Band-Aids. *Perhaps the greatest challenge we face is to use or modify existing national political and economic systems to anticipate and prevent serious long-term problems, many of them global.* We cannot control the future, but we can influence it.

The motivation for balancing short- and long-term interests may come from a rare type of political leader who has the vision and ability to inspire and mobilize people to see and take new paths. Throughout history key acts of political leadership have been those in which the seemingly impossible—or the highly improbable—is made possible.

To paraphrase George Bernard Shaw, "Some see things as they are and say, 'Why?' I dream of things that never were and say, 'Why not?'" These rare individuals practice *anticipatory public politics*. They try to change our institutions and individual actions to prevent anticipated crises. Or they react to crises in ways that may keep them from recurring.

President Abraham Lincoln did this when he led the country to abolish slavery. President Theodore Roosevelt led the first wave of resource conservation (Section 2-4). In the early 1960s President John F. Kennedy motivated people to become involved in changing the world. His legacy continues today as a model of how to be an inspirational leader. To many the most inspirational moral and political leader in this century was Mahatma Gandhi, who showed us how to bring about change by using nonviolent tactics.

Such leaders challenge and prod us to do more than we think we can. They bring out the best in us. This is also what a good teacher does. Such leaders and teachers may not always be appreciated or liked because we have a built-in resistance to change. But later we often realize that these people helped make the world and us better by inspiring us to convert our ideals to realities. Instead of saying something can't be done because it's too idealistic, they say, "Let's do it!"

Role of Private Political and Economic Decisions
Effective anticipatory political leaders don't come along very often. When they do, many people are too scared of change to elect and support them. Indeed, change in a world that is always changing is so threatening that many inspirational leaders, such as Abraham Lincoln, Mahatma Gandhi, John Kennedy, and Martin Luther King, have been assassinated. But their challenges to us to make the world a better place continue to haunt and inspire us.

So we can't sit around and wait for such leadership to inspire us to sustain the earth or for elected leaders to stick their necks out. We have to lead the leaders by practicing personal politics and economics.

For example, the enactment of environmental and resource conservation laws since the mid-1960s (Appendix 2) did not happen primarily because of leadership by elected officials. Instead, the alarm had been sounded in terms that people could understand by a few scientists such as Rachel Carson, Paul Ehrlich, Barry Commoner, and Garrett Hardin. Then the media further explained and showed graphic pictures of environmental damage (Section 2-4).

This led large numbers of citizens to insist that the government do something. Many joined or supported the Sierra Club, Friends of the Earth, the Wilderness Society, Greenpeace, Environmental Defense Fund, Natural Resources Defense Council (see Case Study below), and other environmental and resource conservation groups. This public support helped elected leaders like Senators Gaylord Nelson, Edmund Muskie, and Morris Udall in drafting and passing environmental and conservation legislation in the 1970s.

Without the political actions of millions of individual citizens and organized groups, the air you breathe and the water you drink today would be much more polluted. Leading leaders is not easy. But history shows that it can be done. You can make a difference.

3-5 ECONOMIC AND POLITICAL APPROACHES TO IMPROVING ENVIRONMENTAL QUALITY AND CONSERVING RESOURCES

How Far Should We Go? You, like most people, are probably in favor of a clean environment and resource conservation. But how clean do you want the environment to be?. How far do you believe we should go in requiring resource conservation? How much money are you willing to spend to achieve these goals? What changes in your lifestyle are you willing to make to reach these goals? Are we spending too much on environmental protection? (see Spotlight on p. 64).

Shouldn't our goal always be zero pollution? For most pollutants the answer is no. First, because everything we do produces some potential pollutants, and nature can handle some of our wastes. The trick is not to destroy, degrade, or overload these natural processes. Exceptions are very harmful products that cannot be degraded by natural processes or that break down very slowly in the environment. They should neither be produced nor used except in small amounts with special permits.

CASE STUDY The National Resources Defense Council

The Natural Resources Defense Council (NRDC) was founded in 1970. Since then its teams of scientists, lawyers, and resource specialists have been working on critical environmental and resource problems. These efforts are supported by membership fees and contributions from about 70,000 individuals. The following are some of the many accomplishments of the NRDC:

- 1973—compelled the EPA to establish regulations restricting lead additives in gasoline
- 1975—forced the Nuclear Regulatory Commission to adopt tougher regulations for the storage and disposal of radioactive wastes from uranium mining and processing (mill tailings)
- 1976—led the successful fight to ban the use of chlorofluorocarbons (CFCs) in aerosol products
- 1983—filed a lawsuit that forced the National Steel Company to comply with air

pollution control laws and pay $2.5 million in back penalties; spearheaded a successful campaign to protect 40 million acres of fragile coastal areas in Florida, California, and Massachusetts from an offshore oil leasing program pushed by the Reagan administration
- 1984—filed a lawsuit compelling oil refineries to tighten pollution control and reduce toxic discharges; won a Supreme Court case giving the public the right to obtain chemical industry data on the health effects of pesticides
- 1985—led a coalition of citizen groups in successful negotiations with the chemical industry to strengthen safety provisions of the federal pesticide law; won an appeal against the U.S. Forest Service's 50-year management plans that would have increased environmentally damaging logging in four Colorado national forests

- 1986—launched a history-making agreement with the Soviet Academy of Sciences that will allow scientists to monitor nuclear test sites in both countries; led negotiations with the oil industry to protect environmentally sensitive areas in Alaska's Bering Sea
- 1987—won an environmental penalty of $1.5 million against the Bethlehem Steel Company for polluting the Chesapeake Bay; played a key role in promoting the International Ozone Treaty designed to cut worldwide use of CFCs at least 35% by the end of this century; years of lobbying led to new appliance energy-efficiency standards that will save energy equal to that of 40 large coal-fired or nuclear plants and 1.5 billion barrels of oil and natural gas; won a lawsuit on the disposal of radioactive waste from government and commercial nuclear facilities

---

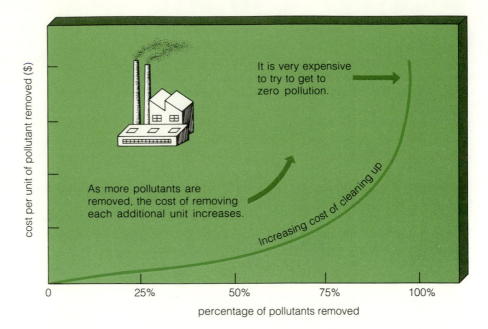

Figure 3-9 The cost of removing each additional unit of pollution rises exponentially.

It is very expensive to try to get to zero pollution.

As more pollutants are removed, the cost of removing each additional unit increases.

Increasing cost of cleaning up

cost per unit of pollutant removed ($)

0   25%   50%   75%   100%

percentage of pollutants removed

Second, we can't afford to have zero pollution for any but the most harmful substances. Removing a small percentage of the pollutants in air, water, or soil is not too costly. But when we remove more, the price per unit multiplies. The cost of removing pollutants follows a J curve of exponential growth (Figure 3-9).

For example, in 1972 the EPA estimated that removing 85% of the pollutants from all industrial and municipal effluents between 1971 and 1981 would cost $62 billion. But to remove all the pollutants would have cost at least $317 billion. It costs five times as much to remove the last 15% as it does to remove the first 85%.

How far do we go? If we go too far in cleaning up, the costs of pollution control will be greater than its harmful effects. This may cause some businesses to go bankrupt. You and others may lose jobs, homes, and savings. If we don't go far enough, however, the harmful external effects will cost us more than reducing the pollution to a lower level would cost. Then you and others may get sick or even die. Getting the right balance is crucial (see Spotlight on p. 66).

How do we do this? We plot a curve of the estimated social costs of cleaning up pollution and a curve of the estimated social costs of pollution. We then add the two curves to get a third curve showing the total costs. The lowest point on this third curve is the optimum level of pollution (Figure 3-10).

On a graph this looks neat and simple. But environmentalists and business leaders often disagree in their estimates of the social costs of pollution. Furthermore, the optimum level of pollution is not the same in different areas. Areas with lots of people and industry have lower optimum pollution levels. Soils

and lakes in some areas are more sensitive to acid deposition than those in other places.

Improving Environmental Quality and Reducing Resource Waste You have seen why preventing pollution and reducing unnecessary resource use and waste require government intervention in the free market. There are four ways the government can intervene:

- *Make harmful actions illegal.* Pass and enforce laws that set pollution standards, regulate harmful activities, and require that certain resources be conserved.

- *Penalize harmful actions.* Levy taxes on each unit of pollution discharged into the air or water and each unit of unnecessary resource waste.

- *Market pollution rights and resource use rights.* Sell rights that allow pollution up to the estimated optimum level; sell the right to harvest or extract a certain amount of resources from public lands or common property resources.

- *Reward beneficial actions.* Use tax dollars to pay subsidies to businesses and individuals that install pollution control equipment and reduce unnecessary resource use and waste by recycling and reusing resources and by inventing more efficient processes and devices.

Often several or all of these methods are needed to deal with environmental and resource problems.

The first three are *polluter-or-resource-waster-pays* approaches that internalize some or most external costs of pollution and resource waste. Because the inter-

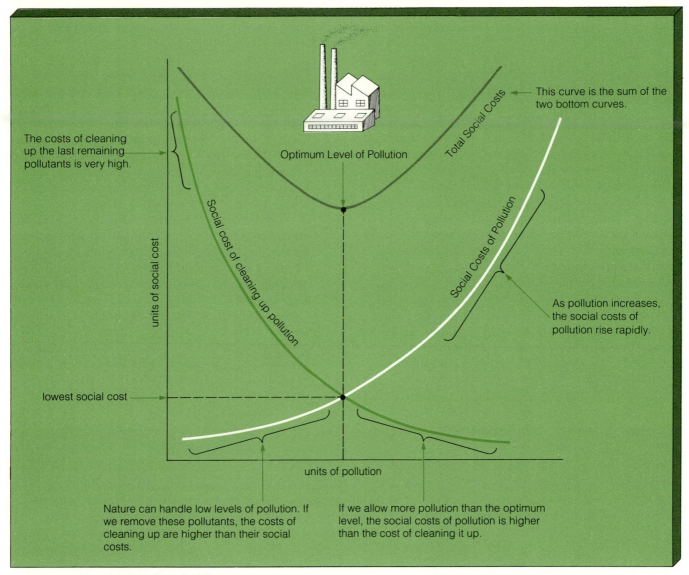

The costs of cleaning up the last remaining pollutants is very high.

Optimum Level of Pollution

Total Social Costs

This curve is the sum of the two bottom curves.

units of social cost

Social cost of cleaning up pollution

Social Costs of Pollution

As pollution increases, the social costs of pollution rise rapidly.

lowest social cost

units of pollution

Nature can handle low levels of pollution. If we remove these pollutants, the costs of cleaning up are higher than their social costs.

If we allow more pollution than the optimum level, the social costs of pollution is higher than the cost of cleaning it up.

Figure 3-10 Finding the optimum level of pollution.

nalized costs are passed on to consumers, these measures make each of us pay directly for the unnecessary pollution added to the environment and the resources wasted in the production of the economic goods we choose to buy.

Most economists prefer the second and third methods because they use the marketplace to control pollution and resource waste and do a better job of internalizing the external costs. Most conservationists favor a combination of the first three methods.

The first three approaches share several disadvantages. Because pollution costs are internalized, the ini-

tial cost of products may be higher unless new, more cost-effective and productive technologies are developed. This can put a country's products at a disadvantage in the international marketplace. Higher initial costs also mean that the poor are left out unless they are given tax relief or other subsidies from public funds. Also, fines and other punishments must be severe enough and enforced quickly enough to deter violations.

The fourth approach is a *taxpayer-pays* approach that does little to internalize external costs. It leads to higher-than-optimum levels of pollution and resource waste. Polluting industries and resource wasters usually prefer this approach. This is understandable. If we have a choice, most of us would rather be paid not to pollute or waste resources than to pay directly for the pollution we create and the resources we unnecessarily waste. Trying to pass external costs to others so that we can maximize short-term profits is natural. But eventually this leads to economic and environmental harm for everyone.

All four approaches are limited by incomplete and disputed information about the short- and long-term effects of pollutants. There are also disputes over estimates of available supplies of nonrenewable resources and sustained yields of renewable resources. All four approaches require greatly increased environmental monitoring to determine how well they work. Widespread monitoring is also necessary to catch violators of antiwaste and antipollution laws.

We need to greatly increase research and monitoring to get better information. But we will never have enough. Lack of information may cause us to make mistakes in our attempts to reduce pollution and resource waste. But not dealing with these problems will be much more harmful and costly in the long run.

Another problem with all four approaches is the potential for international economic blackmail. Multinational companies are based in one country but operate in many countries. If it costs too much to control pollution or conserve resources in one country, a company can close down plants there and open up new ones in countries with less strict environmental and resource use regulations or higher subsidies.

But governments should not use economic blackmail as an excuse for not dealing with environmental and resource problems. Since many of these problems are regional and global, governments must begin to recognize the need for global policies. Table 3-1 summarizes other advantages and disadvantages of the four government approaches.

Cost-Benefit Analysis Comparing the estimated short-term and long-term costs (losses) and benefits (gains) of an economic decision is called **cost-benefit analysis.** If the estimated benefits exceed the estimated costs, the decision to produce or buy an economic good or provide a public good is considered worthwhile. You intuitively make such evaluations when you decide to buy a particular economic good or service.

More formal cost-benefit analysis is often used in evaluating whether to build a large hydroelectric dam, to clean up a polluted river, or to reduce air pollution emissions to an optimum level. Cost-benefit analysis is widely used by government agencies, but its use is controversial.

One problem is that present costs may be fairly easy to estimate, but putting a price tag on future benefits and costs is difficult. Because the future is unknown, all we can do is make educated guesses based on various assumptions about what the future

---

SPOTLIGHT Is Environmental Protection Costing Too Much in Money and Jobs?

Is the United States spending too much on environmental protection? Have our environmental protection standards caused massive unemployment?

Industrialists often argue that the costs of reducing pollution will make their businesses unprofitable and force them to close down plants and lay off employees. They argue that the economic benefits of jobs outweigh the need for stricter environmental control. Environmentalists and conservationists argue that we are spending too little on pollution control.

What are the facts? By 1985 environmental damage was costing the United States an estimated 4% of its GNP. But the country was spending only about 1.6% of its GNP on environmental protec-

tion. U.S. businesses were spending only 2.7% of their capital investments on pollution control.

Moreover, pollution control itself is a rapidly growing beneficial form of economic activity. The pollution control business is growing at about 18% per year—twice the annual growth rate for all U.S. manufacturing.

Pollution control also creates far more jobs than it eliminates. Between 1971 and 1985, U.S. air and water pollution control laws created over 300,000 new jobs. According to the Environmental Protection Agency, during this same period fewer than 52,000 workers were alleged to have lost their jobs because of environmental regulations.

Pollution control expenditures create more jobs and help reduce unemployment more than most other expenditures. Studies have shown that 60,000 to 70,000 jobs are created for each $1 billion spent on pollution control. By comparison, each $1 billion of GNP generates an average of 50,000 jobs, and each $1 billion of military spending creates only 28,000 jobs.

Pollution control also saves industry money in the long run. For example, an $8 million pollution control system installed by the Great Lakes Paper Company reduced the plant's operating cost by $4 million a year and paid for itself in only two years.

value of a resource might be. Using different assumptions gives quite different estimates.

These assumptions are major sources of disagreement between conservationists and business people. Business people give more weight than do conservationists to immediate profits and values over possible future profits and values: "A bird in the hand is worth two in the bush." They worry that inflation will make the value of their earnings less in the future than now. They also fear that innovation or changed consumer preferences will make their product or service obsolete.

Many business leaders and economists also assume that economic growth through technological progress will automatically raise average living standards in the future. So why should the current generation pay higher prices and taxes to benefit future generations who will be better off anyhow? Cost-benefit analyses have a built-in bias against future environmental protection and resource conservation because they weigh future benefits and costs lower than current benefits and costs.

Conservationists put greater emphasis on the future value of resources. They also are not convinced that future economic growth will raise average living standards unless we redirect this growth to reduce the "bads" and increase the "goods" (see Spotlight on p. 56).

Another problem is determining who gets the benefits and who is harmed by the costs. Cost-benefit analysis often fails to include all parties affected by an economic decision. For example, suppose a cost-benefit analysis concludes that it is too expensive to meet certain safety and environmental standards in a manufacturing plant. The owners of the company benefit by not having to spend money on making the plant less hazardous. Consumers may also benefit from lower

Table 3-1 Evaluation of Ways to Improve Environmental Quality and Conserve Resources

Advantages	Disadvantages
Direct Government Regulation	
Helps keep pollution and resource waste below a certain level; internalizes some external costs; having the same emission and resource recycling standards everywhere prevents polluters and resource wasters from moving to parts of the country with lower standards; leaves firms free to decide how best to meet standards; encourages innovation and development of new pollution control and resource conservation technology but this is often not done; only effective way to control emissions and resource waste from cars and home furnaces; easier to get through Congress than other methods	Requiring all pollution emitters and resource wasters to meet the same standards internalizes only part of the external costs; does not take into account differences in the capacity of the local or regional environment to dilute or degrade some pollutants; requiring all producers to use the same control technology discourages development of better and cheaper pollution control and resource conservation technology; can force small producers, without enough capital to install new equipment, out of business; standards tend to be ones that are enforceable rather than optimum; unfair because polluters do not pay for the damages
Pollution Emission and Resource Use Charges	
Internalizes external costs if charges are close to estimated external costs; encourages producers to reduce pollution and resource waste to optimum levels; generates tax revenue rather than having taxpayers pay for external costs; fair because polluters pay for damages; encourages compliance	May take several trials and errors to find right level of fees; inflation can lead to an increase in pollution and resource waste unless charges automatically rise with inflation; hard to get through Congress
Pollution and Resource Use Rights	
Encourages producers to reduce pollution and resource waste to optimum levels; environmental and conservation groups can buy up and hold rights to protect vulnerable areas; generates tax revenue rather than having taxpayers pay for external costs; inflation would automatically raise prices of rights and keep pollution and resource waste from rising; lets market set tax	Requires extensive monitoring and enforcement to make sure that those not buying rights do not pollute, degrade, and waste resources
Economic Incentives	
Decreases production costs and can lead to higher profits, keep prices of goods down, and improve competitiveness in the international marketplace	Does little to internalize external costs; producers tend to lobby for and receive subsidies to increase their output rather than conserve resources and improve pollution control; uses tax revenues instead of generating them; subsidies often go to those with the most influence; difficult to discontinue when no longer needed; takes tax dollars away from other uses

prices. But the workers are harmed by hazardous and unhealthful conditions.

Still another serious limitation of cost-benefit analysis is that many things we value cannot be reduced to dollars and cents. Some of the costs of air pollution, such as extra laundry bills, house repainting, and ruined crops, are fairly easy to estimate. But how do we put meaningful price tags on human life, clean air and water, beautiful scenery, a wilderness area, whooping cranes, and the ability of natural systems to degrade and recycle some of our wastes?

We can assign dollar values to such items, but the values we assign will vary widely because of different assumptions and value judgments. This can lead to a wide range of projected costs and benefits. For example, in 1984 the EPA did a cost-benefit analysis on a proposed revision of the Clean Air Act. The analysis concluded that the net benefits (after deducting the projected costs) ranged from a loss of $1.4 billion to a gain of $110 billion—depending mostly on the monetary value assigned to human life, human health, and a cleaner environment.

Values assigned to a human life in various cost-benefit studies vary from nothing to about $7 million. The most frequently assigned values range from $200,000 to $500,000. If you were asked to put a price tag on your life, you might say it is infinite, or you might contend that making such an estimate would be impossible or even immoral.

You may not want others to place a low monetary value on your own life. But you place a low value on your life if you choose to smoke cigarettes, not eat properly, drive without a seat belt, drive while impaired by alcohol or some other drug, or refuse to pay more for a safer car. In each case you decide that the benefits—pleasure, convenience, or a lower purchase price—outweigh the potential costs—poorer health, injury, or death.

Critics of cost-benefit analysis argue that because estimates of many costs and benefits are so uncertain, they can easily be weighted to achieve the desired outcome by proponents or opponents of a proposed project or action. The experts making or evaluating such analyses have to be paid by somebody, so they often represent the point of view of that somebody.

The difficulty in making cost-benefit analyses does not mean that they should not be made or that they are not useful. At best, they are crude estimates and sometimes they are deliberately distorted. But they can be useful as long as decision makers and the public are aware that they give only rough estimates and guidelines for resource use and management based on a given set of assumptions. They should never be thought of as precise, "bottom-line" numbers.

There have been successes in using cost-benefit analysis for environmental protection and resource conservation. Much of today's environmental protection legislation is based on cost-benefit analyses by

---

CASE STUDY **Preservation Versus Development: The Hell's Canyon Case***

Hell's Canyon is on the Snake River, which separates Idaho and Oregon. The deepest canyon in North America, it provides a spectacular view for visitors and is a habitat for a variety of wildlife. It is also one of the best remaining sites in the United States for a hydroelectric power plant.

During the 1970s a major controversy arose over whether a dam should be built across this canyon to produce hydroelectric power or the canyon should be preserved in its natural state. The dam would create a large lake and change the character of the canyon.

Congress asked Resources for the Future, Inc., a respected Washington think tank, to make a cost-benefit analysis of this project. Economists Anthony Fisher, John Krutilla, and Charles Chicchetti carried out the study.

They found that the demand for recreational use of this unique canyon area was increasing rapidly. Construction of the dam would diminish the value of the site for recreation. On the other hand, electricity produced by the dam would be valuable. They found that the projected electricity demand could be met by other methods, but these methods would be more expensive.

The economists found that the current potential net benefits from producing hydroelectricity were greater than the current recreational benefits of preservation. However, the net benefits from preservation were rising more rapidly over time than the projected net benefits of producing electricity.

The analysis concluded that if the current annual value of recrea-

tional benefits at the canyon site exceeded $80,000, the site should be preserved. The economists estimated that the current annual value of recreational activities at the site was $900,000—over ten times the value needed to justify preservation. They admitted that the $900,000 estimate may have been too high, but they thought it unlikely to be ten times too high.

Thus, they recommended preservation. On the basis of this recommendation and other considerations, Congress voted to protect Hell's Canyon from development.

*Based on material in Tietenberg, Tom. 1988. *Environmental and Resource Economics*, 2nd ed. Glenview, Ill.: Scott, Foresman.

John Krutilla, Anthony Fisher, Charles Chicchetti, Lester Lave, Eugene Seskin, and other economists (see Case Study on p. 66).

Conservationists and economists have suggested ways to improve cost-benefit analysis:

- Require all studies to use a uniform set of standards.

- Clearly state all assumptions.

- Show all projected costs with their estimated range of values based on each set of assumptions.

- Estimate the short- and long-term benefits and costs to all affected population groups.

- Estimate the effectiveness of the project or regulation, instead of assuming (as is often done) that all projects and regulations will be executed with 100% efficiency and effectiveness.

- Open evaluations to public review and challenge.

A Sustainable-Earth Economy Conservationists and a few economists, including Herman Daly, Kenneth Boulding, and Nicholas Georgescu-Roegen, have proposed that the world's countries make a transition to a **sustainable-earth economy** (see Spotlight below).

They believe that the industrial economy in its present form is not a sustainable economy because it is based on depleting and degrading the earth's natural capital. We are running up a massive earth debt—the ultimate debt—that can't be ignored any longer. They call for us to move from an earth-plundering economy to a more sustainable ecological economy.

They see the processes that sustain the earth as the best model for any human economy. The earth's processes use, conserve, and recycle resources with virtually no waste and with far greater efficiency and

---

SPOTLIGHT Characteristics of a Sustainable-Earth Economy

A sustainable-earth economy discourages certain types of economic growth and encourages other types to prevent overloading and degradation of the earth's life-support systems now and in the future.

Discourages

- throwaway and nondegradable products, oil and coal use, nuclear energy, deforestation, overgrazing, groundwater depletion, soil erosion, resource waste, and output pollution control

- creating and satisfying wants that cause high levels of pollution, environmental degradation, and resource waste

Does this by

- using fees and marketable permits to internalize the external costs of goods and services

- removing government subsidies from highly pollution-producing, resource-depleting, and resource-wasting economic activities.

Encourages

- recycling, reuse, solar energy, energy conservation, education,

prevention of health problems, ecological restoration, input pollution control, appropriate technology, and long-lasting, easily repaired products

- consumption of goods and services that satisfy essential needs, not artificially created wants

- growth in productivity—not mere production—of beneficial goods and services (do more with less)

- use of renewable resources at a sustainable rate

- use of locally available matter and energy resources

- decentralization of some production facilities to reduce transportation costs, make better use of locally available resources, enhance national security by spreading out targets, and increase employment

- preservation of biological diversity at local, national, and global levels by setting aside and controlling the use of forests, wetlands, grasslands, soil, and wildlife

- self-sufficiency of families, urban areas, rural areas, and countries

- regulation of human population growth

- global economic and political cooperation to promote peace and sustain the earth's life-support systems for everyone now and in the future

- a fairer distribution of the world's resources and wealth

Does this by

- using government subsidies to encourage pollution reduction and resource-conserving activities and selling marketable permits for resource extraction.

- educating people to understand and value the earth's life-sustaining processes for present and future generations and for all species; following the advice given by a Chinese poet in 500 B.C.: "If you are thinking a year ahead, sow a seed. If you are thinking ten years ahead, plant a tree. If you are thinking a hundred years ahead, educate the people."

Determines progress with indicators that measure

- changes in the quality of life

- sustainable use of renewable resources

- recycling and reuse of nonrenewable resources.

productivity than any economy we have invented so far.

Making the transition to a sustainable-earth economy requires use of the political system to help direct and regulate the economic system. But this won't happen unless enough people adopt a sustainable-earth worldview.

3-6 ACHIEVING A SUSTAINABLE-EARTH SOCIETY: WORLDVIEWS AND ENVIRONMENTAL ETHICS

Throwaway Worldview According to E. F. Schumacher, "Environmental deterioration does not stem from science or technology, or from a lack of information, trained people, or money for research. It stems from the lifestyle of the modern world, which in turn arises from its basic beliefs." Many people, especially in industrialized countries, have a throwaway worldview based on several beliefs:

- We are apart from nature.

- We are superior to other species.

- Our role is to conquer and subdue wild nature to further our goals.

- Resources are unlimited because of our ingenuity in making them available or in finding substitutes—there is always more.

- The more we produce and consume, the better off we are.

- The most important nation is the one that can command and use the largest fraction of the world's resources.

- The ideal person is the self-made individualist who does his or her own thing and hurts no one.

You may not accept all these statements, but most of us act as if we did. And that's what counts.

This worldview emphasizes and justifies short-term self-interest to satisfy as many of our unlimited wants as possible. Short-term self-interest is natural and motivating. It's why most things have been invented, why we work, and why we survive. But there are 5.2 billion people trying to survive and satisfy as many of their unlimited wants as possible. In your lifetime there may be twice this many people trying to do this.

Many analysts fear that continuing devotion to this seductive worldview will turn out to be a fatal attraction. Thomas Berry calls the industrial-consumer society built upon this worldview the "supreme pathology of all history."

We can break the mountains apart; we can drain the rivers and flood the valleys. We can turn the most luxuriant forests into throwaway paper products. We can tear apart the great grass cover of the western plains and pour toxic chemicals into the soil and pesticides onto the fields until the soil is dead and blows away in the wind. We can pollute the air with acids, the rivers with sewage, the seas with oil—all this in a kind of intoxication with our power for devastation. . . . We can invent computers capable of processing ten million calculations per second. And why? To increase the volume and speed with which we move natural resources through the consumer economy to the junk pile or the waste heap. Our managerial skills are measured by our ability to accelerate this process. If in these activities the topography of the planet is damaged, if the environment is made inhospitable for a multitude of living species, then so be it. We are, supposedly, creating a technological wonderworld. . . . But our supposed progress toward an ever-improving human situation is bringing us to a wasteworld instead of a wonderworld.

Sustainable-Earth Worldview Many types of sustainable-earth economies, political systems, and individual lifestyles are possible. But all are based on the following beliefs and guidelines that make up the sustainable-earth worldview:

- We are part of nature (*principle of oneness*).

- We are not superior to other species. In the words of Aldo Leopold, each of us is "to be a plain member and citizen of nature" (*principle of humility*).

- Our role is to understand and work with the rest of nature (*principle of cooperation*).

- Something is right when it tends to maintain the earth's life-support systems and wrong when it tends otherwise; the bottom line is that the earth is the bottom line (*principle of sustainability*).

- Our primary purposes should be to share the earth's finite resources, care for other people and other species, and interfere with nonhuman species only to satisfy vital needs—not frivolous wants. Success is based on the degree to which we achieve these goals (*principle of love, caring, and joy*).

- Resources are limited and must not be wasted—there is a lot, but there is not always more (*principle of limits*).

- All people are entitled to a fair share of the world's resources as long as they are assuming their responsibility for sustaining the earth (*principle of equity*).

- No individual, corporation, or nation has a right to an ever-increasing share of the earth's finite resources. As the Indian philosopher and social activist Mahatma Gandhi said, "The earth provides enough to satisfy every person's need but not every person's greed" (*principle of enoughness*).

- We can never completely "do our own thing." Everything we do has present and future effects on other people and other species. Most of these effects are unpredictable (*principle of ecological backlash*).

- It is wrong to treat people and other living things primarily as factors of production, whose value is expressed only in economic terms. As Aldo Leopold said, "We abuse land because we regard it as a commodity belonging to us. When we see land as a community to which we belong, we may begin to use it with love and respect" (economics is not everything principle).

- Premature extinction of any wild species by human activities is wrong (preservation of wildlife and biodiversity principle).

- Everything we have or will have ultimately comes from the sun and the earth; an exhausted planet is an exhausted economy (respect-your-roots or earth-first principle).

- Don't do anything that depletes the physical, chemical, and biological capital provided by the earth; the earth deficit is the real deficit (balanced earth budget principle).

- To love, cherish, celebrate, and understand the earth and yourself you must take time to experience and sense the air, water, soil, trees, animals, bacteria, and other parts and rhythms of the earth directly, not just indirectly in books, TV images, and ideas (experience is the best teacher principle).

Types of Conflict There are two basic types of conflicts over ways to live our lives and deal with environmental and resource problems. One is a conflict between people with different basic assumptions or worldviews. Conflicts between the throwaway and sustainable-earth worldviews are fundamental. They usually can't be resolved, unless members of one group change their worldview or are required by law to behave in certain ways.

You may not be fully aware of your worldview and how strongly it influences your actions. Education can help you understand your worldview and compare it with other possibilities. But you must also directly listen to and experience the earth with your senses (see Spotlight below).

A second type of conflict occurs between people with the same general worldview. Although they have the same general goals, they differ on the best way to deal with a particular resource or environmental problem. Often they can resolve their disagreements by

---

SPOTLIGHT Listening to the Earth and Ourselves

The essence, rhythms, and pulse of the earth within and around us can only be experienced at the deepest level by our senses and feelings—our emotions. We must tune our senses into the flow of air and water into our bodies; they are absolute needs provided for us by nature at no charge.

We must listen to the soft, magnificent symphony of billions of organisms expressing their interdependency. We must pick up a handful of soil and try to sense its teeming microscopic life forms that keep us alive. We must look at a tree, a mountain, a rock, a bee and try to sense how they are a part of us and we are a part of them.

We must learn to cherish and listen to the gentle sounds of silence within and around us instead of identifying any lack of frantic activity as boredom and loneliness. We must tune in to our urgent yearning to understand and experience ourselves and the rest of nature. Instead, we often cover up this need by seeking a frantic life of motion and artificial things and sensations that only deepen our emotional separation from our inner selves and from the earth.

Michael J. Cohen urges each of us to recognize who we really are by saying,

I am a desire for water, air, food, love, warmth, beauty, freedom, sensations, life, community, place, and spirit in the natural world. These pulsating feelings are the Planet Earth, alive and well within me. I have two mothers: my human mother and my planet mother, Earth. The planet is my womb of life.

We need to stop attaching more feelings of survival and happiness to dollars that we can't eat, breathe, and drink than to the sun, land, air, water, plants, bacteria, and other organisms that really keep us alive. We need to recognize that our technological cocoon and our feeling of self-importance as a species has given us an incredibly distorted picture of what is really important and joyful.

We need to understand that formal education is important but is not enough. Much of it is designed to cut us off from the sense of wonder, joy, and communion with nature within and around us that we had at birth. Much of it is designed to socialize and homogenize us so that we will accept and participate in the worldview that our role is to conquer nature (and not feel guilty about it).

The way to break out of this mental straitjacket is to experience nature directly. This allows you to get in touch with your deepest self that has sensed from birth that when you destroy and degrade natural systems to insulate yourself from nature, you are attacking yourself. Then you will love the earth as part of yourself and live your life in ways that sustain and replenish the earth and thus yourself. Discovering ourselves means discovering the earth. This is true progress.

gathering more information or through analysis, discussion, mediation, and compromise.

Becoming Earth Citizens Sustaining the earth requires each of us to make a personal commitment to live an environmentally ethical life. We must do this not because it is required by law but because it is right. It is our responsibility to ourselves, our children, our neighbors, and the earth. We must avoid some common excuses that lead to indifference and inaction:

- *Gloom-and-doom pessimism:* the belief that the world is doomed by nuclear war or environmental catastrophe, so we should enjoy life while we can.

- *Blind technological optimism:* the belief that human ingenuity will always be able to come up with technological advances that will solve our problems. This is the most seductive and dangerous trap. It is something that we would like to believe—don't worry, be happy, technology will save us.

- *Fatalism:* the belief that whatever will be will be, and that we have no control over our actions and the future.

- *Extrapolation to infinity:* the belief that "If I can't change the entire world quickly, I won't try to change any of it." This rationalization is reinforced by modern society's emphasis on instant gratification and quick results with as little effort as possible.

Making the transition to sustainable-earth societies means that economics and politics must become earth-centered and ethics-centered instead of self-centered. A sustainable-earth economy and political system are based on the beliefs that all people, all other species, and all the earth matter.

Some affluent people in MDCs are adopting a lifestyle of voluntary simplicity, based on doing and enjoying more with less. They are learning that buying more products and luxuries to satisfy artificially created wants doesn't provide security, freedom, or joy. Instead it can lead to insecurity and reduced freedom because *the more things you own, the more you are owned by things.* You have to spend a lot of time and money buying, protecting, repairing, or replacing them.

Many people call for the United States to redefine national security in economic and environmental rather than military terms and cut out massive waste in military spending. They agree with President Dwight D. Eisenhower's warning in the 1960s:

Every gun that is made, every warship launched, every rocket fired, signifies in the final sense a theft from those who are hungry and are not fed, those who are cold and not clothed. This world in arms is not spending money alone. It is spending the sweat of its laborers, the genius of its scientists, and the hopes of its children.

Many ordinary citizens are beginning to work together to find ways out of the arms race and the resource consumption race, rather than leaving the fate of the world up to political leaders. They are educating people to see themselves as members of a global community with ultimate loyalty to the planet, not merely a particular country. They urge individual citizens to think globally and act locally to bring about change.

These earth citizens recognize the powerful forces aligned against such change. But they believe that creative, cooperative efforts can lead us and our leaders to sustain the earth. They are guided by historian Arnold Toynbee's observation: "If you make the world ever so little better, you will have done splendidly, and your life will have been worthwhile," and by George Bernard Shaw's reminder that "indifference is the essence of inhumanity."

Can we do it? Yes—if we care enough to make the necessary commitment and in the process discover that caring for the earth is a never-ending source of joy and inner peace. We must become *earth conservers,* not *earth degraders.* We must become *earth citizens.* No goal is more important, more urgent, and more worthy of our time, energy, creativity, and money.

The ultimate test of our conscience is our willingness to sacrifice something today for future generations whose words of thanks will never be heard.

Gaylord Nelson

DISCUSSION TOPICS

1. What obligations, if any, concerning the environment do you have to future generations? List the major environmental benefits and harmful conditions passed on to you by the last two generations.

2. Some economists argue that only by increasing economic growth will we have enough money to eliminate poverty and protect the environment. Explain why you agree or disagree with this view. If you disagree, how should we deal with these problems?

3. Do you believe that cost-benefit analysis should be used to make all decisions about how limited federal, state, and local government funds are to be used? Explain. If not, what decisions should not be made in this way? How should these decisions be made?

4. What good and bad effects would internalizing the external costs of pollution and unnecessary resource waste have on the U.S. economy? Do you favor doing this? Explain. How might it affect your lifestyle? The lifestyle of the poor? Wildlife?

5. What do you believe are the major strengths and weaknesses of the form of government in the United States (or in any country where you live) for protecting the environment and sustaining the earth? What major changes, if any, would you make in this system?

6. What is your worldview? What things, if any, are you doing to help sustain the earth?

7. If you won ten million dollars in a sweepstakes, how would you live your life differently? Why?

8. List five different ways that your life-style insulates and separates you from directly sensing and experiencing your inner self and the earth. How does this isolation affect your deepest feelings about yourself and your worldview?

FURTHER READINGS

Berger, John J. 1986. *Restoring the Earth*. New York: Alfred A. Knopf.

Berry, Thomas. 1988. *The Dream of the Earth*. San Francisco: Sierra Club Books.

Boulding, Kenneth E. 1985. *The World as a Total System*. Beverly Hills, Calif.: Sage Publications.

Bowden, Elbert V. 1987. *Principles of Economics: Theory, Problems, Policies*, 4th ed.. Cincinnati, Ohio: South-Western.

Bowles, Samuel, et al. 1983. *Beyond the Wasteland*. New York: Anchor Press.

Boyer, William H. 1984. *America's Future: Transition to the 21st Century*. New York: Praeger.

Brown, Lester R. 1981. *Building a Sustainable Society*. New York: W. W. Norton.

Butlin, John A. 1981. *The Economics of Environmental and Natural Resources Policy*. Boulder, Colo.: Westview Press.

Cahn, Robert. 1978. *Footprints on the Planet: A Search for an Environmental Ethic*. New York: Universe Books.

Caldwell, Lynton K. 1984. *International Environmental Policy*. Durham, N.C.: Duke University Press.

Capra, Fritjof. 1983. *The Turning Point*. New York: Bantam.

Clark, W. C. 1986. *Sustainable Development of the Biosphere*. New York: Cambridge University Press.

Cohen, Michael J. 1988. *How Nature Works: Regenerating Kinship with the Planet Earth*. Waldpole, N.H.: Stillpoint.

Collard, David, et al., eds. 1988. *Economics, Growth, and Sustainable Environments*. New York: St. Martin's Press.

Daly, Herman E. 1977. *Steady-State Economics*. San Francisco: W. H. Freeman.

Daly, Herman E., ed. 1980. *Economics, Ecology, and Ethics*. San Francisco: W. H. Freeman.

Daly, Herman E. 1988. "Moving to a Steady-State Economy," in Paul R. Ehrlich and John P. Holdren, eds. *The Cassandra Conference: Resources and the Human Predicament*. College Station: Texas A & M University, pp. 271–285.

Devall, Bill, and George Sessions. 1985. *Deep Ecology: Living As If Nature Mattered*. Salt Lake City, Utah: Gibbs M. Smith.

Dye, Thomas R., and Harmon Zeigler. 1987. *The Irony of Democracy: An Uncommon Introduction to American Politics*, 7th. ed. Monterey, Calif.: Brooks/Cole.

Fisher, Anthony C. 1981. *Resource and Environmental Economics*. New York: Cambridge University Press.

Freedman, Leonard, and Roger A. Riske. 1987. *Power and Politics in America*, 5th ed. Monterey, Calif.: Brooks/Cole.

Freeman, A. Myrick, III. 1982. *Air and Water Pollution Control: A Benefit-Cost Assessment*. New York: John Wiley.

Fritsch, Albert J. 1980. *Environmental Ethics: Choices for Concerned Citizens*. New York: Anchor Books.

Georgescu-Roegen, Nicholas. 1971. *The Entropy Law and the Economic Process*. Cambridge, Mass.: Harvard University Press.

Goldsmith, Edward. 1978. *The Stable Society*. Cornwall, England: Wadebridge Press.

Hamrin, Robert D. 1983. *A Renewable Resource Economy*. New York: Praeger.

Hamrin, Robert D. 1988. *America's New Economy: A Basic Guide*. New York: Franklin Watts.

Hardin, Garrett. 1977. *The Limits of Altruism: An Ecologist's View of Survival*. Bloomington: Indiana University Press.

Hardin, Garrett, and John Bardeen, eds. 1977. *Managing the Commons*. San Francisco: W. H. Freeman.

Henderson, Hazel. 1978. *Creating Alternative Futures*. New York: Putnam.

Henderson, Hazel. 1981. *The Politics of the Solar Age*. New York: Anchor/Doubleday.

Johnson, Warren. 1978. *Muddling Toward Frugality*. San Francisco: Sierra Club.

Krutilla, John V., and Anthony C. Fisher. 1985. *The Economics of Natural Environments*. Washington, D.C.: Resources for the Future.

Maurice, Charles, and Charles W. Smithsonian. 1984. *The Doomsday Myth*. Stanford, Calif.: Hoover Institution Press.

McCay, Bonnie, and James M. Acheson, eds. 1987. *The Question of the Commons: Culture and Ecology of Communal Resources*. Tucson: University of Arizona Press.

McConnell, Campbell R. 1987. *Economics: Principles, Problems, and Policies*, 10th ed. New York: McGraw-Hill.

Mishan, E. J. 1977. *The Economic Growth Debate: An Assessment*. London: Allen & Unwin.

Naess, Arne. 1988. *Ecology, Community, and Lifestyle*. New York: Cambridge University Press.

Nash, Roderick. 1988. *The Rights of Nature: The History of Environmental Ethics*. Madison: University of Wisconsin Press.

Ophuls, William. 1977. *Ecology and the Politics of Scarcity*. San Francisco: W. H. Freeman.

Rolston, Holmes, III. 1988. *Environmental Ethics: Duties to and Values in the Natural World*. Philadelphia: Temple University Press.

Rosenbaum, Walter A. 1985. *Environment, Politics, and Policy*. Washington, D.C.: Congressional Quarterly.

Seymour, John, and Herbert Giradet. 1987. *Blueprint for a Green Planet: Your Practical Guide to Restoring the World's Environment*. Englewood Cliffs, N.J.: Prentice Hall.

Tietenberg, Tom. 1988. *Environmental and Resource Economics*, 2nd. ed. Glenview, Ill.: Scott, Foresman.

Woodward, Herbert N. 1977. *Capitalism Can Survive in a No-Growth Economy*. New York: Brookdale.

CHAPTER 4

Matter and Energy Resources: Types and Concepts

General Questions and Issues

1. What are the major physical and chemical forms of matter and what is matter made of?

2. What scientific law governs changes of matter from one physical or chemical form to another?

3. What are the three major types of nuclear changes that matter can undergo?

4. What are the major types of energy?

5. What two scientific laws govern changes of energy from one form to another?

6. How can the two scientific laws governing changes in energy from one form to another be used to help us evaluate present and future sources of energy?

7. How are the scientific laws governing changes of matter and energy from one form to another related to resource use and environmental disruption?

The laws of thermodynamics control the rise and fall of political systems, the freedom or bondage of nations, the movements of commerce and industry, the origins of wealth and poverty, and the general physical welfare of the human race.

Frederick Soddy, Nobel laureate, chemistry

T his book, your hand, the water you drink, and the air you breathe are all samples of *matter*—the stuff all things are made of. The light and heat streaming from a burning lump of coal and the work you must do to lift this book are examples of *energy*. It is what you and all living things use to move matter around, change its form, or cause a heat transfer between two objects at different temperatures.

All changes of matter and energy from one form to another are governed by certain scientific laws. A **scientific law** summarizes what scientists find happening in nature over and over with the same results. Unlike the social laws people enact, these scientific laws cannot be broken.

This chapter is a brief introduction to what is going on in the world from a physical and chemical standpoint. It describes the major types of matter and energy and the scientific laws governing all changes of matter and energy from one form to another. These laws are used throughout this book to help you understand resource and environmental problems and evaluate proposed solutions. The next two chapters are an introduction to what is going on in the world from an ecological standpoint, based on how key physical and chemical processes are integrated into the biological systems we call life.

4-1 MATTER: FORMS AND STRUCTURE

Physical and Chemical Forms of Matter Anything that has mass (or weight on the earth's surface) and takes up space is **matter. Mass** is the amount of "stuff" in an object. All matter found in nature can be viewed as being organized in identifiable patterns, according to size and function (Figure 4-1).

This section is devoted to a discussion of the three lowest levels of organization of matter—subatomic particles, atoms, and molecules—which make up the basic components of all higher levels. Chapter 5 discusses the five higher levels of organization of matter—organisms, populations, communities, ecosystems, and the ecosphere—the major concern of ecology.

Any matter, such as water, can be found in three *physical forms:* solid (ice), liquid (liquid water), and gas (water vapor). All matter also consists of *chemical forms:* elements, compounds, or mixtures of elements and compounds.

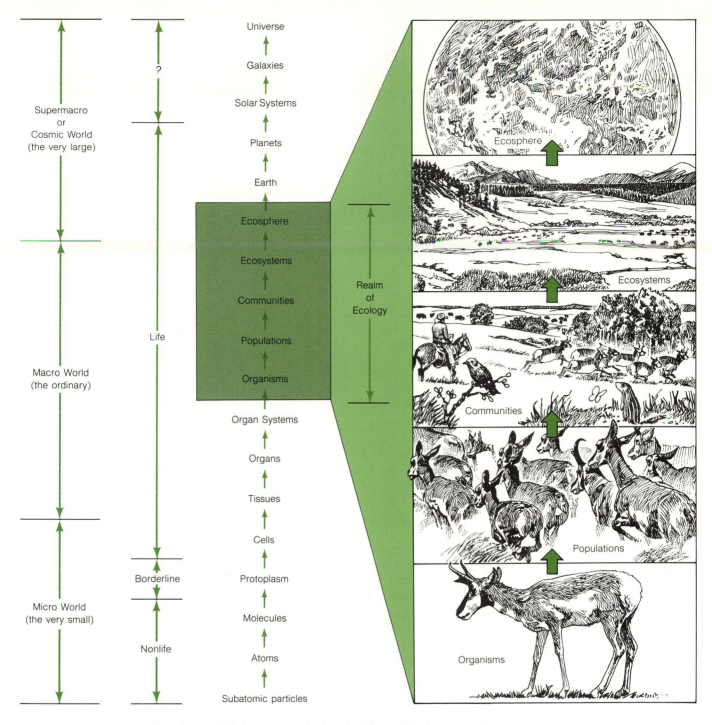

Figure 4-1 Levels of organization of matter. This is one way scientists classify organized patterns of matter found in nature according to size and function.

Elements The 92 **elements** that occur naturally on earth are distinctive forms of matter that make up every material substance. Another 15 elements have been artificially synthesized in laboratories. Examples of these basic building blocks of all matter include hydrogen (represented by the symbol H), carbon (C), oxygen (O), nitrogen (N), phosphorus (P), sulfur (S), chlorine (Cl), fluorine (F), sodium (Na), and uranium (U).

All elements are composed of an incredibly large number of particular types of minute particles called **atoms.** Some elements consist of **molecules,** formed when two or more atoms of the same element combine in fixed proportions. Examples are the nitrogen and

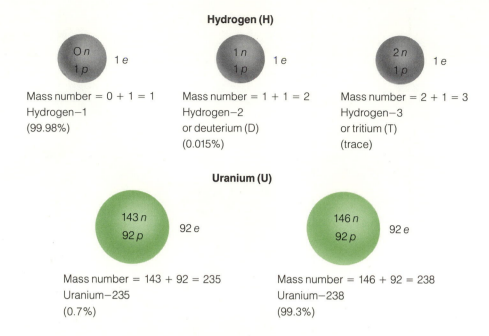

Figure 4-2 Isotopes of hydrogen and uranium. Figures in parentheses show the percent abundance by weight of each isotope in a natural sample of each element.

Hydrogen (H)

Mass number = 0 + 1 = 1
Hydrogen−1
(99.98%)

Mass number = 1 + 1 = 2
Hydrogen−2
or deuterium (D)
(0.015%)

Mass number = 2 + 1 = 3
Hydrogen−3
or tritium (T)
(trace)

Uranium (U)

Mass number = 143 + 92 = 235
Uranium−235
(0.7%)

Mass number = 146 + 92 = 238
Uranium−238
(99.3%)

oxygen gases making up about 99% of the volume of air we breathe. For example, two atoms of nitrogen (N) can combine to form a nitrogen molecule with the shorthand formula N_2 (read as "N-two"). The subscript after the symbol for the element gives the number of atoms of that element in a molecule. Similarly, most of the oxygen gas in the atmosphere exists as O_2 (read as "O-two") molecules. A small amount of oxygen, found mostly in the upper atmosphere (stratosphere), exists as ozone molecules with the formula O_3 (read as "O-three").

All atoms are made up of even smaller **subatomic particles:** protons, neutrons, and electrons. Each atom of an element has a tiny center, or **nucleus.** Each nucleus has a certain number of positively charged **protons** (represented by the symbol p) and uncharged **neutrons** (n). One or more negatively charged **electrons** (e) whiz around somewhere outside each nucleus.

Each atom of the same element always has the same number of positively charged protons inside its nucleus and an equal number of negatively charged electrons outside its nucleus. Because of this electrical balance, each atom as a whole has no net electrical charge. For example, each atom of the lightest element, hydrogen, has one positively charged proton in its nucleus and one negatively charged electron outside. Each atom of a much heavier element, uranium, has 92 protons and 92 electrons (Figure 4-2).

Because an electron has an almost negligible mass (or weight) compared to a proton and a neutron, the approximate mass of an atom is determined by the number of neutrons plus the number of protons in its nucleus. This number is called its **mass number.**

Atoms of the same element must have the same number of protons and electrons. However, they may have different numbers of uncharged neutrons in their nuclei, and thus different mass numbers. These different forms of the same element with different mass numbers, or different numbers of neutrons in their nuclei, are called **isotopes.**

Isotopes of the same element are identified by attaching the mass number to the name or symbol of the element: hydrogen-1, or H-1; hydrogen-2, or H-2 (common name, deuterium); and hydrogen-3, or H-3 (common name, tritium). A natural sample of an element contains a mixture of its isotopes in a fixed proportion or percent abundance by weight (Figure 4-2).

Atoms of some elements can lose or gain one or more electrons to form **ions:** atoms or groups of atoms with one or more net positive (+) or negative (−) electrical charges. The charge is shown as a superscript after the symbol for an atom or group of atoms. Examples of positive ions are sodium ions (Na^+) and ammonium ions (NH_4^+). Common negative ions are chloride ions (Cl^-), nitrate ions (NO_3^-), and phosphate ions (PO_4^{3-}).

Compounds Most matter exists as **compounds**—combinations of atoms or oppositely charged ions of two or more different elements held together in fixed proportions by attractive forces called chemical bonds. Water, for example, is made up of H_2O (read as "H-two-O") molecules, each consisting of two hydrogen atoms chemically bonded to an oxygen atom. Sodium chloride, or table salt, consists of a network of oppositely charged ions (Na^+Cl^-) held together by the forces of attraction that exist between opposite electric charges.

Compounds can be classified as organic or inorganic. Skin, blood, food, vitamins, oil, gasoline, natural gas, cotton, wool, paper, plastics, detergents, aspirin, penicillin, and many other materials important to you and your lifestyle have one thing in common. They all are **organic compounds,** containing atoms of the element carbon, usually combined with itself and with atoms of one or more other elements such as hydrogen, oxygen, nitrogen, sulfur, phosphorus, chlorine, and fluorine.

Examples of the more than 7 million known organic compounds include:

- *Hydrocarbons:* compounds made up of carbon and hydrogen atoms. An example is methane (CH_4)—the major component of natural gas.

- *Chlorinated hydrocarbons:* compounds made up of atoms of carbon, hydrogen, and chlorine. Examples are DDT ($C_{14}H_9Cl_5$), an insecticide, and toxic PCBs (such as $C_{12}H_5Cl_5$), used as insulating materials in transformers, condensers, and other electrical apparatus.

- *Chlorofluorocarbons (CFCs):* compounds made up of atoms of carbon, chlorine, and fluorine. An example is Freon-12 (CCl_2F_2), used as a coolant in refrigerators and air conditioners and in making plastics such as styrofoam.

- *Simple sugars:* certain types of compounds made up of atoms of carbon, hydrogen, and oxygen. An example is glucose ($C_6H_{12}O_6$), which most plants and animals break down in their cells to obtain energy.

Inorganic compounds are combinations of two or more elements other than those used to form organic compounds. Some inorganic compounds you will encounter in this book are sodium chloride (NaCl), water (H_2O), nitric oxide (NO), carbon monoxide (CO), carbon dioxide (CO_2), nitrogen dioxide (NO_2), sulfur dioxide (SO_2), ammonia (NH_3), sulfuric acid (H_2SO_4), and nitric acid (HNO_3).

4-2 CHANGES IN MATTER AND THE LAW OF CONSERVATION OF MATTER

Physical and Chemical Changes Elements and compounds can undergo physical and chemical changes; each change either gives off or requires energy, usually in the form of heat. A **physical change** is one that involves no change in chemical composition. For example, taking a piece of aluminum foil and cutting it into small pieces is a physical change. Each cut piece is still aluminum. Changing a substance from one physical state to another is also a physical change. For example, when solid water, or ice, is melted or liquid water is boiled, none of the H_2O molecules involved are altered; instead they are organized in different spatial patterns.

In a **chemical change,** or **chemical reaction,** a change takes place in the chemical composition of the elements or compounds involved. For example, when

coal (which is mostly carbon, or C) burns, it combines with oxygen gas (O_2) from the atmosphere to form the gaseous compound carbon dioxide (CO_2). In this case energy is given off, explaining why coal is a useful fuel.

The Law of Conservation of Matter: There Is No Away
The earth loses some gaseous molecules to space, and it gains small amounts of matter from space, mostly in the form of stony or metallic bodies (meteorites). However, these losses and gains of matter are minute compared to earth's total mass—somewhat like losing or adding a few grains of sand to the world's beaches.

This means that *the earth has essentially all the matter it will ever have.* Fortunately, over billions of years nature has developed systems for continuously recycling key chemicals back and forth between the nonliving environment (soil, air, and water) and the living environment (plants, animals, and decomposers).

You, like most people, probably talk about consuming or using up material resources. But the truth is that we don't consume any matter. We only use some of the earth's resources for a while. We take materials from the earth, carry them to another part of the globe, and process them into products. These products are used and then discarded, reused, or recycled. For example, we dig up iron ore, transport it to a steel plant, and convert it to various types of iron and steel, which are used to make cars, stoves, and other products. Some worn out cars and stoves are recycled to recover their iron and steel. But many end up as rusting hulks that litter the landscape.

In doing this we may change various elements and compounds from one physical or chemical form to another, but we neither create from nothing nor destroy to nothingness any measurable amount of matter. This fact, based on many thousands of measurements of matter undergoing physical and chemical changes, is known as the **law of conservation of matter.** In other words, *in all physical and chemical changes we can't create or destroy any of the atoms involved. All we can do is rearrange them into different spatial patterns (physical changes) or different combinations (chemical changes).*

The law of conservation of matter means that there is no "away." *Everything we think we have thrown away is still here with us, in one form or another.* We can collect dust and soot from the smokestacks of industrial plants, but these solid wastes must then go somewhere. We can collect garbage and remove solid grease and sludge from sewage, but these substances must be burned (perhaps causing air pollution), dumped into rivers,

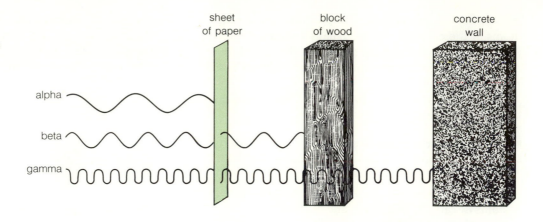

Figure 4-3 The three major types of ionizing radiation emitted by radioactive isotopes vary considerably in their penetrating power.

sheet of paper

block of wood

concrete wall

alpha

beta

gamma

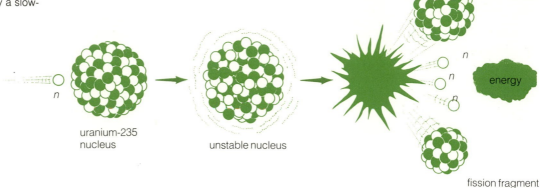

Figure 4-4 Fission of a uranium-235 nucleus by a slow-moving neutron.

fission fragment

n

energy

n

n

uranium-235 nucleus

unstable nucleus

fission fragment

lakes, and oceans (perhaps causing water pollution), or deposited on the land (perhaps causing soil and groundwater pollution). There is no away.

We can make the environment cleaner and convert some potentially harmful chemicals to less harmful or even harmless physical or chemical forms. But the law of conservation of matter means that we will always be faced with pollution and resource degradation of some sort—though we don't have to create nearly as much as we presently do.

Nuclear Changes and Radioactivity In addition to physical and chemical changes, matter can also undergo a third type of change, known as a **nuclear change.** It occurs when nuclei of certain isotopes spontaneously change or are forced to change into one or more different isotopes. The three major types of nuclear change are natural radioactivity, nuclear fission, and nuclear fusion. Unlike physical and chemical changes, nuclear changes involve conversion of a small amount of mass in a nucleus into energy.

Natural radioactivity is a nuclear change in which unstable nuclei spontaneously shoot out "chunks" of mass (usually alpha or beta particles), energy (gamma rays), or both at a fixed rate. An isotope of an atom whose unstable nucleus spontaneously emits fast-moving particles, high-energy electromagnetic radiation, or both is called a **radioactive isotope,** or **radioisotope.**

Radiation emitted by radioisotopes is called **ionizing radiation.** It has enough energy to dislodge one or more electrons from atoms it hits to form positively charged ions, which can react with and damage living tissue. The two most common types of particles emitted by radioactive isotopes are high-speed **alpha particles** (positively charged chunks of matter that consist of two protons and two neutrons) and **beta particles** (negatively charged electrons). The most common form of ionizing electromagnetic radiation released from radioisotopes is high-energy **gamma rays,** which are even more penetrating than X rays. Figure 4-3 shows the relative penetrating power of alpha, beta, and gamma ionizing radiation. Any exposure to ionizing radiation can cause potential harm to tissue in your body.

Nuclear fission is a nuclear change in which nuclei of certain isotopes with large mass numbers (such as uranium-235) are split apart into lighter nuclei when struck by slow- or fast-moving neutrons; this process releases more neutrons and energy (Figure 4-4). The two or three neutrons produced by each fission can be used to split many additional uranium-235 nuclei if enough nuclei are present to provide the **critical mass** needed for efficient capture of these neutrons. These multiple fissions taking place within the critical mass represent a **chain reaction** that releases an enormous amount of energy (Figure 4-5). Damage to living cells can be caused by the ionizing radiation released

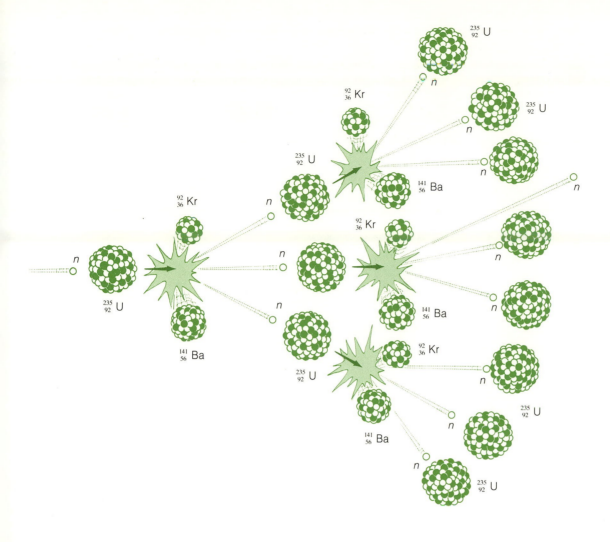

Figure 4-5 A nuclear chain reaction initiated by one neutron triggering fission in a single uranium-235 nucleus. This shows only a few of the trillions of fissions caused when a single uranium-235 nucleus is split within a critical mass of other uranium-235 nuclei.

by radioactive lighter nuclei produced by nuclear fission and by the neutrons released.

In an atomic or nuclear fission bomb, a massive amount of energy is released in a fraction of a second in an *uncontrolled* nuclear fission chain reaction. The reaction is initiated by an explosive charge, which suddenly pushes a mass of fissionable fuel together from all sides, causing the fuel to reach the critical mass for a massive chain reaction almost instantly.

In the nuclear reactor of a nuclear electric power plant, the rate at which the nuclear fission chain reaction takes place is *controlled* so that only one of each two or three neutrons released is used to split another nucleus. In conventional nuclear fission reactors, nuclei of uranium-235 are split apart and release energy. Another fissionable radioisotope is plutonium-239, formed from nonfissionable uranium-238 in breeder nuclear fission reactors, which may be developed in

the future to extend supplies of uranium (see Section 19-6).

Nuclear fusion is a nuclear change in which two nuclei of isotopes of elements such as hydrogen with low mass numbers are forced together at extremely high temperatures until they fuse to form a heavier nucleus, releasing energy in the process. Temperatures of 100 million to 1 billion degrees Celsius (°C) are needed to force the positively charged nuclei (which strongly repel one another) to join together. Fusion is much harder to initiate than fission, but once started, it releases far more energy per gram of fuel than fission. Fusion of hydrogen atoms to form helium atoms is the source of energy in the sun and other stars.

After World War II the principle of *uncontrolled nuclear fusion* was used to develop extremely powerful hydrogen, or thermonuclear, bombs and missile warheads. These weapons involve the D-T fusion reac-

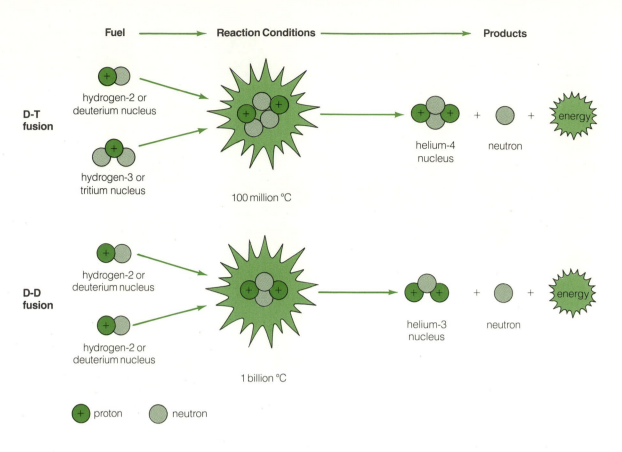

Figure 4-6 The deuterium-tritium (D-T) and deuterium-deuterium (D-D) nuclear fusion reactions, which take place at extremely high temperatures.

tion, in which a hydrogen-2, or deuterium (D), nucleus and a hydrogen-3, or tritium (T), nucleus are fused to form a larger, helium-4 nucleus, a neutron, and energy (Figure 4-6).

Scientists have also tried to develop *controlled nuclear fusion*, in which the D-T reaction is used to produce heat that can be converted into electricity. However, this process is still at the laboratory stage despite 40 years of research. If it ever becomes technologically and economically feasible—a big *if*—it is not projected to be a commercially important source of energy until 2050 or later.

4-3   ENERGY: TYPES AND CHANGES

Types of Energy   Energy, not money, is the real "currency" that the world runs on. We depend on it to grow our food, to keep us and other living things alive, and to warm and cool our bodies and the buildings where we work and live. We also use it to move people and other forms of matter from one place to another and to change matter from one physical or chemical form to another.

Energy is capacity to take action. It is the ability to do work or to cause a heat transfer between two objects at different temperatures. **Work** is what happens when a force is used to push or pull a sample of matter, such as this book, over some distance. Everything going on in and around us is based on work in which one form of energy is transformed into one or more other forms of energy. Scientists classify most forms of energy as either potential or kinetic.

Kinetic energy is the energy that matter has because of its motion and mass. Examples include a moving car, a falling rock, a speeding bullet, and the flow of water or charged particles (electrical energy). **Potential energy** is stored energy that is potentially available for use. A rock held in your hand, a stick of dynamite, still water behind a dam, and nuclear energy stored in the nuclei of atoms all have potential energy. Other examples are the chemical energy stored in the molecules of gasoline and in the carbohydrates, proteins, and fats of the food you eat.

Energy Resources Used by People   We talk about heating buildings by burning oil, gasoline, coal, or wood or by fissioning uranium nuclei to produce electricity. But the truth is that *the direct input of essentially inexhaustible solar energy alone supplies 99% of the energy used to heat the earth and all buildings free of charge.* Were it not for this direct input of energy from the sun, the

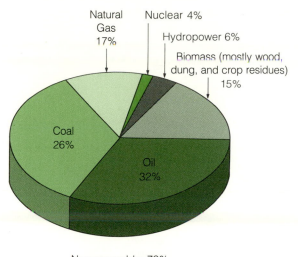

Natural Gas 17%
Nuclear 4%
Hydropower 6%
Biomass (mostly wood, dung, and crop residues) 15%
Coal 26%
Oil 32%

Nonrenewable: 79%
Renewable: 21%

Figure 4-7 World consumption of commercial nonrenewable (shaded) and renewable (unshaded) energy by source in 1986. (Sources: U.S. Department of Energy and Worldwatch Institute)

average temperature would be −240°C (−400°F) and life as we know it would not have arisen.

Most people think of solar energy in terms of direct heat from the sun. But, broadly defined, **solar energy** includes perpetual *direct* energy from the sun and a number of *indirect* forms of energy produced by the direct input. Major indirect forms of solar energy include perpetual wind, perpetual falling and flowing water (hydropower), and renewable biomass (solar energy converted to chemical energy in trees and other plants).

We have learned how to capture and use some of these direct and indirect forms of solar energy. *Passive solar energy systems* capture and store direct solar energy and use it to heat buildings and water without the use of mechanical devices. An example is a well-insulated, airtight house with large double- or triple-paned windows that face the sun.

Direct solar energy can also be captured by *active solar energy systems*. For example, specially designed roof-mounted collectors concentrate direct solar energy; pumps transfer this heat to water or to the interior of a building. We have also developed wind turbines and hydroelectric power plants to convert indirect solar energy in the form of wind and falling or flowing water into electricity.

Natural processes convert direct solar energy to chemical energy as biomass in the tissues of plants and animals. When plants and animals die, their biomass is buried and subjected to tremendous pressures and temperatures over millions of years. This converts the chemical energy stored in biomass to chemical

energy stored in underground deposits of fossil fuels such as natural gas, coal, crude oil, tar sands, and oil shale. This chemical energy is also an indirect form of solar energy.

The problem is that this form of solar energy, stored for us hundreds of millions of years ago, is being used up at such a rapid rate that it is *nonrenewable* on a human time scale. Fossil fuels took millions of years to form, but we are using them up in only a few hundred years.

Human ingenuity has developed a number of ways to use various forms of perpetual, renewable, and nonrenewable energy resources to supplement the direct input of solar energy and sell this energy to users. This supplemental commercial energy makes up the remaining 1% of the energy we use on earth (Figure 4-7).

Worldwide, three-fourths of the commercial energy used to supplement direct solar energy comes from burning nonrenewable fossil fuels to provide heat (oil, coal, natural gas) and produce electricity (mostly coal) and burning gasoline processed from crude oil to move vehicles. A moderate amount comes from burning potentially renewable biomass (wood, dung, crop residues, and trash) to produce heat. A small amount comes from using falling or flowing water—hydropower—and controlled nuclear fission to produce electricity. A very small amount (less than 1%) comes from using heat from the earth's interior (geothermal energy) and wind to produce electricity and solar energy (passive and active systems) to heat buildings and water.

Conserving, or not wasting, all forms of energy saves money and makes nonrenewable energy resources such as oil, coal, natural gas, and uranium last longer. It also reduces the environmental impact from using any form of energy.

At one extreme, the United States, with 4.8% of the world's population, uses 25% of the world's commercial energy. At the other extreme, India, with about 16% of the world's people, uses only about 1.5% of the world's commercial energy. In 1988 the 246 million Americans used more energy for air conditioning alone than 1.09 billion Chinese used for all purposes.

The most important supplemental source of energy for LDCs is potentially renewable biomass—especially fuelwood—the main source of energy for heating and cooking for roughly half the world's population. One-fourth of the world's population in MDCs may soon be faced with shortages of oil, but half the world's population in LDCs already faces a fuelwood shortage.

In 1850 the United States and most other MDCs had a decentralized energy system based on locally available renewable resources, primarily wood. Today they have a centralized energy system based on nonrenewable fossil fuels, especially oil and natural gas, increasingly produced in one part of the world and

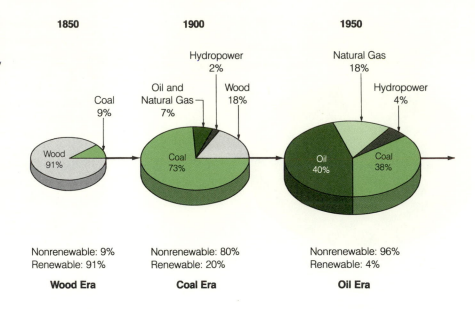

Figure 4-8 Changes in U.S. consumption of commercial nonrenewable (shaded) and renewable (unshaded) energy resources between 1850 and 1986. Relative circle size indicates the total amount of energy used. (Data from U.S. Department of Energy)

1850

Wood 91%
Coal 9%

Nonrenewable: 9%
Renewable: 91%

Wood Era

1900

Hydropower 2%
Oil and Natural Gas 7%
Wood 18%
Coal 73%

Nonrenewable: 80%
Renewable: 20%

Coal Era

1950

Natural Gas 18%
Hydropower 4%
Oil 40%
Coal 38%

Nonrenewable: 96%
Renewable: 4%

Oil Era

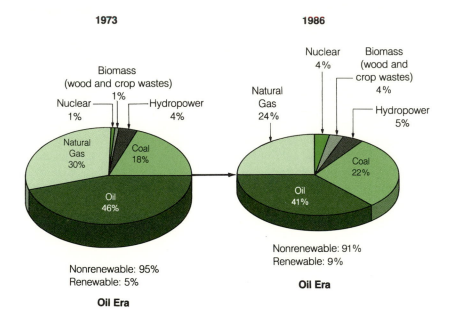

1973

Biomass (wood and crop wastes) 1%
Nuclear 1%
Hydropower 4%
Natural Gas 30%
Coal 18%
Oil 46%

Nonrenewable: 95%
Renewable: 5%

Oil Era

1986

Nuclear 4%
Biomass (wood and crop wastes) 4%
Natural Gas 24%
Hydropower 5%
Coal 22%
Oil 41%

Nonrenewable: 91%
Renewable: 9%

Oil Era

transported to and used in another part. By 1986 about 87% of the commercial energy used in the United States was provided by burning oil, coal, and natural gas, with the largest percentage (41%) coming from oil (Figure 4-8).

4-4 THE FIRST AND SECOND LAWS OF ENERGY

First Law of Energy: You Can't Get Something for Nothing In studying millions of falling objects, physical and chemical changes, and changes of temperature in living and nonliving systems, scientists have observed and measured energy being changed from one form to another. However, they have never been able to detect any creation or destruction of energy in any physical or chemical change.

This important information about what scientists find happening in nature without fail is summarized in the **law of conservation of energy,** also known as the **first law of energy or thermodynamics.** According to this scientific law, in any physical or chemical change, movement of matter from one place to another, or change in temperature, energy is neither created nor destroyed but merely transformed from one form to another. In other words, the energy gained or lost by any living or nonliving *system*—any collection of mat-

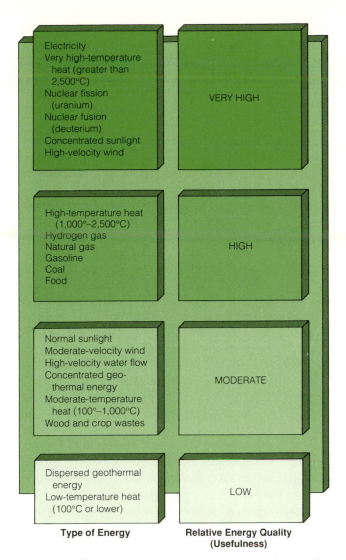

Type of Energy	Relative Energy Quality (Usefulness)
Electricity Very high-temperature heat (greater than 2,500°C) Nuclear fission (uranium) Nuclear fusion (deuterium) Concentrated sunlight High-velocity wind	VERY HIGH
High-temperature heat (1,000°–2,500°C) Hydrogen gas Natural gas Gasoline Coal Food	HIGH
Normal sunlight Moderate-velocity wind High-velocity water flow Concentrated geothermal energy Moderate-temperature heat (100°–1,000°C) Wood and crop wastes	MODERATE
Dispersed geothermal energy Low-temperature heat (100°C or lower)	LOW

Figure 4-9 Generalized ranking of the quality or usefulness of different types of energy.

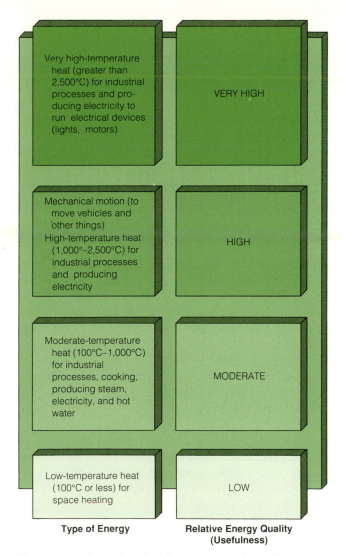

Type of Energy	Relative Energy Quality (Usefulness)
Very high-temperature heat (greater than 2,500°C) for industrial processes and producing electricity to run electrical devices (lights, motors)	VERY HIGH
Mechanical motion (to move vehicles and other things) High-temperature heat (1,000°–2,500°C) for industrial processes and producing electricity	HIGH
Moderate-temperature heat (100°C–1,000°C) for industrial processes, cooking, producing steam, electricity, and hot water	MODERATE
Low-temperature heat (100°C or less) for space heating	LOW

Figure 4-10 General quality of energy needed to perform various energy tasks. To avoid unnecessary energy waste, it is best to match the quality of an energy source (Figure 4-9) fairly close to the quality of energy needed to perform a particular energy task.

ter under study—must equal the energy lost or gained by its *surroundings* or *environment*—everything outside the system.

This law means that we can never get more energy out of an energy transformation process than we put in: *Energy input always equals energy output*. For example, the total amount of chemical energy in a gallon of gasoline exactly equals the output of energy in the form of mechanical energy to move the car, electrical energy to run the radio, heater, and other electrical systems, and heat lost to the environment when the gasoline is burned. The first energy law also means that in terms of energy quantity, *it always takes energy to get energy, and we can't get something for nothing (there is no free lunch)*.

Energy Quality Because the first law of energy states that energy can neither be created nor destroyed, you might think that there will always be enough energy.

Yet if you fill a car's tank with gasoline and drive around or if you use a flashlight battery until it is dead, you have lost something. If it isn't energy, what is it?

The answer involves understanding that energy varies in its *quality* or ability to do useful work. Energy quality is a measure of energy usefulness (Figure 4-9). **High-quality energy** is organized or concentrated and has great ability to perform useful work. Examples of these useful forms of energy are electricity, coal, gasoline, concentrated sunlight, nuclei of uranium-235, and high-temperature heat.

The mechanical energy in a fast-moving hammer held in your hand is high-quality kinetic energy because its atoms are moving in an organized way. Electrical energy is high-quality kinetic energy because it is a highly organized flow of electrons through a wire or other conductor. High-temperature heat is high-quality kinetic energy because it consists of rapidly moving atoms or molecules. Gasoline and a bowl of cereal are forms of high-quality potential energy because chemical energy is concentrated in the chemical bonds of their molecules.

By contrast, **low-quality energy** is disorganized or dilute and has little ability to do useful work. An example is the ambient or low-temperature heat in the air around you or in a river, lake, or ocean. For instance, the total amount of low-temperature heat stored in the Atlantic Ocean is greater than the amount of high-quality chemical energy stored in all the oil deposits in Saudi Arabia. But heat is so widely dispersed in the ocean that we can't do much with it. This dispersed heat like that in the air around us can't be used to move things or to heat things to high-temperatures.

We use energy to accomplish certain tasks, each requiring a certain minimum energy quality (Figure 4-10). Very high-quality electrical energy is needed to run lights, electric motors, and electronic devices. We need high-quality mechanical energy to move a car. But we need only low-temperature heat (less than 100°C) to heat homes and other buildings (space heating). It makes sense to match the quality of an energy source (Figure 4-9) to the quality of energy needed to perform a particular task (Figure 4-10). This saves energy and usually saves money.

Unfortunately, many forms of high-quality energy, such as high-temperature heat, electricity, gasoline, hydrogen gas (a useful fuel that can be produced by heating or passing electricity through water), and concentrated sunlight, do not occur naturally. We must use other forms of high-quality energy such as fossil, wood, and nuclear fuels to produce, concentrate, and store them, or to upgrade their quality so that they can be used to perform certain tasks.

Second Law of Energy: You Can't Break Even

Millions of measurements by scientists have shown that in any conversion of energy from one form to another, there is always a decrease in the amount of useful energy. Some of the initial energy input is always degraded to lower-quality, less-useful energy, usually low-temperature heat that flows into the environment. This summary of what we always find occurring in nature is known as the **second law of energy.** This law of energy quality degradation is also known as the **second law of thermodynamics.** No one has ever found a violation of this fundamental physical law.

Consider three examples of the second energy law in action. First, when a car is driven, only about 10% of the high-quality chemical energy available in its gasoline fuel is converted to mechanical energy to propel the vehicle and electrical energy to run its electrical systems. The remaining 90% is degraded to low-quality heat that is released into the environment and eventually lost into space. Second, when electrical energy flows through filament wires in an incandescent light bulb, it is changed into a mixture of

about 5% useful radiant energy, or light, and 95% low-quality heat that flows into the environment.

Much of modern civilization is built around the internal combustion engine and the incandescent light, which, respectively, waste 90% and 95% of their initial energy input. When oil and other fossil fuels are abundant and cheap, such waste is not considered important—easy come, easy go. But as nonrenewable energy resources become more scarce and expensive, reducing such unnecessary energy waste and finding more efficient substitutes become vital.

A third example of the degradation of energy quality is illustrated in Figure 4-11: A green plant converts solar energy to high-quality chemical energy stored in molecules of glucose and low-quality heat given off to the environment. When you eat a plant food, such as an apple, its high-quality chemical energy is transformed within your body to high-quality electrical and mechanical energy (used to move your body and perform other life processes) and low-quality heat. In each of these energy conversions, some of the initial high-quality energy is degraded into lower-quality heat that flows into the environment and eventually into space.

According to the first energy law, we will never run out of energy because energy can neither be created nor destroyed. But according to the second energy law, the overall supply of concentrated, high-quality energy available to us from all sources is being continually depleted as it is converted to low-quality energy. *Not only can we not get something for nothing in terms of energy quantity (the first energy law), we can't break even in terms of energy quality (the second energy law).* In using energy there is always a decrease in the amount of useful energy.

The second energy law also means that *we can never recycle or reuse high-quality energy to perform useful work.* Once the concentrated, high-quality energy in a piece of food, a gallon of gasoline, a lump of coal, or a piece of uranium is released, it is degraded into dispersed, low-quality heat that flows into the environment. We can heat air or water at a low temperature and upgrade it to high-quality energy. But the second energy law tells us that it will take more high-quality energy to do this than we get back.

4-5 ENERGY LAWS AND ENERGY RESOURCES

Which Energy Resources Should We Develop? The history of energy use since the Industrial Revolution has shown that developing and phasing in the widespread use of any energy resource takes about 50 years. Thus, today's energy research and development will determine the energy resources available to us 50 years from now. Using large amounts of human ingenuity

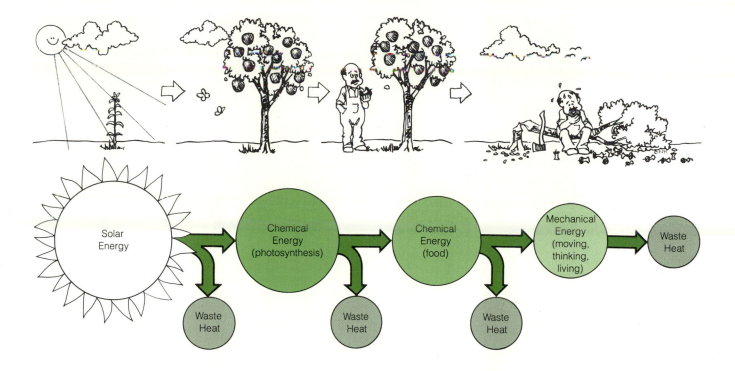

Figure 4-11 The second energy law in action in living systems. When energy is changed from one form to another, some of the initial input of high-quality energy is degraded, usually to low-quality heat, which is added to the environment.

and limited financial capital to develop the wrong mix of future energy resources could be disastrous for people in both MDCs and LDCs. The two energy laws are important tools in helping us decide how to reduce unnecessary energy waste and in evaluating the usefulness of various energy resources.

Increasing Energy Efficiency   Only 16% of all the commercially produced energy that flows through the U.S. economy performs useful work or is used to make petrochemicals (which are used to produce plastics, drugs, and many other products [Figure 4-12]). *This means that 84% of all energy used in the United States is wasted.* About 41% of this energy is wasted automatically because of the energy-quality tax imposed by the second energy law. But 43% of the commercial energy used in the United States is unnecessarily wasted.

One way to cut much of this energy waste and save money, at least in the long run, is to increase **energy efficiency.** This is the percentage of total energy input that does useful work and is not converted to low-quality, essentially useless heat in an energy conversion system. The energy conversion devices we use vary considerably in their energy efficiencies (Figure 4-13). We can reduce waste by using the most efficient processes or devices available and by trying to make them more efficient.

We can save energy and money by buying the most energy-efficient home heating systems, water heaters,

cars, air conditioners, refrigerators, and other household appliances available. The initial cost of the most energy-efficient models is usually higher, but, in the long run they usually save money by having a lower **life-cycle cost:** the initial cost plus lifetime operating costs.

The net efficiency of the entire energy delivery system of a heating system, water heater, or car is determined by finding the efficiency of each energy conversion step in the system. These steps include extracting the fuel, purifying and upgrading it to a useful form, transporting it, and finally using it.

Figure 4-14 shows how net energy efficiencies are determined for heating a well-insulated home **(1)** passively with an input of direct solar energy through south-facing windows and **(2)** with electricity produced at a nuclear power plant, transported by wire to the home, and converted to heat (electric resistance heating). This analysis shows that converting the high-quality chemical or nuclear energy in nuclear fuel to high-quality heat at several thousand degrees, converting this heat to high-quality electricity, and then using the electricity to provide low-quality heat for warming a house to only about 68°F is extremely wasteful of high-quality energy.

Such use of high-quality energy to provide low-quality heat is like using a chain saw to cut butter or using a sledge hammer to kill a fly. It is much less wasteful of high-quality energy to use a passive or

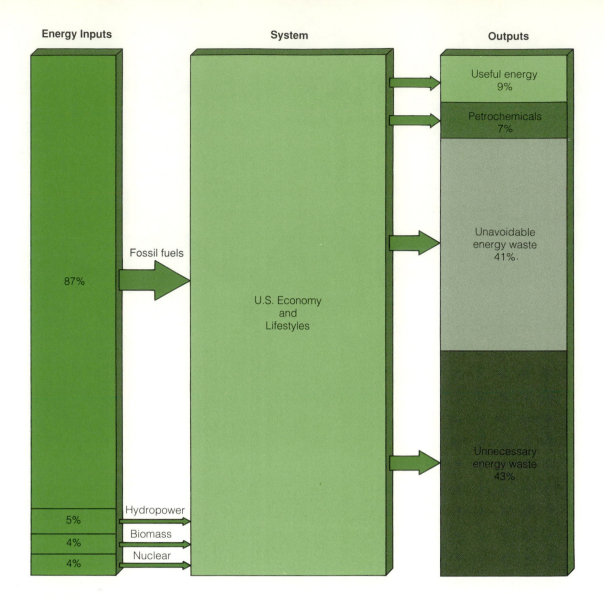

Figure 4-12 Flow of commercial supplemental energy through the U.S. economy. Note that only 16% of all commercial energy used in the United States ends up performing useful tasks (or is converted to petrochemicals). The rest is either automatically wasted because of the second law of energy (41%) or is wasted unnecessarily (43%).

active solar heating system to obtain low-quality heat from the environment and, if necessary, raise its temperature slightly to supply space heating.

This leads to a general rule of energy use called the *principle of matching energy quality to energy tasks:* Don't use high-quality energy (Figure 4-9) to do something that can be done by using lower-quality energy (Figure 4-10). This explains why using electricity to heat a house or to heat water wastes a lot of energy (and usually money) compared to other alternatives.

The cheapest and most energy-efficient way to provide heating, especially in a cold climate, is to build a superinsulated house. Such a house is so heavily insulated and airtight that even in areas where winter temperatures fall to −40°F, all of its space heating can usually be supplied by a combination of passive solar

gain (about 59%), waste heat from appliances (33%), and body heat from occupants (8%).

Passive solar heating, which has been used for thousands of years, is the next most efficient and cheapest method of heating a house, followed by one of the new, 95% efficient, natural gas furnaces. The least efficient, most expensive way to heat a house is with electricity produced by nuclear power plants. For example, in 1987 the average price of obtaining 250,000 kilocalories (1 million British thermal units, or Btus) for heating space or water in the United States was $4.90 using natural gas, $5.40 using fuel oil, and $22.65 using electricity.

Utility companies often run advertisements urging people to buy heat pumps, mostly because their combined heating and air conditioning systems run

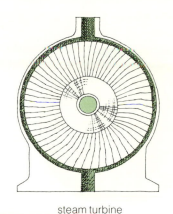
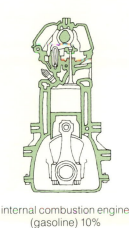

human body
20 to 25%

internal combustion engine
(gasoline) 10%

steam turbine
45%

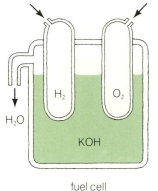

fuel cell
60%

incandescent light
5%

fluorescent light
22%

on electricity. A heat pump is an efficient way to heat a house as long as the outside temperature does not fall below 45°F. But once the temperature falls below 45°F, these devices begin using electric resistance heating—the most expensive, energy-wasting way to heat any space.

Heat pumps are useful in areas with fairly warm climates. But in such areas their main use is for air conditioning. The air conditioning units with most heat pumps are usually much less energy-efficient than many stand-alone units.

A similar analysis of net energy efficiency shows that the least efficient and most expensive way to heat water for washing and bathing is to use electricity produced by nuclear power plants. The most efficient method is to use a tankless, instant water heater fired by natural gas or liquefied petroleum gas (LPG). Such heaters fit under a sink and burn fuel only when the hot water faucet is turned on, heating the water instantly as it flows through a small burner chamber and providing hot water only when and as long as it is needed. In contrast, conventional natural gas and electric resistance heaters keep a large tank of water hot all day and night and can run out after a long shower or two. Tankless heaters are widely used in many parts of Europe and are slowly beginning to appear in the United States. A well-insulated, conventional natural gas or LPG water heater is also efficient.

As mentioned earlier, the net energy efficiency of a car powered with a conventional internal combustion engine is only about 10%. An electric engine with batteries recharged by electricity from a hydroelectric power plant has a net efficiency almost three times that of a gasoline-burning internal combustion engine. But a hydroelectric-powered system cannot be widely used in the United States because favorable hydroelectric sites are found only in certain areas and most have already been developed. In addition, electric cars will not be cost-effective unless scientists can develop cheaper, longer-lasting batteries.

The most efficient nonelectric automobile system is a gasoline-burning turbine engine. American, Japanese, and European carmakers have built prototype turbine engines, but so far we don't know whether they are cost-effective. Thus, for the time being, the best way to save money and gasoline is to use a fuel-efficient car (at least 35 to 50 miles per gallon) and whenever possible use mass transportation, ride a bicycle, or walk.

Using Waste Heat We cannot recycle high-quality energy. But we can slow the rate at which waste heat flows into the environment when high-quality energy is degraded. For instance, in cold weather an uninsulated, leaky house loses heat almost as fast as it is produced. By contrast, a well-insulated, airtight house

Passive Solar   **Electricity from Nuclear Power Plant**

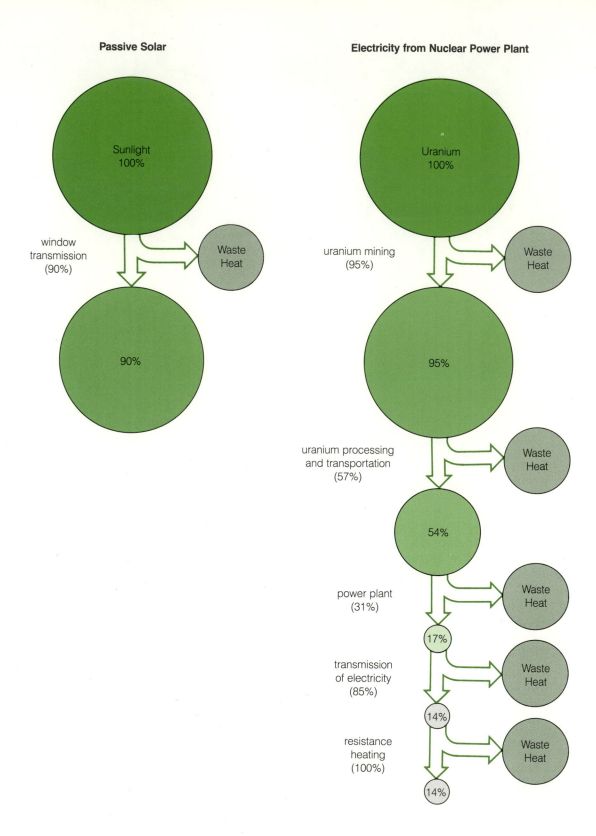

Figure 4-14 Comparison of net energy efficiency for two types of space heating. The cumulative net efficiency is obtained by multiplying the percentage shown inside the circle for each step by the energy efficiency for that step (shown in parentheses). Usually, the greater the number of steps in an energy conversion process, the lower its net energy efficiency.

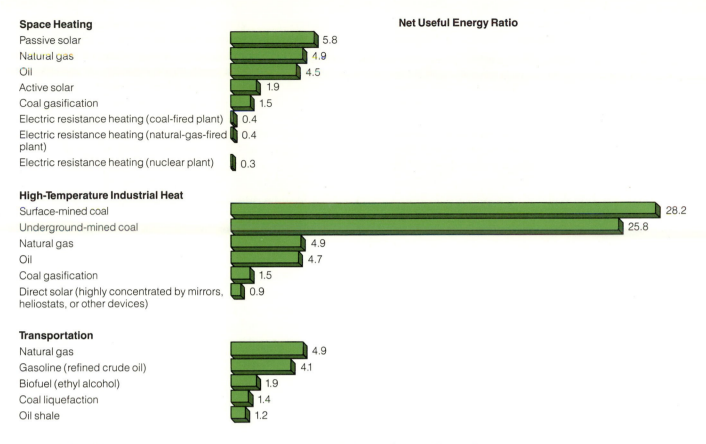

Space Heating

	Net Useful Energy Ratio
Passive solar	5.8
Natural gas	4.9
Oil	4.5
Active solar	1.9
Coal gasification	1.5
Electric resistance heating (coal-fired plant)	0.4
Electric resistance heating (natural-gas-fired plant)	0.4
Electric resistance heating (nuclear plant)	0.3

High-Temperature Industrial Heat

Surface-mined coal	28.2
Underground-mined coal	25.8
Natural gas	4.9
Oil	4.7
Coal gasification	1.5
Direct solar (highly concentrated by mirrors, heliostats, or other devices)	0.9

Transportation

Natural gas	4.9
Gasoline (refined crude oil)	4.1
Biofuel (ethyl alcohol)	1.9
Coal liquefaction	1.4
Oil shale	1.2

Figure 4-15 Net useful energy ratios for various energy systems. (Data from Colorado Energy Research Institute, *Net Energy Analysis*, 1976, and Howard T. Odum and Elisabeth C. Odum, *Energy Basis for Man and Nature*, 3rd ed., McGraw-Hill, 1981)

can retain most of its heat for five to ten hours, and a well-designed, superinsulated house can retain most of its heat up to four days.

Because heat always flows from hot to cold samples of matter, on hot days heat in the outside air spontaneously flows into a building. A well-insulated and airtight building slows down the rate of this flow.

In some office buildings, waste heat from lights, computers, and other machines is collected and distributed to reduce heating bills during cold weather, or exhausted to reduce cooling bills during hot weather. Waste heat from industrial plants and electrical power plants can be distributed through insulated pipes and used as a district heating system for nearby buildings, greenhouses, and fish ponds, as is done in some parts of Europe.

Waste heat from coal-fired and other industrial boilers can be used to produce electricity at half the cost of buying it from a utility company. The electricity can be used by the plant or sold to the local power company for general use. This combined production of high-temperature heat and electricity, known as **cogeneration,** is widely used in industrial plants throughout Europe.

If all large industrial boilers in the United States used cogeneration, they could produce electricity equal to that of 30 to 200 large nuclear or coal-fired power plants (depending on the technology used) at about half the cost. This would reduce the average price of electricity and essentially eliminate the need to build any large electric power plants through the year 2020.

Net Useful Energy: It Takes Energy to Get Energy The usable amount of high-quality energy obtainable from a given quantity of an energy resource is its **net useful energy.** It is the total energy available from the resource over its lifetime minus the amount of energy used (the first energy law), automatically wasted (the second energy law), and unnecessarily wasted in finding, processing, concentrating, and transporting it to a user. For example, if nine units of fossil fuel energy are needed to supply ten units of nuclear, solar, or additional fossil fuel energy (perhaps from a deep well at sea), the net useful energy gain is only one unit of energy.

We can express this relationship as the ratio of useful energy produced to the useful energy used to produce it. In the example just given, the net energy ratio would be 10/9, or 1.1. The higher the ratio, the greater the net useful energy yield. When the ratio is less than 1, there is a net energy loss over the lifetime of the system. Figure 4-15 lists estimated net useful energy ratios for various energy alternatives for space heating, high-temperature heat for industrial processes, and gaseous or liquid fuels for vehicles.

Currently, a fossil fuel such as oil has a relatively high net useful energy ratio because much of it comes from rich, accessible deposits such as those in Saudi Arabia and other parts of the Middle East. When these sources are depleted, however, the net useful energy ratios of fossil fuels will decline and prices will rise. Then more money and high-quality fossil fuel will be needed to find, process, and deliver new fuel from poorer deposits found deeper in the earth and in remote, hostile areas like Alaska, the Arctic, and the North Sea—far from where the energy is to be used.

Conventional nuclear fission energy has a low net energy ratio because large amounts of energy are required to build and operate power plants. Additional energy is needed to take them apart after their 25 to 30 years of useful life and to safely store the resulting highly radioactive wastes.

Large-scale solar energy plants for producing electricity or high-temperature heat for industrial processes also have low net useful energy ratios. This is because the small flow of high-quality solar energy in a particular area must be collected and concentrated to provide the necessary high temperatures. Large amounts of money and high-quality energy are necessary to mine, process, and transport the materials used in vast arrays of solar collectors, focusing mirrors, pipes, and other equipment. On the other hand, passive and active solar energy systems for heating individual buildings and for heating water have relatively high net useful energy ratios because they supply relatively small amounts of heat at moderate temperatures.

4-6 MATTER AND ENERGY LAWS AND ENVIRONMENTAL AND RESOURCE PROBLEMS

Every Little Bit of Waste Heat and Matter Counts   The three scientific laws governing what happens when matter and energy resources change from one form to another can help us understand how to work with nature and reduce the environmental impact of human activities. Because of the law of conservation of matter and the second law of energy, the use of resources by each of us automatically adds some waste heat and waste matter to the environment.

Your individual use of matter and energy resources and your addition of waste heat and waste matter to the environment may seem small and insignificant. But you are only one of the 1.2 billion individuals in industrialized countries using large quantities of the earth's matter and energy resources at a rapid rate. And the 4.0 billion people in less developed countries hope to be able to use more of these resources.

Throwaway Societies   Today's advanced industrialized countries are **throwaway societies,** sustaining ever-increasing economic growth by maximizing the rate at which matter and energy resources are used and wasted (Figure 4-16). The scientific laws of matter and energy tell us that if more and more people continue to use and unnecessarily waste resources at an increasing rate, sooner or later the capacity of the local, regional, and global environments to dilute and degrade waste matter and absorb waste heat will be exceeded.

Because the law of conservation of matter states that we can't destroy any of the matter on earth, some analysts have fallen into the trap of thinking we have infinite matter resources. But not being able to destroy matter is not the same as not being able to destroy a matter resource.

A resource is useful only if it is available at an affordable cost and in a particular form and concentration. When nonrenewable resources are converted to less useful forms (rusted iron, for example) and widely dispersed as litter and junk, they can become too expensive to collect and recycle. Similarly, when potentially renewable resources such as groundwater, trees, and wildlife are exploited faster than they are renewed, their supply is depleted.

The scientific laws discussed in this chapter tell us what we can and cannot do in using matter and energy resources. Not knowing these laws and not understanding their implications can lead one to come up with ridiculous ideas (see Spotlight on page 89).

Matter-Recycling Societies   A stopgap solution to this problem is to convert from a throwaway society to a **matter-recycling society.** The goal of such a shift would be to allow economic growth to continue without depleting matter resources and without producing excessive pollution and environmental degradation.

But as we have seen already, there is no free lunch. The two laws of energy tell us that *recycling matter resources always requires high-quality energy, which cannot be recycled.* However, if a recyclable resource such as aluminum or paper is not too widely scattered, recycling often requires less high-quality energy than that needed to find, extract, and process virgin resources.

Nevertheless, in the long run, a matter-recycling society based on indefinitely increasing economic growth must have an inexhaustible supply of affordable high-quality energy. And the environment must have an infinite capacity to absorb and disperse waste heat and to dilute and degrade waste matter.

Experts disagree on how much usable high-quality energy we have. However, supplies of coal, oil, natural gas, and uranium are clearly finite. Affordable supplies of oil, the most widely used supplementary energy resource, may be gone in several decades.

"Ah," you say, "but don't we have a virtually inexhaustible supply of high-quality solar energy flowing to the earth?" The problem is that the amount of solar energy reaching a particular small area of the earth's surface each minute or hour is low, and nonexistent at night.

With a proper collection and storage system, using solar energy to provide hot water and to heat a house to moderate temperatures makes good thermodynamic and economic sense. But to provide the high temperatures needed to melt metals or to produce electricity in a power plant, solar energy may not be cost-effective. Why? Because it has a very low net useful energy ratio (Figure 4-15).

A promising solar energy technology that may get around this problem is the *solar photovoltaic cell*, which converts solar energy directly to electricity in one simple, nonpolluting step. If researchers can improve their energy efficiency and decrease their cost, solar cells, covering roofs or walls facing the sun, could meet all household electricity needs.

The excess electricity produced by the cells during daylight can be stored in deep-cycle batteries (like those used in golf carts and marine vessels) for use when the sun isn't shining. Or the excess could be sold to the local utility company. The excess might also be used to recharge batteries to run your small electric urban car or passed through water to produce hydrogen gas that could be used as a fuel to run your car and heat your house. When the hydrogen gas burns,

it reacts with oxygen in the air to produce water vapor and some nitric oxide (NO). Using hydrogen gas as a fuel eliminates all but one of the air pollutants we now produce by burning fossil fuels and wood. It also produces no carbon dioxide, the major culprit that can make the earth's climate warmer.

Scientists and engineers project that solar cells might be mass-produced at an affordable price sometime in the 1990s or shortly after the turn of the century. If so, most of the large, centralized electric power plants in the United States and the world would quickly become obsolete.

The first country that develops such a technology could rapidly become the dominant economic force in the world. Japan is increasing its already extensive research efforts in this area. In the United States, President Carter greatly expanded government-supported research in photovoltaic cells during the late 1970s. However, the Reagan administration sharply reduced federal funding for such research.

Suppose that solar cells or some other breakthrough were to supply an essentially infinite supply of affordable useful energy. Would this solve our energy problems? No. It would be an important and incredibly useful breakthrough. But the second energy law tells us that the faster we use more energy to transform more matter into products and to recycle these products, the faster large amounts of low-quality heat and waste matter are dumped into the environment. Thus, the more we attempt to "conquer" the earth,

---

SPOTLIGHT Not Knowing Much About Science Can Cost You Money

Some of the key ideas proposed by cornucopian economist Julian Simon (see Guest Essay on p. 24) have been based on an incredible lack of knowledge about science. He once stated that we would never run out of energy because it could be partially recycled. When questioned, he explained he was talking about using waste heat before it flowed into the environment. This is an excellent way to save some money and energy. But it is not a source of *any* high-quality energy, much less an infinite supply.

Another time Simon made what must be one of the most unscientific and uneconomic statements ever published:

Copper can be made from other metals. . . . Even the total weight of the

earth is not a theoretical limit to the amount of copper that might be available to earthlings in the future. Only the total weight of the universe . . . would be such a theoretical limit.

He based his statement on the fact that nuclear reactions can be used to change isotopes of some elements into isotopes of other elements. For example, an isotope of nickel can be converted to an isotope of copper. But such conversions are incredibly difficult and expensive to do. Using extremely optimistic assumptions, two physicists calculated that to produce copper from nickel would cost at least a billion dollars a pound!

Since the 1800s people have come up with various alleged inventions of perpetual motion

machines, which are supposed to put out more high-quality energy than you have to put in—violating both the first and second energy laws. Such schemes have been used to put large amounts of money in the pockets of con artists who rely on people's greedy desire to get something for nothing. Anytime you hear someone say you can get something for nothing, hold on to your pocketbook and run!

Unless everyone acquires at least a basic knowledge of science, we can be duped by people with dumb, costly, and even dangerous ideas.

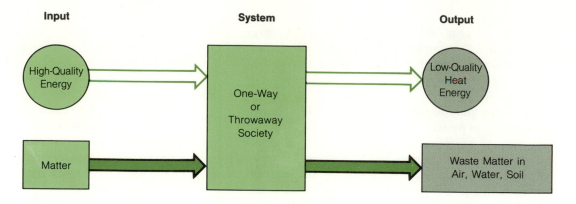

Figure 4-16 The one-way, or throwaway, society in most industrialized countries is based on maximizing the rates of energy flow and matter flow. This rapidly converts the world's high-quality matter and energy resources to trash, pollution, and low-quality heat.

the more stress we put on the environment. Although experts argue over how close we are to reaching overload limits, the scientific laws of matter and energy indicate that such limits do exist.

Sustainable-Earth Societies   The three scientific laws governing matter and energy changes indicate that the best long-term solution is to shift from a throwaway society based on maximizing matter and energy flow (and in the process wasting an unnecessarily large portion of the earth's resources) to a **sustainable-earth society** (Figure 4-17).

Such a society would go a step further than a matter-recycling society. In addition to recycling and reusing much of the matter we now discard as trash, it would emphasize the conservation of matter and energy resources by reducing unnecessary waste and by making things that last longer and are easier to recycle, reuse, and repair.

Just as important, a sustainable-earth society would cut down on the use of resources by regulating population growth. With such an approach, local, regional, and global limits of the environment to absorb low-quality heat and to dilute and degrade waste matter would not be exceeded. Also, depletion of exhaustible resources would be prevented or at least delayed much further into the future.

The matter and energy laws also show us why input approaches for controlling pollution usually make more sense thermodynamically and economically than output approaches. For example, preventing a toxic chemical from reaching underground supplies of

drinking water is much easier and cheaper than trying to remove the chemical once it has contaminated a groundwater deposit.

The three basic scientific laws of matter and energy show that, like it or not, we are all interdependent on each other and on the other parts of nature for our survival. In the next chapter we will apply these laws to living systems and look at some biological principles that can help us learn how to work with nature.

The second law of thermodynamics holds, I think, the supreme position among laws of nature. . . . If your theory is found to be against the second law of thermodynamics, I can give you no hope.

Arthur S. Eddington

DISCUSSION TOPICS

1. Explain why we don't really consume anything, and why we can never really throw matter away.

2. A tree grows and increases its mass. Explain why this isn't a violation of the law of conservation of matter.

3. Use the second energy law to explain why a barrel of oil can be used only once as a fuel.

4. Explain why most energy analysts urge that improving energy efficiency should form the basis of any individual, corporate, or national energy plan. Is it an important part of your personal energy plan or lifestyle? Why or why not?

5. Explain why using electricity to heat a house and to supply household hot water is so expensive and waste-

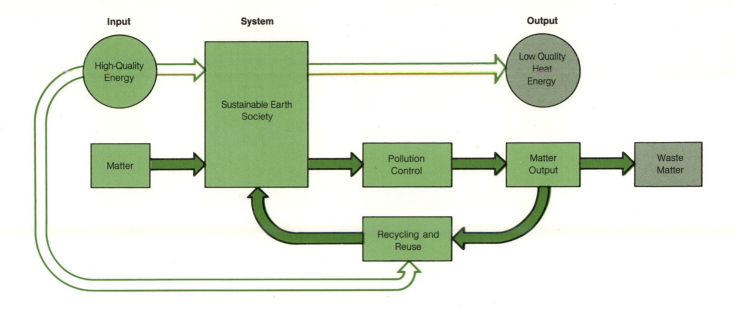

Figure 4-17 A sustainable-earth society based on energy flow and matter recycling. It is characterized by reusing and recycling renewable matter resources, wasting less resources, reducing unnecessary consumption, and controlling population growth.

ful of energy. What energy tasks can be done best by electricity?

6. You are about to build a house. What energy supply (oil, gas, coal, or other) would you use for space heating, cooking food, refrigerating food, and heating water? Consider long-term economic and environmental impact.

7. **a.** Use the law of conservation of matter to explain why a matter-recycling society will sooner or later be necessary.
   b. Use the first and second laws of energy to explain why in the long run a sustainable-earth society, not just a matter-recycling society, will be necessary.

FURTHER READINGS

American Physical Society. 1975. *Efficient Use of Energy.* New York: American Institute of Physics.

Carrying Capacity, Inc. 1987. *Beyond Oil.* New York: Ballinger.

Christensen, John W. 1984. *Global Science: Energy, Resources, and Environment,* 2nd ed. Dubuque, Iowa: Kendall/ Hunt.

Colorado Energy Research Institute. 1976. *Net Energy Analysis: An Energy Balance Study of Fossil Fuel Resources.* Golden, Colo: Colorado Energy Research Institute.

Fowler, John M. 1984. *Energy and the Environment,* 2nd ed. New York: McGraw-Hill.

Hirsch, Robert L. 1987. "Impending United States Energy Crisis." *Science,* vol. 235, 1467–1473.

Lovins, Amory B. 1977. *Soft Energy Paths.* Cambridge, Mass.: Ballinger.

Lynch, Michael. 1987. "The Next Oil Crisis." *Technology Review,* Nov./Dec., 39–45.

Nash, Hugh, ed. 1979. *The Energy Controversy: Soft Path Questions and Answers.* San Francisco: Friends of the Earth.

Odum, Howard T., and Elisabeth C. Odum. 1980. *Energy Basis for Man and Nature.* New York: McGraw-Hill.

Rifkin, Jeremy. 1980. *Entropy: A New World View.* New York: Viking Press.

Schneider, Steven A. 1983. *The Oil Price Revolution.* Baltimore, Md.: Johns Hopkins University Press.

CHAPTER 5

Ecosystems: What Are They and How Do They Work?

General Questions and Issues

1. What two major natural processes keep us and other organisms alive?
2. What is an ecosystem and what are its major living and nonliving components?
3. What happens to energy in an ecosystem?
4. What happens to matter in an ecosystem?
5. What are the habitat requirements and roles of organisms in ecosystems?

If we love our children, we must love the earth with tender care and pass it on, diverse and beautiful, so that on a warm spring day 10,000 years hence they can feel peace in a sea of grass, can watch a bee visit a flower, can hear a sandpiper call in the sky, and can find joy in being alive.

Hugh H. Iltis

W hat plants and animals live in a forest or a pond? How do they get enough matter and energy resources to stay alive? How do these plants and animals interact with one another and with their physical environment? What changes will this forest or pond undergo through time?

Ecology is the science that attempts to answer such questions about how nature works. In 1869 German biologist Ernst Haeckel coined the term *ecology* from two Greek words: *oikos,* meaning "house" or "place to live," and *logos,* meaning "study of."

Literally, then, ecology is the study of living things in their home or **environment**: all the external conditions and factors, living and nonliving, that affect an organism. In other words, **ecology** is the study of the interactions between organisms and their living (biotic) and nonliving (abiotic) environment. The key word is *interactions.* Scientists usually carry out this study by examining different **ecosystems**: forests, deserts, grasslands, rivers, lakes, oceans, or any set or organisms interacting with one another and with their nonliving environment.

This chapter will consider the major nonliving and living components of ecosystems and how they interact. The next chapter will consider major types of ecosystems and the changes they can undergo because of natural events and human activities.

5-1 THE EARTH'S LIFE SUPPORT SYSTEMS: AN OVERVIEW

The Biosphere and the Ecosphere   The earth has several major parts that play a role in sustaining life (Figure 5-1). You are part of what ecologists call the **biosphere**—the living and dead organisms found near the earth's surface in parts of the atmosphere, hydrosphere, and lithosphere. These organisms are found mostly in a zone extending from about 200 feet below the ocean's surface to about 20,000 feet above sea level.

The living organisms that make up the biosphere interact with one another and with energy from the sun and various chemicals found in parts of the atmosphere, hydrosphere, and lithosphere. This collection of living and dead organisms (the biosphere) interacting with one another and their nonliving environment (energy and chemicals) throughout the world is called the **ecosphere.** If the earth were an apple, the ecosphere would be no thicker than the apple's skin. *The goal of ecology is to learn how the ecosphere works.*

Energy Flow and Matter Recycling   What keeps you, me, and most other organisms alive on this tiny planet as it hurtles through space at a speed of 66,000 miles per hour? The answer to this question is that life on

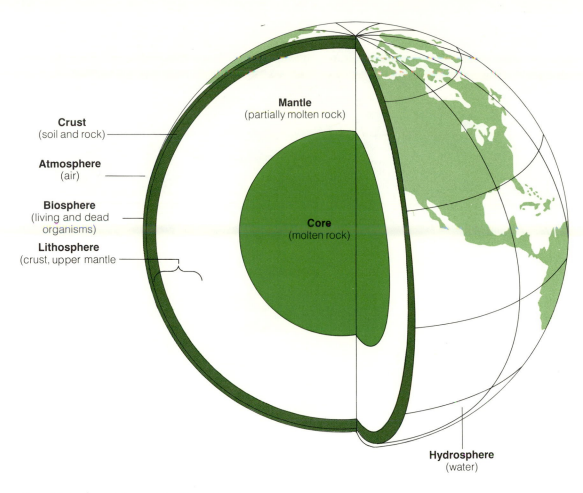

Crust
(soil and rock)

Atmosphere
(air)

Biosphere
(living and dead
organisms)

Lithosphere
(crust, upper mantle

Mantle
(partially molten rock)

Core
(molten rock)

Hydrosphere
(water)

Figure 5-1 Our life support system: the general structure of the earth.

earth depends largely on two fundamental processes (Figure 5-2):

- The *one-way flow of high-quality energy* from the sun, through materials and living things on or near the earth's surface, and eventually into space as low-quality heat

- The *recycling* of chemicals required by living organisms through parts of the ecosphere

The Sun: Source of Energy for Life The source of the radiant energy that sustains life on earth is the sun. It lights and warms the earth and supplies the energy used by green plants to synthesize the compounds that keep them alive and serve as food for almost all other organisms. Solar energy also powers the recycling of key chemicals and drives the climate and weather systems that distribute heat and fresh water over the earth's surface.

Massive amounts of energy are released from the sun into space as a spectrum of ultraviolet light, visible light, infrared radiation, and other forms of *radiant*, or *electromagnetic, energy.* These forms of energy travel outward in all directions through space at a speed of 186,000 miles per second.

Figure 5-3 shows what happens to the solar radiant energy reaching the earth. About 34% is immediately reflected back to space by clouds, chemicals, and dust in the atmosphere and by the earth's surface. Most of the remaining 66% warms the atmosphere and land, evaporates water and cycles it through the ecosphere, and generates winds. A tiny fraction (0.023%) is captured by green plants and used in the process of photosynthesis to make organic compounds that all organisms need to survive.

Most of the radiant energy reaching the earth's surface is in the form of light and near-infrared radiation. Most of the harmful forms of ionizing radiation emitted by the sun, especially ultraviolet radiation, are absorbed by molecules of ozone (O_3) in the upper atmosphere (stratosphere) and water vapor in the lower atmosphere. Without this screening effect, most present forms of life on earth could not exist.

Most of the incoming solar radiation not reflected away is degraded into low-quality heat (far-infrared radiation) in accordance with the second law of energy and flows into space. The amount of energy returning to space as low-quality heat is affected by the presence of molecules such as water, carbon dioxide, methane, and ozone and by some forms of solid particulate

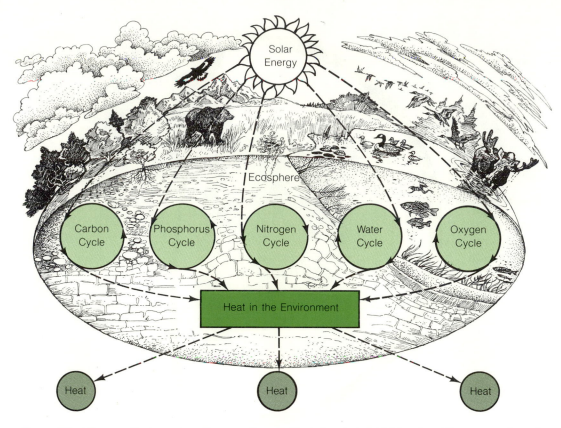

Figure 5-2 Life on earth depends on the recycling of critical chemicals (solid lines) and the one-way flow of energy through the ecosphere (dashed lines). This greatly simplified overview shows only a few of the many chemicals that are recycled.

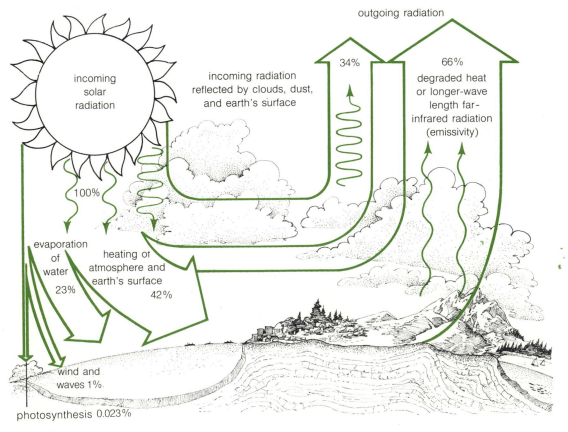

Figure 5-3 The flow of energy to and from the earth.

matter in the atmosphere. These substances, acting as gatekeepers, allow some high-quality forms of radiant energy from the sun to pass through the atmosphere. They also absorb and reradiate some of the resulting low-quality heat back toward the earth's surface.

Scientists are becoming increasingly concerned that human activities are changing global climate patterns by disrupting the rate at which incoming solar energy flows through the ecosphere and returns to space as low-quality heat. Some possible effects of our activities on climate are discussed in Section 7-5.

Biogeochemical Cycles Any element or compound needed by an organism for its survival, growth, and reproduction is called a **nutrient.** Nutrient elements and compounds required by organisms in large amounts are called **macronutrients.** Examples are carbon, oxygen, hydrogen, nitrogen, and phosphorus. These five elements and their compounds make up 97% of the mass of your body and more than 95% of the mass of all living organisms. Other nutrients required by organisms in small, or trace, amounts are called **micronutrients.**

Only a small portion of the earth's chemicals exist in forms useful to the organisms that make up the ecosphere. Fortunately, the essentially fixed supply of elements and compounds required as nutrients for life on earth is continuously recycled through the ecosphere and converted to useful forms by a combination of biological, geological, and chemical processes.

This recycling of nutrients from the environment, to organisms, and then back to the environment takes place in **biogeochemical cycles** (*bio* meaning living, *geo* for water, rocks, and soil, and *chemical* for the changing of matter from one form to another). These nutrient cycles, driven directly or indirectly by incoming energy from the sun, include the carbon, oxygen, nitrogen, phosphorus, and hydrologic (water) cycles (Figure 5-2).

This means that a chemical may be part of an organism at one moment and part of its nonliving environment at another moment. For example, one of the oxygen molecules you just inhaled may be one inhaled previously by you, your grandmother, King Tut thousands of years ago, or a dinosaur millions of years ago. Similarly, some of the carbon atoms in the skin covering your right hand may once have been part of a leaf, a dinosaur hide, or a limestone rock.

5-2 ECOSYSTEMS: TYPES AND COMPONENTS

The Realm of Ecology Ecology is primarily concerned with interactions among five of the levels of organization of matter shown in Figure 4-1 (page 73):

organisms, populations, communities, ecosystems, and the ecosphere. An **organism** is any form of life. Biologists classify the earth's organisms in anywhere from 4 to 20 categories. But in this introductory book it is only necessary to classify organisms as *plants, animals,* or *decomposers.*

Plants range from microscopic, one-celled, floating and drifting plants known as phytoplankton to the largest of all living things, the giant sequoia trees of western North America. Animals range in size from floating and drifting zooplankton (which feed on phytoplankton) to the 14-foot-high, male African elephant and the 100-foot-long blue whale. Decomposers range from microscopic bacteria to large fungi such as mushrooms.

A group of organisms that have similar characteristics is called a **species.** For organisms that reproduce sexually, a species can also be defined as organisms that can potentially interbreed only among themselves. It's estimated that 5 million to 10 million different species exist worldwide. Some biologists put the estimate as high as 50 million species, 30 million of them insects. So far, about 1.7 million of the earth's species have been described and named, and about 10,000 new species are added to the list each year.

Each species is found as **populations**: groups of individual organisms of the same species living in a particular region. Examples of populations are all the sunfish in a pond, gray squirrels in a forest, white oak trees in a forest, people in a country, or people in the world. Populations are dynamic groups of organisms that adapt to changes in environmental conditions by changing their size, distribution among various age groups (age structure), and genetic makeup.

Each organism and population has a **habitat**: the place or type of place where it naturally lives. When several populations of different species live together and interact with one another in a particular place, they make up what is called a **community,** or **biological community.** Examples include all the plants, animals, and decomposers found in a forest, a pond, a desert, a dead log, or an aquarium.

An **ecosystem** is the combination of a community and the chemical and physical factors making up its nonliving environment. It is an ever-changing (dynamic), interdependent network of biological, chemical, and physical interactions that help sustain a community and allow it to respond to changes in environmental conditions. All the earth's ecosystems together make up the ecosphere.

Major Terrestrial and Aquatic Ecosystems Although no two are exactly alike, ecosystems can be classified into general types that contain similar types of organisms. The ecosphere's major land ecosystems such as forests, grasslands, and deserts are called **terrestrial ecosystems,** or **biomes.** The differences among these

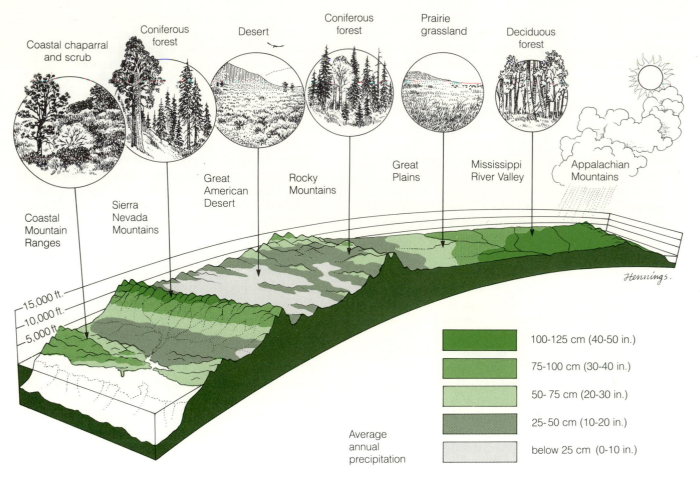

Coastal chaparral and scrub

Coniferous forest

Desert

Coniferous forest

Prairie grassland

Deciduous forest

Coastal Mountain Ranges

Sierra Nevada Mountains

Great American Desert

Rocky Mountains

Great Plains

Mississippi River Valley

Appalachian Mountains

Hennings.

15,000 ft.
10,000 ft.
5,000 ft.

	Average annual precipitation
■	100-125 cm (40-50 in.)
■	75-100 cm (30-40 in.)
■	50- 75 cm (20-30 in.)
■	25- 50 cm (10-20 in.)
■	below 25 cm (0-10 in.)

Figure 5-4 Gradual transition from one major biome to another along the 39th parallel crossing the United States. The major factors causing these transitions are changes in average temperature and precipitation.

land ecosystems in various parts of the world are caused mostly by differences in average temperature and average precipitation (Figure 5-4).

Major ecosystems found in the hydrosphere are called **aquatic ecosystems.** Examples include ponds, lakes, rivers, open ocean, coral reefs, estuaries (mouths of rivers or ocean inlets where salt water and fresh water mix), and coastal and inland wetlands (such as swamps, marshes, and prairie potholes). The major differences between these ecosystems are the result of differences in the amount of various nutrients dissolved in the water environment (salinity), depth of sunlight penetration, and average water temperature. Major terrestrial and aquatic ecosystems are discussed in more detail in Chapter 6.

Whether large or small, biomes and aquatic ecosystems normally don't have distinct boundaries. An ecosystem blends into an adjacent one through a transition zone, called an **ecotone.** An ecotone contains many of the plant and animal species found in both adjacent ecosystems and often has species not found in either of them. As a result, ecotone areas between two ecosystems usually contain a greater diversity of species than their surrounding areas.

Abiotic Components of Ecosystems Ecosystems consist of various nonliving and living components. Figures 5-5 and 5-6 are greatly simplified diagrams showing a few of the components of ecosystems in a freshwater pond and in a field.

The nonliving, or **abiotic,** components of an ecosystem include various physical and chemical factors. Important physical factors are sunlight, shade, precipitation, wind, terrain, temperature, and water currents. The major chemical factors are the nutrient elements and compounds in the atmosphere, hydrosphere, and lithosphere that are required in large or small amounts for the survival, growth, and reproduction of organisms.

Biotic Components of Ecosystems The major types of organisms that make up the living, or **biotic,** components of an ecosystem are usually classified as *producers, consumers,* or *decomposers.* This classification is

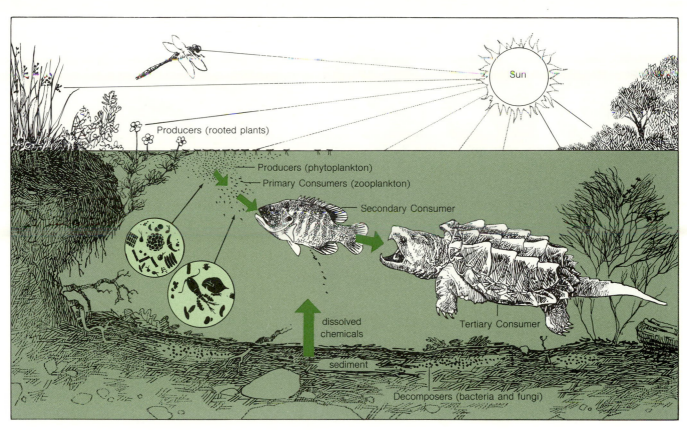

Figure 5-5 The major components of a freshwater pond ecosystem.

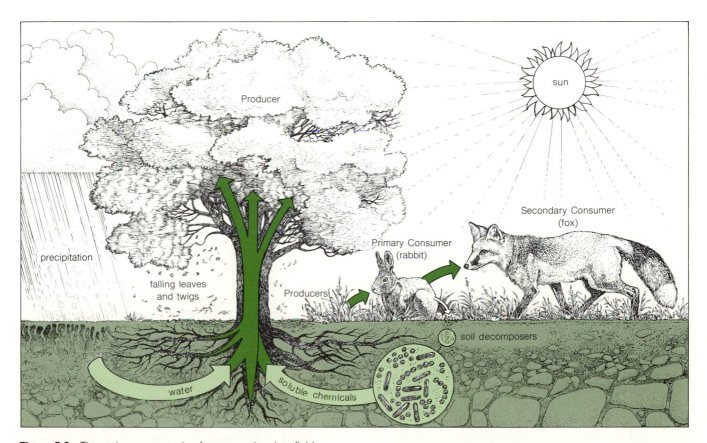

Figure 5-6 The major components of an ecosystem in a field.

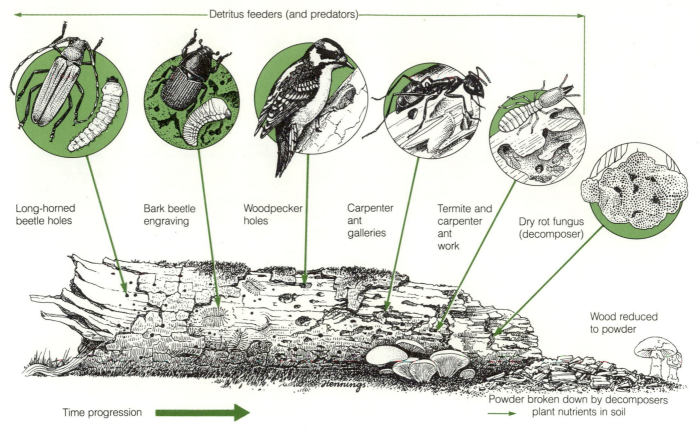

Figure 5-7 Some detritivores, called detritus feeders, directly consume dead organic matter in a fallen tree. Other detritivores, called decomposers, break down complex organic chemicals in the dead wood into simpler nutrient chemicals that are returned to the soil for reuse by plants.

based on the general lifestyles of three types of organisms in ecosystems, especially how they get the nutrients they require for survival.

Producers—sometimes called **autotrophs** (self-feeders)—are organisms that can manufacture the organic compounds they use as sources of energy and nutrients. Most producers are green plants that make the organic nutrients they require through **photosynthesis.** The process begins when sunlight is absorbed by pigments such as chlorophyll in producer plants. The plants then use this energy to combine carbon dioxide (which they get from the atmosphere or water) with water (which they get from the soil or aquatic surroundings) to make carbohydrates—sugars such as glucose, starches, and celluloses. Oxygen gas is also produced by photosynthesis.

carbon dioxide + water + **solar energy** → glucose + oxygen

In essence this complex process converts radiant energy from the sun into chemical energy stored in the chemical bonds that hold glucose and other carbohydrates together.

Some producer organisms, mostly specialized bacteria, can extract inorganic compounds from their environment and convert them to organic nutrients without the presence of sunlight. This process is called **chemosynthesis.** For example, hydrothermal vents in some parts of the ocean floor spew forth large amounts of heated ocean water and rotten-egg–smelling hydrogen sulfide gas. In this pitch-dark, warm environment, teeming clouds of specialized producer bacteria carry out chemosynthesis to convert inorganic hydrogen sulfide to nutrients they require.

Only producers can make their own food. In addition, they provide food for animals and decomposers. You, I, and most other animals get nutrients either by eating plants or by eating animals that feed on plants: All flesh is grass, so to speak.

Organisms that get the nutrients and energy they require by feeding either directly or indirectly on producers are called **consumers,** or **heterotrophs** (other-feeders). Some consumers feed on living plants and animals, and others feed on dead plant and animal matter, called **detritus.**

Depending on their food sources, consumers that feed on *living organisms* fall into three major classes:

- **Herbivores** (plant eaters), *primary consumers,* which feed directly and only on all or part of a living plant. Examples are deer, sheep, grasshoppers, and zooplankton.

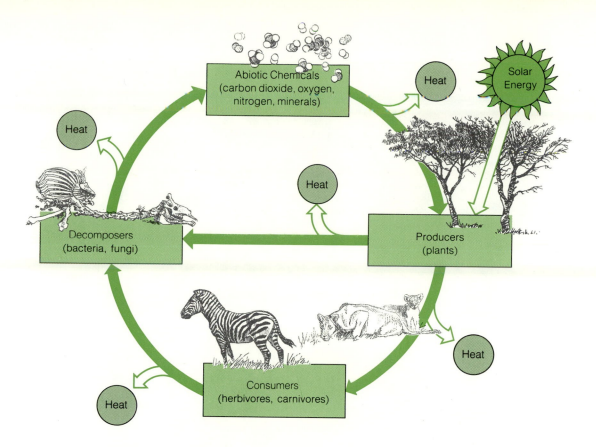

Figure 5-8 Summary of ecosystem structure and function. The major structural components (energy, chemicals, and organisms) of an ecosystem are connected through the functions of energy flow (open arrows) and matter recycling (solid arrows).

- **Carnivores** (flesh eaters), *secondary consumers,* which feed only on plant-eating animals (herbivores), and *tertiary or higher-level consumers,* which feed only on animal-eating animals. Spiders and frogs are secondary consumers. Hawks and sharks are tertiary or higher-level consumers.

- **Omnivores** (plant and meat eaters), which can eat both plants and animals. Examples are pigs, rats, cockroaches, and humans.

Most consumers do not live on or in the organisms they feed on. But some consumers, called **parasites,** feed off other organisms, called their **host,** while living in or on their host. Tapeworms, disease-causing bacteria, and other parasites live inside their host. Lice, ticks, and mistletoe plants attach themselves to the outside of their host.

Consumer organisms that feed on detritus, or dead, organic plant and animal matter are known as **detritivores** (Figure 5-7). There are two major classes of detritivores: detritus feeders and decomposers. **Detritus feeders** directly consume dead organisms and their cast-off parts and organic wastes. Examples are vultures, jackals, termites, earthworms, millipedes, ants, and crabs.

Much of the detritus in ecosystems—especially dead wood and leaves—undergoes decay, rot, or decomposition, in which its complex organic molecules are broken into simpler inorganic compounds containing nutrient elements.

This decomposition process is brought about by the feeding activity of the other type of detritus consumer, **decomposers.** Decomposers consist of two classes of organisms: *fungi* (mostly molds and mushrooms) and microscopic, single-celled *bacteria.* Bacteria and fungi decomposers in turn are an important source of food for organisms such as worms and insects living in the soil and water.

The survival of any individual organism depends on matter flow and energy flow through its body. However, the community of organisms in an ecosystem survives primarily by a combination of matter recycling and energy flow (Figure 5-8).

Figure 5-8 shows that decomposers are responsible for completing the cycle of matter. They carry out waste disposal in nature. They break down organic compounds in organic wastes and dead organisms and return them to the soil, water, and air in forms usable as essential nutrients for producers so that the cycle of life can begin again. Without decomposers, the entire world would soon be knee-deep in plant litter, dead animal bodies, animal wastes, and garbage.

Each species and each individual organism of a species has a particular **range of tolerance** to variations in chem-

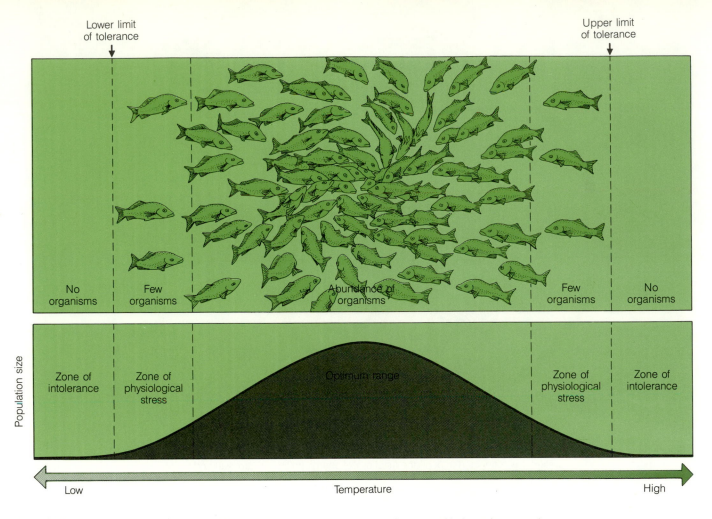

No
organisms

Few
organisms

Abundance of
organisms

Few
organisms

No
organisms

Population size

Zone of
intolerance

Zone of
physiological
stress

Optimum range

Zone of
physiological
stress

Zone of
intolerance

Low

Temperature

High

Figure 5-9 Range of tolerance for a population of organisms of the same species to an abiotic environmental factor—in this case, temperature.

ical and physical factors in its environment, such as temperature (Figure 5-9). The tolerance range includes an *optimum range* of values within which populations of a species thrive and operate most efficiently. The tolerance range also includes values slightly above or below the optimum level of each abiotic factor—values that usually support a smaller population size. When values exceed the upper or lower limits of tolerance, few if any organisms of a particular species survive.

These observations are summarized in the **law of tolerance:** The existence, abundance, and distribution of a species are determined by whether the levels of one or more physical or chemical factors fall above or below the levels tolerated by the species. Organisms of the same species share the same range of tolerance to various abiotic factors. But individual organisms within a large population of a species may have slightly different tolerance ranges because of small differences in their genetic makeup. For example, it may take a little more heat or a little more of a poisonous chemical to kill one frog or one human being than another. This is why the tolerance curve shown in Figure 5-9 represents the response of a population composed of many individuals of the same spe-

cies to changes in an environmental factor such as temperature.

Usually the range of tolerance to a particular stress varies with the physical condition and life cycle of the individuals making up a species. Individuals already weakened by fatigue or disease are normally more sensitive to stresses than healthy ones. For most animal species, tolerance levels are much lower in juveniles (where body defense mechanisms may not be fully developed) than in adults.

Organisms of most species have a better chance of adjusting to an environmental change that takes place gradually. For example, you can tolerate a higher water temperature by getting into a tub of fairly hot water and then slowly adding hotter and hotter water.

This ability to adapt slowly to new conditions is a useful protective device, but it can also be dangerous. With each change, the organism comes closer to its limit of tolerance. Suddenly, without any warning signals, the next small change triggers a harmful or even fatal effect—much like adding the single straw that breaks an already overloaded camel's back.

This **threshold effect** partly explains why many environmental problems seem to arise suddenly even

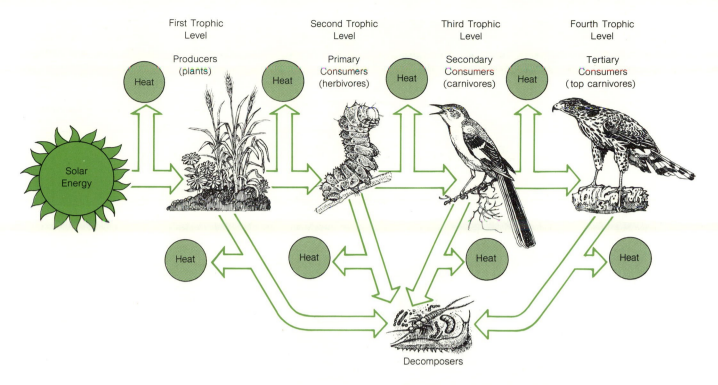

Figure 5-10 A food chain. The arrows show how chemical energy in food flows through various trophic levels, with most of the high-quality chemical energy being degraded to low-quality heat in accordance with the second law of energy.

though they have been building for a long time. For example, trees in certain forests begin dying in large numbers after prolonged exposure to numerous air pollutants. We usually notice the problem only when entire forests die, as is happening in parts of Europe and North America.

Limiting Abiotic Factors in Ecosystems Another ecological principle related to the law of tolerance is the **limiting factor principle**: Too much or too little of any abiotic factor can limit or prevent growth of a population of a species in an ecosystem even if all other factors are at or near the optimum range of tolerance for the species. A single factor found to be limiting the population growth of a species in an ecosystem is called the **limiting factor.**

For example, suppose a farmer plants corn in a field containing too little phosphorus. Even if the corn's needs for water, nitrogen, potassium, and other nutrients are met, the corn will stop growing when it has used up the available phosphorus. In this case, availability of phosphorus is the limiting factor that determines how much corn will grow in the field. Similarly, even with plenty of food and air, you will die in a relatively short time without enough water. Growth can also be limited by the presence of too much of a particular abiotic factor. For example, plants can be killed by too much water or by too much fertilizer.

In aquatic ecosystems, **salinity** (the amounts of various salts dissolved in a given volume of water) is the limiting factor. It determines the species found in marine ecosystems, such as oceans, and freshwater ecosystems, such as rivers and lakes. Three major limiting factors determining the numbers and types of organisms at various layers in aquatic ecosystems are temperature, sunlight, and **dissolved oxygen content** (the amount of oxygen gas dissolved in a given volume of water at a particular temperature), as discussed in Chapter 6.

5-3 ENERGY FLOW IN ECOSYSTEMS

Food Chains and Food Webs *There is no waste in functioning natural ecosystems.* All organisms, dead or alive, are potential sources of food for other organisms. A caterpillar eats a leaf; a robin eats the caterpillar; a hawk eats the robin. When the plant, caterpillar, robin, and hawk die, they are in turn consumed by decomposers.

A series of organisms, each eating or decomposing the preceding one, is called a **food chain** (Figure 5-10). Food chains are channels for the one-way flow of a tiny part of the sun's high-quality energy captured by photosynthesis through the living components of ecosystems and back into space as low-quality heat.

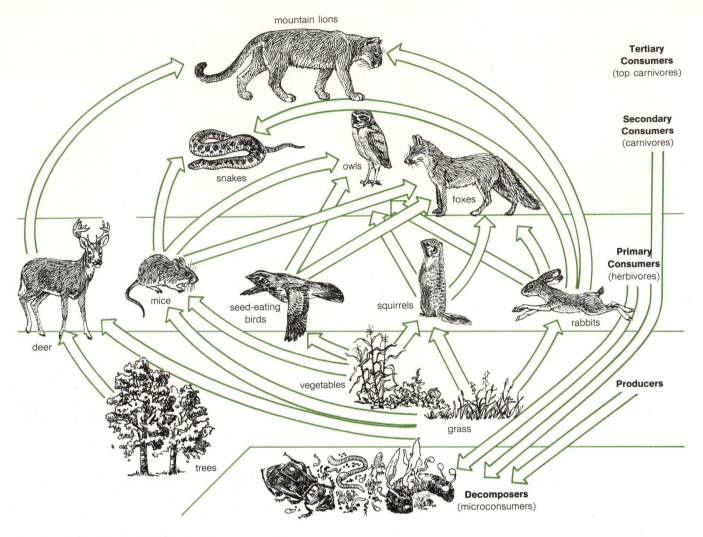

Tertiary Consumers (top carnivores)

Secondary Consumers (carnivores)

Primary Consumers (herbivores)

Producers

Decomposers (microconsumers)

mountain lions

snakes

owls

foxes

deer

mice

seed-eating birds

squirrels

rabbits

vegetables

grass

trees

Figure 5-11 Greatly simplified food web for a terrestrial ecosystem.

Food chains are also pathways for the recycling of nutrients from producers, ordinary consumers (herbivores, carnivores, and omnivores), and decomposers back to producers (Figure 5-9).

All organisms that share the same general types of food in a food chain are said to be at the same **trophic level** (from the Greek *trophos,* feeder). As shown in Figure 5-10, all producers belong to the first trophic level; all primary consumers, whether feeding on living or dead producers, belong to the second trophic level; and so on.

The food chain concept is useful for tracing chemical recycling and energy flow in an ecosystem, but simple food chains like the one shown in Figure 5-10 rarely exist by themselves in nature. Very few herbivores or primary consumers feed on just one kind of plant, nor in turn are they eaten by only one type of carnivore or secondary consumer. In addition, omnivores eat several different kinds of plants and animals at several trophic levels.

This means that the organisms in a natural ecosystem are involved in a complex network of many interconnected food chains, called a **food web.** A simplified food web in a terrestrial ecosystem is diagrammed in Figure 5-11, which shows that trophic levels can be assigned in food webs just as in food chains.

Energy flows through ecosystems by means of two interconnected types of food webs: grazing and detritus (Figure 5-12). In **grazing food webs,** herbivores consume living plant tissue and are then consumed by an array of carnivores and omnivores. In **detritus food webs,** detritus feeders and decomposers break down organic waste products and the remains of dead plants and animals to simple inorganic compounds for recycling by plants.

Predation   The most obvious form of species interaction in food chains and webs is **predation**: An individual organism of one species, known as the **predator,** captures and feeds on parts or all of an organism of another species, the **prey.** Together, the two organisms involved are said to have a **predator–prey relationship.** Sharks are one of the most important

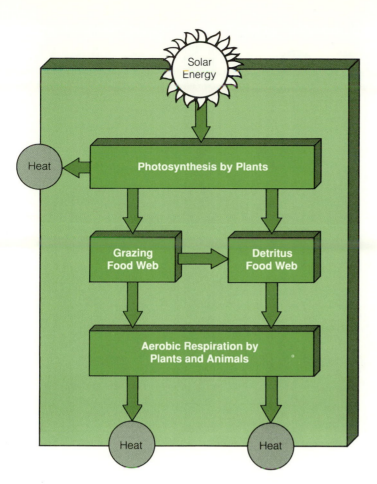

Figure 5-12 Generalized model of the main pathways for the one-way flow of energy through ecosystems via grazing and detritus food webs.

predators in the world's oceans (see Case Study on p. 105).

Prey species have various protective mechanisms. Otherwise, they would easily be captured and eaten. Some can run or fly fast. Others have thick skins or shells. Still others have camouflage colorings or the ability to change color so that they can hide by blending into their environment.

A carnivore generally has to chase and catch its food; a herbivore doesn't. One way a carnivore can get enough food is to be able to run fast like the cheetah. Another way is to cooperate by hunting in packs as spotted hyenas, lions, wolves, and Cape hunting dogs do. A third way to kill animals for food is to invent weapons and traps and learn how to domesticate animals as humans do.

Energy Flow Pyramids At each transfer from one trophic level to another in a food chain or web, work is done, low-quality heat is given off to the environment, and the availability of high-quality energy to organisms at the next trophic level is reduced. This reduction in high-quality energy available at each trophic level is the result of the inevitable energy quality tax imposed by the second law of energy.

The percentage of available high-quality energy transferred from one trophic level to another varies

from 2% to 30%, depending on the types of species involved and the ecosystem in which the transfer takes place. In the wild, ecologists estimate that an average of about 10% of the high-quality chemical energy available at one trophic level is typically transferred and stored in usable form as chemical energy in the bodies of the organisms at the next level. The rest of this energy is used to keep the organisms alive and most is eventually degraded and lost as low-quality heat to the environment in compliance with the second law of energy. Some of it is transferred to decomposers who in turn use a small amount to stay alive and degrade the rest to low-quality heat.

Figure 5-13 illustrates this loss of usable high-quality energy at each step in a simple food chain. The **pyramids of energy flow and energy loss** in this diagram show that the greater the number of trophic levels or steps in a food chain or web, the greater the cumulative loss of usable high-quality energy.

This loss of available high-quality energy leads to an important principle affecting the ultimate population size of an omnivorous species such as human beings: *The shorter the food chain or web, the less the loss of usable high-quality energy.*

The energy-flow pyramid explains why a larger population of people can be supported if people shorten the food chain by eating grains directly (for example,

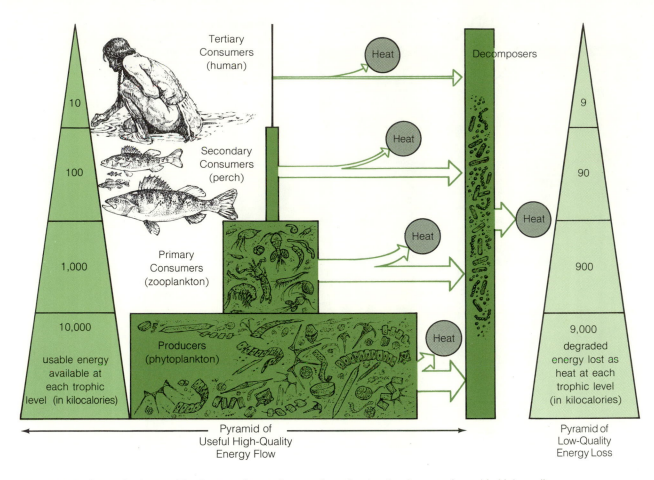

Figure 5-13 Generalized pyramids of energy flow and energy loss showing the decrease in usable high-quality energy available at each succeeding trophic level in a food chain or web.

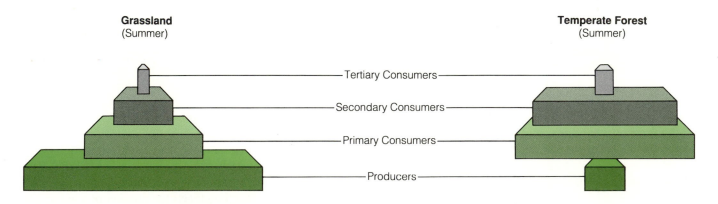

Figure 5-14 Generalized pyramids of numbers in ecosystems.

rice → human) rather than eating animals that fed on grains (grain → steer → human). To prevent protein malnutrition, such a vegetarian diet must include a variety of plants that provide enough of the ten nitrogen-containing amino acid molecules used to make proteins that our bodies cannot synthesize. Poor people surviving on a plant diet often don't have enough

money to grow or purchase the variety of plants needed to avoid protein malnutrition.

Pyramids of Numbers and Biomass We can collect samples of organisms in ecosystems and count the number of each type found at each trophic level. This information can then be used to construct **pyramids of numbers** for ecosystems (Figure 5-14). For example, a million phytoplankton in a small pond may support 10,000 zooplankton, which in turn may support 100 perch, which might feed one person for a month or so.

The energy flow pyramid means there must either be many fewer plant eaters than plants or the plant eaters must be very small (like insect herbivores) so as not to require much plant tissue. Pyramids of numbers for a grassland and many other ecosystems taper off in going from the producer level to the higher trophic levels (Figure 5-14, left).

But in some ecosystems the number pyramids have different shapes and can take on an inverted form. For example, in a forest a small number of large trees, such as redwoods (the producers), support a larger number of mostly small, herbivorous insects and birds (the primary consumers) that feed on and from the trees (Figure 5-14, right).

The dried weight of all organic matter contained in the organisms in an ecosystem is called its **biomass.** Each trophic level in a food chain or web contains a certain amount of biomass. This can be estimated by harvesting several randomly selected patches or narrow strips in an ecosystem. The organisms in the samples are then sorted according to known trophic levels, dried, and weighed. These data are then used to plot a **pyramid of biomass** for the ecosystem (Figure 5-15).

For most land ecosystems, the total biomass at each successive trophic level of a food chain or web usually decreases. This yields a pyramid of biomass with a large base of producers, topped by a series of increasingly small trophic levels of consumers (Figure 5-15, left).

In aquatic ecosystems, however, the pyramid of biomass can be upside down, with the biomass of consumers exceeding that of producers (Figure 5-15, right). Here the producers are tiny phytoplankton that grow and reproduce rapidly, not large plants that grow and reproduce slowly.

CASE STUDY Sharks: The Oceans' Most Important Predator

Influenced by movies and popular novels, most people see sharks as people-eating monsters. This is far from the truth. Sharks have lived in the oceans for over 400 million years, long before dinosaurs appeared. During their long history, sharks have evolved into more than 350 species, whose size, behavior, and other characteristics differ widely.

Some sharks, called "cookie cutters," are about one foot long. They survive by taking bites out of the sides of other fish. At the other end of the scale is the whale shark, the world's biggest fish. It can grow to 45 feet. The angel shark is as flat as a flounder. The tail of the thresher shark is as long as its body.

Sharks have extremely sensitive sense organs. They can detect the scent of decaying fish or blood even when it is diluted to only one part per million parts of seawater. They have superb hearing and better night vision than we do. They also sense the electrical impulses radiated by the muscles of animals, making it difficult for their

prey to escape detection. They are powerful and rapid swimmers. Because their bodies are denser than seawater, they must always keep moving in order not to sink.

Sharks are the key predators in the world's oceans, helping control the number of many other ocean predators. Without sharks the oceans would be overcrowded with dead and dying fish and depleted of many healthy ones that we rely on for food. Eliminating sharks would upset the ecological balance of ocean ecosystems.

Yet this is precisely what we are in danger of doing. Every year we catch nearly 100 million sharks, mostly for food. Others are killed for sport and out of fear. Some shark species, such as edible thresher and mako sharks, are being commercially exploited and could face extinction. Sharks are vulnerable to overfishing because they mature slowly and produce only a few offspring.

Each year a few types of shark injure about 100 people and kill perhaps 25. With hundreds of millions of people swimming in the

ocean each year, the chances of being killed by a shark are minute—about 1 in 5 million. You are thousands of times more likely to get killed when you drive a car.

Furthermore, sharks help save lives. In addition to providing people with food, they are helping us learn how to fight cancer, bacteria, and viruses. Sharks are incredibly healthy and have aging processes similar to ours. Their highly effective immune system allows wounds to heal quickly without becoming infected. A chemical extracted from shark cartilage is also being used as an artificial skin for burn victims. Sharks are among the few animals in the world that almost never get cancer and eye cataracts. Understanding why can help us improve human health.

Sharks are needed in the world's ocean ecosystems. They don't need us, but we need them.

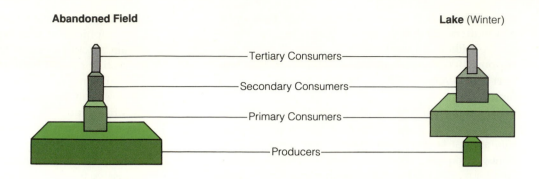

Figure 5-15 Generalized pyramids of biomass in ecosystems. The size of each tier represents the dry weight per square meter of all organisms at that trophic level.

5-4 MATTER RECYCLING IN ECOSYSTEMS

Carbon Cycle Carbon is the basic building block of the carbohydrates, fats, proteins, nucleic acids such as DNA and RNA, and other organic compounds necessary for life. Most land plants get their carbon by absorbing carbon dioxide gas, which makes up about 0.04% of the gaseous atmosphere, through pores in their leaves. Phytoplankton, the microscopic plants that float in aquatic ecosystems, get their carbon from atmospheric carbon dioxide that has dissolved in water. These producer plants then carry out *photosynthesis.*

carbon dioxide + water + **solar energy** → glucose + oxygen

Aerobic (oxygen-consuming) organisms change part of the glucose and other, more complex compounds they synthesize (producers), eat (consumers), or decompose (decomposers) back into carbon dioxide and water by the process of **cellular aerobic respiration.**

glucose + oxygen → carbon dioxide + water + **energy**

This process is not the same as the breathing process, which is also called *respiration.* Aerobic respiration is a sort of carefully controlled, slow-burning of organic compounds that takes place in the cells of living organisms. The chemical energy released in this process is stored in other molecules such as ATP and ADP and released as needed to drive the life processes of organisms.

As it is used, most of this chemical energy is degraded to low-temperature heat that flows into the environment. This explains why you continually radiate heat into the environment at about the same rate as a 100-watt light bulb. The carbon dioxide released by aerobic respiration is returned to the atmosphere and water for reuse by plant producers.

This linkage between photosynthesis and aerobic respiration circulates carbon in the ecosphere and is a major part of the **carbon cycle** shown in greatly sim-

plified form in Figure 5-16. The diagram shows some of the ways plants, animals, and decomposers in the biosphere depend on one another for survival. Oxygen and hydrogen, which (along with carbon) are the other elements in glucose and other carbohydrates, cycle almost in step with carbon.

Figure 5-16 also shows that some of the earth's carbon is tied up for long periods in fossil fuels—coal, petroleum, natural gas, peat, oil shale, tar sands, and lignite—formed over millions of years in the lithosphere. The carbon in these mineral deposits remains locked deep in the earth's crust until it is released to the atmosphere as carbon dioxide when fossil fuels are extracted and burned.

In aquatic ecosystems, some carbon and oxygen combine with calcium to form insoluble calcium carbonate in shells and rocks. When shelled organisms die, they sink and their shells become buried in bottom sediments.

Carbon in these sediment deposits reenters the cycle as carbon dioxide very slowly, often over millions of years. This happens by slow dissolution into ocean water to form dissolved carbon dioxide gas that can enter the atmosphere, melting of rocks in long-term geological processes, and volcanic eruptions. Also movements of the earth's crust that uplift these deposits to form an island or continent expose the carbonate rock to chemical attack and conversion to carbon dioxide gas.

Another part of the carbon cycle not shown in Figure 5-16 involves *anerobic respiration* that takes place without the presence of oxygen. In this process, various types of anaerobic bacteria convert organic compounds to methane (CH_4) gas and other compounds that can flow into the atmosphere. This type of respiration takes place mostly in swamps and bogs. It also occurs underground in landfills where we bury trash.

We have intervened in the carbon cycle in two major ways, especially since 1950 as world population and resource use have increased rapidly:

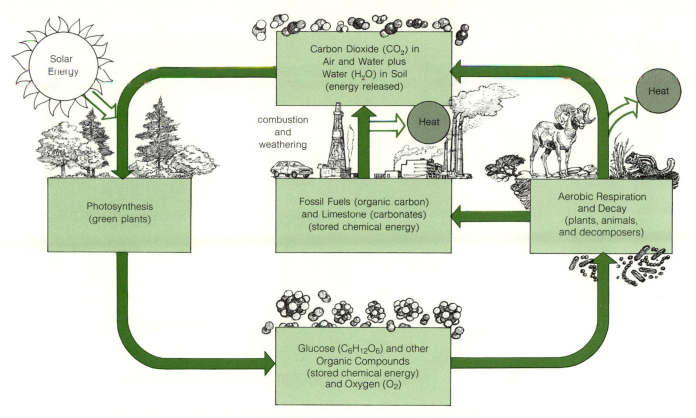

Figure 5-16 Simplified diagram of a major portion of the carbon cycle, showing matter recycling (solid arrows) and one-way energy flow (open arrows). This cyclical movement of matter through ecosystems and the ecosphere is also an important part of the oxygen and hydrogen cycles.

■ Removal of forests and other vegetation without sufficient replanting. This adds additional carbon dioxide to the atmosphere when some nonharvested wood and plant debris decays and organic matter and roots in the exposed soil react with oxygen in the atmosphere.

■ Burning carbon-containing fossil fuels and wood. This produces carbon dioxide that flows into the atmosphere. Scientists project that this "extra" CO_2 (plus other chemicals we are adding to the atmosphere) will warm the earth's atmosphere in coming decades and disrupt global food production.

Nitrogen Cycle Organisms use nitrogen in various chemical forms to make proteins and genetically important nucleic acids such as DNA. The nitrogen gas (N_2) that makes up about 78% of the volume of the earth's atmosphere is useless to most organisms. Fortunately, nitrogen gas is converted into water-soluble ionic compounds containing nitrate ions (NO_3^-) and ammonium ions (NH_4^+), which are taken up by plant roots as part of the **nitrogen cycle,** shown in simplified form in Figure 5-17.

The conversion of atmospheric nitrogen gas into other chemical forms useful to plants is called **nitrogen fixation.** It is carried out by blue-green algae and certain kinds of bacteria in soil and water and by rhizobium bacteria living in small swellings called nodules on the roots of alfalfa, clover, peas, beans, and other legume plants. Lightning converts nitrogen gas and oxygen gas in the atmosphere to nitric oxide and nitrogen dioxide gas. These gases react with water vapor in the atmosphere and are converted to nitrate ions that return to the earth as nitric acid dissolved in precipitation and as particles of nitrate salts.

Plants convert inorganic nitrate ions and ammonium ions obtained from soil water into proteins, DNA, and other large, nitrogen-containing organic compounds they require. Animals get most of their nitrogen-containing nutrients by eating plants or other animals that have eaten plants.

Decomposers convert the nitrogen-containing organic compounds found in the wastes of living plants and animals, discarded parts, and the bodies of dead organisms into inorganic compounds such as ammonia gas and water-soluble salts containing ammonium ions (NH_4^+). Other specialized groups of bacteria then convert these inorganic forms of nitrogen back into nitrate ions in the soil and into nitrogen gas, which is released to the atmosphere to begin the cycle again.

We intervene in the nitrogen cycle in three major ways:

■ Emitting large quantities of nitric oxide (NO) into the atmosphere when wood or any fossil fuel is

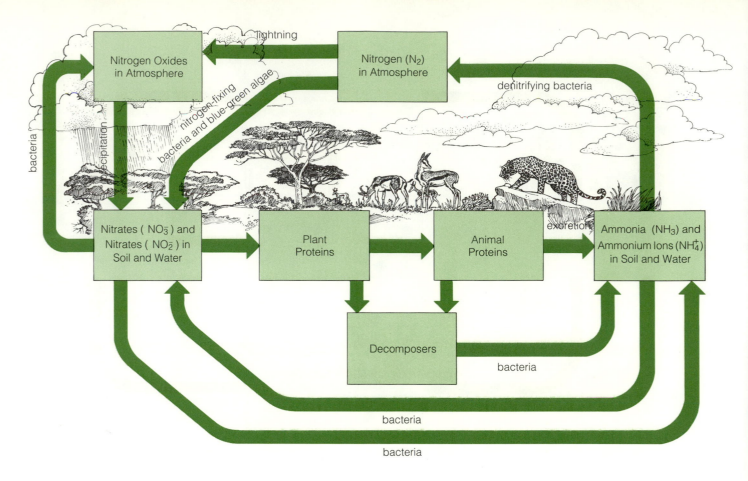

Figure 5-17 Greatly simplified diagram of the nitrogen cycle.

burned. The nitric oxide then combines with oxygen gas in the atmosphere to form nitrogen dioxide (NO_2) gas, which can react with water vapor in the atmosphere to form nitric acid (HNO_3). This acid is a component of acid deposition that is damaging trees and killing fish in parts of the world.

- Mining mineral deposits of compounds containing nitrate and ammonium ions for use as commercial fertilizers.

- Adding excess nitrate ions and ammonium ions to aquatic ecosystems in runoff of animal wastes from livestock feedlots, runoff of commercial nitrate fertilizers from cropland, and discharge of untreated and treated municipal sewage. This excess supply of plant nutrients can stimulate rapid growth of algae and other aquatic plants. Aerobic decomposers breaking down dead algae can deplete the water of dissolved oxygen gas and cause massive fish kills.

Phosphorus Cycle Phosphorus, mainly in the form of phosphate ions (PO_4^{3-} and HPO_4^{2-}), is an essential nutrient of both plants and animals. It is a part of DNA molecules that carry genetic information, ATP and ADP molecules used to store chemical energy for use by organisms, certain fats in the membranes that encase plant and animal cells, and bones and teeth in animals.

Various forms of phosphorus are cycled through the lower atmosphere, water, soil, and living organisms by the **phosphorus cycle,** shown in simplified form in Figure 5-18. The phosphorus cycle is different from the carbon and nitrogen cycles in that very little phosphorus is cycled through the atmosphere. Instead it cycles from phosphate deposits on land and shallow ocean sediments to living organisms and back to the land and ocean.

Some phosphates released by the slow breakdown, or weathering, of phosphate rock deposits are dissolved in soil water and taken up by plant roots. However, most soils contain only small amounts of phosphates because phosphate compounds are fairly insoluble in water and are found only in certain kinds of rocks.

Animals get their phosphorus by eating plants or animals that have eaten plants. Animal wastes and the decay products of dead animals and plants return much of this phosphorus to the soil, rivers, and eventually to the ocean bottom as insoluble deposits of phosphate rock.

Some phosphate is returned to the land as *guano*—the phosphate-rich manure from fish-eating birds such as pelicans, gannets, and cormorants (Figure 5-19).

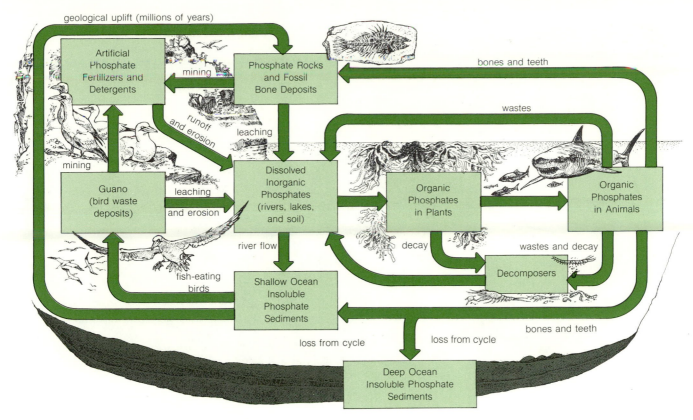

Figure 5-18 Greatly simplified diagram of the phosphorus cycle.

But this return is small compared to the much larger amounts of phosphate eroded from the land to the oceans each year by natural processes and human activities.

Over millions of years geologic processes may push up and expose the seafloor, forming islands and other land surfaces. Weathering then slowly releases phosphorus from the exposed rocks and allows the cycle to begin again.

We intervene in the phosphorus cycle in two major ways:

- Mining large quantities of phosphate rock to produce commercial inorganic fertilizers and detergent compounds.

- Adding excess phosphate ions to aquatic ecosystems in runoff of animal wastes from livestock feedlots, runoff of commercial phosphate fertilizers from cropland, and discharge of untreated and treated municipal sewage. As with nitrate and ammonium ions, an excessive supply of this plant nutrient causes explosive growth of blue-green algae and other aquatic plants that disrupt life in aquatic ecosystems.

Hydrologic, or Water, Cycle The **hydrologic cycle,** or **water cycle,** which collects, purifies, and distributes

Figure 5-19 "Guano islands" off the coast of Peru are kept as sanctuaries for fish-eating birds whose droppings (guano) are rich in nitrates and phosphates. The birds return some of these chemicals from the sea to the land as part of the phosphorus and nitrogen cycles.

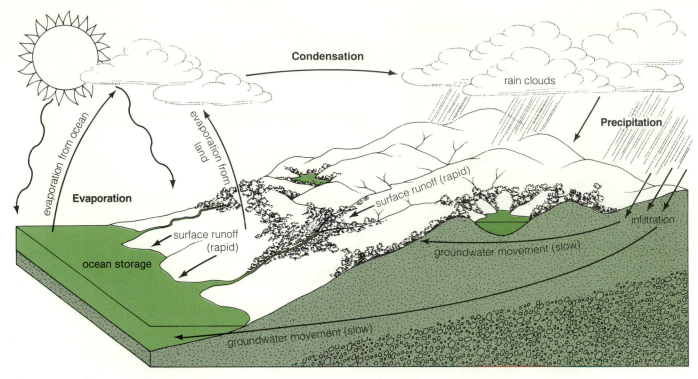

Figure 5-20 Greatly simplified diagram of the hydrologic cycle.

the earth's fixed supply of water, is shown in simplified form in Figure 5-20. Solar energy and gravity continuously move water among the ocean, air, land, and living organisms. The main processes in this cycle are evaporation (conversion of water to water vapor), condensation (conversion of water vapor to droplets of liquid water), precipitation (rain, sleet, hail, snow), and runoff back to the sea to begin the cycle again.

Incoming solar energy evaporates water from oceans, rivers, lakes, soil, and vegetation into the atmosphere. Winds and air masses transport this water vapor over various parts of the earth's surface. Drops in temperature in parts of the atmosphere cause the water vapor to condense and form tiny droplets of water. Eventually these droplets combine and become heavy enough to fall to the land and bodies of water as *precipitation* in the forms of rain, sleet, hail, and snow.

Some of this fresh water returning to the earth's surface as precipitation becomes locked in glaciers. Much of it collects in puddles and ditches and runs off into nearby streams, rivers, and lakes, which carry water back to the oceans, completing the cycle. This *runoff* of fresh water from the land also causes erosion of soil.

A large portion of the water returning to the land seeps deep into the ground. There it is stored as *groundwater* in *aquifers*—spaces in and between rock formations. Underground springs and streams eventually return this water to the surface and to rivers,

lakes, and surface streams where it evaporates or returns to the ocean. Fresh water percolates downward through the soil to replenish most aquifers. However, this underground circulation loop of water is extremely slow compared to that on the surface and in the atmosphere.

We intervene in the water cycle in two major ways:

■ Withdrawing large quantities of fresh water from rivers, lakes, and underground aquifers. In heavily populated or heavily irrigated areas, withdrawals have led to groundwater depletion or intrusion of ocean salt water into underground water supplies.

■ Clearing vegetation from land for agriculture, mining, roads, parking lots, construction, and other activities. This increases the rate of surface runoff, which increases soil erosion, reduces seepage that recharges groundwater supplies, and increases the risk of flooding.

5-5 HABITAT QUALITY AND ROLES OF ORGANISMS IN ECOSYSTEMS

Habitat Quality As mentioned before, an organism's habitat is the place where it lives—its address in the ecosphere. Even if enough habitat is available, it will not support individuals and the minimum breeding population of a species unless it also has sufficient quality. **Habitat quality** refers to how well a habitat

Figure 5-21 Long grasses provide a nesting site and protective cover for this bobwhite quail in southern Illinois.

supplies the physical, chemical, and biological needs of an individual organism.

Habitat quality is usually described in terms of the availability of adequate food, water, cover, and, for some species, the ecotones (or edges) between two different habitat types. One of these factors may seem more important at times than another. But all are required if an individual or a population of a species is to survive.

The maximum number of individuals of a particular species that can be supported by a given area of habitat over a given period of time is called the **carrying capacity** of that area. The factors determining habitat quality act together to determine the carrying capacity for each species occupying the area.

Food Good habitat quality for plants means that enough but not too many of the nutrients they need are in the soil or water. Good habitat quality for animals means that enough plants and animals are available to supply them with the nutrients they require for survival, growth, and reproduction. Often the availability of enough protein or the right kinds of protein are limiting factors that can weaken animals and make them susceptible to disease.

Bears, pigs, people, most bird species, and other animals with *simple stomachs* get protein by eating certain plants and animals. The protein food intake of such animals must have ten essential amino acids, which cannot be synthesized by the animal. Other-

wise, the animal cannot make certain proteins it needs and suffers from protein deficiency.

Herbivorous animals such as deer, elk, mountain sheep, gazelles, and camels have *compound stomachs.* Specialized bacteria in their digestive tracts synthesize the amino acids they require by breaking down bulky, fibrous plant materials.

Catching a meal is harder for carnivores than for herbivores. But once caught, the meal is far higher in nutrition. If carnivores can find and catch enough prey, they usually get enough vitamins and proteins. This means that meat eaters normally spend much less of their time eating than plant eaters. For example, meat-eating species such as the leopard, lion, polar bear, cheetah, wolf, and hunting dog spend only 5% to 10% of their time eating. Herbivores spend 18% to 70% of their time feeding.

Plants are a less balanced source of vitamins and proteins than meat. Thus, without a sufficient variety of plants, herbivores are more likely than carnivores to suffer from vitamin and protein deficiencies. The bigger the herbivore, the more time it must spend feeding simply to stay alive. For example, a plant-eating monkey spends about 18% of its time feeding compared to 55% for a rhino and 70% for an elephant.

The mineral content of wild plants, which directly feed herbivores and indirectly feed carnivores, is dependent on soil type. Most nutrient-rich, highly fertile soils are used for crop production and livestock grazing. Thus, many wild animals eat plants grown on nutrient-deficient soils and can suffer from mineral deficiencies.

The susceptibility of animals to nutritional deficiencies also depends on their feeding habits. Generalist animals can avoid or minimize such deficiencies by feeding on a variety of food. For example, the red fox eats mice throughout the year. It supplements this food source with grapes, wild cherries, and grasshoppers in the fall; frozen apples, and rotting meat from dead animal carcasses in winter; and turtle eggs, snakes, blackberries, and raspberries in spring and summer. Bobwhite quail (Figure 5-21) mainly eat seeds, but insects may make up one-fourth of their diet in the summer.

An animal species with a specialized diet is more vulnerable to nutritional deficiency disorders and starvation when its usual food source becomes scarce during seasonal changes or is eliminated by habitat changes, destruction, or degradation. For example, the critically endangered black-footed ferret feeds on prairie dogs and pocket gophers. But these species are often eliminated on grazing land by ranchers who don't want them to compete with livestock for grass.

Water All wild species require water for their survival, but they vary greatly in the amount they need and the way they get it. In desert areas, animals such as the white-tailed wood rat get much of their water from cacti and other succulent plants. Desert carnivores such as the desert fox, rattlesnake, bobcat, and prairie falcon get much of their water from the blood and body fluids of their prey. The kangaroo rat, which lives only on dry seeds, has metabolic processes that break down fats and proteins in its body to produce all the water it needs.

Most wild animal species, however, must get water directly from standing or flowing bodies of water, dew, or snow on a regular basis in order to survive. Species that need to drink only once every few days can use habitats farther from water than those that must drink daily. Because birds can fly quickly over long distances, they can use habitats far from water supplies.

The regular need for water ties many wild animal species to water sources available throughout the year, particularly in dry regions and during drought periods. On African grasslands, for example, the greatest wildlife numbers and species diversity are found close to water holes, rivers, and lakes. Predators are attracted to watering areas not only by water but also by the abundance of prey.

Cover Any physical or biological feature of the habitat that gives an animal protection from weather, concealment and escape from its predators, concealment while it is stalking prey, a safe place to breed and rear young, or simply a place to rest is called **cover.** It may be tall grass (Figure 5-21), dense woods, tree foliage, an underground burrow, a rock pile, a crevice in a cliff face, a cave, or a hole in a dead or dying tree.

Most species require several different types of vegetation as cover during their life cycles. For example, a sage grouse needs bare ground when it struts during courtship but usually feeds in stands of sagebrush.

Deer, which prefer to feed near open areas, may seek deep shelter in dense, bushy thickets when threatened by natural predators or human hunters. This explains why deer hunters either create or seek edges or ecotone areas between forestland and open meadows in order to increase their chances of finding and killing deer. Bobwhite quail (Figure 5-21) also prefer edge habitats.

Ecological Niche The **ecological niche** (pronounced "nitch") is a description of all the physical, chemical, and biological factors that a species needs to survive, stay healthy, and reproduce in an ecosystem. It describes an organism's role in an ecosystem.

A common analogy is that an organism's habitat is its "address" in an ecosystem, whereas its ecological niche is its "occupation" and "lifestyle." For example, the habitat of a robin includes such areas as woodlands, forests, parks, pasture lands, meadows, orchards, gardens, and yards. Its ecological niche includes other factors such as nesting and roosting in trees, eating insects, earthworms, and fruit, and dispersing fruit and berry seeds in its droppings.

Each species has important roles to play in its ecosystem. Some ecologists have found evidence indicating that certain species play key roles in ecosystems that can affect many other organisms. The demise of such a *keystone species* may trigger a cascade of sharp population drops and extinctions of other species that depend on them for certain services. Many keystone species are little known and not cute, cuddly, or glamorous like many of those that get the lion's share of wildlife conservation funds. Examples are the gopher tortoise and the alligator (see Case Study on p. 114).

The gopher tortoise is found in sandhill areas of Florida and other southern states. Each of these slow-moving, dinner-plate size animals digs a 30-foot burrow. In this hot, inhospitable ecosystem, these holes become cool refuges for some 40 other species. They include the gray fox, opossum, indigo snake, and many insects. In areas where the gopher tortoise has been hunted to extinction or near extinction for its tasty meat, many other species depending on this species no longer exist.

Information about ecological niches helps people manage domesticated and wild plant and animal species as sources of food or other resources. It also helps us predict the effects of either adding or removing a species to or from an ecosystem.

But determining the interacting factors that make up an organism's ecological niche is very difficult. As we learn more about ecosystems, we may learn that all or most species are keystone. Meanwhile, we need to protect those that have been identified as playing key roles in ecosystems.

Specialist and Generalist Niches The niche of an organism can be classified as specialized or generalized, depending primarily on its major sources of food, the extent of its habitat, and its tolerance to temperature and other physical and chemical factors. Most species of plants and animals can tolerate only a narrow range of climatic and other environmental conditions and feed on a limited number of different plants or animals. Such species have a *specialized niche,* which limits them to fairly specific habitats in the ecosphere.

The giant panda, for example, has a highly specialized niche because it obtains 99% of its food by consuming bamboo plants. The destruction and mass die-off of several species of bamboo in parts of China, where the panda is found, has led to its near extinction.

In a tropical rain forest, an incredibly diverse array of plant and animal life survives by occupying a variety of specialized ecological niches in distinct vertical layers of the forest's vegetation (Figure 5-22). The widespread clearing of such forests is dooming millions of specialized plant and animal species to extinction.

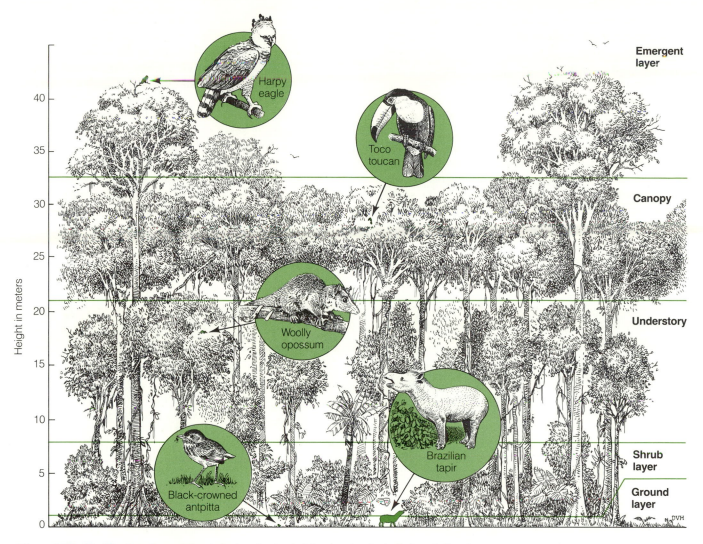

Figure 5-22 Stratification of specialized plant and animal niches in a tropical rain forest. Species occupy specialized niches in the various layers of vegetation.

Species with a *generalist niche* are very adaptable. They can live in many different places, eat a wide variety of foods, and tolerate a wide range of environmental conditions. This explains why they are usually in less danger of extinction than species with a specialized niche. Examples of generalist species include flies, cockroaches, mice, rats, and human beings.

In terms of cultural history, the fairly recent shift of most humans from hunter-gatherer societies to a mix of agricultural and industrial societies (Figure 2-17, p. 43) represents a trend toward increasing specialization. Today people in agricultural and industrial societies depend on a much smaller number of crop and livestock species than their hunter-gatherer ancestors. Today's industrial societies also depend on massive use of a small number of nonrenewable metallic minerals and a few nonrenewable energy resources—primarily oil, coal, and natural gas.

A catastrophic loss of human life and life quality would take place if supplies of any of this fairly small

number of food, mineral, and energy resources were cut off or sharply reduced. Such a crisis could be caused by widespread conventional or nuclear war, excessive pollution and environmental degradation, or natural or human-induced regional or global climate change.

This is a major reason why conservationists call for us to reduce our present overspecialization by shifting to a more diverse and less vulnerable array of crop and livestock species, metallic minerals, and perpetual and renewable energy resources. Not putting all or most of our eggs in one basket is an insurance policy against disaster.

Competition Between Species As long as commonly used resources are abundant, different species can share them. But when two or more species in the same ecosystem attempt to use the same scarce resources, they are said to be engaging in **interspecific competition.** The scarce resource may be food, water, carbon dioxide, sunlight, soil nutrients, space, shelter, or anything required for survival.

One species can gain an advantage over competing species in the same ecosystem in several ways. It can produce more young, get more food or solar energy, defend itself better, or tolerate a wider range of temperature, light, water salinity, or concentrations of certain poisons.

Populations of some animal species avoid or reduce competition with more dominant species by moving to another area, switching to a less accessible or less readily digestible food source, or hunting for the same food source at different times of the day or in different places. For example, hawks and owls feed on similar prey, but hawks hunt during the day and owls hunt at night. Where lions and leopards occur together, lions take mostly larger animals as prey and leopards take smaller ones.

This chapter has shown that the essential feature of the living and nonliving parts of individual terrestrial and aquatic ecosystems and of the global ecosystem, or ecosphere, is interdependence and connectedness, as summarized in the Guest Essay on p. 115. Without the services performed by diverse communities of plants, animals, and decomposers, we would be starving, gasping for breath, and drowning in our own wastes. The next chapter shows how this interdependence is the key to understanding the earth's major types of terrestrial and aquatic ecosystems and how such ecosystems change in response to natural and human stresses.

CASE STUDY Ecological Importance of the American Alligator

People tend to divide plants and animals into "good" and "bad" species and to assume that we have a duty to wipe out the villains. One species that we drove to near extinction in many of its marsh and swamp habitats is the American alligator (Figure 5-23).

Alligators have no natural predators, except people. Hunters once killed large numbers of these animals for their exotic meat and supple belly skin used to make shoes, belts, and other items. Between 1950 and 1960, hunters wiped out 90% of the alligators in Louisiana. The alligator population in the Florida Everglades also was threatened.

Many people might say, "So what?" But they are overlooking the key role the alligator plays in subtropical, wetland ecosystems such as the Everglades. Alligators dig deep depressions, or "gator holes," which collect fresh water during dry spells. These holes are refuges for aquatic life and supply fresh water and food for birds and other animals.

Large alligator nesting mounds also serve as nest sites for birds such as herons and egrets. As alligators move from gator holes to nesting mounds, they help keep waterways open. They also eat large numbers of gar, a fish which

preys on other fish. This means that alligators help maintain populations of game fish such as bass and bream.

In 1967 the U.S. government placed the American alligator on the endangered species list. Protected from hunters, by 1975 the alligator population had made a comeback in many areas. Indeed, it had reestablished its population too successfully in some places. Some people began finding alligators in their backyards and swimming pools.

In 1977 the U.S. Fish and Wildlife Service reclassified the American alligator from endangered to threatened in Florida, Louisiana, and Texas, where 90% of the animals live. In 1987 this reclassification was extended to seven other states.

As a threatened species, alligators are still protected from excessive harvesting by hunters. However, limited hunting is allowed in some areas to keep the population from growing too large. Florida, with an estimated 1 million alligators, permits 7,000 kills a year. The protection and comeback of the American alligator is an important wildlife conservation success story.

Figure 5-23 In 1967 the American alligator was classified as an endangered species in the United States. This protection allowed the population of this species to recover to the point where its status has been changed from endangered to threatened.

Edward J. Kormondy

Edward J. Kormondy is Chancellor and professor of biology at University of Hawaii-Hilo/West Oahu College. He has taught at the California State University at Los Angeles, University of Southern Maine, the University of Michigan, Oberlin College, and Evergreen State College. Among his many research articles and books are Concepts of Ecology *and* Readings in Ecology *(both published by Prentice-Hall). He has been a major force in biological education and for several years was director of the Commission on Undergraduate Education in the Biological Sciences.*

Energy flows—but downhill only in terms of its quality; chemical nutrients circulate—but some stagnate; populations stabilize—but some go wild; communities age—but some age faster. These dynamic and relentless processes are as characteristic of ecosystems as are thermonuclear fusion reactions in the sun and other stars.

Thinking one can escape the operation of these and other laws of nature is like thinking one can stop the earth from rotating and revolving or make rain fall up. Yet we have peopled the earth only for hundreds of millions to endure starvation and malnutrition, deliberately dumped wastes only to ensure contamination, purposefully simplified agricultural systems only to cause widespread crop losses from pest invasions. Such actions suggest that we believe that energy and food automatically increase as people multiply, that things stay where they are put, that simplification of ecosystems aids in their productivity. Such actions indicate that we have ignored basic, inexorable, and unbreakable physical laws of ecosystems. We have proposed, but nature has disposed, often in unexpected ways counter to our intent.

We proposed more people, more mouths to be fed, more space to be occupied. Nature disposed by placing an upper limit on the rate at which the earth's plants can produce organic nutrients for themselves and for the people and other animals that feed on them. It also disposed by using and degrading energy quality at and between all trophic levels in the biosphere's intricate food webs and by imposing an upper limit on the total space that is available and

which can be occupied by humans and other species.

Ultimately, the only way there can be more and more people is for each person to have less and less food and fuel and less and less space. Absolute limits to growth are imposed both by thermodynamics and space. We may argue about what these limits are and when they will be reached, but there are limits and if present trends continue they will be reached. The more timely question then becomes a qualitative one. What quality of life will we have within these limits? What kind of life do you want?

We proposed exploitative use of resources and indiscriminate disposal of wastes generated by people and technology. Nature disposed, and like a boomerang, the consequences of our acts came back to hit us. On the one hand, finite oil, coal, and mineral resource supplies are significantly depleted—some nearing exhaustion. On the other hand, air, water, and land are contaminated, some beyond restoring.

Nature's laws limit each resource; some limits are more confining than others, some more critical than others. The earth is finite, and its resources are therefore finite. Yet another of nature's laws is that fundamental resources—elements and compounds—circulate, some fully and some partially. They don't stay where they are put. They move from the land to the water and the air, just as they move from the air and water to the land. Must not our proposals for using resources and discharging wastes be mindful of ultimate limits and the earth's chemical recycling processes? What about your own patterns of resource use and waste disposal?

We proposed simplification of our agricultural and to some extent our aquatic food-producing systems to ease the admittedly heavy burden of cultivation and harvest. Nature has disposed otherwise, however. Simple ecosystems such as a cornfield are youthful ones, and like our own youth, are volatile, unpredictable, and unstable. Young ecosystems do not conserve nutrients, and agricultural systems in such a stage must have their nutrients replaced artificially and expensively by adding commercial inorganic fertilizers. Young agricultural systems essentially lack resistance to pests and disease and have to be protected artificially and expensively by pesticides. These systems are also more subject to the whims of climate and often have to be expensively irrigated. Must not our proposals for managing agricultural systems be mindful of nature's managerial strategy of providing biological diversity to help sustain most complex ecosystems? What of your own lawn?

The take-home lesson is a rather straightforward one: We cannot propose without recognizing how nature disposes of our attempts to manage the earth's resources for human use. We are shackled by basic

(continued)

ecological laws of energy flow, chemical recycling, population growth, and the aging process of biological communities. We have plenty of freedom within these laws, but like it or not we are bounded by them. You are bounded by them. What do you propose to do? And what might nature dispose in return?

Guest Essay Discussion

1. List the patterns of your life that are in harmony with the laws of energy flow and chemical recycling and those that are not.

2. Set up a chart with examples of "we propose" and "nature disposes," but add a third column based on using ecological principles to work with nature titled "we repropose."

We sang the songs that carried in their melodies all the sounds of nature—the running waters, the sighing of winds, and the calls of the animals. Teach these to your children that they may come to love nature as we love it.

Grand Council Fire of American Indians

DISCUSSION TOPICS

1. **a.** A bumper sticker asks, "Have you thanked a green plant today?" Give two reasons for appreciating a green plant.
   b. Trace the sources of the materials that make up the sticker and see whether the sticker itself is a sound application of the slogan.
   c. Explain how decomposers help keep you alive.

2. **a.** How would you set up a self-sustaining aquarium for tropical fish?
   b. Suppose you have a balanced aquarium sealed with a clear glass top. Can life continue in the aquarium indefinitely as long as the sun shines regularly on it?
   c. A friend cleans out your aquarium and removes all the soil and plants, leaving only the fish and water. What will happen?

3. Using the second law of energy, explain why there is such a sharp decrease in high-quality energy as energy flows through a food chain or web. Doesn't an energy loss at each step violate the first law of energy? Explain.

4. Using the second law of energy, explain why many poor people in less developed countries exist mostly on a vegetarian diet. How can people on such a diet avoid malnutrition? Why are many poor people on a plant diet unable to avoid malnutrition?

5. Using the second law of energy, explain why a pound of steak costs more than a pound of corn.

6. Why are there fewer lions than mice in an African ecosystem supporting both types of animals?

7. Compare the ecological niches of people in a small town and in a large city; in a more developed country and in a less developed country.

FURTHER READINGS

Andrewartha, H. G., and L. C. Birch. 1984. *The Ecological Web.* Chicago: University of Chicago Press.

Colinvaux, Paul A. 1986. *Ecology.* New York: John Wiley.

Ehrlich, Anne H., and Paul R. Ehrlich. 1987. *Earth.* New York: Franklin Watts.

Ehrlich, Paul R. 1986. *The Machinery of Life: The Living World Around Us and How It Works.* New York: Simon & Schuster.

Ehrlich, Paul R., and Jonathan R. Roughgarden. 1987. *The Science of Ecology.* New York: Macmillan.

Gates, David M. 1985. *Energy and Ecology.* Sunderland, Mass.: Sinauer.

Kormondy, Edward J. 1984. *Concepts of Ecology,* 3rd ed. Englewood Cliffs, N.J.: Prentice-Hall.

Krebs, Charles J. 1985. *Ecology,* 3rd ed. New York: Harper & Row.

Odum, Eugene P. 1983. *Basic Ecology.* Philadelphia: Saunders.

Rickleffs, Robert E. 1976. *The Economy of Nature.* Portland, Ore.: Chiron Press.

Smith, Robert L. 1985. *Elements of Ecology,* 2nd ed. New York: Harper & Row.

Tudge, Colin. 1988. *The Environment of Life.* New York: Oxford University Press.

Watt, Kenneth E. F. 1982. *Understanding the Environment.* Newton, Mass.: Allyn & Bacon.

CHAPTER 6

Ecosystems: What Are the Major Types and What Can Happen to Them?

General Questions and Issues

1. What are the major types of terrestrial ecosystems (biomes), and how does climate influence the type found in a given area?

2. What are the major types of aquatic ecosystems, and what major factors influence the kinds of life they contain?

3. What are the major effects of environmental stress on living systems?

4. How can populations of plant and animal species adapt to natural and human-induced stresses?

5. How can communities and ecosystems adapt to small- and large-scale natural and human-induced stresses to preserve their overall stability and sustainability?

6. What major impacts do human activities have on ecosystems?

When we try to pick out anything by itself, we find it hitched to everything else in the universe.

John Muir

The ecosphere, in which all organisms are found, contains an astonishing variety of *terrestrial ecosystems*, such as deserts, grasslands, and forests, and *aquatic ecosystems*, such as lakes, reservoirs, ponds, rivers, and oceans. Each ecosystem has a characteristic plant and animal community adapted to certain environmental conditions.

Ecosystems, however, are dynamic, not static. Their populations of various organisms are always changing and adapting in response to major and minor changes in environmental conditions. Some of these changes occur because of natural events such as climate change, floods, and volcanic eruptions. Others are caused by land clearing, emissions of various pollutants, and other human activities.

6-1 MAJOR TYPES OF TERRESTRIAL ECOSYSTEMS

Climate and Terrestrial Ecosystems Why is one area of the earth a desert, another a grassland, and another a forest? Why are there different types of deserts, grasslands, and forests? What determines the types of life found in these biomes?

The general answer to these questions is differences in **climate**: the average of the day-to-day weather conditions in a region, usually over a 30-year period or longer. Many factors affect the climate of an area, as discussed in Section 7-1. However, the two most important are its *average temperature* and *average precipitation*.

There are three major types of large terrestrial ecosystems, or biomes: deserts, grasslands, and forests. Each type has a distinctive set of climatic conditions, organisms and, often, general soil type. An estimated 90% of the earth's species live in terrestrial ecosystems. The map inside the back cover shows the general distribution of the major types of desert, grassland, and forest biomes throughout the world. Biomes don't have sharp borders. Each biome gradually blends into neighboring communities.

Effects of Precipitation and Temperature on Plant Types With respect to plants, *precipitation generally is the limiting factor that determines whether the biomes of most of the world's land areas are desert, grassland, or forest.* A **desert** is an area where evaporation exceeds precipitation and the average amount of precipitation is less than ten inches a year. Such areas have little vegetation or have widely spaced, mostly low vegetation.

Figure 6-1 Average precipitation and average temperature act together over a period of 30 years or more as limiting factors that determine the type of desert, grassland, or forest ecosystem found in a particular area.

Because vegetation is sparse and skies are usually clear, the heat stored in desert soil during the day is quickly lost at night. Thus, deserts undergo large changes in temperature between day and night.

Grasslands are regions where the average annual precipitation is great enough to allow grass to prosper yet so erratic that periodic drought and fire prevent large stands of trees from growing. Undisturbed areas with moderate- to high-average annual precipitation tend to be covered with **forest,** containing various species of trees and smaller forms of vegetation.

Average precipitation and average temperature, along with soil, are the major factors determining the particular type of desert, grassland, or forest found in a given area. Acting together, these factors lead to *tropical*, *temperate*, and *polar* deserts, grasslands, and forests (Figure 6-1).

If you travel from the equator to either of the earth's poles, you will encounter different climates and different zones of vegetation adapted to each climate (see Figure 6-2).

As elevation above sea level increases, the climate becomes wetter and colder. Thus, if you climb a tall mountain from its base to its summit, you will find changes in plant life similar to those you would find in traveling from the equator to one of the earth's poles (Figure 6-2). That is why high mountains with permanent ice or snow exist in the tropics.

Major Types of Deserts Deserts cover some 15% of the earth's land surface and are located mainly between the tropics and subtropical regions (see map inside back cover). You may think that all deserts are hot during the day and consist of vast expanses of sand dunes dotted with a few oases. Such deserts do exist. But they are only one of three major types of deserts that occur because of combinations of low average precipitation with different average temperatures: tropical, temperate, and cold. (Figure 6-1).

Tropical deserts, such as the southern Sahara, make up about one-fifth of the world's desert area. They typically have few plants and a hard, windblown surface strewn with rocks and some sand. Sand dunes cover about 10% of these deserts. Temperatures are hot year-round. In *temperate deserts,* such as the Mojave in southern California, daytime temperatures are hot in summer and cool in winter. In *cold deserts,* such as the Gobi lying south of Siberia, winters are cold and summers are warm or hot.

Plants and animals in all deserts are adapted to capture and conserve scarce water. Plants in temperate and cold deserts usually are widely spaced, minimizing competition for water. Thorny bushes and shrubs like mesquite and salt cedar have roots reaching deep into the soil to tap groundwater. Others, such as the evergreen creosote bush, have wax-coated leaves, which reduce the amount of water lost by evaporation. Shrubs like ocotillo drop their leaves and survive in a dormant state during long dry spells and then grow new ones within a week after a rain.

Fleshy-stemmed cacti are either short (prickly pear) or tall (saguaro) and have shallow but widespread root systems that absorb water quickly (Figure 6-3). They store water in their tissues and have thick skins that prevent water loss. After a brief spring rain, wildflowers and grasses grow swiftly, produce seed, and die within a few weeks. Their seeds lie in the sand awaiting the next spring rain.

Most desert animals escape the daytime heat by staying underground in burrows during the day and being active at night. If you visit an Arizona or California desert during the day, you will probably see only a few insects, lizards, and birds such as hawks and roadrunners that prey on lizards. At night, however, the desert is alive with rodents and their predators such as rattlesnakes and owls.

Desert animals also have special adaptations to help them conserve water. The nocturnal kangaroo rat, for example, doesn't drink water. It gets the water it needs from its food and cellular respiration. It also conserves water by excreting dry feces and thick, nearly solid urine. Insects and reptiles have thick outer skin coverings to minimize water loss through evaporation. Some desert animals become dormant during periods of extreme heat or drought.

In some desert areas the soil is low in nutrients, whereas in other areas it is fairly rich in nutrients. In these areas, only the lack of water prevents the growth of plants found in other wetter biomes. Humans have converted desert into productive farmland by bringing in water for irrigation from other areas or by drawing on deep pools of groundwater underneath the desert surface.

The slow growth rate of plants, low species diversity, and shortages of water make deserts fragile biomes. For example, vegetation destroyed by human activities such as livestock grazing, motorcycling, and other off-road driving may take decades to grow back.

Major Types of Grasslands *Tropical grasslands,* or *savannas,* are found in areas with high average temperatures, two prolonged dry seasons during winter and summer, and abundant rain the rest of the year. They occur in a wide belt on either side of the equator beyond the borders of tropical rain forests (see map inside back cover).

Some of these biomes, such as Africa's Serengeti Plain, consist mostly of open plains covered with low or high grasses. Others contain grasses along with varying numbers of widely spaced, small, mostly deciduous trees and shrubs such as palms, acacias, and baobab. These plants shed their leaves during the dry season and avoid excessive water loss.

Savanna herbivores have specialized eating habits. Giraffes eat leaves and twigs found high up on the scattered trees, elephants eat leaves and branches further down, and gazelles, antelopes, and zebras graze on grasses of different heights and coarseness. Grasses grow out from the bottom instead of at the top so that their stems can survive being nibbled off by grazing animals.

Savannas have a larger number and variety of hoofed animal species than any other biome. In African savannas vast herds of wildebeests, gazelles, zebras, giraffes, antelopes, and other large herbivores graze in different areas depending on water and soil conditions. During the dry season, fires often sweep savannas, and the massive herds of grazing animals migrate in search of food. Some of these herbivores and their large predators such as lions, leopards, and cheetahs are disappearing rapidly except in a few protected areas because of ranching, farming, hunting, poaching, and other human activities.

Temperate grasslands are found in large, interior areas of continents, especially North America, South America, Europe, and Asia (see map inside back cover). Average temperatures are moderate. Precipitation is more evenly distributed throughout the year and winters are longer and colder than in tropical grasslands. Summers are hot and dry. Winds blow almost continuously and evaporation is rapid. As long as it is not plowed up, the soil is held in place by the thick network of roots of its grasses.

The soil is highly fertile and supports large populations of decomposers. Beetles, spiders, grasshoppers, and other insects live in the grasses in huge numbers and varieties. Prairie dogs, pocket gophers, deer mice, ground squirrels, prairie chickens, and other small herbivores are found in the American grasslands. Most of these animals live in underground burrows. Most large grazing animals live in herds, which afford them protection against predators.

Examples of temperate grasslands are the *tall-grass* and *short-grass prairies* of the midwestern and western United States and Canada, the *pampas* of South Amer-

Figure 6-2 Different biomes with similar types of vegetation occur primarily as a result of changes in climate in traveling from the equator toward the earth's poles or up mountain slopes. Similar types of animals live in each of these vegetation belts or life zones by adapting to similar environmental conditions.

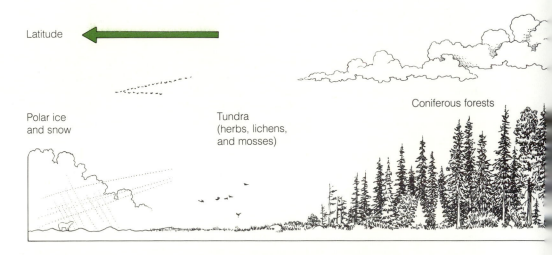

Latitude

Polar ice and snow

Tundra (herbs, lichens, and mosses)

Coniferous forests

Figure 6-3 Typical view of saguaro, a succulent cacti, and other desert vegetation in Pinal County, Arizona.

Soil Conservation Service/B. Brixner

ica, the *veld* of southern Africa, and the *steppes* that stretch from central Europe into Siberia (see map inside back cover). Temperate grasslands are often populated by herds of grazing animals. At one time, for example, vast herds of bison and pronghorn antelope roamed the prairies of North America. But these wild herbivores have been replaced by domesticated herbivores such as cattle and sheep. Wolves, cougars, coyotes and other animals that preyed on wild herbivores have largely been killed or driven away because they are a threat to livestock.

Only about 1% of the original tall-grass prairies that once thrived in the midwestern United States and Canada remain. Because of their highly fertile soils, most have been cleared for crops such as corn, wheat, and soybeans and for hog farming.

The short-grass prairies of the western United States are covered with low perennial grasses. They have too

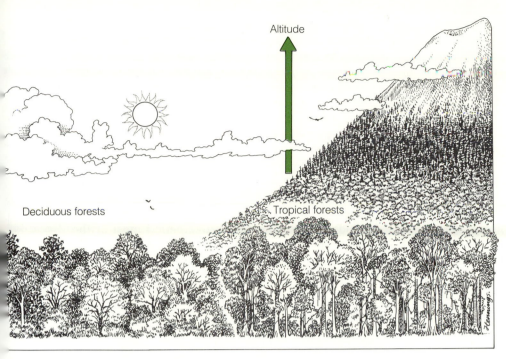

Altitude

Mountain
ice and snow

Tundra (moss,
lichen, herbs)

Coniferous
forests

Deciduous
forests

Tropical
forests

Deciduous forests

Tropical forests

little precipitation and soils too low in some plant nutrients to support taller grasses. They are widely used to graze unfenced cattle and in some areas to grow wheat and irrigated crops. Mismanagement of the short-grass prairies plus periodic, prolonged droughts led to severe erosion and loss of topsoil in the 1930s—a condition called the Dust Bowl (see Case Study on page 227).

Polar grassland or *Arctic tundra* is found in areas just below the Arctic ice region (see map inside back cover). During most of the year this biome is bitterly cold with icy galelike winds and is covered with ice and snow. Winters are long and dark, and average annual precipitation is low (less than five inches) and occurs mostly as snow.

The Arctic tundra is an enormous biome, covering a fifth of the earth's land surface. It is carpeted with a thick, spongy mat of low-growing plants such as lichens (growths of algae and fungi), sedges (grasslike plants often growing in dense tufts in marshy places), mosses, grasses, and low shrubs. These hardy plants are adapted to the lack of sunlight and water, freezing temperatures, and constant high winds in this harsh environment. Because of the cold temperatures, decomposition is slow. Partially decomposed organic matter accumulates as soggy masses of peat.

One effect of this biome's extreme cold is the presence of **permafrost**—water permanently frozen year-round in thick underground layers of soil. During the six- to eight-week summer, when sunlight persists almost around the clock, the surface layer of soil thaws. But the layer of permanent ice a few feet below the surface prevents the water from seeping deep into the

ground. As a result, during summer the tundra turns into a soggy landscape dotted with shallow lakes, marshes, bogs, and ponds. During this summer thaw hordes of mosquitoes, deerflies, blackflies, and other insects thrive in the shallow surface pools. They serve as food for large colonies of migratory birds, especially waterfowl, which migrate from the south to nest and breed in the bogs and ponds.

Most of the tundra's permanent animal residents are small herbivores such as lemmings, hares, and voles, and ground-squirrels, which burrow under the ground to escape the cold. Few species are present in large numbers. Musk-oxen are the only large herbivores that live all year in the tundra. Caribou in North America and reindeer, a similar species in Eurasia, spend the summer in the Arctic tundra but migrate south into northern coniferous forests for the rest of the year.

Populations of lemmings in the tundra rise and fall, depending on how good the summer season is for plants they eat. The lemming populations, in turn, regulate the numbers of their predators, such as the lynx, arctic fox, arctic wolf, weasel, and snowy owl. Many of these animals have white coats in winter, which make them hard to see against the winter snow.

Only Laplanders in northern Finland and Scandinavia live in the harsh tundra. However, discoveries of oil and gas have led to the building of pipelines through the North American tundra. The low rate of decomposition, shallow soil, and slow growth rate of plants make the Arctic tundra perhaps the earth's most fragile biome. Wheel ruts left by a single wagon crossing over tundra soil 100 years ago are still visible. Vegetation destroyed by this and other human activities can take decades to grow back. Buildings, roads, pipelines, and railroads must be built over bedrock, on insulating layers of gravel, or on deep-seated pilings. Otherwise, the structures melt the upper layer of permafrost and tilt or crack as the land beneath them shifts and settles.

Major Types of Forests *Tropical rain forests,* found in certain areas near the equator (see map inside back cover), have a warm but not hot annual mean temperature that varies little either daily or seasonally. They have high humidity and heavy rainfall almost daily. These biomes are dominated by evergreen trees, which keep most of their leaves or needles throughout the year and thus can use photosynthesis to produce organic nutrients all year.

The almost unchanging climate in rain forests means that water and temperature are not limiting factors as they are in other biomes. In this biome, nutrients from the often nutrient-poor soils are the major limiting factors.

A mature rain forest has a greater diversity of plant and animal species per unit of area than any other biome. More species of animals can be found in a single tree in a tropical forest than in an entire forest at higher latitudes. Although tropical forests cover only about 7% of the earth's land surface, they contain almost half of the world's growing wood and at least half of its different species of plants and animals.

These diverse forms of plant and animal life occupy a variety of ecological niches in distinct layers (Figure 5-22, p. 113). Much of the animal life, particularly insects, bats, and birds, is found in the sunny canopy layer with its abundance of shelter, fruits, and other foods. The tangled vegetation and the leaves on the lower canopy of smaller trees block out most of the sunlight so that the forest floor is dark, humid, and relatively free of vegetation.

Monkeys, geckos, iguanas, snakes, chameleons, and other animals move up and down the trunks and vines to feed on insects and fruits. A great variety of tiny animals live on the ground, where there are also vast populations of termites and other decomposers. Because of the moist warm conditions, the rate of decomposition is very rapid, explaining why there is so little litter on the ground.

Most of the nutrients in this biome are found in the vegetation, not in the upper layers of soil as in most other biomes. Once the vegetation is removed, the soils rapidly lose the few nutrients they have and cannot grow crops for more than a few years without large-scale use of commercial fertilizers. Furthermore, when vegetation is cleared, the heavy rainfall washes away most of the thin layer of topsoil. This means that regenerating a mature rain forest on large cleared areas is almost impossible.

These unique and valuable forests are being cleared at an alarming rate to harvest timber and to plant crops and graze livestock on mostly unsustainable soils. Some ecologists project that if the clearing of tropical rain forests continues at the present rate, within 50 years only a few of these diverse ecosystems will remain. Many thousands of animal and plant species with highly specialized niches in these forests will also vanish. Such clearing may also accelerate the warming of the earth's atmosphere as a result of the greenhouse effect.

Other types of tropical forests (see map inside back cover) get most of their rainfall during monsoon periods. During the annual dry period most of the trees in these monsoon forests shed their leaves.

Temperate deciduous forests occur in areas with moderate average temperatures that change significantly during four distinct seasons (see map inside back cover). They are found in areas with long summers, not very severe winters, and abundant precipitation spread fairly evenly throughout the year.

These biomes are dominated by a few species of broadleaf deciduous trees such as oak, hickory, maple, poplar, sycamore, and beech. These plants survive during winter by dropping their leaves and going into an inactive state. Each spring they sprout buds that grow into deep green leaves that change in the fall into a beautiful array of colors before dropping. In most mature deciduous forests, as in tropical forests, the vegetation is found in distinct layers: a canopy of leaves in the tops of the tallest trees, an understory of shorter, shade-tolerant trees, a layer of shrubs, and a layer of ferns and other low-growing plants on the forest floor.

This layering of vegetation supplies a diversity of ecological niches for animal life. Hawks and owls nest in the canopy. They play an important ecological role by keeping down populations of mice and other small rodents, which would otherwise destroy much of the vegetation on the forest floor. Woodcocks and black bears nest and feed on the ground, and squirrels regularly commute between the canopy and the forest floor.

Once the deciduous forests in the eastern United States were home for large predators such as bears, wolves, foxes, and mountain lions. Today most of these predators have been killed or displaced. Today large numbers of plant-eating whitetail deer are found in most of these forests. Warblers, robins, and a number of other bird species migrate to the forests during the summer to feed and breed.

Temperate forests have nutrient-rich soil (helped by the annual fall of leaves) and valuable timber and are located near settled areas. This explains why all but about 0.1% of the original stands of temperate forests in North America have been cleared for farms, orchards, timber, and urban development.

Northern coniferous forests, also called *boreal forests* and *taigas*, are found in regions with a subarctic climate. Winters are long and dry with light snowfall and short days. Temperatures range from cool to extremely cold. Summers are short with mild to warm temperatures, but the sun typically shines for 19 hours each day.

These coniferous forests form an almost unbroken belt just south of the Arctic tundra across North America, Asia, and Europe (see map inside back cover). They are dominated by a few species of coniferous (cone-bearing) evergreen trees such as spruce, fir, cedar, and pine. The needle-shaped, waxy-coated leaves of these trees conserve heat and water during the long, cold, dry winters. Plant diversity is low in these forests because few species can survive the winters, when soil moisture is frozen. Parts of the forests are dotted with wet bogs, or *muskegs.*

The crowded needles of the evergreen trees block out much of the light. Beneath the dense stands of trees, a carpet of fallen needles and leaf litter covers the nutrient-poor soil, making the soil acidic and preventing most other plants from growing on the forest floor. During the brief summer the soil becomes waterlogged.

For all or part of the year, taigas are home for large herbivores such as mule deer, elk, caribou, and moose and small herbivores such as porcupines, snowshoe hares, squirrels, and chipmunks. They also contain medium to large predators such as grizzly bears, black bears, wolverines, foxes, lynxes, martens, and wolves. Insect pests thrive during the warm summer months. They are fed upon by birds that migrate from the south for the breeding season.

In settled areas of this biome in North America, farmers and ranchers have essentially eliminated large predators, such as timber wolves, which can prey on livestock. However, this has allowed populations of moose, caribou, and mule deer to increase and devastate taiga vegetation. In the long run this reduces the ability of the land to support grazing livestock. Loggers have cut the trees from large areas of taiga in North America. Much fur trapping has also taken place in this biome.

6-2 AQUATIC ECOSYSTEMS

Limiting Factors of Aquatic Ecosystems Five main factors affect the types and numbers of organisms found in aquatic ecosystems. One is *salinity:* the concentration of dissolved salts, especially sodium chloride, in a body of water. The others are the depth to which sunlight penetrates, amount of dissolved oxygen, availability of plant nutrients, and water temperature.

Salinity levels are used to divide aquatic ecosystems into two major classes. Those with high to very high salinity levels are *marine* or *saltwater ecosystems.* They include oceans, estuaries (where fresh water from rivers and streams mixes with seawater), coastal wetlands, and coral reefs. *Freshwater ecosystems* have low salinity. Examples are inland bodies of standing water (lakes, reservoirs, ponds, and inland wetlands) and flowing water (streams and rivers).

Most producers need sunlight to carry out photosynthesis. Thus, the depth to which sunlight penetrates determines the abundance of plant life (and thus animal life) found in various parts of aquatic ecosystems.

On land oxygen is easily available from the atmosphere to oxygen-consuming animals. In aquatic ecosystems, however, oxygen is dissolved by exposure of the water to the atmosphere and through photosynthesis in aquatic plants. Oxygen is often scarce in the bottom layers of nonflowing aquatic ecosystems, which are not exposed to the atmosphere and sunlight.

Marine Aquatic Ecosystems: Why Are the Oceans So Important? As landlubbers, we tend to think of the earth in terms of land. It is more accurately described, however, as the "water planet" because 71% of its surface is covered by water. The oceans make up 97% of that water, and they play a key role in the survival of life on earth.

The oceans are the ultimate receptacle for terrestrial water flowing from rivers. Because of their size and mixing, the oceans dilute many human-produced wastes to less harmful or harmless levels. They play a major role in regulating the climate of the earth by helping distribute solar heat through ocean currents and evaporation as part of the hydrologic cycle. They also participate in other major biogeochemical cycles.

In addition, the oceans serve as a gigantic reservoir of carbon dioxide, which helps regulate the temperature of the atmosphere. Oceans provide habitats for about 250,000 species of marine plants and animals, which are food for many organisms, including human beings. They also serve as a source of iron, sand, gravel, phosphates, lime, magnesium, oil, natural gas, and many other valuable resources.

Major Ocean Zones Each of the world's oceans can be divided into two major zones: coastal, and open sea (Figure 6-4). The **coastal zone** is the relatively warm, nutrient-rich, shallow water that extends from the high-tide mark on land to the edge of a shelflike extension of the continental land mass known as the *continental shelf.* The coastal zone, representing less than 10% of the total ocean area, contains 90% of all ocean plant and animal life and is the site of most of the major commercial marine fisheries. It contains some of the earth's most important ecosystems (see Spotlight on p. 125).

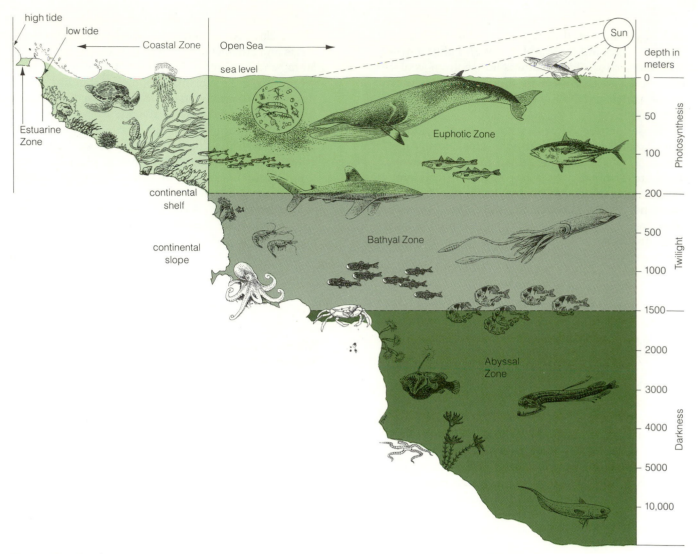

Figure 6-4 Major zones of life in an ocean or marine ecosystem. Actual depths of zones may vary. The lighted upper zone where photosynthesis takes place supports scattered populations of microscopic, drifting producers (mostly algae and bacteria) called phytoplankton (plant plankton). They are fed upon by slightly larger, more mobile zooplankton (animal plankton). These herbivores in turn are eaten by commercially important herrings, sardines, anchovies, and other small fish that feed in the surface layer. These secondary consumers are then eaten by larger predators such as tuna, mackerel, and swordfish.

The sharp increase in water depth at the edge of the continental shelf marks the separation of the coastal zone from the **open sea** (Figure 6-4). This marine zone contains about 90% of the total surface area of the ocean but only about 10% of its plant and animal life. The open sea is divided into three zones (Figure 6-4).

The Coastal Zone: A Closer Look   The coastal zone includes a number of different habitats. **Estuaries** are coastal areas where fresh water from rivers, streams, and runoff from the land mixes with salty seawater. Estuaries provide aquatic habitats with a lower average salinity than the waters of the open ocean. They, along with inland swamps and marshes and tropical rain forests, produce more plant biomass per square foot each year than any of the world's other ecosystems.

Land that is flooded all or part of the year with fresh or salt water is called a **wetland.** Wetlands extending inland from estuaries and covered all or part of the year with salt water are known as **coastal wetlands.** In temperate areas coastal wetlands usually consist of a mix of bays, lagoons, and salt marshes, where grasses are the dominant vegetation. In areas with warm tropical climates, we find swamps dominated by mangrove trees.

These nutrient-rich areas are among the world's most productive ecosystems. Only about 5% of all wetlands in the United States are coastal wetlands. The other 95% are inland wetlands covered with fresh water during all or part of the year.

The coastal zones of warm tropical and subtropical oceans, with water temperatures above 20°C, often

SPOTLIGHT Why Is the Coastal Zone So Important?

Many people view estuaries and coastal wetlands as desolate, mosquito-infested, worthless lands. They believe that these ecosystems should be drained, dredged, filled in, built on, or used as depositories for human-generated pollutants and waste materials.

Nothing could be further from the truth. These highly productive areas provide us and many other species with a remarkable variety of benefits. They supply food and serve as spawning and nursery grounds for many species of marine fish and shellfish (Figure 6-5). They are also breeding grounds and habitats for waterfowl and other wildlife, including many endangered species. Each year millions of people visit coastal zones for whale or bird watching, waterfowl hunting, and other recreational activities.

In the United States, estuaries and coastal wetlands are spawning grounds for 70% of the country's seafood, including shrimp, salmon, oysters, clams, and haddock. The $15-billion-a-year commercial and recreational marine fishing industry, taking place mostly in the coastal zone, provides jobs for millions of people.

Coastal areas also dilute and filter out large amounts of waterborne pollutants, helping protect the quality of waters used for swimming, fishing, and wildlife habitats. It is estimated that one acre of tidal estuary substitutes for a $75,000 waste treatment plant and is worth a total of $83,000 when its production of fish for food and recreation is included. By comparison one acre of prime farmland in Kansas has a top

value of $1,200 and an annual production value of $600.

Estuaries and coastal wetlands, along with barrier islands and the sand dunes of barrier beaches, help protect coastal areas. They absorb damaging waves caused by violent storms and hurricanes and serve as giant sponges to absorb floodwaters.

Clearly, estuaries and coastal wetlands are among our most productive and important natural ecosystems. But they are also among our most intensely populated, used, and stressed ecosystems. Human activities are increasingly impairing or destroying some of the important, free services these ecosystems provide (see Case Study on p. 126).

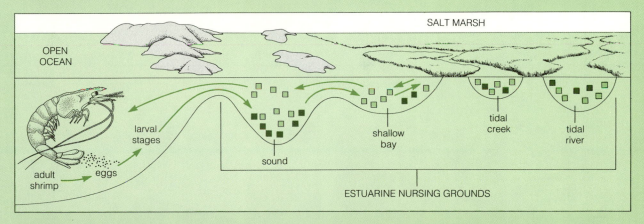

Figure 6-5 Life history of shrimp that use the coastal zone as nursery grounds. Adult shrimp spawn offshore and the larva of their offspring move into semi-enclosed estuaries. There they find the food and protection they need for rapid growth during their young (dark green boxes) and adolescent (light green boxes) stages. As they mature, the shrimp move into deeper coastal waters and then into the open ocean. (Adapted with permission from Cecie Starr and Ralph Taggart, *Biology: The Unity and Diversity of Life*, 4th ed., 1987, Belmont, Calif.: Wadsworth)

contain *coral reefs*. They consist mostly of deposits of insoluble calcium compounds secreted by photosynthesizing red and green algae and small coral animals. Because of their complexity and diversity, coral reefs support at least one-third of all marine fish species as well as numerous other marine organisms. They are also believed to be important in maintaining ocean salinity levels.

Along some steep, western coasts of continents, almost constant trade winds blow offshore and push

surface water away from the shore. This outwardly moving surface water is replaced by an **upwelling** of cold, nutrient-rich bottom waters. This upwelling brings plant nutrients from the deeper parts of the ocean to the surface and supports large populations of plankton, fish, and fish-eating seabirds. Although they make up only about 0.1% of the world's total ocean area, upwellings are highly productive. However, periodic changes in climate and ocean currents can reduce their high productivity and cause sharp drops in the annual

About 55% of the U.S. population lives along the coastlines of the Atlantic Ocean, the Pacific Ocean, and the Great Lakes. Two out of three Americans live within an hour's drive of these shores. By 1995, three out of four will live in or near the country's coastal zones.

Nine of the country's largest cities, most major ports, about 40% of the manufacturing plants, and two out of three nuclear and coal-fired power plants are located in coastal counties. The coasts are also the sites of large numbers of motels, hotels, condominiums, beach cottages, and other developments (Figure 6-6). To meet energy, irrigation, and flood control needs, most of the country's major rivers have been dammed or diverted. This changes the normal flow of fresh water into estuaries and modifies their nutrient supplies and food webs.

Because of these multiple uses and stresses, nearly 50% of the estuaries and coastal wetlands in the United States have been destroyed or damaged, primarily by dredging and filling and contamination by wastes. For example, garbage slicks laden with harmful bacteria and viruses and toxic chemicals have caused massive fish kills and closed beaches in New Jersey. Only about 58% of U.S. shellfish waters are now clean enough to produce edible seafood.

Fortunately, about half of the country's estuaries and coastal wetlands remain undeveloped, but each year additional areas are developed. Some coastal areas have been purchased by federal and state governments and by private conservation agencies. Such purchases are designed to help protect key areas from development and to allow most of them to be used as parks and wildlife habitats.

The National Coastal Zone Management Acts of 1972 and 1980 gave federal aid to the 37 coastal and Great Lakes states and territories to help them develop voluntary programs for protecting and managing coastlines not under federal protection. By 1988, more than 90% of the country's coastal areas in all but six of the eligible states had federally approved state coastal management plans.

These plans, however, are voluntary, and many are vague and don't provide enough enforcement authority. Since 1981 their implementation has also been hindered by federal budget cutbacks. California and North Carolina are considered to have the strongest programs, but developers and other interests make continuing efforts to weaken them.

The Water Quality Act of 1987 is a step in the right direction. It established the National Estuary Program with the goal of identifying nationally significant estuaries, protecting and improving their water quality, and enhancing their living resources. What else, if anything, do you think should be done to protect the country's remaining undeveloped coastal ecosystems?

Bob Graeber/Airflite

Bob Graeber/Airflite

Figure 6-6   Development of Port of Los Angeles between 1972 (left) and 1988 (right).

catch of some important marine fish species, such as anchovies.

Some coasts have gently sloping *barrier beaches* at the water's edge. If not destroyed by human activities, one or more rows of sand dunes on such beaches serve as the land's first line of defense against the ravages of the sea (Figure 6-7). When coastal developers remove the dunes or build behind the first set of dunes, minor hurricanes and sea storms can flood and even sweep away houses and other buildings. Coastal dwellers mistakenly call these human-assisted disasters natural disasters. Other coasts contain steep *rocky shores* pounded by waves. Many organisms live in the numerous intertidal pools in the rocks.

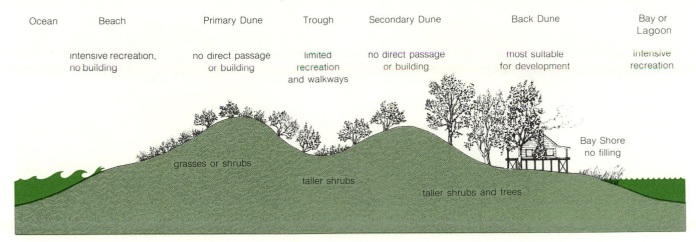

Ocean	Beach	Primary Dune	Trough	Secondary Dune	Back Dune	Bay or Lagoon
intensive recreation, no building	no direct passage or building	limited recreation and walkways		no direct passage or building	most suitable for development	intensive recreation

grasses or shrubs

taller shrubs

taller shrubs and trees

Bay Shore no filling

Figure 6-7 Primary and secondary dunes on a barrier beach. Ideally, construction and development should be allowed only behind the second strip of dunes, with walkways to the beach built over the dunes to keep them intact. This helps protect human structures from being damaged and washed away by wind, high tides, beach erosion, and flooding from storm surges. Protection of barrier beaches is rare, however, because the short-term economic value of limited oceanfront land is considered much higher than its long-term ecological and economic value.

Strings of thin *barrier islands* in some coastal areas (such as portions of North America's Atlantic and Gulf coasts) help protect the mainland, estuaries, lagoons, and coastal wetlands by dispersing the energy of approaching storm waves. People build cottages and other structures on these slender ribbons of sand with water on all sides, but sooner or later most of these structures are damaged or destroyed. The islands are flooded and eroded by major storms and hurricanes and are slowly but continually moved toward the mainland by currents and winds. As they move, the islands relocate with no net loss of beach. But human structures built near the original high-tide line are gradually undermined.

Freshwater Lakes and Reservoirs Lakes are large natural bodies of standing fresh water formed when precipitation, land runoff, or flowing groundwater fills depressions in the earth. Causes of such depressions include glaciation (the Great Lakes of North America), earthquakes (Lake Nyasa in East Africa), and volcanic activity (Lake Kivu in Africa). Lakes normally consist of four distinct zones (Figure 6-8), which provide a variety of ecological niches for different species.

Lakes can be divided into three categories, based on their supply of plant nutrients. A lake with a small supply of plant nutrients (mostly nitrates and phosphates) is called an **oligotrophic lake** (Figure 6-9). Such a lake is usually deep and has crystal-clear water with cool to cold temperatures. It has small populations of phytoplankton and fish such as smallmouth bass and lake trout. Crater Lake in Oregon is an oligotrophic lake.

A lake with a large or excessive supply of plant nutrients is called a **eutrophic lake** (Figure 6-9). This type of lake is usually shallow and has cloudy, warm water. It has large populations of phytoplankton (especially algae) and zooplankton, and diverse populations of fish, particularly bullhead, catfish, and carp. In warm summer months the bottom layer of a eutrophic lake is often depleted of dissolved oxygen. Lake Erie is a eutrophic lake. Many lakes fall somewhere between the two extremes of nutrient enrichment and are called **mesotrophic lakes.**

Eutrophication is the physical, chemical, and biological changes that take place after a lake receives inputs of plant nutrients from the surrounding land basin from natural erosion and runoff over a long period of time. Near urban or agricultural centers the natural input of plant nutrients to a lake can be greatly increased by human activities. This **accelerated,** or **cultural, eutrophication** is caused mostly by nitrate- and phosphate-containing effluents from sewage treatment plants, runoff of fertilizers and animal wastes, and accelerated soil erosion.

Reservoirs are fairly large and deep, human-created bodies of standing fresh water. They are often built behind a dam to collect water running down from mountains into streams and rivers (Figure 6-10). Often reservoirs are incorrectly called lakes. For example, I live not too far from a massive reservoir in central North Carolina called Jordan Lake.

Reservoirs are built primarily to store and release water in a controlled manner. The released water may be used for hydroelectric power production at the dam site. Water can also be released over the dam and diverted into irrigation canals to grow crops on dry

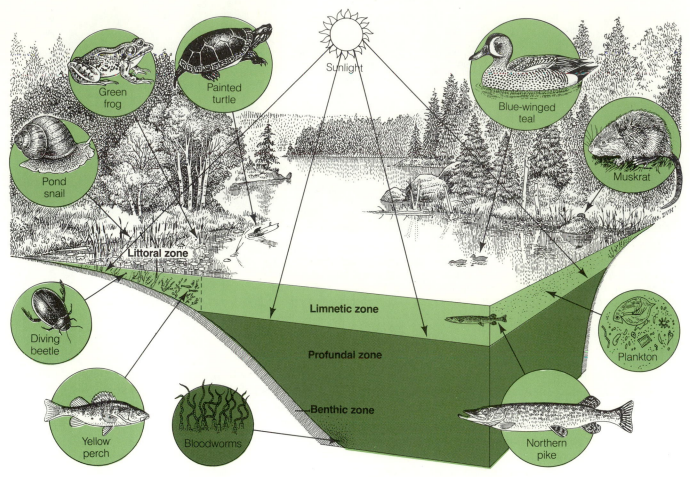

Figure 6-8 Four major zones of life in a lake. The *littoral zone* includes the shore and the shallow, nutrient-rich waters near the shore, in which sunlight penetrates to the lake bottom. It contains a variety of free-floating producers, rooted aquatic plants, and other forms of aquatic life such as frogs, snails, and snakes. The *limnetic zone* is the open water surface layer that gets enough sunlight for photosynthesis to take place. It contains varying amounts of floating phytoplankton, plant-eating zooplankton, and fish, depending on the supply of plant nutrients. The *profundal zone* is the deep, open water where it is too dark for photosynthesis to take place. It is inhabited by fish adapted to its cooler, darker water. The *benthic zone* at the bottom of a lake is inhabited mostly by large numbers of decomposers and detritus-feeding clams and wormlike insect larvae. These detritivores feed mostly on dead plant debris, animal remains, and animal wastes that descend from above.

but otherwise fertile land. It can be stored and released slowly to prevent flooding and diverted into aqueducts and carried to towns and cities for use by homes, businesses, and industries. Reservoirs are also used for recreation such as swimming, fishing, and boating.

Freshwater Streams and Rivers Precipitation that doesn't infiltrate into the ground or evaporate remains on the earth's surface as *surface water.* This water becomes *runoff,* which flows into streams and rivers and eventually downhill to the oceans for reuse in the hydrologic cycle (Figure 5-20, p. 110). The entire land area that delivers the water, sediment, and dissolved substances via streams to a major river, and ultimately to the sea, is called a **watershed** or **drainage basin.** Some streams are fed mostly by groundwater flow instead of surface runoff.

The downward flow of water from mountain highlands to the sea takes place in three phases (Figure 6-11). First, narrow headwater or mountain highland streams with cold, clear water rush down steep slopes. As this turbulent water flows and tumbles downward over waterfalls and rapids, it dissolves large amounts of oxygen from the air. Most fish that thrive in this environment are cold-water fish, such as trout, which require a high level of dissolved oxygen.

In the second phase various headwater streams merge to form wider, deeper, lower-elevation streams that flow down gentler slopes and meander through wider valleys. Here the water is warmer and usually less turbulent. It can support a variety of cold-water and warm-water fish species with slightly lower oxygen requirements.

Gradually these streams coalesce into wider and deeper rivers that meander across broad, flat valleys.

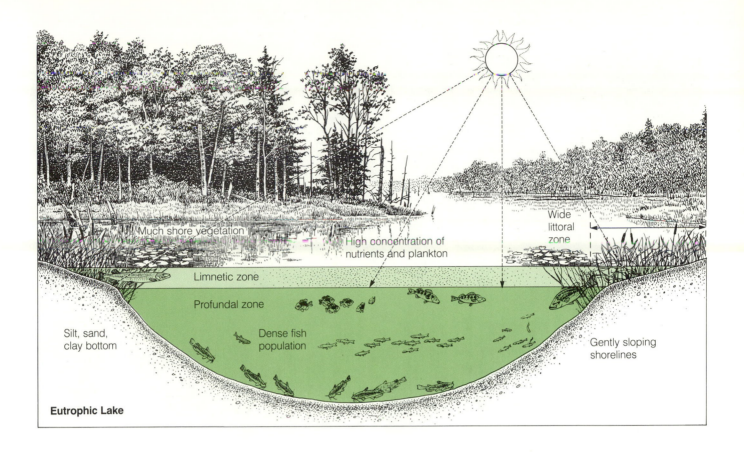

Much shore vegetation

High concentration of nutrients and plankton

Wide littoral zone

Limnetic zone

Profundal zone

Silt, sand, clay bottom

Dense fish population

Gently sloping shorelines

Eutrophic Lake

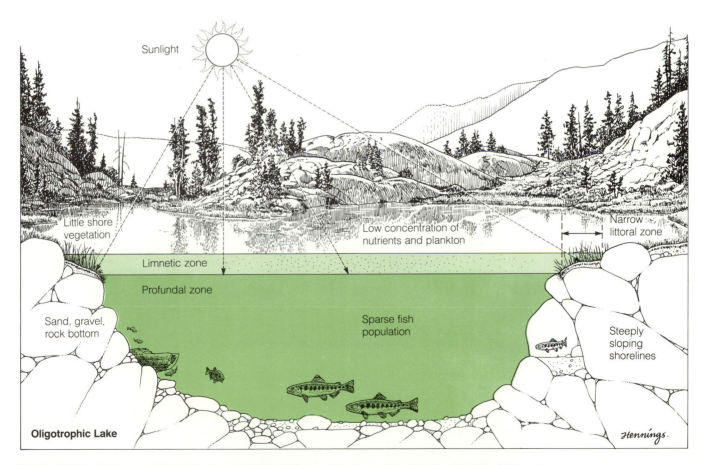

Sunlight

Little shore vegetation

Low concentration of nutrients and plankton

Narrow littoral zone

Limnetic zone

Profundal zone

Sand, gravel, rock bottom

Sparse fish population

Steeply sloping shorelines

Oligotrophic Lake

Hennings

Figure 6-9 Eutrophic, or nutrient-rich lake, and oligotrophic, or nutrient-poor lake. Mesotrophic lakes fall between these two extremes of nutrient enrichment.

Figure 6-10 Reservoir formed behind Shasta Dam on the Sacramento River north of Redding, California.

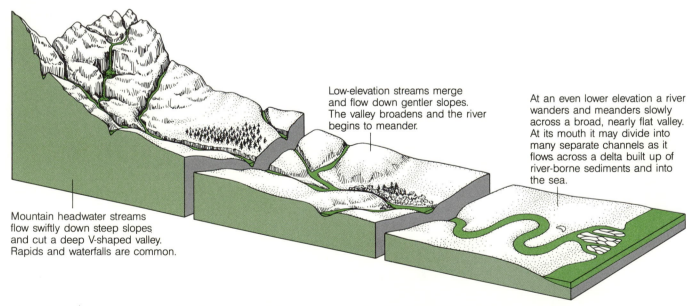

Low-elevation streams merge and flow down gentler slopes. The valley broadens and the river begins to meander.

At an even lower elevation a river wanders and meanders slowly across a broad, nearly flat valley. At its mouth it may divide into many separate channels as it flows across a delta built up of river-borne sediments and into the sea.

Mountain headwater streams flow swiftly down steep slopes and cut a deep V-shaped valley. Rapids and waterfalls are common.

Figure 6-11 Three phases in the flow of water downhill from mountain headwater streams to wider, lower-elevation streams to rivers, which empty into the ocean.

The main channels of these rivers support a distinctive variety of fish, whereas their backwaters support species similar to those found in lakes. At its mouth a river may divide into many channels as it flows across a *delta*—a built-up deposit of river-borne sediments—and coastal wetlands and estuaries where river water mixes with ocean water.

Inland Wetlands Lands covered with fresh water all or part of the year and located away from coastal areas

Figure 6-12 Prairie potholes and cropland in Minnesota.

Grant Heilman

are called **inland wetlands.** They include inland bogs, marshes, swamps, mud flats, river-outflow lands, prairie potholes (Figure 6-12), and the wet tundra during summer. Shallow marshes and swamps are among the most productive ecosystems in the world.

In the United States, inland wetlands in the lower 48 states are roughly equivalent in total area to the state of California. Almost twice this area of inland wetlands is found in Alaska—58% of the state is covered with wetlands. Most of the waterfowl harvested in North America are produced in wetland habitats of Canada. Inland wetlands are important ecosystems that are being rapidly destroyed and degraded (see Spotlight on p. 132).

Connections Between Terrestrial and Aquatic Ecosystems Distinguishing between land and water ecosystems is useful. At the same time, however, understanding how these ecosystems are linked is also important.

One important connection is the runoff of plant nutrients, mostly as nitrates and phosphates, from the land into aquatic ecosystems. These nutrients help support plant life in rivers, lakes, and estuaries, which in turn support aquatic animal life. Runoff of decaying organic matter into aquatic ecosystems is a source of food for aquatic detritivores. When soil erodes into lakes and slow-moving rivers, it builds up bottom sediments. These sediments gradually change the types of aquatic life that can thrive and eventually convert an aquatic ecosystem to a terrestrial ecosystem.

Natural events and human activities can drastically change the rates at which plant nutrients, detritus, and soil are transferred from land to water. For example, flooding and land clearing increase the rate at which materials move to aquatic ecosystems, often overloading them with plant nutrients. This can cause explosive growth, or blooms, of algae. When the algae die and are broken down by oxygen-consuming decomposers, the water is depleted of dissolved oxygen, killing fish and other organisms.

Conversely, matter resources also flow from aquatic to terrestrial ecosystems. Fish and shellfish are sources of food for many land-dwelling animals such as seabirds, bears, eagles, and people. When seabirds deposit their wastes on land (Figure 5-19, p. 109), they return some of these nutrients from the sea to the land as part of the nitrogen and phosphorous cycles.

6-3 RESPONSES OF LIVING SYSTEMS TO ENVIRONMENTAL STRESS

Effects of Environmental Stress Table 6-1 (p. 133) summarizes what can happen to organisms, populations, and ecosystems if one or more environmental factors fall above or below the levels tolerated by various species (Figure 5-9, p. 100). The stresses that can

SPOTLIGHT **Why Are Inland Wetlands So Important?**

In addition to providing habitats for a variety of fish and other wildlife, inland wetlands store and regulate stream flow. Thus, they reduce flood frequency, flood levels, and river bank erosion. The wetlands also improve water quality by trapping stream sediments and absorbing, diluting, and degrading many toxic pollutants.

By holding water, many wetlands allow increased ground infiltration, thus helping recharge groundwater supplies. They are also used for recreation, especially waterfowl hunting, and to grow crops such as blueberries, cranberries, and rice. Wetlands also play significant roles in the global cycles of carbon, nitrogen, and sulfur.

Because people are often unaware of their ecological importance, inland wetlands are dredged or filled in and used as croplands, garbage dumps, and sites for urban and industrial development. They are viewed as wastelands.

Altogether, about 56% of the original coastal and inland wetland acreage in the lower 48 states has been destroyed—enough to cover an area four times the size of Ohio. About 80% of this loss was due to draining and clearing of wetlands for agriculture. Most of the rest were used for real estate development and highways. Wetland destruction has greatly reduced the habitat of birds and other wildlife that live on or near these ecosystems, threatening some species with extinction.

Iowa has lost 95% of its natural marshes and California has lost 90% of its wetlands. Almost all southern bottomland hardwood wetlands are gone. It is estimated that each year the United States is still losing 300,000 to 450,000 acres of wetlands.

Attempts have been made to slow the rate of wetland loss. The Farm Act of 1985 has a "swampbuster" provision that withholds agricultural subsidies from landowners who convert wetlands to croplands. The Emergency Wetlands Resource Act raises about $20 million a year for federal wetland acquisition. A federal permit is now required to fill or deposit polluting material in wetland areas. The North American Waterfowl Management Plan should help acquire and restore massive wetland areas in the next 15 years.

A major problem is that only about 8% of inland wetlands is under federal protection. Also federal, state, and local protection of wetlands is still quite weak. Existing laws are poorly enforced and subsidies and tax incentives are still given to developers who drain, dredge, drain, fill, and destroy wetlands. What do you think should be done?

---

cause the changes shown in the table may result from natural hazards (such as earthquakes, volcanic eruptions, hurricanes, drought, floods, and fires) or from human activities (industrialization, warfare, transportation, and agriculture).

Stability of Living Systems Organisms, populations, communities, and ecosystems all have some ability to withstand or recover from externally imposed changes or stresses—provided these external stresses are not too severe. In other words, they have some degree of *stability*. This stability is maintained, however, only by constant dynamic change.

Although an organism maintains a fairly stable structure over its life span, it is continually gaining and losing matter and energy. Similarly, in a mature tropical rain forest ecosystem some trees will die, others will take their place. Some species may disappear, and the number of individual species in the forest may change. But unless it is cut, burned, or blown down, you will recognize it as a tropical rain forest 50 years from now.

It is useful to distinguish between two aspects of stability in living systems. **Inertia,** or **persistence,** is the ability of a living system to resist being disturbed or altered. **Resilience** is the ability of a living system to restore itself to an original condition after being exposed to an outside disturbance that is not too drastic.

Nature is remarkably resilient. For example, human societies have survived natural disasters and devastating wars. Rapidly producing insect populations can alter their genetic structure to survive massive doses of pesticides and ionizing radiation. Plants recolonize areas devastated by volcanoes, retreating glaciers, mining, bombing, and farming—although such natural restoration usually takes a long time on a human time scale.

6-4 POPULATION RESPONSES TO STRESS

Changes in Population Size and Structure Populations of organisms that make up ecosystems respond in various ways to changes in environmental conditions, such as an excess or a shortage of food or other critical nutrients. The major changes are an increase or decrease in population size (Figure 6-13, p. 134).

Also, the structure of the population in terms of the distribution of individuals of different ages and

Table 6-1	Some Effects of Environmental Stress

Organism Level

Physiological and biochemical changes
Psychological disorders
Behavioral changes
Fewer or no offspring
Genetic defects in offspring (mutagenic effects)
Birth defects (teratogenic effects)
Cancers (carcinogenic effects)
Death

Population Level

Population increase or decrease
Change in age structure (old, young, and weak may die)
Survival of strains genetically resistant to a stress
Loss of genetic diversity and adaptability
Extinction

Community—Ecosystem Level

Disruption of energy flow
    Decrease or increase in solar energy input
    Changes in heat output
    Changes in trophic structure in food chains and food webs

Disruption of chemical cycles
    Depletion of essential nutrients
    Excessive addition of nutrients

Simplification
    Reduction in species diversity
    Reduction or elimination of habitats and filled ecological niches
    Less complex food webs
    Possibility of lowered stability
    Possibility of ecosystem collapse

sex may change. For example, old, very young, and weak members may die. The remaining population is then better equipped to survive such stresses as a more severe climate, an increase in predators, or an increase in disease organisms. Some animal species can reduce their population by leaving one area and migrating to another area with favorable environmental conditions and resource supplies. The continual changes in the size and composition of a population are called **population dynamics.** Wildlife managers can use knowledge about population dynamics to help manage various wildlife species.

Species Characteristics Influencing Birth Rate

Several major characteristics of an animal species affect its birth rate. One is the number of live young hatched or born to a female at the end of the birthing period. For example, female California condors lay only one or two eggs during each breeding period. This makes the species more vulnerable to extinction than birds, such as ducks and grouse, that lay and incubate 8 to 15 eggs at one time.

The birth rate of a species is also affected by the number of times a female goes through a complete breeding cycle each year and by the length of the gestation period before hatching or birth occurs. The meadow vole (a small rodent), with a gestation period of only 21 days, can produce large numbers of young in a short period. In contrast, the African elephant has a gestation period of almost two years and does not breed while its offspring is nursing heavily. Thus, it produces at most one young every 2.5 years, and usually at longer intervals.

When the population density of a species in a particular area is too low, individuals may have trouble finding mates, so that the birth rate may be lower than normal. The birth rate can also decline when the population density becomes too high, due to the poorer health of breeding individuals caused by lack of food. Under overcrowded and stressful conditions some species, such as rats, reduce their birth rate even when plenty of food is available.

Major Factors Influencing Death Rate A major characteristic that affects the death rate and age structure of a species is the chances individuals in various age groups have for survival. We can construct a *survivorship curve* for a particular species by plotting the number or percentage of individuals in a particular population still alive at various ages. Studies have shown that most species tend to have one of three general types of survivorship curves (Figure 6-14, p. 135).

In addition to survivorship, other factors can affect the death rate of a species. One is *interspecific competition:* competition between members of two or more *different* species for scarce food and other resources. Another is *intraspecific competition:* competition between members of the *same* species for scarce resources. Still other factors affecting the death rate include predation by other species including humans, diseases and parasites, stress from overcrowded conditions, loss or degradation of habitat as a result of human activities, and catastrophic natural events such as drought, earthquakes, hurricanes, fires and floods.

J and S Curves: Idealized Model of Population Dynamics With unlimited resources and ideal environmental conditions, a species can produce offspring at its maximum rate. Such growth starts off slowly and then increases rapidly to produce an exponential, or J-shaped, curve of population growth (Figure 6-15). Species such as bacteria, insects, and mice can produce many offspring in a short time. Larger species such as elephants and humans take a long time to produce only a few offspring.

The maximum population size of each species that an ecosystem can support *indefinitely* under a given set of environmental conditions is called that ecosys-

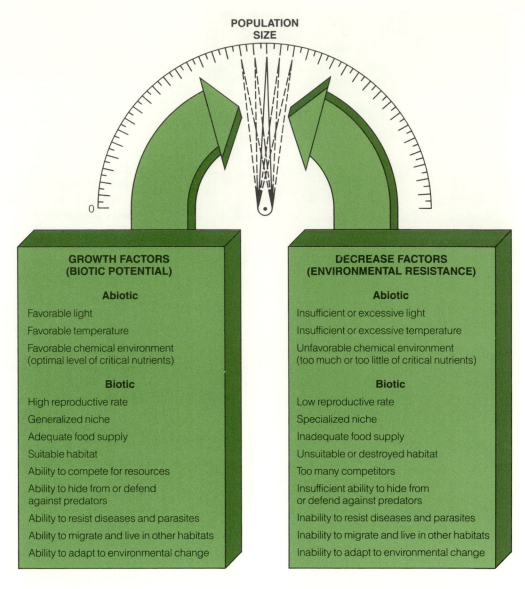

Figure 6-13 Population size is a balance between factors that increase numbers and factors that decrease numbers.

POPULATION SIZE

GROWTH FACTORS (BIOTIC POTENTIAL)	DECREASE FACTORS (ENVIRONMENTAL RESISTANCE)
Abiotic	**Abiotic**
Favorable light	Insufficient or excessive light
Favorable temperature	Insufficient or excessive temperature
Favorable chemical environment (optimal level of critical nutrients)	Unfavorable chemical environment (too much or too little of critical nutrients)
Biotic	**Biotic**
High reproductive rate	Low reproductive rate
Generalized niche	Specialized niche
Adequate food supply	Inadequate food supply
Suitable habitat	Unsuitable or destroyed habitat
Ability to compete for resources	Too many competitors
Ability to hide from or defend against predators	Insufficient ability to hide from or defend against predators
Ability to resist diseases and parasites	Inability to resist diseases and parasites
Ability to migrate and live in other habitats	Inability to migrate and live in other habitats
Ability to adapt to environmental change	Inability to adapt to environmental change

tem's **carrying capacity.** Environmental conditions are usually less than ideal and resources are normally limited. As a result, factors such as predation, competition within and between species, food shortages, disease, adverse climatic conditions, and lack of suitable habitat usually act to reduce the growth rate of a population below its maximum rate.

Without unlimited resources the population size of a species is limited, and its J-shaped curve of a population growth bends away from its steep incline and eventually levels off to form an S-shaped curve (Figure 6-15). Then the population size typically fluctuates slightly above and below the carrying capacity of the environment.

This transition can occur fairly smoothly or with a sharp drop in population size known as a *population crash* (Figure 6-16). A crash occurs when a rapidly reproducing population of a species overshoots the carrying capacity of its environment or when a change in conditions suddenly lowers the carrying capacity.

Large numbers of individuals then die if they cannot migrate to other areas.

Crashes have occurred in the human populations of various countries throughout history. Ireland, for example, experienced a population crash after a fungus infection ruined the potato crop in 1845. Dependent on the potato for a major portion of their diet, by 1900 half of Ireland's 8 million people had died of starvation or emigrated to other countries.

In spite of such local and regional disasters, the overall human population on earth has continued to grow. Human beings have made technological, social, and other cultural changes that have extended the earth's carrying capacity for their species (Figure 6-17)*. The human species has been able to alter its

---

*The curve shown in Figure 6-17 is plotted by a different mathematical method (a plot of the logarithm of population size versus the logarithm of time) from the method (a plot of population size versus time) used in Figure 1-1, p. 4.

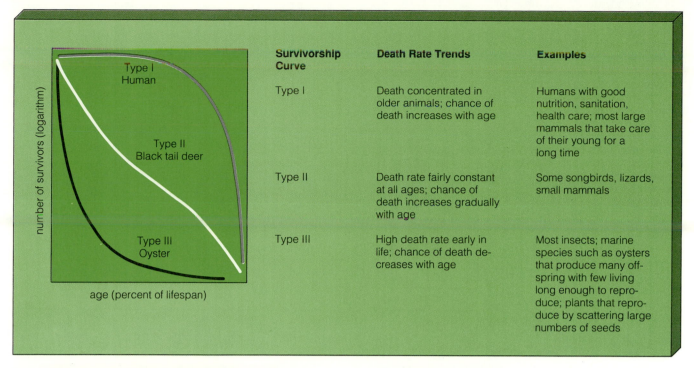

Survivorship Curve	Death Rate Trends	Examples
Type I	Death concentrated in older animals; chance of death increases with age	Humans with good nutrition, sanitation, health care; most large mammals that take care of their young for a long time
Type II	Death rate fairly constant at all ages; chance of death increases gradually with age	Some songbirds, lizards, small mammals
Type III	High death rate early in life; chance of death decreases with age	Most insects; marine species such as oysters that produce many offspring with few living long enough to reproduce; plants that reproduce by scattering large numbers of seeds

Figure 6-14 The three generalized types of survivorship curves for populations of different species.

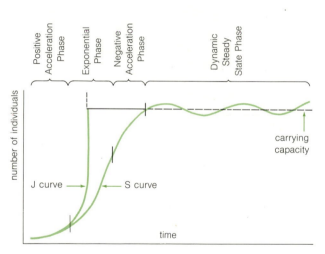

Figure 6-15 The J-shaped curve of population growth of a species is converted to an S-shaped curve when the population growth is limited by one or more environmental factors.

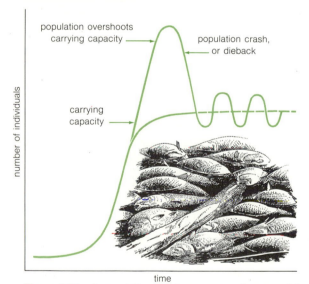

Figure 6-16 A population crash can occur when a rapidly expanding population overshoots its carrying capacity or a change in environmental conditions lowers the carrying capacity of its environment.

ecological niche by increasing food production, controlling disease, and using large amounts of energy and matter resources to make normally uninhabitable areas of the earth inhabitable.

The idealized J- to S-shaped mathematical model of population dynamics accurately represents the situation found in nature for many species. It is widely used by wildlife managers to estimate the carrying capacity and the maximum sustained yield for a species in a particular habitat. However, this simplified model does not always apply to populations of bird and mammal species because it assumes that environmental conditions remain the same and that every individual in a population is the same.

Patterns of Population Dynamics in Nature Decades ago Aldo Leopold classified wildlife population fluctuations into three general categories: relatively stable, irruptive, and cyclic (Figure 6-18). Species whose numbers remain about the same from year to year

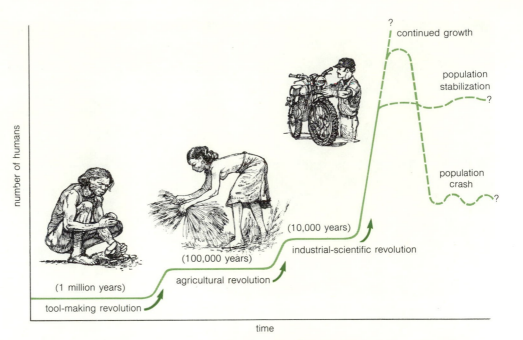

Figure 6-17 Human beings have expanded the earth's carrying capacity for their species through technological innovation, leading to several major cultural changes. Dashed lines represent possible future changes in human population size: continued growth, population stabilization, and continued growth followed by a crash and stabilization at a much lower level. (These curves are generalized log-log plots not drawn to scale.)

once they have reached the environmental carrying capacity have *relatively stable populations*. Such stability is characteristic of many populations of wildlife found in undisturbed tropical rain forests, where average temperature and rainfall don't change much from day to day and year to year.

Some species, such as the raccoon, normally have a fairly stable population, but occasionally their numbers rise sharply, or irrupt, to a high peak and then crash to a relatively stable lower level. Such species have *irruptive populations* (Figure 6-19). The sudden population rise is due to some factor that temporarily increases the carrying capacity for the population, such as favorable change in weather, an increase in the food supply, or a sharp reduction of predators, including human hunters and trappers. After soaring past its new, higher carrying capacity, the population experiences high death rates and decreases its size.

Some species undergo sharp increases in their numbers followed by crashes every 3 to 4 years, every 10 years, or at other regular intervals. These species have *cyclic populations* (Figure 6-20). The factor or mix of factors responsible for this pattern is still poorly understood.

Biological Evolution and Natural Selection   In addition to changing its size, a population of a particular species can also adapt to a change in environmental conditions by changing its genetic composition, or **gene pool.** All individuals of a population do not have exactly the same genes. This genetic diversity helps protect a species from extinction. It helps to ensure that some individuals in the population can withstand a particular environmental change, such as exposure of an insect population to a pesticide like DDT.

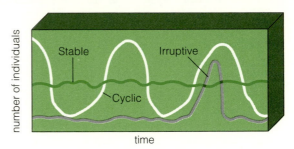

Figure 6-18   Basic types of population curves for living species.

Individuals with a protective genetic composition generally produce more offspring than those that don't have these traits and pass these favorable genetic traits to their offspring. For example, the few surviving insects in a population that have genetic resistance to DDT continue to reproduce rapidly. The more the insect population is exposed to a particular pesticide, the more genetically resistant it becomes to that chemical.

The gene pool of the population then becomes more adaptable to a particular environmental stress. This ability of individuals with adaptive genetic traits to reproduce more offspring than individuals without such traits is called **differential reproduction.**

The resulting change in the genetic composition of a population exposed to new environmental conditions because of differential reproduction is called **biological evolution** or simply **evolution.** If this process continues, the entire population of a species can undergo such marked genetic changes that it is considered to be a new species incapable of naturally breeding with members of the earlier species. This process is called **speciation.**

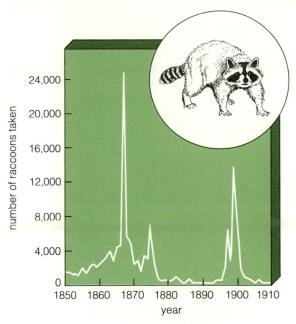

Figure 6-19 Irruptive population changes in a raccoon population, based on the number of pelts taken in the same general area and purchased by the Hudson's Bay Company over a period of 60 years. These irruptive changes were caused by occasional improvements in the weather followed by returns to less favorable conditions.

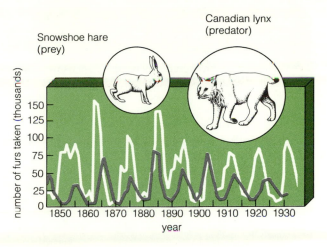

Figure 6-20 The nine- to ten-year population cycles of the snowshoe hare and its major predator, the Canadian lynx, based on the number of pelts taken in the same general area and purchased by the Hudson's Bay Company over a period of 90 years. Notice the time lag between the cyclic population curves for the predator and prey populations.

The process by which some genes and gene combinations in a population are reproduced more than others is called **natural selection.** Charles Darwin, who proposed this idea in 1858, described natural selection as meaning "survival of the fittest." This phrase has often been misinterpreted to mean survival of the strongest, biggest, or most aggressive. Instead, *fittest* means that individuals with the genetic traits best-adapted to environmental conditions on the average produce the most offspring in a given generation.

Species differ widely in how rapidly they can undergo evolution through natural selection. Some species have many offspring and short generation times. Others have few offspring and long generation times. Those that can quickly produce a large number of tiny offspring with short average life spans (weeds, insects, and rodents) can adapt to a change in environmental conditions through natural selection in a short time. For example, in only a few years many species of insects have become genetically resistant to DDT and other pesticides. Also, many species of bacteria have become genetically resistant to widely used antibiotics, such as penicillin.

Other species, such as elephants, horses, tigers, white sharks, and humans, have long generation times and a small number in each litter. This means that they cannot reproduce a large number of offspring rapidly. For such species, adaptation to an environmental stress by natural selection typically takes thousands to millions of years.

The human species used its intelligence to develop cultural mechanisms for controlling and adapting to environmental stresses. We have also learned to bring about genetic change in other species at a fast rate—first through crossbreeding and recently through genetic engineering (see Pro/Con on p. 138).

Speciation and Extinction The earth's present inventory of perhaps 5 to 10 million different species is believed to be the result of a combination of two processes taking place over billions of years. One is **speciation:** A new species, adapted to changes in environmental conditions, originates as a result of natural selection. The other is **extinction:** A species ceases to exist because it cannot genetically adapt and successfully reproduce under new environmental conditions.

Speciation can occur from changes within a single genetic line over a long period of time, often because of long-term changes in climate (Figure 6-21). It can also take place by the gradual splitting of lines of descent into two or more new species in response to new environmental conditions. This type of speciation is believed to occur when a population of a particular species becomes distributed over areas with quite different climates, food sources, soils, and other environmental conditions for long periods—typically for 1,000 to 100,000 generations. For example, different populations of the same species may be geographically isolated when floods, hurricanes, earthquakes, or other geological processes break up a single land mass into separate islands, change a river's course, thrust mountains upward from the seafloor, or submerge parts of dry land.

Populations of some animal species also split up when part of the group migrates in search of food (Figure 6-22). Eventually, the isolated populations

For many decades humans have selected and crossbred different genetic varieties of plants and animals to develop new varieties with certain desired qualities for many reasons. Today "genetic engineers" have learned how to splice genes and recombine sequences of existing DNA molecules in organisms to produce DNA with new genetic characteristics (recombinant DNA).

In other words, they use laboratory techniques to transfer traits from one species to another to make new genetic combinations instead of waiting for nature to evolve new genetic combinations through natural selection. This new biotechnology, just beginning to emerge from the laboratory, in the near future may give us greatly increased control over the course of evolution of the earth's living species.

This increasingly real possibility excites some scientists. They see it as a way to increase crop and livestock yields and to produce plants and livestock that have greater resistance to diseases, pests, frost, and drought and that provide greater quantities of nutrients such as proteins. They hope to develop bacteria that can destroy oil spills and degrade toxic wastes and to develop new vaccines, drugs, and therapeutic hormones. Gene therapy would also be used to eliminate certain genetic diseases and other genetic afflictions.

Already genetic engineering has produced a drug to arrest heart attacks and agents to fight diabetes, hemophilia, and some forms of cancer. It has also been used to diagnose AIDS and cancer. Genetically altered viruses have been used to manufacture more effective vaccines.

In agriculture gene transfers have been used to develop strawberries that resist frost and smaller cows that produce more milk. Also, toxin-producing genes have been transferred from bacteria to plants, giving the plants better immunity from insect attack.

Genetic technology has also produced edible fish that grow faster and bigger than conventional varieties.

Other people are horrified by this prospect. Most of these critics recognize that it is essentially impossible to stop the development of genetic engineering, which is already well under way. But they believe that this technology should be kept under strict control.

They are particularly concerned that it may be used to reduce the natural genetic diversity among individuals of a single species. It could also reduce the biological diversity represented by the world's variety of species. Genetic and species diversity are essential to the long-term functioning and adaptability to change of ecosystems and the ecosphere. These critics do not believe that people have enough understanding of how nature works to be trusted with such great control over the genetic characteristics of humans and other species.

Critics also fear that unregulated biotechnology could lead to the development of "superorganisms." If such organisms were released deliberately or accidentally into the environment, they could cause unpredictable, possibly harmful health and ecological effects. Most would probably be safe, but some would inevitably turn out to be dangerous.

Since many organisms, especially bacteria, are capable of rapidly reproducing and spreading to new locations, any problems that develop could be widespread. For example, genetically altered bacteria designed to clean up ocean oil spills by degrading the oil might multiply rapidly and eventually degrade the world's remaining oil supplies—including the oil in cars and trucks.

In addition to being able to reproduce and rapidly proliferate, genetically engineered organisms can also mutate and change their

form and behavior. Unlike defective cars and other products, these living organisms can't be recalled once they are in the environment.

The risks of this or other catastrophic events resulting from biotechnology are quite small. But critics contend that biotechnology is a potential source of such enormous profits that without strict controls greed—not ecological wisdom and restraint—will take over.

Genetic scientists answer, however, that it is highly unlikely that the release of genetically engineered species would cause serious and widespread ecological problems. To have a serious effect, such organisms would have to be outstanding competitors and resistant to predation. In addition, they would have to be capable of becoming dominant in ecosystems and in the ecosphere. But critics point out that this is what has happened many times when we have accidentally or deliberately introduced alien organisms into various biological communities.

Some genetic scientists contend that the introduction of a well-characterized DNA molecule into the genes of organisms is *safer* than the more random alteration of genetic strains by mutation and natural selection. But other proponents of biotechnology acknowledge that some genetically engineered organisms might contribute to localized or temporary ecological disasters. They join the critics in calling for strict control over this emerging technology.

This controversy illustrates the difficulty of balancing the actual or potential benefits of a technology with its actual or potential risks of harm. What do you think?

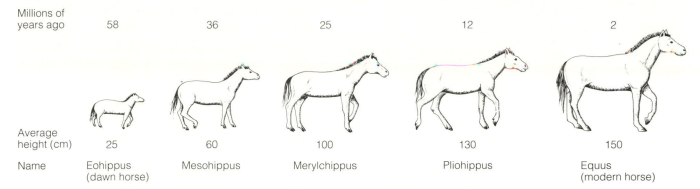

Figure 6-21 Speciation of the horse through natural selection along the same genetic line into different equine species.

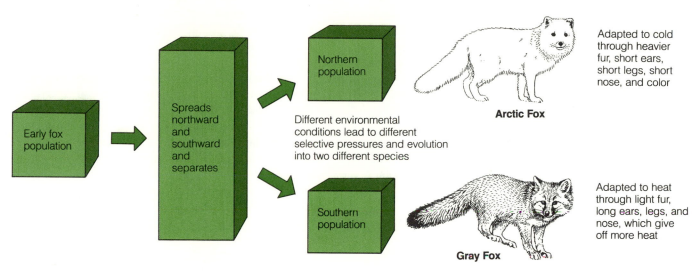

Adapted to cold through heavier fur, short ears, short legs, short nose, and color

Arctic Fox

Different environmental conditions lead to different selective pressures and evolution into two different species

Adapted to heat through light fur, long ears, legs, and nose, which give off more heat

Gray Fox

Figure 6-22 Speciation of an early species of fox into two different species as a result of migration of portions of the original fox population into areas with different climates.

become so genetically different that they are no longer capable of successfully interbreeding should they subsequently come to occupy the same area again.

In some rapidly producing organisms, speciation may take place in thousands or even hundreds of years. In most cases, however, it takes from tens of thousands to millions of years.

Over billions of years these processes have produced the planet's most valuable resource: **biological diversity.** It is made up of two related concepts: genetic diversity and species diversity. **Genetic diversity** is the genetic variability among individuals within a single species. **Species diversity** is the number of different species within a community of organisms.

This diversity within and among species has provided new sources of food, energy, raw materials, industrial chemicals, and medicines. It also provides us and other species with free resource recycling and purification services. Every species here today represents stored genetic information that allows the species to adapt to certain changes in environmental con-

ditions. This biodiversity is nature's "insurance policy" against disasters. It must be preserved and sustained (see Spotlight on p. 140).

6-5 COMMUNITY-ECOSYSTEM RESPONSES TO STRESS

Responses to Small and Moderate Stress Communities and ecosystems are so complex and variable that ecologists have little understanding of how they maintain their inertia and resilience. One major problem is the difficulty of conducting controlled experiments. Identifying and observing even a tiny fraction of the interacting variables found in simple ecosystems are virtually impossible.

In addition, ecologists cannot run long-term experiments in which only one variable in a natural ecosystem is allowed to change. Greatly simplified ecosystems can be set up and observed under laboratory conditions. But extrapolating the results of such experiments to more complex, natural ecosystems is difficult if not impossible.

At one time, it was believed that the higher the species diversity of an ecosystem, the greater its stability. According to this idea, an ecosystem with a diversity of species has more ways to respond to most environmental stresses because it does not "have all its eggs in one basket." However, research indicates that there appear to be many exceptions to this intuitively appealing idea.

Does an ecosystem need both high inertia and high stability to be considered stable? Evidence indicates that some ecosystems have one type of stability but not the other. For example, California redwood forests and tropical rain forests have high species diversity and high inertia. This means that they are hard to alter significantly or destroy through natural processes. However, once large tracts of these diverse ecosystems are completely cleared, they have such low resilience that restoring them is nearly impossible.

On the other hand, grasslands, with much lower species diversity, burn easily and thus have low inertia. However, because most of their plant matter consists of roots beneath the ground surface, these ecosystems have high resilience, allowing them to recover quickly. A grassland can be destroyed only if its roots are plowed up and wheat or another crop is planted in its soil or its grasses are severely overgrazed.

Clearly, we have a long way to go in understanding how the factors involved in natural ecosystems interact. But considerable evidence indicates that simplifying an ecosystem by the intentional or accidental removal of a species often has unpredictable short- and long-term harmful effects (see Spotlight on p. 141).

Responses to Large-Scale Stress: Ecological Succession Most ecosystems can adapt not only to small and moderate changes in environmental conditions but also to quite severe changes. Sometimes, for example, little vegetation and soil are left as a result of a natural environmental change (retreating glaciers, fires, floods, volcanic eruptions, earthquakes) or a human-induced change (fires, land clearing, surface mining, flooding to create a pond or reservoir, pollution).

After such a large-scale disturbance, life usually begins to recolonize a site in a series of stages. First, a few hardy *pioneer species* invade the environment and start creating soil or, in aquatic ecosystems, sediment. Eventually these pioneer species change the soil or bottom sediments and other conditions so much that the area is less suitable for them and more suitable for a new group of plants and animals with different ecological niche requirements.

Gradually, these new invaders alter the local environment still more by changing the soil, providing shade, and creating a greater variety of ecological niches. This paves the way for invasion by a third wave of plants and animals. Each successive invasion makes the local environment more suitable for future invaders and less suitable for previous communities. This process, in which communities of plant and animal species are replaced over time by a series of different and usually more complex communities, is called **ecological succession.**

If not severely disrupted, ecological succession usually continues until the community becomes much more self-sustaining and stable than the preceding ones. When this happens, what ecologists call the

---

SPOTLIGHT How Do We Protect Biological Diversity?

Preserving the planet's biological diversity is vital. How can we do this? Because it is a *public good*, we cannot rely on the private sector or market to do it. There is little or no profit in it.

Taking up a collection will help. Private conservation organizations can raise funds to buy land and protect its biological diversity or pay governments to do so. This is very important. But it won't supply enough money to preserve the desired level. Why? Because money contributed by a few to supply this public good benefits everyone, so others have little incentive to participate.

This means that the governments must play a major role in protecting this public good. One way to do this is to protect vital areas from all forms of development. But this is expensive and hard to enforce. It can also deprive local people living near such areas from using the biological income produced by these communities. Without local cooperation, no large preserved ecosystem can be protected from poaching.

The other way is for governments to work with private businesses, conservation groups, and local people to develop and finance plans for the *sustainable use and development* of biologically diverse ecosystems throughout the world. Some areas and parts of areas would be protected from all development. But other parts could be used on a sustainable basis. How much would you be willing to pay in taxes and donate to private organizations·each year to preserve the world's biological diversity?

mature, or **climax, community** occupies the site. Depending primarily on the climate, climax terrestrial communities may be various types of mature grasslands, forests, or deserts (Figure 6-1, p. 118).

Ecologists recognize two types of ecological succession: primary and secondary. Which type takes place depends on the conditions at a particular site at the beginning of the process. **Primary succession** is the sequential development of biotic communities in a bare area. Examples of such areas include the rock or mud exposed by a retreating glacier or mudslide, cooled volcanic lava, a new sandbar deposited by a shift in ocean currents, and surface-mined areas from which all topsoil has been removed. On such barren surfaces, primary succession from bare rock to a mature forest may take hundreds to thousands of years.

The more common type of succession is **secondary succession.** This is the sequential development of communities in an area where the natural vegetation has been removed or destroyed, but the soil or bottom sediment has not been destroyed. Examples of areas that can undergo secondary succession include abandoned farmlands, burned or cut forests, land stripped of vegetation for surface mining, heavily polluted streams, and land that has been flooded naturally or to produce a reservoir or pond. Because some soil or sediment is present, new vegetation can usually sprout within only a few weeks.

In the central (Piedmont) region of North Carolina, European settlers cleared away the native oak and hickory climax forests and planted the land in crops. Figure 6-23 shows how this abandoned farmland, covered with a thick layer of soil, has undergone secondary succession over a period of about 150 years until the area is again covered with a mature oak and hickory forest. Newly created lakes, reservoirs, and ponds also undergo secondary succession: As they gradually fill up with bottom sediments, they are eventually converted to terrestrial ecosystems, which then undergo secondary ecological succession.

Comparison of Immature and Mature Ecosystems

Pioneer, or immature, ecosystems and climax, or mature, ecosystems have strikingly different characteristics, as summarized in Table 6-2. Immature communities at the early stages of ecological succession consist of only a few species (low species diversity). They also have fairly simple food webs, made up mostly of producers fed upon by herbivores and relatively few decomposers.

Most of the plants are small annuals that grow close to the ground. They use most of their energy to produce large numbers of small seeds for reproduction rather than to develop large root, stem, and leaf systems. They receive some matter resources from other ecosystems, because they are too simple to hold and recycle many of the nutrients they receive.

In contrast, the community in a mature ecosystem has a high species diversity, relatively stable populations, and complex food webs dominated by decomposers that feed on the large amount of dead vegetation and animal wastes. Most plants in mature ecosystems are larger herbs and trees that produce a small number of large seeds. They use most of their energy and matter resources to maintain their large root, trunk, and leaf systems rather than to produce large numbers of new plants. They also have the complexity necessary to entrap, hold, and recycle most of the nutrients they need.

SPOTLIGHT **Ecosystem Interference Is Full of Surprises!**

Malaria once infected nine out of ten people in North Borneo, now known as Brunei. In 1955 the World Health Organization (WHO) began spraying dieldrin (a pesticide similar to DDT) to kill malaria-carrying mosquitoes. The program was so successful that the dreaded disease was almost eliminated from the island.

But other, unexpected things happened. The dieldrin killed other insects, including flies and cockroaches, living in houses. The islanders applauded. But then small lizards that also lived in the houses died after gorging themselves on dead insects. Then cats began dying after feeding on the dead lizards. Without cats, rats flourished and overran the villages. Now people were threatened by sylvatic plague carried by the fleas on the rats. The situation was brought under control when WHO parachuted healthy cats onto the island.

Then roofs began to fall in. The dieldrin has killed wasps and other insects that fed on a type of caterpillar that either avoided or was not affected by the insecticide.

With most of its predators eliminated, the caterpillar population exploded. The larvae munched their way through one of their favorite foods, the leaves used in thatching roofs.

In the end, the Borneo episode was a success story; both malaria and the unexpected effects of the spraying program were brought under control. But it shows the unpredictable results of interfering in an ecosystem.

annual weeds

Time ——→

perennial weeds and grasses

shrubs

young pine forest

mature oak forest

canopy

lower canopy trees

tall shrub understory

Figure 6-23 Secondary ecological succession of plant communities on an abandoned farm field in North Carolina over about 150 years. Succession of animal communities is not shown.

Table 6-2	Ecosystem Characteristics at Immature and Mature Stages of Ecological Succession	
Characteristic	**Immature Ecosystem**	**Mature Ecosystem**
Ecosystem Structure		
Plant size	Small	Large
Species diversity	Low	High
Trophic structure	Mostly producers, few decomposers	Mixture of producers, consumers, and decomposers
Ecological niches	Few, mostly generalized	Many, mostly specialized
Community organization (number of interconnecting links)	Low	High
Ecosystem Function		
Food chains and webs	Simple, mostly plant → herbivore with few decomposers	Complex, dominated by decomposers
Efficiency of nutrient recycling	Low	High
Efficiency of energy use	Low	High

6-6 HUMAN IMPACTS ON ECOSYSTEMS

Human Beings and Ecosystems In modifying ecosystems for our use, we simplify them. For example, we bulldoze and plow grasslands and forests. Then we replace the thousands of interrelated plant and animal species in these ecosystems with a greatly simplified, single-crop, or monoculture, ecosystem or with structures such as buildings, highways, and parking lots.

Modern agriculture is based on deliberately keeping ecosystems in early stages of succession, where the biomass productivity of one or a few plant species (such as corn or wheat) is high (Figure 6-24). But such simplified ecosystems are highly vulnerable.

Figure 6-24 Modern, industrialized agriculture uses large inputs of fossil fuels—mostly oil—to plant, protect, and harvest vast fields of one crop (monoculture). These greatly simplified ecosystems are highly vulnerable to disruption from weeds, pests, and crop diseases.

Table 6-3	Comparison of a Natural Ecosystem and a Simplified Human System
Natural Ecosystem (marsh, grassland, forest)	**Simplified Human System (cornfield, factory, house)**
Captures, converts, and stores energy from the sun	Consumes energy from fossil or nuclear fuels
Produces oxygen and consumes carbon dioxide	Consumes oxygen and produces carbon dioxide from the burning of fossil fuels
Creates fertile soil	Depletes or covers fertile soil
Stores, purifies, and releases water gradually	Often uses and contaminates water and releases it rapidly
Provides wildlife habitats	Destroys some wildlife habitats
Filters and detoxifies pollutants and waste products free of charge	Produces pollutants and waste, which must be cleaned up at our expense
Usually capable of self-maintenance and self-renewal	Requires continual maintenance and renewal at great cost

A major problem is the continual invasion of crop fields by unwanted pioneer species, which we call *weeds* if they are plants, *pests* if they are insects or other animals, and *disease* if they are harmful microorganisms such as bacteria, fungi, and viruses. Weeds, pests, or disease can wipe out an entire monoculture crop unless it is artificially protected with pesticides such as insecticides (insect-killing chemicals) and herbicides (plant-killing chemicals) or by some form of biological control.

When quickly breeding species develop genetic resistance to these chemicals, farmers must use ever-stronger doses or switch to a new product. Persistent, broad-spectrum insect poisons kill not only the pests but also species that prey on the pests. This further simplifies the ecosystem and allows pest populations to expand to even larger sizes.

Thus, in the long run every pesticide increases the rate of natural selection of the pests to the point that the effectiveness of the chemical is eventually lost. This illustrates biologist Garrett Hardin's **first law of ecology:** We can never do merely one thing. Any intrusion into nature has numerous effects, many of which are unpredictable.

Cultivation is not the only way that people simplify ecosystems. Ranchers, who don't want bison or prairie dogs competing with sheep for grass, eradicate these species, as well as wolves, coyotes, eagles, and other predators that occasionally kill sheep. Far too often, ranchers allow livestock to overgraze grasslands until excessive soil erosion helps convert these ecosystems to simpler and less productive deserts.

The cutting of vast areas of diverse tropical rain forests is causing the irreversible loss of many plant and animal species. People also tend to overfish and overhunt some species to extinction or near extinction, another way of simplifying ecosystems. The burning of fossil fuels in industrial plants, homes, and vehicles creates atmospheric pollutants that fall to the earth as acidic compounds. These chemicals simplify forest ecosystems by killing trees and aquatic ecosystems by killing fish.

It is becoming increasingly clear that the price we pay for simplifying, maintaining, and protecting such stripped-down ecosystems is high: It includes time, money, increased use of matter and energy resources, loss of genetic diversity, and loss of natural landscape (Table 6-3). There is also the danger that as the human population grows, we will convert too many of the world's mature ecosystems to simple, young, productive, but highly vulnerable forms. The challenge is to maintain a balance between simplified, human ecosystems and the neighboring, more complex, natural ecosystems our simplified systems depend on.

Some Environmental Lessons It should be clear from the brief discussion of principles in this and the preceding chapter that living systems have six major features: *interdependence, diversity, resilience, adaptability, unpredictabilty,* and *limits.* Understanding this does not mean that we should stop growing food, building cities, and making other changes that affect the earth's biological communities. But we do need to recognize that such human-induced changes have far-reaching and unpredictable consequences. This calls for wisdom, care, and restraint as we alter the ecosphere.

Our environmental and resource problems result from our arrogance toward nature. Somehow we must tune our senses to how nature really works and sustains itself, sensing in nature fundamental rhythms we can trust and cooperate with even though we may never fully understand them.

What has gone wrong, probably, is that we have failed to see ourselves as part of a large and indivisible whole. For too long we have based our lives on a primitive feeling that our "God-given" role was to have "dominion over the fish of the sea and over the fowl of the air and over every living thing that moveth upon the earth." We have failed to understand that the earth does not belong to us, but we to the earth.

Rolf Edberg

DISCUSSION TOPICS

1. List a probable limiting factor for each of the following ecosystems: **(a)** a desert, **(b)** the surface layer of the open sea, **(c)** the Arctic tundra, **(d)** the floor of a tropical rain forest, and **(e)** the bottom of a deep lake.

2. If possible, visit a nearby lake. Would you classify it as oligotrophic, mesotrophic, or eutrophic? What are the major factors contributing to its nutrient enrichment? Which of these are related to human activities?

3. Since the deep oceans are vast, self-sustaining ecosystems located far away from human habitats, why not use them as a depository for essentially all of our radioactive and other hazardous wastes? Give your reasons for agreeing or disagreeing with this proposal.

4. Why are coastal and inland wetlands considered to be some of the planet's most important ecosystems? Why have so many of these vital ecosystems been destroyed by human activities? What factors in your lifestyle contribute to the destruction and degradation of wetlands?

5. Someone tells you not to worry about air pollution because the human species through natural selection will develop lungs that can detoxify pollutants. How would you reply?

6. Are human beings or insects such as flies and mosquitoes better able to adapt to environmental change? Defend your choice and give the major way each of these species can adapt to environmental change.

7. Explain how a species can change local conditions so that the species becomes extinct in a given ecosystem. Could human beings do this to themselves? Explain.

FURTHER READINGS

Attenborough, David. 1984. *The Living Planet.* Boston: Little, Brown.

Brown, J. H., and A. C. Gibson. 1983. *Biogeography.* St. Louis: C. V. Mosby.

Clapham, W. B., Jr. 1984. *Natural Ecosystems,* 2nd ed. New York: Macmillan.

Daiber, Franklin C. 1988. *Conservation of Tidal Marshes.* New York: Van Nostrand Reinhold.

Ehrlich, Paul R. 1980. "Variety Is the Key to Life." *Technology Review,* Mar./Apr., 599–568.

Endler, John A. 1986. *Natural Selection in the Wild.* Princeton, N.J.: Princeton University Press.

Greenland, David. 1983. *Guidelines for Modern Resource Management: Soil, Land, Water, Air.* Columbus, Ohio: Charles E. Merrill.

Hardin, Garret. 1985. "Human Ecology: The Subversive, Conservative Science." *American Zoologist,* vol. 25, 469–476.

McArthur, Robert H. 1972. *Geographical Ecology: Patterns in the Distribution of Species.* New York: Harper & Row.

Maltby, Edward. 1986. *Waterlogged Wealth.* Washington, D.C.: Earthscan.

Mitsch, William J., and James G. Gosselink. 1986. *Wetlands.* New York: Van Nostrand Reinhold.

Odum, Eugene P. 1969. "The Strategy of Ecosystem Development." *Science,* vol. 164, 262–270.

Parker, Henry S. 1985. *Exploring the Oceans.* Englewood Cliffs, N.J.: Prentice-Hall.

Pilkey, Orin H., Sr., et al. 1984. *Coastal Design, A Guide for Builders, Planners, & Homeowners.* New York: Van Nostrand Reinhold.

Slobodkin, Laurence B. 1980. *Growth and Regulation of Animal Populations.* New York: Dover Press.

Tiner, Ralph W., Jr. 1984. *Wetlands of the United States: Current Status and Recent Changes.* Washington, D.C.: U.S. Government Printing Office.

Tudge, Colin. 1988. *The Environment of Life.* New York: Oxford University Press.

Wallace, David. 1987. *Life in the Balance.* New York: Harcourt Brace Jovanovich.

Wilson, E. O. 1984. *Biophilia.* Cambridge, Mass.: Harvard University Press.

Wilson, E. O., ed. 1988. *Biodiversity.* Washington, D.C.: National Academy Press.

Woodwell, G. M. 1970. "Effects of Pollution on the Structure and Physiology of Ecosystems." *Science,* vol. 168, 429–433.

PART TWO

Renewable Air, Water, and Soil Resources: Degradation and Management

Air pollution over Denver, Colorado   U.S. Department of Interior, Bureau of Reclamation

I am utterly convinced that most of the great environmental struggles
will be either won or lost in the 1990s, and that by the next century
it will be too late to act.

Thomas E. Lovejoy

CHAPTER 7

Air Resources

General Questions and Issues

1. What are the major components of the atmosphere, and what role does it play in determining climate?

2. What are the major types and sources of air pollutants?

3. What is smog, an urban heat island, and acid deposition?

4. What undesirable effects can air pollutants have on people, other species, and materials?

5. What undesirable effects can certain air pollutants have on the ozone layer and global climate?

6. What legal and technological methods can be used to reduce air pollution?

I thought I saw a blue jay this morning. But the smog was so bad it turned out to be a cardinal holding its breath.

Michael J. Cohen

The chemical content and physical properties of the atmosphere play a key role in the biogeochemical cycles that sustain living organisms and in local, regional, and global climate. About 99% of the air you must inhale to stay alive is gaseous nitrogen and oxygen.

Each breath you inhale also has trace amounts of other gases and *particulate matter:* minute droplets of various liquids and tiny particles of various solids. Most of these chemicals come from cars, trucks, power plants, factories, cigarettes, cleaning solvents, and other sources related to human activities. Repeated exposure to trace amounts of many of these chemicals, known as *air pollutants,* can damage lung tissue, plants, buildings, metals, and other materials. Changes in the chemical content of the atmosphere from human activities can also alter local, regional, and global climate.

7-1 THE ATMOSPHERE AND CLIMATE

Our Air Resources The **atmosphere,** a thin envelope of gases surrounding the earth, is divided into several spherical layers—much like the successive layers of skin on an onion (Figure 7-1). About 95% of the mass of the air is found in the innermost layer known as the **troposphere,** extending only 11 miles (17 kilometers) above the earth's surface. If the earth were an apple, our vital air supply would be no thicker than the apple's skin.

About 99% of the volume of clean, dry air in the troposphere consists of two gases: nitrogen (78%) and oxygen (21%). The nitrogen gas is a key chemical in the nitrogen cycle (Figure 5-17, p. 108), and the oxygen is necessary for cellular respiration in plants and animals as part of the carbon cycle (Figure 5-16, p. 107). The remaining volume of air in the troposphere has slightly less than 1% argon and about 0.035% carbon dioxide. Air in the troposphere also holds water vapor in amounts varying from 0.01% by volume at the frigid poles to 5% in the humid tropics.

Large masses of air in the troposphere are constantly churning and swirling as air heated by the sun rises and is replaced by cooler air. The physical processes causing these movements throughout the troposphere are a key factor determining the earth's climate and weather. Air movements and turbulence also help dilute potential pollutants. Long-lived pollutants are transported great distances before they return to the earth's surface as solid particles, liquid droplets, or chemicals dissolved in precipitation. Air

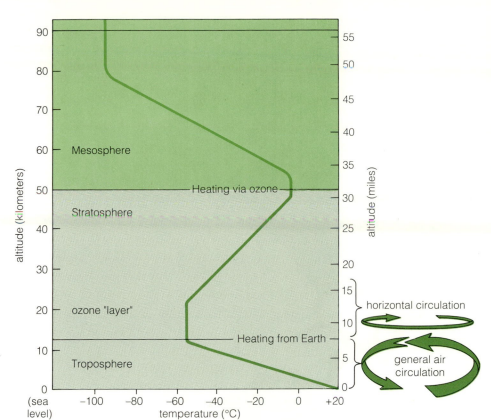

Figure 7-1 The earth's atmosphere. About 95% of the planet's air circulates in the troposphere, where temperatures decrease rapidly with altitude. Most ultraviolet radiation from the sun is absorbed by small amounts of ozone (O$_3$) in the stratosphere, where temperatures rise with increasing altitude. Most of this ozone is found in what is called the ozone layer between 11 and 16 miles (17 and 26 kilometers) above sea level.

pollution does not respect the political boundaries we draw on maps.

The second layer of the atmosphere, extending from 11 to 30 miles (17 to 48 kilometers) above the earth's surface, is called the **stratosphere** (Figure 7-1). It contains small amounts of gaseous ozone (O$_3$) that filters out about 99% of the incoming harmful ultraviolet (UV) radiation. By preventing large amounts of UV radiation from reaching the earth's surface, the thin gauze of ozone in the stratosphere protects people from increased sunburn, skin cancer, eye cancer, and eye cataracts. This global sunscreen also prevents damage to some plants and aquatic organisms.

By filtering out high-energy UV radiation, stratospheric ozone also keeps much of the oxygen in the troposphere from being converted to ozone. The trace amounts of ozone that do form in the troposphere as a component of urban smog damage plants, the respiratory systems of people and other animals, and materials such as rubber. Thus, our good health depends on having enough "good" ozone in the stratosphere and as little as possible "bad" ozone in the troposphere. Unfortunately, our activities are decreasing ozone in the stratosphere and increasing it in the troposphere.

Weather and Climate Every moment and every day, there are changes in temperature, barometric pressure, humidity, precipitation, sunshine (solar radia-

tion), cloudiness, wind direction and speed, and other conditions in various parts of the troposphere. These short-term changes in the properties of the troposphere from place to place are what we call **weather.**

Climate, in contrast, is the general pattern of atmospheric or weather conditions, seasonal variations, and weather extremes in a region, usually over a long period—at least 30 years. Climate is the weather you might expect to occur at a particular time and place, on the basis of past experience. Weather is the atmospheric conditions you actually experience at a given moment.

The physical properties and chemical composition of the atmosphere, along with the daily input of energy from the sun, are the major factors determining the weather and climate of different parts of the earth. Climate in turn is a key factor determining the types and numbers of plants and animals in various ecosystems, especially on land (Figure 6-1, p. 118).

The two most important factors determining the climate of an area are its *average temperature* and *average precipitation.* Figure 7-2 shows the global distribution of the major types of climate based on these two factors.

Climate and the Global Circulation of Air Five major factors determine the uneven patterns of average temperature and average precipitation shown in Figure 7-2 and thus the climates of the world:

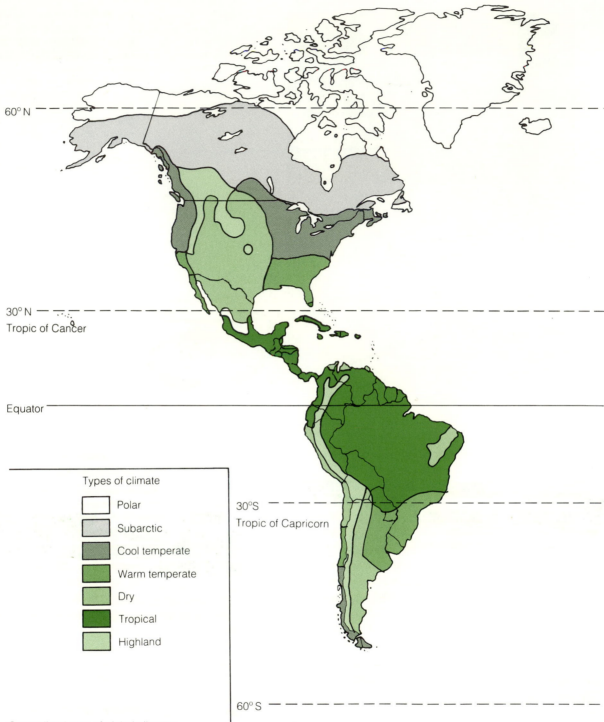

Types of climate

◻ Polar

▨ Subarctic

▨ Cool temperate

▨ Warm temperate

▨ Dry

▨ Tropical

▨ Highland

Figure 7-2 Generalized map of global climates.

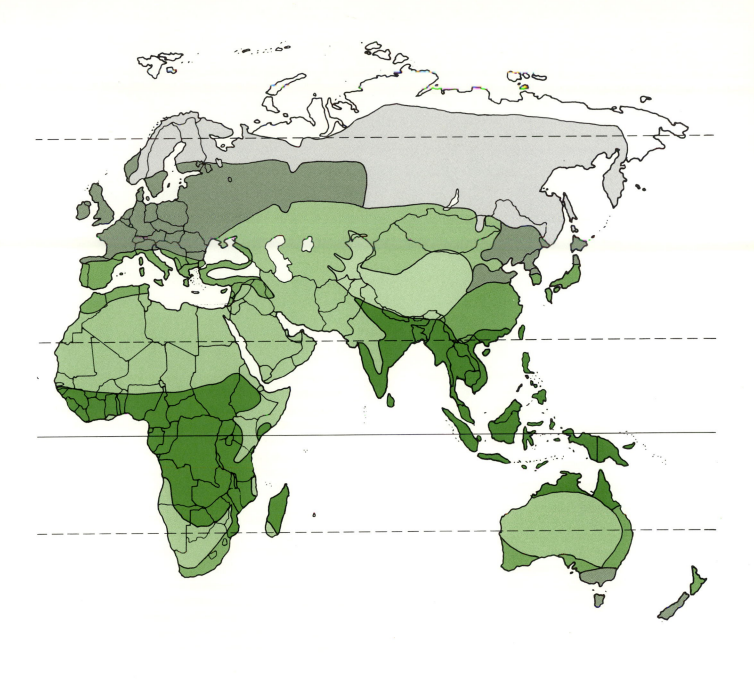

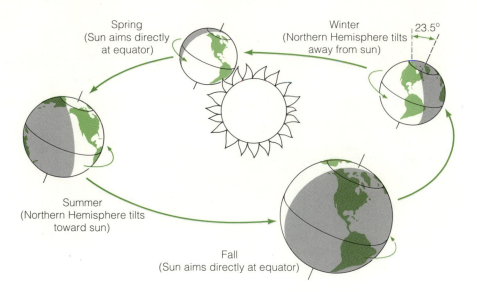

Figure 7-3 The seasons (shown here for the Northern Hemisphere only) are caused by variations in the amount of incoming solar energy as the earth makes its annual rotation around the sun on an axis tilted 23.5 degrees.

Spring
(Sun aims directly at equator)

Winter
(Northern Hemisphere tilts away from sun)

23.5°

Summer
(Northern Hemisphere tilts toward sun)

Fall
(Sun aims directly at equator)

- variations in the amount of incoming solar energy striking different parts of the earth
- the earth's annual orbit around the sun and its daily rotation around its axis—the imaginary line connecting the North and South poles
- chemical content of the atmosphere
- distribution of the continents and oceans
- topographical features such as mountains

The amount of incoming solar energy reaching the earth's surface varies with *latitude*—the distance north or south from the equator. Air in the troposphere is heated more at the equator (zero latitude), where the sun is almost directly overhead, than at the high-latitude poles, where the sun is lower in the sky and strikes the earth at a low angle.

The large input of heat at and near the equator causes large masses of warm air to rise because warm air has a lower density (mass per unit of volume) than cold air. As these warm air masses rise, they spread northward and southward, carrying heat from the equator toward the poles.

At the poles the warm air cools and sinks downward because cool air is denser than warm air. These cool air masses then move back toward the equator to fill the void left by rising warm air masses. The general *global air circulation pattern* in the troposphere leads to warm average temperatures near the equator, cold average temperatures near the poles, and moderate or temperate average temperatures at the middle latitudes between the two regions (Figure 7-2).

However, these general average temperature patterns vary with the seasons in all parts of the world away from the equator. Seasonal changes in climate

are caused by two major factors. One is the earth's annual orbit around the sun. The other is the earth's daily, eastward rotation around its axis, which is tilted 23.5 degrees from its plane of revolution around the sun. When the north pole leans toward the sun, its rays strike the Northern Hemisphere in a more direct and concentrated manner per unit of area, bringing summer to the northern half of the earth. At the same time, the south pole is angled away from the sun, bringing winter conditions over the Southern Hemisphere (Figure 7-3). As the earth makes its annual rotation around the sun, these conditions shift and cause seasonal changes.

The rotation of the earth around its axis and the tilt of its axis also deflect and change the general movement of large air masses from the equator to the poles and back. These conditions break the general air circulation pattern into three separate belts of moving air, or *prevailing surface winds*, north and south of the equator (Figure 7-4).

The general circulation of air masses in the troposphere and the prevailing surface winds affect the distribution of precipitation over the earth. The larger input of solar energy near the equator evaporates huge amounts of water from the oceans, inland water sources, soil, and vegetation in this region into the troposphere. The moisture-holding capacity of air (humidity) increases when it is warmed and decreases when it is cooled. As warm and humid tropical air rises, it cools rapidly and loses most of its moisture as rain near the equator. This abundant rainfall and the constant warm temperatures give rise to the world's tropical rain forests (see map inside back cover).

By the time these air masses have moved 30 degrees in latitude north and south of the equator (around the

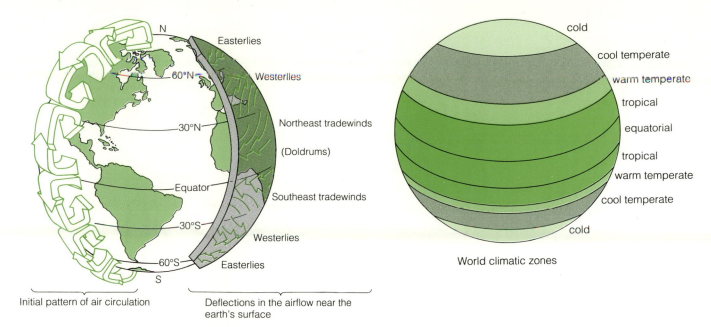

Initial pattern of air circulation

Deflections in the airflow near the earth's surface

World climatic zones

Figure 7-4 Formation of belts of prevailing surface winds. The twisting motion caused by the earth's rotation on its axis causes the airflow in each hemisphere to break up into three separate belts of prevailing winds. This is an important factor affecting the types of climate in different areas.

Tropic of Cancer and the Tropic of Capricorn), they have lost most of their moisture. The low precipitation of these regions explains why most of the world's large deserts are found there (see map inside back cover).

In flowing over these desert and semiarid areas, the air is warmed again. As it continues northward and southward, this warm air picks up some moisture. By the time it reaches latitudes about 60 degrees north and south of the equator, it begins rising and cooling again. Enough moisture is released in these mid-latitudes to support temperate forests and grasslands (see map inside back cover). The fairly dry air then descends toward the poles and cools, producing zones with very low precipitation.

Climate and the Chemical Content of the Atmosphere   The chemical content of the troposphere and stratosphere is another factor determining the earth's average temperatures and thus its climates. In the troposphere, carbon dioxide, water vapor, and trace amounts of ozone, methane, nitrous oxide, and chlorofluorocarbons play a key role in this temperature regulation process.

These gases, known as **greenhouse gases,** act somewhat like a pane of glass in a greenhouse. They let in visible light from the sun but prevent some of the resulting infrared radiation, or heat, from escaping back into space. They reradiate it back toward the earth's surface (Figure 7-5). The resulting heat buildup raises the temperature of the air in the troposphere, a warming action called the **greenhouse effect.** It is one of the best documented and most accepted theories in the atmospheric sciences.

The atmosphere's greenhouse gases make the earth a livable, air-conditioned planet. If these gases vanished tomorrow, overnight the earth would become a frozen and lifeless planet like Mars. If levels of these gases rose significantly, the earth would be like Venus with temperatures high enough to boil your blood.

Scientists expect increases in levels of carbon dioxide and other greenhouse gases from human activities to raise the average temperature of the troposphere several degrees within your lifetime. Unless we take action now to slow down our inputs of greenhouse gases into the atmosphere, global climate and food-producing patterns will change, causing economic, ecological, and social chaos.

The ozone content of the stratosphere also affects climate. Absorption of UV radiation by ozone molecules creates warm layers of air high in the stratosphere (Figure 7-1). These layers prevent the churning gases in the troposphere from entering the stratosphere. This thermal cap is an important factor in determining the average temperature of the troposphere and thus the earth's climates. Any human activities that decrease the average amount of ozone in the stratosphere can have far-reaching effects on climate and human health.

Climate and Ocean Currents   The earth's rotation, inclination, prevailing winds, and differences in water density cause *ocean currents* and *surface drifts* that gen-

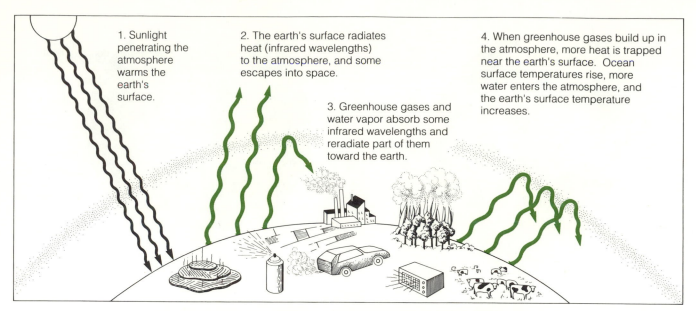

1. Sunlight penetrating the atmosphere warms the earth's surface.

2. The earth's surface radiates heat (infrared wavelengths) to the atmosphere, and some escapes into space.

3. Greenhouse gases and water vapor absorb some infrared wavelengths and reradiate part of them toward the earth.

4. When greenhouse gases build up in the atmosphere, more heat is trapped near the earth's surface. Ocean surface temperatures rise, more water enters the atmosphere, and the earth's surface temperature increases.

Figure 7-5 The greenhouse effect. (Adapted with permission from Cecie Starr and Ralph Taggart. 1989. *Biology: The Unity and Diversity of Life,* 5th ed., Belmont, Calif.: Wadsworth)

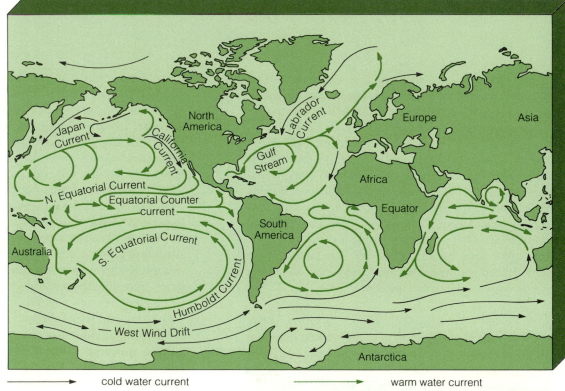

Figure 7-6 Major warm and cold currents and surface drifts of the world's oceans. These water movements are produced by the earth's winds and modified by its rotational forces. They circulate water in the oceans in great surface gyres and have major effects on the climate of adjacent lands.

cold water current   warm water current

erally move parallel with the equator (Figure 7-6). Tradewinds push surface ocean waters westward in the Atlantic, Pacific, and Indian oceans until these waters bounce off the nearest continents. This causes two large, circular water movements, called *gyres,* that turn clockwise in the northern hemisphere and counterclockwise in the southern hemisphere. These large circular eddies move warm waters to the north and south of the equator.

Warm and cold currents and surface drifts in the world's oceans affect the climates of nearby coastal areas. For instance, without the warm Gulf Stream, which transports 50 times more water than all the world's rivers, the climate of northwestern Europe would be more like that in the sub-Arctic. Ocean currents and drifts also help mix ocean waters and distribute the nutrients and dissolved oxygen needed by aquatic organisms.

Climate and Topography Mountains, valleys, and other topographical features of the earth's surface also affect the climate of certain areas. Because of their higher

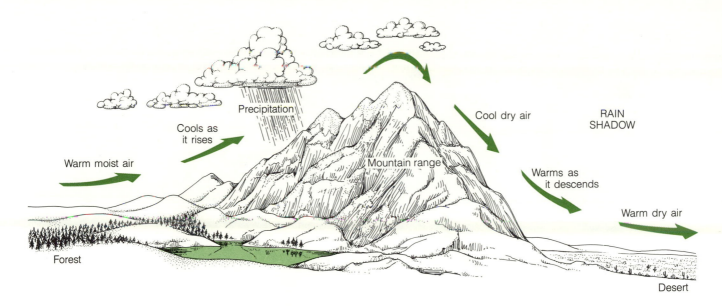

Figure 7-7 When a mountain range lies across the direction of prevailing wind the upwind movement of air on the windward side of the range is cooled and precipitates its moisture as rain. The terrain on the leeward side receiving a flow of dry air is in the "rain shadow" of the range and has a dry climate.

elevation, mountain highlands tend to be cooler, windier, and wetter than bordering valleys. For instance, although Mount Kilimanjaro, Africa's highest peak, stands just south of the equator, its summit is always covered with snow.

Mountains interrupt the flow of prevailing surface winds and the movement of storms. When prevailing winds blowing inland from an ocean reach a mountain range, the moist air cools as it is forced to rise and expand. This causes the air to lose most of its moisture as rain and snow on the windward (wind-facing) slopes. As the drier air flows down the slopes of the leeward sides (not facing the wind), it is compressed and becomes warmer. Then it flows over the arid and semiarid land beyond.

This drop in air moisture and the resulting semiarid and arid conditions on the leeward side of high mountains is called the **rain shadow effect** (Figure 7-7). The Mojave Desert east of the Sierra Nevada mountains parallel to the coast of California is the result of the rain shadow effect. Rain shadows also produce arid and semiarid lands near the Himalayan mountain ranges of Asia and the Andes of South America.

7-2 OUTDOOR AND INDOOR AIR POLLUTION

Types and Sources of Outdoor Air Pollution As clean air moves across the earth's surface, it collects various chemicals produced by natural events and human activities. Once in the troposphere, these potential air pollutants mix vertically and horizontally and often react chemically with each other or with natural components of the atmosphere.

There are hundreds of potential air pollutants in the troposphere. However, nine major classes of pollutants cause most outdoor air pollution:

1. *carbon oxides:* carbon monoxide (CO) and carbon dioxide (CO_2)

2. *sulfur oxides:* sulfur dioxide (SO_2) and sulfur trioxide (SO_3)

3. *nitrogen oxides:* nitric oxide (NO), nitrogen dioxide (NO_2), and nitrous oxide (N_2O)

4. *volatile organic compounds (VOCs):* hundreds of compounds such as methane (CH_4), benzene (C_6H_6), and chlorofluorocarbons (CFCs)

5. *suspended particulate matter (SPM):* thousands of different types of *solid particles* such as dust (soil), soot (carbon), asbestos, and lead, arsenic, cadmium, nitrate (NO_3^-) and sulfate (SO_4^{2-}) salts and *liquid droplets* of chemicals such as sulfuric acid (H_2SO_4), oil, PCBs, dioxins, and DDT, malathion, and other pesticides

6. *photochemical oxidants:* ozone (O_3), PANs (peroxyacyl nitrates), hydrogen peroxide (H_2O_2), hydroxy radicals (OH), and aldehydes such as formaldehyde (CH_2O) formed in the atmosphere by the reaction of oxygen, nitrogen oxides, and volatile hydrocarbons under the influence of sunlight

7. *radioactive substances:* radon-222, iodine-131, strontium-90, plutonium-239, and other radioisotopes that enter the atmosphere as gases or suspended particulate matter

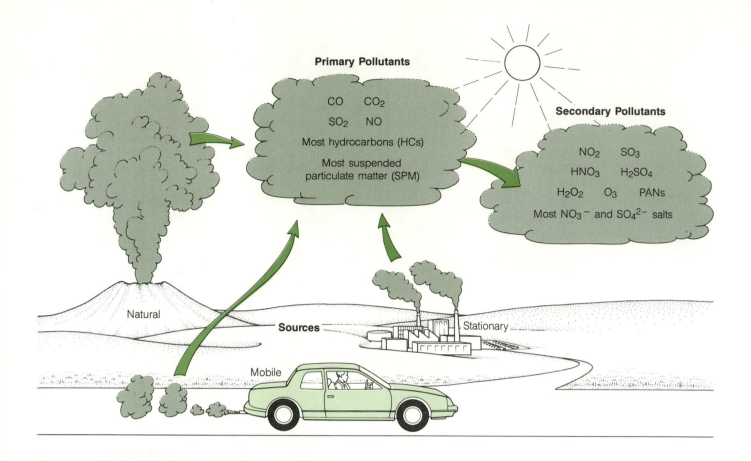

Primary Pollutants

CO   CO$_2$

SO$_2$ NO

Most hydrocarbons (HCs)

Most suspended particulate matter (SPM)

Secondary Pollutants

NO$_2$ SO$_3$

HNO$_3$ H$_2$SO$_4$

H$_2$O$_2$ O$_3$ PANs

Most NO$_3^-$ and SO$_4^{2-}$ salts

Natural

Sources

Stationary

Mobile

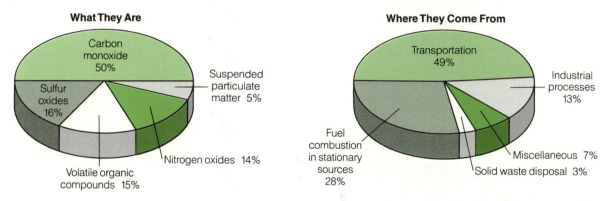

What They Are

Carbon monoxide 50%

Suspended particulate matter 5%

Sulfur oxides 16%

Nitrogen oxides 14%

Volatile organic compounds 15%

Where They Come From

Transportation 49%

Industrial processes 13%

Fuel combustion in stationary sources 28%

Miscellaneous 7%

Solid waste disposal 3%

Figure 7-9 Emissions of major outdoor air pollutants in the United States. (Data from Environmental Protection Agency)

8. *heat:* produced when any kind of energy is transformed from one form to another—for example, when fossil fuels are burned in cars, factories, homes, and power plants

9. *noise:* produced by motor vehicles, airplanes, trains, industrial machinery, construction machinery, lawn mowers, vacuum cleaners, food blenders, sirens, earphones, radios, casette players, and live concerts

Each of these chemicals or forms of energy (heat and noise) can be classified as either a primary or sec-ondary air pollutant. A **primary air pollutant,** such as sulfur dioxide, is one that directly enters the air as a result of natural events or human activities. A **secondary air pollutant,** such as sulfuric acid, is one that is formed in the air through a chemical reaction between two or more air components (Figure 7-8).

Most atmospheric emissions from widely scattered natural sources are diluted and dispersed throughout the atmosphere and rarely reach concentrations high enough to cause serious damage. Exceptions are massive injections of sulfur dioxide and suspended particulate matter (SPM) into the atmosphere from large

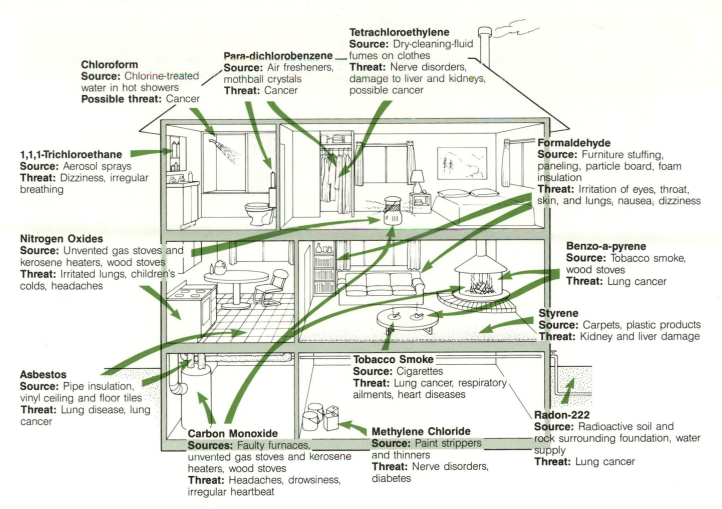

Chloroform
Source: Chlorine-treated water in hot showers
Possible threat: Cancer

Para-dichlorobenzene
Source: Air fresheners, mothball crystals
Threat: Cancer

Tetrachloroethylene
Source: Dry-cleaning-fluid fumes on clothes
Threat: Nerve disorders, damage to liver and kidneys, possible cancer

1,1,1-Trichloroethane
Source: Aerosol sprays
Threat: Dizziness, irregular breathing

Formaldehyde
Source: Furniture stuffing, paneling, particle board, foam insulation
Threat: Irritation of eyes, throat, skin, and lungs; nausea; dizziness

Nitrogen Oxides
Source: Unvented gas stoves and kerosene heaters, wood stoves
Threat: Irritated lungs, children's colds, headaches

Benzo-a-pyrene
Source: Tobacco smoke, wood stoves
Threat: Lung cancer

Styrene
Source: Carpets, plastic products
Threat: Kidney and liver damage

Asbestos
Source: Pipe insulation, vinyl ceiling and floor tiles
Threat: Lung disease, lung cancer

Carbon Monoxide
Sources: Faulty furnaces, unvented gas stoves and kerosene heaters, wood stoves
Threat: Headaches, drowsiness, irregular heartbeat

Tobacco Smoke
Source: Cigarettes
Threat: Lung cancer, respiratory ailments, heart diseases

Methylene Chloride
Source: Paint strippers and thinners
Threat: Nerve disorders, diabetes

Radon-222
Source: Radioactive soil and rock surrounding foundation, water supply
Threat: Lung cancer

Figure 7-10 Some major indoor air pollutants.

volcanic eruptions and buildup of radioactive radon-222 gas inside buildings.

About 90% of the most widely recognized outdoor air pollution in the United States is caused by five groups of pollutants: carbon monoxide, nitrogen oxides, sulfur oxides, volatile organic compounds (mostly hydrocarbons), and suspended particulate matter (Figure 7-9). Most of these and other pollutants are added to the troposphere as a result of human activities, mainly the burning of fossil fuels in power and industrial plants (*stationary sources*) and in motor vehicles (*mobile sources*).

So far most air pollution control efforts have concentrated on reducing emissions of six *conventional outdoor air pollutants:* carbon monoxide, nitrogen oxides, sulfur dioxide, medium to large SPM, lead particles, and ozone. Recently it has been recognized that hundreds, perhaps thousands, of *unconventional outdoor air pollutants* may be a long-term threat to human health when inhaled over long periods. They include various toxic volatile organic compounds and different types of SPM (especially fine particles of toxic metals and asbestos) found in the atmosphere in trace amounts. The EPA estimates that these pollutants also cause about 1,500 cases of cancer a year in the United States. Little effort has been made to control most of these pollutants.

Types and Sources of Indoor Air Pollution High concentrations of toxic air pollutants can also build up indoors, where most people spend 90% to 98% of their time (Figure 7-10). Indeed, scientists recently have found that the air inside many homes, schools, office buildings, factories, cars, and airliners is more polluted and dangerous than outdoor air on a smoggy day. Indoor air pollution poses an especially high risk for the elderly, the very young, the sick, and factory workers who spend a large amount of time indoors.

In 1985 the EPA reported that toxic chemicals found in almost every home are three times more likely to cause some type of cancer than outdoor air pollutants. Other air pollutants found in buildings produce dizziness, headaches, coughing, sneezing, burning eyes, and flulike symptoms in many people—a health problem called the "sick building syndrome." An estimated one-fifth to one-third of all U.S. buildings, including the EPA headquarters, are now considered "sick."

Smoking tobacco causes more death and suffering by far among adults than any other environmental factor (Figure 7-11). More than a billion of the world's people—one of every five—smoke. Worldwide, 2 million to 2.5 million smokers die prematurely each year of heart disease, lung cancer, bronchitis, and emphysema—all related to smoking. In the United States tobacco is estimated to cause 325,000 deaths each year—one of every five deaths. This annual death toll is about seven times that of the nine-year Vietnam War.

Each cigarette smoked reduces one's average life span by five and a half minutes. Overwhelming statistical evidence from more than 30,000 studies shows that smoking causes an estimated one-third of all cancer deaths in the United States, 30% of all heart disease deaths, and three-fourths of all lung cancer deaths in American men. People who smoke two packs of cigarettes a day increase their risk of getting lung cancer 15 to 25 times over nonsmokers. Fires caused by cigarettes kill 2,000 to 4,000 Americans each year.

The nicotine in tobacco is a highly addictive drug that, like heroin and crack, can quickly hook its victims. A British government study showed that adolescents who smoke more than one cigarette have an 85% chance of becoming smokers. Other studies have shown that a child is about twice as likely to become a smoker if either parent smokes and that 75% of smokers who quit start smoking again within six months.

Nicotine is not classified as an illegal drug. Yet, it kills and harms more people each year in the United States than all illegal drugs and alcohol (the second most harmful drug), automobile accidents, suicide, and homicide combined (Figure 7-11).

Smokers are not the only ones harmed by smoke from cigarettes and other tobacco products. About 86% of nonsmoking Americans involuntarily inhale smoke from other people's cigarettes, amounting to an average of about one cigarette a day. People working in smoky bars or living with a chain-smoker passively smoke the equivalent of 14 cigarettes a day.

A 1985 study by the EPA indicated that passive smoke kills as many as 5,000 Americans a year. According to a 1986 study by the National Research Council, nonsmoking spouses of smokers have a 30% greater chance of getting lung cancer than spouses of nonsmokers. Children of smokers have a 20% to 80% higher risk of respiratory problems than children of nonsmokers.

There is some good news, however. After about one year, an ex-smoker's chances of developing heart disease are about the same as a nonsmoker's assuming all other heart disease risk factors are equal. Studies also show that 10 to 15 years after smokers quit, they have about the same risk of dying from lung cancer as those who never smoked. In the United States the percentage of the population that smokes dropped from 41% in 1965 to 24% in 1987. But this still means that one of every four Americans smokes.

On a strictly economic basis, tobacco's costs to society exceed its economic benefits to tobacco farmers and employees of tobacco companies by more than two to one. In the United States, smoking costs society $38 billion to $95 billion a year in increased health care and insurance costs, lost work because of illness, and other economic losses. Smokers cost their employers at least $650 a year more in health insurance, lost work time, and cleanup costs than nonsmokers. These external costs amount to an average cost to society of $1.25 to $3.15 per pack of cigarettes sold.

In 1986 the American Medical Association called for a total ban on cigarette advertising in the United States, the prohibition of the sale of cigarettes and other tobacco products to anyone under 21, and a ban on cigarette vending machines—a program already in effect in Sweden. By 1988, at least 42 states and more than 300 cities and counties had passed laws that limit or ban smoking in public places. Almost 40% of all U.S. companies restrict or ban smoking in the workplace—actions approved of by 87% of both smokers and nonsmokers polled.

Health advocates have suggested that government subsidies to U.S. tobacco farmers and tobacco companies (amounting to $123 million in 1986) be eliminated and that these farmers be given aid and subsidies to grow more healthful crops. Others have suggested that cigarettes be taxed at $1.25 to $3.15 a pack. This would discourage smoking and make smokers—not nonsmokers—pay for the health and productivity losses now borne by society as a whole. What do you think should be done?

Figure 7-11 Annual deaths in the United States related to tobacco use and other causes in 1986. (Data from National Center for Health Statistics)

Cause of Death	Annual Deaths
Tobacco use	325,000
Alcohol use	150,000
Automobile accidents	50,000
Hard drug use	30,000
Suicides	27,500
Homicides	19,000

A study of commuter autos on a Los Angeles freeway found levels of harmful air pollutants inside cars 3 to 5 times higher than levels outside. The EPA has found that the air in some office buildings is 100 times more polluted than the air outside. Each year exposure to pollutants inside factories and businesses in the United States kills up to 210,000 workers prematurely.

According to the EPA and public health officials, cigarette smoke (see Case Study on p. 156), radioactive radon-222 gas (see Case Study on p. 158), and asbestos are the three most dangerous indoor air pollutants. Asbestos is a group of minerals made up of tiny fibers that can easily become airborne and inhaled into the lungs. Evidence indicates that exposure to a small amount of asbestos fibers can cause lung cancer or mesothelioma (cancer of the chest and abdominal lining) 15 to 40 years later. The EPA estimates that exposure to asbestos in U.S. schools, shopping malls, office and apartment buildings causes 3,000 to 12,000 cancer cases a year. Workers who smoke and are exposed to asbestos have a much greater chance of dying from lung cancer than those who don't smoke.

In 1988 the EPA estimated that more than 484,000—one of every seven—commercial and public buildings in the United States contain easily broken asbestos. So far little is being done to remove this hazard.

7-3 SMOG, URBAN HEAT ISLANDS, AND ACID DEPOSITION

Smog: Cars + Sunlight = Tears A mixture of certain primary pollutants and secondary pollutants formed when some of the primary pollutants interact under the influence of sunlight is called **photochemical smog** (Figure 7-13, p. 160). Virtually all modern cities have photochemical smog, but it is much more common in those with sunny, warm, dry climates and lots of motor vehicles. Cities with serious photochemical smog include Los Angeles, Denver, Salt Lake City (see photo on p. 145), Sydney, Mexico City, and Buenos Aires. The worst episodes of photochemical smog tend to occur in summer.

The first step in the formation of photochemical smog occurs during the early morning rush hours. Nitric oxide from automobile exhaust builds up and reacts with atmospheric oxygen to produce nitrogen dioxide, a yellowish-brown gas with a pungent, choking odor.

Then, as the sun rises, its ultraviolet rays cause a series of complex chemical reactions involving NO_2 and hydrocarbons that produce the other components of this type of smog—nitric acid, peroxyacyl nitrates (PANs), aldehydes, and ozone (Figure 7-13). Traces of these secondary pollutants build up to peak levels by early afternoon on a sunny day, irritating people's eyes and respiratory tracts. People with asthma and other respiratory problems and healthy people who exercise outdoors between 11 A.M. and 4 P.M. are especially vulnerable. The hotter the day, the higher the levels of ozone and other components of photochemical smog.

Thirty years ago, cities like London, Chicago, and Pittsburgh burned large amounts of coal and heavy oil, which contain sulfur impurities, in power and industrial plants and for space heating. During winter such cities suffered from **industrial smog,** consisting mostly of a mixture of sulfur dioxide, suspended droplets of sulfuric acid formed from some of the sulfur dioxide, and a variety of suspended solid particles. Today coal and heavy oil are burned only in large boilers with reasonably good control so that industrial smog is rarely a problem. However, in China and in some eastern European countries, such as Poland and Czechoslovakia, large quantities of coal are burned with inadequate controls.

Local Climate, Topography, and Smog The frequency and severity of smog in an area depend on the local climate and topography, the density of population and industry, and the major fuels used in industry, heating, and transportation. In areas with high average annual precipitation, rain and snow help cleanse the air of pollutants. Winds also help sweep pollutants away and bring in fresh air, but may transfer some pollutants to distant areas.

Hills and mountains tend to reduce the flow of air in valleys below and allow pollutant levels to build up at ground level. Buildings in cities also slow wind speed and reduce dilution and removal of pollutants.

During the day the sun warms the air near the earth's surface. Normally this heated air expands and rises, diluting low-lying pollutants and carrying them higher into the troposphere. Air from surrounding high-pressure areas then moves down into the low-pressure area created when the hot air rises (Figure 7-14, left, p. 161). This continual mixing of the air helps keep pollutants from reaching dangerous levels in the air near the ground.

But sometimes weather conditions trap a layer of dense, cool air beneath a layer of less dense, warm air in an urban basin or valley. This is called a **temperature inversion,** or **thermal inversion** (Figure 7-14, right, and Figure 7-15, p. 161). In effect, a warm-air lid covers the region and prevents pollutants from escaping in upward-flowing air currents. Usually these inversions last for only a few hours, but sometimes they last for several days when a high-pressure air mass stalls over an area. Then, air pollutants at ground level build up to harmful and even lethal levels.

In 1948 a lengthy thermal inversion over Donora, an industrial town in Pennsylvania, killed 20 people and made 6,000 of the town's 14,000 inhabitants sick. A prolonged thermal inversion over New York City in 1963 killed 300 people and injured thousands.

Radon-222 is a colorless, odorless, tasteless naturally occurring radioactive gas produced by the radioactive decay of uranium-238. Small amounts of radon-producing uranium-238 are found in most soil and rock. But this isotope is much more concentrated in underground deposits of uranium, phosphate, granite, and shale rock.

When radon gas from such deposits percolates upward to the soil and is released outdoors, it disperses quickly in the atmosphere and decays to harmless levels. However, when the gas seeps or is drawn into buildings through cracks and drains in basements or into water in underground wells over such deposits, it can build up to high levels (Figure 7-12). Stone and other building materials obtained from radon-rich deposits can also be a source of indoor radon contamination.

Radon-222 gas quickly decays into solid particles of radioactive elements that can be inhaled, exposing lung tissue to a large amount of alpha-ionizing radiation. Smokers are especially vulnerable because the inhaled radioactive particles tend to adhere to tobacco tar deposits in the lungs and upper respiratory tract. Repeated exposure to these radioactive particles over 20 to 30 years can cause lung cancer. Physicist Bernard Cohen disputes the connection between radioactive radon and lung cancer, but most other radiation experts argue that Cohen's conclusions are based on inadequate data.

Data from a sampling of indoor radon levels mostly in basements or crawl spaces of houses in 30 states indicate that at least one of every ten American homes—perhaps as many as one of every three—may contain harmful levels of this gas. The highest levels of surveyed homes were found in North Dakota, Minnesota, Colorado, Pennsylvania, Wisconsin, Wyoming, Indiana, and Massachusetts. In Pennsylvania radon levels in the home of one family created a cancer risk equal to having 455,000 chest X rays a year. So far the highest radon levels in well water were found in Maine.

According to studies by the EPA and the National Research Council, prolonged exposure to high levels of radon over a 70-year lifetime is second to smoking as a cause of lung cancer. It causes up to 20,000 of the 136,000 lung cancer deaths each year in the United States, with 85% of these being due to a combination of radon and smoking. Radon released from water obtained from groundwater near radon-laden rock and then heated and used for showers and washing clothes may be responsi-ble for 50 to 400 of these premature deaths.

Because radon hot spots can occur almost anywhere, it is impossible to determine which buildings have unsafe levels of radon without carrying out tests. In 1988 the EPA and the U.S. Surgeon General's Office recommended that everyone living in a detached house, town house, trailer, basement, or in a first-floor or second-floor apartment test for radon.

Unsafe levels can build up easily in a superinsulated or airtight home unless the building has an air-to-air heat exchanger to change indoor air without losing much heat. Some tests also indicate higher levels in houses with electric heat. Homeowners with wells should also have their water tested for radon.

Individuals can measure radon levels in their homes or other buildings with radon detection kits that can be bought in many hardware stores and supermarkets or from mail-order firms for $10 to

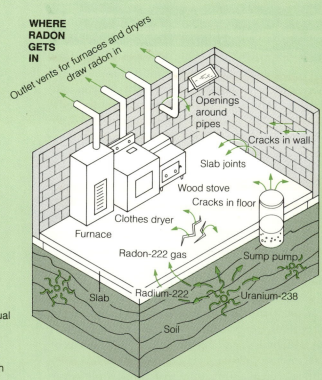

WHERE RADON GETS IN

Outlet vents for furnaces and dryers draw radon in

Openings around pipes

Cracks in wall

Slab joints

Wood stove

Cracks in floor

Clothes dryer

Furnace

Radon-222 gas

Sump pump

Slab

Radium-222

Uranium-238

Soil

Figure 7-12 Sources of indoor radon-222 gases and comparable risks of exposure to various levels of this radioactive gas for a lifetime of 70 years. Levels are those in an actual living area, not a basement or crawl space where levels are much higher. Smokers have the highest risk of getting lung cancer from a combination of prolonged exposure to cigarette smoke and radon-222 gas. (Data from Environmental Protection Agency)

$25. Pick one that is EPA-approved. Detectors are usually left in basement and first-floor levels for a few days—ideally during winter when houses are sealed up. Then they are mailed to an EPA-certified testing laboratory to get the test results.

If testing reveals an unacceptable level (over four picocuries of radiation per liter of air), the EPA recommends several ways to reduce radon levels and health risks.* The first is to stop all indoor smoking or at least confine it to a well-ventilated room. Cracks in basement walls and floors should be sealed and crawl spaces should be vented. Air-to-air heat exchangers ($500 to $2,000) can be installed to remove radon if radiation levels are not above 10 picocuries per liter of air. These devices also remove most other indoor air pollutants.

For houses with serious radon gas problems, special venting systems usually have to be installed below the foundations at a cost of $1,000 to $2,500. To remove radon from contaminated well water, a special type of activated carbon filter can be added to holding tanks at a cost of about $1,000. Contact the state radiological health office or regional EPA office to get a list of approved contractors and avoid unscrupulous radon testing and repair firms.

In Sweden no house can be built until the lot has been tested for radon. If the reading is high, the builder must follow government-mandated construction procedures to ensure that the house won't be contaminated.

Environmentalists urge enactment of a similar building-code program for all new construction in the United States. They also suggest that before buying a lot to build a new house, individuals should have the soil tested for radon.

Similarly, no one should buy an existing house unless it has been tested by certified personnel, just as houses must now be inspected for termites. People building a new house should insist that the contractor use relatively simple construction practices that prevent harmful buildup of radon and add only $100 to $1,000 to the construction cost. Has the building where you live been tested for radon?

*A free copy of *Radon Reduction Methods* can be obtained from the Environmental Protection Agency, 401 M St., S.W., Washington, D.C. 20460. A free copy of *Radon Reduction in New Construction* is available from state radiation-protection offices or the National Association of Home Builders, Attention: William Young, 15th and M Streets, N.W., Washington, D.C. 20005.

POSSIBLE RISKS

Exposure (picocuries per liter of air)*	Lung-cancer Deaths per 1,000 People Exposed (for a lifetime of 70 years)	Comparable Lifetime Risk (70 years)	Recommended Action
200	440–470		**20–200 picocuries** Lower levels within several months. If higher than 200, remedy within a few weeks or move out until levels are reduced.
		Smoking 4 packs of cigarettes a day	
100	270–630		
		2,000 chest X-rays a year	
40	120–380		
		Smoking 2 packs of cigarettes a day	
20	60–210		**4–20 picocuries** You've got a few years to make changes, but do it sooner if you're at the top of the scale.
		Smoking 1 pack of cigarettes a day	
10	30–120		
		5 times the lung-cancer risk of a nonsmoker	
4	13–50		
		200 chest X-rays a year	**Below 4 picocuries** Once you get around 4, it's nearly impossible to bring levels below 4.
2	7–30		
		Same lung-cancer risk as a nonsmoker	
1	3–13		
		20 chest X-rays a year	
0.2	1–3		

*A picocurie is a trillionth of a curie, a standard measure of ionizing radiation.

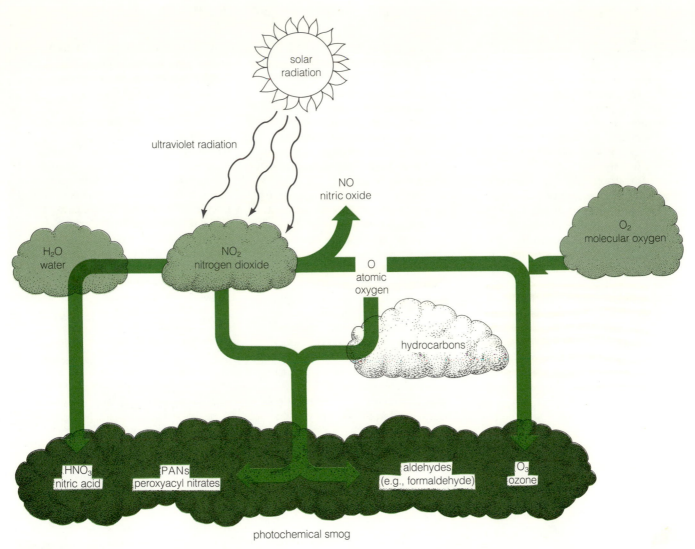

Figure 7-13 Simplified scheme of the formation of photochemical smog.

Thermal inversions occur more often and last longer over towns or cities located in valleys surrounded by mountains (Donora, Pennsylvania), on the leeward sides of mountain ranges (Denver, see photo on p. 145), and near coasts (New York City). A city with several million people and automobiles in an area with a sunny climate, light winds, mountains on three sides, and the ocean on the other, has the ideal conditions for photochemical smog worsened by frequent thermal inversions. This describes the Los Angeles basin. It has almost daily inversions, many of them prolonged during the summer months, 12 million people, 8 million cars, and thousands of factories. Despite having the world's toughest air pollution control program, Los Angeles is the air pollution capital of the United States.

Urban Heat Islands and Dust Domes According to the second energy law, when energy is converted from one form to another, low-quality heat is added to the atmosphere. In the United States, energy use is so high that each of the 246 million Americans continuously injects heat into the atmosphere equal to that from one hundred 100-watt light bulbs.

The effect of this atmospheric heating is felt in large cities, which are typically like islands of heat surrounded by cooler suburban and rural areas. This climatic effect is known as an **urban heat island** (Figure 7-16, p. 162).

This dome of heat also traps pollutants, especially SPM, and creates a **dust dome** above urban areas. As a result, concentrations of SPM over urban-industrial areas may be a thousand times higher than those over rural areas. If wind speeds increase, the dust dome elongates downwind to form a dust plume, which spreads the city's pollutants to rural areas and other urban areas up to hundreds of miles away. As cities grow and merge into vast urban regions, the heat and dust from the cities can combine to form *regional heat islands*, which affect regional climates and prevent polluted air from being effectively diluted and cleansed.

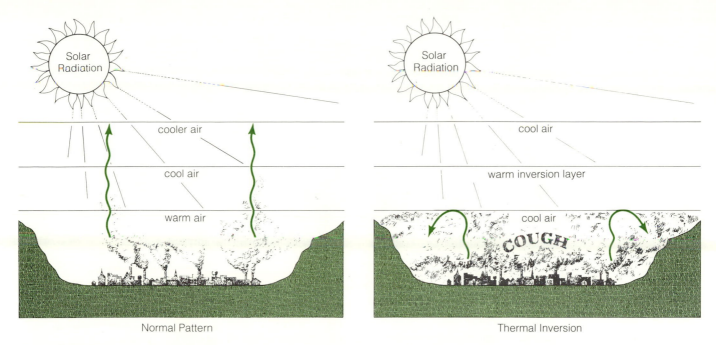

Normal Pattern

Thermal Inversion

Figure 7-14 Thermal inversion traps pollutants in a layer of cool air that cannot rise to carry the pollutants away.

New York Daily News/Courtesy EPA

Figure 7-15 Two faces of New York City. The almost clear view was photographed on a Saturday afternoon (November 26, 1966). The effect of more cars in the city and a thermal inversion is shown in the right-hand photograph, taken the previous day.

Acid Deposition When electric power plants and industrial plants burn coal and oil, their smokestacks emit large amounts of sulfur dioxide, suspended particulate matter, and nitrogen oxides. Power plants and factories emit 90% to 95% of the sulfur dioxide and 57% of the nitrogen oxides in the United States.

As sulfur dioxide and nitric oxide emissions from stationary sources are transported long distances by winds, they form secondary pollutants such as nitrogen dioxide, nitric acid vapor, and droplets containing solutions of sulfuric acid and sulfate and nitrate salts. These chemicals descend to the earth's surface in wet

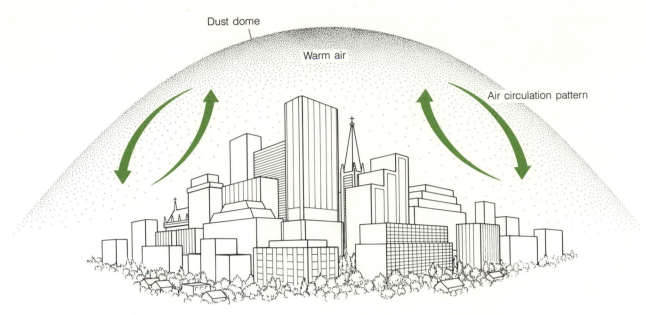

Figure 7-16 An urban heat island causes air circulation patterns that create a dust dome over the city. Winds elongate the dome toward downwind areas. A strong cold front can blow the dome away and lower pollution levels.

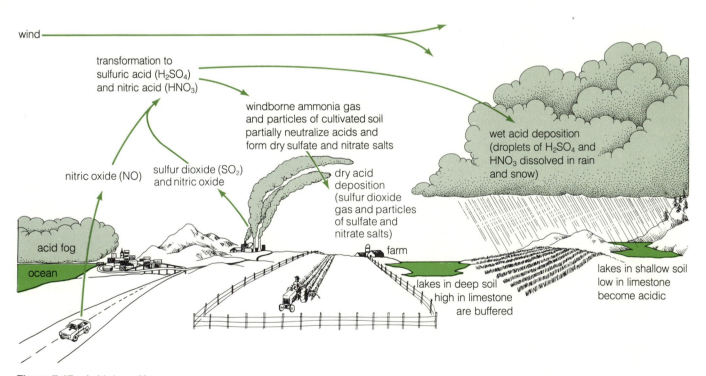

Figure 7-17 Acid deposition.

form as acid rain or snow and in dry form as gases, fog, dew, or solid particles. The combination of dry deposition and wet deposition of acids and acid-forming compounds onto the surface of the earth is known as **acid deposition,** commonly called acid rain (Figure 7-17). Other contributions to acid deposition come from emissions of nitric oxide from massive numbers of automobiles in major urban areas.

Different levels of acidity and basicity of water

solutions of substances are commonly expressed in terms of **pH** (Figure 7-18). A neutral solution has a pH of 7; one with a pH greater than 7 is basic, or alkaline; and one with a pH less than 7 is acidic. The lower the pH below 7, the more acidic the solution. Each whole-number decrease in pH represents a tenfold increase in acidity.

Natural precipitation varies in acidity but has an average pH of 5.6. Acid deposition with a pH value

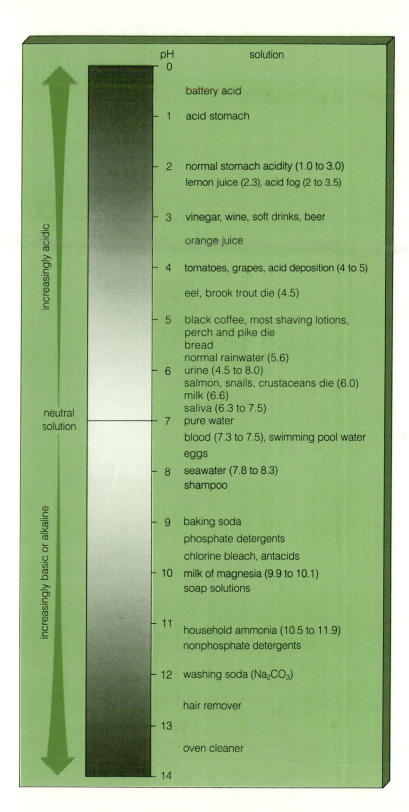

Figure 7-18 Scale of pH, used to measure acidity and alkalinity of water solutions. Values shown are approximate.

pH	solution
0	battery acid
1	acid stomach
2	normal stomach acidity (1.0 to 3.0) lemon juice (2.3), acid fog (2 to 3.5)
3	vinegar, wine, soft drinks, beer / orange juice
4	tomatoes, grapes, acid deposition (4 to 5) / eel, brook trout die (4.5)
5	black coffee, most shaving lotions, perch and pike die / bread / normal rainwater (5.6)
6	urine (4.5 to 8.0) / salmon, snails, crustaceans die (6.0) / milk (6.6) / saliva (6.3 to 7.5)
7	pure water / blood (7.3 to 7.5), swimming pool water / eggs
8	seawater (7.8 to 8.3) / shampoo
9	baking soda / phosphate detergents / chlorine bleach, antacids
10	milk of magnesia (9.9 to 10.1) / soap solutions
11	household ammonia (10.5 to 11.9) / nonphosphate detergents
12	washing soda (Na_2CO_3) / hair remover
13	oven cleaner
14	

increasingly acidic

neutral solution

increasingly basic or alkaline

less than 5.6 has a number of harmful effects, especially when the pH falls below 5.1:

- damage to statues, buildings, metals, and car finishes

- killing fish, aquatic plants, and microorganisms in lakes and streams

- reducing the ability of salmon and trout to reproduce when the pH falls below 5.5

- killing and reducing productivity of many species of phytoplankton when the pH is below their optimum range of 6 to 8

- disruption of the nitrogen cycle in lakes with a pH of 5.4 to 5.7

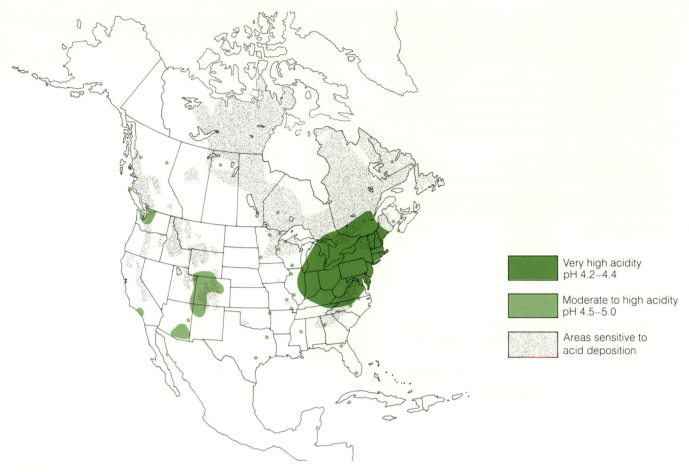

Figure 7-19 Average acidity of acid deposition and areas with soils sensitive to acid deposition in North America in 1984. (Data from Environmental Protection Agency)

- weakening or killing trees, especially conifers at high elevations, by leaching calcium, potassium, and other plant nutrients from soil

- damaging tree roots and killing many kinds of fish by releasing ions of aluminum, lead, mercury, and cadmium from soil and bottom sediments

- weakening trees and making them more susceptible to attacks by diseases, insects, drought and fungi and mosses that thrive under acidic conditions

- stunting the growth of crops such as tomatoes, soybeans, snap beans, tobacco, spinach, carrots, broccoli, and cotton

- increasing populations of giardia, a protozoan that is associated with a severe gastrointestinal disease that afflicts hikers and mountain climbers who drink water from seemingly clear mountain-stream waters

- leaching toxic metals such as copper and lead from city and home water pipes into drinking water

- causing and aggravating many human respiratory diseases and leading to premature death

Acid deposition illustrates the threshold effect. Most soils, lakes, and streams contain alkaline or basic chemicals that can react with a certain amount of acids and thus neutralize them. But repeated exposure to acids year after year can deplete most of these acid-buffering chemicals. Then suddenly large numbers of trees start dying and most fish in a lake or stream die when exposed to the next year's input of acids. When this happens it is ten to twenty years too late to prevent serious damage.

Acid deposition is already a serious problem in northern and central Europe, the northeastern United States, southeastern Canada, and parts of China. It is emerging as a problem in heavily industrialized parts of Asia, Latin America, and Africa. A large portion of the acid-producing chemicals produced in one country is exported to others by prevailing surface winds. For example, over three-fourths of the acid deposition in Norway, Switzerland, Austria, Sweden, the Netherlands, and Finland is blown to those countries from industrialized areas of western and eastern Europe.

More than half the acid deposition in heavily populated southeastern Canada and in the eastern United States originates from emissions from the heavy concentration of coal- and oil-burning power and industrial plants in seven central and upper Midwest states—Ohio, Indiana, Pennsylvania, Illinois, Missouri, West Virginia, and Tennessee (Figure 7-19). The acidity of the precipitation falling over much of eastern North America has a pH of 4.0 to 4.2. This is 30 to 40 times greater than the acidity of the normal precipitation that fell on these areas several decades ago. The flow of acid deposition from the United States to Canada is straining relations between the two countries.

According to the National Academy of Sciences, damage from acid deposition already costs the United States $5 billion a year, and costs will rise sharply unless action is taken now. The cost of reducing these pollutants runs from $1.2 billion to $20 billion, depending on the extent of cleanup and the technology used. New technology may make the costs a fraction of what utility companies wishing to avoid stricter controls have projected.

Soils in some areas contain limestone and other alkaline substances that can neutralize the acids. But acidic, thin soils in other areas have little ability to neutralize acid (Figure 7-19). Also repeated exposure of any soil to large inputs of acids can eventually deplete its acid-neutralizing chemicals. Acid runoff in these sensitive areas can kill many forms of aquatic life in nearby lakes and streams.

7-4 EFFECTS OF AIR POLLUTION ON LIVING ORGANISMS AND MATERIALS

Damage to Human Health Your respiratory system has a number of defense mechanisms that help protect you from air pollution. Hairs in your nose filter out large particles. Sticky mucus in the lining of your upper respiratory tract captures small particles and dissolves some gaseous pollutants. Automatic sneezing and coughing mechanisms expel contaminated air and mucus when your respiratory system is irritated by pollutants. Your upper respiratory tract is lined with hundreds of thousands of tiny, mucus-coated hairs, called cilia. They continually wave back and forth, transporting mucus and the pollutants it traps to your mouth, where it is either swallowed or expelled.

Years of smoking and exposure to air pollutants can overload or deteriorate these natural defenses, causing or contributing to a number of respiratory diseases such as *lung cancer, chronic bronchitis,* and *emphysema.* Fine particles are particularly hazardous to human health because they are small enough to penetrate the lung's natural defenses. They can also bring with them droplets or other particles of toxic or cancer-causing pollutants that become attached to their surfaces. Smoking is considered the leading cause of lung cancer, but the disease has also been linked to inhalation

of a number of other air pollutants, such as asbestos fibers.

Emphysema is an incurable condition that reduces the ability of the lungs to transfer oxygen to the blood so that the slightest exertion causes acute shortness of breath. Prolonged smoking and exposure to air pollutants can cause emphysema in anyone. However, about one-fourth of the population is much more susceptible to emphysema because of a hereditary condition that reduces the elasticity of the air sacs of the lungs. Anyone with this condition, for which testing is available, should not smoke and should not live or work in a highly polluted area.

Elderly people, infants, pregnant women, and persons with heart disease, asthma, or other respiratory diseases are especially vulnerable to air pollution. One of every three persons in the United States falls into one or more of these groups. Air pollution costs the United States at least $110 billion annually in health care and lost work productivity. About $100 billion of this is caused by indoor air pollution. Scientists at the University of California at Davis estimate that the use of gasoline and diesel fuel in the United States causes up to 30,000 premature deaths a year, especially among those suffering from respiratory ailments.

In Athens, Greece, air pollution kills as many as six people a day. Cities with the world's worst air pollution problems include Mexico City, Mexico; Cairo, Egypt; New Delhi and Calcutta, India; and Cubatao and São Paulo, Brazil (see Spotlight on p. 167). An estimated 60% of the people living in Calcutta suffer from respiratory diseases related to air pollution. Breathing the air in Mexico City is roughly equivalent to smoking two packs of cigarettes a day.

Damage to Plants Some gaseous pollutants, such as sulfur dioxide, nitrogen oxides, ozone, and PANs, cause direct damage to leaves of crop plants and trees when they enter leaf pores (stomata). Chronic exposure of leaves and needles to air pollutants can also break down the waxy coating that helps prevent excessive water loss and damage from diseases, pests, drought, and frost. In the midwestern United States crop losses of wheat, corn, soybeans, and peanuts from damage by ozone and acid deposition amount to about $5 billion a year.

Chronic exposure interferes with photosynthesis and plant growth, reduces nutrient uptake, and causes leaves or needles to turn yellow or brown and drop off. Coniferous trees, especially at high elevations, are highly vulnerable to the effects of air pollution because of their long life spans and the year-round exposure of their needles to polluted air.

In addition to causing direct leaf and needle damage, acid deposition can leach vital plant nutrients such as calcium, magnesium, and potassium from the soil

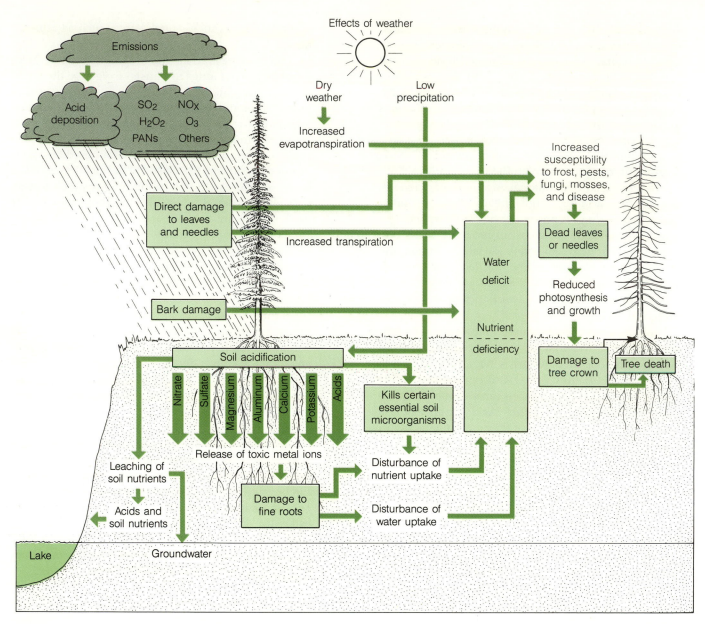

Figure 7-20 Harmful effects of air pollutants on trees.

and kill essential soil microorganisms. It also releases aluminum ions, which are normally bound to soil particles, into soil water. There they damage fine root filaments, reduce uptake of water and nutrients from the soil, and make trees more vulnerable to drought, frost, insects, fungi, mosses, and disease (Figure 7-20). Prolonged exposure to high levels of multiple air pollutants can kill all trees and vegetation in an area (see the Case Study on p. 167).

The effects of chronic exposure of trees to multiple air pollutants may not be visible for several decades. Then suddenly large numbers begin dying off because of soil nutrient depletion and increased susceptibility to pests, diseases, mosses, fungi, and drought.

That is what is happening to almost one-fourth of the forests in Europe. The phenomenon, known as *waldsterben* (forest death), turns whole forests into stump-studded meadows. For example, 8% of the trees in West German forests were found to be dead or damaged in 1982. One year later the figure was 34%, and by 1986 the toll stood at about 53% (Figure 7-22). This has caused a $10 billion loss of commercially important trees such as spruce, fir, pine, beech, and oak. The diebacks have also eliminated habitats for many types of wildlife.

Similar damage is occurring in at least 15 other European countries. The trees damaged or killed by chronic exposure to air pollutants will not be replaced for up to 100 years.

So far, similar diebacks in the United States have occurred primarily in stands on higher-elevation slopes facing moving air masses. The most seriously affected

The air pollution capital of the world may be Cubatao, an hour's drive south of São Paulo, Brazil. This city of 100,000 people lies in a coastal valley that has frequent thermal inversions. Residents call it "the valley of death."

In this heavily industrialized city scores of plants spew thousands of tons of pollutants a day into the frequently stagnant air.

More babies are born deformed there than anywhere else in Latin America.

In one recent year 13,000 of the 40,000 people living in the downtown core area suffered from respiratory disease. One resident says, "On some days if you go outside, you will vomit." The mayor refuses to live in the city. Most residents would like to live somewhere else, but they need the jobs available in the city and they cannot afford to move. The government has begun some long overdue efforts to control air pollution but has far to go. Meanwhile the poor continue to pay the price of this form of economic progress: bad health and premature death.

CASE STUDY   The Deaths of Ducktown and Copperhill, Tennessee

Between 1855 and 1907 a large copper smelter operated near the towns of Ducktown and Copperhill, Tennessee. Sulfur dioxide and other fumes from the smelter killed the luxurious forest once growing on this land, leaving a desert of dry, red-clay hills with no signs of life (Figure 7-21).

Between 1930 and 1970 efforts to restore vegetation on the 56-square-mile area were unsuccessful. In the 1970s, however, new reforestation techniques were used, and today about two-thirds of what used to be desert sprouts some kind of vegetation. With an expenditure of $6 million the remaining desert could be covered with vegetation in 10 to 20 years.

Copper mines continued to operate in the area until 1986 and were the leading employer of the almost 1,000 people living in Ducktown and Copperhill. As the ecological health of the area slowly improves, these mining towns now face economic death.

Figure 7-21   Sulfur dioxide and other fumes from a copper smelter that operated for 52 years near Ducktown and Copperhill, Tennessee, killed the forest once found on this land and left a desert in its place. After decades of replanting, some vegetation has returned to the area.

A. Keith, U.S. Geological Survey

In Sudbury, Ontario, an area three times larger than that in Tennessee was also ravaged by copper mining and smelting since 1886. Like Ducktown and Copperhill, this land is slowly being revived and reforested. At the same time, however, new ecologically devastated areas are being created around mining and smelting operations in Mexico, Brazil, and other LDCs with inadequate environmental controls.

---

areas are the Appalachian Mountains from Georgia to New England. In New York, Vermont, and New Hampshire, air pollution has killed 60% of high-elevation red spruce trees. By 1988 most spruce, fir, and other conifers atop North Carolina's Mt. Mitchell, the highest peak in the East, were dead from being bathed in ozone and acid fog for years. The soil was so acidic that new seedlings could not survive.

Plant pathologist Robert Bruck warns that damage to mountaintop forests is an early warning that many tree species at lower elevations may soon die or be damaged by prolonged exposure to air pollution, as has happened in Europe. Many scientists fear that elected officials in the United States will continue to delay establishing stricter controls on major forms of air pollution until it is too late to prevent a severe loss

Figure 7-22 This dead coniferous forest in West Germany is believed to be the result of long-term exposure to multiple air pollutants, which made the trees more vulnerable to disease and drought.

Phototake/Bernd Uhlig

Table 7-1 Harmful Effects of Air Pollution on Materials

Material	Effects	Principal Air Pollutants
Stone and concrete	Surface erosion, discoloration, soiling	Sulfur dioxide, sulfuric acid, nitric acid, solid particulates
Metals	Corrosion, tarnishing, loss of strength	Sulfur dioxide, sulfuric acid, nitric acid, solid particulates, hydrogen sulfide
Ceramics and glass	Surface erosion	Hydrogen fluoride, solid particulates
Paints	Surface erosion, discoloration, soiling	Sulfur dioxide, hydrogen sulfide, ozone, solid particulates
Paper	Embrittlement, discoloration	Sulfur dioxide
Rubber	Cracking, loss of strength	Ozone
Leather	Surface deterioration, loss of strength	Sulfur dioxide
Textile fabrics	Deterioration, fading, soiling	Sulfur dioxide, nitrogen dioxide, ozone, solid particulates

of valuable forest resources like that happening in Europe.

Damage to Aquatic Life Acid deposition has a severe harmful impact on the aquatic life of freshwater lakes in areas where surrounding soils have little acid-buffering capacity (Figure 7-19). Much of the damage to aquatic life in the Northern Hemisphere is a result of *acid shock*. Acid shock is caused by the sudden runoff of large amounts of highly acidic water (along with toxic aluminum leached from the soil) into lakes when snow melts in the spring or when heavy rains follow a period of drought. The aluminum leached from the soil and lake sediment kills fish by clogging their gills.

In Norway and Sweden 68,000 lakes either contain no fish or have lost most of their acid-buffering capacity because of excess acidity. About 25% of the lakes in New York's Adirondack Mountains are so acidic they cannot support fish life. Another 20% have lost most of their acid-neutralizing capacity. In Ontario, Canada, at least 1,600 lakes are fishless because of excess acidity. Aquatic life in 48,000 more of Canada's lakes is also threatened. The Pennsylvania Fish Commission estimates that half the state's streams will not be

Figure 7-23 This marble monument in Rome has been damaged by exposure to acidic air pollutants.

able to support fish populations by the year 2000 unless acid deposition declines.

A 1988 study by the Environmental Defense Fund indicated that excess nitrate input from acid deposition is a major threat to many types of aquatic plants and fish in lakes and estuaries, such as the Chesapeake Bay. Nitrate plant nutrients stimulate the overgrowth of algae and other phytoplankton, which cloud the water and prevent light from filtering down to plants on the lake bottom. When the algae die, their decomposition by oxygen-consuming bacteria depletes the water of dissolved oxygen, suffocating fish and other aerobic organisms.

Damage to Materials Each year air pollutants cause tens of millions of dollars in damage to various materials (Table 7-1). The fallout of soot and grit on buildings, cars, and clothing requires costly cleaning. Irreplaceable marble statues, historic buildings, and stained-glass windows throughout the world have been pitted and discolored by air pollutants (Figure 7-23).

7-5 EFFECTS OF AIR POLLUTION ON STRATOSPHERIC OZONE AND GLOBAL CLIMATE

Chlorofluorocarbons, Halons, and Depletion of Ozone in the Stratosphere In 1974 chemists Sherwood Roland and Mario Molina theorized that human-made chlorofluorocarbons (CFCs) are lowering the average concentration of ozone in the stratosphere. No one suspected such a possibility when CFCs were developed in 1930. These stable, odorless, nonflammable, nontoxic, and noncorrosive chemicals were a chem-

ist's dream. Soon they were widely used as coolants in air conditioners and refrigerators and as propellants in aerosol spray cans. They are also used in cleaning electronic parts, hospital sterilants, and as blowing agents to puff liquid plastic into styrofoam and other plastic foams used for insulation and packaging.

Since 1945 the use of the four major types of CFCs has increased sharply. Bromine-containing CFCs, called *halons*, are also widely used, mostly in fire extinguishers.

Since 1978 the use of CFCs in aerosol cans has been banned in the U.S., Canada, and most Scandinavian countries. But worldwide nonaerosol uses have risen sharply, along with aerosol use in western Europe. Aerosols are still the largest use, accounting for 25% of global CFC use. Spray cans, discarded or leading refrigeration and air conditioning equipment, and the burning of plastic foam products release CFCs into the atmosphere. Depending on the type, these chemicals stay in the atmosphere for 22 to 111 years.

Over several decades they gradually move up to the stratosphere. There, under the influence of high-energy UV radiation, they break down and release chlorine atoms, which speed up the breakdown of ozone into oxygen gas. Over time a single chlorine atom can convert as many as 10,000 molecules of O_3 to O_2. CFCs are also greenhouse gases that contribute to global warming.

In 1988 the National Aeronautics and Space Administration (NASA) released a study showing that stratospheric ozone has decreased by as much as 3% over the most populous areas of North America, Europe, China, and Japan since 1969 (Figure 7-24). Over Scandinavia and Alaska the average loss during winter months is 6%.

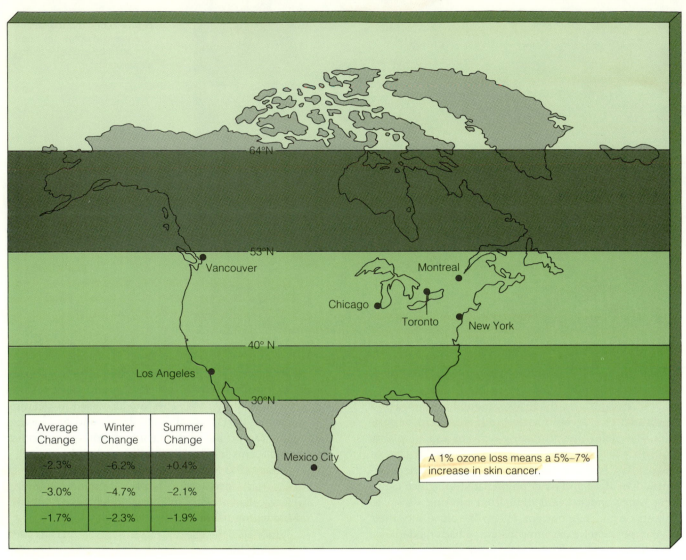

	Average Change	Winter Change	Summer Change
	-2.3%	-6.2%	+0.4%
	-3.0%	-4.7%	-2.1%
	-1.7%	-2.3%	-1.9%

A 1% ozone loss means a 5%–7% increase in skin cancer.

Figure 7-24 Average drops in ozone levels in the stratosphere above parts of the earth between 1969 and 1986, based on data gathered from satellites and ground stations. (Data from NASA)

In 1987 the ozone level in the upper stratosphere over the Antarctic dropped 60% from September through November. The amount in the lower stratosphere above this region dropped 95%. This annual decrease, known as the *Antarctic ozone hole*, has been increasing since 1978 and covers an area the size of the continental United States. Measurements indicate that this large annual decrease in ozone over the South Pole is caused by the presence of ice clouds that make ozone-destroying CFCs more active. There are also signs that an ozone hole about the size of Greenland opens over the North Pole for a few months each year.

Large volcanic eruptions and natural climatic processes such as cyclic changes in solar output can alter stratospheric ozone levels. However, there is considerable and growing evidence that CFCs are a major cause of ozone depletion. Between 1989 and 1991 an increase in solar output is expected to cause a slight increase in average levels of ozone in the strat-

osphere. After that, ozone levels are projected to decrease as a result of increasing levels of CFCs in the stratosphere.

Effects of Ozone Depletion With less ozone in the stratosphere, more UV radiation can reach the earth's surface. Each 1% drop in stratospheric ozone allows 2% more UV to reach the ground, increasing future cases of skin cancer by 5% to 7%. The EPA estimates that a 5% ozone depletion would cause

- an additional 940,000 cases annually of basal-cell and squamous-cell skin cancers—both disfiguring but usually not fatal cancers if treated in time

- an additional 30,000 cases annually of often-fatal melanoma skin cancer, which now kills almost 8,000 Americans each year

- a sharp increase in eye cataracts and severe sunburn in people and eye cancer in cattle

- suppression of the human immune system, which would reduce our defenses against a variety of infectious diseases

- an increase in eye-burning photochemical smog, highly damaging ozone, and acid deposition in the troposphere

- decreased yields of important food crops such as corn, rice, soybeans, and wheat

- damage to some aquatic plant species essential to ocean food webs

- a loss of perhaps $2 billion a year from degradation of plastics and other polymer materials

- increased global warming (greenhouse effect) leading to changes in climate, agricultural, and forest productivity, and wildlife survival

Protecting the Ozone Layer Models of atmospheric processes indicate that just to keep CFCs at 1987 levels would require an immediate 85% drop in total CFC emissions throughout the world. Analysts believe that the first step toward this goal should be an immediate worldwide ban on the use of CFCs in aerosol spray cans and in producing plastic foam products. Cost-effective substitutes are already available for these uses.

The next step would be to phase out all other uses of CFCs, halons, and carbon tetrachloride (a cleaning solvent) by 1995. Substitute coolants in refrigeration and air conditioning will probably cost more. But compared to the potential economic and health consequences of ozone depletion, such cost increases would be minor.

Some progress has been made. In 1987, 46 countries producing CFCs signed a treaty to reduce production of the eight most widely used and most damaging CFCs. If carried out, it will reduce total emissions of CFCs into the atmosphere by about 35% between 1989 and 2000.

However, the agreement allows LDCs signing the treaty to increase their production or use of these CFCs between 1989 and 1999 by as much as 10% a year. The treaty also makes no provisions for the retrieval and destruction of the millions of tons of CFCs that will escape from presently running refrigerators and air conditioners when they wear out or develop leaks. Also, it does not decrease use of halons, carbon tetrachloride, and methyl chloroform that can also deplete ozone.

Most scientists agree that the treaty is an important symbol of global cooperation but that it does not go far enough to prevent significant depletion of the ozone layer. They call for phasing out all uses of these chemicals by 1995, as Sweden has agreed to do.

Even if all CFCs were banned tomorrow, it would take about 100 years for the planet to recover from the present ozone depletion and that to come from CFCs already in the atmosphere. The key question is whether MDCs can agree to sacrifice short-term economic gain by quickly kicking their present addiction to CFCs and halons to protect life on earth in coming decades.

Global Warming from an Enhanced Greenhouse Effect A buildup of one or several greenhouse gases in the atmosphere would cause the average temperature of the earth's lower atmosphere to rise as a result of an enhanced greenhouse effect (Figure 7-5, p. 152). This appears to be what is happening, mostly because of gases we are putting into the atmosphere (Figure 7-25).

Between 1860 and 1988 the average global level of carbon dioxide in the atmosphere increased 25%, with a sharp rise since 1958 (Figure 7-25a). About 80% of this rise is due to the burning of fossil fuel. Deforestation, especially the wholesale clearing and burning of tropical forests, is believed to account for about 20% of the increase in carbon dioxide levels. Levels of other greenhouse gases have also been increasing (Figure 7-25b, c, d).

Since 1880, average global temperatures have risen about 1.2°F (0.7°C) (Figure 7-26). Climate experts believe that normal climatic fluctuations caused about one third of this increase, with the greenhouse effect causing the rest. Many climate experts expect the enhanced greenhouse effect caused by our activities to begin accelerating in the 1990s.

Climatic models project that the earth's average atmospheric temperature will rise 3°F to 8°F (1.5°C to 4.5°C) between 2030 and 2050 if greenhouse gases continue to rise at the current rate. Temperatures at middle and high latitudes will rise two to three times the average increase. If these changes take place, the atmosphere will be warmer than it has been at any time during the past 100,000 years. Changes caused by this warming could last for hundreds to thousands of years.

Effects of Global Climate Changes At first glance a warmer average climate might seem desirable. It could lead to lower heating bills and longer growing seasons in middle and high latitudes. Crop yields might increase 60% to 80% in some areas because more carbon dioxide in the atmosphere can increase the rate of photosynthesis.

But other factors could offset potential gains in crop yields. Damage from insect pests might increase because warmer temperatures would boost insect breeding. Higher temperatures would also increase plant aerobic respiration rates and reduce water availability. Also soils in some of the new food-growing areas would not be useful for growing key crops. Much of Canada, for example, does not have the optimum type of soil for growing wheat and corn.

A 7°F rise in temperature would change world-

Figure 7-25 Increases in average concentrations of greenhouse gases in the atmosphere. They are projected to increase the global warming trend shown in Figure 7-26. (Data from Electric Power Research Institute). (Adapted by permission from Cecie Starr and Ralph Taggart, 1989, *Biology: The Unity and Diversity of Life,* 5th ed. Belmont, Calif.: Wadsworth)

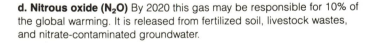

a. Carbon dioxide (CO$_2$) By the year 2020 this gas is expected to be responsible for 50% of the global warming trend. Major sources are fossil fuel burning (80%) and deforestation (20%).

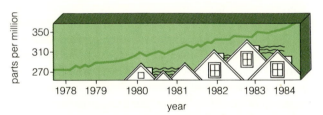

b. Chlorofluorocarbons (CFCs) By 2020 these gases will probably be responsible for about 25% of the global warming trend. Major sources are leaking air conditioners and refrigerators, evaporation of industrial solvents, production of plastic foams, and propellants in aerosol spray cans (in some countries).

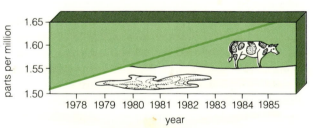

c. Methane (CH$_4$) By 2020 this gas may be responsible for 15% of the global warming trend. It is produced by natural bacterial decay processes in swamps, bogs, rice fields, and landfills and by biomass burning. Some also leaks from natural gas wells, pipelines, storage tanks, furnaces, dryers, and stoves.

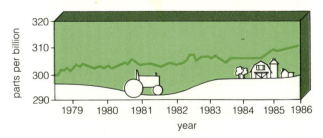

d. Nitrous oxide (N$_2$O) By 2020 this gas may be responsible for 10% of the global warming. It is released from fertilized soil, livestock wastes, and nitrate-contaminated groundwater.

wide patterns of precipitation, winds, storms, and ocean currents. There would be major shifts in areas where crops could be grown, with each 1.8°F rise pushing climatic zones 62 to 93 miles northward. Iowa could become a desert and Alberta, Canada a breadbasket.

Giant hurricanes, with 50% more destructive potential than those today, would hit farther north and during more months of the year. The spread of tropical climates from the equator would bring malaria and other insect-borne diseases to formerly temperate zones. Extreme heat waves would occur more frequently. Rainfall would increase in Africa and India. The mountain snow that supplies much of California's water would dwindle. Rain instead of snow in the mountains would cause winter floods followed by

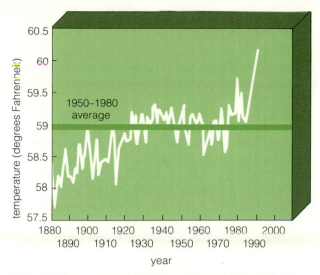

Figure 7-26 Average global temperatures, 1880–1988. Note the general increase since 1880 and the sharp rise in the 1980s. The baseline is the global average temperature from 1950 to 1980. (Data from National Academy of Sciences and National Center for Atmospheric Research)

summer droughts that would disrupt food production and water supplies, especially for already arid southern California.

The growth rates of commercially important tree species might be lowered by a rise in average temperature. Stress to trees from pests and disease microorganisms would increase because they are able to adapt to climate change faster than trees. The number of devastating fires in drier forest areas and grasslands would increase. Many wildlife species would disappear.

Global warming would also raise average sea levels. Warmer temperatures would expand the upper layers of the ocean and perhaps cause partial melting of the Greenland and West Antarctic ice sheets. Present models indicate that raising the average atmospheric temperature by 7°F would raise the average global sea level by between one and four feet over the next hundred years.

This would flood major cities such as Shanghai and Cairo and large areas of agricultural lowlands and deltas in Bangladesh, India, and China, where much of the world's rice is grown. Low-lying islands like the Marshall Islands in the Pacific, the Maldives off the west coast of India, and some Caribbean nations would disappear. Such flooding would threaten the homes of up to 50 million people, including the poor in Bangladesh and the rich in Malibu, California.

Coastal wetlands that are nurseries for most commercially important fish species would also be flooded. In the United States 50% to 80% of coastal wetlands would be lost. If most of the West Antarctic ice sheet melted, as happened during a warm period 120,000 years ago, sea levels would gradually raise as much as 20 feet over the next several hundred years.

In the United States even a modest 1-foot rise would flood major portions of Louisiana and Florida and erode Atlantic and Gulf Coast beaches at least 98 feet. It would also flood tanks storing hazardous chemicals along the Gulf and Atlantic coasts and cause intrusion of saltwater into groundwater supplies. Aquifers that supply water for large numbers of people in Florida and Long Island would become too salty to use.

Hundreds of billions of dollars would have to be spent to build dikes to keep cities like Manhattan, Atlantic City, Boston, New Orleans, and Galveston from flooding, or these cities would have to be abandoned. (A comedian joked that he was planning to buy land in Kansas because it would probably become valuable beach-front property.)

There are poorly understood natural fluctuations in climate and weather that periodically bring abnormal droughts and flooding to various areas. For this reason, most atmospheric scientists are reluctant to say that the droughts and heat waves that blistered much of the United States in 1988 were caused by an enhanced greenhouse effect. But they agree that these conditions could become routine weather if we don't mount a crash program to slow down the rate of global warming.

There is widespread agreement that any significant change in world climate would cause a sharp increase in food prices, famine, severe economic losses, and economic, ecological, and social chaos. The faster the climate change, the greater these problems.

Dealing with Global Warming Basically there are two ways to deal with global warming: slow it down and adjust to its effects. Many atmospheric scientists believe that past emissions of greenhouse gases will automatically raise average atmospheric temperatures 1°F to 3°F, even if we stop burning fossil fuels tomorrow. But slowing down the rate of change can help prevent economic and social chaos and buy time to switch to other energy alternatives.

We can slow down the rate of global warming by

- banning emissions of CFCs and halons

- cutting fossil fuel use by at least 20% by 2000 and by 50% by 2015, mostly by placing heavy taxes on gasoline and all fossil fuels and using the revenue to develop energy alternatives to replace fossil fuels, improve energy efficiency, and plant trees worldwide

- sharply reducing the use of coal, which emits 60% more carbon dioxide per unit of energy produced than any other fossil fuel

- using scrubbers to remove carbon dioxide from the smokestack emissions of coal-burning power and industrial plants and from vehicle exhausts; but present methods remove only about 30% of the CO$_2$ and are too expensive

- improving energy efficiency
- doubling average gas mileage in new cars from 26 miles per gallon to 50 miles per gallon by 2005 to cut lifetime CO_2 emissions from vehicles in half
- requiring new homes to have the most efficient heating and cooling systems available
- greatly increasing use of solar energy, wind power, and geothermal energy
- increasing use of natural gas during the transition from the present fossil fuel age to a new solar age
- greatly slowing down the clearing and degradation of tropical forests
- planting trees worldwide; an acre of trees absorbs enough carbon dioxide each year to offset that produced by driving a car 26,000 miles
- slowing population growth

Achieving these goals will require countries to draw up and abide by a Global Law of the Atmosphere.

We could also increase use of nuclear power if a new generation of much safer reactors can be developed and the problem of how to store nuclear waste safely for thousands of years can be solved. But to make a real contribution to slowing global warming we would need thousands of reactors. Also using nuclear energy to produce electricity is very inefficient (Figure 4-15, p. 87), and electricity cannot be used to run cars unless much better batteries are developed. This method would be very expensive in comparison to other options. Improving energy efficiency is quicker and reduces emissions of CO_2 per dollar invested 2.5 to 10 times more than nuclear power can.

Many observers doubt that countries will agree to reduce fossil fuel use and deforestation in time to prevent significant global warming. Countries likely to have a more favorable climate after global warming will resist severe restrictions, whereas countries likely to suffer from reduced food-growing capacity may favor taking immediate action. Sharply restricting fossil fuel use, no matter how desirable from a long-term environmental and economic viewpoint, would cause major short-term economic and social disruptions that most countries would find unacceptable.

Thus, some analysts suggest that while attempting to reduce fossil fuel use and deforestation to buy time, we should also begin to prepare for the effects of long-term global warming. Their suggestions include

- increasing research on the breeding of food plants that need less water and plants that can thrive in water too salty for ordinary crops
- building dikes to protect coastal areas from flooding, as the Dutch have done for hundreds of years
- moving storage tanks of hazardous materials away from coastal areas

- banning new construction on low-lying coastal areas
- storing large supplies of key foods throughout the world as insurance against disruptions of food production

But making such changes would take 20 years and cost hundreds of billions of dollars. For example, adjusting the world's irrigation systems alone could take $200 billion. There is no free lunch.

Changing the global climate by our activities can be viewed as the ultimate tragedy of the commons. In 1975, anthropologist Margaret Mead said, "The atmosphere is the key symbol of global interdependence. If we can't solve some of our problems in the face of threats to this global commons, then I can't be very optimistic about the future of the world."

7-6 CONTROLLING AIR POLLUTION

U.S. Air Pollution Legislation   Air pollution or any other type of pollution can be controlled by laws to establish desired standards and by technology to achieve the standards. In the United States Congress passed the Clean Air Acts of 1970 and 1977, which gave the federal government considerable power to control air pollution.

These laws required the EPA to establish **national ambient air quality standards (NAAQS)** for seven major outdoor pollutants found in almost all parts of the country: SPM, sulfur oxides, carbon monoxide, nitrogen oxides, ozone, hydrocarbons, and lead. Each standard specifies the maximum allowable level, averaged over a specific time period, for a certain pollutant in outdoor (ambient) air.

The EPA has also established a policy of *prevention of significant deterioration (PSD)*. This policy is designed to prevent a decrease in air quality in regions where the air is cleaner than required by the NAAQS for SPM and sulfur dioxide. Otherwise, industries would move into these areas and gradually degrade air quality to the national standards for these two major pollutants.

The EPA is also required to establish *national emission standards* for less common air pollutants capable of causing serious harm to human health at low concentrations. Scientists have identified at least 600 potentially hazardous air pollutants. However, by 1988 the EPA had established emission standards for only seven hazardous pollutants.

Part of the problem is the difficulty of getting accurate scientific data on the effects of specific pollutants on human health. Economic and political pressures also hamper the EPA's work. Since 1981, Congress slashed EPA budgets, and the Reagan administration reduced enforcement of air pollution laws.

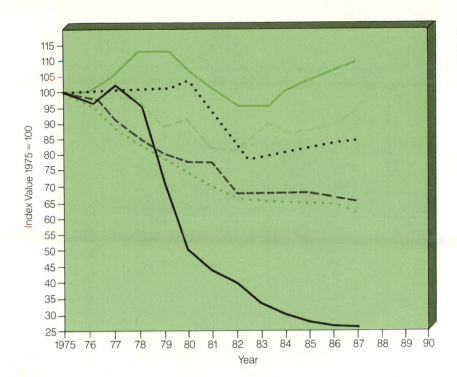

Figure 7-27 Trends in U.S. outdoor air quality for six pollutants, 1975–1986. (Data from Environmental Protection Agency)

Legend:
- Suspended particulate matter ··············
- Nitrogen oxides ——————
- Lead ——————
- Sulfur dioxide — — — — —
- Ozone ————
- Carbon monoxide ··············

Congress set a timetable for achieving certain percentage reductions in emissions of carbon monoxide, hydrocarbons, and nitrogen oxides from motor vehicles. Although significant progress has been made, a series of legally allowed extensions has pushed deadlines for complete attainment of most of these goals into the future.

Trends in U.S. Outdoor Air Quality In the United States between 1975 and 1986, average outdoor concentrations of most major pollutants, except nitrogen oxides, dropped as a result of air pollution control laws, economic recession, and higher energy prices (Figure 7-27). Lead made the sharpest drop because of the gradual phaseout of leaded gasoline.

Between 1976 and 1987 there was a sharp drop in the number of days in which the air was classified as hazardous, very unhealthful, or unhealthful in most major urban areas. New York, Chicago, and Cleveland showed considerable improvement, while Los Angeles, Houston, and Dallas-Fort Worth showed relatively little improvement. In 1987 the five large metropolitan areas with the dirtiest air according to the EPA were Denver, Colorado; San Bernardino, California; El Paso, Texas; St. Louis, Missouri; Los Angeles, California; and Phoenix, Arizona.

Except for Sweden, the United States has made more progress in reducing air pollution than any other country. However, there is still much to be done because the increase in new vehicles and other emission sources gradually overwhelms pollution control efforts. Between 1982 and 1986, for example, average outdoor

levels of major pollutants other than lead either stayed the same or climbed slightly (Figure 7-27).

Cities were supposed to meet NAAQS standards for the six pollutants shown in Figure 7-27 by 1977 or be ineligible to receive federal funds for construction, highways, and sewers. As 100 major cities failed to meet these goals, Congress extended the deadlines to 1982, then to 1987, and now to 1994. Many cities have become dependent on receiving extensions and have failed to take enough action.

One out of three Americans lives in 70 major cities where average ozone levels regularly exceed safe levels. The worst is Los Angeles where ozone levels exceeded the standard for 141 days during 1987. Other cities where the ozone standard is typically exceeded 15 to 43 days a year are New York, Hartford, New Haven, Philadelphia, Houston, Bakersfield, Fresno, San Diego, Modesto, Visalia, and Atlanta. One out of four Americans lives in 59 cities with too much carbon monoxide.

Many scientists believe that the sulfur and nitrogen-containing components of acid deposition, along with ozone and other air pollutants, are causing severe health, ecological, and economic effects. They warn that failure to reduce these pollutants will eventually lead to massive losses of forests, aquatic life, metals and buildings, and other economically and ecologically important resources.

Despite such warnings, politicians in the United States and most MDCs have continued to call for more research. They have delayed setting stricter standards for sulfur dioxide and SPM emissions from coal-burning plants and for nitrogen oxide emissions from motor

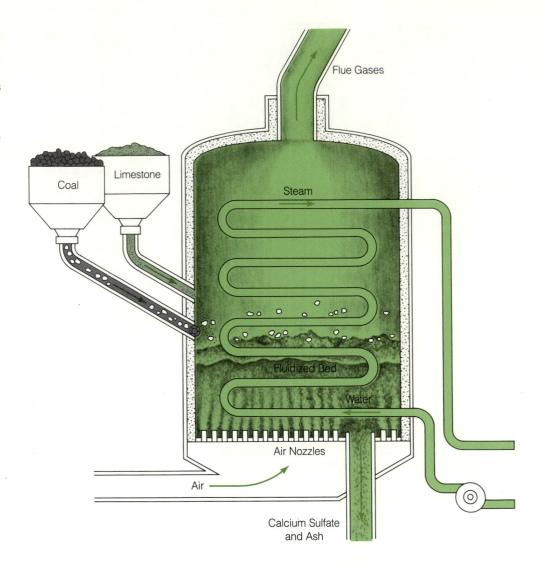

Figure 7-28 Fluidized-bed combustion of coal. A stream of hot air is blown into a boiler to suspend a mixture of powdered coal and crushed limestone. This removes most of the sulfur dioxide, sharply reduces emissions of nitrogen oxides, and burns coal more efficiently and cheaply than conventional combustion methods.

Flue Gases

Coal

Limestone

Steam

Fluidized Bed

Water

Air Nozzles

Air

Calcium Sulfate and Ash

vehicles. In contrast, Sweden has set an example for other countries. By 1995 its government plans to reduce sulfur dioxide emissions by 65% and nitrogen oxide emissions by 95%.

In the 1970s most Western European countries, Canada, Australia, Japan, and South Korea established automobile emissions standards similar to those in the United States, although some European countries lag behind. Brazil will have similar standards by 1997. Little, if any, attempt is made to control vehicle emissions in India, Mexico, Argentina, China, the Soviet Union, and Eastern European countries.

Methods of Pollution Control Once a pollution control standard has been adopted, two general approaches can be used to prevent levels from exceeding the standard. One is *input control,* which prevents or reduces the severity of the problem. The other is *output control,* which treats the symptoms. Output control methods, especially those that attempt to remove the pollutant once it has entered the environment, tend to be expensive and difficult.

Input methods are usually easier and cheaper in the long run. The five major input control methods for reducing the total amount of pollution of any type from reaching the environment are:

- regulating population growth
- reducing unnecessary waste of metals, paper, and other matter resources through increased recycling and reuse and by designing products that last longer and are easy to repair
- reducing energy use
- using energy more efficiently
- switching from coal to natural gas, which produces less pollution and carbon dioxide when burned
- switching from fossil fuels to energy from the sun, wind, and flowing water (hydropower) or nuclear power

These input methods are the most effective and least costly ways (except nuclear power) to reduce air, water, and soil pollution. They are the only cost-effective methods for reducing the rate of buildup of carbon dioxide and other greenhouse gases in the atmosphere. However, they are rarely given serious consideration in national and international strategies for pollution control.

Control of Sulfur Dioxide Emissions from Stationary Sources Environmentalists in the United States and Canada call for a 50% reduction in sulfur dioxide emissions from U.S. coal-burning plants over the next ten years. The cost of doing this is estimated at $2 billion to $7 billion a year. In addition to the general input control methods mentioned earlier, the following approaches can lower sulfur dioxide emissions or reduce their effects:

Sulfur Dioxide Input Control Methods

1. *Burn low-sulfur coal.* Especially useful for new power and industrial plants located near deposits of such coal; Midwest power plants could switch to low-sulfur coal strip-mined in the West. But this would put 20,000 or more miners in Illinois, Kentucky, Ohio, and West Virginia out of work.

2. *Remove sulfur from coal.* Fairly inexpensive; removes only 20% to 50%.

3. *Convert coal to a gas or liquid fuel.* Low net energy yield.

4. *Remove sulfur during combustion by fluidized-bed combustion (FBC)* (Figure 7-28). Removes up to 90%; should be commercially available for small to medium plants in the 1990s.

5. *Remove sulfur during combustion by limestone injection multiple burning (LIMB).* Still in the development and testing stage.

Sulfur Dioxide Output Control Methods

1. *Use smokestacks tall enough to pierce the thermal inversion layer.* Can decrease pollution near power or industrial plants but increases pollution levels in downwind areas.

2. *Remove pollutants after combustion by using flue gas desulfurization (FGD), or scrubbing* (Figure 7-29d). Removes up to 95% of SO_2 and 99.9% of SPM (but not the more harmful fine particles); can be used in new plants and added to most existing large plants but is very expensive.

3. *Add a tax on each unit emitted.* Encourages development of more efficient and cost-effective methods of emissions control; opposed by industry because it costs more than tall smokestacks and requires polluters to bear more of the external costs.

By 1987 the Soviet Union and 21 European countries had signed a treaty agreeing to reduce their annual emissions of sulfur dioxide from 1980 levels by at least 30% by 1993. The United States and Great Britain refused to participate in this historic agreement, citing scientific uncertainty over the harmful effects of sulfur dioxide.

Control of Emissions of Nitrogen Oxides from Stationary Sources About half the emissions of nitrogen oxides in the United States come from the burning of fossil fuels at stationary sources, primarily electric power and industrial plants. The rest comes mostly from motor vehicles.

So far little emphasis has been placed on reducing emissions of nitrogen oxides from stationary sources because control of sulfur dioxide and particulates was considered more important. Now it is clear that nitrogen oxides are a major contributor to acid deposition and that they increase tropospheric levels of ozone and other photochemical oxidants that can damage crops, trees, and materials. The following approaches can be used to decrease emissions of nitrogen oxides from stationary sources:

Input Control Methods for Nitrogen Oxides

1. *Remove nitrogen oxides during fluidized-bed combustion* (Figure 7-28). Removes 50% to 75%.

2. *Remove during combustion by limestone injection multiple burning (LIMB).* Removes 50% to 60%.

3. *Reduce by decreasing combustion temperatures.* Well-established technology that reduces production of these gases by 50% to 60%.

Output Control Methods for Nitrogen Oxides

1. *Use tall smokestacks.*

2. *Add a tax for each unit emitted.*

3. *Remove after combustion by reburning.* Removes 50% or more but is still under development for large plants.

4. *Remove after burning by reacting with isocyanic acid (HCNO).* Removes up to 99% and breaks down into harmless nitrogen and water; will not be available commercially for at least ten years.

In 1988 representatives from 24 countries, including the United States, signed an agreement that would freeze emissions of nitrogen oxides at 1987 levels by 1995. Twelve West European countries agreed to cut emissions of nitrogen oxide by 30% between 1987 and 1997.

Control of Particulate Matter Emissions from Stationary Sources The only input control method for SPM is to convert coal to a gas or liquid, a method that is expensive and low in net energy yield. The following output approaches can be used to decrease emissions of SPM from stationary sources:

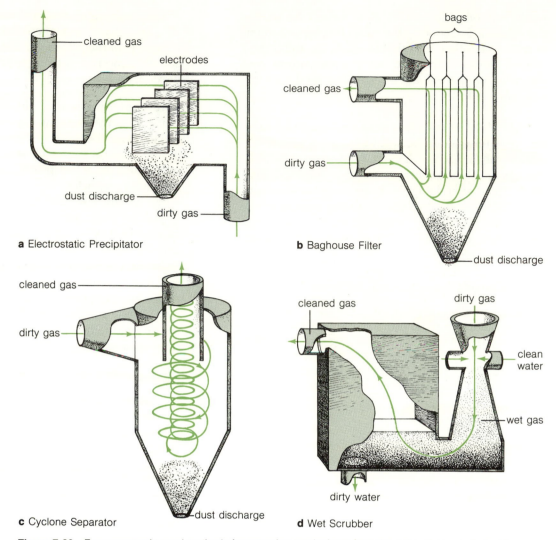

a Electrostatic Precipitator

b Baghouse Filter

c Cyclone Separator

d Wet Scrubber

Figure 7-29 Four commonly used methods for removing particulates from the exhaust gases of electric power and industrial plants. The wet scrubber is also used to reduce sulfur dioxide emissions.

SPM Output Control Methods

1. *Use tall smokestacks.*

2. *Add a tax on each unit emitted.*

3. *Remove particulates from stack exhaust gases.* The most widely used method in electric power and industrial plants. Several methods are in use: **(a)** electrostatic precipitators (Figures 7-29a and 7-30); **(b)** baghouse filters (Figure 7-29b); **(c)** cyclone separators (Figure 7-29c); and **(d)** wet scrubbers (Figure 7-29d). Except for baghouse filters, none of these methods removes many of the more hazardous fine particles; all produce hazardous solid waste or sludge that must be disposed of safely; except for cyclone separators, all methods are expensive.

Control of Emissions from Motor Vehicles   The following approaches can be used to decrease emissions of carbon monoxide, nitrogen oxides, SPM, and lead from motor vehicles:

Motor Vehicle Input Control Methods

1. *Rely more on mass transit, bicycles, and walking.*

2. *Shift to less-polluting automobile engines* such as steam or electric engines. Presently these engines are not as good as the internal combustion engine in performance, fuel economy, durability, and cost. Electric cars would increase use of electricity produced by coal-burning or nuclear power plants and trade one set of environmental hazards for another.

3. *Shift to less-polluting fuels* such as natural gas, alcohols, and hydrogen gas. Supplies of natural gas may be limited; alcohol is still too costly but may become competitive when oil prices rise; hydrogen gas has a negative net useful energy yield and requires greatly improved fuel cells.

4. *Improve fuel efficiency.* A quick and cost-effective approach. Present U.S. fuel-efficiency standards for new cars should be increased from 26.5 miles per gallon in 1988 to 40 miles per gallon by 2000.

Figure 7-30 The effectiveness of an electrostatic precipitator in reducing particulate emissions is shown by this stack, with the precipitator turned off (left) and with the precipitator operating.

5. *Modify the internal combustion engine to reduce emissions.* Burning gasoline using a lean, or more air-rich, mixture reduces carbon monoxide and hydrocarbon emissions but increases emissions of nitrogen oxides; a new lean-burn engine that reduces emissions of nitrogen oxides by 75% to 90% may be available in about ten years.

6. *Raise annual registration fees on older, more polluting cars or offer owners an incentive to retire such cars.*

7. *Add a charge on all new cars based on the amount of the three major pollutants emitted by the engine according to EPA tests.* This would prod manufacturers to reduce emissions and encourage consumers to buy less-polluting cars.

Motor Vehicle Output Control Methods

1. *Use emission control devices.* Most widely used approach; engines must be kept well tuned for such devices to work effectively; three-way catalytic converters now being developed can decrease pollutants by 90% to 95% and should be available within a few years.

2. *Require car inspections twice a year and have drivers exceeding the standards pay an emission charge based on the grams emitted per mile and the number of miles driven since the last inspection.* This would encourage drivers not to tamper with emission control devices and to keep them in good working order. About 48% of U.S. cars and light trucks have malfunctioning emissions equipment.

Control of Troposphere Ozone Levels Ozone levels in the troposphere are affected primarily by emissions of nitrogen oxides and hydrocarbons coupled with sunlight (Figure 7-13). Thus, decreasing ozone levels involves combining the input and output methods already discussed for nitrogen oxides and for motor vehicles.

It also involves decreasing hydrocarbon emissions. For cities with high ozone levels this requires control or relocation of petroleum refining, dry cleaning, auto painting, printing, baking and other industries that release large quantities of hydrocarbons. Also aerosol propellants, paints, household cleaners, and consumer products that release hydrocarbons would have to be banned or reformulated. Gas stations can be required to sell low-volatile fuel and to use a hydrocarbon vapor recovery system on gas pumps.

Trees in urban areas have a number of benefits, including helping control air pollution. But trees also emit hydrocarbons that are even more reactive than most of those emitted by human-related sources. In sunny southeastern cities with large areas of trees, emissions of hydrocarbons from vegetation may equal or exceed those from human sources. For example, about 60% of the Atlanta urban area is forested. In such areas the only way to reduce ozone levels is to sharply reduce emissions of nitrogen oxides.

Control of Indoor Air Pollution Despite the seriousness of indoor air pollution, Congress, the EPA, and state legislatures have been reluctant to establish mandatory indoor air quality standards. For most people, indoor air pollution poses a much greater threat to their health than outdoor air pollution. Yet, the EPA spends $200 million a year trying to reduce outdoor air pollution and only $2 million a year on indoor air pollution.

Part of the problem with monitoring and controlling indoor air pollution is that more than 100 million homes and buildings are involved. In addition, many home and building owners would resent having their indoor air tested. Many would also oppose being required to reduce excessive pollution levels, even if the indoor air were making them sick or threatening them and their families with premature death. Some couldn't afford to reduce the pollution. In the workplace, however, employers should be required to provide safe indoor air for employees.

One way to prevent buildup of most indoor air pollutants is to install air-to-air heat exchangers, which maintain a flow of fresh air without causing major heating or cooling losses. Indoor levels of formaldehyde and several other toxic gases can be sharply reduced by house plants such as the spider or airplane plant (the most effective), golden pathos, syngonium, and philodendron. Other remedies include changing air filters regularly and not storing gasoline, solvents, and other volatile hazardous chemicals inside a home or attached garage.

People building and remodeling homes should not use particleboard and plywood—found in roughly 80 million houses and mobile homes in the United States. These materials can emit high levels of formaldehyde for several months to several years. Consumers should not use room deodorizers and air fresheners, and they should properly dispose of or store partially used containers of paints, solvents, cleaners, cosmetics, and pesticides.

Smokers can reduce exposure to others by smoking outside or in a closed room vented to the outside. If many indoor pollution sources cannot be eliminated, whole-house electrostatic air cleaners and charcoal filters can be attached to central heating and air conditioning equipment. Humidifiers, however, can load indoor air with bacteria, mildew, and viruses.

What Needs to Be Done From this chapter's overview of the earth's air resources, we see that any human activities that affect the physical properties or chemical composition of the atmosphere can cause serious problems. Changes in the atmosphere can damage plants and animals and set into motion long-term changes in the earth's climate, food-growing areas, and average sea levels.

Many MDCs have made important progress in reducing atmospheric emissions of six major conventional outdoor pollutants. But MDCs and newly industrialized LDCs must make much greater reductions of these pollutants. And all industrial countries must sharply reduce emissions of CFCs, carbon dioxide, and hundreds of toxic compounds found in trace amounts in the atmosphere. We also need to put much greater emphasis on control of indoor air pollutants.

Changing our resource consumption patterns and environmental bad habits to prevent long-term climate changes and to make indoor and outdoor air healthier for people, other animals, and plants is one of the greatest political, economic, and ethical challenges we face!!

Are we really moving into a wonderland so magnificient that it is worth our destruction of the natural world? Is this the only way or the best way to survive, to provide food and shelter and clothing and energy we need? . . . . What have we gained? . . . . What benefit is worth giving up the purity of the air we breathe, the water we drink, the life-giving soil in which our food is grown?

Thomas Berry

DISCUSSION TOPICS

1. Rising oil and natural gas prices and environmental concerns over nuclear power plants could force the U.S. to depend more on coal, its most plentiful fossil fuel, for producing electric power. Comment on this in terms of air pollution. Would you favor a return to coal instead of increased use of nuclear power? Explain.

2. Evaluate the pros and cons of the statement, "Since we have not proven absolutely that anyone has died or suffered serious disease from nitrogen oxides, present federal emissions standards for this pollutant should be relaxed."

3. Should all uses of CFCs be banned in the U.S., including their use in refrigeration and air conditioning units? Explain.

4. Should MDCs set up a world food bank to store several years' supply of food to reduce the harmful effects of a loss in food production caused by a change in climate? How would you decide who gets this food in times of need?

5. What topographical and climate factors either increase or decrease air pollution in your community?

6. Do you favor or oppose requiring a 50% reduction in emissions of sulfur dioxide and nitrogen oxides by fossil-fuel-burning electric power and industrial plants and a 50% reduction in emissions of nitrogen oxides by motor vehicles in the U.S. over the next ten years? Explain.

7. Should all tall smokestacks be banned? Explain.

8. Do buildings in your college or university contain asbestos? If so, what is being done about this potential health hazard?

9. Should standards be set and enforced for most major indoor air pollutants? Explain.

FURTHER READINGS

Brouder, Paul. 1985. *Outrageous Misconduct: The Asbestos Industry on Trial.* New York: Pantheon Books.

Brown, Michael. 1987. *The Toxic Cloud.* New York: Harper & Row.

Cogan, Douglas G. 1988. *Stones in a Glass House.* Washington, D.C.: Investor Responsibility Research Center.

Cohen, Bernie. 1988. *Radon: A Homeowner's Guide to Detection and Control.* Mt. Vernon, N.Y.: Consumer Report Books.

Environmental Protection Agency. 1989. "The Greenhouse Effect: How It Can Change Our Lives." *EPA Journal,* Vol. 15, no. 1, 1–50.

Environmental Protection Agency. 1988. *The Potential Effects of Global Climate Change on the United States.* Washington, D.C.: Environmental Protection Agency.

Flavin, Christopher. 1988. "The Heat Is On." *World Watch,* Nov./Dec., 10–20.

Lafavore, Michael. 1987. *Radon: The Invisible Threat.* Emmaus, Penn.: Rodale.

Lovins, Amory B., et al. 1981. *Least-Cost Energy: Solving the CO_2 Problem.* Andover, Mass.: Brick House.

MacKenzie, James J., and Mohamed El-Ashry. 1988. *Ill Winds: Airborne Pollution's Toll on Trees and Crops.* Holmes, Penn.: World Resources Institute Publishing.

McKormick, John. 1985. *Acid Earth: The Global Threat of Acid Pollution.* Washington, D.C.: Earthscan.

Mello, Robert A. 1987. *Last Stand of the Red Spruce.* Covelo, Calif.: Island Press.

Mintzer, Irving M. 1987. *A Matter of Degrees: The Potential for Controlling the Greenhouse Effect.* Washington, D.C.: World Resources Institute.

Mohnen, Volker A. 1988. "The Challenge of Acid Rain." *Scientific American,* vol. 259, no. 2, 30–38.

National Academy of Sciences. 1983. *Changing Climate.* Washington, D.C.: National Academy Press.

National Academy of Sciences. 1986. *Acid Deposition: Long-Term Trends.* Washington, D.C.: National Academy Press.

Navara, John G. 1979. *Atmosphere, Weather, and Climate: An Introduction to Meteorology.* Philadelphia: Saunders.

Office of Technology Assessment. 1985. *Acid Rain and Transported Air Pollutants: Implications for Public Policy.* New York: Unipub.

Pawlick, Thomas. 1986. *A Killing Rain: The Global Threat of Acid Precipitation.* San Francisco: Sierra Club Books.

Postel, Sandra. 1984. *Air Pollution, Acid Rain, and the Future of Forests.* Washington, D.C.: Worldwatch Institute.

Postel, Sandra. 1986. *Altering the Earth's Chemistry: Assessing the Earth's Risks.* Washington, D.C.: Worldwatch Institute.

Shea, Cynthia Pollock. 1988. *Protecting Life on Earth: Steps to Save the Ozone Layer.* Washington, D.C.: Worldwatch Institute.

Turiel, Issac. 1985. *Indoor Air Quality and Human Health.* Stanford, Calif.: Stanford University Press.

Wark, K., and C. F. Warner. 1986. *Air Pollution: Its Origin and Control,* 3rd ed. New York: Harper & Row.

CHAPTER 8

Water Resources

General Questions and Issues

1. How much usable fresh water is available for human use and how much of this supply are we using?
2. What are the major water resource problems in the world and in the United States?
3. How can water resources be managed to increase the supply and reduce unnecessary waste?
4. What are the major types and sources of water pollutants?
5. What are the major pollution problems of rivers, lakes, oceans, and groundwater aquifers?
6. What legal and technological methods can be used to control water pollution?

If there is magic on this planet, it is in water.

Loren Eisley

W ater is our most abundant resource, covering about 71% of the earth's surface. This precious film of water—about 97% salt water and the remainder fresh—helps maintain the earth's climate and dilutes environmental pollutants. Essential to all life, water makes up 50% to 97% of the weight of all plants and animals and about 70% of your body. Water is also a vital resource for agriculture, manufacturing, transportation, and countless other human activities.

Because of differences in average annual precipitation, some areas of the world have too little fresh water and others too much. With varying degrees of success, we have attempted to correct some of these imbalances. We have captured fresh water in reservoirs behind dams, transferred fresh water in rivers and streams from one area to another, tapped underground supplies, and attempted to reduce water use, waste, and contamination.

Despite these efforts, water is one of the most poorly managed resources on earth. We waste it and pollute it. We also charge too little for making it available, thus encouraging even greater waste and pollution of this potentially renewable resource.

8-1 SUPPLY, RENEWAL, AND USE OF WATER RESOURCES

Worldwide Supply and Renewal The world's fixed supply of water in all forms (vapor, liquid, and solid) is enormous. If we could distribute it equally, every person on earth would have 74 billion gallons. However, about 97% of the earth's water is found in the oceans and is too salty for drinking, growing crops, and most industrial uses except cooling.

The remaining 3% is fresh water. However, all but 0.003% of this supply is highly polluted, lies too far under the earth's surface to be extracted at an affordable cost, or is locked up in glaciers, polar ice caps, atmosphere, and soil. To put this in measurements that we can understand, if the world's water supply were only 26 gallons (100 liters), our usable supply of fresh water would be only about one-half teaspoon (0.003 liter) (Figure 8-1).

That tiny fraction of usable fresh water still amounts to an average of 2.2 million gallons for each person on earth. This supply is continually collected, purified, and distributed in the natural *hydrologic (water) cycle*

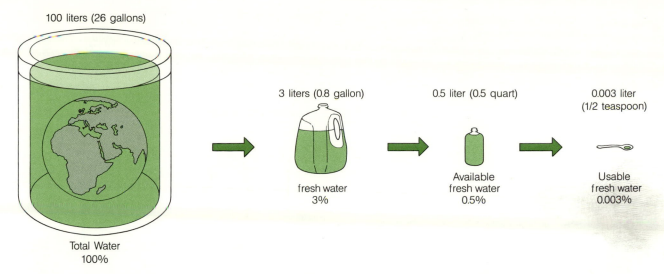

100 liters (26 gallons)

3 liters (0.8 gallon)

0.5 liter (0.5 quart)

0.003 liter
(1/2 teaspoon)

fresh water
3%

Available
fresh water
0.5%

Usable
fresh water
0.003%

Total Water
100%

Figure 8-1 Only a tiny fraction of the world's water supply is available as fresh water for human use.

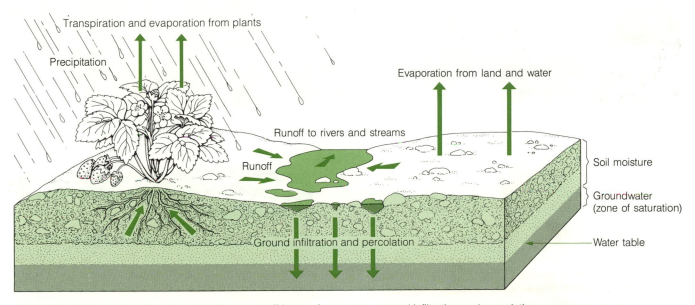

Transpiration and evaporation from plants

Precipitation

Evaporation from land and water

Runoff to rivers and streams

Runoff

Soil moisture

Groundwater
(zone of saturation)

Ground infiltration and percolation

Water table

Figure 8-2 Major routes of local precipitation as runoff into surface waters, ground infiltration and percolation into aquifers, and evaporation and transpiration into the atmosphere.

(Figure 5-20, p. 110). This natural recycling and purification process works as long as we don't pollute water faster than it is replenished or overload it with slowly degradable and nondegradable wastes.

Surface-Water Runoff The fresh water we use comes from two sources: groundwater and surface-water runoff (Figure 8-2). Precipitation that does not infiltrate into the ground or return to the atmosphere is called **surface water** and becomes **runoff**—fresh water that flows on the earth's surface into nearby streams, rivers, lakes, wetlands, and reservoirs. This flow of water is renewed every 12 to 20 days in areas with average precipitation. The land area that delivers run-off, sediment, and water-soluble substances to a major river and its tributaries is called a **watershed** or **drainage basin**.

Surface water can be withdrawn from streams, rivers, lakes, and reservoirs for human activities, but only part of the total annual runoff is available for use. Some of it flows in rivers to the sea too rapidly to be captured, and some must be left in streams for wildlife and to supply downstream areas. In some years the amount of runoff is reduced by below average precipitation.

Groundwater Some precipitation seeps into the ground. Some of this accumulates as **soil water** and

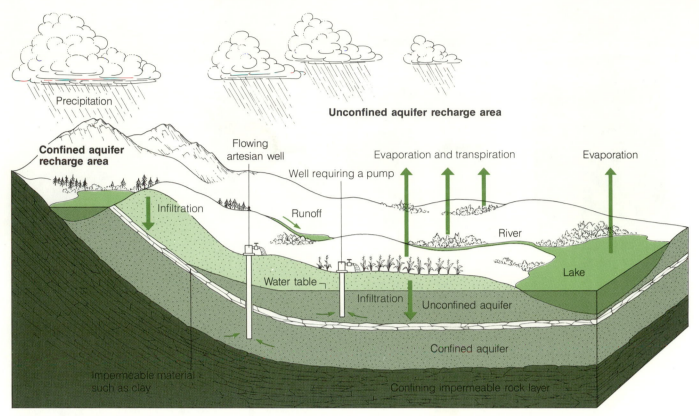

Figure 8-3 The groundwater system.

partially fills pores between soil particles and rocks within the upper soil and rock layers of the earth's crust (Figure 8-2). Most of this water is eventually lost to the atmosphere by evaporation from the upper layers of soil and transpiration from leaves.

Under the influence of gravity, some infiltrating water slowly percolates through porous materials deeper into the earth. There it fills pores and fractures in spongelike, or permeable, layers of sand, gravel, and porous rock such as sandstone. This area where all available pore spaces are filled by water is called the *zone of saturation*. These porous, water-bearing layers of underground rock are called **aquifers**, and the water in them is known as **groundwater** (Figure 8-3).

Aquifers are recharged or replenished naturally by precipitation, which percolates downward through soil and rock in what is called a **recharge area**. The recharge process is usually quite slow (decades to hundreds of years) compared to the rapid replenishment of surface water supplies. If the withdrawal rate of an aquifer exceeds its recharge rate, the aquifer is converted from a slowly renewable resource to a nonrenewable resource on a human time scale. This is called groundwater mining.

There are two types of aquifers: confined and unconfined. An **unconfined**, or **water-table, aquifer** forms when groundwater collects above a layer of impermeable rock or compacted clay. The top of the water-saturated portion of an unconfined aquifer is called the **water table** (Figures 8-2 and 8-3). Thus, groundwater is the part of underground water in the zone of saturation below the water table. Soil water is the part of underground water above the water table, sometimes called the *zone of aeration*. This water is found within the root zones of most plants. Shallow, unconfined aquifers are recharged by water percolating downward from soils and materials directly above the aquifer.

To get water from an unconfined aquifer, a water table well is drilled below the water table and into the unconfined aquifer. Then a pump must be used to bring water to the surface. The water table in an area rises during prolonged wet periods and falls during prolonged drought. The water table also falls when water is pumped out by wells faster than the natural rate of recharge, called overdrafting. This creates a waterless volume known as a *cone of depression* (Figure 8-4).

A **confined aquifer** forms when groundwater is sandwiched between two layers of impermeable rock, such as clay or shale (Figure 8-3). This type of aquifer is saturated with water under a pressure greater than that of the atmosphere. In some cases pressure from the weight of water higher in the aquifer is so great

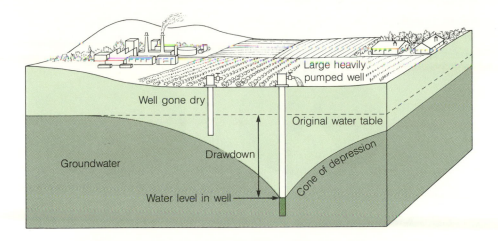

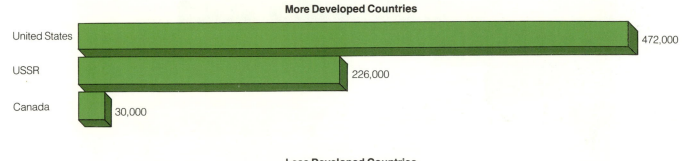

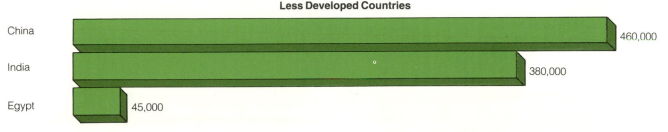

Figure 8-5 Total water withdrawal in selected countries in 1984 in billions of liters. (Data from Worldwatch Institute and World Resources Institute)

that when a well is drilled into the confined aquifer, water is pushed to the surface without the aid of a pump. Such a well is called a *flowing artesian well*.

With other confined-aquifer wells, called *nonflowing artesian wells*, pumps must be used because there isn't enough pressure to force the water all the way to the surface. Recharge areas for confined aquifers can be hundreds of miles away from wells where water is withdrawn. Thus, the rate of natural recharge for such aquifers is not based on local precipitation at the point of withdrawal as it is for unconfined aquifers. These aquifers are also polluted only in their recharge areas.

World and U.S. Water Use Two common measures of water use are withdrawal and consumption. **Water withdrawal** involves taking water from a groundwater or surface water source and transporting it to a place of use. **Water consumption** occurs when water that has been withdrawn is not available for reuse in the area from which it is withdrawn. Some seeps into the ground. Some evaporates into the atmosphere. Some becomes contaminated with salts dissolved from the soil.

Annual total water withdrawal and annual average water withdrawal per person vary considerably among various MDCs and LDCs (Figure 8-5). Worldwide, almost three-fourths of the water withdrawn each year is used for irrigation. The rest is used in industrial processing, in cooling electric power plants, and in homes and businesses (public use). However, the uses of withdrawn water vary widely from one country to another (Figure 8-6).

In the United States about three-fourths of the fresh water withdrawn each year comes from rivers, lakes, and reservoirs. The rest comes from groundwater aquifers. Almost 80% of the water withdrawn in the United States is used for cooling electric power plants and for irrigation. Producing food and manufacturing

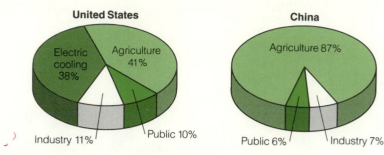

Figure 8-6 Use of water in the United States and China. (Data from Worldwatch Institute and World Resources Institute)

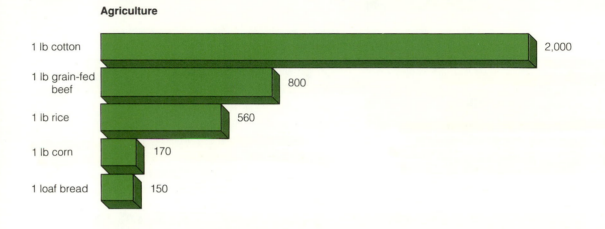

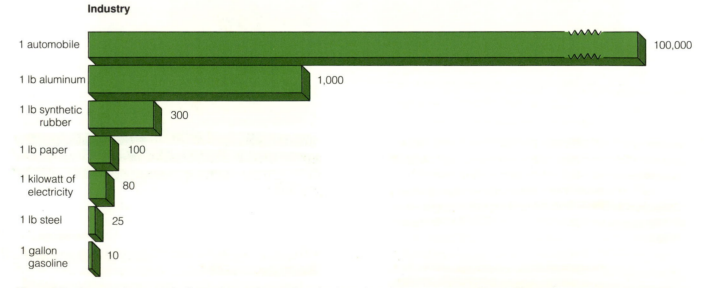

Figure 8-7 Amount of water typically used to produce various foods and products in the United States. (Data from U.S. Geological Survey)

various products require large amounts of water (Figure 8-7), although in most cases much of this water could be conserved and reused.

Since 1950 total water withdrawal in the United States has more than doubled. This increase was caused by increases in population, urbanization, and economic activity, and by government-subsidized, low water prices that discourage conservation and reuse. Each day water withdrawal used directly or indirectly averages 1,400 gallons per person. Average per capita use, however, ranges from 152 gallons per day in Rhode Island to 22,200 gallons per day in Idaho, where large amounts of water are used for irrigation.

About one-fourth of the water withdrawn in the

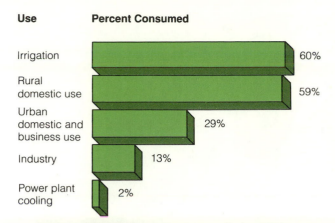

Use	Percent Consumed	
Irrigation		60%
Rural domestic use		59%
Urban domestic and business use		29%
Industry		13%
Power plant cooling		2%

Figure 8-8 Percentage of water consumed by different uses in the United States. (Data from U.S. Geological Survey)

United States is consumed. The other three-fourths returns to surface-water or groundwater supplies. Water consumption varies with different types of use (Figure 8-8). It also varies in different regions. For example, the average consumption rate per person in the mostly arid and semiarid West is ten times that in the East.

Worldwide, up to 90% of all water withdrawn from rivers and lakes is returned to them for potential reuse. However, about 75% of the water supplied for irrigation is consumed. Between 1985 and 2020 worldwide withdrawal of water for irrigation is projected to double, primarily because of increasing population in LDCs. Withdrawal for industrial processing and cooling electric power plants is projected to increase twentyfold because of increasing industrialization in LDCs. Withdrawal for public use in homes and businesses is expected to increase fivefold.

8-2 WATER RESOURCE PROBLEMS

Too Little Water A number of experts consider the availability of enough fresh water to meet human needs among the most serious long-range problems confronting many parts of the world and the United States. During the 1970s, major drought disasters affected an average of 24.4 million people and killed over 23,000 a year—a trend continuing in the 1980s. A drought occurs when an area does not get enough water because of lower than normal precipitation, higher than normal temperatures that increase evaporation, or both.

At least 80 arid and semiarid countries, where nearly 40% of the world's people live, have serious periodic droughts. These countries, mostly in Asia and Africa, have great difficulty growing enough food to support their populations. A prolonged drought affected much of Africa between 1982 and 1986 (Figure 8-9). It led to widespread starvation and disease and forced at least 10 million people to abandon their homes in a desperate search for food and water.

In many LDCs poor people must spend a good part of their waking hours fetching water, often from polluted streams and rivers. Many women and children walk 10 to 15 miles a day, carrying heavy, water-filled jars.

Reduced average annual precipitation, higher than normal temperatures, or both usually trigger a drought. But rapid population growth and poor land use intensify its effects. In many LDCs large numbers of poor people have no choice but to try to survive on drought-prone land. To get enough food and fuelwood, they strip the land of trees, cultivate poor soils, let their livestock overgraze grasslands, and grow crops at higher, more erosion-prone elevations. This land degradation increases the severity of long-term drought by reducing the amount of rainfall absorbed and slowly released by vegetation and soils.

In arid and semiarid parts of MDCs, where periodic drought is to be expected, networks of canals and tunnels are often used to withdraw water from rivers and transport it to urban and industrial areas. However, during a prolonged drought the flow of water in the rivers supplying these urban oases is sharply reduced. The resulting water supply crisis is often viewed as a natural disaster. But it is actually a human-caused disaster—the result of trying to support too many people in areas that normally have droughts.

Water scarcity is a source of conflict between countries, especially in the arid Middle East. Israel went to war in 1967 partly because Arabian countries were trying to divert surface water from the Jordan River. Part of the reason that Israel continues to occupy the Golan Heights and the West Bank is to ensure its access to water from this river.

Almost 150 of the world's 200 major river systems are shared by at least two countries. Together these countries contain 40% of the world's population, and they often clash over water rights. For example, India and Bangladesh dispute the water rights to the Ganges River, and India and Pakistan dispute water rights to the Indus River.

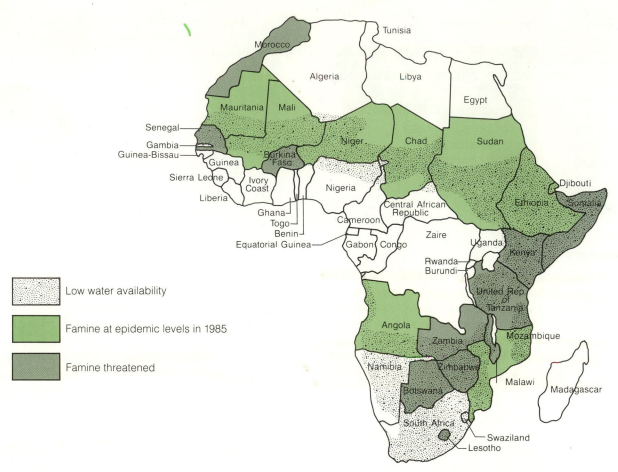

Figure 8-9 African countries suffering from low per capita food production, famine, and poor water availability. These conditions are caused by a combination of rapid population growth, prolonged drought, land misuse, war, and ineffective water and soil resource management. (Data from UN Food and Agriculture Organization)

Too Much Water Some countries have enough annual precipitation but get most of it at one time of the year. In India, for example, 90% of the annual precipitation falls between June and September—the monsoon season. This downpour runs off so rapidly that most of it cannot be captured and used. The massive runoff also causes periodic flooding.

During the 1970s, major flood disasters affected 15.4 million people, killed an average of 4,700 people a year, and caused tens of billions of dollars in property damages. This trend continued in the 1980s.

Floods, like droughts, are usually called natural disasters. But human activities have contributed to the sharp rise in flood deaths and damages since the 1960s. Cultivation of easily erodible land, deforestation, overgrazing, and mining have removed water-absorbing vegetation and soil (see Case Study on p. 189). Urbanization also increases flooding, even with moderate rainfall. It replaces vegetation and soil with highways, parking lots, shopping centers, office buildings, homes, and numerous other structures that lead to rapid runoff of rainwater.

Many poor people have little choice but to live on land subject to severe flooding. Many other people in LDCs and MDCs believe that the benefits of living in flood-prone areas outweigh the risks. Urban areas and croplands often are located on **floodplains**—flat areas along the banks of rivers naturally subject to periodic flooding. These usually are level areas with highly fertile topsoil deposited by the rivers. They are also close to water supplies and water transportation routes and are widely used for outdoor recreation.

Since 1925 the U.S. Army Corps of Engineers, the Soil Conservation Service, and the Bureau of Reclamation have spent more than $8 billion on flood control projects. They have straightened and deepened stream channels (stream channelization) and built dams, reservoirs, levees, and seawalls. These projects stimulate development on flood-prone land. As a result, property damage from floods in the United States has increased from about $0.5 billion a year in the 1960s to about $3 billion a year in the 1980s.

There are a number of effective ways to prevent or reduce flood damage. Vegetation can be replanted in disturbed areas to reduce runoff. In urban areas ponds can be built to retain rainwater and release it slowly to rivers. Rainwater can be diverted through storm sewers to holding tanks and ponds for use by industry.

Natural and Unnatural Flooding in Bangladesh

Bangladesh is one of the world's most densely populated countries. More than 110 million people—almost half the population of the United States—are packed into a country roughly the size of Wisconsin. It is also one of the world's poorest countries with an average per capita income of about $160.

The country is located on a vast, low-lying delta of shifting islands of silt at the mouths of the Ganges, Brahmaputra, and Meghna Rivers. Its people are accustomed to flooding after water deposited by annual monsoon rains in the Himalayan mountain ranges of India, Nepal, Bhutan, and Tibet flows downward through rivers to Bangladesh and into the Bay of Bengal.

Bangladesh depends on this annual flooding to grow rice, its major source of food. The annual deposit of silt in the delta basin also helps maintain soil fertility. Thus, the people of this country are used to moderate annual flooding and need it for their survival.

But massive flooding is disastrous. In the past, major floods occurred only once every fifty years or so. But since 1950 the number of large-scale floods has increased sharply. During the 1970s and 1980s the country has had major floods on average once every four years. After a flood in 1974, an estimated 300,000 people died in a famine.

In the 1980s floods have become even more severe. In 1988 a massive flood covered 80% of the country's land mass. At least 1,500 people were killed by drowning and snakebite and 30 million people—almost one out of four—were left homeless. Hundreds of thousands more contracted diseases such as cholera and typhoid fever from contaminated water and food supplies. Hundreds of thousands will probably die from famine, even with massive international aid.

We usually think of such floods as unpreventable natural disasters. But the increased severity of flooding in Bangladesh is primarily an unnatural disaster caused by human activities.

Bangladesh's flooding problems begin in the Himalayan watershed, where people depend on wood for fuel. There, a combination of rapid population growth, deforestation, overgrazing, and unsustainable farming on easily erodible steep mountain slopes have greatly diminished the ability of soil in this mountain watershed to absorb water. Instead of being absorbed and released slowly, water from the annual monsoon rain runs off mountainsides rapidly. Then heavier than normal monsoon rains cause massive flooding in Bangladesh. This deluge of water also carries with it the unprotected soil vital to the survival of people in the Himalayas.

Floodplains should be clearly identified, and zoning regulations should prohibit their use for certain types of development. Sellers of property in these areas should be required to provide prospective buyers with information about average flood frequency. In the United States floodplain zoning is now a national policy.

Water in the Wrong Place   In some countries the largest rivers, which carry most of the runoff, are far from agricultural and population centers where the water is needed. South America has the largest average annual runoff of any continent. But 60% of this runoff flows through the Amazon—the world's largest river—in areas far from where most people live.

Contaminated Drinking Water   Drinking contaminated water is the most common hazard to people in much of the world. In 1983 the World Health Organization estimated that in LDCs 61% of the people living in rural areas and 26% of the urban dwellers did not have access to safe drinking water (Figure 8-10). WHO estimated that at least 5 million people die every year from cholera, dysentery, diarrhea, and

United Nations

Figure 8-10   About two out of three rural people and one out of four city dwellers in LDCs lack ready access to uncontaminated water. These children in Lima, Peru, are scooping up drinking water from a puddle.

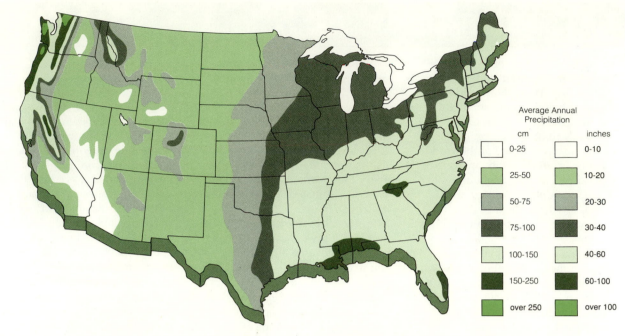

Figure 8-11 Average annual precipitation in the continental United States. (Data from Water Resources Council)

Average Annual Precipitation

cm	inches
0-25	0-10
25-50	10-20
50-75	20-30
75-100	30-40
100-150	40-60
150-250	60-100
over 250	over 100

other preventable waterborne diseases. Every day these diseases prematurely kill an average of 13,700 people. Most of these deaths could be prevented at little cost.

In 1980 the United Nations proclaimed this the International Drinking Water Supply and Sanitation Decade. UN officials called for MDCs and LDCs to spend $300 billion over ten years to supply all the world's people with clean drinking water and adequate sanitation by 1990. The $30-billion-a-year cost of this program would be roughly equal to what the world spends every ten days for military purposes. Some progress has been made. But by 1988 the program had fallen far short of its goal because of lack of funding and lack of commitment by MDCs and LDCs.

The U.S. Situation Overall, the United States has plenty of fresh water. But much of the country's annual runoff is not in the desired place, occurs at the wrong time, or is contaminated from agricultural and industrial activities. Average annual precipitation throughout the United States varies widely. Most of the eastern half of the country usually has ample precipitation, while much of the western half has too little (Figure 8-11).

Many major urban centers in the United States are located in areas that don't have enough water or are projected to have water shortages by 2000 (Figure 8-12). Because water is such a vital resource, you might find Figure 8-12 useful in deciding where to live in coming decades. Several of the fastest growing states, especially California and Arizona, have severe periodic water shortages.

In many parts of the eastern United States the major water problems are flooding, inability to supply enough water to some large urban areas, and increasing pollution of rivers, lakes, and groundwater. For example, 3 million residents of Long Island, New York, must draw all their water from an underground aquifer. This aquifer is becoming severely contaminated by industrial wastes, leaking septic tanks and landfills, and ocean salt water, which is drawn into the aquifer when fresh water is withdrawn faster than it is replaced by natural recharge.

The major water problem in arid and semiarid areas in the western half of the country is a shortage of runoff. This is caused by low and variable average annual precipitation, high rates of evaporation, prolonged periodic drought, and rapidly dropping water tables as farmers and cities deplete groundwater aquifers faster than they are recharged.

Because most areas in the region have too little precipitation to grow crops without irrigation, 85% of the western water supply is used in agriculture. Federally subsidized dams, reservoirs, and water transfer projects provide water to farms and cities at such low prices that there is little incentive for conservation. Experts project that present water shortages and conflicts over water supplies will get much worse as more industries and people migrate west and compete with farmers for scarce water.

8-3 WATER RESOURCE MANAGEMENT

Methods for Managing Water Resources Although we can't increase the earth's supply of water, we can

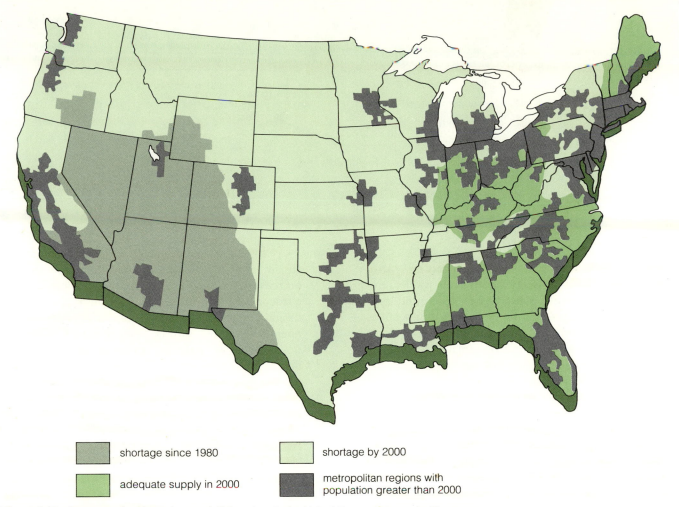

▨ shortage since 1980	▨ shortage by 2000
▨ adequate supply in 2000	▨ metropolitan regions with population greater than 2000

Figure 8-12 Present and projected water deficit regions in the United States compared with present metropolitan regions with populations greater than 1 million. (Data from U.S. Water Resources Council and U.S. Geological Survey)

manage what we have better to reduce the impact and spread of water resource problems. The two general approaches to water resource management are to increase the usable supply and to decrease unnecessary loss and waste (Table 8-1). Most water resource experts believe that any effective plan for water management should combine these approaches.

Water problems and available solutions often differ between MDCs and LDCs. LDCs may or may not have enough water, but they rarely have the money needed to develop water storage and distribution systems. Their people must settle where the water is.

In MDCs people tend to live where the climate is favorable and then bring in water through expensive water diversion systems. Some settle in a desert and expect water to be brought to them at a low price.

Others settle on a floodplain and expect the government to keep flood waters away.

Constructing Dams and Reservoirs Rainwater and water from melting snow that would otherwise be lost can be captured and stored in large reservoirs behind dams built across rivers (Figure 6-10, p. 130). Damming increases the annual supply by collecting fresh surface water during wet periods and storing it for use during dry periods.

By controlling river flow, dams reduce the danger of flooding in downstream areas and allow people to live on the fertile floodplains of major rivers below the dam. They also provide a controllable supply of water for irrigating arid and semiarid land below the dam. Hydroelectric power plants, which use the energy of

Table 8-1	Methods for Managing Water Resources
Increase the Supply	**Reduce Unnecessary Loss and Waste**
Build dams and reservoirs	Decrease evaporation of irrigation water
Divert water from one region to another	Redesign mining and industrial processes to use less water
Tap more groundwater	Encourage the public to reduce unnecessary water waste and use
Convert salt water to fresh water (desalinization)	Increase the price of water to encourage water conservation
Tow freshwater icebergs from the Antarctic to water-short coastal regions	Purify polluted water for reuse
Seed clouds to increase precipitation	

water flowing from dam reservoirs, generate more than 20% of the world's electricity, This is a renewable, non-polluting source of electricity. Reservoirs behind large dams can also be used for outdoor recreation such as swimming, boating, and fishing. Dams may also give developers and residents in a floodplain a false sense of safety from major floods that can overwhelm the ability of a dam to control flood waters.

But the benefits of dams and reservoirs must be weighed against their costs (see Case Study on p. 193). They are expensive to build. The reservoirs fill up with silt and become useless in 20 to 200 years, depending on local climate and land-use practices. The permanent flooding of land behind dams to form reservoirs displaces people and destroys vast areas of valuable agricultural land, wildlife habitat, white-water rapids, and scenic natural beauty. Millions of people have been uprooted to make way for the world's more than 13,000 dams of more than 50 feet in height. China's massive Three Gorges Dam project will submerge ten cities and partially flood another eight. Over 3.3 million people will have to be resettled.

The storage of water behind a dam also raises the water table. The higher water table often waterlogs the soil on nearby land, decreasing its crop or forest productivity. A dam can decrease rather than increase the available supply of fresh water, especially in semiarid areas. This happens because water that would normally flow in an undammed river evaporates from the reservoir's surface or seeps into the ground below the reservoir. Evaporation also increases the salinity of reservoir water by leaving salts behind, decreasing its usefulness for irrigation. The sheer weight of the water impounded in reservoirs can contribute to earthquakes by increasing the likelihood of fault movements.

By interrupting the natural flow of a river, a dam disrupts the migration and spawning of some fish, such as salmon. Dams have been a major factor in the 90% drop in the salmon population in the northwestern United States. By trapping silt that would normally be carried downstream, dams deprive down-stream areas and estuaries of vital nutrients and decrease their productivity. In the opinion of some outdoor sports enthusiasts, a dam replaces more desirable forms of water recreation (white-water canoeing, kayaking, rafting, stream fishing) with less desirable, more "artificial" forms (motorboating, sailboating, lake fishing).

In rural areas of some LDCs, dams reduce the natural flow of water that sweeps away snails carrying tiny worms that can infect people with schistosomiasis. This, painful, incurable, and often fatal disease affects 200 million people around the world. It makes people too weak to work and kills about 800,000 people a year. After decades of research, scientists have yet to develop a vaccine to prevent this disease. Mosquitoes carrying malaria also thrive in the newly irrigated areas below dams.

Faulty construction, earthquakes, sabotage, or war can cause dams to fail, taking a terrible toll in lives and property. In 1972 a dam failure in Buffalo Creek, West Virginia, killed 125 people. Another in Rapid City, South Dakota, killed 237 and caused more than $1 billion in damages. According to a 1986 study by the Federal Emergency Management Agency, the United States has 1,900 unsafe dams in populated areas. The agency reported that the dam safety programs of most states are inadequate because of weak laws and budget cuts.

Water Diversion Projects In MDCs local governments often increase the supply of fresh water in water-poor populated areas by transferring it from water-rich areas. One such project in the United States is the California Water Plan. It transports water from water-rich parts of northern California to heavily populated parts of northern California and to mostly arid and semiarid, heavily populated southern California (Figure 8-13).

Although several large urban areas use lots of water, about 80% of the water withdrawn in California is used by agriculture throughout the state. The major farm-

The billion-dollar Aswan High Dam on the Nile River in Egypt shows what can happen when a large-scale dam and reservoir project is built without adequate consideration of long-term environmental effects and costs. The 369-foot-high, 2-mile-long dam was built in the 1960s to provide flood control and irrigation water for the lower Nile basin and electricity for Cairo and other parts of Egypt. This water was badly needed because only 5% of Egypt is arable land. The rest is desert.

These goals have been partially achieved. Today the dam supplies about one-third of Egypt's electrical power. This is down from the 53% supplied in 1974 because of increased demand for electricity. The dam saved Egypt's rice and cotton crops during the droughts of 1972 and 1973. Year-round irrigation has increased food production. It allows farmers below the dam to harvest crops three times a year on land that was previously harvested only once a year. Irrigation has also brought about 1 million acres of desert land under cultivation.

Since the dam opened in 1964, it has had a number of undesirable ecological effects. The dam ended the yearly flooding that had fertilized the Nile basin with silt, flushed mineral salts from the soil, and swept away snails that can infect humans with schistosomiasis—a disease that causes pain, weakness, and premature death. Cropland in the Nile basin now has to be treated with commercial fertilizer at a cost of over $100 million a year to make up for plant nutrients once available at no cost. The country's new fertilizer plants use up much of the electrical power produced by the dam.

Salts have built up in the soil of this once-productive cropland. This salinization has offset three-fourths of the gain in food production from new, less productive land irrigated by water from the reservoir. Today 90% of the irrigated land in Egypt is affected by salinization.

Since the dam opened, cases of schistosomiasis among farmers wading in irrigation ditches has risen somewhat but not as much as expected because of increased education and sanitation measures.

The dam was expected to increase the amount of cropland. However, because of rapid population growth, the country now has less arable land than when the dam was built. Urbanization has taken over much of Egypt's short supply of arable land.

Because of a drop in sediment, the clearer river has eroded its bed and undermined numerous bridges and smaller dams downstream. To remedy this problem, the government proposes to build ten barrier dams. The projected cost is $250 million—one-fourth of what the dam cost. Also, without the Nile's annual discharge of sediment, the sea is eroding the delta and advancing inland, reducing productivity on many acres of agricultural land.

Now that the nutrient-rich silt no longer reaches the waters at the river's mouth, Egypt's sardine, mackerel, shrimp, and lobster industries have all but disappeared. This has led to losses of approximately 30,000 jobs, millions of dollars annually, and an important source of protein for Egyptians. Eventually, these losses are expected to be replaced by a new fishing industry based on taking bass, catfish, and carp from the massive reservoir, called Lake Nasser, behind the dam.

The reservoir uprooted 125,000 people. It was supposed to be full by 1970 and to have enough water to meet the needs of Egypt and the Sudan during a prolonged drought. But seepage of water into the underlying sandstone and evaporation have been much greater than projected. Today the reservoir is only about half full. Most authorities believe that the level will not rise much more in the next 100 years.

Excessive siltation due to high rates of soil erosion from deforested highlands supplying water to the Nile River is filling the reservoir and cutting the dam's projected lifespan in half. In 1981 the area around the dam suffered a fairly severe earthquake, despite being a low-risk area. Scientists believe the quake was triggered by the weight of the water in Lake Nasser.

Some analysts believe that in the long run the benefits of the Aswan Dam will outweigh its costs. Others consider it an economic, ecological, and hydrological disaster.

---

ing region is the Central Valley, made up of the Sacramento and San Joaquin valleys in the northern and central parts of the state. This area receives too little precipitation for most crops to be grown without irrigation.

For decades, northern and southern Californians have been feuding over how the state's water should be allocated under the California Water Plan. In 1982 voters rejected a proposal to expand the system by building a $1 billion canal to divert to southern California much of the water that now flows into San Francisco Bay.

Opponents of this proposal called it a costly and unnecessary boondoggle that would degrade the Sacramento River, threaten fishing, and reduce the flushing action that helps clean San Francisco Bay of pollutants. They also argued that much of the water already sent south is wasted and that an increase of only 10%

Figure 8-13 California Water Plan and Central Arizona Project for large-scale transfer of water from one area to another. Arrows show general direction of water flow.

in irrigation efficiency would provide enough water for domestic and industrial uses in southern California. Supporters of the expansion contended that without more water a prolonged drought would bring economic ruin to much of southern California. The issue of how water should be allocated in California is far from dead.

A related project is the federally financed $3.9 billion Central Arizona Project. It began pumping water from the Colorado River uphill to Phoenix in 1985 and is expected to deliver water to Tucson by 1991 (Figure 8-13). When the first part of this project was completed in 1985, southern California, especially the arid and booming San Diego region, began losing up to one-fifth of its water. Until then this water had been diverted from the Colorado River to southern California by the Colorado River Aqueduct.

Since 1922 Arizona has been legally entitled to one-fifth of the Colorado River's annual flow. However, until the Central Arizona Project was in place, the state had no way to get more than half its share. The surface water diverted from the Colorado will partially replace groundwater overdrafts that have led to falling water tables in many parts of Arizona during the past 50 years.

Tucson, for example, is the largest city in the United States that relies entirely on groundwater. Each year it pumps five times as much water out of the ground as nature puts back in. Yet its population continues to grow at a rapid rate. Without the Central Arizona Project the aquifers supplying Tucson with water would be exhausted within 100 years.

Another example of large-scale water diversion is in Soviet Central Asia, where so much water has been diverted from the Aral Sea for irrigation that the lake bed has dried up. Now massive amounts of salt and sand are blown into the air by winds, disrupting agriculture as far away as India. According to Soviet scientists, this project may be one of the world's greatest human-caused ecological disasters.

Tapping Groundwater Another solution to water supply problems is to rely on groundwater. In the United States about half of the drinking water (96% in rural areas and 20% in urban areas), 40% of the irrigation water, and 23% of all fresh water used is withdrawn from underground aquifers.

Overuse of groundwater, however, can cause or intensify several problems: aquifer depletion, subsidence (sinking of land when groundwater is withdrawn), intrusion of salt water into aquifers, and groundwater contamination (Figure 8-14). Aquifer depletion occurs when groundwater is withdrawn faster than it is recharged by precipitation. Currently, about one-fourth of the groundwater withdrawn in the United States is not replenished. In the arid and semiarid Texas Gulf region up to 77% of the groundwater withdrawn is not replenished. The major groundwater overdraft problem is in parts of the huge Ogallala Aquifer, extending under the farm belt from northern Nebraska to northwestern Texas (see Case Study on p. 196).

Groundwater levels often can recover when withdrawals are reduced. For example, replacement of groundwater with imported surface water in the Mendota area of California's Central Valley allowed groundwater levels to rise 850 feet between 1968 and 1983.

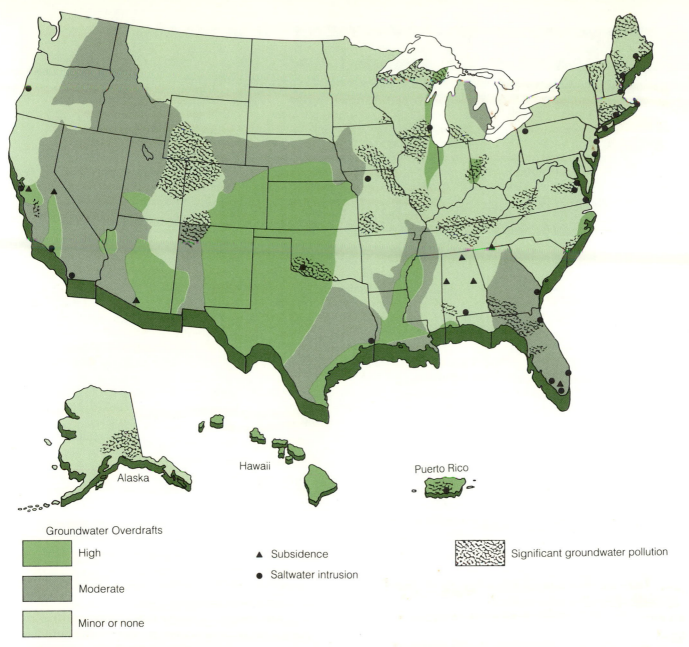

Groundwater Overdrafts

High

Moderate

Minor or none

▲ Subsidence

● Saltwater intrusion

Significant groundwater pollution

Figure 8-14 Major areas of aquifer depletion, subsidence, saltwater intrusion, and groundwater contamination in the United States. (Data from U.S. Water Resources Council and U.S. Geological Survey)

Aquifer depletion is also a serious problem in northern China, Mexico City, and parts of India. The most effective solution is to reduce the amount of groundwater withdrawn by wasting less irrigation water and by not growing crops in arid and semiarid areas.

When groundwater in an unconfined aquifer is withdrawn faster than it is replenished, the soil becomes compacted and the land overlying the aquifer sinks, or subsides. Widespread subsidence in the San Joaquin Valley of California has damaged houses, factories, pipelines, highways, and railroad beds. Some areas have sunk almost 30 feet. Shanghai, China, has sunk almost 9 feet.

When fresh water is withdrawn from an aquifer near a coast or an inland deposit of saline water faster

than it is recharged, salt water intrudes into the aquifer (Figure 8-16). *Saltwater intrusion* threatens to contaminate the drinking water of many towns and cities along the Atlantic and Gulf coasts (Figure 8-14) and in the coastal areas of Israel, Syria, and the Arabian Gulf states. Another growing problem in the United States and many other MDCs is groundwater contamination from agricultural and industrial activities, septic tanks, underground injection wells, and other sources, as discussed in Section 8-5.

Desalination Removing dissolved salts from ocean water or brackish (slightly salty) groundwater is an appealing way to increase freshwater supplies because of the huge volume of sea water adjacent to coastal

Water withdrawn from the vast Ogallala Aquifer (Figure 8-15) is used to irrigate one-fifth of all U.S. cropland in an area too dry for rainfall farming. It supports $32 billion of agricultural production a year—mostly wheat, sorghum, cotton, corn, and 40% of the country's grain-fed beef cattle.

The Ogallala Aquifer contains a massive amount of water. However, it has an extremely low natural recharge rate because it underlies a region with fairly low average annual precipitation (Figure 8-11). Today the overall rate of withdrawal from this aquifer is eight times faster than its natural recharge rate. Even higher withdrawal rates, sometimes 100 times the recharge rate, are taking place in parts of the aquifer that lie beneath Texas, New Mexico, Oklahoma, and Colorado.

Water resource experts project that at the present rate of withdrawal, much of this aquifer will be dry by 2020, and much sooner in areas where it is only a few yards deep. Long before this happens, however, the high energy cost of pumping water from rapidly dropping water tables will force many farmers to grow crops that need much less water such as wheat and cotton instead of profitable but thirsty crops such as corn and sugar beets. Some farmers will have to go out of business.

The amount of irrigated land already is declining in five of the seven states using this aquifer because of the high energy cost of pumping water from depths as great as 6,000 feet. If farmers in the Ogallala region began using water conservation measures and switched to crops with low water needs, depletion of the aquifer would be delayed—but not prevented in the long run. Unfortunately, the tragedy of the commons shows us that most farmers are likely to continue withdrawing as much water as possible from this shared resource to increase short-term profits.

To prevent depletion of the Ogallala Aquifer and still allow the growing of crops, some people have called for diversion of surface water from the Great Lakes. But this could lower water levels in the lakes and reduce their usefulness for nearby heavily populated urban areas. What do you think should be done?

Figure 8-15 Ogallala Aquifer.

---

cities. Distillation and reverse osmosis are the two most widely used desalination methods. Two other methods are to freeze salt water or to pass electric current through it.

Distillation involves heating salt water until it evaporates and condenses as fresh water, leaving salts behind in solid form. In *reverse osmosis*, high pressure is used to force salt water through a thin membrane whose pores allow water molecules but not dissolved salts to pass through. Desalination plants in arid parts of the Middle East and North Africa produce about two-thirds of the world's desalinated water.

The basic problem with all desalination methods is that they use large amounts of energy and therefore are expensive. Desalination can provide fresh water for coastal cities in arid regions, where the cost of getting fresh water by any method is high. But desalinated water will probably never be cheap enough to irrigate conventional crops or to meet much of the world's demand for fresh water. It might be useful, however, for irrigating new genetically engineered strains of crop plants that can grow in partially salty water.

Another problem is that even more energy and money would be needed to pump desalinated water uphill and inland from coastal desalination plants. Also, a vast network of desalination plants would produce mountains of salt to be disposed of. The easiest and cheapest solution would be to dump the salt in the ocean near the plants. But this would increase the salt concentration in seawater near the coasts, threatening food resources in estuarine waters.

Cloud Seeding Several countries, particularly the United States, have been experimenting for years with seeding clouds with chemicals to produce more rain over dry regions and snowpack over mountains. Cloud seeding involves finding a large, suitable cloud and injecting it with a powdered chemical such as silver iodide from a plane or from ground-mounted burners. Small water droplets in the cloud clump together around tiny particles of the chemical and form drops or ice particles large enough to fall to the earth as precipitation.

Cloud seeding, however, is not useful in very dry areas, where it is most needed, because rain clouds

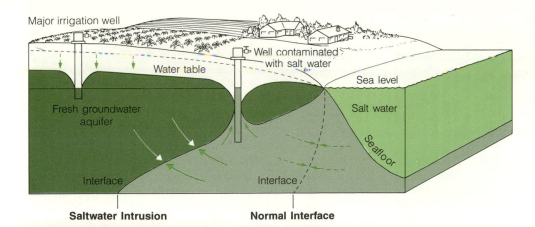

Figure 8-16 Saltwater intrusion along a coastal region. When the water table is lowered from over-pumping, the normal interface (dotted line) between fresh and saline groundwater moves inland (solid line).

are rarely available. Large-scale use could also change snowfall and rainfall patterns and alter regional or even global climate patterns in unknown and perhaps undesirable ways. And widespread cloud seeding would introduce large amounts of silver iodide into soil and water systems, possibly with harmful effects on people, wildlife, and agricultural productivity.

Another obstacle to cloud seeding is legal disputes over the ownership of water in clouds. For example, during the 1977 drought in the western United States, the attorney general of Idaho accused officials in neighboring Washington of "cloud rustling" and threatened to file suit in federal court.

Unnecessary Water Waste *An estimated 30% to 50% of the water used in the United States is unnecessarily wasted.* This explains why many water resource experts consider water conservation the quickest and cheapest way to provide much of the additional water needed in dry areas.

A major cause of water waste in the United States is that elected officials have kept water prices artificially low, hoping to stimulate economic growth and get reelected by keeping consumers happy. Until the late 1970s, federal funds were used to build large dams and water transfer projects, especially in the arid and semiarid West. These subsidized projects provide low-cost water for farms, industries, and homes. Outdated laws governing the use of water resources also encourage unnecessary water waste (see Spotlight on p. 198).

Low-cost water is the only reason that farmers in Arizona can grow water-thirsty crops like alfalfa in the middle of the desert. It also allows people in Palm Springs, California, to keep their lawns and 74 golf courses green.

However, there is no free lunch. Water subsidies are paid for by all taxpayers in the form of higher taxes. Because these indirect costs don't show up on monthly water bills, consumers have little incentive to conserve. Raising the price of water to reflect its true cost would provide powerful incentives for water conservation.

Another reason that water waste in the United States is greater than necessary is that the responsibility for water resource management in a particular water basin is divided among many state and local governments rather than being handled by one authority. For example, the Chicago metropolitan area has 349 separate water supply systems, divided among some 2,000 local units of government over a six-county area.

In sharp contrast is the regional approach to water management used in England and Wales. The British Water Act of 1973 replaced more than 1,600 separate agencies with 10 regional water authorities based on natural watershed boundaries. In this successful approach, each water authority owns, finances, and manages all water supply and waste treatment facilities in its region. The responsibilities of each authority include water pollution control, water-based recreation, land drainage and flood control, inland navigation, and inland fisheries. Each water authority is managed by a group of elected local officials and a smaller number of officials appointed by the national government.

Reducing Irrigation Losses Since irrigation accounts for the largest fraction of water use and waste, more efficient use of even a small amount of irrigation water frees water for other uses. Most irrigation systems distribute water from a groundwater well or a surface canal by gravity flow through unlined field ditches (Figure 8-17). This method is cheap as long as farmers in water-short areas don't have to pay the real cost of making this water available. But it provides far more water than needed for crop growth, and at least 50% of the water is lost by evaporation and seepage. Farmers could prevent seepage by placing plastic, concrete, or tile liners in irrigation canals. But as long as federally subsidized water is available at low cost, they have little incentive to conserve it or to switch to crops that need less water.

Figure 8-17 Gravity flow systems like this one in California's San Joaquin Valley irrigate most of the world's irrigated cropland. About half the water applied is consumed by seepage and evaporation.

U.S. Bureau of Reclamation/J. C. Dahilig

Many farmers served by the dwindling Ogallala Aquifer have switched from gravity flow canal systems to center-pivot sprinkler systems (Figure 8-19), which reduce water waste from 50% or more to 30%. Some farmers are switching to new, precision-application sprinkler systems, which spray water downward, closer to crops, rather than high into the air. These systems cut water waste by 2% to 5% and energy use by 20% to 30%.

In the 1960s highly efficient trickle or drip irrigation systems were developed in arid Israel. A network of perforated piping, installed at or below the ground surface, releases a small volume of water and fertilizer close to the roots of plants, minimizing evaporation and seepage. These systems are expensive to install but are economically feasible for high-profit fruit, vegetable, and orchard crops. But as long as western U.S.

SPOTLIGHT Water Rights in the United States

Laws regulating water access and use differ in the eastern and western parts of the United States (Figure 8-18). In most of the East water use is based on the doctrine of **riparian rights**. Basically this system of water law gives anyone whose land adjoins a flowing stream the right to use water from the stream as long as some is left for downstream landowners.

This approach works well in regions where there are numerous surface streams and rivers with reliable supplies of water. However, as population and water-intensive land uses grow, there is often not enough water to meet the needs of all the people along a stream.

In the arid and semiarid West the riparian system does not work because large amounts of water are needed in areas far from major surface water sources. In most of the West the principle of **prior appropriation** regulates water use. In this first-come-first-served approach, the first user of water from a stream establishes a legal right for continued use of the amount originally withdrawn. Some areas of the United States have a combination of riparian and prior appropriation water rights (Figure 8-18).

One problem with the prior appropriation system is that later water users consider it unfair because they have little access to the resource, especially during droughts. Another problem is that it causes unnecessary use and waste. To hold on to their rights, users must keep on withdrawing and using a certain amount of water even if they don't need it— a use-it-or-lose-it approach.

Different laws also apply to the allocation of groundwater resources. Most groundwater use is based on common law that holds that subsurface water belongs to whoever owns the land above such water. This means that landowners can withdraw as much as they want to use on their land.

When many users tap the same aquifer, that aquifer becomes a common property resource. The multiple users remove water at a faster rate than it is replaced by natural recharge. The largest users have little incentive to conserve. Large withdrawals by a few users deplete supplies for other users. This has led to legal disputes over groundwater rights. In recent years courts in some areas have tended to restrict massive withdrawals by a few users and have distributed groundwater supplies among various landowners using the same aquifer.

Conservationists and many economists call for a change in laws allocating rights to surface and groundwater supplies. They believe that farmers and other users should be free to sell or lease their water rights. Profit motives would then raise the price of scarce water and provide a powerful incentive for water conservation. In parts of Arizona such buying and selling of water rights has made some farmers rich, raised water prices, encouraged conservation, and made more water available for cities and industries.

Conservationists also propose that users of water provided by federal and state projects be charged a much higher price for this water. In addition to a higher base price per gallon, charges should rise sharply with the amount of water used.

There are several other unresolved issues about water rights: How should the true value of water be determined? Who should decide what is the best use of available water? Who should decide how water should be distributed among competing interests such as farmers and urban dwellers?

farmers can get water at an abnormally low cost, they don't find it profitable to invest in drip irrigation systems.

Irrigation efficiency can also be improved by computer-controlled systems that set water flow rates, detect leaks, and adjust the amount of water to soil moisture and weather conditions. Farmers can switch to new, hybrid crop varieties that need less water or that tolerate irrigation with saline water. Since 1950, Israel has used many of these techniques to decrease waste of irrigation water by about 84%, while expanding the country's irrigated land by 44%.

Wasting Less Water in Industry Most manufacturing processes can use recycled water or can be redesigned to use and waste less water. For example, depending on the process used, manufacturing a ton of steel can use as much as 52,800 gallons or as little as 1,320 gallons of water. To produce a ton of paper, a paper mill in Hadera, Israel, uses one-tenth as much water as most paper mills. Manufacturing a ton of aluminum from recycled scrap rather than virgin ores can reduce water needs by 97% percent.

Industry is the largest conserver of water. But the potential for water recycling in U.S. manufacturing industries has hardly been tapped because much of the cost of water to many industries is subsidized by taxpayers through federally financed water projects. Thus, industries have little incentive to recycle water, which typically accounts for only about 3% of total manufacturing costs. A higher, more realistic price would greatly stimulate water reuse and conservation in industry.

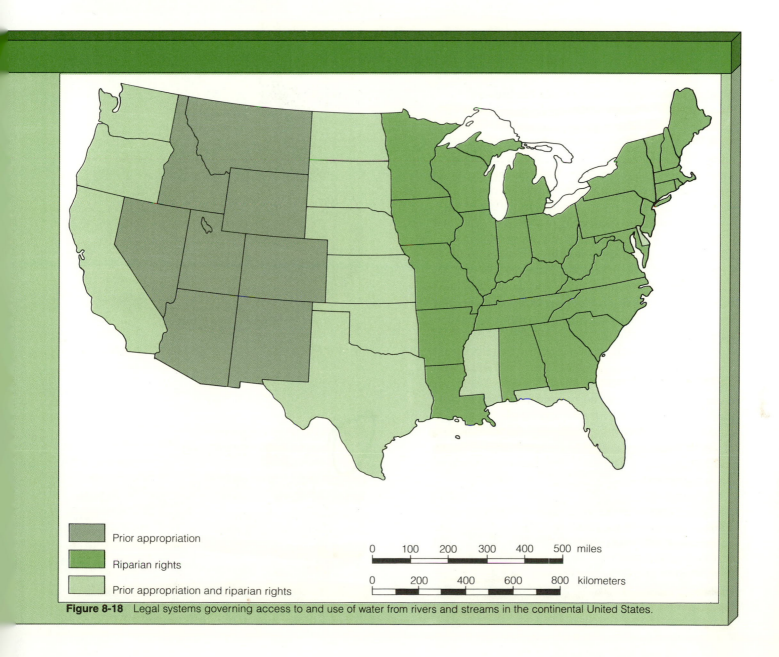

Prior appropriation

Riparian rights

Prior appropriation and riparian rights

0 100 200 300 400 500 miles

0 200 400 600 800 kilometers

Figure 8-18 Legal systems governing access to and use of water from rivers and streams in the continental United States.

Figure 8-19 Center-pivot irrigation systems like this one in the Ogallala Aquifer area can reduce water consumed by seepage and evaporation to about 30%.

Wasting Less Water in Homes and Businesses

Flushing toilets, washing hands, and bathing account for about 77% of the water used in a typical home in the United States (Figure 8-20). Much of this water is unnecessarily wasted (Figure 8-21). Leaks in pipes, water mains, toilets, bathtubs, and faucets waste an estimated 20% to 35% of water withdrawn from public supplies.

Because water costs so little, in most places leaking water faucets are not repaired and large quantities of water are used to clean sidewalks and streets and to irrigate lawns and golf courses. Instead of being a status symbol, a green lawn in an arid or semiarid area should be viewed as a major ecological and economic wrong and replaced with types of natural vegetation adapted to a dry climate.

Many cities offer even less incentive to reduce leaks and waste. In New York, for example, 95% of the residential units don't have water meters. Users are charged flat rates, with the average family paying less than $100 a year for virtually unlimited use of high-quality water. In Boulder, Colorado, the introduction of water meters reduced water use by more than one-third. Appendix 3 lists ways that each of us can conserve water and save money.

Commercially available systems can be used to purify and completely recycle wastewater from houses, apartments, and office buildings. Such a system can be installed in a small shed outside a residence and serviced for a monthly fee about equal to that charged by most city water and sewer systems. In Tokyo, Japan, all the water used in Mitsubishi's 60-story office building is purified for reuse by an automated recycling system.

Figure 8-20 Domestic uses of water. (Data from U.S. Geological Survey)

8-4 MAJOR FORMS OF WATER POLLUTION

Major Types and Sources of Water Pollutants

Although fresh water is a potentially renewable resource, it can become so contaminated by human activities that it is no longer useful for many purposes. The following are eight common types of water pollutants:

1. *disease-causing agents:* bacteria, viruses, protozoa, and parasitic worms that enter water from domestic sewage and animal wastes.

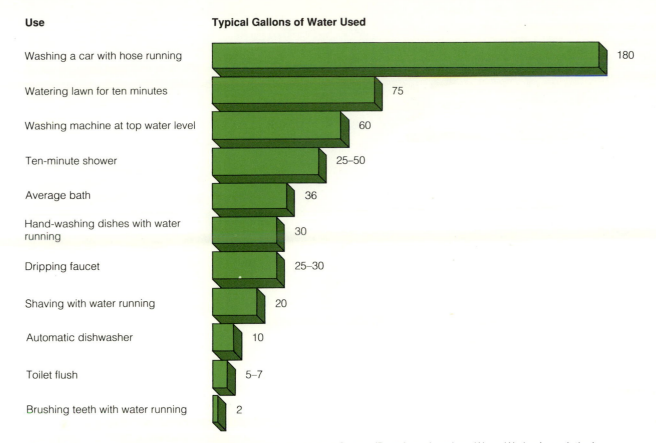

Figure 8-21 Some ways domestic water is wasted in the United States. (Data from American Water Works Association)

2. *oxygen-demanding wastes:* organic wastes, which when degraded by oxygen-consuming bacteria, can deplete water of dissolved oxygen gas. The amount of oxygen-demanding wastes in water is usually determined by measuring **biological oxygen demand (BOD)**—the amount of dissolved oxygen needed by aerobic decomposers to break down the organic materials in a given volume of water at a certain temperature over a specified time period.

3. *water-soluble inorganic chemicals:* acids, salts, and compounds of toxic metals such as lead and mercury. High levels of such dissolved solids can make water unfit to drink, harm fish and other aquatic life, depress crop yields, and accelerate corrosion of equipment that uses water.

4. *inorganic plant nutrients:* water-soluble nitrate and phosphate compounds that can cause excessive growth of algae and other aquatic plants, which then die and decay, depleting water of dissolved oxygen and killing fish.

5. *organic chemicals:* oil, gasoline, plastics, pesticides, cleaning solvents, detergents, and many other water-soluble and insoluble chemicals that threaten human health and harm fish and other aquatic life.

6. *sediment or suspended matter:* insoluble particles of soil, silt, and other solid inorganic and organic

materials that become suspended in water. They cloud the water, reduce photosynthesis by aquatic plants, disrupt aquatic food webs, and carry pesticides, bacteria, and other harmful substances. Many rivers and streams have always carried high sediment loads because of natural erosion occurring in their watersheds. But in most rivers sediment loads have risen sharply because of accelerated erosion from cropland, rangeland, forestland, and construction and mining sites.

7. *radioactive substances:* radioisotopes that are water soluble or capable of being biologically amplified in food chains and webs.

8. *heat:* excessive inputs of heated water used to cool electric power plants. The resulting increases in water temperatures lower dissolved oxygen content and make aquatic organisms more vulnerable to disease, parasites, and toxic chemicals.

Point and Nonpoint Sources For purposes of control and regulation it is useful to distinguish between point sources and nonpoint sources of water pollution from human activities. **Point sources** discharge pollutants at specific locations through pipes, ditches, or sewers into bodies of surface water (Figure 8-22). Examples include factories, sewage treatment plants (which remove some but not all pollutants), electric power plants, active and abandoned underground coal mines,

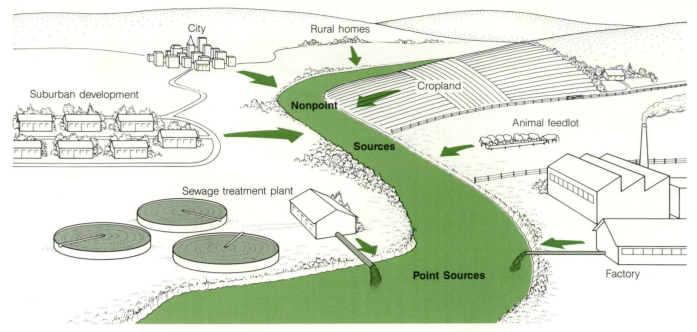

Figure 8-22 Point and nonpoint sources of water pollution.

and offshore oil wells. So far most water pollution control efforts have concentrated on reducing discharges to surface water from industrial and municipal point sources because they are easy to identify.

Nonpoint sources are big land areas that discharge pollutants into surface and underground water over a large area (Figure 8-22). Examples include runoff into surface water and seepage into groundwater from croplands, livestock feedlots, logged forests, urban and suburban lands, septic tanks, construction areas, parking lots, roadways, and atmospheric deposition. Little progress has been made in the control of nonpoint water pollution because of the difficulty and expense of identifying and controlling discharges from so many diffuse sources.

8-5 POLLUTION OF RIVERS, LAKES, OCEANS, AND GROUNDWATER

Rivers and Oxygen-Consuming Wastes Because they flow, most rivers recover rapidly from some forms of pollution—especially excess heat and degradable oxygen-demanding wastes—as long the rivers are not overloaded. Slowly degradable and nondegradable pollutants, however, are not eliminated by natural dilution and degradation processes.

Just below the area where large quantities of oxygen-demanding wastes are added to a river, dissolved oxygen levels in the water drop sharply and the biological oxygen demand rises as aerobic bacteria begin decomposing the wastes (Figure 8-23). As these degradable wastes continue to be decomposed further

downstream, the dissolved oxygen content near the original discharge point returns to its normal level.

The depth and width of the *oxygen sag curve* (Figure 8-23) and thus the time and distance a river takes to recover depend on the river's volume, flow rate, and the volume of incoming degradable wastes. Slow-flowing rivers can easily be overloaded with oxygen-demanding wastes, as can normally rapid-flowing rivers whose volume and flow-rate are reduced during hot summer months or drought. Similar oxygen sag curves occur when heated water from power plants is discharged into rivers.

Along many rivers, water for drinking is removed *upstream* from a city, and the city's industrial and sewage wastes are discharged *downstream*. This pattern is usually repeated hundreds of times along a river as it flows toward the sea. A river or stream receiving heavy loads of oxygen-demanding wastes or toxic wastes along most or all of its path can suffer from severe oxygen depletion, loss of most fish, and high levels of disease-carrying human and animal wastes and toxic substances.

Requiring each city to withdraw its drinking water downstream rather than upstream would dramatically improve the quality of river water. Each city would be forced to clean up its own waste outputs rather than passing them on to downstream areas. However, political and economic pressures work against this input approach for pollution control. It is fought by upstream users, who have the use of fairly clean water without high cleanup costs.

River Water Quality Throughout the World Water pollution control laws enacted in the 1970s have greatly

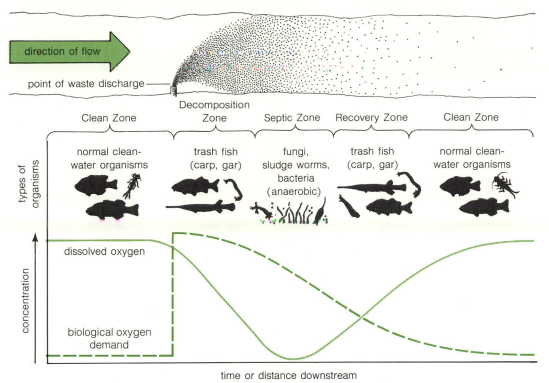

Figure 8-23 The oxygen sag curve (solid) versus oxygen demand (dashes). Depending on flow rates and the amount of pollutants, rivers recover from oxygen-demanding wastes and heat if given enough time and if they are not overloaded.

increased the number and quality of sewage treatment plants in the United States. Laws have also required industries to reduce or eliminate point source discharges into surface waters.

Since 1972 these efforts have enabled the United States to hold the line against increased pollution of most of its rivers and streams by disease-causing agents and oxygen-demanding wastes. This is an impressive accomplishment, considering the rise in economic activity and population since 1972.

Pollution control laws have also led to improvements in dissolved oxygen content in many rivers and streams in Canada, Japan, and most western European countries since 1970. Many rivers in the Soviet Union, however, have become more polluted with industrial wastes as industries have expanded without adequate pollution controls.

Despite progress in improving river quality in most MDCs, large fish kills and contamination of drinking water still occur. Most of these disasters are caused by accidental or deliberate releases of toxic inorganic and organic chemicals by industries, malfunctioning sewage treatment plants, and nonpoint runoff of pesticides from cropland.

Available data indicate that pollution of rivers and streams from massive discharges of untreated or inadequately treated sewage and industrial wastes is a growing problem in most LDCs. Currently more than two-thirds of India's water resources are polluted. Of the 78 rivers monitored in China, 54 are seriously polluted. In Latin America and Africa many rivers are severely polluted.

Pollution Problems of Lakes and Reservoirs The flushing and changing of water in lakes and large reservoirs can take from one to a hundred years, compared to several days to several weeks for rivers. The dilution of pollutants is less effective in lakes than in rivers because lakes have little flow and contain layers that undergo little vertical mixing (Figure 6-8, p. 128). For the same reasons, lakes contain lower levels of dissolved oxygen, especially in bottom layers, and the replenishment of dissolved oxygen in the surface layer is slower than in most rivers.

Thus, lakes are more vulnerable than rivers to contamination with plant nutrients, oil, pesticides, and toxic substances that can destroy bottom life and kill fish. Runoff of acids into lakes is a serious problem in areas subject to acid deposition (Figure 7-19, p. 164). In the Soviet Union, Lake Baikal—the world's largest and deepest body of fresh water—is threatened with pollution, as discussed in the Guest Essay ending this chapter.

Cultural eutrophication is a major pollution problem for shallow lakes and reservoirs, especially near urban or agricultural centers (Figure 8-24). This stepped-up addition of phosphates and nitrates as a result of human activities can produce in a few decades the

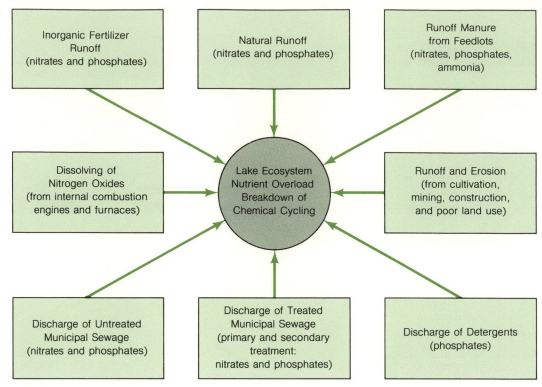

Figure 8-24 Major sources of nutrient overload, or cultural eutrophication, in lakes, slow-flowing rivers, and estuaries.

Inorganic Fertilizer Runoff (nitrates and phosphates)

Natural Runoff (nitrates and phosphates)

Runoff Manure from Feedlots (nitrates, phosphates, ammonia)

Dissolving of Nitrogen Oxides (from internal combustion engines and furnaces)

Lake Ecosystem Nutrient Overload Breakdown of Chemical Cycling

Runoff and Erosion (from cultivation, mining, construction, and poor land use)

Discharge of Untreated Municipal Sewage (nitrates and phosphates)

Discharge of Treated Municipal Sewage (primary and secondary treatment: nitrates and phosphates)

Discharge of Detergents (phosphates)

National Archives

Figure 8-25 Mass of dead and dying algae from cultural eutrophication of a lake.

same degree of plant nutrient enrichment that takes thousands to millions of years by natural processes.

Overloading shallow lakes with plant nutrients during the summer produces dense growths of rooted plants such as water chestnuts and water hyacinths near the shore. It also causes algal blooms—population explosions of floating algae, especially the blue-green species. They make the water look like green soup and release substances that make the water taste and smell bad.

Dissolved oxygen in the surface layer of water near the shore and in the bottom layer is depleted when large masses of algae die, fall to the bottom, and are decomposed by aerobic bacteria (Figure 8-25). Then important game fish such as lake trout and small-mouth bass die of oxygen starvation, leaving the lake populated by carp and other less desirable species that need less oxygen.

About one-third of the 100,000 medium to large lakes and about 85% of the large lakes near major population centers in the United States suffer from some degree of cultural eutrophication. The Great Lakes, for example, receive massive inputs of plant nutrients, as well as numerous toxic water pollutants, from point and nonpoint sources (see Case Study on p. 206).

The solution to cultural eutrophication is to use input methods to reduce the flow of nutrients into lakes and reservoirs and output methods to clean up lakes that suffer from excessive eutrophication. As with other forms of pollution, input approaches are the most effective and usually the cheapest in the long run.

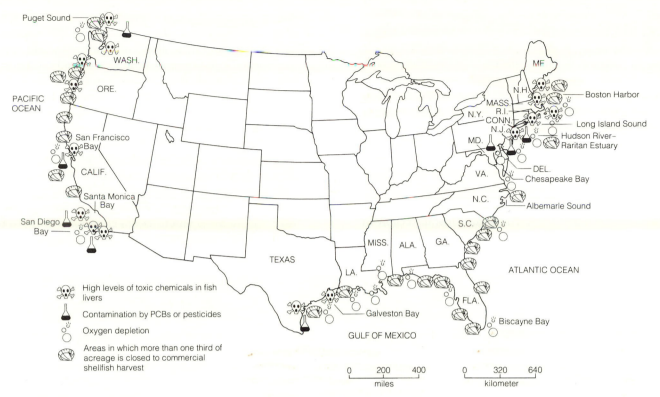

Figure 8-26 Chemical assault on major U.S. coastal areas. (Date from National Oceanic and Atmospheric Administration)

Major input methods include advanced waste treatment, bans or limits on phosphates in household detergents and cleansers, and soil conservation and land-use control to reduce nutrient runoff. Major output methods are dredging bottom sediments to remove nutrient buildup, removing excess weeds, controlling undesirable plant growth with herbicides and algicides, and bubbling air into lakes to avoid oxygen depletion.

Ocean Pollution Marine explorer Jacques Cousteau has warned that "the very survival of the human species depends upon the maintenance of an ocean clean and alive, spreading all around the world. The ocean is our planet's life belt." Oceans are the ultimate sink for much of the waste matter we produce. In addition to natural runoff, the world's oceans receive agricultural and urban runoff, atmospheric fallout, garbage and untreated sewage from ships, accidental oil spills from tankers and offshore oil drilling platforms, and untreated or inadequately treated sewage and industrial wastes from coastal urban and industrial areas.

Barges and ships also dump industrial wastes, sewage sludge (a gooey mixture of toxic chemicals and settled solids removed from wastewater at sewage treatment plants) and dredge spoils (often toxic-laden materials scraped from the bottoms of harbors and rivers to maintain shipping channels). Coastal areas, especially vital estuaries and wetlands, in the United States and other coastal countries bear the brunt of these massive inputs of wastes (Figure 8-26). This can overwhelm the natural dilution and degradation processes of these areas and destroy vital sources of food and recreational pleasure.

During the summer of 1988 several beaches along the east coast from Maryland to New York and New Jersey were temporarily closed when hypodermic needles, blood sample vials, and other debris washed ashore. Under intense public pressure in an election year, Congress passed legislation banning all ocean sludge dumping by 1992. However, pressure from some political leaders in coastal states may delay this ban because of the financial burden of finding other ways to dispose of massive amounts of sludge.

A ban on ocean sludge dumping may help aquatic creatures living 50 to 100 miles from shore, but it will not do much for the beaches. Much of the debris and pollution on New York and New Jersey beaches comes from overflows of combined sewers that mix storm runoff with municipal waste, urban runoff, wastewater discharges, atmospheric fallout, and illegal dumping of hazardous wastes.

Crude petroleum (oil as it comes out of the ground) and refined petroleum (fuel oil, gasoline, and other products obtained by distillation and chemical processing of crude petroleum) are accidentally or deliberately released into the environment from a number of sources. Tanker accidents and blowouts (oil escaping under high pressure from a borehole in the ocean floor) at offshore drilling rigs receive most of the publicity. However, almost half (some experts estimate 90%) of the oil reaching the oceans comes from the land as a result of runoff and dumping of waste oil by cities and industries.

The effects of oil on ocean ecosystems depend on a number of factors: type of oil (crude or refined), amount released, distance of release from shore, time of year, weather conditions, and ocean and tidal currents. Volatile organic hydrocarbons in oil immediately kill a number of aquatic organisms, especially in their larval forms. Floating oil coats the feathers of marine birds and the fur of marine mammals such as seals and sea otters. This oily coating destroys the animals' natural insulation and buoyancy, and most drown or die of exposure from loss of body heat. It is estimated that 150,000 to 450,000 marine birds in the North Sea and North Atlantic regions are killed each year by chronic oil pollution, mostly from routine releases by oil tankers.

Heavy oil components that sink to the ocean floor or wash into estuaries can kill bottom-dwelling organisms such as crabs, oysters, mussels, and clams. Those that survive can't be eaten because of their oily taste and smell. Most forms of marine life recover from exposure to large amounts of crude oil within three years. However, recovery of marine life from exposure

CASE STUDY The Great Lakes

The five interconnected Great Lakes contain at least 95% of the surface fresh water in the United States and 20% of the world's fresh water (Figure 8-27). The massive watershed around these lakes has thousands of industries and over 60 million people—one-third of Canada's population and one-eighth of the U.S. population. The lakes supply drinking water for 24 million people. About 40% of U.S. industry and half of Canada's industry are located in this watershed.

Despite their enormous size, these lakes are especially vulnerable to pollution from point and nonpoint sources because less than 1% of the water entering the Great Lakes flows out the St. Lawrence River each year. Although Lake Erie is flushed out once about every 2.7 years, the flushing time for Lake Superior is 182 years and that for Lake Michigan is 105 years. The Great Lakes also receive large quantities of acids, pesticides, and other toxic chemicals by deposition from the atmosphere.

By the 1960s many areas of the Great Lakes were suffering from severe cultural eutrophication, massive fish kills, and contamination with bacteria and other wastes. Many bathing beaches had to be closed, and there was a sharp drop in commercial and sport fishing.

Although all five lakes were affected, the impact on Lake Erie was particularly intense. It is the shallowest of the Great Lakes and has the smallest volume of water. Also, its drainage basin is heavily industrialized and has the largest population of any of the lakes. At one time in the mid-1960s, massive algal blooms choked off oxygen to 65% of Lake Erie's bottom. By 1970 the lake had lost nearly all its native fish. Lake Ontario's small size and shallowness also made it vulnerable to cultural eutrophication and other forms of water pollution.

Since 1972 a joint $15 billion pollution control program has been carried out by Canada and the United States. It has led to significant decreases in levels of phosphates, coliform bacteria, and many toxic industrial chemicals. Algal blooms have also decreased, and dissolved oxygen levels and sport and commercial fishing have increased. By 1988 only 8 of 516 swimming beaches remained closed because of pollution.

These improvements were mainly the result of decreased point source discharges, brought about by new or upgraded sewage treatment plants and improved treatment of industrial wastes. Also, phosphate detergents, household cleaners, and water conditioners were banned or their phosphate levels were lowered in many areas of the Great Lakes drainage basin.

The runoff of phosphates from nonpoint sources is still a problem in some areas of the basin. But the most serious problem today is contamination from toxic wastes flowing into the lakes from land runoff, rivers, and atmospheric deposition. Most toxic "hot spots" are found in harbors or near the mouths of tributaries emptying into the lakes, especially Lake Erie and Lake Ontario. For example, there are 164 toxic-waste disposal sites in a three-mile strip along the U.S. side of the Niagara River.

In 1978 the U.S. and Canada signed a new agreement with the goal of virtual elimination of discharges of about 360 toxic chemicals. However, recent studies indicate that much of the input of toxic chemicals—more than 50% in Lake Superior—comes from the atmosphere, a source not covered by the agreement. Despite significant progress, much more needs to be done to improve water quality in the Great Lakes.

to refined oil, especially in estuaries, may take ten years or longer.

Oil slicks that wash onto beaches can have serious economic effects on coastal residents, who lose income from fishing and tourist activities, as shown by the massive oil spill in 1989 near Valdez, Alaska (see frontispiece). Beaches washed by strong waves or currents are cleaned up fairly rapidly, but those in sheltered areas remain contaminated for several years.

Input methods for reducing oil pollution include using and wasting less oil, collecting and reprocessing used oils and greases for reuse, and strictly regulating the construction and operation of oil tankers, offshore oil rigs, and oil refineries. Output methods include using mechanical barriers to keep oil from reaching the shore and then vacuuming it up, soaking it up with pillows filled with chicken feathers, or using helicopters equipped with lasers to ignite and burn as much as 90% of an oil spill in a few seconds. But the Valdez, Alaska spill showed that oil companies have been lax in dealing with this problem.

Oceans can dilute, disperse, and degrade large amounts of sewage and some industrial wastes. But massive discharges can overload these natural purifying systems (see Case Study on p. 208). Natural ocean processes also can't readily degrade many of the plastics, pesticides, and other chemicals we have made.

Groundwater Pollution Groundwater is a vital resource that supplies drinking water for one out of two

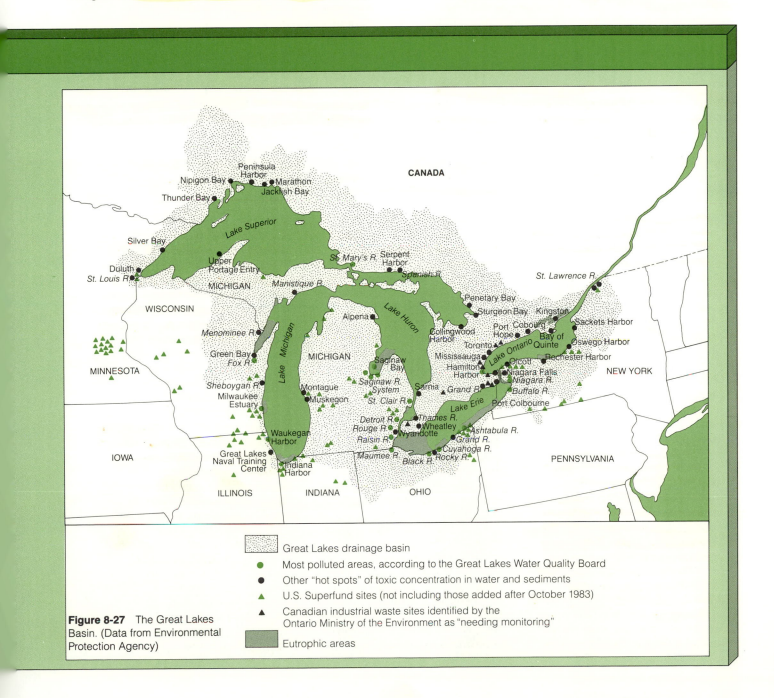

Figure 8-27 The Great Lakes Basin. (Data from Environmental Protection Agency)

- Great Lakes drainage basin
- ● Most polluted areas, according to the Great Lakes Water Quality Board
- ● Other "hot spots" of toxic concentration in water and sediments
- ▲ U.S. Superfund sites (not including those added after October 1983)
- ▲ Canadian industrial waste sites identified by the Ontario Ministry of the Environment as "needing monitoring"
- Eutrophic areas

Americans and 95% of those in rural areas. About 75% of American cities depend on groundwater for all or most of their supply of drinking water.

Little is known about the quality of groundwater in the United States, despite the importance of this resource. Only limited testing has been done. By 1988 only 38 of the several hundred chemicals found in groundwater were covered by federal water quality standards and routinely tested for in municipal drinking water supplies.

In a 1982 survey the EPA found that 45% of the large public water systems served by groundwater were contaminated with synthetic organic chemicals that pose potential health threats. The most common are solvents such as trichloroethylene (TCE), carbon tetrachloride, and chloroform. The EPA has documented groundwater contamination by 74 pesticides in 38 states. In California, 57 different pesticides have been detected in various groundwater supplies.

Another EPA survey in 1984 found that two-thirds of the rural household wells tested violated at least one federal health standard for drinking water. The most common contaminants were nitrates from fertil-izers and pesticides used to kill nematode worms. In Florida, where 90% of the population relies on groundwater, more than 1,000 wells have been closed due to pollution by a cancer-causing worm killer.

Groundwater can be contaminated from a number of point and nonpoint sources (Figure 8-29). EPA surveys indicate that by 1990 up to 58% of the 2 million underground tanks used to store gasoline, solvents, and other hazardous chemicals throughout the United States will be leaking their contents into groundwater. A gasoline leak of just one gallon a day can seriously contaminate the water supply for 50,000 persons. Seepage of hazardous organic chemicals and toxic heavy metal compounds from landfills, abandoned hazardous-waste dumps, and industrial-waste storage lagoons located above or near aquifers is also a serious problem.

Another concern is accidental leaks into groundwater aquifers from deep wells used to inject almost 60% of the country's hazardous wastes deep underground. Laws regulating deep-well injection are weak and poorly enforced. Reporting of the types of wastes injected is not required, and no national inventory of

---

CASE STUDY The Chesapeake Bay: An Estuary in Trouble

The Chesapeake Bay (Figure 8-28) is the largest estuary in the United States and one of the world's most productive estuaries. It is home for about 200 species of fish and shellfish. It is the largest single source of oysters in the United States and the largest producer of blue crabs in the world. The bay is also important for shipping, recreational boating, and sport fishing. Between 1940 and 1987 the number of people living close to the bay grew from 3.7 million to 13.2 million and is projected to reach 15 million by 2000.

The 200-mile-long estuary receives wastes from point and nonpoint sources scattered throughout a massive drainage basin that includes 9 large rivers and 141 smaller rivers and creeks in parts of six states. It has become a massive pollution sink because only 1% of the waste entering the bay is flushed into the Atlantic Ocean.

Levels of phosphate and nitrate plant nutrients have risen sharply in many parts of the bay, causing algal blooms and oxygen depletion. Studies have shown that point sources, primarily sewage treatment plants, contribute most of the phosphates. Nonpoint sources, mostly runoff from urban and suburban areas and agricultural activities, are the major sources of nitrates. However, a 1988 study by the Environmental Defense Fund found that one-fourth of the nitrates come from the atmosphere as acid deposition.

Additional pollution comes from nonpoint runoff of large quantities of pesticides from cropland and urban lawns. Point source discharge of numerous toxic wastes by industries, often in violation of their discharge permits, is also a problem.

Commercial harvests of oysters, crabs, and several commercially important fish such as striped bass (rockfish) have fallen sharply since 1960. For example, oyster catches dropped 50% between 1965 and 1985, and rockfish catches by 90% between 1970 and 1985. However, populations of bluefish, men-haden, and other species that spawn in salt water and feed around algae blooms have increased.

In many areas of the bay underwater grasses have virtually disappeared. These plants help control erosion, filter pollutants, and are a vital link in the bay's food webs.

Since 1983 over $650 million in federal and state funds have been spent on a Chesapeake Bay cleanup program that will ultimately cost several billion dollars. Between 1980 and 1987, discharges of phosphates from point sources dropped by about 20%, but there is a long way to go to reverse severe eutrophication in many areas. Bans on phosphate-containing detergents and cleaning agents will probably have to be enacted throughout the six-state drainage basin. Forests and wetlands around the bay also must be protected from development. Halting the deterioration of this vital estuary will require the prolonged, cooperative efforts of citizens, officials, and industries.

active and abandoned wells is kept. Operators are not required to monitor nearby aquifers and are not liable for any damages from leaks once a disposal well is abandoned and plugged. Environmentalists believe that all deep-well disposal of hazardous waste in the United States should be banned. (Safer alternatives are discussed in Section 9-4.)

Once contaminants reach groundwater, they are usually not effectively diluted and dispersed because the movement of water in most aquifers is slow and not turbulent. Degradable organic wastes are not broken down as readily as in rapidly flowing surface waters exposed to the atmosphere because groundwater has little dissolved oxygen and fairly small populations of anerobic decomposing bacteria and dissolved oxygen. This means that it can take hundreds to thousands of years for contaminated groundwater to cleanse itself of degradable wastes. Slowly degradable and nondegradable wastes can permanently contaminate aquifers.

Groundwater pollution is much more difficult to detect and control than surface water pollution. Monitoring groundwater pollution is expensive (up to $10,000 per monitoring well), and many monitoring wells must be sunk. Because of its location deep underground, pumping polluted groundwater to the surface, cleaning it up, and returning it to the aquifer is usually too expensive.

Therefore, preventing contamination is generally viewed as the only effective way to protect groundwater resources. In 1984 the EPA suggested that each state classify its groundwater resources into one of three categories for different degrees of protection:

- *Class I* contains irreplaceable sources of drinking water and ecologically vital sources that should be given the highest protection.

- *Class II* includes all other groundwater currently in use or potentially available for drinking water or for other beneficial uses. These areas would be given the next highest level of protection.

- *Class III* groundwater is not a potential source of drinking water and is of limited beneficial use, usually because it is already too contaminated.

Essentially all disposal of hazardous wastes in landfills and deep wells would have to be banned except

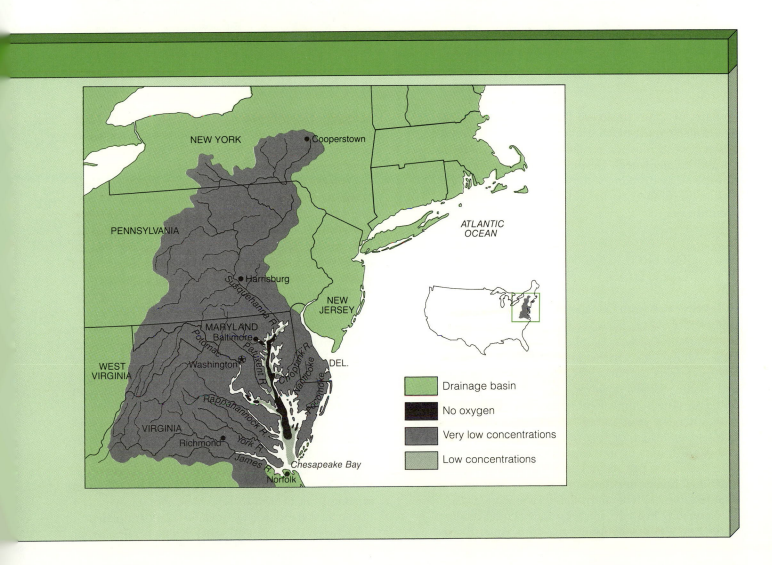

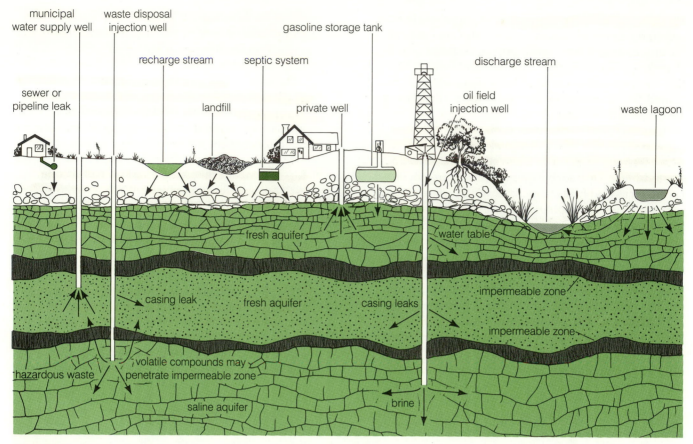

Figure 8-29 Major sources of groundwater contamination in the United States.

perhaps in Class III areas. Protecting groundwater would also require much stricter controls on the application of pesticides and fertilizers by millions of farmers and home owners. Despite the seriousness of the threat to U.S. drinking water supplies, by 1988 there was no comprehensive federal law designed to protect groundwater.

8-6 CONTROLLING WATER POLLUTION

U.S. Water Pollution Legislation The Safe Drinking Water Act of 1974 requires the EPA to establish national drinking water standards, called *maximum contaminant levels (MCLs)*, for any pollutants that "may" have adverse effects on human health. Environmentalists and health officials, however, have criticized the EPA for being slow in implementing this law. By 1986—12 years after the original legislation was passed—the EPA had set MCLs for only 26 of at least 700 potential pollutants found in municipal drinking water supplies. However, privately owned wells for millions of individual homes in suburban and rural areas are not required to meet federal drinking water standards.

According to a 1988 study by the National Wildlife Federation, 26 million Americans drink water that is contaminated with too many bacteria. About 10 million drink water contaminated with excessive radioactivity and 7 million drink water contaminated with other chemicals, mostly pesticides.

The Federal Water Pollution Act of 1972, the Clean Water Act of 1977 (along with amendments in 1981 and 1987), and the 1987 Water Quality Act form the basis of U.S. efforts to control pollution of the country's surface waters. These acts require the EPA to establish *national effluent standards* and to set up a nationwide system for monitoring water quality.

These effluent standards limit the amounts of conventional and toxic water pollutants that can be discharged into surface waters from factories, sewage treatment plants, and other point sources. Each point source discharger must get a permit specifying the amount of each pollutant that facility can discharge.

By 1988 nearly 90% of the country's publicly owned sewage treatment plants complied with national effluent limits set by the Clean Water Act, and about 80% of all industrial dischargers were officially in compliance with their discharge permits. But studies by the General Accounting Office have shown that most industries periodically violate their permits. Also 500 cities ranging from Boston to Key West, Florida, have not met federal standards for sewage treatment plants.

Between 1972 and 1987 water quality has improved,

in some cases dramatically, in 11% of the miles of streams and rivers surveyed for levels of several conventional pollutants. During the same period, however, roughly two-thirds of the stream miles and lakes surveyed showed no change in water quality. And about 2% of the stream miles and 10% of the lake areas monitored have deteriorated since 1972. According to a 1987 survey by the Fund for Renewable Energy and the Environment, the three states with the best surface water protection programs were North Carolina, Georgia, and Iowa.

Scientists point out, however, that many rivers, streams, and lakes are polluted to an unknown degree by a variety of unconventional toxic pollutants not monitored and controlled by present laws. Even the data on conventional surface water pollutants are inadequate because measurements are made at widely separated, fixed points.

Control of Nonpoint Source Pollution The primary reason that water quality in most systems has not improved has been the absence until recently of any national strategy for controlling conventional and unconventional water pollutants from nonpoint sources. Such a strategy would require greatly increased efforts to control soil erosion through conservation and land-use control for farms, construction sites, and suburban and urban areas.

The leading nonpoint source of water pollution is agriculture. Farmers can sharply reduce fertilizer runoff into surface waters and leaching into aquifers in several ways. They should avoid using excessive amounts of fertilizer and should use none on steeply sloped land. They can use slow-release fertilizers and periodically plant fields with soybeans or other nitrogen-fixing plants to reduce the need for fertilizer. Farmers should also be required to have buffer zones of permanent vegetation between cultivated fields and nearby surface water.

Similarly, farmers can reduce pesticide runoff and leaching by applying no more pesticide than needed and by applying it only when needed. They can reduce the need for pesticides by using biological methods of pest control (see Enrichment Study on p. 295).

Livestock growers can control runoff and infiltration of animal wastes from feedlots and barnyards by several methods. They should control animal density and should not locate feedlots on land sloping toward nearby surface water. They can divert runoff of animal wastes into detention basins from which the nutrient-rich water can be pumped and applied as fertilizer to cropland or forestland.

Control of Point Source Pollution: Wastewater Treatment In many LDCs and some parts of MDCs, sewage and waterborne industrial wastes from point sources are not treated. Instead, they are discharged into the nearest waterway or into a storage basin such as a cesspool or lagoon.

In MDCs, however, most of the wastes from point sources are purified to varying degrees. In rural and suburban areas with suitable soils, sewage from each house is usually discharged into a **septic tank** (Figure 8-30). It traps greases and large solids and discharges the remaining wastes over a large drainage field. As these wastes percolate downward, the soil filters out some potential pollutants, and soil bacteria decompose the degradable materials.

In many small urban areas and throughout many LDCs, sewage is transported to a series of **wastewater lagoons**. These are large ponds, three to five feet deep, where air, sunlight, and microorganisms break down wastes, allow solids to settle out, and kill some disease-causing bacteria. Water typically remains in a lagoon for 30 days. Then it is treated with chlorine and pumped out for use by a city or farms. Lagoons are also widely used to handle wastes from animal feedlots.

In larger urban areas in MDCs most waterborne wastes from homes, businesses, factories, and storm runoff flow through a network of sewer pipes to wastewater treatment plants. When sewage reaches a treatment plant, it undergoes up to three levels of purification, depending on the type of plant and the degree of purity desired. The three possible levels of sewage treatment are classified as primary, secondary, and advanced.

Primary sewage treatment is a mechanical process that uses screens to filter out debris such as sticks, stones, and rags. Then suspended solids settle out as sludge in a settling tank (Figure 8-31). **Secondary sewage treatment** is a biological process that uses aerobic bacteria to remove up to 90% of degradable, oxygen-demanding organic wastes (Figure 8-32). In the United States, combined primary and secondary treatment must be used in all communities served by wastewater treatment plants.

Combined primary and secondary treatment, however, still leaves about 10% of the oxygen-demanding wastes and suspended solids, 50% of the nitrogen (mostly as nitrates), 70% of the phosphorus (mostly as phosphates), and 30% of most toxic metal compounds and synthetic organic chemicals in the wastewater discharged from the plant. Virtually none of any long-lived radioactive isotopes and persistent organic substances such as pesticides are removed by these two processes.

Advanced sewage treatment is a series of specialized chemical and physical processes that lower the quantity of specific pollutants still left after primary and secondary treatment (Figure 8-33). Types of advanced treatment vary depending on the contaminants in specific communities and industries. Except

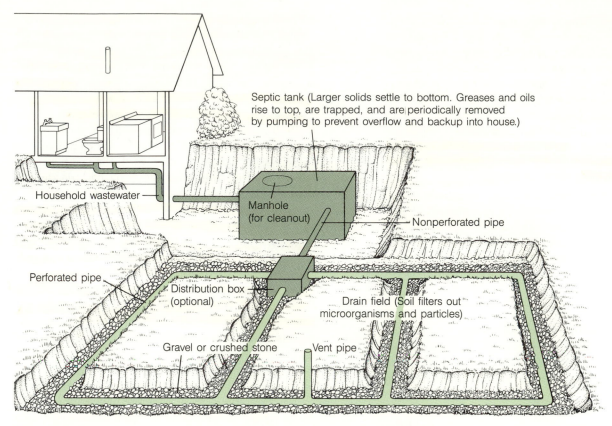

Septic tank (Larger solids settle to bottom. Greases and oils rise to top, are trapped, and are periodically removed by pumping to prevent overflow and backup into house.)

Household wastewater

Manhole (for cleanout)

Nonperforated pipe

Perforated pipe

Distribution box (optional)

Drain field (Soil filters out microorganisms and particles)

Gravel or crushed stone

Vent pipe

Figure 8-30 Septic tank system used for disposal of domestic sewage and wastewater in rural and suburban areas.

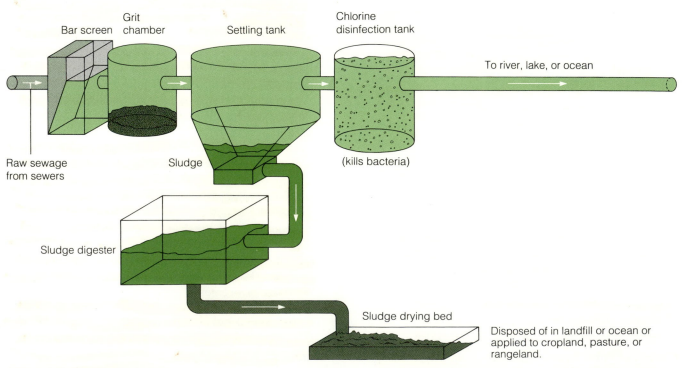

Bar screen

Grit chamber

Settling tank

Chlorine disinfection tank

To river, lake, or ocean

Raw sewage from sewers

Sludge

(kills bacteria)

Sludge digester

Sludge drying bed

Disposed of in landfill or ocean or applied to cropland, pasture, or rangeland.

Figure 8-31 Primary sewage treatment.

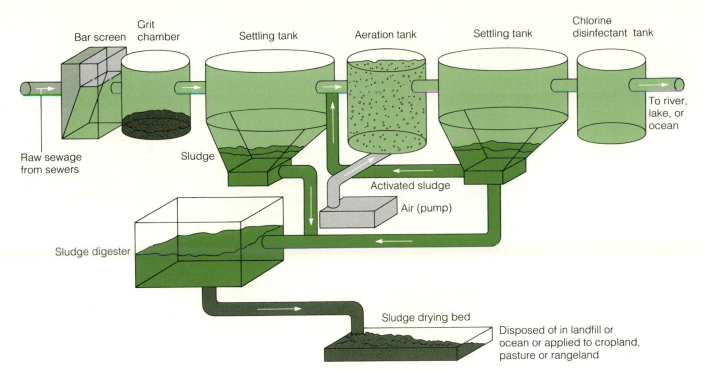

Figure 8-32 Secondary sewage treatment.

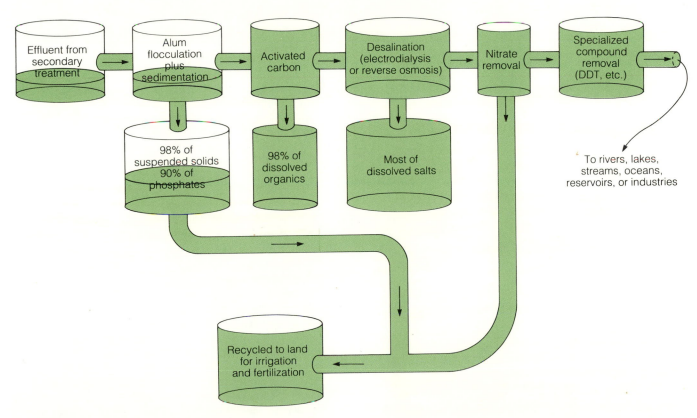

Figure 8-33 Advanced sewage treatment.

in Sweden, Denmark, and Norway, advanced treatment is rarely used because the plants cost twice as much to build and four times as much to operate as secondary plants.

One of the last steps in any form of sewage treatment is to disinfect the water before it is discharged into nearby waterways or applied to land for further filtering and use as fertilizer. Disinfection removes water coloration and kills disease-carrying bacteria and some (but not all) viruses. The usual method is chlorination. A problem is that chlorine reacts with organic materials in the wastewater or in surface water to form small amounts of chlorinated hydrocarbons. Some of these, such as chloroform, are known carcinogens. Several other disinfectants, such as ozone and UV light are being tested, but are more expensive than chlorine.

Without expensive advanced treatment, effluents from primary and secondary sewage treatment plants contain enough nitrates and phosphates to contribute to accelerated eutrophication of lakes and slow-moving rivers. Sewage treatment also produces large volumes of sludge that must be disposed of, usually by incineration or dumping in the ocean or a landfill. In 1988 a pilot plant for testing a new process went into operation. If successful, this process will reduce the volume of sludge normally produced by sewage treatment plants by 80%, and most of the remaining sludge will be converted to diesel fuel.

An alternative is to return the nitrate and phosphate plant nutrients in sewage sludge to the land as fertilizers. By 1986 about 25% of all U.S. municipal sludge was returned to the land as fertilizer at more than 2,600 sites.

Several methods can be used to avoid or minimize contamination of food and groundwater with the bacteria, viruses, toxic metals, and hazardous synthetic organic chemicals found in sludge and sewage plant effluent. Before it is applied, sludge can be heated to kill harmful bacteria and treated to remove toxic metals and organic chemicals. Untreated sludge can be applied to land not used for crops or livestock in areas where groundwater is already contaminated or is not used as a source of drinking water. Examples include forests, surface-mined land, golf courses, lawns, and highway medians.

Future Water Quality Goals Environmentalists and conservationists believe that future water pollution control efforts in the United States should focus on three major goals. First, existing laws controlling discharge of conventional and toxic pollutants into surface waters from point sources should be strictly enforced and not weakened. Second, new legislation for sharply reducing runoff of conventional and toxic

GUEST ESSAY Economics Versus Ecology in the USSR: The Case of Lake Baikal

Philip R. Pryde

Philip R. Pryde is a specialist in land-use planning, water resources, energy resources, and environmental impact analysis in the Department of Geography at San Diego State University. He is also a leading U.S. expert on environmental problems and resource conservation in the USSR. He has served on the San Diego County Planning Commission and San Diego's Growth Management Review Task Force, and he is a director of the San Diego County Water Authority. In addition to numerous articles, he is the author of Nonconventional Energy Resources *(Wiley, 1983) and* Conservation in the Soviet Union *(Cambridge University Press, 1972).*

Lake Baikal is perhaps the most remarkable lake in the world. It is located in the Soviet Union just north of the border with Mongolia and contains the world's largest volume of fresh water. At 5,311 feet, it is also the world's deepest body of fresh water. It stretches for about 435 miles between steep mountain ranges, in a geological depression called a *graben*. The geological faults that produced the graben also subject the entire region to severe earthquakes.

However, the lake's uniqueness is not limited to just its size. In Lake Baikal's unusually clear waters can be found about 800 species of plants and about 1,550 species of animal life. About three-quarters of these species occur nowhere else on earth. Among them are the world's only freshwater seal and freshwater sponge. Because of its uniqueness and scientific value, controversy over the potential pollution of Lake Baikal has drawn considerable interest, not just within the Soviet Union, but throughout the world.

Timber cutting and small industrial facilities have existed in the Lake Baikal basin for decades. But in the 1960s, plans were prepared for two new wood-processing plants to be built on its shores. To keep them supplied with timber, large increases were planned in the logging activities on the surrounding mountain slopes. This would not only be an eyesore but could also result in considerable soil erosion.

Wood-processing plants of the type proposed produce large amounts of potential water pollutants. A debate began almost immediately over whether the proposed wastewater treatment plants at the two factories would be adequate to preserve the quality of Lake Baikal's waters. This debate was noteworthy, as it was the first major environmental issue to be widely publicized in the Soviet press.

pollutants into surface waters from nonpoint sources should be enacted and funded. Finally, new laws should be enacted, funded, and strictly enforced to protect the country's groundwater drinking supplies from pollution by point and nonpoint sources.

Water is more critical than energy. We have alternative sources of energy. But with water there is no other choice.
Eugene Odum

DISCUSSION TOPICS

1. How do human activities increase the harmful effects of prolonged drought? How can these effects be reduced?

2. How do human activities contribute to flooding? How can these effects be reduced?

3. In your community:
   a. What are the major sources of the water supply?
   b. How is water use divided among agricultural, industrial, power plant cooling, and public uses? Who are the biggest consumers of water?
   c. What has happened to water prices during the past 20 years? Are they too low to encourage water conservation and reuse?
   d. What water supply problems are projected?
   e. How is water being wasted?
   f. How is drinking water treated?
   g. Has drinking water been analyzed recently for the presence of synthetic organic chemicals, especially chlorinated hydrocarbons? If so, were any found and are they being removed?
   h. What are the major nonpoint sources of contamination of surface water and groundwater?

4. Explain why dams and reservoirs may lead to more flood damage than had they not been built. Should all proposed large dams and reservoirs be scrapped? What criteria would you use in determining desirable projects?

5. Should the price of water for all uses in the United States be increased sharply to encourage water conservation? Explain. What effects might this have on the economy, on you, on the poor, on the environment?

Despite the pleas of many leading Soviet scientists, artists, and writers, there was at that time little likelihood that the plans for the factories would be abandoned. The most feasible goal of the protesters was to ensure that the highest possible degree of protection would be provided for the lake. And indeed, in addition to more advanced wastewater treatment plants, several other safeguards to protect the lake were adopted.

A special decree was passed on the need to protect Lake Baikal, and a commission was appointed to monitor water quality in the lake. A later decision required that the wood pulp manufactured by the plants be transported to other industrial centers for processing to prevent further addition of pollutants to Lake Baikal. Finally, natural reserves and other types of protected areas have been established around the lake.

As a result of all this controversy, planning, and replanning, could people feel confident that Lake Baikal had been saved from pollution? Unfortunately, the differences of opinion went on. The industrial planners continued to defend their operations, claiming no serious harm had come to the lake, that the treatment facilities were adequate, and that the lake itself could act as a purifier of pollutants.

But the chief Soviet scientist in charge of protecting the lake stated in the early 1980s that he still had serious doubts that the steps taken were sufficient. The problem is that even a small amount of pollution, an amount that might be acceptable in an ordinary lake or river, could do irreversible harm in such a unique water body as Lake Baikal. Not all of the pollutants discharged into the lake are degradable and some are highly toxic. Further, it is known that wastewater purification facilities at the wood-processing plants have been closed down on more than one occasion for improvements.

Finally, in 1987, another decree was enacted that converted one paper mill to furniture manufacturing, which involves much less pollution. A closed cycle water system was required at the other paper mill. Further reductions in timber cutting were also ordered.

Thus, after decades of controversy, Lake Baikal's amazing storehouse of biotic treasures, including many that are quite rare, may today be in somewhat less jeopardy.

The Lake Baikal saga shows clearly that environmental pollution is a worldwide phenomenon inherent in any country experiencing large-scale industrial development. Its cure involves a combination of increased funding for improved pollution abatement facilities and the political determination to see that they are used effectively.

Guest Essay Discussion

1. Do you think that Soviet officials have done enough to protect Lake Baikal? Explain.

2. Compare these efforts with those to protect the Great Lakes in the United States (see Case Study on p. 206).

6. List ten major ways to conserve water on a personal level. Which, if any, of these practices do you now use or intend to use (see Appendix 4)?

7. Explain how a river can cleanse itself of oxygen-demanding wastes. Under what conditions will this natural cleansing system fail?

8. Give your reasons for agreeing or disagreeing with the idea that we should deliberately dump most of our wastes in the ocean because it is a vast sink for diluting, dispersing, and degrading wastes, and if it becomes polluted, we can get food from other sources. Explain why banning ocean dumping alone will not stop ocean pollution.

9. Should the injection of hazardous wastes into deep underground wells be banned? Explain.

FURTHER READINGS

Ashworth, William. 1986. *The Late, Great Lakes: An Environmental History.* New York: Alfred A. Knopf.

Borgese, Elisabeth Mann. 1986. *The Future of the Oceans.* New York: Harvest House.

Conservation Foundation. 1987. *Groundwater Pollution.* Washington, D.C.: Conservation Foundation.

Cousteau, Jacques-Yves, et al. 1981. *The Cousteau Almanac: An Inventory of Life on Our Water Planet.* Garden City, N.Y.: Doubleday.

D'Elia, Christopher R. 1987. "Nutrient Enrichment of the Chesapeake Bay." *Environment,* vol. 29, no. 2, 6–11, 30–35.

Environmental Protection Agency. 1984. *A Ground-Water Protection Strategy.* Washington, D.C.: Government Printing Office.

Goldsmith, Edward, and Nicholas Hidyard, eds. 1986. *The Social and Environmental Effects of Large Dams.* 3 vols. New York: John Wiley.

Golubev, G. N., and A. K. Biswas. 1985. *Large Scale Water Transfers: Emerging Environmental and Social Experiences.* Oxford, England: Tycooly.

Hunt, Constance Elizabeth. 1988. *Down by the River: The Impact of Federal Water Projects and Policies on Biological Diversity.* Covelo, Calif.: Island Press.

King, Jonathan. 1985. *Troubled Water: The Poisoning of America's Drinking Water.* Emmaus, Penn.: Rodale Press.

Lahey, William, and Michael Connor. 1983. "The Case for Ocean Waste Disposal." *Technology Review,* Aug.-Sept., 61–68.

Loer, Raymond C. 1984. *Pollution Control for Agriculture,* 2d ed. New York: Academic Press.

Marx, Wesley. 1981. *The Oceans: Our Last Resource.* San Francisco: Sierra Club Books.

Mather, J. R. 1984. *Water Resources Distribution, Use, and Management.* New York: Wiley.

National Academy of Sciences. 1984. *Groundwater Contamination.* Washington, D.C.: National Academy Press.

National Academy of Sciences. 1985. *Ocean Disposal Systems for Sewage Sludge and Effluent.* Washington, D.C.: National Academy Press.

National Academy of Sciences. 1985. *Oil in the Sea.* Washington, D.C.: National Academy Press.

National Academy of Sciences. 1986. *Drinking Water and Health.* Washington, D.C.: National Academy Press.

Office of Technology Assessment. 1984. *Protecting the Nation's Groundwater from Contamination.* Washington, D.C.: Government Printing Office.

Patrick, R., E. Ford, and J. Quarles, eds. 1987. *Groundwater Contamination in the United States.* Philadelphia: University of Pennsylvania Press.

Postel, Sandra. 1985. *Conserving Water: The Untapped Alternative.* Washington, D.C.: Worldwatch Institute.

Pringle, Laurence. 1982. *Water—The Next Great Resource Battle.* New York: Macmillan.

Rice, Rip G. 1985. *Safe Drinking Water: The Impact of Chemicals on a Limited Resource.* Chelsea, Mich.: Lewis Publishers.

Sheaffer, John, and Leonard Stevens. 1983. *Future Water.* New York: William Morrow.

Simon, Anne W. 1985. *Neptune's Revenge: The Ocean of Tomorrow.* New York: Franklin Watts.

Watson, Lyall. 1988. *The Water Planet.* New York: Crown.

Wijkman, Anders, and Lloyd Timberlake. 1984. *Natural Disasters: Acts of God or Acts of Man?* Washington, D.C.: Earthscan.

Worster, Donald. 1985. *Rivers of Empire: Water, Aridity, and the Growth of the American West.* New York: Pantheon.

CHAPTER 9

Soil Resources

General Questions and Issues

1. What are the major components and types of soil, and what properties make a soil best suited for growing crops?

2. How serious is the problem of soil erosion in the world and in the United States?

3. What are the major methods for reducing erosion and nutrient depletion of topsoil?

4. How can soil and underlying groundwater become contaminated with hazardous chemicals, and how can such contamination be prevented?

Below that thin layer comprising the delicate organism known as the soil is a planet as lifeless as the moon.

G. Y. Jacks and R. O. Whyte

Unless you are a farmer you probably think of soil as dirt—something you don't want on your hands, clothes, or carpet. You are acutely aware of your need for air and water. But you may be unaware that your life and that of other organisms depend on soil—especially the upper portion known as topsoil.

The nutrients in the food you eat come from soil. A more accurate version of the saying that "all flesh is grass" would be "all flesh is soil nutrients." Soil also provides you with wood, paper, cotton, gravel, and many other vital materials. Soil helps purify the water you drink.

As long as it is held in place by vegetation, soil stores water, releasing it in a nourishing trickle instead of a devastating flood. Soil's decomposer organisms recycle the key chemicals we and most other forms of life need. Bacteria in soil decompose degradable forms of garbage you throw away. The buildings and roads you use are all built upon and supported by soil. Soil is truly the base of life and civilization.

Yet since the beginning of agriculture we have abused this vital, potentially renewable resource. Entire civilizations have collapsed because they mismanaged the topsoil that supported their populations (see Case Study on p. 30).

Today we have escalated soil abuse to an all-time high. We remove vegetation from vast areas of soil to grow food, to supply us with wood, to extract min-erals, and to build homes, office buildings, shopping centers, and roads. Many of these activities expose topsoil to erosion by wind and flowing water. Soil run-off pollutes water with massive amounts of sediment. This sediment fills up irrigation ditches and canals. It also fills reservoirs behind dams that we have built to supply irrigation water, control flooding, and produce electricity. This transfer of plant nutrients from land to water removes nutrients needed to grow food and trees and overfertilizes aquatic ecosystems.

Wind erosion pollutes the air with particles of soil nutrients and pesticides we have dumped on the soil. You are now breathing some of these particles. When some of these airborne particles return to the earth, they pollute and overfertilize aquatic ecosystems.

We irrigate soil to grow food. But this often pollutes the soil with salts (salinization) and too much water (waterlogging) and decreases the ability of soil to grow food.

Our solution to the mountains of garbage and hazardous chemicals we produce is to bury or dump most of it in the soil—out of sight, out of mind. Some of these chemicals kill soil microorganisms and pollute groundwater that we drink and use to irrigate crops. There is no away.

You, me, everyone must become involved in protecting the life-giving resource we call soil. In saving the soil, we save ourselves and other forms of life.

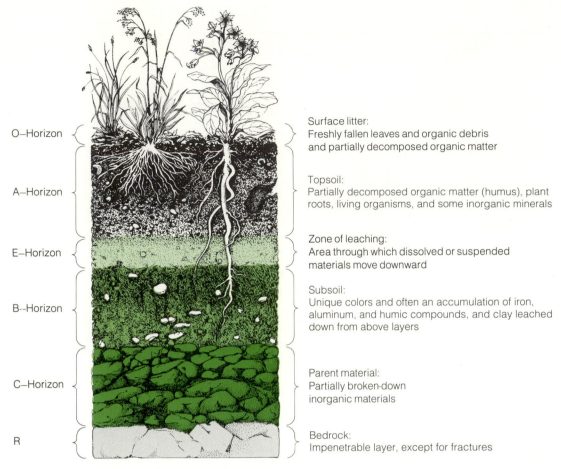

O–Horizon — Surface litter:
Freshly fallen leaves and organic debris and partially decomposed organic matter

A–Horizon — Topsoil:
Partially decomposed organic matter (humus), plant roots, living organisms, and some inorganic minerals

E–Horizon — Zone of leaching:
Area through which dissolved or suspended materials move downward

B–Horizon — Subsoil:
Unique colors and often an accumulation of iron, aluminum, and humic compounds, and clay leached down from above layers

C–Horizon — Parent material:
Partially broken-down inorganic materials

R — Bedrock:
Impenetrable layer, except for fractures

Figure 9-1 Generalized profile of soil. Layers vary in number, composition, and thickness, depending on the type of soil.

9-1   SOIL: COMPONENTS, TYPES, AND PROPERTIES

Soil Layers and Components   Pick up a handful of soil and notice how it feels and looks. The **soil** you hold in your hand is a complex mixture of inorganic minerals (mostly clay, silt, and sand), decaying organic matter, water, air, and billions of living organisms.

The components of mature soils are arranged in a series of layers called **soil horizons** (Figure 9-1). Each horizon has a distinct thickness, color, texture, and composition that vary with different types of soils. A cross-sectional view of the horizons in a soil is called a **soil profile**. Most mature soils have at least three of the six possible horizons. But some new or poorly-developed soils don't have horizons.

The top layer, the *surface-litter layer (O-horizon)*, consists mostly of freshly-fallen and partially decomposed leaves, twigs, animal waste, fungi, and other organic materials. It is usually brown to black in color. The underlying *topsoil layer (A-horizon)* is usually a porous mixture of partially decomposed organic matter (humus), living organisms, and some inorganic mineral particles. It is usually darker and looser than

deeper layers. The roots of most plants and most of a soil's organic matter are concentrated in these two upper soil layers (Figure 9-1).

The two top layers of most soils are teeming with bacteria, fungi, earthworms, and small insects. It is also home for larger, burrowing animals such as moles and gophers. All these soil organisms interact in complex food webs (Figure 9-2). Most are bacteria and other decomposer microorganisms—billions in every handful of soil. They partially or completely break down some of the complex inorganic and organic compounds in the upper layers of soil into simpler nutrient compounds that dissolve in soil water. Soil water carrying these dissolved nutrients is drawn up by the roots of plants and transported through stems and into leaves (Figure 9-3).

Some organic compounds in the two upper layers are broken down slowly and form a dark-colored mixture of organic matter called **humus**. Much of the humus is not soluble in water and it remains in the topsoil layer. It helps retain water and water-soluble plant nutrients so they can be taken up by plant roots. A fertile soil, useful for growing high yields of crops, has a thick topsoil layer containing a high content of

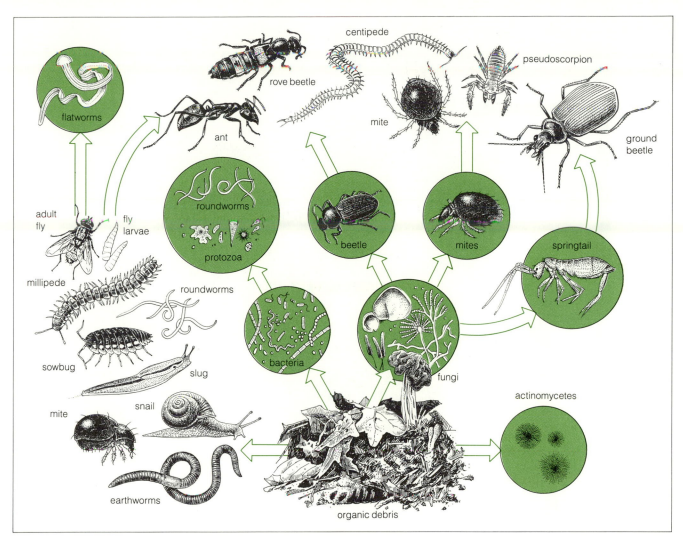

Figure 9-2 Greatly simplified food web of living organisms found in soil.

humus. When soil is eroded, it is the vital surface litter and topsoil layers that are lost.

The color of the topsoil layer tells us a lot about how useful a soil is for growing crops. For example, dark brown or black topsoil has a large amount of organic matter and is nitrogen-rich. Gray, bright yellow, or red topsoils are low in organic matter and will require nitrogen fertilizer to increase their fertility.

The B- and C-horizons contain most of a soil's inorganic matter. Most of this broken-down rock is in the form of varying mixtures of sand, silt, clay, and gravel. These and other soil layers sit atop a base of bedrock (Figure 9-1).

The spaces, or pores, between the solid organic and inorganic particles in the upper and lower soil layers contain varying amounts of two other key inorganic components: air (mostly oxygen and nitrogen gas) and water. The oxygen gas, concentrated in the topsoil, is used by the cells in plant roots to carry out cellular respiration. Some nitrogen gas is also pro-

duced from nitrates in soil by specialized bacteria as part of the nitrogen cycle (Figure 5-17, p. 108).

Some of the rain falling on the soil surface percolates downward through the soil layers and occupies some of the pores. As this water seeps downward, it dissolves and picks up various soil components in upper layers and carries them to lower layers—a process called **leaching**. Most materials leached from upper layers accumulate in the B horizon, if one has developed.

Major Types of Soil Mature soils in different biomes of the world vary widely in color, content, pore space, acidity (pH), and depth. These differences can be used to classify soils throughout the world into ten major types, or orders. Five important soil orders are mollisols, alfisols, spodosols, oxisols, and aridisols, each with a distinct soil profile (Figure 9-4). Most of the world's crops are grown on grassland mollisols and on alfisols exposed when deciduous forests are cleared.

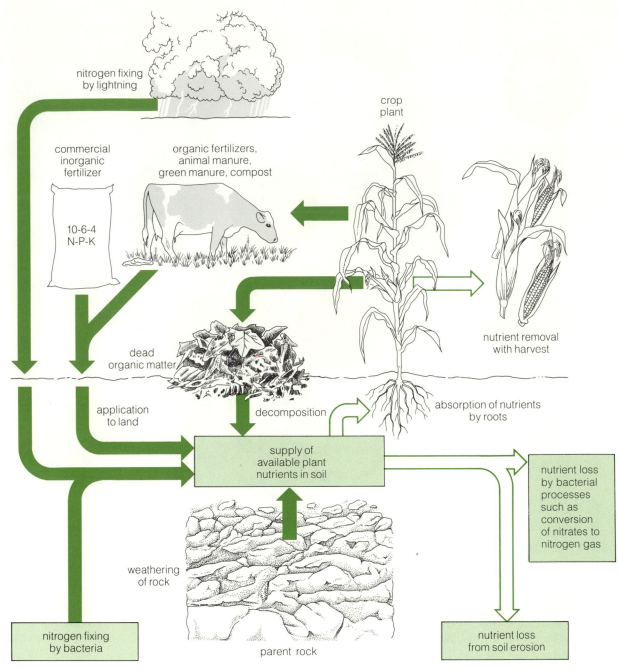

Figure 9-3 Addition and loss of plant nutrients in soils.

Soil Formation Most soil begins as bedrock. Exposure of this rock to the elements gradually breaks it down into small bits and pieces that make up most of the soil's parent inorganic material. These physical and chemical processes are called **weathering**. Other soils develop from the weathering of sediments that have been deposited on bedrock by wind, water (alluvial soils), volcanic eruptions, or melting glaciers.

Physical weathering is the breaking down of rock mostly by temperature changes and the physical action of moving ice, water, and wind. For example, rocks eventually crack and shatter when they expand and contract after being exposed to hot and cold temper-

atures. Growing roots can also exert enough pressure to enlarge cracks in solid rock, eventually splitting the rock. Plants such as mosses and lichens penetrate into rock and loosen particles.

Chemical weathering is the dissolution of rock by chemical reactions from exposure to various chemicals. They include oxygen gas in the atmosphere (oxidation), acidic rainwater, and acidic secretions of bacteria, fungi, roots, and lichens. Where average temperatures and moisture levels are high, these chemical reactions take place rapidly; in colder and drier regions they take place at a slower rate.

The slope of the land also affects the type of soil

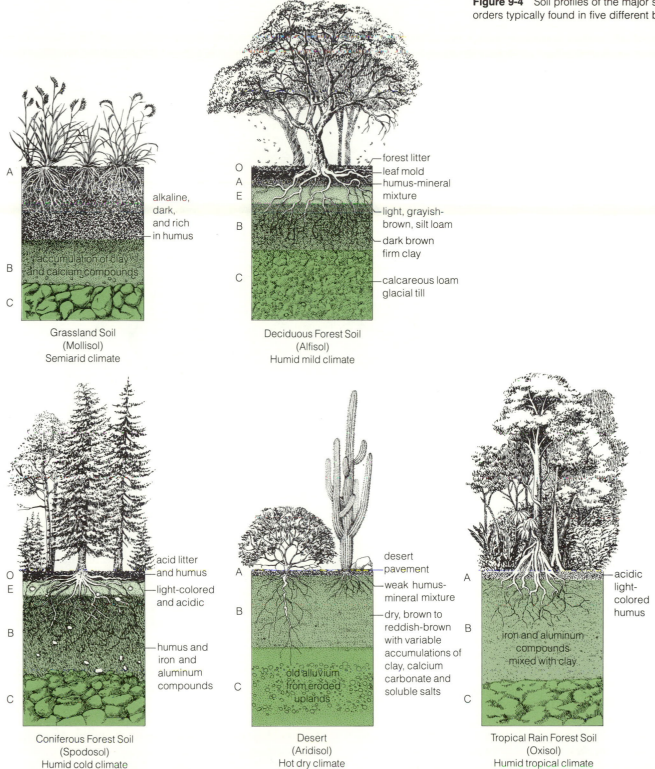

Figure 9-4 Soil profiles of the major soil orders typically found in five different biomes.

Grassland Soil
(Mollisol)
Semiarid climate

- A — alkaline, dark, and rich in humus
- B — accumulation of clay and calcium compounds
- C

Deciduous Forest Soil
(Alfisol)
Humid mild climate

- O — forest litter
- A — leaf mold
- E — humus-mineral mixture
- B — light, grayish-brown, silt loam
- — dark brown firm clay
- C — calcareous loam glacial till

Coniferous Forest Soil
(Spodosol)
Humid cold climate

- O — acid litter and humus
- E — light-colored and acidic
- B
- C — humus and iron and aluminum compounds

Desert
(Aridisol)
Hot dry climate

- A — desert pavement
- — weak humus-mineral mixture
- B — dry, brown to reddish-brown with variable accumulations of clay, calcium carbonate and soluble salts
- C — old alluvium from eroded uplands

Tropical Rain Forest Soil
(Oxisol)
Humid tropical climate

- A — acidic light-colored humus
- B — iron and aluminum compounds mixed with clay
- C

and the rate at which it forms. When the slope is steep, the actions of wind, flowing water, and gravity tend to quickly erode the soil. That is why soils on steep slopes often are thin and infertile. By contrast, valley soils, which receive mineral particles, nutrients, water, and organic matter from adjacent slopes, are often fertile and highly productive if not too wet.

Soil Texture and Porosity   Soils vary in their content of clay (very fine particles), silt (fine particles), sand (coarse particles), and gravel (large particles). The relative amounts of the different sizes and types of particles determine **soil texture.** Figure 9-5 shows how clay, silt, and sand content can be used to group soils into textural classes.

Figure 9-5 Soil texture depends on the percentages of clay, silt, and sand particles in the soil. Soil texture affects soil porosity—the average number and spacing of pores or spaces in a volume of soil. Loams are the best soils for growing most crops. (Data from USDA Soil Conservation Service)

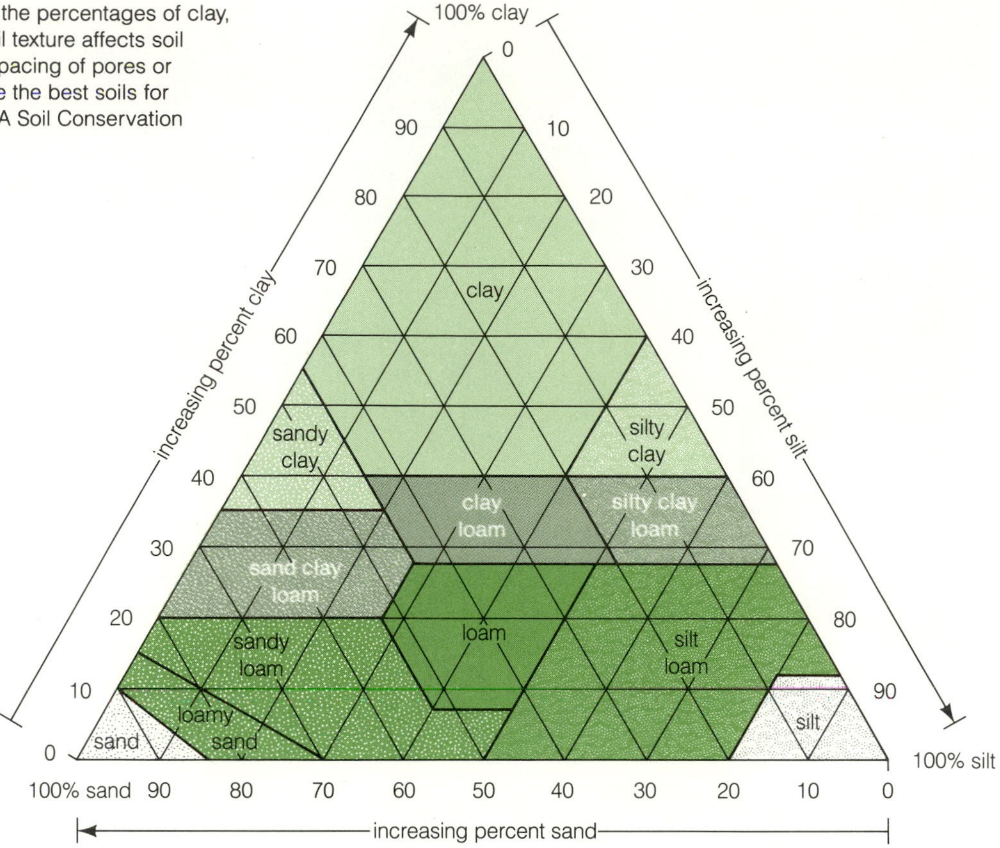

Soil texture helps determine **soil porosity**—a measure of the volume of voids or pores a volume of soil has and the average distances between these spaces. A soil with a high porosity can hold more water and air than one with a lower porosity. Average pore size determines *soil permeability*, the rate at which the soil transmits water and air from upper to lower layers. Soil porosity is also influenced by *soil structure*—how the particles that make up a soil are organized and clumped together.

Soils fall into three broad textural classes: loams, sandy, and clay. Soils, called *loams*, contain almost equal amounts of sand and silt and somewhat less clay. They are the best for growing most crops because such soils can retain a fairly large amount of water that is not held too tightly for plant roots to absorb.

Sandy soils are easy to work and have less pore space per total volume of soil (lower porosity) than other soils. However, sandy soils have a high permeability because their pores are larger than those in most other soils. This explains why water flows rapidly through sandy soils. They are useful for growing irrigated crops or those without large water requirements, such as peanuts and strawberries.

The particles in *clay soils* are very small and easily packed together when compacted from above. When these soils get wet, they form large, dense clumps. That is why wet clay is so easy to mold into bricks and

pottery. Clay soils have more pore space per volume and a greater water-holding capacity than sandy soils. But the pore spaces are so small that these soils have a low permeability. Little water can infiltrate to lower levels and the upper layers of these soils can easily become too waterlogged to grow most crops.

To get a general idea of a soil's texture, take a small amount of topsoil, moisten it, and rub it between your fingers and thumb. A gritty feel means that it contains a lot of sand. A sticky feel means that it has a high clay content. You should also be able to roll such soil into a clump. Silt-laden soil feels smooth (like flour). A loam topsoil best suited for plant growth has a texture between these extremes. It has a crumbly, spongy feeling, and many of its particles are clumped loosely together.

Soil Acidity (pH) The acidity or alkalinity of a soil is another factor determining the types of crops it can support. Scientists use pH as a simple measure of the degree of acidity or alkalinity of a solution. A solution with a pH of less than 7 is acidic; one with a pH of 7 is neutral; and one with a pH greater than 7 is basic, or alkaline (Figure 7-18, p. 163). Each whole-number change in pH represents a tenfold increase or decrease in acidity.

The five types of soils shown in Figure 9-4 vary in acidity. The most acidic are spodosols, which support

Figure 9-6 Wind eroding soil from Iowa farmland in 1930. If grass had been planted between crops, most of this loss of valuable topsoil could have been prevented.

Figure 9-7 Severe soil erosion and gully formation caused by flowing water on a North Carolina farm.

coniferous forests, and to a lesser extent oxisols, which underlie tropical rain forests. Mollisols found in grasslands and alfisols, which typically support deciduous forests, are slightly acidic. The aridisols found in deserts are slightly basic.

Crops vary in the pH ranges they can tolerate. For example, wheat, spinach, peas, corn, and tomatoes grow best in slightly acidic soils; potatoes and berries do best in very acidic soils; and alfalfa and asparagus in neutral soils. When soils are too acidic for the desired crops, the acids can be partially neutralized by an alkaline substance such as lime. But adding lime speeds up the undesirable decomposition of organic matter in the soil, so manure or another organic fertilizer should also be added to maintain soil fertility.

In areas of low rainfall, such as the semiarid valleys in the western and southwestern United States, calcium and other alkaline compounds are not leached away. Soils in the region may be too alkaline (pH above 7.5) for some crops. If drainage is good, irrigation can reduce the alkalinity by leaching the alkaline compounds away. Adding sulfur, which is gradually converted to sulfuric acid by soil bacteria, is another way to reduce soil alkalinity. Soils in areas affected by acid deposition are becoming increasingly acidic (Figure 7-19, p. 164).

9-2 SOIL EROSION

Natural and Human-Accelerated Soil Erosion Soil does not stay in one place indefinitely. **Soil erosion** is the movement of soil components, especially topsoil, from one place to another. The two main forces causing soil erosion are wind (Figure 9-6) and flowing water (Figure 9-7). Some soil erosion always takes place because of natural water flow and winds. But the roots of plants generally protect soil from excessive erosion.

Agriculture, logging, construction, and other human activities that remove plant cover greatly accelerate the rate at which soil erodes.

Soil scientists distinguish between three types of erosion by water: sheet, rill, and gully. **Sheet erosion** occurs when surface water moves down a slope or across a field in a wide flow. Because it erodes topsoil evenly, it may not be noticeable until much damage has been done. In **rill erosion** the surface water forms rivulets that flow at high velocities through miniature valleys. In **gully erosion** the rivulets join together, forming large, high-velocity flows (Figure 9-7).

Excessive erosion of topsoil reduces both the fertility and the water-holding capacity of a soil. The resulting sediment, the largest single source of water pollution, clogs irrigation ditches, navigable waterways, and reservoirs.

Soil, especially the topsoil or A-horizon (Figure 9-1), is classified as a renewable resource because it is continually regenerated by natural processes. However, if the average rate of topsoil erosion exceeds the rate of topsoil formation on a piece of land, the topsoil on that land becomes a nonrenewable resource being depleted.

In tropical and temperate areas the renewal of one inch of soil takes an average of 500 years (with a range of 220 to 1,000 years). Worldwide annual erosion rates for agricultural land are 18 to 100 times this natural renewal rate. Table 9-1 compares the major properties that affect soil nutrient accumulation and soil renewability in natural and cultivated ecosystems.

Soil erosion also occurs in forestland and rangeland but is not as severe as that in the more exposed soil of agricultural land (Figure 9-8). However, soil erosion in managed forests is a major concern, because the soil re-formation rate of forests is two to three times slower than that of cropland. A logging project in Oregon quadrupled the sediment washed into

Table 9-1 Characteristics That Affect Soil Nutrient Content and Soil Erosion in Natural and Cultivated Terrestrial Ecosystems

Factor	Natural	Cultivated
Abiotic		
Water infiltration rate	High	Low
Water runoff rate	Low	High
Soil erosion rate	Low	High
Leaching losses	Low	High
Mineral loss rate	Low	High
Soil organic matter	High	Low
Soil temperature	Low	High
Biotic		
Structural diversity of plants	High	Low
Plant and animal species diversity	High	Low
Plant reproductive potential	High	Low

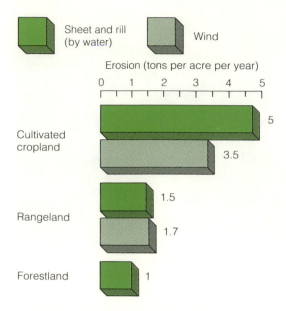

Figure 9-8 Average annual erosion rates on various types of land in the United States. These average values mask much higher rates on many parcels of heavily used land. An erosion rate of five tons per acre per year amounts to a loss of about one inch every thirty years. Natural replacement of an inch of topsoil in temperate areas typically takes 500 years. (Data from U.S. Soil Conservation Service)

nearby streams, and surface mining in Wyoming caused an elevenfold increase in erosion.

Construction sites usually have the highest erosion rates by far. After bulldozers remove all or most of the vegetation from a construction site, most developers and builders do little to prevent erosion of the bare soil. Studies have found that highway construction in Virginia accelerated erosion 200 times the natural rates, while a shopping center development in Maryland boosted erosion rates 100 times. In a few years off-road vehicles have eroded soil off parts of California that nature will take 1,000 years to replace.

The World Situation Today topsoil is eroding faster than it forms on about one-third of the world's cropland. The amount of topsoil washing and blowing into the world's rivers, lakes, and oceans each year would fill a train of freight cars long enough to encircle the planet 150 times. At this rate the world is losing about 7% of its topsoil from potential cropland each decade. The situation is worsening as cultivation is extended into areas unsuited for agriculture to feed the world's growing population. Such mining of the soil converts a potentially renewable resource into a nonrenewable resource.

In mountainous areas, such as the Himalayas on the border between India and Tibet and the Andes near the west coast of South America, farmers traditionally built elaborate systems of terraces (Figure 9-9). This allowed them to cultivate steeply sloping land that would otherwise rapidly lose its topsoil. Today farmers in some areas cultivate steep slopes without terraces, causing a total loss of topsoil in 10 to 40 years. Although most poor farmers know that cultivating a steep slope without terracing causes a rapid loss of topsoil, they often have too little time and too few workers to build terraces.

Since the beginning of agriculture, people in tropical forests have successfully used slash-and-burn, shifting cultivation (Figure 2-2, p. 29) to provide food for relatively small populations. In recent decades, growing population and poverty have caused cultivators in many tropical forest areas to reduce the fallow period to as little as 2 years instead of the 10 to 30 years needed to allow the soil to regain its fertility. The result has been a sharp increase in the rate of topsoil erosion and nutrient depletion.

Overgrazing and poor logging practices also cause heavy losses of topsoil. Intense grazing has turned many areas of North Africa from grassland to desert (See Case Study on p. 225). Once-forested hills in many LDCs have been stripped bare of trees by poor people as a source of firewood for cooking and heating, and by timber companies for use in MDCs. Because new trees are seldom planted, the topsoil quickly erodes away.

In MDCs, where large-scale industrialized agriculture is practiced, many farmers have replaced traditional soil conservation practices with massive inputs of commercial inorganic fertilizers and irrigation water. But the tenfold increase in fertilizer use and the tripling of the world's irrigated cropland between 1950

Figure 9-9 Crop terraces in Pisac, Peru, reduce soil erosion. They also increase the amount of usable land in steep terrain.

Ira Kirschenbaum/Stock, Boston

and 1988 have only temporarily masked the effects of erosion and nutrient depletion.

Commercial inorganic fertilizer is not a complete substitute for naturally fertile topsoil; it merely hides for a time the gradual depletion of this vital resource. Nor is irrigation a long-term solution. Repeated irrigation of cropland without sufficient drainage eventually decreases or destroys its crop productivity as a result of waterlogging and salt buildup (salinization).

Severe erosion accelerated by human activities is most widespread in India, China, the Soviet Union, and the United States, which together account for over half the world's food production and contain almost half the world's people. In China, for example, at least 34% of the land is severely eroded, and river siltation is now a nationally recognized threat. Soil erosion and river siltation are also major problems in India, with erosion affecting one-quarter of the country's land area. The Worldwatch Institute estimates that the Soviet Union, which has the world's largest cropland area, may be losing more topsoil than any other country.

The U.S. Situation According to surveys by the Soil Conservation Service (SCS), about one-third of the original topsoil on U.S. croplands in use today has already been washed or blown into rivers, lakes, and oceans. Surveys also show that the average rate of erosion on cultivated land in the United States is about seven times the rate of natural soil formation.

CASE STUDY Desertification: A Serious and Growing Problem

More than one-third of the earth's land—inhabited by 850 million people—is classified as arid or semiarid desert (see map inside back cover). In drier parts of the world, desert areas are increasing at an alarming rate from a combination of natural processes and human activities.

The conversion of rangeland (uncultivated land used for animal grazing), rain-fed cropland, or irrigated cropland to desertlike land with a drop in agricultural productivity of 10% or more is called **desertification**.

Moderate desertification causes a 10% to 25% drop in productivity, and severe desertification causes a 25% to 50% drop. Very severe desertification causes a drop of 50% or more and usually results in formation of massive gullies and sand dunes.

Most desertification occurs naturally at sites near the edges of existing deserts. It is caused by dehydration of the top layers of soil during prolonged drought and increased evaporation because of hot temperatures and high winds.

However, natural desertification is greatly accelerated by practices that leave the soil on land used for agriculture and forestry vulnerable to erosion by water and wind. These topsoil depletion processes include:

- overgrazing of rangeland by having too many livestock on too little land area
- improper soil and water resource management that leads to increased erosion, salinization, and waterlogging of soil

- cultivation of land with unsuitable terrain or soils
- deforestation and strip mining without adequate replanting

It is estimated that about 2 billion acres—an area ten times the size of Texas—have become desertified during the past 50 years (Figure 9-10). At least 50 million people, half of them in Africa, have not been able to feed themselves because of desertification. Another 400 million people in moderately desertified areas have a reduced capacity to support themselves.

Each year an estimated 14.8 million acres of new desert are formed. Most of it is in sub-Saharan Africa, between North Africa's barren Sahara desert

(continued)

But an average national soil erosion rate masks much higher rates of soil erosion in heavily farmed regions, especially the corn belt and Great Plains. Some of the country's most productive agricultural lands, such as those in Iowa, have lost about half their topsoil. Among major crops, land used for cotton has the highest average annual erosion rate, followed by soybean-, corn-, and wheat-growing lands.

Enough topsoil erodes away each day in the United States to fill a line of dump trucks 3,500 miles long. Two-thirds of this soil comes from less than one-fourth of the country's cropland. The plant nutrient losses from this erosion are worth at least $18 billion a year. This erosion also causes $4 billion a year in damages when silt, plant nutrients, and pesticides are carried into rivers, lakes, and reservoirs.

Soil erosion is also bad for wildlife. A drop in soil fertility means less food. This can affect the size and health of animal populations. Excessive silt washing into lakes and streams can reduce—even eliminate— some fish populations.

Unless soil conservation efforts are increased, projected soil erosion may destroy productivity on U.S. cropland acreage equal to the combined areas of the

---

CASE STUDY (Continued)

and the plant-rich land to its south. In 1983, the southern edge of the Sahara moved almost 180 miles south, a massive increase in desert land.

According to the UN Environmental Programme, one-fifth of the world's people now live in areas that may become desertified over the next 20 years. Mali may be the first country to become uninhabitable because of spreading desertification. Many of its 8.7 million people begin each day by shoveling the night's accumulation of sand from their doors.

The spread of desertification can be halted or sharply reduced by improved management of rangeland, forest, soil and water resources. Also, much presently desertified land can be reclaimed. The total cost of such prevention and rehabilitation would be about $141 billion—only five and one-half times the estimated $26 billion annual loss in agricultural productivity from desertified land. Thus, once this potential productivity is restored, the costs of the program could be recouped in five to ten years. What do you think should be done?

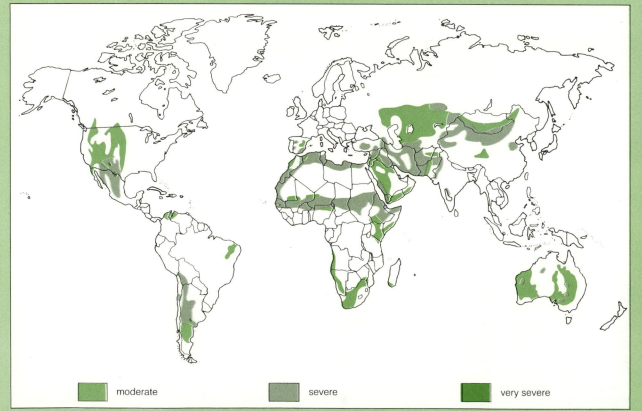

moderate   severe   very severe

Figure 9-10 Desertification of arid and semiarid lands. (Data from UN Environmental Programme and Harold E. Dregnue)

states of New York, New Jersey, Maine, New Hampshire, Massachusetts, and Connecticut over the next 50 years.

At present, soil conservation is practiced on only about half of all U.S. farmland and on less than half of the country's most erodible cropland. Increased soil conservation is particularly important in the fertile midwestern plains, which are subject to high rates of erosion from continuous high winds and periodic prolonged drought (see Case Study below).

9-3 SOIL CONSERVATION AND LAND-USE CONTROL

Conservation Tillage   The practice of **soil conservation** involves using various methods to reduce soil erosion, to prevent depletion of soil nutrients, and to restore nutrients already lost by erosion, leaching, and excessive crop harvesting. Most methods used to control soil erosion involve keeping the soil covered with vegetation.

CASE STUDY   The Dust Bowl: Will It Happen Again?

The Great Plains of the United States stretch through ten states, from Texas through Montana and the Dakotas. The region is normally dry and very windy and periodically experiences long, severe droughts.

Before settlers began grazing livestock and planting crops in the 1870s, the extensive root systems of prairie grasses held the topsoil of these mollisol soils in place (Figure 9-4). When the land was planted in crops, these perennial grasses were replaced by annual crops with less extensive root systems. In addition, the land was plowed up after each harvest and left bare part of the year. Overgrazing also destroyed large areas

of grass, leaving the ground bare. The stage was set for crop failures during prolonged droughts, followed by severe wind erosion.

The droughts arrived in 1890 and 1910 and again with even greater severity between 1926 and 1934, the driest year in this century. In 1934, hot, dry windstorms created dust clouds thick enough to cause darkness at midday in some areas (Figure 9-11). The danger of breathing this dust-laden air was revealed by the dead rabbits and birds left in its wake.

During May 1934 the entire eastern half of the United States was blanketed with a massive dust cloud of topsoil blown off the Great Plains from as far as 1,500

miles away. Ships 200 miles out in the Atlantic Ocean received deposits of midwestern topsoil. These events gave a portion of the Great Plains a tragic new name: the Dust Bowl (Figure 9-12).

About 9 million acres of cropland were destroyed and 80 million acres severely damaged. Thousands of displaced farm families from Oklahoma, Texas, Kansas, and other states migrated to California or to the industrial cities of the Midwest and East. Most found no jobs because the country was in the midst of the Great Depression. These migrants, who once grew food for themselves and others, joined massive numbers of unemployed people waiting in line

(continued)

Figure 9-11   Dust storm approaching Prowers County, Colorado, in 1934.

USDA/Soil Conservation Service

Figure 9-12   The Dust Bowl, the Great Plains area where a combination of periodic severe drought and poor soil conservation practices led to massive losses of topsoil, primarily from wind erosion, in the mid-1930s.

In **conventional-tillage farming**, the land is plowed, disked several times, and smoothed to make a planting surface. If plowed in the fall so that crops can be planted in the spring, the soil is left bare during the winter and early spring months—a practice that makes it vulnerable to erosion.

To lower labor costs, save energy, and reduce erosion, an increasing number of U.S. farmers are using **conservation-tillage farming**, also known as minimum-tillage or no-till farming, depending on the degree to which the soil is disturbed. Farmers using this method disturb the soil as little as possible in planting crops.

For the minimum-tillage method, special tillers break up and loosen the subsurface soil without turning over the topsoil, previous crop residues, and any cover vegetation. For no-till farming, special planting machines inject seeds, fertilizers, and weed killers (herbicides) into slits made in the unplowed soil (Figure 9-13).

In addition to reducing soil erosion, conservation tillage reduces fuel and tillage costs, water loss from the soil, and soil compaction and increases the number of crops that can be grown during a season (multiple cropping). Yields are as high as or higher than yields from conventional tillage. Depending on the soil type, this approach can be used for three to seven years before more extensive soil cultivation is needed

USDA/Soil Conservation Service

Figure 9-13 No-till farming. A specially designed machine plants seeds and adds fertilizers and weed killers at the same time with almost no disturbance of the soil.

to prevent crop yields from declining. Conservation tillage, however, requires increased use of herbicides to control weeds that compete with crops for soil nutrients.

This type of tillage may also benefit wildlife if problems from use of herbicides and pesticides can be eliminated by using other alternatives (see Enrichment Study at end of Chapter 11). By leaving cover

---

CASE STUDY (Continued)

for free food to keep themselves and their families alive.

In May 1934 Hugh Bennett of the U.S. Department of Agriculture (USDA) addressed a congressional hearing, pleading for new programs to protect the country's topsoil. Lawmakers in Washington took action when dust blown from the Great Plains began seeping into the hearing room.

In 1935 the United States established the Soil Conservation Service as part of the Department of Agriculture. With Bennett as its first head, the SCS began promoting good conservation practices in the Great Plains and later in every state. Soil conservation districts were established throughout the country, and farmers and ranchers were given technical assistance in setting up soil conservation programs.

These efforts, however, did not completely stop human-accelerated erosion in the Great Plains. The basic problem is that the climate of much of the region makes it better suited for grazing than for farming. Farmers have had to relearn this ecological lesson several times since the 1930s. For example, because of severe drought and soil erosion in the 1950s, the federal government had to provide emergency relief funds to many Great Plains farmers.

Because periodic, prolonged droughts are a natural part of the Great Plains, their effect on agriculture should not be viewed as a natural disaster. Instead, they are disasters caused by people insisting on trying to grow crops in an area that is not suitable for long-term, sustainable agriculture.

In 1975 the Council of Agricultural Science and Technology warned that severe drought could again create a dust bowl in the Great Plains. The council pointed out that despite large expenditures for erosion control, topsoil losses in the 1970s were 2.5% worse than in the 1930s.

So far, these warnings have not been heeded. Great Plains farmers, many of them debt-ridden because of low crop prices, have continued to stave off bankruptcy by maximizing production and minimizing expenditures for soil conservation. If the greenhouse effect makes this region even drier, farming will have to be abandoned. What do you think should be done about this situation?

USDA/Soil Conservation Service

Figure 9-14 On this gently sloping land, contoured rows planted with alternating crops (strip cropping) reduce soil erosion.

on the ground, conservation tillage can provide more nesting habitat for wildlife, especially birds.

But conservation tillage is no cure-all. It requires farmers to be better managers. Planting and applications of herbicides and pesticides must be more carefully timed than with most other types of cultivation.

By 1987 conservation tillage was used on about 30% of U.S. croplands and is projected to be used on over half by 2000. The USDA estimates that using conservation tillage on 80% of U.S. cropland would reduce soil erosion by at least half. So far the practice is not widely used in other parts of the world.

Contour Farming, Terracing, and Strip Cropping Soil erosion can be reduced 30% to 50% on gently sloping land through **contour farming**—plowing and planting along rather than up and down the sloped contour of the land (Figure 9-14). Each row planted at a right angle to the slope of the land acts as a small dam to help hold soil and slow the runoff of water.

Terracing can be used on steeper slopes. The slope is converted into a series of broad, nearly level terraces with short vertical drops from one to another (Figure 9-9). Some of the water running down the vegetated slope is retained by each terrace. Thus, terracing provides water for crops at all levels and decreases soil erosion by reducing the amount and speed of water runoff. In areas of high rainfall, diversion ditches must be built behind each terrace to permit adequate drainage.

In **strip cropping**, a series of rows of one row crop, such as corn or soybeans, is planted in a wide strip; the next strip is planted with a cover crop, such as alfalfa, which completely covers the soil and thus reduces erosion (Figure 9-14). The alternating strips of row crops and cover crops also reduce water runoff and help prevent the spread of pests and plant dis-

eases from one strip to another. They also help restore soil fertility when nitrogen-rich legumes such as soybeans or alfalfa are planted in some of the strips. On sloping land, strip cropping can reduce soil losses up to 75% when combined with terracing or contour farming.

Gully Reclamation and Windbreaks Water runoff quickly creates gullies in sloping land not covered by vegetation (Figure 9-7). Such land can be restored by **gully reclamation** (Figure 9-15). Small gullies can be seeded with quick-growing plants such as oats, barley, and wheat to reduce erosion. In deeper gullies, small dams can be built to collect silt and gradually fill in the channels. Then, rapidly growing shrubs, vines, and trees can be planted to stabilize the soil. Channels built to divert water away from the gully will prevent further erosion.

Erosion caused by exposure of cultivated lands to high winds can be reduced by **windbreaks**, or **shelterbelts**. These are long rows of trees planted in a direction to partially block wind flow over cropland (Figure 9-16). They are especially effective if land not under cultivation is kept covered with vegetation. Windbreaks also provide habitats for birds, pest-eating and pollinating insects, and other animals. Unfortunately, many of the windbreaks planted in the upper Great Plains following the Dust Bowl disaster of the 1930s have been destroyed to make way for large irrigation systems and farm machinery.

In their struggle to stay solvent, many farmers have stopped rotating crops to give fields a rest. They have also eliminated strip cropping and farmed land subject to high erosion rates. The problem is that farmers who spend money and time protecting their soil from erosion don't get a dime more for their crops than farmers who exploit their soil. In the long run such

USDA/Soil Conservation Service

Figure 9-15 Gully reclamation on a farm in Gilmore County, Minnesota. The severely eroded gully (left) was planted with vegetation, primarily locust trees. After five growing seasons the trees had grown enough to control erosion (right). They also provided habitats for wildlife.

Figure 9-16 Windbreaks, or shelterbelts, reduce erosion on this farm in Trail County, North Dakota. They also reduce wind damage, help hold soil moisture in place, supply some wood for fuel, and provide a habitat for wildlife.

USDA/Soil Conservation Service

short-term exploitation of the soil leads to drops in crop productivity and income. But to stay in business this year and the next, debt-ridden farmers feel compelled to degrade their soil. Many farmers not having serious financial problems also degrade their land to increase short-term income.

Land-Use Classification and Control To encourage wise land use and reduce erosion, the Soil Conservation Service has set up the classification system summarized in Table 9-2 and illustrated in Figure 9-17. An obvious land-use approach to reducing erosion is to prohibit the planting of crops or the clearing of vegetation on marginal land (classes V through VIII in Table 9-2). Such land is highly erodible because of

a steep slope, shallow soil structure, high winds, periodic drought, or other factors.

Since World War II, the typical pattern of suburban housing development in the United States has been to bulldoze a tract of woods or farmland and build rows of houses, each standard house on a standard lot (Figure 9-18). By removing most vegetation, this approach increases soil erosion during and after construction. Someone noted that the United States is where they cut down the trees and eliminate most of the wildlife in an area and then name the streets and developments after them—*Oak Lane*, *Cedar Drive*, *Pheasant Run*, *Fox Fields*.

In recent years, there has been increased use of a new pattern, known as *cluster development* or *planned*

Table 9-2 Land Capability Classification According to the Soil Conservation Service

Land Class	Characteristics	Primary Uses	Secondary Uses	Conservation Measures
Land Suitable for Cultivation				
I	Excellent flat, well-drained land	Agriculture	Recreation Wildlife Pasture	None
II	Good land has minor limitations such as slight slope, sandy soil, or poor drainage	Agriculture Pasture	Recreation Wildlife	Strip cropping Contour farming
III	Moderately good land with important limitations of soil, slope, or drainage	Agriculture Pasture Watershed	Recreation Wildlife Urban industry	Contour farming Strip cropping Waterways Terraces
V	Fair land, severe limitations of soil, slope, or drainage	Pasture Orchards Limited agriculture Urban industry	Pasture Wildlife	Farming on a limited basis Contour farming Strip cropping Waterways Terraces
Land Not Suitable for Cultivation				
V	Rockiness; shallow soil, wetness, or slope prevents farming	Grazing Forestry Watershed	Recreation Wildlife	No special precautions if properly grazed or logged; must not be plowed
VI	Moderate limitations for grazing and forestry	Grazing Forestry Watershed Urban industry	Recreation Wildlife	Grazing or logging should be limited at times
VII	Severe limitations for grazing and forestry	Grazing Forestry Watershed Recreation-Aesthetics Wildlife Urban industry		Careful management required when used for grazing or logging
VIII	Unsuitable for grazing and forestry because of steep slope, shallow soil, lack of water, too much water	Recreation-Aesthetics Watershed Wildlife Urban industry		Not to be used for grazing or logging

unit development. Houses, townhouses, condominiums, and garden apartments are built on only part of the tract. The rest of the area is left as open space, either in its natural state or modified for recreation (Figure 9-19). This approach helps reduce soil erosion by preserving medium-size blocks of open space and natural vegetation.

In rapidly expanding urban areas local governments can control the rate of development by limiting the number of building permits, sewer hookups, roads, and other services. State and federal governments can take any of the following measures to protect cropland, forestland, wetlands, and other nonurban lands near expanding urban areas from development and degradation:

- tax breaks to landowners who agree to use land only for specified purposes such as agriculture, wilderness, wildlife habitat, or nondestructive forms of recreation

- direct purchase and protection of ecologically valuable land by a public agency (or by a private interest such as the Nature Conservancy or the Audubon Society)

- purchase by public agencies of land development rights that restrict the way land can be used (for example, to preserve prime farmland near cities from development)

- assigning a limited number of transferable development rights to a given area of land

LAND CAPABILITY CLASSES			
SUITABLE FOR CULTIVATION		NO CULTIVATION - PASTURE, HAY, WOODLAND AND WILDLIFE	
I	REQUIRES GOOD SOIL MANAGEMENT PRACTICES ONLY	V	NO RESTRICTIONS IN USE
II	MODERATE CONSERVATION PRACTICES NECESSARY	VI	MODERATE RESTRICTIONS IN USE
III	INTENSIVE CONSERVATION PRACTICES NECESSARY	VII	SEVERE RESTRICTIONS IN USE
IV	PERENNIAL VEGETATION - INFREQUENT CULTIVATION	VIII	BEST SUITED FOR WILDLIFE AND RECREATION

USDA/Soil Conservation Service

Figure 9-17 Classification of land according to capability; see Table 9-2 for description of each class.

USDA/Soil Conservation Service

Figure 9-18 A typical suburban housing tract. Note that all trees have been removed. Such areas have very high erosion rates during and after construction.

- requiring environmental impact analysis for proposed private and public projects such as roads, industrial parks, shopping centers, and suburban developments; canceling harmful projects unless they are revised to minimize harmful environmental impact

- subsidies to farmers for taking highly erodible cropland out of production (see Spotlight on p. 233)

Maintaining and Restoring Soil Fertility Organic fertilizers and commercial inorganic fertilizers can be applied to soil to partially restore and maintain plant nutrients lost by erosion, leaching, and crop harvesting and to increase crop yields (Figure 9-3). Three major types of **organic fertilizer** are animal manure, green manure, and compost. **Animal manure** includes the dung and urine of cattle, horses, poultry, and other farm animals. In some LDCs human manure, sometimes called night soil, is used to fertilize crops.

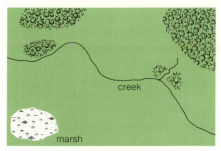

Undeveloped Land

Typical Housing Development

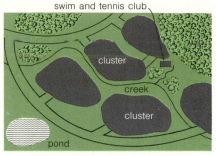

Cluster Housing Development

Figure 9-19 Conventional and planned unit developments as they would appear if constructed on the same land area. The plan on the right sharply reduces soil erosion, provides wildlife habitats and outdoor recreational opportunities, and gives residents a more beautiful place to live.

Application of animal manure improves soil structure, increases organic nitrogen content, and stimulates the growth and reproduction of soil bacteria and fungi. It is particularly useful on crops of corn, cotton, potatoes, cabbage, and tobacco.

Despite its effectiveness, the use of animal manure in the United States has decreased. One reason is that separate farms for growing crops and animals have replaced most mixed animal- and crop-farming operations. Animal manure is available at feedlots near urban areas, but transporting it to distant rural crop-growing areas usually costs too much. In addition, tractors and other motorized farm machinery have replaced horses and other draft animals that naturally added manure to the soil.

Green manure is fresh or growing green vegetation plowed into the soil to increase the organic matter and humus available to the next crop. It may consist of weeds in an uncultivated field, grasses and clover in a field previously used for pasture, or legumes such as alfalfa or soybeans grown for use as fertilizer to build up soil nitrogen.

Compost is a rich natural fertilizer; farmers produce it by piling up alternating layers of carbohydrate-rich plant wastes (such as cuttings and leaves), animal manure, and topsoil. This mixture provides a home for microorganisms that aid the decomposition of the plant and manure layers.

Today, especially in the United States and other industrialized countries, farmers partially restore and maintain soil fertility by applying **commercial inorganic fertilizers**. The most common plant nutrients in these products are nitrogen (as ammonium ions, nitrate ions, or urea), phosphorus (as phosphate ions), and potassium. Other plant nutrients may also be present in low or trace amounts. Farmers can have their soil and harvested crops chemically analyzed to determine the mix of nutrients that should be added.

Inorganic commercial fertilizers can be easily transported, stored, and applied. Throughout the world their use increased tenfold between 1950 and 1988. By 1988 the additional food they helped produce fed one of every three persons in the world.

Commercial inorganic fertilizers, however, have some disadvantages. They do not add humus to the soil. Unless animal manure and green manure are added to the soil along with commercial inorganic fertilizers, the soil's organic matter content and thus its ability to hold water will decrease. If not supplemented by organic fertilizers, inorganic fertilizers cause the soil to become compacted and less suitable for crop growth. By decreasing its porosity, inorganic fertilizers also lower the oxygen content of soil and prevent added fertilizer from being taken up as efficiently. In addition, most commercial fertilizers do not contain many of the nutrients needed in trace amounts by plants.

Water pollution is another problem caused by the

CASE STUDY How to Manage Soil for Homesites and Home Gardens

Unless instructed otherwise, most builders remove the topsoil from a homesite and sell it to increase their profits. This leaves the home owner with a hard subsoil that contains little organic matter and is not fertile enough to support most plants.

The home owner can rebuild topsoil gradually by planting a crop of grass or other ground cover, plowing it up, turning it into the soil as green manure, and then repeating the process with another crop. Another option is to buy enough good-quality topsoil (examine it carefully before purchase) to cover the ground with four to five inches of soil.

If you are building a home, you can avoid this problem by requiring the contractor not to disturb any topsoil unless necessary, to save and replace any topsoil that must be removed, and to set up barriers to catch any soil eroded during construction. Some type of rapidly growing grass or ground cover should be planted on all areas of exposed soil as soon as possible after construction is complete.

After moving into a new or existing house, you need to determine the site's soil type and its suitability for growing various types of vegetation such as crops, grass, flowers, and trees. If the topsoil was not removed during construction, start by finding out if the site has been included on a soil survey map published for about 1,700 counties of the United States. Copies are available in most county libraries, the county agricultural extension office, or the nearest U.S. Soil Conservation Service office. There is a small charge.

If no soil survey is available or if you have purchased new topsoil, use a spade, soil auger, or posthole digger to dig down three to four feet a few inches at a time at several locations. Examine each layer for texture, color, and rock content, using the information in Section 9-1 to determine the soil's generalized mixture of clay, sand, and silt.

A dark brown or red soil usually indicates good drainage. A black top layer indicates a high content of organic matter. Pale soil may mean that the topsoil was removed. Soil containing patches of different colors usually means that the water table is near the surface during certain times of the year. Gray, mixed with yellow or red, indicates that drainage is probably poor.

You can also ask the county agricultural extension agent to have the soil analyzed to determine what type of organic or inorganic fertilizers are needed and whether the soil acidity needs to be adjusted. An inexpensive home kit for testing soil acidity is also available.

You can improve and maintain soil fertility by covering the ground around plants with a mulch of animal manure or other organic materials. You can use leaves, shredded bark, sawdust, straw, peanut hulls, food refuse, egg shells, black-and-white newspaper (colored paper contains harmful dyes and sometimes toxic lead compounds) as mulch. Don't use pine needles because they decay too slowly. Mulch also retains soil moisture, reduces soil erosion, suppresses weed growth, and keeps soil from getting too hot under intense sunlight.

The best way to produce high-quality mulch is to build a simple *compost bin*. Fill the bin with alternating layers consisting of one inch of thoroughly moistened organic material and a one- to two-inch mixture of garden soil, inorganic fertilizer, and lime (Figure 9-20). Leave a depression at the top center of the pile to collect rainwater. Turn the pile over every month or so.

Home gardeners can use the same soil conservation techniques as farmers. For example, if your garden site is on a slight slope, use contour planting (Figure 9-14) to retain rainwater and reduce soil erosion. On steeply sloping land, use a small version of the terraces shown in Figure 9-9.

You can also use a manual method of no-till cultivation to reduce labor and soil erosion and to save money. If you use conventional tillage, leave small trenches

---

p. 240). The publicity surrounding this event made the public and elected officials aware of dangers from the large amounts of hazardous waste we produce each day, as well as from wastes buried in the soil in the past.

Hazardous-Waste Production: Present and Past The total quantity of hazardous wastes produced throughout the world or even in one country is nearly impossible to estimate accurately. It is clear, however, that the United States leads the world in hazardous-waste production. Depending on how hazardous wastes are defined, estimates of the amount produced each year in the United States range from 292 million tons to 400 million tons—an average of 1.1 to 1.6 tons per person per year.

About 95% of this waste is generated and either stored or treated on site by large companies—chemical producers, petroleum refineries, and manufacturers. The remaining 5% is handled by commercial facilities that take care of hazardous waste generated by others.

Texas, Ohio, Pennsylvania, California, Illinois, and Louisiana produce the most hazardous waste each year. However, in terms of population density and the amount of waste produced, residents of New Jersey, Rhode Island, Connecticut, and Massachusetts have the highest levels of risk from exposure to hazardous waste.

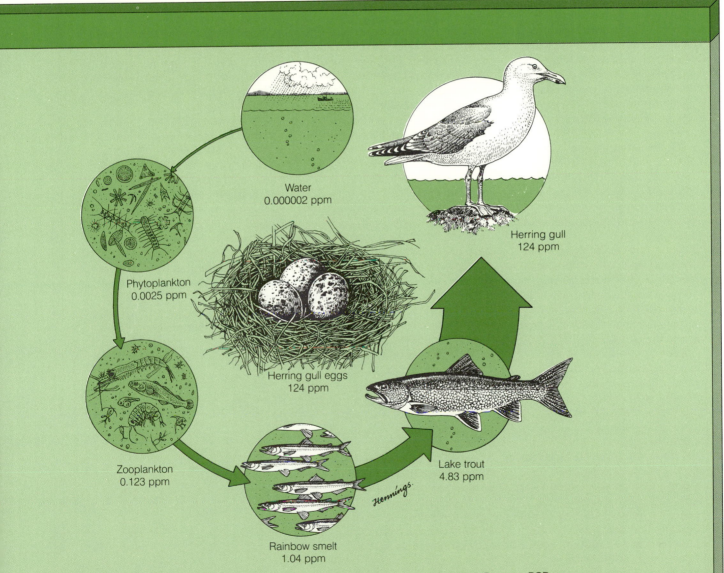

Figure 9-23 Biological amplification of PCBs in an aquatic food chain in the Great Lakes. Because PCBs are insoluble in water and soluble in fats, they are stored in the fatty tissues of animals. This means that their concentrations are greatly increased, or amplified, at each subsequent trophic level in a food chain or web.

In 1977, residents of a suburb of Niagara Falls, New York, discovered that "out of sight, out of mind" often does not apply. Hazardous industrial waste buried decades earlier bubbled to the surface, found its way into groundwater, and ended up in backyards and basements.

Between 1942 and 1953, Hooker Chemicals and Plastics Corporation dumped almost 22,000 tons of highly toxic and cancer-causing chemical wastes (mostly in steel drums) into an old canal excavation, known as the Love Canal. In 1953 Hooker Chemicals covered the dump site with clay and topsoil and sold the site to the Niagara Falls school board for one dollar. The deed specified that the company would have no future liability for any injury or property damage caused by the dump's contents.

An elementary school, playing fields, and a housing project, eventually containing 949 homes, were built in the Love Canal area. Residents began complaining to city officials in 1976 about chemical smells and chemical burns received by children playing in the canal, but these complaints were ignored. In 1977 chemicals began leaking from the badly corroded steel drums into storm sewers, gardens, and basements of homes next to the canal.

Informal health surveys conducted by alarmed residents revealed an unusually high incidence of birth defects, miscarriages, assorted cancers, and nerve, respiratory, and kidney disorders among people who lived near the canal. Complaints to local officials had little effect.

Continued pressure from residents and unfavorable publicity eventually led state officials to conduct a preliminary health survey and tests. They found that women in one area near the canal had a miscarriage rate four times higher than normal. They also found that the air, water, and soil of the canal area and the basements of nearby houses were contaminated with a number of toxic and carcinogenic chemicals.

In 1978 the state closed the school, permanently relocated the 238 families whose homes were closest to the dump, and fenced off the area around the canal. On May 21, 1980, after protests from the outraged 711 families still living fairly close to the landfill, President Carter declared Love Canal a federal disaster area and had these families relocated. Federal and New York state funds were then used to buy the homes of those who wanted to move permanently.

Since that time the school and the homes within a block and a half of the canal have been torn down and the state has purchased 570 of the remaining homes. About 45 families have remained in the desolate neighborhood, unwilling or unable to sell their houses and move.

The dump site has been covered with a clay cap and surrounded by a drain system that pumps leaking wastes to a new treatment plant. Local officials have pressed the federal government for a clean bill of health so that the state can resell the homes it bought from fleeing home owners and begin rehabilitating the neighborhood.

But cleanup proved to be difficult and expensive, with total cleanup costs of almost $250 million. Two-thirds of the area is supposed to be safe enough to live in again by 1990. The rest of the neighborhood near the old dump site may never be safe.

As yet no conclusive study has been made to determine the long-term effects of exposure to hazardous chemicals on former Love Canal residents. All studies made so far have been criticized on scientific grounds. In 1988 an informal survey was made of families that once lived in a group of ten houses next to the canal. All but one had some cancer cases; there were also two suicides and three cases of birth defects among grandchildren.

The psychological damage to evacuated families is enormous. For the rest of their lives they will wonder whether a disorder will strike and will worry about the possible effects of the chemicals on their children and grandchildren.

In 1985 former Love Canal residents received payments from a 1983 out-of-court settlement from Occidental Chemical Corporation (which bought Hooker Chemicals in 1968), the city of Niagara Falls, and the Niagara Falls school board. The payments ranged from $2,000 to $400,000 for claims of injuries ranging from persistent rashes and migraine headaches to cancers and severe mental retardation.

In 1979 the EPA filed a suit against Occidental Chemical to recover the estimated $250 million cleanup costs. In 1988 a U.S. district court ruled that Occidental must pay the cleanup costs. Although the company is protected by insurance, it announced its intention to appeal this ruling.

The Love Canal incident is a vivid reminder that we can never really throw anything away, that wastes don't stay put, and that preventing pollution is much safer and cheaper than cleaning it up.

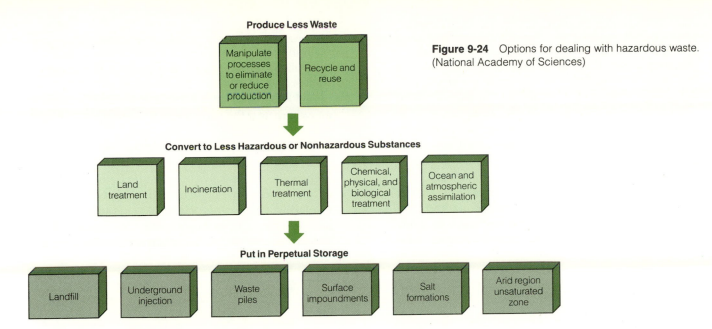

Figure 9-24 Options for dealing with hazardous waste. (National Academy of Sciences)

Most experts consider even the highest estimate of hazardous waste produced in the United States much too low. The official estimates do not include radioactive waste and household toxic waste—none of which is currently regulated by the EPA. The National Academy of Sciences estimates that there is no information available on the acute and chronic toxic effects of 79% of the 48,500 chemicals listed in the EPA's inventory of potentially toxic substances.

A serious problem facing the United States and most industrialized countries is what to do with the tens of thousands of dumps where large quantities of hazardous wastes were disposed of in an unregulated manner in the past. Even with adequate funding, effective cleanup is difficult because officials don't know what chemicals have been dumped and where all sites are located. West Germany alone is estimated to have 35,000 problem sites.

Control and Management of Hazardous Waste In addition to dealing with wastes deposited in the past, countries must develop plans to manage and reduce the wastes presently being produced in increasing amounts. Otherwise, new threats will replace old ones like the Love Canal.

There are three basic ways of dealing with hazardous waste, as outlined by the National Academy of Sciences (Figure 9-24). The first and most desirable method is an input, or waste prevention, approach. Its goal is to reduce the amount of waste produced by modifying industrial or other processes and by reusing or recycling the hazardous wastes that are produced. So far no country has implemented an effective program for achieving this goal.

The EPA estimates that at least 20% of the hazardous materials currently generated in the United States could be recycled, reused, or exchanged so that one industry's waste becomes another's raw material. Presently, however, only about 5% of such materials are managed in this manner. Yet, the EPA's 1988 budget request for waste reduction, recycling, and reuse was only about 0.03% of its total budget.

Firms trying the waste prevention approach have found that waste reduction and pollution prevention save them money. Since 1975 the Minnesota Mining and Manufacturing Company (3M) has had a program that by 1987 had cut its waste production in half and saved over $300 million. U.S. Chemicals rewards employees who suggest effective ways to reduce waste with a share of the money saved. By 1986 the company had given employees $70,000 for projects saving $500,000. The EPA estimates that an expanded program could reduce the amount of hazardous waste produced by U.S. industries by 15% to 30%.

However, most firms have little incentive to reduce their output of waste because waste management makes up only about 0.1% of the total value of the products they ship. Placing a tax of only about $1 on each ton of hazardous waste generated would provide enough money to support a strong program for reducing, recycling, and reusing hazardous waste.

North Carolina has taken the lead in encouraging waste reduction. The state's $600,000-a-year Pollution Prevention Pays Program offers technical assistance, a database of information, and matching grants to small and large companies and communities wanting to implement waste reduction and recycling projects. California, New York, Pennsylvania, Illinois, Wisconsin, Minnesota, and Tennessee also have waste reduction programs. Developing such programs in all states would be an important step.

The second phase of a hazardous-waste management program is to convert any waste remaining after waste reduction, recycling, and reuse to less hazardous or nonhazardous materials (Figure 9-24). Conversion methods include spreading degradable wastes on the land, burning them on land or at sea in specially designed incinerators, thermally decomposing them, or treating them chemically or physically.

The Netherlands incinerates about half its hazardous waste. The EPA estimates that about 60% of all U.S. hazardous waste could be incinerated. With proper air pollution controls, incineration is potentially the safest method of disposal for most types of hazardous waste. But it is also the most expensive method. The ash that is left must be disposed of and often contains toxic metals, and the gaseous and particulate combustion products emitted can be health hazards if not controlled. Another problem is that not all hazardous wastes are combustible. Moreover, most citizens vigorously oppose locating a hazardous waste incinerator anywhere near their community—summarized by the not-in-my-backyard (NIMBY) slogan.

Denmark, which relies almost exclusively on groundwater for drinking water, has the most comprehensive and effective program for detoxifying most of its hazardous waste. Each municipality has at least one facility that accepts paints, solvents and other hazardous wastes from households. Toxic waste from industries is delivered to 21 transfer stations scattered

CASE STUDY The Global Hazardous Waste Trade

To save money, cities and waste-disposal companies in the United States and other MDCs have shipped hazardous waste to other countries. Each year at least 250,000 tons of hazardous waste produced in western Europe are shipped to eastern Europe, where at least 90% of all hazardous waste is disposed of in landfills, many lacking any environmental controls. West Germany exports about one-fourth of its hazardous waste to East Germany.

Great Britain is a major importer of hazardous waste from many MDCs, especially the Netherlands, Ireland, and Belgium. In 1987, U.S. firms legally shipped 100,000 tons of hazardous waste abroad. Most of it went to Canada. All U.S. firms have to do to ship hazardous waste to other countries is notify the EPA of their intent to ship, get written permission from the recipient country, and file an annual report with the EPA.

Officially recorded shipments may be only the tip of the iceberg. There is evidence of a growing trade in illegal shipments of hazardous wastes from one country to another.

It is often easy to ship hazardous wastes illegally. Customs officials in the United States and other countries are not trained to detect illegal shipments. Sometimes exported wastes are labeled as materials to be recycled and then dumped after reaching their destination. Hazardous wastes have also been mixed with wood chips or sawdust and shipped legally as burnable material. Mexican officials have become increasingly concerned about illegal exports from Southern California, where all existing hazardous waste landfills have been filled.

Waste disposal firms can charge high prices for picking up hazardous wastes. If they can then dispose of them in other countries at low costs, they pocket huge profits. Officials of poor LDCs often find it hard to resist the income from receiving these wastes.

In 1987 a Detroit attorney set himself up as a hazardous-waste trade broker and persuaded officials of the African country Guinea-Bissau to accept 15 million tons of hazardous waste over a five-year period. The government would receive $600 million—more than 35 times the total value of its annual exports and twice its foreign debt. The attorney stood to make a profit of as much as $400 million in just one year. After newspapers exposed the deal, government officials abandoned the project.

In 1987 an Italian businessman worked out a scheme to make a $4.3 million profit in the illegal toxic waste trade. He paid various individuals $100 a month to store several thousand barrels of PCBs and other hazardous wastes in their backyards and other sites around the remote Nigerian fishing village off Koko. Nineteen people died from rice contaminated by chemicals from leaking barrels and many others became ill. In 1988 Nigerian officials arrested 54 people and called for their execution. The government has decreed that the 5,000 residents of the contaminated village must be evacuated and have made Italy take back the wastes.

The United Nations Environmental Program and the Organization for Economic Cooperation and Development are trying to work on treaties that would regulate international trade in hazardous waste. Some conservationists and members of the U.S Congress have called for the United States to ban all exports of hazardous waste to other countries. They believe that if we produce the waste, we have the obligation to take care of it. Others would allow exports but only to countries that require it to be handled in ways equal to or more stringent than those in effect in the United States.

Stricter regulations and international treaties are needed. But even the most stringent regulation will not end legal and illegal trade of these wastes. The profits to be earned are simply too great. What do you think should be done?

throughout the country. All waste is then transferred to a large treatment facility in the town of Nyborg on the island of Fyn near the country's geographic center. There about 75% of the waste is detoxified and the rest is buried in a carefully designed and monitored landfill. The West German state of Bavaria has a similar system in operation and South Korea is developing a system based on the Danish approach.

The third phase of waste management involves placing any waste left after detoxification in containers and storing them in specially designed secured landfills. Ideally, such landfills should be located in a geologically and environmentally secure place that is carefully monitored for leaks. In 1983, however, the Office of Technology Assessment concluded that sooner or later any secured landfill will leak hazardous chemicals into nearby surface water and groundwater.

With disposal costs running from $60 to $200 per 50-gallon drum, toxic waste disposal and management firms can make huge profits. The industry is expanding by 20% to 30% a year. Law enforcement officials warn that large profits and generally lax law enforcement have led to increased involvement of organized crime in the hazardous-waste disposal industry, especially in New York, New Jersey, Ohio, and Florida. Waste disposal firms in the United States and several other industrialized countries have shipped hazardous wastes to other countries, especially LDCs in Asia, Africa, and Latin America (see Spotlight on p. 242).

U.S. Hazardous-Waste Legislation In 1976 Congress passed the Resource Conservation and Recovery Act. This law requires the EPA to identify hazardous wastes, set standards for their management, and provide guidelines and financial aid to establish state waste management programs. The law also requires all firms that store, treat, or dispose of more than 220 pounds of hazardous wastes per month to have a permit stating how such wastes are to be managed.

To reduce illegal dumping, hazardous-waste producers granted disposal permits by the EPA must use a "cradle-to-grave" manifest system to keep track of waste transferred from point of origin to approved off-site disposal facilities. EPA administrators, however, point out that this requirement is almost impossible to enforce. The EPA and state regulatory agencies do not have enough personnel to review the documentation of more than 750,000 hazardous-waste generators and 15,000 haulers each year, let alone to verify them and prosecute offenders. If caught, however, violators are subject to large fines.

In 1980 Congress passed the Comprehensive Environmental Response, Compensation and Liability Act, known as the Superfund program. The act established a $1.6 billion fund, financed jointly by federal and state governments and taxes on chemical and petrochemical industries, for the cleanup of abandoned or inactive hazardous-waste dump sites.

In 1986 amendments to the Superfund act authorized $8.5 billion more for cleanup of sites between 1987 and 1994 and $500,000 for cleanup of leaking underground tanks. The EPA is authorized to collect fines and sue the owners of abandoned sites (if they can be found and held responsible) to recover up to three times the cleanup costs.

By July 1988 the EPA had placed 1,177 sites on a priority cleanup list because of their threat to nearby populations. The largest number of these sites are in New Jersey, followed by New York, Pennsylvania, Michigan, and California. Many are located over major aquifers and pose a serious threat to groundwater.

By early 1989, the EPA had spent $4 billion to clean up only 43 sites. In 1985 the Office of Technology Assessment estimated that the final list may include at least 10,000 sites, with cleanup costs amounting to as much as $300 billion over the next 50 years–roughly $1,200 for every U.S. resident.

In 1984 Congress amended the 1976 Resource Conservation and Recovery Act to make it national policy to minimize or eliminate land disposal of hazardous waste by 1990 unless the EPA has determined that it is an acceptable or the only feasible approach for a particular hazardous material. Even then, each chemical is to be treated to the fullest extent possible to reduce its toxicity before land disposal of any type is allowed. Although the 1990 deadline may not be met, this policy represents a much more ecologically sound approach to dealing with hazardous waste.

However, a 1988 study by the OTA showed that the EPA was not following that policy at 10 of the 100 Superfund sites examined. Phasing out land disposal is hampered by a shortage of facilities to treat and handle hazardous waste in safer ways, an inexperienced EPA staff with rapid turnover, lack of funds, and too little emphasis on waste reduction, recycling, and reuse.

In 1989 the Office of Technology Assessment concluded that the Superfund program was so poorly run and managed that its budget should be slashed for several years until it can be reorganized.

What Can You Do? You can help reduce inputs of hazardous waste into the environment. Use pesticides and other hazardous chemicals only when absolutely necessary and in the smallest amount possible. Use less hazardous (and usually cheaper) cleaning products (Table 9-3).

Don't mix household chemicals, because many of them react and produce deadly chemicals. For example, when ammonia and household bleach are combined or even get near one another, they react to pro-

Table 9-3 Alternatives for Some Hazardous Household Chemicals

Chemical	Alternative
Oven cleaner	Use baking soda for scouring. For baked-on grease, apply ¼ cup of ammonia in oven overnight to loosen; scrub the next day with baking soda.
Drain cleaner	Pour ½ cup salt down drain, followed by boiling water; flush with hot tap water.
Glass polish	Use ammonia and soap.
Wall and floor cleaner containing organic solvents	Use detergents to clean large areas and then rinse with water.
Toilet bowl, tub, and tile cleaner	Mix borax and lemon juice in a paste. Rub on paste and let set two hours before scrubbing.
Mildew stain remover and disinfectant cleaner	Chlorine bleach
Furniture polish	Melt 1 pound carnauba wax into 2 cups of mineral oil. For lemon oil polish, dissolve 1 teaspoon of lemon oil into 1 pint of mineral oil.
Shoe polish	Use polishes that do not contain methylene chloride trichloroethylene, or nitrobenzene.
Spot removers	Launder fabrics when possible to remove stains. Also try cornstarch or vinegar.
Carpet and rug shampoos	Cornstarch
Detergents and detergent boosters	Washing soda and soap powder
Water softeners	Washing soda
Pesticides (indoor and outdoor)	Use natural biological controls (see Enrichment Study at end of Chapter 11); boric acid for roaches.
Mothballs	Soak dried lavender, equal parts of rosemary and mint, dried tobacco, whole peppercorns, and cedar chips in real cedar oil and place in a cotton bag.

duce deadly poisonous chloramine gas. Hazardous household chemicals should also not be flushed down the toilet, poured down the drain, buried in the yard, or dumped down storm drains.

Also don't throw such chemicals away in the garbage, because they will end up in a landfill where they can contaminate drinking water supplies. Instead, contact your local health department or environmental agency for information on what do with leftover pesticides, paint solvents, cleaning compounds, and other hazardous chemicals.

Becoming Earth Healers Instead of Earth Abusers

Industrialized societies have failed to take seriously the **second law of ecology**: Everything is connected to and intermingled with everything else. We have not recognized that air, water, and soil are interrelated. Degrade one of these resources and you also abuse the others. We understand only a few of these complex interactions. But we have enough evidence to know they exist.

It is becoming increasingly clear that the earth's potentially renewable air, water, and soil resources must be protected from further degradation by a comprehensive program rather than the present piecemeal approach. We need to integrate air, water, and soil laws into a comprehensive *clean ecosphere act*, administered in each country by a cabinet level ecosphere protection agency. At the international level, countries must cooperate in these efforts.

Pollution control will continue to play an important role. But a clean ecosphere act would be built around the idea that the best and cheapest approach is pollution prevention. It would recognize that most things should be recycled and reused instead of being discarded into the air, water, and soil. It would also encourage and support restoration of degraded ecosystems. It would recognize that ecosphere security—not military security—is the ultimate security for everyone.

Carrying out such a program will be scientifically, economically, and politically difficult. In the long run, however, it will be cheaper and more effective than treating resource and environmental problems in isolation with output, or end-of-pipe, approaches.

There is justifiable moral outrage at child abuse and abuse of women. No one is in favor of pollution, but where is the moral outrage at air abuse, water abuse, and soil abuse? This ultimate form of abuse kills tens of thousands of people—half of them children—every day and harms many more. Earth abuse is self-abuse and life abuse.

We must demand that earth abuse halt and be replaced with earth-healing and earth-renewal. We must insist that earth-abuse by anyone will not be tolerated and begin by changing our own earth-abusing lifestyles. We must see that limited financial and human resources are redirected to earth healing. Each person, school, business, community, and government agency must respect, reward, and cherish earth healers and earth protectors as the world's true heroes.

This transformation in the way we think and act is not idealistic. It is absolutely necessary.

Civilization can survive the exhaustion of oil reserves, but not the continuing wholesale loss of topsoil.

Lester R. Brown

DISCUSSION TOPICS

1. Why should everyone, not just farmers, be concerned with soil conservation?

2. Explain how a plant can have ample supplies of nitrogen, phosphorus, potassium, and other essential nutrients and still have stunted growth.

3. What are the key properties of a soil that is good for growing most crops?

4. Describe briefly the Dust Bowl phenomenon of the 1930s and explain how and where it could happen again. How would you try to prevent a recurrence?

5. Explain how contour farming, terracing, strip cropping, and no-tillage farming can reduce soil erosion.

6. Visit rural or mostly undeveloped areas near your campus and classify the lands according to the system shown in Figure 9-17 and Table 9-2. Look for examples of land being used for purposes to which it is not best suited.

7. What are the major advantages and disadvantages of using commercial inorganic fertilizers to help restore and maintain soil fertility? Why should organic fertilizers also be used on land treated with inorganic fertilizers?

8. Would you oppose locating a secured landfill in your community for the storage of hazardous waste? Would you oppose an incinerator to detoxify such waste? Explain. If you oppose both of these alternatives, how would you propose that the hazardous waste generated in your community and state be managed?

9. Give your reasons for agreeing or disagreeing with each of the following proposals for dealing with hazardous waste in the United States: **(a)** reduce the production of hazardous waste and encourage recycling and reuse of such materials by levying a tax or fee on producers for each unit of waste generated; **(b)** ban all land disposal of hazardous waste to encourage recycling, reuse, and treatment and to protect groundwater from contamination; **(c)** provide low-interest loans, tax breaks, and other financial incentives to encourage industries that produce hazardous waste to recycle, reuse, treat, destroy, and reduce generation of such waste; **(d)** ban the shipment of hazardous waste from the United States to any other country.

10. Visit several homesites in your community and evaluate their use of natural vegetation to reduce soil erosion and enhance natural biological diversity as discussed in the Case Study on p. 234. Also, evaluate the planting of your own homesite and various areas of your campus.

FURTHER READINGS

Batie, Sandra S. 1983. *Soil Erosion: Crisis in America's Croplands?* Washington, D.C.: Conservation Foundation.

Block, Alan A., and Frank R. Scarpitti. 1984. *Poisoning for Profit: The Mafia and Toxic Waste in America.* New York: William Morrow.

Brady, Nyle C. 1974. *The Nature and Properties of Soils.* New York: Macmillan.

Brown, Lester R., and Edward C. Wolf. 1984. *Soil Erosion: Quiet Crisis in the World Economy.* Washington, D.C.: Worldwatch Institute.

Crosson, Pierre R., and Anthony T. Stout. 1983. *Productivity Effects of Cropland Erosion in the United States.* Washington, D.C.: Resources for the Future.

Dregnue, Harold. E. 1983. *Desertification of Arid Lands.* New York: Academic Press.

Dregnue, Harold. E. 1985. "Aridity and Land Degradation." *Environment*, vol. 27, no. 8, 33–39.

Environmental Defense Fund. 1985. *To Burn or Not to Burn.* New York: Environmental Defense Fund.

Environmental Protection Agency. 1987. *The Hazardous Waste System.* Washington, D.C.: EPA.

Epstein, Samuel S., et al. 1982. *Hazardous Waste in America.* San Francisco: Sierra Club Books.

Gibbs, Lois. 1982. *The Love Canal: My Story.* Albany, N.Y.: State University of New York Press.

Goldman, Benjamin A., et al. 1986. *Hazardous Waste Management: Reducing the Risk.* Washington, D.C.: Island Press.

Gordon, Wendy, and Jane Bloom. 1985. *Deeper Problems: Limits to Underground Injection as a Hazardous Waste Disposal Method.* New York: Natural Resources Defense Council.

Grainger, Alan. 1983. *Desertification: How People Make Deserts, How People Can Stop and Why They Don't.* Washington, D.C.: Earthscan.

Huisingh, Donald, et al. 1986. *Proven Profits From Pollution Prevention: Case Studies in Resource Conservation and Waste Reduction.* Washington, D.C.: Institute for Local Self-Reliance.

Institute for Local Self-Reliance. 1986. *Environmental Review of Waste Incineration.* Washington, D.C.: Institute for Local Self-Reliance.

Muir, Warren, and Joanna Underwood. 1987. *Promoting Hazardous Waste Reduction.* New York: INFORM, Inc.

National Academy of Sciences. 1984. *Toxicity Testing: Strategies to Determine Needs and Priorities*. Washington, D.C.: National Academy Press.

North Carolina Pollution Prevention Pays Program. 1986. *Accomplishments of North Carolina Industries*. Raleigh, N.C.: North Carolina Department of Natural Resources and Community Development.

Office of Technology Assessment. 1983. *Technologies and Management Strategies for Hazardous Waste Controls*. Washington, D.C.: Government Printing Office.

Office of Technology Assessment. 1986. *Serious Reduction of Hazardous Waste*. Washington, D.C.: Government Printing Office.

Office of Technology Assessment. 1987. *From Pollution to Prevention*. Washington, D.C.: Government Printing Office.

Piasecki, Bruce, and Gary Davis. 1987. *America's Future in Toxic Waste Management: Lessons from Europe*. New York: Quorum Books.

Postel, Sandra. 1987. *Defusing the Toxics Threat: Controlling Pesticides and Industrial Waste*. Washington, D.C.: Worldwatch Institute.

Sheridan, David. 1981. *Desertification of the United States*. Washington, D.C.: Resources for the Future.

Sophen, C. D., and J. V. Baird. 1982. *Soils and Soil Management*. Reston, Va.: Reston Publishing.

Tolba, M. K. 1986. "Desertification in Africa," *Land Use Policy*, vol. 3, 260–268.

Wilson, G. F. et al. 1986. *The Soul of the Soil: A Guide to Ecological Soil Management*, 2nd ed. Quebec: Gaia Services.

PART THREE

Renewable Living Resources and Their Management

It is the responsibility of all who are alive today to accept the trusteeship of wildlife and to hand on to posterity, as a source of wonder and interest, knowledge, and enjoyment, the entire wealth of diverse animals and plants. This generation has no right by selfishness, wanton or intentional destruction, or neglect, to rob future generations of this rich heritage. Extermination of other creatures is a disgrace to humankind.

—*World Wildlife Charter*

CHAPTER 10

Human Population
Dynamics

General Questions and Issues

1. How is population size affected by birth rates, death rates, migration rates, and fertility rates?

2. How is population size affected by the percentage of men and women at each age level?

3. How is the world's population distributed between rural and urban areas, and how do transportation systems affect population distribution?

4. What methods can be used to control the size and the rate of change of the human population?

5. What success have the world's two most populous countries, China and India, had in trying to control the rate of growth of their populations?

The population of most less developed countries is doubling every twenty to thirty years. Trying to develop into a modern industrial state under these conditions is like trying to work out the choreography for a new ballet in a crowded subway car.

Garrett Hardin

ount slowly to sixty.

During the minute it took you to do this, 171 more people entered the world to be fed, clothed, educated, and housed. By this time tomorrow there will be 247,000 more people on our planetary home. Each day we are now adding more people than at any time in human history.

The good news is that we have used our ingenuity to increase world food supplies, improve health and average life expectancy, and raise average living standards for many people. This has lowered the world's average death rate and saved millions of lives.

But the bad news is that there are more hungry people today than at any time in the past. By this time tomorrow at least 55,000 and perhaps 110,000 people—half of them children under age 5—will have died from preventable malnutrition and diseases.

The reason that the world's population continues to grow rapidly is simple. There are many more births than there are deaths. We have brought average death rates and birth rates down, but death rates have fallen more sharply than birth rates.

This explains why we add about one billion more people every ten years. If this continues, one of two things will happen during your lifetime: **(1)** the number of people on earth will double or **(2)** the world will

experience an unprecedented population crash with billions of people dying prematurely.

In the late 1970s a series of newspaper headlines such as "Population Time Bomb Fizzles," "Another Non-Crisis," and "Population Growth May Have Turned Historic Corner" falsely implied that world population growth had almost stopped. What actually happened was not a halt in net population growth. Instead, the annual rate at which the world's population was growing decreased from a high of 2% in the mid-1960s to around 1.7% in the mid-1980s. This slowdown in the annual growth rate is encouraging. But it is like learning that a truck heading straight at you has slowed down from 100 miles per hour to 85 miles per hour.

When the world's population was growing at 2% in 1969, this added 70 million people. But since then the population base has increased to 5.2 billion people. In 1988 a 1.75% growth rate of this bigger population base added 90 million people—more than in any previous year in human history. This is the nature of exponential growth (see Spotlight on p. 3). Most of this rapid growth is taking place in LDCs where food and many other resources are already stretched.

Basically there are two ways to deal with population growth: the death rate solution or the birth rate solution. The first option is to do little to slow popu-

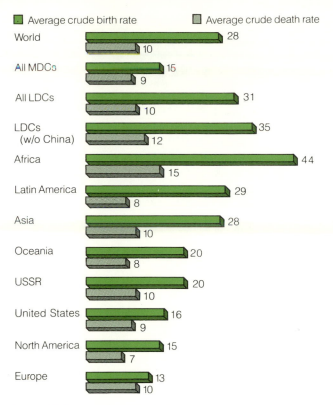

Figure 10-1 Average crude birth rates and crude death rates per 1,000 persons of various groups of countries in 1988. (Data from Population Reference Bureau)

lation growth and let billions die as we shoot way past the earth's carrying capacity for people. The other option is to mount a global crash program to bring birth rates down to prevent a catastrophic and unnecessary loss of life. If we don't sharply lower birth rates, we are deciding by default to raise death rates. Not to decide is to decide.

This chapter is devoted to an overview of *human population dynamics*. It is concerned with the major factors affecting the number of people in the world and its countries, the number of people in each age group, how the world's people are distributed between urban and rural areas, and what methods can be used to control the rate of human population growth or decline.

10-1 MAJOR FACTORS AFFECTING HUMAN POPULATION SIZE

Births, Deaths, and Annual Population Change Rates
The study of population characteristics and changes in the world and parts of the world is called **demography**. In the world or in a country experiencing little if any migration, changes in population size are determined by the difference between the number of people born and the number that die each year. World population grows as long as the number of live births is greater than the number of deaths.

Demographers, or population specialists, nor-

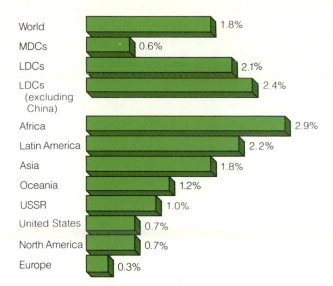

Figure 10-2 Average annual population growth rate in various groups of countries in 1988. (Data from Population Reference Bureau)

mally use the annual crude birth rate and crude death rate rather than total live births and deaths to describe the population change in such cases. The **crude birth rate** is the annual number of live births per 1,000 persons in a population. The **crude death rate** is the annual number of deaths per 1,000 persons in a population. Figure 10-1 shows the crude birth rates and death rates for the world and various groups of countries in 1988.

The annual rate at which the size of a population changes is called the **annual rate of natural change.** It is usually expressed as a percentage representing the difference between the crude birth rate and the crude death rate divided by 10. It indicates how fast the population size of the world or other region (assuming no migration) is growing or decreasing. When the crude death rate equals the crude birth rate, the population size remains stable (assuming no migration). This condition is known as **zero population growth (ZPG)**. When the crude death rate is higher than the crude birth rate, population size decreases.

Figure 10-2 gives the average annual population growth rates in major parts of the world. In 1988 population change rates ranged from a *growth rate* of 4.1% in Kenya in eastern Africa to a *decline rate* of −0.2% in Hungary.

An annual population growth rate of 1% to 3% may seem small, but such rates lead to enormous increases in population size over a 100-year period. For example, Nigeria, the most populous country in Africa, had 112 million people and a growth rate of 3.3% in 1988. By the end of the next century its population is projected to grow to more than half a billion—nearly equal to the present population size of all Africa. A sharp increase in death rates, however, may prevent such a long-range projection from becoming a reality.

The impact of such exponential population growth on population size is much greater in countries with a large existing population base. In sheer numbers, China and India dwarf all other countries, making up 37% of the world's population (Figure 10-3).

Rapid population growth in LDCs creates pressures on their physical and financial resources, making it difficult to raise average living standards. Consider the plight of Bangladesh, a country with 110 million people trying to survive in an area about the size of the state of Wisconsin (see Case Study on p. 189). In 1988 its 2.7% growth rate was the highest of the ten most populous countries (Figure 10-3).

Rapid population growth has also helped widen the differences in average income among rich and poor countries (Figure 1-8, p. 14). Population growth in both LDCs and MDCs also contributes to resource depletion and degradation (Table 1-1, p. 13).

Migration   The annual rate of population change for a particular country, city, or other area is also affected by the movement of people into (*immigration*) and out of (*emigration*) that area.

population change rate =
(births + immigration) − (deaths + emigration)

Most countries control their rates of population growth to some extent by restricting immigration. Only a few countries in the world annually accept a large number of immigrants or refugees. This means that population change for most countries is determined mainly by the differences between their crude birth rates and crude death rates.

However, migration within countries, especially from rural to urban areas, plays an important role in the population dynamics of cities, towns, and rural areas. This migration affects the way population is distributed within countries, as discussed in Section 10-3.

Major Factors Affecting Birth Rates and Fertility Rates
In addition to the crude birth rate, two types of fertility rates affect the population of a country.

Replacement-level fertility is the number of children a couple must have to replace themselves. You might think that two parents need have only two children to replace themselves. The actual average replacement-level fertility rate, however, is slightly higher, primarily because some female children die before reaching their reproductive years. In MDCs the average replacement-level fertility is 2.1 children per couple or woman. In LDCs with high infant mortality rates (deaths of children under age 1), the replacement level may be as high as 2.5 children per couple or woman.

The most useful measure of fertility for projecting future population change is the **total fertility rate (TFR)**.

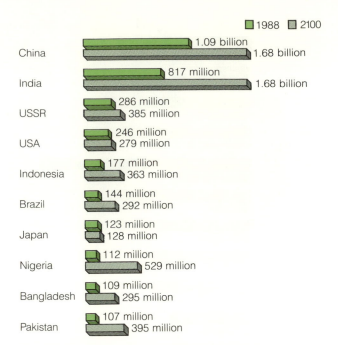

Figure 10-3   The world's ten most populous countries in 1988 with projections of their population size in 2100. (Data from World Bank)

It is an estimate of the number of live children the average woman will bear if she passes through all her childbearing years (ages 15–44) conforming to age-specific rates of a given year. In 1988 the average total fertility rate was 3.6 children per woman for the world as a whole, 1.9 in MDCs, and 4.1 in LDCs. TFRs ranged from a low of 1.4 in West Germany to a high of 8.5 in Rwanda.

In LDCs average TFRs dropped from about 6 births per woman in the mid-1960s to 4.0 by 1989. But during the same period, the TFR in the 41 poorest LDCs has remained at around 6.5.

Since 1972 the United States has had a TFR of around 1.8—below the replacement level (Figure 10-4). A TFR below replacement level doesn't necessarily mean that a country's population has stabilized or is declining. The U.S. population, for example, continues to grow, although its rate of growth has decreased (see Case Study on p. 252).

A number of socioeconomic and cultural factors affect a country's average birth rate and total fertility rate. The following are the most significant factors:

■ *Average levels of education and affluence:* Birth rates and total fertility rates are usually lower in MDCs, where both of these factors are high.

■ *Importance of children as a part of the family labor force:* Birth rates and TFRs tend to be high in LDCs (especially in rural areas). They are lower in countries where a compulsory mass education system removes children from the family labor force during most of the year.

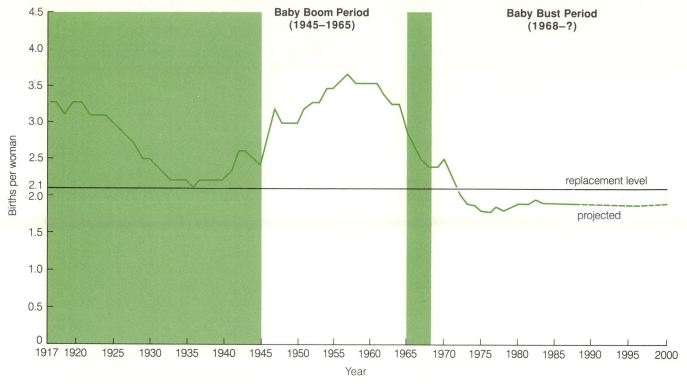

Figure 10-4 Total fertility rate for the United States between 1917 and 1988 and projected rate (dashed line) to 2000. (Data from Population Reference Bureau and U.S. Bureau of the Census)

- *Urbanization:* People living in urban areas tend to have lower birth and fertility rates than those living in rural areas, where children are needed to help in growing food, collecting firewood and water, and other survival tasks.

- *High costs of raising and educating children:* Birth rates and TFRs tend to be low in MDCs and other countries where school is mandatory and child labor is generally illegal. Raising children is much more costly because they don't enter the labor force until their late teens or early twenties.

- *Educational and employment opportunities for women:* Birth rates and TFRs tend to be high when women have limited access to education and to paid employment outside the home.

- *Infant mortality rates:* Birth rates and TFRs tend to be very high in areas with high infant mortality rates. Because children in such areas are often an important part of the family labor force, parents have a strong incentive to replace those that have died.

- *Average marriage age* (or, more precisely, the average age at which women give birth to their first child): Birth rates and TFRs tend to be much lower in countries where the average marriage age of women is at least 25. This reduces the typical childbearing years (ages 15–44) by ten years and cuts the prime reproductive period (ages 20–29), when most women have children, by about half.

- *Availability of private and public pension systems:* In MDCs with pension systems birth rates and TFRs

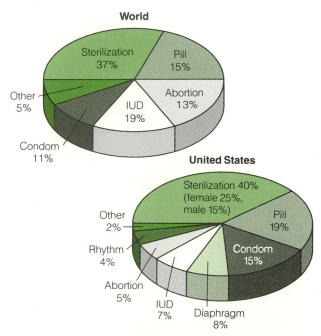

Figure 10-5 Estimated use of various birth control methods by couples of reproductive age in the world and the United States in 1986. (Data from UN Population Division, Population Crisis Committee, and U.S. National Center for Health Statistics)

tend to be low. Pensions eliminate the need for parents to have many children to support them in old age.

- *Availability of reliable methods of contraception* (Figure 10-5): Widespread availability tends to reduce

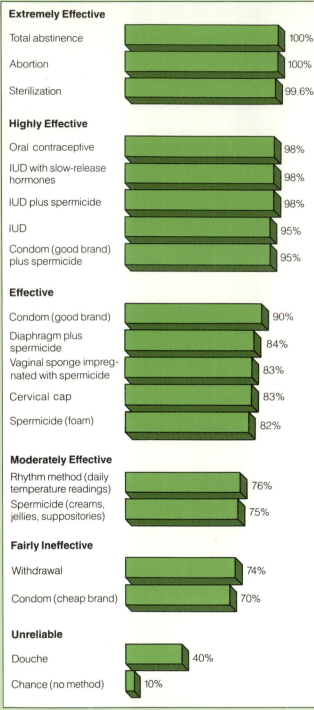

Extremely Effective

Total abstinence — 100%

Abortion — 100%

Sterilization — 99.6%

Highly Effective

Oral contraceptive — 98%

IUD with slow-release hormones — 98%

IUD plus spermicide — 98%

IUD — 95%

Condom (good brand) plus spermicide — 95%

Effective

Condom (good brand) — 90%

Diaphragm plus spermicide — 84%

Vaginal sponge impregnated with spermicide — 83%

Cervical cap — 83%

Spermicide (foam) — 82%

Moderately Effective

Rhythm method (daily temperature readings) — 76%

Spermicide (creams, jellies, suppositories) — 75%

Fairly Ineffective

Withdrawal — 74%

Condom (cheap brand) — 70%

Unreliable

Douche — 40%

Chance (no method) — 10%

Figure 10-6 Typical effectiveness of birth control methods in the United States. (Data from Allan Guttmacher Institute)

The total fertility rate in the United States has oscillated wildly (Figure 10-4). At the peak of the post–World War II baby boom (1945–65) in 1957, the average TFR reached 3.7 children per woman. Since then the average TFR has generally declined and has been at or below replacement level since 1972.

Various factors contributed to this decline:

- Widespread use of effective birth control methods (Figure 10-6).
- Availability of legal abortions.
- Social attitudes favoring smaller families.
- Greater social acceptance of childless couples.
- Rising costs of raising a family ($125,000–$175,000 to raise one child born in 1987 to age 18).
- Increases in the average marriage age between 1950 and 1986 from 20.3 to 23.6 for women and from 22.8 to 25.8 for men.
- An increasing number of women working outside the home. By 1987 more than 70% of American women of childbearing age worked outside the home and had a childbearing rate one-third of those not in the paid labor force.

The United States has not reached zero population growth (ZPG) in spite of the dramatic drop in average total fertility rate. The major reasons for this are

- the large number of women still moving through their childbearing years
- high levels of annual legal and illegal immigration
- an increase in the number of unmarried young women (including teenagers) having children

In 1988 the U.S. population grew by 0.9%. This added 2.5 million people: 1.7 million because births were greater than deaths, 600,000 legal immigrants, and an estimated 200,000 illegal immigrants.

Given the erratic history of fertility rates in the United States (Figure 10-4), no one knows whether or how long the country's total fertility rate will remain below replacement level. The Census Bureau and the World Bank have made various projections of future U.S. population growth, assuming different average total fertility rates, life expectancies, and annual net legal immigration rates (Figure 10-7).

However, no one knows whether these assumptions will hold up. Fertility could rise unexpectedly as it did in the 1950s. New medical discoveries could extend average life expectancy. New laws and more effective enforcement could sharply reduce illegal and legal immigration.

Some demographers project somewhat less growth, based on the assumption that the present TFR of 1.8 will be maintained. If so, legal and illegal immigration will account for all U.S. population growth by the 2030s. Or the country could decide to increase immigration to provide more young workers for an aging population.

Others believe that an annual net migration rate (including both legal and illegal immigration) of 800,000 to 1.1 million is more likely than the 500,000 (400,000 legal and 100,000 illegal) used by the Census Bureau. Still others project a higher population size because of a future rise to a TFR above 1.9.

You and all other Americans will play a role in determining which of these and other demographic possibilities becomes a reality. Assuming you are able to have children, you will decide whether or not to have children and how many to have.

You will also play a key role in determining how long you live. To increase their life spans, many Americans have given up smoking, reduced or eliminated alcohol use and reduced their exposure to sun. Many also exercise more frequently, pay more attention to what they eat, and fasten their seat belts while driving.

On average, Americans move 13 times in their lives. How many times people move and where they move determine what areas gain or lose people. The migrations of people also affect demands on air, water, soil, recreation, and other resources. What role do you intend to play in determining the country's future demographic history?

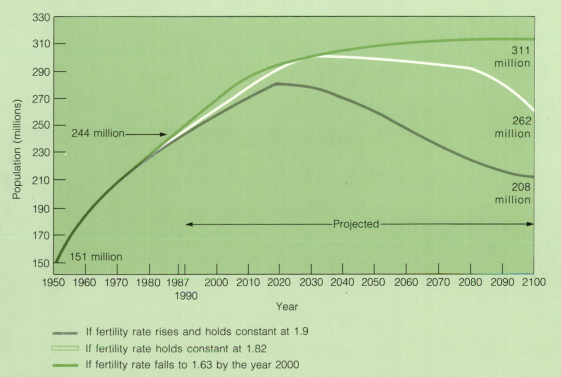

Figure 10-7 Projections of changes in U.S. population size. (Data from U.S. Bureau of the Census and World Bank)

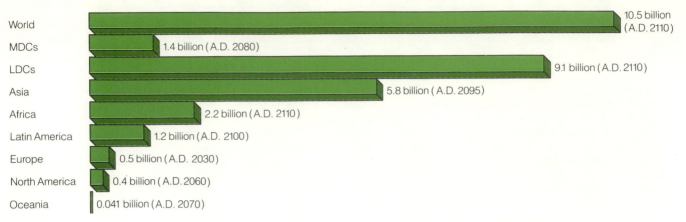

Figure 10-8 United Nations medium projections for stable population size and year of stabilization (shown in parentheses) of various groups of countries.

Figure 10-9 Changes in crude birth and death rates for the more developed and less developed countries between 1775 and 1988 and projected rates (dashed lines) to 2000. (Data from Population Reference Bureau and United Nations)

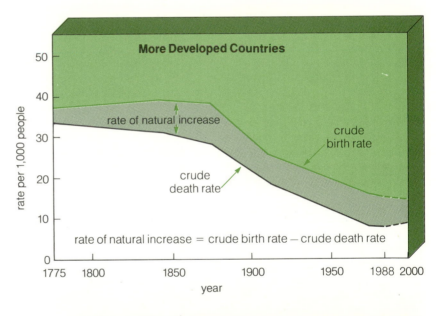

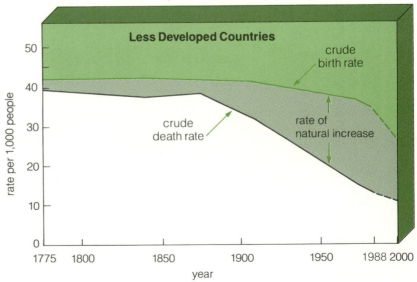

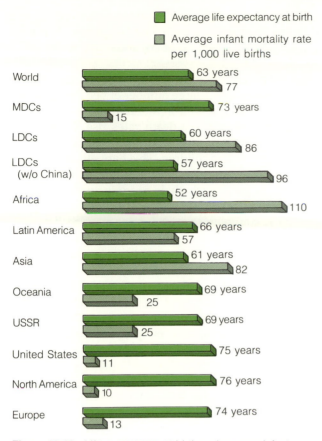

■ Average life expectancy at birth

■ Average infant mortality rate per 1,000 live births

World	63 years	77
MDCs	73 years	15
LDCs	60 years	86
LDCs (w/o China)	57 years	96
Africa	52 years	110
Latin America	66 years	57
Asia	61 years	82
Oceania	69 years	25
USSR	69 years	25
United States	75 years	11
North America	76 years	10
Europe	74 years	13

Figure 10-10 Life expectancy at birth and average infant mortality rate for various groups of countries in 1988. (Data from Population Reference Bureau)

birth rates and TFRs. However, this factor can be counteracted by religious beliefs that prohibit or discourage the use of abortion or certain forms of contraception.

■ *Cultural norms that influence the number of children couples want to have.*

Figure 10-8 projects the size and year of population stabilization for different groups of countries. These projections are based on the UN's medium assumptions—usually considered the most likely—about fertility rates, mortality rates, and international migration patterns. These projections also assume that the worldwide average fertility rate will drop to the replacement level of 2.1 births per woman by 2035. Most demographers see little chance that this will happen. Indeed, by 1988 the loss of momentum in population control programs in some LDCs indicated that future population growth may be closer to the high UN projection of about one billion more people every ten years.

No one really knows whether any of these projections will prove accurate. Demography, like economics, is a notoriously inexact social science. Demo-

graphic projections are not predictions of what will necessarily take place. Instead, they represent possibilities based on present trends and on certain assumptions about people's future reproductive behavior. Despite their uncertainty, demographic projections help us focus our energies on converting the most desirable possibilities into reality.

Major Factors Affecting Death Rates The rapid growth of the world's population over the past 100 years did not happen because of a rise in crude birth rates. Rather, it is due largely to a decline in crude death rates—especially in the LDCs (Figure 10-9).

The major interrelated reasons for this general drop in death rates are:

■ better nutrition because of increased food production and better distribution

■ reduced incidence and spread of infectious diseases because of improved personal hygiene and improved sanitation and water supplies

■ improvements in medical and public health technology through the use of antibiotics, immunization, and insecticides

Two useful indicators of overall health in a country or region are **life expectancy**—the average number of years a newborn infant can be expected to live—and the **infant mortality rate**—the number of babies out of every 1,000 born that die before their first birthday (Figure 10-10).

By 1988, 112 countries, with 67% of the world's population, had achieved an average life expectancy of 60 years or more, mostly because of a drop in childhood deaths. Average life expectancy at birth ranged from a low of 35 years in Sierra Leone in western Africa to a high of 78 years in Japan. In the world's 41 poorest countries, mainly in Asia and Africa, average life expectancy is only 47 years. Between 1900 and 1988, average life expectancy at birth increased sharply in the United States from 42 to 75.

A high infant mortality rate usually indicates a lack of enough food (undernutrition), poor nutrition (malnutrition), and a high incidence of infectious disease (usually from contaminated drinking water). In 1988 infant mortality rates ranged from a low of 5.2 deaths per 1,000 live births in Japan to a high of 183 deaths per 1,000 live births in Afghanistan in southwestern Asia. Nearly one in five children in LDCs dies before the age of five. The average infant mortality rate in the United States is much higher than it should be in a country of such wealth and technology (see Spotlight on p. 256).

10-2 POPULATION AGE STRUCTURE

Age Structure Diagrams   Why will world population probably keep growing for at least 60 years after the average world total fertility rate has reached or dropped below replacement-level fertility of 2.1? The answer to this question lies in an understanding of the **age structure**, or age distribution, of a population. The age structure is the percentage of the population, or the number of people of each sex, at each age level in a population.

Demographers make a population age structure diagram by plotting the percentages or numbers of males and females in the total population in three age categories: *preproductive* (ages 0–14), *reproductive* (ages 15–44), and *postproductive* (ages 45–85+). Figure 10-11 shows the age structure diagrams for countries with rapid, slow, and zero growth rates.

Mexico and most LDCs with rapidly growing populations have pyramid-shaped age structure diagrams. This indicates a high ratio of children under age 15 to adults over age 65. In contrast, the diagrams for the U.S., Sweden, and most MDCs undergoing slow or no population growth have a narrower base. This shows that such countries have a much smaller percentage of population under age 15 and a larger percentage above 65 than countries experiencing rapid population growth.

MDCs such as Sweden that have achieved zero population growth have roughly equal numbers of people at each age level. Hungary, West Germany, and Denmark, which are experiencing a slow population decline, have roughly equal numbers of people at most age levels but lower numbers under age 5.

Age Structure and Population Growth Momentum
Any country with a large number of people below age 15 has a powerful built-in momentum to increase its population size unless death rates rise sharply. The number of births rises even if women have an average of only one or two children. This happens because the number of women who can have children increases greatly as girls reach their reproductive years. The population of a country with a large number of people under 15 continues to grow for one average lifetime—roughly 60 to 70 years—after the average total fertility rate of its women has dropped to replacement level or lower.

In 1988 one-third of the people on this planet were under 15 years old. In LDCs the number is even higher—37% compared to 22% in MDCs. Figure 10-12 shows the massive momentum for population growth in LDCs because of their large number of people under age 15. This powerful force for continued population growth will only be slowed by a crash program to reduce birth rates or a catastrophic rise in death rates.

Making Projections from Age Structure Diagrams   A baby boom took place in the United States between 1945 and 1965. This 75-million-person bulge will move upward through the country's age structure during

---

SPOTLIGHT Why Are U.S. Infant Mortality Rates Higher Than They Should Be?

In 1988 27 countries had lower infant mortality rates than the 11 deaths per 1,000 live births in the United States (18 for blacks and 9 for whites). This meant that 38,300 U.S. babies died in 1988 before they reached their first birthday—as many as all American deaths from AIDS since 1981.

Why is the infant mortality rate in the United States higher than in many other MDCs? One reason is lack of adequate health care for poor women during pregnancy and for their babies after birth. By contrast, such care is encouraged and subsidized in most Western European countries.

The high infant death rate points up the urgent need for bet-ter medical and nutritional programs for poor women who are pregnant and for the infants born to them. Also needed is improved sex education to discourage unwanted pregnancies.

Another factor raising the average infant mortality rate and lowering average life expectancy in the United States is a high birth rate for teenage women. Their babies are more likely to have a low birth weight (under 5.5 pounds)—the most important factor in infant deaths.

Mostly because of a lack of early and effective sex education, the United States has the highest teenage-pregnancy rate of any MDC, ten times higher than Japan's and three times higher than most European countries. Every year in the United States about 900,000 teenage women—1 in every 10—become pregnant. About 560,000 of these young women give birth. The remaining 340,000 have abortions, accounting for about one of every four abortions performed in the United States.

Almost half of the babies born to teenagers depend on welfare to survive. Each of these babies costs taxpayers an average of $15,600 over the 20 years following its birth.

What do you think should be done?

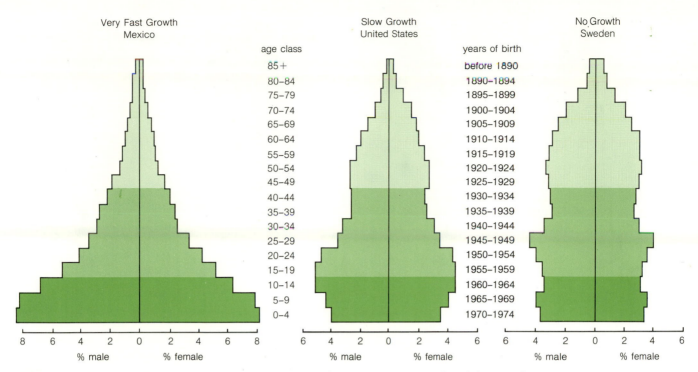

Figure 10-11 Population age structure diagrams for countries with rapid, slow, and zero population growth rates. Dark portions represent preproductive years (0–14), medium portions represent reproductive years (15–44), and light portions represent postproductive years (45–85+). (Data from Population Reference Bureau)

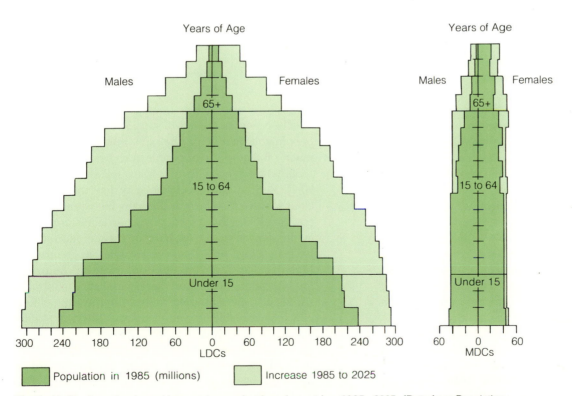

Figure 10-12 Age structure of less and more developed countries, 1985–2025. (Data from Population Reference Bureau)

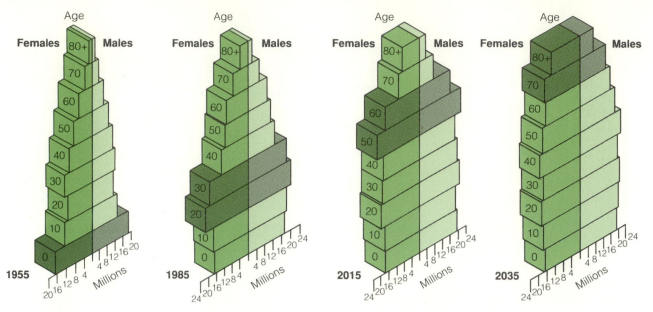

Figure 10-13 Tracking the baby-boom generation. Age structure of the U.S. population in 1955, 1985, 2015, and 2035. (Data from Population Reference Bureau and U.S. Bureau of the Census)

the 80-year period between 1945 and 2025 as baby boomers move through youth, young adulthood, middle-age, and old age (Figure 10-13).

Between 1967 and 1988 the median age of the U.S. population rose from 28 to 32.5 and is projected to reach 39.3 by 2020 and 41.8 by 2030. This is happening for three reasons. One is that the large baby boom generation is now approaching middle age. In 1985 the first baby boomers reached age 40, and all baby boomers will have passed that milestone by 2005. Second, U.S. fertility is so low that the proportion of children in the population is declining. Third, the proportion of the elderly is increasing, in part due to increased longevity. By 2030, when all living members of the baby boom generation are senior citizens, about 21% of the projected population will consist of people 65 and older, compared to 12% in 1985 (Figure 10-14).

Today baby boomers make up nearly half of all adult Americans. In sheer numbers they dominate the population's demand for goods and services. Later they will put strains on the Social Security System and elderly health care services. Between 1970 and 1984 large numbers of baby boomers flooded the job market, raising unemployment rates of teenagers and young adults. Baby boomers, who made up an estimated 60% of registered voters in 1988, will play an increasingly important role in deciding who gets elected and what laws are passed between 1988 and 2030.

During their working years baby boomers will create a large surplus of funds in the Social Security Trust Fund. However, even if elected officials resist the temptation to dip into these funds for balancing the budget or other purposes, the large number of retired baby boomers will quickly use up this surplus.

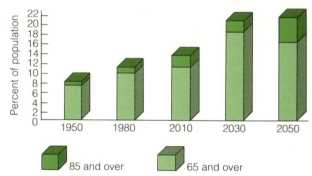

Figure 10-14 Percentage of people age 65 and older in the United States, 1950–2050. (Data from U.S. Bureau of the Census)

The economic burden of supporting so many retired people will then be on the baby bust generation, the much smaller group of people born between 1968 and 1988, when average fertility rates fell sharply (Figure 10-4). Retired baby boomers may use their political clout to force members of the baby bust generation to pay greatly increased income and Social Security taxes.

In many respects, the baby bust generation should have an easier time than the baby boom generation. Much smaller numbers of people will be competing for education, jobs, and services. Labor shortages should also drive up their wages. But three out of four new jobs available between 1990 and 2010 will require education or technical training beyond high school. People without such training may face economic hard times. With a shortage of young adults, the armed forces might find it hard to meet recruiting levels. This could lead the baby boom generation to use its political power to reinstate the draft.

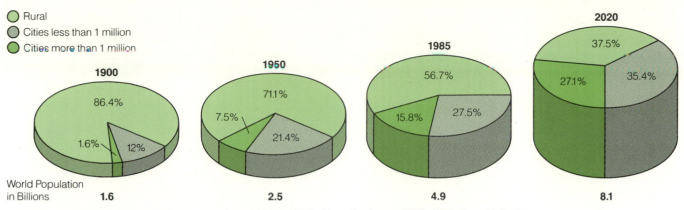

Figure 10-15 Patterns of world urbanization from 1900 to 1985 with projections to 2030. (Data from United Nations and Population Reference Bureau)

Although they will probably have no trouble getting entry-level jobs, the baby bust group may find it hard to get job promotions as they reach middle age because most upper-level positions will be occupied by the much larger baby boom group. Many baby boomers may delay retirement because of improved health and the need to build up adequate retirement funds. From these few projections, we see that any baby boom bulge or baby bust indentation in the age structure of a population creates a number of social and economic changes that ripple through a society for decades.

10-3 POPULATION DISTRIBUTION: URBANIZATION AND URBAN GROWTH

The World Situation Economic, environmental, and social conditions are affected not only by population growth and age structure but also by how population is distributed geographically in rural or urban areas. For several thousand years cities have been recognized as centers of civilization. They support important industrial and commercial activities and serve as centers of innovation, trade, the arts, and culture. Urban social and cultural activities can also enrich the lives of people who live far from city boundaries. Thus, it is not surprising that the percentage of the world's people living in cities continues to increase.

The definition of an **urban area** varies in different parts of the world. In the United States and in this book it is defined as a village or city with a population of more than 2,500 people. It is important to distinguish between the degree of urbanization and urban growth. A country's **degree of urbanization** is the percentage of its population living in areas with a population of more than 2,500 people. **Urban growth** is the rate of growth of urban populations.

Between 1900 and 1985 the percentage of the world's population living in urban areas rose from 14% to 43% (Figure 10-15). By the year 2000, one-half of the world's population is expected to be living in urban areas and one-fourth of these city dwellers will be homeless. By 2020 almost two out of three people on earth will probably live in urban areas. Accommodating the 2.9 billion more people in urban areas by 2020 will be a monumental task.

Most countries are experiencing an increase in both degree of urbanization and urban growth. Today in most MDCs the rate of urban growth is declining. But in LDCs, where three quarters of the world's people live, the number of people living in cities is increasing rapidly. LDCs are simultaneously experiencing high rates of natural population increase and rapid internal migration of people from rural to urban areas. Each of these factors contributes about equally to the urban growth in these countries.

Unprecedented urban growth in MDCs and LDCs has given rise to a new concept—the supercity, an urban area with a population of more than 10 million. In 1985 there were ten supercities, most of them located in MDCs. The United Nations projects that by 2000 there will be twenty-five supercities, most of them in LDCs.

In LDCs more than 20 million rural people migrate to cities each year. Several factors are responsible for this population shift. Part is caused by the pull of urban job opportunities. But much of this migration is caused by rural poverty. Modern mechanized agriculture decreases the need for farm labor and allows large landowners to buy out small-scale, subsistence farmers who cannot afford to modernize. Without jobs or land these people are forced to move to cities.

Urban growth in LDCs is also caused by government policies that distribute most income and social services to urban dwellers at the expense of rural dwellers. For example, in many LDCs where 70% of

The world's most populous urban area is Mexico City, Mexico. In 1988, with an estimated population of 19.2 million people, it was suffering from severe air pollution, massive unemployment, and a soaring crime rate. Slums without running water or electricity have mushroomed almost everywhere, and many residents are losing hope.

With at least 5 million people living without sewage facilities, tons of human waste are left in gutters and vacant lots every day. About half of the city's garbage is left in the open to rot, attracting armies of rats.

Over 3 million cars, 7,000 diesel buses, and 130,000 factories spew massive amounts of air pollutants into the atmosphere. Air pollution is intensified because the city lies in a basin surrounded by mountains and has frequent thermal inversions. The city's air and water pollution cause an estimated 100,000 premature deaths a year. Even so, Mexico City looks good to the estimated 1,500 poverty-stricken rural peasants who pour into the city every day.

These problems, already at crisis levels, will be intensified to horrendous levels if this urban area, as projected, grows to 26.3 million people by the end of this century. This projected population increase may be averted, however, by a lack of water.

Because of its elevated site and lack of nearby water, since 1982 the city has pumped water 1,100 feet uphill from a site 62 miles away. In the 1990s the city will have to pump additional water 2,200 feet uphill from a site 124 miles away. This pumping will require electricity equal to that from six 1,000-megawatt power plants—prohibitively expensive if energy costs rise as projected. The Mexican government is industrializing other parts of the country in an attempt to slow migration to Mexico City.

---

the population is rural, only about 20% of the national budget goes to the rural sector. This encourages rural-to-urban migration.

Most rural-to-urban migrants in LDCs do not find jobs. Instead, they overwhelm already inadequate city services and budgets. For most of these migrants, as well as the urban poor in MDCs, the city becomes a poverty trap, not an oasis of economic opportunity and cultural diversity (see Case Study above). Those few fortunate enough to get a job must work long hours for low wages. To survive they often have to take jobs that expose them to dust, hazardous chemicals, excessive noise, and dangerous machinery.

Many of the urban poor in LDCs are forced to live on the streets (Figure 1-2, p. 5). Others crowd into slums and shantytowns, made from corrugated steel, plastic sheets, tin cans, and packing boxes, which ring the outskirts of most cities in these countries. Because many of these settlements spring up illegally on unoccupied land, their occupants live in constant fear of eviction or of having their makeshift shelters destroyed by bulldozers. Many shantytowns are located on land subject to landslides, floods, or tidal waves or in the most polluted districts of inner cities. Fires are common because most residents use kerosene stoves or fuelwood for heating and cooking.

In most large cities in LDCs, shantytown populations double every five to seven years—four to five times the population growth rate of the entire city. Most cities refuse to provide shantytowns and slums with adequate drinking water, sanitation, food, health care, housing, schools, and jobs. Not only lacking the money, officials also fear that such improvements will attract even more of the rural poor.

Despite joblessness and squalor, shantytown residents cling to life with resourcefulness, tenacity, and hope. Most are convinced that the city offers, possibly for themselves and certainly for their children, the only chance of a better life. Most do have more opportunities and are better off than the rural poor they left behind. With better access to family planning programs, they tend to have fewer children because there is no room for them.

The U.S. Situation In 1988 almost three out of four (74%) Americans lived in the nation's 281 urban areas, and two out of three lived in the country's 15 largest urban regions (Figure 10-16).* About 41% of the country's urban dwellers lived in central cities and 59% lived in suburbs.

Since 1800 several major internal population shifts have taken place in the United States. The major shift has been from rural to urban areas as the country industrialized and needed fewer farmers to produce sufficient food (Figure 10-17).

Since 1970, however, many people have moved from large cities to suburbs and to smaller cities and

---

*Each of these areas, known as a Metropolitan Statistical Area (MSA), is a county or group of counties that contains either a city of at least 50,000 people or an urbanized area with 50,000 or more people and a total population of 100,000 or more. A Consolidated Metropolitan Statistical Area (CMSA) is a large urban area with a population of 1 million or more.

Figure 10-16 Major urban regions in the United States. These areas represent the gradual merging of cities into massive "supercities."

1 **Bosman** (Boston–Manchester)
2 **Mega York** (New York–Philadelphia)
3 **Philwil** (Philadelphia–Wilmington)
4 **Washbalt** (Washington–Baltimore)
5 **Pittyoung** (Pittsburgh–Youngstown)
6 **Miamilaud** (Miami-Fort Lauderdale)
7 **Hougalbeau** (Houston–Galveston–Beaumont)
8 **Dalworth** (Dallas–Fort Worth)
9 **Denboul** (Denver–Boulder)
10 **San Angeles** (Los Angeles–San Diego)
11 **San Franjose** (San Francisco–San Jose)
12 **Seatac** (Seattle–Tacoma)
13 **Chimilgar** (Chicago–Milwaukee–Gary)
14 **Detanntol** (Detroit–Ann Arbor–Toledo)
15 **Clevak** (Cleveland–Akron)

rural areas, primarily because of the large numbers of new jobs in such areas. Since 1980 about 80% of the population increase in the United States has occurred in the South and West (Figure 10-18), particularly near the coasts. Most of this increase is due to migration from the North and East.

This shift is projected to continue, with the South having the largest population increase between 1987 and 2010, followed by the West. During this period the four fastest growing states are expected to be Arizona, New Mexico, Nevada, and Florida.

Population Distribution and Transportation Systems

When there is not enough suitable rural land for conversion to urban land, a city tends to grow upward rather than outward, occupy a fairly small area, and have a high population density. People living in such *compact cities* tend to walk or use energy-efficient mass transit rather than using an automobile to go almost everywhere. They also tend to live in high-rise apartment buildings with shared walls that have an insulating effect, reducing heating and cooling costs.

Compact cities can use energy-efficient district heating systems such as those found in Scandinavian cities. Automobile use is also reduced in compact cities such as Hong Kong, Tokyo, and Singapore. Thus, they are more energy efficient than the spread-out, or dispersed, cities that have developed in the United States since 1945.

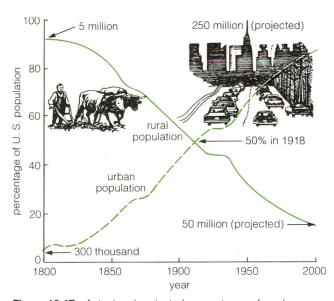

Figure 10-17 Actual and projected percentages of rural and urban populations in the United States between 1800 and 2000. (Data from U.S. Bureau of the Census)

A combination of automobiles, cheap gasoline, and a large supply of rural land suitable for urban development tends to result in a *dispersed city* with a low population density. Most people in such cities live in single-family houses whose unshared walls lose and gain heat rapidly unless they are well insulated. Dis-

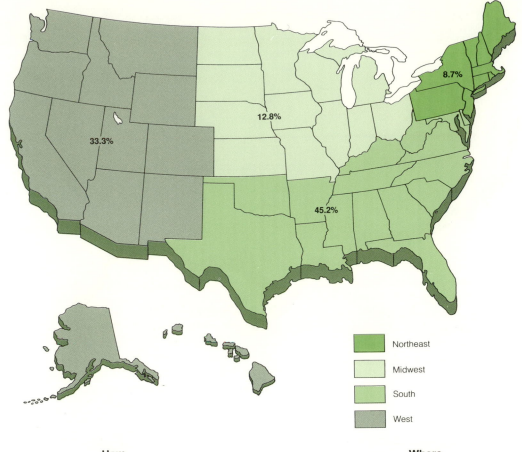

Figure 10-18 Regional shares of U.S. population growth, 1960–1985. (Data from U.S. Bureau of the Census)

8.7%

12.8%

33.3%

45.2%

- Northeast
- Midwest
- South
- West

Figure 10-19 How people in the United States go to and from work. (Data from U.S. Bureau of the Census)

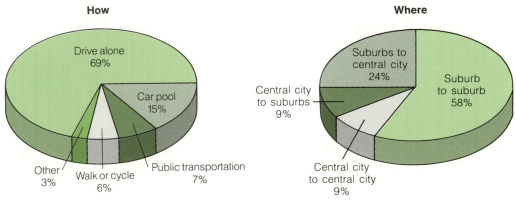

How

Drive alone
69%

Car pool
15%

Other
3%

Walk or cycle
6%

Public transportation
7%

Where

Suburbs to central city
24%

Suburb to suburb
58%

Central city to suburbs
9%

Central city to central city
9%

persed cities and urban areas are unable to take advantage of energy-saving district heating systems.

Most people living in dispersed cities rely on cars with low energy efficiencies for transportation within the central city, to and from its suburbs, and within its suburbs (see Case Study on p. 263). In the United States the car is now used for about 98% of all urban transportation, 85% of all travel between cities, and 84% of all travel to and from work (Figure 10-19).

In the United States the number of motor vehicles—181 million in 1988—has grown twice as fast as the population since 1960. With only 4.8% of the world's people, the United States has one-third of the world's cars. No wonder British author J. B. Priestly remarked, "In America, the cars have become the people." By contrast, China and India, with 37% of the world's people, have only 0.5% of its cars.

Resource and Environmental Vulnerability of Urban Areas Urban areas are not self-sufficient. They survive only by importing large quantities of food, water, energy, minerals, and other resources from ecosystems both near and far beyond their boundaries. The concentrated waste matter and heat output of even a small city can overwhelm the absorption and dilution capacity of its atmosphere and local terrestrial and aquatic ecosystems (Figure 10-20).

As urban areas grow, their resource input needs and pollution outputs put increasing stress on distant aquifers, wetlands, estuaries, forests, croplands, rangelands, wilderness, and other ecosystems. In the words of Theodore Roszak:

The supercity . . . stretches out tentacles of influence that reach thousands of miles beyond its already sprawling parameters. It sucks every hinterland and wilderness into its technological metabolism. It forces rural populations off the land and replaces them with vast agroindustrial combines. Its investments and technicians bring the roar of the bulldozer and oil derrick into the most uncharted quarters. It runs its conduits of transport and communication, its lines of supply and distribution through the wildest landscapes. It flushes its waste into every nearby river, lake, and ocean or trucks them away into desert areas. The world becomes its garbage can.

Making Urban Areas More Sustainable One of our goals in coming decades should be to make urban areas more self-sufficient and sustainable (see Case Study on p. 265). The following are the main methods by which we can make urban areas more ecologically sustainable:

- Recycling effluents and sludge from sewage treatment plants and organic wastes to the land as fertilizer (Section 8-6).

CASE STUDY Advantages and Disadvantages of the Automobile

The automobile has many advantages. Above all, it offers people freedom to go where they want to go, when they want to go there. In addition, much of the world's economy is built around producing and supplying roads, services, and repairs for the world's 425 million motor vehicles, with 33 million new ones produced each year.

In spite of their advantages, motor vehicles have many harmful effects on human lives and on air, water, and land resources. Worldwide, cars and trucks kill an average of 200,000 people, maim 500,000, and injure 10 million a year. On the average an automobile-related death occurs about every 3 minutes, and a disabling injury occurs every 20 seconds.

Each year in the United States motor vehicle accidents kill around 48,000 people and seriously injure at least 300,000. Since the automobile was introduced, almost 2 million Americans have been killed on the highways—about twice the number of Americans killed in all U.S. wars. Auto accidents are the leading cause of death for Americans under age 35. These accidents cost society about $60 billion annually in lost income and in insurance, administrative, and legal expenses.

By providing almost unlimited mobility, automobiles and highways have been a major factor in urban sprawl. This dispersal has made it increasingly difficult for subways, trolleys, and buses to be economically feasible alternatives to the private car. Although the total population has increased, the number of riders on all forms of mass transit in the United States has dropped drastically: from 24 million in 1945 to about 8 million since 1980. Mass transit systems work best in compact cities, such as most European cities, and along heavily populated corridors within urban areas.

Motor vehicles use up large areas of land. The automobile has laced U.S. cities and countryside with almost 4 million miles of roads. Roads and parking space take up 65% percent of the total land area in Los Angeles, more than half of Dallas, and more than one-third of New York City and the nation's capital. Worldwide, at least a third of the average city's land is devoted to roads and parking.

Instead of reducing automobile congestion, the construction of roads has encouraged more automobiles and travel, causing even more congestion. As economist Robert Samuelson put it, "Cars expand to fill available concrete." In 1987 almost two-thirds of all rush-hour traffic on urban interstates was rated as congested. Nationwide traffic congestion wasted an estimated 3 billion gallons of gasoline in 1987. Such energy waste is projected to soar to 7.3 billion gallons by 2005.

In 1907 the average speed of horse-drawn vehicles through the borough of Manhattan was 11.5 miles per hour. Today, cars and trucks with the potential power of 100 to 300 horses creep along Manhattan streets at an average speed of 5.2 miles per hour. In Los Angeles, traffic on the Hollywood Freeway slows to 20 miles per hour for about 14 hours every day. By 2000 the average speed on this freeway is projected to drop to about 7 miles per hour. In London average auto speeds are about 8 miles per hour, and even lower in Tokyo.

In the United States motor vehicles travel almost 2 trillion miles a year and account for 63% of the country's oil consumption. They produce at least 50% of the country's air pollution, even though U.S. emission standards are as strict as any in the world.

Cars are supposed to provide unlimited freedom of movement. Instead, many Americans and people in car-clogged urban areas in other countries are experiencing traffic gridlock. They are spending hours of their daily lives locked in a metal prison moving along at turtle-like speeds along jam-packed freeways and bottlenecked bridges and tunnels. Companies are losing billions of dollars as many of their employees arrive at work late, tired, and frustrated. What do you think should be done?

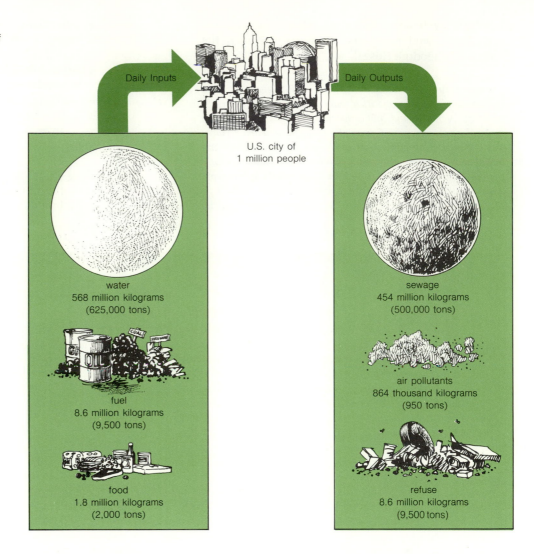

Figure 10-20 Typical daily input and output of matter and energy for a U.S. city of I million people.

Daily Inputs

U.S. city of
1 million people

Daily Outputs

water
568 million kilograms
(625,000 tons)

fuel
8.6 million kilograms
(9,500 tons)

food
1.8 million kilograms
(2,000 tons)

sewage
454 million kilograms
(500,000 tons)

air pollutants
864 thousand kilograms
(950 tons)

refuse
8.6 million kilograms
(9,500 tons)

■ Growing more of their own food in abandoned lots, community garden plots, rooftop gardens, apartment window boxes, and aquaculture ponds for cultivating fish and shellfish. At least six cities in China produce 85% of their vegetable needs within their boundaries, using recycled human waste and garbage as fertilizer.

■ Not keeping urban food prices artificially low. Fixed low prices discourage food production in rural areas and eventually cause urban food shortages, greater dependence on imported food, external debts, and rural-to-urban migration.

■ Giving food and other subsidies only to the neediest people on an equal basis in urban and rural areas. Giving more subsidies to urban residents encourages rural people to migrate to urban areas.

■ Recycling and reusing solid waste and hazardous waste.

■ Using ecological land-use planning and controls.

■ Establishing greenbelts of undeveloped forestland and other forms of open space within and around

urban areas and preserving nearby wetlands and agricultural land. In the United States, for example, Oregon has a statewide strategy to preserve greenbelts around its cities.

■ Planting large numbers of trees in greenbelts, on unused lots, and along streets to reduce urban air pollution and noise and to provide recreational areas and wildlife habitat.

■ Discouraging excessive dependence on motor vehicles within urban areas by providing efficient bus and trolley service and bike lanes; charging car commuters fees to enter cities and to park their vehicles. Virtually all European cities have enacted some restrictions on downtown auto use.

■ Getting more energy from locally available resources. Many cities can increase the energy they get from perpetual and renewable energy resources by relying more on firewood (with adequate reforestation and pollution control for wood stoves), solar energy, small-scale hydroelectric plants, farms of wind turbines, geothermal deposits, methane gas from landfills, and waste heat from power and industrial plants (cogeneration).

- Enacting building codes that require energy conservation and water conservation in new and existing buildings.

- Encouraging water conservation by installing water meters in all buildings and raising the price of water to reflect its true cost.

- Enacting and enforcing strict noise control laws to reduce stress from rising levels of urban noise.

- Discouraging industries that produce large quantities of pollution and use large amounts of water.

- Balancing urban and rural needs by increasing investments and social services in rural areas.

10-4 METHODS FOR CONTROLLING POPULATION CHANGE

Controlling Births, Deaths, and Migration A government can influence the size and rate of growth or decline of its population by encouraging a change in any of the three basic demographic variables: births, deaths, and migration.

Governments of most countries in the world achieve some degree of population control by allowing little immigration from other countries. Some governments also encourage emigration to other countries to reduce population pressures. Only a few countries, chiefly Canada, Australia, and the United States (see Case Study on p. 266), allow large annual increases in their population from immigration.

Increasing death rates is not an acceptable way to slow population growth. Thus, decreasing the birth rate is the focus of most efforts to control population growth. In 1960 only two countries, India and Pakistan, had official policies to reduce their birth rates. By 1988 about 93% of the world's population and 91% of the people in LDCs lived in countries with programs to reduce their fertility rates. However, the effectiveness and funding of these programs vary widely from country to country. Few governments spend more than 1% of the national budget on them.

Three general approaches to decreasing birth rates are *economic development*, *family planning*, and *socioeconomic change*. There is controversy over which approach is best. But increasing evidence shows that a combination of economic development and family planning, and in some cases of all three methods, offers a country the best way to reduce its birth rate and thus its rate of population growth.

Economic Development and the Demographic Transition Demographers examined the birth and death rates of western European countries that industrialized during the nineteenth century. On the basis of these data they developed a hypothesis of population change known as the **demographic transition**. Its basic idea is that as countries become industrialized, they have declines in death rates followed by declines in birth rates. As a result, they move from fast growth, to slow growth, to zero growth, and eventually to a slow decline in population.

This transition takes place in four distinct phases (Figure 10-22). In the *preindustrial stage* harsh living conditions lead to a high birth rate (to compensate for high infant mortality) and a high death rate, and the population grows slowly, if at all. The *transitional stage* begins shortly after industrialization begins. In this phase the death rate drops, mostly because of increased food production and improved sanitation and health.

CASE STUDY **Sustainable Living in Davis, California**

Davis, California, has ample sunshine, a flat terrain, and about 38,000 people. Its citizens and elected officials have committed themselves to making it an ecologically sustainable city.

The city's building codes encourage the use of solar energy to provide space heating and hot water and require all new homes to meet high standards of energy efficiency. When any existing home is sold, it must be inspected and the buyer must bring it up to the energy conservation standards for new homes. The community also has a master plan for planting deciduous trees, which provide shade and reduce heat gain in the summer and allow solar gain in the winter.

The city has adopted several policies that discourage the use of automobiles and encourage the use of bicycles. Some streets are closed to automobiles, and people are encouraged to work at home. A number of bicycle paths and lanes have been built and some city employees are given bikes. Any new housing tract must have a separate bicycle lane. As a result, 28,000 bikes account for 40% of all in-city transportation and much less land is needed for parking spaces. This heavy dependence on the bicycle is made possible by the city's warm climate and flat terrain.

Davis also limits the type and rate of growth and development and maintains a mix of homes for people with low, medium, and high incomes. Development of the fertile farmland surrounding the city for residential or commercial use is restricted. What things are being done to make the area where you live more sustainable?

The United States, founded by immigrants and their children, has admitted more immigrants and refugees than any other country in the world. Between 1820 and 1988 the United States admitted almost twice as many immigrants as all other countries combined.

The number of legal immigrants entering the United States since 1820 has varied during different periods as a result of changes in immigration laws and economic growth (Figure 10-21). Between 1820 and 1960 most legal immigrants came from Europe. Since then most have come from Asia and Latin America.

Between 1960 and 1988 the number of legal immigrants admitted per year more than doubled from 250,000 to 610,000. Each year another 200,000 to 500,000 people enter the country illegally, mostly from Mexico and other Latin American countries. This means that in 1988 legal and illegal immigrants increased the U.S. population by 800,000 to 1.1 million people, accounting for almost 40% of the country's population growth. If birth and death rates and immigration rates continue at present levels, soon immigration will be the major factor increasing the population of the United States.

Some analysts have called for an annual ceiling of no more than 450,000 for all categories of legal immigration, including refugees, to reduce the intensity of some of the country's social, economic, and environmental problems and reach zero population growth sooner. In polls taken in 1985 half of those surveyed favored lower legal immigration levels.

In 1986 Congress passed a new immigration law designed to control illegal immigration. This law included an amnesty program for some illegal immigrants. Those who entered the United States before January 1, 1982, and who could provide evidence that they have lived here continuously since then were eligible to become temporary residents and apply for citizenship after 6.5 years. By the May 4, 1988, deadline about 2.1 million of the estimated 5 million illegal aliens had signed up for the amnesty program.

The 1986 law also prohibits the hiring of illegal immigrants. Employers must examine the identity documents of all new employees. Employers who knowingly hire illegal aliens will be subject to fines of $250 to $10,000 per violation, and repeat offenders can be sentenced to prison for up to six

months. The bill also authorized funds to beef up the border patrol staff by 50%, to increase efforts to detect employers violating the new law, and to deport illegal aliens.

Critics of the law contend that illegals can get around the law with readily available fake documents. Employers are not responsible for verifying the authenticity of documents or for keeping copies. By 1988 the Immigration and Naturalization Service (INS) had failed to vigorously enforce sanctions against most employers who knowingly and repeatedly hired illegal aliens. Only 100 employers had been fined by 1988.

Even with more personnel it is essentially impossible for the INS to patrol more than a fraction of the 1,950-mile U.S.-Mexico border. With nearly 60% of Mexico's labor force unemployed or underemployed, many Mexicans think being caught and sent back is a minor risk compared to remaining in poverty. What, if anything, do you think should be done about legal and illegal immigration into the United States?

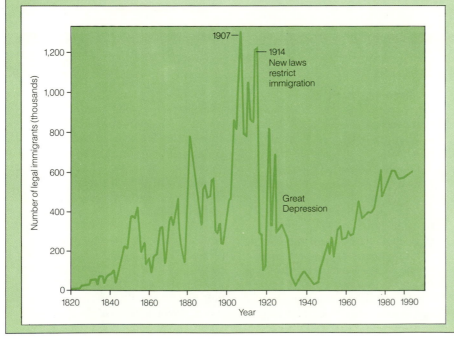

Figure 10-21 Legal immigration to the United States: 1820–1988. (Data from U.S. Immigration and Naturalization Service)

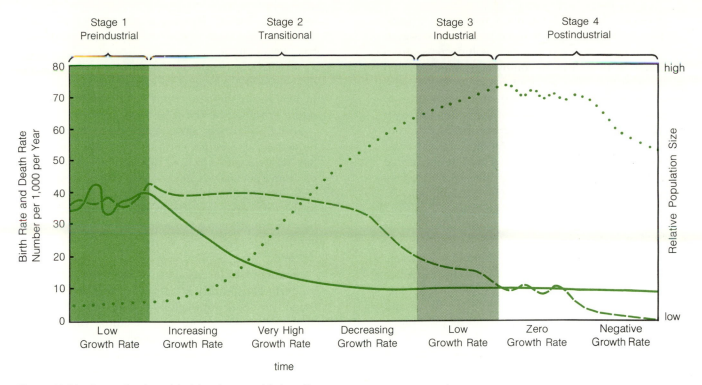

Figure 10-22 Generalized model of the demographic transition.

But the birth rate remains high, and the population grows rapidly (typically about 2.5% to 3% a year).

In the *industrial stage* industrialization is widespread. The birth rate drops and eventually approaches the death rate. The major reason for this is that couples who have jobs in cities realize that children are expensive to raise and that having too many children hinders them from taking advantage of job opportunities in an expanding economy. Population growth continues but at a slower and perhaps fluctuating rate, depending on economic conditions. The United States, Japan, the Soviet Union, Canada, Australia, New Zealand, and most industrialized western European countries are now in this third phase.

In the fourth phase, the *postindustrial stage*, the birth rate declines even further, equaling the death rate, and the population reaches zero population growth. The birth rate falls below the death rate and population size slowly decreases. By 1988, fourteen countries—Austria, Belgium, Bulgaria, Czechoslovakia, East Germany, Finland, Greece, Italy, Luxembourg, Norway, Portugal, Sweden, Switzerland, and the United Kingdom—had reached or were close to ZPG. Three countries—Denmark, Hungary, and West Germany—were experiencing population declines. Together these 17 countries have almost 6% of the world's population.

Can Most of Today's LDCs Make the Demographic Transition? In most LDCs today death rates have fallen more than birth rates. In other words, these LDCs are still in the transitional phase, halfway up

the economic ladder, with high population growth rates. Some economists believe that LDCs will make the demographic transition over the next few decades without increased family planning efforts.

But many population analysts fear that the rate of economic growth in many LDCs will never exceed their high rates of population growth. Without rapid and sustained economic growth, LDCs could become stuck in the transitional stage of the demographic transition.

Also, some of the conditions that allowed today's MDCs to develop are not available to today's LDCs. For example, even with large and growing populations, many LDCs do not have enough skilled workers to produce the high-technology products needed to compete in today's economic environment. Most low- and middle-income LDCs also lack the capital and resources needed for rapid economic development. And the amount of money being given or lent to LDCs—struggling under tremendous debt burdens—has been decreasing since 1980. LDCs face stiff competition from MDCs and recently industrialized LDCs in selling products on which their economic growth depends.

Should MDCs Be Concerned about Population Decline? Slowing population growth is the major concern of leaders in most of the world's countries. But leaders in a few countries, such as West Germany and Hungary, now undergoing a slow population decline are trying to find ways to raise birth rates.

For example, if West Germany maintains its present total fertility rate of 1.4 and does not allow significant immigration, its population will decrease from 61 million in 1988 to 45 million by 2050. West German leaders fear that there will be too few workers to support continued economic growth and to pay taxes to support the increasing portion of the population over age 65. An alternative is to increase immigration of workers from other countries. As other MDCs enter the postindustrial stage, some may become concerned with increasing their birth and fertility rates to reduce their rate of population decline (see Pro/Con below).

Family Planning Recent evidence suggests that improved and expanded family planning programs may bring about a more rapid decline in the birth rate and at a lower cost than economic development alone. **Family planning** programs provide educational and clinical services that help couples choose how many children to have and when to have them.

Such programs vary from culture to culture. But most provide information on birth spacing, birth control, breast-feeding, and pre-natal care and distribute contraceptives. In some cases they also perform abortions and sterilizations, often without charge or at low rates. With the exception of China (discussed in Section 10-5), family planning programs in most countries have not tried to convince or coerce couples to have fewer children.

In MDCs in 1988 about 70% of women in the reproductive period practiced some form of birth control. In LDCs only 49% practiced birth control, with the figure dropping to 39% if China is excluded.

Family planning saves a government money by reducing the need for various social services. It also has health benefits. In LDCs about one million women die from pregnancy-related causes. Half of these deaths could be prevented by effective family planning and health care programs. Family planning programs also help control the spread of acquired immune deficiency syndrome (AIDS) and other sexually transmitted diseases.

Family planning has been a major factor in reducing birth and fertility rates in China, Indonesia, and Brazil with large populations and in some LDCs with moderate to small populations. Examples include Barbados, Cuba, Colombia, Costa Rica, Fiji, Hong Kong, Jamaica, Mauritius, Mexico, Thailand, Singapore, South Korea, Sri Lanka, Taiwan, and Venezuela. These successful programs have been based on committed leadership, local implementation, and wide availability of contraceptive services.

But family planning has had moderate to poor

PRO/CON Is a Birth Dearth Good or Bad?

In 1987 social thinker and cornucopian Ben J. Wattenberg wrote a book titled *The Birth Dearth* (see Further Readings). He warned that if present fertility rates continue to remain below replacement level as projected, the share of the world's population in the United States and other western democracies will decline from 15% in 1985 to 9% in 2025.

Wattenberg and cornucopians like Julian Simon (see Guest Essay on p. 24) urge the United States and other MDCs to increase their populations to maintain their economic growth and power. Wattenberg believes that the U.S. government could encourage more births by paying each couple $2,000 a year for 16 years for each child they have.

Without more babies, he believes, the country will face a shortage of workers, taxpayers, scientists and engineers, con-sumers, and soldiers needed to maintain healthy economic growth, national security, and global power and influence. He also contends that an aging U.S. society will be less innovative and dynamic.

Critics of the proposal counter that the influence of democratic ideals is not based on numbers of people but on the effectiveness of democracies in making life better for people. Critics also point out that technological innovation—not sheer numbers of people—is the key to military and economic power in today's world. Using Wattenberg's reasoning, England and Japan, with fairly small populations, should have little global power and China should rule the world.

History does not show that an older society is necessarily more conservative and less innovative than one dominated by younger people. A society with a higher average age tends to have a larger pool of collective wisdom based on experience. Indeed, the most conservative and least innovative societies in the world today are LDCs with a large portion of their populations under age 29.

Critics also argue that adding millions to the U.S. population will intensify many environmental and social problems by increasing resource use, environmental degradation, and pollution. Instead of encouraging more births, they believe that the United States should establish an official goal of stabilizing its population by 2025. This would help reduce environmental stress in the United States and throughout the world. It would also set a good example for other countries, especially LDCs. What do you think?

results in more populous LDCs such as India, Brazil, Bangladesh, Pakistan, and Nigeria. Results have also been poor in 79 less populous LDCs—especially in Africa and Latin America—where population growth rates are usually very high. For example, only 3% to 10% of couples in most African countries use contraception.

The Population Crisis Committee estimates that between 1978 and 1983, family planning programs reduced world population by 130 million and saved at least $175 billion in government expenditures for food, shelter, clothing, education, and health care. Despite these efforts, the delivery of family planning services in much of the less developed world is still woefully inadequate, particularly in rural areas. The momentum of family planning in many major LDCs has slowed in recent years.

An estimated 400 million women in LDCs want to limit the number and determine the spacing of their children but lack access to such services. Extending family planning services to these women and those who will soon be entering their reproductive years could prevent an estimated 5.8 million births a year and more than 130,000 abortions a day. By 2100 this would mean 2.7 billion fewer people—over half of the world's present population—needing food, water, shelter, and health services.

Family planning could be provided in LDCs to all couples who want it for about $7 billion a year—about two days of world military spending. Currently only about $3 billion is being spent. If MDCs provided half of the $7 billion, each person in the MDCs would spend only 34 cents a year (compared to 3 cents now) to help reduce world population by 2.7 billion.

But even the present inadequate level of expenditure for family planning is decreasing. The United States has sharply curtailed its funding of international family planning agencies since 1985, mostly as a result of political pressure by pro-life activists (see Pro/Con below). Instead of cutting back on international family planning assistance, the United States and other MDCs need to increase contributions. This will help prevent an unnecessary loss of life.

Economic Rewards and Penalties Some population experts argue that family planning, even coupled with economic development, cannot lower birth and fertility rates fast enough. Why? Because most couples in LDCs want 3 or 4 children—well above the 2.1 fertility rate needed to bring about eventual population stabilization.

These experts call for increased emphasis on bringing about socioeconomic change to help regulate population size. Births would be discouraged by using economic rewards and penalties. Fertility would be reduced by increasing rights, education, and work opportunities for women.

About 20 countries offer small payments to individuals who agree to use contraceptives or to be sterilized. They also pay doctors and family planning workers for each sterilization they perform and each IUD they insert. For example, in India a person receives about $15 for being sterilized, the equivalent of about two weeks' pay for an agricultural worker.

Such payments, however, are most likely to attract people who already have all the children they want. Although payments are not physically coercive, they have been criticized as being psychologically coercive. In some cases the poor feel they have to accept them in order to survive.

Some countries, such as China, penalize couples who have more than a certain number of children— usually one or two. Penalties may be extra taxes and other costs or not allowing income tax deductions for a couple's third child (as in Singapore, Hong Kong, Ghana, and Malaysia). Families who have more chil-

---

PRO/CON **Should Federal Funds Be Given to Family Planning Clinics That Tell Clients Abortion Is an Option?**

In 1988 the Reagan administration cut off U.S. contributions to the United Nations Fund for Population Activities and the International Planned Parenthood Federation because these organizations inform women that abortion is one of their alternatives to pregnancy. Between 1988 and 1991 this cutoff could result in 310,000 additional births, 1,200 maternal deaths, and 69,000 more pregnancies that end in abortion.

In 1988 the Reagan administration also cut off federal funding to U.S. family planning clinics that even mention to pregnant women that abortion is an option. If this rule stands, it will affect 4.3 million women—including 1.5 million teenagers—who visit the clinics. Without federal funding many clinics will be forced to close.

These clinics help prevent 800,000 unwanted pregnancies a year, especially for poor women.

They also reduce the number of legal abortions in the United States by 433,000 a year. For every $1 invested, this program saves taxpayers $2 to $3 the following year in health and welfare costs. What do you think about these executive decisions?

dren than the desired limit may also suffer reduced free health care, decreased food allotments, and loss of job choice.

Like economic rewards, economic penalties can be psychologically coercive for the poor. Programs that withhold food or increase the cost of raising children punish innocent children for actions by their parents.

Experience has shown that economic rewards and penalties designed to reduce fertility work best if they:

- nudge rather than push people to have fewer children

- reinforce existing customs and trends toward smaller families

- do not penalize people who produced large families before the programs were established

- increase a poor family's income or land

However, once population growth is out of control, a country may be forced to use coercive methods to prevent mass starvation and hardship. This is what China has had to do.

Changes in Womens' Roles   Another socioeconomic method of population regulation is to improve the condition of women. Today women do almost all of the world's domestic work and child care, mostly without pay. They also do more than half the work associated with growing food, gathering fuelwood, and hauling water. Women also provide more health care with little or no pay than all the world's organized health services put together.

Despite their vital economic and social contributions, most women in LDCs don't have a legal right to own land or to borrow money to increase agricultural productivity. Although women work two-thirds of all hours worked in the world, they get only one-tenth of the world's income and own a mere 1% of the world's land.

At the same time, women make up about 60% of the world's almost 900 million adults who can neither read nor write. Women also suffer the most malnutrition, because men and children are fed first where food supplies are limited.

Women make up one-third of the world's paid labor force. But they have many of the lowest-paid jobs and earn about 75% less than men who do similar work. In the United States, women earn 30% less than men doing similar work, with women workers ages 21 to 29 earning 17% less.

Numerous studies have shown that increased education is a strong factor leading women to have fewer children. Educated women are more likely than uneducated women to be employed outside the home rather than to stay home and raise children. They marry later, thus reducing their prime reproductive years,

and lose fewer infants to death, a major factor in reducing fertility rates.

Giving more of the world's women the opportunity to become educated and to express their lives in meaningful, paid work and social roles outside the home will require some major social changes. But making these changes will be difficult because of the long-standing political and economic domination of society by men throughout the world. In addition, competition between men and women for already scarce jobs in many countries should become even more intense by 2000, when another billion people will be looking for work.

10-5   CASE STUDIES: POPULATION REGULATION IN INDIA AND CHINA

India   India started the world's first national family planning program in 1952, when its population was nearly 400 million. In 1988, after 35 years of population control effort, India was the world's second most populous country, with a population of 817 million.

In 1952 it was adding 5 million people to its population each year. In 1988 it added 17 million. India is expected to become the world's most populous country around 2015. Its population is projected to more than double to 1.6 billion before leveling off early in the twenty-second century.

In 1988 India's average per capita income was about $280 a year. At least one-third of its population had an annual income per person of less than $80 a year. To add to the problem, nearly half of India's labor force is unemployed or can find only occasional work. Each week 100,000 more people enter the job market, and for most of them jobs do not exist.

Without its long-standing family planning program, India's numbers would be growing even faster. But the results of the program have been disappointing. Factors contributing to this failure have been poor planning, bureaucratic inefficiency, the low status of women (despite constitutional guarantees of equality), extreme poverty, and too little administrative and financial support.

But the roots of the problem are deeper. More than 3 out of every 4 people in India live in 560,000 rural villages, where crude birth rates are still close to 40 births per 1,000 people. The overwhelming economic and administrative task of delivering contraceptive services and education to the mostly rural population is complicated by an illiteracy rate of about 71%, with 80% to 90% of the illiterate being rural women.

For years the government has provided information about the advantages of small families. Yet Indian women still have an average of 4.3 children because most couples believe they need many children as a source of cheap labor and old-age survival insurance. This belief is reinforced by the fact that almost one-third of all Indian children die before age 5.

In 1976 Indira Gandhi's government started a mass sterilization program, primarily for men in the civil service who already had two or more children. The program was supposed to be voluntary, with financial incentives given to those who volunteered to be sterilized. But officials allegedly used coercion to meet sterilization quotas in a few rural areas. The resulting backlash played a role in Gandhi's election defeat in 1977.

In 1978 the government took a new approach, raising the legal minimum age for marriage from 18 to 21 for men and from 15 to 18 for women. The 1981 census, however, showed that there was no drop in the population growth rate between 1971 and 1981. Since then the government has increased family planning efforts and funding, with the goal of achieving replacement-level fertility by 2000. Whether such efforts will succeed remains to be seen.

The United Nations projects that 2015 is the earliest India can expect to reach replacement-level fertility. If this happens, its population would still grow significantly for 60 to 70 years because of the number of people under age 15.

Although effective population control still lags behind, India's agricultural production has improved dramatically between the mid-1960s and 1983. However, since 1983 its grain production has not increased. There is a good chance that by the end of this century India will again be unable to produce enough food to feed its population.

China   Between 1958 and 1962 an estimated 30 million people died from famine in China. Since 1970, however, the People's Republic of China has made impressive efforts to feed its people and bring its population growth under control.

Today China has enough grain both to export and to feed its population of 1.1 billion. Between 1972 and 1985 China achieved a remarkable drop in its crude birth rate, from 32 to 18 per 1,000 population and its total fertility rate dropped from 5.7 to 2.1 children per woman.

To accomplish a sharp drop in fertility, China has established the most extensive and strictest population control program in the world, with an outlay of about $1 per person annually. Its major features include:

- strongly encouraging couples to postpone marriage
- expanding educational opportunities
- providing married couples with easy access to free sterilization, contraceptives, and abortion
- giving couples who sign pledges to have no more than one child economic rewards such as salary bonuses, extra food, larger pensions, better housing, free medical care and school tuition for their child, and preferential treatment in employment when the child grows up
- requiring those who break the pledge to return all benefits
- exerting pressure on women pregnant with a third child to have abortions
- requiring one of the parents in a two-child family to be sterilized
- using mobile units and paramedics to bring sterilization, family planning, health care, and education to rural areas
- training local people to carry on the family planning program
- expecting all leaders to set an example with their own family size

By 1987, however, China's birth rate had risen slightly to 21, and its total fertility rate had increased to 2.5. Births rose from 18 million in 1984 to 25 million in 1987. The major reasons for this rise were the large number of women moving into their childbearing years, some relaxation of the government's stringent policies, and a strong preference for male children who, by custom, help support their parents as they grow old.

China's leaders have a goal of reaching ZPG by 2000 with a population at 1.2 billion, followed by a slow decline to 0.6 to 1.0 billion by 2100. Achieving this goal will be very difficult because 34% of the Chinese people are under age 15. As a result, the United Nations projects that the population of China may be around 1.4 billion by 2020.

Most countries cannot or do not want to use the coercive elements of China's program. Other parts of this program, however, could be used in many LDCs. Especially useful is the practice of localizing the program, rather than asking the people to go to distant centers. Perhaps the best lesson that other countries can learn from China's experience is not to wait to curb population growth until the choice is between mass starvation and coercive measures.

Many LDCs hope to slow their population growth. But China is the first and only country in the world to set a goal of *reducing* its population size.

Population programs aren't simply a matter of promoting smaller families. They also mean guaranteeing that our children are given the fullest opportunities to be educated, to get good health care, and to have access to the jobs and careers they eventually want. It is really a matter of increasing the value of every birth, of expanding the potential of every child to the fullest, and of improving the life of a community.

Pranay Gupte

DISCUSSION TOPICS

1. Why are falling birth rates not necessarily a reliable indicator of future population growth trends?

2. Explain the difference between achieving replacement-level fertility and achieving zero population growth (ZPG).

3. How many children do you plan to have? Why?

4. Project what your own life may be like at ages 25, 45, and 65 on the basis of the present population age structure of the country in which you live. What changes, if any, do such projections make in your career choice and in your plans for children?

5. List the advantages and disadvantages of living in (a) the downtown area of a large city, (b) suburbia, (c) a small town in a rural area, (d) a small town near a large city, and (e) a rural area. Which would you prefer to live in? Why? Which will you probably end up living in? Why?

6. What conditions, if any, would encourage you to rely less on the automobile? Would you regularly travel to school or work in a car pool, on a bicycle or motor scooter, on foot, or by mass transit? Explain.

7. Should world population growth be controlled? Explain.

8. Debate the following resolution: The United States has a serious consumption overpopulation problem and should adopt an official policy to stabilize its population and reduce unnecessary resource waste and consumption as rapidly as possible.

9. Do you believe that the demographic transition hypothesis applies to most of today's LDCs? Explain.

10. a. Should the number of legal immigrants and refugees allowed into the United States each year be sharply reduced? Explain.
    b. Should illegal immigration into the United States be sharply decreased? Explain. If so, how would you go about achieving this?

11. Why has China been more successful than India in reducing its rate of population growth? Do you agree with China's present population control policies? Explain. What alternatives, if any, would you suggest?

FURTHER READINGS

Bouvier, Leon F. 1984. "Planet Earth 1984–2034: A Demographic Vision." *Population Bulletin*, vol. 39, no.1, 1–39.

Brown, Lester R. 1981. *Building a Sustainable Society*. New York: W. W. Norton.

Brown, Lester R., and Jodi Jacobson. 1986. *Our Demographically Divided World*. Washington, D.C.: Worldwatch Institute.

Brown, Lester R., and Jodi Jacobson. 1987. *The Future of Urbanization: Facing the Ecological and Economic Restraints*. Washington, D.C.: Worldwatch Institute.

Crewdson, John. 1983. *The Tarnished Door*. New York: New York Times Books.

Croll, Elisabeth, et al. 1985. *China's One-Child Family Policy*. New York: St. Martin's Press.

Formos, Werner. 1987. *Gaining People, Losing Ground: A Blueprint for Stabilizing World Population*. Washington, D.C.: Population Institute.

Gupte, Pranay. 1984. *The Crowded Earth: People and the Politics of Population*. New York: W. W. Norton.

Hardin, Garrett. 1982. *Naked Emperors, Essays of a Taboo Stalker*. San Francisco: William Kaufman.

Hartmann, Betsy. 1987. *Reproductive Rights and Wrongs: The Global Politics of Population Control and Contraceptive Choice*. New York: Harper & Row.

Haupt, Arthur, and Thomas T. Kane. 1985. *The Population Handbook*, 2d ed. Washington, D.C.: Population Reference Bureau.

Hernandez, Donald J. 1985. *Success or Failure? Family Planning Programs in the Third World*. Westport, Conn: Greenwood Press.

Jacobs, Jane. 1984. *Cities and the Wealth of Nations*. New York: Random House.

Jacobsen, Jodi L. 1987. *Planning the Global Family*. Washington, D.C.: Worldwatch Institute.

Lamm, Richard D., and Gary Imhoff. 1985. *The Immigration Time Bomb*. New York: Dutton.

Loup, Jacques. 1983. *Can the Third World Survive?* Baltimore: Johns Hopkins University Press.

McHarg, Ian L. 1969. *Design with Nature*. Garden City, N.Y.: Natural History Press.

Menken, Jane, ed. 1986. *World Population and U.S. Policy: The Choices Ahead*. New York: W. W. Norton.

Morris, David. 1982. *Energy and the Transformation of Urban America*. San Francisco: Sierra Club Books.

Population Reference Bureau. Annual. *World Population Data Sheet*. Washington, D.C.: Population Reference Bureau.

Population Reference Bureau. 1986. *Women in the World: The Women's Decade and Beyond*. Washington, D.C.: Population Reference Bureau.

Register, Richard. 1987. *Ecocity Berkeley: Building Cities for a Healthy Future*. Berkeley, Calif.: North Atlantic Books.

Renner, Michael. 1988. *Rethinking the Role of the Automobile*. Washington, D.C.: Worldwatch Institute.

Ryn, Sin van der, and Peter Calthorpe. 1986. *Sustainable Communities: A New Design Synthesis for Cities, Suburbs, and Towns*. San Fransisco: Sierra Club.

Simon, Julian L. 1981. *The Ultimate Resource*. Princeton, N.J.: Princeton University Press.

Teitelbaum, Michael, and Jay M. Winter. 1985. *The Fear of Population Decline*. Orlando, Fla.: Academic Press.

UNICEF. 1988. *The State of the World's Children*. New York: United Nations.

Wattenberg, Ben J. 1987. *The Birth Dearth*. New York: Pharos Books.

Weber, Susan, ed. 1988. *USA by Numbers: A Statistical Portrait of the United States*. Washington, D.C.: Zero Population Growth.

Weeks, John R. 1989. *Population: An Introduction to Concepts and Issues*, 4th ed. Belmont, Calif.: Wadsworth.

CHAPTER 11

Food Resources

General Questions and Issues

1. What types of agricultural systems provide food from domesticated crops and livestock throughout the world?
2. What are the world's major food problems?
3. Can increasing crop yields and cultivating more land solve the world's major food problems?
4. What government policies can increase food production?
5. What can giving food aid and redistributing land to the poor do to help solve world food problems?
6. How can agricultural systems in MDCs and LDCs be designed to be ecologically and economically sustainable?

7. What are the pros and cons of using pesticides to help protect crops from damage and loss, and what are the alternatives to using pesticides?

Hunger is a curious thing: At first it is with you all the time, working and sleeping and in your dreams, and your belly cries out insistently, and there is a gnawing and a pain as if your very vitals were being devoured, and you must stop it at any cost. . . . Then the pain is no longer sharp, but dull, and this too is with you always.

Kamala Markandaya

What uses more of the earth's land, water, soil, plant, animal, and energy resources and causes more pollution and environmental degradation than any other human activity? Agriculture. Each day, the world has 247,000 more people to feed, clothe, and house. By 2020 the world's population is expected to reach at least 8 billion. To feed these people, we must produce as much food during the next 30 years as we have produced since the dawn of agriculture about 10,000 years ago.

Producing enough food to feed the world's population, however, is only one of a number of complex, interrelated food resource problems. Another major problem is food quality—eating food with enough proteins, vitamins, and minerals to avoid malnutrition. We must also have enough storage facilities to keep food from rotting or being eaten by pests after it is harvested. An adequate transportation and retail outlet system must be available to distribute and sell food throughout a country and the world.

Poverty is the leading cause of hunger and premature death from lack of food quantity and quality. It is the main reason that one out of five people on earth today are not adequately fed. Making sure the poor have enough land or income to grow or buy enough food is the key to reducing deaths from malnutrition. Farmers must also have economic incentives to grow enough food to meet the world's needs. Finally, the world's agricultural systems must be managed to minimize the harmful environmental impacts of producing and distributing food.

11-1 WORLD AGRICULTURAL SYSTEMS: HOW IS FOOD PRODUCED?

Plants and Animals That Feed the World   Although about 80,000 species of plants throughout the world are edible, only about 30 crops feed the world. Four

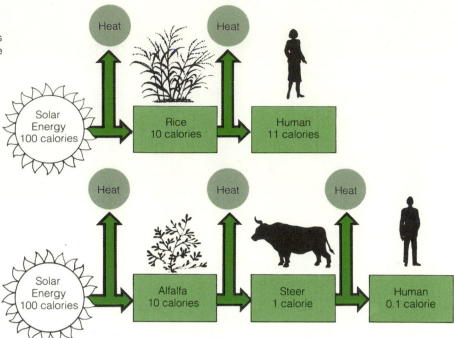

Figure 11-1 Food chain energy losses. The second law of energy causes a sharp drop in available calories of energy at each step. This explains why most people in the world survive on a grain diet.

crops—wheat, rice, corn, and potato—make up more of the world's total food production than all others combined.

The rest of the food people eat is mainly fish, meat, and animal products such as milk, eggs, and cheese. Most of these foods come from just nine groups of domesticated livestock: cattle, sheep, swine, chickens, turkeys, geese, ducks, goats, and water buffalo.

Meat and animal products are too expensive for most people, primarily because of the loss of usable energy when an animal trophic level is added to a food chain (Figure 11-1). Poor people can get more food energy per unit of money or labor from grain than from meat and animal products.

However, as incomes rise, people consume more grain *indirectly*, in the form of meat and products from grain-fed domesticated animals. In MDCs, almost half of the world's annual grain production (especially corn and soybeans) is fed to livestock. Also about one-third of the world's annual fish catch is converted to fish meal and fed to livestock.

Major Types of Agriculture Two major types of agricultural systems are used to grow crops and raise livestock throughout the world: industrialized agriculture and subsistence agriculture (see Spotlight on p. 275). **Industrialized agriculture** produces large quantities of a single type of crop or livestock for sale within the country where it is grown and to other countries. This is done by supplementing solar energy with large amounts of energy from fossil fuels, mostly oil and natural gas.

Industrialized agriculture is widely used in MDCs and since the mid-1960s has spread to parts of some LDCs (Figure 11-3). It is supplemented by **plantation agriculture**, in which specialized crops such as bananas, coffee, and cacao are grown in tropical LDCs primarily for sale to MDCs.

Traditional **subsistence agriculture** produces enough crops or livestock for survival and in good years to have some left over to sell or put aside for hard times. This is done by supplementing solar energy with energy from human labor and draft animals. The three major types of subsistence agriculture are shifting cultivation of small plots in tropical forests (Figure 2-2, p. 29), intensive crop cultivation on relatively small plots of land in other areas, and nomadic herding of livestock. These forms of agriculture are practiced by about 2.6 billion people—one of every two persons on earth—who live in rural villages in LDCs.

The relative inputs of land, human and animal labor, fossil fuel energy, and capital needed to produce one unit of food energy by various types of agriculture are shown in Figure 11-4. It shows that industrialized agriculture is capital and energy intensive, whereas intensive subsistence agriculture is labor intensive, and shifting cultivation and nomadic herding are land intensive. An average of 63% of the people in LDCs work in agriculture, compared to only 10% in MDCs.

Industrialized Agriculture and Green Revolutions
Food production is increased either by cultivating more land or by getting higher yields from existing cropland. Since 1950 most of the increase in world food

Industrial Farmers	Subsistence Farmers

Crop Production

Grow large quantities of food for sale by investing a large amount of money, usually borrowed.

Grow enough food to feed their families, investing little if any money.

Buy scientifically bred hybrid seeds of a single crop variety and plant them as a monoculture on a large field (Figure 6-24, p. 143).

Plant a diversity of naturally available crop seeds on a small plot (Figure 2-2, p. 29).

Buy expensive equipment that is costly to operate, repair, or replace.

Make or buy simple equipment that costs little to run, repair, or replace.

Often farm on flat, easily cultivated fields with fertile soil.

Often farm on easily erodible, hard to cultivate, mountainous highlands, drylands with fragile soils, and tropical forests with low-fertility soils.

Increase crop yields by using irrigation and commercial inorganic fertilizers.

Increase crop yields by making efficient use of natural inputs of water and organic fertilizers.

Plant one crop and use chemicals to kill pest species along with a variety of predators of pest species.

Plant a diversity of crops to provide numerous habitats for natural predators of pest species.

Work against nature by using large amounts of fossil fuel energy to keep a monoculture at an early stage of ecological succession.

Work with nature by allowing a diversity of crops to undergo guided ecological succession.

Do most work with fossil-fuel-powered farm machinery.

Do most work by hand or with help from draft animals.

Meat and Animal Product Production

Produce large quantities of a single type of meat or animal product for sale by investing a large amount of money, usually borrowed.

Produce enough meat and animal products to feed their families, investing little money.

Use animal **feedlots** to raise hundreds to thousands of domesticated livestock in a small space (Figure 11-2). Give animals antibiotics and growth hormones to encourage rapid weight gain and to achieve efficient, factorylike production.

Use natural rangeland, grassland, or forests and fields as sources of food and water for small groups of livestock. Often move flocks from one place to another to provide enough food and water.

Produce fatty meat that most consumers like but is considered unhealthful in large amounts.

Produce lean meat that is more healthful than fatty meat.

Use massive inputs of energy by burning fossil fuels for heating, cooling, pumping water, producing feed, and transporting supplies and livestock.

Use human and animal labor with no inputs of fossil fuels.

Produce large concentrations of animal wastes, which can wash into nearby surface water and contaminate it with disease-causing bacteria and excess plant nutrients (cultural eutrophication).

Return nutrient-rich animal wastes to the soil where animals roam, or collect it and use it as organic fertilizer for growing crops, or dry it and burn it as a fuel for heating and cooking.

Figure 11-2 Feedlots like this huge one for cattle near Greeley, Colorado, increase production efficiency. However, they concentrate massive amounts of animal wastes, which, without proper controls, can pollute groundwater with excessive levels of nitrates and contribute to cultural eutrophication of nearby lakes and slow-moving rivers. Beef cattle are usually moved to feedlots to be fattened a few weeks before slaughter. Other types of livestock, such as chickens and pigs, are kept in automated feedlots from birth to death.

Environmental Protection Agency

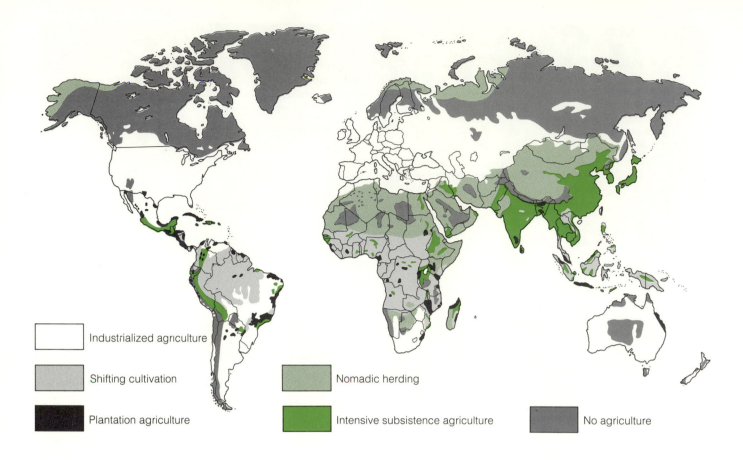

	Industrialized agriculture		
	Shifting cultivation		Nomadic herding
	Plantation agriculture		Intensive subsistence agriculture		No agriculture

Figure 11-3 Generalized location of the world's major types of agriculture.

production has come from increasing the yield per acre by what is called a **green revolution.** It involves planting monocultures of scientifically bred plant varieties and applying large amounts of inorganic fertilizer, irrigation water, and pesticides.

Between 1950 and 1970 this approach led to dramatic increases in yields of major crops in the United States and most other industrialized countries, a phenomenon sometimes known as the *first green revolution* (Figure 11-5). In 1967, after 30 years of genetic research and trials, a modified version of the first green revolution began spreading to many LDCs. New high-yield, fast-growing dwarf varieties of rice and wheat, specially bred for tropical and subtropical climates, were introduced into several LDCs in what is known as the *second green revolution*.

The shorter, stronger, and stiffer stalks of the new varieties allow them to support larger heads of grain without toppling over (Figures 11-6). With large inputs of fertilizer, water, and pesticides, wheat and rice yields of these new varieties can be two to five times those of traditional varieties. The fast-growing varieties allow farmers to grow two and even three consecutive crops a year (multiple cropping) on the same parcel of land.

Nearly 90% of the increase in world grain output in the 1960s and about 70% of that in the 1970s were the result of the second green revolution. In the 1980s

and 1990s at least 80% of the additional production of grains is expected to be based on improved yields of existing cropland through the use of green revolution techniques.

These increases, however, depend heavily on fossil fuel inputs, principally oil. On average it now takes 1.2 barrels of oil to produce a ton of grain, twice the amount of oil used in 1960. Since 1950, agriculture's use of fossil fuels has increased sevenfold, the number of tractors has quadrupled, irrigated area has tripled, and fertilizer use has risen tenfold. Agriculture, like other parts of industrialized societies, has become addicted to oil, now using about one-twelfth of the world oil output.

Industrialized Agriculture in the United States
Since 1940, U.S. farmers have more than doubled crop production while cultivating about the same amount of land. They have done this through industrialized agriculture coupled with a favorable climate and fertile soil. They have increased crop yields per acre by massive inputs of fossil fuel energy, irrigation water, commercial inorganic fertilizers, and pesticides (see Pro/Con on p. 279).

Less than 1% of the U.S. work force is engaged in farming. Yet the country's 2.1 million farmers—with only 650,000 working full time at farming—produce

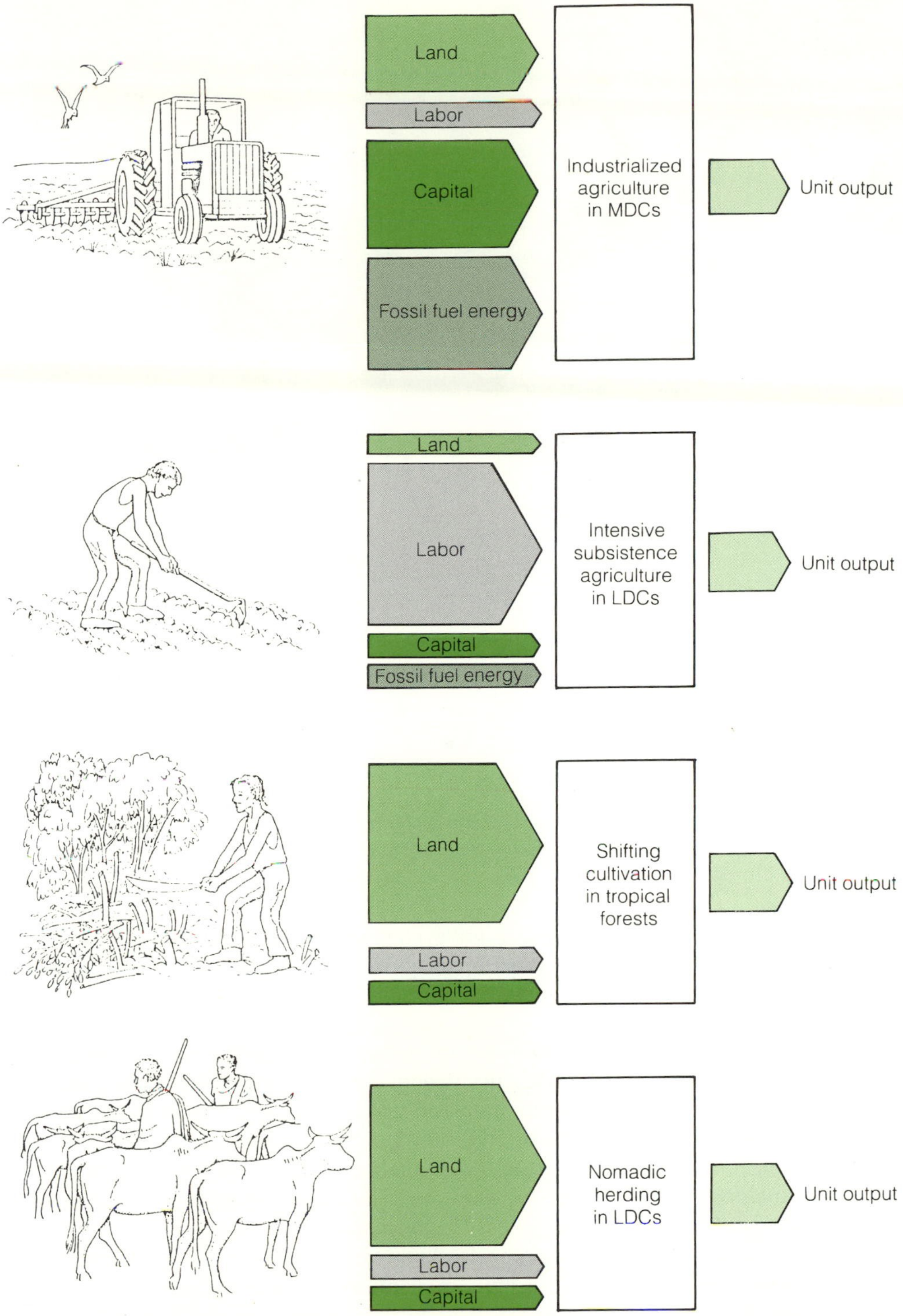

Figure 11-4 Relative inputs of land, labor, capital, and fossil fuel energy into major types of agricultural systems.

enough food to feed most of their fellow citizens better and at a lower percentage of their income than do farmers in any other country. Americans spend an average of 11% to 15% of their disposable income on food, while people in much of the world spend 40% or more. In addition, U.S. farmers produce large amounts of food for export to other countries.

About 23 million people—20% of the U.S. work force—are involved in the U.S. agricultural system in activities ranging from growing and processing food to selling it at the supermarket. In terms of total annual sales, the agricultural system is the biggest industry in the United States—bigger than the automotive, steel, and housing industries combined. In 1987, however, farmers got an average of only 25 cents of every dollar spent on food in the United States.

The gigantic agricultural system consumes about 17% of all commercial energy used in the United States

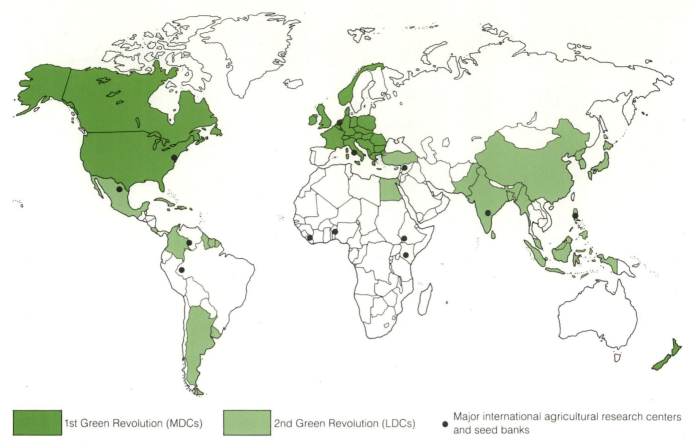

| 1st Green Revolution (MDCs) | 2nd Green Revolution (LDCs) | ● Major international agricultural research centers and seed banks |

Figure 11-5 Countries achieving increases in crop yields per unit of land area during the two green revolutions. The first took place in MDCs between 1950 and 1970, and the second in LDCs with enough rainfall or irrigation capacity between 1967 and 1988. Thirteen agricultural research centers and genetic storage banks play a key role in developing high-yield crop varieties.

each year (Figure 11-7). Most of this energy comes from oil. Most plant crops in the United States provide more food energy than the energy (mostly from fossil fuels) used to grow them. But raising animals for food requires much more fossil fuel energy than the animals provide as food energy.

Energy efficiency is much worse if we look at the entire U.S. food system. Counting fossil fuel energy inputs used to grow, store, process, package, transport, refrigerate, and cook all plant and animal food, *an average of about ten units of nonrenewable fossil fuel energy is needed to put one unit of food energy on the table— an energy loss of nine units per unit of food energy produced*. By comparison, every unit of energy from the human labor of subsistence farmers may provide ten units of food energy.

Suppose everyone in the world ate a typical American diet with the food produced by industrialized agriculture. If the world's known oil reserves were used only for producing this food, these reserves would be depleted in 12 years.

Suppose that fossil fuel, especially oil, suddenly becomes and remains scarce or much more expensive, as most energy experts believe will happen sometime between 1995 and 2010. The present industrialized agricultural system in MDCs would collapse, with a sharp drop in world food production and a rise in food prices, malnutrition, and famine.

Examples of Subsistence Agriculture Farmers in LDCs use various forms of subsistence agriculture to grow crops on about 60% of the world's cultivated land (Figure 11-3). Many subsistence farmers imitate nature by simultaneously growing a variety of crops on the same plot. This biological diversity reduces their chances of losing most or all of their year's food supply from pests, flooding, drought, or other disasters.

Common planting strategies include:

- **Polyvarietal cultivation,** in which a plot of land is planted with several varieties of the same crop.

- **Intercropping,** in which two or several different crops are grown at the same time on a plot—for example, a carbohydrate-rich grain that depletes soil nitrogen and a protein-rich legume that adds nitrogen to the soil.

- **Agroforestry,** a variation of intercropping in which crops and trees are planted together. For example, a grain or legume crop might be planted around fruit-bearing orchard trees or in rows

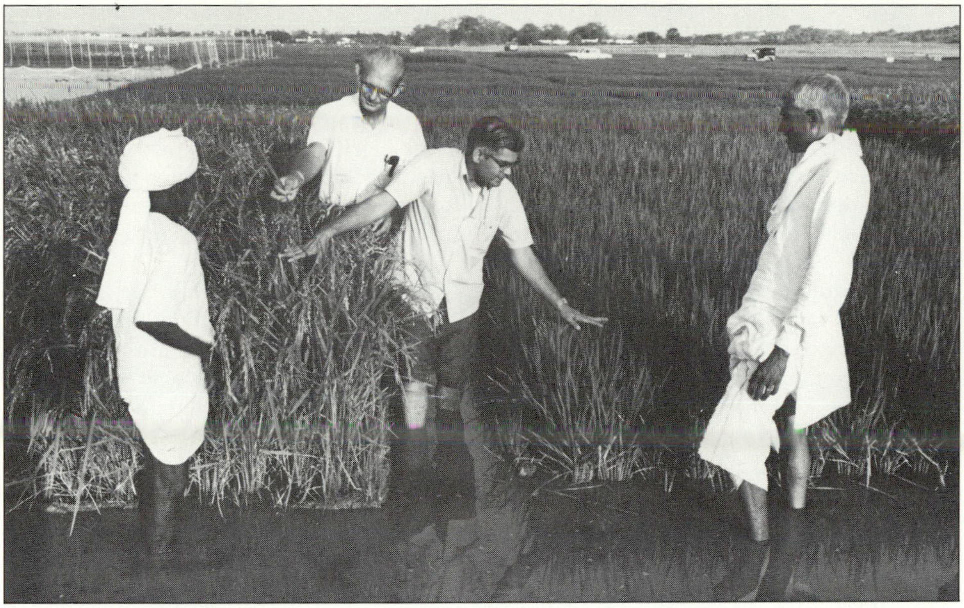

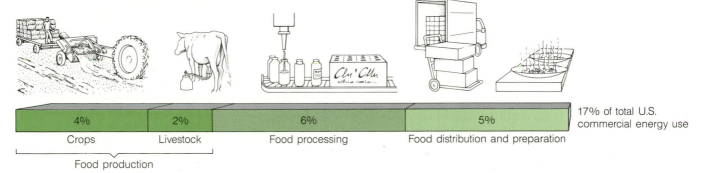

Figure 11-6 Scientists and two Indian farmers compare an older, full-size variety of rice (left) and a new, high-yield dwarf variety, grown in the second green revolution.

4%	2%	6%	5%
Crops	Livestock	Food processing	Food distribution and preparation

17% of total U.S. commercial energy use

Food production

Figure 11-7 Commercial energy use by the U.S. industrialized agriculture system.

PRO/CON The Pesticide Controversy

In the United States about 700 active ingredients and 900 inert ingredients are mixed to make some 50,000 individual pesticide products. U.S. pesticide use rose from 200,000 pounds per year in the 1940s to more than 1 billion pounds today. Each year an average of 5 pounds of these products is used for each American, with 77% used on crops.

The most widely used types of pesticides are:

- **herbicides,** to kill weeds, unwanted plants that compete with crop plants for soil nutrients (accounting for 88% of all pesticide use by U.S. farmers)

- **insecticides,** to kill insects that consume crops and food and transmit diseases to humans and livestock
- **fungicides,** to kill fungi that damage crops

Four crops—corn, cotton, wheat, and soybeans—account for about 70% of the insecticides and 80% of the herbicides used on crops.

About 92% of all U.S. households use pesticides indoors (for example, bug sprays and ant and roach poisons) and outdoors on lawns and gardens and to preserve wood. The average home owner applies about five times more pesticide per unit of land area than do farmers.

Since the middle 1960s there has been much controversy over the widespread use of pesticides, especially insecticides such as DDT and herbicides such as 2,4,5-T. By the mid-1970s the use of 2,4,5-T and most slowly degradable, chlorinated hydrocarbon insecticides (such as DDT and dieldrin) was banned or severely restricted in the United States and most MDCs.

These chemicals have been replaced by a number of more rapidly degradable pesticides. But

(continued)

many of these compounds are more toxic to birds, people, and other mammals and more likely to contaminate groundwater than the longer-lived compounds they replaced.

Pesticide manufacturers and a number of agricultural scientists argue that the benefits of pesticides far exceed their threats to wildlife and human health. Pesticides have reduced outbreaks of insect-transmitted diseases such as malaria and saved millions of people from illness and premature death. They have also increased crop yields by reducing losses to pests. This increase in food production has reduced illness and premature deaths from malnutrition, kept food prices low, and increased profits for farmers.

Environmentalists and conservationists, however, contend that the harmful effects of these chemicals outweigh their benefits. Pesticides threaten human health and wildlife, and in the long run they don't work and may even make matters worse. Moreover, they cost more than safer, natural methods.

Pesticides eventually cause larger, more damaging outbreaks of the pests they are supposed to

control when the pests develop genetic resistance to the pesticides and their natural predators are wiped out. The widespread killing of predator species allows prey species that were not pests or were only minor pests to multiply rapidly and become major pests.

Farmers attempt to control new outbreaks by applying pesticides more frequently, using larger doses, or switching to new (usually more expensive) chemicals. This puts farmers on a **pesticide treadmill**, in which the cost of using pesticides increases while their effectiveness decreases.

Environmentalists point out that pests are basically an ecological problem—not a chemical problem—and thus must be controlled primarily by methods that work with nature. For example, pest infestations can be reduced by *cultivation techniques*. An example is crop rotation, in which the types of crops planted in fields are changed from year to year so that populations of pests that attack a particular crop don't have time to multiply to uncontrollable sizes. Also, rows of hedges can be planted in or around crop fields to act as barriers to pests and to pro-

vide habitats for their natural predators and parasites. A *biological control method* is used to introduce pest predators and parasites in fields where most predators and parasites have been killed by pesticides.

An increasing number of experts believe that in most cases the best method of pest control is a carefully designed ecological approach known as **integrated pest management (IPM)**. In IPM, each crop and its major pests are considered an ecological system. A control program is developed that uses a variety of biological, chemical, and cultivation methods in proper sequence and timing. Small amounts of pesticides are applied only when absolutely necessary, and a variety of chemicals are used to retard development of genetic resistance. The overall aim of IPM is to keep pest populations just below the size at which they can cause economic loss (Figure 11-8).

The pros and cons of using pesticides and alternatives to their use are discussed in more detail in the Enrichment Study near the end of this chapter.

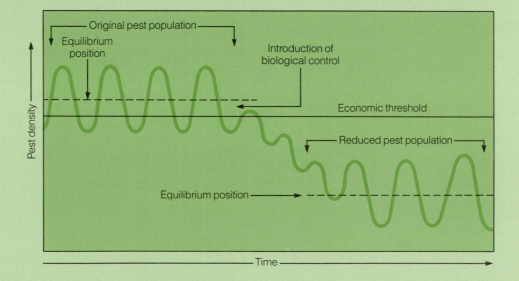

between fast-growing trees that can be used for fuelwood or to add nitrogen to the soil.

- **Polyculture,** a more complex form of intercropping in which a large number of different plants maturing at different times are planted together (see Case Study below).

Perhaps the most impressive success in food production has taken place in China. It is able to feed its people by supplementing labor-intensive subsistence agriculture with several forms of modern agricultural technology (see Case Study on p. 282).

11-2 MAJOR WORLD FOOD PROBLEMS

The Good News About Food Production World food production increased by 140% between 1950 and 1988 and kept ahead of the rate of population growth on all continents except Africa and Latin America. As a result, average food production per person increased by more than 25% between 1950 and 1988, even though world population increased by nearly 2 billion.

During the same period, average food prices adjusted for inflation dropped by 25%, and the amount of food traded in the world market quadrupled. Most of the increase in food production since 1950 came from increases in crop yields per acre by means of improved labor-intensive subsistence agriculture in LDCs and energy-intensive industrialized agriculture in North America, Europe, Australia, New Zealand, and parts of Asia.

The Bad News About Food Production The impressive increases in world food production disguise the fact that average food production per person declined between 1950 and 1988 in 43 LDCs (22 in Africa) containing 1 of every 7 people on earth. The largest declines have occurred in Africa, where average food production per person dropped 21% between 1960 and 1988 and is projected to drop another 30% during the next 25 years (see Case Study on p. 283).

When China, which produces 35% of the world's food, is removed from the calculation, food production gains in most other LDCs since 1950 barely matched their population growth. Average per capita food production has been falling in Africa since 1967 and in Latin America since 1982.

CASE STUDY **Small-Scale, Ecologically Sustainable Polyculture in the Philippines***

In parts of the Philippines many subsistence-farming families use small-scale polyculture to feed themselves. Typically, they harvest crops throughout the year by planting a 0.1-acre plot with a mixture of fast-maturing grains and vegetables, slow-maturing perennials such as papaya and bananas, and slow-maturing tubers such as cassava, taro, and sweet potatoes.

The diverse root systems at different depths beneath the ground capture soil nutrients and soil moisture efficiently and reduce the need for supplemental organic fertilizer (typically home-generated chicken manure) and irrigation water. Year-round coverage with plants also protects the soil from wind and water erosion.

The diversity of habitats for natural predators means that crops don't need to be sprayed with insecticides to control pests. Weeding is reduced and herbicides are unnecessary because weeds have difficulty in competing for plant

nutrients with the multitude of crop plants.

The various crops are harvested all year, so there is always something to eat or sell. Crop diversity also provides insurance against unexpected weather changes. If one crop fails because of too much or too little rain, another crop may survive or even thrive. This approach also spreads the need for labor throughout the growing season.

Most of the crops produced in this particular system have little market value because they are high in starch and low in protein. Nevertheless, using their own hand labor, a typical Filipino farming family can supply most of the food they need with this system.

Yields can vary with site, weather, crop combinations, and management. But measurements revealed that the total yield per year on one family's typical polyculture plot was 26 times that of nearby Philippine fields planted

the same year with high-yield, hybrid varieties of rice and using large amounts of irrigation water, commercial inorganic fertilizer, insecticides, herbicides, mechanized equipment, fossil fuels, and borrowed money. The polyculture plot needed none of these inputs, and the family did not have to borrow any money.

Although small-scale farmers using mechanized, green revolution agriculture can sell their crops, many of them have such large debts that they go bankrupt. They then lose their land and can no longer feed their families by farming. Between 1966 and 1974, for example, the number of landless rural households in the Philippines increased from 30% to 45% of the total population.

*The information in this case study is based on research carried out by geographer David L. Clawson at the University of New Orleans, Louisiana (see Further Readings).

China has one-fifth of the people on earth and less agricultural land than the United States. Yet since 1975 it has been able to grow enough food to feed its 1.1 billion people, double its grain production using 8% less cropland, raise per capita food consumption by 50%, and largely eliminate malnutrition.

This is one of the most spectacular increases in food production in human history. The Chinese accomplished it by combining subsistence agriculture with several modern agricultural methods to increase yields per acre and to grow as many as 12 crops annually on some plots of land. Key elements in this system are:

■ expansion of traditional labor-intensive, subsistence agriculture

■ widespread use of human and other animal wastes, garbage, pond mud, algae and other aquatic plants, and crop residues as organic fertilizer

■ using ducks, frogs, and insects for biological control of insect pests

■ using **aquaculture**, or fish farming, to produce high yields of fish in ponds fertilized by natural runoff and by leaves dropping from nearby plants (Figure 11-9)

■ equitable distribution of land-holdings and food production

■ shifting in 1978 from a centrally planned, state-controlled agricultural system to a market-oriented system largely in the hands of individual families

■ investing heavily in rural agriculture

■ restricting rural-to-urban migration

■ instituting a comprehensive and effective program to sharply reduce the country's population growth rate (p. 271)

■ more than doubling the use of commercial inorganic fertilizer between 1978 and 1988 to supplement organic fertilizer and to help restore severely degraded land

■ using scientifically developed, hybrid strains of crops, including several rice varieties that

produce as much as 180% more per acre than a standard American strain

China has shown that labor-intensive cultivation of small plots produces higher yields per unit of land area than large plots cultivated with expensive, mechanized, industrialized agriculture. Indeed, in terms of output per acre China's farmers are the most efficient in the world.

China is also one of the few LDCs that has managed to regulate urban growth. Whether China can continue to feed its growing population depends on its ability to maintain control of its population growth, halt widespread soil erosion and salinization, and restore degraded cropland. Since 1984, China's food production has fallen slightly.

Figure 11-9 Harvesting silver carp in an aquaculture farm near Chang-Chow, China.

U.N. Food and Agriculture Organization/F. Mattoli

Another disturbing trend is that the rate of increase in world average food production per person has been steadily declining during each of the past three decades. It rose 15% between 1950 and 1960, 7% between 1960 and 1970, and only 4% between 1970 and 1980. Between 1985 and 1988, average per capita food production fell. This trend is caused by a combination of population increase, a decrease in yields per unit of land area for some crops cultivated by industrialized agriculture, sharp drops in food production in some countries, and widespread drought in 1987 and 1988.

According to the UN Food and Agriculture Organization, failure to increase crop yields and to slow population growth in the poorest LDCs will worsen this already serious situation. By the year 2000, at least 64 of the world's 117 LDCs—29 in Africa—will be unable to feed their projected populations from their own water and land resources or from resource exports.

Food Quantity and Quality: Undernutrition, Malnutrition, and Overnutrition Poor people who cannot grow or buy enough food for good health and survival suffer from **undernutrition.** Survival and good health also require that people consume food containing the proper amounts of protein, carbohydrates, fats, vitamins, and minerals. Most poor people are forced to live on a low-protein, high-starch diet of grains such as wheat, rice, or corn. As a result, they often suffer from **malnutrition,** or deficiencies of protein and other key nutrients.

Many of the world's desperately poor people suffer from both undernutrition and malnutrition. Such people barely survive on just two bowls of boiled rice (150 calories) and boiled green vegetables (10 calories) a day. Victims become weak, confused, listless, and unable to work. Disease kills most before they starve. Most of those who die are women and children.

CASE STUDY Africa: A Continent in Crisis

A tragic breakdown of life-support systems has been taking place in Africa where thousands die every day from malnutrition and hunger-related diseases. Since 1985 one of every four Africans has been fed with grain imported from abroad—a dependence likely to increase.

Average per capita food production is lowest in most of the African countries south of the Sahara desert, an area known as *sub-Saharan Africa* (Figure 8-9, p. 188). Famine has been especially severe in a zone known as the *Sahel* (an Arabic word meaning edge of desert), which runs horizontally through the seven countries nearest the desert.

This worsening situation in much of Africa is caused by a number of interacting factors:

- the fastest population growth rate of any continent (Figure 10-2, p. 249), with 1 million more mouths to feed every three weeks
- a 17-year drought
- poor natural endowment of productive soils in many areas
- overgrazing, deforestation, soil

erosion, and desertification in many areas (Figure 9-10, p. 226)
- poor food distribution systems
- governments that keep food prices low to prevent urban unrest, giving rural farmers little incentive to grow more crops
- frequent wars within and between countries
- increasing dependence on food imports that has helped raise Africa's foreign debt eightfold between 1974 and 1988 to $200 billion—equal to nearly half the continent's annual income
- severe underinvestment and lack of interest by African governments and by MDCs and international aid agencies in rural agriculture and family planning
- government policies designed to subsidize urban dwellers at the expense of the rural poor, who make up 75% of Africa's population

Sahelian farmers and herders have developed a number of strategies to survive during the prolonged periodic droughts of the

region. Farmers use intercropping and polyvarietal systems and a number of water conservation measures to decrease the risk of crop failure. Herders diversify their herds and lend or lease breeding animals to one another to regenerate herds when catastrophe strikes.

The basic problem is not lack of knowledge about how to survive drought but lack of money to buy extra food in hard times. During drought poor herders have to sell many of their animals to buy enough grain to survive. Usually, this livestock is bought by wealthy farmers, who then lease the animals to other herders. Poor farmers often have to borrow grain at high interest rates or sell some or all of their land to survive.

Unless African governments and donors of foreign aid address this complex mix of environmental, political, and economic problems, the likelihood of reducing famine is slight. What do you think should be done?

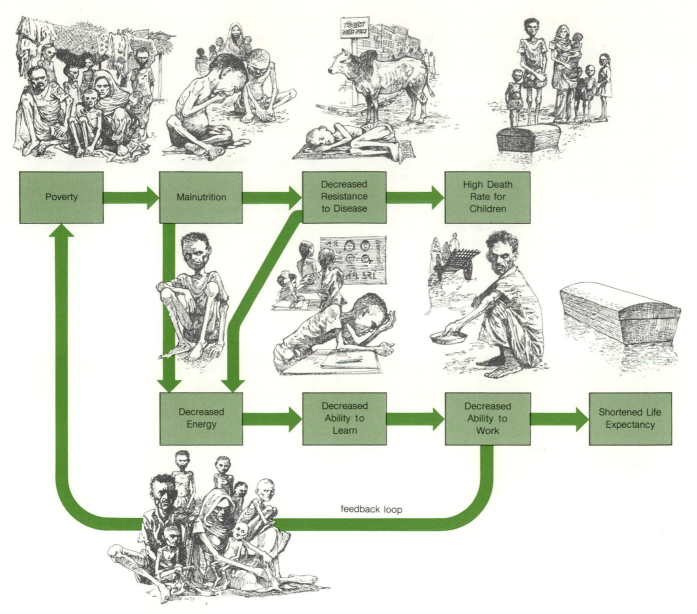

Figure 11-10 Interactions among poverty, malnutrition, and disease form a tragic cycle that perpetuates such conditions in succeeding generations of families.

Each year 20 million to 40 million people—half of them children under age 5—die prematurely from undernutrition, malnutrition, or normally nonfatal infections and diseases, such as diarrhea, measles, and flu, worsened by these nutritional deficiencies. The World Health Organization estimates that diarrhea alone kills at least 5 million children under age 5 a year.

Adults suffering from chronic undernutrition and malnutrition are vulnerable to diseases and too weak to work productively or think clearly. As a result, their children are also underfed and malnourished. If these children survive to adulthood, many are locked in a tragic *malnutrition-poverty cycle* that continues these conditions in each succeeding generation (Figure 11-10).

The two most widespread nutritional-deficiency diseases are marasmus and kwashiorkor. **Marasmus** (from the Greek "to waste away") occurs when a diet is low in both total energy (calories) and protein. Most victims of marasmus are infants in poor families in which children are not breast-fed or in which food quantity and quality are insufficient after the children are weaned. A child suffering from marasmus typically has a bloated belly, thin body, shriveled skin, wide eyes, and an old-looking face (Figure 11-11, left). If the child is treated in time with a balanced diet, most of these effects can be reversed (Figure 11-11, right).

Kwashiorkor (meaning "displaced child" in a West African dialect) occurs in infants and children 1 to 3 years old who suffer from severe protein deficiency.

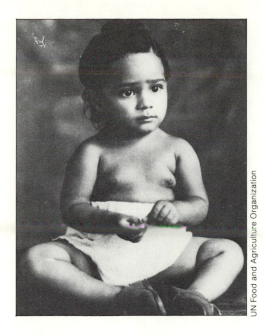

UN Food and Agriculture Organization

Figure 11-11 Most effects of severe marasmus can be corrected if victims are treated in time. This 2-year-old Venezuelan girl suffered from marasmus but recovered after 10 months of treatment and proper nutrition.

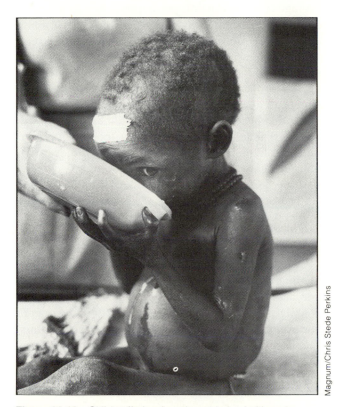

Magnum/Chris Stede Perkins

Figure 11-12 Child suffering from kwashiorkor in Uganda, Africa.

Typically, kwashiorkor afflicts a child whose mother has a younger child to nurse and whose diet changes from highly nutritious breast milk to grain or sweet potatoes, which provide enough calories but not enough protein. Children suffering from kwashiorkor have skin swollen with fluids, a bloated abdomen, lethargy, liver damage, hair loss, diarrhea, stunted growth, possible mental retardation, and irritability

(Figure 11-12). If such malnutrition is not prolonged, most of the effects can be cured with a balanced diet.

Each of us must have a daily intake of small amounts of vitamins that cannot be made in the human body. Otherwise, we will suffer from various effects of vitamin deficiencies. Although balanced diets, vitamin-fortified foods, and vitamin supplements have greatly reduced the number of vitamin deficiency diseases in MDCs, millions of cases occur each year in LDCs. For example, each year more than 500,000 children in LDCs are partially or totally blinded because their diet lacks vitamin A.

Other nutritional-deficiency diseases are caused by the lack of certain minerals, such as iron and iodine. Too little iron causes anemia. Anemia causes fatigue, makes infection more likely, increases a woman's chance of dying in childbirth, and increases an infant's chances of dying from infection during its first year of life. In tropical regions of Asia, Africa, and Latin America, iron-deficiency anemia affects about 10% of the men, more than one-half the children, two-thirds of the pregnant women, and about half of the other women.

Too little iodine in the diet can cause goiter, an abnormal enlargement of the thyroid gland in the neck (Figure 11-13), a condition that leads to deafness if untreated. It affects up to 80% of the population in the mountainous areas of Latin America, Asia, and Africa, where soils are deficient in iodine.

UNICEF officials estimate that between half and two-thirds of the worldwide annual childhood deaths from undernutrition, malnutrition, and associated infections and diseases could be prevented at an average annual cost of only $5 to $10 per child. This life-saving program would involve the following simple measures:

Figure 11-13 People with goiters, an enlargement of the thyroid gland, caused by insufficient dietary iodine.

- immunization against childhood diseases such as measles

- encouraging breast-feeding

- preventing dehydration from diarrhea by giving infants a solution of a fistful of sugar and a pinch of salt in a glass of water

- preventing blindness by giving people a small vitamin A capsule twice a year at a cost of about 75 cents per person

- providing family planning services to help mothers space births at least two years apart

- increasing female education with emphasis on nutrition, sterilization of drinking water, and child care

While 15% of the people in LDCs suffer from undernutrition and malnutrition, about 15% of the people in MDCs suffer from **overnutrition.** This is an excessive intake of food that can cause obesity, or excess body fat, in people who do not suffer from glandular or other disorders that promote obesity. Overnourished people exist on diets high in calories, cholesterol-containing saturated fats, salt, sugar, and processed foods, and low in unprocessed fresh vegetables, fruits, and fiber. Partly because of these dietary choices, overweight people have significantly higher than normal risks of diabetes, high blood pressure, stroke, and heart disease.

Poverty: The Geography of Hunger If all the food currently produced in the world were divided equally among the earth's people, there would be enough to keep 6 billion people alive. However, if this food were used to give everyone the typical diet of a person in a developed country, it would support only 2.5 billion people—half the present world population. The world's supply of food, however, is not now distributed equally among the world's people, nor will it be, because of differences in soil, climate, average income, and economic and political power throughout the world.

Poverty—not lack of food production—is the chief cause of hunger, malnutrition, and premature death throughout the world. The world's 1 billion desperately poor people do not have access to land where they can grow enough food of the right kind, and they do not have the money to buy enough food of the right kind no matter how much is available. About two-thirds of these people live in Asia and one-fifth in sub-Saharan Africa.

Increases in worldwide total food production and average food production per person often hide widespread differences in food supply and quality between and within countries. For example, about one-third of the world's hungry live in India, even though it is self-sufficient in food production. And although total and per person food supplies have increased in Latin America, much of this gain has been confined to Argentina and Brazil. In more fertile and urbanized southern Brazil, the average daily food supply per person is high. However, in Brazil's semiarid, less fertile northeastern interior many people are severely underfed. Overall, almost two out of three Brazilians suffer from malnutrition.

Food is also unevenly distributed within families. In poor families the largest part of the food supply goes to men working outside the home. Children (ages 1–5) and women (especially pregnant women and nursing mothers) are the most likely to be underfed and malnourished.

MDCs also have pockets of poverty and hunger. For example, a 1985 report by a task force of doctors estimated that at least 20 million people—1 out of every 11 Americans—were hungry, mostly because of cuts in food stamps and other forms of government aid since 1980. Half of these people were children.

Without a widespread increase in income and access to land, the number of chronically hungry and malnourished people in the world could increase to at least 1.5 billion by 2000—one out of every four people in the world's projected population at that time.

Environmental Effects of Producing More Food

Both industrialized agriculture and subsistence agriculture have a number of harmful impacts on the air, soil, and water resources that sustain all life (see Spotlight on p. 287).

11-3 METHODS OF INCREASING WORLD FOOD PRODUCTION

Increasing Crop Yields Agriculture experts expect most future increases in crop production to come from increased yields per acre on existing cropland and from the expansion of green revolution technology to other parts of the world. Agricultural scientists are working to create new green revolutions by using genetic engineering and other forms of biotechnology. Over the the next 20 to 40 years they hope to breed new high-yield plant strains that have greater resistance to insects and disease, thrive on less fertilizer, make their own nitrogen fertilizer, do well in slightly salty soils, withstand drought, and make more efficient use of solar energy during photosynthesis.

Seed companies, however, see little profit in developing low-cost crops to be grown by the world's poor subsistence farmers. Therefore, such research must be funded by private organizations and by governments, especially those of MDCs.

If even a small fraction of this research and development is successful, the world could experience rapid and enormous increases in crop production in the early

---

SPOTLIGHT Major Environmental Impacts of Industrialized and Subsistence Agriculture

Industrialized Agriculture

- soil erosion and loss of soil fertility through poor land use, failure to practice soil conservation techniques, and too little use of organic fertilizers to maintain soil structure and fertility (Section 9-3)
- salinization and waterlogging of heavily irrigated soils (Figure 9-21, p. 236), reduction in the number and diversity of nutrient-recycling soil microorganisms due to the heavy use of pesticides and commercial inorganic fertilizers, and soil compaction by large tractors and other farm machinery
- air pollution by dust blown from cropland not kept covered with vegetation and from overgrazed rangeland
- air pollution by droplets of pesticide sprayed from planes or by ground sprayers and blown into the air from plants and soil
- air pollution caused by the extraction, processing, transportation, and combustion of massive amounts of fossil fuels used to support industrialized agriculture
- pollution of estuaries and deep ocean zones with oil from offshore wells and tankers, and from improper disposal of oil, the main fossil fuel used to support industrialized agriculture
- pollution of rivers, lakes, and estuaries and killing of fish and shellfish from pesticide runoff

- depletion of groundwater aquifers by excessive withdrawals for irrigation (Figure 8-14, p. 195)
- pollution of groundwater caused by leaching of water-soluble pesticides, nitrates from commercial inorganic fertilizers, and salts from irrigation water
- accelerated eutrophication of lakes and slow-moving rivers caused by runoff of nitrates and phosphates in commercial inorganic fertilizers, livestock animal wastes, and food processing wastes (Figure 8-24, p. 204)
- sediment pollution of surface waters caused by erosion and runoff from farm fields and animal feedlots
- loss of genetic diversity of plants caused by clearing biologically diverse grasslands and forests and replacing them with monocultures of single crop varieties (Figure 6-24, p. 143)
- endangered and extinct animal wildlife due to loss of habitat when grasslands and forests are cleared, and wetlands drained, for farming (Section 16-2)
- depletion and extinction of commercially important species of fish caused by overfishing (Section 12-3)
- threats to human health from nitrates in drinking water and pesticides in drinking water, food, and the atmosphere

Subsistence Agriculture

- soil erosion and rapid loss of soil fertility caused by clearing and cultivating steep mountain highlands without terracing, using shifting cultivation in tropical forests without leaving the land fallow long enough to restore soil fertility, overgrazing of rangeland (Section 13-2), and deforestation to provide cropland or fuelwood (Section 14-3)
- increased frequency and severity of flooding in lowlands when mountainsides are deforested
- desertification caused by cultivation of marginal land with unsuitable soil or terrain, overgrazing, deforestation, and failure to use soil conservation techniques (Figure 9-10, p. 226)
- air pollution by dust blown from cropland not kept covered with vegetation and from overgrazed rangeland
- sediment pollution of surface waters caused by erosion and runoff from farm fields and overgrazed rangeland
- endangered and extinct animal wildlife caused by loss of habitat when grasslands and forests are cleared for farming
- threats to human health from flooding intensified by poor land use and from human and animal wastes discharged or washed into irrigation ditches and sources of drinking water

part of the next century. But some analysts point to several factors that have limited the spread and long-term success of the green revolutions:

- Without massive doses of fertilizer and water, green revolution crop varieties produce yields no higher and often lower than those from traditional strains.

- Areas without enough rainfall or irrigation water or with poor soils cannot benefit from the new varieties; that is why the second green revolution has not spread to many arid and semiarid areas (Figure 11-5).

- Increasingly greater and thus more expensive inputs of fertilizer, water, and pesticides eventually produce little or no increase in crop yields, as has happened to sorghum and corn crops in the United States. This diminishing-returns effect, however, typically takes 20 to 30 years to develop, so yields in LDCs using second green revolution varieties are projected to increase for some time. Scientists hope to overcome this limitation by developing improved varieties through cross-breeding and genetic engineering.

- Without careful land use and environmental controls, degradation of water and soil can limit the long-term ecological and economic sustainability of green revolutions (see Spotlight on p. 287).

- The loss of genetic diversity caused when a diverse mixture of natural crop varieties is replaced with monoculture crops limits the ability of plant scientists to use crossbreeding or genetic engineering to develop new strains for future green revolutions. For example, a perennial variety of wild corn that replants itself each year, is resistant to a number of viruses, and grows well on wet soils was discovered several years ago. Unfortunately, the few thousand plants known to exist were growing on a Mexican hillside that was being plowed up. To help preserve genetic variety, some of the world's native plants and strains of food crops are being collected and stored in 13 genetic storage banks and agricultural research centers around the world (see Figure 11-5 and Spotlight on this page).

Cultivating More Land Some agricultural experts have suggested that the world's cropland could be more than doubled by clearing tropical forests and irrigating arid lands, mostly in Africa, South America, and Australia (Figure 11-14). Others believe only a small portion of these potentially farmable (arable) lands can be cultivated because most are too dry or too remote or lack productive soils. Even if more cropland is developed, much of the increase would offset the projected loss of almost one-third of today's cultivated cropland and rangeland from erosion, overgrazing, waterlogging, salinization, mining, and urbanization.

Location, Soil, and Insects as Limiting Factors
About 83% of the world's potential new cropland is in the remote rain forests of the Amazon and Orinoco river basins in South America and in Africa's rain forests (see map inside back cover). Most of the land is located in just two countries, Brazil and Zaire.

Cultivation would require massive capital and energy investments to clear the land and to transport the harvested crops to distant populated areas. The resulting deforestation would greatly increase soil erosion. It would also reduce the world's precious genetic diversity by eliminating vast numbers of unique plant and animal species found only in these biomes.

Tropical rain forests have plentiful rainfall and long or continuous growing seasons. However, their soils often are not suitable for intensive cultivation. About 90% of the plant nutrient supply is in ground litter and vegetation above the ground rather than in the

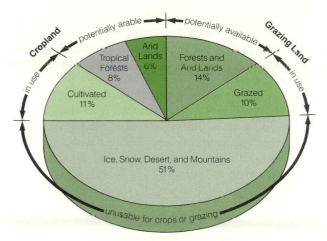

Figure 11-14 Classification of the earth's land. Theoretically, the world's cropland could be doubled in size by clearing tropical forests and irrigating arid lands. But converting this marginal land to cropland would destroy valuable forest resources, cause serious environmental problems, and usually not be cost-effective.

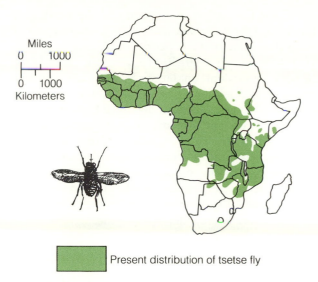

☐ Present distribution of tsetse fly

Figure 11-15 Region of Africa infested by the tsetse fly. Its bite can infect livestock and people with incurable sleeping sickness.

soil. By comparison, as little as 3% of the nutrients in temperate-zone forests are stored above the ground.

Nearly 75% of the Amazon basin, roughly one-third of the world's potential new cropland, has highly acidic and infertile soils. In addition, an estimated 5% to 15% of tropical soils (4% of those in the Amazon basin), if cleared, would bake under the tropical sun into brick-hard surfaces called laterites, useless for farming.

Some tropical soils can produce up to three crops of grain per year if massive quantities of fertilizer are applied at the right time, but costs are high. The warm temperatures, high moisture, and year-round growing season also support large populations of pests and diseases that could devastate monoculture crops. Research has shown that crops grown in the tropics are attacked by up to ten times more species of insects and plant diseases than those grown in temperate zones. Weeds are especially troublesome, sometimes reducing monoculture crop yields to zero. Massive doses of pesticides could be used, but the same conditions that favor crop growth also favor rapid development of genetic resistance in pest species.

In Africa, potential cropland larger in area than the United States cannot be used for farming or livestock grazing because it is infested by 22 species of the tsetse fly, whose bite can give both people and livestock incurable sleeping sickness (Figure 11-15). A $120 million eradication program has been proposed, but many scientists doubt it can succeed.

Researchers hope to develop new methods of intensive cultivation in tropical areas. Some scientists, however, argue that it makes more ecological and economic sense not to use intensive cultivation in the tropics. Instead, farmers should use shifting cultiva-tion with fallow periods long enough to restore soil fertility. Scientists also recommend plantation cultivation of rubber trees, oil palms, and banana trees, which are adapted to tropical climates and soils.

Water, Money, and Environmental Disruption as Limiting Factors Much of the world's potentially arable land lies in dry areas, where water shortages limit crop growth. Large-scale irrigation in these areas would be very expensive, requiring large inputs of fossil fuel to pump water long distances. Irrigation systems would deplete many groundwater supplies and require constant and expensive maintenance to prevent seepage, salinization, and waterlogging. Unfortunately, Africa, the continent that needs irrigation the most, has the lowest potential for it because of the remote location of its major rivers and its unfavorable topography and rainfall patterns.

Do the Poor Benefit? Whether present and future green revolutions reduce hunger among the world's poor depends on how the new technology is applied. In LDCs the major resource available to agriculture is human labor. When green revolution techniques are used to increase yields of labor-intensive subsistence agriculture on existing or new cropland in countries with equitable land distribution, the poor benefit, as has occurred in China (see Spotlight on p. 282).

In most LDCs, however, farmers have been encouraged to combine green revolution techniques with a shift from small-scale, labor-intensive subsistence cultivation to larger-scale, machine-intensive industrialized agriculture. Most poor farmers, however, don't have enough land, money, or credit to buy the seed, fertilizer, irrigation water, pesticides, equipment, and fuel that the new plant varieties need. This means that the second green revolution has bypassed more than 1 billion poor people in LDCs.

Switching to industrialized agriculture makes LDCs heavily dependent on large, MDC-based multinational companies for expensive supplies, increasing the LDCs' foreign debts. It also makes their agricultural and economic systems more vulnerable to collapse from increases in oil and fertilizer prices and reduces their rates of economic growth by diverting much of their capital to pay for imported oil and other agricultural inputs. Finally, mechanization displaces many farm workers, thus increasing rural-to-urban migration and overburdening the cities.

11-4 MAKING FOOD PRODUCTION PROFITABLE, GIVING FOOD AID, AND DISTRIBUTING LAND TO THE POOR

Government Agricultural Policies Governments can influence crop and livestock prices, and thus the supply of food in several ways:

- Keep food prices artificially low. This makes consumers happy but can decrease food production by reducing profits for farmers.

- Give farmers subsidies to keep them in business and encourage them to increase food production.

- Eliminate price controls and subsidies, allowing market competition to determine food prices and thus the amount of food produced.

Governments in many LDCs keep food prices in cities low to prevent political unrest. But low prices discourage farmers from producing enough to feed the country's population, and the government must use limited funds or go into debt to buy imported food. With food prices higher in rural areas than in cities, more rural people migrate to urban areas, aggravating urban problems and unemployment. These conditions increase the chances of political unrest, which the price control policy was supposed to prevent.

LDCs with large foreign debts often encourage farmers to produce various crops for export instead of food crops for their own people. About 14% of all cropland in LDCs is used to grow export crops such as coffee, cocoa, rubber, tea, tobacco, and fibers. Increases in the production of such crops has led to lower prices and reduced the income of LDCs depending on these sales.

Governments can stimulate crop and livestock production, guaranteeing farmers a certain minimum yearly return on their investment. If governments offer adequate but not excessive financial incentives, pro-

duction will increase, and in LDCs the rate of migration of displaced farmers to urban areas will decrease.

However, if government price supports are too generous and the weather is good, farmers may produce more food than can be sold. Food prices and profits then drop because of the oversupply. The resulting availability of large amounts of food for export or food aid to LDCs depresses world food prices. The low prices reduce the financial incentive for farmers to increase domestic food production. Unless even higher government subsidies are provided to prop up farm income by buying unsold crops or paying farmers not to grow crops on some of their land, a number of debt-ridden farmers go bankrupt. This is what happened in the United States during the 1980s. Excessive subsidies can also promote cultivation of marginal land, resulting in increased soil erosion, nutrient depletion, salinization, waterlogging, desertification, and water pollution.

Government price supports and other subsidies make farmers and agribusiness executives happy. They are also popular with most consumers, because they make food prices seem low. Politicians like this approach because it increases their chances of staying in office. What most consumers don't realize is that they are paying higher prices for their food indirectly in the form of higher taxes to provide the subsidies. There is no free lunch.

In the United States the government pays farmers billions of dollars each year not to grow food. At the same time, it provides food stamps for 19 million Americans who are too poor to buy enough food. Eliminating all price controls and agricultural subsidies and allowing market competition to determine food prices and production is a great idea on paper. In practice, however, individuals and companies with excessive economic and political influence use such power to avoid true competition.

The U.S. Farm Situation The farm debt crisis of the 1980s has torn the social and economic fabric of middle-class rural America. Between 1980 and 1988 over 500,000 part-time and full-time U.S. farmers quit farming or went bankrupt. Today at least another 100,000 are still in trouble.

Farm supply and farm machinery and general businesses in farm towns have also suffered severe economic losses. Many went bankrupt. For example, 20% of the grocery stores in rural Iowa closed between 1979 and 1987. Many rural towns and counties have suffered sharp drops in population and tax revenues, causing school closings and reductions in services.

The U.S. farm crisis occurred because the government encouraged farmers to grow food to help fight world hunger and to increase food exports to offset the mounting bill for imported oil after the 1973 OPEC oil embargo. Most farmers responded by expanding their operations. Many borrowed heavily at high interest rates to buy more land and equipment. Their greatly increased debt was backed by the rapid rise in the value of their cropland and the belief that farm income would increase sharply. Many farmers also began farming marginal land with highly erodible soils.

In the 1980s, however, the bottom dropped out for farmers who had borrowed heavily and gambled on increased food demand to keep cropland values and crop prices high. Between 1981 and 1987 the average value per acre of farmland dropped by 33% (40% to 55% in some midwestern states), and net farm income and exports fluctuated. Tax-supported federal subsidies to farmers rose from $7 billion in 1980 to a record $26.5 billion in 1986. To keep even more farmers from going bankrupt, the government used these funds to buy up surplus production and to pay farmers not to grow food.

Two major factors contributed to the drop in the value of cropland. First, overproduction lowered crop prices, reducing the income farmers needed to pay off their debts and plant a new crop. Second, U.S. food exports declined due to increases in food production in many countries because of the second green revolution and cheap farm labor. Also, many debt-ridden LDCs were unable to buy the food they needed. Many other countries were able to sell surplus crops for less because a stronger dollar and high federal price supports made U.S. crop exports more expensive.

According to most food experts, the U.S. agricultural system is too successful for its own good. It produces so much food that the government must pay farmers not to produce or must buy up and store the unneeded crops. This encourages farmers to produce even more to get higher payments and keeps more farmers in business than are needed. A number of analysts believe that the only way out of this dilemma is to gradually wean U.S. farmers from all federal subsidies and let them respond to market demand.

The first step would be to see that federal subsidies go only to poor and middle-class farmers in financial trouble who have the experience and managerial skills to stay in the farming business (see Pro/Con on this page). Next the government would phase out farm subsidies over several years. Some of the money saved would be used to help needy but capable farmers pay off their debts. However, they would be eligible for such subsidies only if they agreed to use an approved soil and water conservation program or to use new, sustainable-earth agricultural methods on some or all of their land (Section 11-5).

Once all federal subsidies were eliminated, all farmers would respond to the demands of the market. Only those who were good farmers and financial managers would be able to stay in business. The elimination of subsidies would decrease the environmental impact of agriculture by limiting production to only

PRO/CON Who Should Get Tax-Supported Farm Subsidies?

The U.S. farm subsidy program is supposed to help struggling middle-class farmers. Yet each year at least $2 billion of taxpayers' money spent on such subsidies goes to investors, big agribusiness companies, and others not in economic trouble.

For example, in 1986 the crown prince of Liechtenstein, a Texas landowner, received more than $2 million in federal aid intended for struggling farmers. During the same year, Commonwealth Edison, one of the country's largest electric utility companies, and the Travelers Insurance Company each received several hundred thousand dollars in farm subsidies. Tyson Foods, the nation's largest poultry producer, is classified as a family farm under the tax code. In 1986 this allowed the company to avoid paying $37.5 million in federal taxes.

By law no farm is supposed to get more than $50,000 a year in federal subsidies. But many big farmers, agribusiness companies, and off-farm investors have gotten around the law. They divide ownership of their acreage among several corporations or people (usually relatives), each eligible for the maximum subsidy.

Those receiving such payments contend that they stimulate national economic growth, help reduce unemployment, and help keep food prices low by lowering business costs. They also argue that tax funds shouldn't be used to keep farmers who are poor managers in business.

Critics contend that tax dollars designated to help needy farmers shouldn't be used to increase profits of those who don't need or deserve such welfare from the general public. They also point out that if this money went only to needy but capable farmers, it would stimulate economic growth, reduce unemployment, help keep food prices low, and help preserve middle-class rural life. What do you think?

what can be sold and by discouraging farmers from growing crops on marginal land.

However, phasing out all farm subsidies is not easy. Large corporate farmers, whose profits are higher and financial risks are lower because of subsidies, use their considerable political influence to maintain them. In addition, many small- and medium-size part- and full-time farmers have become dependent on federal subsidies that now provide one-third to one-half of their income regardless of how much they grow. Farmers and owners of farm-related businesses usually have enough votes to elect congressional representatives opposed to phasing out all farm subsidies.

International Aid Since 1945 the United States has been the world's largest donor of nonmilitary foreign aid. Some of this, known as *bilateral aid*, is donated directly to countries. Some, known as *multilateral aid*, is given to international institutions such as the World Bank for distribution to countries. These forms of aid are used mostly for agriculture and rural development, food relief, population planning, health, and economic development.

In addition to helping other countries, foreign aid stimulates U.S. economic growth and provides Americans with jobs. Seventy cents of every dollar the U.S. gives directly to other countries is used to purchase American goods and services. Today 21 of the 50 largest buyers of U.S. farm goods are countries that once received free U.S. food.

Despite the humanitarian benefits and economic returns of such aid, the percentage of the U.S. gross national product used for nonmilitary foreign aid has dropped from a high of 1.6% in the 1950s to only 0.25% in 1987—an average of only $34 per American.

Private charity organizations such as CARE and Catholic Relief Services and funds from benefit music concerts and record sales provide at least $2 billion a year of additional foreign aid. Some people call for greatly increased food relief for starving people from government and private sources, while others question the value of such aid (see Pro/Con below).

Distributing Land to the Poor An important step in reducing world hunger, malnutrition, poverty, and land degradation is land reform. Land reform involves giving the landless rural poor in LDCs ownership or free use of enough arable land to produce at least enough food for their survival and ideally to produce a surplus for emergencies and for sale.

Such reform would increase agricultural productivity in LDCs and reduce the need to farm and degrade marginal land. It would also help reduce the flow of poor people to overcrowded urban areas by creating employment in rural areas.

China and Taiwan have had the most successful land reforms. Many of the countries with the most unequal land distribution are in Latin America, especially Brazil and Guatemala. Unfortunately, land reform is difficult to institute in countries where government leaders are unduly influenced by wealthy and powerful landowners.

11-5 SUSTAINABLE-EARTH AGRICULTURE

Sustainable-Earth Agricultural Systems Many conservationists and environmentalists believe that there are clear signs that today's agricultural systems are unsustainable. Topsoil is being depleted and degraded, forests are disappearing, desert area is increasing, grasslands are being overgrazed, wetlands are disappearing, and thousands of wild species are being driven to premature extinction (Table 1-1, p. 13)

In effect, we are feeding ourselves at the expense of our children and other species who share the planet

---

PRO/CON Is Food Relief Helpful or Harmful?

Most people view food relief as a humanitarian effort to prevent people from dying prematurely. However, some analysts contend that giving food to starving people in countries where population growth rates are high does more harm than good in the long run. By encouraging population growth, and not helping people grow their own food, it condemns even greater numbers to premature death in the future.

Biologist Garrett Hardin has suggested that we use the concept of *lifeboat ethics* to decide which countries get food aid. He starts with the belief that there are already too many people in the lifeboat we call earth. If food aid is given to countries that are not reducing their population, this adds more people to an already overcrowded lifeboat. Sooner or later the boat will sink and kill most of the passengers.

Massive food aid can also depress local food prices, decrease food production, and stimulate mass migration from farms to already overburdened cities. It discourages the government from investing in rural agricultural development to enable the country to grow enough food for its population on a sustainable basis.

Another problem is that much food aid does not reach hunger victims. Transportation networks and storage facilities are inadequate, so that some of the food rots or is devoured by pests before it can reach the hungry.

Typically, some of the food is stolen by officials and sold for personal profit. Some must often be given to officials as a bribe for approving the unloading and transporting of the remaining food to the hungry.

Critics of food relief are not against foreign aid. Instead, they believe that such aid should be given to help countries control population growth, grow enough food to feed their population, or develop export crops to help pay for food they can't grow. Temporary food aid should be given only when there is a complete breakdown of an area's food supply because of natural disaster. What do you think?

---

with us. In the United States, for example, the World-watch Institute estimates that one-sixth of annual grain production is based on unsustainable use of soil and water.

The key to reducing world hunger and the harmful environmental impacts of industrialized and traditional subsistence agriculture is to develop a variety of **sustainable-earth agricultural systems**. In these systems appropriate parts of existing industrialized and subsistence agricultural systems and new agricultural techniques would be combined to take advantage of local climates, soils, resources, and cultural systems.

A sustainable-earth agricultural system does not require large inputs of fossil fuels, promotes polyculture instead of monoculture, conserves topsoil and builds new topsoil with organic fertilizer, conserves irrigation water, and controls pests with little, if any, use of pesticides. Its most important ingredient is farmers with an ethical commitment to sustaining the land. The following are general guidelines for sustainable-earth agriculture:

- *Emphasize small- to medium-scale intensive production of a diverse mix of fruit, vegetable, and fuelwood crops and livestock animals, rather than large-scale monoculture production of a single crop or livestock animal.* Such biologically diverse food-producing systems can be used at a number of levels: window box planters and rooftop gardens in urban apartment and office buildings, raised bed gardens on unused urban lots and in backyards, small or large solar greenhouses, small to medium farms using low-till and no-till cultivation, organic fertilizers, and integrated pest management.

- *Emphasize intense cultivation of traditional and nontraditional varieties of plants, and ranching of selected wild animals (especially in LDCs) adapted to local conditions to reduce vulnerability to pests, parasites, and disease.* Modern crossbreeding and genetic engineering techniques should be used to improve such varieties as needed, with strict controls and testing to minimize ecological disruption. Farmers should cultivate more perennial crops that replant themselves rather than relying only on annual crops whose seeds must be bought or saved and replanted each year. Farmers should learn to cultivate little-known nontraditional plants and to raise wild grazing animals as livestock.

- *Whenever possible, matter inputs should be obtained from locally available, renewable biological resources and used in ways that preserve their renewability.* Examples include using organic fertilizers from animal and crop wastes, planting fast-growing trees to supply fuelwood and add nitrogen to the soil, and building simple devices for capturing and storing rainwater for irrigating crops. Commercially produced inputs such as inorganic fertilizers and pesticides should be used only when needed and in the smallest amount possible.

- *Minimize use of fossil fuels; use locally available perpetual and renewable energy resources such as sun, wind, flowing water, and animal and crop wastes to perform as many functions as possible.* Examples include passive solar water heaters, solar ponds, solar greenhouses, and compost piles. Biogas digesters can convert animal and crop wastes to methane gas for use as fuel and leave a nutrient-rich residue for use as fertilizer. Wind machines, small-scale hydroelectric systems, and solar photovoltaic cells can provide electricity for pumping irrigation water from nearby surface water supplies and from underground aquifers. Crops can be watered by water-saving trickle or drip irrigation systems.

- *Have parts of the agricultural system perform multiple functions.* For example, a solar greenhouse can be used to prepare crops for planting, to grow certain types of crops year-round, and to provide space heating for an attached building. It can capture solar energy passively to heat water for use in household or farm tasks, and to heat water in large, fiberglass aquaculture tanks to raise fish. The warm, nutrient-rich water in the fish tanks can be used for drip irrigation of greenhouse vegetable crops or hydroponic crops—crops grown without soil in nutrient solutions.

  Animals also serve multiple functions. For example, geese control weeds and grasses in orchards and eat fallen fruit, which, if not removed, will attract pests and plant disease organisms. Geese supply manure for soil fertilization and act as security guards by honking loudly to warn of approaching people or predators. Of course, they also provide eggs, goose down, and, finally, meat.

- *Governments must develop agricultural development policies that include economic incentives to encourage farmers to grow enough food to meet the demand using sustainable-earth agricultural systems.* LDCs should give small- and medium-scale farmers using such systems various subsidies, price supports, access to credit at reasonable interest rates, and technical help. Organizations like the World Bank and FAO should give loans and aid on the basis of the sustainability of proposed agricultural projects.

In MDCs, such as the United States, a shift from large-scale industrialized agriculture to small- to medium-scale sustainable-earth agriculture is difficult. It would be strongly opposed by agribusiness companies, by successful farmers with large investments in industrialized agriculture, and by specialized farmers who are unwilling to learn the demanding managerial skills and agricultural knowledge needed to run a diversified farm.

The shift, however, could be brought about gradually over 10 to 20 years by a combination of methods:

- Greatly increased government support of research and development of sustainable-earth agricultural methods and equipment

- Setting up demonstration projects in each county so farmers can see how sustainable systems work

- Establishing training programs for farmers, county farm agents, and Department of Agriculture personnel

- Establishing curricula for sustainable-earth agriculture for colleges

- Giving subsidies and tax breaks to farmers using sustainable agriculture and to agribusiness companies developing products for this type of farming

Switching from unsustainable agriculture to sustainable-earth agriculture must be coupled with other sustainable-earth policies. These include controlling air pollution (Section 7-6), conserving water (Section 8-3), controlling water pollution (Section 8-6), conserving soil (Section 9-3), and slowing population growth (Section 10-4). Doing this involves practicing sustainable-earth economics (Section 3-5) and ethics (Section 3-6). Everything is connected.

The sustainable farm gives farmers more control over their livelihood, their land, and their future. By producing a variety of field crops, tree crops, fruits, nuts, livestock, and fish (in aquaculture ponds), such farmers can buffer their operations from the turmoil of the international marketplace and changes in weather. Instead of having to buy their food in the grocery store, they can produce most of what they eat. They can cut costs and dependence on outside suppliers by using organic fertilizer produced by their own livestock and by using natural pest control and soil conservation techniques. They can also get more for the food they produce by marketing much of it themselves. The good news is that 50,000 to 100,000 of the 650,000 full-time farmers in the United States have shifted partially or completely away from conventional industrialized agriculture.

What Can You Do? The first step you can take to achieve a sustainable-earth agricultural system is to learn more about world food problems and their possible solutions. Next, you should look at your lifestyle to find ways to reduce your unnecessary use and waste of food, fertilizers, and pesticides.

Today about one-third of all U.S. households grow some of their own food—worth about $10 billion—compared to 47% in 1981. However, most of this food is grown with larger amounts of commercial fertilizers and pesticides per unit of land than are used on most commercial cropland.

Instead, you can use sustainable-earth cultivation techniques to grow some of your own food in backyard plots, window planters, rooftop gardens, or cooperative community gardens. Spending $31 to plant a 15 × 20 foot garden can give you vegetables worth about $250—a better return than almost any financial investment you can make. Fertilize crops primarily with organic fertilizer produced in a compost bin (Figure 9-20, p. 235). Use small amounts of commercial inorganic fertilizer only when supplies of certain plant nutrients are inadequate.

Control pests by a combination of cultivation and biological methods (see pp. 299–301). Use carefully selected chemical pesticides in small amounts only when absolutely necessary. Don't use electricity-wasting and noisy electronic zappers to kill bugs. Cut down insect attacks by not wearing colognes and perfumes outdoors during summer. Take baths in Avon's Skin-So-Soft bath oil to keep bugs away.

Help reduce the use of pesticides on agricultural products by asking grocery stores to stock fresh produce and meat produced by organic methods (without the use of commercial fertilizers and pesticides). Organically grown fruits and vegetables may have a few holes, blemishes, or frayed leaves. But they taste just as good and are just as nutritious as more perfect-looking products (on which pesticides were used). Eating organically grown food is also a form of health insurance. You won't be ingesting small amounts of pesticides, whose long-term potential threats to your health are still largely unknown.

Reduce your indoor use of pesticides. Instead, use biological control methods, keep your kitchen clean, and eat food in only one room. For example, ants can be controlled by boric acid or powdered red pepper. Make sure screens don't have holes, caulk cracks around doors and windows (also saves energy), and try to overcome the tendency to think that the only good bug is a dead bug. Most bugs help control the populations of one or more other types of bugs or plants (including those we call weeds).

Reduce unnecessary waste of food and fertilizer resources. Put no more food on your plate than you intend to eat, and ask for smaller portions in restaurants. Eat lower on the food chain by eliminating or reducing meat consumption. Also, recycle your garbage in compost piles to produce organic fertilizer for growing your own food, and feed food wastes to pets.

Exert pressure on candidates for public office and elected officials to improve and strictly enforce laws designed to protect the public and the environment from the harmful effects of pesticides. Also support policies designed to develop and encourage sustainable-earth agricultural systems in the United States and throughout the world.

The most important fact of all is not that people are dying from hunger, but that people are dying unnecessarily. . . . We have the resources to end it; we have proven solutions for ending it. . . . What is missing is the commitment.
World Hunger Project

THE CASE FOR PESTICIDES

Proponents of pesticides believe that the benefits of pesticides outweigh their harmful effects. They point out the following benefits:

- *Pesticides save lives.* Since World War II, DDT and other chlorinated hydrocarbon and organophosphate insecticides have probably prevented the premature deaths of at least 7 million people from insect-transmitted diseases such as malaria (carried by the *Anopheles* mosquito), bubonic plague (rat fleas), typhus (body lice and fleas), and sleeping sickness (tsetse fly).

- *They increase food supplies and lower food costs.* Each year about 45% of the world's potential food supply is lost to pests before (30%) and after harvest (15%). This amounts to a loss of $20 billion a year. Proponents argue that without pesticides these losses would be much higher and food prices would increase (for example, by 30% to 50% in the United States).

- *They increase profits for farmers.* In the United States 42% of the annual potential food supply is destroyed by pests before and after harvest. Pesticide companies estimate that every $1 spent on pesticides leads to an increase in crop yield worth $3 to $5 to farmers.

- *They work faster and better than other alternatives.* Compared to alternative methods of pest control, pesticides can control most pests quickly and at a reasonable cost, have a relatively long shelf life, are easily shipped and applied, and are safe when handled properly. When genetic resistance occurs in pest insects and weeds, farmers can usually keep them under control by switching to other pesticides.

- *Safer and more effective products are continually being developed.* Pesticide company scientists are continually developing pesticides that are safer to use and that cause less ecological damage. For example, pyrethroid insecticides are not highly toxic to mammals and are effective at low doses, thus slowing the rate at which genetic resistance develops. Their use in small quantities helps compensate for their high cost. These insecticides contain pyrethrum obtained from the heads of flowers such as chrysanthemums (Figure 11-16) or synthetic pyrethroids made from pyrethrum.

U.N. Food and Agriculture Organization

Figure 11-16 The heads of these pyrethrum daisy flowers being harvested in Kenya, Africa, are ground into a powder. It is then used directly as commercial insecticide or converted to other pyrethroid insecticides.

THE CASE AGAINST PESTICIDES

Opponents of the widespread use of pesticides argue that their harmful effects and costs exceed their benefits. The following are the major problems associated with their use:

- *Genetic resistance and elimination of natural predators:* Eventually all widely used pesticides fail and usually lead to even larger populations of pest species, especially insects with large numbers of offspring and short generation times. In temperate regions most insects develop genetic resistance to any chemical poison within five years, and much sooner in tropical areas. By 1988 over 500 major insect pest species had developed genetic resistance to one or more insecticides. At least 20 species are apparently immune to all insecticides. It is estimated that by the year 2000 virtually all major insect pest species will show some form of genetic resistance. To make matters worse, pesticides kill off most of a pest's natural predators and parasites, which develop genetic resistance more slowly.

Because of genetic resistance, most widely used insecticides no longer protect people from insect-transmitted diseases in many parts of the world, leading to even more serious disease outbreaks. For example, between 1970 and 1988 there was an almost 40-fold increase in malaria in tropical and subtropical countries where it had been almost eradicated by widespread use of pesticides.

Weeds also develop genetic resistance to herbicides, but not as quickly as most insects. By 1988 at least 70 weed species had developed resistance to one or more herbicides.

■ *Creation of new pests:* Using broad-spectrum chemical poisons for pest control kills a variety of natural predators and parasites. This allows organisms that were not pests or that were only minor pests to greatly increase in numbers and become major pests.

■ *Pesticide treadmill of increasing costs and decreasing effectiveness:* Pesticide company representatives urge farmers to overcome genetic resistance and the creation of new pests by applying pesticides more often, using stronger doses, or switching to different (usually more expensive) pesticides. This locks farmers into a situation in which they pay more and more for a pest control program that becomes less and less effective.

This pesticide treadmill is an example of the law of diminishing returns in action. For example, although insecticide use in the United States increased tenfold between 1940 and 1980, crop losses from insects during the same period almost doubled from 7% to 13%. Worldwide, insects and weeds reduce crop production by about 30%, about the same as before modern pesticides were used. The development of new chemicals by pesticide companies to reduce the spread of genetic resistance lags far behind the development of such resistance.

David Pimentel, an expert in insect ecology, estimates that when the environmental and other external costs of insecticides are included, they end up saving U.S. farmers somewhere between nothing and $2.40 for each $1 invested. This is much lower than the pesticide companies' estimate of $3 to $5 saved for each $1 invested.

■ *Mobility, biological amplification, and threats to wildlife:* Pesticides don't stay put. Only 1% to 10% of pesticides applied to crops by airplane spraying or ground spraying reaches the target pests. The remaining 90% to 99% ends up in the air, drinking water, food, and nontarget organisms, including people and even penguins in the Antarctic. Pesticide runoff from cropland is a major cause of fish kills in the United States.

Concentrations of fat-soluble, slowly degradable pesticides such as DDT can be biologically amplified thousands to millions of times in food chains and webs. High levels can kill birds and other forms of wildlife feeding at high trophic lev-

els or interfere with their reproduction (see Spotlight on p. 297). The shift to more rapidly degradable pesticides has reduced this threat to wildlife. However, in some vulnerable species of wildlife, levels of DDT and other banned, slowly degradable pesticides have increased recently. Illegal use of these chemicals may be the cause.

■ *Short-term threats to human health:* Each year at least 1 million people are poisoned by pesticides and 3,000 to 20,000 of them die. Most are farmers in LDCs, but an estimated 313,000 U.S. farm workers become seriously ill from exposure to pesticides each year.

Human injuries and deaths from pesticides have increased since 1974, primarily because of a shift to more rapidly degradable insecticides, especially *organophosphates* (such as malathion and methyl parathion) and *carbamates* (such as Sevin and Temik). Most of these compounds are much more toxic to birds, fish, people, and other mammals than the chlorinated hydrocarbons they replaced.

They also more readily leach into groundwater because they are more water-soluble than chlorinated hydrocarbons. For example, in 1988 the EPA reported that traces of 74 different pesticides were found in groundwater supplies in 38 states. In Iowa 75% of the wells tested were contaminated with pesticides. Because most of these chemicals are biodegraded fairly rapidly, farmers apply them more frequently. This means they are present in the environment almost continuously, like the slowly degradable pesticides they replaced. A shift to pyrethroids, which are less toxic to humans, will reduce health threats but will still eventually fail because of genetic resistance and creation of new pests.

Each year, more than 250,000 Americans, the majority children, become sick because of unsafe use or storage of pesticides in and around the home. Pesticides are the second most frequent cause of poisoning in young children in the United States.

Accidents and unsafe practices in pesticide plants can expose workers, their families, and sometimes the general public to harmful levels of pesticides or chemicals used in their manufacture. For example, in 1984 the world's worst industrial accident occurred at a Union Carbide plant in Bhopal, India. A highly toxic gas, used in the manufacture of pesticides, leaked from a storage tank. Almost 3,000 people were killed and up to 20,000 people suffered from blindness, sterility, kidney and liver infections, tuberculosis, brain damage, and other serious disorders. About a dozen of these people die every month because of their injuries, with the total death toll projected to reach almost 5,000 by 1991. Another 200,000 people suffered some sort of illness. Union Carbide probably could have prevented this tragedy by spending no more than a million dollars to improve plant safety. India has filed a $3.3 billion

Biological Amplification of Pesticides in Food Chains and Webs

A factor affecting the survival of some individual organisms and populations of organisms is **biological amplification**. It happens when concentrations of certain chemicals soluble in the fatty tissues of organisms feeding at high trophic levels in a food chain or web are drastically higher than concentrations of these chemicals found in organisms feeding at lower trophic levels.

Some synthetic chemicals, such as the pesticide DDT, PCBs, some radioactive materials, and some toxic mercury and lead compounds, have the three properties needed for biological amplification. They are insoluble in water, soluble in fat, and are slowly degraded or not degraded by natural processes. This means that they become more concentrated in the fatty tissues of organisms at successively higher trophic levels in food chains and webs.

Figure 11-17 shows the biological amplification of DDT in a five-step food chain of an estuary ecosystem adjacent to Long Island Sound near New York City. If each phytoplankton in such a food chain concentrates one unit of water-insoluble DDT from the water, a small fish eating thousands of phytoplankton will store thousands of units of fat-soluble DDT in its fatty tissue. Then a large fish that eats ten of the smaller fish will receive and store tens of thousands of units of fat-soluble DDT. A bird or a person that eats several large fish can ingest hundreds of thousands of units of DDT.

High concentrations of DDT or other slowly degraded, fat-soluble chemicals can reduce populations of such species in several ways. It can directly kill the organisms, reduce their ability to reproduce, or weaken them so that they are more vulnerable to diseases, parasites, and predators. Biological amplification of certain chemicals helps explain why dilution is not always the answer to some forms of pollution.

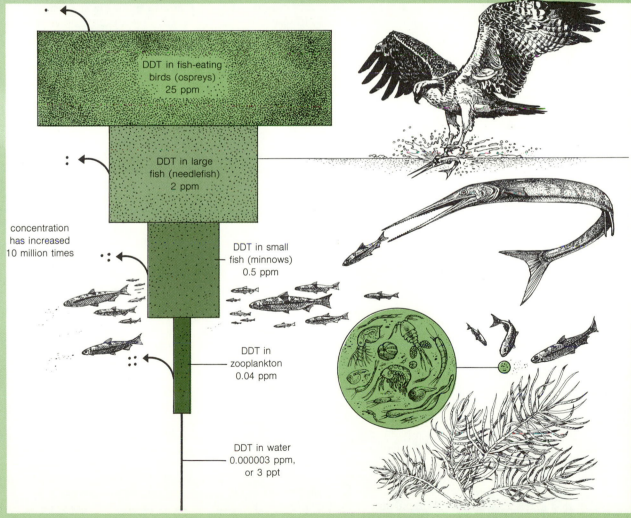

DDT in fish-eating birds (ospreys)
25 ppm

DDT in large fish (needlefish)
2 ppm

concentration has increased 10 million times

DDT in small fish (minnows)
0.5 ppm

DDT in zooplankton
0.04 ppm

DDT in water
0.000003 ppm, or 3 ppt

Figure 11-17 The concentration of DDT in the fatty tissues of organisms was biologically amplified about 10 million times in this food chain of an estuary adjacent to Long Island Sound near New York City. Dots represent DDT and arrows show small losses of DDT through respiration and excretion.

lawsuit against the company to compensate the victims and their families.

- *Long-term threats to human health:* Because of biological amplification and the mobility of slowly degradable, fat-soluble pesticides, essentially all people in the world have traces of DDT and other pesticides in their fatty tissues. A number of scientists are concerned about possible long- term health effects of continuous, long-term, low-level exposure to pesticides. Traces of almost 500 of the 700 active ingredients used in pesticies in the United States show up in the food most people eat. Pesticide residues are especially likely to be found in tomatoes, grapes, apples, lettuce, oranges, potatoes, beef, and dairy products.

In 1987 the National Academy of Sciences reported that 90% of all fungicides, 60% of all herbicides, and 30% of all insecticides may cause cancer in humans. According to the worst-case estimate in this study, exposure to pesticides in food causes 20,000 cases of cancer a year in the United States.

- *Inadequate protection of the public:* According to a recent report by the National Academy of Sciences (NAS), federal laws regulating the use of pesticides in the United States are inadequate and poorly enforced by the Food and Drug Administration (FDA) and the EPA (see Spotlight below). According to another NAS study, by 1984 only 10% of the 700 active ingredients and none of the

---

SPOTLIGHT   Inadequate Federal Regulation of Pesticides in the United States

Numerous studies by the National Academy of Sciences and the General Accounting Office have shown that the weakest and most poorly enforced U.S. environmental law is the Federal Insecticide, Fungicide, and Rodenticide Act (FIFRA) of 1972 and its subsequent amendments. It is the only U.S. environmental law that allows a chemical known to cause cancer or other harmful effects to people and the environment to be used when its economic benefits (estimated by the pesticide manufacturer) exceed its estimated harmful health and environmental effects (also estimated by the pesticide manufacturer).

The FIFRA also allows the EPA to leave inadequately tested pesticides on the market and to license new chemicals without full health and safety data. It also gives the EPA unlimited time to remove a chemical when its health and environmental effects are shown to outweigh its economic benefits. The appeals and procedures built into the law often allow a dangerous chemical to remain on the market for up to ten years.

Pesticide companies can make and export to other countries pesticides that have been banned in the United States or that have not been submitted to the EPA for approval. The U.S. leads the world in pesticide exports, followed by West Germany and the United

Kingdom. In what environmentalists call a circle of poison, residues of some of these exported pesticides often return to the United States on imported coffee, fruits, and vegetables. Many LDCs encourage the importation and overuse of pesticides by not controlling pesticide use and by subsidizing as much as 89% of the cost of pesticides for farmers.

The EPA can immediately cancel the use of a chemical on an emergency basis. But the law then requires the EPA to use its already severely limited funds to compensate pesticide manufacturers for their remaining inventory and for all the costs of storing and disposing of the banned pesticide.

This provision makes it very difficult for the EPA to cancel a chemical quickly. It also encourages pesticide companies to submit inadequate and even false safety data to get new chemicals approved.

A company has little to lose because it can still sell unsafe chemicals for years and is reimbursed for all costs if the chemical is banned on an emergency basis. This amounts to an insurance policy for the pesticide industry paid for by taxpayers—something not provided for any other product regulated by the government. By 1988 repeated attempts to remove this provision had failed.

The FIFRA also has a loophole

that allows the sale in the United States of a number of insecticide products containing as much as 15% DDT by weight, classified as an impurity. These products, along with others smuggled into the United States (mostly from Mexico), are believed to be responsible for increases in DDT levels in some vulnerable forms of wildlife and on some fruits and vegetables grown and sold in the United States (especially in California).

Studies by the General Accounting Office have have shown that a significant portion of domestic and imported fresh fruits and vegetables contain unsafe levels of pesticides, including DDT and other insecticides banned in the United States. Although selling foods containing unsafe levels of pesticides is illegal, enforcement is lax.

FDA inspectors test only about 12,000 samples of domestic and imported food each year for pesticide contamination. Furthermore, the routine testing procedures used by FDA laboratories cannot detect 40% of the pesticides classified by the EPA as having moderate to high health hazards. Most foods found to be contaminated have already been sold and consumed during the average of 28 days it takes FDA laboratories to complete the analysis. What, if anything, do you think should be done?

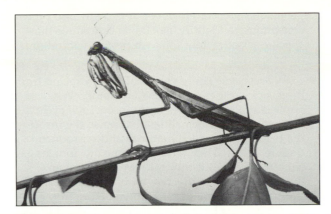

Figure 11-18 The praying mantis (left) and the ladybug (eating an aphid) are used to control insect pests.

U.S. Department of Agriculture

900 inert ingredients used in U.S. pesticide products had been tested well enough to determine their potential for producing cancer, genetic mutations, and birth defects in humans. Since 1972, environmentalists and conservationists have repeatedly tried to have pesticide control laws improved and more strictly enforced and FDA inspection procedures strengthened. By mid-1989 none of these efforts had succeeded because of vigorous congressional lobbying by the powerful agricultural chemicals industry.

ALTERNATIVES TO PESTICIDES

Opponents of the widespread use of pesticides argue that there are many safer, and in the long-run cheaper and more effective, alternatives to the use of pesticides by farmers and home owners. Major alternatives include the following:

- *Cultivation methods:* The type of crop grown in a field can be changed each year (crop rotation) and planting times can be changed so that most major pests starve to death before the crop is available or are consumed by their natural predators. Rows of hedges can be planted in and around fields to act as barriers to insect invasions and to create refuges for natural enemies of pests. Crops can be grown in areas where their major pests do not exist. Farmers can also switch from monocultures to modernized versions of intercropping, agroforestry, and polyculture that use plant diversity to help control pests.

- *Artificial selection, crossbreeding, and genetic engineering:* Varieties of plants and animals that are genetically resistant to certain pest insects, fungi, and diseases can be developed. New varieties usually take a long time (10 to 20 years) to develop by conventional methods and are costly. However, they may be developed much more rapidly by new genetic engineering techniques.

- *Biological pest control:* Various natural predators (Figure 11-18), parasites, and pathogens (disease-causing bacteria and viruses) can be introduced or imported to regulate the populations of various pests. Worldwide, more than 300 biological pest control projects have been successful, especially in China and the Soviet Union. Recently a tiny wasp was used to stop devastation of cassava crops in Africa by a mealybug. The wasps saved this crucial crop for 200 million people in 35 countries.

  In the United States biological control has saved farmers an average of $25 for every $1 invested, compared to the estimated maximum of $2.50 saved for every $1 invested in pesticides. For example, spending about $750,000 in the 1940s to find and introduce a European beetle to control a toxic range weed in California has saved livestock ranchers more than $100 million. The use of fungi, bacteria, and other disease-causing agents has great potential to sharply reduce the use of herbicides for controlling weeds.

- *Livestock guard dogs:* Various breeds of dogs have been used to protect livestock from predators in Europe and Asia for thousands of years. Guard dogs are more effective and cost less than erecting fences and shooting, trapping, and poisoning predators, which sometimes kill nontarget organisms, including people.

- *Ducks:* Ducks are experts at finding and devouring insects and slugs. However, they sometimes damage vegetables, especially leafy greens, and should be kept out of these parts of gardens.

- *Geese:* Geese are useful in weeding orchards, eating fallen and rotting fruit (often a source of pest problems), and controlling grass in gardens and nurseries. They also warn of approaching predators or people by honking loudly.

- *Chickens:* Chicken devour newly planted crops. But they can be used to control insects and weeds and to increase the nitrogen content of the soil in orchards or in gardens after plants have become well established.

Figure 11-19 Chemical hormones can prevent insects from maturing completely and make it impossible for them to reproduce. Compare the normal mealworm (left) with one that failed to develop an adult abdomen after being sprayed with a synthetic hormone.

- *Birds:* Farmers and home owners can provide habitats and nesting sites that attract insect-eating bird species such as woodpeckers, purple martens, chickadees, barn swallows, and nuthatches.

- *Allelopathic plants:* Plants that naturally produce chemicals that are toxic to their weed competitors can be established. For example, certain varieties of barley, wheat, rye, sorghum, and Sudan grass can be grown in gardens or orchards to suppress weeds. Their clippings can also be used as weed-suppressing mulches. Plant combinations that help protect against various insect pests include cassavas and beans, potatoes and mustard greens, and a mixture of sunflowers, maize, oats, and sesame.

- *Insect control by sterilization:* Males of an insect species can be raised in the laboratory and sterilized by radiation or chemicals. Then they can be released in large numbers in an infested area to mate unsuccessfully with fertile wild females. Problems include seeing that sterile males are not overwhelmed numerically by nonsterile males, preventing reinfestation by new nonsterile males, and high costs.

- *Insect sex attractants:* These chemicals are extracted from an insect pest species or synthesized in the laboratory. They are then used in minute amounts to lure pests into traps containing toxic chemicals or to attract natural predators of insect pests into crop fields. Sex attractants are now commercially available for use against 30 major pests. These chemicals work only on one species, are effective in trace amounts, and have little chance of causing

genetic resistance. However, it is costly and time consuming to identify, isolate, and produce the specific sex attractant for each pest or natural predator species.

- *Insect hormones:* These chemicals are extracted from insects or synthesized in the laboratory. When applied at certain stages in an insect's life cycle, they produce abnormalities that cause the insect to die before it can reach maturity and reproduce (Figure 11-19). They have the same advantages as sex attractants. But they take weeks to kill an insect, are often ineffective with a large infestation, and sometimes break down before they can act. They must be applied at exactly the right time in the life cycle of the target insect. Like sex attractants, they are difficult and costly to produce.

INTEGRATED PEST MANAGEMENT

Pest control is basically an ecological problem, not a chemical problem. That is why using large quantities of broad-spectrum chemical poisons to kill and control pest populations eventually fails and ends up costing more than it is worth.

The solution is to replace this ecologically and economically unsustainable chemical approach with an ecological approach. One such approach is a carefully designed integrated pest management (IPM) program, in which pest populations are controlled by a combination of cultivation, biological, and chemical methods in proper sequence and timing.

Over the past 35 years, there have been almost 50 successful IPM programs. China, Brazil, and the United States have led the world in the use of IPM, especially to protect cotton and soybeans. By 1984, IPM programs were being used for nearly 40 crops in 15 states on about 8% of U.S. cropland. Farmers using these programs saved $579 million more than they would have otherwise.

These experiences have shown that a well-designed IPM program can **(1)** reduce inputs of fertilizer and irrigation water, **(2)** reduce preharvest pest-induced crop losses by 50%, **(3)** reduce pesticide use and pest control costs by 50% to 90%, and **(4)** increase crop yields and reduce crop production costs. IPM, however, requires expert knowledge about each specific pest problem and is slower acting and more labor intensive than the use of conventional pesticides.

So far the potential of IPM has barely been tapped. Switching to IPM in the United States is very difficult. First, it is strongly opposed by the politically and economically powerful agricultural chemical companies, who would suffer from a sharp drop in pesticide sales. They see little profit to be made from most alternative pest control methods, except insect sex attractants and hormones.

Second, farmers get most of their information about pest control from pesticide salespeople. They also get information from USDA county farm agents, who have supported pesticide use for decades and rarely have adequate training in the design and use of IPM.

IPM methods will have to be developed and introduced to farmers by federal and state agencies. However, current federal funding of IPM in the United States is only about $20 million a year—less than it costs to develop one new chemical pesticide.

Environmentalists urge the USDA to promote IPM by setting up a federally supported IPM demonstration project on at least one farm in every county. USDA field personnel and all county farm agents should be trained in IPM so they can help farmers use this alternative. The government should provide subsidies and perhaps crop loss insurance to farmers who use IPM or approved alternatives. Once a variety of IPM methods are available, subsidies to farmers who depend almost entirely on pesticides should be gradually phased out.

Indonesia has led the way. In 1986 the Indonesian government banned the use of 57 pesticides on rice and launched a nationwide program to switch to integrated pest management. By 1987 extension workers had trained 31,000 farmers in IPM techniques. This should have far-reaching benefits for Indonesia and serve as a model for other rice-growing countries.

DISCUSSION TOPICS

1. What are the major advantages and disadvantages of (a) labor-intensive subsistence agriculture, (b) energy-intensive industrialized agriculture, and (c) sustainable-earth agriculture?

2. Explain why most people who die from lack of a sufficient quantity or quality of food do not starve to death.

3. Explain why you agree or disagree with the following statement: There really isn't a severe world food problem because we already produce enough food to provide everyone on earth more than the minimum amount needed to stay alive.

4. Summarize the advantages and limitations of cultivating more land by clearing tropical jungles and irrigating arid lands to increase world food supplies and reduce hunger over the next 30 years.

5. What specific actions should the following groups take to reduce the poverty that is the leading cause of hunger, malnutrition, and greatly increased chances of premature death for one out of five people living in LDCs: (a) governments of LDCs, (b) the U.S. government, (c) private international aid organizations, (d) individuals such as yourself, and (e) the poor?

6. Should price supports and other federal subsidies paid to U.S. farmers out of tax revenues be eliminated? Explain. Try to have one or more farmers discuss this problem with your class.

7. Is sending food to famine victims helpful or harmful? Explain. Are there any conditions you would attach to sending such aid? Explain.

8. Should tax breaks and subsidies be used to encourage more U.S. farmers to switch to sustainable-earth farming? Explain.

9. Environmentalists argue that because essentially all pesticides eventually fail, their use should be phased out and farmers should be given economic incentives for switching to integrated pest management. Explain why you agree or disagree with this proposal.

10. Should U.S. companies continue to be allowed to export pesticides, medicines, and other chemicals that have been banned or severely restricted in the United States to other countries? Explain.

11. What changes, if any, do you think should be made in federal pesticide laws to ensure that the public is better protected from known or potential threats to human health and the environment?

FURTHER READINGS

Aliteri, Miguel A. 1983. *Agroecology: The Scientific Basis of Alternative Agriculture.* Berkeley, Calif.: Division of Biological Control, University of California, Berkeley.

Barrons, Keith C. 1981. *Are Pesticides Really Necessary?* Chicago: Regnery Gateway.

Bennett, Jon. 1987. *The Hunger Machine: The Politics of Food.* New York: Basil Blackwell.

Bezdicek, D. F., ed. 1984. *Organic Farming: Current Technology and Its Role in a Sustainable Agriculture.* Washington, D.C.: American Society of Agronomy.

Brown, Larry. 1987. "Hunger in America." *Scientific American*, vol. 256, no. 2, 37–41.

Brown, Lester R. 1988. *The Changing World Food Prospect: The Nineties and Beyond.* Washington, D.C.: Worldwatch Institute.

Brown, Lester R. 1988. "The Vulnerability of Oil-Based Farming." *World Watch*, Mar.–Apr., 24–29.

Carson, Rachel. 1962. *Silent Spring.* Boston: Houghton Mifflin.

Clawson, David L. 1985. "Small-Scale Polyculture: An Alternative Development Model." *Philippines Geographical Journal*, vol. 29, nos. 3 & 4, 1–12.

Dover, Michael J. 1985. *A Better Mousetrap: Improving Pest Management for Agriculture.* Washington, D.C.: World Resources Institute.

Dover, Michael J., and Lee M. Talbot. 1988. "Feeding the Earth: An Agroecological Solution." *Technology Review*, Feb.–Mar., 27–35.

Editorial Research Reports. 1988. *How the U.S. Got into Agriculture and Why It Can't Get Out.* Washington, D.C.: Congressional Quarterly.

Ehrlich, Anne H. 1988. "Development and Agriculture" in Paul R. Ehrlich and John P. Holdren, eds. *The Cassandra Conference: Resources and the Human Predicament.* Texas Station: Texas A & M University Press, pp. 75–100.

Forbes, Malcolm H., and Lois J. Merrill, eds. 1986. *Global Hunger: A Look at the Problem and Potential Solutions.* Evansville, Ind.: University of Evansville Press.

Fuhoka, Masanbou. 1985. *The Natural Way of Farming: The Theory and Practice of Green Farming.* New York: Japan Publications.

Gabel, Medard. 1986. *Empty Breadbasket: The Coming Challenge to America's Food Supply and What We Can Do About It.* Emmaus, Penn.: Rodale.

Gips, Terry. 1987. *Breaking the Pesticide Habit.* Minneapolis, Minn.: IASA.

Granatstein, David. 1988. *Reshaping the Bottom Line: On-farm Strategies for a Sustainable Agriculture.* Stillwater, Minn.: Land Stewardship Project.

Hallenback, William H., and Kathleen M. Cunningham-Burns. 1985. *Pesticides and Human Health.* New York: Springer-Verlag.

Hendry, Peter. 1988. "Food and Population: Beyond Five Billion." *Population Bulletin*, Apr., 1–55.

Hunger Project. 1985. *Ending Hunger: An Idea Whose Time Has Come.* New York: Praeger.

Huessy, Peter. 1978. *The Food First Debate.* San Francisco: Institute for Food and Development Policy.

Hussey, N. W., and N. Scopes. 1986. *Biological Pest Control.* Ithaca, N.Y.: Cornell University Press.

Jackson, Wes. 1980. *New Roots for Agriculture.* San Francisco: Friends of the Earth.

Jackson, Wes et al., eds. 1985. *Meeting the Expectations of Land: Essays in Sustainable Agriculture and Stewardship.* Berkeley, Calif.: North Point Press.

Lappé, Francis M., and Joseph Collins. 1977. *Food First.* Boston: Houghton Mifflin.

Lappé, Francis M., et al. 1988. *Betraying the National Interest.* San Francisco: Food First.

Marco, G. J., et al. 1987. *Silent Spring Revisited.* Washington, D.C.: American Chemical Society.

McKinney, Tom. 1987. *The Sustainable Farm of the Future.* Old Snowmass Colo.: Rocky Mountain Institute.

Mollison, Bill. 1988. *Permaculture: A Designer's Manual.* Davis, Calif.: AgAccess.

Mott, Lawrie, and Karen Snyder. 1987. *Pesticide Alert: A Guide to Pesticides in Fruits and Vegetables.* San Francisco: Sierra Club Books.

National Academy of Sciences. 1986. *Pesticide Resistance: Strategies and Tactics for Management.* Washington, D.C.: National Academy Press.

Nicholaides, J.J., et al. 1985. "Agricultural Alternatives for the Amazon Basin." *BioScience*, vol. 35, no. 5, 279–284.

Office of Technology Assessment. 1988. *Enhancing Agriculture in Africa.* Washington, D.C.: Office of Technology Assessment.

Paddock, Joe et al. 1986. *Land Stewardship and the Future of American Agriculture.* San Francisco: Sierra Club Books.

Parr, J. F., et al. 1983. "Organic Farming in the United States: Principles and Perspectives." *Agro-Ecosystems*, vol. 8, 183–201.

Phipps, Tim T., Pierre R. Crosson, and Kent A. Price. 1986, eds. *Agriculture and the Environment.* Washington, D.C.: Resources for the Future.

Pimentel, David. 1987. "Down on the Farm: Genetic Engineering Meets Ecology." *Technology Review*, Jan., pp. 24–30.

Pimentel, David. 1988 "Industrialized Agriculture and Natural Resources" in Paul R. Ehrlich and John P. Holdren, eds. *The Cassandra Conference: Resources and the Human Predicament.* Texas Station: Texas A & M University Press, pp. 53–74.

Poincelot, Raymond P. 1986. *Toward a Sustainable Agriculture.* Westport, Conn.: AVI Publishing.

Postel, Sandra. 1987. *Defusing the Toxics Threat: Controlling Pesticides and Industrial Waste.* Washington, D.C.: Worldwatch Institute.

Sanchez, Pedro A., et al. 1982. "Amazon Basin Soils: Management for Continuous Crop Production." *Science*, vol. 216, 821–827.

Solkoff, Joel. 1985. *The Politics of Food.* San Francisco: Sierra Club Books.

Strange, Marty. 1988. *Family Farming.* Lincoln: University of Nebraska Press.

Timberlake, Lloyd. 1985. *Africa in Crisis.* Washington, D.C.: Earthscan.

Todd, Nancy J., and John Todd. 1984. *Bioshelters, Ocean Arks, City Farming: Ecology as a Basis for Design.* San Francisco: Sierra Club Books.

Tudge, Colin. 1988. *Food Crops for the Future: Development of Plant Resources.* Oxford, Eng.: Blackwell.

van den Bosch, Robert. 1978. *The Pesticide Conspiracy.* Garden City, N.Y.: Doubleday.

van den Bosch, Robert, and Mary L. Flint. 1981. *Introduction to Integrated Pest Management.* New York: Plenum Press.

Withers, Leslie, and Tom Peterson, eds. 1987. *Hunger Action Handbook: What You Can Do and How to Do It.* Decatur, Ga: Seeds Magazine.

Witter, Sylvan, et al. 1987. *Feeding a Billion: Frontiers of Chinese Agriculture.* East Lansing: Michigan State University Press.

Wolf, Edward C. 1986. *Beyond the Green Revolution: New Approaches for Third World Agriculture.* Washington, D.C.: Worldwatch Institute.

Marine and Freshwater Fishery Resources

General Questions and Issues

1. How are fish and shellfish resources used and harvested?

2. What factors affect the distribution and number of fish and shellfish in different habitats?

3. How much can the world harvest of fish and shellfish be increased?

4. How can marine fish be managed to increase yields and to protect species from being depleted?

5. How can freshwater fish be managed to increase yields and to protect species from being depleted?

There are not all that many fish in the sea, after all. Fisheries production has grown much more slowly than the population since about 1970. What growth there has been has come primarily from exploiting less-desirable stocks as the more desirable ones have declined from overfishing, pollution, and disruption of habitat.

Anne H. Ehrlich and Paul R. Ehrlich

As land animals, we view our planet as a series of continents and islands separated by ocean barriers, and we call the planet Earth. A more accurate name would be Ocean or Water. A glance at a world map shows that the planet is a giant ocean ecosystem with a few land masses separating it into smaller ocean ecosystems (Figure 12-1).

Less than a third of the earth's surface is land. Freshwater ecosystems—lakes, rivers, streams, ponds, marshes, swamps—dot and weave through the land masses we call home. Each year hundreds of millions of people enter these aquatic environments to catch fish for sale, for food, and for fun.

12-1 FISHERY RESOURCES: USES AND REMOVAL

Major Uses of Living Aquatic Resources We use fish and shellfish as food and as feed for livestock. About 91% of the weight of the annual catch is fish such as herring, anchovy, tuna, salmon, trout, bass, and perch. The rest of the catch is mostly shellfish, including lobsters, shrimps, crabs, clams, oysters, mussels, squid, and octopuses.

We get about 20% of the animal protein in our food directly from fish and shellfish and another 5% indirectly from fish meal fed to livestock. The animal protein we get from these sources is more than that from beef, twice as much as from eggs, and three times the amount from poultry. In most Asian coastal and island countries, fish and shellfish supply 30% to 90% of the animal protein eaten by people. Japan, for instance, relies on the oceans for 60% of its animal protein supply—explaining why it's the world's leading fishing nation.

Huge numbers of ornamental freshwater fish, such as goldfish, carp, and many exotic tropical species, are used in aquariums and garden ponds. However, about three-fourths of all wild tropical fish kept as pets die within a year from stress, disease, and improper care.

Freshwater fish are also good indicators of water quality. Populations of sensitive species decrease or are wiped out in waters polluted with oxygen-consuming organic wastes, pesticides, acids, and other toxic chemicals. For example, trout are found in clear,

This chapter was coauthored by Donald M. Baltz, Coastal Fisheries Institute, Louisiana State University; Peter B. Moyle, Department of Wildlife and Fisheries Biology, University of California Davis; and G. Tyler Miller, Jr.

cold, unpolluted water, whereas common carp usually thrive in highly polluted waters. Fish kills are often the first visible sign that water is severely polluted.

Aquatic mammals, such as seals, muskrats, and beavers, are killed for their furs (see Case Study below). Other aquatic mammals include whales, porpoises, otters, and dolphins (not to be confused with species of marine fish also called dolphins).

Harvesting Fish and Shellfish The two methods of harvesting fish and shellfish are fishing and aquaculture. Fishing supplies 92% by weight of these resources,

Ocean Hemisphere

Land-Ocean Hemisphere

Figure 12-1 The ocean planet. About 71% of the earth's surface is covered with water. About 97% of this water is in the interconnected oceans that cover 90% of the planet's ocean hemisphere and 50% of its land-ocean hemisphere.

CASE STUDY The Fate of Fur Seals

The Bering Sea and the Pribilof Islands in U.S. waters off the Alaskan coast are home for 71% of the estimated total world population of northern fur seals (Figure 12-2). Between 1867 and 1911, Russians, Americans, Japanese, and Canadians harvested tens of thousands of helpless young seals by clubbing them to death. Their population dropped from 2.5 million to below 300,000, low enough to threaten the species with extinction in this part of the world.

In 1911 Russia, Japan, Canada, and the United States signed one of the first agreements designed to protect a marine resource from extinction. The four countries agreed not to take any of these seals at sea. They also set annual quotas for harvesting young male

seals from their Pribilof Island breeding area. By 1940 the population had increased to over one million, and the annual quotas were raised to over 60,000 young males.

Since 1940 the size of the breeding population of the species on the Pribilof Islands has dropped sharply. Reducing the annual quota to 30,000 between 1950 and 1988 didn't halt the decline. By 1988 the Pribilof population was half what it was in 1950.

Since 1985 the U.S. government has banned commercial hunting of these seals on the Pribilof Islands. Alaskan Eskimos, however, can take 3,200 to 9,800 seals a year at sea or on the islands to meet their survival needs. Despite the ban, the breeding population continues to drop at an annual rate of 4% to 8%.

Entanglement in discarded fishing nets and plastic garbage plays an important role in this decline, killing at least 30,000 of the seals each year. If the decline continues, less than 400,000 northern fur seals will be left by the turn of the century, and the species will again be threatened with extinction.

Conservationists call for a ban or sharply reduced quotas on the annual harvest of these and other fur seals worldwide. They believe people can easily do without fur coats or should get furs from animals not in danger of extinction. They also call for a ban on the disposal of plastic items by fishing boats, a ban on certain types of net fishing in the Bering Sea, and laws providing payments for the recovery of lost nets. What do you think should be done?

Karl W. Kenyon/National Audubon Society/
Photo Researchers

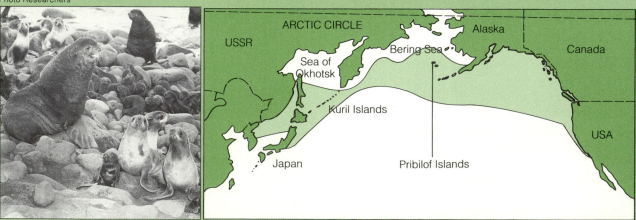

Figure 12-2 Range (shaded area of map) of the northern fur seal. This species breeds on the Pribilof Islands in U.S. waters and on the Kuril Islands in Soviet waters. Each year commercial hunters kill an estimated 20,000 young male seals on the Kuril Islands. In 1985 the U.S. government banned all commercial killing of these seals on the Pribilof Islands attempting to halt a sharp drop in the number of pups born each year since 1940.

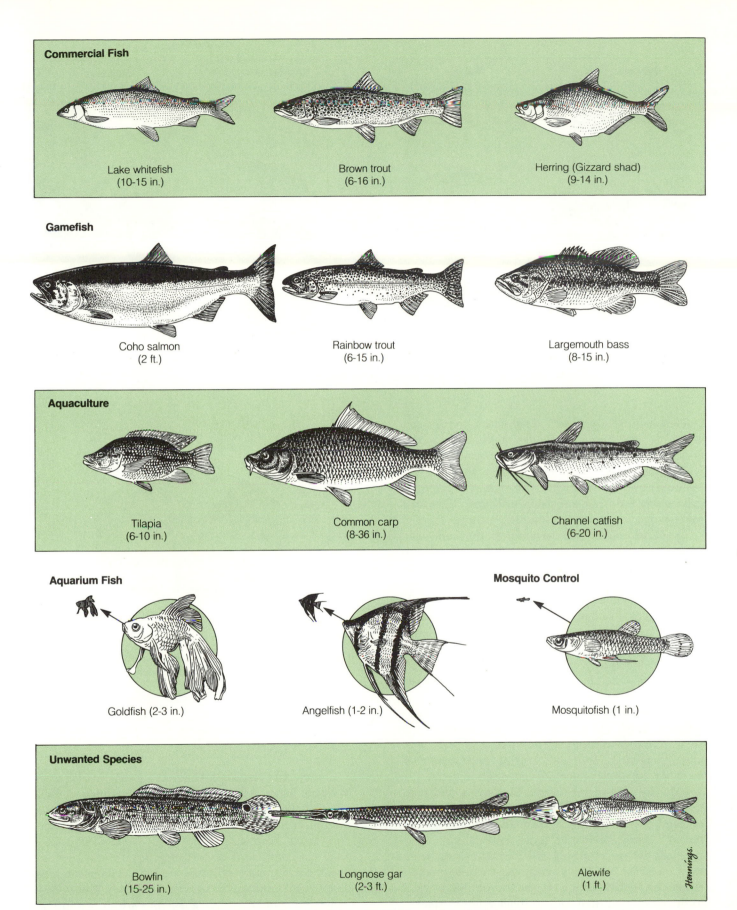

Commercial Fish

Lake whitefish
(10-15 in.)

Brown trout
(6-16 in.)

Herring (Gizzard shad)
(9-14 in.)

Gamefish

Coho salmon
(2 ft.)

Rainbow trout
(6-15 in.)

Largemouth bass
(8-15 in.)

Aquaculture

Tilapia
(6-10 in.)

Common carp
(8-36 in.)

Channel catfish
(6-20 in.)

Aquarium Fish

Goldfish (2-3 in.)

Angelfish (1-2 in.)

Mosquito Control

Mosquitofish (1 in.)

Unwanted Species

Bowfin
(15-25 in.)

Longnose gar
(2-3 ft.)

Alewife
(1 ft.)

Hennings.

Figure 12-3 Some important types of freshwater fish. Typical sizes of adult fish are shown in parentheses.

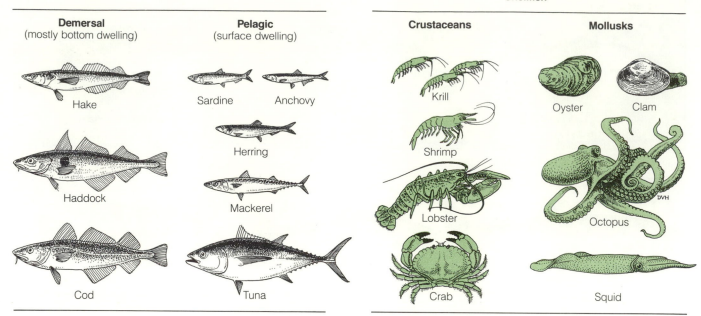

Figure 12-4 Some major types of commercially harvested marine fish and shellfish.

and aquaculture supplies 8%. **Fishing** is a hunting and gathering operation in which desirable species of fish and shellfish are found and captured. Fish is the only type of food of economic importance that we still get by hunting and gathering. People engage in **commercial fishing** for profit, **subsistence fishing** to get food for survival, and **sport fishing** for recreation.

Aquaculture, or fish farming, is the controlled raising and harvesting of fish and shellfish. Freshwater aquaculture is typically carried out in ponds (Figure 11-9, p. 282), irrigation ditches, or tanks. Marine aquaculture (sometimes called mariculture) is usually carried out in fenced-in areas or floating cages in coastal lagoons and estuaries.

Only about 40 of the 30,000 known species of fish are harvested in large quantities. Some of the important species of fish in freshwater and marine habitats are shown in Figures 12-3 and 12-4.

Marine demersal species feed mostly on or near ocean bottoms and usually don't range over a wide area. Examples include cod, flounder, haddock, sole, lobster, crawfish, and crab. **Marine pelagic species** usually feed near the surface and often migrate over a wide area. Most are fast, active swimmers with torpedo-shaped bodies. Examples are tuna, herring, pilchard (whose young are canned and sold as sardines), anchovy, mackerel, squid, and salmon.

Most fish are classified as either marine or freshwater species. But some pelagic species are **anadromous fish,** which after birth move from fresh water to the ocean and then back to fresh water to spawn. This group includes salmon, sturgeon, smelt, and shad.

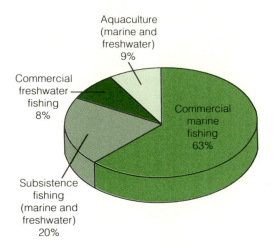

Figure 12-5 Estimated sources of the world's annual harvest of fish and shellfish. (Data from UN Food and Agriculture Organization)

Eels are **catadromous species**, which live in fresh water but breed at sea.

Commercial Fishing About 71% of the world's harvest of fish and shellfish is taken by commercial fishing (Figure 12-5). The oceans supply about 87% of the annual commercial catch. The rest is taken from inland bodies of fresh water.

Concentrations of particular aquatic species suitable for commercial harvesting in a given ocean area or inland body of water are called **fisheries**. The world's major commercial marine fisheries are shown in Figure 12-6; those in the United States, in Figure 12-7.

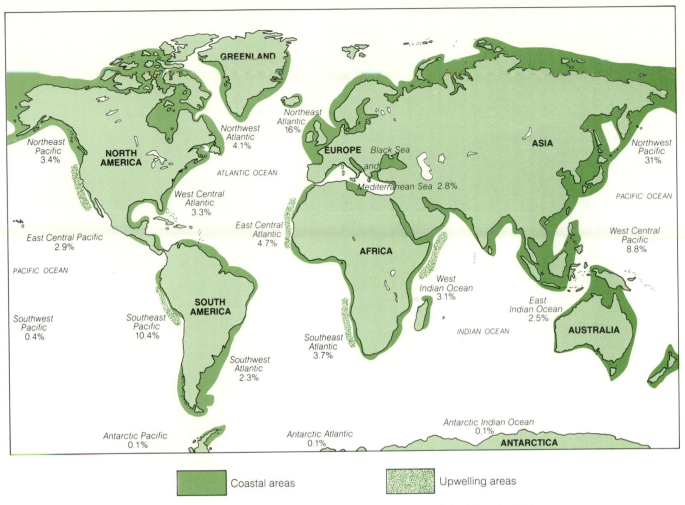

Figure 12-6 Location of the world's major commercial fisheries and distribution of the catch by fishery in 1984. (Data from UN Food and Agriculture Organization)

Almost 99% of the world marine catch is taken from plankton-rich waters within 200 nautical miles (230 statute miles) of coastlines. Most of this catch comes from estuaries and upwellings, where deep, nutrient-rich waters are swept up to the surface. These highly productive areas receive large inputs of plant nutrients either from the land and rivers or from the ocean bottom. However, this vital coastal zone is being disrupted and polluted at an alarming rate (see Case Study on p. 126).

Much of the annual commercial catch from the oceans consists of small, pelagic fish, such as herring, menhaden, and anchovies. Most of these oily fish are processed into fish oil used in edible products and into fish meal used as livestock feed. These species travel in large groups or schools and feed on phytoplankton and zooplankton. These small fish are eaten by larger, commercially valuable pelagic fish, such as mackerel and tuna (Figure 12-8).

Almost half of the world's commercial marine catch is taken by only five countries: Japan (16% of the catch),

the USSR (13%), China (7%), the United States (6%), and Chile (6%). To get large catches, modern commercial fishing boats use sonar, radar, temperature measurement, and other electronic devices to find schools of fish. Some larger boats and fishing fleets use helicopters and aerial photography to spot large schools. Lights and electrodes are used to attract fish.

Fishing boats, called trawlers, catch demersal fish by dragging a funnel-shaped net held open at the neck along the ocean bottom (Figure 12-9). The large mesh of the net allows most small fish to escape. This method, known as **trawler fishing,** is used to catch cod and other bottom-feeding fish and bottom-dwelling shrimp. Each year thousands of harp seals drown when they're caught in trawler cod nets. At least 12,000 endangered and threatened sea turtles are also killed each year when they get tangled in shrimp nets in the Atlantic and Gulf shrimp fishery.

Pelagic species, such as tuna, which feed in schools near the surface or in shallow areas, are often caught by using **purse-seine fishing.** After a school is found,

Figure 12-7 Major commercial marine fisheries of the United States.

it's surrounded by a purse-seine net (Figure 12-10). The bottom of the net is then closed to trap the fish and the catch is hauled aboard. Nets used to capture yellowfin tuna in the eastern tropical Pacific Ocean also kill many dolphins (see Case Study on p. 311).

The world's major marine fishing countries—especially Japan and the USSR—use large, distant-water fishing fleets to capture fish and then to can or freeze their catches at sea. These fleets can stay at sea for months or even years to harvest the world's most productive ocean fisheries. Most fleets use **driftnet fishing** to capture huge quantities of fish, mostly pelagic, at various depths (Figure 12-11). Weighted at the bottom and floated at the top, these massive nets drift in the water and catch fish when their gills become entangled in the mesh (see Spotlight on p. 313).

Commercial fishing boats consume huge amounts of diesel fuel and gasoline. Because 30% to 40% of the operating costs of fishing boats is spent on fuel, energy inputs for each unit of food energy obtained from most

marine species are enormous (Figure 12-12). Therefore, the higher the price of oil, the higher the price of seafood.

Subsistence Fishing   Worldwide, an estimated 8 million to 10 million people provide food for their families and gain some income from subsistence fishing. Subsistence fishing is carried out mostly on inland bodies of fresh water and near ocean coastlines. Fish are caught with spears, fishing poles, small nets, and traps. Subsistence fishing boats often are powered by human muscle energy. Because most of the catch is eaten by families or sold fresh in the local village, it isn't counted in world commercial fishery statistics. But fishery experts estimate that the annual catch from subsistence fishing adds about 25% to the world's officially reported commercial catch.

Sport Fishing   In sport fishing, anglers usually use rods and reels to catch certain species of fish, known

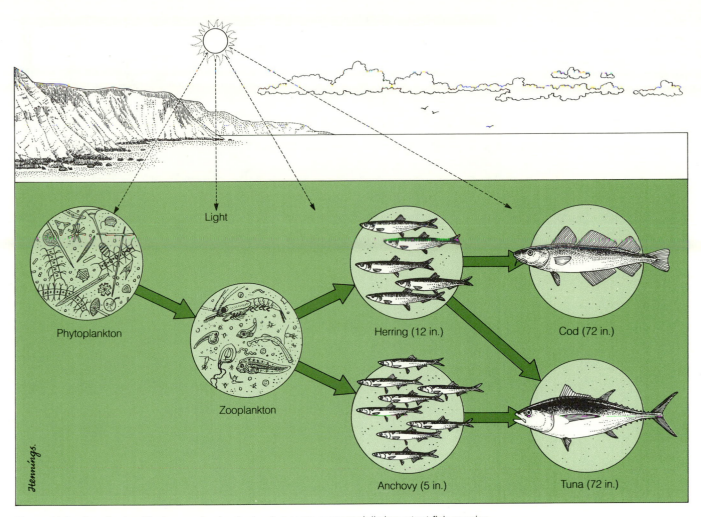

Figure 12-8 Greatly simplified ocean food web showing some commercially important fish species.

as **game fish** (Figure 12-3). Because it's fun and isn't strenuous, sport fishing appeals to people of all ages. Several important game fish caught in U.S. coastal waters are flounder, bluefish, spotted sea trout, king and Pacific mackerel, salmon, halibut, and striped bass. Other prized marine game fish caught in small numbers are swordfish, sailfish, and marlin.

Tens of millions of people engage in sport fishing in Europe, Canada, and the United States. They spend large sums of money on fishing gear, boats, depth finders, life vests, bait, clothing, and other items. They also spend large sums on travel to favorite fishing spots. Many resort areas exist largely because of their attraction to anglers.

Each year over 58 million anglers dip their lines into lakes, reservoirs, streams, and farm ponds throughout the United States, with black bass being the most popular target species. Anglers spend over $3 billion a year, and the U.S. sport fishing industry provides over 800,000 jobs.

In the United States and Canada, sport fisheries are managed by state and federal agencies. Much of the money used by these agencies comes from the sale of fishing licenses and from taxes on fishing gear and boats.

Aquaculture Aquaculture supplies about 6% of the total world catch (including subsistence fishing) and 8% of the world's commercial harvest. There are two major types of aquaculture. **Fish farming** involves cultivating fish in a controlled environment and harvesting them when they reach the desired size. Fish farming is used to grow fish and shellfish that are not very mobile. **Fish ranching** involves holding species in captivity for the first few years of their lives and then harvesting the adults when they return to spawn. Ranching is useful for anadromous species such as salmon and ocean trout (see Spotlight on p. 314).

Fish can be farmed in ponds on low-lying land not suitable for growing crops. In estuaries and fenced-

Figure 12-9 Stern-trawler fishing. After sonar on the trawler finds the fish, they're captured by a trawl net towed along the bottom. Boards angled to the water flow keep the net's mouth open.

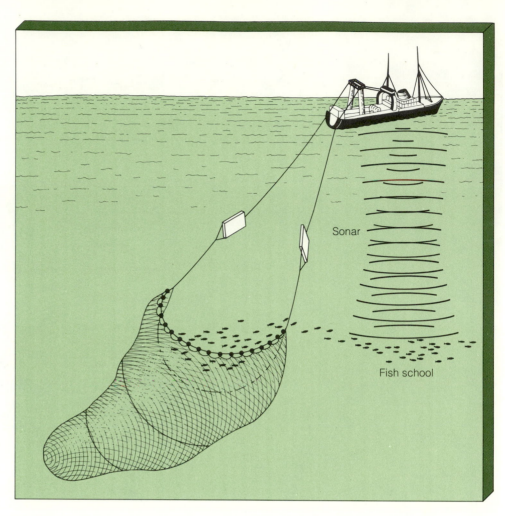

Sonar

Fish school

Figure 12-10 Purse-seine fishing of yellowfin tuna using a technique to release most of the dolphin used to locate the tuna.

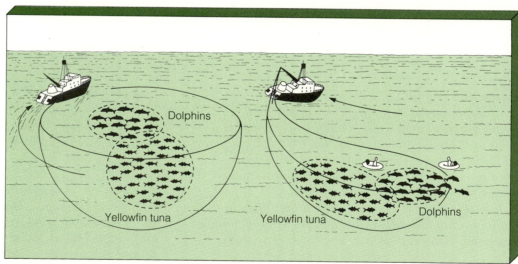

Dolphins

Yellowfin tuna

Yellowfin tuna

Dolphins

off bays large tanks or floating cages are used to produce large yields of shrimps, lobsters, oysters, mussels, and other valuable food species. Aquaculture is not practical for large ocean fish, such as tuna, that migrate over long distances.

Aquaculture of inexpensive species is a major source of low-cost animal protein for the poor in many LDCs, especially in Asia. Almost three-fourths of the world's annual aquaculture catch comes from 71 LDCs. China alone produces 48% of this harvest. Species cultivated in LDCs include carp, tilapia, milkfish, clams, and oysters, which feed low in food webs on phytoplankton and other forms of aquatic plants.

Herbivorous species can be fed easily and cheaply.

The pilot of a helicopter sent up from a tuna-fishing boat spots a large group of dolphins off the coast of southern California. Within a few minutes, half a dozen powerful speedboats are lowered over the side of the 250-foot, $10 million boat. The small boats soon overtake the hundreds of fleeing dolphins and surround them with a mile-long, 450-foot deep purse-seine net. The mother ship then hauls in a line to pull the bottom of the net together (Figure 12-10, left) and the catch is hauled aboard.

The object of this hunt isn't the dolphins but a large school of yellowfin tuna. These valuable fish are found over a 7-million-square-mile area, stretching in the eastern tropical Pacific from southern California, south to Chile, and west to Samoa. They are hunted by a fleet of almost 100 boats mostly from Mexico, the United States, Venezuela, Panama, and Costa Rica. Most of Mexico's catch is imported to the United States.

Partly to avoid complying with U.S. laws reducing the allowed annual dolphin kill, two-thirds of the American tuna fleet began operating under foreign flags in the 1980s. Other reasons included cheaper labor costs and lower insurance and fuel costs.

Yellowfin tuna, for mysterious reasons, often swim under schools of spotted, spin, and common species of dolphin. Many of the air-breathing dolphins drown when they panic and get tangled in the net. Every year at least 100,000 dolphins—an average of 300 a day—are killed by the Pacific tuna fishing fleet.

Before 1959, such deaths were rare because yellowfin were usu-ally caught by throwing out bait (chum) and pulling in the tuna on unbaited hooks. In 1959 the U.S. tuna fishing industry began using purse-seine fishing to increase the catch. Since then U.S. and foreign tuna-fishing fleets have killed at least 6 million dolphins in the eastern tropical Pacific. It is estimated that stocks of some dolphin species have been reduced as much as 80%.

Protests over this slaughter led Congress to pass the Marine Mammal Protection Act of 1972. It requires the U.S. tuna-fishing industry to reduce dolphin kills to "levels approaching zero."

Today nets with small meshes prevent dolphins from catching their pointed snouts in the nets. Nets are pulled into a drawn-out shape. Then workers in rubber rafts help the dolphins spill out over the net into the open sea, leaving the tuna behind (Figure 12-10, right). But this technique requires great experience and skill, especially in rough seas.

The National Marine Fisheries Service (NMFS) has set maximum annual quotas for dolphin kills. U.S. tuna boats must carry an NMFS observer to see that federal regulations are obeyed and to estimate how many dolphins are killed each year.

Between 1976 and 1981, the annual number of dolphins that could be killed by the U.S. tuna fishing fleet was reduced from 78,000 to 20,500. However, three federal observers have signed sworn statements charging the U.S. tuna industry with harassment, intimidation, and bribery of observers on U.S. tuna boats. They estimate that the annual number of dolphins killed by the U.S. fleet is at least twice the officially reported figure.

Since 1981, conservationists have pushed, without success, to have the annual quota for dolphin kills reduced well below 20,500, as required by the Marine Mammal Protection Act. They have lobbied Congress, brought lawsuits against the NMFS and the Department of Commerce for failure to enforce the Marine Mammal Protection Act, and organized consumer boycotts of canned tuna. By 1988 they succeeded in having Congress ban purse seine fishing at night, which kills two to four times more dolphins than setting the nets during the day. Also, federal observers are now required on all U.S. tuna boats.

In 1984 Congress required foreign countries exporting tuna to the United States to have dolphin kill quotas comparable to those in this country. But it was not until 1988 that the NMFS got around to implementing this law. Even then the NMFS defined *comparable* in a way that allows foreign dolphin kills (many by former U.S.-flagged boats) as much as 75% higher than the U.S. fleet's quota.

Conservationists see no need for the continuing annual slaughter of at least 100,000 of these playful, intelligent, and slow-to-reproduce mammals. They call for strict regulation of all yellowfin tuna fishing in U.S. waters to reduce dolphin kills to almost zero. Other goals are banning the use of underwater explosives in tuna fishing and expanding the consumer boycott of canned tuna to the cat and dog food business until the dolphin killing is stopped. What do you think should be done?

Typically, a small pond is fertilized with sewage waste-water, livestock animal wastes, or fish wastes to produce large quantities of phytoplankton. With an ample food supply, large numbers of a plant-eating species, such as carp, grow rapidly. After reaching the desired size, they're easily harvested (Figure 11-9, p. 282).

In MDCs aquaculture is used mostly to raise expensive fish and shellfish and to stock lakes and rivers with game fish. This benefits anglers who fish for sport and is highly profitable for aquaculture farmers and companies. But it does little to increase food and protein supplies for the poor.

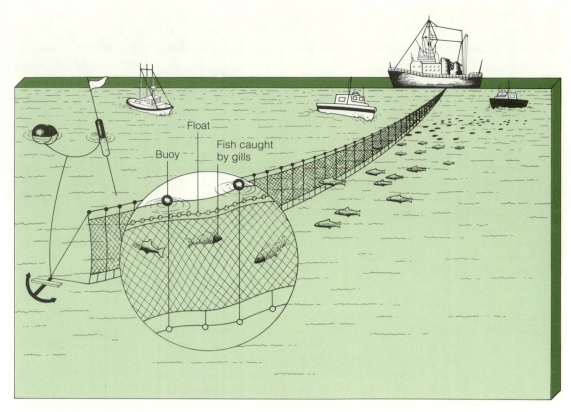

Figure 12-11 Driftnet fishing by a distant-water fishing fleet. Typically such a fleet has several huge factory ships that use sophisticated electronic detection devices, helicopters, and aerial photography to find large schools of fish. Each ship then launches 20 to 50 fast, small catcher boats to set hundreds to thousands of miles of driftnets, weighted down to stay at the wanted depth. After drifting overnight, the nets are hauled in by the factory ships. The catch is then processed on the ship by canning or freezing.

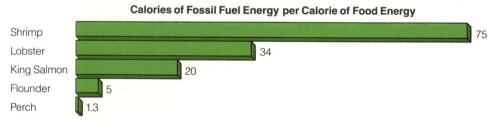

Figure 12-12 Average energy input needed to produce one unit of food energy from some commercially desirable types of fish and shellfish.

Japan, the United States, and some European countries use aquaculture to raise high-priced seafood species such as shrimps, oysters, scallops, mussels, lobsters, crabs, trout, catfish, sea bass, and salmon. Fish farmers produce high yields of catfish and trout in freshwater ponds by feeding the fish grain. This feed is supplemented with soy meal or fish meal, produced from processing less valuable fish. Farmers recover the high feeding costs because catfish and trout command high prices. Fish farming is an efficient way to produce animal protein. Although it takes 7 pounds of grain to produce a pound of beef, only 1.7 pounds are needed to produce a pound of fish.

In the United States, fish farms supply 40% of the oysters and most of the catfish, crawfish, and rainbow trout consumed as food (Figure 12-13). Between 1976 and 1987 the number of farm-raised catfish in the United States increased over 15-fold from 19 million pounds to 282 million pounds—well over a pound for every American. Most of the catfish come from aquaculture ponds in Mississippi, followed by Alabama, Georgia, and Louisiana.

Bait minnow farming (especially in the middle of the country) and goldfish farming (in the middle states and California) are important businesses. Federal and state aquaculture hatcheries also produce minnows,

Figure 12-13 Trout hatcheries and farms, like this one in Moscow, Idaho, use aquacultural methods to raise trout for food or for release in local streams for anglers to catch.

trout, northern pike muskie, walleye, and sunfish for stocking lakes and other bodies of fresh water with game fish.

Aquaculture has a number of advantages. It can produce high yields per unit of area and is limited only by the land and water areas available for such cultivation. Large amounts of fuel are not required, so yields and profits are not closely tied to the price of oil, as they are in commercial fishing. Another advantage is that the fishery is a private property resource. Thus, the owner is motivated to invest in the operation and manage the system to get the highest possible yield without overharvesting.

Maintaining and increasing aquaculture yields depend largely on the control of water quality. Most species require clean, well-oxygenated water. In freshwater ponds and coastal areas, runoff of pesticides and other toxic chemicals can wipe out aquaculture fish. One of the limitations on aquaculture in the United States is that bodies of water are treated as common property resources. Without cooperative management, this leads to overfishing, pollution, and low profits.

Bacterial and viral infections of aquatic species can also limit aquaculture yields. Multimillion-dollar aquaculture operations have been wiped out by dis-

ease. Antibiotics can control bacterial infections, but viral infections usually can't be cured. Without adequate pollution control, waste outputs from shrimp farming and other large-scale aquaculture operations can also pollute nearby surface water and groundwater.

Aquaculture is expected to grow in importance as a source of animal protein. As common property fish resources become more scarce from overfishing and pollution, fish will become more expensive. This means that aquaculture will become more widespread and profitable.

12-2 DISTRIBUTION AND ABUNDANCE OF MARINE AND FRESHWATER FISH

Limiting Factors Most fish and shellfish have an extremely high reproductive capacity. Females of different freshwater fish species, for example, may produce 5,000 to 225,000 eggs. Marine fish generally have an even higher reproductive capacity, probably because the chances of survival in the oceans are poorer than in most freshwater habitats.

Unlike fish and shellfish, whales, seals, and other aquatic mammals typically produce only one or two offspring each year. These mammal species can become extinct if too many of the offspring die before they can reproduce.

The distribution and abundance of species of marine and freshwater fishes are affected by a mix of environmental factors:

- *physical factors*, such as temperature, current, light, bottom type, hiding and cover spaces, and siltation

- *chemical factors*, such as salinity, supply of plant nutrients (mostly nitrates and phosphates), dissolved oxygen concentration, and acidity or alkalinity (pH)

- *biological factors*, such as predation (p. 102) and interspecific competition (p. 113)

Information about these factors is useful in finding a particular species in fishing and in farming or ranching commercially important species. Such information can also be used to prevent overfishing of commercially important species, to manage game fish, and to protect endangered fish.

Temperature   Water temperature is probably the key factor affecting the numbers and distribution of aquatic life. Although each aquatic species has a range of temperatures within which it can survive (Figure 5-9, p. 100), the ranges for best growth and reproduction are much narrower.

Scientists use water temperature and currents to classify three major regions of the oceans:

- *cold-water oceans* at the earth's Arctic and Antarctic poles

- *cool-water oceans* in the southern temperate and northern temperate zones

- *warm-water oceans* in regions with tropical and subtropical climates

In a broad sense, average water temperature similarly separates marine fish into cold (salmon and pollock), cool (haddock), and warm (tuna and swordfish) species.

A combination of average temperature and plant nutrient supply can be used to categorize lakes in three major types (Figure 6-9, p. 129). *Eutrophic lakes* are generally warm, shallow, and nutrient rich. Unless they suffer from excessive eutrophication, these lakes support large and varied populations of fish. In North America they typically have such species as sunfish, largemouth bass, white and yellow bass, catfish, suckers, common carp, and minnows (Figure 12-3). *Mesotrophic lakes* are cool and moderately deep and contain modest supplies of nutrients. They're good habitats

SPOTLIGHT   Salmon Ranching and Farming

Salmon have a natural cycle that involves living part of their lives in fresh water and part in the ocean (Figure 12-14). They hatch in freshwater streams, develop for one to two years, and then migrate to the ocean to feed. When they reach sexual maturity after two to six years at sea, the salmon return to the gravel beds of the rivers or streams where they were born to spawn (deposit eggs). Apparently, each river or stream has unique chemical properties the fish can detect.

In salmon ranching, fish ranchers modify the natural cycle of the salmon by hatching their eggs in hatcheries and then keeping the newly hatched fish (called fry) in pens or tanks for about two years until they reach the smolt stage (Figure 12-14). Then they're released into nearby rivers and streams for their journey to the ocean.

After two to six years, the 1% or more of smolts that survive and reach sexual maturity return to breed in the rivers and streams where they were released. They can then be harvested by placing nets across the streams or diverting them in chutes directly into canneries. For financial success, a salmon-ranching operation must have at least a 1% rate of return of adults released as smolts, about equal to the natural return rate. Average return rates for salmon-ranching operations in Japan and the United States are 2% to 3%.

Japan is the world leader in salmon ranching, followed by the Soviet Union and the United States. Salmon ranching is also becoming popular in Iceland, Canada, Sweden, and France. The main expenses of salmon ranching are running the hatchery and the processing plant.

Another approach is salmon farming. Salmon are raised in floating cages and pens in coastal areas. This is more expensive because the salmon must be fed through their entire life cycle. However, the extra cost is offset by the much lower rate of loss of the newly hatched fish. Norway is the leader in salmon farming, followed by Ireland, Chile, and Scotland. Atlantic salmon are the principal species raised in salmon farms because they take to captivity better than Pacific salmon.

Fishing still accounts of about 63% of the world salmon catch. But if present trends continue, salmon ranching and farming will overtake the hunting and gathering of salmon before the year 2000.

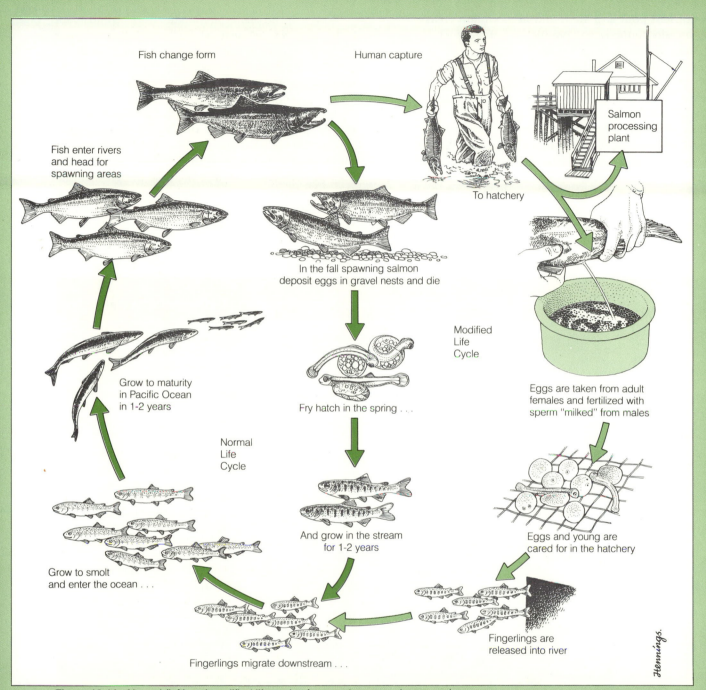

Fish change form

Human capture

To hatchery

Salmon processing plant

Fish enter rivers and head for spawning areas

In the fall spawning salmon deposit eggs in gravel nests and die

Modified Life Cycle

Eggs are taken from adult females and fertilized with sperm "milked" from males

Grow to maturity in Pacific Ocean in 1-2 years

Fry hatch in the spring . . .

Normal Life Cycle

Eggs and young are cared for in the hatchery

And grow in the stream for 1-2 years

Grow to smolt and enter the ocean . . .

Fingerlings are released into river

Fingerlings migrate downstream . . .

Figure 12-14 Normal (left) and modified life cycle of an anadromous salmon species.

for prized game fish such as as walleye, northern pike, and smallmouth bass, and many mesotrophic lakes are used for recreation. *Oligotrophic lakes* are deep, cold, and nutrient poor and are found in mountain areas. They usually contain small populations of fish such as lake trout and whitefish.

Fish communities adapted to a particular lake or slow-moving river environment usually change when they receive large inputs of hot water from electric power plants. Temperature also increases when overarching trees and streamside vegetation are removed.

Fish kills caused by such thermal pollution in lakes, slow-moving rivers, and estuaries are common. For example, trout need cool water temperatures and are particularly vulnerable to thermal pollution. Higher water temperatures reduce the water's capacity to dissolve oxygen, and they increase the amount of oxygen

fish need to survive. Thermal pollution also increases bacterial growth while decreasing the resistance of fish to bacterial infection.

New fish and plant communities develop and adapt to the warmer water near the discharge outlets of power plants. However, when the power plants shut down for refueling or repairs, the water temperature drops suddenly. This thermal shock can cause massive fish kills.

Inputs of heated water aren't always harmful. Heated water can promote the growth of game fish, such as the coho salmon found in Lake Michigan. In cold areas it can keep streams ice-free. Heated water from power plants can also increase the growth rate of warm-water species in aquaculture ponds and canals.

Recurring changes of global climate and weather can change water temperatures and currents, which

---

SPOTLIGHT   Fish Populations, Regional Climate, and El Niño-Southern Oscillation Effect

High atmospheric pressure in the eastern Pacific and low pressure in the west drive trade winds. As these winds blow along the coast of South America and then westward along the equator, they drag surface water away from the coast of Latin America. The warm water removed by these westward-flowing currents is replaced by cooler water upwelling from below the *thermocline*—the buffer zone of gradual temperature change between warm surface water and frigid deep water (Figure 12-15, left).

The resulting upwelling off the coast of Peru is one of the largest in the world. These nutrient-rich waters produce massive blooms of phytoplankton, which support large numbers of zooplankton. They in turn provide enough food for large populations of anchovy and other fish. Large populations of seabirds then dive into the surface water and feed on the fish.

Much of the warm surface water transported to the western Pacific evaporates and feeds torrential rains. High above, the air slowly returns to the east (Figure 12-15, left). This air and water loop is called the Walker Circulation.

Each two to seven years, near the end of December, winds push

a warm current southward along the coasts of Ecuador and Peru. It mixes with the upwelling cold water, warming it slightly and depressing the thermocline (Figure 12-15, right). The warmer water no longer cools the air above it as effectively. The westward surface winds stop or even reverse, disrupting the Walker Circulation.

This irregular increase in water temperature is called *El Niño* (the Christ child) because it usually takes place during the Christmas season. This effect acts jointly with the *Southern Oscillation*, a periodic change in the climate around the equator that affects Indonesia, northern Australia, and the southeastern Pacific. This oscillation is caused by changes in atmospheric pressure, which alter and speed up surface winds in the western equatorial Pacific.

Sometimes this combined El Niño-Southern Oscillation (ENSO) is mild. It then ceases in a few months when there's no longer enough warm water to sustain the shift. Once in a while—at least nine times in the last 40 years—the combined effect is severe and lasts one to two years. When this happens, there's not enough cold, nutrient-rich water to sustain large

plankton populations. The fish that feed on them either die or migrate to colder, deep water. Seabirds that feed on the anchovy and other fish in the surface waters then starve or migrate to other areas.

During such times massive numbers of fish, squid, sea turtles, and seabirds die. As the creatures decay, they release hydrogen sulfide into the water, triggering another effect. It's called *El Pintor* (the painter) by people in South America but is known elsewhere as red tide. The water turns shades of yellow, brown, and red when it becomes filled with microscopic plants called dinoflagellates. Dense blooms of these plankton give off chemicals that kill many kinds of fish and shellfish.

A strong El Niño-Southern Oscillation combination can also trigger massive weather changes over at least two-thirds of the globe, especially in the Pacific and Indian Ocean regions. During 1982–1983 a destructive ENSO—maybe the worst in recorded history—drenched Peru and Ecuador with the heaviest rains in their history. In Peru, areas with a normal rainfall of 6 inches received 11 feet. Parts of the western coast of the

---

in turn affect the supply of nutrients needed to support the phytoplankton that fish populations depend on (see Spotlight below).

Light Light is necessary for photosynthesis by phytoplankton at the bases of aquatic food webs (see Case Study on p. 318). This explains why light availability is a key factor determining the types and numbers of fish found at different depths in oceans (Figure 6-4, p. 124), lakes (Figures 6-8, p. 128, and 6-9, p. 129), reservoirs, rivers, and ponds. Light also gives fish cues about when to feed and when to gather together in large groups, or schools, for protection. Schooling fish usually scatter at night and resume schooling at dawn.

Seabed Types and Fish Migration Patterns Types of seabeds affect the distribution of many commercially important bottom-oriented fish. For example, haddock are usually found near seabeds of gravel, pebbles, clay, sand, and broken shell. Cod prefer rocky ledges, and hake are usually found near soft seabeds.

Fish migration patterns play a role in the population size of some species. Fish usually migrate either to spawn or to feed. Trout, shad, and salmon travel up streams to spawn. Dolphins, tuna, jacks, swordfish, and several types of shark move southward to warmer waters in winter to find food and then travel back north in spring. Cod and mackerel also migrate to warmer, deeper waters in winter.

Many species of whales move to Antarctic waters during the summer months to feed on the abundance of krill produced there. Each day squid and shrimps travel from the ocean depths to the surface to feed. In the Black Sea, anchovies stay in deep waters during

United States were also heavily flooded.

Meanwhile, India got little of its vital monsoon rains. Australia, Africa, and Indonesia suffered from severe droughts, brush fires, and dust storms. Many typhoons occurred in the western Pacific. These severe weather shifts caused 1,300 to 2,000 deaths and $8 billion in property damage and job losses.

Another major ENSO took place between 1986 and 1987. It dried out India by weakening the monsoon rains. The ENSO effect coupled with the greenhouse effect from rising carbon dioxide levels made 1987 the warmest year, on average, around the globe in the 100 years since such temperatures have been recorded.

After climatic conditions return to normal, fish and seabird populations normally recover. However, if a species of fish is harvested in excessive numbers before a severe ENSO hits, its population may take a long time to recover.

Sometimes an ENSO warming of Pacific waters is followed by a one- or two-year cooling effect called *La Niña*. Such an effect began in 1988. Some scientists link it to the 1988 summer drought in the United States, flooding in Bangladesh, and an abnormally cold winter in Alaska and western Canada.

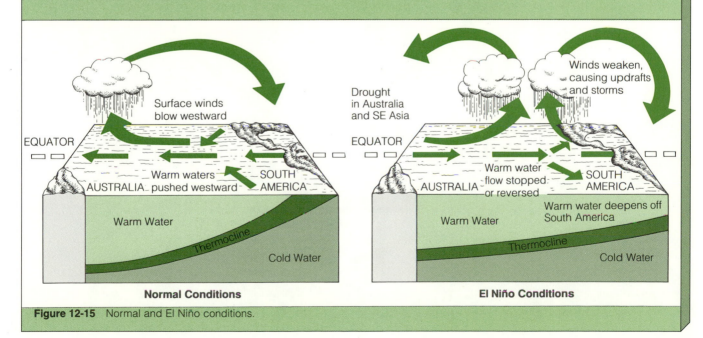

Figure 12-15 Normal and El Niño conditions.

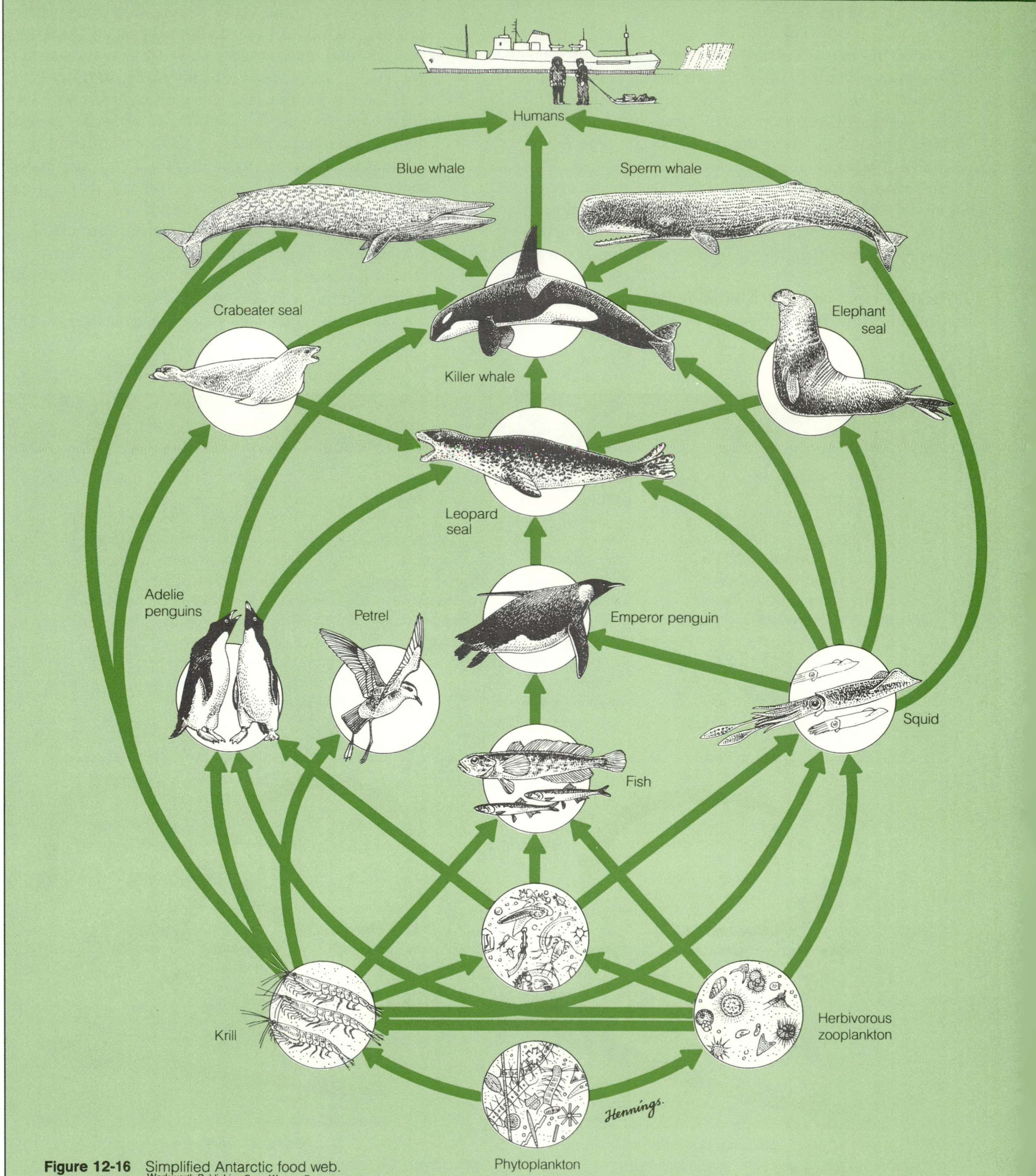

Figure 12-16 Simplified Antarctic food web.
Wadsworth Publishing Co.   W-   F-

Arctic and Antarctic waters near the earth's north and south poles have only a brief summer season with almost constant sunlight and an abundance of plant nutrients. These conditions support massive populations of phytoplankton eaten by a variety of herbivores and carnivores, especially marine birds and mammals. But plant productivity drops drastically during the long winter, when little light is available.

Strong currents and temperature barriers keep most fish species from migrating into the Arctic region. Despite this limitation, around 10% of the world's commercial fish catch comes from the Arctic seas. Large quantities of cod, haddock, and Pacific pollack are caught by commercial fishing ships. The region also has large numbers of northern fur seals, hooded seals, and harp seals harvested for their furs (see Case Study on p. 304).

In the Antarctic region only a few fish species are harvested commercially. Examples include the Antarctic cod toothfish, the Patagonian hake, and various species of krill. Currents sweep nutrient-rich water to the surface. During summer these upwellings support massive amounts of phytoplankton, which in turn support tremendous swarms of krill. These shrimplike crustaceans are important sources of food for various species of seals, penguins, squid, whales, and other species in Antarctic food webs (Figure 12-16).

Soviet and Japanese trawlers harvest many species of krill and use them as a supplement in livestock feed. There's interest in harvesting more krill, but overfishing could deplete their numbers. Then the remaining populations of krill-eating whales, such as the nearly extinct blue whale, and other species that feed on krill would decline.

the day to avoid being eaten by seabirds. Then at night they go to the surface to feed.

Fish with regular migration patterns are usually vulnerable to a variety of predators, especially people. Whales, for example, are easily killed when they congregate in Antarctic waters during the summer to feed. Osprey, bears, gulls, people, and other predators kill large numbers of salmon as they migrate from the ocean to freshwater streams to spawn. Others die when they can't migrate over logjams, dams, and other barriers. Many young salmon also die from pollution and from nitrogen intoxication, when they're exposed to high levels of nitrogen gas dissolved in the turbulent waters below dams.

Cover Spaces and Salinity   Some fish and shellfish need cover spaces to protect themselves from predators. Such spaces also give some predators the concealment they need to catch their prey. Cover spaces such as crevices and rock ledges can shield trout and other cold-water species from heat during the day. In turbulent water they also provide shelter, resting places, and spawning areas. Estuaries and coastal wetlands provide conditions of salinity, temperature, and cover needed by shrimps and other species during different parts of their life cycle (Figure 6-5, p. 125).

As we have seen, aquatic species are divided into those that survive chiefly in saltwater ecosystems and those that survive in freshwater ecosystems. The numbers and distribution of marine species are also affected by differences in salinity levels within ocean ecosystems. For example, seawater salinity varies in shallow waters and is stable in deep waters, where less mixing and turbulence occurs. Because of tidal flows and nutrient inputs from inland areas, average salinity levels in estuaries vary widely throughout each day and season.

Nutrients   The coastal zone (Figure 6-4, p. 124) occupies only about 10% of the total ocean area. Yet 98% of the ocean's fish and shellfish is produced there. This abundance results from a combination of high levels of plant nutrients and light penetration in these shallow waters. The most productive areas of the coastal zone are its nutrient-rich estuaries, coral reefs, and upwellings (Figure 12-15). Although upwelling areas occupy only about 0.1% of the total surface area of the world's oceans, they account for 44% of the ocean's fish production.

The open ocean occupies 90% of the total ocean area but provides only about 2% of the ocean's fish and shellfish. This low productivity is caused by a lack of plant nutrients in many parts of the open ocean's surface layer and too little sunlight in its bottom layer. The lack of plant nutrients in the surface layer is especially severe in tropical waters, where a permanent thermocline limits the flow of nutrients from cold, deep waters to the warmer surface zone.

Despite the lack of light, deep sea habitats support at least 11% of the known fish species. Most of these fish, however, are too small, too bony, and too hard to capture. Some fish in this dark zone have luminescent organs that can help them find food and mates. Others swim to the surface to feed.

Nutrient levels vary greatly in lakes (Figure 6-9, p. 129). Many receive massive inputs of plant nutrients because of human activities (see Figure 8-24, p. 204 and Case Study on p. 206). Such cultural eutrophication can deplete oxygen levels and cause massive fish kills.

Oxygen   Most aquatic plants and animals need oxygen for cellular respiration. They obtain most of it from oxygen dissolved in water. The **dissolved oxygen (DO) level** is the amount of oxygen gas dissolved in a given quantity of water at a particular temperature and pressure. Dissolved oxygen is increased by winds and currents that cause turbulence and mix bottom and surface layers. That is why rapidly flowing mountain headwater streams and the surface waters of the open ocean usually contain high levels of dissolved oxygen.

Dissolved oxygen decreases with increasing depth and temperature. It also decreases in the presence of large amounts of oxygen-demanding wastes, such as sewage and other organic wastes. Massive fish kills have been caused by the discharge of organic wastes from pulp and paper mills, breweries, tanneries, and food-processing factories. Trout and other species that need high levels of dissolved oxygen disappear first. Some species, such as carp and mosquitofish, can gulp oxygen from the atmosphere if the water is depleted of oxygen.

By lowering water levels, drought and excessive withdrawal of surface water also lower dissolved oxygen levels. For example, a 1983 national fisheries survey reported that low water levels were adversely affecting fish communities in 68% of U.S. inland bodies of water.

In the tropics high temperatures frequently deplete dissolved oxygen in the water. Hence, many tropical fish such as lungfish and walking catfish have special, air-breathing organs. In 1969 a dozen walking catfish escaped from a collection of exotic fish in Florida. Today they've become a widespread pest in Florida and number at least 12 million. These fish are hard to eliminate. They can use their two spiny pectoral fins to "walk" away from water where fish poisons have been applied, and they can stay out of water for as long as 80 days. They're crowding other fish out of their habitats, threatening Florida's $500 million a year sport fishing industry.

In northern areas, icy winters cover lakes with ice and snow. This prevents sunlight from penetrating into surface waters and stops photosynthesis. Oxygen levels then drop and can cause winter fish kills, especially in shallow, eutrophic lakes. Summer fish kills also happen in shallow lakes and ponds when high temperatures lead to oxygen depletion.

The downward flow of water from mountain highlands to the sea creates three major types of habitats (Figure 6-11, p. 130). These habitats vary in their temperature, turbulence, dissolved oxygen, sediment load, flow, salinity, and levels of other dissolved substances. Shallow mountain headwater streams are cold, clear, oxygen-rich, and turbulent. They support salmon, trout, and other cold-water species that need a high level of dissolved oxygen. At lower elevations rivers are wider, deeper, warmer, and less turbulent. They support bass, perch, carp, and other warm-water species that need less oxygen. Shallow, nutrient-rich coastal wetlands and estuaries contain a variety of marine fish and shellfish species.

Acidity and Alkalinity   The acidity or alkalinity of water, usually measured in pH (Figure 7-18, p. 163), is especially important in maintaining fish in freshwater lakes and rivers. Although most species of fish can tolerate a pH range of 5 to 8, they grow best in slightly alkaline water with a pH of 7.1 to 7.5. The growth and reproduction rates of most fish species drop in moderately acidic water with a pH of 5 to 6. When the pH drops below 5, fish can't reproduce; waters with a pH of less than 4 usually have no fish.

The first sign of increasing acidity is reduced growth rates of acid-sensitive fish species as they use some of their energy to combat acid-induced stress. Next, the fish have problems reproducing, leading to scarcity of young fish and egg-bearing females. Then the more acid-sensitive and shorter-lived species disappear, leaving mainly large and old individuals of the more tolerant species.

A lake that has become too acidic to support any fish usually has sparkling, clear water due to the lack of phytoplankton, or yellow or coffee-colored water due to dissolved organic substances. Such lakes are as sterile as a chlorinated backyard swimming pool.

Long stretches of some rivers and streams contain no fish because of inputs of highly acidic water from coal mines. Acid deposition has also killed all or most forms of life in many mountain lakes downwind of major power plants and industrial centers (Figure 7-19, p. 164). Many lakes in the northeastern United States, southeastern Canada, and northwestern Europe (especially Scandinavian countries) have no fish because of high acidity and high levels of aluminum released from bottom sediments and nearby soil by exposure to acid deposition (Section 7-4).

Figure 12-17 Surveys in the North Sea show that half the individuals of some bottom-dwelling species have pollution-induced cancers or other lesions. This flounder, caught in coastal waters near the mouth of the Elbe River, West Germany, has lesions due to bacterial or viral infections caused by living in polluted water.

Figure 12-18 Sea lions (seen here) and seals die by the thousands each year after becoming entangled in plastic debris, especially broken and discarded fishing nets.

Toxic Chemicals Large numbers of fish are killed by toxic chemicals, which sometimes enter aquatic ecosystems because of accidental discharges. Fish and shellfish are also killed by runoff of pesticides from cropland. Some fish develop lesions after exposure to toxic chemicals (Figure 12-17). According to a 1983 national fisheries survey, fish populations in 10% of the U.S. surface waters surveyed were contaminated with toxic chemicals.

There is little life in ocean areas where large amounts of toxic sewage sludge are dumped. Release of oil into oceans also disrupts mating and feeding patterns and kills fish, shellfish, aquatic mammals, and seabirds, as shown by the massive oil spill near Valdez, Alaska, in 1989.

By 1988 about 27% of U.S. coastal waters around the lower 48 states was closed to shellfish harvesters because of pollution and habitat disruption. This loss of marine resources costs the United States about $80 million a year.

Plastics Plastics and other debris thrown in oceans and streams are a growing threat to fish, marine mammals, and seabirds. It's estimated that merchant ships dump over 500,000 plastic containers into the ocean every day. Plastic articles now make up more than half of all human-made debris at sea and on coastlines.

Fish are deformed or killed when they swallow or get caught in beverage can pull tabs and plastic holders for beverage six-packs. Studies by marine biologists indicate that 30% of the fish in the world's oceans and individuals of 50 of the world's 280 species of seabirds have tiny pieces of plastic in their stomachs that interfere with their digestion and often kill them. Fish and seabirds can also be killed by the toxic chemicals in some plastics. Large numbers of sea turtles, including endangered green turtles, starve to death after eating plastic bags that they mistake for prey.

Each year, lost or discarded plastic fishing nets, traps, and fishing tackle entangle and kill large numbers of diving seabirds and marine mammals, especially seals and sea lions (Figure 12-18). By the 1970s lightweight, strong, and durable fishing lines, ropes, and fine-mesh nets had virtually replaced those made of natural materials such as cotton, hemp, and linen.

Marine mammals, turtles, and diving birds rarely became entangled in nets made from natural materials because the size of the net fibers made them easy for the animal to detect. Lost nets would sink quickly to the bottom and decompose within months. In contrast, the strands of fine-mesh plastic nets are almost invisible and easily entrap mammals and seabirds. Nets and other plastic fishing gear take hundreds of years to degrade, and sink only when they entrap and kill a heavy load of fish, birds, or mammals.

Conservationists urge that fishing boats be required to recover nets that have broken away. Setting up a fund to pay bounties for recovered nets would also help. Another protective measure would be to ban all ships from dumping garbage at sea. But such a ban would be hard to enforce. Garbage that can be dumped at sea free of charge can cost 25 cents to 50 cents a pound to dispose of at a port—costing a typical ship $500 to $1,000 each time it docks. Most ship owners will continue dumping at sea and risk getting caught and paying small fines to avoid such costs.

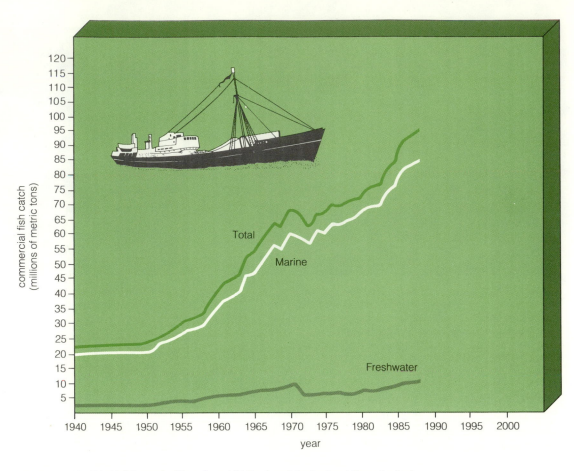

Figure 12-19 World fish catch. (Data from UN Food and Agricultural Organization)

Sedimentation Sediment discharged into rivers and lakes by runoff is a serious threat to many fish. Some sediment comes from natural runoff, but most comes from erosion of soil from farmlands, surface mining and logging operations, and construction sites.

Sediment blocks the gills of fish and kills them by asphyxiation. It also destroys sand and gravel spawning beds and the habitats of bottom-dwelling insects, which are the food supply for trout and other stream fishes. Shallow lakes can gradually become filled with so much sediment that they change from aquatic to terrestrial ecosystems.

12-3 CATCHING AND CULTIVATING MORE FISH: POTENTIAL AND PROBLEMS

Trends in the World Fish Catch Between 1950 and 1970 the annual commercial fish catch increased over threefold from 23 million metric tons to 68 million metric tons (Figure 12-19). This increase was larger than that of any other human food source during the same period. This led to widespread optimism that the catch soon could be expanded to 100 million metric tons a year, the estimated maximum sustainable harvest.

That hasn't happened, however. By 1986 the annual catch had reached about 91 million metric tons (or 84 million metric tons if production from aquaculture is subtracted). Meanwhile, world population continued to grow. This meant that between 1970 and 1986 the average fish catch per person declined in spite of slight increases in the annual harvest (Figure 12-20). Because of overfishing, pollution, population growth, and increased demand for fish, it's projected to drop back to the 1960 level by the year 2000.

Sustainable and Optimum Yields Commercially important species of fish are potentially renewable resources—as long as the annual harvest leaves enough breeding stock to renew the species for the next year. Ideally, an annual **sustainable yield** figure should be established for each species to avoid depleting the stock. The sustainable yield is the size of the annual catch that could be harvested indefinitely without a decline in the population of a species. This is reached when the catch equals the growth rate of the population.

Determining sustainable yields is difficult because we know so little about the aquatic frontiers that surround us. To find the sustainable yield for a species, we must know the size of the population, how many

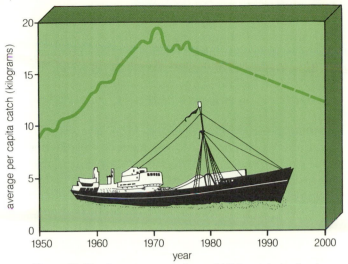

Figure 12-20 Average per capita world fish catch declined in most years since 1970. It's projected to drop further by the end of this century. (Data from United Nations and Worldwatch Institute)

young are born each year, how long it takes the young to reach reproductive age, how long an individual can reproduce, and the average life expectancy of each age group.

Counting aquatic populations isn't easy because they disappear beneath the water. And sustainable yields change from year to year because of changes in climate, pollution, and other factors. Unraveling these and other complexities of the world's aquatic ecosystems is an urgent and challenging task.

Many marine scientists believe that the annual harvest for each species should be based on an **optimum yield.** This is the amount of fish that can be economically harvested on a sustained basis; it is usually less than the sustainable yield. Using the optimum yield as a limit is the best way to prevent overfishing and still supply enough fish for reasonable profit.

Overfishing and Declining Fish Stocks **Overfishing** occurs when so many fish are taken that too little breeding stock is left to prevent a drop in numbers. In other words, the sustainable yield is exceeded because the catch level is greater than the rate at which the population is replenishing itself. Several factors lead to overfishing (see Spotlight above).

Overfishing rarely causes biological extinction because commercial fishing becomes unprofitable before that point. That is, prolonged overfishing leads to **commercial extinction**, the point at which the stock of a species is so low that it's no longer profitable to hunt and gather the remaining individuals in a specific fishery. Fishing fleets then move to a new species or to a new region, hoping that the overfished species will eventually recover.

There are several signs of overfishing. The most obvious is a decrease in the annual catch despite increased fishing efforts. The average size of the fish caught also decreases because the catch includes an increasing number of juvenile fish. An overfished species also may lose its ecological niche to another species. For example, when the anchovy is overfished, its niche may be taken over by the sardine.

By the time all these signs of overfishing appear, it's too late—the sustainable yield has already been exceeded. However, setting and enforcing quotas at the first sign of overfishing can prevent further depletion and allow the stock to recover. Unfortunately, the fishing industry seldom follows that sensible course. Instead, when the catch begins to drop, the industry sends out more boats and more efficient equipment and fishes longer to maintain the catch. This makes the situation worse and hastens the onset of commercial extinction. Overfishing also intensifies conflicts over the rights to common fisheries (see Spotlight below).

Some Examples of Overfishing During the last 75 years many species have become commercially extinct from overfishing. For example, in the 1930s huge numbers of the Pacific sardine were harvested off the west coast of North America. This commercial fishery then ranked first in North America in pounds of fish caught and third in the value of the catch. In addition to being canned for human consumption, sardines went into canned pet food, fish bait, fish oil, and fertilizer.

In the 1940s the annual catch began dropping, but the industry refused to limit the take. By 1953 the annual catch had decreased so much that commercial fishing was no longer profitable. A thriving industry had put itself out of business by removing too many fish to sustain the catch. Sardine-fishing fleets were sold, canneries closed down, and thousands of people were out of work. Today, more than 35 years later, the Pacific sardine fishery has still not recovered.

By the early 1980s overfishing had depleted stocks of 25 valuable fisheries. Examples include Atlantic cod

and herring in the North Atlantic, salmon and Alaskan king crab in the northwest Pacific, and Peruvian anchovy in the southeast Pacific (see Case Study on p. 325). Today 255 of the 280 fish stocks on which the Food and Agriculture Organization keeps records are moderately to heavily exploited.

Decline of the Whaling Industry Whales vary in size from the 3-foot porpoise to the giant 50- to 100-foot blue whale. They can be divided into two major groups, toothed whales and baleen whales (Figure 12-22). **Toothed whales**, such as the porpoise, sperm whale, and killer whale, bite and chew their food. They feed mostly on squid, fish, octopus, and other marine animals and often dive to great depths in search of their prey. Most are fairly small.

Baleen whales, such as the blue, gray, humpback, bowhead, and finback, are filter feeders. Instead of teeth, several hundred horny plates made of baleen, or whalebone, extend downward from their upper jaws. These plates filter small plankton organisms, especially krill, from seawater. Baleen whales are the most abundant group of whale species.

Since the late 1800s whales have been hunted for their flesh, blubber, skin, bones, and oil (used in toilet soaps, household paints, and cosmetics). Substitutes now exist for all these products. Although whales sup-

---

SPOTLIGHT Conflicts Over Fishing Rights

In the North Atlantic, where overfishing has been worst, Iceland and Great Britain have clashed over rights to cod stocks. The Icelandic government threatened to close the U.S. military base at Keflavik if the United States didn't back Iceland in this dispute.

This is only one of many serious clashes over fishery rights. Fishing vessels of the United States and Peru have skirmished over tuna off the coast of Ecuador and Peru. Japan has clashed with the Soviet Union, and Malaysia with Thailand. In many of these "fishery wars" the government of one country seizes foreign vessels fishing in its territorial waters. In 1987 a long-standing conflict between Canada and the United States over the Newfoundland fishery had to be settled by the International Court of Justice.

Fishing rights incite domestic strife as well as international con-

flict. For years U.S. commercial and sport fishing interests have argued over catch levels of king mackerel in the southeast Atlantic and the Gulf of Mexico. Such disputes over ocean fishing rights could become even more common if overfishing and pollution continue to limit yields from the world's major commercial fisheries.

In the Pacific Northwest and the Great Lakes states, fishing conflict centers around the legal interpretation of treaties made 100 to 150 years ago between Native American (Indian) nations and the United States. Native Americans claim that these treaties give them unrestricted rights to the fish resources in rivers and lakes running through or near their lands. They use these resources as important sources of food and income.

State officials and sport fishing groups accuse Native Americans of

depleting populations of fish such as salmon, lake trout, walleye, and muskellunge. They contend that the states have an obligation to prevent overfishing. They also argue that most of the fisheries belong to everyone in the state because they were stocked or planted by state fishery officials.

This dispute raises important economic, political, and moral questions. Should Native Americans have to surrender their legal right to fishery resources so that commercial and sport fishing can have a larger share? What rights, if any, do the states have in this controversy? Should Congress submit to political pressure from constituents and revoke earlier treaties made with Native American nations? Should the federal government require that Native Americans manage these fisheries in ways that prevent overfishing? What do you think?

---

ply about 10% of the meat eaten by Japanese, most whale meat is fed to dogs, cats, ranch mink, and ranch fox in North America and Europe.

In 1900 an estimated 4.4 million whale mammals swam the ocean. Today only about 1.1 million are left. Since 1900 most whaling has taken place in Antarctic waters, where the whales congregate in summer to feed. The whale harvest increased with the development of huge whaling vessels, on which the catch is processed, and electronic equipment and aircraft to find the whales.

Overharvesting has caused a sharp drop in the populations of almost every whale species of commercial value (Figure 12-23). The pattern of the whal-ing industry has been to hunt one species until it becomes commercially extinct and then turn to another species. Today, the populations of 8 of the 11 major species of whales once hunted by the whaling industry have been reduced to commercial extinction. This devastation has happened because of the tragedy of the commons and because whales are more vulnerable to biological extinction than fish species (see Case Study on p. 328).

In 1946 the International Whaling Commission (IWC) was established to regulate the whaling industry. Since 1949 the IWC has set annual quotas to prevent overfishing and commercial extinction. However, these quotas often were based on inadequate

---

CASE STUDY Collapse of the Peruvian Anchovy Fishery

In 1953, Peru began fishing for anchovy in nutrient-rich upwellings off its western coast. The size of the fishing fleet increased rapidly. Factories were built to convert the small fish to fish oil and fish meal for sale to MDCs for use as livestock feed. Between 1965 and 1971, harvests of the Peruvian anchovy made up about 20% of the world's annual commercial fish catch (Figure 12-21).

Between 1971 and 1978, however, the Peruvian anchovy became commercially extinct and did not begin recovering slightly until 1983. The collapse of this fishery is an example of how biology, geography, economics, and politics interact and often clash in fishery management.

At unpredictable intervals the productivity of the upwellings off the coast of Peru drops sharply because of a natural weather change, called the El Niño-Southern Oscillation, or ENSO (see Case Study on p. 316). The numbers of anchovy, other fish, seabirds, and marine mammals in food webs based on phytoplankton then drop sharply. Normally, after each major ENSO, the

anchovy population gradually recovers.

But UN Food and Agriculture Organization biologists warned that during seven of the eight years between 1964 and 1971 the anchovy harvest exceeded the estimated sustainable yield. Peruvian fishery officials ignored these warnings. Peru's fishing industry was financed largely by short-term loans that had to be paid off. Government officials decided to risk the collapse of the fishery to pay off these loans and avoid putting thousands of people out of work. They also believed that a slight drop in the anchovy catch would be beneficial: it would cause shortages and raise the price of fish meal.

Disaster struck in 1972, when a strong ENSO arrived. The anchovy population, already at dangerously low levels due to overfishing, could not recover quickly from the effects of the ENSO. By putting short-term economics above biology, Peru lost a major source of income and jobs and had to increase its foreign debt.

The country has made some economic recovery by harvesting the Peruvian sardine, which took over the niche once occupied by the anchovy. The catches of mackerel, bonita, and hake have also increased. Since 1983 the Peruvian anchovy fishery has been making a slow recovery.

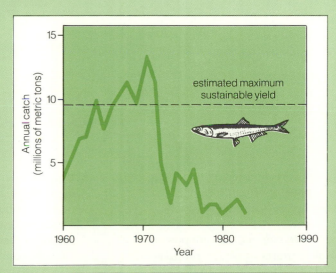

Figure 12-21 Peruvian anchovy catch, showing the combined effects of overfishing and periodic El Niño-Southern Oscillations. (Data from UN Food and Agricultural Organization)

Figure 12-22 Relative sizes of major species of whale.

Polar bear

Walrus

Dall porpoise

feeding on krill

Beluga whale

Bowhead whale

Humpback whale and calf

Minke whale

B

All species on this chart are to scale

scientific information or were ignored by whaling countries. Without any powers of enforcement, the IWC has been unable to stop the decline of most whale species.

In 1970 the United States stopped all commercial whaling and banned all imports of whale products into the country. Since then, conservation groups and the governments of many countries, including the United States, have called for a ban on all commercial whaling. Annual whale quotas have been reduced sharply, but most cutbacks came only after a species had already been hunted to commercial extinction.

In 1982, after ten years of meetings and delays, the IWC established a five-year halt on commercial whal-

Killer whale

White-sided dolphin

Pilot whale

Bottlenosed dolphin

Gray whale

Right whale

Fin whale

False killer whale

Cuvier's beaked whale

Sei whale

Pygmy sperm whale

Baird's beaked whale

Sperm whale

10	20	30	40	50	60	70	80	90	100 feet
5		10		15		20		25	30 meters

ing, starting in 1986. Japan, the Soviet Union, and Norway announced their plans to continue whaling, despite the ruling. However, under pressure from the United States and other countries, the Soviet Union and Norway agreed to end commercial hunting of whales in 1987.

Japan says it needs whale meat to supply its pop-ulation with low-cost protein and that eliminating its whaling industry, in which it has a large financial investment, would force it to import vast quantities of more expensive beef. Under harsh criticism and a threat by the United States to limit fishing in U.S. waters, Japan reluctantly agreed to honor the IWC's five-year moratorium beginning in 1988.

The blue whale is the world's largest animal. A baby blue whale weighs 5 tons at birth and gains about 100 pounds a day. Fully grown, it's more than 100 feet long and weighs 150 tons. The heart of an adult is as big as a Volkswagen "bug" and its brain weighs four times more than a human's. The blue whale is a mammal and shows signs of great intelligence.

Blue whales spend about eight months of the year in Antarctic waters. There they find an abundant supply of shrimplike krill (Figure 12-16), which they filter from seawater. During the colder winter months they migrate to warmer waters, where their young are born.

Once an estimated 200,000 blue whales roamed the Antarctic

waters. Today the species has been hunted to near biological extinction for its oil, meat, and bone. The annual catch of blue whales reached a peak of almost 30,000 in 1930. After that the annual catch dropped sharply and fell nearly to zero by 1964 (Figure 12-23). Less than 1,000 blue whales may be left today.

This decline was caused by a combination of prolonged overfishing and certain natural traits of the blue whale. Their huge size made them easy to spot. They were caught in large numbers because they grouped together in their Antarctic feeding grounds. Also, they take 25 years to mature sexually and have only one offspring every 2 to 5 years. This low reproduction rate makes it hard for

the species to recover once its population has been reduced to a low level.

Blue whales haven't been hunted commercially since 1964 and are classified as an endangered species. Despite this protection, some marine experts believe that not enough blue whales are left for the species to recover. If so, each year there will be fewer blue whales until they disappear forever.

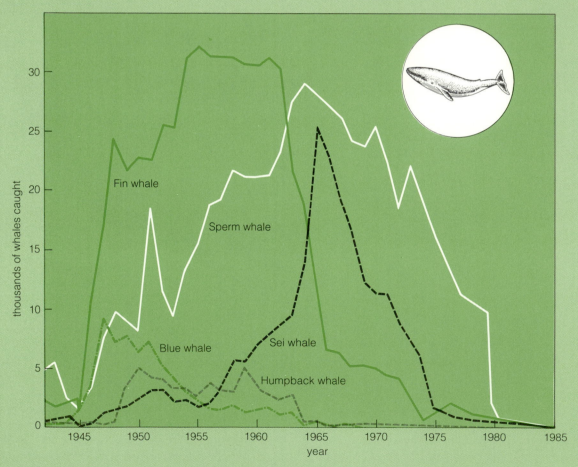

Figure 12-23 Whale harvests, showing the signs of overfishing. (Data from International Whaling Commission)

Japan announced, however, that it will take 875 whales each year for "scientific" purposes. Norway and Iceland announced similar plans. Then they sold most of the meat from whales they had captured for "research" purposes to Japan. Roger Payne and Sidney Holt, two of the world's most prominent marine mammal scientists, view these actions as a thinly disguised continuation of commercial whaling. In 1988 the IWC rejected requests from Japan, Iceland, and Norway for permits to harvest whales for scientific purposes.

Countries violating IWC regulations risk a ban on commercial fishing in U.S. waters. Imports of fishery products into the United States from these countries could also be restricted. In 1987 the United States opposed scientific whaling. This changed in 1988 when the United States supported limited scientific whaling by Iceland to get building permits for the U.S. air base at Keflavik, Iceland. This weakening of the U.S. anti-whaling stance was a key factor leading Japan, Iceland, and Norway to defy the IWC and continue scientific whaling in 1988.

It appears that commercial whaling will stop for a few years, although some whales are still be taken illegally for research purposes. But large-scale commercial whaling may resume when the present moratorium ends. Conservationists are also worried that some newer IWC nonwhaling countries that supported the whaling ban may resign from the commission. They might feel that the job is done and that continued membership is too expensive. This would leave IWC politics to the whaling countries.

Potential for Increasing the Global Catch   Some scientists believe that several methods can be used to increase the world's annual commercial catch of fish and shellfish to at least 100 million metric tons a year. A key step would be to enact and strictly enforce laws preventing overfishing and protecting spawning grounds and estuaries from physical destruction and pollution. One hopeful sign was the signing of the 1982 United Nations Convention on the Law of the Sea by 140 countries. This treaty gives all coastal countries the legal right to control fishing by their own fishing fleets and by foreign ships within 200 nautical miles of their coasts. If enforced, this treaty can sharply reduce overfishing. However, by 1987 fishery scientists found little recovery of many heavily exploited fish stocks.

Most fishing boats hunt and gather only one or two species. Other potentially useful fish species caught in their nets are thrown back because they're not valuable enough to take up the limited storage space in fishing vessels. This wastes one-fifth of all fish caught. Keeping and selling these fish would increase the annual catch by as much as 20%. More refrigerated storage at sea and on land to prevent spoilage would also increase the catch.

Genetic engineering has great potential to increase yields of desirable species. For example, in 1988 scientists were able to transfer a growth hormone gene from rainbow trout into carp to produce bigger, faster-growing fish.

Another way to expand the catch is to harvest more squid, octopus, lantern fish, Antarctic krill, and other unconventional species. Greatly expanded harvesting of krill, however, could lead to sharp declines in the populations of certain whales and other species dependent on krill (Figure 12-16). Krill can be processed into fish meal for use as livestock and aquaculture feed. But food scientists haven't been able to process krill into foods tasty enough for people to eat.

Another approach would be to switch some of the fish now sold mostly as animal feed (such as herrings and sardines) into the market for human consumption. Less expensive soybean meal could replace fish meal as animal feed.

Experts project that annual freshwater and saltwater aquaculture production can be increased more than threefold between 1986 and 2000. The Food and Agriculture Organization estimates that only one-tenth of the area suitable for aquaculture is currently being used.

Other fishery experts believe that further increases in the annual marine catch may be limited by overfishing and pollution and destruction of estuaries and aquaculture ponds. Another factor that may limit the commercial fish catch from the world's oceans is the projected rise in the price of oil—and thus of boat fuel—between 1995 and 2015. Unless more seafood is produced by aquaculture, consumers may find seafood prices too high.

12-4   MANAGEMENT OF MARINE FISHERIES

Conflicting Pressures in Fisheries Management
Fishery managers try to increase harvests of commercial and sport fish and at the same time to prevent overfishing. However, much of the information needed for wise fishery management isn't available.

Even with good information it's often hard to convince the fishing industry of the need for management to prevent overfishing. Without some form of governmental or international regulation, users have little incentive to protect these common property resources for future generations.

Fishery managers must deal with social, economic, and political pressures that often conflict with ideal biological management of fisheries. This means that fishing regulations and other forms of fisheries management are compromises between conservation and economic exploitation.

Management Techniques Since the 1930s many fishery commissions, councils, and advisory bodies have been established. They set quotas for harvesting fish and marine mammals and regulate conflicts over fishery resources in certain regions of the oceans. They consist of members from countries having a common interest in preserving a fishery that they jointly harvest.

These groups use various strategies to prevent overfishing. Often they set sustainable yields based on research they or other groups conduct. They use these estimates to determine the optimum yield for a fishery. Then they establish rules for dividing the allowable annual catch among the countries participating in the fishery.

Sometimes commissions declare closed seasons to limit the catch, especially to protect populations of overfished species. Several commissions also regulate the type of fishing gear that can be used. Enforcement is possible only if there are observers on all fishing vessels and the size and composition of fish catches sold at docks are monitored.

Fishery commissions are important in protecting fishery resources from abuse. As voluntary associations, however, they don't have any legal authority to compel member states to follow their rules. Nor can they compel all countries fishing in a region to join the commission and submit to its rules.

Considering Variations Between Species Differences between species should be considered in plans for managing fisheries. Examples include differences in life span, age at maturity, number of eggs or young, number of spawning events per year, reproductive life span, average adult size, and length of the larval period.

Because prey and predators compete in aquatic food webs, it's impossible to maximize the harvest of all or several species in the same food web at the same time. For example, the harvest of baleen whales in Antarctic waters can be increased by not harvesting the krill they eat. Conversely, the krill harvest can be increased by eliminating whales, seals, and other animals that compete with human beings for the krill (Figure 12-16). The marketplace and the desire for maximum short-term profit—not biology—usually determine which species in an ocean food web is harvested at the highest rate.

Controlling Fishing Efficiency Fishery managers set gear restrictions and size limits to prevent overfishing or to allow a depleted species to recover. **Gear restrictions** are regulations which limit the kind or size of gear that can be used to harvest a particular fish species. For example, in the northeast Atlantic fishery the size of the mesh in fishing nets must be large enough to let smaller, younger individuals escape. This allows enough individuals to reach sexual maturity so that the population can be sustained. Fishing techniques such as dynamiting and poisoning are outlawed.

Size limits make it illegal to keep fish above or below a certain size, usually the average length of the particular fish species when it first reproduces. Such a limit is aimed at preventing excessive harvesting of the breeding population. However, there's little evidence that size limits affect the reproductive rate of small fish species. Such limits are rarely used in commercial marine fisheries, except the commercial hook-and-line fisheries of salmon, halibut, and crab.

Gear restrictions and size limits increase the cost of fishing. The fishing industry can compensate for these restrictions by using more gear or by fishing longer.

Setting Quotas and Restricting Access Another way to prevent overfishing is to set annual harvest quotas. Commercial fishing licenses can be used to limit use of a fishery; each licensee is permitted to take only a certain share of the allowable catch. A tax can be put on each pound of fish caught to discourage overfishing by reducing the rewards of increased fishing. Fishing seasons can be limited. In extreme cases, such as in the Pacific halibut fishery, seasons have been as short as a few days and even hours. Proponents claim that these approaches are easier and cheaper to manage than gear restrictions and size limitations.

Often, a combination of approaches is used. For example, U.S. fishery managers use several methods to prevent overfishing of salmon. Salmon traps and nets can't be placed near the mouths of spawning streams, and only certain types of boats and fishing gear are allowed. The number of salmon that can be taken each season and the number of people licensed to take them are limited. These measures help prevent overfishing, but they force the fishing industry to make larger expenditures of capital and labor to catch the allowed quota of fish. This is economically inefficient and produces smaller profits than unrestricted fisheries are earning on the same yield of fish.

Resource economists contend that the best approach for most fisheries is to set a quota on the number of fish that can be taken. An efficient quota system has three characteristics: (1) the total amount of fish removed should not exceed the sustainable yield; (2) each user is allowed to catch a specified weight of fish; (3) individual quotas are freely transferable among users of the fishery.

However, quotas do pose some problems. It's difficult to get the accurate data on species populations needed to set quotas. Quotas are also hard to enforce over the entire range of mobile species such as tuna and whales.

Switching to Other Species The fishing industry can relieve pressure on overfished species by switching to species previously considered of little commercial value. For example, monk fish were considered "trash fish" only a few years ago. Now they're sold commercially and served in restaurants. Fishery managers can encourage such shifts by supporting research to identify substitutes for overfished species. Three underutilized species are octopus, squid, and krill.

Extending Offshore Fishing Zones Ocean areas beyond the legal jurisdiction of any country are known as the **high seas**. Any limits on the use of the living and mineral common property resources in these areas are set by international maritime law and international treaties. **Territorial seas** are ocean areas extending a certain distance from coastal countries, in which these countries have jurisdiction over all living and mineral resources and transportation.

By the 1970s large fishing fleets from several countries were overharvesting many fisheries on the high seas within 200 nautical miles of shores. In response, many countries met and developed an international treaty to manage ocean resources for the benefit of all the world's people (see Spotlight below). One provision of the treaty extended the outer limits of territorial seas of coastal countries from 3 nautical miles (3.4 statute miles) to 200 nautical miles (230 statute miles) from their shores.

In the United States, the Fisheries Conservation and Management Act of 1976 regulates all fisheries, except tuna, in marine waters to 200 nautical miles offshore. All marine resources within this EEZ are the common property of the country. They are to be managed partly by individual coastal states and partly by the federal government. The goal is to prevent overfishing and sustain populations of living resources for present and future generations.

Coastal states have the primary authority for regulating fishing in the territorial seas extending 3 nautical miles from their shores. From 3 to 200 nautical miles, the National Marine Fisheries Service (NMFS) and eight regional councils share responsibility for managing fishing activities.

Members of each regional council are appointed by federal and state governments. They include state and federal officials and private citizens, including representatives from the commercial and sport fishing industries. Advised by a committee of fishery scientists, the regional councils develop and submit fishery management plans for domestic and foreign fishing in U.S. waters to the secretary of commerce for approval. If a state's action or inaction in its territorial seas adversely affects implementation of an approved federal fishery management plan for the rest of the EEZ, the secretary of commerce can take over regulation of that fishery in state waters.

The results of the Fisheries Conservation and Management Act of 1976 have been mixed. Foreign fishing in U.S. waters has been reduced, although it still accounts for one-fourth of the catch within the EEZ. A 1986 study by the U.S. Department of Com-

---

SPOTLIGHT The Law of the Sea Treaty

In 1974 over 160 countries began working on a treaty for managing the living and mineral resources of the world's oceans. After much work and controversy, the final version of the United Nations Convention on the Law of the Sea (LOS) was finished in 1982. By 1988 more than 140 countries had signed all or most parts of this treaty, and it became legally binding.

The agreement gives any coastal country legal rights over all marine fishery resources and ocean mineral resources in an **exclusive economic zone (EEZ)**. This zone extends 200 nautical miles from the shores of coastal countries (Figures 12-6 and 12-7). Foreign fishing and mining opera-

tions for oil, natural gas, and other minerals are allowed in these zones only with permission and licensing from the government of each coastal country.

The treaty provides for the regulation of ocean pollution and the conservation of living resources, including increased protection of marine mammals. Coastal countries agree to manage the living resources in their EEZs so that they'll be sustained.

By setting up the 200-mile EEZs, the treaty places 40% of the world's oceans under the control of individual coastal countries. Resources in the high seas making up the remaining 60% of the world's oceans are recognized as common property to be shared by

the entire world and managed by the United Nations under international law. The treaty allows any country to remove minerals from the deep seabeds outside EEZs. However, the resources or the profits from them are supposed to be shared by all people.

Several countries, including the United States, West Germany, and the United Kingdom, oppose this provision. They argue that it forces private enterprises to share profits with other countries and threatens the national security of countries by limiting their take of strategic minerals. Therefore, these countries haven't signed this section of the Law of the Sea Treaty. Do you think the United States should sign it?

---

merce identified 19 groups of fish and shellfish that were being overfished in U.S. waters despite being covered by management plans developed under the 1976 act. Between 1982 and 1987 the harvest from waters off New England fell by 18%, and that off the southeastern states by 42%. These losses are the results of overfishing, destruction of coastal wetlands, and pollution.

Building Artificial Reefs Since 1965 the United States, Japan, the Virgin Islands, and several other countries have built artificial reefs to provide food and cover for commercial and game fish species. Some reefs, such as one off Fire Island, New York, are built from boulders and construction debris. Others are built from junk cars, sunken ships, and tires. Offshore rigs also serve as reefs. Most of the artificial reefs have attracted many species of game fish, much to the joy of anglers.

Multispecies Ecological Management So far fishery management has emphasized controlling populations of fish on a single-species basis. But different species in ocean food webs interact in complex ways that significantly affect population levels. Population levels are also affected by natural and human-influenced changes in climate, ocean currents, temperature, pollution, and other environmental factors over large ocean areas.

Managing these species interactions and environmental factors is important in sustaining the populations of commercially important species. Such *multispecies ecological management* must involve large marine ecosystems, not just smaller areas containing important commercial fisheries. The concept of management of large marine regions is being used by the United Nations Environmental Program, in which coastal countries have agreed to cooperate in controlling pollution in ten regional seas.

Three major problems hinder management of large marine ecosystems. First, it's difficult to determine the boundaries of such large ecosystems. Second, we know too little about the ecological relationships within these ecosystems. Third, various parts of many large marine ecosystems are controlled by different countries. Regional agreements and cooperative oceanographic research among the countries involved will be needed for effective management of these ecosystems.

12-5 MANAGEMENT OF FRESHWATER FISHERIES

Brief History of Management in the United States When the early settlers came to North America, they found clear streams filled with fish. As settlers spread across the continent, they converted forests and grasslands to cropland. This led to soil erosion

that choked many lakes and streams with sediment, killing many fish populations. Later, pollution from factories, mills, and towns wiped out many freshwater fisheries.

By 1870 the deterioration of fish resources had become so serious that the federal government established the Bureau of Fisheries to help restore and improve fisheries. Later this bureau became the U.S. Fish and Wildlife Service. Many state governments also formed fish conservation agencies and commissions.

These federal and state agencies began conserving fish resources by enacting laws to restrict catches and by controlling wild predators. Fishing regulations included limits on fishing gear, seasons, and the number and size of fish that could be caught legally.

Later the Fish and Wildlife Service established hatcheries to artificially propagate desirable species and to restock depleted streams and lakes. Sport species that were successful in one area were transplanted to depleted areas. Some conservationists, however, have complained that the hatchery program has eliminated too many species of wild fish. Experience has also shown that some lakes, heavily stocked with hatchery fish, produce less than similar lakes that weren't stocked.

In the last few decades freshwater fishery managers have begun using ecological approaches. These include protecting and improving habitats for game and commercial fish and for endangered species and conducting research on the causes of fishery depletion.

Management Priorities Federal and state agencies manage most streams and lakes with the goal of increasing populations of game fish. This isn't surprising because much of the funding for these agencies comes from the sale of fishing licenses and from taxes on sport fishing equipment. Many streams and lakes would be more polluted if state and federal legislators didn't respond to the demands of anglers.

Catering to the demands of anglers has also created problems. When species of game fish are introduced, they sometimes wipe out populations of native fish. For example, importing the brown trout from Europe has caused sharp drops in the populations of many native species of trout and nongame fish. Efforts by conservationists to have more state and federal fishery money allocated to the preservation of wild and threatened species have been only partly successful.

Improving Fish Habitats Fishery biologists now recognize that protecting and improving fish habitats is the best long-term way to improve commercial and sport fishing and to protect endangered species. Methods of achieving this goal include (1) protecting and creating spawning sites, (2) building reservoirs and farm ponds, **(3)** controlling water pollution (Section 8-6), **(4)** controlling aquatic weeds, **(5)** fertilizing lakes and ponds, **(6)** reducing oxygen depletion, and **(7)** protecting and creating cover spaces.

Protecting and Creating Spawning Sites In Minnesota, Wisconsin, and Iowa, federal money has been used to buy and protect marshes that serve as breeding and spawning sites for northern pike. Elsewhere, streams with sand and gravel beds, which some species such as bass and trout need for spawning, are being protected.

Where spawning beds don't exist or have been destroyed, sand or gravel can be used to create artificial spawning sites. Nylon mats have been placed in streams as spawning sites for largemouth bass and lake trout. Concrete rubble is used to protect the eggs of lake sturgeon from mud puppies (salamanders).

Building Reservoirs and Farm Ponds Large and small reservoirs now serve as major habitats for prized species of freshwater sport fish in the United States. These waters draw many anglers from urban areas, especially since they often replace heavily fished sections of rivers. The introduction of striped bass (Figure 12-3, p. 305) and coho salmon into reservoirs is highly successful if the fish are restocked as needed.

However, the dams that create reservoirs prevent fish such as salmon from migrating upstream to spawn. Ladders and special channels allow migrating fish to bypass low dams (Figure 12-24). But such devices can't be used with high dams, such as Grand Coulee in Washington and Shasta in California (Figure 6-10, p. 130). Many young fish die when they go over dams on their trip downstream.

Small farm ponds can be built and stocked with fish for recreation and food. Aquaculture ponds can also provide income. But ponds are usually small and shallow and have an unreliable supply of water. They also tend to fill with soil, leaves, and debris from the surrounding land. With this large input of plant nutrients, sunlight stimulates excessive growth of phytoplankton and other aquatic plants. Such excessive eutrophication can kill fish populations in hot weather. To be free of these problems, ponds must be at least nine feet deep.

Good management is needed to maintain enough game fish in a pond. Every few years the pond should be drained and aquatic plants and excess bottom sediment removed. It should then be refilled and restocked with balanced populations of fish.

Controlling Water Pollution Since 1965 important progress has been made in improving the water quality in some U.S. rivers, lakes, and streams and preventing a drop in water quality in others (section 8-6). However, poor logging, farming, mining, and con-

Figure 12-24 Fish ladder on the John Day Dam in Oregon allows salmon to migrate up the Columbia River over the dam to upstream spawning grounds.

struction practices still choke many streams with sediment. The runoff of pesticides from cropland into streams and lakes is still a major hazard for fish. Irrigation canals are also hazardous to fish. Where possible, canals should be screened off to keep fish from entering and dying. Because of high installation and maintenance costs, such screens are rarely installed.

Industries and cities also continue to add trash, debris, organic wastes, and a variety of toxic chemicals to rivers, lakes, and streams. In addition to killing fish or their prey, PCBs, DDT, mercury compounds, and other toxic chemicals can be biologically amplified in fish, making them harmful for people to eat (Figure 9-23, p. 239). Little has been done to control acid deposition (Section 7-3), another source of surface water pollution. Protecting the earth's aquatic resources will require that we strengthen and integrate laws that govern land use, water pollution, and air pollution.

Controlling Aquatic Vegetation Aquatic vegetation provides cover, food, spawning sites, and dissolved oxygen for fish. But some aquatic plants, such as water chestnut, lotus, hydrilla, and water hyacinth, tend to take over waterways (see Case Study on p. 334). These plants deplete the water of nutrients and choke off streams.

During summer the decay of plant matter on lake bottoms can deplete dissolved oxygen and contribute to fish kills. The removal of excess aquatic vegetation improves habitats for many game fish. People can remove vegetation by mechanical cutting, by applying herbicides, or by introducing new species that feed on

If you visit Florida and other southeastern states, you may admire the beauty of the mats of leaves and purple flowers that cover many freshwater lakes and streams. These are water hyacinths (Figure 12-25), native to Central and South America. They were brought to the United States in the 1880s for an exhibition in New Orleans. One plant was taken from the exhibition and planted in the yard of a house in Florida. Within ten years the colorful plant was a public menace.

The fast-growing plant can double its population in only two weeks. Unchecked by natural enemies and thriving on Florida's nutrient-rich water, water hyacinths rapidly displaced native aquatic plants. They also blocked boat traffic in many streams, canals, and rivers. Then they spread to waterways in other southeastern states, aided by canals that crisscross the region.

In 1898 the U.S. Army Corps of Engineers tried to cut away the plants. Failing that, they tried to kill the plants by spraying them with sodium arsenite. This method helped get rid of some of the plants but was abandoned in the 1930s because the deadly arsenic found its way into the food of spray boat crews. In the mid-1940s a combination of mechanical removal and the herbicide 2,4-D was used, but the water hyacinth continued to spread.

Next, scientists looked hopefully at the Florida manatee, or sea cow, which feeds on aquatic weeds. Large numbers of manatee can control the growth and spread of water hyacinths in inland waterways more effectively than mechanical or chemical methods. But these gentle and playful mammals, each weighing as much as two tons, are threatened with extinction. They're so trusting that they swim too close to powerboats. Even with protection, large numbers of the animals die each year when they are slashed by powerboat propellers, entangled in fishing gear, or hit on the head by oars. Only about 800 to 1,000 manatees now exist in Florida.

In recent years scientists have brought in other natural predators to help control the hyacinth. For example, a species of weevil that feeds only on hyacinths has been imported from Argentina. Results look promising, but it's too early to evaluate this experiment. A species of water snail from Puerto Rico has also been introduced. However, it's less effective than the weevil, and it can also feed on other, more desirable plants.

The grass carp, or white amur, brought in from the Soviet Union, is also being used to control water hyacinths and hydrilla. This fish species, with individuals weighing as much as 100 pounds, may solve water hyacinth and hydrilla problems, but it could easily become a major pest itself. If its population grows, the grass carp may eat nearly every aquatic plant, including desirable species.

There is some good news, however. Research by the National Aeronautic and Space Administration (NASA) has shown that water hyacinths can be used in several beneficial ways. They can be introduced in sewage treatment lagoons to absorb toxic chemicals. They can be converted by fermentation to a biogas fuel similar to natural gas, added as a mineral and protein supplement to cattle feed, and applied to the soil as fertilizer. They can also be used to clean up polluted ponds and lakes—if their population size can be kept under control.

USDA/Soil Conservation Service

Figure 12-25   Water hyacinths can rapidly cover and choke off a waterway, such as this one near Jacksonville, Florida.

Figure 12-26 Lakes and reservoirs can be aerated to increase dissolved oxygen.

certain aquatic plants. For example, various species of tilapia and green carp have been used for weed control in farm ponds and artificial lakes in warm climates, where these fish thrive.

Fertilizing Lakes and Ponds and Reducing Oxygen Depletion

Nutrient-poor lakes and ponds can be fertilized with artificial fertilizer, fish meal, and animal wastes. Fertilization is widely used in aquaculture to produce high yields of catfish and other species.

In cold climates snowplows can be used to scrape snow from frozen lakes. This allows sunlight to penetrate the ice and support aquatic vegetation needed to prevent winter oxygen depletion. Air can also be pumped into frozen lakes through dozens of holes drilled through the ice. During hot summer months small lakes and ponds can be aerated by machine to prevent oxygen depletion (Figure 12-26). However, aeration is too expensive except for small ponds or lakes used to raise expensive table fish.

Protecting and Creating Cover Spaces

Many streams and rivers have been dredged, straightened, and changed in other ways. These changes often destroy the cover spaces many fish need for survival.

Shelters built of rocks or logs can correct this situation, helping fish escape predators and providing shade from the sun (Figure 12-27). Large boulders can be placed in a trout stream to provide a less turbulent area in midstream. Small dams can be built to create deep pools where trout can find refuge from predators. Vegetation can be planted along banks to increase cover, maintain cooler temperatures, and reduce erosion. In lakes, piles of brush can be anchored near the shore to provide cover and hiding spaces.

Raising and Transplanting Species

Today hatcheries are used in the United States mostly to stock streams and lakes with trout and salmon (Figure 12-14). Streams and lakes are supplied with hatchery-raised fish by a method known as put-and-take stocking. For example, trout are reared in cement troughs and fed food pellets until they reach a legally catchable size, usually eight to ten inches (Figure 12-13). Then they're released in heavily fished lakes and streams before the fishing season starts.

Because these hatchery fish aren't adapted for survival in the wild streams, they die of starvation or other causes if not caught within several days. Heavily fished areas may be restocked several times during a season.

Some fishery managers have extended upstream ranges of trout by planting them in headwater streams and fishless lakes above natural barriers. In the western United States, most mountain lakes had no fish until people introduced various species of trout into them in the last 100 years.

Efforts to restore the Atlantic salmon have been encouraging. The population of this species had dropped sharply because of impassable dams, water pollution, overfishing, and acidic water. Several methods have been used to bring back the species: restricting the take from sport fishing, restoring access to spawning and nursery habitats, and establishing artificial propagation programs.

In contrast, the chinook salmon population that enters the Sacramento River to spawn each year has fallen from 84,000 in 1967 to about 2,800 today. This drop was caused by the completion of a diversion dam, drought, and poor feeding conditions during the 1982–1983 and 1986–1987 El Niño-Southern Oscilla-

CHAPTER 12 Marine and Freshwater Fishery Resources **335**

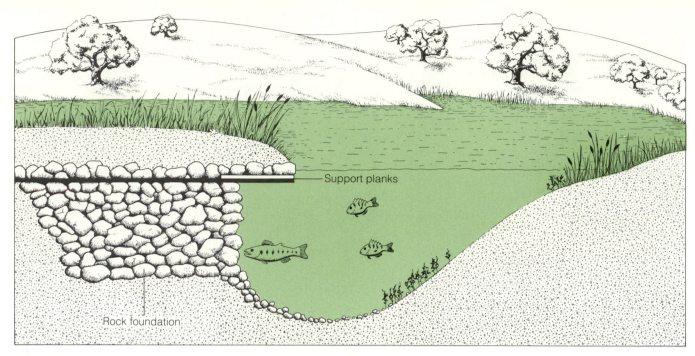

Figure 12-27 Improving fish habitat by building an artificial cover area.

tions. Any new difficulty could wipe the species out in the Sacramento River.

In 1985 several conservation groups asked the NMFS to protect the chinook salmon under the Endangered Species Act. In 1988, after the agency had still not acted, these groups filed suit to force government protection of this threatened species.

Controlling Predators and Introducing New Species

Anglers and commercial fishing interests often assume that wild predators compete with humans for game fish and commercially important fish. They believe that if the predators were removed, their catches of desirable fish would increase.

The true situation is rarely that simple, but the idea of predator control is so appealing that it has persisted. For example, until the mid-1960s the state of Alaska paid bounties on seals to halt a decline in salmon that was actually caused by overfishing and habitat destruction. There is no evidence that reducing the seal population made any difference.

Fishery managers are sometimes successful in introducing a game fish species in a lake or river. But sometimes a fish species accidentally or deliberately introduced into an aquatic ecosystem displaces valued game fish or commercial fish. Fishery managers may then try to eliminate the unwanted species, often by applying the poison rotenone to the affected water system to kill all fish present. Then they make a fresh start by restocking the water with the desired species. Rotenone is chosen because it affects mainly species with gills and is usually harmless to terrestrial vertebrates.

Setting Size and Bag Limits

Fishery managers usually set size limits for rainbow trout at 6 to 8 inches, and for largemouth bass at 12 inches. In some wild trout streams, anglers are allowed to keep only fish longer than 12 inches (to increase spawning) and shorter than 18 inches (to protect large females). Managers also control the size of fish taken in commercial freshwater fisheries by setting a minimum size for hooks or net mesh.

Bag limits specify how many fish an angler can keep in a day of fishing. Bag limits are especially useful for largemouth bass, muskellunge, northern pike, and other popular species that take a long time to reach catchable size. In heavily fished trout streams, a bag limit of 1 or 2 fish per day is common. In contrast, some warm-water fish are so abundant that bag limits aren't needed. Examples include sunfish, catfish, bluegills, crappies, and rock bass. Sometimes, however, bag limits of 25 to 50 fish per day are placed on them simply to prevent waste.

Restricting Fishing Gear and Fishing Seasons

As sport fishing became popular in the nineteenth and twentieth centuries, nets, traps, explosives, bright lights, poisons, and other "efficient" methods of fishing were banned. Sometimes restrictions are placed on gear to reduce the chance of overfishing. For example, the use of live bait might be prohibited or restricted to certain kinds. However, better artificial flies and worms are continually being developed. If these artificial lures become too effective, certain types may have to be banned to prevent overfishing of prized species.

Authorities prohibit fishing for some species during spawning times to increase their ability to reproduce. Many anglers don't consider it sporting to catch fish during the breeding season, when fish defending their nests will bite at anything that passes over them. Some anglers, fishing primarily for enjoyment, carefully release fish they have caught.

In most cases, restricting the fishing season seems to have little effect on reproductive success. Environmental factors that affect the survival of young fish in the first few weeks of their lives are generally more important. However, establishing fishing seasons may reduce the total catch and help prevent overfishing.

Limiting Commercial Fisheries Today freshwater commercial fisheries in the United States are limited, mostly because of protests from sport anglers seeking the same species. A major exception is the Great Lakes (see Case Study below). A few commercial fisheries are also allowed in other large lakes and on Indian reservations.

CASE STUDY   Fisheries in the Great Lakes

Since 1800 the commercial and sport fisheries of the five Great Lakes (Figure 8-27, p. 207) have undergone some remarkable changes. Several valuable species, such as trout and salmon, have become commercially extinct because of overfishing, pollution, and invasions by natural predators. Until the 1960s, fish stocks of the Great Lakes were used mostly for commercial fishing. Today the emphasis is on sport fishing, a $2 billion-a-year industry.

The problems of the lower lakes (Erie and Ontario) differ from those of the upper lakes (Michigan, Huron, and Superior). In the 1800s Ontario was the first of the Great Lakes to suffer declines in fish populations. These losses occurred partly because of the buildup of Toronto, Syracuse, Buffalo, Rochester and other large cities around its shores.

Until the early 1800s, Ontario was also the only Great Lake open to invasion by the sea lamprey and other predators via the St. Lawrence River. The sea lamprey is a parasite that attaches itself to the body of soft-skinned fish and sucks out blood and other body fluids (Figure 12-28).

The other lakes, however, became open to such invasions in the early 1800s, when several canals were built for ocean ships. The canals allowed marine species such as the sea lamprey to invade Lake Erie and then the upper Great Lakes. By the 1920s the population of sea lampreys had become large enough to sharply reduce populations of lake trout, whitefish, and herring.

Lake Erie is the shallowest and most highly nourished of the Great Lakes. Today, even with massive urbanization around its shore and huge pollution inputs, Lake Erie is the major fish spawning ground in the entire Great Lakes system.

Commercial fishing in Lake Erie for valuable trout, whitefish, and herring was carried out on a small scale before 1850. But more efficient nets and other improvements in fishing technology led to overfishing of the herring population. By 1925 it became commercially extinct in Lake Erie and has still not recovered. Chemical pollution in the 1950s was the final blow. By 1935 the whitefish also became commercially extinct in Lake Erie from overfishing and invasion by the sea lamprey.

Populations of trout in Lake Erie and the three upper Great Lakes dropped to the point of commercial extinction by the mid-1940s. Although overfishing played a role, the major factor in this decline was invasion by the sea lamprey. In the 1950s the commercial fish catch was made up mostly of perch, smelt, catfish, chub, and other smaller and less valuable fish.

In the 1930s the upper Great Lakes, especially Lake Michigan, were invaded by the small, plankton-eating alewife. With its natural predators removed by the sea lamprey and commercial overfishing, the alewife population exploded. By the 1950s it had taken over spawning grounds and food supplies for chub, perch, smelt, and several other species.

(continued)

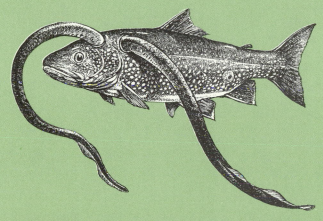

Figure 12-28 The two sea lampreys shown are parasites that attach themselves to the body of soft-skinned fish such as lake trout and salmon. They then open a hole in the skin of their host and suck out its blood and other body fluids. An 18-inch sea lamprey can kill 40 pounds of fish a year. Between 1940 and 1960 these parasites devastated many important fish stocks in the Great Lakes. Since 1960 they have been kept under control by a poison that kills their larvae.

Protecting Species from Extinction In the United States, the Endangered Species Act of 1973 authorizes the National Marine Fisheries Service to identify and list marine species in danger of becoming extinct. It also authorizes the development of programs to help endangered and threatened species recover. This act is discussed in more detail in Section 17-1.

Because of their high reproductive capacity, most

CASE STUDY Continued

After spawning every spring, millions of alewives died, creating a smelly nuisance for swimmers, anglers, and lake front property owners. By the mid-1950s the dominant species in the upper Great Lakes were the parasitic sea lamprey and the economically worthless alewife.

In 1954 a selective poison was found that could kill the larvae of sea lampreys. By the 1960s this poison had caused a sharp decline in lamprey populations. In 1964 a massive program was launched to introduce species of large predators to help control alewives and remaining sea lampreys and to restore predator fish stocks.

Fishery managers decided to shift emphasis from commercial to sport fishing. They believed sport fishing would have greater economic and social benefits for the 50 million people living within a day's drive of some part of the lakes. In 1964 almost 2 million coho and chinook salmon eggs produced in West Coast hatcheries were introduced into the upper Great Lakes. These species were chosen because they're heavy feeders that grow fast, reaching maturity in just a few years (Figure 12-3). They're also hard-fighting, good eating, and easy to catch with sporting tackle.

By the early 1970s millions of salmon populated the upper Great Lakes. Today the upper Great Lakes sport fisheries add more than $1 billion to the economies of surrounding states and provide pleasure for half a million sport anglers. Alewives no longer die and pile up on the beaches in the spring. The successful restoration of these fishery resources has been proclaimed one of North America's most outstanding fish management achievements. Pollution control efforts have also brought about a fantastic recovery in the populations of perch and walleye in western Lake Erie.

Since the early 1980s, however, the sea lamprey has begun breeding in large rivers near the lakes. These rivers are harder to treat with poisons. Unless other control methods are developed, the lamprey may again decimate the populations of desirable game fish in the Great Lakes.

CASE STUDY Protecting the Owens Pupfish

The Owens pupfish is a one- to two-inch fish that once lived in marshes in the arid Owens Valley in southern California. It was an obscure North American fish, not recognized as a distinct species until 1948. By the time it was identified, it was considered extinct, a loss regretted mainly by a few fish specialists, environmentalists, and conservationists.

The pupfish was once abundant in the Owens Valley. Its ability to eat mosquito larvae in the marshes is one reason the valley was so free from mosquitoes when first settled. However, mosquitoes became a problem as the pupfish populations declined because of predation and competition from introduced fishes, such as carp, largemouth bass, and mosquitofish. Mean-while, habitats for this fish became scarce as marshes were drained for farming and the water was piped to arid Los Angeles.

In the 1960s an increase in environmental concern, including concern for obscure desert fish, began to grow. Hence, the discovery in 1964 of a swamp pool containing 200 Owens pupfish generated interest among several California scientists.

These scientists began making plans for the construction of a refuge for this fish previously believed extinct. The difficult task involved convincing several government agencies that this novel project was worth spending time and money on. While the refuge was being planned and built, the pool containing the pupfish began to dry up. Luckily, a graduate student noticed this, and most of the fish were rescued and placed in the refuge in 1970. Two other refuges were built later.

The Owens pupfish was later declared an endangered species by the state of California and by the federal government. The history of the Owens pupfish is significant because it tells of one of the first major efforts to protect an endangered fish species of no obvious value to humans. The fish was protected solely because a few people didn't want to see a small part of the earth's unique living heritage disappear. Today the Owens pupfish lives because people cared.

---

fish species aren't endangered. However, this isn't the case with some freshwater fish found in unique stream or marsh habitats (see Case Study on p. 338).

The ocean offers abundant resources to sustain us. But through ignorance and misunderstanding we're placing this wealth in jeopardy—causing gross impoverishment of many fisheries, near extinction for most large whales, widespread pollution of fish-rich waters, and degradation and disruption of many coastal habitats.

Norman Myers

DISCUSSION TOPICS

1. Describe the factors leading to the collapse of the anchovy fishery off the coast of Peru. How could the collapse of similar fisheries be prevented?

2. Should the annual harvesting of krill in Antarctic waters be increased significantly? Explain.

3. Why have the populations of most whale species been severely depleted? What natural biological factors make the blue whale so vulnerable to commercial and biological extinction?

4. What are gear restrictions and size limits and why are they sometimes ineffective in reducing overfishing?

5. Salmon and trout are among the most valued fishery resources in the United States. Why then are overfishing and destruction of their habitats such continuing problems? How could these problems be overcome?

6. National parks are supposed to give Americans a taste of wilderness as it once was. This means that they're supposed to be managed to conserve native plant and animal species. Trout aren't native to most high mountain lakes in such national parks as Yosemite, Kings Canyon, Sequoia, and Rocky Mountain. Yet, they've been transplanted there for so long that most visitors expect to be able to catch them in those lakes. Do you think the planting of hatchery-raised trout should be continued in national park lakes? Explain.

7. If a large, warm-water reservoir were built in a fishless watershed, what kinds of fish would you plant in the reservoir? Explain.

8. You're placed in charge of restoring the fishery of a lake or stream that once was famous for its game fish but is now dominated by nongame fish. What actions, if any, would you take to correct this imbalance?

9. Examine the fishing regulations that apply to a local body of water. Why do you think they exist? Are they needed to protect the fishery? List any changes you'd make in these regulations.

FURTHER READINGS

Bagenal, T., ed. 1984. *Methods for the Assessment of Fish Production in Freshwaters.* IBP Handbook No. 3, 3rd. ed. London: Blackwell's.

Becker, G. C. 1983. *Fisheries of Wisconsin.* Madison: University of Wisconsin Press.

Browning, R. J. 1980. *Fisheries of the North Pacific.* Anchorage: Alaska Northwest.

Courtenay, W. R., Jr., and J. R. Stauffer, Jr., eds. 1984. *Distribution, Biology, and Management of Exotic Fishes.* Baltimore: Johns Hopkins University Press.

Credlund, Arthur G. 1983. *Whales and Whaling.* New York: Seven Hills Books.

Evans, Peter G. H. 1987. *The Natural History of Whales and Dolphins.* Washington, D.C.: Facts on File.

Everhart, W. H. et al. 1981. *Principles of Fishery Science,* 2nd ed. Ithaca, N.Y.: Comstock.

Food and Agriculture Organization of the United Nations. 1988. *1986 Yearbook of Fishery Statistics.* New York: United Nations.

Gaskin, D. E. 1982. *The Ecology of Whales and Dolphins.* London: Heinemann.

Goldman, C., and A. Horne. 1983. *Limnology.* New York: McGraw-Hill.

Greenbough, Joseph J., and J. W. Greenbough. 1979. *International Management of Tuna, Porpoise, and Billfish: Biological, Legal, and Political Aspects.* Seattle: University of Washington Press.

Klausner, A. 1985. "Food From the Sea." *Biotechnology,* vol. 3, no. 1, 27–32.

Lackey, R. T., and L. A. Nielson. 1980. *Fisheries Management.* New York: John Wiley.

Linburg, Peter R. 1981. *Farming the Waters.* New York: Beaufort Books (Scribner).

Lowe, Marcia D. 1988. "Salmon Ranching and Farming Net Growing Harvest." *World Watch,* Jan.–Feb., 28–32.

Moyle, P. B., and J. J. Cech. 1982. *Fisheries: An Introduction to Ichthyology.* Englewood Cliffs, N.J.: Prentice-Hall.

Ono, R. D. et al. 1983. *Vanishing Fishes of North America.* Washington, D.C.: Stone Wall Press.

Rothschild, B. J. 1981. "More Food From the Sea?" *BioScience,* Mar., 216–220.

Rounsefell, G. A. 1975. *Ecology, Utilization, and Management of Marine Fisheries.* Saint Louis, Mo: C. V. Mosby.

Steiner, Todd et al. 1986. *The Tragedy Continues: Killing of Dolphins by the Tuna Industry.* San Francisco: Earth Island Institute.

Walker, M., ed. 1971. *Sport Fishing USA.* Washington, D.C.: U.S. Fish and Wildlife Service.

CHAPTER 13

Rangeland Resources

General Questions and Issues

1. What are the major ecological characteristics of rangeland plants and animals?

2. How are the world's rangelands distributed and used?

3. How are rangelands in the United States distributed, owned, and used?

4. How can rangelands be managed to produce meat and other products, to protect wildlife, and to prevent overgrazing?

All flesh is grass.

Isaiah XL, 3

L and that supplies vegetation as food for grazing or browsing animals is called **rangeland** or **range**. Most of this arid and semiarid land is unsuited to rainfed crop cultivation, industrial forestry, protected forests, or urbanization.

Unless these lands are irrigated and fertilized at great cost, their best use is for livestock and wildlife production. They are potentially renewable resources that require little or no commercial energy input to produce meat, milk, cheese, wool, hide, and animal fat (tallow) used to make soap, candles, and margarine. In rural areas of LDCs, rangelands supply people with fuelwood, edible fruits and leaves, roof thatch, and fencing materials. Animal manure from livestock and wild animals is used as organic fertilizer, building material, and fuel.

The vegetation on these lands is mostly grasses, grasslike plants, and shrubs. These plants, known as **forage,** supply food for deer, giraffes, wildebeests and other wild animals and for sheep, cattle, goats, and other domesticated animals. Some of these foraging animals graze on grass. Others browse on twigs, leaves, and tender shoots.

13-1 GRASSLAND ECOLOGY

Types of Grasslands Most rangelands are grasslands, found in areas of the world where there is not enough rainfall to support large stands of trees but enough to support various grasses, shrubs, and forbs (broadleafed flowering plants). Grasslands are classi-

fied as tropical, temperate, and polar depending on average annual temperature (Figure 6-1, p. 118, and map inside back cover). Other rangelands, besides grasslands, are desert shrublands, shrub woodlands such as chaparral, temperate forests, and tropical forests.

In tropical regions grasslands occur as *savanna,* a mixture of grass, shrubs, and scattered small trees. In Brazil they are called *campos,* and in Venezuela, *llanos.*

In temperate areas a variety of grasslands are found in the interior of continents. In North America they include *short-grass prairies* and *tall-grass prairies* (Figure 13-1a) . They also include *steppes* in Eurasia (Figure 13-1b), *pampas* in Argentina (Figure 13-1c), *veld* in Africa, and *pastures* in Australia and Europe (Figure 13-1d). In cold areas grasslands occur as *Arctic tundra* and *alpine meadows.*

Once, vast herds of large herbivores roamed the world's temperate grasslands. They included bison and pronghorn antelopes in North America (Figure 2-7, p. 34), kangaroos in Australia, and horses, asses, and saiga antelopes in Europe and Asia. The temperate grasslands also had a rich variety of other mammals and birds adapted to the vegetation.

Today, most large, wild herbivores on these grasslands have been killed or driven away. In areas without enough rainfall to grow crops, temperate grasslands are now used to graze livestock. In wetter areas these fertile grasslands have been plowed up and planted with grain for consumption by humans and livestock.

Growing crops usually costs too much on most of

a

b

c

d

Figure 13-1 Examples of temperate grasslands. **a.** Tall-grass prairie in the Midwest. **b.** Steppe in the USSR. **c.** Pampa in Argentina. **d.** Pasture in southern Australia.

the world's polar and tropical grasslands. Crop production is limited by a lack of water (tropical grasslands), poor soil (tropical, arctic, and alpine grasslands), and low temperatures (arctic and alpine grasslands). Since the beginnings of agriculture these two types of grasslands have been used mainly by wild grazing animals and livestock.

Plant Biomass Productivity and Food Webs The rate at which grassland plants produce plant biomass (Section 5-3) varies with the average annual temperature and precipitation. The rate of biomass production is highest in tropical savannas and lowest in tundra.

The high rate of biomass production in African savanna supports large numbers of zebras, wildebeests, and antelopes. Most of these and other grazers and browsers specialize in eating selected parts of grassland vegetation. For example, giraffes feed on the foliage and young shoots of trees, and rhinoceroses feed on bushes. Wildebeests eat young leaves, and zebras eat only young shoots and older leaves.

Much of the plant biomass on rangeland is consumed by insects and microorganisms. For example,

in rangelands of the southwestern United States, termites consume ten times more biomass than livestock. Locusts and grasshoppers eat nearly all the green vegetation under certain climate conditions in African savannas and in grasslands of the southwestern United States. Rodents and rabbits also eat more above-ground biomass than livestock. Six to eight rabbits, for instance, eat as much grass as one sheep.

The rate of plant biomass production on the tundra is low, and the biomass is available mostly during the short summer. Furthermore, most of this biomass is in underground roots and isn't available to herbivores. Such conditions support only small populations of large grazing mammals. Examples are reindeer in Eurasia and caribou in Canada.

Characteristics of Rangeland Vegetation Four important types of rangeland plants are grasses; grasslike plants (sedges and rushes) with fibrous root systems; forbs; and shrubs usually with a single taproot. Most of the world's grasslands are in areas with semiarid climates, where there's too little rain to support forests and most crops. Grasses and woody shrubs can grow

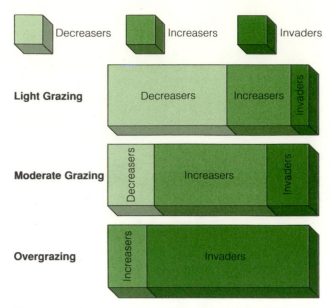

Figure 13-2 Effects of grazing on three major types of grassland plants.

U.S. Department of Agriculture

Figure 13-3 Invasion of severely grazed rangeland in Cotulla, Texas, by prickly cactus and brush.

and reproduce in the short wet season of semiarid areas. The dry climate also increases the likelihood of fires set by lightning or people. These periodic fires prevent trees from dominating these ecosystems.

The amount of grass on rangeland in semiarid areas varies annually and seasonally. Most of the grasses are perennials, which continue to live from year to year. They have deep, complex root systems, known as fibrous root systems. Many grasses cover large areas by putting out runners that form new root systems.

The multiple branches of their roots make these grasses hard to uproot, helping prevent soil erosion. The complex root systems mean that most of the biomass of range grass is underground. By contrast, many rangeland forbs and woody shrubs have a single taproot, which makes them easier to uproot.

When the leaf tip of most plants is eaten, the leaf stops growing. But each leaf of rangeland grass grows from its base, not its tip. When the upper half of the shoot and leaves of grass is eaten, the plant can grow back quickly. However, the lower half of the plant, known as the **metabolic reserve,** must remain if the plant is to survive and grow new leaves. As long as only the upper half is eaten, rangeland grass is a renewable resource that can be grazed again and again.

Range plants vary in their ability to survive and reproduce when heavily grazed. Some species can survive trampling by hoofed animals, while others can't. Grazing intensity depends not only on the number of herbivores but also on how long grazing animals feed in an area.

Rangeland ecologists and managers classify plants in particular range areas as decreasers, increasers, and invaders according to their response to grazing (Figure 13-2). Although this classification applies to graz-

ing by wild herbivores, it's usually used to describe the effects of grazing by domesticated livestock on rangeland plants.

Grass species that are easily depleted even when moderately grazed are called **decreasers.** They're usually the plants grazing animals prefer. Some are also easily killed by trampling. Plant species present before grazing that increase in numbers under heavy grazing are called **increasers.** Some thrive because they are not appetizing to grazing animals. Others flourish because they can get more of the available water and soil nutrients once decreasers have been eaten. Plants that infest severely overgrazed or undergrazed land, such as prickly cactus, are called **invaders** (Figure 13-3). This classification isn't rigid. For example, mesquite is an increaser in some rangelands in the American Southwest and an invader in others that have been heavily grazed.

Types of Grazing Animals You and most other animals can't digest rangeland grasses and shrubs. But grazing and browsing animals can. These **ruminant animals** have a three- or four-chambered stomach that digests the cellulose in the vegetation. Their bodies convert this carbohydrate into protein-rich meat and milk that other animals and most people can digest. This simple food chain, grass → grazing animals → humans, is an important source of the protein we need. Ruminant animals are also a major source of the greenhouse gas methane (Figure 7-25, p. 172). Nonruminant livestock animals, such as pigs and chickens, can't feed on rangeland vegetation.

Herbivores have three general types of grazing styles. Nibblers (like many small African antelope such as duiker and steenbox) have narrow mouths and feed by nipping off a leaf here or there on a plant. Most nibblers do not feed in herds and control their population by some form of breeding inhibition that occurs because of population stress when numbers rise above certain densities. Nibblers generally do not overgraze.

A second type of grazer has a broad mouth and feeds by the mouthful: bison, cattle, horses, zebras, elephants, and hippos. Most of these animals feed in herds. Unlike nibblers, their populations are not self-regulating. Instead, population size is regulated by predation and accidents and by parasitism, disease, and starvation if predation is inadequate. They tend to defoliate plants severely. If these animals remain in an area long enough to bite a plant twice before the plant has had time to recover from the first bite, overgrazing occurs.

Between these two groups are grazing animals who nip several leaves at a time: sheep, goats, deer, pronghorn, impala, and other herding antelope. Like mouthful eaters, they usually feed in herds, do not self-regulate their population size, and can overgraze if they remain in an area too long.

Browsers, which include giraffe, buffalo, elephants, and goats, feed on woody plants and forbs in open grasslands and on trees in savanna and some forests. Note that some animals such as elephants and goats are both grazers and browsers. Goats, for example, are highly destructive. Besides feeding on a variety of ground vegetation, they can jump into trees and browse on branches and foliage. Large populations of goats can kill trees and strip rangeland of most other types of vegetation.

Ecological Stability Grasslands have a remarkable ability to survive and regenerate as long as they're not severely overgrazed, undergrazed, or plowed up and planted with crops. Periodic fire is one factor that helps keep grasslands intact. The other key factor is grazing by a large number and variety of wild animals.

Sometimes fires set by lightning sweep through arid grasslands and burn off the grass and shrubs. However, the roots of the grasses and other plants lie safely below the surface. This allows the plants to spring up during the next growing season, with their growth fertilized by minerals in the ashes of the burned vegetation.

Then migrating herds of wild grazing animals come. Each species grazes on certain types or on chosen parts of plants. This selective feeding and the movement of the animals from one area to another help prevent overgrazing. Their wastes also fertilize the soil. Below the surface, rodents, rabbits, and other burrowing animals turn over and fertilize the soil. The vast underground network of grass roots helps keep the soil from blowing or washing away. Any natural or human-caused changes in the types and numbers of grazing animals can have widespread effects (see Case Study below).

Rangeland Carrying Capacity Each type of grassland has a limited herbivore **carrying capacity**—the maximum number of herbivores a given area can support without consuming the metabolic reserve needed for grass renewal. Carrying capacity is influenced by season of the year, range condition, annual climatic

---

CASE STUDY Changes in the Serengeti Savanna

Savanna ecosystems are easily disrupted. The Serengeti National Park in Tanzania is a 5,000-square-mile savanna ecosystem, about the size of Connecticut. Since the late 1800s it's had several major ecological upsets.

In the 1880s an epidemic of rinderpest swept through the Serengeti plains. This infectious disease killed huge numbers of wild grazing animals and domesticated cattle. Thousands of animals that had preyed on the wild grazing animals starved to death. Hungry lions began attacking humans. Large areas of grassland were replaced by dense woody shrubs and some trees.

After 50 years the rinderpest was finally eliminated, setting in

motion a new series of ecological changes. With the rinderpest gone, the population of wildebeests exploded and trampled moist grasses in wooded areas. This destroyed a major source of food for buffalo, and their numbers fell sharply.

On the plains the wildebeests ate huge quantities of grass, thus encouraging the growth of herbs favored by Grant's gazelles. Their numbers rose sharply and led to an increase in cheetahs, which feed on the gazelles. The increase in wildebeests also created soil conditions that allowed acacia trees to grow. Giraffes, which browse on acacia vegetation, were then able to grow in numbers.

Savanna vegetation can be overgrazed at the height of the dry season by excessive populations of elephants, antelopes, and other large herbivores. Hunting and livestock grazing have forced large numbers of elephants and other large herbivores into small protected areas such as the Serengeti National Park. Then vegetation is grazed longer and more intensely than it would be if grazing animals had more freedom of movement.

During prolonged dry seasons, when forage is scarce, elephants can fell trees. They also kill trees by eating their bark. Everything is connected to everything in ecosystems, often in ways that we can't predict.

Table 13-1 Percent Utilization of Rangeland Vegetation by Various Livestock Animals

Vegetation	Percent Utilization			
	Cattle	Sheep	Goats	Horses
Grasses	60	30	30	80
Forbs	20	40	30	10
Browse	20	30	40	10

USDA/Soil Conservation Service

Figure 13-4 Lightly grazed (left) and severely overgrazed rangeland.

conditions, past grazing use, soil type, kinds of grazing animals (Table 13-1), and how long animals graze in an area.

Rangeland carrying capacity is sometimes expressed as the quantity of herbivore biomass that can be supported per area of rangeland. Rangeland carrying capacity can be exceeded if the vegetation is removed by too many wild or domesticated herbivores feeding too long in a particular area. Grazing intensity is often expressed in an **animal unit equivalent**, a measure of how much vegetation each type of animal eats during a certain time, usually a month. An **animal unit month**, the standardized measure, is the amount of forage needed to feed a 1,000-pound animal for a month. The following are the accepted animal unit equivalents:

1 steer = 1.0 animal unit month
5 sheep = 1.0 animal unit month
5 goats = 1.0 animal unit month
4 deer = 1.0 animal unit month
1 horse = 1.25 animal unit month
1 bull = 1.25 animal unit month
1 elk = 0.67 animal unit month

This means that five sheep or five goats eat as much as one steer; a 1,000-pound horse eats 25% more than a 1,000-pound steer.

One way to avoid exceeding the carrying capacity of a range is to graze animals at the time of year when the range can be grazed without harming the growth and development of important forage plants. This is called the concept of *range readiness*.

Effects of Human Activities on Grassland Stability and Diversity

Human activities can disrupt the ecological stability of grasslands and decrease the diversity of plant and animal species they contain. When people plow up natural grasslands and plant them with crops, they destroy these diverse ecosystems. They replace the grasses with plants whose roots are less effective in holding the soil in place. Instead of being naturally fertilized by wild grazing animals, croplands must be fertilized by livestock wastes or commercial fertilizers. The Dust Bowl in the Great Plains is a tragic example of what can happen when dry grasslands are plowed up and planted with crops without effective soil conservation (see Case Study on p. 227).

Light to moderate grazing is necessary for the health of grasslands: It maintains grass root vigor. By not exposing the soil, normal grazing maintains water and nutrient cycling needed for healthy grass growth, hinders soil erosion, and encourages buildup of organic soil matter. Such grazing also increases energy flow by promoting vigorous leaf growth and healthier root systems, which support microorganisms and other underground soil life. Remove too many grazers from natural grasslands, and the grasses are replaced by forbs and woody shrub species (Figure 13-3). Increase grazers too much, and the grassland turns into desert.

Overgrazing occurs when too many grazing animals feed too long and exceed the carrying capacity of a grassland area. Large populations of wild herbivores can overgraze range in prolonged dry periods. But most overgrazing is caused by excessive numbers of livestock feeding too long in a particular area.

Overgrazing changes ecological succession by shifting from fibrous-root grasses to tap-root woody plants and forbs. It reduces water and nutrient cycling by exposing soil, reducing litter production, and decreasing soil porosity and organic content. Overgrazing also cuts energy flow by reducing leaf growth, root health, and exposure of the soil to the atmosphere.

Rangeland owned by Navajo Native Americans in Arizona and New Mexico has been severely overgrazed. This resource degradation is caused by a large number of poor people trying to survive on a 15-million acre reservation with poor-quality rangeland.

Since 1900 the land the Navajo people live on has tripled in size, but their population size has increased tenfold. The Navajo's sheep population is at least 1.5 million. These animals graze on reservation land with an estimated carrying capacity of only 600,000 sheep. The result is severe overgrazing.

Poverty and 60% unemployment are factors pushing the Navajo to keep grazing large herds on these marginal lands. Sheep and cattle are the main source of income for many Navajo, so reducing their herds would threaten their survival.

On the other hand, continuing to exceed the range's carrying capacity will lead to long-term disaster. If severe overgrazing continues, little vegetation will be left. Livestock will starve and herds will be reduced. Then the Navajo will be even poorer. What do you think should be done?

Figure 13-4 compares normally grazed and *severely overgrazed* grassland. Heavy overgrazing converts continuous grass cover to patches of grass and makes the soil more vulnerable to erosion, especially by wind. Then forbs and woody shrubs, such as mesquite and prickly cactus (Figure 13-3) invade and take over.

Sometimes overgrazing is so severe that all vegetation disappears, leaving the land barren and highly vulnerable to erosion. Severe overgrazing combined with prolonged drought can convert potentially productive rangeland to desert (see Case Study on p. 225).

Undergrazing can also damage rangeland as a source of food for livestock and many wild herbivores. Undergrazing leaves much leaf and stem to become old. This chokes off grass growth and shifts succession from grasses to woody plants and forbs. Undergrazing or excessive plant rest, like overgrazing, leads to reduced nutrient and water cycling and increased soil erosion and degradation. It also causes grasshopper outbreaks.

Dune buggies, motorcycles, and other off-road vehicles also degrade vegetation on rangeland and other types of land. Sometimes political, economic, or cultural factors play an important role in rangeland degradation (see the Case Study above).

13-2 EXTENT AND USE OF RANGELANDS

The World's Rangeland Resources Almost half of the earth's ice-free land is rangeland. Most of these grasslands are in semiarid areas too dry for rainfed cropland. About half are in LDCs. Most of these lands aren't natural grasslands. Many were created when people cleared or burned forests.

We have no comprehensive survey of the world's grasslands, despite their importance. Part of the problem is the overlapping definitions of range, grassland, pasture, and other types of land that produce forage. The distribution of grasslands, shrub lands, and open forests sometimes classified as rangeland is uneven (Figure 13-5).

Only about 42% of the world's rangeland is used for grazing livestock. With proper management, some of the remaining 58% of this land could be used for livestock. Much of it, however, is too dry, cold, or remote from population centers to be grazed by large numbers of livestock animals.

Range Livestock Production Worldwide, there are about 10 billion ruminant and nonruminant domesticated animals—twice the number of people on earth. About 3 billion of these animals are cattle, sheep, goats, buffalo, and other ruminants (Figure 13-6). Three-fourths of these ruminants forage on rangeland vegetation. The rest are fed mostly in feedlots (Figure 11-2, p. 275). Seven billion pigs, chickens, and other nonruminant livestock animals feed mostly on cereal grains grown on cropland.

Worldwide, more than 200 million people use rangelands for some form of livestock (pastoral) production. At least 30 million nomadic and pastoral people are wholly dependent on livestock grazing on rangelands. Most of these people live in LDCs in Africa (55%) and Asia (29%).

The United States, with less than 5% of the world's people, has 9% of the world's 1.2 billion cattle. Some meat-exporting countries, such as Australia and Argentina, have more cattle than people. The global investment in livestock is more than $400 billion.

Livestock graze on one-third of the land in North America. More than half of U.S. croplands are planted with livestock feed. Most of this is eaten by cattle reared in feedlots (Figure 11-2, p. 275) for several weeks before they're slaughtered. Livestock production also uses more than half of the water consumed in the United States. It takes 5 pounds of grain and 2,500 pounds of water to produce 1 pound of meat on a steer fattened in a feedlot.

Cattle, Sheep, and Goats Cattle are the most numerous domesticated range animals. They supply beef,

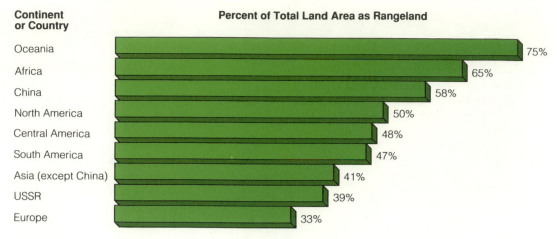

Figure 13-5 Distribution of the world's rangelands. (Data from UN Food and Agriculture Organization)

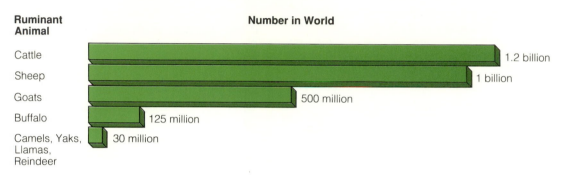

Figure 13-6 Major types of livestock feeding on rangeland. (Data from UN Food and Agriculture Organization)

veal, milk, butter, cheese, and leather. In the meat packinghouse, cattle provide hormones and vitamin extracts, bone meal for feed and fertilizer, and high-protein concentrates for livestock feeding.

The five countries with the largest number of cattle are, in order, India, Brazil, the Soviet Union, the United States, and China. Grasslands in India support 16% of the world's cattle. However, most people of India consider cattle sacred. Thus, instead of being slaughtered for food, cattle provide milk, cheese, manure and other animal products.

Sheep are the world's second most numerous livestock animals. In order, the five countries with the most sheep are the Soviet Union, Australia, New Zealand, Turkey, and India. The United States ranks thirteenth. Sheep raising is especially important in parts of the world where conditions are too harsh for cattle or where people cannot afford to raise cattle. Meat provides about 78% of the total income from sheep, with the rest coming from the sale of wool and hides.

Goats are the world's third most numerous livestock animals. About 85% of the income of the goat industry comes from the sale of mohair cut from angora goats. Of the world's estimated 500 million goats, about 2.5 million are in the United States.

Condition of the World's Rangelands An estimate of how close a particular rangeland is to its productive potential is called **range condition**. The estimate evaluates the site's soil, rainfall, evaporation, transpiration, and other characteristics. Range condition is usually classified in the following manner:

- *Excellent:* Range has more than 75% of its native plant species, and forage production is more than 80% of its potential.

- *Good:* Range has 50% to 75% of its native plant species, and forage production is 50% to 80% of its potential.

- *Fair:* Range has 26% to 74% of its native plant species, and forage production is 21% to 49% of its potential.

- *Poor:* Range has no more than 25% of its native plant species, and its rate of forage production is no more than 20% of its potential.

Except in North America, there's been no comprehensive survey of rangeland conditions. However, data from surveys in various countries indicate that most of the world's rangelands have been degraded to some degree (see Spotlight on p. 347).

North America

Since 1936, evaluations of public and private rangelands in the United States have shown that general range conditions have improved. For example, public rangeland in excellent and good condition increased from 16% to 36% between 1936 and 1986 (Figure 13-7). During the same period, public rangeland in fair and poor condition decreased from 84% to 64%, with 20% in poor condition. Privately owned rangeland showed similar improvements. Despite this improvement, there's a long way to go with almost two-thirds of the country's rangeland in poor and fair condition. Partial surveys indicate that Canada's rangelands have followed a similar pattern of gradual improvement.

South America

No detailed evaluation has been made of this continent's rangelands. However, partial surveys show that many rangelands in Argentina, Brazil, Uruguay, and Paraguay have been degraded from overstocking. Rangeland in Mexico has followed a pattern of abuse with gradual improvement.

Europe

About 33% of Europe's land area is rangeland, 18% classified as permanent pasture. These lands receive adequate rainfall and are intensively managed like cropland. Most of the continent's rangelands are in excellent or good condition and are among the most productive in the world.

Australia

The history of range use in Australia is similar to that of the United States (Figure 13-7). About three-fourths of the country's rangelands are in regions with an arid climate. This makes them particularly vulnerable to overgrazing and wind erosion during periods of prolonged drought. Some areas have been overgrazed by wild rabbits, camels, horses, and water buffalo. In recent decades the general condition of the country's rangelands has improved.

Africa

About 65% of Africa's total land area is rangeland. Most is in the arid Sahel region near the Sahara desert of West Africa and in the countries bordering the semiarid areas of east and southern Africa (see map inside back cover). Overgrazing and decreased forage production have occurred in the north African countries of Algeria, Egypt, Libya, Morocco, and Tunisia. Desertification is increasing in Morocco. Large areas of rangeland in Zambia and Zimbabwe are severely overgrazed. In Zambia, livestock numbers are ten times higher than the carrying capacity of its rangeland. Range is rapidly deteriorating and desertification is increasing in Sudan, Africa's largest country in area. The nine countries in the Sahel region of West Africa report severe overgrazing and an increase in desertification. In these countries livestock numbers exceed rangeland carrying capacity by 50% to 100%.

India

Much of the rangeland is degraded or overgrazed. However, for many years India has had a rangeland improvement program through transferring land to private ownership, applying fertilizers, and introducing improved forage plants.

Middle East

Range is a large percentage of the land area in these west Asian countries. Most of these lands are in areas with arid climates, rough terrain, and barren soils. Many people make their living from nomadic herding of livestock. After being grazed continuously for centuries, rangelands are in poor condition—particularly in parts of Iraq, Syria, Jordan, Iran, Oman, and Pakistan.

China

About 58% of China's land area is rangeland and pasture. During the past 50 years about one fourth of this land has been severely degraded, mostly because of population increase and unsound land use. In northern China much of the rangeland is overgrazed, while in southern China much of the rangeland is undergrazed.

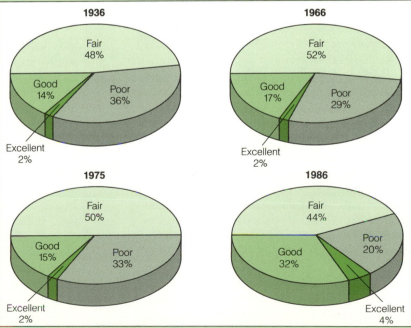

Figure 13-7 Quality of public rangeland in the United States, 1936–1986. (Data from U.S. Bureau of Land Management and U.S. Forest Service)

Figure 13-8 Black-tailed prairie dog at its burrow entrance. Once found in large numbers on western rangeland, these rodents usually live in "towns" containing several hundred individuals. Their underground passages aerate grassland soils and their droppings add fertilizer to the soil. Sometimes cattle and horses trip on prairie dog burrow mounds and break their legs. For this reason, livestock ranchers have used poisons to eliminate prairie dogs from most rangeland in the western United States. This has upset the ecological balance in these ecosystems by eliminating the black-footed ferret (now almost extinct), prairie falcon, and burrowing owl, all of which fed on prairie dogs.

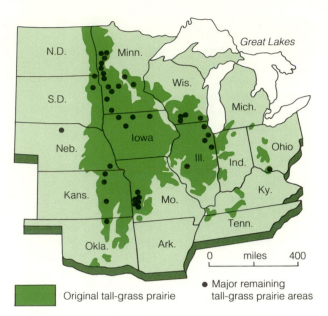

Figure 13-9 Only about 1% of the original tall-grass prairie in the United States is left. (Data from U.S. Departments of Agriculture and the Interior)

13-3 RANGELAND RESOURCES IN THE UNITED STATES

Brief History of Range Use in the United States

Before European settlers arrived in North America, American bison, pronghorn antelope, and other wild herbivores roamed the vast ranges of the continent at will. Their selective grazing and migration patterns helped prevent overgrazing. Predation and competition within and between species helped adjust the numbers of wild ruminants to the carrying capacity of the land. Vast numbers of rodents, such as prairie dogs, fed on the abundant grasses (Figure 13-8).

As settlers began grazing livestock, the relationship between grazing animals and the vegetation base changed drastically. Many wild herbivores were killed or driven from rangelands to reduce their competition with livestock. For example, between 1500 and 1906 the wild American bison was eliminated from most of its vast range and nearly driven to extinction (Figure 2-7, p. 34).

Natural predators that preyed on livestock were also destroyed or driven out. Prairie dogs had to go because they competed with livestock for grass and because their burrows sometimes made cattle and

horses stumble and break their legs. This prolific rodent once was found from the U.S.-Canadian border to northern Mexico. Today only a few isolated populations are left.

Before European settlers came, vast tall-grass and short-grass prairies stretched across the midwest. Today only 1% of the original tall-grass prairie is left, mostly in small patches (Figure 13-9). The rest has been destroyed and replaced with cropland, roads, towns, and cities. Much of the short-grass prairie remains as rangeland in the west and southwest.

The North American range livestock industry had its beginnings in the early 1500s, when Spaniards introduced horses, cattle, sheep, and burros into the southwestern United States. Cattle were important economically because they supplied hides and tallow. Meat production was important only locally because there was no way to preserve it and ship it to population centers.

After the Civil War ended in 1865 and railroads spanned the continent in 1869, cattle and sheep populations in the southwestern prairies expanded rapidly. Between 1870 and 1890 the cattle population rose from 5 million to almost 27 million. Although hides were still important, emphasis shifted to raising cattle for their meat. Between 1850 and 1890 the estimated sheep population in the western U.S. rose from half a million to over 20 million.

In their rush to get rich by selling beef and wool, cattle barons and sheep ranchers ruthlessly took over and overstocked much of the rangeland. The land they claimed wasn't legally theirs, but no one was responsible for settling competing claims for land and water supplies and for seeing that these common property resources weren't overgrazed.

In 1873 an effective type of barbed wire was developed. This allowed farmers ("sod busters") to build fences to keep cattle from trampling their crops. Angry livestock ranchers, used to doing what they pleased on the western range, cut and pulled down the fences. Many farmers who fought against the ranchers were killed or driven from their land. Ranchers and farmers also fought and killed one another over access to limited water.

By 1900 many rangelands had been heavily grazed by cattle, sheep, and horses for more than 50 years. Farmers also degraded rangeland by plowing areas too dry to grow crops without irrigation. After they abandoned these farms, the grass that once prevented soil erosion grew back too slowly to prevent severe erosion.

The condition of some public rangelands improved after 1905, when the U.S. Forest Service was created. This agency tried to control livestock grazing on lands in the national forests.

Severe abuse from uncontrolled grazing on other public rangelands continued until 1934, when Congress passed the Taylor Grazing Act. This law established the Grazing Service and led to the first detailed evaluation of the condition of public rangelands in the western United States. This survey, finished in 1936, confirmed that many of these rangelands had been damaged because of poor management. About 84% were in only fair or poor condition (Figure 13-7). The Taylor Act also organized public rangelands into grazing districts to be managed jointly by the Grazing Service and local stock raisers.

But enforcement of this law was hindered by political opposition from western ranchers. Proponents of states rights also fought to have the law repealed or weakened. Although all Americans jointly own public rangelands, these people felt that rangelands should be under the control of state governments. As a result, many ranchers with grazing permits continued to misuse and abuse public rangelands, and 81% of these lands were in only fair or poor condition in 1966 (Figure 13-7).

In 1976 the situation began to change when Congress passed the Federal Land Policy and Management Act. This law gave the Bureau of Land Management (BLM) authority to manage all public rangelands not in national forests or national parks. The BLM is required to prevent overgrazing and to ensure that damaged lands recover.

During the late 1970s stricter government control of public rangelands prompted western ranchers and others wanting more access to energy and mineral resources on these lands to launch a political campaign known as the sagebrush rebellion. Its first goal was to remove most western public lands from public ownership and return them to the states. Then, supporters of this movement hoped to influence state legislatures to transfer much of this land from state to private ownership.

This cause was helped in 1981, when President Ronald Reagan, a declared sagebrush rebel, placed Robert Burford, a sagebrush rebel and rancher with a public grazing permit, in charge of the BLM. Burford's changes in grazing regulations and policies, staffing, and budget priorities increased the livestock industry's influence on the use of public rangeland, despite strong objections by conservationists.

Distribution, Ownership, and Use About 29% of the total land area of the United States is rangeland. Most of this is short-grass prairies in the arid and semiarid western half of the country (Figure 13-10). Crops can't be grown on most of this rangeland because of a lack of moisture, high evaporation and transpiration, topography, severe temperatures, and poor soils.

Today rangeland grazing plays a small but important role in U.S. cattle and sheep production. Most beef production involves raising calves to maturity on western rangeland or on planted pastureland. Then the animals are shipped to feedlots (Figure 11-2, p. 275) where they're fed grain and protein-rich feed to fatten them for slaughter. Three-fourths of the country's public and privately owned rangeland is grazed by livestock at some time during each year. However, range vegetation supplies only about 16% of the food these animals eat during their lifetime.

About two-thirds of the rangeland in the United States is privately owned. Governments place few limits on how private owners manage their lands. Exceptions are local zoning ordinances and laws regulating pollution from pesticides and livestock wastes.

The remaining one-third of U.S. rangeland is owned by the general public and managed by the federal government, mostly by the Forest Service and the Bureau of Land Management. Some 96% of BLM lands outside Alaska are classified as rangeland. Most of this public rangeland is in the country's 17 western states.

Government agencies are required by law to manage public rangelands according to the principle of multiple use. Thus, besides grazing, these lands are used for mining, energy resource development, watershed protection, soil conservation, wildlife conservation, and recreation.

The Bureau of Land Management and the Forest Service issue permits allowing about 2% of the country's private ranchers (7% of those in the West) to graze their herds on public range. For years ranchers and conservationists have battled over how much ranchers should be charged for the privilege of grazing their livestock on public lands (see Pro/Con on p. 351).

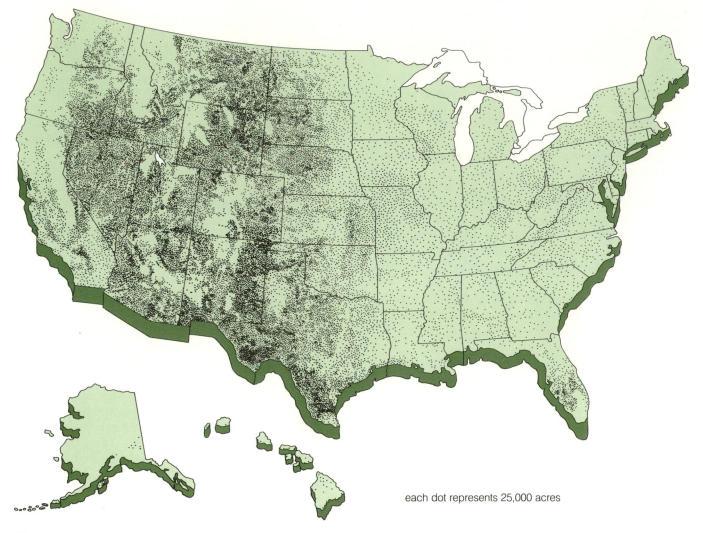

each dot represents 25,000 acres

Figure 13-10 Rangelands in the United States. (Source: Council on Environmental Quality)

13-4 RANGELAND MANAGEMENT

Objectives of Range Management Range management is an interdisciplinary field. It can be viewed as a form of applied ecology using inputs from soil science, agronomy, animal and wildlife sciences, hydrology, economics, politics, and other related disciplines.

The major goal of range management is to maximize livestock productivity without degrading grassland quality. The first step in sound management is to determine the carrying capacity of each area of range. This estimate is then used to control the number and kind of animals grazing on the land so that it's not overgrazed. Stock must be distributed over the land and rotated from one area to another to prevent overgrazing.

Other aspects of range management include suppressing growth of undesirable vegetation, encouraging growth of desirable vegetation, and fertilizing and reseeding severely depleted rangeland. Several

scientists have been able to restore virgin prairie. Controlling populations of wild herbivores that compete with livestock for vegetation and controlling populations of livestock predators are also parts of many range management programs. Experiments in raising wild herbivores as sources of meat have been encouraging.

Controlling the Number and Kind of Grazing Animals The most widely used way to prevent overgrazing is to control the **stocking rate,** the number of a particular kind of animal grazing on a given area, so that it doesn't exceed the carrying capacity. But determining the carrying capacity of a range site is difficult. It requires detailed knowledge of the plant species, the wild herbivores, and the wild carnivores found there. Knowledge of local ecological succession is necessary for predicting how plant species will respond to grazing and what invaders may appear. Information on climate, soil type, and slope is also necessary.

Most ranchers are unwilling to pay for the detailed

studies needed to determine range carrying capacity. Even when carrying capacity is known, it can change due to drought, invasions by new species, and other environmental factors.

On arid and semiarid ranges livestock operators must be prepared for periods of drought lasting for several months to several years. During a drought the stocking rate should be reduced, or livestock should be given supplements of hay or other forage to prevent overgrazing. Feed supplements, however, are costly and can't be used very long as a substitute for range forage. With less food, livestock weigh less and bring less money when sold. So instead of selling them, ranchers often keep excessive numbers of livestock on a range, hoping that the next year will bring more rainfall and higher meat prices.

Grazing Systems Designing a grazing system that supports high levels of livestock production while protecting or improving vegetation resources is the key to successful range management. Grazing management systems have two common features: **(1)** a period of rest that allows range forage plants to grow without being grazed and **(2)** a schedule of systematic grazing on different parts of the range. The objectives of a grazing system are to:

- allow plants to produce seed
- obtain more uniform range utilization
- restore forage plant vigor
- prevent invasion by shrub and woody species
- increase livestock production

PRO/CON Grazing Fees on Public Rangeland

Over 26,000 ranchers lease rights to graze on public range from the BLM and pay a grazing fee for this privilege. In 1981 the Reagan administration set grazing fees at $1.35 per animal unit month (the amount of forage it takes to feed one livestock animal in one month). This fee has been maintained despite the fact that a 1986 study by the Forest Service and the BLM appraised the average market value of federal grazing lands at $6.35 per animal unit month. Fees owners charge for grazing on private grazing land are also much higher, ranging from $4 to $12 per animal unit month.

This means that U.S. taxpayers give the small percentage of ranchers with federal grazing permits subsidies amounting to about $75 million a year—the difference between the fees collected and the actual value of grazing on this land. Each year the government also spends hundreds of millions of tax dollars to maintain these public rangelands. Present grazing fees don't come close to covering these costs, with the government collecting only about $1 from ranchers for every $10 spent on range management.

Conservationists argue that the present system of fees does not give the public a fair return on its

land and thus violates the Federal Land Policy and Management Act. Low fees also encourage overgrazing and degradation. Conservationists call for the fees to be raised to the $6.35 per animal unit month found by the BLM and the Forest Service to be a fair market value for use of this land. Higher fees would also provide more money for improvement of range condition, wildlife conservation, and watershed management.

Conservationists contend that any rancher with a permit who can't stay in business without government subsidies shouldn't be in the ranching business. The 98% of the country's ranchers without federal permits have to survive without such subsidies. Earl Sandvig, formerly administrator of the grazing program for the Forest Service, has suggested that grazing rights be sold by competitive bidding, as is the case with timber cutting rights in national forests.

Ranchers with permits fiercely oppose higher grazing fees and competitive bidding. Grazing rights on public land raise the value of their livestock animals by $1,000 to $1,500 per head. This means that a permit to graze 500 cattle on public land can be worth $500,000 to $750,000 a year to the rancher. The economic value of a

permit is considered a rancher's private property. It's included in the overall worth of the ranches and can be used as collateral for a loan.

Ranchers contend that overgrazing on public rangeland is also caused by increasing numbers of elk and other grazing wildlife. The government is forcing ranchers to reduce overgrazing but is not requiring game and fish departments to reduce excessive wildlife numbers.

Most ranchers who can't get a grazing permit favor open bidding for grazing rights on public land. They believe that the permit system gives politically influential ranchers an unfair economic advantage at the expense of taxpayers.

Some conservationists believe that all commercial grazing of livestock on all or most public lands should be banned. As a minimum, they call for grazing bans on the 64% of public range judged to be in poor or fair condition until that land has recovered. Since only about 4% of the country's livestock graze on public range, such a ban wouldn't have a significant effect on overall livestock production. What do you think should be done?

Continuous grazing is year-long or season-long grazing on a given area. It's used in many range areas with favorable climatic conditions, especially in the southwestern United States. This method is popular because it's easy to manage and it reduces costs by requiring little livestock handling and fencing. It can be used successfully if stocking rates are properly adjusted to forage availability and animals are free to move so that they don't stay in an area too long.

But continuous grazing has several disadvantages. First, when livestock are left to their own ways, they tend to overgraze flat areas and areas near water supplies. Second, livestock tend to overgraze desirable species of forage grass, prompting invasion by less desirable forms of vegetation. Continuous grazing also tends to produce a mosaic of overgrazed and undergrazed patches in an area. For these reasons, continuous grazing is usually the least desirable system.

A common grazing system is **deferred-rotation grazing**, which involves moving livestock between two or more range areas (Figure 13-11). This allows perennial grasses to recover from the effects of grazing. Although this method requires closer management than continuous grazing, it's usually a better way to protect and improve range quality. A more recent system, receiving considerable attention is *holistic grazing management*, also known as the *Savory Grazing Method* (see Case Study below).

CASE STUDY Holistic Rangeland Management

Holistic rangeland management is an ecological approach to sustaining rangeland and livestock productivity. It is based on understanding how grazing affects ecological succession, chemical or nutrient cycling, water cycling, and energy flow in a particular area of rangeland. This approach is based on research and practical range management experience by André Vosin and Allan Savoy.

It begins with the observation that overgrazing occurs when a plant is bitten severely in the growing season and then gets severely bitten again before it recovers from the first bite. This happens when the plant is exposed to grazing animals too long or when they move to another area but return before the plant has been able to recover from the first bite.

The normal approach to preventing overgrazing is to control the number of animals grazing an area. Holistic range management questions this approach. Research and experience by Vosin and Savoy shows that overgrazing is not caused primarily by the number of animals grazing an area but by the length of time the animals graze an area. If animals move or are moved before plants are bitten twice, overgrazing doesn't occur. Using larger stocking rates and keeping animals moving also prevents the undergrazing that occurs with low stocking rates.

A holistic grazing system involves confining fairly large numbers of grazing animals in small paddocks or cells and allowing them to graze for a short time before being moved to another paddock (Figure 13-12). This prevents most grass from being bitten twice during the growing season and allows the grass time to rest and recover after being bitten once. Grazing times are so short that holistic range managers must use animal unit days rather than animal unit months to control stocking rates and rotation times. Paddocks can also be set up in wedges instead of rectangles (Figure 13-13).

Rotation times for movement from one paddock to another are not as rigid as in other grazing systems. Instead, they are based on observation of the condition of the types of grasses favored by the type of livestock being managed. To move herds, holistic managers often use whistles instead of more expensive wranglers on horseback or helicopters.

Holistic range management also sharply reduces the use of fire to control range vegetation. Fire exposes the soil and invigorates growth of many woody plants instead of grasses.

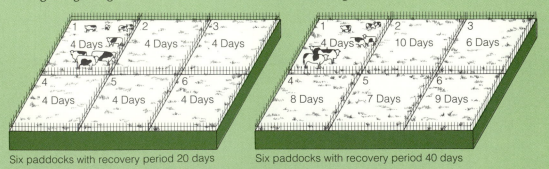

Six paddocks with recovery period 20 days   Six paddocks with recovery period 40 days

Figure 13-12   Schedule for holistic management of a herd of livestock in six paddocks to give two different recovery periods. (Data from Savoy, Allan. 1988. *Holistic Resource Management*, Covelo, Calif.: Island Press)

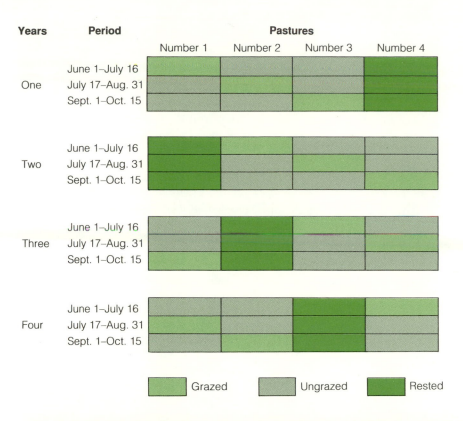

Years	Period	Pastures			
		Number 1	Number 2	Number 3	Number 4
One	June 1–July 16				
	July 17–Aug. 31				
	Sept. 1–Oct. 15				
Two	June 1–July 16				
	July 17–Aug. 31				
	Sept. 1–Oct. 15				
Three	June 1–July 16				
	July 17–Aug. 31				
	Sept. 1–Oct. 15				
Four	June 1–July 16				
	July 17–Aug. 31				
	Sept. 1–Oct. 15				

Grazed   Ungrazed   Rested

Figure 13-11 Schedule for a one-herd, four-pasture, four-year deferred-rotational grazing system on a range in Wyoming managed by the U. S. Forest Service.

Most grazing systems assume that trampling by livestock damages both plants and soils. Prolonged and repeated trampling does do this. But holistic management recognizes that periodic, short-term trampling by a large number of animals can be beneficial. It can be used to:

■ remove dead material in undergrazed areas and shift succession toward grasses instead of woody plants and forbs

■ create a firebreak through almost any type of country without causing soil erosion by spraying a strip of vegetation with a very dilute molasses or salt solution, thus avoiding the use of herbicides or machinery

■ restore land with severe gully erosion by disturbing the soil enough to create conditions for growth of soil-stabilizing plants through natural succession

■ remove thick brush that clogs

grassland, disturbing the soil enough to allow grasses to flourish

■ break the hard soil on overgrazed desert land so that plants can become established

The key is to control the time factor. A high trampling impact for a short time can be beneficial. Periodic short-term trampling from high animal impact promotes growth of grasses on bare eroding land and prevents a shift from grasses to woody plants and forbs on grassland. It also usually improves water and nutrient cycling and energy flow.

Larger herds can also be maintained with holistic management. High density use of a grassland for a short period also gives a more even distribution of animal dung, reducing or eliminating the need to apply expensive commercial inorganic fertilizers to maintain range grasses.

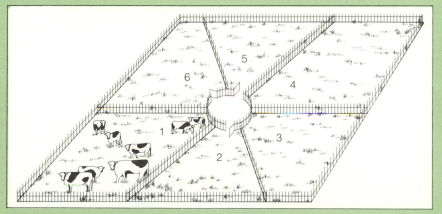

Figure 13-13 Holistic grazing paddocks can also be arranged in wedges. Herds can be driven into a central holding pen and then moved to another paddock.

Figure 13-14 Livestock on this ranch in Cherry County, Nebraska, tend to congregate and overgraze around water sources unless they're moved to other areas of a range.

USDA/Soil Conservation Service

Controlling Distribution of Grazing Animals Moving livestock from place to place is a way to prevent overgrazing and to allow overgrazed areas to recover. Sheep, for example, crop grass very close to the ground. If not kept moving, they can uproot grass and disturb the soil surface with their sharp hooves. To prevent such damage, shepherds and sheepdogs must accompany the herds.

Cattle don't need such close supervision. Herds are usually moved from one fenced area to another on a rotating schedule (Figures 13-11 and 13-12). On unfenced range, cattle herds must be watched more closely and moved as needed to protect vegetation.

Placing water holes and salt blocks in strategic places is an effective way to distribute livestock over rangeland (Figure 13-14). Livestock need both salt and water, but not together. If salt blocks are placed in ungrazed areas away from water sources, livestock are forced to spend some time in these areas. However, some methods used to supply water for livestock have had harmful ecological effects (see Spotlight above). Another way to distribute livestock over a range is to supply supplemental feed at various sites.

Controlling Vegetation People often manipulate range vegetation to suppress the growth of unwanted plants while encouraging wanted plants. Methods used to control weeds and woody vegetation on rangeland include spraying with herbicides, biological control (see Enrichment Study near the end of Chapter 11) controlled burning, and short-term trampling by livestock herds. Care must be taken that methods for controlling unwanted vegetation don't destroy desirable forage plants.

In the southwestern United States inedible woody plants such as sagebrush, mesquite, and tumbleweed

SPOTLIGHT Tube Wells, Overgrazing, and Desertification

In many of the world's arid regions, bore holes have been drilled to provide water for livestock and irrigation. Unfortunately, the widespread use of these tube wells to fill water holes can contribute to desertification and reduce populations of wild grazing animals.

Traditionally, nomadic tribes drive their herds away from the more arid regions during the dry season to find a better supply of water. But when tube wells are available, they abandon this ecologically sound system of livestock rotation.

As a result, tens of thousands of domestic livestock, as well as wild animals, congregate around the artificial water holes on a 24-hour basis at the height of the dry season. The sparse vegetation around the water holes is then so severely trampled and overgrazed that the land is converted to desert. By closing the tube wells and returning to nomadic herding during dry seasons, the nomadic herders can prevent further increase in the world's desert.

(Figure 13-15) have overrun vast areas of dry prairie rangelands because of undergrazing and overgrazing (see Spotlight on p. 355). Herbicides, such as 2,4,5-T, have been sprayed from airplanes to defoliate and kill these invaders. But because of the expense involved and their possible threats to human health, herbicides are now rarely used to control range vegetation in the United States.

Goats, camels, and predatory insects have been introduced to rangeland for the biological control of unwanted plants. This method is usually less expensive than others, but establishing the new species is sometimes difficult. This method is ineffective when the unwanted plants grow in sparse stands.

Controlled burning is another method of removing unwanted plants and encouraging growth of desirable grasses. The fire destroys invader species and removes dead grass, which hinders new plant growth. Roots and seeds of grasses beneath the soil survive the blaze. Such fires must be carefully controlled, and range management after the fire is essential.

Concern about air pollution has restricted the use of fires for vegetation control in the United States in recent years. Fires can also cause a shift from grasses to woody shrubs and forbs. Because it makes the soil bare, burning can also increase soil erosion and reduce soil moisture. Holistic managers often use short-term trampling by large numbers of animals instead of fire to control vegetation.

Figure 13-15 The tumbleweed invaded many areas of rangeland in the United States after it was accidentally introduced from Europe about 100 years ago.

How livestock are managed before and after unwanted vegetation is removed can influence the results. For example, for improved seed production of desirable plants after weed treatment, livestock should be prevented from grazing on land during the growing season before treatment. After removal of the unwanted plants, livestock should not graze on the site until the desirable plants have become established.

Reseeding and Fertilizing Sometimes applying fertilizer leads to significant increases in rangeland productivity, but this method is usually too costly. On the other hand, reseeding is an excellent way to restore severely degraded rangeland and increase its carrying capacity. Ranchers usually reseed an area with grass species favored by livestock. However, seed mixes that provide grass species favored by both domesticated and wild herbivores can be used.

Effective seeding involves:

- reducing or eliminating unwanted species that can prevent slower-growing desirable species from becoming established

- using native or adapted species suited to local soil and climatic conditions

- seeding when rainfall and temperature conditions are favorable

- using equipment such as mechanical seeders or helicopters to broadcast seeds over a large area

- protecting seeded range from grazing by animals and invasions by undesirable plants until the desired species are well established

Several dedicated scientists, with the help of many volunteers, have had remarkable success at restoring prairie grasslands (see Case Study on p. 356).

(see Case Study on p. 356)

SPOTLIGHT Invasion by the Tumbling Tumbleweed

If you are a cowboy-movie fan, you know about the tumbleweed growing on much of the rangeland in the American West. It might surprise you to learn that the western tumbleweed is not a native American plant. Instead, seeds of this plant probably came to the United States about 100 years ago in a sack of flax from Europe. These seeds probably came from the steppes of southern Russia, where this invader plant is known as tartar thistle.

Since its accidental introduction the tumbleweed has fed prairie fires, crowded out crops, and ripped the skin of horses' legs. All attempts to eradicate the plant have failed.

Now researchers are trying to find uses for it. University of Arizona botanists showed that the tumbleweed could be compacted into fireplace logs with a fuel value comparable to low-grade coal. Thus, the tumbleweed may help us in the next energy crisis. Researchers at New Mexico University suggest that we can eat this plant. They say it is fairly nutritious. They have learned how to liquefy the plant, extract its nutritious components, and turn what is left into vitamins, drugs, and fibers for making sanitary napkins. This research illustrates the statement that a weed is a plant whose value hasn't been discovered.

Controlling Rodents and Livestock Predators Rodents and rabbits compete with livestock and with large, wild grazing animals for range vegetation. They cause more damage to desirable range plants than cattle do because they graze more closely to the ground. During dry periods, they even dig up the plants.

Trying to control rabbits and rodents by poisoning, trapping, and shooting usually gives only temporary relief and is rarely worth the cost. These animals have high reproduction rates and their populations can usually recover in a short time. Experience has shown that vegetation management is a better way to protect the range than attempting to control rodents and rabbits.

Predation is a special problem for sheep and goat raisers in the United States and many other countries. Traditionally, ranchers have shot, trapped, and poisoned wild animals that prey on livestock. For decades U.S. sheep and goat raisers have considered the coyote (Figure 13-16) a serious threat to their livestock. Hunting and habitat loss have eliminated most of the coyote's natural enemies. Without some type of predator control, its numbers can increase rapidly.

U.S. Fish and Wildlife Service

Figure 13-16 The coyote sometimes preys on sheep and goats. Conservationists and livestock raisers disagree over whether poisons should be used to control coyote populations.

Bears, mountain lions, bobcats, foxes, and golden eagles also prey on livestock. However, hunting and loss of habitat have sharply reduced the impact of these species on livestock populations. Livestock predator control is a controversial issue (see Pro/Con on p. 357).

Domesticating Wild Herbivores   Recently there's been renewed interest in wild game ranching in arid and semiarid rangelands, especially in Africa. Some ecologists have suggested that wild herbivores, such as eland, oryx, and Grant's gazelles, should be raised in ranches on these hot, dry grasslands. Because wild herbivores have a more diversified diet than cattle, they can make more efficient use of the available vegetation.

Most wild herbivores need less water than cattle. Eland, oryx, and Grant's gazelles may even get all the water they need from the vegetation they eat. The addax, an antelope kept by ancient Egyptians, does not need to drink and is better adapted to the desert than the camel.

CASE STUDY   **Prairie Restoration**

Scientists at the University of Wisconsin-Madison's Arboretum have worked since 1936 to restore the nearby Curtis Prairie. The project began when ecologist Aldo Leopold hired Theodore Sperry, a young prairie ecologist, to restore a 60-acre field to its native prairie condition. By 1941 Sperry had transplanted sod from patches of remaining prairies and reestablished 42 prairie plant species.

Between 1950 and 1955 botanist David Archbald took over the project and introduced more than 150 prairie species to the plot. By 1980, after nearly 50 years of painstaking work and research, parts of the Curtis Prairie were comparable to the native prairie once found on the site.

Another pioneer in prairie restoration is Ray Schulenberg, curator of plant collections for the Morton Arboretum at Lisle, Illinois, near Chicago. In 1962 Schulenberg began reestablishing a prairie on a plot of land at the Morton Arboretum. He collected seeds from remnants of prairie in the area, raised

seedlings in a greenhouse, and then planted them on the plot.

For two years teams of workers removed weeds by hand. After the prairie grasses became established, controlled burning was used each spring to remove weeds and encourage the growth of perennial prairie plants. Today this site is covered with healthy plants. It is used for educational purposes and as a refuge for endangered species of local plants and insects.

The largest prairie restoration project is being carried out in Illinois on land at the Fermi National Accelerator Laboratory. With the help of Schulenberg, this project was started and supervised by Robert Betz, a biology professor at Northeastern Illinois University in Chicago. Schulenberg and Betz found remnants of virgin Illinois prairies in old cemeteries, on embankments, and on other patches of land. In 1972 they transplanted plants by hand from the prairie remnants to a four-hectare patch at the Fermi Laboratory site.

Each year 10 to 20 more hectares of land were carefully prepared and sown with virgin prairie plants and weeded manually. This work was done by more than 100 volunteers. Because of the size of the plot, Betz developed mechanical methods to do some of the work.

By 1982 about 184 hectares of the plot had been planted with prairie plants. So far the site has about 50 species. New plant species are introduced each year and by 1988 there were also over 200 species of birds, coyotes, beavers, and other animals.

Ecosystem restoration isn't easy. To achieve their goals, dedicated scientists like Sperry, Archbald, Schulenberg, and Betz spent decades digging up and transplanting plants and weeding plots by hand. Their efforts and those of the volunteers who helped them are important and inspiring examples of people caring for the earth.

In contrast, cattle, sheep, and goats must walk daily to a water supply to drink. This back and forth movement requires much energy and reduces the rate at which the animals gain weight. It also degrades rangeland by trampling desirable grasses and compacting the soil.

Native herbivores are also more resistant than cattle to animal diseases found in savanna grasslands. The eland, the largest antelope species, is extremely tolerant of heat and drought. It can be domesticated and milked. Since 1900 a domesticated herd of eland has been maintained at Askaniya Nova in the southern Ukraine.

Domesticated red deer are a major source of meat in New Zealand and a minor source in Scotland. In mountainous areas with poor vegetation, llamas and vicunas can be an important source of meat. Moose supply meat for many Finns and Russians. Several experiments have shown that domesticating wild herbivores can be successful (see Case Study on p. 358).

Future Directions for Range Management A nomadic cattle herder in Kenya, Africa, a commercial cattle rancher in Texas, and a sheep rancher in Australia—each operates under different, locally determined conditions and restraints. This means that each manager of a ranch or a rangeland must consider the short- and long-term implications of a unique set of environmental, economic, social, and political factors.

Many actions by nomadic herders and commercial ranchers are motivated by the powerful drive for short-term survival and economic gain. But, too much emphasis on short-term gain can lead to long-term economic and ecological ruin. For long-term success, livestock production must be based on ecological principles that sustain the soil and vegetation resource base.

Livestock production in LDCs is among the world's most inefficient industries. Studies indicate that available knowledge could be used to increase beef cattle population on tropical grasslands in Africa four to five times without degrading the grassland base. A sustainable grassland economy based on sound ecological principles would reduce food deficits and foreign debts for developing African countries.

But the goal of sound range management isn't just to produce food and other livestock products for short-

---

PRO/CON Livestock Predator Control in the United States

Each year sheep and goat raisers in Texas claim they lose 190,000 animals, valued at $9 million, to wild predators. Some ranchers in other western states say they've lost over 25% of their lambs from predation. Conservationists, however, question the accuracy of such estimates. They contend that ranchers exaggerate their losses.

Most western stock raisers have promoted the use of poisons, trapping, and shooting to kill off livestock predators. Between 1940 and 1972 a controversial and largely unsuccessful control program was waged by western ranchers and the U.S. Department of the Interior against livestock predators, especially the coyote. Because coyotes are too numerous and too crafty to be hunted effectively, emphasis was placed on poisoning them.

Poisons were spread from planes, trail bikes, pickup trucks, and snowmobiles. Livestock carcasses were laced with poison. Traps were baited with poisoned meat and set with explosive charges. The most popular poison was sodium fluoroacetate—known as compound 1080. One ounce of this compound is enough to kill 200 people or 20,000 coyotes. In 1963 alone, federal poisoning programs killed an estimated 90,000 coyotes, 21,000 bobcats and lynx, 300 mountain lions, and at least 73,000 other wild carnivores.

A 1972 report by the government-appointed Advisory Committee on Predator Control recommended that all poisoning of predators by the federal government be halted. The committee also urged that poisons no longer be used to kill predators because poisons can accidentally kill non-target animals including eagles, other endangered species, and people.

After receiving the report, President Richard M. Nixon issued an executive order banning predator poisoning on public lands or by government employees anywhere. The Environmental Protection Agency then prohibited the use of several poisons, including 1080, even on private land.

Since 1972, western ranchers have tried to have this ban lifted. In 1985, under pressure from ranchers, western congressional representatives, and the Reagan administration, the EPA approved the use of compound 1080 in livestock collars. These poison-filled rubber collars are placed around the necks of sheep, goats, and other livestock. Coyotes and other predators are poisoned when they bite the neck of their prey. In 1987, government agents shot, poisoned, and trapped 16,726 coyotes, 675 bobcats, 473 red foxes, and an assortment of other wild carnivores. These efforts have hardly made a dent in the coyote population.

Conservation and environmental groups strongly oppose the use of compound 1080. They argue that the poison, dribbling down the neck of a sheep after it's been killed by a coyote, could kill

(Continued)

golden eagles, vultures, and other scavengers feeding on the sheep carcass. Carcasses of poisoned coyotes could also kill such scavengers. Conservationists also fear that some ranchers might illegally extract the poison from collars and use it to bait livestock carcasses.

Because the coyote is so adaptable and prolific, conservationists argue that any poisoning program is doomed to failure and is a waste of tax dollars. Because the average cost of killing a coyote is at least $1,000, it would cost taxpayers less to pay ranchers for each sheep or goat killed by a coyote. Even if poisoning or other programs did succeed in killing most coyotes, conservationists cite evidence that this would decrease livestock productivity and increase overgrazing.

If coyote populations are reduced, the populations of rodents and rabbits they eat and keep under control can explode. These small herbivores then will compete with livestock for rangeland vegetation, reducing livestock productivity and causing rangeland degradation. In the long run, drastic reduction of coyote populations can cause larger economic losses for ranchers than the losses of livestock killed by these predators.

Conservationists suggest that fences, repellants, and trained guard dogs be used to keep predators away. For example, guard dogs have eliminated predation on some Oregon ranches that once suffered heavy lamb losses. Some Texas ranchers are also using various guard dog species.

By using a mix of these methods, sheep producers in Kansas have one of the country's lowest rates of livestock losses to coyotes. The annual cost of their predator control program is only 5% of what neighboring Oklahoma spends on a predator control program of poisoning and trapping. The philosophy of the Kansas program is summed up by its director:

You can't control coyote numbers. You can train people who raise sheep how to avoid coyote losses. But if you tell them they can call in a government trapper to kill coyotes whenever they have a problem, they won't use a prevention program like ours.

In 1986 Department of Agriculture researchers reported that predation can be sharply reduced by penning young lambs and cattle together for 30 days and then allowing them to graze together on the same range. During the penning period the cattle and sheep develop a strong need to mingle. When predators attack, cattle will butt and kick them, and in the process protect themselves and the sheep. The two species coexist nicely on the same range because cattle eat mainly grasses and sheep prefer broadleafed plants. Llamas and donkeys, also tough fighters against predators, can be used in the same way to protect sheep.

Conservationists point out that only a few coyotes and other predators prey on livestock. They suggest concentrating on killing or removing the rogue individuals rather than all coyotes or other predators. The present mass eradication program is like randomly killing large numbers of people when a murder is committed in the hopes of killing the murderer. What do you think should be done?

CASE STUDY Game Ranching in Africa

Since 1978 an important game ranching experiment has been carried out by David Hopcraft on a 20,000-acre ranch on the Athi Plains near Nairobi. The ranch is stocked with a variety of native grazers and browsers, including antelope, zebras, giraffes, and ostriches. Some cattle are also being raised for comparison but are gradually being phased out. The yield of meat from the native herbivores has been rising steadily and the condition of the range has also improved.

Costs are much lower than those for raising cattle in the same region. Because the wild herbivores need less water than cattle do, less money is spent on wells, dams, and piping. Money is also saved because, unlike cattle, wild herbivores don't have to be dipped or inoculated against local animal parasites and diseases. Best of all, the average yield of lean meat per area of grazed land from the wild herbivores is at least twice that from cattle on the same rangeland.

term profit. Good management also allows the multiple use of rangelands. Above all, it maintains, conserves, and where possible improves this vital renewable resource for both humans and wildlife.

If we sell you our land, love it as we've loved it. Care for it as we've cared for it. Hold in your mind the memory of the land as it is when you take it. And with all your strength, with all your might, and with all your heart, preserve it for your children.

Chief Sealth of the Duwamish Tribe of the state of Washington in a letter sent to President Franklin Pierce in 1855 about the proposed government purchase of the tribe's land.

DISCUSSION TOPICS

1. What effect did the passage of the Taylor Grazing Act of 1934 have on the use and abuse of rangelands in the United States? Why were many potential benefits of this legislation not realized until the 1970s?

2. What are the major causes of overgrazing in Africa? On public rangelands in the United States? In each case, devise a general plan for range management that would decrease overgrazing and restore much of the degraded rangeland.

3. Under what conditions can continuous grazing be used? When is it more desirable to use deferred-rotation grazing or holistic grazing?

4. Should fees for grazing on public rangelands in the United States be eliminated and replaced with a competitive bidding system? Explain. Why would making such a change be politically difficult?

5. Should fees for grazing on public rangelands in the United States be increased to the point where they equal the fair market value estimated by the Bureau of Land Management and the Forest Service? Explain.

6. Should compound 1080 or other poisons be used in livestock collars to poison coyotes that prey on livestock? Explain. What are the alternatives?

7. Should poisoning and hunting of livestock predators be allowed on public rangelands? Explain? Try to have both a rancher and a wildlife scientist present to your class their viewpoints on this controversial issue.

8. Should trail bikes, dune buggies, and other off-road vehicles be banned from public rangeland to reduce damage to vegetation and soil? Explain.

FURTHER READINGS

Bell, H. M. 1973. *Rangeland Management for Livestock Production*. Norman: University of Oklahoma Press.

Blonston, G. 1982. "Coyote." *Science 82*, vol 3, no. 8, 62–71.

Defenders of Wildlife. 1982. *1080: The Case Against Poisoning Our Wildlife*. Washington, D.C.: Government Printing Office.

Ferguson, Denzel, and Nancy Ferguson. 1983. *Sacred Cows and the Public Trough*. Bend, Ore: Maverick Publications.

Francis, John G., and Richard Ganzel, eds. 1984. *Western Public Lands: The Management of Natural Resources in a Time of Declining Federalism*. Totowa, N.J.: Rowman and Allanheld.

Gray, J. R., et al. 1982. "Characteristics of Grazing Systems." New Mexico Agricultural Experimental Station Research Report 467, March.

Harris, Robert. 1980. *State of the Range Resource*. Proceedings of the National Conference on Renewable Natural Resources, American Forestry Association, Washington, D.C., Nov. 30–Dec. 3.

Heady, H. F. 1975. *Rangeland Management*. New York: McGraw-Hill.

Libecap, Gary D. 1986. *Locking Up the Range: Federal Land Control and Grazing*. San Francisco: Pacific Institute for Public Policy Research.

Martin, S. C. 1975. "Ecology and Management of Southwestern Semidesert Grass-Shrub Ranges: The Status of Our Knowledge." Forest Service, U.S. Department of Agriculture Research Paper RM-156.

Ramadé, Francois. 1984. *Ecology of Natural Resources*. New York: John Wiley.

Savory, Allan. 1988. *Holistic Rangeland Management*. Covelo, Calif.: Island Press.

Schuster, Joseph L. 1984. "The Importance of Rangeland and Rangeland Conservation." *Rangelands*, vol. 6, no. 5, 14–24.

Sheridan, D. 1981. "Western Rangelands: Overgrazed and Undermanaged." *Environment*, vol 23, no. 4, 37–39.

Stoddart, L. A., et al. 1975. *Range Management*, 3rd. ed. New York: McGraw-Hill.

U.S. Department of Agriculture. 1980. *An Assessment of the Forest and Range Situation in the United States*. Washington, D.C.: U.S. Department of Agriculture.

U.S. Department of Interior. 1984. *50 Years of Public Land Management: 1934–1984*. Washington, D.C.: Bureau of Land Management, U.S. Department of Interior.

Vosin, André. 1988. *Grass Productivity*. Covelo, Calif.: Island Press.

World Resources Institute and International Institute for Environment and Development. Annual. *World Resources*. New York: Basic Books.

Forest, Wilderness, and Park Resources

General Questions and Issues

1. What are the major ecological benefits and characteristics of forests?

2. How are the world's forests distributed and used?

3. Why is tropical deforestation one of the world's most serious environmental and resource problems?

4. What are the major types and uses of public lands and forests in the United States?

5. Why and how should we preserve wilderness?

6. What problems do parks face and what should be done?

Forests precede civilizations, deserts follow them.

François-Auguste-René de Chateaubriand

T hroughout recorded history people have worshiped, feared, and cut down forests, usually with little regard for their renewal. Since agriculture began about 10,000 years ago, the earth's forest cover has been reduced by at least one-third.

Today potentially renewable forest resources still cover about one-third of the earth's land surface (see map inside back cover). These forests are of major ecological and economic importance.

Worldwide, however, forests are disappearing faster than any other ecosystem. The world's remaining tropical forests are being removed ten times faster than they're being replaced by natural regrowth and human replanting. Every second an area of tropical forest the size of a football field is cleared and another area the same size is degraded.

During the last 75 years forest management and conservation have increased forest productivity and prevented deforestation in many MDCs. Air pollution and disease, not deforestation, are now the major threats to forests in Europe and North America.

Some forests and other types of ecosystems have been protected from development and degradation by being set aside as wilderness areas and parks. As population and economic development grow, these oases of biological diversity are coming under increasing stress.

In this chapter we will look at the uses and conditions of forests, wilderness, and parks in the world and in the United States. The next chapter is devoted to a study of methods for managing forest resources.

14-1 FOREST ECOLOGY

Ecological Importance of Forests Forests have important ecological functions that many people are unaware of. As biologist René Dubos reminds us, "Trees are the great healers of nature."

Forested watersheds act like giant sponges. They regulate the flow of water from mountain highlands to croplands and urban areas. They absorb, hold, and gradually release water that recharges springs, streams, and groundwater aquifers. The absorption and slow release of water help control soil erosion, the severity of flooding, and the amount of sediment washing into rivers, lakes, and reservoirs.

Forests also play an important role in local, regional, and global climate. For example, about 50% to 80% of the moisture in the air above tropical forests comes from trees by transpiration and evaporation. If large areas of these forests are cleared, average annual precipitation decreases and the region's climate gets hotter and drier. Rain that does fall runs off the bare soil rapidly instead of being absorbed and slowly released by vegetation. As the climate gets even hotter and drier, soil moisture and fertility drop further. Eventually these changes can convert a diverse tropical forest into a sparse grassland or even a desert.

The world's tropical forests help stabilize global climate by absorbing much of the solar radiation reaching the earth's surface near the equator. Clearing large areas of these forests produces "shinier" land that reflects more of the sun's incoming energy back into space (Figure 5-3, p. 94). Consequently, wind currents, precipitation, and temperatures change in areas far beyond the tropics.

Forests also play an important role in the global carbon and oxygen cycles. Through photosynthesis trees help cleanse the air by absorbing carbon dioxide and adding oxygen. When trees are harvested and burned, the carbon they contain is released to the atmosphere as carbon dioxide. Removing tree cover also leads to the release of some of the carbon stored in the exposed soil.

Increased clearing of forests for fuelwood could add to the greenhouse effect (Figure 7-5, p. 152). Rising temperatures from higher levels of carbon dioxide and other greenhouse gases could lead to further release of carbon dioxide by increasing the respiration rates of trees and soil microorganisms. But some scientists speculate that higher carbon dioxide levels might enhance the growth of trees, which would remove more carbon dioxide from the atmosphere.

Forests provide habitats for a larger number of wildlife species than any other biome, making them the planet's major reservoir of biological diversity. They also absorb noise and some air pollutants and nourish the human spirit by providing solitude and beauty.

Too often economists and timber company managers evaluate forests only on the short-term market value of the fuelwood, timber, paper, and other products they provide. Such cost-benefit analysis rarely considers the value of the ecological benefits that support economic activities and help sustain the biosphere.

According to one calculation, a typical tree that lives 50 years provides $196,250 worth of ecological benefits. Sold as timber, this tree is worth only about $590. In its 50-year lifetime, the tree produces $31,250 worth of oxygen, $62,500 in air pollution reduction, $31,250 in soil fertility and erosion control, $37,500 in water recycling and humidity control, $31,250 in wildlife habitat, and $2,500 worth of protein.

Such a calculation is a general estimate, not reflecting actual values that can be recovered in the marketplace. However, it illustrates dramatically the ecological benefits that are often neglected in making decisions about forest harvesting and management.

Types of Tree Species and Forests The major structural parts of a tree are the roots, trunk, and crown

(Figure 14-1). Roots help hold the tree in place and contain millions of minute root hairs that absorb water and nutrients from the soil. The crown consists of branches and leaves and is the zone where almost all photosynthesis takes place. The trunk carries nutrients between roots and crown and contains a series of concentric rings, each representing a one-year period of growth.

For commercial purposes trees are grouped into two broad categories: hardwoods and softwoods. **Hardwoods** are heavy in weight per unit of volume and are hard to saw, plane, or carve. They're usually broadleafed and deciduous trees, such as oak, maple, mahogany, and hickory, which shed their leaves seasonally. Timber from hardwood trees is used mostly for flooring, furniture, and veneer.

Softwoods are usually lighter in weight per unit of volume (less dense) and generally are easier to saw, plane, or carve than hardwoods. Some softwoods, however, are harder than some species classified as hardwoods. Most softwoods are conifers, such as pine, fir, spruce, cedar, redwood, and other needle-bearing trees, which grow their seeds in cones. Softwoods generally grow more rapidly and have longer trunks and fewer limbs than hardwoods. Thus, they are easier to harvest and mill than most hardwoods. These properties also make them useful for construction lumber, plywood, and paper products (paper, rayon, cellophane).

Forests are also classified as closed or open. A forest where the crowns of trees touch and form a closed canopy during all or part of the year is called a **closed forest**. These forests make up about 62% of the earth's forested area. Almost two-thirds of these forests are broadleafed; the rest are coniferous. An area where trees are abundant but their crowns don't form a closed canopy is known as an **open forest** or **woodland**.

It's also useful to distinguish between secondary and old-growth forests. **Secondary forests** are stands of trees resulting from secondary ecological succession (Figure 6-23, p. 142). Most forests in the United States and other temperate areas are secondary forests that developed after the logging of virgin forests or the abandonment of agricultural lands.

Old-growth forests are uncut, virgin forests containing massive trees that are often hundreds, sometimes thousands, of years old (Figure 14-2). Examples include forests of Douglas fir, western hemlock, giant sequoia, and coastal redwoods in the western United States (Figure 2-6, p. 33); loblolly pine in the Southeast; and most tropical forests. The definition of an old-growth forest varies with the dominant tree species: 250 years for Douglas fir and 80 years for loblolly pine.

Generally, old-growth forests have a greater diversity of plant and animal life than secondary forests. The various understory zones and other vegetation in

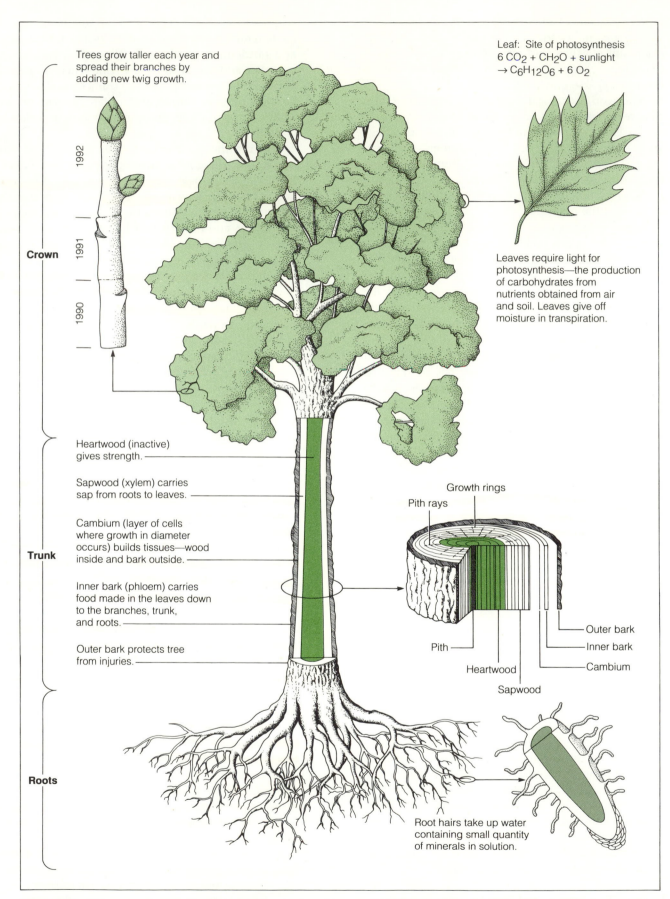

Trees grow taller each year and spread their branches by adding new twig growth.

1992

1991

1990

Crown

Leaf: Site of photosynthesis
$6 CO_2 + CH_2O + sunlight$
$\rightarrow C_6H_{12}O_6 + 6 O_2$

Leaves require light for photosynthesis—the production of carbohydrates from nutrients obtained from air and soil. Leaves give off moisture in transpiration.

Heartwood (inactive) gives strength.

Sapwood (xylem) carries sap from roots to leaves.

Cambium (layer of cells where growth in diameter occurs) builds tissues—wood inside and bark outside.

Inner bark (phloem) carries food made in the leaves down to the branches, trunk, and roots.

Outer bark protects tree from injuries.

Trunk

Growth rings

Pith rays

Pith

Heartwood

Sapwood

Outer bark

Inner bark

Cambium

Roots

Root hairs take up water containing small quantity of minerals in solution.

Figure 14-1 Major parts of a tree. The buds, root tips, and cambium are the only growing parts. The tree takes in oxygen over most of its surface through pores on its leaves, twigs, branches, trunk, and roots.

Figure 14-2 This stand of old-growth northern hardwood in Great Smoky Mountains National Park is a remnant of the vast virgin forests that once extended over much of the eastern half of the United States.

in diameter in only 11 years. In Siberia, Alaska, or northern Canada, however, it may take 100 years for a loblolly pine to grow to commercial log size.

Tree stands typically go through several distinct growth phases. The volume of very young trees (seedlings) increases slowly, although their height may increase significantly. This initial, slow-growth phase is followed by a period of rapid growth with a large increase in volume and height. Then, as the trees mature, their growth rates level off.

Forest quality means different things to different people. To a commercial logger a high-quality forest is one that will produce commercially harvestable timber as quickly as possible. To an ecologist or conservationist a high-quality forest is one with the maximum biological diversity needed to sustain the ecological services it provides.

Climate and Soil Type   Each tree species grows best within a certain range of temperature and moisture. With adequate moisture the average annual temperature determines whether a forest is tropical, temperate, or polar (see map inside back cover and Figure 6-1, p. 118).

Figure 14-3 shows the distribution of forests throughout the world, and Figure 14-4 shows the major types of forests in the lower 48 states of the United States. Forests with humid, cold climates are often dominated by softwood conifers, and those in humid, mild climates by deciduous hardwoods. Other areas contain a mixture of softwoods and hardwoods. Most of the world's remaining hardwood forests are located in the humid tropics.

Climate changes with increasing elevation and drainage is affected by slope. These factors affect the types, sizes, and growth rates of trees (Figure 6-2, p. 120). Soil type also affects the types, sizes, and growth rates of trees on a site. Soils capable of supporting coniferous forests are significantly different from soils that support deciduous forests (Figure 9-4, p. 221).

In coming decades the greatest threat to forests, especially temperate and boreal forests, is expected to be shifts in vegetation from changes in regional climate brought about by global warming. This will disrupt the economic and ecological values of many forests and result in mass extinction of many forms of wildlife. These effects and possible ways to slow down global warming are discussed in Section 7-5.

Tolerance to Shade   Trees are often classified according to their ability to grow and reproduce in shade, mostly in their early growth stages (Table 14-1). **Shade-intolerant tree species** need lots of sunlight in their early growth stages and thrive in forest openings. They are usually pioneer species that dominate the early stages of ecological succession (Figure 6-23, p. 142).

old-growth forests provide a variety of ecological niches for different plants and animals (Figure 5-22, p. 113). These forests also have large numbers of standing dead trees (snags) and fallen logs (boles), which are habitats for a variety of plants and animals. Their decay returns nutrients to the soil.

Ecological Factors Affecting Forest Type and Growth

Forest quality is determined by the types of trees that grow in the forest and the rate of their growth. Each tree species has certain properties that determine how well it can grow and reproduce in a particular climate and soil. They include seeding and germination habits, pattern of growth and growth rate, tolerance to shade, space requirements, size at maturity, and resistance to fire, disease, insects, and pollution.

Since environmental conditions can vary widely, there are tremendous differences in the growth of trees of the same type from stand to stand. For example, in the southeastern United States a loblolly pine tree can grow to pulp size—the size useful for paper making—in 10 to 12 years. After 20 years it can reach log size (about 8 inches in diameter) for use as construction timber. In Brazil the same species can grow to 16 inches

Craig Lorimer, University of Wisconsin

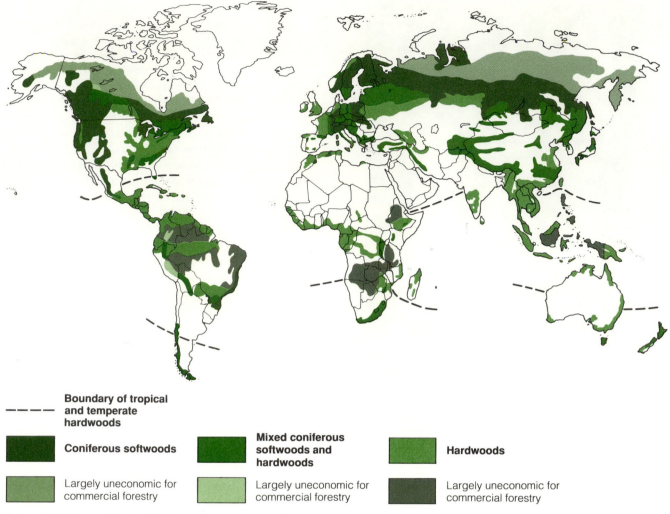

Figure 14-3 The world's forests. (Data from UN Food and Agriculture Organization and U.S. Forest Service)

Legend:

-- -- -- **Boundary of tropical and temperate hardwoods**

Coniferous softwoods

Mixed coniferous softwoods and hardwoods

Hardwoods

Largely uneconomic for commercial forestry

Largely uneconomic for commercial forestry

Largely uneconomic for commercial forestry

Many commercially important species are shade intolerant and do best when grown under full sunlight in even-aged stands, where all trees are planted naturally or artificially as seeds or seedlings at the same time.

Shade-tolerant tree species grow in dim or moderate light under the crown cover of larger trees. They usually dominate in the last stages of ecological succession. Because of variations in shade tolerance, the number and size of openings in a forest determine the type, size, and quality of the trees in various species.

Interactions with Other Species The growth of each tree species is affected by its interactions with the animals and other plants at its forest site. The major factor governing the interactions among trees and other plants is competition for space and other resources. Trees growing too close together compete for limited soil nutrients, moisture, and light; as a result their growth will be stunted (Figure 14-5).

Selective thinning, whereby only certain trees are removed, reduces crowding and improves forest qual-

ity. Unwanted weeds and other pioneer species must also be controlled to reduce competition with planted species.

Interactions between forests and animal life are often critical. For example, birds and squirrels disperse tree seeds, and insects are essential for the pollination of plants. When people eliminate the natural predators of deer in a forest, the deer population can explode and destroy many tree seedlings.

Ecological Succession Natural ecological succession produces a sequence of tree and other plant species best adapted to existing climate and soil conditions (Figure 6-23, p. 142). To sustain the maximum biological diversity of a forest, people usually should not change its natural species mix. This is especially important for protecting a forest's wildlife and water-holding capacity and for enhancing its aesthetic and recreational values.

Managing a forest primarily for timber production involves some human control of natural ecological succession. For example, selected trees may be cut to

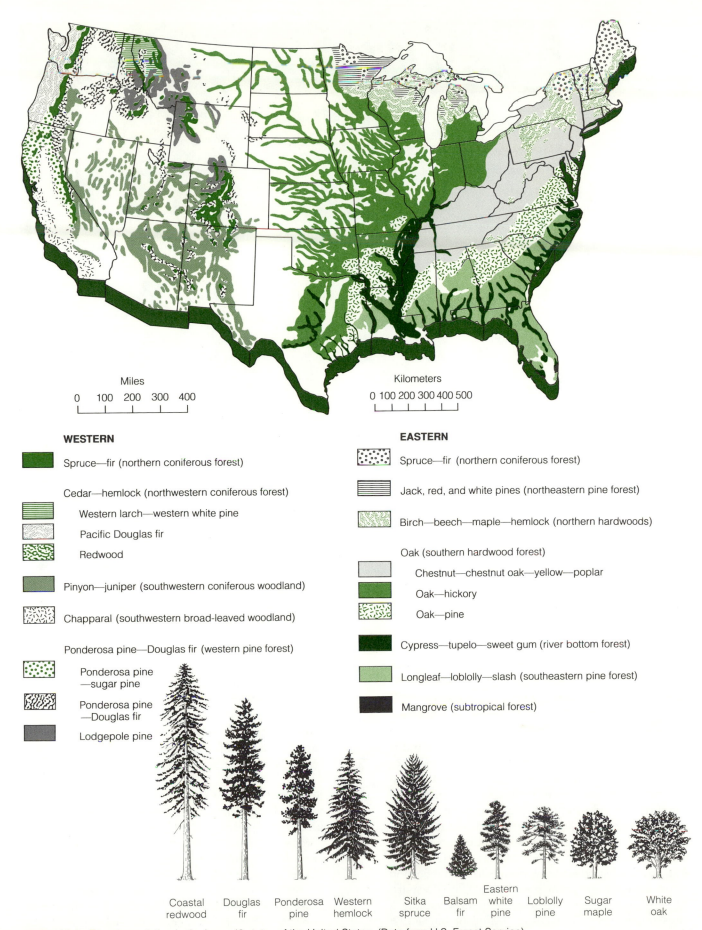

WESTERN

■ Spruce—fir (northern coniferous forest)

Cedar—hemlock (northwestern coniferous forest)

≡ Western larch—western white pine

Pacific Douglas fir

Redwood

Pinyon—juniper (southwestern coniferous woodland)

Chapparal (southwestern broad-leaved woodland)

Ponderosa pine—Douglas fir (western pine forest)

Ponderosa pine —sugar pine

Ponderosa pine —Douglas fir

Lodgepole pine

EASTERN

Spruce—fir (northern coniferous forest)

Jack, red, and white pines (northeastern pine forest)

Birch—beech—maple—hemlock (northern hardwoods)

Oak (southern hardwood forest)

Chestnut—chestnut oak—yellow—poplar

Oak—hickory

Oak—pine

Cypress—tupelo—sweet gum (river bottom forest)

Longleaf—loblolly—slash (southeastern pine forest)

Mangrove (subtropical forest)

Coastal redwood   Douglas fir   Ponderosa pine   Western hemlock   Sitka spruce   Balsam fir   Eastern white pine   Loblolly pine   Sugar maple   White oak

Figure 14-4 Forest vegetation in the lower 48 states of the United States. (Data from U.S. Forest Service)

Table 14-1 Shade-Intolerant and Shade-Tolerant Tree Species of the United States

Shade-Intolerant (need much sunlight)	Shade-Tolerant (need little sunlight)	Moderately Shade-Tolerant (need moderate sunlight)
Black cherry	Sugar maple	Red cedar
White birch	Beech	Yellow birch
Sitka spruce	White spruce	Hickory
Lodgepole pine	Hemlock	White pine
Ponderosa pine	Dogwood	Loblolly pine
Douglas fir	Balsam fir	White and red oak
All aspens	Coast redwood	Black walnut

Too Many Trees
Yearly growth:
None
Spacing: 5 ft. X 5 ft.
(1700 trees per acre)

Not Enough Trees
Yearly growth:
1 cord per acre
Spacing: 15 ft. X 15 ft.
(170 trees per acre)

Right Number of Trees
Yearly growth:
2 cords per acre
Spacing: 10 ft. X 10 ft.
(425 trees per acre)

Figure 14-5 Effect of tree spacing and competition for nutrients on annual tree growth as shown by growth rings. These three trees of the same species grew in the same general type of soil and climate and were ten years old when they were cut. (Data from U.S. Soil Conservation Service)

U.S. Forest Service

Figure 14-6 Monoculture tree farm of white pine near Asheville, North Carolina.

maintain early or intermediate successional stages for favored species such as pine, birch, and aspen.

Sometimes all or most trees are cut from a diverse, old-growth or secondary forest. Then the site is replanted with an even-aged stand of a single species (monoculture) of faster growing softwoods (Figure 14-6). Stands of one or only a few tree species, known as **tree farms,** need intensive management. Close supervision and expensive inputs of fertilizers and pesticides are often needed to protect the pioneer species from diseases and insects.

Once the trees reach maturity, the entire stand is harvested and the area is replanted with seeds or seedlings. Genetic crossbreeding and genetic engineering can be used to improve both the quality and quantity of wood produced from tree farms.

Replacing old-growth forests and natural woodlands with tree farms increases production of commercially desirable softwoods. However, this interference with ecological succession leads to a net reduction in forest quality and in the planet's biological diversity.

Ecological succession determines how rapidly a forest regenerates after being cleared or burned. If

undisturbed, most temperate forests restore themselves in 100 to 200 years. The regeneration of tropical rain forests on cleared land takes 150 to 400 years. However, clearing a large area of tropical rain forest can change the soil and climate so much that the area will no longer support a diverse tropical forest.

Fire Fire was once believed to be always harmful to forests. Today scientists recognize that fires are a natural and important part of many forest ecosystems. Forests that benefit most from periodic fire grow in areas with a long dry season but enough rainfall to permit abundant plant growth.

For millions of years fires started by lightning have caused many tree species to develop genetic adaptations that allow rapid regeneration after fires. Some

Figure 14-7 Surface fire in a California forest.

Figure 14-8 Effects of a highly destructive crown fire in Hunts Gulch, Idaho.

species, especially conifers such as pines and red-woods, have thick, fire-resistant bark. Most conifers benefit from periodic fires. Besides removing competing plants, fires release nutrients in the ground litter of needles, and they kill harmful fungi. The seeds of some conifers, such as the giant sequoia and jack pine, are released or germinate only after being exposed to intense heat.

In evaluating the effects of fire on forest ecosystems, it's important to distinguish between three kinds of forest fires: surface, crown, and ground. **Surface fires** are low-level fires that usually burn only undergrowth and leaf litter on the forest floor (Figure 14-7). Surface fires kill seedlings and small trees but don't kill most mature trees. But they can scar and weaken mature trees, making them more vulnerable to diseases and insects and to being blown down by wind. Wildlife can usually escape from these fairly slow-burning fires.

In areas without excessive ground litter, a surface fire every five years or so burns away flammable material and helps prevent more destructive crown and ground fires. Surface fires also release and recycle valuable mineral nutrients tied up in slowly decomposing litter and undergrowth, increase the activity of nitrogen-fixing bacteria, stimulate the germination of certain tree seeds, and help control diseases and insects. Some wildlife species, such as deer, moose, elk, muskrat, woodcock, and quail, depend on periodic surface fires to maintain their habitats and to provide food in the form of vegetation that sprouts after fires.

Most surface fires burn themselves out or can be put out if caught in time. However, a combination of dry weather, high winds, and a large buildup of surface litter can convert a surface fire into a more damaging crown or ground fire.

Crown fires are extremely hot fires that burn ground vegetation and tree tops (Figure 14-8). They usually occur in forests where all fire has been prevented for several decades, allowing the buildup of dead wood, leaves, and other flammable ground litter that can burn intensely enough to ignite tree tops. In such forests an intense surface fire driven by a strong wind can spread to tree tops. These rapidly burning fires can destroy all vegetation, kill wildlife, and accelerate erosion.

Sometimes surface fires become **ground fires**, which burn decayed leaves or peat deep below the ground surface. Such fires, common in northern bogs, may smolder for days or weeks before being detected. They are very difficult to put out.

For decades U.S. forestry officials attempted to protect forests from all fires. But this allowed highly flammable debris to build up in some forests, increasing the chances of more severe damage from crown fires. Today forest managers deliberately set surface fires to help prevent crown fires, to kill unwanted plants that compete with commercial species for plant nutrients, and to prevent the spread of harmful diseases and insects. Such **prescribed burning** must be carried out only under certain weather conditions and then must be carefully controlled.

Figure 14-9 Tree bark affected by a white pine blister rust fungus.

Figure 14-10 Bark beetles kill pine trees by boring numerous channels in the cambium layer and loosening the bark.

Diseases Throughout the world, diseases and insects cause more losses of commercial timber than fires. The most destructive tree diseases are caused by parasitic fungi, a form of plant life transmitted from tree to tree as spores (reproductive cells) through the air or by insects (Figure 14-9).

Fungi are decomposer organisms. Some fungi kill trees by growing through the bark (chestnut blight and white pine blister rust) or by attacking the roots (root rot and little-leaf). Others, such as the heart rot fungus, convert the heartwood of a tree to a useless, rotten mass. Some retard tree growth by attacking needles (brown spot needle blight) or leaves (oak wilt).

Other diseases are caused by viruses, bacteria, nematodes (parasitic worms), and dwarf mistletoes (parasitic shrubs). Most tree diseases begin by attacking weak or injured trees or young seedlings.

Through millions of years of natural selection, most trees have developed defense mechanisms against many diseases and insects. In a healthy, diverse forest, tree diseases rarely get out of control and seldom destroy many trees.

But a tree farm of one species has few natural defenses and is vulnerable to attack by diseases and insects. Moreover, diseases that are under control in their native forest communities can be accidentally introduced into forest communities where such controls don't exist. In the United States three highly damaging tree diseases were introduced accidentally from other countries: chestnut blight (from China), Dutch elm disease (from Asia via Europe), and white pine blister rust (from Europe). Chestnut blight has almost eliminated the once-abundant and valuable chestnut tree from eastern hardwood forests. Dutch elm disease has killed more than two-thirds of the elm trees in the United States.

Insects Most of the thousands of insect species that can damage trees are kept under control by other species. However, a few insect species can cause severe damage, especially in tree farms or ecosystems where natural controls don't exist.

For example, bark beetles bore channels through the cambium layer beneath the bark of spruce, fir, and pine trees, loosening the bark and eventually killing the tree (Figure 14-10). These insects have killed large areas of forest in the western and southern United States. Wood borers eat into the sapwood and heartwood and render the wood useless for commercial purposes. They also destroy cut logs and wood products such as plywood.

The larvae (worms, grubs, nymphs, and caterpillars) of defoliators, or leaf eaters, such as spruce budworm and gypsy moth, eat the needles or leaves of trees. Repeated attacks over several years can kill trees by eliminating the foliage they need to carry out photosynthesis and produce food. Other insects suck the sap from trees (aphids and scale insects), and some feed on and kill tip buds (white pine weevil and European pine shoot moth).

Pollution Air pollution is a growing threat to many forests, especially in MDCs. Forests at high elevations and forests downwind from urban and industrial centers are exposed to a variety of air pollutants that can harm trees, especially conifers, in many ways (Figures

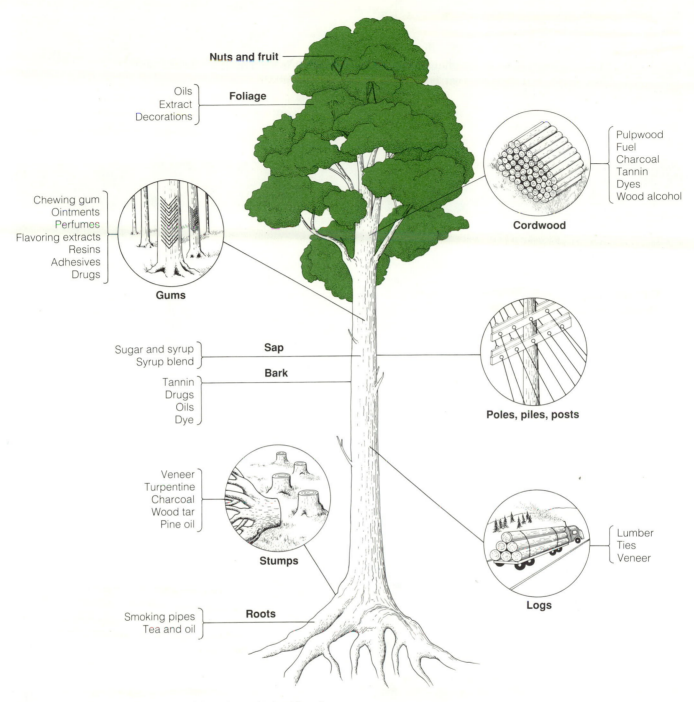

Nuts and fruit

Oils
Extract   **Foliage**
Decorations

Pulpwood
Fuel
Charcoal
Tannin
Dyes
Wood alcohol

Cordwood

Chewing gum
Ointments
Perfumes
Flavoring extracts
Resins
Adhesives
Drugs

Gums

Sugar and syrup
Syrup blend   **Sap**

Bark

Tannin
Drugs
Oils
Dye

Poles, piles, posts

Veneer
Turpentine
Charcoal
Wood tar
Pine oil

Stumps

Lumber
Ties
Veneer

Smoking pipes
Tea and oil   **Roots**

Logs

Figure 14-11 Some of the many useful products obtained from trees.

7-20 and 7-22, pp. 166 and 168). Large-scale forest degradation from air pollution has occurred in Poland, Czechoslovakia, Great Britain, France, East and West Germany, Switzerland, Scandinavia, and eastern North America.

14-2 EXTENT AND USES OF THE WORLD'S FORESTS

Extent of the World's Forests   Today about 34% of the world's land area is covered with open and closed forests (Figure 14-3). Four countries have 58% of the world's closed forests: the USSR (28%), Brazil (13%), Canada (9%), and the United States (7%). Most of Africa and Asia and some parts of Central and South America have little forest.

Commercial Importance of Forests   Forests supply us with lumber, fuelwood, paper pulp, medicines, and many other products worth over $150 billion a year (Figure 14-11). Many forestlands are also used for mining, grazing livestock, and recreation.

Worldwide, about one-half the world's timber cut each year is used as fuel for heating and cooking, especially in LDCs. Some of this is burned directly as firewood, and some is distilled to make charcoal fuel. One-third of the world's annual harvest is sawlogs that are converted to lumber, veneer, panels, plywood, hardboard, particleboard, and chipboard. One-sixth, mostly softwoods, is converted to pulp used in a variety of paper products. Sawlogs and wood pulp are the major uses of timber in MDCs.

In many MDCs the use of throwaway paper products is hastening the deforestation of softwood forests and adding to the growing problem of solid waste. Sharply increasing the recycling of paper is a key to preventing the degradation of forests and reducing unnecessary waste (see Case Study below).

CASE STUDY Recycling Wastepaper

Conservationists estimate that at least 50% of the world's wastepaper could be recycled by the end of this century. But only about 25% is now recycled (Figure 14–12). The Netherlands and Mexico have the highest paper recycling rates because they are sparsely forested. During World War II, when paper drives and recycling were national priorities, the United States recycled about 45% of its wastepaper.

Today the United States leads the world in paper consumption and waste. Directly or indirectly, each American uses an average of about 639 pounds of paper per year—about 8 times the world average and 40 times the average in LDCs. Only about 26% of the wastepaper in the United States is recycled.

Product overpackaging is a major contributor to paper use and waste. Packages inside packages and oversized containers are designed to trick consumers into thinking they're getting more for their money. Product packaging uses 65% of the paper and 15% of the wood produced in the United States. Nearly $1 of every $10 spent for food in the United States goes for throwaway packaging.

Besides saving trees and land, recycling paper saves 30% to 55% of the energy needed to produce paper from virgin pulpwood. It also reduces air pollution from pulp mills by up to 95%, conserves water, and saves landfill space. Recycling half the wastepaper discarded in the United States would save enough energy to supply 10 million people with electrical power each year.

Requiring people to separate paper from other waste materials is a key to increased recycling. Otherwise, paper becomes so contaminated with other trash that wastepaper dealers won't buy it. Slick paper magazines, magazine sections, and advertising supplements cause contamination and must not be included. Today over 200 U.S. cities require residences and businesses to sort out newspapers and cardboard for pickup and recycling.

Tax subsidies and other financial incentives that make it cheaper to produce paper from trees than from recycling hinder wastepaper recycling in the United States. Widely fluctuating prices and a lack of demand for recycled paper products also make recycling wastepaper a risky financial venture.

If the demand for recycled paper products increased, recycled paper would be cheaper and the price paid for wastepaper would rise. One way to increase demand is to require federal and state governments to use recycled paper products whenever possible. The federal government alone uses 2% of all paper products sold in the United States. Half of the trash the government throws away is paper.

In the mid-1970s Congress passed a law calling for federal agencies to buy as many recycled products as practical. But this law has failed because it contains so many exemptions that almost nothing has to be recycled.

In 1977 Maryland enacted a similar but better law. Since then, recycled paper stock bought by the state has increased by 25%. Simple measures like asking teachers to instruct their students to write on both sides of the paper would also reduce unnecessary paper waste and increase environmental awareness. Conservationists call for a national policy designed to recycle half of the wastepaper in the United States by 2000. What do you think?

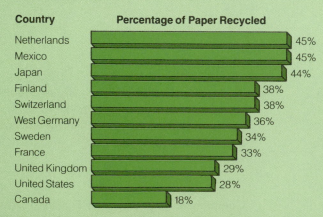

Figure 14-12 Percentage of wastepaper recycled in various countries. (Data from Organization for Economic Cooperation and Development)

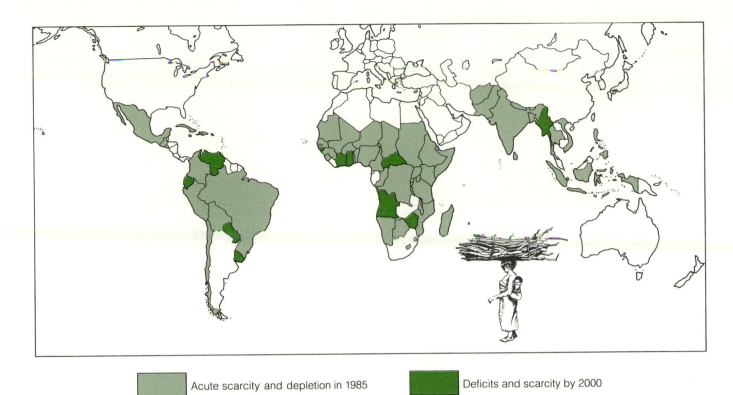

| | Acute scarcity and depletion in 1985 | | Deficits and scarcity by 2000 |

Figure 14-13 Generalized areas of the world experiencing fuelwood scarcity and deficits, 1985 and 2000 (projected). (Data from UN Food and Agriculture Organization)

Taurus Photo

Figure 14-14 Making fuel briquettes from cow dung in India.

The Fuelwood Crisis in LDCs Almost 70% of the people in LDCs rely on wood or charcoal produced from wood for heating and cooking. Half the wood harvested in the world and about 80% of the wood cut in LDCs is used for fuel.

By 1985 about 1.5 billion people—almost one out of every three persons on earth—in 63 LDCs faced a fuelwood crisis (Figure 14-13). They couldn't get enough fuelwood to meet their basic needs, or they were forced to meet their needs by consuming wood faster than it was being replenished. In some areas people have caused shortages of fuelwood by clearing forests to raise cattle and plantation crops for export to MDCs.

The UN Food and Agriculture Organization projects that by the end of this century 3 billion people in 77 LDCs will experience a fuelwood crisis (Figure 14-13). About 500 million people will face acute fuelwood scarcity and 2.5 billion will be depleting remaining supplies to survive.

Fuelwood scarcity has several harmful effects. It places an additional burden on the poor, especially women. Often, they must walk long distances to find and carry home small bundles of fuelwood. Buying fuelwood or charcoal can take 40% of a poor family's meager income. Boiling water for cooking often is an unaffordable luxury.

City dwellers rely more on charcoal than wood because charcoal's light weight makes it easier to transport from the countryside to the city. But when wood is converted to charcoal, more than half the original energy content is lost. This means that villagers who move to a city and switch from wood to charcoal double their consumption of wood—if they can afford it.

Poor families who can't get enough fuelwood often burn dried animal dung and crop residues for cooking and heating (Figure 14-14). This keeps these natural fertilizers from reaching the soil and reduces cropland productivity.

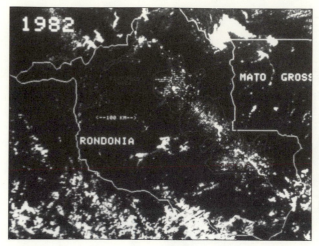
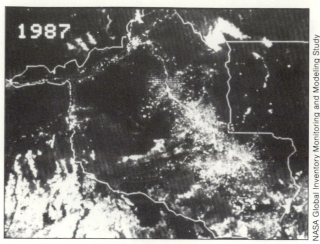

NASA Global Inventory Monitoring and Modeling Study

Figure 14-15 Satellite photos of increased Amazon rain forest destruction in Brazil between 1982 and 1987. The white dots are fires. Such photographs showed that in 1987, 170,000 to 350,000 fires burned over 77,000 square miles of the Brazilian part of the Amazon basin, an area one and one-half times the size of the state of New York. These fires alone may have accounted for as much as 10% of global input of carbon dioxide into the atmosphere during 1987. The fires closely follow the route of the newly constructed Cuiaba-Port Velho highway, built as part of a World Bank-financed development scheme for the Brazilian state of Rondonia. An estimated 20% of Rondonia's forest is gone, and at present rates of destruction it will be totally wiped out in 25 years.

14-3   TROPICAL DEFORESTATION

Why Should You Care About Tropical Forests?

Almost half of the world's original area of tropical moist forests has been cleared for timber, cattle grazing, fuelwood, and farming. The remaining tropical moist forests are found on both sides of the equator in Latin America, Africa, and Southeast Asia (see map inside back cover). If deforestation and degradation of these forests continues at the current rate, almost all of them will be gone in 30 years or so.

Conservationists and ecologists consider this destruction one of the world's most serious environmental and resource problems. Why? There are two major reasons. One is that these incredibly diverse forests are of immense economic and ecological importance to you and everyone else on earth (see Guest Essay near the end of this chapter). The other reason is ethical. Regardless of the importance of tropical forests to us, sustainable-earth conservationists believe that this destruction must be stopped because it is *wrong* (Section 3-6).

Tropical moist forests cover only about 7% of the earth's land surface, but they contain almost half of the world's growing wood. Tropical rain forests account for about two-thirds of all tropical moist forests. Tropical rain forests are by far the earth's most biologically diverse biomes, providing homes for 50% to 80% of the earth's species.

Two-thirds of the plant and animal species and as much as 80% of the plant nutrients in a tropical rain forest are in the canopy (Figure 5-22, p. 113). Hence, removing all or most trees in a forest destroys the habitat and food supply of most of its plant and animal life. This is also causing declines in population of songbird species in North America and other temperate areas, which migrate to tropical areas during cold months. Deforestation also exposes the land's nutrient-poor soil to drying by the hot sun and to erosion by torrential rains.

Tropical moist forests supply half of the world's annual harvest of hardwood. They are also sources of thousands of other materials used in modern industrialized societies. Food products derived from tropical forests include coffee, cocoa, spices, sweeteners, Brazil nuts, and tropical fruits.

Latexes, gums, resins, dyes, waxes, tannins, and essential oils are among the many industrial materials we get from tropical forests. These substances are used in ice cream, toothpaste, shampoo, lipstick, deodorant, sunscreen lotion, perfume, varnish, phonograph records, glossy magazines, tires, tennis rackets, jogging shoes, and hundreds of other products.

The raw materials in one-fourth of the over-the-counter and prescribed drugs we use come from plants growing in tropical rain forests. Aspirin, probably the world's most widely used drug, is made according to a chemical "blueprint" supplied by a compound extracted from the leaves of tropical willow trees.

Surgeons often use a drug called curare to relax patients' muscles. This compound, which can't be made in the laboratory, is extracted from the bark of a tree growing in South American tropical forests. The venom of the Brazilian pit viper is used to make Capoten, a drug for high blood pressure. Future newspapers may be printed in kenaf, an African plant that can produce five times more pulp per acre than the trees normally cut to make newsprint.

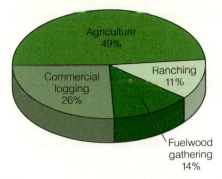

Figure 14-17   Major direct causes of deforestation and degradation of tropical forests. (Data from Norman Myers)

Figure 14-16   Ground level view of tropical forest destruction in the Amazon basin in Brazil.

According to scientists at the National Cancer Institute, 70% of the promising anticancer drugs come from plants in tropical rain forests. Only a few of the millions of plant species found in these forests have been evaluated for their potential as medicines. While you are reading this page, a plant species that might cure a type of cancer that you or someone you love may get could be wiped out forever.

Ecologists warn that the degradation and loss of these extremely diverse biomes could cause the premature extinction of 1 million plant and animal species by the beginning of the next century. Many of these species may be important in the development of hybrid and genetically engineered food plants needed to support future green revolutions (Section 11-3). Throwing these forests away for short-term survival and economic gain is like throwing away unopened presents.

Widespread tropical deforestation can change regional climates and convert large areas of cleared forestland to grassland, or even to desert. It can also affect global climate, food production, and sea levels by making the earth warmer (Section 7-5).

This gives you a glimpse of how tropical forests help support the lifestyle and help protect the health of you and other people in MDCs. But tropical forests are even more important to people living in LDCs. They are home for 250 million people who survive by means of shifting cultivation. Development and degradation of these forests causes loss of indigenous tribal peoples and cultures.

These forests also protect watersheds and regulate water flow for other farmers, who grow food for over 1 billion people in LDCs. Unless there is a halt to the destruction of tropical forests, the Environmental Pol-

icy Institute estimates that as many as 1 billion persons may starve to death during the next 30 years.

How Fast Are We Losing Tropical Forests?   Estimates of the rate at which the world's remaining tropical forests and woodlands are being cleared and degraded vary because of a lack of data and the tendency of some governments to understate the problem for political reasons. However, surveys made by remote-sensing satellites (Figure 14-15), indicate that at least 24,000 square miles and perhaps 60,000 square miles are completely cleared each year. About 99% of all tropical deforestation is taking place in 42 tropical LDCs, with Brazil, Indonesia, Colombia, and Mexico accounting for 47% (Figures 14-15 and 14-16).

It is estimated that at least another 60,000 square miles of tropical forest is degraded each year when more than 30% of the canopy is removed by selective cutting. Felling large trees often damages other trees, and the increase in sunlight dries the forest floor and disrupts the fragile ecosystem. Some experts estimate that the rate of removal and degradation is almost two times higher. Either way the loss is staggering.

Causes of Tropical Deforestation   There are four direct causes of tropical deforestation and degradation: clearing for crop production; commercial logging, mostly for export to MDCs; fuelwood gathering (Figure 14-13); and livestock grazing, mostly to produce beef for export to MDCs (Figure 14-17).

There are also several indirect causes of this destruction of one of the earth's most important life-support systems. They include rapid population growth, widespread poverty, ownership of much of the arable land by a few wealthy people, and the failure of governments to prevent destructive commercial logging and fuelwood gathering.

The population of tropical areas has doubled since 1950 and is projected to double again in the next 35 years to 5 billion—equal to the entire world population today. About 40% of the people now in these countries are living in absolute poverty. The combination of rapid population growth, staggering national debts, and sluggish economies in tropical LDCs creates a massive momentum for an increase in the already devastating clearing and degradation of tropical forests.

Population Growth, Poverty, Land Ownership Patterns, and Government Policies Rapid population growth and poverty push landless people to clear and cultivate forestland and to cut trees for fuelwood. With little land available for subsistence farming, poor people often feel that the only way they can survive is to head for the forests—the only remaining "free land."

In many countries, especially in Latin America, these problems are intensified by land ownership patterns that favor the wealthy. In Latin America 93% of the arable land is owned by a mere 7% of the population, and most people in rural areas have little or no land. Most of the arable land is used for export-oriented ranching or plantation agriculture. The wealthy landowners use their influence to have the government encourage landless peasants to clear tropical forests for cultivation. This helps defuse political pressures for more equitable land distribution.

Policies of MDCs and international lending and aid agencies also encourage tropical deforestation. The mass migration of poor people to tropical forests would not be possible without the highway, logging, mining, ranching, and large dam-building projects that open up these usually inaccessible areas. Many of these projects have been financed by loans from the World Bank, the International Monetary Fund, and other international lending agencies whose policies are dictated by MDCs.

Only recently, after much criticism from conservationists, have these agencies paid much attention to the potentially harmful environmental effects of such projects. Not until 1987, for example, did the World Bank set up a department to review the environmental impacts of its projects. How influential this department will be remains to be seen.

Environmentally Destructive Cultivation Driven by poverty and political forces beyond their control, landless peasants flood into accessible tropical forest areas. Upon arrival they clear patches of tropical forest to grow enough food to survive by shifting, slash-and-burn cultivation (Figure 2-2, p. 29). According to the UN Food and Agriculture Organization, slash-and-burn cultivation is responsible for 70% of closed forest clearing in tropical Africa, 50% in tropical Asia, and 35% in tropical Latin America.

Many of the new cultivators of the tropical forests lack experience in farming these fragile soils. They clear and replant abandoned plots after only a few years instead of waiting the 10 to 25 years needed for restoration of soil fertility. This overcropping exhausts soil nutrients and eventually converts the land to shrubland.

Planting cash crops for export has also played a role in tropical deforestation. In Ethiopia, massive crop plantations have stripped forests in the Awash Valley. About 60% of this land is used to grow cotton and another 22% is devoted to sugar—both primarily for export.

Destructive Commercial Logging Another cause of tropical forest degradation is the failure of governments in tropical LDCs to regulate timber cutting by multinational and national timber companies and to require these companies to replant cleared areas. Increased demand for tropical hardwoods, especially by Japan, the United States, and Great Britain, has encouraged governments of many tropical LDCs to deplete their forests for short-term economic gain. Japan alone consumes 40% of the world's annual harvest of tropical hardwoods, despite the fact that two-thirds of Japan is covered with forests.

In diverse tropical forests only about 10% of the trees are valuable timber species. These are the trees usually cut by loggers. But when these giant trees come crashing down, they pull down 30% to 60% of the other trees, disturbing the forest canopy. The construction of logging roads opens up forests to invasion by the landless poor, ranchers, and plantation growers and accelerates the degradation process.

Many countries have so depleted and degraded their tropical forests that for the foreseeable future timber has become a nonrenewable resource in these countries. For example, in 1960 Nigeria was a leading exporter of tropical logs. By 1985 its forests had been depleted to the point where it spent 27 times more on imports of forest products than it got from exporting such products.

Haiti was once covered with lush rain forests. When the forests were cut, the topsoil on the hills washed away, and with it Haiti's ability to grow enough food to feed its people. Today, Haiti is the poorest country in the Western Hemisphere.

Malaysia, currently the world's leading exporter of tropical logs, is cutting down trees four times faster than they are being replenished and has lost half of its forests during the past 20 years. If this continues, the country will have no forests left in 16 years. As the remaining supply of tropical timber in Asia is depleted in the 1990s, timber cutting in tropical forests will shift to Latin America and Africa. If present trends continue, by 2020 most of the world's tropical hardwoods will be depleted.

A 1988 study by the World Resources Institute shows that deforestation does not make economic sense on a short- or long-term basis. Tropical LDCs have lost billions of dollars by selling their timber too cheaply and by not insisting that their forests be harvested on a sustainable basis. Most LDCs have spent more on tax benefits and other inducements to encourage development and settlement of tropical forests than they have received from the sale of timber, beef, and crops produced on forestland.

To reduce demand and harmful logging practices, conservation groups call for tropical LDCs to double the world price of exportable timber. But this idea is vigorously opposed by Japan and the United States, the world's two largest importers of tropical hardwoods.

Cattle Raising   Each year at least 6 million acres of tropical forest in Central America and in the Amazon basin in Brazil are cleared of trees. Between 1965 and 1983, satellite photos showed that cattle ranches were responsible for 30% of the total deforestation in the Amazon basin. Most of this land is used by wealthy

ranchers to raise beef for export, mostly to the United States, Canada, and western European countries (see Pro/Con below).

Most Latin American ranchers could easily double their output of beef on existing pastures by running their operations more efficiently. However, economic incentives and government inducements make it more profitable for them to clear areas of tropical forests instead.

14-4 PUBLIC LANDS AND FOREST RESOURCES IN THE UNITED STATES

U.S. Public Lands: An Overview   About 42% of all U.S. land consists of public lands owned jointly by all

---

PRO/CON   Should the United States Stop Importing Beef from Tropical Countries?

During the past 25 years almost two-thirds of Central America's tropical forests and woodlands have been cleared and converted to cropland and pastureland. In the 1970s about 40% of the low-cost beef raised on this land was exported to the United States.

Because the Central American cattle graze on grass instead of more expensive grain crops, the beef they produce typically costs only about half as much as beef produced in the United States. This range-fed beef is also tougher and leaner than the feedlot-finished beef produced in the United States. The imported beef is sold mostly to fast-food chains for hamburger meat and to food-processing companies for use in pet foods, baby foods, luncheon meats, chili, stews, and frozen dinners.

For each quarter-pound hamburger made from meat imported from Central America, an area of tropical forest roughly the size of a small kitchen (55 square feet) has been lost. Each of these forest plots was the home of thousands of different plant and animal species.

As tropical forest expert Norman Myers (see Guest Essay near the end of this chapter) points out, Americans eating hamburgers from fast-food outlets that import

beef from tropical countries "indirectly have their hands on the chain saws and bulldozers that are clearing many tropical forests."

After being grazed for five to ten years, these tropical pastures become so degraded and weed infested that they can no longer be used for cattle. Often the land is so depleted of soil nutrients that it can no longer naturally regenerate as forest. Ranchers then move to another area and repeat the process. This destructive "shifting ranching" is often encouraged by government tax subsidies.

By 1985 only 19% of the beef produced in Central America was exported to the United States. This decline in beef imports resulted from a drop in U.S. beef consumption, declining production in Central America caused by pasture degradation, escalating warfare in El Salvador and Nicaragua, and pressure from environmental and consumer groups.

The reduction of U.S. beef imports helps decrease the rate of tropical deforestation. But some conservationists believe that the United States should phase out imports of all beef produced on cleared tropical forestland. Because such beef makes up only 6% of the country's beef imports, a ban would have no noticeable effect on beef supplies.

In the 1980s, environmental and consumer groups (especially the Rainforest Action Network in San Francisco) have organized boycotts of hamburger chains buying beef imported from Latin America. Because of these efforts, many large chains claim they no longer buy beef from tropical countries. However, such claims are virtually impossible to verify because once the imported beef enters the domestic market, it cannot be distinguished from U.S.-raised beef.

The basic question is whether importing beef from tropical countries to cut the cost of a pound of hamburger by a nickel is worth the destruction and degradation of the planet's greatest storehouse of biological diversity.

The best solution would be for Central American governments to require ranchers to produce additional beef on already deforested pasture land. Numerous studies have shown that with improved management the sustainable output of beef from a typical Central American ranch could be doubled or tripled. This solution would provide low-cost beef for export to other countries and not harm Central American economies without causing any deforestation. What do you think?

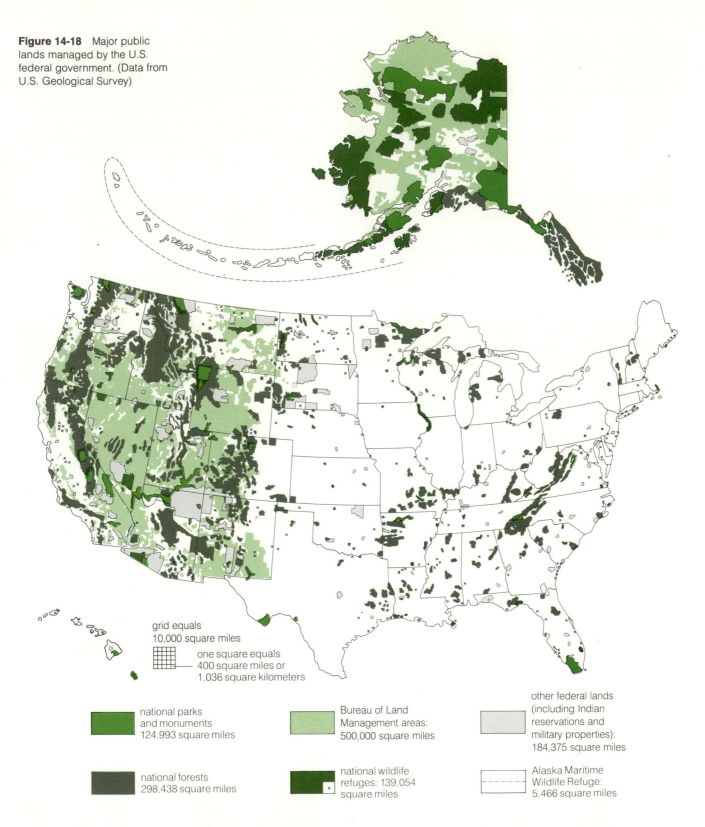

Figure 14-18 Major public lands managed by the U.S. federal government. (Data from U.S. Geological Survey)

grid equals
10,000 square miles

one square equals
400 square miles or
1,036 square kilometers

national parks
and monuments
124,993 square miles

national forests
298,438 square miles

Bureau of Land
Management areas:
500,000 square miles

national wildlife
refuges: 139,054
square miles

other federal lands
(including Indian
reservations and
military properties):
184,375 square miles

Alaska Maritime
Wildlife Refuge:
5,466 square miles

citizens, and managed for them by federal, state, and local governments. Over one-third (35%) of the country's land is managed by the federal government (Figure 14-18). About 95% of this public land is in Alaska (73%) and in western states (22%).

These public lands have been divided by Congress into different units administered by several federal agencies. The allowed uses of these lands vary (see Spotlight on p. 377).

Federally administered public lands contain a large portion of the country's timber, grazing land, and energy resources (Figure 14-19) and most of its copper, silver, asbestos, lead, molybdenum, beryllium, phosphate, and potash. Through various laws Congress

Multiple-Use Lands

National Forests.

The forest system includes 156 national forests and 19 national grasslands managed by the *Forest Service.* Excluding the 15% of this land protected as wilderness areas, this system is managed according to the principles of *sustained yield* and *multiple use.* The lands are used for timbering, grazing, agriculture, mining, oil and gas leasing, recreation, sport hunting, sport and commercial fishing, and conservation of watershed, soil, and wildlife resources.

National Resource Lands.

These lands are mostly grassland, prairie, desert, scrub forest, and other open spaces located in the western states and Alaska. They are managed by the *Bureau of Land Management* under the principle of *multiple use.* Emphasis is on providing a secure domestic supply of energy and strategically important nonenergy minerals and on preserving the renewability of rangelands for livestock grazing under a permit system. Presently about 10% of these lands are being evaluated for possible designation as wilderness areas.

Moderately-Restricted-Use Lands

National Wildlife Refuges.

This system includes 437 refuges and various ranges managed by the *Fish and Wildlife Service.* About 24% of this land is protected as wilderness areas. The purpose of most refuges is to protect habitats and breeding areas for waterfowl and big-game animals in order to provide a harvestable supply for hunters. A few refuges have been set aside to save specific endangered species from extinction. These lands are not officially managed under the principles of multiple use and sustained yield. Nevertheless, sport hunting, trapping, sport and commercial fishing, oil and gas development, mining (old claims only), timber cutting, livestock grazing, and farming are permitted as long as the Secretary of the Interior finds such uses compatible with the purposes of each unit.

Restricted-Use Lands

National Parks.

This system consists of 341 units. They include 49 major parks (mostly in the West) and 292 national recreation areas, monuments, memorials, battlefields, historic sites, parkways, trails, rivers, seashores, and lakeshores. All are managed by the *National Park Service.* Its management goals are to preserve scenic and unique natural landscapes, preserve and interpret the country's historic and cultural heritage, provide protected wildlife habitats, protect wilderness areas within the parks, and provide certain types of recreation. National parks can be used only for camping, hiking, sport fishing, and motorized and nonmotorized boating. Motor vehicles are permitted only on roads, and off-road vehicles are not allowed. In addition to the activities permitted in the parks, national recreation areas can be used for sport hunting, new mining claims, and new oil and gas leasing. About 49% of the land in the National Park System is protected as wilderness areas.

National Wilderness Preservation System.

This system includes 456 roadless areas within the national parks, national wildlife refuges, and national forests. They are managed, respectively, by the National Park Service, the Forest Service, and the Fish and Wildlife Service. These areas are to be preserved in their essentially untouched condition "for the use and enjoyment of the American people in such a manner as will leave them unimpaired for future use and enjoyment as wilderness." Wilderness areas are open only for recreational activities such as hiking, sport fishing, camping, nonmotorized boating, and in some areas sport hunting and horseback riding. Roads, timber harvesting, grazing, mining, commercial activities, and human-made structures are prohibited, except where such activities occurred before an area's designation as wilderness. Motorized vehicles, boats, and equipment are banned except for emergency uses such as fire control and rescue operations. Aircraft, however, can land in Alaskan wilderness areas.

---

has allowed private individuals and corporations to harvest or extract many of these resources—often at below market prices. Because of the economic value of these resources, there has been a long and continuing history of conflict between various groups over management and use of these public lands, as discussed in Section 2-4.

Extent of U.S. Forests Since the first colonists arrived at Jamestown in 1607, the United States has lost about 45% of its original forested area. Since 1920, however, the country's total forested area has remained about the same.

Today forests cover about one-third of the land area in the lower 48 states (Figure 14-4). About three-fourths of the forests lie east of the Great Plains. Most are secondary-growth forests. The remaining forests are mostly old-growth forests in the Rocky Mountain and Pacific Coast regions. There are also large areas of old-growth coniferous forests in Alaska.

Nearly two-thirds of the country's forests are classified as commercial forestland. Because of modern

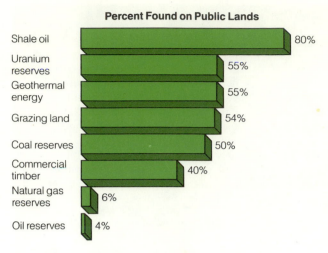

Percent Found on Public Lands

- Shale oil — 80%
- Uranium reserves — 55%
- Geothermal energy — 55%
- Grazing land — 54%
- Coal reserves — 50%
- Commercial timber — 40%
- Natural gas reserves — 6%
- Oil reserves — 4%

Figure 14-19 Estimated percentages of key resources on U.S. public lands. (Data from U.S. Geological Survey)

forestry management, today the average annual growth per acre on U.S. commercial forestland is 3.5 times what it was in 1920. Most of the remaining one-third of U.S. forestland is not capable of producing commercially valuable timber or is set aside as parks, wildlife refuges, or wilderness.

About 58% of the commercial forestland in the United States is owned by about 4 million farmers and other private landowners, especially in the South. Most of the woodlots are small—typically 20 to 40 acres per owner. They supply about half of the country's annual timber harvest.

The rest of the country's commercial forests are owned by forest industries (14%) and local, state, and federal governments (28%). Generally, the forests owned by industry and government are better managed and more productive than the small woodlots owned by private landowners.

Will There Be Enough Wood? Presently the United States is the world's number one consumer of industrial wood products. The average per person use of lumber and paper in the United States is greater than in any other country or region of the world.

Although domestic production satisfies 95% of U.S. wood consumption, the country is still one of the largest importers of forest products. These imports put stresses on forests in other areas of the world. Two-thirds of the imports come from Canada. Much of the rest is tropical hardwoods imported from Asia.

Since 1950 the United States has kept up with the demand for wood and wood products without serious depletion of its commercial forestlands. But according to the U.S. Forest Service, domestic consumption of forest products is projected to double between 1980 and 2030. Some officials and conservationists question

whether the country's forests can meet this demand. Several factors could hinder the greatly increased timber production necessary:

- Forest depletion in some areas. For example, in the Pacific Coast region, annual harvests have exceeded annual growth since 1952.

- Loss of commercial timberland to cropland, pastureland, urban development, and other uses.

- Stunting and destruction of trees by acid deposition and other air pollutants (Figure 7-20, p. 166).

- Difficulty in increasing productivity of the small, privately owned forests that make up 58% of the country's commercial forestland. Most owners are not interested in investing the time and money needed to increase their timber harvest because it takes decades before they get any financial return. Government subsidies and management help for owners of small forest plots could increase yields up to 60%.

- Lack of wastepaper recycling. More paper recycling would decrease the need to harvest softwoods (see Spotlight on p. 370).

Importance and Use of National Forests About 18% of the country's commercial forest area is located within the country's 156 national forests, managed by the U.S. Forest Service (Figure 14-20). These forests are unmatched among federal lands in their importance for wildlife conservation, recreation, and commercial timber production.

They contain 84% of the wilderness areas in the lower 48 states. They're home to over 3,000 species of fish and animal wildlife, including half of the country's big-game animals. Some of these lands are also essential to the survival and recovery of many threatened and endangered species, such as the grizzly bear and the gray wolf.

More than 3 million cattle and sheep graze on national forest lands each year. National forests receive more recreational visits than any other federal public lands—more than twice as many as the National Park System.

Almost half of national forest lands are open to commercial logging. They supply about 15% of the country's total annual timber harvest—enough wood to build about 1 million homes. Each year private timber companies bid for rights to cut a certain amount of timber from areas designated by the Forest Service.

The Forest Service is required by law to manage the forests according to the principles of sustained yield and multiple use. But since the 1960s there has been controversy over how well the agency is doing this, as discussed in the next chapter. Besides managing this vast system, the Forest Service provides technical help for the management of private forest and rangelands throughout the country.

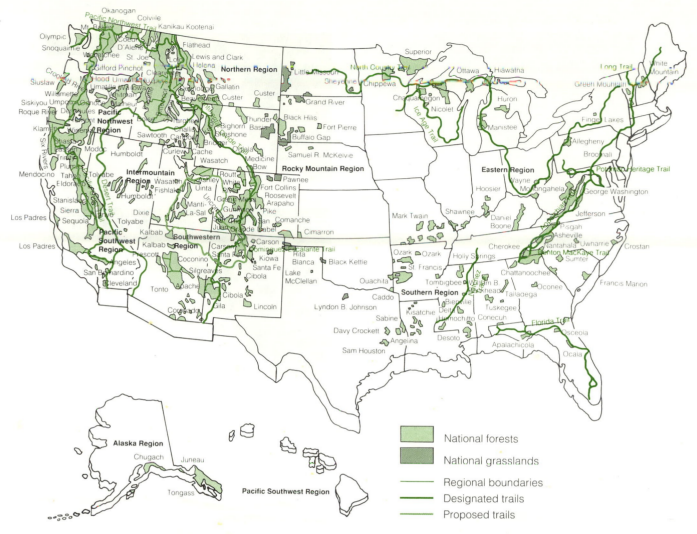

Figure 14-20 National forests and national grasslands in the United States. This map also shows the National Trails System. (Data from U.S. Forest Service)

Legend:
- National forests
- National grasslands
- Regional boundaries
- Designated trails
- Proposed trails

14-5 WILDERNESS PRESERVATION

What Is Wilderness? According to the Wilderness Act of 1964, **wilderness** consists of those areas "where the earth and its community of life are untrammeled by man, where man himself is a visitor who does not remain." It is wild land with no roads, power lines, or other signs of modern civilization.

Preservationists Aldo Leopold and Robert Marshall founded the Wilderness Society in 1935. They suggested that a wilderness area should be large enough for backpackers to travel in for two weeks "without crossing their own tracks." Such an area would have to be at least 1 million acres in size. Without large blocks surrounded by buffer zones, wilderness areas can be degraded by air pollution, water pollution, and noise pollution from nearby mining, oil and natural gas drilling, timber cutting, industry, and urban development.

How Much Wild Land Is Left? In 1987 the Sierra Club sponsored a survey of the world's remaining wild lands in blocks of at least 1 million acres. It revealed that only about 34% of the earth's land area is undeveloped wilderness. Much of it is in Antarctica, Greenland, and a broad band running across the northern latitudes of Alaska, Canada, and the Soviet far north. Large wild areas are also found in desert and other arid lands in Africa, the Middle East, and Australia and in the tropical forests of South America (Figure 14-21). Little wilderness is left in Europe and in the lower 48 states of the United States.

We often think of wilderness as forests. Forests do make up 30% of the earth's remaining wild lands (Figure 14-22). Much of this is tropical forests which are being rapidly cleared and degraded. Tundra and desert make up 64% of the world's remaining wild lands. These two types of biomes are vulnerable to disruption by even minor development. If they were not so

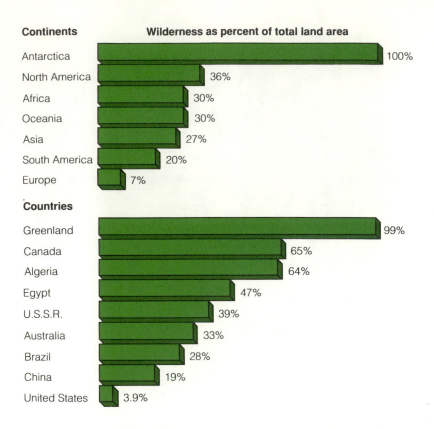

Figure 14-21 Wilderness areas by major geographical areas. (Data from J. Michael McCloskey and Heather Spalding. 1987. "A Reconnaissance-Level Inventory of the Wilderness Remaining in the World," Sierra Club)

Continents — **Wilderness as percent of total land area**

- Antarctica 100%
- North America 36%
- Africa 30%
- Oceania 30%
- Asia 27%
- South America 20%
- Europe 7%

Countries

- Greenland 99%
- Canada 65%
- Algeria 64%
- Egypt 47%
- U.S.S.R. 39%
- Australia 33%
- Brazil 28%
- China 19%
- United States 3.9%

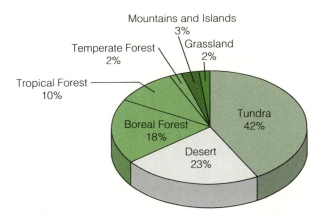

Mountains and Islands 3%
Grassland 2%
Temperate Forest 2%
Tropical Forest 10%
Boreal Forest 18%
Tundra 42%
Desert 23%

Figure 14-22 Wilderness areas by major biomes. (Data from J. Michael McCloskey and Heather Spalding. 1987. "A Reconnaissance-Level Inventory of the Wilderness Remaining in the World," Sierra Club)

hot and dry or cold, these biomes would have been intensely developed.

Why Preserve Wilderness?   There are many reasons. We need wild places where we can experience majestic beauty and natural biological diversity. We need places where we can enhance our mental health by getting away from noise, stress, and large numbers of people. Wilderness preservationist John Muir advised:

Climb the mountains and get their good tidings. Nature's peace will flow into you as the sunshine into the trees. The winds will blow their freshness into you, and the storms their energy, while cares will drop off like autumn leaves.

Wilderness areas provide recreation for growing numbers of people. They produce economic benefits for the booming outdoor-gear and tourist industries. They also are a savings account of resources that can be used later in a true emergency situation, rather than now for short-term economic gain.

Wilderness also has important ecological values. It provides undisturbed habitats for wild plants and animals, maintains diverse biological reserves protected from degradation, and provides a laboratory in which we can discover how nature works. It is an ecological insurance policy against eliminating too much of the earth's natural biological diversity. In the words of Henry David Thoreau: "In wildness is the preservation of the world." On ethical grounds wilderness should be preserved because the wild species it contains have a right to exist without human interference.

U.S. Wilderness Preservation System   In the United States preservationists have been trying to keep wild areas from being developed since 1900 (Section 2-4). They have fought timber, mining, oil, and natural gas companies, as well as scientific conservationists (see Spotlight on p. 38).

Mostly they have fought a losing battle. It was not until 1964 that Congress passed the Wilderness Act. It allows the government to protect undeveloped tracts

Officials of the timber, mining, and energy industries and ranchers operating on public lands say we already have too much wilderness. Conservationists say we don't have enough.

Resource industries argue that resources on and under any public lands should be used now and in the future to promote economic growth and provide mineral and energy resources to enhance national security. Between 1980 and 1988 this position was strongly supported by the Reagan administration.

Preservationists point out that wilderness is irreplaceable. It cannot be reestablished once the land has been developed. They urge Congress to add more area to the wilderness system, especially in the lower 48 states, where little wilderness land is left.

Since 1972 government agencies have made several reviews of remaining roadless areas in public lands. These studies show that an additional 5% of the total land area in the lower 48 states could qualify for wilderness designation.

Preservationists call for virtually all this land to be added to the wilderness system. They argue that nondestructive recreation and biological diversity far outweigh the short-term benefits of extracting resources from the land. They contend that this potential wilderness would not add much to the country's timber, mineral, and energy resources. For example, studies in 1982 by the Wilderness Society and the General Accounting Office indicated that designated wilderness areas contain only about 1% of the country's potential onshore oil and natural gas reserves.

Preservationists also point out that 60% of U.S. public lands are already managed officially or unofficially for multiple use, which includes some resource development. These lands along with private lands should supply enough resources to enhance national security and promote economic growth.

What do you think?

of public land from development as part of the National Wilderness Preservation System. Establishing this system was a vital step in wilderness preservation. But by 1964 much of the country's land was already developed. And since then resource developers have vigorously fought almost every proposal for adding more land to the system.

Only 3.9% of the U.S. land area is protected in the system. Almost two-thirds of this is in Alaska. Even in Alaska only 9 of 43 wilderness areas consist of more than 1 million acres. Only 1.7% of the land area of the lower 48 states is protected in the wilderness system. Of the 413 wilderness areas there, only 4 consist of more than 1 million acres.

Between 1970 and 1988 the amount of land in the National Wilderness Preservation System increased eightfold, from 11 million acres to 90 million acres, with most of the increase in Alaska. Nearly 60 million acres were added between 1970 and 1980. The pace slowed between 1981 and 1988, with only 10.6 million acres added to the system.

There remain almost 100 million acres of public lands that could qualify for designation as wilderness. Preservationists urge that these remaining roadless areas be added to the wilderness system. Resource developers lobby elected officials and government agencies to build roads in these areas so that they can't be designated wilderness (see Pro/Con above).

Use and Abuse of Wilderness Areas   In 1988 people made an estimated 15 million recreational visits to U.S. wilderness areas—about three times the number in 1970. Two-thirds of this recreational use is concentrated on 10% of the wilderness lands in the lower 48 states, especially in California, North Carolina, and Minnesota.

Popular wilderness areas are visited by so many people that their wildness is threatened. Fragile vegetation is damaged, soil is eroded from trails and campsites, water is polluted from bathing and dishwashing, and litter is scattered along trails. Instead of quiet and solitude, visitors sometimes face the noise and congestion they are trying to escape.

Wilderness areas are also being degraded by air, water, and noise pollution from nearby grazing, logging, oil and gas drilling, factories, power plants, and urban areas. In 1985 the National Park Service reported that scenic views in 64 wilderness areas within national parks were obscured by haze from air pollutants at least 90% of the time.

Global warming from the greenhouse effect is expected to be the biggest threat to wilderness, parks, forests, rangelands, croplands, estuaries, and inland wetlands during your lifetime. In a warmer world, vegetation zones will shift away from the equator and toward the pole. Many inland wetlands will dry up while many coastal wetlands will be flooded. This will alter and disrupt many wilderness and other protected areas. Then they will no longer be able to serve the purpose for which they were established, even with the best management possible.

Wilderness Management   To protect the most popular areas from damage, wilderness managers have had to limit the number of people hiking or camping at any one time. They have also designated areas where camping is allowed.

Another approach is to teach people how to use the wilderness without degrading it. Managers have increased the number of wilderness rangers to patrol vulnerable areas and enlisted volunteers to pick up trash discarded by thoughtless users.

Conservationists call for Congress to require agencies administering wilderness to prepare comprehensive guidelines for the management of individual areas. The public should have the opportunity to participate in this process.

Historian and wilderness expert Roderick Nash suggests that wilderness areas be divided into three categories. The easily accessible, popular areas would be intensively managed and have trails, bridges, hiker's huts, outhouses, assigned campsites, and extensive ranger patrols. Large, remote wilderness areas would not be intensively managed. They would be used only by people who get a use permit by demonstrating their wilderness skills. A third category would consist of large, biologically unique areas. They would be left undisturbed as genetic pools of plant, and animal species, with no human entry allowed.

National Wild and Scenic Rivers System In 1968 Congress passed the National Wild and Scenic Rivers Act. It allows rivers and river segments with outstanding scenic, recreational, geological, wildlife, historical, or cultural values to be protected in the National Wild and Scenic Rivers System.

These waterways are to be kept forever free of development. They cannot be widened, straightened, dredged, filled, or dammed along the designated lengths. The only activities allowed are camping, swimming, nonmotorized boating, sport hunting, and sport and commercial fishing. New mining claims, however, are permitted in some areas.

By 1988 the Wild and Scenic River System protected 116 rivers and river segments. They make up about 0.2% of the country's 3.5 million miles of rivers. Conservationists have urged Congress to add 1,500 additional eligible river segments to the system by the year 2000. If this goal is achieved, about 2% of the country's unique rivers would be protected from further development.

One problem is that Congress must pass a separate act to have a river or river segment studied as a possible candidate for the system. Conservationists want Congress to make a five-year nationwide study of all rivers and river segments currently eligible for designation as a wild or scenic river. During this period they want none of the candidate rivers to be developed in any way that might affect its ecological integrity.

Conservationists urge that a permanent federal administrative body be established to manage the Wild and Scenic River System. It would develop management plans for each unit in the system. They also urge states to develop their own wild and scenic river programs.

National Trails System In 1968 Congress passed the National Trails Act. It protects scenic and historic hiking trails in the National Trails System (Figure 14–20). By 1988 almost 24,000 miles of trails were included in this system. Another 8,000 miles of recreation trails have been established. However, no designated scenic or historic trail is complete.

In 1921 volunteers began working on the Appalachian Trail, running from Maine to Georgia. Despite 68 years of work and inclusion of the trail in the National Trails System in 1968, the government must still purchase easements for almost 300 miles to make it an unbroken footpath.

The Trails System has a low priority and gets little funding. In 1989 the Forest Service requested only $15.7 million for long neglected trail maintenance and no funds for trail construction. Conservationists propose that the government take the following measures:

- Place the Trails System under the management of a single agency.

- Make a comprehensive study of present and future trail needs.

- Complete the present system within ten years.

- Add new trails to achieve the goal of a network of trails throughout the country by the year 2000.

14-6 PARKS: TYPES, USE, AND ABUSE

Types of Parks The world's first parks, established many centuries ago in the Middle East and in Europe, were areas set aside for hunting by kings or other members of the ruling elite. The general public was excluded.

The world's first national park, Yellowstone, was set aside by an act of Congress in 1872. It was the first park established for the benefit and enjoyment of the general public.

Today there are over 1000 national parks in more than 120 countries. Since 1972 the number of national parks has increased 47% and their land area has increased 82%. This is an important achievement in the global conservation movement.

But these parks are increasingly threatened. In MDCs many national parks are threatened by nearby industrial development, urban growth, air and water pollution, roads, noise, invasion by alien species, and loss of natural species. Some of the most popular national parks are also threatened by overuse.

In LDCs the problems are worse. Plant and animal life in national parks are being threatened by local people who desperately need wood, cropland, and other resources. Poachers kill animals and sell their parts, such as rhino horns, elephant tusks, and furs. Most park services in these countries have too little money and staff to fight these invasions, either through enforcement or public education programs.

Most national parks in MDCs and LDCs are too small to sustain many of their natural species, especially larger animals. National parks are essentially islands of biological diversity surrounded by different types of ecosystems and often by developed areas. A national park is large enough if it can support its top predators in numbers that allow them to play their ecological roles. Most national parks flunk this test.

In addition to national parks, the public has access to state, county, and city parks. Virtually every state in the United States has at least one state park and many have several. Most state parks provide outdoor recreation for the public. Many are located near urban areas and thus are used more heavily than national parks. On less than one-seventh the acreage of national parks, state parks have twice the number of visitors.

The hundreds of county parks in the United States are used mostly for picnicking and camping. The thousands of urban parks vary widely in size and features. They are heavily used for recreation, education, and escape from urban stress.

Most urban parks are modest in size. Three large and well-known ones are Central Park in New York City, Golden Gate Park in San Francisco, and Griffith Park in Los Angeles. Some small urban spaces have been transformed into miniparks to serve the needs of local residents and passersby. In New York City a number of vest-pocket parks have been developed on small vacant lots between buildings.

U.S. National Parks The National Park System is dominated by 49 national parks found mostly in the West (Figure 14-18). These repositories of majesty, beauty, and biological diversity have been called America's crown jewels. But most of the Park System's 341 units are culture-oriented areas such as national historic sites and national battlefields.

During the 1970s several national recreation areas, seashores, lakeshores, and other units, usually located close to heavily populated urban areas, were added to bring national parks closer to the people. Since they opened in the 1970s, the Golden Gate National Recreation Area near San Francisco and the Gateway National Recreation Area near New York City have been two of the most widely used units in the National Park System.

Nature walks, guided tours, and other educational services provided by Park Service employees have provided many Americans with a better understand-

Figure 14-23 A National Park Service guide leads visitors through Redwood National Park.

ing of how nature works (Figure 14-23). Some conservationists urge that this effective educational program be expanded to show citizens ways to work with nature in their own daily lives. They have proposed that all park buildings and other facilities be designed as or converted to systems that demonstrate energy-efficient, low-polluting methods of heating, cooling, water purification, waste handling, transportation, and recycling.

Internal Stresses on Parks The major problems of national and state parks stem from their spectacular success. Because of more roads, cars, and affluence, annual recreational visits to National Park System units increased twelvefold and visits to state parks sevenfold between 1950 and 1988.

In 1988 more than 300 million visitors used the 49 national parks and other Park System units. The top draw, with 10.4 million visitors, was the Great Smoky Mountains National Park in Tennessee and North Carolina. Other popular national parks are Maine's oceanside Acadia (4.3 million), Arizona's Grand Canyon (3.5 million), California's Yosemite ((3.1 million), Washington's Olympic (2.8 million), and Yellowstone (2.6 million). Annual visits to national park system units is expected to double to 600 million by 2020.

The recreational use of state and national parks and other public lands is expected to increase even more in the future, putting additional stress on many already overburdened parks. Under the onslaught of people during the peak summer season, the most popular national and state parks are often overcrowded with cars and trailers and plagued by noise, traffic jams, litter, vandalism, deteriorating trails, polluted water, drugs, and crime. The theft of timber and cacti from national parks is a growing problem. At Grand Canyon National Park 50,000 small-plane and helicopter flights per year for tourists have turned the area into a noisy flying circus.

Park Service rangers are now trained more in law enforcement than in resource conservation and management. They must wear guns and spend an increasing amount of their time acting as park police officers. Popular parks spend more than half their meager budgets on removing garbage and maintaining rest rooms.

Populations of wolves, bears, and other large predators in and near various parks have dropped sharply or disappeared because of excessive hunting, poisoning by ranchers and federal officials, and the limited size of some parks. This decline has allowed populations of remaining prey species to increase sharply, destroy vegetation, and crowd out other native animal species. Park Service officials are trying to decide what to do about this problem (see Pro/Con below).

The movement of alien species into parks is also a threat. Wild boars are a major threat to vegetation in part of the Great Smoky Mountains National Park. The Brazilian pepper tree has invaded Florida's Everglades National Park. Mountain goats in Washington's Olympic National Park trample native vegetation and accelerate soil erosion.

External Threats to Parks The greatest danger to many parks today is from human activities in nearby areas. Wildlife and recreational values are threatened by mining, timber harvesting, grazing, coal-burning power plants, water diversion, and urban development. In 1988 the Wilderness Society identified the ten most endangered national park units (Figure 14-24).

To take one example, the amount and diversity of plant and animal life in the Everglades National Park in southern Florida have dropped sharply. Much of the water that once flowed southward into this swampland wildlife preserve has been diverted for irrigation and urban development. The decrease in water, the resulting increased salinity of the swamp, and the spread of nearby housing developments have reduced the wading-bird population in the park by 90%, down from 2.5 million in the 1930s to 250,000 now.

Park Management: Combining Conservation and Sustainable Development Because of increasing internal and external stresses, many park managers are rethinking ways to manage parks. Some managers, especially in LDCs, are developing integrated management plans that combine conservation and sustainable development of the park and, where possible, surrounding areas.

PRO/CON Should Wolves Be Reintroduced into Yellowstone?

During the 1920s the federal government launched a successful program to kill all the wolves in Yellowstone National Park. They were considered too great a threat to populations of elk, deer, and other large grazing animals.

Wolves were also killed by ranchers and federal officials to protect livestock in most other areas of the lower 48 states. Some 5,000 wolves still live in Alaska. But the lower 48 states now contain only about 1,200 wolves in Minnesota and 50 in Wisconsin and Michigan. In 1987 four pairs of red wolves, which feed mostly on rabbits, were introduced into the Alligator River National Wildlife Refuge in North Carolina.

Since 1930, when the wolf was exterminated from Yellowstone, the elk population has exploded. The herd, which now numbers 25,000, is depleting vegetation needed as food by other species.

To prevent further decline in other plant and animal species, park officials are considering three alternatives: controlling the elk population by reintroducing wolves into Yellowstone, allowing sport hunters to kill excess elk, or not interfering at all and allowing large die-offs of elk as they exceed their food supplies.

Conservationists favor returning the wolf to Yellowstone, in keeping with the goal of national parks to preserve natural ecosystems. Some oppose increased hunting. And waiting for the elk to die off could endanger many other plant and animal species native to Yellowstone.

Sheep and cattle ranchers strongly oppose reintroducing wolves. They fear that some of them will leave the park to prey on livestock. Conservationists respond that only 0.2% of the 12,000 farms in Minnesota wolf country lose even one animal per year to wolves. Also, under the proposed plan, wolves could be easily tracked because they would wear radio collars. If found on ranchlands, they could be captured or shot. What do you think should be done?

1 Yosemite
- Logging and road building in nearby national forests
- Nearby mining and geothermal energy development
- Nearby urban development

2 Olympic
- Offshore oil drilling
- Logging and road building in surrounding national forest
- Non-native goats

3 Glacier
- Nearby residential and commercial development
- Oil drilling, logging, and road building in nearby national forests
- Wolf-killing program

4 Yellowstone
- Logging and road building, oil and gas drilling, and geothermal energy development in nearby national forests
- Nearby residential development and ski runs
- Building up to 9 dams on Clarks Fork River

5 Manassas National Battlefield
- Proposed adjacent shopping mall

6 Great Smoky Mountain
- Logging and road building in nearby national forests
- Air pollution
- Non-native wild boars

7 Everglades
- Nearby urban development
- Water pollution
- Military use

8 Rocky Mountain
- Nearby condominiums and urban sprawl
- Overcrowding
- Logging and road building on nearby national forest

9 Grand Canyon
- Tourist planes
- Nearby uranium mining
- Damage to beaches and fish from upstream Glen Canyon Dam

10 Santa Monica Recreation Area
- Only one third of proposed recreation area purchased within last 10 years
- Increasing private development within the area

Figure 14-24 The ten most endangered units of the National Park System. (Data from the Wilderness Society)

In such a plan the inner core and especially vulnerable areas of the park are protected from development and treated as wilderness. Controlled numbers of people are allowed to use these areas for hiking, nature study, ecological research, and other nondestructive recreational and educational activities. In other areas controlled commercial logging and hunting and fishing by local natives are allowed. Thus, local people can use park resources on a sustainable basis. Money spent by park visitors also adds to local income.

By involving local people in developing park management plans, managers help them see the park as a vital resource they need to sustain. They become protectors instead of abusers of the park.

Park managers can also survey the land surrounding a park to identify areas that threaten the park's wildlife. Sometimes these areas can be added to the park. If not, managers may be able to persuade developers or local people to use less critical areas for certain types of development. However, the greatest threat to many of the world's parks within your lifetime is regional climate change from global warming, regardless of how well parks are managed.

An Agenda for U.S. National Parks The National Park Service faces difficult problems. It has two goals that increasingly conflict. One is to preserve nature in parks. The other is to make nature more available to the public. The Park Service must accomplish these goals with a small budget at a time when park usage and external threats to the parks are increasing.

In 1988 the Wilderness Society and the National Parks and Conservation Association published the results of studies they had made of the National Park System. Their blueprint for the future of this system included the following proposals:

- Educate the public about the urgent need to protect, mend, and expand the system.

- Establish the National Park Service as an independent agency responsible to the president and Congress. This would make it less vulnerable to the shifting political winds of the Interior Department.

GUEST ESSAY Tropical Forests and Their Species: Going, Going . . .?

Norman Myers

Norman Myers is an international consultant in environment and development with emphasis on conservation of wildlife species and tropical forests. He has served as a consultant for many development agencies and research organizations, including the U.S. National Academy of Sciences, the World Bank, the Organization for Economic Cooperation and Development (OECD), various UN agencies, and the World Resources Institute. Among his recent publications (see Further Readings) are The Sinking Ark *(1979), Conversion of Tropical Moist Forests (1980), A Wealth of Wild Species (1983), The Primary Source (1984), and The Gaia Atlas of Planet Management (1985).*

Tropical forests still cover an area roughly equivalent to the "lower 48" United States. Climatic and biological data suggest they could have once covered an area at least twice as large. So we have already lost half of them, mostly in the recent past. Worse, remote-sensing surveys show that we are now destroying the forests at a rate of at least 1.25% a year, and we are grossly degrading them at a rate of at least another 1.25% a year—and both rates are accelerating. Unless we act now to halt this loss, within just another few decades at most, there could be little left, except perhaps a block in central Africa and another in the western part of the Amazon basin. Even these remnants may not survive the combined pressures of population growth and land hunger beyond the middle of the next century.

This means that we are imposing one of the most broad-scale and impoverishing impacts on the biosphere that it has ever suffered throughout its 4 billion years of existence. Tropical forests are the greatest celebration of nature to appear on the face of the planet since the first flickerings of life. They are exceptionally complex ecologically, and they are remarkably rich biotically. Although they now account for only 7% of the earth's land surface, they still are home for half, and perhaps three-quarters or more, of all the earth's species of plant and animal life. Thus, elimination of these forests is by far the leading factor in the mass extinction of species that appears likely over the next few decades.

Already, we are certainly losing several species every day because of clearing and degradation of tropical forests. The time will surely come, and come soon, when we shall be losing many thousands every year. The implications are profound, whether they be scientific, aesthetic, ethical—or simply economic. In medicine alone, we benefit from myriad drugs and pharmaceuticals derived from tropical forest plants. The commercial value of these products worldwide can be reckoned at $20 billion each year.

By way of example, the rosy periwinkle from Madagascar's tropical forests has produced two potent drugs against Hodgkin's disease, leukemia, and other

---

- Block the mining, timbering, and other threats to national parks that are taking place near park boundaries on land managed by the U.S. Forest Service and the Bureau of Land Management.

- Acquire new parkland near threatened areas. Within the next decade expand 200 of the 341 national park units by 10 million acres and add at least 75 new parks. In 1978 the federal budget for purchase of new parkland was $681 million, but in 1989 only $17 million was requested for this purpose.

- Locate commercial park facilities (such as restaurants) *outside* park boundaries.

- Wherever feasible, place visitor parking areas outside the park areas. Use low-polluting vehicles to carry visitors to and from parking areas and for transportation within the park.

- Greatly expand the Park Service budget for maintenance and science and conservation programs. According to the General Accounting Office, at least $1.9 billion is needed for long-neglected road repair. Funding is also needed for inventories of park wildlife species and for gathering adequate data on the ecological health of parks.

- Require the Park Service and Forest Service to develop integrated management plans so that activities in nearby national forests don't degrade national parklands.

Sustaining forests, wilderness, rivers, trails, and parks is an urgent task. It will cost a great deal of money and require strong support from the public. But it will cost our civilization much more if we do not protect these resources from degradation and destruction.

blood cancers. Madagascar has—or used to have—at least 8,000 plant species, of which more than 7,000 could be found nowhere else. Today Madagascar has lost 93% of its virgin tropical forest. The U.S. National Cancer Institute estimates that there could be another 10 plants in tropical forests with potential against various cancers—provided pharmacologists can get to them before they are eliminated by chain saws and bulldozers.

We benefit in still other ways from tropical forests. Elimination of these forests disrupts certain critical environmental services, notably their famous "sponge effect" by which they soak up rainfall during the wet season and then release it in regular amounts throughout the dry season. When tree cover is removed and this watershed function is impaired, the result is a yearly regime of floods followed by droughts, which destroys property and reduces agricultural production. There is also concern that if tropical deforestation becomes wide enough, it could trigger local, regional, or even global changes in climate. Such climatic upheavals would affect the lives of billions of people, if not the whole of humankind.

All this raises important questions about our role in the biosphere and our relations with the natural world around us. As we proceed on our disruptive way in tropical forests, we—that is, political leaders and the general public alike—give scarcely a moment's thought to what we are doing. We are deciding the fate of the world's tropical forests unwittingly, yet effectively and increasingly.

The resulting shift in evolution's course, stemming from the elimination of tropical forests, will rank as one of the greatest biological upheavals since the dawn of life. It will equal, in scale and significance, the development of aerobic respiration, the emer-

gence of flowering plants, and the arrival of limbed animals, taking place over eons of time. But whereas these were enriching disruptions in the course of life on this planet, the loss of biotic diversity associated with tropical forest destruction will be almost entirely an impoverishing phenomenon brought about entirely by human actions. And it will all have occurred within the twinkling of a geologic eye.

In short, our intervention in tropical forests should be viewed as one of the most challenging problems that humankind has ever encountered. After all, we are the first species ever to be able to look upon nature's work and to decide whether we should consciously eliminate it or leave much of it untouched.

So the decline of tropical forest is one of the great sleeper issues of our time. Yet we can still save much of these forests, and the species they contain. Should we not consider ourselves fortunate that we alone among all generations are being given the chance to preserve tropical forests as the most exuberant expression of nature in the biosphere—and thereby to support the right to life of many of our fellow species and their capacity to undergo further evolution without human interference?

Guest Essay Discussion

1. What obligation, if any, do you as an individual have to preserve a significant portion of the world's remaining tropical forests?

2. Should MDCs provide most of the money to preserve remaining tropical forests in LDCs? Explain.

3. What can you do to help preserve some of the world's tropical forests? Which, if any, of these actions do you plan to carry out?

If people in general could be got into the woods, even for once, to hear the trees speak for themselves, all difficulties in the way of forest preservation would vanish.

Sierra Club Bulletin, 1896

DISCUSSION TOPICS

1. List the major ecological roles of forests. How might your life and lifestyle change if these services continue to be drastically reduced by human activities, including your own use of forestry products?

2. Why do people rarely take into account the important ecological services provided by forests when considering whether to log a forest? How would you correct this situation?

3. How would your life and lifestyle change if wood products were unavailable or became much more expensive?

4. What difference could the loss of essentially all the remaining tropical forests have on your life and on the life of any child you might have?

5. Why are tropical forests especially vulnerable to widespread slash-and-burn clearing for agriculture?

6. Explain how eating a hamburger in some U.S. fast-food chains indirectly contributes to the destruction of tropical forests?

7. Should more wilderness areas and wild and scenic rivers be preserved in the United States? Explain.

8. If significant deposits of oil, coal, or key metallic minerals are found under land designated as wilderness or proposed for wilderness designation, would you favor allowing these resources to be extracted now? Explain.

9. Explain why you agree or disagree with each of the following suggestions concerning national parks in the United States:
   a. Entrance, activity, and private concessionaire fees should be raised so that they pay for 25% of the costs of operating the National Park System.
   b. All private vehicles should be kept out.
   c. Campgrounds, lodges, and other commercial facilities in parks should be moved to nearby areas outside the parks.
   d. The annual federal budget for restoration of existing national parks and purchase of more parkland should be sharply increased.

FURTHER READINGS

Allin, Craig W. 1982. *The Politics of Wilderness Preservation*. Westport, Conn.: Greenwood Press.

Borman, F. H. 1985. "Air Pollution and Forests: An Ecosystem Perspective," *BioScience*, vol. 35, no. 7, 434–441.

Brown, Lester R., et al. Annual. *State of the World*. New York: W. W. Norton.

Caufield, Catherine. 1985. *In the Rainforest*. New York: Alfred A. Knopf.

Chase, Alston. 1986. *Playing God in Yellowstone: The Destruction of America's First National Park*. New York: Atlantic Monthly Press.

Clawson, Marion. 1983. *The Federal Lands Revisited*. Washington, D.C.: Resources for the Future.

Clawson, Marion. 1975. *Forests for Whom and for What?* Baltimore: Johns Hopkins University Press.

Conservation Foundation. 1985. *National Parks and the New Generation*. Washington, D.C.: Conservation Foundation.

Eckholm, Erik, et al. 1984. *Fuelwood: The Energy Crisis That Won't Go Away*. Washington, D.C.: Earthscan.

Hartzog, George B., Jr. 1988. *Battling for the National Parks*. New York: Mayer Bell.

Hendee, John, et al., eds. 1977. *Principles of Wilderness Management*. Washington, D.C.: Government Printing Office.

Hewett, Charles E., and Thomas E. Hamilton, eds. 1982. *Forests in Demand: Conflicts and Solutions*. Boston: Auburn Publishing House.

Jordan, Carl F. 1982. "Amazon Rain Forests," *American Scientist*, vol. 70, July–Aug., 394–400.

Kelly, David. 1988. *Secrets of the Old Growth Forest*. Layton, Utah: Gibbs Smith.

McConneely, Jeffery A., and Kenton R. Miller, eds. 1984. *National Parks, Conservation, and Development*. Washington, D.C.: Smithsonian Institution Press.

Mello, Robert A. 1987. *Last Stand of the Red Spruce*. Covelo, Calif.: Island Press.

Myers, Norman. 1984. *The Primary Source: Tropical Forests and Our Future*. New York: W. W. Norton.

Myers, Norman, ed. 1984. *Gaia: An Atlas of Planet Management*. Garden City, N.Y.: Anchor Press/Doubleday.

Nash, Roderick. 1982. *Wilderness and the American Mind*. 3d ed. New Haven, Conn.: Yale University Press.

National Parks and Conservation Association. 1988. *Blueprint for National Parks* (9 vols). Washington, D.C.: National Parks and Conservation Association.

Postel, Sandra. 1984. *Air Pollution, Acid Rain, and the Future of Forests*. Washington, D.C.: Worldwatch Institute.

Runte, Alfred. 1987. *National Parks: The American Experience*. 2d ed. Lincoln: University of Nebraska Press.

Sierra Club. 1982. *Our Public Lands: An Introduction to the Agencies and Issues*. San Francisco: Sierra Club Books.

Spurr, Stephen H., and Buron V. Barnes. 1980. *Forest Ecology*. 3d ed. New York: Ronald Press.

World Resources Institute and International Institute for Environment and Development. Annual. *World Resources*. New York: Basic Books.

Zaslowsky, Dyan, and The Wilderness Society. 1986. *These American Lands*. New York: Henry Holt.

CHAPTER 15

Management and Conservation
of Forest Resources

General Questions and Issues

1. What are the major principles of forest resource management and conservation?

2. What methods can be used to manage and conserve forest resources?

3. How should national forests in the United States be managed and used?

4. How can we deal with the fuelwood crisis and tropical deforestation?

What do forests bear? Soil, water, and pure air.
Motto of the Chipko Tree Preservation Movement in India

M anaging forests to produce a sustainable supply of timber is not easy. Although crops can be harvested annually, trees take 20 to 1,000 years to mature. A delicate balance must be established between commercial harvesting and other uses of forests such as watershed protection, wildlife habitat, and recreation. Halting the conversion of potentially renewable forest resources into nonrenewable resources and reforesting depleted lands are urgent and challenging tasks.

15-1 PRINCIPLES OF FOREST RESOURCE MANAGEMENT AND CONSERVATION

Silviculture and Forest Management The art and science of growing trees to provide a renewable supply of timber is called **silviculture** (from the Latin word *silva* for forest). It covers only biological considerations.

Forest conservation involves managing or protecting forests to sustain commercial tree populations, wildlife populations, biological diversity, watershed protection, and other ecological services. **Forest management** blends silviculture with economic considerations to determine how a stand of trees is to be harvested and regenerated. Ideally, the management of forest resources should be based on biological or silvicultural principles. In practice, the management of

forests, like that of any resource, also involves economic, political, legal, and ethical factors. Often these factors are at odds with sound scientific principles of forest management.

Economics and Politics of Commercial Forestry
Sustainable forestry is not a very lucrative business because it takes a long time to grow timber. Tree farms can grow timber in sizes useful for pulp, rough lumber, and plywood in 20 to 30 years. But to grow high-quality timber in useful sizes for lumber takes 75 to 150 years. To grow high-quality wood for fine furniture and musical instruments takes 150 to 1,000 years.

The average annual return on the investment in a tree farm in the United States ranges from 2.5% to 5%, far less than the 10% to 15% average return for most other industries. The average return on the sustained yield of an uneven-aged, old-growth forest is only about 1% to 2% of the cash value of its entire inventory.

Since timber companies are in business to make a profit, they naturally want to get a return on their investment as quickly as possible. So they usually prefer to cut and sell the timber on uneven-aged, old-

---

This chapter was coauthored by Carl H. Reidel, Director of the Environmental Program, University of Vermont, and G. Tyler Miller, Jr.

Table 15-1 Compatibility of Various Multiple Uses of Forests

Primary Use	Secondary Multiple Uses (degree of compatibility with the primary use)						
	Attractive Environment	Recreation Opportunity	Wilderness	Wildlife	Watershed	General Conservation	Wood Production and Harvest
Maintain an attractive environment	-----	Moderate unless intense	Good	Good for most	Fully	Fully	Limited; affects amount of harvest
Recreation opportunity	Moderate unless intense	-----	Poor	Fair	Depends on intensity	Moderate	Limited, but manageable
Wilderness	Fully	Poor; can't tolerate heavy use	-----	Good for most; not for some	Fully	Fully	Completely incompatible
Wildlife	Generally compatible	Limited; use must be limited	Good for most	-----	Fully	Fully	Generally good with limits on harvesting
Natural watershed	Fully	Moderate; limit intensity	Good	Good	-----	Fully	Moderate if harvesting is limited
General conservation	Fully	Moderate	Fair	Generally good	Fully	-----	Good with modification
Wood production and harvest	Good if harvest method strictly controlled	Fair to moderate	Not compatible	Good if methods controlled	Good if methods controlled	Good if methods controlled	-----

Adapted with permission, from *Forests for Whom and for What?* by Marion Clawson. Copyright © 1975 by Johns Hopkins University Press.

growth forests and replace them with even-aged tree farms that can be harvested every 20 to 30 years.

This economic decision makes sense for a forest industry concerned with producing a single product like timber on land that it owns or has leased. But developing a management plan for harvesting timber from public lands is much more complex and controversial. Public forestry agencies are often required by law to manage public forests so as to produce timber on a sustainable basis while also preserving these forests for other values.

Besides economic efficiency, people want to know who gains and who loses in forest management decisions involving public lands. One question is to what degree the external costs of harvesting timber on public land should be internalized (Section 3-3). Should the external costs be internalized by requiring private timber companies to bear all costs of road building, site preparation, site restoration, and site protection incurred by any timber harvesting they are allowed to carry out on public land? Or should taxpayers subsidize many of these costs, as they now do? Should all timber sales on public land at least break even in terms

of the estimated market value of the timber and any harvesting costs borne by taxpayers? Or should sales be allowed at below market prices, as now occurs in many national forests?

Three public-forest management policies designed to integrate ecological, political, economic, and other social factors are scientific conservation, multiple use, and sustained yield.

Scientific Conservation Scientific conservation involves using forest resources to provide economic and social benefits for people without destroying or degrading these resources for future generations. Despite continuing controversy (Section 2-4), most public forests in the United States are managed according to the principle of scientific conservation in combination with the principles of multiple use and sustained yield.

Multiple Use According to the Multiple-Use Sustained-Yield Act of 1960, public forests are to be managed to allow timber harvesting, outdoor recreation, livestock grazing, watershed protection, and protection of wildlife and fish habitat *on the same land, at the same time*. Thus, the U.S. Forest Service must perform a delicate balancing act in managing the country's 156 national forests.

The 1976 National Forest Management Act updates some elements of national forest management. But it also states six times that its provisions must be carried out in a manner consistent with the Multiple-Use Sustained-Yield Act.

Some competing uses of public forests are incompatible (Table 15-1). This means that managing a public forest for balanced multiple use is difficult and sometimes impossible. It usually involves making trade-offs that don't satisfy all the special-interest groups wanting different things from the forest.

In the United States, conservationists and timber company officials have argued over multiple-use management of public forests for decades. In practice, many public forests and areas of these forests are now managed for dominant use instead of multiple use. Many areas are managed primarily for commercial timber harvesting. Others are managed with emphasis on conservation of wildlife, watersheds, and outdoor recreation.

Sustained Yield   The policy of managing forests to ensure their continued productivity is the heart of forest resource conservation. In the Multiple-Use, Sustained-Yield Act of 1960, Congress defined **sustained yield** as follows:

Sustained yield of the several products and services means the achievement and maintenance in perpetuity of high-level annual or regular periodic output of the various renewable resources of the National Forests without impairment of the productivity of the land.

This definition is subject to a broad range of controversial interpretations. For example, should entire national forests or only certain parts of such forests be managed on an annual sustained-yield basis? Should the sustained-yield cycle be longer than a year?

In later legislation Congress changed the concept of sustained yield by adding the concept of **nondeclining even flow** to help ensure a continuous flow of timber from the national forests. This policy calls for setting a total periodic harvest from each national forest that will rise or stay level over time, but will never decline.

Strictly interpreted, this policy prevents the Forest Service from allowing timber cutting in any national forest that exceeds its sustained yield. However, Congress provided a loophole that allows the sustained yield in a particular national forest to be exceeded temporarily if this leads to a higher future yield of timber.

Despite many problems, conflicts, and competing interests, the basic principles of scientific conserva-

tion, multiple use, and sustained yield are remarkably good guidelines for the practical management of public-forest resources. Most controversies are not over the principles themselves but how they are applied.

15-2   METHODS OF FOREST MANAGEMENT AND CONSERVATION

Types of Forest Management   There are two basic forest management systems: even-aged management and uneven-aged management. With **even-aged management** trees in a given stand, covering an extensive area, are maintained at about the same age and size, harvested all at once, and replanted naturally or artificially so that a new even-aged stand will grow. Emphasis is on mass production of low-quality wood with the goal of maximizing economic return on investment in as short a time as possible. It is basically a short-term, economics-centered approach.

With **uneven-aged management** trees in a given stand are maintained at many ages and sizes to permit continuous natural regeneration. Here the primary goal is to sustain biological diversity, sustain long-term production of high-quality timber, provide a reasonable economic return, and allow multiple use of a forest stand. It is a long-term, ecology- and economics-centered approach.

The Forest Management Process   Forest management consists of a cycle of decisions and events (Figure 15-1). Each cycle of management between planting and harvesting is called a *rotation*. The major steps in this cycle include making an inventory of the site, developing a forest management plan, preparing the site for harvest, harvesting commercially valuable timber, and regenerating and managing the site before the next harvest.

Making an Inventory   The forest management process begins with an inventory of a proposed site. The purpose of an inventory is to get information about past growth, site quality, and projected future growth. A survey is made to determine the species present, age classes, relationships of commercial species with other plant and animal species, and soil conditions. A small hole is bored in selected trees and a core or plug is removed. This core contains a cross section of growth rings that indicate tree age and rate of growth and can help foresters project future growth. Site index measurements of tree height and age can be used to identify the most productive sites.

During the inventory foresters also consider the best sites for logging roads and evaluate their effects

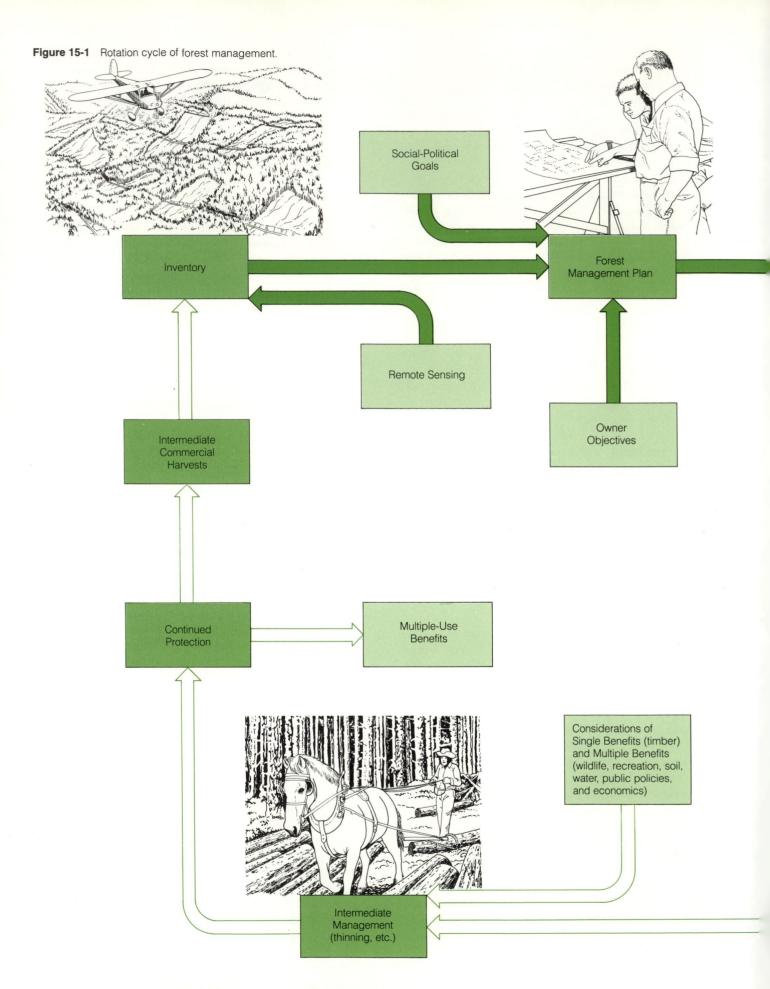

Figure 15-1 Rotation cycle of forest management.

Social-Political Goals

Inventory

Forest Management Plan

Remote Sensing

Owner Objectives

Intermediate Commercial Harvests

Continued Protection

Multiple-Use Benefits

Considerations of Single Benefits (timber) and Multiple Benefits (wildlife, recreation, soil, water, public policies, and economics)

Intermediate Management (thinning, etc.)

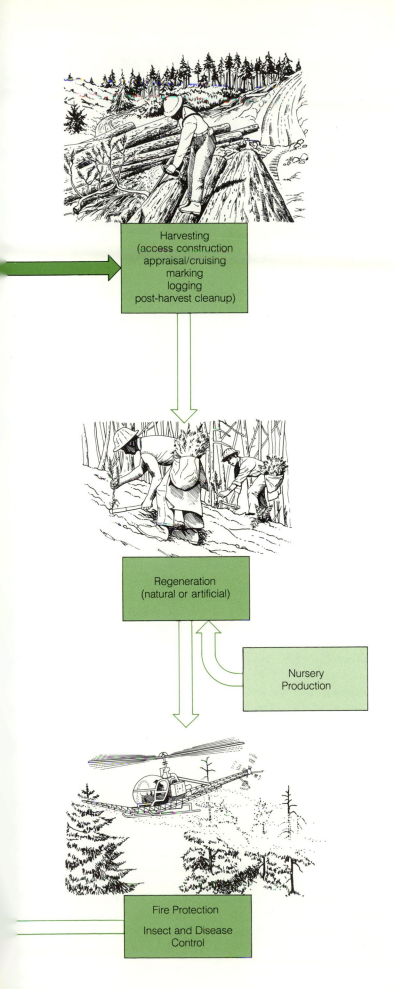

Harvesting
(access construction
appraisal/cruising
marking
logging
post-harvest cleanup)

Regeneration
(natural or artificial)

Nursery
Production

Fire Protection

Insect and Disease
Control

on scenic and historical resources. Roads must be built with as little as possible erosion and other forms of forest damage. In areas where roads are not possible or would be too environmentally harmful, another method of log removal must be planned. Examples include lifting logs out by balloon or helicopter, sliding logs down skid trails, and building a cable system to transport logs to lower elevations.

The technology of conducting forest inventories has changed dramatically with the development of computer-aided remote-sensing capabilities. Photographs and infrared images taken from aircraft or satellites allow foresters to view land in three dimensions. Tree height, canopy height, and species groups can be measured with a high degree of accuracy from three-dimensional photos. These data can be fed into a computer to generate maps of sites. Using these measurements and on-site ground checks, the forester can produce remarkably accurate vegetation maps and estimates of the harvestable volumes of wood. The same photos can be used with topographic maps to find existing roads or to pick the best locations for new roads and work sites.

Forest Management Plan The next step in forest management is to use the inventory data to develop a forest management plan. The plan includes the owner's goals, the primary desired product or use, other uses to be served by the area, and ecological restraints.

Most forests are managed to obtain the maximum possible profit from timber harvesting. So the key parts of most management plans deal with how to gain access to the harvestable timber, the type of harvesting to be used, a harvesting schedule, how the site will be regenerated, and how it is to be managed between harvests.

The volume of wood produced by a forest varies as it goes through various stages of growth and ecological succession (Figure 15-2). If the goal is to produce a large quantity of fuelwood or fiber for paper production in the shortest time, the forest is usually harvested on a short rotation cycle before their rate of growth begins to decline (point A of Figure 15-2). Harvesting when the trees reach their peak growth gives the maximum yield of wood (point B of Figure 15-2). But if the goal is quality of growth for fine furniture or veneer, managers use longer rotations to take advantage of the high-quality wood in larger, older-growth trees (point C of Figure 15-2).

Ecological and aesthetic values often can be best served by never harvesting a forest stand. Ecological restraints and noncommercial uses of forests can be important factors in developing management plans for some public and private forests. However, they are only secondary goals in forests where commercial wood production is the major goal.

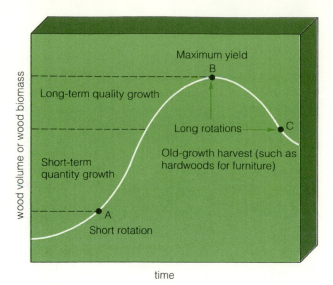

Figure 15-2   The cycle of forest productivity.

The graph shows wood volume or wood biomass (y-axis) versus time (x-axis), with an S-shaped curve. Labels include: Maximum yield at point B, Long-term quality growth, Long rotations, Old-growth harvest (such as hardwoods for furniture) at point C, Short-term quantity growth, Short rotation at point A.

Figure 15-3   Selective cutting of ponderosa pine in Deschutes National Forest, an old-growth forest near Sisters, Oregon.

Preparation for Harvest   Before a forest area is harvested, foresters go to the site and estimate the volume and grade of standing timber. This on-site survey is called a *cruise*. Then a timber-marking crew marks individual trees to be cut and marks the boundary of areas to be cut.

Data from the cruise are used to draw up a timber sales contract. It specifies what trees and areas are to be cut, the harvesting method, how cut logs are to be removed, where roads or skid trails are to be built, and how the area is to be regenerated. It also specifies all other obligations of the seller and buyer, how the operation will be supervised, and penalties and fines for violations of the contract. Usually the contract is then sent out for open bidding.

Tree Harvesting   The method chosen for harvesting depends on whether uneven-aged or even-aged forest management is being used. It also depends on the tree species involved, the nature of the site, and the objectives and resources of the owner.

In **selective cutting**, intermediate-aged or mature trees in an uneven-aged forest are cut singly or in small groups (Figure 15-3). This reduces crowding, encourages the growth of younger trees, and maintains an uneven-aged stand with trees of different species, ages, and sizes. Over time the stand will regenerate itself.

If done properly, selective cutting helps protects the site from soil erosion and tree damage and destruction by the wind. Because slash (debris left on the ground after cutting) is scattered, the fire hazard is usually low. This harvesting method is favored by those who wish to use forests for multiple uses and wish to preserve biological diversity.

Selective cutting of individual trees is used primarily in mixed northern and tropical hardwood forests. In such forests the forester can regulate the amount of cutting and can select species to encourage growth of favored commercial species. Selective cutting of small groups of trees can be used to harvest ponderosa pine, Douglas fir, oak, hickory, and loblolly pine.

But selective cutting is costly unless the value of the trees removed is high. It's not useful for shade-intolerant species (Table 14-1, p. 366), which require full sunlight for seedling growth. Selective cutting of small groups of trees, however, can reduce logging costs and provide enough sunlight for many shade-tolerant species. The need to reopen roads and trails periodically for selective harvests can cause erosion of certain soils. Maintaining a good mixture of tree ages and sizes takes considerable planning and skill.

One type of selective cutting, not considered a sound forestry practice, is *high grading*, or *creaming*—removing the most valuable trees without considering the quality or distribution of the remaining trees needed for regeneration. Many loggers in tropical forests in LDCs use this destructive form of selective cutting.

Some tree species do best when grown in full or moderate sunlight in forest openings or in large cleared and seeded areas. Even-aged stands or tree farms of such shade-intolerant species are usually harvested by shelterwood cutting, seed-tree cutting, or clearcutting.

Figure 15-4 First stage of shelterwood cutting of red pine in a 140-year stand in Minnesota.

U.S. Forest Service/Paul J. Zahngraff

Figure 15-5 Seed trees left after the seed-tree cutting of a stand of longleaf pine in Florida. About ten trees per hectare are left to reseed the area.

Department of Forestry, University of Florida, Gainesville

Shelterwood cutting is the removal of all mature trees in an area in a series of cuttings typically over a period of ten years. This technique can be applied to even-aged or uneven-aged stands. In the first harvest—called the *preparatory cutting*—selected mature trees, unwanted tree species, and dying, defective, and diseased trees are removed. This "sanitation-salvation cut" opens up the forest floor to light. It also leaves the best trees to cast seed and provide shelter for growing seedlings (Figure 15-4).

After a number of seedlings have taken hold, a second cutting—called the *seed cutting*—removes more of the remaining mature trees. Some of the best mature trees are left to provide shelter for the growing young trees. After the young trees are well established, a third cutting—the *removal cutting*—removes the remaining mature trees and allows the even-aged stand of young trees to grow to maturity.

This method allows natural reseeding from the best seed trees and protects seedlings from being crowded out. The trees left standing in the first and second cuttings help accelerate the growth of young trees.

Shelterwood cutting leaves a fairly natural-looking forest that can be used for a variety of purposes. It also helps reduce soil erosion and provides good habitat for wildlife. It is particularly useful for northern red oak, yellow poplar, hickories, white ash, northeastern spruce-fir, loblolly pine, ponderosa pine, white pine, Douglas fir, and Sitka spruce.

Without careful planning and supervision, however, loggers may take too many trees in the initial cutting, especially the most valuable trees. Shelterwood cutting is also more costly and takes more skill and planning than clearcutting.

Seed-tree cutting harvests nearly all the trees on a site in one cutting, leaving a few seed-producing, wind-resistant trees uniformly distributed as a source of seed to regenerate a new crop of trees (Figure 15-5).

Figure 15-6 Forest Service clearcut on Prince of Wales Island, Alaska. All trees in the area are removed and the area is reseeded.

Southeast Alaska Conservation Council

Figure 15-7 Patch clearcutting Kootenai National Forest, Montana.

U.S. Forest Service

In most cases at least five to ten seed trees must be left per hectare, singly or in groups. After the new trees have become established, the seed trees are sometimes harvested.

By allowing a variety of species to grow at one time, seed-tree cutting leaves an aesthetically pleasing forest useful for recreation, deer hunting, erosion control, and wildlife conservation. Leaving the best trees for seed can also lead to genetic improvement in the new stand.

Seed-tree cutting is a popular technique for harvesting and regenerating southern pine tree species, such as loblolly, longleaf, shortleaf, and slash pines. However, it's not used for species with shallow roots, such as northeastern spruce and fir, lodgepole pine, Douglas fir, Sitka spruce, and western hemlock. These trees can be blown down by wind or toppled over by ice before a new stand becomes established. If the mature seed trees are harvested, they can fall on and damage some of the young trees.

Clearcutting is the removal of all trees from a given area in a single cutting to establish a new, even-aged stand or tree farm. Usually these are stands of only one or two fast-growing species that need large or moderate amounts of sunlight for germination of the seed and development of the seedlings. Species often harvested by clearcutting include Douglas fir, jack pine, lodgepole pine, Sitka spruce, western hemlock, northeastern spruce and fir, black walnut, and black cherry.

The clearcut area may consist of a whole stand (Figure 15-6), a group, a strip, or a series of patches (Figure 15-7). After all trees are cut, the site is reforested naturally from seed released by the harvest, or foresters broadcast seed over the site, or plant genetically superior seedlings raised in a nursery.

Currently, almost two-thirds of the annual U.S. timber production is harvested by clearcutting. Timber companies prefer this method because it usually gives them the maximum economic return. It is the

Figure 15-8 Whole-tree harvesting. After being cut or pulled up, a tree is fed into a chipper, which deposits wood chips into the truck at right.

Weyerhauser, Inc., Tacoma, Wash.

simplest and crudest method and requires much less skill and planning than other harvesting methods. Clearcutting increases the volume of timber harvested per acre, reduces road building, often permits reforesting with genetically improved stock, and shortens the time needed to establish a new stand of trees. Small clearcut areas and their edges improve forage and habitat for some herbivore game species, such as deer, elk, and some shrubland birds.

Clearcutting is an effective way to remove a stand of trees heavily infested with damaging insects or disease. Usually the infested trees can be salvaged for commercial use. Clearcutting is also used on shallow-rooted species or trees growing in exposed places where there is danger that the whole stand will be blown down by the wind.

Large-scale clearcutting has become the subject of controversy in many parts of the world, especially the United States, Canada, Australia, and the tropical forests of Asia, Africa, Indonesia, and Latin America. When used on steeply sloped land, it leads to severe soil erosion, sediment water pollution, flooding from melting snow and heavy rains, and landslides when the exposed roots decay.

Repeated clearcutting on any site causes severe damage to forest soil and impairs the future productivity of the land. It promotes compaction of the soil by heavy logging equipment. In wet climates the exposed topsoil can be severely eroded by rainfall. In dry climates the exposed topsoil can easily be eroded by wind and dried out by the sun and wind.

Clearcutting leaves ugly and unnatural forest openings that take decades to regenerate (Figures 15-6 and 15-7) and reduces the recreational value of the forest. It also reduces the number and types of wildlife habitats and thus reduces biological diversity.

If flammable slash is not removed, the area is more vulnerable to damage from fire.

Clearcutting an old-growth forest replaces a diverse, uneven-aged stand of tree species with a monoculture more vulnerable to attack from disease, insects, and fire. It liquidates high-quality, old-growth timber and replaces it with faster-growing, lower-quality timber. Once a site has been clearcut, it is hard to break the cycle and wait 100 to 400 years for an uneven-aged stand to regrow through secondary ecological succession.

To avoid or minimize some of these problems, loggers can clearcut forests in small strips and patches. They can preserve the appearance of a forest by making irregularly shaped, small clearcuts that blend into the landscape. Small clearcuts allow natural seeding from nearby uncut forest, reduce logging debris, and create more edge zones, which are valuable to some types of wildlife.

Conservationists and ecologically oriented foresters recognize that clearcutting can be useful for some species if it's properly done. This means not clearcutting large areas or steeply sloped sites and making sure that the area is reseeded or replanted and protected until the next harvest.

The problem is that when timber companies harvest wood from public land, they understandably want to get as much timber as possible at the lowest cost. They have a built-in economic incentive to use large-scale clearcutting, often on species that could be harvested by less environmentally destructive methods. Without an adequate budget to pay for careful and competent supervision of timber company operations, and without effective fines and punishment, government agencies fight a losing battle in protecting public forests from abuse.

Two variations of clearcutting are whole-tree harvesting and coppicing. In **whole-tree harvesting** a machine cuts each tree at ground level. In some cases the entire tree is then transported to a chipping machine, in which massive blades reduce the wood to small chips in about one minute (Figure 15-8). Some whole-tree harvesting machines pull up the entire tree so that roots are also converted to wood chips.

This approach is used primarily to harvest stands for use as pulpwood or fuelwood. A whole-tree harvesting operation can clear about 12 acres of forest a day. Chips are then hauled to a pulp mill or wood-burning plant where they are burned to produce heat. Whole-tree harvesting removes and uses all wood materials from a stand, including defective trees and dead standing timber. As a result, it can increase the yield of wood materials per acre from a temperate forest by as much as 300%.

Many foresters and ecologists, however, oppose this method because the periodic removal of all tree materials eventually depletes the soil of plant nutrients.

The soil can be restored somewhat by commercial fertilizers, but they are usually too expensive. The removal of standing dead timber and fallen logs also removes numerous wildlife habitats. Research is under way to determine how whole-tree harvesting methods might be modified to reduce such harmful environmental effects.

Coppicing is a type of regeneration after clearcutting used only on oaks, aspens, and other species that sprout easily from their stumps and roots. Instead of reseeding or replanting, foresters rely on sprouting to produce a new stand on a clearcut area. It is especially useful for regeneration of some types of fuelwood trees in arid areas.

Forest Regeneration Trees can be regenerated on a harvested site naturally or artificially. In natural regeneration the forest regrows without human intervention. New trees develop from seedlings and seed that remain after harvest or that invade the site from nearby stands, or from sprouts on stumps and roots. Timber companies usually prefer natural regeneration because it's cheaper than artificial methods.

When a large area of a diverse, old-growth or secondary forest is clearcut, growers often artificially regenerate the site as a tree plantation by planting seeds or young trees (seedlings) started in a nursery. Artificial seeding is usually done from an airplane or a helicopter. Planting seedlings by hand is more widely used than artificial seeding because tree survival rates are higher and tree density is easier to control.

Increasingly, plant scientists are developing genetically improved seedlings, sometimes called supertrees. These species are bred to grow faster and straighter and to produce higher-quality timber than natural seedlings. Species can also be bred with increased resistance to fire, disease, and insects.

Intermediate Management After a new forest stand is established, it must be managed and protected during the period before the next commercial harvest. Usually this involves making several *intermediate cuttings* to remove weak and diseased trees and increase the rate of growth of healthier trees. This process, called *timber stand improvement*, also includes weeding and pruning.

Weeding is often needed to protect tree seedlings from being crowded out by fast-growing pioneer plant species. *Pruning* is the cutting of lower branches to reduce knots and improve the quality of timber used as sawlogs. *Thinning* reduces competition and accelerates the growth of the healthiest trees (Figure 14-6, p. 366). Thinning cuts are made mostly in even-aged stands of overcrowded young trees. The trees removed can be used for posts, fuelwood, and pulpwood.

In stands containing a mix of desirable and undesirable trees, an *improvement cutting* may be made to favor the growth of trees desirable for timber, wildlife habitat, aesthetic appeal, or recreation. A *sanitation cutting* removes trees that have been damaged by insects or disease to protect remaining trees. A *salvage cutting* harvests damaged but still partially usable trees, thus reducing economic losses after windstorm, fire, ice storm, insect attack, or widespread disease.

Protecting stands from damage by fire, disease, insects, and air pollution is also an important part of intermediate forest management. In the United States, for example, it's estimated that up to one-fourth of the net annual growth of commercially usable timber is lost to such damage.

Protecting Forests from Diseases and Insects The best and cheapest way to prevent insect damage is to preserve forest biological diversity, which naturally controls most insect populations. However, natural control may not be effective on tree farms or in cases of accidental introduction of alien insect species, such as the highly destructive gypsy moth caterpillar (see Case Study on p. 399).

Other methods for controlling insects and tree diseases include

- banning imported timber that might carry harmful parasites
- removing vegetation that acts as a host for disease organisms during some part of their life cycle
- treating diseased trees with antibiotics
- developing disease-resistant species
- identifying and removing dead and infected trees
- clearcutting infected areas and removing or burning all debris
- applying insecticides and fungicides (pp. 295–299).
- using biological control (p. 299)
- using integrated pest management (p. 300)

Protecting Forests from Fires Wildfires started by lightning or people are the best-known threat to forests. According to the U.S. Forest Service, about 85% of all forest fires are started by humans, either deliberately or accidentally through carelessness. Fires are especially damaging during dry, windy weather, which enables them to spread fast and become crown fires (Figure 14-8, p. 367).

The protection of forest resources from fire involves four phases: prevention, prescribed burning, presuppression, and suppression. *Prevention* of forest fires is the most important and cheapest method. It is primarily an educational process. The Smokey-the-Bear educational campaign of the Forest Service and the National Advertising Council has been successful in preventing many forest fires in U.S. forests. Since it began in the 1940s, this program has been credited with saving many lives and avoiding losses of billions of dollars. Some ecologists, however, contend that it also caused harm by allowing litter buildup in some forests that increased the likelihood of highly destructive crown fires.

Other methods of fire prevention include requiring burning permits and closing all or parts of a forest to travel and camping during periods of drought and high fire danger. Other regulations to reduce fire hazards include requiring spark arresters on logging and railroad equipment, allowing no smoking during logging operations, and requiring slash, rubbish, and other flammable debris to be removed.

Prescribed surface fires can be an effective method for preventing crown fires by reducing litter buildup. They are also used to control outbreaks of tree diseases and pests. These fires are started only by well-trained personnel when weather and forest conditions are ideal for control and proper intensity of burning. Prescribed fires are also timed to keep levels of air pollution as low as possible.

Presuppression involves trying to reduce the spread and damage of a wildfire before it starts. To help confine fires and allow access by fire-fighting equipment, vegetation is cleared to form fire breaks and fire roads, and brush and trees are cleared along existing roads.

Personnel are trained to detect fires at an early stage. Lookout towers, once widely used for fire detection, have been largely replaced by airplane patrols, a much cheaper method. Aircraft often carry infrared systems that detect small fires, especially at night, before they get out of control. Helicopters are used for observation and to carry fire fighters to remote fires within minutes of detection.

Once a wildfire starts, fire fighters have a number of methods for fire *suppression*. They use specially designed bulldozers and breaker plows to quickly establish fire breaks. They pump water onto the fire from tank trucks, and they drop water or fire retardant chemicals from aircraft. Trained personnel use controlled backfires to create burned areas to confine fires. Fire suppression efforts are coordinated with sophisticated electronic detection and communications equipment.

Burned forests are planted with grass and seedlings as soon as possible to reduce flooding and erosion (Figure 15-9). In some parts of western national forests and parks, officials allow surface fires set by lightning to burn without human intervention. However, fire fighters carefully monitor these fires and suppress them if they pose a danger to people or property or threaten to become crown fires (see Pro/Con on p. 401).

Protecting Forests from Air Pollution   Massive tree kills and tree damage in parts of Europe, the United States, and Canada have been attributed primarily to the prolonged exposure of trees to numerous air pollutants (Figure 7-22, p. 168). In addition to direct harm, prolonged exposure to multiple air pollutants makes trees much more vulnerable to diseases and insects (Figure 7-20, p. 166). The only solution is to sharply reduce emissions of the offending pollutants from coal-burning power plants, industrial plants, and cars (Section 7-6).

Sustainable-Earth Forestry   All aspects of forest management must be integrated into plans based on sound ecological principles. Such *sustainable-earth for-*

CASE STUDY   Forest Damage from the Gypsy Moth

Gypsy moths are a major threat to several species of U.S. trees, especially in the Northeast and Middle Atlantic regions. In their caterpillar stage, which lasts from late April through early July, they can defoliate entire forests.

Accidentally introduced into Massachusetts in 1869, gypsy moths have now spread to 15 states from Maine to Virginia. In 1985 the caterpillars chewed their way through an estimated 1.7 million acres of U.S. forestland.

Oak leaves are their favorite food. But they also eat the leaves of many other trees, including sweet gum, linden, willow birch, alder, apple, and hawthorn. Healthy trees can usually recover from one defoliation, but they die if attacked several years in a row.

So far no way has been found to eradicate or effectively control these destructive pests. However, people can reduce damage by tying a strip of burlap or tar paper around the base of a tree. This

keeps the caterpillars from climbing up the trunk for their evening meal. Traps containing sex attractants can be used to attract and kill the male moths.

As a last resort, susceptible trees can be sprayed with insecticides. Although this is the most widely used method, in the long run it often makes the problem worse (see Enrichment Study, pp. 295–300).

Grass seed is dropped directly into ash by helicopter or plane in critical areas. Grass helps soil stay in place and absorbs rain.

Crews scrape dirt across logs placed perpendicular to slope to capture water and allow it to soak into soil rather than running off.

Debris may be removed from stream channels to prevent dams from forming. Culverts may be enlarged or fitted with debris screens.

1- to 2-year-old seedlings are planted, mostly by hand.

Most burned timber is salvaged within 2 years, before it deteriorates.

Figure 15-9 Reforesting burned forest land to minimize flood and erosion. (U.S. Forest Service)

est management treats a forest as a complex ecosystem providing us and other species with valuable services. It is multiple-use, sustained-yield forest management that emphasizes uneven-aged management.

Sustainable-earth forestry recognizes that a biologically diverse forest ecosystem is the best protection against soil erosion, flooding, sediment water pollution, and tree loss from fire, wind, insects, and diseases. A diverse ecosystem also provides natural forest regeneration, habitats for a wide variety of fish and wildlife, and many recreational opportunities for people. This is the type of forestry that is practiced in Switzerland, West Germany, and several other West European countries.

PRO/CON Should Natural Fires Be Allowed To Burn in National Parks?

Periodic natural fires (fires set by lightning) are part of the ecological cycle of forests. They help revitalize old-growth forests by cleaning out the accumulation of dead trees and debris and destroying weak and diseased trees and other plants. This promotes new plant growth through secondary ecological succession and helps maintain a diversity of wildlife habitats and species.

In spite of these ecological benefits, all fires are fought immediately in national forests (except in wilderness areas) because these forests are used for logging, energy development, hunting, and other uses.

Between 1920 and 1972 the Park Service had the same policy of fighting all fires in national parks.

But this allowed the buildup of ground litter and small plants, greatly increasing the chance of destructive crown fires (Figure 15-10).

Since 1972 Park Service policy has been to allow most lightning-caused fires to burn themselves out as long as they don't threaten human lives, park facilities, or private property. This policy was put to a severe test during the hot, dry summer of 1988. In seven western states 25,000 fire fighters tried to contain 30 major fires that blackened nearly 1.5 million acres—the worst year of wildfires since 1919.

The summer of 1988 was the driest and hottest the region had experienced in 112 years. This severe drought plus high winds made fighting the fires a losing battle. Thousands of firefighters could at best slightly alter the paths of the major fires and put out small fires.

Yellowstone National Park is probably the most intact ecosystem in the lower 48 states. The dry and cold climate of the park dramatically slows decomposition. Dead grasses, branches, fungi, and dead trees pile up faster than they can be broken down by bacteria and fungi. With this type of climate, periodic major fires occur every 200 to 300 years and play an important role in maintaining the park's plant and animal life. Without such fires, growing plants would deplete the soil faster than decaying plants could replenish it.

(continued)

U.S. National Park Service

U.S. National Park Service/Dan Taylor

Figure 15-10 A grove of trees in Yosemite National Park. Left photo shows area in 1890 before the government had a policy of suppressing all fires. Right photo shows buildup of ground litter and small plants at the site in 1970 after 50 years of fire suppression.

This type of forest management emphasizes:

- growing and harvesting a diversity of high-quality timber, instead of short-term pulpwood production

- growing timber on long rotations, generally from 100 to 200 years, depending on the species and the soil quality

- selective cutting of individual trees or small groups of most tree species

- extreme precautions to protect topsoil, the base upon which all present and future forest productivity depends

- methods of road building and logging that minimize soil erosion and compaction

- small, lightweight equipment for logging

- building roads and skid trails with the contour of the land rather than cutting them into the land

- clearcutting only in small patches of less than 15 acres and never on steeply sloped land (more than a 15- to 20-degree slope)

- leaving standing dead trees and fallen timber to maintain diverse wildlife habitats and enhance nutrient recycling

- leaving slash, tree tops, and branches to help restore soil fertility, unless it causes too much build-up of dry fuel on the ground or hinders reseeding of some desirable species

PRO/CON (continued)

During the 1988 summer fires, the media gave the impression that most of Yellowstone was devastated by fire. But infrared photographs taken from NASA aircraft revealed that fire affected only about 20% of the park. These blazes moved quickly through some areas, jumped over some tree stands, and killed most trees in others. This skipping from one area to another left a diverse mosaic of black areas and green areas—like a blanket with holes burned in it.

In most areas, heat from the flames damaged only the top inch of the soil on the forest floor. Seeds, grass roots, and plant bulbs underneath this layer began sprouting during the spring of 1989. Less than 1% of the area burned so intensely hot that the soil was severely damaged. Less than 0.1% of the park's area was affected so badly that it won't recover. The bulldozers used to fight the fires did more damage to the park's delicate soils than the searing heat.

Angry residents criticized the Park Service for not fighting the fires earlier. Many in nearby towns feared they would lose money from a drop in tourism. Nearby ranchers and farmers were concerned that bison and elk without enough winter forage would seek food on their lands. Overblown

media reports of devastation led many people to call for a reversal of park policy to let most natural fires burn.

Park officials insisted that they fought the major fires vigorously from the beginning to protect park property and nearby private property. But the record drought and high winds meant they could not put out the fires. Park biologists believe that tourism will increase as people come to see how this ecosystem regenerates itself, just as tourists flocked to see Mount St. Helens after its volcanic eruption.

Biologists contend that damage was more widespread than it should have been because the earlier park policy of fighting all fires had allowed buildup of flammable ground litter and small plants. A return to the previous policy of fighting all fires in Yellowstone and other national parks would eventually cause a far greater ecological disaster than the fires of 1988.

Biologists estimate that the 1988 fire will lead to a 30-fold increase in Yellowstone's plant species. The ash provides mineral nutrients for new plant growth. A few weeks after the fire, grasses and other small pioneer plants began coming up.

The fire did reduce vegetation for elk and bison to feed on during the winter season after the fire.

But ecologists pointed out that the drought had a much larger effect on vegetation than the fires. This will help reduce the elk herd from about 20,000 to 15,000, the area's estimated carrying capacity.

By the spring of 1989 visitors were able to see a profusion of wildflowers and other plant life. New populations of bluebirds, woodpeckers, and squirrels found refuge and food in insect-infested dead trees. Seedlings of lodgepole pine had begun sprouting from the seeds released from pine cones by the extreme heat of the fire. With fewer mature trees and shrubs, it is easier for visitors to see wildlife such as elk, moose, bison, black bears, grizzly bears, and rare trumpeter swans.

In three to five years the burned areas will be covered with a lush mat of grasses, flowers, and shrubs. Aspen, fir, pine, and spruce trees will be well established, and deer, elk, bear, and most bird populations will be abundant. Indeed, the abundance of new vegetation may help preserve some threatened animal species.

In a century or so, if no new natural fires occur, the forest will again be mature and ready to repeat the natural ecological fire cycle. Do you agree with the present fire policy in U.S. national parks?

- relying on natural controls to protect the forest from most diseases and pests

- controlling occasional severe pest outbreaks by using natural predators (biological control) and integrated pest management (p. 300)

Sustainable-earth forestry does not mean that tree farms or even-aged management should never be used. But it does mean that their use should be severely limited on public land. On private land they should be regulated to prevent excessive soil erosion and water pollution from runoff of sediment, fertilizers, and pesticides (see Pro/Con below).

15-3 MANAGEMENT AND CONSERVATION OF NATIONAL FORESTS IN THE UNITED STATES

Conflicting Demands on National Forests Between 1905, when the U.S. Forest Service was created, and 1960, the national forests were managed mainly by the principles of sustained yield and multiple use as set down by Gilbert Pinchot in 1905. Until about 1950, demands on U.S. national forests were low and conflicts between competing uses were relatively rare.

Since 1950, however, there have been greatly increased demands on national forests for timber sales (Figure 15-11), development of mineral and energy resources, recreation, wilderness protection, and wildlife conservation. The economic boom during and after World War II caused the depletion of many private forests. Consequently, timber companies, particularly in the West, increasingly looked to the national forests to supply timber for their mills.

Because of these growing and often conflicting demands on national forest resources, the management policies of the Forest Service have been the subject of heated controversy since the 1960s. Timber company officials complain that they aren't allowed to buy and cut enough timber on public lands, especially in remaining old-growth forests in California and the Pacific-Northwest.

Conservationists charge that the Forest Service has bowed to political pressure. Increasingly it has replaced multiple use and uneven-aged management of national

---

PRO/CON Responsible Forestry: Monocultures or Mixed Cultures?

Tree farms or plantations are found on only about 2% of the world's forest area. Two-thirds of these industrial forests are in the Soviet Union (24%), China (19%), the United States (13%), and Japan (10%). Between 1985 and 2000 the total area of tree farms is projected to more than double.

There's controversy over this trend. Most commercial foresters believe that tree farms are the best way to meet the increasing demand for wood and wood products and to increase short-term profits for timber companies. They believe that these intensively managed forests can be harvested and regenerated in ways that conserve these potentially renewable resources for future generations.

High yields from tree farms can reduce pressure to clear large areas of old-growth forests. Planting a tree farm is also the quickest way to reforest degraded land and prevent soil erosion and desertification.

Other foresters and many ecologists are concerned that planting vast forest monocultures will lead to environmental degradation of soil and watersheds and to a decline in forest quality and wildlife diversity. These critics are not completely against this form of forest management, but they believe that it should be limited.

The German experience in forestry between 1840 and 1918 shows the long-term harmful effects of monoculture forestry. Around 1840, German foresters decided to clearcut diverse natural forests and replace them with pine and spruce plantations to increase the output of wood per acre. These trees were harvested every 20 to 30 years to provide low-quality timber and pulp. Deciduous hardwood and true fir species became nearly extinct.

Yields of pine and spruce increased for a time. But the monoculture plantations depleted the soil of plant nutrients. After the second or third generation, the yield of the pine and spruce stands declined and the general quality of the wood decreased.

Many trees were stunted, and the number killed by pests and diseases and blown down by storms increased.

After 1918, German forestry officials began shifting to a more natural type of forestry management. Monoculture stands were replanted with uneven-aged mixtures of commercially valuable species. Hardwood species were interplanted with softwood species. Instead of cutting all the trees in an area (clearcutting), loggers harvested only certain economically important trees in a stand (selective cutting).

The result was an increase in timber production and an improvement in soil quality. Today German foresters are appalled to see the United States and other countries making the same mistakes their predecessors made in sacrificing long-term, sustainable productivity for short-term nonrenewable gain. What do you think?

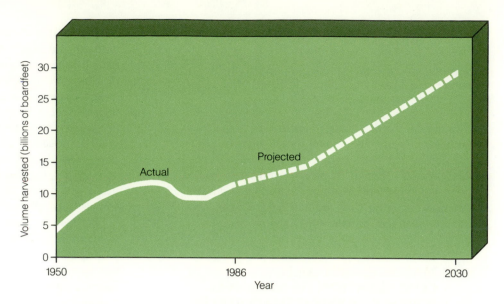

Figure 15-11 Timber harvested in national forests, 1950–1986, and projected to 2030. (Data from U.S. Forest Service)

forests with dominant use and even-aged management based on excessive clearcutting. They argue that this policy violates the principle of balanced multiple use.

They also suspect that cutting on public forests, often at below market prices and with government subsidies, is designed to protect U.S. timber companies from increased competition and lower prices of imported timber, mostly from Canada and LDCs. Instead of lowering wood prices for consumers, such protectionism tends to keep prices high.

Clearcutting and the National Forest Management Act Before 1950 clearcutting in national forests was done only in Douglas fir regions. But in the 1950s, 1960s, and early 1970s clearcutting became widespread in the national forests. Conservationists charged that this violated the multiple-use principle of management by degrading soil, water, and wildlife resources. The argument wasn't whether clearcutting should be banned in the national forests, but how much should be allowed and under what conditions.

Congress eased the controversy by passing the National Forest Management Act (NFMA) of 1976, after conservation and environmental groups had won several key court decisions. This law sets certain limitations on clearcutting and other timber-harvesting methods in national forests. Clearcut areas are to be restricted in size and contoured to the terrain. Some dead trees must be left standing. Fallen logs and other undergrowth must also be left to provide food and habitats for plants and animals. These restrictions, however, are weakened by numerous exemptions and exceptions written into the law at the urging of timber company interests.

In 1987 the controversy was renewed when a report by the Wilderness Society charged the Forest Service with widespread and regular violations of the NMFA. Violations included excessive clearcutting, logging on physically and economically unsuitable lands, and failure to maintain biological diversity in many national forests, especially in the Northwest.

The Wilderness Society surveyed the 19 national forests in the Pacific Northwest from airplanes and compared Forest Service maps with the types of forests actually found in these areas. The survey showed that the Forest Service had greatly overestimated the amount of old-growth forest still left, had underreported the amount of clearcutting, and had counted mature second-growth forest as old-growth virgin forest. In Oregon and Washington only 33% to 50% of the sample tracts listed as old growth were still forested.

How Much Timber Should Be Harvested from National Forests? The NFMA began a new era of long-range planning for use of the national forests. It requires the Forest Service to prepare 50-year management plans for each national forest region. Congress ordered that the plan for each forest area was to be developed with active participation by local citizens and conservation organizations.

But conservationists charge that such participation has not been able to offset the influence of the timber industry on the way national forests are managed by the Forest Service. They accuse the Forest Service of emphasizing commercial logging at the expense of other uses, and thus violating the agency's responsibility to manage these lands for multiple use.

Conservationists are also alarmed because the Forest Service has proposed doubling the timber harvest on national forests between 1986 and 2030 at the urging of the Reagan administration and the timber industry (Figure 15-11). The shift toward greatly increased timber harvesting in the national forests began in 1981 when President Reagan appointed John Crowell assistant secretary of agriculture in charge of national forests. Crowell was formerly employed by Louisiana Pacific, a major timber company. His view of the national forests is that "from an economic stand-point, these trees are doing nothing but standing there rotting. We could get more value by cutting them down and growing a new crop."

Under Crowell's direction, the Forest Service has also proposed the building of 240,000 miles of new roads in the national forests over the next 50 years to give timber companies access to the trees needed to double the harvest. The proposed new roads are six times the 40,000 miles of roads in the entire interstate highway system. If these roads are added to the 346,000 miles of roads already in the national forests, the system will be long enough to reach to the moon and back and still circle the globe four times.

Conservationists charge that expanded logging and road building in national forests will damage watersheds and fisheries, reduce biological diversity, and destroy and fragment wildlife habitats. They also fear that plans to build roads in inaccessible areas are designed to disqualify these areas from inclusion in the National Wilderness Preservation System. Parts of national forests that are still roadless in the 1990s will come up for consideration as wilderness areas. About 20% of the proposed new roads to be built between 1985 and 1995 will be in roadless areas. By 1988 a number of these roads had been built.

In 1988 the draft long-range management plans for the 19 national forests in the Pacific Northwest projected high levels of logging and extensive road build-ing to open up remote areas for logging. In 5 of the 19 national forests, the plans proposed cutting more timber than would be replaced by new growth.

Conservationists have also accused the Forest Service of poor financial management of public forests (see Pro/Con below).

Forestry experts and conservationists have suggested several ways to reduce exploitation of publicly owned timber resources and provide true multiple use of national forests as required by law:

- Cut the present annual harvest of timber from national forests in half instead of doubling it as proposed by the timber industry and the Forest Service.

- Keep 15% to 25% of remaining old-growth timber in any national forest from being cut.

- Require that timber from national forests be sold at a price that includes the costs of roads, site preparation, and site regeneration.

- Require that all timber sales in national forests yield a profit for taxpayers based on the fair market value of any timber sold.

- Use a much larger portion of the Forest Service budget to improve management and increase timber yields of the country's privately owned commercial forestland to take pressure off the national forests.

PRO/CON Should Sales of Timber on Public Land Lose Money?

Timber sales from some public forests make money, but sales from many public forests do not.

By law the Forest Service must sell timber for no less than the cost of reforesting the land it was harvested from. The cost of building roads to make the timber accessible is not included in this price. Most of these roads are built by the timber purchaser, and the road-building costs are deducted from the price of the timber. In essence, the government exchanges timber for roads, with taxpayers paying for the roads used by private timber companies.

Studies have shown that between 1975 and 1985 timber from 79 national forests was sold below the amount the Forest Service spent on roads and preparing the trees for sale. During this period Forest Service timber sales lost $2.1 billion.

In Alaska's Tongass National Forest, the country's largest national forest, the Forest Service spent $50 million in 1987 to subsidize the logging of timber, for which it received only $1 million. Two nearby pulp mills have 50-year contracts with the Forest Service that allow them to buy timber for 1% or less of its appraised value.

The Wilderness Society projects that losses from harvests in the national forests could reach another $2 billion between 1985 and 1995. Conservationists oppose such subsidies for private timber companies at taxpayers' expense.

Industry representatives argue that such subsidies help taxpayers by keeping lumber prices down. But conservationists note that each year taxpayers already give the lumber industry tax breaks almost equal to the cost of managing the entire National Forest System.

Forest Service officials argue that timber harvesting shouldn't be subject to strict cost-accounting requirements. They point out that some expenses, such as road building, help prevent forest fires and provide more opportunities for hiking, hunting, and other recreational activities by the general public.

Conservationists respond that most people using national forests for recreation would rather hike woodland trails than logging roads. What do you think?

DEALING WITH THE FUELWOOD CRISIS AND TROPICAL DEFORESTATION

Reducing the Fuelwood Crisis LDCs can reduce the severity of the fuelwood crisis by a combination of methods: increasing the supply of fuelwood by planting more trees and reducing the demand for fuelwood by burning wood more efficiently or switching to other fuels. The governments of China, Nepal, Senegal, and South Korea (see Case Study right) have established successful tree-planting programs at the village level.

Experience has shown that planting projects are most successful when local people are involved in their planning and implementation. Typically, government foresters supply villagers with seed or seedlings of fast-growing fuelwood trees and shrubs and provide advice on the planting and care of the trees. Villagers are encouraged to plant these species in fields along with crops (agroforestry), on unused patches of land around homes and farmland, and along roads and waterways.

Programs work best when village farmers own the land or are given ownership of any trees grown on common resource land (see Case Study, p. 407). This gives them a strong incentive to plant and protect trees for their own use and for sale. Many reforestation projects have failed because women, who do most of the firewood gathering, were excluded from planning and carrying them out.

Agroforestry, in which trees are grown among crops or on pasture land, is a promising approach to increasing supplies of food and fuelwood, especially in the tropics. Successful projects have been instituted in a number of countries, including Kenya, India, Thailand, Costa Rica, China, Tanzania, Burma, Nepal, India, and Nigeria.

Agroforestry has a number of advantages. Trees planted with crops can supply fuelwood, timber, nuts, fruits, fertilizer for crops, and food for cattle. The trees also increase crop yields by increasing soil moisture, reducing soil erosion, restoring soil nutrients, crowding out weeds, and shielding crops from damaging wind and excessive sunlight. Agroforestry also usually costs less than establishing fuelwood plantations.

Trees used in agroforestry should be fast growing and have fairly thin crowns to allow enough sunlight to reach food plants nearer the ground. Ideal trees include the leucaena (Figure 15-12), acacia, and gliricidia, which thrive in many tropical areas. The leucaena, which can grow 20 feet in its first year, has many uses. Its leaves are excellent fodder for livestock; the seed pods are a nutritious food; its wood is clean burning and hard enough for furniture and construction; and its roots fertilize the soil with nitrogen.

Agroforestry and most tree-planting programs, however, do little to help the millions of rural people

---

CASE STUDY Preventing Fuelwood Shortages in South Korea

In the early 1970s South Korea began a massive village fuelwood program to increase its fuelwood supplies. Village forest authorities, made up of local villagers, were established throughout the country. These groups coordinated programs to increase fuelwood supplies in and near each village. The government also exerted strong pressure on private landowners to plant fuelwood trees on land not used to grow crops.

These efforts paid off. More than 740,000 acres of new woodlots were established in about 11,000 villages. Twice as many acres of existing fuelwood lots near villages were brought under more intensive management.

The government also began efforts to improve the efficiency of traditional wood-burning heating and cooking devices. The government-supported Forest Research Institute developed an improved version of the traditional under-floor heating system. The new system, now in widespread use, decreases fuelwood consumption by about 30%.

---

who don't own their own land. They usually have to collect wood from common lands or steal it from protected forest reserves.

Several countries have started programs to encourage rural and urban people to switch from energy-wasting open fires to more-efficient cook stoves and to other fuels. Villagers in Burkina Faso in West Africa have been shown how to make a stove from mud and dung that cuts wood use by 30% to 70%. It can be made by villagers in half a day at virtually no cost. New types of stoves must be designed to make use of locally available materials and to provide both heat and light like the open fires they replace.

Despite encouraging success in some countries, most LDCs suffering from fuelwood shortages have inadequate forestry policies and budgets and lack trained foresters. Such countries are planting 10 to 20 times fewer trees than needed to offset forest losses and meet increased demands for fuelwood and other forest products.

Reducing the Destruction and Degradation of Tropical Forests In 1985 the World Resources Institute, the World Bank, the UN Food and Agriculture Organization, the UN Development Program, the U.S. Agency for International Development, and representatives from most tropical countries developed a global Tropical Forestry Action Plan. The plan called for $8 billion to be spent over five years to help tropical LDCs

CASE STUDY Providing Fuelwood for the Landless Poor

The government of West Bengal, India, allowed landless families to grow trees for their use and for sale on over 12,000 acres of treeless land. Instead of having title to the land, families were given ownership of any trees they planted and grew.

The Forest Department supplied families with free seedlings, technical assistance, fertilizer, and insecticide. Small payments were also made for all trees surviving after three years.

While the trees matured, families collected twigs and branches to meet their own fuel needs. After five years the trees were large enough to be harvested and sold as fuelwood. Most families made enough money to buy small parcels of land suitable for growing their own food and fuelwood.

This innovative project converted degraded land into productive land. It also supplied the landless poor with fuelwood and enough income to buy their own land and break the vicious cycle of poverty, malnutrition, and poor health.

Figure 15-12 Leucaena. This fast-growing tree adds nitrogen to the soil and can be used for fuelwood and reforestation in much of the tropics. Another tree species, acacias, can grow to heights of 27 to 42 feet in four years.

Comstock/Russ Kinne

protect and renew their forests. International development organizations, such as the World Bank, are to provide half these funds. The rest is to come from national governments, especially MDCs, and the private sector. The funds would be used to:

- provide financial incentives to villagers and village organizations for establishment of fuelwood trees and tree farms on abandoned and degraded land with suitable soils

- improve management practices in natural forests to increase yields and reduce forest degradation

- set aside 14% of the world's tropical forests as reserves and parks protected from unsustainable development

- restore degraded tropical forests and watersheds

- strengthen forestry research, training, and extension services in tropical LDCs

Because of favorable growing conditions, tree farms in most tropical areas can produce 10 to 20 times more wood per acre than most of the world's natural forests. Greatly increasing the area of tree farm sites in tropical countries can reduce pressures to log large areas of natural tropical forest. But governments must encourage tree plantations only on abandoned cropland or pastureland or other degraded land—not in natural forest areas.

Despite their potential for increasing wood supplies, there are some problems with tree farms in the tropics. Tree species must be carefully selected (see Spotlight on p. 408). Tree growing can deplete already deficient tropical soils of nutrients. Expensive applications of fertilizers are needed to help maintain a site's productivity.

Monoculture tree farms in the tropics are also more vulnerable to attack by insects and disease than those in temperate areas. Tropical climates and habitat diversity support a much larger number of rapidly multiplying insects and plant diseases than temperate climates.

Sustainable production of commercial wood can also be increased by better management of natural tropical forests. Foresters can remove undesirable competing plants and trees and cut small openings in the canopy to promote the growth of commercially valuable species. They can supplement natural regeneration of valuable species by planting seeds or seedlings of these trees. Governments can reduce over-harvesting of choice species by helping develop markets for lesser-known tree species.

Government-sponsored research should identify which tropical forest soils are best suited for various purposes on a renewable basis. Then a zoning system can be used to concentrate forestry, agriculture, and livestock grazing in areas suitable for each use. Governments should establish networks of nurseries to provide seeds and seedlings for planting tree farms in suitable areas and for restoring natural forests.

Governments can ban creaming, the selective-cutting practice in which only the most valuable trees are harvested. Commercial loggers should be required to take down and remove large trees in ways that minimize destruction of nearby trees. They can also be required to replant harvested areas as part of doing business. Prices for exported wood can be raised sharply to provide more income and reduce forest degradation.

Logging concessions should be auctioned competitively. Concession periods should be extended to at least 70 years. This would reduce logging intensity by providing loggers with two cutting cycles of 35 years each.

In 1982, Dr. Ira Rubinoff, director of the Smithsonian Tropical Research Institute, proposed that governments of MDCs and tropical LDCs work together to establish a network of protected tropical forest reserves. He proposed that 1,000 reserves, averaging 250,000 acres each, be set aside in the 48 tropical forest countries.

In return for this aid, participating tropical countries would agree to act as custodians for the reserves, with an annual inspection made by an international agency. Each country would get an annual payment based on the area being protected—averaging about $3 million per reserve. If the country failed to maintain the reserve, no payment would be made. Rubinoff's idea was included in the 1985 Tropical Forestry Action Plan.

Several conservation groups have urged that the following measures be added to this plan:

- placing emphasis on debt-for-nature swaps that allow LDCs to exchange some of their massive foreign debt for agreeing to protect large areas of their tropical forests from destruction and degradation (see Case Study on p. 410)

- initiating a massive reforestation program with trees selected primarily for their ecological rather than their commercial value

- phasing out dams, plantations, ranches, roads, and colonization programs that threaten tropical forests

- initiating ecologically sustainable forestry and agriculture development projects designed to satisfy local needs rather than to cater to international markets

- including indigenous tribal peoples, women, and private local conservation organizations in the planning and execution of tropical forestry plans

- developing national zoning plans to achieve a sustainable mix of preservation and economic development

- preventing banks and international lending agencies from lending money for environmentally destructive projects

By 1988 progress toward the goals of the Tropical Forestry Action Plan was slow. Between 1984 and 1988 foreign aid for tropical forestry increased from $606

SPOTLIGHT **Are Fast-Growing Eucalyptus Trees The Answer?**

Most of Australia's fairly small forest area is dominated by various species of eucalyptus trees. Forests of these trees grow rapidly on very poor soils, are superbly adapted to frequent fire, and tolerate a wide range of ecological conditions.

Australia's eucalyptus forests are being clearcut at a rapid rate and converted into tree farms. The harvested eucalyptus trees are converted to small wood chips, most of which are exported to Japan and used to make paper pulp. The loss of the eucalyptus forests has destroyed the habitats of many forms of wildlife.

While eucalyptus trees are being cut in Australia, they are being used to reforest areas threatened by desertification and to establish fuelwood plantations in other parts of the world. Because these species grow fast even on poor soils, you might think this is a good idea.

But conservationists now see it as an ecological disaster. In their native Australia these trees thrive in areas with good rainfall. However, when planted in arid areas, the trees suck up so much of the scarce soil water that most other plants can't grow. This means farmers don't have fodder to feed their livestock and groundwater is not replenished. The eucalyptus trees also deplete the soil of nutrients and produce toxic compounds that are not flushed from the soil because of low rainfall.

In Karnata, India, villagers became so enraged over a government-sponsored project to plant these trees that they uprooted the saplings. Furthermore, at least 20 species of trees native to India grow faster than eucalyptus. Even with good intentions, transplanting species from one ecosystem to another is a risky and often unpredictable venture. It should be done only after careful research, testing, and consultation with local people where the trees will be planted.

million to $1.1 billion. This is an important trend but funding is still far below the levels needed. Several international meetings have been held and forestry specialists were conducting surveys in 50 tropical countries throughout Africa, Asia, and Latin America. The information from such surveys will be used to develop integrated, long-range tropical forestry plans for each country.

Debt-for-Nature Swaps Most banks believe that many LDCs will be unable to pay back much of their $1.2 trillion debt to public and private lending institutions. To recoup some of their money, banks are often willing to sell these debts to conservation organizations for 5 cents to 60 cents on each dollar owed. Banks are also being encouraged to donate some of their debts to conservation organizations and obtain a full tax write-off.

The conservation organizations can then work out debt-for-nature swaps with tropical LDCs. In exchange for not having to repay the part of its national debt held by a conservation organization, a tropical LDC agrees to protect or rehabilitate a certain number of acres of tropical forest.

Debt-for-nature swaps have many benefits. They allow banks and international lending institutions to get rid of bad loans and free up bank funds for new investment. They allow tropical countries to reallocate government spending from interest payments to protection and management of tropical forests and other natural resources. Countries that have worked out debt-for-nature swaps include Ecuador, the Philippines, Mexico, Peru, Jamaica, Bolivia, and Costa Rica (see Case Study on p. 410).

This approach will put only a small dent in the problem of protecting some of the world's remaining tropical forests. But it is an important and innovative step in the right direction. This mechanism is expected to relieve only 1% to 2% of Latin America's $409 billion debt, most of which is owed to U.S. commercial banks. It will affect even less of Africa's and Asia's debts, most of which are owed to the World Bank, International Monetary Fund, and regional development banks.

So far, only private debt has been exchanged for protection of tropical forests and other ecosystems. However, legislation pending in the U.S. Congress would push for such exchanges for debts owed to the World Bank and the African Development Bank. West German Chancellor Helmut Kohl has also called for governments of MDCs to forgive debts to LDCs in exchange for protection of forests and other ecosystems.

Planetary Reforestation Slowing destruction and degradation of tropical forests in LDCs and preventing further damage to forests in MDCs from air pol-

lution are urgent tasks. At the same time, however, we must launch a global program to rehabilitate degraded forestland and plant new trees.

The goal should be to reforest at least 5 billion acres of land over the next ten years. The number of trees that can be planted per acre varies with the site from about 200 to 1,500. Assuming an average of 300 trees per acre, then we need to plant 1.5 trillion trees during the next decade—an average of 150 billion trees a year.

To do this we would need about 6.25 million people planting an average of 400 trees a day during the average two-month tree planting season. This would be an excellent way to give part-time employment to some of the 1.7 billion people worldwide who are unemployed or underemployed. It would also be a good way to utilize some of the 77 million people in the armed services of the world for two months a year. We need to mobilize a global Conservation Corps similar to the Peace Corps.

How much would such a planetary reforestation project cost? Assuming that the average cost for raising, planting, protecting, and tending a tree is $1, it would cost $1.5 trillion to reforest 5 billion acres—an average of $150 billion a year. This is only about one-fourth of the world's annual military budget and would provide much more security from global problems, such as climate change and economic chaos resulting from conversion of renewable resources into nonrenewable resources.

Can it be done? Yes. Will it be done? That depends on you, me, and millions of other sustainable-earth citizens who recognize that protecting and renewing the earth is the only form of long-term security for all people and for other species on this planet.

Getting Involved in Forest Conservation Sustaining the earth's resources instead of depleting them for short-term economic gain is not a popular cause in affluent and not-so-affluent societies dedicated to economic growth at almost any cost. Nevertheless, this cause is so important that it demands our attention and involvement.

Some women in India have set an example by starting the nonviolent Chipko (an Indian word for "hug" or "cling to") movement. Women and children go into nearby forests, link their hands together, and encircle trees to prevent commercial loggers from cutting them down. During the past two decades the Chipko movement has widened its efforts from embracing trees to embracing mountains and water threatened with destructive forms of development. Today the women who guarded trees from loggers also plant trees, prepare village forestry plans, and build walls to stop soil erosion.

In Malaysia, Penan tribesmen armed with blowguns have joined forces with environmentalists in an effort to halt destructive logging. In Brazil, 500 conservation organizations have organized a coalition to preserve Brazil's remaining tropical forests. In the United States, members of Earth First! have perched in the tops of giant Douglas firs and put their bodies in front of logging trucks and bulldozers to prevent trees in national forests from being cut down.

You also have an important role to play. Begin by looking at how forests around you are managed. If you or your loved ones own forested land, develop a sustainable-earth management and conservation plan for these resources. Above all, try to plant and nurture several trees a year and encourage others to do so. In addition to helping conserve soil, water, and wildlife

---

CASE STUDY Preservation, Restoration, and Sustainable Use of Tropical Forests in Bolivia and Costa Rica

The first debt-for-nature swap was announced in 1987. The Weeden Foundation provided Conservation International (a U.S. organization) with a grant of $100,000. The organization used this money to buy $650,000 of Bolivia's $5.7 billion foreign debt from a Swiss bank.

In exchange for forgiveness of this part of its debt, Bolivia agreed to protect 3.7 million acres of tropical forest around its existing Beni Biosphere Reserve from harmful forms of development. This land is to be a model of how conservation of forest and wildlife resources can be mixed with sustainable economic development (Figure 15-13).

The core of this land is a virgin tropical forest to be set aside as a 350,000-acre biological reserve. It will be surrounded by a protective buffer of savanna to be used for sustainable grazing of livestock.

Controlled commercial logging, as well as hunting and fishing by local natives, will be permitted in 1.6 million acres of forest in the tract (Figure 15-13). Logging will not be allowed in the mountain area above the tract to protect the area's watershed and to prevent erosion.

Costa Rica is a small country about the size of West Virginia. Today it leads all tropical countries in efforts to protect remaining tropical forests and restore degraded areas. Dense forests once formed a canopy over virtually the entire country. Today only about 2% of the country is still forested and less than 1% of these forests is protected.

In the mid-1970s, Costa Rica established a system of national parks and reserves that presently protect 13% of the country's land area. Since Oscar Arias was elected president of the country in 1986, these conservation efforts have increased sharply. Besides establishing long-range plans and obtaining outside funding, Arias has appointed knowledgeable people to key conservation posts. The country's plan is to combine conservation and sustainable economic development and to expand protected areas to 25% of the country's land by the end of this century.

A rugged mountainous region with a tropical rain forest contains the Guanacaste National Park and has been designated an international biosphere reserve. It is located near the Nicaraguan border, where Costa Rica's mountains descend to the Pacific Ocean. One of the country's most visible projects is the restoration of the dry tropical forest in this park, the world's first project of this kind.

Daniel Janzen, professor of biology at the University of Pennsylvania in Philadelphia, has helped galvanize international support for restoration in this 203,000-acre reserve. He has conducted ecological research in the area for 27 years and serves as ecological adviser for the restoration project.

His vision is to make the nearly 40,000 local people who live near the park an integral part of the restoration project—a concept he calls *biocultural restoration*. By actively participating in the project, local residents will reap enormous educational, economic, and environmental benefits. Local farmers have been hired to plant hundreds of acres with tree seeds and seedlings started in Janzen's lab.

The essence of the program is to make the park a living classroom. Students in elementary schools, high schools, and universities will study the ecology of the park in the classroom and go on field trips in the park itself. There will also be educational programs for civic groups and tourists from Costa Rica and elsewhere. These visitors and activities will stimulate the local economy.

The project will also serve as a training ground in tropical forest restoration for Costa Rican and other scientists throughout the world. Research scientists working on the project will give guest lectures in classrooms and lead some of the field trips.

Already dozens of students in the region visit the park each day. Plans call for several thousand elementary and high school students in the region to visit the park for a full day of field biology at least once a year.

Janzen recognizes that in 20 to 40 years these children will be running the park and the local political systems. If they understand the biology and importance of their local environment, they are more likely to protect and sustain its resources. The project will cost about $50 million over 10 years— about $50 a species.

CHAPTER 16

Depletion and Extinction
of Wild Plants and Animals

General Questions and Issues

1. Why are wild species important to us and to the biosphere?

2. What human activities cause wild species to become depleted, endangered, and extinct?

3. What natural traits make some wild species vulnerable to extinction from our activities?

The mass of extinctions which the Earth is currently facing is a threat to civilization second only to the threat of thermal nuclear war.

National Academy of Sciences

In the 1850s Alexander Wilson, a prominent ornithologist, watched a single migrating flock of passenger pigeons darken the sky for over four hours. He estimated that this flock consisted of more than 2 billion birds and was 240 miles long and 1 mile wide.

By 1914 the passenger pigeon (Figure 16-1) had disappeared forever. How could the species that was once the most numerous bird in North America become extinct in only a few decades?

The answer is people. The major reasons for the extinction of this species were uncontrolled commercial hunting and loss of habitat and food supplies as forests were cleared for farms and cities.

Passenger pigeons were good to eat and widely used for fertilizer. They were easy to kill because they flew in gigantic flocks and nested in long narrow colonies. People captured one pigeon alive and tied it to a perch called a stool. Soon a curious flock landed beside this "stool pigeon." They were then shot or trapped by nets that might contain more than 1,000 birds.

Beginning in 1858, the massive killing of passenger pigeons became a big business. Shotguns, fire, traps, artillery, and even dynamite were used. Birds were also suffocated by burning grass or sulfur below their roosts. Live birds were used as targets in shooting galleries. In 1878 one professional pigeon trapper made $60,000 by killing 3 million birds at their nesting grounds near Petoskey, Michigan.

By the early 1880s commercial hunting ceased because only several thousand birds were left. Recovery of the species was essentially impossible because these birds laid only one egg per nest. Many of the remaining birds died from infectious disease and from severe storms during their annual fall migration to Central and South America.

By 1896 the last major breeding colony had vanished, and by 1900 only a few small, scattered flocks were left. In 1914 the last known passenger pigeon on earth—a hen named Martha after Martha Washington—died in the Cincinnati Zoo. Her stuffed body is now on view at the National Museum of Natural History in Washington, D.C.

Since all species eventually become extinct, does it matter that we hastened the extinction of the passenger pigeon and many other species? Between 1975 and 2000 we will probably have hastened the extinction of as many as 1 million species.

Reducing this premature loss of the earth's biological diversity and restoring species that we have helped deplete are vital tasks. We have little chance of succeeding in this effort unless we first understand why the earth's wild species are important and how we are depleting the earth's genetic savings account.

This chapter was coauthored by Jack R. Nelson, Department of Forestry and Range Management, Washington State University; Jack Ward Thomas, Pacific Northwest Forest and Range Experiment Station, USDA-Forest Service; and G. Tyler Miller, Jr.

Figure 16-1 The extinct passenger pigeon. The last known passenger pigeon died in the Cincinnati Zoo in 1914.

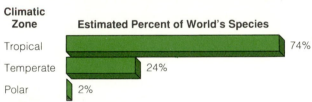

Climatic Zone	Estimated Percent of World's Species	
Tropical		74%
Temperate		24%
Polar		2%

Figure 16-2 Percentage of world's wild species found in major climatic zones. (Data from International Union for Conservation of Nature and Natural Resources and World Resources Institute)

This chapter is devoted to these topics. The next chapter discusses what we can do to prevent premature extinction of wild species.

16-1 WHY PRESERVE WILD PLANT AND ANIMAL SPECIES?

How Many Species Exist? We share this planet with perhaps 5 million to 50 million different species of plants and animals, most of them insects. So far scientists have identified only about 1.8 million species—two-thirds of them insects.

Almost three-fourths of the world's known and unknown plant and animal species are believed to live only in areas with tropical climates (Figure 16-2). Many of these are found only on particular mountains, islands, riverbanks, and other limited and often unique habitats. Biologists estimate that at least 50% of the world's species live in tropical forests, which are being rapidly cleared and degraded (Figure 14-15, p. 372). In one tree in a tropical forest in Peru scientists found

as many species of ants as have been identified in the entire British Isles.

Wildlife is usually defined as consisting only of vertebrates (animals with backbones) such as mammals and birds. This definition excludes species of plants and the vast number of invertebrates (animals without backbones), mostly insects.

In this book the terms **wildlife** and **wild species** are defined more broadly to include all free, undomesticated animals, plants, and microorganisms. (This definition doesn't include animals in zoos and plants in botanical gardens because they are not free). This chapter and the one that follows deal primarily with all forms of wildlife except fish and marine mammals, which were discussed in Chapter 12.

Protecting Biological Diversity Why should we care about the loss of wildlife? What difference does it make if the natural world that surrounds us becomes less diverse? It makes a great difference for a number of economic, aesthetic, recreational, scientific, ecological, and ethical reasons.

The 5 million to 50 million species and the billions of genetically distinct populations that exist today can be thought of as a giant genetic library of successful survival strategies developed over several billion years. They are the source of all future biological evolution through natural selection or genetic engineering (see Pro/Con on p. 138).

Sooner or later all species become extinct. However, we have become a major factor in the premature extinction of an increasing number of species. Protecting the biological diversity—*biodiversity* for short—in these millions of species and the genetic variability within each species is one of the most important and challenging tasks we face.

Biodiversity is the foundation of the ecosystem services upon which we and other species depend. Eliminating a species damages the earth's biological fabric in ways we don't understand and can't predict.

The basic problem is that biological diversity is a common property resource. Since no one owns a species, any wild species found to be useful or in the way of human activities is in danger of being exploited or driven to the point of extinction.

Economic and Medical Importance Certain wild species are important because of their actual or potential economic value to people. These species are called **wildlife resources**. They are potentially renewable resources, if not driven to extinction or near extinction by our activities.

Most of the plants that supply 90% of the world's food today were domesticated from wild plants found in the tropics. Existing wild plant species, most of them still unclassified and unevaluated, will be needed by agricultural scientists to develop new crop strains that have higher yields and increased resistance to diseases, pests, heat, salinity, and drought.

Wild animal species are another largely untapped source of food. Wildlife biologists have suggested that African grazing animals such as wildebeests, antelopes, buffaloes, and warthogs be herded and raised as human food. These presently undomesticated species produce higher yields of meat with fewer environmental problems than cattle (see Case Study on p. 358).

Pollination by insects is essential for many food and nonfood plant species. In some parts of the world insects are eaten as a source of protein. They may become an even more important food source in the future.

During the last few decades we have learned about the ecological limitations and dangers of commercial pesticides (see Enrichment Study near the end of Chapter 11). As a result, farmers are learning to use predatory insects (Figure 11-18, p. 299), parasites, and disease-causing bacteria and viruses for biological control of various weeds and insect pests. In Florida, for instance, citrus growers have been saving about $35 million a year by spending only $35,000 to import three tropical species of parasitic wasps that feed on citrus crop pests.

Various sex attractant chemicals and hormones (Figure 11-19, p. 300) are extracted from insects and used to control insect pests. Plants are also sources of natural insecticides, such as pyrethrum (Figure 11-16, p. 295).

Since the beginning of recorded history thousands of wild plant species have been used as medicines. Today in China 1,700 plants, and in India at least 2,500 plants, are used for medicinal purposes. About 80% of the people in LDCs rely on natural herbs and other plants for most of their health care.

Roughly half of the prescription and nonprescription drugs used in the world and 25% of those used in the United States have active ingredients extracted from wild organisms. About one-fourth of these ingredients are extracted from plants found in tropical forests. Annual sales of drugs based on naturally derived chemicals are at least $40 billion worldwide and $20 billion in the United States.

Quinine, used to treat malaria, is derived from the cinchona tree. Penicillin is produced by a fungus. Certain species of bacteria produce other lifesaving antibiotics such as tetracycline and streptomycin. In 1988 a scientist discovered a natural antibiotic produced by the African clawed frog that is likely to revolutionize the treatment of infections from burns and other causes. A key ingredient in today's widely used contraceptive pills is derived from a compound found in a wild Mexican yam. Materials extracted from an endangered

Figure 16-3 The nine-banded armadillo is used in research to find a cure for leprosy.

species of evening primrose have the potential to treat coronory heart disease, multiple sclerosis, schizophrenia, eczema, and possibly alcoholic hangovers.

At least 1,400 plant species of tropical forests are believed to contain anticancer chemicals. And this estimate is based on a preliminary screening of only 1 in 10 known tropical plants, and intensive screening of only 1 in 100 such plants. A chemical that causes leaves to change color in the fall is being studied as a possible cure for colon cancer. In addition to foods and medicines, trees and other plants, many of them found in tropical forests, supply us with an enormous variety of materials (Figure 14-11, p. 369).

Medical scientists use many wild animal species to test drugs, vaccines, chemical toxicity, and surgical procedures and to increase their understanding of human health and disease. In the United States alone about 71 million animals—mice, rats, dogs, cats, primates, birds, frogs, guinea pigs, rabbits, and hamsters—are used each year for research and teaching.

Elephants under stress are used to study the causes of heart disease. The nine-banded armadillo (Figure 16-3) is being used to study leprosy and prepare a vaccine for this disease. Chimpanzees are used to test the safety of various hepatitis vaccines. Rhesus monkeys are used to test vaccines for smallpox, measles, mumps, and polio. In the 1940s, before the polio vaccine was developed, polio killed some 30,000 people annually and crippled thousands of children.

Mice, rats, chimpanzees, and rhesus monkeys are used to test for possible cancer-causing agents and toxic chemicals. By working with such animals, researchers increased the cure rate for children suffering from acute lymphocytic leukemia from 4% in 1965 to 70% today. The Florida manatee, an endangered mammal, is being used in hemophilia research.

Work with dogs and other animals led to the discovery of insulin, used to control diabetes, and to the development of techniques for open-heart surgery and organ transplants. These are only a few of the thousands of ways wild plants and animals help improve our health. However, animal rights activists are protesting the use of animals in medical and biological research (see Pro/Con below).

Wild animals also supply us with silk, glue, soap (from animal fats), leather, musk, down, wool, and other materials. Trees and other plants not presently used may become future sources of paper and energy. For example, kenaf, a fast-growing wild plant found in Kenya and Tanzania, can grow in the southern United States and be used to make paper. It can grow to maturity in 150 days and produce 3 to 5 times more paper pulp a year per acre at about half the cost.

Soon fast-growing trees and bushes may be planted in large biomass energy plantations and harvested as fuel to supplement or replace the world's dwindling oil supplies. Scientists have suggested planting "petroleum plantations" of species such as the tropical copaiba tree and some of the 2,000 varieties of *Euphorbia* plants. These plants produce an oil-like material that can be extracted and used directly to fuel vehicles or refined to produce gasoline.

Despite their potential importance, less than 10% of the earth's 250,000 identified plant species have been thoroughly studied for their possible usefulness to us. We know nothing about the 300,000 to 400,000 plants that remain to be discovered. As tropical forests are cleared and degraded, many potentially useful plants and any animals that depend on them will be wiped out before we can find out what value they have to the biosphere and to us.

Aesthetic and Recreational Importance Wild plants and animals are a source of beauty, wonder, joy, and recreational pleasure for large numbers of people. Observing leaves change color in autumn, smelling wildflowers, seeing a robin feeding its young, watch-

---

PRO/CON Should Animals Be Used for Research and Teaching?

The controversy between laboratory researchers and a growing number of animal rights advocates has been heating up recently, especially in the United States and other MDCs. Today there are some 7,000 animal-protection groups in the United States, with combined memberships of 10 million. Advocates of animal rights believe that much of the use of animals for research and teaching is unnecessary and inhumane.

They would like to see most or all animal testing halted and replaced with other methods. They also call for much stricter laws and better enforcement of existing laws controlling how test animals are to be treated.

Because of the value of animal experimentation in medicine and science, most scientists feel that such protection can go too far. They argue that this research is vital for human welfare. Most scientists, however, favor laws requiring humane treatment for lab animals.

Scientists point out that 85% of the animals used annually for medical research in the United States are mice, rats, and other rodents. Advocates of animal rights answer that this still amounts to the use of 180,000 dogs, 50,000 cats, 61,000 nonhuman primates, 539,000 guinea pigs, and 554,000 rabbits a year for medical research.

Researchers believe that animals would benefit more if animal rights advocates concentrated on preventing people from abandoning 200,000 dogs and cats *each week* in the United States because of pet overpopulation and the throwaway mentality. Each year U.S. pounds and animal shelters have to kill about 12 million unwanted cats and dogs. By contrast, about 200,000 dogs and cats are killed each year for research and teaching purposes. Most of these animals are obtained from pounds and shelters where they have been condemned to die anyway.

Scientists point out that animals themselves have benefited from animal research. Animals that people cherish as companions can have cataracts removed, undergo open-heart surgery, or wear a pacemaker because of animal research performed to benefit humans. Animals benefit from vaccines for rabies, distemper, anthrax, tetanus, and feline leukemia— all developed through animal re-

search in veterinary medicine.

Under intense pressure from animal rights groups, scientists are trying to find testing methods that do not cause animals to suffer or— better yet—that do not use animals at all. Promising alternatives include the use of cell and tissue cultures, simulated tissues and body fluids, and bacteria. Computer-generated models can also be used to estimate the toxicity of a compound from knowledge of its chemical structure and properties.

Computer simulations of animals under anesthesia can be used to teach veterinary medical students. Videotapes can replace live demonstrations on animals for biology and veterinary medical students.

But researchers point out that such techniques cannot replace all animal research. Cell cultures, for example, do not have bones and therefore cannot be used to test treatments for arthritis or other bone and joint diseases. They argue that live animals are still needed to help perfect new surgical techniques and to test many lifesaving drugs and vaccines. What do you think?

ing an eagle soar overhead or a porpoise glide through the water are only a few of the pleasurable experiences provided for us by wild species. Wild **game species** provide recreation in the form of hunting and fishing.

Outdoor recreation involving wildlife is not only fun, it's a big and growing business. Each year, almost one of every two Americans participates in some form of outdoor recreational activity involving wildlife, and in the process these people spend $37 billion. Each year 95 million Americans observe, feed, or photograph wild plants and animals. Another 54 million fish and 16 million hunt.

Wildlife tourism is important to the economy of some LDCs. Kenya, for example, netted $300 million from 500,000 tourists in 1985. One wildlife economist estimated that one male lion living to seven years of age in Kenya leads to $515,000 of expenditures by tourists. If the lion were killed for its skin, it would be worth only about $1,000.

Scientific Importance Most people, especially scientists, have a compelling urge to understand how the world around them works. Scientists seek to discover, classify, and name all living species on the planet. They also try to understand their ecological roles, as well as their anatomy, physiological processes, genetic makeup, and chemical composition. In this sense science can be defined as the search for order in the natural world around us.

Each species has scientific value because it can help scientists understand how life has evolved and will continue to evolve on this planet. Such investigations can give us a better understanding of ourselves and the role of each species in sustaining life on earth.

Ecological Importance The most important contributions of wild species may be their roles in maintaining the health, integrity, and adaptability of the world's ecosystems. These ecosystem services supply us and other species with food from the soil and the sea, recycle nutrients essential to agriculture, and help produce and maintain fertile soil.

Wild species also produce and maintain oxygen and other gases in the atmosphere, moderate the earth's climate, help regulate water supplies, and store solar energy as chemical energy in food, wood, and fossil fuels. They also filter and detoxify poisonous substances, decompose wastes, control most potential crop pests and carriers of disease, and make up a vast gene pool from which we and other species can draw.

All species have ecological roles, but some may be especially vital to the workings of their ecosystems. Examples include large herbivores that significantly change vegetation, large carnivores that regulate predator–prey relationships, organisms that pollinate plants, plants that bear fruit at times when few others

do, and animals that provide habitats for other species (see Case Study on p. 114).

How many of us appreciate the role of hawks, owls, foxes, and coyotes in keeping rodent populations down, and the importance of vultures and other scavengers in removing and recycling dead animal carcasses? How often do we think about the crucial roles fungi, bacteria, and other decomposers play in recycling nutrients needed by all life forms? Instead of looking at wetlands as free sewage treatment plants and highly productive ecosystems, many people see them as places to be filled and used as sites for houses and condominiums.

Once a species is extinct because of natural causes or human activities, it is gone forever. From an ecological and long-term economic point of view, we should not hasten the extinction of any species as we manipulate and modify nature to suit our purposes. As conservationist Aldo Leopold said, "To keep every cog and wheel is the first precaution of intelligent tinkering."

Ethical Importance So far, the reasons given here for preserving wildlife are based on the actual or potential usefulness of plants, animals, and decomposers as resources for people. This view is based on the human-centered (anthropocentric) belief that we are the most important species on the planet. According to this worldview, we have the right, and according to some the duty, to use the world's resources as we please.

Many ecologists and conservationists believe that wild species will continue to disappear at an alarming rate until we replace this human-centered view of wildlife and the environment with either a life-centered (biocentric) or an ecosystem-centered (ecocentric) view (pp. 68–70).

The biocentric worldview sees the human species as no more important than any other species. Each wild species has inherent value completely apart from whatever worth they have to humans. Thus, each wild species has an inherent right to exist—or at least the right to *struggle* to exist—equal to that of any other species.

According to this view, it is ethically wrong for us to hasten the extinction of any species. As environmental historian Roderick Nash put it, "We must be concerned about conservation and environmental responsibility not because it is profitable or beautiful, and not even because it promotes our survival, but because it is right."

Some believe that each individual wild creature has a right to survive without human interference, just as each human being has the right to survive. Some distinguish between the survival rights of plants and those of animals. The poet Alan Watts once commented that he was a vegetarian "because cows scream louder than carrots."

Time Period	Average Annual Extinction Rate of Mammal and Bird Species
8000 B.C.–A.D.1600	0.001, or 1 species every 1,000 years
1600–1900	0.25, or 1 species every 4 years
1900–1975	1 a year

Figure 16-4 Estimated average annual extinction rate of mammal and bird species between 8000 B.C. and 1975 A.D. (Data from E. O. Wilson and Norman Myers)

Many people make ethical distinctions for various types of animals. For instance, they think little about killing a fly, mosquito, cockroach, or sewer rat, or about catching and killing fish they don't eat. The same people, however, might deplore the killing of game animals such as deer, squirrels, or rabbits.

Others distinguish between the rights of wild and domesticated animals. People with a biocentric worldview focus mostly on the inherent rights of all wild animal, plant, and microorganism species to exist. Animal rights advocates focus only on animals but extend their ethical concern to each individual animal. They call for wild and domesticated animals to be given legal protection from being subjected to unnecessary pain, suffering, and killing (see Pro/Con on p. 416).

Most of us are involved in the violent deaths of domesticated animals every day. When we buy meat or any animal product, including leather, we are paying others to kill cows, calves, lambs, and chickens for us in slaughterhouses. Some ask whether this violence toward life is any more justified than killing wild animals.

One factor hindering ethical concern for wildlife preservation, especially in MDCs, is that most people are urban dwellers. People living in and around cities are largely cut off from the natural world of plants and animals. Naturalist John Livingston summarizes this feeling of isolation from nature:

I think that the extraordinary boom in the house plant business these days is a very good indication of a fundamental problem. I do not see it so much as a decorative fad as the expression of a deep and primal need—a biological imperative. To be alive means to maintain contact with something—anything—that is alive. It is the most fundamental part of being. The geranium on the tenement windowsill is both an offering to the mysterious tidal pull of some distant biological memory, and a heartbreaking cry for help.

Decades ago conservationist Aldo Leopold pointed out the important link between direct experience with wild species and ethical concern about these species: "We can be ethical only in relation to something we can see, feel, understand, love, or otherwise have faith in" (see Spotlight on p. 69).

The ecocentric worldview stresses the importance of not degrading or impairing ecosystems, rather than focusing only on individual species or on individual organisms. It is based on the ethical principle that something is right when it tends to maintain the earth's life-support systems for us and other species and wrong when it tends otherwise. Here the emphasis is on preserving biodiversity—species diversity and genetic diversity within species—by preserving entire ecosystems.

16-2 HOW SPECIES BECOME DEPLETED AND EXTINCT

Extinction Before the Dawn of Agriculture The species found on earth today are the result of two biological processes taking place since life emerged on earth several billion years ago. One is **speciation**, the formation of new species from existing ones through natural selection in response to changes in environmental conditions (Figure 6-21 and Figure 6-22, p. 139). The other is **extinction**, the process in which a species ceases to exist because its members cannot adapt and reproduce under new environmental conditions.

During the last 4.6 billion years the earth has been home for an estimated 500 million species of plants and animals. Only 5 million to 50 million of those species exist today. This means that up to 98% of the earth's species have either become extinct or have evolved into a form different enough to be identified as a new species.

Fossil remains and other evidence suggest that over the past 500 million years there have been five or six catastrophic extinctions of life, mostly numerous species of animals. We probably will never know the exact cause of past mass extinctions. We do know, however, that humans caused none of these extinction spasms.

Extinction of Species Today Extinction is a natural process. However, since agriculture began about 10,000 years ago, the rate of species extinction has increased sharply as human settlements have expanded worldwide.

Rough estimates indicate that between 8000 B.C. and 1975 A.D. the average extinction rate of mammal and bird species increased about 1,000-fold (Figure 16-4). If the extinction rates of plant and insect species are included, the estimated extinction rate in 1975 was several hundred species a year (Figure 16-5).

Since then the rate of extinction has accelerated. Biologist Edward O. Wilson estimated that by 1985 the

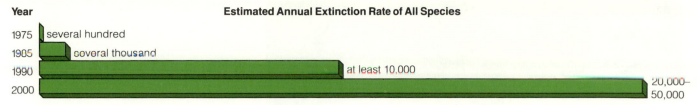

Year   **Estimated Annual Extinction Rate of All Species**

1975   several hundred

1985   several thousand

1990   at least 10,000

2000   20,000–50,000

Figure 16-5 Estimated annual extinction rate of all species between 1975 and 2000. These estimates assume that there are 10 million species worldwide. If there are 30 million to 50 million insect species in tropical forests alone, then the extinction rates for 1990 and 2000 will be much higher. (Data from E. O. Wilson and Norman Myers)

extinction rate had increased at least tenfold to several thousand species per year.

Wilson, Norman Myers (see Guest Essay at the end of Chapter 14), and other biologists are alarmed at this situation. They warn that if deforestation (especially of tropical forests), desertification, and destruction of wetlands and coral reefs continue at their present rates, then at least 500,000 and perhaps 1 million species will become extinct because of human activities between 1975 and 2000. Most of these species will be plants and insects that have yet to be classified and evaluated for their value to humans and their roles in ecosystems.

Using the lower estimate of 500,000 extinctions, by the year 2000 an average of 20,000 species a year would become extinct because of our activities. This is an average of 1 species every 30 minutes—a 200-fold increase in the extinction rate in only 25 years.

Animal extinctions get the most publicity. But plant extinctions are more important ecologically because most animal species depend directly or indirectly on plants for food. It is estimated that about 10% of the world's plant species are threatened with extinction today. By the year 2000, from 16% to 25% of all plant species face extinction.

Some analysts contend that the projected species extinction rate for the year 2000 is only a wild guess and that it may greatly overstate the situation. But even if the average extinction rate is only 1,000 per year by the end of this century, the total loss will still rival the great mass extinctions of the past.

There are important differences between the present mass extinction and those in the past. First, the present "extinction spasm" is being caused by us. Such extinction cannot be balanced by speciation because it takes between 2,000 and 100,000 generations for new species to evolve. Second, it is taking place in only a few decades rather than over several million years. Third, plant species are disappearing as rapidly as animal species, thus threatening many animal species that otherwise would not become extinct at this time.

Threatened and Endangered Species Today   Private conservation organizations and government conservation agencies often classify species heading toward extinction as either endangered or threatened. An

endangered species is one having so few individual survivors that the species could soon become extinct over all or most of its natural range. Examples of endangered species are given in Table 16-1.

A **threatened species** is still abundant in its natural range but is declining in numbers and likely to become endangered. Examples are the African elephant, Utah prairie dog, bald eagle, and grizzly bear.

The International Union for the Conservation of Nature (IUCN) regularly compiles lists of the world's threatened and endangered species. In 1988 the IUCN listed 4,600 species as being threatened or endangered. Many thousands of others are being evaluated for listing. Some will become extinct before this process is completed. Thousands of other species—mostly plants and insects—disappear before they are even found and recognized as species by biologists. More than 1,000 of the world's 9,000 species of birds are now at risk of extinction.

Endangered and threatened species in the United States and other parts of the world are listed and given federal protection by the Office of Endangered Species of the U.S. Department of the Interior's Fish and Wildlife Service. By January, 1988 the Office of Endangered Species had listed 1,037 species as endangered or threatened, with 531 of them found in the United States. Several states also have lists of endangered and threatened species.

About 3,000 plant species in the United States have been identified as endangered. Only 149 were under federal protection in early 1989. In 1988 the Center for Plant Conservation, a consortium of 19 botanical gardens and arboreta, estimated that 680 of the 25,000 native plant species in the United States could disappear from the wild by the year 2000, mostly because of habitat loss to agriculture and urbanization. Nearly three-fourths of the most critically endangered plant species occur in Hawaii, California, Texas, Florida, and Puerto Rico. Scientists at the center are developing emergency conservation plans to protect these critically endangered species in their natural habitats, cultivate them in botanical gardens and arboreta, and store their seeds in seed banks.

Focusing solely on species loss hides the importance of other indicators of the condition of the world's wildlife. Many wild species are not in danger of extinc-

Table 16-1 Some of the World's Endangered Animal Species

Species	Remaining Habitat	Estimated Number Left in the Wild
California condor	Mountains near Los Angeles	0
Black-footed ferret	Meeteetse, Wyoming	0
Ivory-billed woodpecker	Cuba and Texas	2–5
Gray wolf	U.S., Mexico	100
White rhinoceros	Sub-Saharan Africa	100
Key deer	Florida Keys	250–300
Giant panda	Central China mountains	1,000
Florida manatee	Southeast U.S. to South America	1,000
Black rhinoceros	Sub-Saharan Africa	3,500
Snow leopard	Central Asia	2,500
Galapagos tortoise	Ecuador	13,000
Cheetah	Africa, India	15,000
Gorilla	Central and western Africa	15,000

U.S. Fish and Wildlife Service

Figure 16-6 The whooping crane is an endangered species in the United States, with only about 200 birds surviving in the wild in 1989. This migratory bird makes its winter home in Arkansas Pass, Texas, and its summer home at a lake in northern Canada.

tion, but their populations have been sharply reduced locally or regionally. Because such number losses are occurring much faster and more frequently than extinctions, they may be a better sign of the condition of wildlife and entire ecosystems. This could allow scientists to prevent species extinction rather than responding mostly to emergency situations.

Habitat Loss and Disturbance The greatest threat to most wild species is destruction, fragmentation, and degradation of their habitats. As we increase in numbers and affluence, we increase our use of the earth's land and water resources at the expense of other creatures.

We build cities and suburbs, clear forests, drain and fill wetlands, plow up grasslands and plant them with crops, and strip the land by mining. Such disruption of natural communities threatens wild species by destroying migration routes, breeding areas, and food sources. Deforestation, especially of tropical forests, is probably the single greatest cause of the decline in global biological diversity (Section 14-3).

A UN study found that two-thirds of the original wildlife habitat in tropical Africa and in much of Southeast Asia has been lost or severely degraded. Bangladesh, the world's most densely populated large country, has lost 95% of its wildlife habitat.

In the United States forests have been reduced by 33%, tall-grass prairies by 98%, and wetlands by 50%. Furthermore, much of the remaining wildlife habitat is being fragmented and polluted at an alarming rate. Habitat disturbance was a major factor in the extinction of American bird species such as the heath hen. Loss or degradation of habitat is also the key factor in the near extinction of Atwater's prairie chicken, the whooping crane (Figure 16-6), and the California condor. The American bald eagle is endangered in some areas mostly because of loss of habitat.

Many rare and threatened species live in vulnerable, specialized habitats such as small islands or single trees in tropical forests. About 75% of the mammals and birds that have become extinct in recent history were island-dwelling species. For example, 99% of the known animal species and 95% of the flowering plants on the isolated chain of islands that make up Hawaii are found nowhere else. The loss of species in Hawaii from deforestation and urbanization has been staggering.

An island is usually defined as a land mass surrounded by water. From an ecological viewpoint, any habitat area surrounded by different habitats is considered a habitat island. Human alterations of ecosystems fragment wildlife habitats into patches or habitat islands, which are often too small to support the minimum number of individuals needed to sustain a population. Fragmenting of habitat can also cause inbreeding, which produces genetically inferior offspring that are vulnerable to extinction. Remaining individuals and species in such habitat islands are also highly vulnerable to being killed by human activities, floods, and other disasters.

In Florida the diversion of water to supply a rapidly increasing human population has shortened the wet season and lengthened the dry season in the Everglades. This has caused a 90% drop in populations of wading birds in the Everglades.

Plant species unique to a small locality can be eliminated from the earth by a single bulldozer, as can the animals that feed on them. For example, as many as 90 unique plant species were lost when the forest on top of an isolated ridge in western Ecuador was cleared to plant subsistence crops. Such unintentional extinctions are common.

The removal of large dead and dying trees from forests, city parks, and suburban areas eliminates important wildlife habitats. The holes and cavities in such trees are nesting sites for hundreds of bird species and for squirrels, raccoons, and other animals.

The Puerto Rican parrot, for instance, is close to extinction because few suitable nest holes remain in its native forest. Another bird very close to extinction in the United States is the ivory-billed woodpecker. Its food source is insects on standing dead timber in old-growth hardwood forests in the southeastern United States. As these forests have been cut down and replaced by plantations of even-aged trees, this woodpecker species has lost most of its habitat and food supply.

The loss or displacement of such cavity-nesting birds has important ecological consequences. Most of these birds help control nuisance insects such as mosquitoes and flies, and they help protect forests from being ravaged by insects such as gypsy moths and wood-boring beetles.

Migratory birds are vulnerable to habitat loss at each end of their routes (see Case Study below).

According to Harvard biologist Edward O. Wilson:

The one process ongoing in the 1980s that will take millions of years to correct is the loss of genetic and species diversity by

---

CASE STUDY Loss of North American Songbirds

Nearly half of all species of wild birds in North America are migratory songbirds—warblers, flycatchers, thrushes, and others. Each year these birds spend six or seven months in the tropical forests of Mexico, Central America, South America, and the Caribbean Islands feeding on insects.

Having gained the necessary fat, they then fly to North America in the spring. During the three or four months the birds spend in temperate-zone woodlands, they breed, raise their young, and prepare to fly south again. Many do not survive this hazardous journey, which may take four to six weeks each way (with resting stops).

Many of these birds are now threatened with extinction, mostly by loss or degradation of habitat in their summer and winter homes. The naturally short lives of all songbirds makes them especially vulnerable to habitat loss. Clearing and fragmentation of forests and woodlands in the United States and the clearing of tropical forests in South America have led to a sharp decline in the numbers of hundreds of migrating species of songbirds.

When forests are reduced to small, scattered fragments, songbirds are forced to nest and breed near the edge of these communities. This makes them more susceptible to predation and parasit-

ism. Raccoons, skunks, possums, crows, and bluejays raid songbird nests for eggs and chicks. Nest parasites, especially cowbirds, lay their eggs in songbird nests and destroy many of the eggs and chicks of songbirds. The larger, stronger cowbird young grab most of the food, starving out many of the remaining songbird chicks.

Why should you care about these birds? In addition to adding beauty and magnificent sounds, the declining songbirds are very efficient insect eaters. They have as much right to exist as we do.

the destruction of natural habitats. This is the folly our descendants are least likely to forgive us.

Commercial Hunting   There are three major types of hunting: commercial, subsistence, and sport. **Commercial hunting** involves killing animals for profit from sale of their furs or other parts. The killing of animals to provide enough food for survival is called **subsistence hunting**. **Sport hunting** is the killing of animals for recreation.

Subsistence hunting once caused the extinction of many animal species. In the early 1880s, for instance, the eastern elk became extinct in the United States mostly because it was hunted for food and hides. Today, however, subsistence hunting has declined sharply in most parts of the world because of the decrease in hunting-and-gathering societies.

Sport hunting is now closely regulated in most countries. Game species are endangered by such hunting only when protective regulations do not exist or are not enforced. No animal in the United States, for instance, has become extinct or endangered because of regulated sport hunting.

Worldwide, legal and illegal commercial hunting threatens many species of large animals. The jaguar, tiger, snow leopard, and cheetah are hunted for their furs. Rhinoceroses are hunted for their horns (see Case Study on p. 423), and elephants for their tusks.

Commercial hunting in the United States was an important factor in the extermination of the American passenger pigeon (Figure 16-1). It also played a key role in the near extermination of the American bison (Figure 2-7, p. 34), the snowy egret (Figure 2-8, p. 35), and the heath hen once found from Massachusetts to the Potomac River. Today commercial hunting is not legal in the United States, except for fur trapping, mostly of raccoon, muskrat, and beaver.

Illegal hunting, however, does occur. In 1988 and 1989, U.S. Fish and Wildlife officials arrested 66 people for allegedly killing black bears in Appalachia and several northeastern states. The bears were killed for their tennis-sized gallbladders, sold for $50 to $150 each for use in Asia as an aphrodisiac. However, there is no evidence that a ground-up gallbladder of a bear, the horn of a rhino, the antler of a deer, the phallus of the tiger, or the tail of a seal sought by many Asians have any physical effect on sexual desire.

Annual commercial trade in wild plants and animals has an estimated value of at least $5 billion. One-fourth to one-third of this trade is illegal. Most wildlife traded in this global market comes from tropical and subtropical regions of Africa, Southeast Asia, and South America. The largest importers of wildlife and wildlife products are the United States, Canada, China, Japan, Taiwan, Singapore, Hong Kong, and western European countries. It is not surprising that Bengal tigers face extinction, when a coat made from their fur sells

for $100,000 in Tokyo. For similar reasons, only about 300 wild Siberian tigers and less than 2,500 wild snow leopards are left. The U.S. Fish and Wildlife Service estimates that illegal wildlife imports into the United States are worth $100 million to $250 million a year.

Predator and Pest Control   Extinction or near extinction can also occur when people attempt to exterminate pest and predator species that compete with humans for food and game. Fruit farmers exterminated the Carolina parakeet in the United States around 1914 because it fed on fruit crops. The species was easy to exterminate because when one member of a flock was shot, the rest of the birds hovered over its body, making themselves easy targets.

As animal habitats have shrunk, farmers have killed large numbers of African elephants to keep them from trampling and eating food crops. Carnivore predators that sometimes kill livestock and game are shot, trapped, and poisoned. Since the 1930s predator control programs by ranchers, hunters, and government agencies have sharply reduced populations of the timber wolf, grizzly bear, and mountain lion over most of the continental United States.

Since 1929 ranchers and government agencies have poisoned prairie dogs (Figure 13-8, p. 348) because their mounds sometimes cause horses and cattle to stumble and break their legs. This poisoning has led to the near extinction of the black-footed ferret, which preyed on the prairie dog (see Case Study on p. 424). Other species whose populations have been greatly reduced by prairie dog poisoning campaigns include burrowing owls, swift foxes, and prairie falcons. These species help control rodents such as ground squirrels, which also compete with livestock for range grass.

Pets and Decorative Plants   Each year large numbers of threatened and endangered animals are smuggled into the United States and other countries. Most are sold as pets. Many of these animals die during shipment. After purchase many are mistreated, killed, or abandoned by their owners.

Worldwide, over 6 million live wild birds are sold each year. Most of them end up in pet-loving countries such as the United States, Great Britain, and Germany. Because of this trade, at least nine bird species are now listed as threatened or endangered.

Exotic-bird collectors may pay $10,000 for a threatened hyacinth macaw smuggled out of Brazil. Bird collectors in the United States and Europe will pay as much as $12,000 for a pair of rare parakeets.

Collectors have also endangered some species of butterflies. For example, the only remaining non-breeding habitats of monarch butterflies in North America are a few sites along the Pacific coast in the United States and in the mountains of central Mexico.

The North American population of monarchs could soon become extinct because these sites are jeopardized by farming and housing developments.

Some species of exotic plants, especially orchids and cacti, are also endangered because they are gathered, often illegally. They are then sold to collectors and used to decorate houses, offices, and landscapes. A collector may pay $5,000 for a single rare orchid.

Nearly one-third of the cactus species native to the United States, especially those in Texas and Arizona, are thought to be endangered because they are collected and sold for use as potted plants. For instance, a rare 19-ft-high crested saguaro cactus removed illegally from an Arizona site turned up in a Las Vegas nursery with a $15,000 price tag. To reduce losses from cactus rustlers, Arizona has put 222 species under state protection with penalties of up to $1,000 and jail sentences up to one year. However, only seven people are assigned to enforce this law over the entire state.

Medical Research   Most test animal species are not endangered. However, medical and biological research

CASE STUDY   Near Extinction of the Rhinoceros

The rhinoceros is one of the earth's oldest animals, dating back some 55 million years. There are five surviving wild rhino species. Two of these—black rhinos (Figure 16-7) and white rhinos—live in northern and southern African grasslands. The other three—Sumatran, great Indian, and Javan—inhabit rain forests in Asia. All five species are threatened with extinction because of loss of habitat and poachers who kill them for their horns, each worth $40,000 to $112,000.

Importing rhino horn is illegal in most countries. However, an illegal $3 million a year trade flourishes in the Middle East and eastern Asia. In the Middle East Asian rhino horn, the most prized, can fetch as much as $16,000 a pound—over twice the price of gold.

In North Yemen the horns are carved into dagger handles that sell for $500 to $12,000. These ornate daggers are worn as a sign of masculinity and virility. North Yemen has been responsible for about half of the world's consumption of rhino horn since 1970.

In China and other parts of Asia rhino horns are ground into a powder and used for reducing fever and other medicinal purposes for which its effectiveness has not been verified by medical science. Some Asians believe the powder is an aphrodisiac. If this were true, human hair and fingernails (which consist of the same substance—keratin—as rhino horn) would be a much cheaper, readily available sexual stimulant.

Since 1970 about 85% of the world's population of wild rhinos has disappeared largely because of poaching in Africa and habitat loss and poaching in Asia. By 1988 there were probably no more than 11,000 wild rhinos, down from 125,000 two decades ago. By 1988 the Javan rhino was down to about 50 animals, the Sumatran rhino to 700, and the great Indian rhino to about 1,300. Less than 100 northern white rhinos, 4,900 southern white rhinos, and 3,500 black rhinos were left in Africa.

Illegal killing continues. Poacher gangs usually outnumber and sometimes outgun rangers patrolling protected areas. If poaching continues at present rates, no rhinos will be left in the wild within a decade.

In Zimbabwe government park rangers patrol around the clock to protect the remaining black rhinos from extinction. They have orders to shoot poachers on sight. Since 1985 they have killed more than 30 poachers and taken over 20 prisoners.

Private and government conservationists are trying to protect rhinos from further poaching by creating fenced or heavily guarded sanctuaries and private ranches, relocating some to protected areas, and building up captive breeding populations for all species. This has led to a slow increase in numbers in protected areas and in captivity.

National Geographic Society

Figure 16-7   Only about 3,500 black rhinos are left in Africa. This and other species of rhinoceros face extinction because they are illegally killed for their valuable horns.

The black-footed ferret can be distinguished from other members of the weasel family by its black-masked face, black feet, and black-tipped tail (Figure 16-8). At one time it lived in over 100 million acres of grasslands that once covered much of central and western North America (Figure 16-9). A nocturnal animal that feeds mostly on prairie dogs, the black footed ferret lives and raises its young in prairie dog burrows.

In 1890 an estimated 5 billion prairie dogs lived in North America. About 99% of that population has been destroyed by massive poisoning campaigns on behalf of the livestock industry.

These poisons, coupled with loss of prey and habitats, also killed black-footed ferrets. In 1981 zoologists thought the species might be extinct. Today none of these animals are known to exist in the wild. A $5,000 reward is offered to anyone who finds one or more of these animals living in the wild.

About 60 black-footed ferrets live in captivity in research facilities in Wyoming, Nebraska, and Virginia. The survival of this species will depend on whether the captured animals can produce enough offspring to be relocated in the wild and on finding a suitable habitat.

Figure 16-8 The black-footed ferret is one of the most endangered mammals in North America. None are known to exist in the wild. About 60 live in captivity in Virginia, Nebraska, and Wyoming.

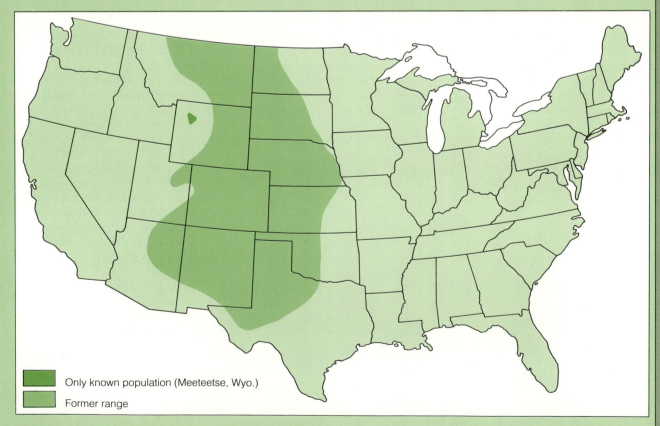

■ Only known population (Meeteetse, Wyo.)

■ Former range

Figure 16-9 Drastically reduced range of the black-footed ferret. (Data from Defenders of Wildlife)

coupled with habitat loss is a serious threat to endangered wild primates such as the chimpanzee and the orangutan. As many as six chimpanzees die during capture and shipment for each one that ends up in a laboratory. Primates are especially useful for medical research and drug testing because of their anatomical, physiological, and genetic similarities to humans.

In 1975 the United States banned all imports of primates for pets. But they can still be imported for research and for display in zoos. Annual imports of primates into the United States have dropped from over 200,000 in the 1950s and 1960s to about 35,000 in the 1980s. But some members of the 60 threatened and endangered primate species are captured and smuggled into the United States each year.

In response to petitions from the World Wildlife Fund and the Humane Society of the United States, the Fish and Wildlife Service changed the status of wild chimpanzees from threatened to endangered in 1988. This will sharply reduce the importing of wild chimps for research purposes. Captive populations of chimps living and born in research facilities are still classified as threatened.

Pollution Changes in climate from global warming and depletion of the ozone layer are major threats to wildlife. Toxic chemicals degrade wildlife habitats and kill some plants and animals.

Industrial wastes, mine acids, and excess heat from electric power plants have wiped out some species of fish, such as the humpbacked chub, in local areas. Slowly degradable pesticides have caused populations of some bird species to decline (see Spotlight below).

Selenium dissolved in irrigation water has contaminated water supplies in California's Kesterson National Wildlife Refuge. This metallic substance has caused large numbers of birth defects in waterfowl and failure of their eggs to hatch.

Introduction of Alien Species As people travel around the world, they sometimes pick up plants and animals intentionally or accidentally and introduce these species to new geographical regions. Many of these alien species have provided food, game, and beauty, and have helped control pests in their new environments.

However, some alien species have no natural predators and competitors in their new habitats. Thus, they

---

SPOTLIGHT Effects of DDT on Wildlife Populations

During the 1950s and 1960s, populations of ospreys, cormorants, Eastern and California brown pelicans (Figure 2-11, p. 37), and bald eagles (Figure 2-16, p. 41) declined drastically. These birds feed mostly on fish at the top of long, aquatic food chains and webs. As a result, the birds ingest large quantities of biologically amplified DDT in their prey (Figure 11-17, p. 297).

Populations of predatory birds such as prairie falcons, sparrow hawks, Bermuda petrels, and peregrine falcons (Figure 16-10) also dropped when they ate animal prey containing DDT. These birds control populations of rabbits, ground squirrels, and other crop-damaging, small mammals. Only about 1,000 peregrine falcons are left in the lower 48 states.

Research has shown that these population declines occurred because DDE, a chemical produced by the breakdown of DDT, accu-mulates in the bodies of the affected bird species. This chemical reduces the amount of calcium in the shells of their eggs. As a result, the shells are so thin that many of them break, and the unborn chicks die.

Since the U.S. ban on DDT in 1972, populations of most of these bird species have made a comeback. In 1980, however, it was discovered that levels of DDT and other banned pesticides were rising in some areas and in some species such as the peregrine falcon and the osprey.

These species may be picking up biologically amplified DDT and other chlorinated hydrocarbon insecticides in Latin American countries where the birds live during winter. In these countries the use of such chemicals is still legal. Illegal use of DDT and other banned pesticides in the United States may also play a role.

Glen Elkmiller/The Peregrine Fund

Figure 16-10 The peregrine falcon is endangered in the United States, mostly because of exposure to DDT. The insecticide caused many of its young to die before hatching because their eggshells were too thin to protect them.

Table 16-2 Damage Caused by Plants and Animals Imported into the United States

Name	Origin	Mode of Transport	Type of Damage
Mammals			
European wild boar	Russia	Intentionally imported (1912), escaped captivity	Destruction of habitat by rooting; crop damage
Nutria (cat-sized rodent)	Argentina	Intentionally imported, escaped captivity (1940)	Alteration of marsh ecology; damage to levees and earth dams; crop destruction
Birds			
European starling	Europe	Intentionally released (1890)	Competition with native songbirds; crop damage; transmission of swine diseases; airport interference
House sparrow	England	Intentionally released by Brooklyn Institute (1853)	Crop damage; displacement of native songbirds
Fish			
Carp	Germany	Intentionally released (1877)	Displacement of native fish; uprooting of water plants with loss of waterfowl populations
Sea lamprey	North Atlantic Ocean	Entered via Welland Canal (1829)	Destruction of lake trout, lake whitefish, and sturgeon in Great Lakes (see p. 337)
Walking catfish	Thailand	Imported into Florida	Destruction of bass, bluegill, and other fish
Insects			
Argentine fire ant	Argentina	Probably entered via coffee shipments from Brazil (1918)	Crop damage; destruction of native ant species
Camphor scale insect	Japan	Accidentally imported on nursery stock (1920s)	Damage to nearly 200 species of plants in Louisiana, Texas, and Alabama
Japanese beetle	Japan	Accidentally imported on irises or azaleas (1911)	Defoliation of more than 250 species of trees and other plants, including many of commercial importance
Plants			
Water hyacinth	Central America	Intentionally introduced (1884)	Clogging waterways; shading out other aquatic vegetation (see p. 334)
Chestnut blight (a fungus)	Asia	Accidentally imported on nursery plants (1900)	Destruction of nearly all eastern American chestnut trees; disturbance of forest ecology
Dutch elm disease, *Cerastomella ulmi* (a fungus, the disease agent)	Europe	Accidentally imported on infected elm timber used for veneers (1930)	Destruction of millions of elms; disturbance of forest ecology

From *Biological Conservation* by David W. Ehrenfeld. Copyright © 1970 by Holt, Rinehart and Winston, Inc. Modified and reprinted by permission.

can dominate their new ecosystems by preying on, outcompeting, and outproducing many native species. Eventually, they can cause the extinction, near extinction, or displacement of native species (see Table 16-2 and the Case Study on p. 427).

For example, the fast-growing water hyacinth, accidentally introduced into Florida, has displaced native plants in Florida waterways (see Case Study on p. 334). In the mid-1800s, house sparrows and starlings were intentionally introduced into the United States from Europe. They have now displaced many native songbirds from their preferred habitats.

The kudzu vine was imported into the southeastern United States from Africa to help control soil erosion. It does control erosion, but it is so prolific that it has also covered hills, trees, houses, roads, stream banks (Figure 16-11), and even entire patches of forest. It has displaced some natural plant species. People have dug it up, cut it up, burned it, and tried to kill it with herbicides, all without success.

Figure 16-11 Kudzu overgrowing stream banks and a patch of forest. No one has found a way to stop the spread of this prolific and hearty plant throughout the southeastern United States.

USDA Soil Conservation Service

CASE STUDY **Effects of Importing Wild European Hares to Australia**

In 1859 a farmer in southern Australia imported a dozen pairs of wild European hares as game animals. Within six years the 24 hares had mushroomed to 22 million and by 1907 had reached every corner of the continent. By the 1930s their population had reached an estimated 750 million.

They competed with sheep for the best grass and in many areas cut the sheep population in half. They also outcompeted native species, such as kangaroos and wallabies, for vegetation. The hares devoured food crops, gnawed young trees, fouled water holes (Figure 16-12), and accelerated soil erosion.

In the early 1950s about 90% of the hare population was killed by a viral disease deliberately introduced by humans. Now scientists are concerned that succeeding

Figure 16-12 European wild hares around a water hole in Australia.

Australian Information Service

generations of the remaining hare population will develop immunity to this disease through natural selection. Then the hares could again become the scourge of Australian farmers and ranchers.

16-3 CHARACTERISTICS OF EXTINCTION-PRONE SPECIES

Why Are Some Species More Vulnerable to Extinction than Others? Some species have natural traits that make them more vulnerable than others to premature extinction (Table 16-3). Each animal species also has a critical population density and size, below which survival may be impossible because males and females have a hard time finding each other. Once the population reaches its critical size, it continues to decline even if the species is protected, because its death rate exceeds its birth rate. The remaining small population can easily be wiped out by fire, flood, landslide, dis-

Table 16-3 Characteristics of Extinction-prone Species

Characteristic	Examples
Low reproduction rate	Blue whale, polar bear, California condor, Andean condor, passenger pigeon, giant panda, whooping crane
Specialized feeding habits	Everglades kite (eats apple snail of southern Florida), blue whale (krill in polar upwelling areas), black-footed ferret (prairie dogs and pocket gophers), giant panda (bamboo), Australian koala (certain types of Eucalyptus leaves)
Feed at high trophic levels	Bengal tiger, bald eagle, Andean condor, timber wolf
Large size	Bengal tiger, African lion, elephant, Javan rhinoceros, American bison, giant panda, grizzly bear
Limited or specialized nesting or breeding areas	Kirtland's warbler (nests only in 6- to 15-year-old jack pine trees), whooping crane (depends on marshes for food and nesting), orangutan (now found only on islands of Sumatra and Borneo), green sea turtle (lays eggs on only a few beaches), bald eagle (prefers habitat of forested shorelines), nightingale wren (nests and breeds only on Barro Colorado Island, Panama)
Found in only one place or region	Woodland caribou, elephant seal, Cooke's kokio, and many unique island species
Fixed migratory patterns	Blue whale, Kirtland's warbler, Bachman's warbler, whooping crane
Preys on livestock or people	Timber wolf, some crocodiles
Certain behavioral patterns	Passenger pigeon and white-crowned pigeon (nest in large colonies), redheaded woodpecker (flies in front of cars), Carolina parakeet (when one bird is shot, rest of flock hovers over body), Key deer (forages for cigarette butts along highways—it's a "nicotine addict")

ease, or some other catastrophic event. Species with low reproductive rates, such as the California condor (see Case Study on p. 429) are particularly vulnerable.

When an isolated population of a species is reduced below its critical size, extinction can be hastened by inbreeding. Inbreeding increases the number of individuals in the population susceptible to birth defects and disease. As a general rule, the remaining wild population of an animal species must have at least 500 individuals to allow some degree of evolution by natural selection.

A specialist feeder, an animal species that depends on a single food source, is much more vulnerable to extinction than one that can feed on several different foods. For example, the giant panda feeds almost exclusively on bamboo. The clearing of bamboo forests in China has made this animal a highly endangered species (Table 16-1).

Predatory birds and large carnivores that feed at high trophic levels in food webs need a large home range because their food supplies are widely dispersed, making them particularly vulnerable to loss of habitat. Many are also highly susceptible to poisons

such as DDT, which can accumulate to high levels in their bodies (Figure 11-17, p. 297). Large animals are easy victims to professional hunters and poachers seeking skins, horns, or other valuable body parts and to sport hunters seeking trophies.

Species with limited or specialized nesting or breeding areas are very susceptible to habitat loss or disturbance. This is particularly true for species found only on small islands or in any isolated habitat.

Species with fixed migratory patterns are vulnerable to habitat loss at both ends of their routes and at stopover areas along their routes. For example, the endangered Kirtland's warbler spends its summers in Michigan in habitats that are now protected. However, it winters in the northern Bahamas on two formerly pine-covered islands that have been almost completely cleared by American companies.

Other species are vulnerable because of behavioral patterns that put them in jeopardy from cars, hunters, and various human activities (Table 16-3). Some species, such as bats, are vulnerable to extinction for a combination of reasons (see Case Study on p. 430).

We can avoid the mass extinction that our activities

On April 19, 1987, for the first time in 600,000 years, no wild California condors (Figure 16-13) soared through the California skies.

The landings and takeoffs of this large vulture with a wrinkled head are clumsy. But once it is airborne, it soars on wings that can span nine feet. With one flap of its wings, it can travel ten miles.

This scavenger once flourished from Canada to Baja California. In earlier times it fed on the carcasses of the millions of large animals that roamed the western half of North America. In recent decades it has had to survive on the carcasses of sheep, cattle, and large predators—many of them laced with predator poisons or poisonous lead shot.

In 1967, when this species was placed on the endangered species list, 40 wild individuals remained, living mainly in a mountainous sanctuary north of Los Angeles. Despite considerable efforts to protect the species, by 1985 only 15 wild birds were left. During the winter of 1985 six died, victims of land development and poisoning from animal carcasses.

In 1987 the U.S. Fish and Wildlife Service, the California Fish and Game Department, and the Audubon Society decided to take the few remaining birds into protective custody at the San Diego Wild Animal Park. By April no condors remained in the wild.

Since 1982 the San Diego Wild Animal Park and the Los Angeles Zoo have had a captive breeding program. By May 1988 there were 28 condors in captivity. Most of them were hatched in the zoos from eggs removed from nests in the wild. Several one-year-old chicks were also taken from the wild and are being reared in the zoos. On April 29, 1988, the first California condor conceived in captivity hatched. The goal of the $200,000-a-year program is to breed at least 200 condors so that some can be returned to the wild in 20 to 40 years. DNA fingerprints have been taken on all captive condors to help make pairing decisions and reduce weakening the gene pool by inbreeding.

Why is the California condor on the brink of extinction? Part of the answer is the condor's large size. Being big, the condor was an easy target for shooters, who prized its long feathers. Many birds were killed by ranchers and farmers, who wrongly blamed them for the deaths of lambs, calves, and chickens, not knowing that these birds fed only on animal carcasses.

Another characteristic that makes the California condor vulnerable is its low reproduction rate. Condor pairs are monogamous partners for life and usually produce only one offspring every two years. Chicks fail to hatch when human activities and noise scare the parents away from the nest during the 42-day incubation period. For example, a person standing 500 yards away can keep a condor from its nest. A newborn chick depends on its parents for up to two years and dies if prematurely abandoned. Finally, it takes a condor six to seven years to reach reproductive age.

Condors need a large, undisturbed habitat and often fly 100 miles a day between nesting and feeding areas. Only about 10% of the species' remaining habitat in California is under federal protection. The rest is on private land that is being threatened by development.

In 1987 the federal government bought several thousand acres of condor habitat to be added to a national wildlife refuge in California. Conservationists hope there will be a large enough, undisturbed habitat left when the captive birds are ready to be returned to the wild.

Figure 16-13 California condor breeding pair in captivity at the San Diego Zoo. None of these birds once found in the thousands are left in the wild.

are now bringing about without an unacceptably high cost, as discussed in the next chapter. But we have no time to waste in such efforts.

Love the animals, love the plants, love everything. If you love everything, you will perceive the divine mystery in

things. Once you perceive it, you will begin to comprehend it better every day. And you will come at last to love the whole world with an all-embracing love.

Fyodor *Dostoevsky*, The Brothers Karamazov

CASE STUDY Bats: Misunderstood, Feared, and Vulnerable

The world's nearly 1,000 species of bat make up one-fourth of all mammal species. These small, nocturnal creatures form the largest populations of any warm-blooded animal. They are found in all but the most extreme polar and desert areas of the earth.

Despite their variety and distribution, bats have several traits that make them vulnerable to extinction from human activities. They reproduce very slowly compared to other mammals and nest in huge breeding colonies in accessible places such as caves, where people can easily destroy them by blocking the entrances.

They are also specialized feeders. Some bats feed only on certain types of nectar, others on certain types of fruit, and others on various night-flying insects.

People kill bats in large numbers because of misinformed fears based on vampire movies and folklore. Most people also falsely believe that bats are dangerous creatures that attack and infect humans and livestock with rabies and other diseases and destroy fruit crops.

Because of such fears and misinformation, some countries have begun massive bat eradication programs, and others are considering such programs. A number of species have been driven to extinction and others are threatened in Australia, Southeast Asia, and the South Pacific.

Most bat species are harmless to people, livestock, and crops. Less than half of one percent of bats get rabies, and these individuals rarely become aggressive and

transmit rabies to wildlife or people. The few people who are bitten by a bat are those who foolishly pick up a sick bat, which bites in self-defense, as almost any sick, wild animal would.

In all of Asia, Europe, Australia, and the Pacific Islands, only two people have been suspected of dying from bat-transmitted rabies. No people in these areas are known to have died of any other bat-transmitted disease. By comparison, in India some 15,000 people die each year from rabies transmitted by other animals, mostly dogs.

In the United States only 10 people have died of bat-transmitted disease in four decades of record keeping. More Americans die each year from dog attacks, falling coconuts, or food poisoning contracted at church picnics.

Because of such unwarranted fear and misunderstanding, Americans spend millions of dollars annually to have pest-control companies exterminate bats. In Europe and the USSR, where there is greater recognition of their economic and ecological benefits, bats receive legal protection.

Bats are of great ecological and economic importance to us. Bats disperse seeds and pollinate trees and shrubs and thus are crucial for the survival of tropical rain forests. In Thailand, for example, a cave-dwelling, nectar-eating bat species is the only known pollinator of durian trees, whose fruit crops are worth $90 million per year.

Many people are unaware that bananas, guavas, mangoes, avocados, dates, figs, and many other

tropical fruits are heavily dependent on nectar-eating and fruit-eating bats for pollination and seeding. Only fruit that is too ripe to harvest and worthless to farmers is consumed by fruit-eating bats.

The pollinating and seeding activities of bats also play an important role in producing many other materials we get from tropical forests. They include prized timber used for furniture, kapok filler used for life preservers and surgical bandages, tequila, hemp fibers for rope, beads for jewelry, and hundreds of other commercially important materials.

Insectivorous bats are the only major predators of night-flying insects. They help control many insects that damage human crops. A single cave colony of insect-eating bats can devour 250,000 pounds or more of insects each night.

In parts of Asia families earn a living by periodically scraping bat droppings, or guano, from bat caves and selling it for fertilizer. Bats are also valuable to medicine and science. Research on bats has contributed to the development of birth control and artificial insemination methods, drug testing, studies of disease resistance and aging, production of vaccines, and development of navigational aids for the blind.

We need to see bats as valuable allies—not enemies—before we destroy them and lose their important benefits to us and other species.

DISCUSSION TOPICS

1. Discuss your gut-level reaction to the statement: "It doesn't really matter that the passenger pigeon is extinct and the blue whale, whooping crane, bald eagle, grizzly bear, and a number of other plant and animal species are endangered." Be honest about your reaction, and give arguments for your position.

2. Why should an urban dweller be concerned about preservation of wildlife and wildlife habitat?

3. Make a log of your own consumption and use of food and other products for a single day. Relate your consumption to the increased destruction of wildlife and wildlife habitats in the United States and in tropical forests.

4. Do you accept the ethical position that each species has the inherent right to survive without human interference, regardless of whether it serves any useful purpose for humans?

5. Do you believe that the species listed below have an inherent right to exist? Explain.
   a. Anopheles mosquitoes, which transmit malaria
   b. Tigers that roam the jungle along the border between India and Nepal and have killed at least 105 persons between 1978 and 1983
   c. Bacteria that cause smallpox or other infectious diseases
   d. Rats, which compete with humans for food
   e. Rattlesnakes, which sometimes kill people

6. Do you believe that each individual of an animal species has an inherent right to survive? Explain. Would you extend such rights to individual plants and microorganisms? Explain.

7. Do you believe that laws should be passed making it illegal to inflict pain, suffering, or unnecessary killing on some or all animals? Explain. What types of killing, if any, would you consider necessary and thus legally allowed? What species, if any, would you omit from such protection?

8. Discuss the idea that because up to 98% of the species that have existed on earth have become extinct by natural selection, we should not be concerned about the several hundred animal species and thousands of plant species that have become extinct primarily because of human activities.

9. Use Table 16-3 to predict a species that may soon be endangered. What, if anything, is being done for this species? What pressures is it being subjected to? Try to work up a plan for protecting it.

10. Do you think that the human species will someday become extinct? Explain. List in order of importance the five major actions individuals and governments throughout the world should take to help prevent such a possibility from becoming a reality.

FURTHER READINGS

Clark, Stephen R. L. 1984. *The Moral Status of Animals*. New York: Oxford University Press.

Davis, Steven, et al. 1986. *Plants in Danger: What Do We Know?* Cambridge, U.K.: Conservation Monitoring Centre, International Union for Conservation of Nature and Natural Resources.

Ehrlich, Paul, and Anne Ehrlich. 1981. *Extinction*. New York: Random House.

Elliot, David K. 1986. *Dynamics of Extinction*. New York: Wiley.

Elton, Charles S. 1958. *The Ecology of Invasions by Plants and Animals*. London: Methuen.

Hoage, R. J., ed. 1985. *Animal Extinctions: What Everyone Should Know*. Washington, D.C.: Smithsonian Institution.

Huxley, Anthony. 1984. *Green Inheritance*. Garden City, N.Y.: Anchor/Doubleday.

Koopowitz, Harold, and Hilary Kaye. 1983. *Plant Extinctions: A Global Crisis*. Washington, D.C.: Stone Wall Press.

Livingston, John A. 1981. *The Fallacy of Wildlife Conservation*. Toronto: McClelland and Stewart.

Midgley, Mary. 1984. *Animals and Why They Matter*. Athens: University of Georgia Press.

Myers, Norman. 1983. *A Wealth of Wild Species: Storehouse for Human Welfare*. Boulder, Colo.: Westview Press.

Norton, B. G., ed. 1986. *The Preservation of Species*. Princeton, N.J.: Princeton University Press.

Passmore, John. 1974. *Man's Responsibility for Nature*. New York: Charles Scribner's.

Prescott-Allen, Robert, and Christine Prescott-Allen. 1982. *What's Wildlife Worth?* Washington, D.C.: Earthscan.

Reagan, Tom. 1982. *All that Dwell Within: Animal Rights and Environmental Ethics*. Berkeley: University of California Press.

Reagan, Tom, and P. Singer. 1976. *Animal Rights and Human Obligation*. Englewood Cliffs, N.J.: Prentice-Hall.

Regenstein, L. 1975. *The Politics of Extinction*. New York: Macmillan.

Rolston, Holmes, III. 1988. *Environmental Ethics: Duties to and Values in the Natural World*. Philadelphia: Temple University Press.

Roots, Clive. 1976. *Animal Invaders*. New York: Universe Books.

Singer, Peter. 1975. *Animal Liberation: A New Ethics for Our Treatment of Animals*. New York: New York Review of Books.

Tuttle, Merlin D. 1988. *America's Neighborhood Bats: Understanding and Learning to Live in Harmony with Them*. Austin: University of Texas Press.

U.S. Fish and Wildlife Service. 1988. *Endangered and Threatened Wildlife and Plants*. Washington, D.C.: U.S. Fish and Wildlife Service.

Wilson, E. O. 1984. *Biophilia*. Cambridge, Mass.: Harvard University Press.

Wilson, E. O., ed. 1988. *Biodiversity*. Washington, D.C.: National Academy Press.

World Resources Institute and International Institute for Environment and Development. Annual. *World Resources*. New York: Basic Books.

CHAPTER 17

Wildlife Protection and Management

General Questions and Issues

1. How can endangered and threatened wild species be protected from premature extinction caused by human activities?

2. How can we save endangered species and prevent species from becoming endangered by protecting and restoring their habitats?

3. How can populations of large game be managed to have enough animals available for sport hunting without endangering the long-term survival of the species?

4. How can populations of game birds be managed to have enough available for sport hunting without endangering the long-term survival of the species?

Harmony with land is like harmony with a friend; you cannot cherish his right hand and chop off his left. . . . you cannot love game and hate predators. . . . The land is one organism.

Aldo Leopold

Our increasing population and our ability to modify and disrupt the planet to satisfy our short-term needs and wants have led to the present age of wildlife extinction. One of our greatest challenges is to embark on a new path that preserves and sustains the earth's biological and genetic diversity.

This challenge calls for us to slow down or stop the human-accelerated extinction of wildlife and to protect and restore the wildlands needed as habitats by the earth's wild species. To accomplish these goals, we will have to learn how to combine development and conservation, and we will have to greatly increase the effort and the funds we put into wildlife conservation and management.

This chapter was coauthored by Jack R. Nelson, Department of Forestry and Range Management, Washington State University; Jack Ward Thomas, Pacific Northwest Forest and Range Experiment Station, USDA-Forest Service; and G. Tyler Miller, Jr.

17-1 PROTECTING WILDLIFE FROM EXTINCTION: THE SPECIES APPROACH

Wildlife Conservation and Management The activity of protecting, preserving, managing, and studying wildlife and wildlife resources is called **wildlife conservation**. **Wildlife management** is a part of wildlife conservation. It involves the manipulation of wildlife populations (especially game species) and habitats for their welfare and for human benefit, the preservation of endangered and threatened wild species, the introduction of exotic wild species into ecosystems, and wildlife law enforcement.

Wildlife conservation and management require an understanding of the ecological niches of wildlife (Section 5-4) and their habitat requirements. These habitat requirements include habitat quality, food, water, cover, and edge availability (Section 5-5). Wildlife managers also need to know how wildlife populations change in response to stress (Section 6-4) and how ecological succession affects wildlife species and habitats (Section 6-5).

Another part of wildlife conservation is **wildlife education**. It involves educating and training wildlife scientists and managers in colleges and universities and providing the general public and decision makers with information about wildlife. It is the key to having enough competent wildlife scientists and to getting political and economic support for wildlife conservation.

Methods of Wildlife Protection Governments use several methods to protect endangered and threatened wildlife and to keep other wild species from becoming endangered. One is to establish treaties and pass laws to protect species of wildlife. Another is to set aside wildlife refuges to protect critical wildlife habitats from destruction and degradation.

Public and private gene banks, zoos, research centers, and botanical gardens preserve critically endangered species in artificial habitats. Zoos and research centers also breed individuals of critically endangered species for eventual return to the wild.

All of these methods protect individual species. Ecologists know, however, that the cheapest and best way to keep plant and animal species from becoming extinct is to preserve a network of the world's representative ecosystems, the approach discussed in Section 17-2.

Treaties Organizations such as the International Union for the Conservation of Nature and Natural Resources (IUCN), the International Council for Bird Preservation (ICBP), and the World Wildlife Fund (WWF) have identified threatened and endangered species and led efforts to protect them. The IUCN, for example, compiles lists of threatened and endangered species and publishes them in *The Red Data Book*.

Many species have populations in more than one country or populations that migrate from one country to another. The countries involved can enter into treaties to protect such species. One international conservation agreement is the 1979 Convention on Conservation of Migratory Species of Wild Animals, now signed by 23 countries. Six other treaties between countries protect migratory birds passing through these countries. Thirty-four countries have signed the Convention on Wetlands of International Importance, which helps protect 279 wetland sites throughout the world.

Another important treaty is the 1975 Convention on International Trade in Endangered Species (CITES), developed by the IUCN and administered by the UN Environment Program (see Spotlight below).

Laws Many countries have passed laws to protect endangered or threatened species. Canada, the United States, and the Soviet Union have the most strictly enforced wildlife protection laws.

The United States controls imports and exports of endangered wildlife and wildlife products with two important laws. One is the Lacey Act of 1900, which prohibits transporting live or dead wild animals or their parts across state borders without a federal permit.

The other law is the Endangered Species Act of 1973 (including amendments in 1982 and 1988), one of the world's toughest environmental laws. This act makes it illegal for the United States to import or to carry on trade in any product made from an endangered species unless it is used for an approved sci-

---

SPOTLIGHT **The Convention on International Trade in Endangered Species (CITES)**

By 1988 the CITES treaty had been signed by 96 countries. It now lists 675 species that cannot be commercially traded as live specimens or wildlife products because they are endangered or threatened. Another 27,000 species—about 2,300 animals and 24,000 plants—may be traded commercially only under certain conditions and with special permits.

This treaty has reduced illegal traffic in some endangered wild species, especially crocodiles, turtles, and some large cat species whose skins are used for furs. But enforcement is spotty, and convicted violators often pay only small fines. In 1979, for example, a Hong Kong fur dealer illegally imported 319 Ethiopian cheetah skins valued at $43,900. The dealer was caught, but was fined only $1,540.

Much of the $1 billion to $2 billion a year illegal trade in wildlife and wildlife products goes on in countries, such as Singapore, that have not signed CITES. Some countries—Bolivia, for example—have signed the treaty but do little to enforce its provisions. Many Bolivian dealers use forged and stolen CITES permits to export wildlife smuggled into Bolivia from other countries.

Another problem is that countries can exclude certain species when they sign the treaty. For example, Japan claims 12 exemptions including the endangered hawksbill sea turtle (to convert its shell into jewelry and figurines). Despite these drawbacks, CITES is considered one of the most successful international wildlife treaties because it is so vigorously enforced in many countries.

Figure 17-1 Confiscated products derived from endangered species. Because of a lack of funds and too few inspectors, probably no more than one-tenth of the illegal wildlife trade in the United States is discovered. The situation is much worse in most other countries.

Steve Hillebrand/U. S. Fish and Wildlife Service

CASE STUDY The Snail Darter Controversy

In 1975 conservationists filed suit against the Tennessee Valley Authority to stop construction of the $137 million Tellico Dam on the Little Tennessee River in Tennessee. The reason for the suit was that the area to be flooded by the resulting reservoir threatened the only known breeding habitat of an endangered fish species, the snail darter, a three-inch-long fish. Although the dam was 90% completed, construction was halted for several years by the courts.

In 1978 Congress amended the Endangered Species Act to allow a seven-member review committee to grant an exemption if it believed that the economic benefits of a project would outweigh the potential harmful ecological effects. At its first meeting the review committee denied the request to exempt the Tellico Dam project on the grounds that it was an economically unsound, "pork barrel" project.

Despite this decision, political influence by members of Congress from Tennessee and others afraid of losing present and future projects in their states prevailed. In 1979 Congress passed special legislation exempting the Tellico Dam from the Endangered Species Act.

The dam's reservoir is now full of water. The snail darters that once lived there were transplanted to nearby rivers.

In 1981 snail darter populations were found in several remote tributaries of the Little Tennessee River. This led the FWS in 1983 to downgrade the status of the snail darter from endangered to threatened.

entific purpose or to enhance the survival of the species. To make control more effective, all commercial shipments of wildlife and wildlife products must enter or leave the country through one of nine designated ports.

Unfortunately, many illegal shipments of wildlife slip by. Permits have been falsified and some government inspectors have been bribed. Only 60 Fish and Wildlife Service inspectors must check more than 90,000 reported wildlife shipments a year. Only one in four of the wildlife shipments that enter and leave the United States each year is physically examined by an inspector (Figure 17-1), often not thoroughly. Many violators are not prosecuted, and convicted violators often pay only a small fine.

The Endangered Species Act of 1973 also provides protection for endangered and threatened species in the United States and abroad. It authorizes the National Marine Fisheries Service (NMFS) of the Department of Commerce to identify and list endangered and threatened marine species. The Fish and Wildlife Service (FWS) identifies and lists all other endangered and threatened species. These species cannot be hunted, killed, collected, or injured in the United States. Any decision by either agency to add or remove a species from the list must be based only on biological grounds without economic considerations.

The Endangered Species Act also prohibits federal agencies from carrying out, funding, or authorizing projects that would jeopardize endangered or threatened species or destroy or modify their critical habitats. This last provision has been highly controversial (see Case Study on this page).

Once a species is listed as endangered or threatened in the United States the FWS or the NMF is supposed to prepare a plan to help it recover. However,

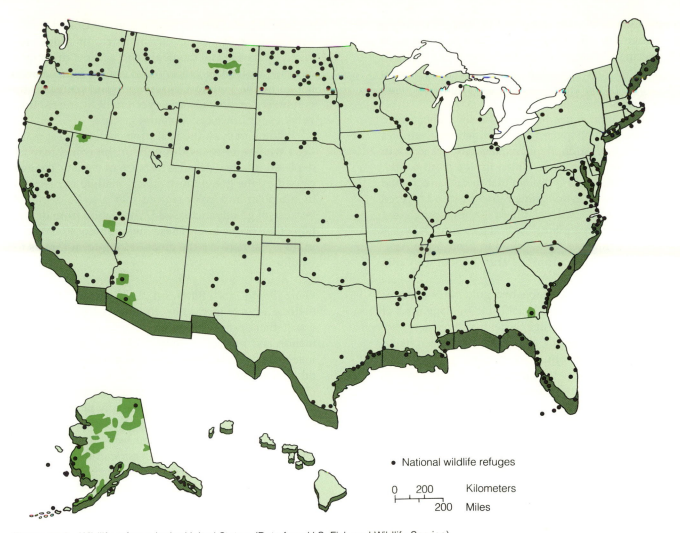

Figure 17-2 Wildlife refuges in the United States. (Data from U.S. Fish and Wildlife Service)

• National wildlife refuges

because of a lack of money about half of these plans exist only on paper. Between 1978 and 1988 the annual federal budget for endangered species stayed around $25 million when adjusted for inflation—about equal to the cost of 12 Army bulldozers.

In 1988 Congress reauthorized the Endangered Species Act. New provisions authorize funding to more than double to $56 million in 1989 and rise to $66 million by 1992. It also includes stiffer penalties for violators and more protection for endangered plants.

Even at these increased funding levels, it will take the Fish and Wildlife Service 20 years to evaluate the species presently under consideration for listing. Many species will probably disappear before they can be protected. Some have already disappeared.

State Responsibilities The federal government has the main responsibility for managing migratory species, endangered species, and wildlife on federal lands. States are responsible for the management of all other wildlife.

Funds for state game management programs are provided by the sale of hunting and fishing licenses and federal taxes on hunting and fishing equipment (see Guest Essay at the end of this chapter). Two-thirds of the states also have checkoffs on state income tax returns that allow individuals to contribute money to state wildlife programs.

Most of these funds are spent on the management of game species. Only 10% of all U.S. wildlife dollars are spent to understand or benefit the nongame species that make up nearly 90% of the country's wildlife species.

Wildlife Refuges In 1903 President Theodore Roosevelt established the first U.S. federal wildlife refuge at Pelican Island on the east coast of Florida to protect the endangered brown pelican (Figure 2-11, p. 37). By 1989 the National Wildlife Refuge System had 437 refuges (Figure 17-2). About 85% of the area included in these refuges is in Alaska.

Over three-fourths of the refuges are wetlands for protection of migratory waterfowl. Many other species are also protected in these refuges. Most of the species on the U.S. endangered list have habitats in the refuge system. Some refuges have been set aside for specific endangered species. These have helped endangered species such as the key deer, the brown pelican of southern Florida, and the trumpeter swan to recover.

Several other countries have also set aside areas to protect individual species from extinction. Examples include the tiny Addo Elephant National Park in South Africa and ten reserves in China for the giant panda.

Conservationists complain that there has been too little emphasis on establishing refuges for endangered plants. Not until 1980 was the first refuge purchased to save endangered plants. This is the Antioch Dunes Refuge in California, established to protect the Antioch Dunes evening primrose and the Contra Costa wallflower.

Congress has not established guidelines (such as multiple use or sustained yield) for management of the National Wildlife Refuge System, as it has for other public lands. As a result, the FWS has allowed many refuges to be used for hunting, fishing, trapping, timber cutting, grazing, farming, oil and gas development, mining, and recreational activities. The Reagan administration encouraged expansion of commercial activities in refuges to provide some of the money for their operation. By 1988 more than 60% of the refuges were open to hunting and almost 50% were open to fishing.

Conservationists charge that the commercial activities in the refuges are not always controlled properly and can interfere with wildlife protection. Development of oil, gas, and other resources can destroy or degrade wildlife habitats through road building, well and pipeline construction, oil and gas leaks, and pits filled with brine or drilling muds (see Pro/Con on p. 437). The FWS has not had enough money or foresight to acquire the rights to gas, oil, coal, or other minerals that may exist under 80% of the country's refuges.

Pollution is also a problem in a number of refuges. A 1986 study by the FWS estimated that one in five federal refuges is contaminated with toxic chemicals. Most of this pollution comes from old toxic waste dump sites and runoff from nearby agricultural land. A 1983 FWS survey showed that 86% of the federal refuges had water quality problems and 67% had air quality and visibility problems.

No thorough studies have been made of the effects of pollution on state refuges, which outnumber federal ones. Presumably a large number of state refuges also suffer from pollution.

Private groups also play an important role in conserving wildlife in refuges and other protected areas. For example, since 1951 the Nature Conservancy has been able to preserve over 2.5 million acres of forests, marshes, prairies, islands, and other areas of unique ecological or aesthetic significance in the United States. The organization purchases some areas by funds provided by its 435,000 members and accepts donations of other areas. The preserved areas are either maintained by the Nature Conservancy and managed by volunteers or donated to government agencies, universities, or other conservation groups.

Wildlife in even the best protected and best managed wildlife reserves throughout the world may be depleted in a few decades because of climatic change caused by the greenhouse effect. Wildlife in reserves in sub-polar and polar regions may also be depleted because of greatly increased UV-radiation from depletion of the ozone layer. These human-induced changes in the ecosphere are the greatest long-term threats to wildlife.

Gene Banks and Botanical Gardens A last-ditch method to save a critically endangered plant species is to gather or capture some of its remaining wild population and protect these individuals or their genetic material in a gene bank, a botanical garden, or some other artificial habitat.

Gene banks preserve genetic information by storing seeds of plants. Dry seeds of many plant varieties can be stored for long periods in a refrigerated environment with low humidity. Gene banks of most known and many potential varieties of agricultural crops and other plants now exist throughout the world (see Spotlight on p. 288). Scientists have urged that many more be established.

Despite their importance, gene banks have drawbacks. Some species cannot be stored and others suffer genetic damage during long-term storage. Many seeds rot and must be replaced. A fire, power failure, cut in funding, or poor administrator can cause the loss of irreplaceable specimens. Species that are refrigerated do not continue to evolve. This means that stored species become less fit to be reintroduced into their native habitats, which may have undergone various changes.

The world's botanical gardens help preserve some of the genetic diversity found in the wild. However, the gardens have too little capacity and too little money to maintain all of the world's threatened plants.

Egg Pulling and Captive Breeding in Zoos and Animal Research Centers Zoos and animal research centers are increasingly being used to preserve a representative number of individuals of critically endangered animal species. Two techniques for preserving such species are egg pulling and captive breeding.

Egg pulling involves collecting eggs produced in the wild by the remaining breeding pairs of a critically endangered bird species and hatching them in zoos or research centers. Removing these eggs sometimes causes parents to nest again and lay more eggs, increasing the number of eggs that can be hatched in the wild and in captivity. In 1983 scientists began an egg-pulling program to help save the critically endangered California condor (see Case Study on p. 429).

For **captive breeding** some or all of the individuals of a critically endangered species still in the wild are captured and placed in zoos or research centers to breed in captivity. Scientists hope that after several

---

PRO/CON Should There Be Oil and Gas Development in the Arctic National Wildlife Refuge?

The 19-million-acre Arctic National Wildlife Refuge sits on Alaska's North Slope near the Canadian border (Figure 17-3). This refuge, the second largest in the system, is home for a herd of over 180,000 caribou. It is also home for many other species, including polar bears, grizzly bears, musk oxen, wolves, snow geese, golden eagles, and peregrine falcons.

The refuge is the last place in North America where a complete range of arctic and subarctic ecosystems remains intact. Its coastal plain is the only stretch of Alaska's 1,060-mile Arctic coast that has not been opened to oil and gas development.

That could change. Energy companies have asked Congress to open 1.5 million acres of the coastal plain of this refuge to drilling for oil and natural gas. In 1987 the Secretary of the Interior joined forces with energy developers in this request.

Officials of energy companies and the Interior Department argue that the area might contain oil and natural gas deposits that would reduce U.S. reliance on foreign oil. These energy resources would enhance national security, provide a better trade balance, and increase economic growth.

Conservationists oppose this plan and want Congress to designate the entire coastal plain as wilderness. They point to Interior Department estimates that there is only a 21% chance of finding any economically recoverable large deposits of oil in this area. They do not believe that it's worth degrading a priceless and irreplaceable wildlife resource for the remote possibility of providing the United States with only a six-month supply of oil. They point

out that we could save twice as much oil in only two years merely by raising the average gas mileage requirements from 27.5 mpg in 1989 to 30 mpg by 1991.

Roughly 91% of the country's known, easily recoverable oil reserves lie outside this refuge and other wilderness areas. Conservationists believe that that these should be used to supply more oil.

Officials of oil companies claim they have developed the Prudhoe Bay oil fields, just 60 miles west of the Arctic National Wildlife Refuge, without significant harm to wildlife. They argue that their 15 years of experience with this project should enable them to do an even better job of protecting wildlife in the Arctic Refuge.

However, according to a preliminary report leaked from the FWS in 1988, oil drilling at Alaska's Prudhoe Bay has caused much more air and water pollution than was estimated before drilling began in 1972. In 1985 oil production activi-

ties on the North Slope released 36 million gallons of waste water into the fragile tundra environment.

In 1989 the massive oil spill near Valdez weakened support for oil exploration in the refuge. It also destroyed public confidence in safety claims made by oil company officials.

The drilling activity also destroyed 11,000 acres of vegetation used by wildlife—almost double the amount predicted. This has caused decreases in the populations of bears, wolves, other predators, and 100 bird species.

According to the FWS, oil development in the coastal plain could cause the loss of 20% to 40% of the area's caribou herd, 25% to 50% of the 476 musk oxen still left, 50% or more of the wolverines, and 50% of the snow geese that winter in this area. Do you think that oil and gas development should be allowed in the Arctic National Wildlife Refuge?

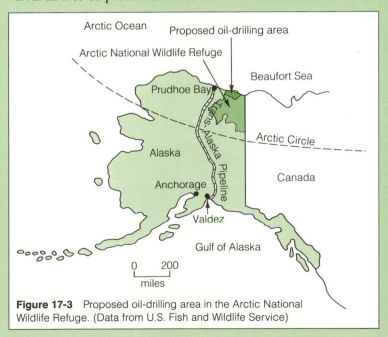

Figure 17-3 Proposed oil-drilling area in the Arctic National Wildlife Refuge. (Data from U.S. Fish and Wildlife Service)

decades of captive breeding and egg pulling the captive population of an endangered species will be large enough that some individuals can be successfully reintroduced into protected wild habitats.

Some species, such as the panda, bats, cheetahs, and whooping cranes don't breed well in captivity. In such cases, females may be artificially inseminated with collected male sperm. Embryos may also be collected from wild or captive females, frozen, and then transplanted to captive females or surrogate mothers. For example, at the London Zoo a young zebra was born after its embryo was transplanted to a Welsh pony mare.

Some captive species have difficulty or show little interest in raising their young. To overcome this problem, wildlife scientists have used foster parenting;

adults of a related species raise the new offspring of parents of an endangered species. Often, a variety of approaches is used to save an endangered species— the whooping crane, for example (see Case Study below).

By the mid-1960s, the peregrine falcon was headed for extinction in the lower 48 states, mostly from eggshell thinning caused by absorption of pesticides such as DDT and dieldrin (Figure 16-10, p. 425). In 1970 a captive breeding program was begun at Cornell University by Professor Thomas J. Cade. By 1987 more than 850 captivity-bred peregrines had been released into the wild in the eastern United States. In 1978 James C. Roush set up another captive breeding program at the University of California's Santa Cruz campus to help restore peregrine populations in

---

CASE STUDY Saving the Whooping Crane

Whooping cranes are the tallest birds in North America. They stand as much as five feet tall and have wing spans of up to seven feet (Figure 16-6, p. 420). These omnivorous birds eat frogs, minnows, berries, insects, acorns, and sometimes grains. They roost overnight by standing in water about five to eight inches deep, thus protecting themselves from coyotes and other nocturnal predators.

Whooping cranes have a low reproduction rate and a fixed migration pattern. These traits make them vulnerable to extinction (Table 16-3, p. 428).

When European settlers first arrived in North America, there were probably no more than 1,400 individuals of this species. By 1890 an estimated 500 to 700 birds were left. Mostly because of illegal shooting and loss of habitat, the number of whooping cranes in the wild dropped to only 15 by 1941. The species was on the brink of extinction.

By 1967 protection of its habitat had raised the number to about 44. Between 1967 and 1989 the number of whooping cranes increased to 200, primarily because of a recovery program directed by the U.S. Fish and Wildlife Service.

About 149 of these birds make up two wild populations that winter in national wildlife refuges in

New Mexico and Texas. Each spring they migrate to breeding grounds in Idaho and Wood Buffalo National Park in Alberta, Canada. The remaining birds are in captive breeding programs in Idaho and in Maryland at the federal Patuxent Endangered Wildlife Research Center.

The $5 million-a-year recovery program for this species uses a combination of habitat preservation, egg pulling, captive breeding, and foster parenting. Habitats for these birds are burned, cut, or grazed to control vegetation height and increase insect availability. Corn and other crops the birds eat are planted at many wildlife refuges used by the cranes. Fresh water is pumped in to decrease chances of diseases such as avian cholera and botulism.

During migration many whooping cranes die when they collide with electric power lines. To reduce this hazard, wildlife officials have asked utility companies to attach bright marker balls to the lines to make them more visible.

In Canada eggs are removed from nests of wild breeding pairs and flown to the Patuxent Research Center, where they are artificially incubated and hatched. This egg pulling induces wild whooping cranes to increase the two eggs they normally lay per

season to as many as eleven. Wild birds are also captured for breeding in captivity through artificial insemination.

Newly hatched chicks produced by captive birds or by egg pulling are then transferred to sandhill-crane nests in Grays Lake National Wildlife Refuge in Idaho. The closely related but more abundant wild sandhill cranes act as foster parents for whooping crane chicks. Whooping cranes raised by sandhill cranes return with their foster parents to wintering areas in New Mexico.

It has taken almost 50 years of painstaking effort to increase the number of whooping cranes from 15 to 200. Wildlife scientists hope to raise the number to the point where the species can be moved from the endangered to the threatened category by the year 2000 and removed from the protected list by 2020.

Critics have questioned the spending of millions of dollars each year to protect the whooping crane. Proponents of the program argue that we have an ethical duty to protect any species from premature extinction. Also, each year almost 100,000 people visit refuges to view this bird. Do you think this program should be continued?

the western United States. By 1982 more than 100 captivity-bred birds were released in California.

Captive breeding programs at zoos in Phoenix, San Diego, and Los Angeles have saved the nearly extinct Arabian oryx (Figure 17-4). This large antelope species once lived throughout the Middle East. However, by the early 1970s it had disappeared from the wild after being hunted by people using jeeps, helicopters, rifles, and machine guns. Since 1980 small numbers of these animals bred in captivity have been returned to the wild in protected habitats in the Middle East.

These are only a few of the successes in using zoos and research centers to save wildlife species from premature extinction. But such efforts are limited by money, space, and other factors (see Spotlight below).

Limitations of the Species Approach The species approach has been successful in protecting and allowing populations of a number of threatened or endangered species to increase, especially in the United States (Table 17-1).

Because of limited money and trained personnel, however, only a few of the world's endangered and threatened species can be saved by treaties, laws, wildlife refuges, and zoos. This means that wildlife experts must decide which species out of thousands of candidates should be saved. This decision is similar

© Zoological Society of San Diego, 1985

Figure 17-4 The Arabian oryx barely escaped extinction in 1969 after being overhunted in the deserts of the Middle East. Captive breeding programs in zoos in Arizona and California have been successful in saving this antelope species from extinction.

to the difficult decisions physicians must make about which individuals will receive transplants of scarce organs from donors.

Many experts suggest that the limited funds for preserving threatened and endangered wildlife be

---

Table 17-1 Animal Wildlife Conservation Successes in the United States		
	Populations	
Species	1900	1988
Pronghorn antelope	13,000	1 million
White-tailed deer	500,000	13 million
Rocky Mountain elk	41,000	1 million
Trumpeter swan	73	900
Canada goose	1 million	2.3 million
Wild turkey	30,000	3.8 million

concentrated on those species that **(1)** have the best chance for survival, **(2)** have the most ecological value to an ecosystem, and **(3)** are potentially useful for agriculture, medicine, or industry.

Some critics go further and question the use of limited funds to protect a few critically endangered species. They argue that more wildlife would be saved if we used limited funds to protect endangered wildlife habitats such as tropical forests and wetlands.

17-2 PROTECTING WILD SPECIES FROM EXTINCTION: THE ECOSYSTEM APPROACH

Saving Habitats by Ecosystem Preservation Most wildlife biologists believe that the best way to prevent the loss of wild species is to establish and maintain a worldwide system of reserves, parks, and other protected areas. The system should consist of at least 10% of the world's land area. The goal would be to conserve and manage entire ecosystems instead of the present species-centered approach to wildlife preservation.

This ecosystem approach would protect the earth's existing biological and genetic diversity. It would prevent species from becoming endangered by human activities and reduce the need for human intervention to prevent extinction. The reserves would be natural habitats for endangered species now in zoos and other artificial habitats. They can also be used for wildlife research and education.

Using reserves and parks to help prevent extinction of many species is cheaper than managing endangered species one by one. For example, the 17,800-acre Sacramento National Wildlife Refuge contains tens of thousands of individuals of hundreds of plant and animal species. The roughly $1 million spent each year to manage this system is less than the amount spent

each year on the recovery effort for the critically endangered California condor.

Certain parts of reserves and parks can also be used for photographic safaris, school field trips, and other nondestructive activities. Fees for these activities would provide money for managing these areas and for educating local people and tourists about the need to conserve wildlife.

By 1988, there were more than 3,600 major protected areas throughout the world, totaling almost 1.7 million square miles. This is an important beginning, but it represents only about 3.2% of the earth's land area and 7.2% of the land in the United States. Less than 5% of the world's remaining virgin forests are protected within parks and reserves. Futhermore, many of the world's ecosystem types have not been included in reserves or are too small to protect their populations of wild species.

Biosphere Reserves In 1981 UNESCO proposed that at least one, and ideally five or more, biosphere reserves be set up in each of the earth's 193 biogeographical zones. Each reserve should be large enough to prevent gradual species loss as occurs on most isolated islands. By 1988 there were 267 biosphere reserves worldwide.

The core of a reserve should be given the most protection. The core should be surrounded by two buffer zones (Figure 17-5). These zones would be used for recreation, hunting, grazing, logging, and other purposes on a sustainable basis. Biosphere reserves can combine conservation with sustainable forms of development (see Case Study on p. 410).

Rarely can wild places and the species they contain be saved merely by leaving them untouched. Most have to be actively managed. Otherwise they become degraded by global pollution, by poaching, and by urbanization, farming, and other activities on nearby lands.

For example, because of habitat loss elephants have crowded into many of the national parks of South Africa. A single elephant can eat as much as a small herd of cattle, and elephants have no natural predators (except people). To prevent them from uprooting trees and destroying the vegetation needed by other wild animals, park managers must harvest some of the elephants periodically to keep the population within sustainable limits. Usually managers harvest old, weak, or especially dangerous individuals.

If local people are involved in the planning and managing of each reserve, the protected area will cause less disruption of local cultures. Feeling a sense of responsibility for protecting the area, local people will not be likely to engage in poaching. The local community also benefits from the sale of wildlife meat and other products, licenses for sport hunting, and tourism.

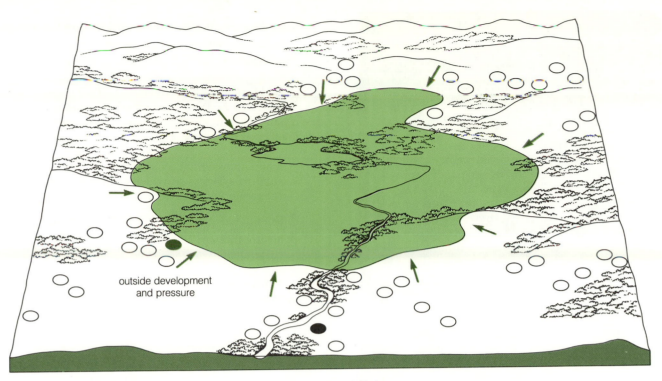

Traditional Wildlife Park

outside development
and pressure

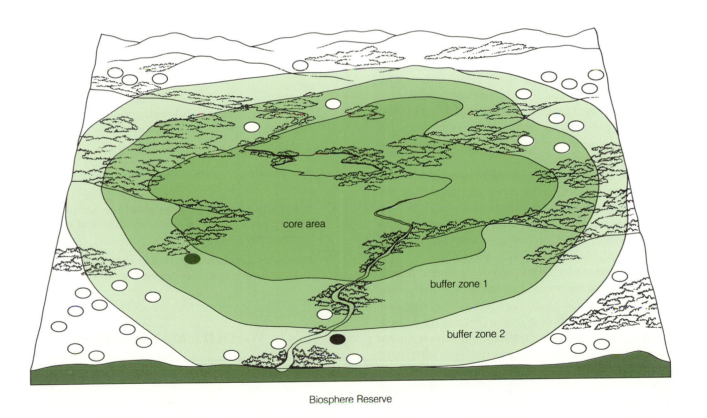

core area

buffer zone 1

buffer zone 2

Biosphere Reserve

human settlements   research station   tourism and
education center

Figure 17-5 Comparison of a traditional wildlife park or refuge, threatened by outside development, and a well-designed biosphere reserve.

In 1981 and 1982, for example, the necessary culling of 1,500 elephants from the herd in Africa's Chizaria National Park and Safari Area provided almost $1 million for local schools, health clinics, and transportation. This revenue reduced the need for game wardens because local people no longer had a reason to poach.

UNESCO, the IUCN, and the President's Council on Environmental Quality have proposed that the world's MDCs set up an international fund to help LDCs protect and manage biosphere reserves. The program would cost $100 million a year—about what the world spends on arms every 90 minutes.

Research is under way to answer questions about the size and management of reserves (see Case Study above).

The often difficult first step in setting up an ecological reserve is acquiring the land. Most reserves are set aside by governments, but governments often need persuading. Conservation groups and other organizations can buy up foreign debts of LDCs from banks and swap this debt for agreements by the governments to set up and protect reserves. Such debt-for-nature swaps are being used in Costa Rica, Bolivia, and several other countries (see Case Study on p. 410).

Income tax deductions can be given to private landowners who donate land for reserves or agree to add easements to their property titles that allow the land to be used only for wildlife conservation. Gov-

ernments can also give free technical assistance to private landowners wishing to preserve land for wildlife conservation.

World Conservation Strategy   In 1980 the IUCN, the UNEP, and the WWF developed a World Conservation Strategy, a long-range plan for conserving the world's biological resources. The goals of this plan are to:

- maintain essential ecological processes and life-support systems on which human survival and economic activities depend
- preserve species diversity and genetic diversity
- ensure that any use of species and ecosystems is sustainable

This strategy is not based on protecting large parts of the earth from use by humans. Instead, it is based on combining wildlife conservation with sustainable development (see Case Study on p. 410).

By 1988 forty countries had planned or established national conservation programs. If MDCs provide enough money and scientific assistance, the world conservation strategy offers a glimmer of hope for preserving much of the world's biological and genetic diversity.

In 1988 a new global conservation strategy, called *World Conservation Strategy II*, was being developed for publication in 1990. Some proposals for this strategy are:

- including women and indigenous people in the development of conservation plans
- monitoring the sustainability of development
- promoting an ethic that includes protection of plants and animals as well as people
- encouraging the recognition of the harmful environmental effects of armed conflict and economic insecurity
- encouraging rehabilitation of degraded ecosystems upon which humans depend for food and fiber

17-3   WILDLIFE MANAGEMENT

Management Approaches   The first step in wildlife management is to decide which species or groups of species are to be managed in a particular area. This often involves the evaluation of competing interests.

Ecologists stress preservation of biological diversity. Wildlife conservationists are concerned about endangered species. Bird watchers want the greatest diversity of bird species. Hunters want large populations of game species for harvest each year during hunting season.

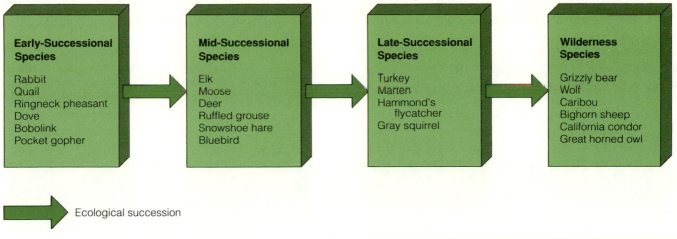

Early-Successional Species	Mid-Successional Species	Late-Successional Species	Wilderness Species
Rabbit	Elk	Turkey	Grizzly bear
Quail	Moose	Marten	Wolf
Ringneck pheasant	Deer	Hammond's flycatcher	Caribou
Dove	Ruffled grouse	Gray squirrel	Bighorn sheep
Bobolink	Snowshoe hare		California condor
Pocket gopher	Bluebird		Great horned owl

→ Ecological succession

Figure 17-6 Preferences of some wildlife species for habitats at different stages of ecological succession.

Difficult choices must be made; in any wildlife management scheme some wildlife species will benefit and others will be harmed. One option is to protect a wilderness or other undisturbed area from most human activities. Another approach is to control population sizes and habitats to maintain a diversity of species in an area. A third option is to manipulate population sizes and habitats to favor a single species, usually a game species or an endangered species.

In the United States most wildlife management is devoted to the production of harvestable surpluses of game animals. The principal big-game animals of the United States are white-tailed deer, black-tailed deer, and mule deer. Other big-game animals, harvested in smaller numbers, include pronghorn, elk, moose, bears, and mountain lions.

Game birds are often divided into upland game birds and waterfowl. Important upland game birds in the United States are doves, wild turkeys, ringneck pheasants, bobwhite quails (Figure 5-21, p. 111), and other species of quail and pheasant. Ducks and geese are the major waterfowl game birds (Section 17-4).

After goals have been set, the wildlife manager must develop a management plan. Ideally, the plan should be based on principles of ecological succession (Section 6-5), wildlife population dynamics (Section 6-4), and an understanding of the cover, food, water, space, and other habitat requirements of each species to be managed (Section 5-5). The manager must also consider the number of potential hunters, their success rates, and the regulations available to prevent excessive harvesting.

This ecological information is difficult, expensive, and time consuming to get. Often it is not available or reliable. That is why wildlife management for many species is as much an art as a science. In practice it involves much guesswork and trial and error. Management plans must also be adapted to political pressures from conflicting groups and to budget constraints.

Manipulation of Habitat Vegetation Wildlife managers can encourage the growth of plant species that are the preferred food and cover for a particular animal species by controlling the ecological succession of vegetation in various areas (Figure 6-23, p. 142).

Animal wildlife species can be classified into four types according to the stage of ecological succession at which they are most likely to be found: wilderness, late-successional, midsuccessional, and early-successional (Figure 17-6). **Wilderness species** flourish only in fairly undisturbed, climax vegetational communities such as large areas of old-growth forest, tundra, grasslands, and deserts. Their survival depends largely on the establishment of large state and national wilderness areas and wildlife refuges (see Case Study on p. 444).

Late-successional species need old-growth and mature forest habitats to produce the food and cover on which they depend (Figure 17-6). These animals require the establishment and protection of moderate-sized, old-growth forest refuges.

Midsuccessional species are found around abandoned croplands and partially open areas. Such areas are created by the logging of small stands of timber, controlled burning, and clearing of vegetation for roads, firebreaks, gas pipelines, and electrical transmission lines.

Such openings of the forest canopy promote the growth of vegetation favored as food by midsuccessional mammal and bird species. It also increases the amount of edge habitat, where two communities such as a forest and field come together. This transition zone allows animals such as deer to feed on vegetation in clearings and quickly escape to cover in the nearby forest.

However, when vegetation is managed to increase populations of deer and other midsuccessional species, the populations of other wild species may be eliminated or severely reduced. For example, squirrels could become scarce in such areas. They require mature forests that produce the nuts and acorns they eat and the hollow trees they use as dens. Similarly, partial clearing of forests can increase the nesting sites for resident birds, but it can reduce the nesting area for migratory birds.

Early-successional species find food and cover in weedy pioneer plants. These plants invade an area that has been cleared of vegetation for human activities and then abandoned.

Habitat Improvement Various types of habitat improvement can attract and encourage the population growth of a desired species. Improvement techniques include artificial seeding, transplanting certain types of vegetation, and building artificial nests.

CASE STUDY   Protecting the Grizzly Bear

The grizzly bear has humped shoulders, long, curved front claws, and a somewhat concave face (Figure 17-7). In Alaska adult male grizzlies can be six feet tall and weigh 1,400 pounds. In the lower 48 states adult males range from 300 to 850 pounds. Despite their size, adult bears can run at speeds up to 25 miles per hour.

The grizzly bear is an opportunistic omnivore. Up to 90% of its food consists of green plants, roots and tubers, fruits, and pine cone nuts. About 10% of its diet comes from dead animal carcasses (carrion), ground squirrels, deer, elk, and trout. Along the Alaskan coast, salmon is a major food source.

The grizzly hibernates for five to six months in winter. During this period the dormant bears don't eat, drink, urinate, or defecate. To store fat reserves needed for survival during hiberation, the bears must eat enormous amounts of food during summer and fall.

To find enough food, the grizzly travels over a very large home range, sometimes 1,100 square miles. Thus, the species is vulnerable to loss of habitat from logging, mining, and oil and gas development. The grizzly also has one of the lowest reproduction rates of all mammals. Together, these factors make the grizzly highly vulnerable to premature extinction.

Once this species roamed half the North American continent (Figure 17-8). One hundred years ago there were perhaps 100,000 grizzlies in the western United States and Mexico.

Today only 700 to 900 grizzlies survive, mostly in northern Montana and northwestern Wyoming, on only 2% of their original range in the lower 48 states. Since 1975 the grizzly has been listed as a threatened species in the lower 48 states. However, about 50,000 of these animals survive in Alaska and western Canada.

Even with protection, grizzlies are killed by poachers, ranchers protecting their livestock, and hunters mistaking them for black bears not on the endangered list. Some have had to be killed after becoming so used to surviving on human foods and garbage that they were a threat to campers and hikers in national parks and forests.

For more than 50 years bears in Yellowstone National Park in Wyoming and Glacier National Park in Montana were allowed to feed in garbage dumps near visitor areas. In 1967 all dumps in these parks were closed after two young women were killed by grizzlies in Glacier campgrounds. Today these parks have bear-proof dumpsters.

Some wildlife scientists opposed this action. They recommended that the bears be weaned from garbage over several years. Otherwise, the bears, already dependent on human foods, would go into campgrounds and pose an even greater threat to people. Then a large number of bears would have to be killed.

As these scientists predicted, grizzlies did move into the campgrounds to find food, and many had to be killed. In 1983 a camper was killed by a grizzly in the Gallatin National Forest on the western edge of Yellowstone. The Park Service first tried relocating the bears in the backcountry, but the bears wouldn't stay there.

Between 1968 and 1988 the grizzly bear population in Yellowstone dropped from 400 to 200. Glacier National Park now has only about 200 grizzlies. Because Yellowstone National Park is an isolated ecosystem, ecologists fear that within a few decades no grizzlies will be left there.

To help protect the grizzly, some bear habitats in the parks are now closed year-round to humans. Others are closed seasonally. Certain streams in Yellowstone are closed during spawning periods to allow bears to feed undisturbed on fish.

Presently, the Park Service provides no food for grizzlies. Some wildlife conservationists have urged park officials to provide supplemental feeding for grizzlies by dumping animal carcasses in areas not open to people. They believe

Figure 17-7   The grizzly bear.

Nest boxes, artificial roosts, and brush piles attract various species of birds. Standing dead trees, logs, and debris also serve as habitats for wildlife (Figure 17-9).

Wildlife managers working for state fish and wildlife agencies often have little or no authority over wildlife habitat on private land or on land managed by other agencies. The only tools these managers can use to improve wildlife habitats are education and incentive programs.

Fire as a Wildlife Management Tool Prescribed burning is widely used by wildlife managers and forest managers to encourage the growth of vegetation preferred by game species such as deer and elk. It has

that this would reduce attempts by grizzlies to feed in campgrounds. It could also help keep the bears within park boundaries, where they are less likely to be killed by poachers. Other suggestions include banning sheep grazing near bear habitat areas and prohibiting black-bear hunting in nearby forests to prevent the accidental killing of grizzlies.

Visitors, hearing stories of people killed by grizzlies, push for the bears to be eliminated from the parks. Yet a visitor to Glacier National Park is far more likely to be hurt or killed in a traffic or climbing accident in the park. In Yellowstone, bison injure far more people than grizzlies.

Some people question whether it makes sense to spend more than $2 million a year—more than on any other endangered or threatened species—to keep a few grizzlies in western national parks. They believe the species has a much better chance of surviving in Alaska and Canada. What do you think should be done?

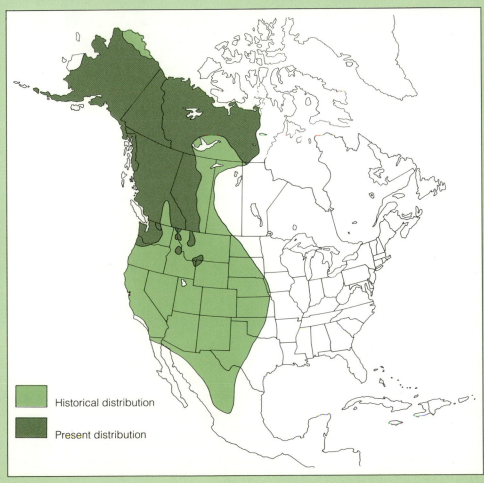

Figure 17-8 Once the grizzly bear was found in much of the western half of North America. Today it is found in Alaska, Canada, and only a few areas of the lower 48 states, where it is classified as a threatened species. (Data from U.S. Fish and Wildlife Service)

Historical distribution

Present distribution

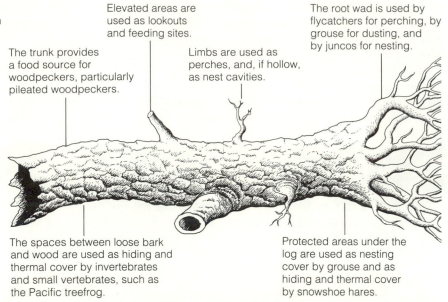

Figure 17-9 Some wildlife habitats provided by a decaying log. (Data from U.S. Forest Service)

The trunk provides a food source for woodpeckers, particularly pileated woodpeckers.

Elevated areas are used as lookouts and feeding sites.

Limbs are used as perches, and, if hollow, as nest cavities.

The root wad is used by flycatchers for perching, by grouse for dusting, and by juncos for nesting.

The spaces between loose bark and wood are used as hiding and thermal cover by invertebrates and small vertebrates, such as the Pacific treefrog.

Protected areas under the log are used as nesting cover by grouse and as hiding and thermal cover by snowshoe hares.

CASE STUDY **Using Prescribed Burning to Protect the Kirtland's Warbler**

The Kirtland's warbler (Figure 17-10) is an endangered species, mostly because it requires a unique habitat. This small, colorful bird nests only in young jack pine trees about the size of Christmas trees. Stands of these trees are found only in seven counties in north-central Michigan, near the town of Mio.

Fire is essential to maintaining the ecosystem needed by this bird. The pine trees have tightly closed cones, which open and release their seeds only when exposed to the intense heat of fire. The young trees used as nesting cover by the Kirtland's warbler become established after a fire.

Fire prevention was the major factor threatening the warbler.

Attempts to control wildfire led to a sharp drop in suitable nesting trees.

The tiny songbird now clings to life through the cooperative efforts of the Michigan department of Natural Resources and the U.S. Forest Service. Since 1957 these agencies have used prescribed burning about every 15 years to remove old jack pine trees. This allows younger trees to grow and provide the low-branch nesting cover needed by the Kirtland's warbler.

Despite this successful program, the species is still vulnerable to extinction from the loss and degradation of its winter habitat in the Bahamas.

Michigan Department of Natural Resources

Figure 17-10 The Kirtland's warbler is an endangered species that nests only in young jack pine trees in one small area of Michigan's Lower Peninsula.

---

also been used to help protect the Kirtland's warbler from extinction (see Case Study above).

Prescribed burns are also carried out on grasslands to promote the growth of taller plants useful as habitat for nesting ducks, quail, prairie chickens, and other wild species.

Water Impoundments Wildlife managers often create or improve ponds and lakes in wildlife refuges to provide water, food, and habitat for waterfowl and other wild animals. A water impoundment created for livestock or recreational activities can also provide habitats for eagles, osprey, amphibians, and marsh animals living around its edges. Deer, raccoons, and snakes can also find food along the shores of impoundments.

In arid areas wildlife managers use various kinds of water catchments, usually called "guzzlers," to gather water during wet seasons for later use during dry seasons. Guzzlers are used by game birds, pronghorn antelope, mule dear, desert bighorn sheep, and other wild species found in arid areas in western states.

Figure 17-11 Deer starvation during winter in Wisconsin. Overpopulation caused the deer to exceed the winter carrying capacity of their habitat.

Wisconsin Department of Natural Resources

Population Management by Controlled Hunting

Wildlife managers usually use controlled hunting to manipulate the number, gender distribution, and age distribution of populations of wild game species. Deer, rabbits, squirrels, quails, ducks, and several other game animals reproduce rapidly. Without effective control by natural predators or hunting by human predators, such species will exceed the carrying capacity of their habitat.

For example, a deer population can more than double every two years. As the number of deer exceeds the carrying capacity of their range, vegetation is destroyed and their habitat deteriorates. Without enough food many deer become weakened and die of diseases or starvation during winter (Figure 17-11).

People have eliminated most natural predators of deer, but carefully regulated hunting can keep the deer population within the carrying capacity of the available habitat. Ideally, each year wildlife managers should survey the land under their control to determine habitat conditions and the numbers, reproduction rates, age structures, and sex ratios of game animals. They should use this information to set annual hunting season regulations to achieve the following objectives:

- Provide an annual surplus for harvesting by hunters.
- Keep animal numbers within the carrying capacity of the habitat.
- Regulate the harvest to ensure that there are enough females of reproductive age to reestablish the population.
- Harvest enough males so that an appropriate sex ratio is maintained.

The United States and most MDCs use hunting laws to manage populations of game animals. Hunters must have licenses and hunting is allowed only during certain months of the year to protect animals during mating season. Only certain types of hunting equipment, such as bows and arrows, shotguns, and rifles, are allowed.

Managers use annual estimates of game populations to set the length of hunting seasons for each species. They control annual harvests by setting limits on the size, number, and sex of animals allowed to be killed and on the number of hunters allowed in a game refuge.

But close control of hunting is often not possible. Accurate data on game populations may not exist and may cost too much to get. People in communities near hunting areas, who benefit from money spent by hunters, may push to have hunting quotas raised.

Severe restriction of hunting in an area causes a drop in income from the sale of hunting licenses and decreases funds available for carrying out wildlife management programs. Also, some individuals and conservation groups are opposed to sport hunting and exert political pressure to have it banned or sharply curtailed (see Pro/Con on p. 448).

Population Management by Chemical Fertility Control

Considerable research has been carried out since the 1950s on the use of various antifertility agents for population management of wildlife such as red foxes, coyotes, white-tailed deer, starlings, Norway rats, and wild horses. Animals receive such agents in baited food or in small darts shot from tranquilizer guns.

This approach has several advantages. It causes little discomfort to the animal and is more humane

Sport hunters, hunting groups, and state game officials believe that Americans should be free to hunt as long as they obey state and local game regulations and don't damage wildlife resources. They argue that carefully regulated sport hunting by human predators is needed because we have eliminated most of the natural predators of deer and other large game animals. Without hunting, populations of game species will exceed the carrying capacity of their habitats and destroy vegetation they and other species need.

Sport hunting also provides recreational pleasure for millions of people (17 million in the United States) and stimulates local economies. In south and central Texas, for example, income from hunting now exceeds that from livestock ranching.

Defenders of sport hunting also point out that sales of hunting licenses and taxes on firearms and ammunition have provided more than $1.6 billion since 1937. This money has been used to buy, restore, and maintain wildlife habitats and to support wildlife

research in the United States (see Guest Essay near the end of this chapter).

Conservation groups such as the Sierra Club and Defenders of Wildlife also consider hunting an acceptable management tool to keep numbers of game animals in line with the carrying capacity of their habitats. They see this as a way of preserving biological diversity by helping prevent depletion of other native species of plants and animals.

But some individuals and groups such as the Humane Society oppose sport hunting. They believe that it inflicts unnecessary pain and suffering on animals, few of which are killed to supply food needed for survival. In the 1970s statewide and nationwide surveys showed that about half of the American public opposed hunting.

The Humane Society has filed suit to block all hunting in national wildlife refuges on the grounds that state game commissions often set hunting limits to cater to hunters' demands, not to keep wildlife in balance. The Humane Society also points out that sport hunting

tends to reduce the genetic quality of remaining wildlife populations because hunters are most likely to kill the largest and strongest trophy animals. In contrast, natural predators tend to improve population quality by eliminating weak and sick individuals.

Hunting opponents also argue that game managers deliberately create a surplus of game animals by eliminating their natural predators such as wolves. Then, having created the surplus, game managers claim that the surplus must be harvested by hunters to prevent habitat degradation. Instead of eliminating natural predators, say opponents, wildlife managers should reintroduce them to reduce the need for sport hunting.

But hunting supporters point out that populations of many game species such as deer are so large that predators such as the wolf cannot possibly control them. Also, because most wildlife habitats are fragmented, introduction of predators can lead to loss of nearby farm animals. What do you think?

---

than hunting or trapping. When administered by dart guns, the agents cannot affect nontarget species. The use of these chemicals can be stopped for one or more breeding seasons to allow population size to increase if it becomes too low.

However, some problems must be solved. Better methods must be developed for disguising or encapsulating antifertility agents so that certain target animals will accept the bait. A method is also needed for reducing or eliminating unwanted effects in target animals and nontarget animals who might consume the agents in baited food. Finally, this approach is expensive and time consuming.

17-4 MIGRATORY BIRD PROTECTION AND MANAGEMENT

Special Needs of Migratory Waterfowl Migratory waterfowl such as ducks, geese, and swans require some special management approaches. In North

America many of these species nest in Canada during the summer. During the fall hunting season they migrate to the United States and Central America along generally fixed routes called **flyways** (Figure 17-12).

Populations of waterfowl can drop sharply because of destruction or degradation of their winter and summer habitats and stopover areas along their migration routes, and because of excessive hunting in these areas. The North American countries—Canada, the United States, and Mexico—have signed agreements to prevent habitat destruction and overhunting.

The primary aim of waterfowl management in North America is to produce and maintain a surplus of harvestable game birds, especially ducks and geese. Hunting seasons must be arranged in each country so that these game birds are not shot during the breeding season.

Maintaining a harvestable surplus of these birds depends largely on maintaining adequate habitats over their entire range. As suitable breeding and wintering habitats decrease, the size of the allowable kill by hunters must also be reduced.

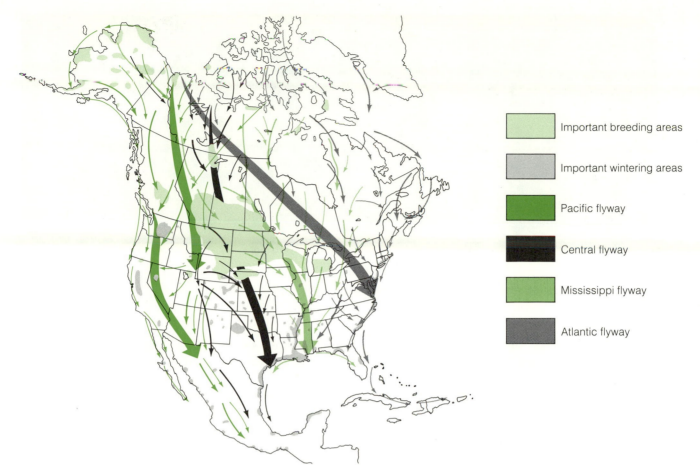

Figure 17-12 Major breeding and wintering areas and fall migration flyways used by migratory waterfowl in North America.

Legend:
- Important breeding areas
- Important wintering areas
- Pacific flyway
- Central flyway
- Mississippi flyway
- Atlantic flyway

Other migratory birds, such as trumpeter swans and whooping cranes, which are not game species, must also be protected from extinction (see Case Study on p. 438). In the United States 16 species of migratory birds are listed as threatened or endangered throughout their range. Another 25 species are threatened or endangered in part of their range.

Loss of Habitat and Pollution   As with most species, loss of habitat is a major threat to migratory bird species. So far there has been little destruction of waterfowl habitats in the far north of Canada, where much of the breeding occurs. Efforts have been made by the Canadian government and private organizations to prevent draining of wetlands, small ponds, and lakes that provide nesting grounds for birds. New water impoundments have also been created along the flyways in Canada. However, some of these habitats are in jeopardy because of plans for increased logging, recreation, and hydropower development.

More than half of the original coastal and inland wetlands in the United States have been lost to farming and other development (see Case Studies on p. 125 and p. 132). Each year tens of thousands of additional acres of wetlands vanish. About half of North America's ducks are hatched in the prairie pothole region stretching from Iowa to Alberta (Figure 17-12). The wet potholes (Figure 6-12, p. 131) that pock-mark this terrain have been rapidly disappearing as farmers have drained and filled them to create more cropland.

About 90% of the wetlands once found along the Pacific flyway have been drained and converted to cropland and human settlements. Probably 60% of all ducks and geese in the Pacific flyway winter in the Central Valley of California. More than 95% of this valley's original wetlands have been destroyed. Urban development and wetland drainage have also removed large areas of wintering grounds for waterfowl along the central, Mississippi, and Atlantic flyways.

The remaining wetlands are used by dense flocks of ducks and geese. This crowding makes them more prone to diseases such as avian cholera and botulism. It also makes them more vulnerable to predators such as skunks, foxes, coyotes, minks, and raccoons and to being shot by hunters. Many species are forced to find food in nearby rice and barley fields and other croplands. To protect their crops, many farmers drain these wetlands.

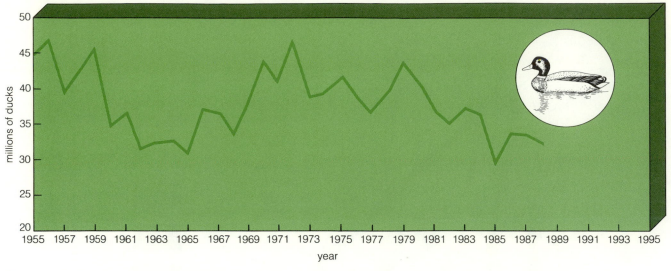

Figure 17-13 Estimated duck breeding population in North American survey areas. (Data from U.S. Fish and Wildlife Service)

Waterfowl in wetlands near croplands are also exposed to pollution from pesticides and other chemicals in the irrigation runoff they drink. For example, toxic selenium leached from the soil by irrigation water in California's San Joaquin Valley has caused birth defects in young birds hatched in the nearby Kesterson National Wildlife Refuge. Water pollution from oil kills at least 100,000 waterfowl a year in North America. Preliminary research also shows that acid deposition may be decreasing waterfowl production, breeding success, and duckling survival on acidic waters.

Ducks in North America are in trouble. Since 1979 their estimated breeding populations have been declining in the areas surveyed (Figure 17-13). In 1985 breeding populations of mallard and pintail ducks were the lowest ever recorded for these species. There was a modest increase in duck numbers in 1987, but numbers fell again in 1988. The major reasons for this decrease are prolonged drought in key breeding areas and degradation and destruction of wetland and grassland breeding habitats by farmers.

Hunting and Lead Poisoning Each year hunters in Canada and the United States kill about 20 million ducks (12 million in the United States). Another 20 million ducks die each year from disease, predation, and accidents. Hunting also causes lead poisoning of an estimated 2 million to 3 million ducks and geese. These birds die when they ingest the shotgun lead that fall into bodies of water where waterfowl feed.

For over 20 years conservation groups pressured elected officials and the U.S. Fish and Wildlife Service to enact a nationwide ban on the use of lead shot for waterfowl hunting and to require hunters to use less-harmful steel shot. Some hunting groups and a few state wildlife agencies opposed such a ban. They argued

that steel shot is more costly, does more damage to gun barrels, and cripples more waterfowl than lead shot.

Conservation groups went to court and charged the FWS with violating the endangered species act by failing to ban lead shot. This long-standing controversy ended in 1986, when the FWS announced a nationwide ban on lead shot for waterfowl hunting. Its use is to be phased out from 1987 to 1992. The ban will also protect endangered species such as the bald eagle, which dies from lead poisoning after feeding on waterfowl that contain lead pellets. However, lead shot already deposited in wetlands will continue to kill waterfowl for decades.

Waterfowl hunting provides funds for managing game and nongame species. The sale of duck stamps, the federal excise tax on guns and ammunition, and the purchase of hunting licenses raise at least $45 million a year for wetlands acquisition and waterfowl research.

Methods of Waterfowl Management Wildlife officials manage waterfowl by regulating hunting, protecting existing habitats, and developing new habitats. More than 75% of the federal wildlife refuges in the United States are wetlands used for migratory birds (Figure 17-2). Other waterfowl refuges have been established by local and state agencies and private conservation groups such as Ducks Unlimited, the Audubon Society, and the Nature Conservancy. Building artificial nesting sites, ponds, and nesting islands is another method of establishing protective habitats for breeding populations of waterfowl (Figure 17-14).

A new device is being used to keep predators away from nesting waterfowl: a three-foot-high chicken wire fence with several strands of electrified wire along its

Figure 17-14 Artificial nesting island for Canada geese in Alberta, Canada.

Ducks Unlimited, Canada

Congress has also created other sources of revenue for this fund. They include direct appropriations, refuge entrance fees, and import duties on firearms and ammunition. In 1988 the FWS collected over $37 million from all sources for this fund. In 1986 Congress passed the Emergency Wetlands Resources Act. One of its provisions doubles the price of a duck stamp between 1987 and 1991 and greatly increases the amount of money available for buying migratory-bird habitats.

The Federal Farm Act of 1985 contains a provision designed to reduce the conversion of wetlands to cropland. Under this law's so-called swampbuster provision, farmers who convert wetlands to cropland that produces a cash crop after December 23, 1985, lose federal farm benefits on all their land. But verifying and enforcing this provision is difficult.

Individual Action We are all involved, at least indirectly, in the excessive destruction of wildlife any time we buy or drive a car, build a house, consume almost anything, and waste electricity, paper, water, or any other resource. All these activities contribute to the destruction or degradation of wildlife habitats or to the killing of one or more individuals of some plant or animal species.

We all have a role to play in preventing the premature extinction of wildlife and in protecting and restoring ecosystems that have been harmed by human activities. To help prevent and heal the earth, we can try to improve the habitat on a patch of the earth in our immediate environment. We can improve our backyards, abandoned city lots, campus areas, and streams clogged with debris. We can develop a wildlife protection and management plan for any land that we own.

We can also support politicians and groups that fight for wildlife conservation. One goal should be to pressure Congress to pass a National Biological Diversity Act and to encourage the development of an international treaty to preserve biological diversity at the ecosystem, species, and gene levels. The United States should also develop a national conservation program as part of the World Conservation Strategy.

top and bottom. A solar-powered energizer delivers a 5,000-volt shock that repels predators without killing them. Nesting success in such enclosures has climbed to 100%, compared to only 10% in unprotected areas. This approach costs less per duckling than most other duck management methods.

In 1986 the United States and Canada agreed on a plan to spend $1.5 billion over a 15-year period with the goal of almost doubling the continental duck breeding population to 62 million birds. The key elements in this program will be the purchase, improvement, and protection of an additional 5.6 million acres of waterfowl habitat (1.9 million acres in the United States and 3.7 million acres in Canada) in five priority ranges.

Since 1934 the Migratory Bird Hunting and Conservation Stamp Act has required waterfowl hunters to buy a duck stamp each season they hunt. Revenue from these sales go into a fund to buy land and easements for the benefit of waterfowl.

Every part of this earth is sacred to my people. Every shining pine needle, every sandy shore, every mist in the dark woods, every clearing and humming insect is holy in the memory and experience of my people. . . . To harm the earth is to heap contempt on its creator.

Chief Sealth of the Duwamist Tribe of the state of Washington in a letter sent to President Franklin Pierce in 1855 concerning the proposed purchase of the tribe's land, the heart of which now contains the city of Seattle.

Robert Leo Smith

Robert Leo Smith is professor of wildlife ecology at West Virginia University. In addition to numerous research articles and papers on forest and wildlife management, he is the author of three ecology texts (see Further Readings for Chapter 5) Ecology and Field Biology, 4th ed. (1990), Elements of Ecology, 2d ed. (1986), and Ecology of Man: An Ecosystem Approach, 2d ed. (1976). He has also served as a consultant to government agencies on wildlife habitat assessment and other environmental issues.

If you were to ask people, both hunters and nonhunters, how it is we have an abundance of white-tailed deer and wild turkey when they were threatened or endangered species just 50 years ago, few would know why. The answer is the Federal Aid in Wildlife Restoration Act of 1937, better known as the Pittman-Robertson, or P-R, Act. Born out of the depression and dust bowl (pp. 227–28) of the 1930s, this one piece of legislation is most responsible for pulling many forms of North American wildlife from the brink of extinction and for providing the foundation of modern scientific wildlife management.

U.S. animal wildlife was in a desperate situation in the 1930s. Populations of wild game species such as white-tailed deer, pronghorn antelope, bighorn sheep, wild turkey, and wood duck had been drastically reduced by years of uncontrolled hunting and habitat destruction (Table 16-1, p. 420).

Alarmed that game animals might disappear, a group of people who liked to hunt organized and began lobbying for wildlife conservation measures. One of the group's prominent leaders was Jay N. "Ding" Darling, a nationally syndicated cartoonist for the *Des Moines Register*. His cartoons hit hard at commercial hunters and greedy sport hunters and exploiters of natural resources. His leadership in promoting wildlife conservation prompted President Franklin D. Roosevelt to appoint him as director of the Bureau of Biological Survey, forerunner of today's U.S. Fish and Wildlife Service.

In 1936 Darling advocated a national wildlife policy that would declare the survival of game animals in the national interest and would place wildlife management by states and the federal government on a scientific basis. This was a bold step forward because in the 1930s most wildlife management officials were political appointees with no special training or expertise and often with little interest in their job.

To provide for trained wildlife biologists, Darling proposed that wildlife research units be established at land-grant universities. These units would provide graduate-level training for wildlife scientists and conduct much-needed research. To finance such a program and aid states in undertaking projects to restore wildlife populations, Darling proposed a federal excise tax on the sale of sporting firearms and ammunition. It would be a "user-pay" program in which hunters paid the bill for the conservation and management of wildlife.

In 1937, a bill to this effect, sponsored by conservationists Senator Key Pittman of Nevada and Representative (later Senator) Willis Robertson of Virginia, was passed and signed into law. The P-R Act had three major provisions. It provided states with a portion of the tax revenues from firearm and ammunition sales on a matching basis (75% federal and 25% state) based on each state's size and number of licensed hunters. It prohibited use of these federal revenues for any purpose other than wildlife conservation. And no state could receive funds provided by P-R tax revenues unless it passed a law requiring all income from sale of state hunting license fees to be used for support of its state fish and wildlife department.

Since 1937 the P-R law has provided more than $1.6 billion to the states for wildlife conservation, to which has been added over $500 million in state matching funds. Nearly half the money distributed to states has been used to develop, maintain, and operate wildlife management areas which benefit most forms of wildlife. The remainder has been used for wildlife research and surveys (25%), land acquisition (13%), and hunter safety and education (9%).

Funds provided by the P-R law have helped restore population of many birds and animals. Although emphasis has been on game species, in recent years about 12% to 13% of the revenues (a smaller percentage in earlier years) have been spent on the conservation of nongame species. The act has also enabled states to purchase over 4 million acres of wildlife habitats used by game and nongame species. Perhaps the most important and least visible result from the P-R Act has been development of the science of wildlife management, which has helped in the restoration of many game and nongame species of wildlife.

The success of the P-R act led to the passage of the Dingell-Johnson, or D-J, Act in 1950, cosponsored by Representative John Dingell of Michigan and Senator Edwin Johnson of Colorado. Similar to P-R funding, it provides money for restoration and conservation of fish species with a sport or recreational value through a federal excise tax on fishing equipment including rods, reels, lines, and artificial lures, baits, and flies. Since 1951 the D-J Act has raised almost $700 million for state fishery conservation efforts.

The money is apportioned to each state on the basis of its total acreage and number of paid fishing licenses. This law has been especially useful in restoring and maintaining species favored by anglers, such as bass, trout, catfish, and other pan fish. In 1984 Congress passed an amendment to the D-J Act that established a trust fund for fish restoration and more than tripled the amount of money available under the D-J Act, primarily by imposing taxes on additional types of domestic and imported fishing equipment and pleasure boats and yachts.

Attempts to pass federal legislation that would place an excise tax on bird seed, binoculars, certain camera equipment, and other items associated with wildlife-related recreation and to use the resulting revenues for restoration and conservation of nongame wild species have failed. In 1980, however, Congress enacted the Fish and Wildlife Conservation Act, also known as the Nongame Act. It authorizes funding by means of general appropriations from the treasury to encourage states to prepare and carry out plans for the conservation of nongame wildlife species. However, between 1980 and 1988 this program was not funded because the Reagan administration did not request any appropriations for this purpose.

Antihunting factions have opposed excise taxes on hunting and fishing equipment under the P-R and D-J acts on the grounds that they sacrifice wildlife in order to increase revenues for state wildlife and fishery departments and increase profits for the sporting equipment industry. However, these critics fail to recognize that for several decades sport hunting and fishing has promoted and financed the restoration of much of the country's wildlife. It is because of these laws that we still have an abundance of wildlife, from bears and deer to bobwhite quail and songbirds. In 1985 revenues collected under the P-R and D-J acts also accounted for 21% of the U.S. Fish and Wildlife Service budget.

In spite of such funding and a wealth of knowledge available on the management of wildlife resources, many species of wildlife face a precarious future because of problems money cannot solve. This results from the relentless destruction and fragmentation of wildlife habitat by an expanding human population—leaving many forms of wildlife without a place to live.

Guest Essay Discussion

1. What do you believe would be the condition of game and nongame wildlife in the United States if Congress had not passed the P-R and D-J acts?

2. Do you agree or disagree with the claim by antihunting factions that these acts have sacrificed wildlife to increase profits for the sporting equipment industry? Explain.

3. Should the Nongame Act passed in 1980 be funded? Explain. Should this act be funded from general appropriations (as is presently the case) or by an excise tax on certain wildlife-related recreational items? Explain.

DISCUSSION TOPICS

1. Since 1981 funds available to federal agencies charged with protecting and managing wildlife on publicly owned lands have been sharply decreased. Do you agree or disagree with this action? Explain. If you believe that funding for these programs should be sharply increased, then what federal expenditures would you cut in order to provide more money for wildlife protection and management?

2. Describe two methods a wildlife manager might use to increase the harvestable surplus of a game population such as deer. Give the major advantages and disadvantages of each method.

3. Should state and federal agencies be required to shift to the use of chemical antifertility agents as the major method for controlling wild species? Explain.

4. Make a survey of your campus and local community to identify examples of habitat destruction or degradation that have had harmful effects on the populations of various wild plant and animal species. Develop a management plan for the rehabilitation of these habitats and wildlife.

5. What hunting regulations exist in your local area? How well are they enforced? What changes, if any, should be made in these regulations? Explain. You might invite state or federal wildlife conservation officials and hunters to discuss this issue with your class.

6. Are you for or against sport hunting? Explain.

7. Find out how much revenue your state fish and game department receives each year from taxes and from the sale of fishing and hunting licenses. Also find out how this money is used.

FURTHER READINGS

See also the Readings for Chapter 16.

Anderson, S.H. 1985. *Managing Our Wildlife Resources.* Columbus, Ohio: Charles Merrill.

Bailey, J. A. 1984. *Principles of Wildlife Management.* New York: John Wiley.

Baker, Ron. 1985. *The American Hunting Myth.* New York: Vantage Press.

Dasmann, Raymond F. 1981. *Wildlife Biology,* 2d ed. New York: John Wiley.

Durrell, Lee. 1986. *State of the Ark: An Atlas of Conservation in Action.* Garden City, N.Y.: Doubleday.

Gassett, Jose Ortega. 1972. *Meditations on Hunting.* New York: Scribner.

Gilbert, Frederick, and Donald G. Dodds. 1987. *The Philosophy and Practice of Wildlife Management.* Malabar, Fla.: Robert E. Krieger.

Giles, R.H. 1978. *Wildlife Management.* San Francisco: W.H. Freeman.

Hall, L. K., ed. 1984. *White-Tailed Deer—Ecology and Management.* Harrisburg, Penn.: Stackpole Books.

International Union for Conservation of Nature and Natural Resources. 1980. *World Conservation Strategy.* New York: Unipub.

Kaufman, Les, and Kenneth Mallory, eds. 1986. *The Last Extinction.* Cambridge, Mass.: MIT Press.

Leopold, Aldo. 1933. *Game Management.* New York: Charles Scribner's Sons.

Lund, T. A. 1980. *American Wildlife Law.* Berkeley: University of California Press.

Luoma, Jon. 1987. *A Crowded Ark: The Role of Zoos in Wildlife Conservation.* Boston: Houghton Mifflin.

McNamee, Thomas. 1984. *The Grizzly Bear.* New York: Alfred A. Knopf.

Moen, A. N. 1973. *Wildlife Ecology.* San Francisco: W.H. Freeman.

National Audubon Society. Annual. *Audubon Wildlife Report.* New York: National Audubon Society.

Office of Technology Assessment. 1987. *Technologies to Maintain Biological Diversity.* Washington, D.C.: Government Printing Office.

Robbins, C. T. 1983. *Wildlife Feeding and Nutrition.* New York: Academic Press.

Shaw, J. H. 1985. *Introduction to Wildlife Management.* New York: McGraw-Hill.

Soulé, Michael E., ed. 1987. *Viable Populations for Conservation.* New York: Cambridge University Press.

Soulé, Michael E., and Bruce Wilcox, eds. 1980. *Conservation Biology.* Sunderland, Mass.: Sinauer Associates.

Tudge, Colin. 1988. *The Environment of Life.* New York: Oxford University Press.

Wallace, David Rains. 1987. *Life In the Balance.* New York: Harcourt Brace Jovanovich.

Watkins, T. H. 1988. *Vanishing Arctic: Alaska's National Wildlife Refuge.* New York: Aperture.

Wolf, Edward C. 1987. *On the Brink of Extinction: Conserving the Diversity of Life.* Washington, D.C.: Worldwatch Institute.

PART FOUR

Mineral and Energy Resources and Their Management

Kennecott Copper Corporation

Our entire society rests upon—and is dependent upon—our water, our land, our forests, and our minerals. How we use these resources influences our health, security, economy, and well-being.

John F. Kennedy

CHAPTER 18

Nonrenewable Mineral Resources and Solid Waste

General Questions and Issues

1. How are minerals formed and distributed?

2. How are mineral deposits found and extracted from the earth's crust?

3. What harmful environmental impacts occur from mining, processing, and using minerals?

4. How long will affordable supplies of key minerals last for the world and the United States?

5. How can we increase the supplies of key minerals?

6. How can we make supplies of key minerals last longer?

We seem to believe we can get everything we need from the supermarket and corner drugstore. We don't understand that everything has a source in the land or sea, and that we must respect these sources.

Thor Heyerdahl

W hat do cars, spoons, glasses, dishes, beverage cans, coins, electrical wiring, bricks, and sidewalks have in common? Few of us stop to think that these products and many others we use every day are made from nonrenewable raw materials extracted from the earth's solid crust—the upper layer of the lithosphere (Figure 5-1, p. 93).

Any naturally occurring inorganic substance found in the earth's crust as a crystalline solid is called a **mineral**. Examples include salt, used to season food; clay, to make dishes and bricks; silicates, to make glass; and sand, gravel, limestone, and gypsum, to make concrete.

Other important minerals are metals such as iron, aluminum, copper, and gold. An **ore** is a mineral deposit containing enough of a metallic element to permit it to be extracted and sold at a profit. The higher the concentration of metal in the ore, the higher its grade.

These minerals are part of our nonrenewable heritage, produced by geologic events over millions of years. Without them technological civilization as we know it would not be possible.

Unlike biological resources, minerals cannot be managed to produce a sustained yield. Their supply is limited. We can recycle, reuse, and conserve some minerals to make them last longer. But after the high-grade ores and easy-to-get deposits have been tapped, our supply of these minerals will be economically depleted. It would cost too much to find, process, and use what is left.

18-1 ORIGIN AND DISTRIBUTION OF MINERAL RESOURCES

The Rock Cycle A **rock** is a naturally occurring solid that contains one or more minerals. The largest and slowest of the earth's cyclical processes is the **rock cycle,** which forms and modifies rocks in the earth's crust and mantle (Figure 18-1). Three major types of rocks are formed in this cycle: igneous, sedimentary, and metamorphic (Figure 18-2).

Granite and other **igneous rocks** form when magma (molten rock) wells up from the earth's upper mantle and cools and crystallizes on or beneath the earth's surface. The resulting mounds and mountains of rock are gradually broken into smaller pieces by exposure to water, wind, ice, plant roots, and acid secretions from lichens and mosses that grow on rocks. Sediments formed from these weathering processes are transported by wind, water, gravity, and ice to basins at lower elevations. Sandstone and other rocks formed of compacted sediments collected in basins are called **sedimentary rocks.**

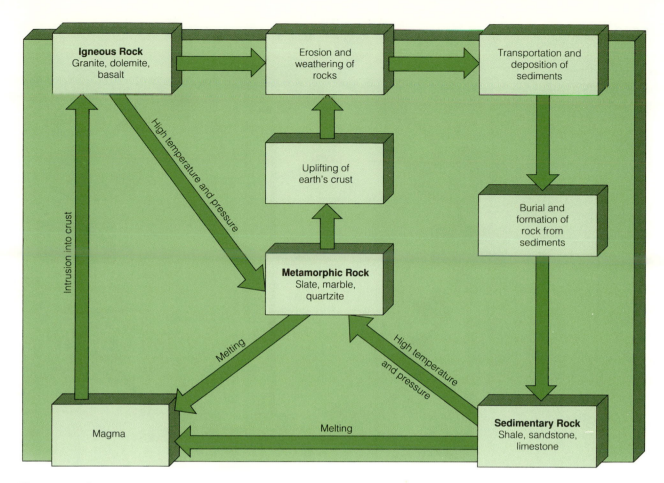

Figure 18-1 The rock cycle.

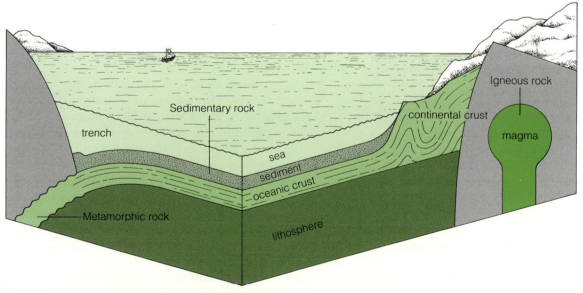

Figure 18-2 Major rock types.

Over millions of years deposits of sedimentary and igneous rocks are buried deeper and deeper in the earth's crust, where high temperatures and great pressures change them into **metamorphic rocks**, such as slate. Some of these rocks may then melt to start the rock cycle over again (Figure 18-1).

The rock cycle is powered by energy from the sun, heat from the earth's interior, wind, flowing water,

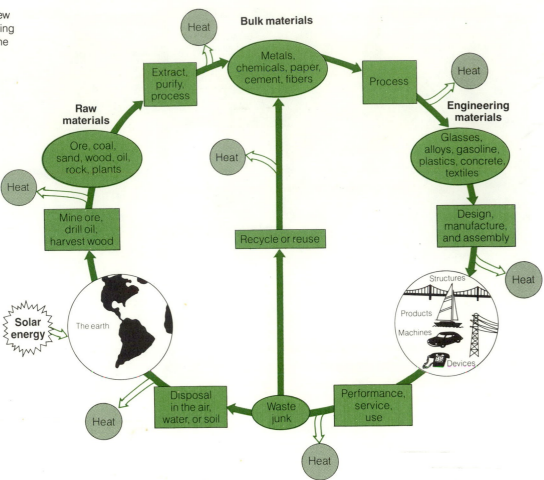

Figure 18-3 Generalized view of the extraction and processing of raw materials to produce the products we use and then discard, recycle, or reuse.

and movements of the earth's crust. Mountains, plains, ocean floors, and other geologic features of the planet are the results of this geological cycle of destruction and creation of the earth's three basic types of rocks.

Mineral Resource Abundance and Distribution We have learned how to find and mine concentrated deposits of more than 100 minerals formed by the rock cycle in the earth's continental and oceanic crusts. We convert these minerals into many of the everyday items we use and then discard, reuse, or recycle (Figure 18-3).

We remove concentrated minerals, process and use them, and often disperse them over parts of the earth's surface. It takes millions of years for these dispersed materials to become concentrated by the rock cycle into useful minerals again. Therefore, on a human time scale we classify these minerals as nonrenewable resources.

A few minerals, such as gold and silver, occur as free elements. But most minerals are compounds of only ten elements that make up 99.3% of the earth's crust (Figure 18-4). Only trace amounts of other elements are found in the earth's crust.

Metallic minerals can be classified according to how abundant they are in the earth's crust. Aluminum,

iron, magnesium, titanium, manganese, and chromium are abundant metals. Scarce metals include lead, copper, zinc, silver, gold, platinum, molybdenum, and mercury.

Iron makes up 95% of the metals extracted from the earth each year. It is used to make steel. Small amounts of other metals, such as cobalt, manganese, nickel, and chromium, are added to steel to make stainless steel and other alloys with certain desired properties.

Over hundreds of millions of years geochemical processes have dissolved, transported, and deposited elements and their compounds unevenly. Consequently, there are great differences between the average crustal abundances of elements shown in Figure 18-4 and how much of an element is found at a particular place. Concentrated deposits of a particular mineral such as iron or copper may exist at some locations. But most deposits contain too little of the desired metal to be economically useable.

Mineral Formation Minerals are formed by several different processes. One is plate tectonics, movements of parts of the earth's crust downward, upward, and across one another (Figure 18-5). Boundaries between the moving plates (faults) are zones where

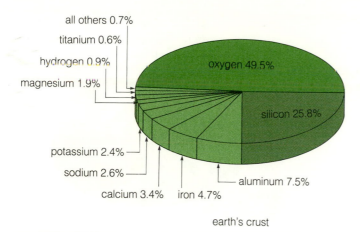

Figure 18-4 Percentage by weight of elements in the earth's crust.

Figure 18-5 Plate tectonics. The earth's crust is divided into rigid plates which move in relation to each other because of movements in the underlying mantle.

earthquakes occur and the sites of active volcanoes. New crust is formed where two plates are drawn apart by movements in the underlying mantle. The theory of plate tectonics explains how the continents have drifted together and apart over hundreds of millions of years and how some mineral deposits were formed.

Most deposits of metallic ores are formed at the boundaries where tectonic plates separate and where they come together. Where plates separate along the ocean floor, molten igneous rock (magma) comes into contact with cold ocean water. The heated water rises through fractured rocks and leaches metals from them. This hot, mineral-laden water spews out of hydrothermal vents on the ocean floor. The dissolved metals are deposited as metal sulfides when the water cools.

At boundaries where tectonic plates come together, igneous rocks saturated with sea water are forced together. The resulting high temperatures and pressures partially melt the rocks to form bodies of magma. This magma may force its way upward into the crust, cool, and allow minerals to crystallize.

Mineral deposits also may form where plate movements allow magma to rise, penetrate the earth's surface, and form active volcanoes. As the molten igneous rock inside the volcano cools, minerals with high densities crystallize first and sink to the bottom. Less dense minerals crystallize later and are found near the top of the rock deposit. Diamonds form when molten rock made up mostly of carbon cools very slowly under enormous pressure.

Many ore deposits are formed by hot waters moving underground within the earth's crust. Hot, circulating groundwater dissolves minerals from deeply buried molten rock. When the water reaches rock in areas above or beyond the molten zone, it cools and leaves deposits of minerals.

Sedimentary processes also concentrate minerals in deposits. The processes that weather and erode igneous rocks and deposit them as sediments can remove unwanted materials and leave behind deposits of useful minerals.

Weathering and erosion deposit materials in ocean and stream beds at lower elevations. Wind and running water separate these rock particles by density, shape, and size. Sand and gravel, for example, are sedimentary deposits of fine-grained rock. Sometimes minerals such as gold are found in placers in streams. Placers are deposits formed when flowing water separates heavier mineral particles from sediment and drops them on stream beds with little water flow and turbulence.

Some mineral deposits are formed when minerals dissolve in water and then crystallize as the water evaporates. For example, vast underground caverns of limestone are formed when calcium carbonate is dissolved by acidic water seeping downward. The water becomes acidic by dissolving carbon dioxide from the air and by passing through some types of soil. As the water evaporates, it leaves deposits of calcium carbonate hanging from the ceiling of a cavern (stalactites) and standing on the floor (stalagmites). Aboveground salt deposits form when the sun evaporates water from shallow pools of seawater.

18-2 LOCATING AND EXTRACTING MINERAL RESOURCES

Making Mineral Resources Available   Several steps are involved in making a mineral resource available for use:

- A deposit with enough of the desired mineral to make removing it profitable must be found.

Figure 18-6 Big Muskie, a giant power shovel used to remove the overburden for the surface mining of coal. The cars behind the shovel look like toys.

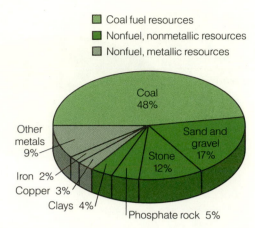

- Coal fuel resources
- Nonfuel, nonmetallic resources
- Nonfuel, metallic resources

Coal 48%

Sand and gravel 17%

Stone 12%

Other metals 9%

Iron 2%

Copper 3%

Clays 4%

Phosphate rock 5%

Figure 18-7 Percentage of surface-mined U.S. land used to extract coal and various mineral resources.

- Some form of mining is used to extract the mineral from the deposit.

- The mineral is processed to remove impurities.

- In some cases (especially metallic ores) the purified mineral is converted to a different chemical form by smelting or other chemical processes. For example, aluminum is found in the earth's crust in ore form as aluminum oxide (Al_2O_3). After the ore is purified and melted, electrical current is passed through the molten oxide to convert it to aluminum metal (Al) and oxygen gas (O_2).

Large amounts of energy are needed to mine and process minerals. As energy prices rise, it costs more to meet our demands for minerals.

Finding Deposits Because concentrated deposits of useful minerals are unevenly distributed in the earth's crust, they are difficult and expensive to find.

Mining companies use several methods to find promising deposits. Geological information about crustal movements and mineral formation helps them find areas for closer study. Photos taken from airplanes or images relayed by satellites sometimes reveal geological features such as mounds or rock formations, often associated with deposits of certain minerals.

Instruments mounted on aircraft and satellites can detect concentrated deposits of minerals that affect the earth's magnetic or gravitational fields. At promising sites samples are taken from test holes, tunnels, or trenches and analyzed for their mineral content.

Extraction of Minerals and Coal Once an economically acceptable deposit of a mineral or coal (Section 19-3) is found, it is removed by surface or subsurface mining. Mineral deposits near the earth's surface are removed by **surface mining**. Giant mechanized equip-

ment is often used to strip away the overlying layer of soil and rock—known as **overburden**—and vegetation.

For example, Big Muskie, a $25 million power shovel for the surface mining of coal, is 32 stories high with a boom as long as a football field (Figure 18-6). It gouges out 325 tons of overburden every 55 seconds and drops this load on a pile one city block away. Then smaller power shovels remove the exposed mineral deposit.

Surface mining extracts about 90% of the metallic and nonmetallic minerals and almost two-thirds of the coal used in the United States. Almost half of the land disturbed by surface mining in the United States has been mined for coal. The rest has been mined for nonmetallic minerals such as sand, gravel, stone, and phosphate rock and metallic minerals such as iron, copper, and aluminum (Figure 18-7).

Several types of surface mining are used, depending on the type of mineral and local topography. In **open-pit surface mining** large machines dig holes in the earth's surface and remove mineral deposits, primarily stone, sand, gravel, iron, and copper (see photo on p. 455). Sand and gravel are removed from thousands of small pits in many parts of the country. Building rocks such as limestone, granite, and marble are taken from larger pits called *quarries*. After the stone is removed, these sites often fill with water.

Area strip mining is carried out on flat or rolling terrain. Bulldozers and power shovels strip away the overburden and dig a trench to remove the mineral deposit. Then a parallel trench is dug and its overburden is placed in the nearby trench from which the mineral deposit has been removed.

Area strip mining is used mostly for mining coal in many western and midwestern states, and phosphate rock, especially in Florida, North Carolina, and Idaho. If the land is not restored, this type of mining leaves a wavy series of highly erodible hills of rubble called spoil banks (Figure 18-8).

National Archives

Figure 18-8 Effects of area strip mining of coal. Although restoration of newly strip-mined areas is now required, many previously mined areas have not been restored.

Figure 18-9 Contour strip mining of coal.

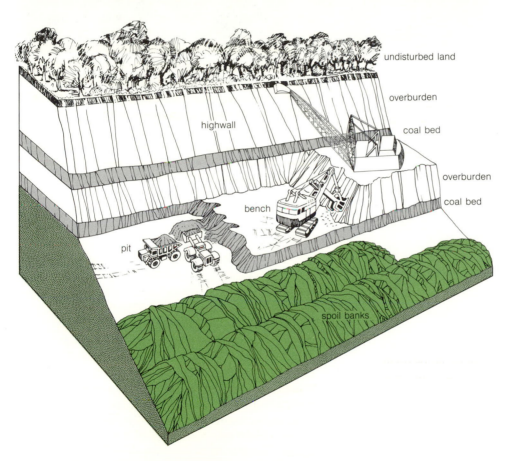

undisturbed land

overburden

highwall

coal bed

overburden

coal bed

bench

pit

spoil banks

Contour strip mining is used in hilly or mountainous terrain. A power shovel cuts a series of terraces into the side of a hill or mountain (Figure 18-9). The overburden from each new terrace is dumped onto the one below. Unless the land is restored, a wall of dirt is left in front of a highly erodible bank of soil and rock, called a highwall (Figure 18-10). In the United States contour strip mining is used mostly for extracting coal in the mountainous Appalachian region.

Some mineral deposits lie so deep in the ground that removing them by surface mining is too expensive. These deep, underground mineral deposits are removed by **subsurface mining**. For coal and some metallic ores miners dig a deep vertical shaft, blast subsurface tunnels and rooms to get to the deposit, and haul the coal or ore to the surface.

In the *room-and-pillar method* as much as half the coal is left in place as pillars to prevent the mine from

Figure 18-10 Severely eroded hillsides on Bolt Mountain, West Virginia, as a result of contour strip mining of coal without proper restoration.

U.S. Department of Agriculture

Department of Energy

Figure 18-11 Longwall mining of coal in southern Illinois.

collapsing. In the *longwall method* a narrow tunnel is created and then supported by movable metal pillars (Figure 18-11). After a cutting machine has removed the coal or ore from part of the mineral seam, the roof supports are moved forward, allowing the earth behind the supports to collapse. No tunnels are left behind after the mining operation has been completed.

18-3 ENVIRONMENTAL IMPACT OF MINING, PROCESSING, AND USING MINERAL RESOURCES

Overall Impact The mining, processing, and use of any nonfuel or fuel mineral resource cause land disturbance, air pollution, and water pollution (Figure 18-12). Most land disturbed by mining can be restored to some degree, and most forms of air and water pollution can be controlled. But these efforts are expensive. They also require energy, which, in being produced and used, pollutes the environment.

Mining Impacts Mining involves removing material from the surface or subsurface of the earth and dumping unwanted rock and other waste materials, called *spoils*, somewhere else. The harmful environmental effects of such land disturbance depend on the type of mineral extracted, the size of the deposit, the method used (surface or subsurface), and the local topography and climate (Figures 18-8 and 18-10).

For each unit of mineral produced, subsurface mining disturbs less than one-tenth as much land as surface mining. Usually subsurface mining produces less waste material than surface mining.

But subsurface mining is more dangerous and expensive than surface mining. Sometimes roofs and walls of underground mines collapse, trapping and killing miners. Explosions of dust and natural gas in mines can also kill and injure miners. Prolonged inhalation of coal dust and other types of mining dust can cause various lung diseases.

Often surfaces above mined areas cave in or subside. Subsidence causes roads to buckle, houses to crack, railroad tracks to bend, sewer lines to crack, and gas mains to break and can disrupt groundwater systems. Longwall mining causes the overlying surface land to collapse several feet.

Compared to agriculture and urbanization, surface mining uses a small amount of the earth's surface. For

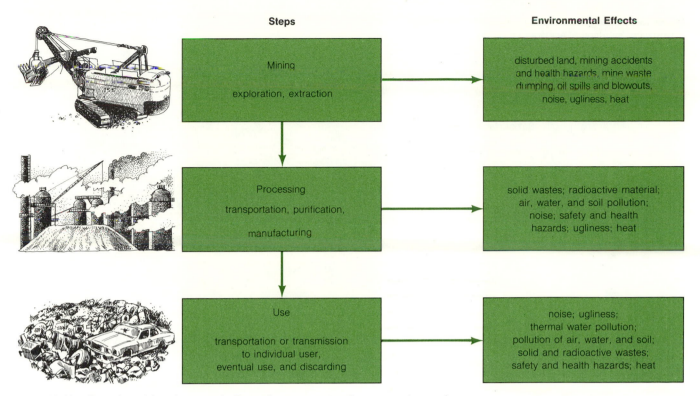

Steps	Environmental Effects
Mining exploration, extraction	disturbed land, mining accidents and health hazards, mine waste dumping, oil spills and blowouts, noise, ugliness, heat
Processing transportation, purification, manufacturing	solid wastes; radioactive material; air, water, and soil pollution; noise; safety and health hazards; ugliness; heat
Use transportation or transmission to individual user, eventual use, and discarding	noise; ugliness; thermal water pollution; pollution of air, water, and soil; solid and radioactive wastes; safety and health hazards; heat

Figure 18-12 Some harmful environmental effects of resource extraction, processing, and use.

example, between 1930 and 1988, only about 0.3% of the total land area of the United States was surface-mined or used to dispose of wastes (spoils) from such mining.

However, in some areas there is a growing conflict between one-time land disruption for mineral or coal extraction and long-term use for food production. For example, much of the strippable coal reserves in the United States are located on highly productive farmlands in areas such as Illinois and Iowa.

Nevertheless, surface mining has a severe environmental impact because the land is stripped bare of vegetation. This destroys or substantially reduces soil fertility and disrupts groundwater systems. Most of the damage cannot be undone by even the best reclamation. Only about 64% of the land area disturbed by coal mining, 26% by nonmetals, and 8% by metals have been restored. The exposed soil and mining wastes can be eroded by wind and water, polluting the atmosphere and nearby aquatic ecosystems.

Restoration of surface-mined land involves three phases. First the excavated area is filled in and graded to restore the original contour. Then the topsoil is replaced and fast-growing vegetation is planted to keep it from blowing or washing away. Restoration costs range from $1,000 to $5,000 an acre.

The success of restoration efforts depends on average precipitation, slope of the land, and how well federal and state surface-mining regulations are enforced. Restoration is simpler and more effective in areas with

U.S. Department of Interior, Office of Surface Mining

Figure 18-13 With the land returned to its original contour and grass planted to hold the soil in place, it is hard to tell that this was once a surface coal-mining site in West Virginia.

more than ten inches of rainfall a year and with flat or slightly rolling topography (Figure 18-13). About three-fourths of the coal in the United States that can be surface-mined is in the West in arid and semiarid regions. There the climate and soil usually prevent full restoration of surface-mined land. For many large open-pit mines and quarries, especially in arid and semiarid regions, there is little hope of restoration.

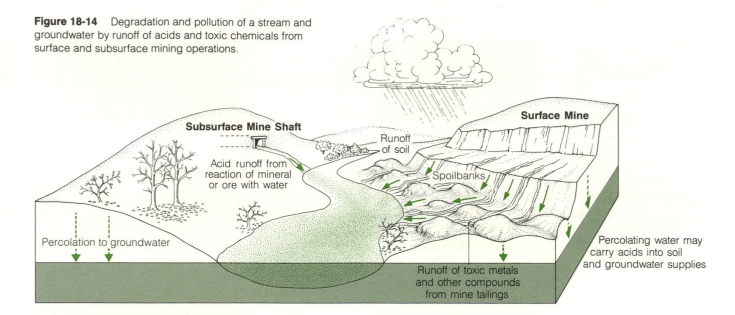

Figure 18-14 Degradation and pollution of a stream and groundwater by runoff of acids and toxic chemicals from surface and subsurface mining operations.

Subsurface Mine Shaft

Acid runoff from reaction of mineral or ore with water

Percolation to groundwater

Surface Mine

Runoff of soil

Spoilbanks

Percolating water may carry acids into soil and groundwater supplies

Runoff of toxic metals and other compounds from mine tailings

Another environmental problem of mining, especially subsurface mining, is runoff of acids, eroded soil (silt), and toxic substances into nearby rivers and streams (Figure 18-14). These pollutants can also percolate downward and contaminate groundwater.

Large-scale mining operations also have social impacts. When mining begins, many workers move into the area and add to the local economy. But this puts stress on areas unprepared for rapid growth. Often, schools, water supplies, rental housing, and sewage and solid waste disposal are inadequate to serve the sudden increase in people. The increased growth can also put stress on nearby recreation and wilderness areas and cause the conversion of forests and cropland to urban development.

Communities may adjust to the increased growth, but mine production varies because of fluctuating mineral prices and demand. Eventually the mines are depleted and shut down, and communities that depended on them for income become ghost towns.

Processing Impacts Some ores contain no more than 0.4% of the desired metal, and few contain more than 30%. Processing extracted mineral deposits to remove impurities produces huge quantities of rock and other waste materials. That is why most processing takes place near mine sites.

The waste materials, called **tailings**, usually are piled on the ground or dumped into ponds near mining and processing sites. Wind blows particles of dust and toxic metals from piles of tailings into the atmosphere, and water leaches toxic substances into nearby surface water or groundwater (Figure 18-14). Laws have forced mining companies to reduce contamination from tailings, but enforcement of these laws is weak.

Without adequate pollution control equipment, mineral-smelting plants emit massive quantities of air

pollutants that can damage vegetation and soils in the surrounding area. Pollutants include sulfur dioxide, soot, and tiny particles of toxic elements and compounds (such as arsenic, cadmium, and lead) found as impurities in many ores. Decades of uncontrolled sulfur dioxide emissions from copper-smelting operations near Copperhill and Ducktown, Tennessee, killed all vegetation for miles around (see Case Study on p. 167).

Smelting plants also cause water pollution and produce liquid and solid hazardous wastes, which must be disposed of safely or converted into less harmful substances. Workers in some smelting industries have an increased risk of cancer. For example, workers in arsenic, cadmium, and lead smelters have a higher than normal incidence of lung cancer.

Solid Waste Huge quantities of solid waste are produced from the extraction, processing, and use of minerals, wood, and other resources. **Solid waste** is any unwanted or discarded material that is not a liquid or a gas.

The United States is first by far in total and per capita waste production. Each year the country produces at least 6.2 billion tons of solid, liquid, and gaseous waste—an average of 50,000 pounds of waste per person. About 51% of that is solid waste. Thus, the average American directly or indirectly produces 26,000 pounds of solid waste a year—or 71 pounds a day. About 89% of this solid waste is produced by agricultural, forestry, and mining activities (Figure 18-15). Most agricultural and silvicultural wastes are left in the field or forest where they were created. If these crop and wood wastes are not carried into streams by storm runoff, they help control soil erosion and fertilize the soil. About 50% of all animal manure is spread on the land as a fertilizer and soil conditioner. Almost

70% of the wood wastes from lumber, plywood, and pulp production are burned for fuel or used as raw material for other products.

Industrial solid waste makes up about 8% of the total produced each year. Much of this is scrap metal, plastics, slag, paper, fly ash from electrical power plants, and sludge from sewage treatment plants. Tougher air and water pollution control laws will produce more fly ash and sewage sludge. Most industrial solid waste is disposed of at the plant site where it is produced.

Municipal solid waste from homes and businesses in or near urban areas makes up the remaining 3% of the solid waste produced in the United States. One year's worth of this waste would fill a bumper-to-bumper convoy of garbage trucks that would encircle the earth almost five times. A 1988 study by the American Public Works Association found that each American directly throws away an average of 7 pounds of trash a day, or 2.5 tons a year. Urban dwellers in most other industrialized countries throw away one-half to one-fourth this amount per day. In Calcutta, India, the daily average per person is about 1 pound.

Roughly 55% of what the typical American throws away as garbage and rubbish is paper and yard waste (Figure 18-16). About 37% of urban solid waste is paper, much of it from overpackaged items (see Case Study on p. 370). Because municipal solid waste is concentrated in highly populated areas, it must be removed quickly to prevent health hazards, infestations by rats and other disease-carrying organisms, and buildup of massive piles of ugly trash.

Another source of solid waste is the litter that people throw out of their cars along roadsides. The release of tens of thousands of helium-filled balloons at sporting events and celebrations is causing widespread litter, suggests to children and adults that it is okay to pollute, and wastes helium—a scarce resource. Environmentalists believe that states should ban balloon releases.

Ways to Deal with Solid Waste What are our options? One is a throwaway approach in which we dump, bury, or burn these wastes. In the United States about 80% of the municipal solid waste is hauled away and buried in landfills, and 9% is burned in municipal incinerators (Figure 18-17).

Another throwaway approach is to burn paper and other combustible types of garbage to generate steam and electricity. Denmark and Sweden burn about half of their waste to produce energy, compared to 9% in the United States. However, burning solid waste encourages people to continue throwing away paper, plastics, and other burnable materials.

A third option is to recycle and reuse much of the paper, bottles, metals, food scraps, yard clippings, and other wastes we throw away. Japan, Denmark, Sweden, and the Netherlands recycle about 50% of their

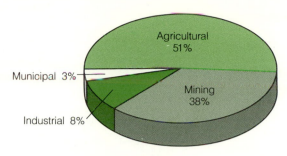

Figure 18-15 Sources of solid waste in the United States. (Data from Environmental Protection Agency)

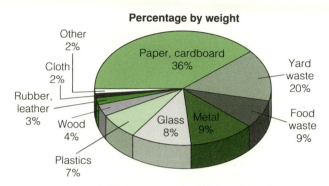

Figure 18-16 Composition by weight of urban solid waste thrown away in a typical day by each American in 1984. Because plastic containers are replacing many glass containers, plastics are expected to make up 10% of urban solid waste by the year 2000. (Data from Environmental Protection Agency)

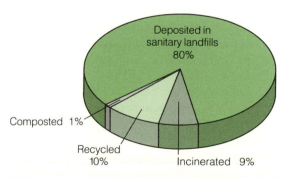

Figure 18-17 Fate of solid waste in the United States. (Data from Environmental Protection Agency)

municipal solid waste. In the United States only 10% is recycled.

A fourth approach is to reduce the amount of solid waste we produce. We can develop manufacturing processes that use as little matter and energy resources as possible. We can also make products that last longer

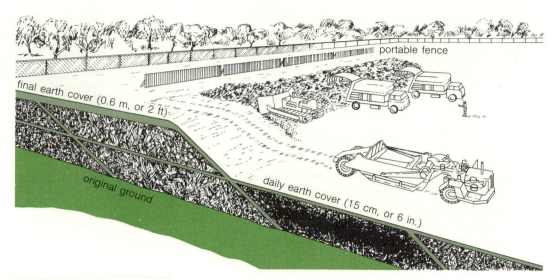

Figure 18-18 A sanitary landfill. Wastes are spread in a thin layer and then compacted with a bulldozer. A scraper (foreground) covers the wastes with a fresh layer of soil at the end of each day. Portable fences catch and hold windblown debris.

and are easy to repair, recycle, and remanufacture. So far no country makes widespread use of waste reduction.

Environmentalists and conservationists believe we should begin shifting from the first two throwaway approaches (Figure 4-16, p. 90) to a sustainable-earth, low-waste approach (Figure 4-17, p. 91) based on increased recycling, reuse, and waste reduction. Most of what we throw away would not be seen as solid waste but as some of our most valuable resources. The low-waste approach would reduce the garbage glut, save energy, save money, and conserve wood, metals, and other raw materials.

Burying Solid Waste in Landfills Until 1976 when the Resource Conservation and Recovery Act (RCRA) was enacted, most trash in the United States was thrown into open dumps or burned in crude incinerators that polluted the air. Open dumps are unsightly health hazards. They also pollute nearby surface water and groundwater, and they often catch fire and pollute the air.

Ocean dumping of solid waste has been limited by the Marine Protection Research and Sanctuaries Act of 1972. But illegal dumping is a problem. During the summer of 1988, illegally dumped medical wastes washed onto beaches from Maine to Florida. The discovery of blood vials (some testing positive for the AIDs virus), syringes and needles, and high bacteria levels led to beach closings in Connecticut, New Jersey, and New York.

The RCRA banned all open dumps and required landfills to be upgraded to sanitary landfills. A **sanitary landfill** is a land waste disposal site in which

wastes are spread out in thin layers, compacted, and covered with a fresh layer of soil each day (Figure 18-18). No open burning is allowed, odor is seldom a problem, and rodents and insects cannot thrive. Sanitary landfills should be located so as to reduce water pollution from runoff and leaching, but this is not always done.

A sanitary landfill can be put into operation quickly, has low operating costs, and can handle a massive amount of solid waste. After a landfill has been filled and allowed to settle for a few years, the land can be graded and used as a park, a golf course, an athletic field, a wildlife area, or some other recreation area (Figure 18-19).

Landfills have drawbacks. While they are in operation, there is much traffic, noise, and dust. Wind can scatter litter and dust before each day's load of trash is covered with soil. That is why most people do not want a landfill nearby, even if it is eventually used as a recreation site. The underground anaerobic decomposition of organic wastes at landfills produces explosive methane gas and toxic hydrogen sulfide gas. These gases can seep into nearby buildings and cause explosions or asphyxiation. This problem can be prevented by equipping landfills with vent pipes to collect these gases so that they can be burned or allowed to escape into the air.

At the Fresh Kills landfill on Staten Island enough methane gas is collected to heat 50,000 homes a year. Besides saving energy, collecting and burning methane gas from all landfills worldwide would lower atmospheric emissions of methane by 6% to 18%. This would help reduce depletion of the ozone layer and global warming from greenhouse gases.

Contamination of groundwater and nearby surface water is also a potential problem, especially for thousands of sanitary landfills filled and abandoned before stricter siting and operating regulations were established. At least 25%—some say 80%—of the landfills in operation today may be polluting surface water and groundwater.

Many cities in the East and Midwest are running out of landfill space. In 1976 there were about 30,000 landfills in the United States. By 1988 there were only about 6,000. Many of the earlier landfills were filled, and those that could not be upgraded to sanitary landfills were closed.

By 1995 half of the existing landfills in the United States will be filled and closed. Most cities are not building new landfills. Either there are no acceptable sites or construction is prevented by citizens who want their trash hauled away but don't want a landfill anywhere near them—the *not in my backyard* attitude.

Soon Chicago and most other cities in Illinois will be out of landfill space. So will Connecticut, New Jersey, Los Angeles, and New York City. New York City's gigantic Fresh Kills landfill already stands 150 feet high. By 1997, when it reaches 500 feet, it will have to be closed because it is in the flight path of Newark International Airport. By 1995 more than 60% of the landfill space in Florida and 75% in Massachusetts will be filled.

Some cities with no more landfill space are shipping their trash elsewhere. Philadelphia ships part of its solid waste to a waste-to-energy incinerator in Baltimore, Maryland. The rest goes to rural areas in Pennsylvania, Ohio, West Virginia, and Kentucky. Between 1980 and 1987 Philadelphia's average disposal costs rose from $20 to $80 a ton. Some East Coast regions without landfill space pay up to $240 a ton to get rid of their trash. Attempts by some cities to ship their trash to Great Britain and to several African and Latin American countries have outraged citizens and officials in those countries.

Some Sunbelt cities like Dallas, Texas, and Phoenix, Arizona, have enough landfill capacity to last well into the next century. But even where landfill space is available, operating costs are rising sharply.

Landfill costs will also rise because of new EPA regulations. By 1991 landfill operators will have to:

- close landfills near airports, flood plains, wetlands, and earthquake zones
- monitor nearby surface and groundwater supplies for contaminants
- install a liner at the bottom of a new landfill to control runoff of contaminated water and a system to collect liquid that does run off
- monitor release of methane gas and install vent pipes to collect methane or vent it to the atmosphere

Figure 18-19   This entertainment center in Mountain View, California, was once a landfill.

- monitor a landfill for at least 30 years after it is closed

In addition to making landfills safer, these regulations are designed to spur local governments to recycle more trash.

Burning Solid Waste   Burning solid waste in incinerators kills disease-carrying organisms and reduces the volume of solid waste by 90% and its weight by 75%. Salvaged metals and glass can be sold for recycling.

In *waste-to-energy incinerators* heat released when trash is burned is used to produce electricity or to heat nearby buildings. Incinerators do not pollute groundwater and add little pollution to the air if equipped with effective pollution control devices. Sweden, which burns half its solid waste, requires such devices.

However, incinerators have some drawbacks. Even with air pollution control devices, incinerators emit small amounts of toxic dioxins and large quantities of fine particulate matter into the atmosphere. For every ten tons of municipal waste fed into an incinerator, one ton of ash is produced. This ash, currently disposed of in landfills, is usually contaminated with toxic metals and dioxins, and may soon be classified as hazardous waste by the EPA.

Construction, maintenance, and operating costs are much higher for incinerators than for landfills, except in areas where land prices are high or waste must be hauled long distances to the landfills. Between 1982 and 1987 the average cost of incinerating a ton of solid waste in the United States rose from $13 to $34. Incineration is not useful in rural areas and small towns that do not generate enough burnable waste to make the operation economical.

Incinerator sites are hard to find because of citizen opposition. But as urban areas run out of acceptable landfills, incineration will become more economically attractive. By the end of this century incinerators are projected to be burning 30% of the solid waste in the United States.

Composting Degradable solid waste from slaughterhouses, food-processing plants, and kitchens and yard waste can be mixed with soil and decomposed by aerobic bacteria to produce **compost**, a soil conditioner and fertilizer. Organic waste produced by food-processing and other industries is collected and degraded in large composting plants. The compost is then bagged and sold. This approach is used in many European countries, including the Netherlands, West Germany, France, Sweden, and Italy. Sweden composts 25% of its solid waste. Kitchen waste, paper, leaves, and grass clippings can be decomposed in backyard compost bins and used in gardens and flower beds (Figure 9-20, p. 235).

Composting cannot be used for mixed urban waste because sorting out the glass, metals, and plastics is too expensive. Composting yard waste would reduce the amount of municipal solid waste in the U.S. by 20%. Currently only 1% of the solid waste produced in the United States is composted.

Locating a city compost next to a landfill would reduce the waste going to the landfill and extend its life. The compost can be used as landfill cover and used by public works departments. Seattle plans to recycle 60% of its urban solid waste by 1990. This strategy includes curbside collection and composting of yard wastes and promotion of backyard composting.

18-4   WILL THERE BE ENOUGH MINERAL RESOURCES?

How Much Is There?   How much of a particular nonrenewable mineral resource exists on earth? How much of it can be found and extracted at an affordable price? Answering these questions is difficult and controversial.

The term **total resources** refers to the total amount of a particular material that exists on earth. It's hard to make useful estimates of total resources because the entire world has not been explored for each resource.

The U.S. Geological Survey estimates actual and potential supplies of a mineral resource by dividing total resources into two broad categories: identified and undiscovered (Figure 18-20). **Identified resources** are deposits of a particular mineral-bearing material of which the location, quantity, and quality are known or have been estimated from geological evidence and measurements.

Undiscovered resources are potential supplies of a particular mineral. They are believed to exist on the basis of geologic knowledge and theory, though specific locations, quality, and amounts are unknown.

These two categories are subdivided into reserves and resources. **Reserves**, or **economic resources**, are identified resources that can be extracted profitably at present prices with current mining technology. **Resources** are all identified and undiscovered deposits, including those that can't be recovered profitably with present prices and technology. They may become reserves when prices rise or mining technology improves.

Reserves are like the money you now have available to spend. Resources are the total income you expect to have during your lifetime. Your cash reserves are certain. But the resources you expect to have may or may not become available for many reasons.

Most published estimates of the available supply of a particular nonrenewable mineral refer to reserves, not resources or total resources. Supplies of a mineral are usually higher than estimates of reserves. Some deposits classified as resources will be converted to reserves. Sometimes new deposits are discovered. Improvements in mining technology or shortages that cause price increases for a mineral may make it profitable to mine lower-grade deposits.

However, a large portion of potentially recoverable resources will not become available because of the law of diminishing returns. Usually the first deposits of a mineral to be exploited are high grade ores found near the earth's surface and near the mineral's point of use. Once these deposits are depleted, the industry must turn to deeper, more remote, and lower-grade deposits. Eventually extracting, transporting, and processing the remaining lower-quality deposits costs more than they are currently worth.

How Fast Are Supplies Being Depleted?   The future supply of a nonrenewable mineral resource depends on two factors: its actual or potential supply and how rapidly this supply is being depleted. We never completely run out of any mineral. Instead of becoming physically depleted, a mineral becomes economically depleted. When this economic limit is reached, we have four choices: recycle or reuse what has already been extracted, cut down on unnecessary waste of the resource, find a substitute, or do without.

Depletion time is how long it takes to use a certain portion—usually 80%—of the known reserves or

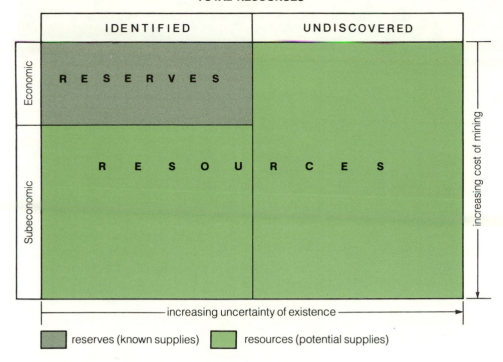

TOTAL RESOURCES

| | IDENTIFIED | UNDISCOVERED |

Figure 18-20 General classification of mineral resources by the U.S. Geological Survey.

reserves (known supplies) resources (potential supplies)

estimated resources of a mineral at an assumed rate of use. Resource experts project depletion times and plot them on a graph by making different assumptions about the resource supply and its rate of use (Figure 18-21).

We can use a mineral resource in three ways: rapid consumption, consumption with increased recycling and exploration, or use with greatly increased recycling, reuse, and reduced consumption. Each choice gives a different estimated depletion time.

For example, we get one estimate of depletion time by assuming that the resource is not recycled or reused, estimated reserves don't increase, and prices rise (curve A, Figure 18-21). We get a longer depletion time estimate by assuming that recycling will extend the life of existing reserves and that improved mining technology, price rises, and new discoveries will expand present reserves by some factor, say 2 (curve B). We get an even longer depletion time estimate by assuming that new discoveries, recycling, reuse, and reduced consumption will expand reserves even more, perhaps five or ten times (curve C).

Finding a substitute for a resource cancels all these curves and requires a new set of depletion curves for the new resource. Figure 18-21 shows why cornucopians and neo-Malthusians disagree over projected supplies of nonrenewable nonfuel and fuel resources (see Pro/Con on p. 20). We get optimistic or pessimistic projections of the depletion time for a nonrenewable resource by making different assumptions.

Who Has the World's Nonfuel Mineral Resources?
Five MDCs—the Soviet Union, the United States,

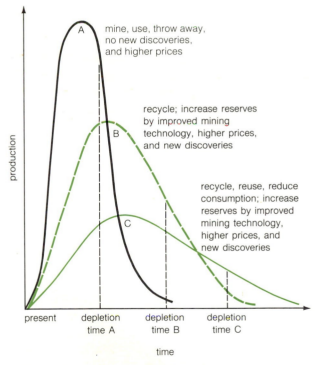

mine, use, throw away, no new discoveries, and higher prices

recycle; increase reserves by improved mining technology, higher prices, and new discoveries

recycle, reuse, reduce consumption; increase reserves by improved mining technology, higher prices, and new discoveries

Figure 18-21 Depletion curves for a nonrenewable resource, using three sets of assumptions. Dashed vertical lines show when 80% depletion occurs.

Canada, Australia, and South Africa—supply most of the 20 minerals that make up 98% of all nonfuel minerals consumed in the world. Exceptions include copper in South America, tin and tungsten in Southeast Asia, aluminum ore in the Caribbean, and cobalt in Zaire.

Table 18-1 U.S. Import Dependence for Selected Key Nonfuel Minerals in 1985

Mineral	Percentage Imported	Major Suppliers	Key Uses
Columbium	100	Brazil, Canada, Thailand	High-strength alloys for construction, jet engines, machine tools
Industrial diamonds	100	South Africa, United Kingdom, Soviet Union	Machinery, mineral services, abrasives, stone and ceramic products
Manganese	99	South Africa, Gabon, France	Alloys for impact-resistant steel, dry-cell batteries, chemicals
Aluminum ore	96	Jamaica, Guinea, Suriname	Aluminum production, building materials, abrasives
Cobalt	95	Zaire, Zambia, Canada	Alloys for tool bits, aircraft engines, high-strength steel
Tantalum	94	Thailand, Malaysia, Brazil	Nuclear reactors, aircraft parts, surgical instruments
Platinum	91	South Africa, United Kingdom, Soviet Union	Oil refining, chemical processing, telecommunications, medical and dental equipment
Graphite	90+	Mexico, China, Brazil	Foundry operations, lubricants, brake linings
Chromium	82	South Africa, Zimbabwe, Soviet Union	Alloys for springs, tools, engines, bearings
Tin	79	Thailand, Malaysia, Indonesia	Cans and containers, electrical products, construction, transportation
Vanadium	41	South Africa, Canada, Finland	Iron and steel alloys, titanium alloys, sulfuric acid production

The United States and the Soviet Union are the world's two largest producers and consumers of nonfuel mineral resources. The Soviet Union is the only country that meets nearly all its mineral resource needs from domestic supplies.

Despite its rich resource base, the United States imports large amounts of many key nonfuel minerals (Table 18-1). Some of these minerals are imported because they are consumed more rapidly than they can be produced from domestic supplies. The U.S. rate of consumption exceeds its domestic production. Other minerals are imported because other countries have higher-grade ore deposits that are cheaper to extract than lower-grade U.S. reserves. Japan and most western European countries are much more dependent on imports of vital nonfuel minerals than the United States is.

The United States stockpiles 93 **strategic materials** vital to industry and defense to cushion against short-term supply interruptions and sharp price rises. Eighty of the strategic materials are nonfuel minerals. Stockpiles are supposed to last through a three-year war, but most supplies are far below this level.

Sometimes countries with most of the world's supply of a resource band together to control supplies and raise prices. OPEC is an example of such a cartel. So far no cartel, single country, or company has been able to control the supply and price of nonfuel minerals. An exception is industrial diamonds, which have been controlled for 50 years by De Beers Consolidated Mines of South Africa.

According to the U.S. Bureau of Mines and the U.S. Geological Survey, the United States has enough domestic reserves of most key minerals to last at least several decades. Exceptions include chromium, cobalt, platinum, manganese, tin, gold, and palladium. However, the Geological Survey estimates that present reserves of most key minerals will not meet U.S. needs for more than 100 years without increased recycling, conservation, and substitutes.

18-5 INCREASING MINERAL RESOURCE SUPPLIES: THE SUPPLY-SIDE APPROACH

Economics and Resource Supply Geologic processes determine how much there is of a mineral resource. Economics, however, determines what part of the total supply will be used.

According to standard economic theory, a competitive free market should control the supply and demand of goods and services (Section 3-2). If a resource becomes scarce, its price rises. If there is an oversupply, the price falls. Cornucopians believe that increased demand will raise mineral prices and stimulate new discoveries and development of more efficient mining technology. Higher prices also will make it profitable to mine ores of increasingly lower grades.

Many economists argue that this theory does not apply to nonfuel mineral resources in most MDCs. In the United States and many other MDCs, industry and government have gained so much control over supply, demand, and prices of mineral raw materials and mineral products that a competitive free market does not exist.

Another problem is that the costs of nonfuel mineral resources make up only a small part of the total cost of most goods. A major reason for this is that the cost of a mineral resource does not include most of the harmful external costs caused by its extraction, processing, and use (Figure 18-12). As a result, scarcities of nonfuel minerals do not raise the final price of products very much. Because product prices do not reflect dwindling mineral supples, consumers have no incentive to reduce demand soon enough to avoid economic depletion. Instead, low prices increase demand and encourage faster resource depletion.

Finding New Land-Based Mineral Deposits

Geologic exploration—guided by better geologic knowledge, satellite surveys, and other new techniques—will increase present reserves of most minerals. Cameras and sensors in orbiting satellites now scan the globe for land, forest, mineral, energy, and water resources.

According to geologists, rich deposits will probably be found in unexplored areas in LDCs. However, in MDCs and many LDCs, most of the easily accessible, high-grade deposits have already been discovered. Remaining deposits are difficult and costly to find and mine and usually are less concentrated.

Exploration for new resources requires a large capital investment and is a risky financial venture. Typically, if geologic theory identifies 10,000 sites where a deposit of a particular resource might be found, only 1,000 sites are worth costly exploration; only 100 justify even more costly drilling, trenching, or tunneling; and only 1 out of the 10,000 will probably be a producing mine.

Even if large new supplies are found, no mineral supply can stand up to continued exponential growth in its use. For example, a 1-billion-year supply of a resource would be exhausted in only 584 years if its rate of use increased 3% a year.

Getting More Minerals from Seawater and the Ocean Floor

Ocean resources are found in three areas: seawater, sediments and deposits on the shallow continental shelf and slope, and sediments and nodules on the deep-ocean floor. Because there is so much seawater, some people view it as an almost inexhaustible source of minerals. But most of the 90 chemical elements found in seawater occur in such low concentrations that recovering them takes more energy and money than they are worth.

For example, to get a mere 0.003% of the annual U.S. consumption of zinc from the ocean, we would have to process a volume of seawater equal to the combined annual flows of the Delaware and Hudson rivers. Only magnesium, bromine, and sodium chloride are abundant enough in seawater to be extracted profitably at present prices with current technology.

Offshore deposits and sediments in shallow waters are already important sources of crude oil, natural gas, sand, gravel, and ten minerals. The main factor limiting extraction of these resources is the increasing cost of the energy needed to find and remove them. Other problems are the harmful effects of oil leaks and spills and mining operations on marine food resources and wild species (see photo at front of book).

At a few sites on the deep-ocean floor, manganese-rich nodules have been found in large quantities. These potato-size rocks contain 30% to 40% manganese, used in certain steel alloys. They also contain small amounts of other strategically important metals such as nickel and cobalt.

These nodules could be scooped up or sucked up from the muds of the ocean floor. Then they would be transported by pipe or by a continuous cable with buckets to a mining ship two to three miles above.

Environmentalists recognize that such seabed mining would probably cause less harm than mining on land. They are concerned, however, that removing nodules from the seabed and dumping back unwanted material will stir up deep ocean sediments. This could destroy seafloor organisms and have unknown effects on poorly understood deep-sea food webs. Surface waters might also be polluted by the discharge of sediments from mining ships and rigs.

Economic uncertainties make it unclear whether seabed nodules will be extracted in the near future. Ample and much cheaper supplies of most of these minerals are expected to be available for many decades. Prices of these metals may not be high enough to return a reasonable profit on large and risky investments in seabed mining for the next 15 to 20 years.

Because most seabed mining sites are located in international waters, various countries are squabbling over ownership of the nodules. Faced with these legal and economic uncertainties, private ocean-mining companies have halted most research and development of seabed minerals since 1984.

Improving Mining Technology and Mining Low-Grade Deposits

Cornucopians talk of improved mining technology that will allow us to drill deeper into the earth to get more minerals. However, the likelihood of obtaining materials from greater depths is slim because finding and extracting these deposits would be very expensive.

Cornucopians also assume that all we have to do to increase supplies of any mineral is to mine lower grades of ore. They point to advances in technology during the past few decades that have allowed the mining of low-grade deposits of copper, for example, without significant cost increases.

Neo-Malthusians point out that several factors limit the mining of lower-grade deposits. As increasingly poorer ores are mined, we eventually reach a point where energy costs drastically increase. Our ability to mine and process increasingly poorer grades of ore depends on having an inexhaustible source of cheap energy. Most energy experts believe that in the future energy will neither be unlimited nor cheap. Today mineral production requires about 20% of the energy used in the United States. By the year 2000 mineral industries are expected to account for one-third of U.S. energy consumption.

Available supplies of fresh water also may limit the supply of some mineral resources because large amounts of water are needed to extract and process most minerals. Many areas with major mineral deposits are poorly supplied with fresh water.

Finally, exploitation of lower grades of ore may be limited by the environmental impact of waste material produced during mining and processing. The production of low-grade ores increases the amount of disturbed land and the amount of air and water pollution. At some point, land restoration and pollution control costs will exceed the value of the minerals produced.

Finding Substitutes Cornucopians believe that even if supplies of key minerals become very expensive or scarce, human ingenuity will find substitutes. They point out that new developments by scientists are already leading to a materials revolution based on clay, sand, and new, high-performance plastics. They argue that these materials, made of silicon and other abundant elements, can be substituted for most scarce metals (see Spotlight below). In 1980 Japan's government saw the development of new materials as a key technology of the future and launched a ten-year, $400 million program of research.

Substitutes can probably be found for many scarce mineral resources, but there are problems. Finding or developing a substitute is costly, and phasing it into a complex manufacturing process requires a long lead time. During the transition period, people may suffer economic hardships as the price of the increasingly scarce mineral being replaced rises sharply. And finding substitutes for some key materials such as helium and phosphates may be extremely difficult, if not impossible.

Some substitutes are inferior to the minerals they replace. Others may become scarce and too expensive because of greatly increased demand or rising energy prices. Aluminum could replace copper in electrical wiring, but the energy cost of producing aluminum is higher than that of copper. And aluminum wiring is more of a fire hazard than copper wiring. Plastic-coated iron plate can substitute for galvanized iron, but the plastic increases energy costs by at least 50%. The materials revolution is an important advance, but it will not meet all of our mineral needs.

18-6 EXTENDING MINERAL RESOURCE SUPPLIES: THE CONSERVATION APPROACH

Advantages of Resource Recovery As mentioned earlier, one way to deal with solid waste is to recycle and reuse it. **Resource recovery**—salvaging usable metals, paper, and glass from solid waste and selling them to manufacturing industries for recycling—is also a way to extend our supplies of mineral resources.

Recycling metals and other nonrenewable mineral resources has many advantages. It extends the supply of minerals by reducing the amount of virgin materials that must be extracted from the earth's crust to meet demand. Recycling usually saves energy, causes less

---

SPOTLIGHT **The Materials Revolution**

Scientists and engineers are rapidly developing new materials that can replace many of the metals we now rely on. Ceramic materials are being used in engines, knives, scissors, batteries, fish hooks, and artificial limbs.

Ceramics are harder, stronger, lighter, and longer-lasting than many metals. Also, they withstand enormous temperatures, and they do not corrode. Because they can burn fuel at higher temperatures than metal engines, ceramic

engines can boost fuel efficiency by 30% to 40%.

High-strength plastics and composite materials strengthened by carbon and glass fibers are likely to transform the automobile and aerospace industries. Many of these new materials are stronger and lighter than metals. They cost less to produce because they require less energy. They don't need painting and can easily be molded into any shape.

Many cars now have plastic body parts, which reduce weight and boost fuel economy. Planes and cars made almost entirely of plastics—held together by new superglues—may be common in the next century.

The materials revolution is even transforming medicine. So-called biomaterials, made of new plastics, ceramics, glass composites, and alloys, are being used in artificial skin, arteries, organs and joints.

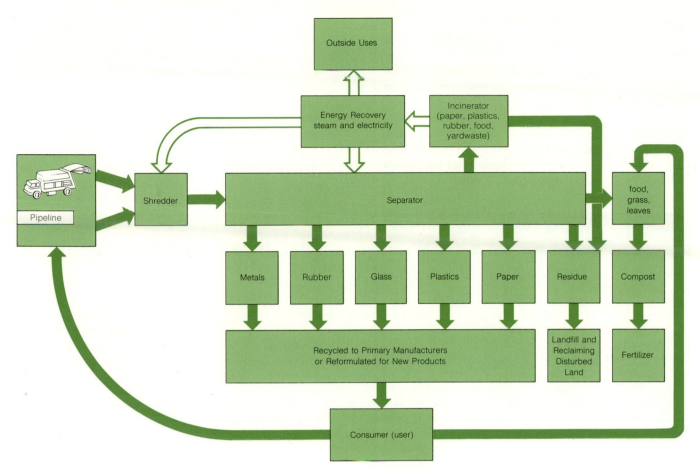

Figure 18-22 Generalized urban resource recovery system.

pollution and land disruption than use of virgin resources, cuts waste disposal costs, and prolongs the life of landfills by reducing the volume of solid waste.

Items containing iron and aluminum account for 94% of all metals used. Using scrap iron instead of iron ore to produce steel conserves iron ore and the coal needed to process the ore. Using scrap iron requires 65% less energy and 40% less water and produces 85% less air pollution and 76% less water pollution. Recycling aluminum produces 95% less air pollution and 97% less water pollution, and requires 95% less energy than mining and processing aluminum ore.

Despite these advantages, only about one-fourth of the world's iron and aluminum is recycled, partly because many discarded items are widely dispersed. Recycling rates vary in different countries. The Netherlands recycles about half of its scrap iron and aluminum, and Japan and the United States recycle about a third of theirs.

High-Technology Resource Recovery In high-technology **resource recovery plants**, machines shred and automatically separate mixed urban waste to recover glass, iron, aluminum, and other valuable materials (Figure 18-22). These materials are then sold to man-

ufacturing industries as raw materials for recycling. The remaining paper, plastics, and other combustible wastes are recycled or incinerated. The heat given off is used to produce steam or electricity to run the recovery plant and for sale to nearby industries or residential developments.

By 1988 the United States had more than 110 waste-incinerating plants, and 210 others were being built or planned. Although a few of these plants separate and recover some iron, aluminum, and glass for recycling, most are merely trash-to-energy incinerators.

One problem with waste-incinerating plants is that they emit dioxins—suspected carcinogens. Proponents of incinerators contend that new pollution control devices can remove 99% of the pollutants emitted. But the United States has no nationwide standards for emissions of most air pollutants, including dioxins, from waste-to-energy incinerators.

Another problem is what to do with the hazardous residue left after the trash is burned. Presently it is hauled off to a landfill. So far, the EPA has not classified incinerator ash as hazardous waste, but pending legislation could change that.

Many environmentalists oppose the widespread use of trash-to-energy incinerators. They encourage people to keep on creating solid waste and discourage recycling programs. Incinerators are also expensive to build and maintain. Environmentalists believe communities' limited tax dollars would be better spent on recycling and other methods that reduce the amount of trash produced.

Low-Technology Resource Recovery Most waste materials recovered in the United States are recycled by a low-technology method. Homes and businesses place various kinds of waste materials—glass, paper, metals, plastics, and yard wastes—into separate containers. Compartmentalized city collection trucks, private haulers, or volunteer recycling organizations pick up the segregated wastes and sell them to scrap dealers, compost plants, and manufacturers. Studies have shown that trash separation takes only 16 minutes a week for the average American family.

A comprehensive low-technology recycling program could save 5% of annual U.S. energy use—more

---

CASE STUDY **Recycling Beverage Containers in the United States**

About 56% of the new aluminum beverage cans used in the United States were recycled in 1988 at more than 5,000 recycling centers set up by the aluminum industry, other private interests, and local governments. People who returned the cans got about a penny a can for their efforts, earning about $700 million. Within six weeks the average recycled aluminum has been melted down and is back on the market as a new can.

Despite this progress almost half the aluminum cans produced each year in the United States are still thrown away. Each is an almost indestructible form of solid waste and its production represents a waste of energy equal to that in half a beverage can of gasoline. Only about one-third of the aluminum produced each year in the United States is recycled.

Beverage container deposit laws can be used to decrease litter and encourage recycling of nonrefillable glass, metal, and plastic containers (refillable containers are discussed later in this chapter). Consumers pay a deposit (usually 5¢ to 10¢) on each beverage container they buy. The deposits are refunded when containers are turned in to retailers, redemption centers, or reverse vending machines, which return cash when consumers put in empty beverage cans and bottles.

By 1988 container deposit laws had been adopted in Sweden, Norway, the Netherlands, the Soviet Union, parts of Australia, Canada, and Japan. In the United

States such laws have been passed in eleven states with about one-fourth of the population.

Such laws work. Experience in the United States has shown that 90% of cans and bottles are turned in for refund. Litter is decreased by 35% to 70%, expensive landfills don't fill up as quickly, energy and mineral resources are saved, and jobs are created. Environmentalists and conservationists believe a nationwide deposit law should be passed by Congress.

So far such a law has been effectively opposed by a well-funded lobby of steel, aluminum, and glass companies, metalworkers' unions, supermarket chains, and most major brewers and soft drink bottlers. Merchants don't like to have returned bottles and cans piling up in their stores.

Labor unions are afraid that some workers in bottle and can manufacturing industries will lose their jobs. Beverage makers fear the extra nickel deposit per container will hurt sales. Some people believe that a nationwide bottle deposit law would be an infringement on states rights. Although they may support deposit laws, they believe that this problem should be dealt with by each state.

"Keep America Beautiful" and other ad campaigns financed by groups opposing deposit laws have helped prevent passage of such laws in a number of states. These groups favor litter-recycling laws, which levy a tax on industries whose products may end up as litter or in landfills. Revenues

from the tax are used to set up and maintain statewide recycling centers. By 1988 seven states, containing about 14% of the U.S. population, had this type of law.

Environmentalists point out that according to surveys litter taxes are not as effective as container deposit laws. Surveys have also shown that a national container deposit law is supported by 73% of the Americans polled. EPA and General Accounting Office studies estimate that such a law would:

- save consumers at least $1 billion annually
- reduce roadside beverage container litter by 60% to 70%
- reduce urban solid waste by at least 1%, saving taxpayers $25 million to $50 million a year in waste disposal costs
- decrease mining and processing of aluminum ore by 53% to 74% and the use of iron ore by 45% to 83%
- reduce air, water, and solid waste pollution from the beverage industry by 44% to 86%
- save energy equal to that needed to supply the annual electrical needs for 2 million to 7.7 million homes
- create 80,000 to 100,000 new jobs because collecting and recycling beverage containers requires more labor than producing new ones

Do you favor passage of such a law?

than the energy generated by all U.S. nuclear power plants—at perhaps one-hundredth of the capital and operating costs. By contrast, burning all combustible urban solid waste in waste-to-energy plants would supply only 1% of the country's annual energy use.

The low-technology approach produces little air and water pollution and has low start-up costs and moderate operating costs. It also saves more energy and provides more jobs for unskilled workers than high-technology resource recovery plants. Another advantage is that collecting and selling cans, paper, and other materials for recycling is an important source of income for many people (especially the homeless and the poor) and for volunteer service organizations.

Recycling in the United States By 1988, more than 3,000 U.S. cities had curbside collection of separated wastes. Eight states—New York, Maryland, New Jersey, Oregon, Connecticut, Pennsylvania, Florida, and Rhode Island—have programs with goals of recycling 25% to 50% of their solid waste sometime before 1995. But more than half of the states currently recycle less than 5% of their municipal solid waste. In some places households are required to put recyclable materials into separate containers for curbside pickup and recycling. If people don't comply, their trash is not picked up. What are your state and community doing?

Hundreds of U.S. cities are recycling 15% to 50% of their solid waste. The recycling honor role includes San Francisco, Seattle, Chicago, Philadelphia, and Minneapolis. Despite these encouraging trends, only about 10% of all potentially recoverable waste material in the United States is recycled (see Case Study on p. 474).

In densely populated and resource-poor countries such as Japan and the Netherlands, about half of urban waste materials are recycled. Much of Japan's success is due to close coordination of national, regional, and local governments in collecting and managing waste.

Recycling rates are also high in some LDCs, including Mexico, India, and China. Small armies of poor people go through urban garbage disposal sites by hand. They remove paper and sell it to paper mills. They sell metal scrap to metal-processing factories, bones to glue factories, and rags to furniture factories for use in upholstery.

The use of plastic bottles and containers in MDCs is growing rapidly. In 1988 plastics made up about 7% of the weight and 30% of the volume of municipal solid wastes in the United States. By 2000, plastics are expected to make up 10% of the weight and 66% of the volume of these wastes (see Spotlight below).

Efforts are under way to recycle some of the 200 million tires that are thrown away each year in the United States. Some are dumped in landfills, but most are piled in junkyards, where they are fire hazards and breeding grounds for mosquitoes.

SPOTLIGHT Degrading and Recycling Plastics

Most plastics used today are non-degradable or slowly degradable. When these plastics are buried in landfills, they remain there for hundreds of years. They also take up lots of space.

Scientists are hard at work trying to develop degradable plastics for use in garbage bags, bottles, fishing nets, and other items. A number of companies are making degradable plastic bags, six-pack yokes, and fast-food containers. But biodegradable plastics still take decades to decompose in landfills. Also, their degradation products may pollute groundwater.

Some companies are also recycling plastics. For example, plastic soda bottles can be collected and turned into plastic chips that can be stuffed into seat cushions, used as insulation in sleeping bags and

jackets, or used to make textiles and carpets. Mixed plastics can be recycled and used to make landscaping ties, park benches, boat docks, and other products. Recycling plastics saves twice as much energy as burning them in a waste-to-energy incinerator.

Despite these promising developments, only 1% of all plastic wastes and 4% of plastics packaging used in the United States are recycled. New York State has a deposit system to encourage the return of plastic soft drink containers. However, in 1985 two-thirds of the containers returned were buried because of poor markets for plastic scrap.

This could change. Recycling plastics is a way to make money. In 1988 scrap dealers were paying 12 cents a pound for high-density

polyethylene jugs and 60 cents a pound for plastic soft drink bottles and other containers. Plastics have become the second most valuable recyclable material after aluminum.

The Plastic Pollution Control Act of 1988 requires that by 1992 all plastic items deemed recyclable by the EPA and the Commerce Department must be recycled. All remaining plastic items would have to be biodegradable.

With proper economic and political incentives, about 43% of the plastic wastes produced in the United States could be recycled by the year 2000. Since most of the raw materials used to make plastics come from petroleum and natural gas, recycling plastics would help reduce waste of these energy resources. But the best solution is to use less plastic.

Figure 18-23 Evidence of the throwaway mentality at the site of an outdoor rock concert.

UPI/Bettmann Newsphotos

Some paper and cement companies are shredding tires and mixing the rubber with coal to burn in their boilers. In Modesto, California, a power plant burns tires to generate enough electricity for 15,000 homes. Next to the plant sits the world's largest pile of tires, 35 million of them.

Other companies are using pulverized tires to make resins for a range of products, including car bumpers and garbage cans. A Canadian firm has developed a process that converts used tires into heating oil and high-octane compounds that can substitute for lead in gasoline. Used tires have also been used to build artificial reefs to attract fish.

Obstacles to Recycling in the United States Several factors hinder recycling in the United States. One is the failure of many U.S. metals industries to modernize. Since 1950, countries such as Japan and West Germany have built modern steel plants that use large amounts of scrap steel, much of it bought from the United States.

During the same period, the U.S. steel industry did not invest much in modernizing and replacing older plants. Instead, it continued to rely heavily on older processes that require virgin iron ore. The industry has now lost much of its business to foreign competitors and no longer has the capital to modernize. This shows how overemphasis on short-term economic gain can lead to long-term economic pain, decline, and loss of jobs for thousands of Americans.

Another problem is that Americans have been conditioned by advertising and example to a throwaway lifestyle (Figure 18-23). The emphasis is on making, using, and replacing more and more items to increase short-term economic growth regardless of the long-term environmental and economic costs.

Waste collection and disposal costs make up a large part of local budgets supported by tax revenues. Consumers pay these costs indirectly in the form of higher taxes rather than directly as part of the cost of any item that is disposed of. Because the true costs of items are not reflected in their prices, consumers have little incentive to recycle and conserve recoverable resources.

The growth of the recycling, or secondary-materials, industry in the United States is hindered by several factors. One is that primary mining and energy industries get huge tax breaks, depletion allowances, and other tax-supported federal subsidies to encourage them to get virgin resources out of the ground as fast as possible.

In contrast, recycling industries get few tax breaks and other subsidies. The lack of large, steady markets for recycled materials makes recycling a risky business. It is typically a boom-and-bust financial venture that does not attract much investment capital. Some states have made efforts to correct this situation. New York, North Carolina, Florida, Oregon, and Wisconsin give tax breaks to businesses that use secondary materials or buy recycling equipment. Based on current costs, it is estimated that an average suburban community with landfill or incineration charges of $45 a ton or more would save money by recycling much of its solid waste.

Overcoming the Obstacles In 1988 the EPA set a goal of recycling 25% of municipal solid waste by 1992. By the year 2000, the United States could easily recycle and reuse 35% of the matter resources it now throws away. By 2012 one-half and perhaps two-thirds of these resources could be recycled or reused. Ultimately perhaps 80% could be recycled and reused. Such a shift could be accomplished through the following measures:

- Enact a national beverage container deposit law.

- Include waste disposal costs in the price of all items and ban disposable plastic items.

- Encourage recycling of waste oil, tires, and CFCs used as coolants for refrigerators and air conditioners.

- Provide federal and state subsidies for secondary-materials industries.

- Decrease subsidies for primary-materials industries.

- Guarantee a large market for recycled items and stimulate the recycling industry by encouraging federal, state, and local governments to require the highest feasible percentage of recycled materials in all products they purchase.

- Use advertising and education to discourage the throwaway mentality.

- Encourage or require consumers to sort household waste for recycling instead of disposal in landfills.

In addition to being economically motivated, people must be educated to understand the need for and the value of recycling. From kindergarten on, children should be taught to call trash cans and garbage dumpsters *resource containers*. Schools can be collection points for recycled materials as they were during World War II. Profits from school and university recycling centers run by students could be used to fund school activities. Students should also take field trips to recycling centers to see how the resources they collect are put back into use.

Reusable Containers   Reuse involves using the same product again and again in its original form. An example is glass beverage bottles that can be collected, washed, and refilled by bottling companies. Until 1975 most beverage containers in the United States were refillable glass. Today they make up only 15% of the market, with nonrefillable aluminum and plastic containers making up the rest.

Another reusable container is the metal or plastic lunch box that most workers and school children once used. Today many people carry their lunches in paper bags. In many European, Asian, and African countries shoppers carry groceries and other items they buy in their own reusable baskets or small carts.

Reuse extends resource supplies and reduces energy use and pollution even more than recycling. Refillable glass bottles are the most energy-efficient beverage container on the market. Three times more energy is needed to crush and remelt a glass bottle to make a new one than to clean and refill it. Cleaning and refilling a bottle also takes much less energy than melting a used aluminum can and making a new one.

If reusable glass bottles replaced the 80 billion throwaway beverage cans produced annually in the United States, enough energy would be saved to supply the annual electricity needs of 13 million people. Denmark has led the way by banning all nonreusable beverage containers.

Reuse is much easier if containers for products that can be packaged in reusable glass are available in only a few sizes. In Norway and Denmark less than 20 different reusable containers for beer and soft drinks are allowed on the market. We can also use reusable cloth diapers instead of disposable ones.

The Low-Waste Society: Beyond Recycling and Reuse
High- and low-technology resource recovery are output approaches—they deal with solid waste already produced. They can be coupled with input approaches, designed to produce less solid waste. Reducing unnecessary waste of nonrenewable mineral resources can extend supplies even more dramatically than recycling and reuse. Reducing waste also saves energy and reduces the environmental impacts of extracting, processing, and using resources (Figure 18-12). Table 18-2 compares the throwaway resource system of the United States, a resource recovery and recycling system, and a sustainable-earth, or low-waste, resource system.

Manufacturers can conserve resources by using less material per product. Smaller and lighter cars, for example, save nonfuel mineral resources as well as energy. Solid-state electronic devices and microwave transmissions have greatly reduced materials requirements. Making a transistor, for example, requires about one-millionth the material needed to make the vacuum tube it replaces. Optical fibers drastically reduce the demand for copper wire in electrical transmission lines.

Another low-waste approach is to make products that last longer. The economies of the United States and most industrial countries are built on the principle of planned obsolescence. Product lives are designed to be much shorter than they could be so that people will buy more things to stimulate the economy and raise short-term profits. Many consumers can empathize with Willy Loman, the main character in Arthur Miller's play *Death of a Salesman:* "Once in my life I would like to own something outright before it's broken! I'm always in a race with the junkyard."

Products should also be easy to repair. Today many items are intentionally designed to make repair impossible or too expensive. Manufacturers should adopt the principle of modular design, which allows circuits in computers and other electronic devices to be easily and quickly replaced without replacing the entire item.

Table 18-2 Three Systems for Handling Discarded Materials

Item	High Waste Throwaway System	Moderate Waste Resource Recovery and Recycling System	Low-Waste Sustainable Earth System
Glass bottles	Dump or bury	Grind and remelt; remanufacture; convert to building materials	Ban all nonreturnable bottles; reuse (not remelt and recycle) bottles
Bimetallic "tin" cans	Dump or bury	Sort, remelt	Limit or ban production; use returnable bottles
Aluminum cans	Dump or bury	Sort, remelt	Limit or ban production; use returnable bottles
Cars	Dump	Sort; remelt	Sort, remelt; tax car lasting less than 15 years, weighing more than 1,800 pounds, and getting less than 35 miles per gallon
Metal objects	Dump or bury	Sort, remelt	Sort, remelt; tax items lasting less than 10 years
Tires	Dump, burn, or bury	Grind and revulcanize or use in road construction; incinerate to generate heat and electricity	Recap usable tires; tax all tires not usable for at least 80,000 miles; recycle to make new tires
Paper	Dump, burn, or bury	Incinerate to generate heat or electricity	Compost or recycle; tax all throwaway items; eliminate overpackaging
Plastics	Dump, burn, or bury	Incinerate to generate heat or electricity	Limit production; use returnable glass bottles instead of plastic containers; tax throwaway items and packaging
Yard wastes	Dump, burn, or bury	Incinerate to generate heat or electricity	Compost; return to soil as fertilizer; use as animal feed

We also need to develop remanufacturing industries that would disassemble, repair or improve, and reassemble used and broken items. New products should be designed to make such remanufacturing easy and affordable.

Some people argue that a shift away from a production-disposal, high-waste society to a service-repair, low-waste society would cause a loss of jobs and an economic decline. This is not true. When a society shifts to automated, machine-intensive production, some factory workers and others lose their jobs. However, studies have shown that this is more than offset by the increase in profits and jobs in labor-intensive service, repair, and recycling businesses.

Individual Action   We all have an important role to play in conserving matter resources. We can support programs that reduce waste production and that treat trash and scrap materials as resources to be recycled and reused. We can push for recycling programs in our communities and schools.

We can produce less waste by not using disposable products when other alternatives are available. We can ask store managers to increase the use of reusable containers. We can choose items that have the least packaging or no packaging. We can carry small loads of groceries and other items in our own reusable baskets and carts like those used in many parts of the world. BYOB (bring your own bag) is a way to save resources and to help protect the earth.

We can buy fast food only in wrappers and containers that are biodegradable or recyclable. We can buy beverages in reusable glass bottles instead of metal and plastic containers, and we should explain to store managers why we are doing this. Best of all, we can buy only things that we need and that last as long as possible.

We can support efforts to ban nondegradable or slowly degradable plastic grocery bags, garbage bags, and plastic packaging for all items. Suffolk County on New York's Long Island has banned plastic grocery bags unless they are degradable. Florida and 14 other states are considering such measures. What is your state doing?

We owe our children, our children's children, and the other species that live on this planet with us a better environmental future. Each of our acts—no matter how small—that helps sustain rather than destroy the earth contributes to this goal.

Solid wastes are only raw materials we're too stupid to use.

Arthur C. Clarke

DISCUSSION TOPICS

1. So far only about 0.3% of the land area of the United States has been surface-mined. Why then should we be concerned about the environmental impact from increasing surface mining?

2. Do you believe that the United States is an overdeveloped country that uses and unnecessarily wastes too many of the world's resources relative to its population size? Explain.

3. Debate each of the following propositions:
   a. The competitive free market will control the supply and demand of mineral resources.
   b. New discoveries will provide all the raw materials we need.
   c. The ocean will supply all the mineral resources we need.
   d. We will not run out of key mineral resources because we can always mine lower-grade deposits.
   e. When a mineral resource becomes scarce, we can always find a substitute.
   f. When a nonrenewable resource becomes scarce, all we have to do is recycle it.

4. Use the second law of energy (thermodynamics) to show why the following options are usually not profitable:
   a. extracting most minerals dissolved in seawater
   b. recycling minerals that are widely dispersed
   c. mining increasingly lower-grade deposits of minerals
   d. using inexhaustible solar energy to mine minerals
   e. continuing to mine, use, and recycle minerals at increasing rates

5. Explain why you support or oppose the following:
   a. eliminating all tax breaks and depletion allowances for extraction of virgin resources by mining industries
   b. passing a national beverage container deposit law
   c. requiring that all beverage containers be reusable

6. Why is it difficult to get accurate estimates of mineral resource supplies?

7. What is the difference between reserves and resources?

8. How is solid waste collected and disposed of in your community? Is the groundwater near any sanitary landfills in your community monitored for contamination?

9. Keep a list for a week of the solid waste materials you dispose of. What percentage is composed of materials that could be recycled, reused, or burned as a source of energy?

10. Would you favor requiring all households and businesses to sort recyclable materials for curbside pickup in separate containers? Explain.

11. Determine whether (a) your college and your city have recycling programs; (b) your college sells soft drinks in throwaway cans or bottles; and (c) your state has, or is contemplating, a law requiring deposits on all beverage containers.

FURTHER READINGS

Borgese, Elisabeth Mann. 1985. *The Mines of Neptune: Minerals and Metals from the Sea*. New York: Abrams.

Clark, Joel P., and Frank R. Field, III. 1985. "How Critical Are Critical Materials?" *Technology Review*, Aug./Sept., 38–46.

Council on Economics and National Security. 1981. *Strategic Minerals: A Resource Crisis*. Washington, D.C.: Council on Economics and National Security.

Dorr, Ann. 1984. *Minerals—Foundations of Society*. Montgomery County, Md.: League of Women Voters of Montgomery County Maryland.

Environmental Protection Agency. 1989. *Solid Waste Disposal in the United States*. Washington, D.C.: Government Printing Office.

Gordon, Robert B., et al. 1988. *World Mineral Exploration: Trends and Issues*. Washington, D.C.: Resources for the Future.

Hershowitz, Allen, and Eugene Salermi. 1987. *Garbage Management in Japan*. New York: INFORM.

Huls, Jon, and Neil Seldman. 1985. *Waste to Wealth*. Washington, D.C.: Institute for Local Self-Reliance.

Husingh, Donald, et al. 1986. *Proven Profits from Pollution Prevention*. Washington, D.C.: Institute for Local Self-Reliance.

Leontief, Wassily, et al. 1983. *The Future of Nonfuel Minerals in the U.S. and World Economy: 1980–2030*. Lexington, Mass.: Lexington (Heath).

Neal, Homer A., and J. R. Schubel. 1987. *Solid Waste Management and the Environment: The Mounting Garbage and Trash Crisis*. Englewood Cliffs, N.J.: Prentice-Hall.

Office of Technology Assessment. 1985. *Strategic Materials: Technologies to Reduce U.S. Import Vulnerability*. Washington, D.C.: Government Printing Office.

Pollack, Cynthia. 1987. *Mining Urban Wastes: The Potential for Recycling*. Washington, D.C.: Worldwatch Institute.

Purcell, Arthur H. 1980. *The Waste Watchers: A Citizen's Handbook for Conserving Energy and Resources*. Garden City, N.Y.: Anchor Press/Doubleday.

Robinson, William D., ed. 1986. *The Solid Waste Handbook*. New York: John Wiley.

Underwood, Joanna D., and Allen Hershkowitz. 1989. *Facts About U.S. Garbage Management: Problems and Practices*. New York: INFORM.

U.S. Bureau of Mines. 1983. *The Domestic Supply of Critical Minerals*. Washington, D.C.: Government Printing Office.

Westing, Arthur H. 1986. *Global Resources and International Conflict*. New York: Oxford University Press.

CHAPTER 19

Nonrenewable Energy Resources:
Fossil Fuels, Geothermal Energy,
and Nuclear Energy

General Questions and Issues

1. How can we evaluate present and future energy alternatives?

2. What are the uses, advantages, and disadvantages of oil and natural gas as energy resources?

3. What are the uses, advantages, and disadvantages of coal as an energy resource?

4. What are the uses, advantages, and disadvantages of geothermal energy as an energy resource?

5. What are the advantages and disadvantages of using conventional nuclear fission, breeder nuclear fission, and nuclear fusion to produce electricity?

We are an interdependent world and if we ever needed a lesson in that, we got it in the oil crisis of the 1970s.

Robert S. McNamara

Useful, high-quality energy is the lifeblood of ecosystems and human societies. The flow of energy through the ecosphere connects all forms of life (Figure 5-2, p. 94). The types and amounts of energy we use determine the economic and environmental health of individuals, countries, and the world.

About 99% of the energy we and other living organisms use comes from the sun and costs us nothing. As we have shifted from hunting-and-gathering societies to agricultural societies to industrialized societies, creative people have found ways to supplement this input of solar energy.

These supplemental energy resources now supply 1% of the energy we use. They have dramatically increased the average amount of energy people in industrialized societies use (Figure 2-3, p. 31). Supplemental energy resources—mostly oil, coal, and natural gas—have supported most of the world's economic growth, especially since 1950. Their use has also greatly increased pollution and environmental degradation.

Most analysts agree that the era of cheap oil is coming to an end. This means we must find substitutes for the oil that now supplies one-third of the world's supplemental energy (40% in the United States and 55% in Japan) and 90% of the energy we use for transportation.

Which supplemental energy alternatives should we use to meet future energy needs? Some say burn more coal and synthetic liquid and gaseous fuels made from coal. Some believe natural gas is the answer. Some think nuclear power is the answer (see Guest Essay on p. 507). Others believe that a combination of energy conservation and increased energy from the sun, wind, flowing water, biomass, and heat from the earth's core (geothermal energy) is the solution (see Guest Essay on p. 509). Each of these energy choices has certain advantages and disadvantages, as discussed in this and the next chapter.

19-1 EVALUATING ENERGY RESOURCES

Experience has shown that it takes about 50 years to phase in new supplemental energy resources on a large scale (Figure 19-1). In deciding which combination of energy alternatives we should use to supplement solar energy in the future, we need to plan for three time periods: the short term (1990 to 2000), the intermediate term (2000 to 2010), and the long term (2010 to 2040).

First we must decide how much we need, or want, of different kinds of energy, such as low-temperature heat, high-temperature heat, electricity, and liquid fuels for transportation. This involves deciding what type and quality of energy (Figure 4-10, p. 81) can best perform each task (see Guest Essay, p. 509). Then we decide which energy sources can meet these needs at the lowest cost and environmental impact by answering four questions about each alternative:

- How much will probably be available during the short term, intermediate term, and long-term?
- What is the estimated net useful energy yield (Figure 4-15, p. 87)?
- How much will it cost to develop, phase in, and use?
- What are its potentially harmful environmental impacts and how can they be reduced?

After answering these questions, we will be ready to develop an energy strategy.

We can use geologic analysis to project how long nonrenewable energy resources such as oil, coal, natural gas, uranium (used to fuel nuclear reactors), and some forms of geothermal energy might last (Figure 18-21, p. 469). The first and second laws of energy can help us evaluate the net useful energy we can get from each energy option (Section 4-4).

We can use economic analysis to help us decide which energy choices are the most cost-effective so that we can make wise use of our limited financial capital (section 3-5). Ecology and environmental science can help us evaluate the environmental impacts of each energy alternative. This is crucial because most of the world's air pollution, water pollution, and land disruption comes from mining, processing, and using fossil fuels (Figure 18-12, p. 463). For example, nearly 80% of all U.S. air pollution is caused by burning fossil fuels in cars, furnaces, industries, and power plants.

Politics also plays a major role in our energy choices. The political influence of energy companies and of individuals help determine how tax dollars are allocated to subsidize the development and use of various energy resources. The choices we make as individuals about the types and amounts of energy we consume are political and economic acts that help shape national energy policy as well as our own economic well-being.

In the United States and most MDCs, government subsidies are used to promote the development and use of fossil fuels and nuclear power. Some people support this approach, others do not. Because we have limited funds and little time to develop and phase in replacements for oil, making the wrong choices could lead to economic and environmental chaos.

Ethics should be the bedrock for making national and individual energy decisions (Section 3-6). The most important question decision makers should ask is What energy choices will do the most to sustain the earth

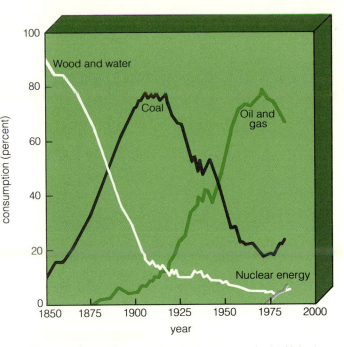

Figure 19-1 Shifts in use of energy resources in the United States since 1850. Shifts from wood to coal and then from coal to oil and natural gas have each taken about 50 years. (Data from U.S. Department of Energy)

for us, for future generations, and for the other species living on this planet? In choosing a lifestyle, each person should ask: How can I live in a way that sustains rather than degrades the earth's life-support systems?

Despite their importance, these ethical questions are rarely considered by government officials, energy company executives, and most people. Changing this situation is probably the most important and difficult challenge we face.

19-2 OIL AND NATURAL GAS

Conventional Crude Oil **Petroleum**, or **crude oil**, is a gooey liquid consisting mostly of hydrocarbon compounds and small amounts of compounds containing oxygen, sulfur, and nitrogen. Crude oil and natural gas deposits are often trapped together deep within the earth's crust on land (Figure 19-2) and beneath the sea floor.

The most valued petroleum, known as light or sweet crude, contains few sulfur impurities and large amounts of components that can be easily refined into gasoline. The lower the sulfur content of oil, the less sulfur dioxide emitted into the atmosphere when the oil is burned. The least valued petroleum is heavy or sour crude. It has higher levels of sulfur impurities and is more difficult and more costly to refine into gasoline than sweet crude.

Figure 19-2 Oil and natural gas are usually found together beneath a dome of impermeable cap rock.

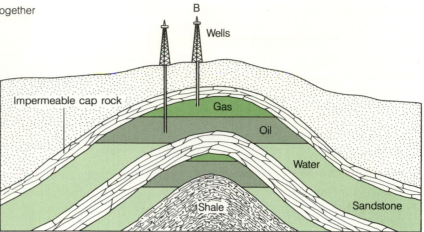

If there is enough pressure from water and natural gas under the dome of rock, some of the crude oil is pushed to the surface when a well is drilled. Such wells, called gushers, are rare. **Primary oil recovery** involves pumping out the oil that flows by gravity into the bottom of the well. Thicker, slowly flowing heavy oil is not removed.

After the flowing oil has been removed, water can be injected into adjacent wells to force some of the remaining thicker crude oil into the central well and push it to the surface. This is known as **secondary oil recovery**. Usually primary and secondary recovery remove only one-third of the crude oil in a well.

For each barrel removed by primary and secondary recovery, two barrels of heavy oil are left in a typical well. As oil prices rise, it may become economical to remove about 10% of the heavy oil by **enhanced oil recovery**. Steam or carbon dioxide can be pumped into the well to soften the heavy oil so that it can be pumped to the surface.

The problem is that enhanced oil recovery is expensive. The net useful energy yield is low because we have to use the energy equivalent of one-third of a barrel of oil to soften and pump each barrel of heavy oil to the surface. Additional energy is needed to increase the flow rate and to remove sulfur and nitrogen impurities before the heavy oil can be pumped through a pipeline to an oil refinery. Recoverable heavy oil from known U.S. crude oil reserves could supply U.S. oil needs for only about seven years at current usage rates.

Once it is removed from a well, most crude oil is sent by pipeline to a refinery. There it is heated and distilled to separate it into gasoline, heating oil, diesel oil, asphalt, and other components. Because these components boil at different temperatures, they are removed at different levels of giant distillation columns (Figure 19-3).

Some components, called **petrochemicals**, are used as raw materials in industrial chemicals, fertilizers,

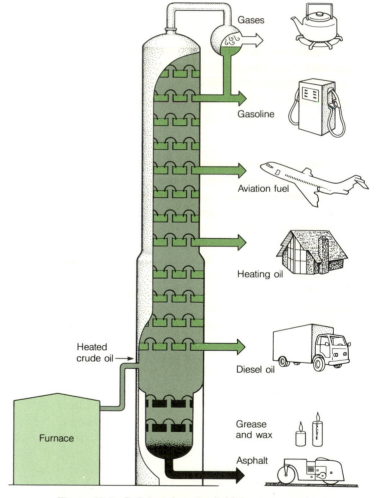

Figure 19-3 Refining of crude oil. Major components are removed at various levels, depending on their boiling points, in a giant distillation column.

pesticides, plastics, synthetic fibers, paints, medicines, and many other products. About 3% of the crude oil extracted throughout the world is used in this way. Thus, the prices of many items we use go up after crude oil prices rise.

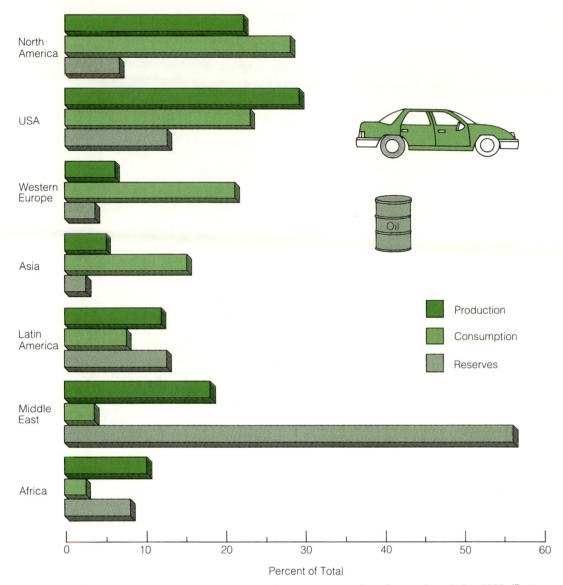

Figure 19-4 Comparison of oil consumption, production, and reserves in various regions during 1985. (Data from British Petroleum Company)

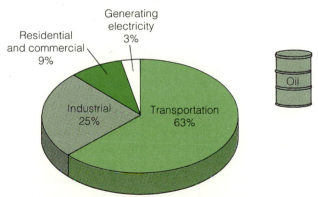

Figure 19-5 How oil was used in the United States in 1986. (Data from U.S. Department of Energy)

How Long Will Supplies of Conventional Crude Oil Last?

Oil is one of the world's most unevenly distributed resources, with 95% of the proven reserves found in only 20 countries. Almost two-thirds of the world's proven oil reserves are in just five countries: Saudi Arabia, Kuwait, Iran, Iraq, and the United Arab Emirates. OPEC countries have 67% of these reserves, with Saudi Arabia having 25%. The Middle East also contains most of the world's undiscovered oil. This explains why OPEC is expected to have long-term control over world oil supplies and prices.

There are also imbalances between oil reserves and where oil is extracted and consumed (Figure 19-4). The Soviet Union is presently the world's largest oil extractor, with an annual output triple that of Saudi Arabia. The United States has less than 3% of the world's oil reserves but uses nearly 30% of the oil extracted each year. Transportation uses almost two-thirds of the 16 billion barrels of oil consumed each day in the United States (Figure 19-5).

Although the United States is the world's second largest oil extractor, it has imported oil since 1950 to

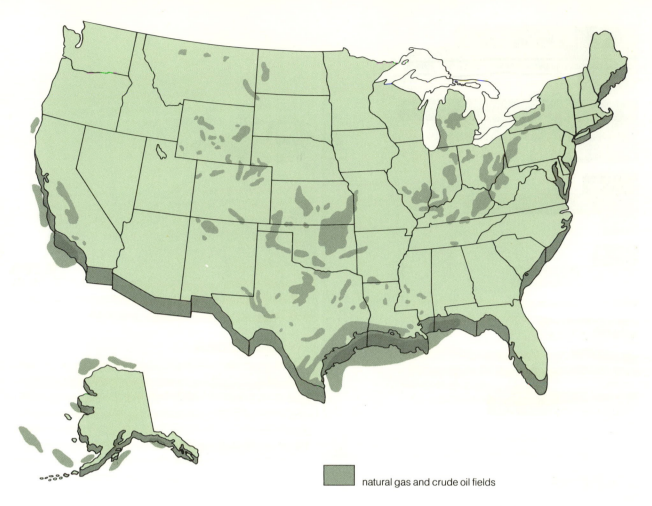

Figure 19-6 Major deposits of natural gas and crude oil in the United States. (Source: Council on Environmental Quality)

natural gas and crude oil fields

help meet demand. Most oil deposits in the Middle East are large and cheap to extract; most in the United States are small and more expensive to tap. Therefore, it has generally been cheaper for the United States to buy oil from other countries than to extract it from its own deposits (Figure 1-8, p. 16). But U.S. military intervention in the Persian Gulf since 1985 means that U.S. oil imports cost $495 a barrel when the military costs are included.

Figure 19-6 shows the locations of the major crude oil and natural gas fields in the United States. Most are in Texas, Louisiana, and Oklahoma and in the continental shelf of the Pacific, Gulf, and Alaskan coasts. U.S. oil extraction has declined steadily since 1970 despite greatly increased exploration and test drilling.

Experts disagree over how long the world's identified and unidentified crude oil resources will last. At present consumption rates, world crude oil reserves will be economically depleted in 33 years and U.S. reserves in 28 years. Cornucopians argue that higher prices will stimulate the discovery and extraction of large new crude oil resources. They also believe we

can extract and upgrade heavy oils from oil shale, tar sands, and enhanced recovery from existing wells.

Some believe that the earth's mantle may contain 100 times more oil than usually thought. But such deposits, if they exist, lie six miles or more below the earth's surface—about twice the depth of today's deepest wells. New and expensive drilling technology would have to be developed to find and tap these deposits. Most geologists do not believe these deposits exist. But if they do, and if they could be tapped at an affordable price compared to other energy options, they would meet human oil needs for centuries.

Neo-Malthusians argue that cornucopians misunderstand the arithmetic and consequences of exponential growth in the use of any nonrenewable resource. Consider the following facts about the world's exponential growth in oil use, assuming that we continue to use crude oil at the current rate:

- Saudi Arabia, with the world's largest known crude oil reserves, could supply all the world's oil needs for only ten years if it were the world's only source.

Figure 19-7 Sample of oil shale rock and the shale oil extracted from it. Major oil shale projects have now been canceled in the United States because of excessive cost.

- Mexico, with the world's sixth largest crude oil reserves, could supply the world's needs for only about three years.

- The estimated crude oil reserves under Alaska's North Slope—the largest deposit ever found in North America—would meet world demand for only six months or U.S. demand for three years.

- Cornucopians who believe that new discoveries will solve world oil supply problems must figure out how to discover the equivalent of a new Saudi Arabian deposit *every ten years* just to keep on using oil at the current rate.

The ultimately recoverable supply of crude oil is estimated to be three times today's proven reserves. Suppose all this new oil is found and developed—which most oil experts consider unlikely—and sold at a price of $50 to $95 a barrel, compared to the 1988 price of about $18 a barrel. About 80% of this oil would be depleted by the year 2073 at the current usage rate and by 2037 if oil use increased 2% a year.

We can see why most experts expect little of the world's affordable crude oil to be left by the 2059 bicentennial of the world's first oil well. Oil company geologists and executives have known this for a long time; thus, most oil companies have become diversified energy companies. To keep making money after oil runs out, these international companies now own much of the world's natural gas, coal, and uranium reserves and have bought many of the companies producing solar collectors and solar cells.

Advantages and Disadvantages of Oil Oil has several important advantages that explain why it is so widely used. It has been and still is fairly cheap, it can easily be transported within and between countries, and it has a high net useful energy yield. It is also a versatile fuel that can be burned to propel vehicles, heat buildings and water, and supply high-tempera-

ture heat for industrial processes and electricity production.

Oil also has some disadvantages. Its burning releases carbon dioxide gas, which could alter global climate, and other air pollutants such as sulfur oxides and nitrogen oxides, which damage people, crops, trees, fish, and other wild species. Oil spills and drilling muds (see photo at front of book) cause water pollution, and the brine solution injected into oil wells can contaminate groundwater. The big disadvantage of oil is that affordable supplies will be depleted within 40 to 80 years. As countries are forced to drill for deeper, more remote deposits, the net useful energy yield of oil will drop and its price will rise sharply.

Heavy Oils from Oil Shale and Tar Sands Oil shale is a fine-grained sedimentary rock (Figure 19-7) that contains varying amounts of a solid, waxy mixture of hydrocarbon compounds called **kerogen**. After being removed by surface or subsurface mining, shale rock is crushed and heated to a high temperature in a large retort to vaporize the solid kerogen (Figure 19-8). The kerogen vapor is condensed, forming a slow-flowing, dark brown, heavy oil called **shale oil**. Before shale oil can be sent by pipeline to a refinery, it must be processed to increase its flow rate and heat content and to remove sulfur, nitrogen, and other impurities.

The world's largest known deposits of oil shale are in Colorado, Utah, and Wyoming. Because 80% of this rock is below public lands, energy companies must get leases from the federal government to exploit these resources. It is estimated that the potentially recoverable heavy oil from oil shale deposits in the United States could meet the country's crude oil demand for 41 years if consumption remains at the current level, and for 32 years if consumption rises 2% a year. Large oil shale deposits are also found in Canada, China, and the Soviet Union.

Environmental problems may limit shale oil production. Shale oil processing requires large amounts of water, which is scarce in the semiarid areas where the richest deposits are found. When the oil is processed and burned, carbon dioxide is released into the atmosphere, along with nitrogen oxides and sulfur dioxide. There would be massive land disruption from the mining and disposal of large volumes of shale rock, which breaks up and expands when heated. Various salts, cancer-causing substances, and toxic metal compounds can be leached from the processed shale rock into nearby water supplies.

One way to avoid some of these environmental problems is to extract oil from shale underground—known as *in situ* (in-place) *processing* (Figure 19-8). But this method is too expensive with present technology and produces more sulfur dioxide emissions than surface processing.

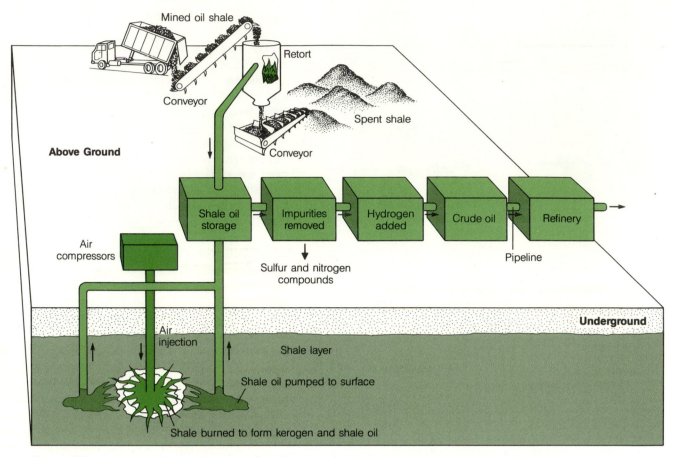

Figure 19-8 Aboveground and underground (in situ) methods for producing synthetic crude oil from oil shale.

The net useful energy yield of shale oil is much lower than that of conventional oil because the energy equivalent of one-third of a barrel of conventional crude oil is needed to produce one barrel of shale oil (Figure 4-15, p. 87). More energy is needed to upgrade and refine shale oil. In 1987, scientists at Lawrence Livermore Laboratory developed a process they claim might produce shale oil for $25 a barrel. Other analysts believe that shale oil will always be too expensive because it takes so much energy to extract, process, and refine it. In 1987 conservationists were outraged when the Reagan administration leased 82,000 acres of public grazing and recreation land in Colorado to an oil-shale consortium for a mere $2.50 an acre.

Tar sand (or oil sand) is a deposit of a mixture of fine clay, sand, water, and varying amounts of **bitumen**, a gooey, black, high-sulfur heavy oil. Tar sand is usually removed by surface mining and heated with steam at high pressure to make the bitumen fluid enough to float to the top. The bitumen is removed and then purified and chemically upgraded into synthetic crude oil suitable for refining into a variety of products, including gasoline (Figure 19-9). So far it is not technically or economically feasible to remove deeper deposits of tar sand by underground mining or to remove bitumen by in situ extraction.

The world's largest known deposits of tar sands lie in a cold, desolate area in northern Alberta, Canada. Oil in these deposits is estimated to exceed the proven oil reserves of Saudi Arabia. Other large deposits are in Venezuela, Colombia, and the Soviet Union. Smaller deposits exist in the United States, mostly in Utah. If developed, they would supply all U.S. oil needs at the current usage rate for only about three months at a price of $48 to $62 a barrel.

Since 1985 two plants have been supplying about 11% to 12% of Canada's oil demand by extracting and processing heavy oil from tar sands at a cost of $12 to $15 a barrel—below the average world oil price between 1986 and 1988. By 2000 tar sands should be supplying 20% of Canada's oil demand. Economically recoverable deposits of heavy oil from tar sands can supply all of Canada's projected oil needs for about 33 years at the current consumption rate. These deposits are an important source of oil for Canada, but they would meet the world's present oil needs for only about 2 years.

Producing synthetic crude oil from tar sands has several disadvantages. The net useful energy yield is low because it takes the energy equivalent of one-third of a barrel of conventional oil to extract and process one barrel of bitumen. Additional energy is needed

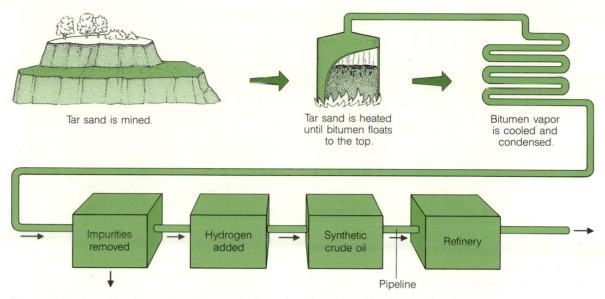

Tar sand is mined.

Tar sand is heated until bitumen floats to the top.

Bitumen vapor is cooled and condensed.

Impurities removed

Hydrogen added

Synthetic crude oil

Refinery

Pipeline

Figure 19-9 Generalized summary of how synthetic crude oil is produced from tar sand.

to remove sulfur impurities and to upgrade the bitumen to synthetic crude oil before it can be sent to an oil refinery. Other problems include the need for large quantities of water for processing and the release of air and water pollutants. Upgrading bitumen to synthetic crude oil releases sulfur dioxide, hydrogen sulfide, and particulates of toxic metals such as lead, chromium, nickel and cadmium.

The two Canadian tar sand processing plants have repeatedly exceeded emissions limits for these pollutants. As a result, the average level of acid deposition in Alberta is twice the Canadian government's estimated safe limit. Environmentalists charge that synthetic crude oil is produced from tar sand at a low price only because these plants are not required to control air pollution emissions. The plants have also created huge ponds filled with mine tailings. The water in these waste disposal ponds is so toxic that scarecrows must be used to keep birds away. Cleaning up these toxic waste dump sites is another external cost not included in the price of crude oil produced from Canadian tar sand.

Conventional Natural Gas In its underground gaseous state, **natural gas** is a mixture of 50% to 90% methane gas and smaller amounts of heavier gaseous hydrocarbon compounds such as propane and butane. Conventional natural gas lies above deposits of crude oil (Figure 19-2). Unconventional natural gas is found by itself in other underground deposits.

When a natural gas deposit is tapped, propane and butane gases are liquefied and removed as **liquefied petroleum gas (LPG)**. LPG is stored in pressurized tanks for use mostly in rural areas not served by natural gas pipelines. The rest of the gas (mostly methane) in the deposit is dried, cleaned of hydrogen sulfide and other impurities, and pumped into pressurized pipelines for distribution.

Natural gas is by far the largest source of heat for residential and commercial buildings in the United States. New natural gas furnaces have energy efficiencies of 90% to 95%. It is also used for drying in many industrial processes. In 1987 about 15% of the electricity generated in the United States was produced by burning natural gas. About 5% of the natural gas used in the United States is imported, mostly by pipeline from Canada.

At a very low temperature natural gas can be converted to **liquefied natural gas (LNG)**. This liquid form of natural gas can then be shipped to other countries in refrigerated tanker ships.

Most U.S. reserves of natural gas are located with the country's deposits of crude oil (Figure 19-6). America's largest known deposits of natural gas lie in Alaska's Prudhoe Bay, thousands of miles from natural gas consumers in the lower 48 states.

How Long Will Natural Gas Supplies Last? Conventional supplies of natural gas are expected to last longer than those of crude oil. Between 1973 and 1984 the world's proven reserves of natural gas doubled, and they now have about the same energy content as the world's petroleum reserves.

Much of this increase came from large discoveries in the Soviet Union, which has 40% of the world's proven reserves and is the world's largest natural gas extractor. Other countries with large proven natural gas reserves are Iran (14%), the United States (6%), Quatar (4%), Algeria (4%), Saudi Arabia (3%), and Nigeria (3%). Geologists expect to find more natural gas deposits, especially in LDCs that have not been widely explored for this resource.

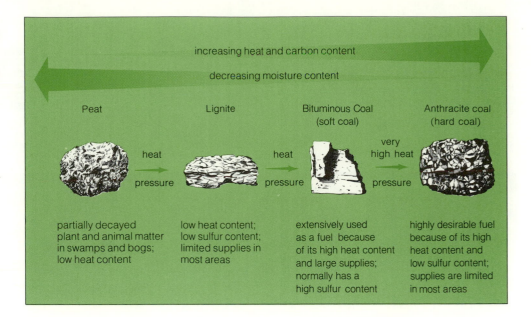

Figure 19-10 Stages in the formation of coal over millions of years. Peat is a humus soil material. Lignite and bituminous coal are sedimentary rocks, and anthracite is a metamorphic rock.

increasing heat and carbon content

decreasing moisture content

Peat	Lignite	Bituminous Coal (soft coal)	Anthracite coal (hard coal)
heat / pressure	heat / pressure	very high heat / pressure	
partially decayed plant and animal matter in swamps and bogs; low heat content	low heat content; low sulfur content; limited supplies in most areas	extensively used as a fuel because of its high heat content and large supplies; normally has a high sulfur content	highly desirable fuel because of its high heat content and low sulfur content; supplies are limited in most areas

U.S. extraction of natural gas has dropped steadily since 1973, despite increased exploration. The known reserves in the United States are projected to last only until 1993 at the current usage rate, but more domestic supplies are expected to be found. However, in 1988 the U.S. Geological Survey reduced its estimate of undiscovered natural gas in the United States by 54% because of unsuccessful exploratory drilling.

The world's identified reserves of natural gas are projected to last until 2045 at the current usage rate and until 2022 if consumption rises 2% a year. Estimated unidentified supplies available at higher prices would last about 200 years at the current rate and 80 years if usage rose 2% a year.

Unconventional Sources of Natural Gas As the price of natural gas from conventional sources rises, it may become economical to drill deeper into the earth and get natural gas from unconventional sources. Such sources include deep underground deposits of tight sands and geopressurized zones that contain natural gas dissolved in hot water. Some natural gas is also found in coal seams and deposits of Devonian shale rock.

Some energy experts doubt that natural gas in such deposits can be recovered at affordable prices. However, if new mining technology and higher prices should make it possible to tap these deposits, they would supply enough natural gas to meet the projected need for several hundred to a thousand years. Natural gas would probably become the most widely used fuel for space heating, industrial processes, producing electricity, and transportation. It would serve as a transition energy resource to avoid economic disruption as oil is phased out and other new energy resources are developed and phased in.

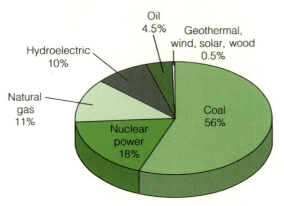

Figure 19-11 Electricity generation methods in the United States in 1987. (Data from U.S. Department of Energy)

Advantages and Disadvantages of Natural Gas
Natural gas burns hotter and produces less air pollution than any fossil fuel. Its burning, however, produces carbon dioxide, although the amount per unit of energy produced is lower than that of other fossil fuels. So far the price of natural gas has been low. It is a versatile fuel, is transported easily over land by pipeline, and has a high net useful energy yield (Figure 4-15, p. 87).

The major problem with natural gas is that it must be converted to liquid natural gas before it can be shipped by tanker from one country to another. Shipping LNG in refrigerated tankers is expensive and dangerous. Massive explosions could kill many people and cause much damage in urban areas near LNG loading and unloading facilities. Conversion of natural gas to LNG also reduces the net useful energy yield by one-fourth.

If large amounts of natural gas can be extracted from unconventional sources at affordable prices, it

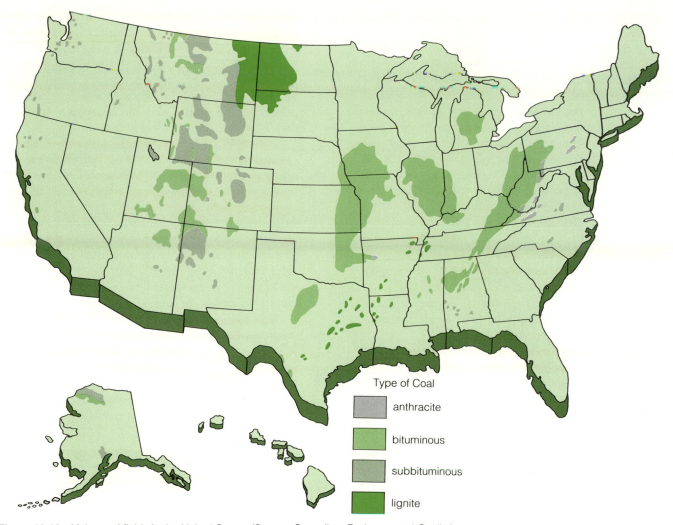

Figure 19-12 Major coal fields in the United States. (Source: Council on Environmental Quality)

Type of Coal

anthracite

bituminous

subbituminous

lignite

will be a key option for making an economically and environmentally acceptable, orderly transition to solar and other energy options as oil is phased out over the next 50 years.

19-3 COAL

Types and Distribution Coal is a solid formed in several stages as the remains of plants are subjected to intense heat and pressure over millions of years. It consists mostly of carbon with varying amounts of water and small amounts of nitrogen and sulfur. Four types of coal are formed at different stages: peat, lignite, bituminous coal, and anthracite (Figure 19-10). The last three types are the most widely used.

About 60% of the coal extracted in the world and 70% in the United States is burned in boilers to produce steam to generate electrical power. Much of the

rest is converted to coke used to make steel. Coal is burned to supply 56% of the electricity generated in the United States (Figure 19-11).

Coal is the world's most abundant fossil fuel. About 68% of the world's proven coal reserves and 85% of the estimated undiscovered coal deposits are located in three countries: the United States, the USSR, and China. These countries extract 60% of the coal used today. China, which recently passed the USSR as the world's largest coal extractor, plans to double its coal consumption between 1987 and 2000.

The major U.S. coalfields are located primarily in 17 states (Figure 19-12). Anthracite, the most desirable form of coal, makes up only 2% of U.S. coal reserves. About 45% of U.S. coal reserves is high-sulfur, bituminous coal with a high fuel value. It is found in the East, mostly in Kentucky, West Virginia, Pennsylvania, Ohio, and Illinois. In 1987 nearly two-thirds of the coal extracted came from states east of the Mississippi River. About half of this was extracted by underground mining (Figure 18-11, p. 462), and the other half by surface mining (Figure 18-8, p. 461).

About 55% of U.S. coal reserves are found west of the Mississippi River. Most of these are deposits of low-sulfur, bituminous and lignite coal. Although only one-third of the country's coal is extracted from these deposits, the output of coal in the West has increased almost eightfold since 1970. Most western coal is removed by surface mining. The problem is that these deposits are far from the heavily industrialized and populated East, where most coal is consumed.

How Long Will Supplies Last?

Identified world reserves of coal should last about 220 years at current usage and 65 years if usage rises 2% a year. The world's unidentified coal resources are projected to last about 900 years at the current rate and 149 years if usage increases 2% a year. During the 1980s world coal consumption has been growing 2.5% a year.

Identified coal reserves in the United States should last about 300 years at the current usage rate. Unidentified U.S. coal resources could extend these supplies at the current rate for perhaps 100 years, at a much higher average cost.

Advantages and Disadvantages of Solid Coal

Coal is the most abundant conventional fossil fuel in the world and in the United States. It has a high net useful energy yield for producing high-temperature heat for industrial processes and for generating electricity (Figure 4-15, p. 87). In countries with adequate coal supplies, burning solid coal is the cheapest way to produce high-temperature heat and electricity.

But using coal as an energy resource has many disadvantages. Coal mining is dangerous. Since 1900 underground mining in the United States has killed more than 100,000 miners and permanently disabled at least 1 million. At least 250,000 retired U.S. miners suffer from black lung disease, a form of emphysema caused by prolonged breathing of coal dust and other particulate matter. Coal mining in the United States is safer than in most other countries, but it could be made safer by stricter enforcement of existing laws and by enactment of tougher new laws.

Coal mining and coal use pollute and degrade the environment in several ways. Acids flushed from abandoned underground coal mines can kill fish and many other forms of aquatic life. In the United States acid mine drainage has degraded over 7,000 miles of streams—90% of them in Appalachia.

Underground coal mining can also cause subsid-

SPOTLIGHT   Surface Mining Legislation in the United States

More than 1 million acres of American land disturbed by surface mining have been abandoned by coal companies and not restored. To control such land disturbance, Congress enacted the Surface Mining Control and Reclamation Act of 1977. Among its requirements:

- Surface-mined land must be restored as closely as possible to its original contour.

- Surface mining is banned on some prime agricultural lands in the West, and farmers and ranchers can veto mining under their lands even though they do not own the mineral rights.

- Mining companies must reduce the effects of their activities on local watersheds and water quality by using the best available technology, and they must prevent acid from entering local streams and groundwater.

- Surface-mined land not reclaimed before 1977 is to be

restored with money provided by a fee on each ton of coal mined.

- States are responsible for enforcing the law except on federally owned lands.

- The Department of the Interior has enforcement power when states fail to act and on federally owned lands.

- The public has the right to observe federal mine inspections and to sue if the law is not being followed.

Many surface-mined areas have been restored as required by this law. But some coal companies found ways to get around the law. One strategy was to divide a strip mine into plots too tiny to be covered by the law and connect them by dirt roads. More than 4,000 of these "string-of-pearl" mines were dug and abandoned without reclamation before Congress closed this loophole in 1987.

Some coal companies have ignored the law and not reclaimed strip-mined land. Others have left a mess and called it reclamation.

How do they get away with such flagrant violations? For one thing, the Reagan administration cut the federal inspection and enforcement staff by 70%. Also, the Office of Surface Mining has failed to collect $200 million in fines owed by mining companies breaking the law.

Lack of money has also limited enforcement in many states. For example, in 1983 Utah state officials were carrying out fewer than half the inspections required by law. In 1988 the Sierra Club and the National Wildlife Federation sued the Department of Interior for failure to enforce the federal surface mining law in West Virginia and Kentucky. What do you think should be done?

---

ence—a depression in the earth's surface—when a mine shaft partially collapses during or after mining. In the United States over 2 million acres of land, much of it in central Appalachia, has subsided because of underground coal mining.

Surface coal mining also can have a devastating impact on land (Figure 18-9, p. 461 and Figure 18-10, p. 462). However, in some areas the disturbed land has been fully restored (Figure 18-13, p. 463) as required by law (see Spotlight on p. 490).

Without effective air pollution control devices, burning coal causes more air pollution than burning other fossil fuels. Burning converts the sulfur and nitrogen impurities in coal to sulfur dioxide and nitrogen oxides. About 70% of the sulfur dioxide emissions and almost one-fourth of the emissions of nitrogen oxides in the United States are produced by coal burning, mostly in electric power plants. These emissions cause much of the acid deposition that damages forests and aquatic ecosystems in the eastern United States and parts of Canada (Figure 7-19, p. 164).

Each year these and other air pollutants emitted when coal is burned kill about 5,000 people in the United States. They also cause 50,000 cases of respiratory disease and several billion dollars in property damage each year. Since 1978 federal law has reduced allowable emissions of sulfur dioxide, nitrogen oxides, and particulate matter by all new coal-burning power and industrial plants in the United States. Requiring all older coal-burning plants to meet the same standards as new plants would reduce the deaths caused by coal burning to about 500 per year. Air pollution laws in most other countries that rely on coal are weaker than those in the United States.

New ways have been developed to burn coal more cleanly and efficiently (see Spotlight below).

To environmentalists one of the most serious problems with coal is that burning it gives off more carbon dioxide per unit of energy produced than burning other

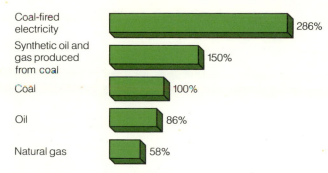

Figure 19-13 Carbon dioxide emissions per unit of energy produced by other fossil fuels as percentages of those produced by coal.

fossil fuels (Figure 19-13). This means that burning more coal to meet energy needs can accelerate the greenhouse effect (Figure 7-5, p. 152). Presently there is no effective and affordable method for preventing carbon dioxide released by fossil-fuel burning from reaching the atmosphere.

Another disadvantage of coal is that its solid form makes it difficult and expensive to transport and unsuitable as a fuel for motor vehicles. Currently most coal is transported by railroad, an expensive mode of transportation. A cheaper method is to transport coal in pipelines as a coal slurry, made by suspending powdered coal in water. But this method requires enormous amounts of water, a scarce resource in the semiarid regions where some major coal deposits are found.

Synfuels: Converting Solid Coal to Gaseous and Liquid Fuels Methods for converting solid coal to gaseous and liquid fuels, called **synfuels**, have been available for many years. **Coal gasification** (Figure 19-14) is the conversion of coal to synthetic natural gas (SNG).

Coal liquefaction is the conversion of coal to a liquid hydrocarbon fuel such as methanol or synthetic gasoline. A commercial coal liquefaction plant supplies 10% of the liquid fuel used in South Africa at a

---

SPOTLIGHT Burning Coal More Cleanly and Efficiently

A mixture of powdered coal and water can be burned more cleanly and efficiently than coal alone. Since 1986 coal-water mixtures have been burned in a few small, experimental power plants in the United States and Canada.

Another promising method for burning coal more efficiently, cleanly, and cheaply than in conventional coal boilers is **fluidized-bed combustion (FBC)** (Figure 7-28, p. 176). Crushed coal is burned on a bed of limestone suspended on a cushion of high-pressure air. Gaseous sulfur dioxide produced when the coal burns reacts with the limestone to produce solid calcium sulfate, which can be disposed of in a landfill.

FBC removes 90% to 98% of the sulfur dioxide gas produced during combustion. It also lowers emissions of nitrogen oxides and CO_2 because the pressurized air provides more oxygen for more complete combustion. FBC boilers also can burn many other fuels. Power plants can convert to FBC by modifying their conventional boilers.

Successful small-scale FBC plants have been built in Great Britain, Sweden, Finland, the Soviet Union, West Germany, and China. In the United States, commercial FBC boilers are expected to begin replacing conventional coal boilers in the mid-1990s.

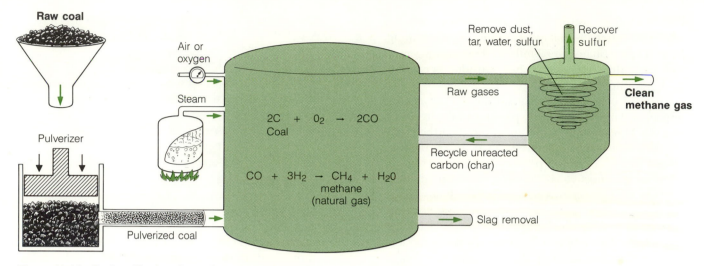

Figure 19-14 Coal gasification. Generalized view of one method for converting solid coal into synthetic natural gas (methane).

cost equal to paying $35 a barrel for oil. When two new plants are completed, the country will be able to meet half of its oil needs from this source. Engineers hope to get the cost down to $25 a barrel.

Advantages and Disadvantages of Synfuels Synfuels can be transported through a pipeline, and they burn more cleanly than solid coal. When oil becomes too scarce and expensive, most petrochemicals now produced from crude oil may be made from SNG produced from coal.

Synfuels are more versatile than solid coal. Besides being burned to produce high-temperature heat and electricity like solid coal, synfuels can be burned to heat houses and water and to propel vehicles.

But synfuels have disadvantages. A synfuel plant costs much more to build and operate than an equivalent coal-fired power plant equipped with air pollution control devices. Synfuels also have low net useful energy yields (Figure 4-15, p. 87). The widespread use of synfuels would accelerate the depletion of world coal supplies because 30% to 40% of the energy content of coal is lost in the conversion process. It would also lead to greater land disruption from surface mining because producing synfuels uses more coal per unit of energy produced than burning solid coal uses.

Producing synfuels requires huge amounts of water, and burning synfuels releases large amounts of carbon dioxide (Figure 19–13). Converting coal to SNG underground would solve or reduce some of these problems (except carbon dioxide emissions, high costs, and low net energy yields). But after years of experimentation, such in situ coal gasification is still not competitive with conventional coal mining and aboveground coal gasification.

The major factor holding back large-scale production of synfuels in the United States is their high cost compared to conventional oil and natural gas. Producing synfuels with current technology is the equivalent of buying oil at $50 to $100 a barrel. Most analysts expect synfuels to play only a minor role as an energy resource until oil prices rise sharply sometime after 2000.

19-4 GEOTHERMAL ENERGY

Nonrenewable Geothermal Energy Heat from the earth's molten core is also a source of energy. At various places in the earth's crust this **geothermal energy** is transferred over millions of years to nonrenewable or very slowly renewable underground deposits of dry steam (steam with no water droplets), wet steam (a mixture of steam and water droplets), and hot water.

If these geothermal deposits are close enough to the earth's surface, wells can be drilled to extract the dry steam, wet steam, or hot water. This thermal energy can be used for space heating and to produce electricity or high-temperature heat for industrial processes.

Currently about 20 countries are tapping geothermal deposits. This energy heats over 2 million homes in cold climates and supplies electricity for over 1.5 million homes with an output equal to that from five large coal-fired or nuclear power plants. The United States accounts for 44% of the electricity produced by geothermal power plants in 18 countries. Figure 19-15 shows that most accessible, high-temperature geothermal deposits in the United States lie in the western states, especially California and the Rocky Mountain states.

Dry-steam deposits are the preferred geothermal resource, but also the rarest. A large dry-steam well near Larderello, Italy, has been producing electricity

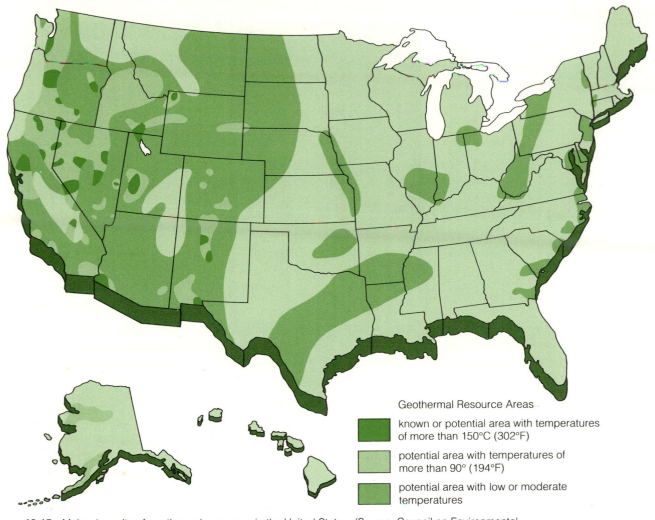

Figure 19-15 Major deposits of geothermal resources in the United States. (Source: Council on Environmental Quality)

Geothermal Resource Areas

- known or potential area with temperatures of more than 150°C (302°F)
- potential area with temperatures of more than 90° (194°F)
- potential area with low or moderate temperatures

since 1904 and is a major source of power for Italy's electric railroads. Two other major dry-steam sites are the Matsukawa field in Japan and the Geysers steam field about 90 miles north of San Francisco.

The Geysers field has been producing electricity since 1960. Currently it supplies more than 6% of northern California's electricity at less than half the cost of a new coal or nuclear plant and largely without government subsidies. This was enough to meet all the electrical needs of a city the size of San Francisco. New units can be added every 2 to 3 years (compared to 6 years for a coal plant and 12 years for a nuclear plant). By 2000 this field may supply one-fourth of California's electricity.

Underground *wet-steam deposits* are more common but harder and more expensive to convert to electricity. The world's largest wet-steam power plant is in Wairaki, New Zealand. Others operate in Mexico, Japan, El Salvador, Nicaragua, and the Soviet Union. The geothermal plants in El Salvador and Nicaragua already produce 17% of the electric power generated in Central America. Four small-scale demonstration plants built in the United States since 1980 are producing electricity at a cost equal to paying $40 a barrel for oil.

Hot-water deposits are more common than dry-steam and wet-steam deposits. Almost all the homes, buildings, and food-producing greenhouses in Reykjavik, Iceland, a city with a population of about 85,000, are heated by hot water drawn from deep geothermal deposits under the city. At 180 locations in the United States, mostly in western states, hot-water deposits have been used for years to heat homes and farm buildings and to dry crops.

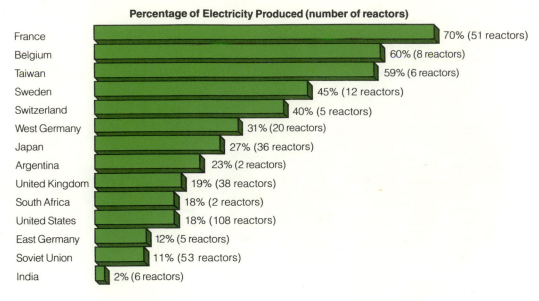

Figure 19-16 Use of nuclear fission reactors to produce electricity in various countries in 1987. (Data from Atomic Industrial Forum and International Atomic Energy Agency)

Percentage of Electricity Produced (number of reactors)

France	70% (51 reactors)
Belgium	60% (8 reactors)
Taiwan	59% (6 reactors)
Sweden	45% (12 reactors)
Switzerland	40% (5 reactors)
West Germany	31% (20 reactors)
Japan	27% (36 reactors)
Argentina	23% (2 reactors)
United Kingdom	19% (38 reactors)
South Africa	18% (2 reactors)
United States	18% (108 reactors)
East Germany	12% (5 reactors)
Soviet Union	11% (53 reactors)
India	2% (6 reactors)

The hot, salty water (brine) pumped up from such wells can also be used to produce electricity. A demonstration system went into operation in 1984 in California's Imperial Valley. The main problem is that the brine corrodes metal parts and clogs pipes. An underground system is being tested as a means to reduce corrosion and wastewater problems. It also leaves water and steam in the well for continual reheating rather than depleting the resource.

A fourth potential source of nonrenewable geothermal energy and natural gas is *geopressurized zones*. These are underground reservoirs of water at a high temperature and pressure, usually trapped deep under ocean beds of shale or clay. With present drilling technology, they would supply geothermal energy and natural gas at a cost equal to paying $30 to $45 a barrel for oil.

Advantages and Disadvantages of Nonrenewable Geothermal Energy The major advantages of nonrenewable geothermal energy include a 100- to 200-year supply of energy for areas near deposits, moderate net useful energy yields for large and easily accessible deposits, and no emissions of carbon dioxide. The cost of producing electricity in geothermal plants is about half the cost of power from new coal plants and one-fourth the cost of power from new nuclear plants.

Two limitations of nonrenewable geothermal energy are the scarcity of easily accessible deposits and our inability to use this energy to power vehicles. Without pollution control, geothermal energy production causes moderate to high air pollution from hydrogen sulfide, ammonia, and radioactive materials. It also causes moderate to high water pollution from dissolved solids (salinity) and runoff of several toxic compounds. Noise, odor, and local climate changes can also be

problems. Most experts, however, consider the environmental effects of geothermal energy to be less or no greater than those of fossil fuel and nuclear power plants.

Perpetual Geothermal Energy There are also three types of vast, potentially perpetual sources of geothermal energy. One is *molten rock* (magma) found near the earth's surface. Another is *hot dry-rock zones,* where molten rock has penetrated the earth's crust from below and heats subsurface rock to high temperatures. The third type is low- to moderate-temperature *warm-rock deposits,* useful for preheating water and geothermal heat pumps for space heating and air conditioning. According to the National Academy of Sciences, the amount of potentially recoverable energy from such deposits would meet U.S. energy needs at current consumption levels for 600 to 700 years.

The problem is developing methods to extract this energy economically. Several experimental projects are in progress, but none has been able to produce energy at a cost competitive with other energy sources.

19-5 CONVENTIONAL NONRENEWABLE NUCLEAR FISSION

A Controversial Fading Dream Originally nuclear power was envisioned as a clean, safe, and cheap source of energy. By the end of this century 1,800 nuclear power plants were supposed to supply as much as 21% of the world's energy and 25% of U.S. energy used to supplement solar energy that supplies 99% of the energy we use.

However, by 1988, after 41 years of development, only 414 commercial nuclear reactors in 33 countries

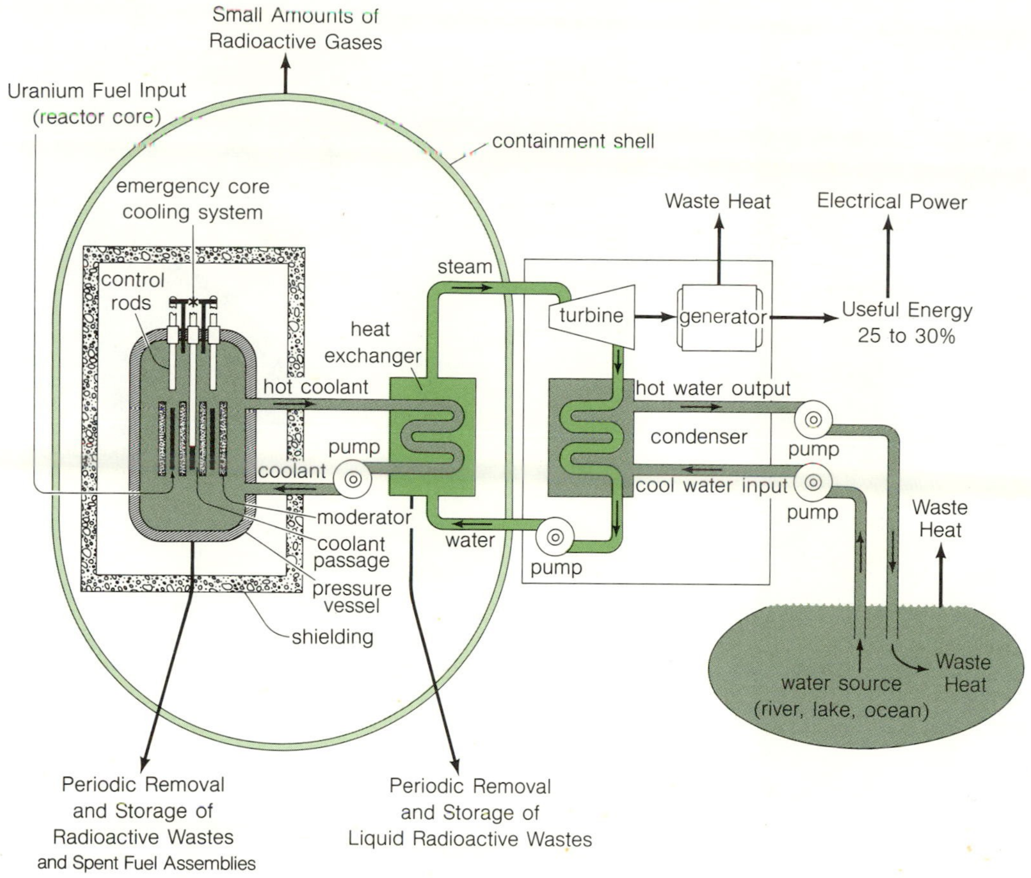

Small Amounts of
Radioactive Gases

Uranium Fuel Input
(reactor core)

containment shell

emergency core
cooling system

control
rods

steam

heat
exchanger

hot coolant

turbine

generator

Waste Heat   Electrical Power

Useful Energy
25 to 30%

hot water output

pump   coolant

condenser

pump

moderator

water

cool water input

pump

coolant
passage

pump

pressure
vessel

Waste
Heat

shielding

water source
(river, lake, ocean)

Waste
Heat

Periodic Removal
and Storage of
Radioactive Wastes
and Spent Fuel Assemblies

Periodic Removal
and Storage of
Liquid Radioactive Wastes

Figure 19-17 Light-water-moderated and -cooled nuclear power plant with a pressurized water reactor.

were producing only 16% of the world's electricity—equal to about 4.5% of the world's supplemental energy (Figure 19-16). The percentage of the world's electricity produced by nuclear power will probably drop between 1990 and 2010, as aging plants are retired.

Industrialized countries like Japan and France, which have few fossil fuel resources, believe that using nuclear power is the best way to reduce their dependence on imported oil. France plans to get 90% of its electricity from nuclear power by the early 1990s. However, both Japan and France already are producing more electricity than they can use and nuclear power cannot be used to run vehicles—the main use of oil (see Guest Essay on p. 509).

Since the Chernobyl nuclear accident in 1986 (see Spotlight on p. 498), most LDCs have scaled back or eliminated their plans to build nuclear power plants. Denmark, Norway, Australia, Greece, Luxembourg, the Netherlands, and New Zealand have decided not to build any nuclear power plants. Sweden plans to shut down 2 of its 12 nuclear reactors by 1996 and close the other 10 by 2010. Austria and the Philippines have decided to dismantle their single nuclear plants. In 1988 Italy and Switzerland decided not to build any more nuclear plants.

In 1989 the United States, with 111 reactors licensed to operate in 34 states, produced 31% of the world's nuclear power and used it to supply only 19% of the country's electricity and 5% of its supplemental energy.

Since 1975, no new nuclear power plants have been ordered in the United States and 108 previous orders have been canceled. During the 1990s, U.S. nuclear capacity is almost certain to decline as aging plants are retired.

What happened to nuclear power? To understand some of the problems with nuclear power, we need to know how a nuclear power plant works.

How Does a Nuclear Fission Reactor Work? When the nuclei of atoms such as uranium-235 and plutonium-239 are split by neutrons, energy is released and converted mostly to high-temperature heat in a nuclear fission chain reaction (Figure 4-5, p. 77). The rate at which this happens can be controlled in the nuclear fission reactor in a nuclear power plant, and the high-temperature heat released can be used to produce electrical energy.

Almost 75% of the world's commercial nuclear reactors (98% in the United States) are *light-water reactors (LWRs)*. Key parts of an LWR are the core, fuel assemblies, fuel rods, control rods, moderator, and coolant (Figure 19-17). The core of an LWR typically contains about 200 fuel assemblies. Each of these contains about 200 long, thin fuel rods (Figure 19-18). Each fuel rod is packed with eraser-sized pellets of uranium oxide fuel that lasts for about 3 to 4 years (Figure 19-19).

About 97% of the uranium in each fuel pellet is

Figure 19-18 Bundles of fuel rods filled with pellets of enriched uranium-235 oxide serve as the fuel core for a conventional nuclear fission reactor.

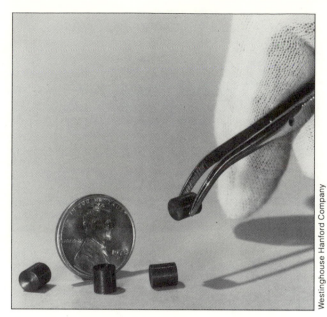

Figure 19-19 Fuel pellets of uranium oxide. They contain about 3% fissionable uranium-235.

uranium-238, an isotope that cannot be fissioned. The other 3% is uranium-235, which can be fissioned. This fuel is produced by increasing (enriching) the uranium-235 found in natural uranium ore (Figure 4-2, p. 74) from 0.7% to 3%. The uranium-235 in each fuel rod produces energy equal to that of three railroad carloads of coal.

Control rods made of materials that absorb neutrons are moved in and out of the reactor to regulate the rate of fission and the amount of power the reactor produces. All reactors place or circulate some type of material between the fuel rods and the fuel assemblies. This material, known as a moderator, slows down the neutrons emitted by the fission process so that the chain reaction can be kept going.

Three-fourths of the world's reactors use ordinary water, called light water, as a moderator. The moderator in about 20% of the world's reactors (50% of those in the Soviet Union, including the ill-fated Chernobyl reactor) is solid graphite, a form of carbon. Graphite-moderated reactors can also be used to produce fissionable plutonium-239 for use in nuclear weapons.

A coolant circulates through the reactor's core. It removes heat to keep fuel rods and other materials from melting and to produce steam that spins generators to produce electricity. Most water-moderated and graphite-moderated reactors use water as a coolant; a

few gas-cooled reactors use an unreactive gas such as helium or argon.

A typical LWR has an energy efficiency of only 25% to 30%, compared to 40% for a coal-burning plant. Graphite-moderated, gas-cooled reactors are widely used in the United Kingdom. Although they are more expensive to build and operate, they are more energy-efficient (38%) than LWRs because they operate at a higher temperature.

Nuclear power plants, each with one or more reactors, are only one part of the nuclear fuel cycle necessary for using nuclear energy to produce electricity (Figure 19-20). *In evaluating the safety and economy of nuclear power, we need to look at the entire cycle—not just the nuclear plant itself.*

After about three years in a reactor, the concentration of fissionable uranium-235 in a fuel rod becomes too low to keep the chain reaction going, or the rod becomes damaged from exposure to ionizing radiation. Each year about one-third of the spent fuel rods in a reactor are removed and stored in large, concrete-lined pools of water at the plant site.

After they have cooled for several years and lost some of their radioactivity, the spent fuel rods are sealed in shielded, supposedly crash-proof casks. These casks can be loaded onto a truck or train and transferred to storage pools away from the reactor or to a permanent nuclear waste repository or dump. Because neither of these options exist in the United States, spent fuel is stored at plant sites, where storage space is rapidly running out.

A third option is to send spent fuel to a fuel-reprocessing plant (Figure 19-20). There, remaining uranium-235 and plutonium-239 (produced as a by-

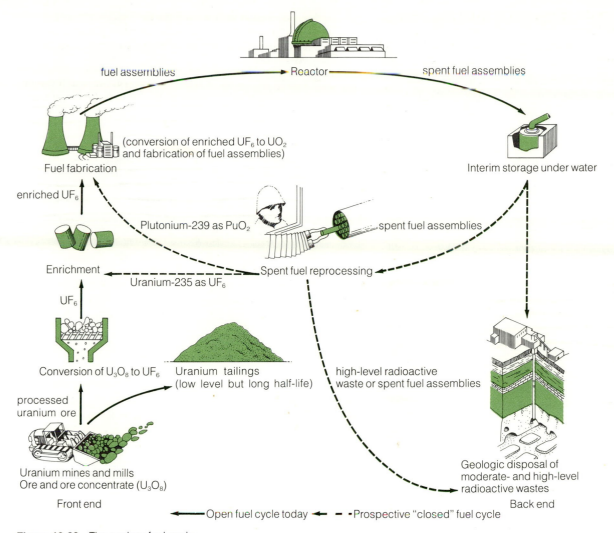

Figure 19-20 The nuclear fuel cycle.

product of the fission process) are removed and sent to a fuel fabrication plant. These recovered isotopes can be used to make new fuel rods for use in a conventional nuclear fission reactor or a breeder nuclear fission reactor.

Two small commercial fuel-reprocessing plants in operation (one in France and one in Great Britain) have had severe operating and economic problems. The United States has delayed development of commercial fuel-reprocessing plants because of technical difficulties, high construction and operating costs, and adequate domestic supplies of uranium. Also, such plants would handle and ship nuclear fuel in a form that could be used directly to make nuclear weapons.

The fission products produced in a nuclear reactor give off radioactivity and heat even after control rods have been inserted to stop all nuclear fission in the reactor core. To prevent a **meltdown** of the fuel rods and the reactor core after a reactor is shut down, huge amounts of water must be kept circulating through the core. A meltdown could release massive quantities of highly radioactive materials into the environment.

How Safe Are Nuclear Power Plants? To greatly reduce the chances of a meltdown and other serious reactor accidents, commercial reactors in the United States (and most countries) have many safety features:

- thick walls and concrete and steel shields surrounding the reactor vessel

- a system for automatically inserting control rods into the core to stop fission under emergency conditions

- a steel-reinforced concrete containment building to keep radioactive gases and materials from reaching the atmosphere because of an accident (ineffective in a complete core meltdown or a massive gas explosion like the one that happened at the Chernobyl plant in 1986)

- large filter systems and chemical sprayers inside the containment building to remove radioactive dust from the air and further reduce chances of radioactivity reaching the environment

- systems to condense steam released from a ruptured reactor vessel and prevent pressure from rising beyond the holding power of containment building walls

- an emergency core-cooling system to flood the core automatically with tons of water within one minute to prevent meltdown of the reactor core

- two separate power lines servicing the plant and several diesel generators to supply backup power for the massive pumps in the emergency core-cooling system

- X-ray inspection of key metal welds during construction and periodically after the plant goes into operation to detect possible sources of leaks from corrosion

- an automatic backup system to replace each major part of the safety system in the event of a failure

Such elaborate safety systems make a complete reactor core meltdown very unlikely. However, a partial or complete meltdown is possible through a series

SPOTLIGHT Some Significant Nuclear Accidents

Winter 1957

Perhaps the worst nuclear disaster in history occurred in the Soviet Union in the southern Ural Mountains around the city of Kyshtym, believed then to be the center of plutonium production for Soviet nuclear weapons. The cause of the accident and the number of people killed and injured remain a secret. However, it is known that a massive amount of radiation was released, allegedly from an explosion of large quantities of radioactive wastes carelessly stored in shallow trenches. Today the area is deserted and hundreds of square miles have been sealed off. A river has been diverted around the area and the names of 30 towns and villages in the region have disappeared from Soviet maps.

October 7, 1957

A water-cooled, graphite-moderated reactor used to produce plutonium for nuclear weapons north of Liverpool, England, caught fire as the Chernobyl nuclear plant did 29 years later. By the time the fire was put out, 200 square miles of countryside had been contaminated with radioactive material. Exposure to high levels of radiation caused an estimated 33 people to die prematurely from cancer.

March 22, 1975

Against regulations, a maintenance worker used a candle to test for air leaks at the Brown's Ferry commercial nuclear reactor near

Decatur, Alabama. It set off a fire that knocked out five emergency core-cooling systems. Although the reactor's cooling water dropped to a dangerous level, backup systems prevented any radioactive material from escaping into the environment. At the same plant, in 1978, a worker's rubber boot fell into a reactor and led to an unsuccessful search costing $2.8 million. Such incidents, based on unpredictable human errors, are common in most nuclear plants. Although they rarely hurt or kill anyone, they add to the already high cost of using nuclear fission to produce electricity.

March 28, 1979

The worst accident in the history of U.S. commercial nuclear power happened at the Three Mile Island (TMI) nuclear plant near Harrisburg, Pennsylvania (Figure 19-21). One of its two reactors lost its coolant water because of a series of mechanical failures and human operator errors not anticipated in safety studies. The reactor's core became partially uncovered. At least 70% of the core was damaged, and about 50% (25 tons) of it melted and fell to the bottom of the reactor. Unknown amounts of ionizing radiation escaped into the atmosphere and 144,000 people were evacuated. Investigators found that if a stuck valve had stayed open for just another 30 to 60 minutes, there would have been a complete meltdown. No one is

known to have died because of the accident. But its long-term health effects on workers and nearby residents are still being debated because data published on the radiation released during the accident are contradictory and incomplete.

The cleanup of the damaged TMI reactor will cost more than $1 billion, compared to the $700 million construction cost of the reactor, and won't be completed until 1990 or later. Confusing and misleading statements about the accident issued by Metropolitan Edison (which owned the plant) and by the Nuclear Regulatory Commission (NRC) eroded public confidence in the safety of nuclear power. Nuclear power critics contend that the TMI accident and hundreds of serious incidents since then have not led to a complete meltdown and breach of a reactor's containment building mostly because of luck. Nuclear industry officials claim that a catastrophic accident has not happened because the industry's multiple-backup safety systems work.

April 26, 1986

At 1:23 A.M. there was a massive explosion inside one of the four graphite-moderated, water-cooled reactors at the Chernobyl nuclear power plant north of Kiev in the Soviet Union. The blast blew the 1,000-ton roof off the reactor building, set the graphite core on fire, and flung radioactive debris sev-

of equipment failures, operator errors, or both. In 1979 a reactor at the Three Mile Island plant in Pennsylvania underwent a partial meltdown because of equipment failures and operator errors (see Spotlight below).

Another highly unlikely but possible danger is a powerful hydrogen gas or steam explosion inside the reactor containment vessel. This could split the containment building open and spew highly radioactive materials high into the atmosphere. Winds could spread this cloud of radioactive materials for thousands of miles as happened in the Chernobyl accident. A worst-case accident could kill and injure hundreds of thousands of people and contaminate large areas with radioactive isotopes for thousands of years.

Many studies of nuclear safety have been made since 1957, when the first commercial nuclear power plant began operating in the United States. However, there is still no officially accepted study of just how safe or unsafe these plants are and no study of the safety of the entire nuclear fuel cycle. Even if engineers can make the hardware 100% reliable, human reliability can never reach 100%. To be human is to

eral thousand feet into the air. Over the next several days winds carried some of these radioactive materials over parts of the Soviet Union and much of eastern and western Europe as far as 1,250 miles from the plant. The accident happened when engineers turned off most of the reactor's automatic safety and warning systems to keep them from interfering with an unauthorized safety experiment (Figure 19-22).

About 135,000 people living within 18 miles of the plant were evacuated by an armada of 1,100 buses and trucks. According to Soviet officials, most of these people will never be able to return to their contaminated homes and farms. By 1989 exposure to high levels of ionizing radiation at the accident site had killed 36 plant workers, fire fighters, and rescue workers. Another 237 people received large doses of radiation and were hospitalized with acute radiation sickness. Many of these people will probably die prematurely from cancer in coming years. Soviet and Western medical experts estimate that 5,000 to 100,000 people in the Soviet Union and the rest of Europe will die prematurely over the next 70 years from cancer caused by exposure to the ionizing radiation release at Chernobyl. Thousands of others

(Continued)

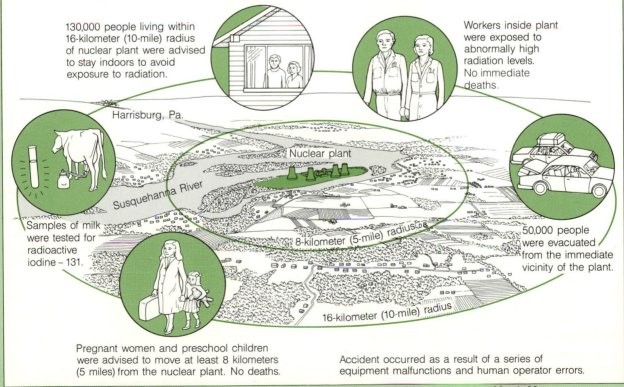

130,000 people living within 16-kilometer (10-mile) radius of nuclear plant were advised to stay indoors to avoid exposure to radiation.

Workers inside plant were exposed to abnormally high radiation levels. No immediate deaths.

Harrisburg, Pa.

Nuclear plant

Susquehanna River

Samples of milk were tested for radioactive iodine – 131.

8-kilometer (5-mile) radius

16-kilometer (10-mile) radius

50,000 people were evacuated from the immediate vicinity of the plant.

Pregnant women and preschool children were advised to move at least 8 kilometers (5 miles) from the nuclear plant. No deaths.

Accident occurred as a result of a series of equipment malfunctions and human operator errors.

Figure 19-21   Three Mile Island (TMI) in eastern Pennsylvania, where a nuclear accident occurred on March 28, 1979.

err, and human behavior is highly unpredictable, as the TMI and Chernobyl accidents showed.

The Nuclear Regulatory Commission estimated that there is a 15% to 45% chance of a complete core meltdown at a U.S. reactor during the next 20 years. The commission also found that 39 U.S. reactors have an 80% chance of containment failure from a meltdown or massive gas explosion. Scientists in West Germany and Sweden projected that, worldwide, there is a 70% chance of another serious core-damaging nuclear accident within the next 54 years.

A 1982 study by the Sandia National Laboratory estimated that a worst-case accident in a reactor near a large U.S. city might cause 50,000 to 100,000 immediate deaths, 10,000 to 40,000 later deaths from cancer, and $100 billion to $150 billion in damages. Most citizens and businesses suffering injuries or property damage from a major nuclear accident would get little if any financial reimbursement. Since the beginnings of commercial nuclear power in the 1950s, insurance companies have refused to cover more than a small part of the possible damages from an accident.

In 1957 Congress enacted the Price-Anderson Act. Until 1988 it limited insurance liability from a nuclear accident in the United States to a maximum of $700 million—less than 1% of the damage that could occur

will be afflicted with thyroid tumors, cataracts, and sterility. The death toll would have been much higher if the accident had happened during the day when people were not sheltered in houses and if the wind had been blowing toward the nearby city of Kiev, with 2.4 million people.

In 1988 Soviet officials revealed that the Chernobyl accident cost $14.4 billion, almost four times their original estimate of damages. Today the reactor is entombed in over 300,000 tons of concrete and metal. The area within a 16-mile radius of the plant is being set aside as a reserve to study the long-term effects of radiation on plants and animals.

In 1987 the United States permanently shut down a Chernobyl-type military reactor at Hanford, Washington, to make safety improvements; 54 serious safety violations had occurred at the plant during 1985 and 1986. The Chernobyl accident eroded public support for nuclear power worldwide and showed people that they need to be concerned about the safety of nuclear plants within and outside the borders of their countries.

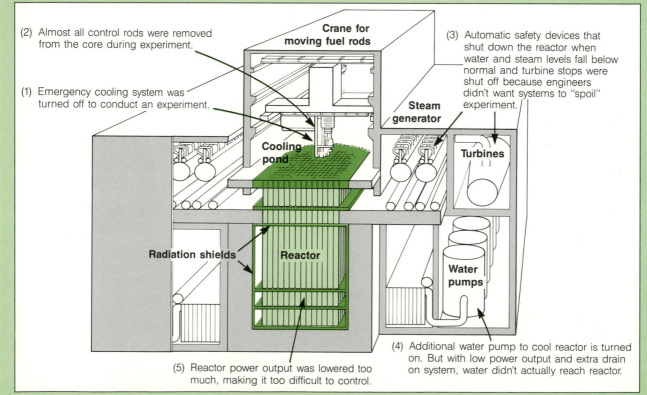

(1) Emergency cooling system was turned off to conduct an experiment.

(2) Almost all control rods were removed from the core during experiment.

(3) Automatic safety devices that shut down the reactor when water and steam levels fall below normal and turbine stops were shut off because engineers didn't want systems to "spoil" experiment.

Crane for moving fuel rods

Cooling pond

Steam generator

Turbines

Radiation shields

Reactor

Water pumps

(4) Additional water pump to cool reactor is turned on. But with low power output and extra drain on system, water didn't actually reach reactor.

(5) Reactor power output was lowered too much, making it too difficult to control.

Figure 19-22 Major events leading to the Chernobyl nuclear power plant accident on April 26, 1986, in the Soviet Union.

from a worst-case accident near a densely populated area. In 1988 Congress extended the law for 20 years and raised the insurance liability to $7 billion—still only 7% of the possible damage from a severe accident.

Without this law the U.S. nuclear power industry would never have developed. Critics charge that the law is an unfair subsidy of the nuclear industry. Also, according to a 1987 General Accounting Office report, the NRC has allowed plants to keep operating even after repeated safety violations. Nuclear critics also contend that nuclear accident evaluation plans in the United States are inadequate (see Pro/Con below).

Disposal and Storage of Radioactive Wastes Each part of the nuclear fuel cycle for military and commercial nuclear reactors produces solid, liquid, and gaseous radioactive wastes (Figure 19-20, p. 497). Some of these, called *low-level radioactive wastes*, give off small amounts of ionizing radiation, usually for a short time. Others are *high-level radioactive wastes*, which give off large amounts of ionizing radiation for a long time.

From the 1940s to 1970 most low-level radioactive waste produced in the United States (and most other countries) was dumped into the ocean in steel drums. Since 1970 low-level radioactive wastes from military activities have been buried at government-run landfills. Three of these have been closed because of leakage. Low-level waste materials from hospitals, universities, industries, and other producers are put in steel drums and shipped to three regional landfills run by federal and state governments.

Most high-level radioactive wastes are spent fuel rods from commercial nuclear power plants and an assortment of wastes from nuclear weapons plants. According to the EPA, spent fuel rods must be stored safely for 10,000 years before they decay to acceptable levels of radioactivity. However, unless plutonium 239 and other very long-lived radioactive isotopes are removed by expensive processing, high-level wastes would have to be stored for at least 240,000 years.

Large amounts of high-level radioactive waste have been stored at government nuclear weapons plants at Hanford, Washington, and Barnwell, South Carolina. Over half a million gallons of these wastes have leaked from single-shell, underground storage tanks built between 1943 and 1968. Storage tanks built after 1968 have a double shell; if the inner wall corrodes, the liquid spills into the space between the two walls, where it can be detected in time to be pumped into another tank.

In 1986 once-secret documents revealed that the Hanford and Barnwell nuclear weapons plants had accidently and deliberately released ionizing radiation for several decades without telling local residents. Environmentalists are worried that radioactive contamination from the Barnwell plant could reach the Tuscaloosa aquifer, which supplies drinking water for South Carolina and several other states.

In 1987 and 1988 government studies revealed that most of the nuclear weapons production plants supervised by the Department of Energy were being operated with gross disregard for the safety of their workers and people in nearby areas. At least 30 serious

---

PRO/CON **How Large Should the Evacuation Zone Around a Nuclear Plant Be?**

After the TMI accident 10-mile evacuation zones were set up around all U.S. commercial reactors. In 1986 nuclear power critics called for extending the evacuation zone to at least the 19 miles Soviet officials found necessary after the Chernobyl accident.

Another problem is that areas around many U.S. reactors are up to ten times more densely populated than those around most Soviet reactors. For example, whereas 135,000 had to be evacuated because of the Chernobyl accident, about 1.5 million people would have to be evacuated if a similar accident occurred at the Indian Point plant near New York City.

Many urban areas near U.S. reactors would be almost impossible to evacuate if an accident happened. Most Americans would get into their cars and clog up evacuation routes. At Chernobyl few people had cars.

Instead of increasing the evacuation zone, the U.S. nuclear industry has have been pushing the NRC to reduce the evacuation area around reactors to as low as one mile. Industry officials contend that new safety studies show that less radiation would escape in the event of an accident than previously thought.

Environmentalists charge that the industry wants to reduce the required size of evacuation zones

to prevent state and local governments from blocking the licensing of new nuclear plants whose evacuation plans are inadequate under the present standard. This is the main reason that New Hampshire's $5.7 billion Seabrook nuclear plant, completed in 1986, was still idle in 1989.

In 1988, just before leaving office, President Ronald Reagan issued an executive order allowing the NRC to give operating permits for nuclear power plants without states or localities approving or participating in an evacuation plan they believe to be inadequate. Do you agree with this executive decision?

incidents between 1957 and 1985 were kept secret. The General Accounting Office estimated that it will cost taxpayers $84 billion to $200 billion over the next 60 years to get these facilities cleaned up and in safe working order, if Congress decides to require this.

Presently, EPA regulations call for high-level radioactive wastes to be stored for 10,000 years. After 32 years of research and debate, scientists still don't agree on a safe method of storing these wastes (see Case Study below). Regardless of the storage method, most U.S. citizens strongly oppose the location of a low- or high-level nuclear waste disposal facility anywhere near them.

In 1982 Congress passed the Nuclear Waste Policy Act. It set a timetable for the Department of Energy to choose a site and build the country's first deep

---

CASE STUDY   **What Can We Do with High-Level, Long-Lived Radioactive Waste?**

Some scientists believe that the long-term safe disposal of high-level radioactive wastes is technically possible. Others say it is impossible to show that any method will work for 10,000 to 240,000 years. The following are some of the proposed methods and their possible drawbacks:

1. *Bury it deep underground.* The currently favored method is to package unreprocessed spent fuel rods and bury them in a deep underground salt, granite, or other stable geological formation that is earthquake resistant and waterproof for 10,000 to 240,000 years (Figure 19-23). Reprocessing the waste before burial is expensive but reduces burial time to 10,000 years. Some geologists question this approach, arguing that the drilling and tunneling to build the repository might cause water leakage and weaken resistance to earthquakes. They also contend that with present geological knowledge scientists cannot make meaningful 10,000-year projections about earthquake probability and paths of groundwater by which drinking supplies could be contaminated with radioactive waste.

2. *Shoot it into space or into the sun.* Even if feasible, costs would be very high. A launch accident (such as the space shuttle *Challenger* explosion) could disperse radioactive wastes over large areas of the earth's surface.

3. *Bury it under the Antarctic ice sheets or the Greenland ice caps.* The long-term stability of the ice sheets is not known. They could be destabilized by heat from the wastes, and retrieval of the wastes would be difficult or impossible if the method failed.

4. *Dump it into downward-descending, deep-ocean sediments.* The long-term stability of these sediments is unknown. Wastes could eventually be spewed out somewhere else by volcanic activity. Waste containers might leak and contaminate the ocean before being carried downward, and retrieval would probably be impossible if the method did not work.

5. *Change it into harmless or less harmful isotopes.* Presently there is no way to do this. Even if a method were developed, costs would probably be extremely high, and resulting toxic materials and low-level radioactive wastes would also have to be disposed of safely.

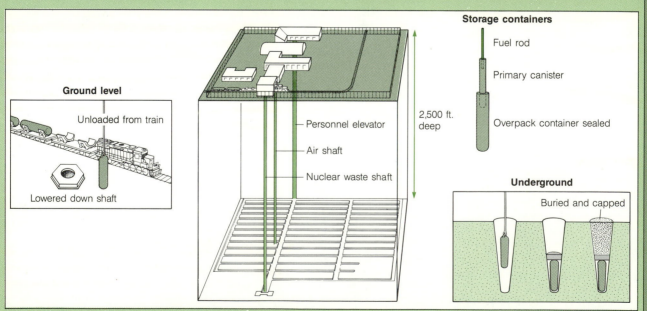

Figure 19-23 Proposed general design for deep underground permanent storage of high-level radioactive wastes from commercial nuclear power plants in the United States. (Source: U.S. Department of Energy)

underground repository in which to store high-level radioactive wastes from commercial nuclear reactors for 10,000 years. In 1985 the Department of Energy announced plans to build the first repository, at a cost of $6 billion to $10 billion, based on the design shown in Figure 19-23.

The repository is to be built in a volcanic rock formation on federal land in the Yucca Mountain desert region, 100 miles northwest of Las Vegas, Nevada. Tests and studies are to be made to determine the likelihood of earthquakes and water penetration at the site over the next 10,000 years. Construction is to begin in 1998 and is supposed to be completed by 2003, but few observers expect this will happen. By 2010 the Department of Energy is to report to Congress on the need for a second repository, probably in the eastern United States.

The government has spent $700 million building the Waste Isolation Pilot Plant (WIPP) for the underground storage of radioactive wastes from nuclear weapons production. It has been carved out in salt beds 2,150 feet below the desert near Carlsbad, New Mexico. In 1988 its opening was delayed indefinitely because of failure to pass safety and environmental reviews.

Decommissioning Nuclear Power Plants and Weapons Facilities   The useful operating life of today's nuclear power plants is hoped to be 30 to 40 years. Because the core and many other parts contain large amounts of radioactive materials, a nuclear plant cannot be abandoned or demolished by a wrecking ball like a worn-out coal-fired power plant.

Decommissioning nuclear power plants and nuclear weapons plants is the last step in the nuclear fuel cycle. Three ways have been proposed:

- *entombment*: covering the reactor with reinforced concrete and putting up a barrier to keep out intruders

- *dismantlement*: decontaminating and taking the reactor apart immediately after shutdown and shipping all radioactive debris to a radioactive-waste burial facility

- *mothballing*: putting up a barrier and setting up a 24-hour security guard system to keep out intruders for several decades to 100 years before dismantlement

Each method involves shutting down the plant, removing the spent fuel from the reactor core, draining all liquids, flushing all pipes, and sending all radioactive materials to approved waste storage sites yet to be built. Presently most U.S. utilities favor dismantlement. Utilities in France, Canada, and West Germany are planning to mothball their reactors for several decades before dismantlement.

Worldwide, more than 20 commercial reactors (4 in the United States) have been retired and are awaiting decommissioning. Another 225 large commercial reactors (70 in the United States) will probably be retired by 2010.

Dismantlement of the first commercial nuclear reactor in the United States near Shippingport, Pennsylvania, began in 1986. This five-year project, involving a small reactor, is expected to cost at least $100 million.

Utility company officials estimate that dismantlement of a typical reactor 10 to 20 times larger than the Shippingport reactor should cost about $170 million. Most analysts consider this figure too low and put the cost at $1 billion to $3 billion per large reactor—roughly equal to the initial construction cost. Decommissioning costs will add to the already high price of electricity produced by nuclear fission. Politicians and nuclear industry officials may be tempted to mothball retired plants and pass dismantlement costs and problems on to the next generation.

Proliferation of Nuclear Weapons   Terrorist groups can make a small atomic bomb by using about 5 pounds of plutonium or uranium-233, or 11 pounds of uranium-235 and commercially available components. Such a bomb would blow up a large building or a small city block and would contaminate a much larger area with radioactive materials for centuries. A handful of trained people could make such a blockbuster if they could get enough fissionable bomb-grade material.

Spent reactor fuel is so highly radioactive that theft is unlikely, but separated bomb-usable plutonium is easily handled. Although plutonium shipments are heavily guarded, it could be stolen from nuclear weapons or reprocessing plants, especially by employees. Each year about 3% of the 142,000 people working in 127 U.S. nuclear weapons facilities are fired because of drug use, mental instability, or other security risks.

Bomb-usable plutonium fuel could also be stolen from a commercial fuel-reprocessing plant or one of the more than 150 research and test reactors operating in 30 countries. Another possibility is to highjack a shipment of this material as it is being transported from a fuel-reprocessing plant to one of Europe's six experimental breeder nuclear fission power plants.

Those who would steal plutonium need not bother to make atomic bombs. They could simply use a conventional explosive charge to disperse the plutonium into the atmosphere from atop any tall building. Dispersed in this way, 2.2 pounds of plutonium oxide powder theoretically would contaminate three square miles with dangerous levels of radioactivity for several hundred thousand years.

An analysis of government reports indicated that by 1988 at least 4.8 tons of bomb-grade plutonium from commercial power plants and government-run weapons and reprocessing plants throughout the world was unaccounted for. This is enough to make 190 to 360 blockbuster nuclear bombs or many much larger nuclear weapons.

Plutonium could be deliberately contaminated with substances to make it not useful as weapons material. But so far no one has come up with a way to do this. Most nuclear experts doubt it can be done. The best ways to slow down the spread of bomb-grade material are to abandon civilian reprocessing of power plant fuel, develop substitutes for highly enriched uranium in research reactors, and tighten international safeguards.

Soaring Costs: The Achilles Heel of Nuclear Power

After the United States dropped atomic bombs on the Japanese cities of Hiroshima and Nagasaki, ending World War II, the scientists who developed the bomb and the elected officials responsible for its use were determined to show the world that the peaceful uses of atomic energy would outweigh the immense harm it had done. One part of this "Atoms for Peace" program was to use nuclear power to produce electricity. American utility companies were skeptical but began ordering nuclear power plants in the late 1950s for four reasons:

- The Atomic Energy Commission and builders of nuclear reactors projected that nuclear power would produce electricity at a very low cost, compared to using coal and other alternatives.

- The nuclear industry projected that nuclear reactors would have an 88% *capacity factor*—a measure of the time a reactor would operate each year at full power.

- The first round of commercial reactors was built with the government paying about one-fourth of the cost and with the reactors provided to utilities at a fixed cost with no cost overruns allowed.

- Congress passed the Price-Anderson Act, which protected the nuclear industry and utilities from significant liability to the general public in case of accidents.

It was an offer utility company officials could not resist. Today many wish they had.

Experience has shown that nuclear power is a very expensive way to produce electricity, even when it is heavily subsidized as partial protection from free market competition by other energy sources. In 1987 new U.S. nuclear power plants produced electricity at an average of 13.5 cents per kilowatt-hour—equal to buying oil at $216 per barrel. These already high costs do not include most of the costs of storing radioactive wastes and decommissioning worn-out plants.

In contrast, new coal plants with the latest air pollution control equipment produced electricity at an average cost of 6 cents per kilowatt-hour in 1987. Producing electricity by cogeneration costs only 5 cents per kilowatt-hour, and saving electricity by improving energy efficiency costs only about 2 to 4 cents per kilowatt-hour. Experts project that sometime in the 1990s wind power and solar photovoltaic cells will be able to produce cheaper electricity than nuclear plants.

Operating costs of nuclear plants have been higher than projected because U.S. pressurized water reactors operate at an average of only 60% of their capacity—far below the 88% capacity projected by proponents of nuclear power in the 1950s. The average capacity factor for PWRs in the United Kingdom is only 51%, and those in Sweden, 54%. Those in other countries are higher: Japan and Canada (71%), France (74%), West Germany (82%), and Switzerland (87%), mostly because of standardized design and better management.

New nuclear plants in France and Japan cost about half as much per kilowatt of power to build as those in the United States because they are better planned and use standardized designs. The higher cost of coal in Europe and Japan also makes it easier to justify building these still expensive nuclear plants. However, France has so much surplus electricity that it is forced to run at partial capacity. It also sells surplus electricity to neighboring countries at bargain prices to help pay the interest on the enormous $39 billion debt used to finance its nuclear industry.

In the United States, where almost every nuclear plant has a different design, poor planning and management and stricter safety regulations since the TMI accident have increased costs and lengthened construction time. New nuclear power plants cost three times as much to build as equivalent coal-fired plants with the latest air pollution control equipment. A 1988 Department of Energy study found that operating costs for American nuclear plants are rising so fast that electric utilities may find it cheaper to close many of them before the end of their useful lives.

Banks and other lending institutions have become skeptical about financing new U.S. nuclear power plants. The Three Mile Island accident showed that utility companies could lose $1 billion or more of equipment in an hour, and at least $1 billion more in cleanup costs, even without any known harmful effects on public health. Lenders' confidence in nuclear power was eroded further in 1988 when it was decided not to open a completed nuclear plant (see Spotlight on p. 505).

The highly regarded U.S. business magazine *Forbes* has called the failure of the U.S. nuclear power program "the largest managerial disaster in U.S. business history." It involves perhaps $1 trillion in wasted investments, cost overruns, and unnecessarily high electricity costs, and production of more electricity than the country needs. Utilities have been trying to have electricity consumers absorb the costs of cancelled nuclear power plants. In 1989, however, the Supreme Court reaffirmed the power of states to force utilities and their shareholders to absorb the costs of abandoned plants.

Is nuclear power dead in the United States and most other MDCs? You might think so because of its high costs and massive public opposition. But powerful economic and political forces strive to maintain and expand the world's nuclear power industry. Officials from private and government-run companies that build nuclear power plants hope to build more in their own countries and also sell them to LDCs. They have mounted public campaigns to restore people's confidence in the safety and need for nuclear power (see Pro/Con on p, 506).

Advantages and Disadvantages of Conventional Nuclear Fission   Using nuclear fission to produce electricity has many advantages. Nuclear plants don't release carbon dioxide, particulate matter, sulfur dioxide, or nitrogen oxides into the atmosphere as do coal-fired plants. Water pollution and disruption of land are low to moderate if the entire nuclear fuel cycle operates normally. Multiple safety systems greatly reduce the likelihood of a catastrophic accident releasing deadly radioactive material into the environment. But the Chernobyl accident showed this can happen because of inability to control human error.

Nuclear power also has many disadvantages. It produces electricity, which cannot be used to run vehicles without the development of affordable, long-lasting batteries to propel electric cars. Construction and operating costs for nuclear power plants in the United States and most countries are high and are rising, even with massive government and consumer subsidies.

Standardized design and mass production can bring costs down. But electricity can still be produced by safer methods at a cost equal to or lower than that of nuclear power. Although large-scale accidents are infrequent, a combination of mechanical failure and human errors, sabotage, or shipping accidents could again release deadly radioactive materials into the environment.

The net useful energy yield of nuclear-generated electricity is low (Figure 4-15, p. 87). Scientists disagree greatly over how high-level radioactive wastes should be stored, and some doubt that an acceptably safe method can ever be developed.

Today's military and commercial nuclear energy programs commit future generations to storing dangerous radioactive wastes for thousands of years even if nuclear fission power is abandoned tomorrow. Perhaps even more dangerous, the existence of nuclear power technology helps spread knowledge and materials that can be used to make nuclear weapons. For these reasons, many people feel that it is unethical to use nuclear power to produce electricity.

19-6   BREEDER NUCLEAR FISSION AND NUCLEAR FUSION

Nonrenewable Breeder Nuclear Fission   At the present rate of use the world's supply of uranium should last at least 100 years and perhaps 200 years. However, some nuclear power proponents project a sharp rise in the use of nuclear fission to produce electricity after the year 2000. They urge the widespread use of breeder nuclear fission reactors (see Guest Essay on p. 507).

Conventional fission reactors use fissionable uranium-235, which makes up only 0.7% of natural uranium ore. **Breeder nuclear fission reactors** convert nonfissionable uranium-238 into fissionable plutonium-239. Since breeders would use over 99% of the uranium in ore deposits, the world's known uranium

---

SPOTLIGHT   New York's Shoreham Nuclear Plant

The Shoreham nuclear power plant on Long Island near New York City was completed in 1984 but will probably never operate. It cost $5.3 billion to build—three times what it was supposed to cost.

Local and state officials have opposed putting the plant into operation. They believe it would not be possible to evacuate most of the people on Long Island in case of a major nuclear accident.

In 1988 the executives of the almost bankrupt utility company that built the plant and state officials worked out a plan to dismantle the plant. The utility executives agreed to sell the plant to the state for $1. The state agreed to spend at least $400 million to dismantle the plant if it can figure out what to do with the radioactive core. Even though the NRC knew the plant had little chance of getting a full operating license, it allowed the utility to load radioactive fuel into the plant to save the company from bankruptcy.

As part of the deal, the state will grant the utility company a series of rate increases to help save the company from bankruptcy. This will force the company's customers to pay part of the $2.5 billion that the utility still owes for the construction of the plant and pay for dismantling the plant. A court must approve this plan. In 1989 the Bush administration filed suit to prevent the plant from being dismantled. What do you think?

reserves would last at least 1,000 years and perhaps several thousand years.

Under normal operation a breeder reactor is considered by its proponents to be much safer than a conventional fission reactor. But if the reactor's safety system should fail, the reactor could lose some of its liquid sodium coolant. This could cause a runaway fission chain reaction and perhaps a small nuclear explosion with the force of several hundred pounds of TNT. Such an explosion could blast open the containment building, releasing a cloud of highly radioactive gases and particulate matter. Leaks of flammable liquid sodium also can also cause fires, as has happened with all experimental breeders built so far.

Since 1966, experimental breeder reactors have been built in the United States, the United Kingdom, the Soviet Union, West Germany, Japan, and France. In December 1986 France began operating a commercial-size breeder reactor, the Superphenix. It cost three times the original estimate to build. The little electric-

ity it has produced is twice as expensive as that generated by France's conventional fission reactors.

In May 1987, shortly after the reactor began operating at full power, it began leaking liquid sodium coolant and was shut down. Repairs may be so expensive that the reactor may not be put back into operation.

Tentative plans to build full-size commercial breeders in West Germany, the Soviet Union, and the United Kingdom may be canceled because of the excessive cost of France's reactor and an excess of electric generating capacity. Studies have suggested that breeders will not be economically competitive with conventional fission reactors for at least 50 years, if then.

Nuclear Fusion Scientists hope someday to use controlled nuclear fusion (Figure 4-6, p. 78) to provide an almost limitless source of energy for producing high-temperature heat and electricity. For 40 years research has focused on the D-T nuclear fusion reaction in which two isotopes of hydrogen-deuterium (D) and tritium (T) fuse at about 100 million degrees—ten times hotter

---

PRO/CON Should More Nuclear Power Plants Be Built in the United States?

Since the Three Mile Island accident, the U.S. nuclear industry and utility companies have financed a massive advertising campaign by the U.S. Council for Energy Awareness. This campaign, with a $340 million budget in 1988, is designed to improve the industry's image, resell nuclear power to the American public, and downgrade the importance of solar energy, conservation, geothermal energy, wind, and hydropower as alternatives to nuclear power.

The campaign's magazine and television ads do not tell readers and viewers that the ads are paid for by the nuclear industry. Most ads use the argument that more nuclear power is needed in the United States to reduce dependence on imported oil.

The truth is that since 1979 only about 5% (3.5% in 1988) of the electricity in the United States has been produced by burning oil, and 95% of this is residual oil that can't be used for other purposes (Figure 19-11). Thus, building more nuclear power plants will not save the country any significant amount of domestic or imported oil.

The nuclear industry points out correctly that nuclear power—unlike coal burning—does not add any carbon dioxide to the atmosphere. They argue that replacing coal-burning power plants with nuclear plants would help delay major climate changes from the greenhouse effect. They hope to convince governments and utility companies to build hundreds of new, "second-generation" plants, allegedly designed to prevent radiation leaks into the environment (see Guest Essay, p. 507).

However, coal-burning plants in the United States account for only 24% of fossil-fuel CO_2 emissions. The largest amounts of CO_2 are emitted into the atmosphere by motor vehicles—a problem that is not affected by building nuclear or any kind of power plant.

It has taken 32 years and $250 billion (plus $1 trillion in federal subsidies) to build the current generation of 111 nuclear power plants in the United States. If we displaced half of the U.S. use of coal to produce electricity by building 200 new nuclear plants at a cost of $1 trillion or more, this would

reduce the world greenhouse effect by only 2%. Just to make this small dent in the CO_2 problem would require completing a large nuclear reactor in the U.S. *every 3 days* for the next 37 years. Worldwide, we would have to build *one reactor a day* for 37 years at a total cost of $23 trillion!

Improvements in energy efficiency—especially requiring all new cars to get at least 50 miles per gallon of gasoline—would result in much greater reductions of CO_2 emissions at a fraction of the cost of building new nuclear plants. Improving energy efficiency by 2% a year could cut CO_2 emission in half in the next 40 years.

Nuclear power critics believe that we do not need much of the electricity we already produce, and even if we did, there are better, quicker, and cheaper ways to produce it (see Guest Essay on p. 509). They also believe that we should not spend a trillion dollars or more to produce electricity, which cannot replace oil for transportation, and would do little to delay global warming. What do you think?

---

than the sun's center. Another possibility is the D-D fusion reaction in which the nuclei of two deuterium atoms fuse together at much higher temperatures. If developed, it would run on virtually unlimited heavy water (D_2O) fuel obtained from seawater at a cost of about 10 cents a gallon.

After 40 years of research, high-temperature nuclear fusion is still at the laboratory stage. Deuterium and tritium atoms have been forced together by using electromagnetic reactors the size of 12 locomotives, 120-trillion watt laser beams, and bombardment with high-speed particles. But so far none of these approaches have produced more energy than they use.

If researchers eventually can get more energy out than they put in, the next step is to build a small fusion reactor and then scale it up to commercial size. This task is considered one of the most difficult engineering problems ever undertaken. The estimated cost of a commercial fusion reactor is at least four times that of a comparable conventional fission reactor. If everything goes right (a very big if), high-temperature fusion might be in widespread commercial use sometime after 2100, if ever.

In 1989 two chemists announced what might be either a spectacular energy breakthrough or merely a fascinating scientific experiment. Preliminary results suggest that they were able to bring about some D-D nuclear fusion at room temperature using a simple apparatus. Two metal electrodes—one, a pencil-thin rod of palladium and the other, a coil of platinum wire surrounding the palladium—were inserted into a jar of heavy water (D_2O) and hooked up to a 12-volt car battery. The electric current decomposed the heavy water into deuterium and oxygen, and the deuterium diffused into the latticelike crystal structure of the palladium electrode. After the cell ran for 2 to 3 weeks, the researchers believe that enough deuterium nuclei were packed into the palladium electrode to overcome their mutual repulsion and fuse at room temperature.

However, these early experiments produced only about one ten-trillionth of the energy needed to run an electric toothbrush. Also, it is not clear whether

GUEST ESSAY Nuclear Power: A Faustian Bargain We Should Accept

Alvin M. Weinberg

Alvin M. Weinberg was a member of the group of scientists that developed the first experimental fission reactors at the University of Chicago in 1941. Since then he has been a leading figure in the development of commercial nuclear power. From 1948 to 1973 he served as director of the Oak Ridge National Laboratory. In 1974 he was director of the Office of Energy Research and Development in the Federal Energy Administration (now the Department of Energy). From 1975 to 1985 he was director of the Institute for Energy Analysis of the Oak Ridge Associated Universities, where he is now a Distinguished Fellow. He has written numerous articles and books on nuclear energy (see Further Readings) and has received many awards for his contributions to the development of nuclear energy.

There are two basically different views of the world's future (see Pro/Con on p. 20). The one most popular in recent years holds that the earth's resources are limited. According to this neo-Malthusian view, nothing except drastic reduction in population, affluence, and certain types of technology can prevent severe environmental degradation.

The other view, held by cornucopians, holds that as scarce materials are exhausted there will always be new, more expensive ones to take their place. According to this view, Spaceship Earth has practically infinite supplies of resources, but it will cost more and more to stay where we are as we use up those resources that are readily available.

The cornucopian view seems to me to be the more reasonable, especially since all of our past experience has shown that as one resource becomes scarce, another takes its place. We do not use whale oil for lighting any more, yet we have better lighting than our ancestors who burned this oil in lamps.

In the long run humankind will have to depend on the most abundant and almost infinitely abundant elements in the earth's crust: iron, sodium, carbon, nitrogen, aluminum, oxygen, silicon, and a few others. Glass, cement, and plastics will perform many more functions than they do now. Our average standard of living will be diminished, but probably no more than by a factor of 2.

Thus, in contrast to what seems to be the prevailing mood, I retain a certain basic optimism about the future. My optimism, however, is predicated on certain assumptions:

1. Technology can indeed deal with most of the effluents of this future society. Here I think I am

(Continued)

some of this energy is coming from unexpected chemical reactions or other nonfusion processes.

The two chemists spent five years and $100,000 of their own money on their cold fusion research, whereas at least $20 billion has been spent over 40 years for high-temperature fusion research. It will probably take 2 to 3 decades to evaluate the commercial feasibility, if any, of cold nuclear fusion.

Even if cold fusion is scientifically possible, there are many problems:

- It may not yield enough heat to drive a turbine and produce electricity. To do this, metals such as palladium, titanium, and nickel that absorb deuterium would have to be heated to over 300°C. But the hydrogen-absorbing ability of these metals declines sharply as temperatures rise above room temperature.

- Converting the apparatus from a tabletop model to a massive commercial plant may not be technically or economically feasible.

- Palladium is expensive and scarce and found mostly in South Africa and the Soviet Union. The palladium probably needed for a large plant would cost $2 billion to $4 billion. Scientists hope cold fusion can occur with other less expensive, more plentiful metals, such as titanium and nickel.

GUEST ESSAY (continued)

on firm ground, for, on the whole, where technology has been given the task and been given the necessary time and funding, it has come through with very important improvements such as reducing air pollution emissions by cars. On the other hand, CO_2, which is the major greenhouse gas, cannot be controlled; this may place a limit on the rate at which we burn fossil fuels.

2. Phosphorus, though essentially infinite in supply in the earth's crust at various locations, has no substitute. Will we be able to so revolutionize agriculture that we can eventually use the "infinite" supply of phosphorus at acceptable cost? This technological and economic question is presently unresolved, although I cannot believe it to be unresolvable.

3. All of this presupposes that we have at our disposal an inexhaustible, relatively cheap source of energy. As I and others now see the technological possibilities, there is only one energy resource we can count on—and this is *nuclear fission*, based on *breeder reactors* to extend the world's supply of fissionable uranium far into the future. This is not to say that nuclear fusion, geothermal energy, or solar energy will never be economically available. We simply do not know now that any of these will ever be available in sufficient quantity and at affordable prices. We know, however, that conventional nuclear fission and breeder reactors are already technologically feasible, and standardized, improved, and that inherently safer reactor designs already being tested or on the drawing boards should bring costs down in the future.

In opting for nuclear fission breeders—and we hardly have a choice in the matter—we assume a moral and technological burden of serious proportion. A properly operating nuclear reactor and its subsystems are environmentally a very benign energy source. In particular, a reactor emits no carbon dioxide.

The issue hangs around the words "properly operating." Can we ensure that henceforth we shall be able to maintain the degree of intellectual responsibility, social commitment, and stability necessary to maintain this energy form so as not to cause serious harm? This is basically a moral and social question, though it does have strong technological components.

It is a Faustian bargain (a pact with the devil) that we strike: in return for this essentially inexhaustible energy source, which we must have if we are to maintain ourselves at anything like our present numbers and our present state of affluence, we must commit ourselves and generations to come—essentially forever—to exercise the vigilance and discipline necessary to keep our nuclear fires well behaved.

As a nuclear technologist who has devoted his career to this quest for an essentially infinite energy source, I believe the bargain is a good one, and it may even be an inevitable one, especially if our concerns about the greenhouse effect are justified. It is essential that the full dimension and implication of this Faustian bargain be recognized, especially by the young people who will have to live with the choices that are being made on this vital issue.

Guest Essay Discussion

1. Do you agree that the resources of the earth are practically infinite? Explain.

2. The author bases his optimism on three assumptions. Do you believe that these assumptions are reasonable? Explain. Are there any other assumptions that should be added?

3. Do you agree that we should accept the Faustian bargain of conventional and breeder nuclear fission? Explain.

4. Do you agree with the author that "we hardly have any choice" in opting for nuclear fission breeder reactors? Explain.

If everything goes right (another very big if), a commercial cold fusion power plant might be built as early as 2030. But even if everything goes right, energy experts don't expect cold or high-temperature nuclear fusion to be a significant source of energy until 2100, if ever. If feasible, a commercial cold nuclear fusion plant, one of the most complicated machines ever built, would create hundreds of times less radioactive waste than a nuclear fission power plant. Also, it wouldn't emit the greenhouse gases and harmful sulfur and nitrogen oxides and particulate matter that coal plants do. Meanwhile, several other quicker, cheaper, and safer ways can be used to produce more electricity than we need, as discussed in the next chapter and in the Guest Essay below.

Nuclear fission energy is safe only if a number of critical devices work as they should, if a number of people in key positions follow all their instructions, if there is no sabotage, no hijacking of the transport, if no reactor fuel processing plant or repository anywhere in the world is situated in a region of riots or guerrilla activity, and no

GUEST ESSAY   Technology Is the Answer (But What Was the Question?)

Amory B. Lovins

Physicist Amory B. Lovins is recognized as one of the world's leading experts on energy strategy. In 1989 he was the first recipient of the Delphi Prize, one of the world's top environmental awards. He is director of research at the Rocky Mountain Institute, which he and his wife cofounded in 1989. He has served as a consultant to several United Nations agencies, the U.S. Department of Energy, the Congressional Office of Technology Assessment, and the U.S. Solar Energy Research Institute. He is active in energy affairs in 15 countries and has published several hundred papers and a dozen books, including the widely discussed Soft Energy Paths *(New York: Harper Colophon, 1979), and the nontechnical version of this work with coauthor L. Hunter Lovins,* Energy Unbound: Your Invitation to Energy Abundance *(San Francisco: Sierra Club Books, 1986).*

The answers you get depend on the questions you ask. But sometimes it seems so important to resolve a crisis that we forget to ask what problem we're trying to solve.

It is fashionable to suppose that we're running out of energy, and that the solution is obviously to get lots more of it. But asking how to get more energy begs the question of how much we need. That depends not on how much we used in the past but on what we want to do in the future and how much energy it will take to do those things.

How much energy it takes to make steel, run a sewing machine, or keep you comfortable in your house depends on how cleverly we use energy, and the more it costs, the smarter we seem to get. It is now cheaper, for example, to double the efficiency of most industrial electric motor drive systems than to get more electricity to run the old ones. (Just this one saving can more than replace the entire U.S. nuclear power program.). We know how to make lights five times as efficient as those presently in use and how to make household appliances that give us the same work as now, using one-fifth as much energy (saving money in the process).

Eight automakers have made good-sized, peppy, safe prototype cars averaging 70 to 120 miles per gallon. We know today how to make new buildings and many old ones so heat-tight (but still well ventilated) that they need essentially no energy to maintain comfort year-round, even in severe climates.

These energy-saving measures are uniformly cheaper than going out and getting more energy. Detailed studies in over a dozen countries have shown that supplying energy services in the cheapest way—by wringing more work from the energy we already have—would let us increase our standard of living while using several times less total energy (and electricity) than we do now.

But the old view of the energy problem included a worse mistake than forgetting to ask how much energy we needed: It sought more energy, in any form, from any source, at any price—as if all kinds of energy were alike. This is like saying, "All kinds of food are alike; we're running short of potatoes and turnips and cheese, but that's OK, we can substitute sirloin steak and oysters Rockefeller."

Some of us have to be more discriminating than that. Just as there are different kinds of food, so there are many different forms of energy, whose different prices and qualities suit them to different uses. There is, after all, no demand for energy as such; nobody wants raw kilowatt-hours or barrels of sticky black goo. People instead want energy services: comfort, light, mobility, ability to bake bread, ability to make cement. We ought therefore to start at that end of the energy problem: to ask, "What are the many different tasks we want energy for, and what is the amount,

(Continued)

revolution or war—even a "conventional one"—takes place in these regions. No acts of God can be permitted.

Hannes Alfven, Nobel Laureate in Physics

DISCUSSION TOPICS

1. Explain why you agree or disagree with the following statements:
   a. We can get all the oil we need by extracting and processing heavy oil left in known oil wells.
   b. We can get all the oil we need by extracting and processing heavy oil from oil shale deposits.
   c. We can get all the oil we need by extracting heavy oil from tar sands.
   d. We can get all the natural gas we need from unconventional sources.

2. Coal-fired power plants in the United States cause an estimated 10,000 deaths a year, mostly from atmospheric emissions of sulfur oxides, nitrogen oxides, and particulate matter. These emissions also damage many buildings and some forests and aquatic systems. Should

---

GUEST ESSAY (continued)

type, and source of energy that will do each task *in the cheapest way?"*

Electricity is a particularly special, high-quality, expensive form of energy. An average kilowatt-hour delivered in the United States in 1987 was priced at about 8 cents, equivalent to buying the heat content of oil costing $128 per barrel—over seven times the average world price during 1987. The average cost of electricity from nuclear plants (including fuel and operating expenses) beginning operation in 1987 was at least 13.5 cents per kilowatt-hour, equivalent on a heat basis to buying oil at about $216 per barrel.

Such costly energy might be worthwhile if it were used only for the premium tasks that require it, such as lights, motors, electronics, and smelters. But those special uses, only 8% of all delivered U.S. energy needs, are already met twice over by today's power stations. Two-fifths of our electricity is already spilling over into uneconomic, low-grade uses such as water heating, space heating, and air conditioning. Yet no matter how efficiently we use electricity (even with heat pumps), we can never get our money's worth on these applications. Electricity is far too expensive to be worthwhile for the 58% of the delivered energy needed in the form of heat in the United States and for the 34% needed to run nonrail vehicles. But these tasks are all that additional electricity could be used for without wasting energy and money, because today's power stations already supply our real electric needs twice over.

Thus, *supplying more electricity is irrelevant to the energy problem that we have.* Even though electricity accounts for almost all of the federal energy research and development budget and for at least half of national energy investment, it is the wrong kind of energy to meet our needs economically. Arguing about what kind of new power station to build—coal, nuclear, solar—is like shopping for the best buy in antique Chippendale chairs to burn in your stove or brandy to put in your car's gas tank. *It is the wrong question.*

Indeed, *any kind of new power station is so uneconomical that if you have just built one, you will save the country money by writing it off and never operating it.* Why? Because its additional electricity can be used only for

low-temperature heating and cooling (the premium, "electricity-specific" uses being already filled up) and is the most expensive way of supplying these services.

The real question is what is the cheapest way to do low-temperature heating and cooling. That means weatherstripping, insulation, heat exchangers, greenhouses, superwindows, window shades and overhangs, trees, and so on. These measures generally cost about half a penny per kilowatt-hour, whereas the running costs *alone* for a new nuclear plant will be nearly 4 cents per kilowatt-hour, so it is cheaper not to run it. In fact, under our crazy U.S tax laws, the extra saving from not having to pay the plant's future subsidies is probably so big that society can also recover the capital cost of having built the plant by shutting it down!

If we want more electricity, we should get it from the cheapest sources first. In approximate order of increasing price, these include:

1. Converting to efficient lighting. This would save the U.S. electricity equal to the output of 120 large power plants plus $30 billion a year in fuel and maintenance costs.

2. Eliminating pure waste of electricity, such as lighting empty offices at headache level.

3. Displacing with good architecture, and with passive and some active solar techniques, the electricity now used for water heating and space heating and cooling. Some U.S. utilities now give low- or zero-interest weatherization loans, which you need not start repaying for 10 years or until you sell your house—because it saves them millions of dollars to get electricity that way compared with building new power plants.

4. Making lights, motors, appliances, smelters, and the like cost-effectively efficient.

Just these four measures can quadruple U.S. electrical efficiency, making it possible to run today's economy, with no changes in lifestyles, using no thermal power plants, whether old or new, and whether fueled with oil, gas, coal, or uranium. We would need only the present hydroelectric capacity, readily available small-scale hydroelectric projects, and a modest

air pollution emission standards for *all* new and existing coal-burning plants be tightened significantly? Explain.

3. Should all coal-burning power and industrial plants in the United States be required to convert to fluidized-bed combustion? Explain. What are the alternatives?

4. Do you favor a U.S. energy strategy based on greatly increased use of coal-burning plants to produce electricity? Explain. What are the alternatives?

5. List the energy services you would like to have, and note which of these must be furnished by electricity.

6. Explain why you agree or disagree with the following statements:

   a. Dry-steam, wet-steam, and hot-water geothermal deposits can supply most needs for electricity in the United States by the year 2010.

   b. Molten rock (magma) geothermal deposits should be able to supply the United States with all the electricity and high-temperature heat it needs by 2025.

   c. Although geothermal energy may not be a major source of energy for the United States over the next few decades, it can supply a significant fraction of

amount of windpower. But if we still wanted more electricity, the next cheapest sources would include:

5. Industrial cogeneration, combined-heat-and-power plants, low-temperature heat engines run by industrial waste heat or by solar ponds, filling empty turbine bays and upgrading equipment in existing big dams, modern wind machines or small-scale hydroelectric turbines in good sites, steam-injected natural gas turbines, and perhaps recent developments in solar cells with waste heat recovery.

It is only after we had clearly exhausted all these cheaper opportunities that we would even consider:

6. Building a new central power station of any kind— the slowest and costliest known way to get more electricity (or to save oil).

To emphasize the importance of starting with energy end uses rather than energy sources, consider a sad little story from France, involving a "spaghetti chart" (or energy flowchart)—a device energy planners often use to show how energy flows from primary sources via conversion processes to final forms and uses. In the mid-1970s energy conservation planners in the French government started, wisely, on the right-hand side of the spaghetti chart. They found that their biggest single need for energy was to heat buildings, and that even with good heat pumps, electricity would be the most uneconomic way to do this. So they had a fight with their nationalized utility; they won; and electric heating was supposed to be discouraged or even phased out because it was so wasteful of money and fuel.

But meanwhile, down the street, the energy supply planners (who were far more numerous and influential in the French government) were starting on the left-hand side of the spaghetti chart. They said: "Look at all that nasty imported oil coming into our country! We must replace that oil. Oil is energy. . . . We need some other source of energy. Voilà! Reactors can give us energy; we'll build nuclear reactors all over the country." But they paid little attention to what would happen to that extra energy, and no attention to relative prices.

Thus, the two sides of the French energy establishment went on with their respective solutions to two different, indeed contradictory, French energy problems: *more energy of any kind*, versus *the right kind to do each task cheapest*. It was only in 1979 that these conflicting perceptions collided. The supply side planners suddenly realized that the only way they would be able to *sell* all that nuclear electricity would be for electric heating, which they had just agreed not to do.

Every industrial country is in this embarrassing position (especially if we include in "heating" air conditioning, which just means heating the outdoors instead of the indoors). Which end of the spaghetti chart we start on, or *what we think the energy problem is*, is not an academic abstraction: It *determines what we buy*. It is the most fundamental source of disagreement about energy policy.

People starting on the left side of the spaghetti chart think the problem boils down to whether to build coal or nuclear power stations (or both). People starting on the right realize that *no* kind of new power station can be an economic way to meet the needs for low- and high-temperature heat and for vehicular liquid fuels that are 92% of our energy problem.

So if we want to provide our energy services at a price we can afford, let's get straight what question our technologies are supposed to provide the answer to. Before we argue about the meatballs, let's untangle the strands of spaghetti, see where they're supposed to lead, and find out what we really need the energy *for*!

Guest Essay Discussion

1. List the energy services you would like to have, and note which of these must be furnished by electricity.

2. Do you agree or disagree that increasing the supply of energy, instead of concentrating on improving energy efficiency, is the wrong answer to U.S. energy problems? Explain.

energy needs in areas where high-quality deposits are found.

7. Do you favor a U.S. energy strategy based on building a large number of better-designed, conventional nuclear fission reactors to produce electricity? Explain.

8. Explain why you agree or disagree with each of the following proposals made by the nuclear power industry:

   a. The licensing time of new nuclear power plants in the United States should be halved (from an average of 12 to 6 years) so that they can be built at less cost and compete more effectively with coal and other renewable energy alternatives.

   b. A major program for developing the nuclear breeder fission reactor should be developed and funded by the federal government to conserve uranium resources and keep the United States from being dependent on other countries for uranium supplies.

9. According to the Department of Energy, commercial nuclear power in the United States received $1 trillion in research and development and other federal subsidies between 1952 and 1988—an average of $9 billion per reactor. Even with these enormous subsidies, nuclear power in the U.S. is not economically competitive with other energy alternatives that have received less or little federal subsidies. Do you believe that U.S. taxpayers should continue subsidizing commercial nuclear power, or should it be required to compete in the marketplace with little if any government subsidies? Explain.

10. Find out what has happened with the possible breakthrough in carrying out nuclear fusion at room temperature, which was announced at the time this book was being printed. If this turns out to be an economically feasible breakthrough that can be developed over the next 30 to 60 years, explain why this will help but still won't solve our energy, mineral resource, pollution, and environmental degradation problems (see p. 89).

FURTHER READINGS

Also see Readings for Chapter 4.

Allar, Bruce. 1984. "No More Coal-Smoked Skies?" *Environment*, vol. 26, no. 2, 25–30.

Campbell, John L. 1988. *Collapse of an Industry: Nuclear Power and the Contradictions of U.S. Policy.* Ithaca, N.Y.: Cornell University Press.

Carter, Luther J. 1987. *Nuclear Imperatives and Public Trust: Dealing with Radioactive Waste.* Baltimore: Resources for the Future.

Clark, Wilson, and Jake Page. 1983. *Energy, Vulnerability, and War.* New York: W. W. Norton.

Cohen, Bernard L. 1983. *Before It's Too Late: A Scientist's Case for Nuclear Power.* New York: Plenum Press.

Congressional Quarterly Editors. 1985. *Energy and Environment: The Unfinished Business.* Washington, D.C.: Congressional Quarterly.

Flavin, Christopher. 1985. *World Oil: Coping with the Dangers of Success.* Washington, D.C.: Worldwatch Institute.

Flavin, Christopher. 1987. *Reassessing Nuclear Power: The Fallout from Chernobyl.* Washington, D.C.: Worldwatch Institute.

Flavin, Christopher. 1988. "The Case Against Reviving Nuclear Power." *World Watch*, July/Aug., 27–35.

Ford, Daniel F. 1986. *Meltdown.* New York: Simon & Schuster.

Hippenheimer, T. A. 1984. *The Man-Made Sun: The Quest for Fusion Power.* Boston: Little, Brown.

Holdren, John. 1982. "Energy Hazards: What to Measure, What to Compare." *Technology Review*, April, 32–38.

Hunt, Charles B. 1984. "Disposal of Radioactive Wastes." *Bulletin of the Atomic Scientists*, April, 44–46.

Kaku, Michio, and Jennifer Trainer. 1982. *Nuclear Power: Both Sides.* New York: W. W. Norton.

League of Women Voters Education Fund. 1985. *The Nuclear Waste Primer.* Washington D.C.: League of Women Voters.

Lidsky, Lawrence M. 1984. "The Reactor of the Future." *Technology Review*, Feb.-Mar., 52–56.

Lovins, Amory B., and L. Hunter Lovins. 1982. *Brittle Power: Energy Strategy for National Security.* Andover, Mass.: Brick House.

Mould, Richard F. 1988. *Chernobyl: The Real Story.* New York: Pergamon.

National Academy of Sciences. 1988. *Geothermal Energy Technology.* Washington, D.C.: National Academy Press.

Office of Technology Assessment. 1984. *Managing the Nation's Commercial High-Level Radioactive Waste.* Washington, D.C.: Government Printing Office.

Patterson, Walter C. 1984. *The Plutonium Business and the Spread of the Bomb.* San Francisco: Sierra Club Books.

Pollack, Cynthia. 1986. *Decommissioning: Nuclear Power's Missing Link.* Washington, D.C.: Worldwatch Institute.

President's Commission on the Accident at Three Mile Island. 1979. *Report of the President's Commission on the Accident at Three Mile Island.* Washington, D.C.: Government Printing Office.

Resnikoff, Marvin. 1987. *Living Without Landfills.* New York: Radioactive Waste Campaign.

Schobert, Harold H. 1987. *Coal: The Energy Source of the Past and Future.* Washington, D.C.: American Chemical Society.

Shahinpoor, Mohsen. 1982. "Making Oil From Sand." *Technology Review*, Feb.-Mar., 49–54.

Taylor, John J. 1989. "Improved and Safer Nuclear Power." *Science* 244, 318–25.

Union of Concerned Scientists. 1985. *Safety Second: A Critical Evaluation of the NRC's First Decade.* Washington, D.C.: Union of Concerned Scientists.

U.S. Department of Energy. 1988. *An Analysis of Nuclear Power Operating Costs.* Washington, D.C.: Government Printing Office.

U.S. Office of Technology Assessment. 1984. *Nuclear Power in an Age of Uncertainty.* Washington, D.C.: Government Printing Office.

Watson, Robert K. 1988. *Fact Sheet on Oil and Conservation Resources.* New York: Natural Resources Defense Council.

Weinberg, Alvin M.. 1985. *Continuing the Nuclear Dialogue.* La Grange Park, Ill.: American Nuclear Society.

CHAPTER 20

Renewable and Perpetual Energy Resources: Conservation, Sun, Wind, Water, and Biomass

General Questions and Issues

1. What are the advantages and disadvantages of improving energy efficiency as a way to reduce unnecessary waste?

2. What are the advantages and disadvantages of capturing and using some of the sun's direct input of solar energy for heating buildings and water and for producing electricity?

3. What are the advantages and disadvantages of using indirect solar energy stored in falling and flowing water (hydropower) for producing electricity?

4. What are the advantages and disadvantages of using indirect solar energy in the form of heat stored in water for producing electricity and heating buildings and water?

5. What are the advantages and disadvantages of using indirect solar energy stored in winds to produce electricity?

6. What are the advantages and disadvantages of using renewable, indirect solar energy stored in plants and organic waste (biomass) for heating buildings and water and for transportation (biofuels)?

7. What are the advantages and disadvantages of producing and using hydrogen gas and fuel cells to produce electricity, to heat buildings and water, and to propel vehicles when oil runs out?

8. What are the best present and future energy options for the United States and what should be the country's long-term energy strategy?

If the United States wants to save a lot of oil and money and increase national security, there are two simple ways to do it: Stop driving petropigs and stop living in energy sieves.

Amory B. Lovins

W hat is our best energy option? The answer is: Cut out unnecessary energy waste. What is our next best energy option? Here there is much disagreement.

Some say: Find and burn more conventional and unconventional forms of oil, natural gas, and coal. Some say: Build more and better conventional nuclear power plants and increase efforts to develop breeder nuclear fission and nuclear fusion. These choices, based on using more of the earth's nonrenewable resources, were evaluated in the last chapter.

Others say: Get more of the energy we need from the sun, wind, flowing water, biomass, and renewable forms of geothermal energy. They urge us to make more use of locally available energy supplies instead of building more large, fossil-fuel and nuclear plants and having them send energy to us. These energy

choices, based on using the earth's perpetual and renewable energy resources, are evaluated in this chapter.

20-1 IMPROVING ENERGY EFFICIENCY: DOING MORE WITH LESS

Reducing Energy Waste: An Offer We Can't Afford to Refuse The easiest and cheapest way to make more energy available with the least environmental impact is to reduce or eliminate unnecessary energy use and waste. There are three general ways we can do this:

- We can reduce energy consumption by changing energy-wasting habits. Examples of such changes include walking or riding a bicycle for short trips, using mass transit instead of cars, wearing a sweater indoors in cold weather to allow a lower thermostat setting, and turning off unneeded lights.

- **We can improve energy efficiency by using less energy to do the same amount of work.** Examples include adding more insulation to houses and buildings, keeping car engines tuned, and switching to more energy-efficient cars, houses, heating and cooling systems, appliances, lights, and industrial processes.

- **We can also use less energy to do more work by developing devices that waste less energy than existing ones.** Examples include solar cells that convert solar energy directly to electricity, aerodynamic vehicle designs that reduce fuel consumption, and more efficient heating and cooling systems, appliances, and vehicle engines.

Improving energy efficiency has the highest net useful energy yield of all energy alternatives. It reduces the environmental impacts of using energy because less of each energy resource is used. It adds no carbon dioxide to the atmosphere and is the best, cheapest, and quickest way to slow down the greenhouse effect. If worldwide energy efficiency improved by 2% a year, major changes in climate from the greenhouse effect would probably be delayed until at least 2075.

Reducing the amount of energy we use and waste makes domestic and world supplies of nonrenewable fossil fuels last longer, buys time for phasing in perpetual and renewable energy resources, and reduces dependence on imported oil. Furthermore, it usually provides more jobs and promotes more economic growth per unit of energy than other energy alternatives. By contrast, each big, new power plant loses the economy about 4,000 jobs by starving other sectors of the capital they need.

Improving energy efficiency also has fewer disadvantages than any energy alternative. One disadvantage is that improving energy efficiency by replacing houses, industrial equipment, and cars as they wear out with more energy-efficient ones takes a long time. For example, replacing most buildings and industrial equipment takes several decades, and replacing the older cars on the road with new ones takes 10 to 12 years. Some of the improvements in automobile gas mileage depend on driving smaller and lighter cars, which some drivers don't like.

Japan, Sweden, and France have the highest energy efficiency of any MDCs. The Soviet Union has the lowest and the United States and Canada fall between these extremes. Because the United States uses more energy than any country and has only moderate energy efficiency, it wastes more energy than any country (see Spotlight below).

Improving Industrial Energy Efficiency In the United States, industrial processes consume more energy than transportation, residences, and commercial buildings

---

SPOTLIGHT The World's Biggest Energy User and Waster

As the world's largest energy user and waster, the United States has more impact on fossil fuel depletion, the greenhouse effect, and acid deposition than any country. At least half of all energy used in the United States is unnecessarily wasted. This waste equals all the energy consumed by two-thirds of the world's population.

Some progress has been made. Between 1975 and 1988, energy efficiency improvements in the United States supplied more new energy (by reducing waste) than all other alternatives combined. This waste reduction has cut the country's energy bills by about $150 billion a year.

On the average, American houses now use 20% less space-heating energy per square foot than they did in 1975. The average new home being built today is 35% more energy-efficient than the typical house built before 1973 and some new houses are 75% more efficient. In 1988 new U.S. autos averaged about 26.5 miles per gallon, nearly double that of new cars in 1973. New refrigerators are now about 72% more efficient than they were in 1972.

Despite these improvements, energy efficiency in the United States is half what it could be. Average gas mileage for new cars and for the entire fleet of cars is below that in most other MDCs. Most U.S. houses and buildings are still underinsulated and leaky. Electric resistance heating is the most wasteful and expensive way to heat a home. Yet it is installed in over half the new homes in the United States.

Known ways to improve the efficiency of electricity use in the United States could replace the electricity produced by 250 large power plants. This would cut the country's annual electricity bill by $100 billion.

The amount the United States spends each year to buy energy would be reduced by $200 billion a year if it used energy as efficiently as Japan or Sweden. This annual savings could be used to pay off the national debt, invest in new improvements in energy efficiency and new energy alternatives, and stimulate the economy. What do you think should be done?

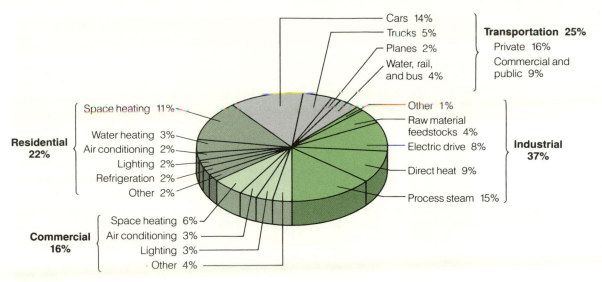

Cars 14%
Trucks 5%
Planes 2%
Water, rail, and bus 4%

Transportation 25%
Private 16%
Commercial and public 9%

Space heating 11%

Residential 22%
Water heating 3%
Air conditioning 2%
Lighting 2%
Refrigeration 2%
Other 2%

Other 1%
Raw material feedstocks 4%
Electric drive 8%
Direct heat 9%
Process steam 15%

Industrial 37%

Commercial 16%
Space heating 6%
Air conditioning 3%
Lighting 3%
Other 4%

Figure 20-1 Distribution of commercial energy use in the United States among various sectors in 1984. (Data from U.S. Department of Energy)

(Figure 20-1). Today American industry uses 70% less energy to produce the same amount of goods as it did in 1973. But American industry still wastes enormous amounts of energy.

Japan has the highest overall industrial energy efficiency in the world. Denmark, France, Italy, Spain, and West Germany also have high industrial energy efficiencies. Japanese products have a 5% average price advantage over American goods simply because of the higher average energy cost of U.S. goods.

Industries that use large amounts of high-temperature heat and electricity can save energy and money by installing *cogeneration units,* which produce both of these types of energy. Today industrial cogeneration in the United States supplies electricity equal to the output of 16 large (1,000-megawatt) power plants. By 2000 cogeneration has the potential to produce more electricity than all of the country's nuclear power plants.

Industry uses almost half of the world's electricity. Massive amounts are used to convert aluminum ore to aluminum metal. A new process for doing this uses 25% less electricity. Using recycled aluminum reduces electricity use by 95%. Despite such enormous savings, the average world aluminum-recycling rate is only 25%. This could easily be doubled or tripled.

About 70% of the electricity used in U.S. industry drives electric motors. Most of these motors run at fixed speeds and voltages regardless of the tasks they perform. Adding variable-speed drives, light dimmers, and other devices that match the output of a motor or other electrical device to power needs would cut U.S. electricity use by one-sixth. This would eliminate the need for all existing U.S. nuclear power plants and save hundreds of millions of dollars a year.

Within 20 years newly discovered superconduc-

tors could save energy and money. Another major way to save energy in industry is to greatly reduce the production of throwaway items. This can be done by increasing recycling and reuse and by making products that last longer and are easy to repair and recycle (see Section 18-6).

Improving Transportation Energy Efficiency One-fourth of the supplemental energy consumed in the United States is used to transport people and goods (Figure 20–1). With 4.8% of the world's people, the United States has 35% of the world's cars and trucks. Each year these vehicles travel almost as many miles as the rest of the world's motor vehicles taken together.

The increased use of the automobile, especially in the United States, has decreased the use of railroads and buses and has led to energy-wasting urban sprawl. About one-tenth of the oil consumed in the world each day is used by American motorists on their way to and from work, two-thirds of them driving alone.

Today transportation consumes 63% of all oil used in the United States—up from 50% in 1973. Transportation also uses much of the oil consumed in other countries: 39% in Japan, 44% in western Europe, and 49% in LDCs.

Thus, the best way to reduce world oil consumption and to slow down the greenhouse effect is to improve vehicle fuel economy (Figure 20-2), make greater use of mass transit (Figure 20-3), and haul freight more efficiently. Denmark had the highest average fuel efficiency for new and existing cars, followed closely by West Germany, Italy, Japan, and the United Kingdom. Canada and the United States have the lowest. Between 1973 and 1988 the average fuel efficiency of new American cars nearly doubled, and the average

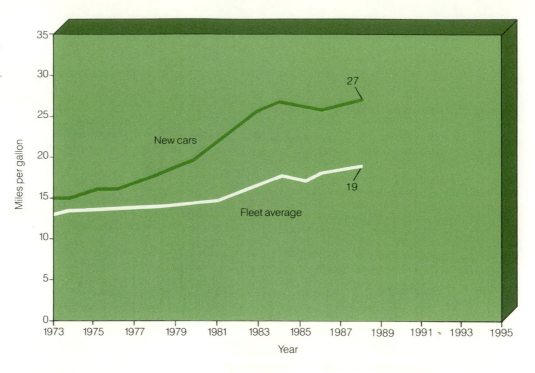

Figure 20-2 Increase in average fuel efficiency of new cars and the entire fleet of cars in the United States between 1973 and 1988. (Data from U.S. Department of Energy and Environmental Protection Agency)

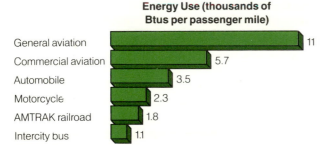

Energy Use (thousands of Btus per passenger mile)

General aviation — 11
Commercial aviation — 5.7
Automobile — 3.5
Motorcycle — 2.3
AMTRAK railroad — 1.8
Intercity bus — 1.1

Figure 20-3 Energy efficiency of various types of domestic transportation.

fuel efficiency of all the cars on the road increased from 13 miles per gallon (mpg) to 20 miles per gallon.

This is an important gain. But it is well below the 30 to 33 mpg fuel efficiency of new cars and the 22 to 25 mpg fuel efficiency of car fleets in Japan and western Europe. Because of lower fuel efficiency and more driving, the average car in the United States and Canada burns twice as much gasoline each year as the average car in Japan and western Europe.

New U.S. cars were supposed to average 27.5 mpg by 1985. But Congress caved in to pressure from carmakers and the Reagan administration and since 1985 has rolled back the average required for new cars from 27.5 mpg to 26 mpg. Environmentalists call this a tragic economic, environmental, and strategic mistake. Each 1-mpg improvement in the car and light truck fleet saves about as much oil as the United States imports each year from the Persian Gulf.

According to the U.S. Office of Technology Assessment, new cars produced in the United States could

easily average between 38 to 55 mpg by 1992, with only $50 to $90 added to the cost of a car. By the year 2000 new U.S. cars could average 51 to 78 mpg for an additional cost of $120 to $330 a car. Replacing the U.S. car and light truck fleet with 60-mpg vehicles would save over 5 million barrels of oil per day, eliminating the need to import any oil.

By 1988 the three leading American car companies had discontinued much of their research and development on small, more fuel-efficient cars. The major reasons for this were the higher profits to be made on larger cars and declining consumer interest in improved fuel efficiency because of the temporary oil glut of the 1980s.

Meanwhile, Japan and some western European countries have increased their research in this area. They want to have fuel-efficient cars ready when the oil crisis of the 1990s replaces the oil glut of the 1980s. The Chevrolet GEO built in Japan by Suzuki has a fuel efficiency of 57 mpg. Prototype models built by Volvo, Volkswagen, Toyota, Peugeot, and Renault get 71 to 124 mpg. The Volvo LCP-2000 gets 63 mpg in the city and 81 mpg on the highway. It seats four, weighs half as much as the average American car, exceeds U.S. crash safety standards, meets U.S. air pollution limits, and has better acceleration than the average American car. It is ready for production and could be mass produced at about the same cost as today's subcompacts. Widespread use of these new designs could raise the average fuel economy of new cars and trucks to between 60 and 100 mpg over the next 20 years.

There are several other ways to make the world's diminishing supply of oil last longer. One is to shift

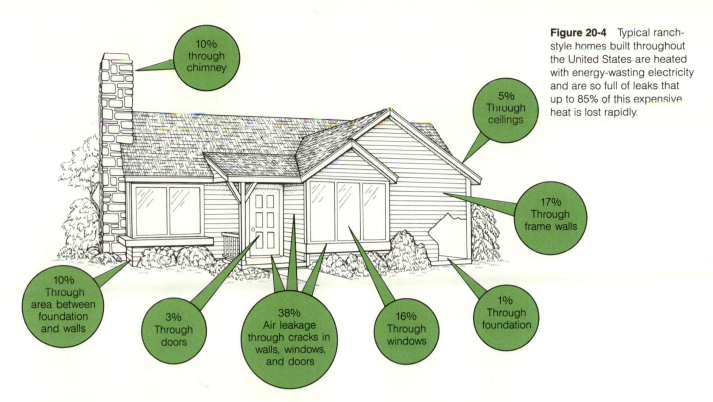

Figure 20-4 Typical ranch-style homes built throughout the United States are heated with energy-wasting electricity and are so full of leaks that up to 85% of this expensive heat is lost rapidly.

10%
through
chimney

5%
Through
ceilings

17%
Through
frame walls

10%
Through
area between
foundation
and walls

3%
Through
doors

38%
Air leakage
through cracks in
walls, windows,
and doors

16%
Through
windows

1%
Through
foundation

more freight from trucks and airplanes to trains (Figure 20-3). Manufacturers can increase the energy efficiency of transport trucks by improving their aerodynamic design and by using turbocharged diesel engines and radial tires. Trucking companies can reduce waste by helping truckers not to return empty after reaching their destination. The energy efficiency of today's commercial jet aircraft fleet could be doubled by improved designs.

Improving the Energy Efficiency of Commercial and Residential Buildings Most commercial and residential buildings in the United States consume much more energy than necessary (Figure 20-4). With existing technology the United States could save 40% to 60% of the energy used in existing buildings and 70% to 90% of the energy used in new buildings.

Sweden and South Korea have the world's toughest standards for energy efficiency in buildings and houses. For example, the average home in Sweden, the world's leader in energy efficiency, consumes about one-third as much energy as an average American home of the same size.

A monument to energy waste is the 110-story, twin-towered World Trade Center in Manhattan, which uses as much electricity as a city of 100,000 persons. Windows in its walls of glass cannot be opened to take advantage of natural warming and cooling. Its heating and cooling systems must run around the clock, chiefly to take away heat from its inefficient lighting.

By contrast, Atlanta's 20-story Georgia Power Company building uses 60% less energy than conventional office buildings. The largest surface of the building is oriented to capture solar energy. Each floor extends over the one below, allowing heating by the low, winter sun and blocking out the higher, summer sun to reduce air conditioning costs. Energy-efficient lights focus on desks rather than illuminating entire rooms. Employees working at unusual hours use an adjoining three-story building so that the larger structure doesn't have to be heated or cooled when few people are at work.

Building a *superinsulated house* is the best way to improve the efficiency of residential space heating and save on lifetime energy costs, especially in cold climates (Figure 20-5). Such a house is heavily insulated and made extremely airtight. Heat from direct solar gain, people, and appliances warms the house, requiring little if any auxiliary heating. An air-to-air heat exchanger prevents buildup of humidity and indoor air pollution.

New superinsulated houses in Sweden, where winters are very cold, stay warm all winter and use only $100 worth of fuel. Currently, there are about 25,000 superinsulated houses in North America, with about 5,000 more built every year. However, this is only about 1% of new housing construction.

Most home buyers look only at the initial price, not the more meaningful lifetime cost. A superinsulated house costs about 5% more to build than a conventional house. But this extra cost is paid back by energy savings within five years and can save a homeowner $50,000 to $100,000 over a 40-year period. Combining energy efficiency measures with existing and emerging technology could greatly increase the energy efficiency of new houses (see Spotlight on p. 519).

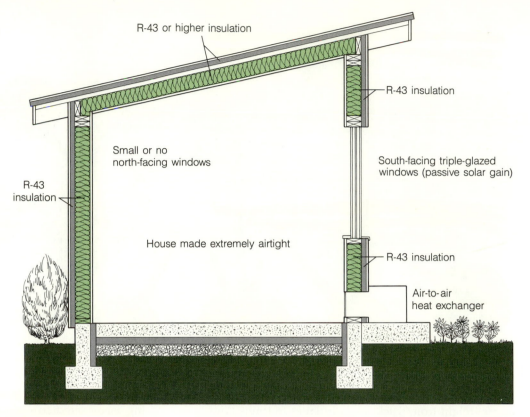

Figure 20-5 Major features of a superinsulated house.

R-43 or higher insulation

R-43 insulation

Small or no north-facing windows

South-facing triple-glazed windows (passive solar gain)

R-43 insulation

R-43 insulation

House made extremely airtight

Air-to-air heat exchanger

Many energy-saving features can be added to existing homes, a process called *retrofitting*. Simply increasing insulation above ceilings can drastically reduce heating and cooling loads. The home owner usually recovers initial costs in two to six years and then saves money each year. Caulking and weatherstripping around windows, doors, pipes, vents, ducts, and wires save energy and money quickly. Switching to new gas furnaces with energy efficiencies of 90% to 95%, compared to 60% to 65% for most conventional gas furnaces, also saves energy and money on a lifetime-cost basis (Figure 4-15, p. 87).

Maintaining a military force in the Persian Gulf to protect oil tankers means that the United States is paying about $485 a barrel for oil imported from the Middle East. If one year's budget for this military force in the Gulf was spent on making U.S. buildings more heat-tight, this would save more oil than the country imports from the Middle East.

One-third of the heat in U.S. homes escapes through closed windows—an energy loss equal to the energy in all the oil flowing through the Alaskan pipeline each year. The heat escapes because a single-pane glass window has an insulating value of only R-1. The R-value of a material indicates its insulating ability. Even double-glazed windows have an insulating value of only R-2 and a typical triple-glazed window has an insulating value of R-4 to R-6.

Two U.S. firms now sell "superinsulating" R-10 to R-12 windows, about the insulating value of a normal outside wall (R-11), which pay for themselves in 2 to 4 years. These superwindows, which cost less than

conventional triple-glazed windows, combine triple-glazing, heat-reflecting films (which let light in without letting much heat out) and inert insulating gases such as argon. If everyone in the United States used these windows, we would save more oil and natural gas each year than Alaska now supplies. The cost of saving this energy is equivalent to buying oil at $2 to $3 a barrel.

Today American homes are responsible for 14% of the carbon dioxide emitted into the atmosphere from burning all fossil fuels. Home energy use also accounts for 25% of sulfur dioxide emissions and 13% of nitrogen oxides emissions—both key causes of acid deposition. Cutting average home energy use in half would also cut these emissions in half.

Communities can also use laws to increase energy conservation in homes and buildings. Building codes can be changed to require that all new houses use 80% less energy than conventional houses of the same size, as has been done in Davis, California (see Spotlight on p. 265). Laws can require that any existing house be insulated and weatherproofed to certain standards before it can be sold, as required in Portland, Oregon, for example.

Using the most energy-efficient appliances available can also save energy and money.* About one-

---

*Each year the American Council for an Energy-Efficient Economy publishes a list of the most energy-efficient major appliances sold in the U.S. For a copy, send $2 to the council at 1001 Connecticut Ave., N.W., Suite 530, Washington, DC 20036.

third of the electricity generated in the United States and other industrial countries is used to power household appliances.

At least 20% of the electricity produced in the United States is used for lighting—about equal to the output of 100 large power plants. Burning one 100-watt light bulb just six hours a day each year consumes energy equal to that in fifteen 55-gallon barrels of oil. Since conventional incandescent bulbs are only 5% efficient, their use wastes enormous amounts of energy and adds to the heat load of houses during hot weather. Using available superefficient lighting can cut energy needs for lighting in the United States by 75%.

Socket-type fluorescent light bulbs that use one-fourth as much electricity as conventional bulbs are now available. Although they cost about $20 a bulb, they last about 13 times longer than conventional bulbs, and save 3 times more money than they cost through lower electricity bills. Switching to these bulbs and other improved lighting equipment would save one-third of the electric energy now produced by all U.S. coal-fired plants or eliminate the need for all electricity produced by the country's 111 nuclear power plants.

The amount of electricity used for lighting could be cut in half by installing more efficient ballasts that regulate the flow of electricity in fluorescent lights and by installing automatic dimmer switches to turn down lights when there is enough sunlight to illuminate building interiors. This would eliminate the need for 50 large power plants.

U.S. refrigerators consume about 7% of the country's electricity, roughly the output of 26 large power plants. If all U.S. households had the most efficient, 17-cubic-foot, frost-free refrigerators now available, they would save enough electricity to eliminate the need for 18 large nuclear or coal-fired power plants. New prototype refrigerators being built in Denmark and Japan cut electricity use by another 50%.

Similar savings are possible with high-efficiency models of other energy appliances such as stoves, hot water heaters, and air conditioners. If the most energy-efficient appliances now available were installed in U.S. homes over the next 20 years, we would save fuel equal to all the oil produced by Alaska's North Slope fields over their 25-year lifetime.

The 1987 National Appliance Energy Conservation Act set minimum energy efficiency standards for major appliances. Within 20 years this law should save energy equal to that in 1.5 billion barrels of oil plus the output of 40 large power plants.

Developing a Personal Energy Conservation Plan

Each of us can develop an individual plan for saving energy and money (see inside back cover for suggestions). Four basic guidelines:

- Don't use electricity to heat space or water.

- Insulate new or existing houses heavily, and caulk and weatherstrip to reduce air infiltration and heat loss.

- Get as much heat and cooling as possible from natural sources—especially sun, wind, geothermal energy, and trees for windbreaks and natural shading.

- Buy the most energy-efficient homes, cars, and appliances available, and evaluate them only in terms of lifetime cost.

SPOTLIGHT The Energy-Efficient House of the Near Future

The energy-efficient house of the near future will be controlled by microprocessors (computer chips), each programmed to do a different job. These microprocessors will monitor indoor temperatures, sunlight angles, and the location of people and will then send heat or cooled air where it is needed. Some will automatically open and close windows and insulated shutters to take advantage of solar energy and breezes and to reduce heat loss from windows at night and on cloudy days.

Windows will have a coating like the light-sensitive glass in some sunglasses, automatically becoming opaque to keep the sunlight out when the house gets too hot. Superinsulating windows (R-10 to R-12) already available mean that a house can have as many windows as the owner wants in any climate without much heat loss. Thinner insulation material will allow roofs to be insulated to R-100 and walls to R-43, far higher than today's best superinsulated houses (Figure 20-5).

Small-scale cogeneration units that run on natural gas or LPG are already available. They can supply a home with all its space heat, hot water, and electricity needs. The units are no larger than a refrigerator and make less noise than a dishwasher. Except for an occasional change of oil filters and spark plugs, they are nearly maintenance-free. Typically, this home-sized power and heating plant will pay for itself in four to five years.

Soon home owners may get all the electricity they need from rolls of solar cells attached like shingles to a roof or applied to window glass as a coating (already developed by Arco). Amory and Hunter Lovins (see Guest Essay, p. 509) have built a large, passively heated, superinsulated, partially earth-sheltered home and offices in Old Snowmass, Colorado.

Table 20-1 Energy Use and Conservation in the United States and Sweden

Use or Method	United States	Sweden
Average per capita use	230,000 kcal/day	150,000 kcal/day
Transportation energy use	High	Moderate
Country size	Large	Small
Cities	Dispersed	Compact
Mass transit use	Low	High
Average car fuel economy	Fair	Good
Gasoline taxes	Low	High to encourage conservation
Tariffs on oil imports	Low	High to encourage conservation
Industrial energy efficiency	Fairly low	High (fuels) to low (electricity)
Nationwide energy-conserving building codes	No	Yes (buildings over twice as efficient as those in U.S., despite colder climate)
Municipally owned district heating systems	None	35% of population
Emphasis on electricity for space heating	High (one-half of new homes)	High (one-half of new homes)
Domestic hot water	Most kept hot 24 hours a day in large tanks	Most supplied as needed by instant tankless heaters
Refrigerators	Mostly large, frost-free	Mostly smaller, non-frost free, using about one-third the electricity of U.S. models
Long-range national energy plan	No	Yes
Government emphasis and expenditures on energy conservation and renewable energy	Low	High
Government emphasis and expenditures on nuclear power	High	Low (to be phased out)

Energy Efficiency Differences Between Countries

Japan, Sweden, and most industrialized western European countries have average standards of living at least equal to and in some cases greater than that in the United States. Yet people in these countries use an average of one-third to two-thirds less energy per person than Americans.

One reason for this difference is that these countries put greater emphasis on improving energy efficiency than the United States does (Table 20-1). Another is that most cities in these countries are more compact than U.S. cities. This means that the average person in these countries drives fewer miles per year than the average American.

20-2 DIRECT SOLAR ENERGY FOR PRODUCING HEAT AND ELECTRICITY

Passive Solar Systems for Space Heating A **passive solar heating system** captures sunlight directly within a structure and converts it to low-temperature heat for space heating (Figure 20-6). It has several design features. Insulating windows or a greenhouse or solarium facing the sun collect solar energy by direct gain. Thermal mass such as walls and floors of concrete, adobe, brick, stone, or tile store the collected solar energy as heat and release it slowly throughout the day and night. Some designs also use water-filled glass or plastic columns, black-painted barrels, and panels or cabinets containing heat-absorbing chemicals to store heat.

Besides collecting and storing solar energy as heat, passive systems must also reduce heat loss. Such structures are heavily insulated and caulked and have insulating windows. Movable, insulated shutters or curtains on windows or superwindows reduce heat loss at night and on days with little sunshine.

Houses with passive solar systems often have an open design to allow the collected and stored heat to be distributed by natural airflow or fans. Buildup of moisture and indoor air pollutants is prevented by an air-to-air heat exchanger, which supplies fresh air without much heat loss or gain. A small backup heating system may be used but is not needed in most well-designed, passively heated, superinsulated houses. A passive solar system can be even more efficient in an earth-sheltered house (see Figure 20-6 and Spotlight on p. 523). Today, about 500,000 homes and 17,000 nonresidential buildings in the United States have passive solar designs.

A series of roof-mounted passive solar water heaters (Figure 20-7) can also supply hot water for a house. The installed cost is $1800 to $4000 in the United States and $1000 in Israel and Japan.

Passively heated buildings must also be designed to stay cool in hot weather. Passive cooling can be provided by deciduous trees, window overhangs, or awnings to block the high summer sun (Figure 20-6). Think of a mature deciduous tree between a house and the summer sun as five window-mounted air conditioners. Windows and fans take advantage of breezes and keep air moving. A foil sheet can be suspended in the attic to block heat from radiating down into the house.

At a depth of 10 to 20 feet, the temperature of the earth stays about 55°F all year long in cold northern climates and about 67°F in warm southern climates. Buried earth tubes can pipe cool and partially dehumidified air into an energy-efficient house at a cost of several dollars a summer (Figure 20-6).

In areas with dry climates, such as the southwestern United States, evaporative coolers can remove interior heat by evaporating water. In hot and humid areas a small dehumidifier or a solar-assisted geothermal heat pump may be needed to lower humidity to acceptable levels. Solar-powered air conditioners have been developed but so far are too expensive for residential use.

Some office buildings in Sweden collect and store so much heat given off by people and equipment that they require little if any auxiliary heating. In Reno, Nevada, some buildings stay cool throughout the hot summer without air conditioning; large, insulated tanks of water chilled by cool nighttime air keep indoor temperatures comfortable during the day.

Active Solar Systems for Heating Space and Water In an **active solar heating system** specially designed collectors concentrate solar energy and store it as heat for space heating and heating water. Several connected collectors are usually mounted on a roof with an unobstructed southern exposure (Figure 20-7).

Solar energy collected as heat is transferred to water, an antifreeze solution, or air pumped through copper pipe inside the collector. The heated solution or air is pumped through and stored in an insulated tank containing water or rocks. Thermostat-controlled fans or pumps distribute this stored heat as needed, usually through conventional heating ducts. In middle and high latitudes with cold winter temperatures and moderate levels of sunlight (Figure 20-8, p. 525), a

small backup heating system is needed during prolonged cold or cloudy periods.

Active solar collectors can also supply hot water. Over 1 million active solar hot water systems have been installed in the United States, especially in California, Florida, and southwestern states with ample sunshine. They save more than 3 million barrels of oil per year. The main barrier to their widespread use in the United States is an initial cost of $3,500 to $5,000.

Solar water heaters are used in 90% of all households in Cyprus. In Israel 65% of all domestic water heating is supplied by simple active solar systems that cost less than $500 per residence. About 12% of the houses in Japan and 37% in Australia use such systems.

Between 1984 and 1988, sales of active solar collectors in the United States dropped by 75%, and 28,000 of the industry's 30,000 employees lost their jobs. This happened because of low oil and natural gas prices and the elimination of federal and most state tax credits for installation of renewable energy systems in residences and businesses.

Advantages and Disadvantages of Solar Energy for Heating Space and Water Using active or passive systems to collect solar energy for low-temperature heating of buildings and water has many advantages. The energy supply is free and naturally available on sunny days, and the net useful energy yield is moderate (active) to high (passive). The technology is well developed and can be installed quickly. No carbon dioxide is added to the atmosphere, and environmental impacts from air pollution and water pollution are low. Land disturbance is also low because passive systems are built into structures and active solar collectors are usually placed on rooftops.

On a lifetime-cost basis good passive solar and superinsulated design is the cheapest way to provide 50% to 100% of the space heating for a home or small building in regions with enough sunlight. Such a system usually adds 5% to 10% to the construction cost but lowers the lifetime cost of a house by 30% to 40% of the cost of conventional houses.

Active systems cost more than passive systems on a lifetime basis because they require more materials to build, they need more maintenance, and eventually they deteriorate and must be replaced. However, retrofitting an existing house with an active solar system is often easier than adding a passive system.

In areas with enough sunlight, an active solar system is a cost-effective way to supply hot water for most homes and buildings. In such areas it may also be a cost-effective way to provide much of the space heating for moderate-size and large buildings with large, unshaded rooftops.

However, there are disadvantages. The energy supply is not available at night and on cloudy days.

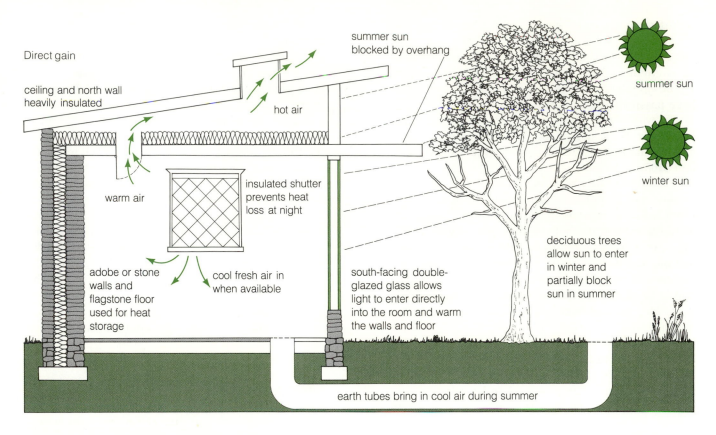

Direct gain

ceiling and north wall
heavily insulated

summer sun
blocked by overhang

summer sun

winter sun

hot air

warm air

insulated shutter
prevents heat
loss at night

deciduous trees
allow sun to enter
in winter and
partially block
sun in summer

adobe or stone
walls and
flagstone floor
used for heat
storage

cool fresh air in
when available

south-facing double-
glazed glass allows
light to enter directly
into the room and warm
the walls and floor

earth tubes bring in cool air during summer

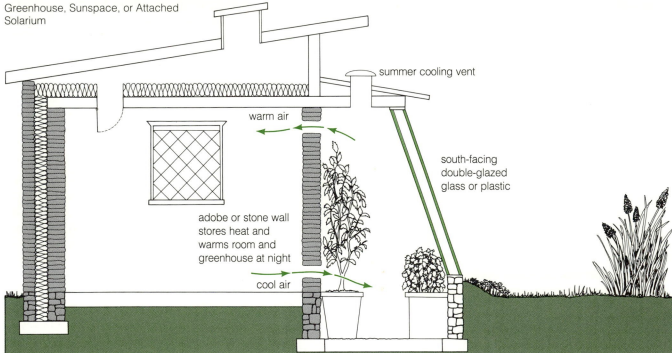

Greenhouse, Sunspace, or Attached
Solarium

summer cooling vent

warm air

south-facing
double-glazed
glass or plastic

adobe or stone wall
stores heat and
warms room and
greenhouse at night

cool air

Figure 20-6 Three examples of passive solar design.

This means that heat storage systems and small backup heating systems are usually needed. Higher initial costs discourage buyers not used to considering lifetime costs and buyers who move every few years to change jobs.

With present technology, active solar systems usually cost too much for heating most homes and small buildings. Better design and mass production techniques could change this. Many people also believe that active solar collectors sitting on rooftops are ugly.

Most passive solar systems require that owners open and close windows and shades to regulate heat flow and distribution, but this can be done by cheap

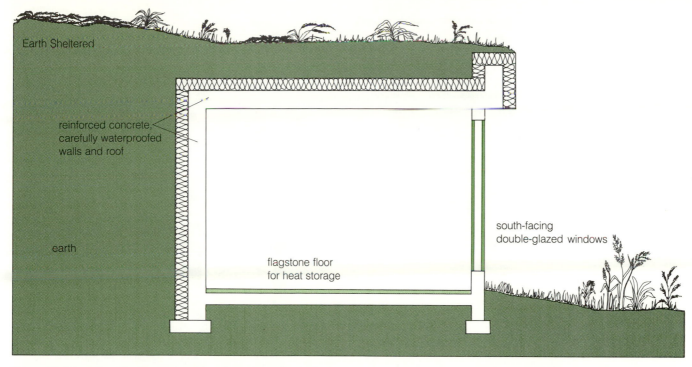

Earth Sheltered

reinforced concrete, carefully waterproofed walls and roof

earth

flagstone floor for heat storage

south-facing double-glazed windows

Figure 20-6 (continued)   Three examples of passive solar design.

SPOTLIGHT Earth-Sheltered Houses

Some people in the United States are building passively heated and cooled houses (Figure 20-6) and commercial buildings partially or completely underground. Such earth-sheltered buildings cost about 15% more to build than a comparable above-ground structure.

The extra cost comes from the large amount of concrete needed to bear the heavy load of earth and the need for careful waterproofing to prevent leaks that would be difficult and expensive to repair. However, a new design using insulated, curved wooden panels that form underground arches has reduced the cost to that of a comparable aboveground structure.

Earth-sheltered houses have much lower heating and cooling requirements. They need no exterior maintenance and painting, and they provide more privacy, quiet, and security from break-ins, fires, hurricanes, tornadoes, earthquakes, and storms than conventional buildings. Thus, they have lower insurance rates. Even with higher initial costs, earth-sheltered houses are cheaper than aboveground houses of the same size on a lifetime-cost basis.

The interior of an earth-sheltered house looks like that of an ordinary house. South-facing, solar-collecting windows, an attached greenhouse, and skylights can provide more daylight than is found in most conventional dwellings.

microprocessors. Owners of solar systems also need laws that prevent others from building structures that block a user's access to sunlight. Such legislation is often opposed by builders of high-density developments.

Concentrating Solar Energy to Produce High-Temperature Heat and Electricity   In experimental systems huge arrays of computer-controlled mirrors track the sun and focus sunlight on a central heat collection point, usually atop a tall tower. This concentrated sunlight can produce temperatures high enough for industrial processes or for making high-pressure steam to run turbines and produce electricity.

The world's largest *solar furnace*, the Odeillo Furnace, has been operating high in the Pyrenees Mountains in southern France since 1970 (Figure 20-9). This system, which produces temperatures up to 5,000°F is used in the manufacture of pure metals and other substances; the excess heat is used to produce steam and generate electricity fed into the public utility grid. Smaller units are being tested in France, Italy, Spain, and Japan.

Active Solar Hot Water Heating System

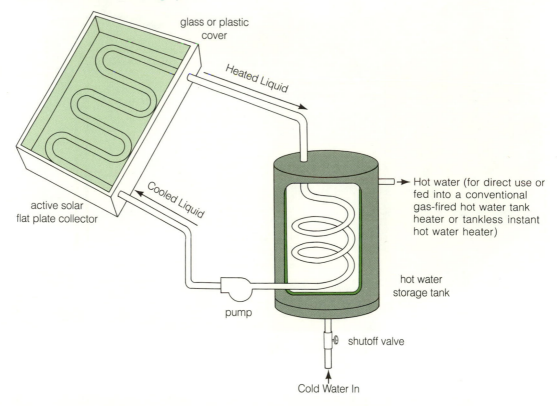

Passive Solar Hot Water Heating System

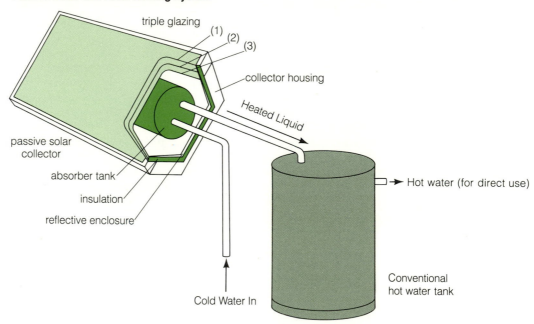

Figure 20-7 Active and passive solar water heaters.

Several private and government-financed experimental *solar power towers*, which produce electricity, have been built in the United States. Five 30-megawatt power towers have been built in the Mojave Desert in southern California and supply enough electricity for 10,000 homes (Figure 20-10). By 1992, at least 14 more of these units are expected to be in operation. New, more efficient designs have also been developed.

The towers take only a year to build and cost about the same per kilowatt as new nuclear plants. The main

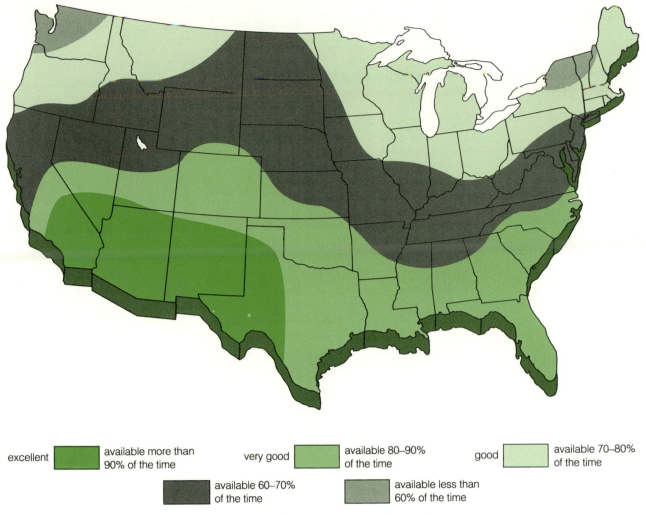

| excellent | available more than 90% of the time | very good | available 80–90% of the time | good | available 70–80% of the time |
| | available 60–70% of the time | | available less than 60% of the time | | |

Figure 20-8 Availability of solar energy during the day in the continental United States. (Data from U.S. Department of Energy and National Wildlife Federation)

use of these small plants will be to supply reserve power to meet daytime peak electricity loads, especially in sunny areas with large air conditioning demands.

Many analysts believe that these systems will make little contribution to overall energy supplies. They have a low net useful energy yield and cost more to build and operate than several other energy alternatives.

Their impact on air and water is low, but their disruption of land is significant because they need large areas for solar collection. Also, they are usually built in sunny, arid, ecologically fragile desert biomes, where there may not be enough water for use in cooling towers to recondense spent steam.

Converting Solar Energy Directly to Electricity: Photovoltaic Cells Solar energy can be converted by **photovoltaic cells**, commonly called **solar cells,** directly into electrical energy. A solar cell consists of a thin wafer of purified silicon, which can be made from inexpensive, abundant sand. Trace amounts of other substances (such as gallium arsenide or cadmium sulfide) are added so that the wafer emits electrons and produces a small amount of electrical current when struck by sunlight (Figure 20-11).

Today solar cells supply electricity for at least 15,000 homes worldwide (6,000 in the United States). Most of these buildings are in isolated areas where it costs too much to bring in electric power lines. Solar cells are also used to switch railroad tracks and to supply power for ocean buoys, lighthouses, and offshore oil-drilling platforms in the sunny Persian Gulf. Some scientists have proposed putting billions of solar cells on large orbiting satellites and beaming the energy back to earth in the form of microwaves. Such schemes, however, are considered far too costly.

Because the amount of electricity produced by a single solar cell is very small, many cells must be wired together in a panel to generate 30 to 100 watts of electric power (Figure 20-11). Several panels are wired together and mounted on a roof or on a rack that tracks the sun to produce electricity for a home or building.

Figure 20-9 Solar furnace near Odeillo in the Pyrenees Mountains of southern France.

Peter Menzel/Stock, Boston

Figure 20-10 Solar 1 power tower used to generate electricity in the Mojave Desert near Barstow, California. This is an expensive way to generate electricity compared to other alternatives.

Sandia National Laboratories, Livermore, California

Massive banks of cells can produce electricity at a small power plant, but this is expensive and has a low net useful energy yield.

Excess electricity produced during daylight can be sold to the local utility company. It can also be stored for use at night and on cloudy days in long-lasting, rechargeable DC batteries like those used in boats and golf carts.

The electricity produced by solar cells is in the form of direct current (DC), not the alternating current (AC) commonly used in households. One option is to use this electricity to power lights and appliances that run on DC current, such as those in most recreational vehicles. Another is to use an electronic inverter to convert direct current to alternating current. In the

future, DC electricity produced by solar cells could be used to decompose water to produce hydrogen gas, which would be used as a fuel for cars and burned in fuel cells to provide space heat, hot water, and electricity (Section 20-7). But it is very wasteful of energy and money to use solar cells (or any form of energy) to supply electricity for heating space and water and running inefficient lights and appliances.

To produce electricity competitively, commercial solar cells must have an energy efficiency of about 15%, enabling them to produce electricity at about 6 cents per kilowatt hour. In 1988 commercially available solar cells, with an efficiency of 7% to 12%, could produce electricity at about 25 to 30 cents per kilowatt-hour. A new type of solar cell tested under laboratory

Single Solar Cell

boron-doped silicon

sunlight

junction

cell

phosphorus-doped silicon

DC electricity

Panel of Solar Cells

Figure 20-11 Use of photovoltaic (solar) cells to provide DC electricity for an energy-efficient home; surplus can be sold to the local power company. Prices should be competitive sometime in the 1990s.

Array of Solar Cell Panels on a Roof

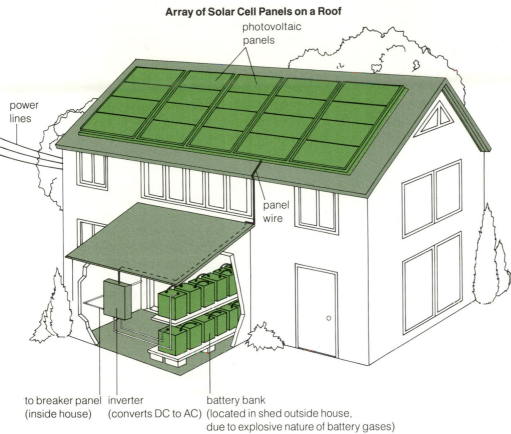

photovoltaic panels

power lines

panel wire

to breaker panel (inside house)

inverter (converts DC to AC)

battery bank (located in shed outside house, due to explosive nature of battery gases)

conditions had an efficiency of 31%, and researchers in Israel have developed a solar cell that can also store energy.

By 1990 Arco is expected to market new solar cells that can produce electricity at about 13 cents per kilowatt hour—cheaper than electricity produced by a new nuclear power plant. The development of more energy-efficient (at least 15%) cells and cost-effective mass-production techniques should allow solar cells to produce electricity at about 6 cents per kilowatt hour by the mid-1990s or shortly after the turn of the century. The potential market for these cells would be $100 billion a year.

Since 1981 the U.S. federal research and development budget for solar cells has been cut by 90%, whereas Japanese government expenditures in this area have tripled. Between 1980 and 1986 Japan's share of the worldwide solar cell market grew from 15% to 46%. By 1989 Japan, West Germany, and Italy were spending more on solar cell research than the United States.

Federal and private research efforts on photovoltaics in the United States need to be increased sharply. Otherwise, the United States may find much of its capital being drained to pay for imports of photovoltaic cells from Japan and other countries. The United States would also lose out on a major global economic market.

Advantages and Disadvantages of Photovoltaic Cells

Solar cells have many advantages. If present projections are correct, they could supply 20% to 30% of the world's electricity by 2050. This would eliminate the need to build large-scale power plants of any type and allow many existing nuclear and coal-fired power plants to be phased out.

Solar cells are also reliable and quiet, have no moving parts, and should last 30 years or more if encased in glass or plastic. They can be installed quickly and easily and need little maintenance other than occasional washing to prevent dirt from blocking the sun's rays.

Most solar cells are made from silicon, the second most abundant element in the earth's crust. They do not produce carbon dioxide during use. Air and water pollution during operation is low, air pollution from manufacture is low, and land disturbance is very low for roof-mounted systems. The net useful energy yield is fairly high and rising with new designs.

However, solar cells have some drawbacks. The present costs of solar cell systems are high but are projected to become competitive in 7 to 15 years. Many people find racks of solar cells on rooftops or in yards ugly. Without tough plastic coating, solar cells can be damaged by hail storms.

The use of solar cells could be limited by an insufficient amount of gallium and cadmium. The widespread use of solar cells might bankrupt utilities with unneeded large power plants and the banks that invested money in them. Without effective pollution control, the manufacture of solar cells can produce moderate water pollution from hazardous wastes.

20-3 INDIRECT SOLAR ENERGY: PRODUCING ELECTRICITY FROM FALLING AND FLOWING WATER

Types of Hydroelectric Power Since the 1700s, kinetic energy in the falling and flowing water of rivers and streams has been used to produce electricity in small- and large-scale hydroelectric plants. In *large-scale hydropower projects,* high dams are built across large rivers to create large reservoirs (Figure 6-10, p. 130). The stored water is then allowed to flow at controlled rates, spinning turbines and producing electricity as it falls downward to the river below the dam.

The electricity produced by water flowing over large dams is an indirect form of the perpetual solar energy that drives the hydrologic cycle. However, the reservoirs behind the dams usually fill with silt and become useless in 30 to 300 years, depending on the rate of natural and human-accelerated soil erosion from land above the dam. This means that large hydroelectric plants are nonrenewable sources of energy.

In *small-scale hydropower projects,* a low dam, with no reservoir or only a small one, is built across a small river or stream. The natural water flow is used to generate electricity. However, electricity production can vary with seasonal changes in stream flow. Under drought conditions there may not be enough water flow to produce any electricity.

Falling water can also be used to produce electricity in *pumped-storage hydropower systems.* Their main use is to supply extra power during times of peak electrical demand. When electricity demand is low, usually at night, electricity from a conventional power plant pumps water uphill from a lake or reservoir to another reservoir at a higher elevation, usually on top of a mountain. When a power company needs more electricity than its plants can produce, water in the upper reservoir is released. On its downward trip, the water flows through turbines and generates electricity. But this is a very expensive method.

Present and Future Use of Hydropower In 1987 hydropower supplied 21% of the world's electricity and 6% of the world's total supplemental energy. Countries or areas with mountainous or plateau regions have the greatest hydropower potential.

Much of the hydropower potential of North America and Europe has been developed. Hydropower supplies Norway with essentially all its electricity, Switzerland 74%, and Austria 67%. Canada gets more than 70% of its electricity from hydropower and exports electricity to the United States.

Africa has harnessed only 5% of its hydropower potential, Latin America 8%, and Asia 9%. In 1987, LDCs got almost 50% of their electricity from hydropower. Between 1981 and 1995, LDCs are projected to add large hydropower plants that will produce electricity equal to that of 225 large nuclear or coal-burning power plants. Half of this new hydropower capacity will be added in Brazil, China, and India.

China, with one-tenth of the world's hydropower potential, is likely to become the world's largest producer of hydroelectricity. There is a controversial proposal for a hydropower dam across the Yangtze River that could produce electricity equal to that of 25 large nuclear or coal power plants. This project, however, would force 2 million people to leave their homes. China has also built almost 100,000 small dams to produce electricity for villages.

The United States is the world's largest producer of electricity from hydropower. Today hydropower produced at almost 1,600 sites supplies 12% of the electricity and 5% of all supplemental energy used by the United States.

U.S. hydroelectric power plants produce electricity more cheaply than any other source. One reason is that most large-scale projects were built from the 1930s to the 1950s, when costs were low and were subsidized by all taxpayers. Another reason is that hydroelectric energy efficiency is high (83% to 93%) and the plants produce full power 95% of the time, compared to 60% for nuclear plants and 65% for coal plants, which are shut down for repairs and maintenance more frequently. This explains why regions such as the Pacific Northwest, where most of the electricity is produced by hydropower, have the lowest electric rates in the country.

By the year 2000, however, hydroelectric power will probably supply only about 5% of the commercial energy used in the United States—the same percentage as today. The large dam-building era in the United states is drawing to a close because of high construction costs and lack of suitable sites. Any new large supplies of hydroelectric power in the United States will be imported from Canada.

By 1988 almost 1,500 small-scale hydroelectric power plants were operating or under construction, mostly in the West and Northeast. They were generating electricity equal to that of three large coal or nuclear power plants. According to the U.S. Corps of Engineers, retrofitting abandoned small and medium-size hydroelectric sites and building new small-scale hydroelectric plants on suitable sites could supply the United States with electricity equal to that of 45 large power plants.

However, since 1985 the development of small-scale hydropower in the United States has fallen off sharply because of low oil prices and the loss of federal tax credits. Many projects have been opposed by local residents and conservationists because the dams reduce stream flow, disrupting aquatic life and preventing some types of recreation.

Advantages and Disadvantages of Hydropower

Hydropower has a number of advantages. Many LDCs have large, untapped potential sites, although many are far from where the electricity is needed. Hydropower has a moderate to high net useful energy yield and fairly low operating and maintenance costs.

Hydroelectric plants rarely need to be shut down, and they produce no emissions of carbon dioxide or other air pollutants during operation. They have life spans two to ten times those of coal and nuclear plants. In addition to producing electricity, large dams can help control flooding and supply a regulated flow of irrigation water to areas below the dam.

Developing small-scale hydroelectric plants by rehabilitating existing dams has little environmental impact, and once rebuilt, the units have a long life. Only a few people are needed to operate them and they need little maintenance.

But hydropower has some drawbacks. Construction costs for new large-scale systems are high, and few suitable sites are left in the United States and Europe. Large-scale projects flood large areas of land to form reservoirs, destroy wildlife habitats, uproot people, decrease natural fertilization of prime agricultural land in river valleys below the dam, and decrease fish harvests below the dam (see Case Study on p. 193). Without proper land-use control, large-scale projects can greatly increase soil erosion and sediment water pollution near the reservoir above the dam. This reduces the effective life of the reservoir.

By reducing stream flow, small hydroelectric projects threaten recreational activities and aquatic life, disrupt scenic rivers, and destroy wetlands. During droughts these plants produce little if any power. Most of the electricity produced by these projects can be supplied at a lower cost and with less environmental impact by industrial cogeneration, improving energy efficiency, and upgrading existing big dams.

Tidal Power Twice a day a large volume of water flows in and out of inland bays or other coastal bodies of water to produce high and low tides because of gravitational attraction between the earth and the moon. In a few places tides flow in and out of a bay with an opening narrow enough to be obstructed by a dam with gates that can be opened and closed. If the difference in water height between high and low tides is large enough, these daily tidal flows can be used to spin turbines to produce electricity.

However, only about two dozen places in the world have these conditions. Since 1968 France has been operating a small commercial tidal power plant at the La Rance estuary, where tides rise and fall up to 44 feet. Although operating costs are low, the project cost about 2.5 times more to build than a conventional hydroelectric power plant further up the Rance River.

The world's largest daily tidal fluctuation—52 feet—occurs in the Bay of Fundy in Nova Scotia. Since 1984 Canada has been operating a small, experimental tidal power plant there. If this project is successful, the plant may be expanded. Two possible locations for experimental tidal power stations in the United States are the Cook Inlet in Alaska and Passamaquoddy Bay between the coasts of Maine and New Brunswick.

Using tidal energy to produce electricity has several advantages. The energy source (tides) is free, operating costs are low, and the net useful energy yield is moderate. No carbon dioxide is added to the atmosphere, air pollution is low, and little land is disturbed.

Most analysts, however, expect tidal power to make only a tiny contribution to world electricity supplies. There are few suitable sites and construction costs are high. The output of electricity varies daily with tidal flows and must have a backup system. The dam and power plant can be damaged by storms, and metal parts are easily corroded by seawater.

Wave Power The kinetic energy in ocean waves, created primarily by wind, is another potential source of energy for producing electricity from moving water. Japan, Norway, Great Britain, Sweden, the United States, and the Soviet Union have built small experimental plants to evaluate this form of hydropower.

None of these plants have produced electricity at a competitive price, but some designs show promise.

Most analysts expect this alternative to make little contribution to world electricity production except in a few coastal areas with the right conditions. Construction costs are moderate to high, and the net useful energy yield is moderate. Equipment could be damaged or destroyed by saltwater corrosion and severe storms.

20-4 INDIRECT SOLAR ENERGY: PRODUCING ELECTRICITY FROM HEAT STORED IN WATER

Ocean Thermal Energy Conversion Ocean water stores huge amounts of heat from the sun. Japan and the United States have been conducting experiments to evaluate the technological and economic feasibility of using the large temperature differences between the cold bottom waters and the sun-warmed surface waters of tropical oceans to produce electricity.

If feasible, a gigantic, floating **ocean thermal energy conversion (OTEC)** power plant, would be anchored in a tropical ocean area no more than 50 miles offshore. Some 62 countries, mostly LDCs in South America and Africa, have suitable sites for such plants. Favorable sites in U.S. waters include parts of the Gulf of Mexico and areas near southern California and the islands of Puerto Rico, Hawaii, and Guam.

In a typical OTEC plant, warm surface water would be pumped through a large heat exchanger and used to evaporate and pressurize a low-boiling fluid such as liquid ammonia. The pressurized ammonia gas would drive turbines to generate electricity. Then, cold bottom water as deep as 3,000 feet below the plant would be pumped to the surface through massive pipes 100 feet in diameter. The water would be used to cool and condense the ammonia back to a liquid state to begin the cycle again. Pumps in a medium-size plant would pump more water than the average flow rate of the Mississippi River.

A large cable would transmit the electricity to shore. Other possibilities include using the electricity produced to desalinate ocean water, extract minerals and chemicals from the sea, or decompose water to produce hydrogen gas, which could be piped or transported to shore for use as a fuel.

Advantages and Disadvantages of OTEC The source of energy for OTEC is limitless at suitable sites, and a costly energy storage and backup system is not needed. No air pollution, except large amounts of carbon dioxide, is produced during operation, and the floating power plant requires no land area. Nutrients brought up when water is pumped from the ocean bottom might be used to nourish schools of fish and shellfish. Advocates believe that with enough research-and-development funding, large-scale OTEC plants could be built to produce electricity equal to that of ten large power plants by the year 2000.

However, most energy analysts believe that the large-scale extraction of energy from ocean thermal gradients may never compete economically with other energy alternatives. Construction costs are high—two to three times those of comparable coal-fired plants. Operating and maintenance costs are also high because of corrosion of metal parts by seawater and fouling of heat exchangers by algae and barnacles. Plants could also be damaged by hurricanes and typhoons.

Other problems include a limited number of sites and a low net useful energy yield. The electricity used by the massive pumps reduces the net useful energy yield by one-third. Pumping large volumes of deep-ocean water to the surface could disrupt aquatic life and release lots of dissolved carbon dioxide into the atmosphere.

Inland Solar Ponds A **solar pond** is a solar energy collector consisting of at least one acre of a lined cavity filled with salt water or with fresh water enclosed in black plastic bags. *Saline solar ponds* can be used to produce electricity and are usually located near inland saline seas or lakes, near deserts with ample sunlight. The bottom layer of water in such ponds stays on the bottom when heated because it has a higher salinity and density (mass per unit volume) than the top layer. Heat accumulated during daylight in the bottom layer can be used to produce electricity in a manner similar to the OTEC process in a tropical ocean.

An experimental saline solar pond power plant on the Israeli side of the Dead Sea has been operating successfully for several years. By 2000, Israel plans to build several plants around the Dead Sea to supply electricity for air conditioning and desalinating water. By 1986, more than a dozen experimental saline solar ponds had been built in the United States. Most were in desert areas near the Salton Sea in California and the Great Salt Lake in Utah.

Freshwater solar ponds can be used as a source of hot water and space heating. A very shallow hole is dug, lined with concrete, and covered with insulation. A number of large, black, plastic bags, each filled with several inches of water, are placed in the hole. The top of the pond is then covered with fiberglass panels, which let sunlight in and keep most of the heat stored in the water during daylight from being lost to the atmosphere.

When a computer-controlled monitoring system determines that the water in the bags has reached its peak temperature in the afternoon, the computer turns on pumps to transfer the hot water to large, insulated tanks for distribution as hot water or for space heating.

The world's largest freshwater solar pond went into operation at Fort Benning, Georgia, in 1985. This $4 million, 11-acre pond supplies hot water for 6,500 service personnel and is expected to save up to $10 million over a 20-year period.

Advantages and Disadvantages of Solar Ponds
Saline and freshwater solar ponds have the same advantages as OTEC systems. In addition, they have a moderate net useful energy yield, moderate construction and operating costs, and need little maintenance. Freshwater solar ponds can be built in almost any sunny area. They may be useful for supplying hot water and space heating for large buildings and small housing developments. Enthusiasts project that with adequate research-and-development support, solar ponds could supply 3% to 4% of U.S. supplemental energy by the year 2000.

Saline solar ponds are feasible only in areas with moderate to ample sunlight, especially ecologically fragile deserts. Operating costs can be high because of saltwater corrosion of pipes and heat exchangers. Unless lined, the ponds can become ineffective when compounds leached from bottom sediment darken the water and reduce sunlight transmission.

20-5 INDIRECT SOLAR ENERGY: PRODUCING ELECTRICITY FROM WIND

Wind Power: Past and Present Since the 1600s prevailing winds, produced indirectly by solar energy, have been used to propel ships, grind grain, pump water, and power many small industrial shops. In the 1700s settlers in the American West used small windmills to pump groundwater for farms and ranches (Figure 20-12). In the 1930s and 1940s small farms beyond the reach of electric utility lines used small wind turbines to produce electricity. By the 1950s cheap hydropower, fossil fuels, and rural electrification had replaced most of these wind turbines.

Since the 1970s small to large modern wind turbines have been developed and are used in 95 countries (Figure 20-12). Experience has shown that these machines can produce electricity at a reasonable cost for use by small communities and large utility companies in areas with average wind speeds of 14 to 24 miles per hour, often found in mountain passes and along coastlines.

Since 1974 more than 60,000 wind turbines have been installed, especially in California and Denmark. Small (10- to 50-kilowatt) and intermediate-size (60- to 1,000-kilowatt) wind turbines are the most widely used. They are easier to mass-produce, are less vulnerable to stress and breakdown, and can produce more power in light winds than large wind turbines.

U.S. Department of Energy

Figure 20-12 An old windmill and a modern, 200-kilowatt wind turbine in Clayton, New Mexico.

Use of wind power in the United States has grown more rapidly since 1981 than any other new source of electricity. More than 70% of the electricity produced by wind energy worldwide and 90% of that in the United States is generated in California in three windy mountain passes. Between 1981 and 1988 almost 17,000 small to intermediate-size wind turbines were installed in California, mostly by private companies. They are grouped together in clusters called *wind farms* (Figure 20-13). By 1988 these turbines produced electricity equal to that of 1.5 large power plants, enough to meet 15% of San Francisco's electrical demand. Economically, it makes more sense to build wind farms to serve entire communities or groups of houses than for individual home owners to install wind power systems.

The California Energy Commission projects that wind power will supply 8% of the state's electricity by 2000. The island of Hawaii gets about 8% of its electricity from wind, and the use of wind power is spreading to the state's other islands. Other countries planning to make increasing use of wind energy include Denmark, China, India, Canada, Spain, Greece, Argentina, the United Kingdom, Sweden, West Germany, Australia, the Netherlands, and the Soviet Union.

Wind power experts project that wind energy could meet 5% to 19% of the officially projected—but probably high—demand for electricity in the United States and as much as 13% of the world's demand by 2000. However, the development of this energy resource in the United States has slowed down since 1986, when federal tax credits and most state tax credits for wind

Figure 20-13 A California wind farm consisting of an array of modern wind turbines in a windy mountain pass. Such farms can produce electricity at competitive prices.

Georg Gerster/Photo Researchers, Inc.

power were eliminated. Also, the federal budget for research and development of wind power was cut by 90% between 1981 and 1988.

Wind power is an unlimited source of energy at favorable sites, and large wind farms can be built in 3 to 6 months. Wind power systems have a moderate to fairly high net useful energy yield, emit no carbon dioxide or other air pollutants during operation, and need no water for cooling. They operate 80% to 95% of the time the wind is blowing. Their manufacture and use produce little water pollution. The land occupied by wind farms can also be used for grazing and other purposes. They don't require water to operate, making them especially well suited for arid and semiarid areas. Wind farms are expected to have an economic advantage over coal and nuclear power plants in the United States and the world by the 1990s and already do at good sites.

But wind power can be used only in areas with sufficient winds. Also, backup electricity from a utility company or from an energy storage system is necessary when the wind dies down, but this is not a problem at suitable sites. Backup could also be provided by linking wind farms with a solar cell or hydropower system, or both. Building wind farms in mountain passes and along shorelines can cause visual pollution. Noise and interference with local television reception have been problems with large turbines but can be overcome with improved design and use in isolated areas.

20-6 INDIRECT RENEWABLE SOLAR ENERGY: BIOMASS

Renewable Biomass as a Versatile Fuel Biomass is organic plant matter produced by solar energy through photosynthesis. Some of this plant matter can be burned as solid fuel or converted to more convenient gaseous or liquid *biofuels* (Figure 20-14). In 1987, biomass, mostly from the burning of wood and manure to heat buildings and cook food, supplied about 15% of the world's supplemental energy (4% to 5% in Canada and the United States).

All biomass fuels have several advantages in common. They can be used in solid, liquid, and gaseous forms for space heating, water heating, producing electricity, and propelling vehicles. Biomass is a renewable energy resource as long as trees and plants are not harvested faster than they grow back—something that is not being done in most places (Sections 14-2 and 14-3).

There is no net increase in atmospheric levels of carbon dioxide as long as the rate of removal and burning of trees and plants and loss of below-ground organic matter does not exceed their rate of replenishment. Burning of biomass fuels adds much less sulfur dioxide and nitric oxide to the atmosphere per unit of energy produced than the uncontrolled burning of coal and thus requires fewer pollution controls.

Biomass fuels also share some disadvantages. Without effective land-use controls and replanting, widespread removal of trees and plants can deplete soil nutrients and cause excessive soil erosion, water pollution, flooding, and loss of wildlife habitat. Biomass resources also have a high moisture content (15% to 95%), which lowers their net useful energy. The added weight of the moisture makes collecting and hauling wood and other plant material fairly expensive. Each type of biomass fuel has other specific advantages and disadvantages.

Burning Wood and Wood Wastes About 80% of the people living in LDCs heat their dwellings and cook their food by burning wood or charcoal made from wood. However, about 1.1 billion people cannot find

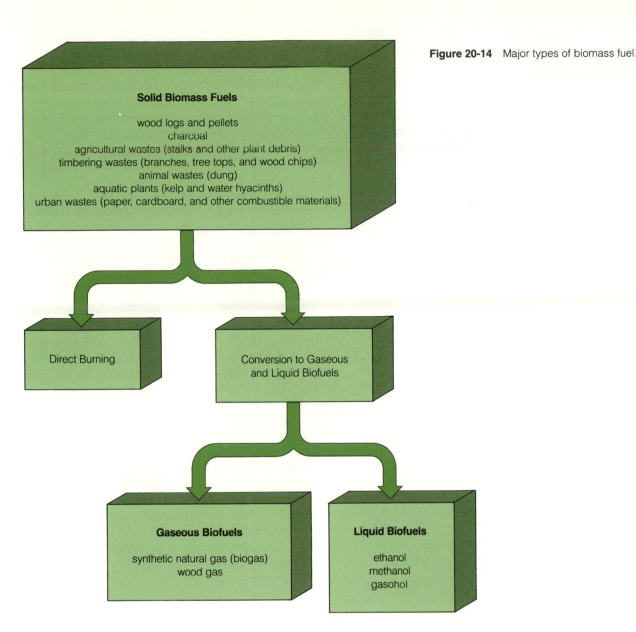

Figure 20-14 Major types of biomass fuel.

Solid Biomass Fuels

wood logs and pellets
charcoal
agricultural wastes (stalks and other plant debris)
timbering wastes (branches, tree tops, and wood chips)
animal wastes (dung)
aquatic plants (kelp and water hyacinths)
urban wastes (paper, cardboard, and other combustible materials)

Direct Burning

Conversion to Gaseous
and Liquid Biofuels

Gaseous Biofuels

synthetic natural gas (biogas)
wood gas

Liquid Biofuels

ethanol
methanol
gasohol

or are too poor to buy enough fuelwood to meet their needs, and this number may increase to 2.5 billion by 2000.

In MDCs with adequate forests, the burning of wood, wood pellets, and wood wastes to heat homes and to produce steam and electricity in industrial boilers increased rapidly during the 1970s because of price increases in heating oil and electricity. Sweden leads the world in using wood as an energy source, mostly for district heating plants.

The forest products industry (mostly paper companies and lumber mills) consumes almost two-thirds of the fuelwood used in the United States. Homes and small businesses burn the rest. In 1985 one of every ten single-family homes (one in six in nonmetropolitan areas) relied entirely on wood for space heating. Almost one-third of other U.S. homes burned wood for some of their space heating.

The largest use of fuelwood is in New England, where wood is plentiful. However, because of market saturation, loss of tax credits, and low oil prices, annual sales of woodstoves in the United States dropped from 3 million to 450,000 between 1980 and 1987.

Wood has a moderate to high net useful energy yield when collected and burned directly and efficiently near its source. But in urban areas where wood must be hauled long distances, it can cost home owners more per unit of energy produced than oil and electricity.

Harvesting and burning wood can cause accidents. Each year in the United States over 10,000 people are injured by chain saws and several hundred are killed in house fires caused by wood stoves.

Burning fuelwood releases carbon monoxide, solid particulate matter, and unburned residues that pollute indoor and outdoor air. According to the EPA, wood burning causes as many as 820 cancer deaths a year in the United States.

This air pollution can be reduced 75% by a $100 to $250 catalytic combustion chamber in the stove or stovepipe. These units also increase the energy efficiency of a typical airtight wood stove from 55% to as high as 81% and reduce the need for chimney cleaning and the chance of chimney fires. However, they must be replaced every four years at a cost of about $100. Recently wood stoves have been developed that are 65% efficient and that emit 90% less air pollution than conventional wood stoves without using catalytic combustion.

In London and in South Korean cities, wood fires have been banned to reduce air pollution. Oregon, Colorado, and Montana have passed laws setting air pollution emission standards for all wood stoves, and 20 other states were considering similar laws. In some areas, especially valleys suffering from frequent thermal inversions (Figure 7-14, p. 161), wood burning is banned when particulate matter in the atmosphere reaches certain levels. By 1990 all new wood stoves sold in the United States will be required by the EPA to meet air pollution emission standards designed to reduce emissions by more than 70%.

Energy Plantations One way to produce biomass fuel is to plant large numbers of fast-growing trees in *biomass-energy plantations* to supply fuelwood. Plantations of oil palms and varieties of Euphorbia plants, which store energy in hydrocarbon compounds (like those found in oil), can also be established. After these plants are harvested, their oil-like material can be extracted and either refined to produce gasoline or burned directly in diesel engines. Both types of energy plantations can be established on semiarid land not needed to grow crops, although lack of water probably would limit productivity.

This industrialized approach to biomass production usually requires the heavy use of pesticides and fertilizers, which can pollute drinking supplies and harm wildlife. Conversion of large areas to monoculture energy plantations also reduces biodiversity. In some areas biomass plantations might compete with food crops for prime farmland. Also, they are likely to have low or negative net useful energy yields, as do most conventional crops grown by industrialized agricultural methods.

Burning Agricultural and Urban Wastes In agricultural areas, crop residues (the inedible, unharvested parts of food crops) and animal manure can be collected and burned or converted to biofuels. By 1985 Hawaii was burning a residue (called bagasse) left after sugarcane harvesting and processing to supply almost 10% of its electricity (58% on the island of Kauai and 33% on the island of Hawaii). Power plants burning rice husks are operating in India, Malaysia, the Philippines, Thailand, Suriname, and India. Other crop residues that could be burned include coconut shells, peanut and other nut hulls, and cotton stalks.

In most areas, however, plant residues are widely dispersed. Unless they are harvested along with crops, they require large amounts of energy to collect, dry, and transport to large, centralized power plants. Also, ecologists argue that it makes more sense to use crop residues to feed livestock, retard soil erosion, and fertilize the soil.

An increasing number of cities in Japan, western Europe, and the United States have built incinerators that burn trash and use the heat released to produce electricity or to heat nearby buildings. The advantages and disadvantages of this approach are discussed in Chapter 18. Some analysts argue that more energy is saved by composting or recycling paper and other organic wastes than by burning them.

Converting Solid Biomass to Liquid and Gaseous Biofuels Plants, organic wastes, sewage, and other forms of solid biomass can be converted by bacteria and various chemical processes into gaseous and liquid biofuels (Figure 20-13). Examples are *biogas* (a mixture of 60% methane and 40% carbon dioxide), *liquid methanol* (methyl, or wood alcohol), and *liquid ethanol* (ethyl, or grain alcohol).

In China, bacteria in an estimated 7 million *biogas digesters* convert organic plant and animal wastes into methane fuel for heating and cooking. After the biogas has been removed, the solid residue left behind can be used as fertilizer on food crops or, if contaminated, on nonedible crops such as trees.

When they work, biogas digesters are very efficient. However, they are slow and unpredictable. They don't work well at low temperatures or when contaminated by acids, heavy metals, synthetic detergents, and other industrial effluents. Development of new, more reliable models could change this.

Methane fuel is also produced by underground decomposition of organic matter in the absence of air (anaerobic digestion) in active and closed landfills. The gas is collected by pipes inserted in landfills. The gas is then purified and burned as a fuel. By 1988 almost 50 landfill gas recovery systems were operating in the United States (mostly in California) and 35 others were under construction. Some 2,000 to 3,000 large U.S. landfills have the potential for large-scale methane recovery. Because methane is a greenhouse gas (Figure 7-25, p. 172), this recovery would also help slow down global warming.

Methane can also be produced by anaerobic digestion of manure and sludge produced at sewage treatment plants. Converting to methane all the manure that U.S. livestock produce each year could provide nearly 5% of the country's total natural gas consumption at the current level. But collecting and transporting manure for long distances to large, centralized power plants takes energy. Recycling this manure to the land to replace commercial inorganic fertilizer, which requires large amounts of natural gas to produce, would probably save more natural gas.

Some analysts believe that methanol and ethanol can be used as liquid fuels to replace gasoline and diesel fuel when oil becomes too scarce and expensive. Both alcohols can be burned directly as fuel without requiring additives to boost octane ratings.

Currently, emphasis is on using ethanol as an automotive fuel. It can be made from sugar and grain crops (sugarcane, sugar beets, sorghum, and corn) by fermentation and distillation. Pure ethanol can be burned in today's cars with little engine modification. Gasoline can also be mixed with 10% to 23% ethanol to make *gasohol*. It burns in conventional gasoline engines and is sold as super unleaded or ethanol-enriched gasoline.

By 1987 ethanol made by fermentation of sugarcane accounted for about half the automotive fuel consumption in Brazil. Almost one-third of existing cars and 90% of new cars produced in Brazil can run on pure ethanol. The rest can run on an unleaded gasoline mixture containing 20% ethanol. The use of ethanol helped Brazil cut its oil imports in half between 1978 and 1984. It also created an estimated 575,000 full-time jobs. The country plans to triple its production of ethanol fuel by 1993. But this may be delayed by the temporary oil glut of the 1980s, which has lowered conventional gasoline prices. Without catalytic converters, cars burning ethanol fuels produce more aldehydes and PANs that kill plants and cause eye irritation than cars burning gasoline.

Super unleaded gasoline containing 90% gasoline and 10% ethanol now accounts for about 8% of gasoline sales in the United States—and more than 30% in some states. The ethanol used in gasohol is made in 150 ethanol production plants built between 1980 and 1985. Excluding federal taxes, it costs about $1.60 to produce a gallon of ethanol, compared to about 50 cents for a gallon of gasoline. However, new, energy-efficient distilleries are lowering the costs of producing ethanol. Soon this fuel may be able to compete with other forms of unleaded gasoline without federal tax breaks, which are scheduled to expire in 1992.

The distillation process used to make ethanol produces large volumes of a waste material known as swill, which if allowed to flow into waterways, kills algae, fish, and plants. Another problem is that the net useful energy yield for producing ethanol fuel is low in older oil- or natural-gas-fueled distilleries. However, the yield is moderate at new distilleries using modern technology and powered by coal, wood, or solar energy.

Some experts are concerned that growing corn or other grains to make alcohol fuel could compete for cropland needed to grow food. For example, 40% of the entire U.S. annual harvest of corn would be needed to make enough ethanol to meet just 10% of the country's demand for automotive fuel.

Another alcohol, methanol, can be produced from wood, wood wastes, agricultural wastes, sewage sludge, garbage, coal, and natural gas at a cost of about $1 to $2 per gallon. High concentrations of methanol corrode conventional engines, but in a properly modified engine methanol burns cleanly without any problems.

A fuel of 85% methanol and 15% unleaded gasoline could reduce emissions of ozone-forming hydrocarbons 20% to 50%. Running cars on pure methanol would reduce these emissions by 90% and carbon monoxide emissions by 30% to 90%. However, cars burning pure methanol emit two to five times more formaldehyde, a suspected carcinogen, than those burning gasoline. Methanol-powered cars emit less carbon dioxide than gasoline-powered cars. But producing the methanol from coal would double carbon dioxide emissions.

Recently chemists at the Solar Energy Research Institute have developed specialized molecules that can remove CO_2 from the air. The recovered carbon dioxide could be converted to methanol and used as a car fuel. If successful, this process could help deal with the greenhouse effect and reduce U.S. dependence on oil.

Diesohol, a mixture of diesel fuel with 15% to 20% methanol by volume, is being tested and could lower emissions of nitrogen oxide pollutants, a drawback of regular diesel fuel. Another alternative fuel for diesel engines is vegetable oil, particularly soybean oil. The oil can be treated chemically to produce a diesel fuel, or it can be blended with ethanol.

Growing more soybeans in the United States could replace as much as 88% of the diesel fuel used by agriculture. The chief problem is cost. Diesel fuel made from soybean oil costs about $1.60 a gallon, almost twice as much as regular diesel fuel. More research could bring the cost down to $1 a gallon and make this a competitive fuel when gasoline prices rise, probably in the 1990s.

20-7 HYDROGEN AS A POSSIBLE REPLACEMENT FOR OIL

Some scientists have suggested that we use hydrogen gas (H_2) to fuel cars, heat homes, and provide hot water when oil and natural gas run out. Hydrogen gas does not occur in significant quantities in nature. However, it can be produced by chemical processes from nonrenewable coal or natural gas or by using heat, electricity, or perhaps sunlight to decompose fresh water or seawater (Figure 20-15).

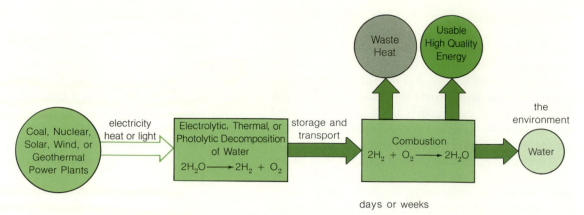

Figure 20-15 The hydrogen energy cycle. The production of hydrogen gas requires electricity, heat, or solar energy to decompose water, thus leading to a negative net useful energy yield.

Hydrogen gas can be burned in a reaction with oxygen gas in a power plant, a specially designed automobile engine, or in a fuel cell that converts the chemical energy produced by the reaction into direct-current electricity. Fuel cells running on a mixture of hydrogen and air have efficiencies of 60% to 80%.

Hydrogen burns cleanly in pure oxygen, yielding only water vapor and no air pollutants. When burned in air, it produces only small amounts of nitrogen oxides, 200 times less than current vehicles. Hydrogen gas can be combined with various metals to produce solid compounds that can be heated to release hydrogen as needed in a specially designed automobile motor. Unlike gasoline, the solid metallic hydrogen compounds would not explode or burn if the tank is ruptured in an accident.

The major problem with using hydrogen as a fuel is that only trace amounts of the gas occur in nature. Producing it uses high-temperature heat or electricity from another energy source, such as nuclear fission, direct solar power, or wind, to decompose water. This is expensive.

Because of the first and second energy laws, hydrogen production by any method will take more energy than is released when it is burned. Thus, its net useful energy yield will always be negative. This means that its widespread use depends on having an abundant and affordable supply of some other type of environmentally acceptable energy.

Another problem is that hydrogen gas is highly explosive. However, most analysts believe we could learn how to handle it safely, as we have for highly explosive gasoline and natural gas. Over two dozen experimental hydrogen-fueled cars are operating in the world today.

Burning hydrogen does not add carbon dioxide to the atmosphere. However, carbon dioxide would be added to the atmosphere if electricity or high-temperature heat from coal or other fossil-fuel-burning power plants were used to decompose water and produce hydrogen. No carbon dioxide would be added if electricity produced by photovoltaic, wind, hydroelectric, geothermal, or nuclear power were used to produce hydrogen.

Scientists are trying to develop cells that use ordinary light or solar energy to split water molecules into hydrogen and oxygen gases with reasonable efficiency. In 1988 construction began on an experimental solar-hydrogen plant in Bavaria, West Germany. If everything goes right, affordable commercial cells for using solar energy to produce hydrogen could become available sometime after 2000.

20-8 DEVELOPING AN ENERGY STRATEGY FOR THE UNITED STATES

Overall Evaluation of U.S. Energy Alternatives

Table 20-2 summarizes the major advantages and disadvantages of the energy alternatives discussed in this and the preceding chapter, with emphasis on their potential in the United States. Energy experts argue over these and other projections, and new data and innovations may change some information in this table. But it does provide a useful framework for making decisions based on presently available information. Four major conclusions can be drawn:

- The best short-term, intermediate, and long-term alternative for the United States and other countries is to reduce unnecessary energy waste by improving the efficiency of energy use (Section 20-1).

- Total systems for future energy alternatives in the world and in the United States will probably have low to moderate net useful energy yields and moderate to high development costs. Since there is not enough financial capital to develop all energy alternatives, projects must be chosen carefully. Otherwise, limited capital will be depleted

Table 20-2 Evaluation of Energy Alternatives for the United States (shading indicates favorable conditions)

Energy Resource	Estimated Availability			Estimated Net Useful Energy of Entire System	Projected Cost of Entire System	Actual or Potential Overall Environmental Impact of Entire System
	Short Term (1990–2000)	Intermediate Term (2000–2010)	Long Term (2010–2040)			
Nonrenewable Resources						
Fossil fuels						
Petroleum	High (with imports)	Moderate (with imports)	Low	High but decreasing	High for new domestic supplies	Moderate
Natural gas	High (with imports)	Moderate (with imports)	Moderate (with imports)	High but decreasing	High for new domestic supplies	Low
Coal	High	High	High	High but decreasing	Moderate but increasing	Very high
Oil shale	Low	Low to moderate	Low to moderate	Low to moderate	Very high	High
Tar sands	Low	Fair? (imports only)	Poor to fair (imports only)	Low	Very high	Moderate to high
Biomass (urban wastes for incineration)	Low	Moderate	Moderate	Low to fairly high	High	Moderate to high
Synthetic natural gas (SNG) from coal	Low	Low to moderate	Low to moderate	Low to moderate	High	High (increases use of coal)
Synthetic oil and alcohols from coal and organic wastes	Low	Moderate	High	Low to moderate	High	High (increases use of coal)
Nuclear energy						
Conventional fission (uranium)	Low to moderate	Low to moderate	Low to moderate	Low to moderate	Very high	Very high
Breeder fission (uranium and thorium)	None	None to low (if developed)	Low to moderate	Unknown, but probably low	Very high	Very high
Fusion (deuterium and tritium)	None	None	None to low (if developed)	Unknown	Very high	Unknown (probably moderate)
Geothermal energy (trapped pockets)	Poor	Poor	Poor	Low to moderate	Moderate	Moderate
Perpetual and Renewable Resources						
Improving energy efficiency	High	High	High	Very high	Very low	Decreases impact of other sources
Water power (hydroelectricity)						
New large-scale dams and plants	Low	Low	Very low	Moderate to high	Moderate to very high	Low to moderate
Reopening abandoned small plants or upgrading big ones	Moderate	Moderate	Low	High	Moderate	Low

(continued)

Table 20-2 (continued)

Energy Resource	Estimated Availability			Estimated Net Useful Energy of Entire System	Projected Cost of Entire System	Actual or Potential Overall Environmental Impact of Entire System
	Short Term (1990–2000)	Intermediate Term (2000–2010)	Long Term (2010–2040)			
Perpetual and Renewable Resources (continued)						
Tidal energy	None	Very low	Very low	Unknown (moderate)	High	Low to moderate
Ocean thermal gradients	None	Low	Low to moderate (if developed)	Unknown (probably low to moderate)	Probably high	Unknown (probably moderate)
Solar energy						
Low-temperature heating (for homes and water)	High	Moderate to high	High	Moderate to high	Moderate (passive) to fairly high (active)	Low
High-temperature heating	Low	Moderate	Moderate to high	Moderate	Very high initially (but probably declining fairly rapidly)	Low to moderate
Photovoltaic production of electricity	Low to moderate	Moderate	High	Fairly high	High initially (but declining fairly rapidly)	Low
Wind energy						
Home and neighborhood turbines	Low	Moderate	Moderate to high	Fairly high	Moderate	Low
Large-scale power plants	None	Very low	Probably low	Low	High	Low to moderate?
Geothermal energy (low heat flow)	Very low	Very low	Low to moderate	Low to moderate	Moderate to high	Moderate to high
Biomass (burning of wood, crop, food, and animal wastes)	Moderate	Moderate	Moderate to high	Moderate	Moderate	Variable
Biofuels (alcohols and natural gas from plants and organic wastes)	Low to moderate?	Moderate	Moderate to high	Low to fairly high	Moderate to high	Variable
Hydrogen gas (from coal or water)	None	Low	Moderate	Variable (depending on energy source used to produce H_2)	Variable	Variable

on energy alternatives that yield too little net useful energy or prove to be economically or environmentally unacceptable.

- We cannot and should not depend mostly on one nonrenewable energy resource like oil, coal, natural gas, or nuclear power. Instead, the world and the United States should rely more on improving energy efficiency and on a mix of perpetual and renewable energy resources.

- We should decrease dependence on coal and nuclear power to produce electricity at large, centralized power plants. Instead, individuals, communities, and countries should get more of the heat and electricity they need from locally available renewable and perpetual energy resources. These nearby energy resources should be tapped on a small scale to meet community or individual needs.

Economics and National Energy Strategy Cost is the major factor determining which commercial energy resources are widely used by consumers. Governments throughout the world use three major economic and political strategies to stimulate or dampen the short- and long-term use of a particular energy resource:

- *not attempting to control the price,* so that its use depends on open, free market competition (assuming all other alternatives also compete in the same way)

- *keeping prices artificially low* to encourage its use and development

- *keeping prices artificially high* to discourage its use and development

Each approach has certain advantages and disadvantages.

Free Market Competition Leaving it to the marketplace without any government interference is appealing in principle. However, free competition rarely exists in practice because businesspeople are in favor of it for everyone but their own companies (Section 3-2).

Most energy industry executives work hard to get control of supply, demand, and price for their particular energy resource, while urging free market competition for any competing energy resources. They try to influence elected officials and help elect those who will give their businesses the most favorable tax breaks and other government subsidies. Such favoritism distorts and unbalances the marketplace.

An equally serious problem with the open marketplace is its emphasis on today's prices to enhance short-term economic gain. This inhibits long-term development of new energy resources, which can rarely compete in their development stages without government support.

One effort to increase free market competition among energy alternatives in the United States is the 1978 Public Utility Regulatory Policies Act (PURPA). This law forces utilities to buy electricity at favorable rates from private firms and individuals producing power by using conventional fuels, cogeneration, or renewables such as wind and hydropower.

Power companies bitterly fought this law in Congress and in the courts. But in 1983 the Supreme Court upheld the law. By 1988 a variety of privately owned firms were generating electricity equal to that from 12 large nuclear power plants. This output is expected to double between 1988 and 1993. Eventually these sources could supply electricity equal to the output of 62 nuclear power plants. This would eliminate the need to build any new nuclear power plants as older ones are retired.

Keeping Energy Prices Artificially Low: The U.S. Strategy Many governments give tax breaks and other subsidies, pay for long-term research and development, and use price controls to keep prices for a particular energy resource artificially low. This is the main approach used by the United States and the Soviet Union.

This approach encourages the development and

use of energy resources getting favorable treatment. It also helps protect consumers (especially the poor) from sharp price increases, and it can help reduce inflation. Because keeping prices low is popular with consumers, this practice often helps leaders in democratic societies get reelected and helps keep leaders in nondemocratic societies from being overthrown.

But this approach also encourages waste and rapid depletion of an energy resource (such as oil) by making its price lower than it should be compared to its true value and long-term supply. This strategy discourages the development of energy alternatives not getting at least the same level of subsidies and price control. Once energy industries such as the fossil fuel and nuclear power industries get government subsidies, they usually have enough clout to maintain this support long after it becomes unproductive. And they often fight efforts to provide equal or higher subsidies for the development of new energy alternatives that would allow more competition in the marketplace.

In 1984 federal tax breaks and other subsidies for the development of energy conservation and perpetual solar-based energy resources in the United States amounted to $1.7 billion. But, these tax breaks were eliminated a year later and have not been restored.

By contrast, during 1984 the nuclear power industry received $15.6 billion, the oil industry $8.6 billion, the natural gas industry $4.6 billion, and the coal industry $3.4 billion in federal tax breaks and subsidies. These subsidies, unlike those for energy conservation and renewable energy, have not been eliminated. Thus, the marketplace is distorted in favor of fossil fuels and nuclear power.

Conservationists are alarmed that an increasing share of the Department of Energy's annual budget is being used to develop nuclear weapons instead of to develop new energy alternatives. Between 1981 and 1989 the share of the department's budget used for making nuclear weapons and developing new ones increased from 38% to 65%.

Only 35% of the 1989 DOE budget was for research and development of energy alternatives. And only 9% of this money (with only 5% proposed for 1990) was spent on research and development of energy conservation and renewable energy resources. The rest was spent mostly on continued development of fossil fuels and nuclear fission and fusion.

Conservationists consider this an upside-down view of reality because using energy conservation and renewable energy resources to reduce dependence on imported oil and decrease CO_2 emissions will be the key to future U.S. economic, environmental, and national security. They call for an entirely new national energy strategy in the 1990s (see Spotlight on p. 540).

Keeping Energy Prices Artificially High: The Western European Strategy Governments keep the price of an energy resource artificially high by withdrawing existing tax breaks and other subsidies or by adding taxes to the price. This encourages improvements in energy efficiency, reduces dependence on imported energy, and decreases use of an energy resource (like oil) whose future supply will be limited.

However, increasing taxes on energy use contribute to inflation and dampen economic growth. They also put a heavy economic burden on the poor unless some of the energy tax revenues are used to help low-income families offset increased energy prices and to stimulate labor-intensive forms of economic growth such as improving energy efficiency. High gasoline and oil import taxes have been imposed by many European governments. That is one reason why those countries use less energy per person and have greater energy efficiency than the United States (Table 20-1).

Why the U.S. Has No Comprehensive Long-Term Energy Strategy
After the 1973 oil embargo, Congress was prodded to pass a number of laws (see Appendix 2) to deal with the country's energy problems. Most energy experts agree, however, that these laws do not represent a comprehensive energy strategy. Indeed, analysis of the U.S. political system reveals why the United States has not been able and will probably never be able to develop a coherent energy policy.

One reason is the complexity of energy issues as revealed in this and the preceding chapter. But the major problem is that the American political process produces laws—not policies—and is not designed to deal with long-term problems. Each law reflects political pressures of the moment and a maze of compromises between competing groups representing industry, conservationists, and consumers. Once a law is passed, it is difficult to repeal or modify drastically until its long-term consequences reach crisis proportions.

Taking Energy Matters into Your Own Hands
While elected officials, energy company executives, and conservationists argue over the key components of a national energy strategy, many individuals and localities have gotten fed up and taken energy matters into their own hands. With or without tax credits, they are insulating, weatherizing, and making other improvements to conserve energy and save money.

Some are building passively heated and cooled solar homes. Others are building superinsulated dwellings or are adding passive solar heating to existing homes. Each of us can develop a personal energy strategy that improves personal and national security and saves money (see Spotlight on p. 541 and inside back cover).

Similarly, local governments in a growing number of cities are developing successful programs to improve energy efficiency and to rely more on locally available energy resources. Across the country, towns are realizing that paying for energy is bleeding them to death

---

SPOTLIGHT A New Energy Strategy for the United States

Conservationists and environmentalists believe that the present U.S. energy strategy will lead to economic and environmental disaster and greatly increase the chances of nuclear and conventional war. They call for greatly increased research-and-development spending on energy conservation and renewable energy in the 1990s.

They also believe that energy conservation and renewable energy alternatives should get at least the same level of federal subsidies as fossil fuels and nuclear power. Another way to allow energy alternatives to compete on a more equal footing would be to eliminate all energy subsidies. However, this would be nearly impossible to do because of the political and economic power of the fossil fuel and nuclear industries.

Conservationists call for Congress to raise the average fuel efficiency requirement of new cars and light trucks to 60 miles per gallon by 2000. Incentives could also be established to encourage consumers to scrap older cars early and buy more efficient ones.

Some conservationists believe that the government should phase in a $1 per gallon gasoline tax over the next five years. This would bring U.S. gasoline prices closer to world levels and help discourage the use of fuel-inefficient vehicles. It would also raise $100 billion of revenue each year to help reduce the national debt and provide funds for energy research aimed at reducing dependence on oil and reducing carbon dioxide emissions.

Another conservation measure the government can take is to give tax writeoffs to consumers who buy new energy efficient houses or who make older ones more energy efficient. The goal would be to cut in half the consumption of oil, gas, and electricity for heating space and hot water over the next 20 years. Much tougher energy efficiency standards should also be set for all major appliances.

Experts also suggest that a climate protection tax be levied on all fossil fuels on the basis of their relative emissions of carbon dioxide to the atmosphere (Figure 19-13, p. 491). Such a tax could delay climate changes from the greenhouse effect and raise at least $53 billion a year for encouraging energy conservation and the development of renewable energy resources. What do you think?

---

economically, with 80% to 90% of the money they spend on energy leaving the local economy forever.

Each of these individual and local initiatives are crucial political and economic actions that are bringing about change from the bottom-up. Multiplied across the country, such actions can shape a sane national energy strategy with or without help from federal and state governments.

Most LDCs can also improve energy efficiency and use renewable and perpetual energy resources to meet much of their energy needs. Most renewable-energy projects have short construction times and provide large numbers of jobs. Countries and communities that depend on energy from locally available renewable resources are less vulnerable to disruptions of fuel supplies and price rises, and their economies are stronger because they spend less on energy imports.

A few countries are leading the way in making the transition from the age of oil to the age of energy efficiency and renewable energy. Sweden leads the world in energy efficiency, followed by Japan. Brazil and Norway get more than half their energy from hydro-

---

SPOTLIGHT Working with Nature: A Personal Progress Report

I am writing this book deep in the midst of some beautiful woods in Eco-Lair, a structure that Peggy, my wife and earthmate, and I designed to work with nature. First, we purchased a 1954 school bus from a nearby school district and sold the tires for the same price that we paid for the bus. We built an insulated foundation, rented a crane for two hours to lift and set the gutted bus on the foundation, placed heavy insulation around the bus, and added a wooden outside frame.

We attached a solar room—a passive solar collector with double-paned conventional sliding glass windows (for ventilation)—to the entire south side of the bus structure (Figure 20-16). The solar room serves as a year-round sitting and work area and contains a small kitchen with a stove and refrigerator that run on liquefied petroleum gas (LPG).

The room collects enough solar energy to meet about 60% of our heating needs during the cold months. A solar-assisted water stove in a small building outside provides backup heat as needed by burning wood. During sunny days active solar collectors store heat in a 500-gallon insulated tank with a built-in firebox. Wood is burned in the firebox in very cold weather to supplement the stored solar energy.

Placing this system in a separate shed eliminates indoor smoke and soot. A pump connected to the water tank circulates heated

Figure 20-16   Eco-Lair. A south-facing solar room collects solar energy passively and distributes it to a well-insulated, recycled school bus. Backup heat is provided by a solar-assisted water stove housed in the separate structure at left. Cooling is provided by earth tubes for about $1 a summer. Electricity bills run about $30 a month.

Ron Sells

water through insulated underground pipes to a heat exchanger before the water is returned to the tank. A fan transfers the heat in the water to air, which is blown through ducts connected to the house. With a conventional thermostat to control indoor temperature, the system eliminates the uneven heating provided by a conventional wood stove. A recycled thermostat-controlled gas burner is attached to the water-stove tank as a backup.

Our hot water is supplied by active solar collectors connected to the water stove. In winter the solar-heated water is heated further as needed by a tankless, instant heater fueled by LPG. Most

of our light bulbs we use last an average of six years and use about 60% less electricity than conventional bulbs.

For the time being we are buying electricity from the power company. But we plan to get our electricity from roof-mounted panels of photovoltaic cells (Figure 20-11) when their price is lower, probably sometime in the 1990s. We hope to be able to sell any excess power we produce back to the power company. Our present monthly electricity bills run around $30.

We cool the structure in moderate weather by opening windows to capture breezes during hot and humid North Carolina summers.

(continued)

---

power, wood, and alcohol fuel. Israel, Japan, the Philippines, and Sweden plan to rely on renewable and perpetual sources for most of their energy.

Countries that have the vision to change from an unsustainable to a sustainable energy strategy will be rewarded with increased security—not just military security but also economic, energy, and environmental security. Those that do not will experience unnecessary economic and environmental hardships and increased human suffering.

In the long run, humanity has no choice but to rely on renewable energy. No matter how abundant they seem today, eventually coal and uranium will run out. The choice before us is practical: We simply cannot afford to make more than one energy transition within the next generation.

Daniel Deudney and Christopher Flavin

SPOTLIGHT (continued)

We get additional cooling from earth tubes, or cool tubes (Figure 20-6). Four plastic pipes were buried about 18 feet underground, extending down a gently sloping hillside until their ends emerge some 100 feet away. The other ends of the tubes come up into the foundation of the bus and connect to a duct system containing a small fan whose speed can be varied by a rheostat. When the fan is turned on, outside air at a temperature of 95°F is drawn slowly through the buried tubes (which are surrounded by earth at about 60°F) and enters the structure at about 72°F. This natural air conditioning costs about $1 per summer for running the fan.

Several large oak trees and other deciduous trees in front of the solar room give us additional passive cooling during summer and drop their leaves to let the sun in during winter. Because of our allergies, we have had to install a recycled conventional air conditioning unit. We turn it on for short periods (typically no more than 30 minutes a day) when excessive pollen or heat and humidity overwhelm our immune systems and the earth tubes. Life always involves some trade-offs.

Eco-Lair is surrounded by natural vegetation, including flowers and low-level ground cover. This means we have no grass to cut and no lawnmower to repair, feed with gasoline, and listen to. To the natural diversity of the landscape we have added plants that repel various insects, so we have few insect pest problems. The surrounding trees and other vegetation also provide habitats for various species of insect-eating birds.

We have reduced water use by installing water-saving faucets and low-flush toilets. We have also experimented with a waterless composting toilet that gradually converts waste and garbage scraps to a dry, odorless powder that can be used as a soil conditioner. Kitchen wastes are composted and recycled to the soil and paper is carried to a recycling center. We store extra furniture, clothes, and other items in three other old school buses and recycle these items to family, friends, and people in need.

Eco-Lair lies near the end of a narrow, one-mile-long dirt road that at times can be traversed only by a four-wheel-drive vehicle. As a result, we have to drive a vehicle that consumes much more gasoline than we would like. We plan to buy a car that gets 80 to 100 mpg and use it for most trips. If the technology becomes available and economically feasible in the future, we hope to have one that runs on hydrogen gas produced by solar photovoltaic cells that decompose water into hydrogen and oxygen gas. Because of laziness and allergies, we get most of our food from the grocery store rather than growing it ourselves.

We feel a part of the piece of land we live on and love. To us, ownership of this land means that we are ethically driven to defend and protect it from degradation.

We feel that the trees, flowers, deer, squirrels, hummingbirds, songbirds, and other forms of wildlife we often see are a part of us and we are a part of them. As temporary caretakers of this small portion of the biosphere, we feel obligated to pass it on to future generations with its ecological integrity and sustainability preserved.

Most of our political activities involve thinking globally but acting locally. They include attempts to prevent an economically unnecessary nuclear power plant from opening about 15 miles away (it opened anyway), to prevent an ecologically unsound development along a nearby river that is already badly polluted (we've been successful so far), to prevent the building of a large, conventional housing development that would double the size of the closest town (successful).

We also financially support numerous environmental and conservation organizations working at the national and global levels. We are not opposed to all forms of development, only those that are ecologically unsound and destructive.

We find that working with nature gives us great joy and a sense of purpose. It also saves us money. We are trying to work with nature in a rural area. But people in cities can also have high-quality lifestyles that conserve resources and protect the environment (see Further Readings).

DISCUSSION TOPICS

1. What are the ten most important things an individual can do to save energy in the home and in transportation (see inside back cover)? Which, if any, of these do you do? Which, if any, do you plan to do? When?

2. Make an energy use study of your school, and use the findings to develop an energy conservation program.

3. Should the United States institute a crash program to develop solar photovoltaic cells? Explain.

4. Explain why you agree or disagree with each of the following statements:
   a. The United States can get most of the electricity it needs by developing solar power plants.
   b. The United States can get most of the electricity it needs by using direct solar energy to produce electricity in photovoltaic cells.
   c. The United States can get most of the electricity it needs by building new, large hydroelectric plants.
   d. The United States can get most of the electricity it needs by building ocean thermal electric power plants.
   e. The United States can get most of the electricity it needs by building wind farms.
   f. The United States can get most of the electricity it needs by building power plants fueled by wood, crop wastes, trash, and other biomass resources.

5. Explain why you agree or disagree with the following propositions suggested by various energy analysts:
   a. The United States should cut average per capita energy use by at least 50% between 1990 and 2010.
   b. A mandatory energy conservation program should form the basis of any U.S. energy policy in order to provide economic, environmental, and military security.
   c. To solve world and U.S. energy supply problems, all we need to do is recycle some or most of the energy we use.
   d. Federal subsidies for all energy alternatives should be eliminated so that all energy choices can compete in a true, free-enterprise market system.
   e. All government tax breaks and other subsidies for conventional fuels (oil, natural gas, coal), synthetic natural gas and oil, and nuclear power should be removed and replaced with subsidies and tax breaks for improving energy efficiency and developing solar, wind, geothermal, and biomass energy alternatives.
   f. Development of solar and wind energy should be left up to private enterprise without help from the federal government, but nuclear energy and fossil fuels should continue to receive federal subsidies (present U.S. energy policy).
   g. To solve present and future U.S. energy problems, all we need to do is find and develop more domestic supplies of conventional and unconventional oil, natural gas, and coal and increase our dependence on nuclear power (present U.S. energy policy).
   h. The United States should not worry about heavy dependence on foreign oil imports because they improve international relations and help prevent depletion of domestic supplies (the "don't drain America first" approach).
   i. A heavy federal tax should be placed on gasoline and imported oil used in the United States.
   j. Between 2000 and 2020 the U.S. should phase out all nuclear power plants.

6. The present government policy in the United States is to keep heating oil, gasoline, natural gas, coal, and electricity prices artificially low by giving massive, tax-supported subsidies to the fossil-fuel and nuclear industries and not imposing higher taxes on gasoline and imported oil. Explain how this policy can (a) discourage exploration for domestic supplies of fossil fuels, (b) increase or at least not significantly decrease dependence on imported oil, (c) lead to higher than necessary unemployment, (d) discourage development of direct and indirect sources of solar energy, and (e) discourage improvements in energy efficiency.

FURTHER READINGS

Also see Readings for Chapters 4 and 19.

Blackburn, John O. 1987. *The Renewable Energy Alternative: How the United States and the World Can Prosper Without Nuclear Energy or Coal.* Durham, N.C.: Duke University Press.

Brown, Lester R., Annual. *State of the World.* New York: W. W. Norton.

Butti, Ken, and John Perlin. 1980. *A Golden Thread—2500 Years of Solar Architecture.* Palo Alto, Calif.: Cheshire Press.

Charlier, Roger Henri. 1982. *Tidal Energy.* New York: Van Nostrand Reinhold.

Clarke, Robin. 1977. *Building for Self-Sufficiency.* New York: Universe Books.

Davidson, Joel. 1987. *The New Solar Electric Home.* Ann Arbor, Mich: Aatec Publications.

Deudney, Daniel, and Christopher Flavin. 1983. *Renewable Energy: The Power to Choose.* New York: W. W. Norton.

Dinga, Gustav P. 1988. "Hydrogen: The Ultimate Fuel and Energy Carrier." *Journal of Chemical Education,* vol. 65, no. 8. 688–691.

Edmonds, Jae, and John M. Reilly. 1985. *Global Energy: Assessing the Future:* New York: Oxford University Press.

Farallones Institute. 1979. *The Integral Urban House: Self-Reliant Living in the City.* San Francisco: Sierra Club Books.

Flavin, Christopher. 1984. *Electricity's Future: The Shift to Efficiency and Small-Scale Power.* Washington, D.C.: Worldwatch Institute.

Flavin, Christopher. 1986. *Electricity for a Developing World: New Directions.* Washington, D.C.: Worldwatch Institute.

Flavin, Christopher, and Alan B. Durning. 1988. *Building on Success: The Age of Energy Efficiency.* Washington, D.C.: Worldwatch Institute.

Gever, John, et al. 1986. *Beyond Oil.* Cambridge, Mass: Ballinger.

Glasner, David. 1986. *Politics, Prices, and Petroleum: The Political Economy of Energy.* San Francisco: Pacific Institute for Public Policy Analysis.

Heede, H. Richard, et al. 1985. *The Hidden Costs of Energy.* Washington, D.C.: Center for Renewable Resources.

Hubbard, H. M. 1989. "Photovoltaics Today and Tomorrow." *Science,* vol. 244, 297–304.

Hughes, Barry B., et al. 1985. *Energy in the Global Arena: Actors, Values, Policies, and Futures.* Durham, N.C.: Duke University Press.

Humphrey, Craig R., and Frederick R. Buttel. 1982. *Environment, Energy, and Society.* Belmont, Calif.: Wadsworth.

Kovarik, Bill. 1982. *Fuel Alcohol: Energy and Environment in a Hungry World.* Washington, D.C.: Earthscan.

Leckie, Jim, et al. 1975. *Other Homes and Garbage: Designs for Self-Sufficient Living.* San Francisco: Sierra Club Books.

Lovins, Amory B. 1989. *Energy, People, and Industrialization.* Old Snowmass, Colo.: Rocky Mountain Institute.

Medsker, Larry. 1982. *Side Effects of Renewable Energy Resources.* New York: National Audubon Society.

Morris, James W. 1980. *The Complete Energy Saving Book for Home Owners.* New York: Harper & Row.

National Academy of Sciences. 1983. *Alcohol Fuels: Options for Developing Countries.* Washington, D.C.: National Academy Press.

Nussbaum, Bruce. 1985. *The World After Oil: The Shifting Axis of Power and Wealth.* New York: Simon & Schuster.

Penny, Terry R., and Desikan Bharathan. 1987. "Power from the Sea." *Scientific American,* vol. 286, no. 1, 86–92.

Pimentel, David, et al. 1984. "Environmental and Social Costs of Biomass Energy." *BioScience,* February, 89–93.

Pryde, Philip R. 1983. *Nonconventional Energy Resources.* New York: John Wiley-Interscience.

Purcell, Arthur. 1980. *The Waste Watchers: A Citizen's Handbook for Conserving Energy and Resources.* Garden City, N.Y.: Anchor Press/Doubleday.

Renner, Michael. 1988. *Rethinking the Role of the Automobile.* Washington, D.C.: Worldwatch Institute.

Rocky Mountain Institute. 1988. *An Energy Security Reader,* 2nd ed. Old Snowmass, Colo.: Rocky Mountain Institute.

Rocky Mountain Institute. 1987. *Resource-Efficient Housing Guide.* Snowmass, Colo.: Rocky Mountain Institute.

Rose, David. 1986. *Learning about Energy.* New York: Plenum.

Rosenbaum, Walter A.. 1987. *Energy, Politics, and Public Policy.* 2d ed. Washington, D.C.: Congressional Quarterly.

Sawyer, Stephen W. 1986. *Renewable Energy: Progress, Prospects.* Washington, D.C.: Association of American Geographers.

Shea, Cynthia Pollack. 1988. *Renewable Energy: Today's Contribution, Tomorrow's Promise.* Washington, D.C.: Worldwatch Institute.

Skelton, Luther W. 1984. *The Solar-Hydrogen Economy: Beyond the Age of Fire.* New York: Van Nostrand Reinhold.

Starr, Gary. 1987. *The Solar Electric Book.* Lower Lake, Calif.: Integral Publishing.

Swan, Christopher C. 1986. *Suncell: Energy, Economy, Photovoltaics.* New York: Random House.

Wade, Herb. 1983. *Building Underground.: The Design and Construction Handbook for Earth-Sheltered Houses.* Emmaus, Penn. Rodale Press.

Achieving a Sustainable-Earth Society

When there is no dream, the people perish.

Proverbs 29:18

T he frontier or throwaway mentality sees the earth as a place of unlimited room and resources, where ever-increasing production, consumption, and technology inevitably lead to a better life for everyone. If we pollute one area, we merely move to another or eliminate or control the pollution through technology. This worldview is based on dominating nature.

Most environmentalists and conservationists believe that over the next 50 years or so we must change from our present throwaway lifestyle to sustainable-earth or conserver lifestyles designed to maintain the earth's vital life-support system for us, future generations, and the other species that inhabit the earth.

A sustainable-earth worldview sees that the earth is a place of limited room and resources. It recognizes that ever-increasing production and consumption put severe stress on the natural processes that renew and maintain the air, water, soil, and biological diversity upon which we and other species depend. Sustaining the earth calls for cooperating with nature, rather than attempting to dominate it. Achieving a sustainable-earth worldview involves working our way through four levels of environmental awareness summarized in the Spotlight on p. 546.

But the sustainable-earth worldview by itself is not enough. It is unrealistic to expect poor people living at the margin of existence to think about the long-term survival of the planet. When people need to burn wood to keep from freezing, they will cut down trees. When their livestock and their families face starvation, they will overgraze grasslands.

Analysts argue that an equally important element in the transition to a sustainable-earth society is generous and effective aid and technical advice from MDCs to LDCs. Such aid should help poorer nations become more self-reliant rather than making them more dependent on MDCs for goods and services.

We can read and talk about environmental and resource problems, but finally it comes down to what you and I are willing to do individually and collectively. We can begin at the individual level and work outward by joining with others to amplify our actions. This is the way the world is changed.

Envision the world as made up of all kinds of matter cycles and energy flows. See these life-sustaining processes as a beautiful and diverse web of interrelationships—a kaleidoscope of patterns and rhythms whose very complexity and multitude of potentials remind us that cooperation, honesty, humility, and love must be the guidelines for our behavior toward one another and the earth.

Make a difference by caring. Care about the air, water, soil. Care about wild plants, wild animals, wild places. Care about people—young, old, black, white, brown—in this generation and generations to come. Let this caring be your guide for doing. Live your life caring about the earth and you will be fulfilled. Live your life this way and know that if the earth that bore and sustained you could speak, it would say: Thank you for caring, thank you for making a difference.

It is not too late. There is time to deal with the complex environmental and resource problems we face if enough of us really care. It's not up to "them," it's up to "us." Don't wait.

The main ingredients of an environmental ethic are caring about the planet and all of its inhabitants, allowing unselfishness to control the immediate self-interest that harms others, and living each day so as to leave the lightest possible footprints on the planet.

Robert Cahn

First Awareness Level: Pollution and Environmental Degradation

We must discover the symptoms. At this level we must point out and try to stop irresponsible acts of pollution, resource waste, and environmental degradation by individuals and organizations and resist being duped by slick corporate advertising. But we must also change our own lifestyles. We have all been working toward our own destruction by "drilling holes in the bottom of the boat." Arguing over who is drilling the biggest hole diverts us from working together to keep the boat from sinking. The problem with staying at the first awareness level is that individuals see their own impacts as too tiny to matter, not realizing that millions of individual impacts acting together threaten our life-support systems. Remaining at this first level of awareness also leads people to see the crisis as a problem comparable to a moon shot, and to look for a quick technological solution: "Have technology fix us up, send me the bill at the end of the month, but don't ask me to change my way of living."

Second Awareness Level: Consumption Overpopulation

We must recognize that the cause of pollution is not just people but their level of consumption and the environmental impact of various types of production (Figure 1-13,

p. 18) At this level the answers seem obvious. One is to control the world's population. But we must also reduce wasteful consumption of matter and energy resources—especially in MDCs, which, with less than 26% of the world's population, account for about 80% of the world's resource consumption and environmental pollution.

Third Awareness Level: Spaceship Earth (Shallow Ecology)

We must become aware that population and resource use will not be controlled until enough world leaders and citizens stress that protecting and preserving the environment must be our primary purpose. The goal at this level is to use technology, economics, and conventional politics to control population growth, pollution and resource depletion to prevent ecological overload. Some argue that the popular view of the earth as a spaceship is a sophisticated expression of our arrogance toward nature—the idea that through technology we can control nature and create artificial environments to avoid environmental overload. They also believe that this approach threatens individual freedom because to protect the life-support systems that are necessary in space, a centralized authority (ground control) must rigidly control astronauts' lives. Instead of novelty, spontaneity, joy, and free-

dom, the spaceship model is based on cultural sameness, social regimentation, artificiality, monotony, and gadgetry. It is also argued that this approach can cause environmental overload and resource depletion in the long run because it is based on the false idea that we understand how nature works. This awareness level does not seriously question economic, political, social, and ethical foundations of modern industrial society, which some see as the major causes of our environmental and resource problems.

Fourth Awareness Level: Sustainable Earth (Deep Ecology)

We must recognize that (1) all living species are interconnected; (2) the role of human beings is not to rule and control nature but to work with nature and to meet human needs on the basis of ecological understanding; (3) because the earth's organisms and their interactions are so diverse, attempts at excessive control will sooner or later backfire; (4) our major goal should be to preserve the ecological integrity, sustainability, and diversity of the life-support systems for all species; (5) the forces of biological evolution, not technological control, should determine which species live or die; and (6) human beings have no right to interfere destructively with nonhuman life except to satisfy vital needs.

Publications

The following publications will help you keep informed and up to date on resource and environmental problems. Subscription prices, which tend to change, are not given. National, state, and local resource and environmental organizations are listed in the *Conservation Directory*, published annually by the National Wildlife Foundation, 1400 16th St. N.W., Washington, DC 20036.

Alternate Sources of Energy, Alternate Sources of Energy, Inc., 107 S. Central Ave., Milaca, MN 56353. Useful source of information on renewable energy alternatives.

American Forests, American Forestry Association, 1516 P St. N.W., Washington, DC 20005. Popular treatment of forest and conservation issues.

Amicus Journal, Natural Resources Defense Council, 122 E. 42nd St., New York, NY 10168. Useful summary of activities and issues.

Annual Review of Energy, Department of Energy, Forrestal Building, 1000 Independence Ave. S.W., Washington, DC 20585. Basic data.

Audubon, National Audubon Society, 950 Third Ave., New York, NY 10022. Popular summaries of conservation and wildlife issues.

Audubon Wildlife Report, National Audubon Society, 950 Third Ave., New York, NY 10022. Annual summary of wildlife agencies, problems, and species; published since 1985; excellent source of data.

BioScience, American Institute of Biological Sciences, 730 11th St. N.W., Washington, DC 20001. Popular and technical coverage of biological aspects of conservation and environmental issues.

CoEvolution Quarterly, P.O. Box 428, Sausalito, CA 94965. Covers a wide range of environmental and self-sufficiency topics.

Conservation Biology, Blackwell Scientific Publications, Inc., 52 Beacon St., Boston, MA 02108. Semitechnical coverage of wildlife conservation.

Conservation Foundation Letter, Conservation Foundation, 1250 24th St. N.W., Washington, DC 20037. Good summaries of key issues.

Conservation News, National Wildlife Foundation, 1400 16th St. N.W., Washington, DC 20036. Popular coverage of wildlife issues.

Demographic Yearbook, Department of International Economic and Social Affairs, Statistical Office, United Nations Publishing Service, United Nations, NY 10017. Basic population data.

Earth Island Journal, Earth Island Institute, 300 Broadway, Suite 28, San Francisco, CA 94133. Nontechnical summaries of national and global conservation and environmental issues.

The Ecologist, Ecosystems Ltd., 73 Molesworth St., Wadebridge, Cornway PL27 7DS, United Kingdom. Wide range of articles on conservation and environmental issues from an international viewpoint.

Ecology, Ecological Society of America, Dr. Duncan T. Patten, Center for Environmental Studies, Arizona State University, Tempe, AR 85281. Professional journal.

Endangered Species UPDATE, School of Natural Resources, The University of Michigan, Ann Arbor, MI 48109. Monthly reprint of the latest U.S. Fish and Wildlife endangered species technical bulletin, a feature article, and technical notes.

Environment, Heldref Publications, 4000 Albemarle St. N.W., Washington, DC 20016. Nontechnical articles on environmental and resource issues.

Environmental Abstracts, Bowker A & I Publishing, 245 West 17th St., New York, NY 10011. Basic bibliographic tool; in most libraries.

Environmental Action, 1525 New Hampshire Ave. N.W., Washington, DC 20036. Popular coverage of environmental and resource issues; emphasis on political and social action.

Environmental Ethics, Department of Philosophy, University of Georgia, Athens, GA 30602. Major journal in the field.

The Environmental Professional, Editorial Office, Department of Geography, University of Iowa, Iowa City, IA 52242. Semitechnical discussion of environmental and resource issues.

Environmental Quality, Council on Environmental Quality, 722 Jackson Place N.W., Washington, DC 20006. Annual report on environmental problems and progress in environmental protection in the United States.

EPA Journal, Environmental Protection Agency. Order from Government Printing Office, Washington, DC 20402. Nontechnical coverage of environmental issues and updates on EPA activities.

Fisheries, American Fisheries Society, 5410 Grosvenor Lane, Bethesda, MD 20814. Professional journal.

The Futurist, World Future Society, P.O. Box 19285, Twentieth Street Station, Washington, DC 20036. Popular coverage of environmental, resource, and social issues with emphasis on the future.

International Wildlife, National Wildlife Federation, 1400 16th St. N.W., Washington, DC 20036. Popular coverage of global wildlife and other resource conservation issues.

Issues in Science and Technology, National Academy of Sciences, 2101 Constitution Ave. N.W., Washington, DC 20077-5576.

Covers a range of issues, including environment and resources.

Journal of Environmental Education, Heldref Publications, 4000 Albemarle St. N.W., Suite 504, Washington, DC 20016. Useful information for teachers.

Journal of Forestry, Society of American Foresters, 5400 Grosvenor Lane, Bethesda, MD 20814. Professional journal.

Journal of Range Management, Society for Range Management, 1839 York St., Denver, CO 80206. Professional journal.

Journal of Soil and Water Conservation, Soil and Water Conservation Society, 7515 NE Ankeny Rd., Ankeny, Iowa 50021. Professional journal.

Journal of Wildlife Management, Wildlife Society, 5410 Grosvenor Lane, Bethesda, MD 20814. Covers basic issues and information.

National Geographic, National Geographic Society, P.O. Box 2895, Washington, DC 20077-9960. Popular coverage of wildlife and environmental issues; beautiful photographs.

National Parks and Conservation Magazine, National Parks and Conservation Association, 1015 31st St. N.W., Washington, DC 20007. Popular coverage of parks and wildlife issues.

National Wildlife, National Wildlife Federation, 1400 16th St. N.W., Washington, DC 20036. Popular coverage of wildlife and other resource conservation issues in the United States.

Natural History, American Museum of Natural History, Central Park West at 79th St., New York, NY 10024. Popular coverage of a broad range of topics, including environmental and resource issues.

Nature, 711 National Press Building, Washington, DC 20045. Summaries of latest research in a range of scientific fields.

New Scientist, 128 Long Acre, London, WC 2, England. Nontechnical coverage of environmental and other issues related to science.

Not Man Apart, Friends of the Earth, 530 Seventh St. SE, Washington, DC 20003. Nontechnical summaries and articles on national and international conservation and environmental issues.

Organic Gardening & Farming Magazine, Rodale Press, 33 E. Minor St., Emmaus, PA 18049. The best guide to organic gardening.

Pollution Abstracts, Cambridge Scientific Abstracts, 7200 Wisconsin Ave., Bethesda, MD 20814. Basic bibliographic tool; in many libraries.

Population and Vital Statistics Report, UN Publications Sales Section, New York, NY 10017. Basic population data.

Population Bulletin, Population Reference Bureau, 777 Fourteenth St. N.W., Suite 800, Washington, DC 20005. In-depth nontechnical articles on population issues.

Science, American Association for the Advancement of Science, 1333 H St. N.W., Washington, DC 20005. Technical articles and popular summaries of scientific issues; in recent years has decreased coverage of environmental and resource issues.

Science News, Science Service, Inc., 1719 N St. N.W., Washington, DC 20036. Popular weekly summaries of scientific developments, including environmental topics.

Scientific American, 415 Madison Ave., New York, NY 10017. Semitechnical articles on science with some coverage of environmental and resource issues.

Sierra, 730 Polk St., San Francisco, CA 94108. Popular coverage of conservation and environmental issues with emphasis on political action.

State of the World, Worldwatch Institute, 1776 Massachusetts Ave. N.W., Washington, DC 20036. Annual summary of environment and resource issues.

Statistical Yearbook, Department of International Economic and Social Affairs, Statistical Office, United Nations Publishing Service, United Nations, NY 10017. Annual summary of data on population, food pro-

duction, resource production and consumption, energy, housing, and forestry.

Technology Review, Massachusetts Institute of Technology, Room E219-430, Cambridge, MA 02139. Popular discussion of scientific and engineering issues, with about half its pages on environment and resource issues.

Transition, Laurence G. Wolf, ed., Department of Geography, University of Cincinnati, Cincinnati, OH 45221. Quarterly journal of the Socially and Ecologically Responsible Geographers.

Wilderness, Wilderness Society, 1400 I St. N.W., 10th Floor, Washington, DC 20005. Nontechnical articles on wilderness and wildlife conservation.

World Development Report, World Bank, Publications Department, 1818 H Street N.W., Washington, DC 20433. Annual summary of economic development.

World Rainforest Report, Rainforest Action Network, 300 Broadway, Suite 28, San Francisco, CA 94133. Summary of problems and progress in protecting rainforests.

World Resources, World Resources Institute, 1735 New York Ave. N.W., Washington, DC 20006. Summary of environment and resource problems; useful source of data; published every two years.

World Watch, Worldwatch Institute, 1776 Massachusetts Ave. N.W., Washington, DC 20036. Bimonthly magazine giving nontechnical summaries of key environmental and resource issues.

Worldwatch Papers, Worldwatch Institute, 1776 Massachusetts Ave. N.W., Washington, DC 20036. Series of nontechnical reports designed to serve as an early warning system on major environmental and resource problems.

Yearbook of World Energy Statistics, Department of International Economic and Social Affairs, Statistical Office, United Nations Publishing Service, United Nations, NY 10017. Annual summary of data on worldwide energy production.

Major U.S. Resource Conservation and Environmental Legislation

General

National Environmental Policy Act of 1969 (NEPA)

International Environmental Protection Act of 1983

Energy

National Energy Act of 1978, 1980

Water Quality

Water Quality Act of 1965

Water Resources Planning Act of 1965

Federal Water Pollution Control Acts of 1965, 1972

Ocean Dumping Act of 1972

Safe Drinking Water Act of 1974, 1984

Clean Water Act of 1977, 1987

Air Quality

Clean Air Act of 1963, 1965, 1970, 1977

Noise Control

Noise Control Act of 1965

Quiet Communities Act of 1978

Resources and Solid Waste Management

Solid Waste Disposal Act of 1965

Resources Recovery Act of 1970

Resource Conservation and Recovery Act of 1976

Toxic Substances

Toxic Substances Control Act of 1976

Resource Conservation and Recovery Act of 1976

Comprehensive Environmental Response, Compensation, and Liability (Superfund) Act of 1980, 1986

Nuclear Waste Policy Act of 1982

Pesticides

Federal Insecticide, Fungicide, and Rodenticide Control Act of 1972, 1988

Wildlife Conservation

Anadromous Fish Conservation Act of 1965

Fur Seal Act of 1966

National Wildlife Refuge System Act of 1966, 1976, 1978

Species Conservation Act of 1966, 1969

Marine Mammal Protection Act of 1972

Marine Protection, Research, and Sanctuaries Act of 1972

Endangered Species Act of 1973, 1982, 1985, 1988

Fishery Conservation and Management Act of 1976, 1978, 1982

Whale Conservation and Protection Study Act of 1976

Fish and Wildlife Improvement Act of 1978

Fish and Wildlife Conservation Act of 1980 (Nongame Act)

Land Use and Conservation

Taylor Grazing Act of 1934

Wilderness Act of 1964

Multiple Use Sustained Yield Act of 1968

Wild and Scenic Rivers Act of 1968

National Trails System Act of 1968

National Coastal Zone Management Act of 1972, 1980

Forest Reserves Management Act of 1974, 1976

Forest and Rangeland Renewable Resources Act of 1974, 1978

Federal Land Policy and Management Act of 1976

National Forest Management Act of 1976

Soil and Water Conservation Act of 1977

Surface Mining Control and Reclamation Act of 1977

Antarctic Conservation Act of 1978

Endangered American Wilderness Act of 1978

Alaskan National Interests Lands Conservation Act of 1980

Coastal Barrier Resources Act of 1982

Food Security Act of 1985

How to Save
Water and Money

Bathroom (65% of residential use; 40% for toilet flushing)

- For existing toilets, reduce amount of water used per flush by putting a tall plastic container weighted with a few stones into each tank, or buy (for about $10) and insert a toilet dam made of plastic and rubber; bricks also work but disintegrate and gum up the water.

- In new houses, install water-saving toilets or, where health codes permit, waterless or composting toilets. Flush only when necessary, using advice found on a bathroom wall in a drought-stricken area: "If it's yellow, let it mellow—if it's brown, flush it down."

- Take short showers—showers of less than 5 minutes use less water than a bath. Shower by wetting down, turning off the water while soaping up, and then rinsing off. If you prefer baths, fill tub well below the overflow drain.

- Use water-saving flow restrictors, which cost less than a dollar and can be easily installed, on all faucets and showerheads.

- Check frequently for toilet, shower, and sink leaks and repair them promptly. A pinhole leak can cost $25 a month in excess water and electricity charges; a fast leak, $50 or more.

- Don't keep water running while brushing teeth, shaving, or washing.

Laundry Room (15%)

- Wash only full loads; use short cycle and fill machine to the lowest possible water level.

- When buying a new washer, choose one that uses the least amount of water and fills up to different levels for loads of different sizes.

- Check for leaks frequently and repair all leaks promptly.

Kitchen (10%)

- Use an automatic dishwasher only for full loads; use short cycle and let dishes air-dry to save energy.

- When washing many dishes by hand, don't let the faucet run. Instead, use one filled dishpan for washing and another for rinsing.

- Keep a jug of water in the refrigerator rather than running water from a tap until it gets cold enough to drink.

- While waiting for faucet water to get hot, catch the cool water in a pan and use it for cooking or to water plants.

- Check for sink and dishwasher leaks frequently and repair them promptly.

- Try not to use a garbage disposal or water-softening system—both are major water users.

Outdoors (10%; higher in arid areas)

- Don't wash your car, or wash it less frequently. Wash the car from a bucket of soapy water; use hose only for rinsing.

- Sweep walks and driveways instead of hosing them off.

- Reduce evaporation losses by watering lawns and gardens in early morning or evening, rather than in the heat of midday or when windy. Better yet, landscape with pebbles, rocks, sand, wood chips, or native plants adapted to local average annual precipitation so that watering is not necessary.

- Use drip irrigation systems and mulch on home gardens to improve irrigation efficiency and reduce evaporation.

Glossary

abiotic Nonliving. Compare *biotic*.

absolute resource scarcity Situation in which there are not enough actual or affordable supplies of a resource left to meet present or future demand. Compare *relative resource scarcity*.

abyssal zone Bottom zone of the ocean, consisting of deep, dark, cold water and the ocean bottom (benthos). Compare *bathyal zone, euphotic zone*.

accelerated eutrophication See *cultural eutrophication*.

acid deposition The falling of acids and acid-forming compounds from the atmosphere to the earth's surface. Acid deposition is commonly known as *acid rain*, a term that refers to only wet deposition of droplets of acids and acid-forming compounds.

acidic See *acid solution*.

acid rain See *acid deposition*.

acid solution Any water solution that has more hydrogen ions (H^+) than hydroxide ions (OH^-); any water solution with a pH less than 7. Compare *basic solution, neutral solution*.

active solar heating system System that uses solar collectors to capture energy from the sun and store it as heat for space heating and heating water. A liquid or air pumped through the collectors transfers the captured heat to a storage system such as an insulated tank of water or a bed of rocks. Pumps or fans then distribute the stored heat or hot water throughout a dwelling as needed. Compare *passive solar heating system*.

advanced sewage treatment Specialized chemical and physical processes that reduce the amount of specific pollutants left in wastewater after primary and secondary sewage treatment. This type of treatment is usually expensive. See also *primary sewage treatment, secondary sewage treatment*.

aerobic organism Organism that needs oxygen to stay alive. Compare *anerobic organism*.

aerobic respiration See *cellular aerobic respiration*.

aesthetic resource Resource valued because of its beauty or ability to give pleasure. Examples are solitude, quiet, and scenic beauty.

age structure (age distribution) Percentage of the population, or the number of people of each sex, at each age level in a population.

agroforestry Planting trees and crops together.

air pollution One or more chemicals or substances in high enough concentrations in the air to harm humans, other animals, vegetation, or materials. Such chemicals or physical conditions (such as excess heat and noise) are called *air pollutants*. See *primary air pollutant, secondary air pollutant*.

algae Simple, one-celled or many-celled plants that usually carry out photosynthesis in rivers, lakes, ponds, oceans, and other surface waters.

algal bloom Population explosion of algae in surface waters due to an increase in plant nutrients such as nitrates and phosphates.

alkaline solution See *basic solution*.

alpha particle Positively charged matter consisting of two neutrons and two protons that is emitted as a form of radioactivity from the nuclei of some radioisotopes. See also *beta particle, gamma rays*.

ambient outdoor

amenity resource See *aesthetic resource*.

anadromous species Species of fish, such as salmon, that after birth move from fresh water to the ocean and then back to fresh water to spawn. Compare *catadromous species*.

anaerobic organism Organism that does not need oxygen to stay alive. Compare *aerobic organism*.

animal manure Dung (fecal matter) and urine of animals that can be used as a form of organic fertilizer. Compare *green manure*.

animal unit equivalent Number representing how much vegetation each type of animal grazing on rangeland eats during a certain time, usually a month. See also *animal unit month*.

animal unit month Amount of rangeland vegetation (forage) needed to feed a 1,000-pound grazing animal for a month. See also *animal unit equivalent*.

annual rate of natural change Annual rate at which the size of a population changes, usually expressed in percent as the difference between crude birth rate and crude death rate divided by 10.

aquaculture Growing and harvesting of fish and shellfish for human use in freshwater ponds, irrigation ditches, and lakes or in cages or fenced-in areas of coastal lagoons and estuaries. See *fish farming, fish ranching*.

aquatic Pertaining to water. Compare *terrestrial*.

aquatic ecosystem Any water-based ecosystem such as a river, pond, lake, or ocean. Compare *biome*.

aquifer Porous layer of underground rock that contains water known as groundwater. See *confined aquifer, unconfined aquifer*.

aquifer depletion Withdrawal of groundwater from an aquifer faster than it is recharged by precipitation.

arable land Land that can be cultivated to grow crops.

area strip mining Cutting deep trenches to remove minerals such as coal and phosphate found near the earth's surface in flat or rolling terrain. Compare *contour strip mining, open-pit surface mining.*

arid Dry. A desert or other area with an arid climate has little precipitation.

artesian aquifer See *confined aquifer.*

atmosphere The whole mass of air surrounding the earth. See *stratosphere, troposphere.*

atoms Minute particles that are the basic building blocks of all chemical elements and thus all matter.

autotroph See *producer.*

average life expectancy at birth See *life expectancy.*

average per capita GNP Annual gross national product (GNP) of a country divided by its total population. See *average per capita real GNP, gross national product.*

average per capita NEW Annual net economic welfare (NEW) of a country divided by its total population. See *average per capita real NEW, net economic welfare.*

average per capita real GNP Average per capita GNP adjusted for inflation.

average per capita real NEW Average per capita NEW adjusted for inflation. See *average per capita NEW, net economic welfare.*

bacteria One-celled organisms. Some transmit diseases. Most act as decomposers that break down dead organic matter into substances that dissolve in water and are used as nutrients by plants.

baleen whales Blue, gray, humpback, finback, and other species of whales that are filter feeders. Several hundred horny plates made of baleen, or whalebone, in the upper jaw filter small plankton organisms, especially krill, from seawater. Compare *toothed whales.*

basic See *basic solution.*

basic solution Water solution with more hydroxide ions (OH⁻) than hydrogen ions (H⁺); water solution with a pH greater than 7. Compare *acidic solution, neutral solution.*

bathyal zone Cold, fairly dark ocean zone below the euphotic zone, in which there is some sunlight but not enough for photosynthesis. Compare *abyssal zone, benthic zone, euphotic zone.*

benthic zone Bottom of a body of water. Compare *abyssal zone, bathyal zone, euphotic zone, limnetic zone, littoral zone.*

beta particle Swiftly moving electron emitted by the nucleus of a radioactive isotope. See also *alpha particle, gamma rays.*

biodegradable Material that can be broken down into simpler substances (elements and compounds) by bacteria or other decomposers. Paper and most organic wastes such as animal manure are biodegradable. Compare *nonbiodegradable.*

biofuel Gas or liquid fuel (such as ethyl alcohol) made from plant material (biomass).

biogeochemical cycle Natural processes that recycle nutrients in various chemical forms from the environment, to organisms, and then back to the environment. Examples are the carbon, oxygen, nitrogen, phosphorus, and hydrologic cycles.

biological amplification Increase in concentration of DDT, PCBs, and other slowly degradable, fat-soluble chemicals in successively higher trophic levels of a food chain or web.

biological community See *community.*

biological diversity Variety of different species and genetic variability among individuals within each species. See *genetic diversity, species diversity.*

biological evolution See *evolution.*

biological oxygen demand (BOD) Amount of dissolved oxygen needed by aerobic decomposers to break down the organic materials in a given volume of water at a certain temperature over a specified time period.

biological pest control Control of pest populations by natural predators, parasites, or disease-causing bacteria and viruses (pathogens).

biomass Total dry weight of all living organisms that can be supported at each trophic level in a food chain; dry weight of all organic matter in plants and animals in an ecosystem; plant materials and animal wastes used as fuel.

biome Large land (terrestrial) ecosystem such as a forest, grassland, or desert. Compare *aquatic ecosystem.*

biosphere The living and dead organisms found near the earth's surface in parts of the lithosphere, atmosphere, and hydrosphere. See also *ecosphere.*

biotic Living. Living organisms make up the biotic parts of ecosystems. Compare *abiotic.*

birth rate See *crude birth rate.*

bitumen Gooey, black, high-sulfur, heavy oil extracted from tar sand and

then upgraded to synthetic fuel oil. See *tar sand.*

breeder nuclear fission reactor Nuclear fission reactor that produces more nuclear fuel than it consumes by converting nonfissionable uranium-238 into fissionable plutonium-239.

calorie Unit of energy; amount of energy needed to raise the temperature of 1 gram of water 1°C. See also *kilocalorie.*

cancer Group of more than 120 different diseases—one for most major cell types in the human body. Each type of cancer produces a tumor in which cells multiply uncontrollably and invade surrounding tissue.

capital goods Tools, machinery, equipment, factory buildings, transportation facilities, and other manufactured items made from land resources and used to produce and distribute consumer goods and services. Compare *labor, natural resources.*

capitalism See *pure market economic system.*

captive breeding Capturing some or all individuals of a critically endangered species still in the wild and placing them in zoos or research centers to breed in captivity.

carbon cycle Cyclic movement of carbon in different chemical forms from the environment, to organisms, and then back to the environment.

carcinogen Chemical or form of high-energy radiation that can directly or indirectly cause a cancer.

carnivore Animal that feeds on other animals. Compare *herbivore, omnivore.*

carrying capacity Maximum population of a particular species that a given area of habitat can support over a given period of time.

cartel Group of countries that work together to control the supply and determine the price of an economic good such as oil. OPEC is an example. See also *monopoly, oligopoly.*

catadromous species Aquatic species such as eels that live in fresh water but breed at sea. Compare *anadromous species.*

cell Basic structural unit of all organisms.

cellular aerobic respiration Complex process that occurs in the cells of plants and animals in which nutrient organic molecules such as glucose ($C_6H_{12}O_6$)

combine with oxygen (O_2) and produce carbon dioxide (CO_2), water (H_2O), and energy. Compare *photosynthesis*.

CFCs See *chlorofluorocarbons*.

chain reaction Series of nuclear fissions taking place within the critical mass of a fissionable isotope that release an enormous amount of energy in a short time.

chemical One of the millions of different elements and compounds found in the universe.

chemical change Interaction between chemicals in which there is a change in the chemical composition of the elements or compounds involved. Compare *physical change*.

chemical reaction See *chemical change*.

chemosynthesis Process in which certain organisms (mostly specialized bacteria) convert chemicals obtained from the environment into nutrient molecules without using sunlight. Compare *photosynthesis*.

chlorinated hydrocarbon Organic compound made up of atoms of carbon, hydrogen, and chlorine. Examples are DDT and PCBs.

chlorofluorocarbons (CFCs) Organic compounds made up of atoms of carbon, chlorine, and fluorine. An example is Freon-12 (CCl_2F_2) used as a refrigerant in refrigerators and air conditioners and in plastics such as Styrofoam. Gaseous CFCs can deplete the ozone layer when they slowly rise into the stratosphere and react with ozone molecules.

clearcutting Method of timber harvesting in which all trees in a forested area are removed in a single cutting. Compare *selective cutting, seed-tree cutting, shelterwood cutting, whole-tree harvesting*.

climate General pattern of atmospheric or weather conditions, seasonal variations, and weather extremes in a region over a long period, usually 30 years or more. Compare *weather*.

climax community See *mature community*.

closed forest Forest where the crowns of trees touch and form a closed canopy during all or part of a year. Compare *open forest*.

coal Solid, combustible material containing 55% to 90% carbon mixed with varying amounts of water and small amounts of compounds containing sulfur and nitrogen. It is formed in several stages as the remains of plants are subjected to intense heat and pressure over millions of years.

coal gasification Conversion of solid coal to synthetic natural gas (SNG) or a gaseous mixture that can be burned as a fuel.

coal liquefaction Conversion of solid coal to a liquid fuel such as synthetic crude oil or methanol.

coastal wetland Land along a coastline, extending inland from an estuary that is flooded with salt water all or part of the year. Examples are marshes, bays, lagoons, tidal flats, and mangrove swamps. Compare *inland wetland*.

coastal zone Relatively warm, nutrient-rich, shallow part of the ocean that extends from the high-tide mark on land to the edge of the continental shelf. Compare *open sea*.

cogeneration Production of two useful forms of energy such as high-temperature heat and electricity from the same process.

commercial extinction Depletion of the population of a wild species used as a resource to a point where it is no longer profitable to harvest the species.

commercial fishing Finding and catching fish for sale. Compare *sport fishing, subsistence fishing*.

commercial hunting Killing of wild animals for profit from sale of their furs or other parts. Compare *sport hunting, subsistence hunting*.

commercial inorganic fertilizer Commercially prepared mixtures of plant nutrients such as nitrates, phosphates, and potassium, applied to the soil to restore fertility and increase crop yields. Compare *organic fertilizer*.

common property resource Resource to which people have virtually free and unmanaged access. Examples are air, fish in parts of the ocean not under the control of a coastal country, migratory birds, and the ozone content of the stratosphere. See *tragedy of the commons*. Compare *private property resource, public property resource*.

commons See *common property resource*.

community Populations of different plants and animals living and interacting in an area at a particular time.

competition Two or more individual organisms of a single species (*intraspecific competition*) or two or more individuals of different species (*interspecific competition*) attempting to use the same scarce resources in the same ecosystem.

competitive exclusion principle No two species in the same ecosystem can occupy exactly the same ecological niche indefinitely.

compost Partially decomposed organic plant and animal matter that can be used as a soil conditioner or fertilizer.

composting Partial breakdown of organic plant and animal matter by aerobic bacteria to produce a material (compost) that can be used as a soil conditioner or fertilizer.

compound Combination of two or more different chemical elements held together by chemical bonds. Compare *element*. See *inorganic compound, organic compound*.

concentration Amount of a chemical in a particular volume or weight of air, water, soil, or other medium.

confined aquifer Groundwater between two layers of impermeable rock, such as clay or shale. Compare *unconfined aquifer*.

conifer See *coniferous trees*.

coniferous trees Cone-bearing trees, mostly evergreens, that have needle-shaped or scale-like leaves. They produce wood known commercially as softwood. Compare *deciduous trees*.

conservation Use, management, and protection of resources so that they are not degraded, depleted, or wasted and are available on a sustainable basis for use by present and future generations. Methods include preservation, balanced multiple use, reducing unnecessary waste, recycling, reuse, and decreased use.

conservationists People who believe that resources should be used, managed, and protected so that they will not be degraded and unnecessarily wasted and will be available to present and future generations. See *preservationists, scientific conservationists, sustainable-earth conservationists*.

conservation-tillage farming Crop cultivation in which the soil is disturbed little (*minimum-tillage farming*) or not at all (*no-till farming*) to reduce soil erosion, lower labor costs, and save energy. Compare *conventional-tillage farming*.

consumer Organism that cannot produce its own food and must get it by eating or decomposing other organisms; generally divided into *primary consumers* (herbivores), *secondary consumers* (carnivores), and *microconsumers* (decomposers). In economics one who uses economic goods.

consumption overpopulation Situation in which people use resources at such a high rate and without sufficient pollution control that significant depletion, pollution, and environmental degradation occur. Compare *people overpopulation*.

consumptive water use See *water consumption*.

continental shelf Shallow undersea land adjacent to a continent.

continuous grazing Allowing livestock animals to graze on rangeland or pasture all year long or during an entire grazing season. Compare *deferred-rotation grazing, holistic grazing management*.

contour farming Plowing and planting across rather than up and down the slope of land to help retain water and reduce soil erosion.

contour strip mining Cutting a series of shelves or terraces on the side of a hill or mountain to remove a mineral such as coal from a deposit found near the earth's surface. Compare *area strip mining, open-pit surface mining*.

contraceptive Physical, chemical, or biological method used to prevent pregnancy.

conventional-tillage farming Making a planting surface by plowing land, disking it several times to break up the soil, and then smoothing the surface. Compare *conservation-tillage farming*.

coppicing Type of regeneration of trees after clearcutting used on oaks, aspens, and other species that sprout easily from their stumps or roots.

cornucopians People, mostly economists, who believe that if present trends continue, economic growth and technological advances will produce a less crowded, less polluted, more resource-rich world in which most people will be healthier, will live longer, and will have greater material wealth. Compare *neo-Malthusians*.

cost-benefit analysis Estimates and comparison of short-term and long-term costs (losses) and benefits (gains) from an economic decision. If the estimated benefits exceed the estimated costs, the decision to buy an economic good or provide a public good is considered worthwhile.

cover Physical or biological feature of a habitat that gives an animal protection from weather, concealment and escape from its predators, concealment while it is stalking prey, and a safe place to breed, rear young, and rest.

critical mass Amount of fissionable isotopes needed to sustain a nuclear fission chain reaction.

crop rotation Planting the same field or areas of fields with different crops from year to year to reduce depletion of soil nutrients. A plant such as corn, tobacco, or cotton, which remove large amounts of nitrogen from the soil, is planted one year. The next year a legume such as soybeans, which add nitrogen to the soil, is planted.

crown fire Extremely hot forest fire that burns ground vegetation and tree tops. Compare *ground fire, surface fire*.

crude birth rate Annual number of live births per 1,000 persons in the population of a geographical area at the midpoint of a given year. Compare *crude death rate*.

crude death rate Annual number of deaths per 1,000 persons in the population of a geographical area at the midpoint of a given year. Compare *crude birth rate*.

crude oil Gooey liquid made up mostly of hydrocarbon compounds and small amounts of compounds containing oxygen, sulfur, and nitrogen. Extracted from underground deposits, it is sent to oil refineries, where it is converted to heating oil, diesel fuel, gasoline, and tar.

cruise Survey of a tree stand to locate and estimate the volume and grade of standing timber for future harvesting.

cultural eutrophication Overnourishment of aquatic ecosystems with plant nutrients (mostly nitrates and phosphates) due to human activities such as agriculture, urbanization, and discharges from industrial plants and sewage treatment plants. See *eutrophication*.

DDT Dichlorodiphenyltrichloroethane, a chlorinated hydrocarbon that has been widely used as a pesticide.

death rate See *crude death rate*.

deciduous trees Trees such as oaks and maples that lose their leaves during part of the year. Compare *coniferous trees*.

decomposers Organisms such as bacteria, mushrooms, and fungi, which get nutrients by breaking down organic matter in the wastes and dead bodies of other organisms into simpler chemicals. Most of these chemicals are returned to the soil and water for reuse by producers. Compare *consumers, detritivores, producers*.

decreasers Grass species that are easily depleted even when moderately grazed. Compare *increasers, invaders*.

deferred-rotation grazing Moving or rotating livestock between two or more range areas to prevent overgrazing. Compare *continuous grazing, holistic grazing management*.

deforestation Removal of trees from a forested area without adequate replanting.

degradable See *biodegradable*.

degree of urbanization Percentage of the population in the world or a country living in areas with a population of more than 2,500 people.

delta Built-up deposit of river-borne sediments at the mouth of a river.

demand See *market demand*.

demographic transition Hypothesis that as countries become industrialized, they have declines in death rates followed by declines in birth rates.

demography Study of characteristics and changes in the size and structure of the human population in the world or other geographical area.

depletion time How long it takes to use a certain fraction—usually 80%—of the known or estimated supply of a non-renewable resource at an assumed rate of use. Finding and extracting the remaining 20% usually costs more than it is worth.

desalination Purification of salt water or brackish (slightly salty) water by removing dissolved salts.

desert Type of land ecosystem (biome) where evaporation exceeds precipitation and the average amount of precipitation is less than ten inches a year. Such areas have little vegetation or have widely spaced, mostly low vegetation.

desertification Conversion of range-land, rain-fed cropland, or irrigated cropland to desertlike land with a drop in agricultural productivity of 10% or more. It is usually caused by a combination of overgrazing, soil erosion, prolonged drought, and climate change.

detritivores Consumer organisms that feed on detritus or dead organic plant and animal matter. The two major types are *detritus feeders* and *decomposers*.

detritus Dead organic plant and animal matter.

detritus feeders Organisms that directly consume dead organisms and the cast-off parts and organic wastes of organisms. Examples are vultures, jackals, termites, earthworms, millipedes, ants, and crabs. Compare *decomposers*.

detritus food web Transfer of energy from one trophic level to another by detritus feeders and decomposers. Compare *grazing food web*.

deuterium (D: hydrogen-2) Isotope of the element hydrogen with a nucleus containing one proton and one neutron, and a mass number of 2. Compare *tritium*.

developed country See *more developed country*.

differential reproduction Ability of individuals with adaptive genetic traits to outreproduce individuals without such traits. See also *natural selection*.

dissolved oxygen (DO) content (level) Amount of oxygen gas (O_2) dissolved in a certain amount of water at a particular temperature and pressure, often expressed as a concentration in parts of oxygen per million parts of water.

diversity Variety. In biology the number of different species in an ecosystem (*species diversity*) or diversity in the genetic makeup of different species or within a single species (*genetic diversity*).

DNA (deoxyribonucleic acid) Large molecules that carry genetic information in living organisms. They are found in the cells of organisms.

drainage basin See *watershed*.

dredge spoils Materials scraped from the bottoms of harbors and rivers to maintain shipping channels. They are often contaminated with high levels of toxic substances that have settled out of the water. See *dredging*.

dredging Type of surface mining in which materials such as sand and gravel are scooped up from seabeds. It is also used to remove sediment from streams, rivers, and harbors to maintain shipping channels. See *dredge spoils*.

driftnet fishing Catching fish in massive nets that drift in the water. Compare *purse-seine fishing, trawler fishing*.

drip irrigation Using small tubes or pipes to deliver small amounts of irrigation water to the roots of plants.

dust dome Dome of heated air that surrounds an urban area and traps pollutants, especially suspended particulate matter. See also *urban heat island*.

early-successional species Wild animal species found in pioneer communities of plants at the early stage of ecological succession. Compare *late-successional species, midsuccessional species, wilderness species*.

ecological land-use planning Method for deciding how land should be used by developing an integrated model that considers geological, ecological, health, and social variables.

ecological niche Description of all the physical, chemical, and biological factors that a species needs to survive, stay healthy, and reproduce in an ecosystem.

ecological succession Process in which communities of plant and animal species in a particular area are replaced over time by a series of different and usually more complex communities. See *primary ecological succession, secondary ecological succession*.

ecology Study of the interactions of living organisms with each other and with their environment; study of the structure and functions of nature.

economic decision Choosing what to do with scarce resources; deciding what goods and services to produce, how to produce them, how much to produce, and how to distribute them to people.

economic depletion Exhaustion of 80% of the estimated supply of a nonrenewable resource. Finding, extracting, and processing the remaining 20% usually costs more than it is worth.

economic good Any service or material item that gives people satisfaction and whose present or ultimate supply is limited.

economic growth Increase in the real value of all goods and services produced by an economy; an increase in real GNP. Compare *productivity*.

economic needs Types and amounts of certain economic goods—food, clothing, water, oxygen, shelter—that each of us must have to survive and to stay healthy. Compare *economic wants*. See also *poverty*.

economic resources Natural resources, capital goods, and labor used in an economy to produce material goods and services. See *capital goods, labor, natural resources*.

economics Study of how individuals and groups make decisions about what to do with scarce resources to meet their needs and wants.

economic system Method that a group of people uses to choose what goods and services to produce, how to produce them, how much to produce, and how to distribute them to people. See *mixed economic system, pure command economic system, pure market economic system, traditional economic system*.

economic wants Economic goods that go beyond our basic economic needs. These wants are influenced by the customs and conventions of the society we live in and by our level of affluence. Compare *economic needs*.

economy System of production, distribution, and consumption of economic goods.

ecosphere Collection of living and dead organisms (biosphere) interacting with one another and their nonliving environment (energy and chemicals) throughout the world. See also *biosphere*.

ecosystem Community of organisms interacting with one another and with the chemical and physical factors making up their environment. See *aquatic ecosystem, biome*.

ecotone Transition zone where one type of ecosystem blends into another type. Ecotones contain many of the plant and animal species found in both ecosystems, and often species not found in either ecosystem. See also *edge*.

ectoparasites Parasites such as lice or ticks that attach themselves to the outside of their host. Compare *endoparasites*. See *parasite*.

edge Area where two different types of plant communities meet.

efficiency Measure of how much output of energy or of a product is produced by a certain input of energy, materials, or labor. See *energy efficiency*.

egg pulling Collecting eggs produced in the wild by pairs of a critically endangered species and hatching the eggs in zoos or research centers.

electron Tiny particle moving around outside the nucleus of an atom. Each electron has one unit of negative charge (–) and almost no mass.

element Chemical, such as hydrogen (H), iron (Fe), sodium (Na), carbon (C), nitrogen (N), and oxygen (O), whose distinctly different atoms serve as the basic building blocks of all matter. There are 92 naturally occurring elements. Another 15 have been made in laboratories. Two or more elements combine to form compounds that make up most of the world's matter. Compare *compound*.

emigration Migration of people out of one country or area to take up permanent residence in another country or area. Compare *immigration*.

endangered species Wild species with so few individual survivors that the species could soon become extinct in all or most of its natural range. Compare *threatened species*.

endoparasites Parasites such as tapeworms and disease-causing bacteria that live inside their host. Compare *ectoparasites*. See *parasite*.

energy Ability to do work by moving matter or by causing a transfer of heat between two objects at different temperatures.

energy conservation Reduction or elimination of unnecessary energy use and waste.

energy efficiency Percentage of the total energy input that does useful work and is not converted into low-temperature, usually useless heat in an energy conversion system or process. See *net useful energy*.

energy quality Ability of a form of energy to do useful work. High-temperature heat and the chemical energy in fossil fuels and nuclear fuels is concentrated high-quality energy. Low-quality energy such as low-temperature heat is dispersed or diluted and cannot do much useful work. See *high-quality energy, low-quality energy*.

enhanced oil recovery Removal of some of the heavy oil left in an oil well after primary and secondary recovery. Compare *primary oil recovery, secondary oil recovery*.

environment All external conditions that affect an organism or other specified system during its lifetime.

environmental degradation Depletion or destruction of a potentially renewable resource such as soil, grassland, forest, or wildlife by using it at a faster rate than it is naturally replenished. If such use continues, the resource can become nonrenewable on a human time scale or nonexistent (extinct). See also *sustainable yield*.

environmentalists People who are primarily concerned with preventing pollution and degradation of the air, water, and soil. See *conservationists*.

EPA Environmental Protection Agency. It is responsible for managing federal efforts in the United States to control air and water pollution, radiation and pesticide hazards, ecological research, and solid waste disposal.

epilmnion Upper layer of warm water with high levels of dissolved oxygen in a stratified lake. Compare *hypolimnion, thermocline*.

erosion See *soil erosion*.

estuarine zone Area near the coastline that consists of estuaries and coastal saltwater wetlands, extending to the edge of the continental shelf.

estuary Zone along a coastline where fresh water from rivers and streams and runoff from the land mix with seawater.

ethics What we believe to be right or wrong behavior.

euphotic zone Surface layer of an ocean, lake, or other body of water, which gets enough sunlight for photosynthesis. Compare *abyssal zone, bathyal zone*.

eutrophication Physical, chemical, and biological changes that take place after a lake, estuary, or slow-flowing river receives input of plant nutrients—mostly nitrates and phosphates—from natural erosion and runoff from the surrounding land basin. See also *cultural eutrophication*.

eutrophic lake Lake with a large or excessive supply of plant nutrients—mostly nitrates and phosphates. Compare *mesotrophic lake, oligotrophic lake*.

evaporation Physical change in which a liquid changes into a vapor or gas.

even-aged management Method of forest management in which trees, usually of a single species, in a given stand are maintained at about the same age and size, then harvested all at once so that a new even-age stand will grow. Compare *uneven-aged management*.

even-aged stand Forest area where all trees are about the same age. Usually such stands contain trees of only one or two species. See *even-aged management, tree farm*. Compare *uneven-aged management, uneven-aged stand*.

evergreen plants Pines, spruces, firs, and other plants that keep some of their leaves or needles throughout the year. Compare *deciduous trees*.

evolution Changes in the genetic composition (gene pool) of a population exposed to new environmental conditions as a result of differential reproduction. Evolution can lead to the splitting of a single species into two or more different species. See also *differential reproduction, natural selection, speciation*.

exclusive economic zone (EEZ) Zone extending outward for 200 nautical miles from the shores of coastal countries. Under international law each coastal country has legal rights over all marine fishery resources and ocean mineral resources in this zone. Compare *high seas, territorial seas*.

exhaustible resource See *nonrenewable resource*.

exponential growth Growth in which some quantity, such as population size, increases by a constant percentage of the whole during each year or other time period; when the increase in quantity over time is plotted, this type of growth yields a curve shaped like the letter *J*.

external benefit Beneficial social effect of producing and using an economic good that is not included in the market price of the good. Compare *external cost, internal cost, true cost*.

external cost Harmful social effect of producing and using an economic good that is not included in the market price of the good. Compare *external benefit, internal cost, true cost*.

externalities Social benefits ("goods") and social costs ("bads") not included in the market price of an economic good. See *external benefit, external cost*. Compare *internal cost, true cost*.

extinction Complete disappearance of a species from the earth. This happens when a species cannot adapt and successfully reproduce under new environmental conditions. Compare *speciation*. See also *endangered species, threatened species*.

factors of production See *economic resources*.

family planning Providing information, clinical services, and contraceptives to help couples choose the number and spacing of children they want to have.

famine Widespread malnutrition and starvation in a particular area because of a shortage of food, usually caused by drought, war, flood, earthquake, or other catastrophic event that disrupts food production and distribution.

feedlot Confined outdoor or indoor space used to raise hundreds to thousands of domesticated livestock. Compare *rangeland*.

fertilizer Substance that adds inorganic or organic plant nutrients to soil and improves its ability to grow crops, trees, or other vegetation. See *commercial inorganic fertilizer, organic fertilizer*.

first law of ecology We can never do merely one thing. Any intrusion into nature has numerous effects, many of which are unpredictable.

first law of energy See *first law of thermodynamics*.

first law of thermodynamics (energy) In any physical or chemical change, any movement of matter from one place to another, or any change in temperature, energy is neither created nor destroyed but merely transformed from one form to another; you can't get more energy out of something than you put in; in terms of energy quantity you can't get something for nothing, or there is no free lunch. See also *second law of thermodynamics*.

fishery Concentrations of particular aquatic species suitable for commercial harvesting in a given ocean area or inland body of water.

fish farming Form of aquaculture in which fish are cultivated in a controlled pond or other environment and harvested when they reach the desired size. See also *fish ranching*.

fishing Finding and capturing a desirable species of fish or shellfish.

fish ranching Form of aquaculture in which anadromous fish such as salmon are held in captivity for the first few years of their lives, released, and then harvested when, as adults, they return to spawn. See also *fish farming*.

fissionable isotope Isotope that can split apart when hit by a neutron or other particle moving at the right speed and thus undergo nuclear fission. Examples are uranium-235 and plutonium-239. Compare *nonfissionable isotope*.

floodplain Land along a river or stream that is periodically flooded when the river or stream overflows its banks.

fluidized-bed combustion (FBC)
Process for burning coal more efficiently, cleanly, and cheaply. A stream of hot air is used to suspend a mixture of powdered coal and limestone during combustion. About 90% to 98% of the sulfur dioxide produced during combustion is removed by reaction with limestone to produce solid calcium sulfate.

flyway Generally fixed route along which waterfowl migrate from one area to another at certain seasons of the year.

food chain Series of organisms, each eating or decomposing the preceding one. Compare *food web*.

food web Complex network of many interconnected food chains and feeding interactions. Compare *food chain*. See *detritus food web, grazing food web*.

forage Vegetation eaten by animals, especially grazing and browsing animals.

forest Terrestrial ecosystem (biome) with enough average annual precipitation (at least 30 inches) to support growth of various species of trees and smaller forms of vegetation. See also *closed forest, open forest*.

forest conservation Managing or protecting forests to sustain commercial tree populations, wildlife populations, bio-

logical diversity, watershed protection, and other ecological services.

forest management Blending silviculture with economic considerations to determine how a stand of trees is to be harvested and regenerated.

forestry Science or profession of forest resource management to provide timber and other wood products without depleting this potentially renewable resource.

fossil fuel Buried deposits of decayed plants and animals that have been converted to crude oil, coal, natural gas, or heavy oils by exposure to heat and pressure in the earth's crust over hundreds of millions of years. See *coal, crude oil, natural gas*.

Freons See *chlorofluorocarbons*.

frontier worldview See *throwaway worldview*.

fungicide Chemical used to kill fungi that damage crops.

fungus Type of decomposer; a plant without chlorophyll that gets its nourishment by breaking down the organic matter of other plants. Examples are molds, yeasts, and mushrooms.

game See *game species*.

game fish Fish that people try to catch for fun and recreation.

game species Type of wild animal that people hunt or fish for fun and recreation.

gamma rays High-energy, ionizing, electromagnetic radiation emitted by some radioisotopes. Like X rays, they readily penetrate body tissues.

gasohol Vehicle fuel consisting of a mixture of gasoline and ethyl or methyl alcohol—typically 10% to 23% alcohol by volume.

gear restrictions Regulations that limit the kind or size of gear that can be used to harvest a particular fish species.

gene pool All genetic (hereditary) information contained in a reproducing population of a particular species.

genes The parts of DNA molecules that control hereditary characteristics in organisms.

genetic adaptation Changes in the genetic makeup of organisms of a species that allow the species to reproduce and gain a competitive advantage under changed environmental conditions.

genetic diversity Genetic variability among individuals within a single species. Compare *species diversity*.

geothermal energy Heat transferred from the earth's molten core to underground deposits of dry steam (steam with no water droplets), wet steam (a mixture of steam and water droplets), hot water, or rocks lying fairly close to the earth's surface.

GNP See *gross national product*.

grassland Terrestrial ecosystem (biome) found in regions where moderate annual average precipitation (10 to 15 inches), is enough to support the growth of grass and small plants but not enough to support large stands of trees.

grazing food web Food web in which herbivores consume living plant tissue and are then consumed by an array of carnivores and omnivores. Compare *detritus food web*.

greenhouse effect Trapping and buildup of heat in the atmosphere (troposphere) near the earth's surface. Some of the heat flowing back toward space from the earth's surface is absorbed by water vapor, carbon dioxide, ozone, and several other gases in the atmosphere and then reradiated back toward the earth's surface. If the atmospheric concentration of these greenhouse gases rises, the average temperature of the lower atmosphere will gradually increase.

greenhouse gases Gases in the earth's atmosphere that cause the greenhouse effect. Examples are carbon dioxide, chlorofluorocarbons, ozone, methane, and nitrous oxide.

green manure Freshly cut or still-growing green vegetation that is plowed into the soil to increase the organic matter and humus available to support crop growth. Compare *animal manure*.

green revolution Popular term for introduction of scientifically bred or selected varieties of grain (rice, wheat, maize) that with high enough inputs of fertilizer and water can greatly increase crop yields.

gross national product (GNP) Total market value in current dollars of all final goods and services produced by an economy during a year. Compare *average per capita GNP, average per capita real NEW, real GNP*.

ground fire Fire that burns decayed leaves or peat deep below the ground surface. Compare *crown fire, surface fire*.

groundwater Water that sinks into the soil and is stored in slowly flowing and

slowly renewed underground reservoirs called aquifers; underground water in the zone of saturation below the water table. See *confined aquifer, unconfined aquifer.*

gully erosion Severe soil erosion caused when high-velocity water flow removes enough soil to form miniature valleys. Compare *rill erosion, sheet erosion.*

gully reclamation Restoring land suffering from gully erosion by seeding gullies with quick-growing plants, building small dams to collect silt and gradually fill in the channels, and building channels to divert water away from the gully.

habitat Place or type of place where an organism or community of organisms lives and thrives.

habitat quality How well a habitat provides the physical, chemical, and biological needs of an organism. It is usually described in terms of availability of enough food, water, cover, and space. For some species it also includes the availability of edges, where two communities come together.

hardwood Tree species whose wood has a high weight per unit of volume (high density) and is hard to saw, plane, or carve. Hardwoods are usually broadleaf and deciduous trees, such as oak, maple, mahogany, and hickory. Compare *softwood.*

hazardous waste Discarded solid, liquid, or gaseous material that can harm people or other species. See also *toxic waste.*

heat Form of kinetic energy that flows from one body to another when there is a temperature difference between the two bodies. Heat always flows spontaneously from a hot sample of matter to a colder sample of matter. This is one way to state the second law of thermodynamics.

heavy oil Black, high-sulfur, tarlike oil found in deposits of crude oil, tar sands, and oil shale.

herbicide Chemical that kills a plant or inhibits its growth.

herbivore Plant-eating organism. Examples are deer, sheep, grasshoppers, and zooplankton. Compare *carnivore, omnivore.*

heterotroph See *consumer.*

high-quality energy Energy that is concentrated and has great ability to perform useful work. Examples are high-temperature heat and the energy in elec-

tricity, coal, oil, gasoline, sunlight, and nuclei of uranium-235. Compare *low-quality energy.*

high seas Ocean areas beyond the legal jurisdiction of any country—beyond the exclusive economic zone. Compare *exclusive economic zone, territorial seas.*

holistic grazing management Ecological approach to sustaining rangeland and livestock productivity based on how grazing affects ecological succession, nutrient cycling, water cycling, and energy flow. Compare *continuous grazing, deferred-rotation grazing.*

host Plant or animal upon which a parasite feeds.

humus Complex mixture of decaying organic matter and inorganic compounds in topsoil. This insoluble material helps retain water and water-soluble nutrients so they can be taken up by plant roots.

hunters-gatherers People who get their food by gathering edible wild plants and other materials and by hunting wild animals and fish.

hydrocarbon Organic compound of hydrogen and carbon atoms.

hydroelectric power plant Structure in which the energy of falling or flowing water spins a turbine generator to produce electricity.

hydrologic cycle Biogeochemical cycle that collects, purifies, and distributes the earth's fixed supply of water from the environment, to living organisms, and back to the environment.

hydropower Electrical energy produced by falling or flowing water. See *hydroelectric power plant.*

hydrosphere All the earth's liquid water (oceans, smaller bodies of fresh water, and underground aquifers), frozen water (polar ice caps, floating ice, and frozen upper layer of soil known as permafrost), and small amounts of water vapor in the atmosphere.

hypolimnion Bottom layer of water in a stratified lake. This layer is colder and more dense than the top or epilimnion layer. Compare *epilimnion, thermocline.*

identified resources Deposits of a particular mineral-bearing material of which the location, quantity, and quality are known or have been estimated from geological evidence and measurements. Compare *total resources.*

igneous rock Rocks that form when magma (molten rock) wells up from the earth's upper mantle and cools or crystallizes on or beneath the earth's surface. Compare *metamorphic rocks, sedimentary rocks.*

immature community Community at an early stage of ecological succession. It usually has a low number of species and ecological niches and cannot capture and use energy and cycle critical nutrients as efficiently as more complex, mature ecosystems. Compare *mature community.*

immigration Migration of people into a country or area to take up permanent residence. Compare *emigration.*

increasers Plant species present before grazing that increase in numbers under heavy grazing. Compare *decreasers, invaders.*

industrialized agriculture Using large inputs of energy from fossil fuels (especially oil and natural gas) to produce large quantities of crops and livestock for domestic and foreign sale. Compare *subsistence agriculture.*

industrial smog Type of air pollution consisting mostly of a mixture of sulfur dioxide, suspended droplets of sulfuric acid formed from some of the sulfur dioxide, and a variety of suspended solid particles. Compare *photochemical smog.*

inertia Ability of a living system to resist being disturbed or altered. Compare *resilience.*

infant mortality rate Annual number of deaths of infants under one year of age per 1,000 live births.

inland wetland Land away from the coast, such as a swamp, marsh, or bog, that is flooded all or part of the year with fresh water. Compare *coastal wetland.*

inorganic compound Combination of two or more elements other than those used to form organic compounds. Compare *organic compound.*

inorganic fertilizer See *commercial inorganic fertilizer.*

input pollution control Method that prevents a potential pollutant from entering the environment or that sharply reduces the amount entering the environment. Compare *output pollution control.*

insecticide Chemical designed to kill insects.

integrated pest management (IPM) Combined use of biological, chemical, and cultivation methods in proper sequence and timing to keep the size of a pest population below the size that causes economically unacceptable loss of a crop or livestock animal.

intercropping Growing two or more different crops at the same time on a plot. For example, a carbohydrate-rich grain that depletes soil nitrogen and a protein-rich legume that adds nitrogen to the soil may be intercropped. Compare *monoculture, polyculture, polyvarietal cultivation.*

intermediate goods See *capital goods.*

internal cost Direct cost paid by the producer and buyer of an economic good. Compare *external cost.*

interspecific competition Members of two or more species trying to use the same scarce resources in an ecosystem. See *competition, intraspecific competition.*

intraspecific competition Two or more individual organisms of a single species trying to use the same scarce resources in an ecosystem. See *competition, interspecific competition.*

invaders Plants such as prickly cactus that infest severely overgrazed land. Compare *decreasers. increasers.*

inversion See *thermal inversion.*

ion Atom or group of atoms with one or more positive (+) or negative (–) electrical charges.

ionizing radiation Fast-moving alpha or beta particles or high-energy radiation (gamma rays) emitted by radioisotopes. They have enough energy to dislodge one or more electrons from atoms they hit, forming charged ions that can react with and damage living tissue.

isotopes Two or more forms of a chemical element that have the same number of protons but different mass numbers or numbers of neutrons in their nuclei.

J-shaped curve Curve with the shape of the letter *J* that represents exponential growth.

kerogen Solid, waxy mixture of hydrocarbons found in oil shale, a fine-grained sedimentary rock. When the rock is heated to high temperatures, the kerogen is vaporized. The vapor is condensed and then sent to a refinery to produce gasoline, heating oil, and other products. See also *oil shale, shale oil.*

kilocalorie (kcal) Unit of energy equal to 1,000 calories. See *calorie.*

kilowatt (kw) Unit of electrical power equal to 1,000 watts. See *watt.*

kinetic energy Energy that matter has because of its motion and mass. Compare *potential energy.*

kwashiorkor Type of malnutrition that occurs in infants and very young children when they are weaned from mother's milk to a starchy diet low in protein. See also *marasmus.*

labor Physical and mental talents of people used to produce, distribute, and sell an economic good. Labor includes workers and entrepreneurs, who assume the risk and responsibility of combining the resources of land, capital goods, and workers to produce an economic good. Compare *capital goods, natural resources.*

lake Large natural body of standing fresh water formed when water from precipitation, land runoff, or groundwater flow fills a depression in the earth created by glaciation, earthquake, volcanic activity, or a giant meteorite. Compare *reservoir.* See *eutrophic lake, mesotrophic lake, oligotrophic lake.*

landfill See *sanitary landfill, secured landfill.*

land-use planning Process for deciding the best use of each parcel of land in an area. See *ecological land-use planning.*

late-successional species Wild animal species found in moderate-size, old-growth and mature forest habitats. Compare *early-successional species, midsuccessional species, wilderness species.*

law of conservation of energy See *first law of thermodynamics.*

law of conservation of matter In any ordinary physical or chemical change, matter is neither created nor destroyed but merely changed from one form to another; in physical and chemical changes existing atoms are either rearranged into different spatial patterns (physical changes) or different combinations (chemical changes).

law of demand If price is the only factor affecting the market demand for an economic good, then as its price rises, demand falls, and as its price falls, demand increases. Compare *law of supply.* See *market equilibrium.*

law of energy degradation See *second law of thermodynamics.*

law of supply If price is the only factor affecting the market supply of an economic good, then as its price rises, suppliers will try to supply more, and as its

price falls, the supply will drop. Compare *law of demand.* See *market equilibrium.*

law of tolerance The existence, abundance, and distribution of a species are determined by whether the levels of one or more physical or chemical factors fall above or below the levels tolerated by the species. See also *tolerance limit.*

LDC See *less developed country.*

leaching Process in which various chemicals in upper layers of soil are dissolved and carried to lower layers and in some cases to groundwater.

less developed country (LDC) Country that has low to moderate industrialization and low to moderate average GNP per person. Most LDCs are located in the tropical (or low) latitudes in Africa, Asia, and Latin America. Compare *more developed country.*

life-cycle cost Initial cost plus lifetime operating costs of an economic good.

life expectancy Average number of years a newborn infant can be expected to live.

light-water reactor (LWR) Nuclear fission reactor in which ordinary water, called light water, is used as a moderator inside the core to slow down neutrons emitted by the fission process and sustain the chain reaction.

limiting factor Single factor that limits the growth, abundance, or distribution of the population of a particular organism in an ecosystem. See *limiting factor principle.*

limiting factor principle Too much or too little of any single abiotic factor can limit or prevent growth of the populations of particular plant and animal species in an ecosystem even if all other factors are at or near the optimum range of tolerance for the species.

limnetic zone Open water surface layer of a lake, away from the shore, where there is enough sunlight for photosynthesis. Compare *benthic zone, littoral zone, profundal zone.*

liquefied natural gas (LNG) Natural gas converted to liquid form by cooling to a very low temperature.

liquefied petroleum gas (LPG) Mixture of liquefied propane and butane gas removed from a deposit of natural gas.

lithosphere Soil and rock in the earth's upper surface or crust and the earth's upper mantle.

littoral zone Shallow waters near the shore of a body of water, in which sunlight penetrates to the bottom. Compare *benthic zone, limnetic zone, profundal zone.*

low-quality energy Energy such as low-temperature heat that is dispersed or diluted and has little ability to do useful work. Compare *high-quality energy.*

LPG See *liquefied petroleum gas.*

macronutrient Chemical that a plant or animal needs in large amounts to stay alive and healthy. Compare *micronutrient.*

magma Molten rock material in the earth's core.

malnutrition Faulty nutrition. Caused by a diet that does not supply an individual with enough proteins, essential fats, vitamins, minerals, or other nutrients needed for good health. See *kwashiorkor, marasmus.* Compare *overnutrition, undernutrition.*

manure See *animal manure, green manure.*

marasmus Nutritional-deficiency disease caused by a diet that does not have enough calories and protein to maintain good health. See *kwashiorkor, malnutrition.*

marine demersal species Fish and shellfish that feed mostly on or near ocean bottoms and usually don't range over a wide area. Examples are cod, flounder, haddock, sole, lobster, crawfish, and crab. Compare *marine pelagic species.*

marine pelagic species Species of fish and shellfish that usually feed near the ocean surface and often migrate over a wide area. Examples are tuna, mackerel, and anchovy. Compare *marine demersal species.*

market demand How much of an economic good consumers are willing and able to buy at a particular price in a given time period. See *law of demand.* Compare *market supply.*

market equilibrium State in which sellers and buyers of an economic good agree on the quantity to be produced and the price to be paid. See *law of demand, law of supply, market demand, market supply.*

market supply How much of an economic good producers are willing and able to produce and sell at a particular price in a given period of time. See *law of supply.* Compare *market demand.*

mass The amount of stuff in matter.

mass number Sum of the number of neutrons and the number of protons in the nucleus of an atom. It gives the approximate mass of that atom.

mass transit Buses, trains, trolleys, and other forms of transportation that carry large numbers of people.

matter Anything that has mass and occupies space; the stuff the world is made of.

matter-recycling society Society that emphasizes recycling the maximum amount of all resources that can be recycled. The goal is to allow economic growth to continue without depleting matter resources and without producing excessive pollution and environmental degradation. Compare *sustainable-earth society, throwaway society.*

mature community Fairly stable, self-sustaining community at an advanced stage of ecological succession. It usually has a diverse array of species and ecological niches and captures and uses energy and cycles critical chemicals more efficiently than simpler, immature communities. Compare *immature community.*

maximum sustainable yield See *sustainable yield.*

MDC See *more developed country.*

meltdown The melting of the core of a nuclear reactor.

mesotrophic lake Lake with a moderate supply of plant nutrients. Compare *eutrophic lake, oligotrophic lake.*

metabolic reserve Lower half of rangeland grass plants; plants can grow back as long as this part is not consumed by herbivores.

metamorphic rock Rock formed from other types of rocks by high temperatures and high pressures. Some of these rocks may then melt to start the rock cycle over again. Compare *igneous rocks, sedimentary rocks.* See *rock cycle.*

microconsumer See *decomposer.*

micronutrient Chemical that a plant or animal needs in small, or trace, amounts to stay alive and healthy. Compare *macronutrients.*

midsuccessional species Wild species found around abandoned croplands and partially open areas at the middle stages of ecological succession. Compare *early-successional species, late-successional species, wilderness species.*

mineral Any naturally occurring inorganic substance found in the earth's crust as a crystalline solid. See *metallic mineral, nonmetallic mineral.*

mineral resource Nonrenewable chemical element or compound in solid form that is used by humans. Mineral resources are classified as metallic (such as iron and tin) or nonmetallic (such as fossil fuels, sand, and salt).

minimum-tillage farming See *conservation-tillage farming.*

mixed economic system Economic system that falls somewhere between pure market and pure command economic systems. Virtually all of the world's economic systems fall into this category, with some closer to a pure market system and some closer to a pure command system. Compare *pure command economic system, pure market economic system, traditional economic system.*

molecule Chemical combination of two or more atoms of the same chemical element (such as O_2) or different chemical elements (such as H_2O).

monoculture Cultivation of a single crop, usually on a large area of land. Compare *polyculture.*

monopoly Complete control over the supply and price of an economic good by a single producer. See also *cartel, oligopoly.*

more developed country (MDC) Country that is highly industrialized and has a high average GNP per person. Compare *less developed country.*

multiple use Principle of managing public land such as a national forest so that it is used for a variety of purposes, such as timbering, mining, recreation, grazing, wildlife preservation, and soil and water conservation. See also *sustainable yield.*

municipal solid waste Solid materials discarded by homes and businesses in or near urban areas.

mutagen Chemical or form of radioactivity that can increase the rate of genetic mutation in a living organism.

nanoplankton Extremely small photosynthetic algae and bacteria. See also *phytoplankton.*

national ambient air quality standards (NAAQS) Maximum allowable level, averaged over a specific time period, for a certain pollutant in outdoor (ambient) air.

natural eutrophication See *eutrophication.*

natural gas Underground deposits of gases consisting of 50% to 90% methane (CH_4) and small amounts of heavier gaseous hydrocarbon compounds such as propane (C_3H_8) and butane (C_4H_{10}).

natural radioactivity Nuclear change in which unstable nuclei of atoms spontaneously shoot out "chunks" of mass, energy, or both at a fixed rate.

natural resources Area of the earth's solid surface, nutrients and minerals in the soil and deeper layers of the earth's crust, water, wild and domesticated plants and animals, air, and other resources produced by the earth's natural processes. Compare *capital goods, labor.*

natural selection Process by which some genes and gene combinations in a population of a species are reproduced more than others when the population is exposed to an environmental change or stress. When individual organisms in a population die off over time because they cannot tolerate a new stress, they are replaced by individuals whose genetic traits allow them to cope better with the stress. When these better-adapted individuals reproduce, they pass their adaptive traits on to their offspring. See also *evolution.*

neo-Malthusians People who believe that if present population, resource use, and environmental trends continue, the world will become more crowded and more polluted, and many resources will be depleted or degraded. They believe that competition for scarce resources will lead to greater political and economic turmoil and increase the threat of nuclear and conventional wars. It is an updated and expanded version of the hypothesis proposed in 1789 by Thomas Robert Malthus: Human population growing exponentially will eventually outgrow food supplies and will be reduced in size by starvation, disease, and war. Compare *cornucopians.*

neritic zone See *coastal zone.*

net economic welfare (NEW) Measure of annual change in quality of life in a country. It is obtained by subtracting the value of all products and services that decrease the quality of life from a country's GNP. See *average per capita NEW.*

net energy See *net useful energy.*

net primary productivity Rate at which all the plants in an ecosystem produce net useful chemical energy. It is equal to the difference between the rate at which the plants in an ecosystem produce useful chemical energy and the rate at which they use some of this energy through cellular respiration.

net useful energy Total amount of useful energy available from an energy resource or energy system over its lifetime minus the amount of energy used (the first energy law), automatically

wasted (the second energy law), and unnecessarily wasted in finding, processing, concentrating, and transporting it to users.

neutral solution Water solution containing an equal number of hydrogen ions (H^+) and hydroxide ions (OH^-); water solution with a ph of 7. Compare *acid solution, basic solution.*

neutron (n) Elementary particle in the nuclei of all atoms (except hydrogen-1). It has a relative mass of 1 and no electric charge.

niche See *ecological niche.*

nitrogen cycle Cyclic movement of nitrogen in different chemical forms from the environment, to organisms, and then back to the environment.

nitrogen fixation Conversion of atmospheric nitrogen gas into forms useful to plants by lightning, bacteria, and blue-green algae; it is part of the nitrogen cycle.

nonbiodegradable Substance that cannot be broken down in the environment by natural processes. Compare *biodegradable.*

nondeclining even flow State in which trees in a forest are periodically harvested so that the amount of timber rises or stays level over time, but never decreases.

nondegradable See *nonbiodegradable.*

nonionizing electromagnetic radiation Forms of radiant energy, such as radio waves, microwaves, infrared light, and ordinary light that do not have enough energy to cause ionization of atoms in living tissue. Compare *ionizing electromagnetic radiation.*

nonmetallic mineral Inorganic substance found in the earth's crust that contains useful nonmetallic compounds. Examples are sand, stone, and nitrate and phosphate salts used as commercial fertilizers. Compare *metallic mineral.*

nonpoint source Large land area, such as crop fields and urban areas, that discharges pollutants into surface and underground water over a large area. Compare *point source.*

nonrenewable resources Resources available in a fixed amount (stock) in the earth's crust. They can be exhausted either because they are not replaced by natural processes (copper) or because they are replaced more slowly than they are used (oil and coal). Compare *perpetual resource, renewable resource.*

no-till cultivation See *conservation-tillage farming.*

nuclear change Process in which nuclei of certain isotopes spontaneously change or are forced to change into one or more different isotopes. The three major types of nuclear change are natural radioactivity, nuclear fission, and nuclear fusion. Compare *chemical change.*

nuclear energy Energy released when atomic nuclei undergo a nuclear reaction such as the spontaneous emission of radioactivity, nuclear fission, or nuclear fusion.

nuclear fission Nuclear change in which the nuclei of certain isotopes with large mass numbers (such as uranium-235 and plutonium-239) split apart into two lighter nuclei when struck by a neutron. This process releases more neutrons and a large amount of energy. Compare *nuclear fusion.*

nuclear fusion Nuclear change in which two nuclei of isotopes of elements with a low mass number (such as hydrogen-2 and hydrogen-3) are forced together at a very high temperature until they fuse to form a heavier nucleus (such as helium-4). This process releases a large amount of energy. Compare *nuclear fission.*

nucleus Extremely tiny center of an atom, making up most of the atom's mass. It contains one or more positively charged protons and one or more neutrons with no electrical charge (except for a hydrogen-1 atom, whose nucleus has one proton and no electrons).

nutrient Element or compound needed for the survival, growth, and reproduction of a plant or animal. See *macronutrient, micronutrient.*

ocean thermal energy conversion (OTEC) Using the large temperature differences between the cold bottom waters and the sun-warmed surface waters of tropical oceans to produce electricity.

oil See *crude oil.*

oil shale Underground formation of a fine-grained sedimentary rock containing varying amounts of a solid, waxy mixture of hydrocarbon compounds known as kerogen. Heating the rock to high temperatures converts the kerogen to a vapor, which can be condensed to form a slow-flowing heavy oil called shale oil. See *kerogen, shale oil.*

old-growth forest Uncut, virgin forest containing massive trees that are often hundreds of years old. Examples include forests of Douglas fir, western hemlock, giant sequoia, and coastal redwoods in the western United States. Compare *secondary forest, tree farm.*

oligopoly   Domination of the supply of an economic good by a few large firms. If these firms agree to set the price of the good, they become a monopoly. See also *cartel, monopoly.*

oligotrophic lake   Lake with a low supply of plant nutrients. Compare *eutrophic lake, mesotrophic lake.*

omnivore   Animal organism that can use both plants and other animals as food sources. Examples are pigs, rats, cockroaches, and people. Compare *carnivore, herbivore.*

open forest (woodland)   An area where trees are abundant but their crowns do not form a closed canopy. Compare *closed forest.*

open-pit surface mining   Removal of materials such as stone, sand, gravel, iron, and copper by digging them out of the earth's surface and leaving a large pit. See also *area strip mining, contour strip mining.*

open sea   The part of an ocean that is beyond the continental shelf. Compare *coastal zone.*

optimum yield   Weight or amount of fish of a particular species that can be economically harvested on a sustainable basis. It is usually less than the sustainable yield.

ore   Mineral deposit containing a high enough concentration of at least one metallic element to permit the metal to be extracted and sold at a profit.

organic compound   Molecule that contains atoms of the element carbon, usually combined with itself and with atoms of one or more other elements such as hydrogen, oxygen, nitrogen, sulfur, phosphorus, chlorine, and fluorine. Compare *inorganic compound.*

organic farming   Producing crops and livestock naturally by using organic fertilizer (manure, legumes, compost) and natural pest control (bugs that eat harmful bugs, plants that repel bugs, and environmental controls such as crop rotation) instead of using commercial inorganic fertilizers and synthetic pesticides and herbicides.

organic fertilizer   Organic material such as animal manure, green manure, and compost, applied to cropland as a source of plant nutrients. Compare *commercial inorganic fertilizer.*

organism   Any form of life.

output pollution control   Method for reducing the level of pollution after pollutants have been produced or have entered the environment. Examples are automobile emission control devices and sewage treatment plants. Compare *input pollution control.*

overburden   Layer of soil and rock overlying a mineral deposit that is removed during surface mining.

overfishing   Harvesting so many fish of a species, especially immature ones, that there is not enough breeding stock left to replenish the species to the point where it is profitable to harvest them.

overgrazing   Consumption of rangeland grass by grazing animals to the point that it cannot be renewed or can be only slowly renewed because of damage to the root system.

overnutrition   Diet so high in calories, saturated (animal) fats, salt, sugar, and processed foods, and so low in vegetables and fruits that the consumer runs high risks of diabetes, hypertension, heart disease, and other health hazards. Compare *malnutrition, undernutrition.*

overpopulation   State in which the life-support systems in the world or a geographic area are impaired because people use nonrenewable and renewable resources to such an extent that the resource base is degraded or depleted and air, water, and soil are severely polluted. See *consumption overpopulation, people overpopulation.*

oxygen cycle   Cyclic movement of oxygen in different chemical forms from the environment, to organisms, and then back to the environment.

oxygen-demanding wastes   Organic materials that are usually biodegraded by aerobic (oxygen-consuming) bacteria if there is enough dissolved oxygen in the water. See also *biological oxygen demand.*

ozone layer   Layer of gaseous ozone (O_3) in the stratosphere that protects life on earth by filtering out harmful ultraviolet radiation from the sun.

PANs   Peroxyacyl nitrates. Group of chemicals found in photochemical smog.

parasite   Consumer organism that feeds on a living plant or animal, known as the host, over an extended period of time. A parasite harms the host organism but does not kill it—at least not immediately, as most other consumers do. See *ectoparasites, endoparasites.*

particulate matter   Solid particles or liquid droplets suspended or carried in the air.

parts per billion (ppb)   Number of parts of a chemical found in one billion parts of a particular gas, liquid, or solid mixture.

parts per million (ppm)   Number of parts of a chemical found in one million parts of a particular gas, liquid, or solid.

passive solar heating system   System that captures sunlight directly within a structure and converts it to low-temperature heat for space heating. Compare *active solar heating system.*

pathogen   Organism that produces disease.

PCBs   See *polychlorinated biphenyls.*

people overpopulation   Situation in which there are more people in the world or a geographic region than available supplies of food, water, and other vital resources can support. It can also occur where the rate of population growth so exceeds the rate of economic growth or the distribution of wealth is so inequitable that a number of people are too poor to grow or buy enough food, fuel, and other important resources. Compare *consumption overpopulation.*

permafrost   Water permanently frozen year-round in thick underground layers of soil in tundra.

perpetual resource   Resource such as solar energy that comes from a virtually inexhaustible source on a human time scale. Compare *nonrenewable resource, renewable resource.*

persistence   See *inertia.*

pest   Unwanted organism that directly or indirectly interferes with human activities.

pesticide   Any chemical designed to kill or inhibit the growth of an organism that people consider to be undesirable. See *fungicides, herbicides, insecticides.*

pesticide treadmill   Situation in which the cost of using pesticides increases while their effectiveness decreases, mostly because the pest species develop genetic resistance to the pesticides.

petrochemicals   Chemicals obtained by refining (distilling) crude oil. They are used as raw materials in the manufacture of most industrial chemicals, fertilizers, pesticides, plastics, synthetic fibers, paints, medicines, and many other products.

petroleum   See *crude oil.*

pH   Numeric value that indicates the relative acidity or alkalinity of a substance on a scale of 0 to 14, with the neutral point at 7. Acid solutions have pH values lower than 7, and basic solutions have pH values greater than 7.

phosphorus cycle Cyclic movement of phosphorus in different chemical forms from the environment, to organisms, and then back to the environment.

photochemical smog Complex mixture of air pollutants produced in the atmosphere by the reaction of hydrocarbons and nitrogen oxides under the influence of sunlight. Especially harmful components include ozone, peroxyacyl nitrates (PANs), and various aldehydes. Compare *industrial smog*.

photosynthesis Complex process that takes place in cells of green plants. Radiant energy from the sun is used to combine carbon dioxide (CO_2) and water (H_2O) to produce oxygen (O_2) and simple nutrient molecules, such as glucose ($C_6H_{12}O_6$). Compare *cellular aerobic respiration, chemosynthesis*.

photovoltaic cell (solar cell) Device in which radiant (solar) energy is converted directly into electrical energy.

physical change Process that alters one or more physical properties of an element or compound without altering its chemical composition. Examples are changing the size and shape of a sample of matter (crushing ice and cutting aluminum foil) and changing a sample of matter from one physical state to another (boiling and freezing water). Compare *chemical change*.

phytoplankton Small, drifting plants, mostly algae and bacteria, found in aquatic ecosystems. See also *nanoplankton*. Compare *plankton, zooplankton*.

pioneer community First integrated set of plants, animals, and decomposers found in an area undergoing primary ecological succession. See *immature community, mature community*.

plankton Small plant organisms (phytoplankton and nanoplankton) and animal organisms (zooplankton) that float in aquatic ecosystems.

plantation agriculture Growing specialized crops such as bananas, coffee, and cacao in tropical LDCs, primarily for sale to MDCs.

plate tectonics Widely accepted theory that parts of the earth's crust move horizontally and vertically and in some cases slide over one another.

point source A single identifiable source that discharges pollutants into the environment. Examples are a smokestack, a sewer, a ditch, and a pipe. Compare *nonpoint source*.

politics See *private politics, public politics*.

pollution A change in the physical, chemical, or biological characteristics of the air, water, or soil that can affect the health, survival, or activities of humans in an unwanted way. Some expand the term to include harmful effects on all forms of life.

polychlorinated biphenyls (PCBs) Group of 209 different toxic, oily, synthetic chlorinated hydrocarbon compounds that can be biologically amplified in food chains and webs.

polyculture Complex form of intercropping in which a large number of different plants maturing at different times are planted together. See also *intercropping*. Compare *monoculture, polyvarietal cultivation*.

polyvarietal cultivation Planting a plot of land with several varieties of the same crop. Compare *intercropping, monoculture, polyculture*.

population Group of individual organisms of the same species living within a particular area.

population crash Large number of deaths over a fairly short time brought about when the number of individuals in a population is too large to be supported by available environmental resources.

population density Number of organisms in a particular population found in a specified area.

population distribution Variation of population density over a particular geographical area. For example, a country has a high population density in its urban areas and much lower population densities in rural areas.

population dynamics Major abiotic and biotic factors that tend to increase or decrease the population size and age and sex composition of a species.

potential energy Energy stored in an object because of its position or the position of its parts. Compare *kinetic energy*.

potentially renewable resource See *renewable resource*.

poverty Inability to meet basic needs. People in different societies differ in what they consider to be basic needs.

ppb See *parts per billion*.

ppm See *parts per million*.

precipitation Water in the form of rain, sleet, hail, and snow that falls from the atmosphere onto the land and bodies of water.

predation Situation in which an organism of one species (the predator) captures and feeds on parts or all of an organism of another species (the prey).

predator Organism that captures and feeds on parts or all of an organism of another species (the prey).

prescribed burning Deliberate setting and careful control of surface fires in forests to help prevent more destructive crown fires and to kill off unwanted plants that compete with commercial species for plant nutrients; may also be used on grasslands. See *crown fire, ground fire, surface fire*.

preservationists People who stress the need to limit human use of parks, wilderness, estuaries, wetlands, and other types of ecosystems primarily to nondestructive recreation, education, and research. Compare *scientific conservationists, sustainable-earth conservationists*.

prey Organism that is captured and serves as a source of food for an organism of another species (the predator).

primary air pollutant Chemical that has been added directly to the air by natural events or human activities and occurs in a harmful concentration. Compare *secondary air pollutant*.

primary consumer See *herbivore*.

primary ecological succession Sequential development of communities in a bare or soilless area that has never been occupied by a community of organisms. Compare *secondary ecological succession*.

primary oil recovery Pumping out the crude oil that flows by gravity into the bottom of an oil well. Compare *enhanced oil recovery, secondary oil recovery*.

primary sewage treatment Mechanical treatment of sewage in which large solids are filtered out by screens and suspended solids settle out as sludge in a sedimentation tank. Compare *advanced sewage treatment, secondary sewage treatment*.

prime reproductive age Years between ages 20 and 29, during which most women have most of their children. Compare *reproductive age*.

principle of multiple use See *multiple use*.

prior appropriation Legal principle by which the first user of water from a stream establishes a legal right to continued use of the amount originally withdrawn. See also *riparian rights*.

private good Economic good that can be owned and enjoyed on a private, or exclusive, basis. It can be produced and sold in units. Compare *public good*.

private politics Process in which people seek to gain power to satisfy their physical and emotional needs and wants within family, workplace, and other non-government groups. Compare *public politics*.

private property resource Resource owned by an individual or group of individuals other than the government. Compare *common property resource, public property resource*.

producer Organism that uses solar energy (green plant) or chemical energy (some bacteria) to manufacture its own organic nutrients from inorganic nutrients. Compare *consumer, decomposer*.

productivity Measure of the output of economic goods and services produced by the input of the factors of production (natural resources, capital goods, labor). Increasing economic productivity means getting more output from less input. Compare *economic growth*.

profundal zone Deep, open-water region of a lake, a region not penetrated by sunlight. Compare *benthic zone, limnetic zone, littoral zone*.

proton (p) Positively charged particle in the nuclei of all atoms. Each proton has a relative mass of 1 and a single positive charge.

public good Economic good that cannot be divided and sold in units, is owned by nobody in particular, and can be enjoyed by anybody. Examples are national defense, clean air, clean water, beautiful scenery, and wild plants and animals (biological diversity). Compare *private good*.

public land resources Land that is owned jointly by all citizens but is managed for them by an agency of the local, state, or federal government. Examples are state and national parks, forests, wildlife refuges, and wilderness areas. Compare *common property resource, private property resource*.

public politics Process through which individuals and groups try to influence or control the policies and actions of governments that affect the local, state, national, and international communities. Compare *private politics*.

public property resource See *public land resource*.

pure capitalism See *pure market economic system*.

pure command economic system System in which all economic decisions are made by the government or other central authority. Compare *mixed eco-*

nomic system, pure market economic system, traditional economic system.

pure competition State in which there are large numbers of independently acting buyers and sellers for each economic good in a pure market economic system. No buyer or seller is able to control the supply, demand, or price of a good. All buyers and sellers are free to enter or leave the market as they please but must accept the going market price.

pure market economic system System in which all economic decisions are made in the market, where buyers and sellers of economic goods freely interact with no government or other interference. Compare *mixed economic system, pure command economic system, traditional economic system*.

purse-seine fishing Catching fish, such as tuna, that feed in schools near the surface or in shallow water by surrounding them with a net whose bottom can be pulled closed. Compare *driftnet fishing, trawler fishing*.

pyramid of biomass Diagram representing the biomass, or total dry weight of all living organisms, that can be supported at each trophic level in a food chain. See also *pyramid of energy flow, pyramid of energy loss, pyramid of numbers*.

pyramid of energy flow Diagram representing the flow of usable, high-quality energy through each trophic level in a food chain. With each energy transfer, only a small part (typically 10%) of the usable energy entering one trophic level is transferred to the next trophic level. See also *pyramid of energy loss*. Compare *pyramid of biomass, pyramid of numbers*.

pyramid of energy loss Diagram showing the amount of low-quality energy, usually low-temperature heat, lost to the environment at each trophic level in a food chain. Typically 90% of the high-quality energy entering a trophic level is converted to low-quality energy and lost to the environment. See *pyramid of energy flow*. Compare *pyramid of biomass, pyramid of numbers*.

pyramid of numbers Diagram representing the number of organisms of a particular type that can be supported at each trophic level from a given input of solar energy at the producer trophic level in a food chain. Compare *pyramid of biomass, pyramid of energy flow*.

radiation Fast-moving particles (particulate radiation) or waves of energy (electromagnetic radiation). See *ionizing radiation, nonionizing radiation*.

radioactive isotope See *radioisotope*.

radioactive waste Radioactive waste products of nuclear power plants, research, medicine, weapons production, or other processes involving nuclear reactions.

radioactivity Nuclear change in which unstable nuclei of atoms spontaneously shoot out "chunks" of mass, energy, or both at a fixed rate. The three major types of radioactivity are gamma rays and fast-moving alpha particles and beta particles.

radioisotope Isotope of an atom whose unstable nuclei spontaneously emit one or more types of radioactivity (alpha particles, beta particles, gamma rays).

rain shadow effect Drop in precipitation on the far side (leeward side) of a mountain when prevailing winds flow up and over a high mountain or range of high mountains. This creates semiarid and arid conditions on the leeward side of a high mountain range.

range See *rangeland*.

range condition Estimate of how close a particular area of rangeland is to its potential for producing vegetation that can be consumed by grazing or browsing animals.

rangeland Land, mostly grasslands, whose plants can provide food (forage) for grazing or browsing animals. Compare *feedlot*.

range of tolerance Range of chemical and physical conditions that must be maintained for populations of a particular species to stay alive and grow, develop, and function normally. See *law of tolerance*.

real GNP Gross national product adjusted for inflation. Compare *average per capita GNP, average per capita real GNP, gross national product*.

recharge area Area in which an aquifer is replenished with water by the downward percolation of precipitation through soil and rock.

recycling Collecting and reprocessing a resource so it can be used again. An example is collecting aluminum cans, melting them down, and using the aluminum to make new cans or other aluminum products. Compare *reuse*.

relative resource scarcity Situation in which a resource has not been depleted but there is not enough available to meet the demand. This can be caused by a war, natural disaster, or other events that disrupt the production and distribution of a resource or by deliberate attempts of its producers to lower production to drive prices up. Compare *absolute resource scarcity.*

renewable resource Resource that normally is replenished through natural processes. Examples are trees in forests, grasses in grasslands, wild animals, fresh surface water in lakes and rivers, most deposits of groundwater, fresh air, and fertile soil. If such a resource is used faster than it is replenished, it can be depleted and converted to a nonrenewable resource. Compare *nonrenewable resource, perpetual resource.*

replacement-level fertility Number of children a couple must have to replace themselves. The average for a country or the world is usually slightly higher than 2 children per couple (2.1 in the the United States and 2.5 in some LDCs), because some children die before reaching their reproductive years. See also *total fertility rate.*

reproductive age Ages 15 to 44, when most women have all their children. Compare *prime reproductive age.*

reserves (economic resources) Identified deposits of a particular resource in known locations that can be extracted profitably at present prices and with current mining technology. Compare *resources.*

reservoir Human-created body of standing fresh water, often built behind a dam. Compare *lake.*

resilience Ability of a living system to restore itself to original condition after being exposed to an outside disturbance that is not too drastic. See also *inertia.*

resource Anything obtained from the environment to meet human needs and wants.

resource conservation See *conservation.*

resource recovery Salvaging usable metals, paper, and glass from solid waste and selling them to manufacturing industries for recycling.

resource recovery plant Facility in which mixed municipal solid waste is shredded and automatically separated to recover glass, iron, aluminum, and other valuable materials. The remaining paper, plastics, and other materials are incinerated to produce steam, hot water, or electricity.

resources Identified and unidentified deposits of a particular mineral that cannot be recovered profitably with present prices and mining technology. Some of these materials may be converted to reserves when prices rise or mining technology improves. Compare *reserves.*

respiration See *cellular aerobic respiration.*

reuse To use a product over and over again in the same form. An example is collecting, washing, and refilling glass beverage bottles. Compare *recycle.*

rill erosion Soil erosion caused when small streams of surface water flow at high velocities over the ground and create miniature valleys when the soil is washed away. Compare *gully erosion, sheet erosion.*

riparian rights System of water law that gives anyone whose land adjoins a flowing stream the right to use water from the stream as long as some is left for downstream users. Compare *prior appropriation.*

rock Naturally occurring solid that contains one or more minerals and is found in the earth's crust and mantle. See *igneous rock, metamorphic rock, rock cycle, sedimentary rock.*

rock cycle Cyclic processes that form and modify rocks in the earth's crust and mantle. See *igneous rock, metamorphic rock, sedimentary rock.*

ruminant animals Grazing and browsing herbivores such as cattle, sheep, goats, and buffalo that have a three- or four-chambered stomach, which digests the cellulose in vegetation they eat.

runoff Fresh water from precipitation and melting ice that flows on the earth's surface into nearby streams, rivers, lakes, wetlands, and reservoirs.

rural area Geographical area with a population of less than 2,500 people. Compare *urban area.*

salinity Amount of various salts (especially sodium chloride) dissolved in a given volume of water.

salinization Accumulation of salts that can eventually make the soil unable to support plant growth.

saltwater intrusion Movement of salt water into freshwater aquifers in coastal and inland areas as groundwater is withdrawn faster than it is recharged by precipitation.

sanitary landfill Land waste disposal site in which waste is spread in thin layers, compacted, and covered with a fresh layer of soil each day. Compare *secured landfill.*

scarcity Situation in which there isn't an unlimited supply of a resource people need or want. See *absolute resource scarcity, relative resource scarcity.*

scientific conservationists People who believe that the findings of science and

technology should be used to manage resources according to the principle of multiple use and the principle of sustainable yield so that they are available for future generations. Compare *preservationists, sustainable-earth conservationists.*

scientific law Summary of what scientists find happening in nature over and over with the same results. See *first law of thermodynamics, second law of thermodynamics, law of conservation of matter.*

secondary air pollutant Harmful chemical formed in the atmosphere by reacting with normal air components or other air pollutants. Compare *primary air pollutant.*

secondary consumer See *carnivore.*

secondary ecological succession Sequential development of communities in an area in which natural vegetation has been removed or destroyed, but the soil or sediment is not destroyed. Compare *primary ecological succession.*

secondary forest Stand of trees resulting from secondary ecological succession. Compare *old-growth forest, tree farm.*

secondary oil recovery Injecting water into an oil well to remove some of the thick crude oil remaining after primary oil recovery. Compare *enhanced oil recovery, primary oil recovery.*

secondary sewage treatment Second step in most waste treatment systems, in which aerobic bacteria break down up to 90% of degradable, oxygen-demanding organic wastes in wastewater. This is usually done by bringing sewage and bacteria together in trickling filters or in the activated sludge process. Compare *advanced sewage treatment, primary sewage treatment.*

second law of ecology Everything is connected to and intermingled with everything else.

second law of energy See *second law of thermodynamics.*

second law of thermodynamics In any conversion of heat energy to useful work, some of the initial energy input is always degraded to a lower-quality, more-dispersed, less useful form of energy, usually low-temperature heat that flows into the environment; you can't break even in terms of energy quality. See *first law of thermodynamics.*

secured landfill Land site for the storage of hazardous solid and liquid wastes. The wastes are placed in containers and buried in a restricted-access area that is continually monitored. Such landfills are located above geologic strata that are supposed to prevent the leaching of wastes into groundwater. Compare *sanitary landfill*.

sediment Insoluble particles of soil, silt, and other solid inorganic and organic materials that become suspended in water and eventually fall to the bottom of a body of water.

sedimentary rock Limestone and other rocks that collect as sediments in basins. Compare *igneous rock, metamorphic rock*. See *rock cycle*.

Seed-tree cutting Removal of nearly all trees on a site in one cutting, with a few seed-producing trees left uniformly distributed to regenerate the forest. Compare *clearcutting, selective cutting, shelterwood cutting, whole-tree harvesting*.

selective cutting Cutting of intermediate-aged, mature, or diseased trees in an uneven-aged forest stand either singly or in small groups. This encourages the growth of younger trees and maintains an uneven-aged stand. Compare *clearcutting, seed-tree cutting, shelterwood cutting, whole-tree harvesting*.

septic tank Underground tank for treatment of wastewater from a home in rural and suburban areas. Bacteria in the tank decompose organic wastes and the sludge settles to the bottom of the tank. The effluent flows out of the tank into the ground through a field of drain pipes.

sewage sludge See *sludge*.

shade-intolerant tree species A tree species that needs lots of sunlight in the early growth stages and thrives in forest openings. Compare *shade-tolerant tree species*.

shade-tolerant tree species A tree species that can grow in dim or moderate light under the crown cover of larger trees. Compare *shade-intolerant tree species*.

shale oil Slow-flowing, dark brown, heavy oil obtained when kerogen in oil shale is vaporized at high temperatures and then condensed. Shale oil can be refined to yield gasoline, heating oil, and other petroleum products. See *kerogen, oil shale*.

sheet erosion Soil erosion caused by surface water moving down a slope or across a field in a wide flow. Because it removes topsoil evenly, it may not be noticeable until much damage has been done. Compare *gully erosion, rill erosion*.

shelterbelt See *windbreak*.

shelterwood cutting Removal of mature, marketable trees in an area in a series of partial cuttings to allow regen-

eration of a new stand under the shade of older trees, which are removed later. Typically this is done by making two or three cuts over a decade. Compare *clearcutting, seed-tree cutting, selective cutting, whole-tree harvesting*.

shifting cultivation Clearing a plot of ground in a forest, especially in tropical areas, and planting crops on it for a few years (typically 2 to 5 years) until the soil is depleted of nutrients or until the plot has been invaded by a dense growth of vegetation from the surrounding forest. Then a new plot is cleared and the process is repeated. The abandoned plot cannot successfully grow crops for 10 to 30 years. See also *slash-and-burn cultivation*.

silviculture Science and art of cultivating and managing forests to produce a renewable supply of timber.

size limits Fishing regulations that make it illegal to keep fish above or below certain sizes.

slash-and-burn cultivation Cutting down trees and other vegetation in a patch of forest, leaving the cut vegetation on the ground to dry, and then burning it. The ashes that are left add plant nutrients to the nutrient-poor soils found in most tropical forest areas. Crops are planted between tree stumps. Plots must be abandoned after a few years (typically 2 to 5 years) because of loss of soil fertility or invasion of vegetation from the surrounding forest. See also *shifting cultivation*.

sludge Gooey solid mixture of bacteria- and virus-laden organic matter, toxic metals, synthetic organic chemicals, and solid chemicals removed from wastewater at a sewage treatment plant.

smog Originally a combination of smoke and fog but now used to describe other mixtures of pollutants in the atmosphere. See *industrial smog, photochemical smog*.

softwood Tree species whose wood is lighter in weight per unit of volume (less dense) and generally easier to saw, plane, or carve than hardwoods. Some softwoods, however, are harder than some species classified as hardwoods. Compare *hardwood*.

soil Complex mixture of inorganic minerals (mostly clay, silt, and sand), decaying organic matter, water, air, and living organisms.

soil conservation Methods used to reduce soil erosion, to prevent depletion of soil nutrients, and to restore nutrients already lost by erosion, leaching, and excessive crop harvesting.

soil erosion Movement of soil components, especially topsoil, from one place to another, usually by exposure to wind, flowing water, or both. This natural process can be greatly accelerated by human activities that remove vegetation from soil. See *gully erosion, rill erosion, sheet erosion*.

soil horizons Horizontal layers that make up a particular mature soil.

soil porosity Measure of the volume of pores, or empty spaces, and the average distances between them in a sample of soil.

soil profile Cross-sectional view of the horizons in a soil.

soil texture Relative amounts of the different types and sizes of particles in a sample of soil.

soil water Underground water that partially fills pores between soil particles and rocks within the upper soil and rock layers of the earth's crust above the water table. Compare *groundwater*.

solar cell See *photovoltaic cell*.

solar collector Device for collecting radiant energy from the sun and converting it into heat. See *active solar heating system, passive solar heating system*.

solar energy Direct radiant energy from the sun. It also includes indirect forms of energy such as wind, falling or flowing water (hydropower), ocean thermal gradients, and biomass, which are produced when direct solar energy interacts with the earth.

solar furnace System for concentrating direct solar energy to produce electricity or high-temperature heat for direct use. Also called a power tower.

solar pond Fairly small body of fresh water or salt water from which stored solar energy can be extracted because of temperature difference between the hot surface layer exposed to the sun during daylight and the cooler layer beneath it.

solid waste Any unwanted or discarded material that is not a liquid or a gas.

speciation Formation of new species from existing ones through natural selection in response to changes in environmental conditions; usually takes thousands to millions of years. Compare *extinction*.

species All organisms of the same kind; for organisms that reproduce sexually, a species is all organisms that can interbreed.

species diversity Number of different species and their relative abundances in a given area. Compare *genetic diversity*.

sport fishing Finding and catching fish mostly for recreation. Compare *commercial fishing, subsistence fishing*.

sport hunting Finding and killing animals mostly for recreation. Compare *commercial hunting, subsistence hunting*.

S-shaped curve Leveling off of an exponential, J-shaped curve when a rapidly growing population encounters environmental resistance.

stability Ability of a living system to withstand or recover from externally imposed changes or stresses. See *inertia, resilience*.

stocking rate Number of a particular kind of animal grazing on a given area of rangeland.

strategic materials Fuel and nonfuel minerals vital to the industry and defense of a country. Ideally, supplies are stockpiled to cushion against supply interruptions and sharp price rises.

stratosphere Second layer of the atmosphere, extending from about 12 to about 30 miles above the earth's surface. It contains small amounts of gaseous ozone (O_3), which filters out about 99% of the incoming harmful ultraviolet (UV) radiation.

strip cropping Planting regular crops and close-growing plants such as hay or nitrogen-fixing legumes in alternating rows or bands to help reduce depletion of soil nutrients.

strip mining See *surface mining*.

subatomic particles Extremely small particles—electrons, protons, and neutrons—that make up the internal structure of atoms.

subsidence Sinking down of part of the earth's crust due to underground excavation, such as a coal mine, or removal of groundwater.

subsistence agriculture Supplementing solar energy with energy from human labor and draft animals to produce enough food to feed oneself and family members; in good years there may be enough food left over to sell or put aside for hard times. Compare *industrialized agriculture*.

subsistence economy Economic system where the major goal is to produce enough goods to meet basic survival needs with little or no surplus left over for sale or trade. It is often a traditional economic system. See *traditional economic system*. Compare *mixed economic system, pure market economic system, pure command economic system*.

subsistence fishing Finding and catching fish to get food for survival. Compare *commercial fishing, sport fishing*.

subsistence hunting Finding and killing wild animals to get enough food and other animal material for survival. Compare *commercial hunting, sport hunting*.

subsurface mining Extraction of a metal ore or fuel resource such as coal from a deep underground deposit. Compare *surface mining*.

succession See *ecological succession*.

succulent plants Plants such as cacti that store water and produce the food they need in the thick, fleshly tissue of their green stems and branches.

superinsulated house House that is heavily insulated and extremely airtight. Typically, active or passive solar collectors are used to heat water, and an air-to-air heat exchanger is used to prevent buildup of excessive moisture and indoor air pollutants.

supply See *market supply*.

surface fire Forest fire that burns only undergrowth and leaf litter on the forest floor. Compare *crown fire, ground fire*.

surface mining Removal of soil, subsoil, and other strata and then extracting a mineral deposit found fairly close to the earth's surface. See *area strip mining, contour strip mining, open-pit surface mining*; compare *subsurface mining*.

surface water Precipitation that does not infiltrate into the ground or return to the atmosphere and becomes runoff that flows into nearby streams, rivers, lakes, wetlands, and reservoirs. Compare *groundwater*. See *runoff*.

sustainable-earth agricultural system Method of growing crops and raising livestock based on organic fertilizers, soil conservation, water conservation, biological control of pests, and minimal use of nonrenewable fossil fuel energy.

sustainable-earth conservationists People who believe that the earth's resources should be protected and sustained not just for human beings but also for other species. They have a life-centered rather than a human-centered approach to managing and sustaining the earth's resources by working with nature, not wasting resources unnecessarily, and interfering with nonhuman species only to meet important human needs. Compare *preservationists, scientific conservationists*.

sustainable-earth economy Economic system in which the number of people and the quantity of goods are maintained at some constant level. This level is ecologically sustainable over time and meets at least the basic needs of all members of the population.

sustainable-earth society Society based on working with nature by recycling and reusing discarded matter, conserving matter and energy resources by reducing unnecessary waste and use, and by building things that are easy to recycle, reuse, and repair. Compare *matter-recycling society, throwaway society*.

sustainable-earth worldview Belief that the earth is a place with finite room and resources so that continuing population growth, production, and consumption inevitably put severe stress on natural processes that renew and maintain the resource base of air, water, and soil that support all life. To prevent environmental overload and resource depletion, people should work with nature by controlling population growth, reducing unnecessary use and waste of matter and energy resources, and not causing the premature extinction of any other species. Compare *throwaway worldview*.

sustainable yield (sustained yield) Highest rate at which a renewable resource can be used without impairing or damaging its ability to be fully renewed. See also *environmental degradation*.

sustained yield See *sustainable yield*.

synfuels Synthetic gaseous and liquid fuels produced from solid coal or sources other than natural gas or crude oil.

synthetic natural gas (SNG) Gaseous fuel containing mostly methane produced from solid coal.

tailings Rock and other waste materials removed as impurities when minerals are mined and mineral deposits are processed. These materials are usually dumped on the ground or into ponds.

tar sand Swamplike deposit of a mixture of fine clay, sand, water, and variable amounts of a tarlike heavy oil known as bitumen. Bitumen can be extracted from tar sand by heating. It is then purified and upgraded to synthetic crude oil. See *bitumen*.

temperature inversion See *thermal inversion*.

teratogen Chemical that, if ingested by a pregnant female, causes malformation of the developing fetus.

terracing Planting crops on a long, steep slope that has been converted into a series of broad, nearly level terraces that follow the slope of the land to retain water and reduce soil erosion.

terrestrial   Pertaining to land. Compare *aquatic*.

terrestrial ecosystem   See *biome*.

territorial seas   Areas extending outward a certain distance from coastal countries in which these countries have jurisdiction over all living and mineral resources and transportation. See *exclusive economic zone*. Compare *high seas*.

tertiary (and higher) consumers   Animals that feed on animal-eating animals. They feed at high trophic levels in food chains and webs. Examples are hawks, lions, bass, and sharks. Compare *carnivores, decomposers, herbivores*.

tertiary sewage treatment   See *advanced sewage treatment*.

thermal enrichment   Beneficial effects in an aquatic ecosystem from a rise in water temperature. Compare *thermal pollution*.

thermal inversion   Layer of dense, cool air trapped under a layer of less dense, warm air, thus reversing the normal situation. In a prolonged inversion air pollution in the trapped layer may build up to harmful levels.

thermal pollution   Increase in water temperature that has harmful effects on an aquatic ecosystem. Compare *thermal enrichment*.

thermocline   Zone of gradual temperature between warm surface water and colder deep water in a lake, reservoir, or ocean.

threatened species   Wild species that is still abundant in its natural range but is likely to become endangered because of a decline in numbers. Compare *endangered species*.

threshold effect   The harmful or fatal effect of a small change in environmental conditions that exceeds the limit of tolerance of an organism, population, or volume of air, water, or soil.

throwaway society   Society found in most advanced industrialized countries, in which ever-increasing economic growth is sustained by maximizing the rate at which matter and energy resources are used, with little emphasis on recycling, reuse, reduction of unnecessary waste, and other forms of resource conservation. Compare *matter-recycling society, sustainable-earth society*.

throwaway worldview   Belief that the earth is a place of unlimited resources.

Any type of resource conservation that hampers short-term economic growth is unnecessary because if we pollute or deplete resources in one area, we will find substitutes, control the pollution through technology, and if necessary get resources from the moon and asteroids in the "new frontier" of space. Compare *sustainable-earth worldview*.

toothed whales   Porpoise, sperm, killer, and other whale species that have teeth that enable them to bite and chew their food. They feed mostly on squid and octopus. Compare *baleen whales*.

total fertility rate (TFR)   Estimate of the number of live children the average woman will bear if she passes through all her childbearing years (ages 15 to 44) conforming to the age-specific fertility rates of each year.

total resources   Total amount of a particular resource material that exists on earth. Compare *identified resources, reserves, resources, undiscovered resources*.

totally planned economy   See *pure command economic system*.

toxic waste   Form of hazardous waste that causes death or serious injury (such as burns, respiratory diseases, cancers, or genetic mutations) to humans. See *hazardous waste*.

traditional economic system   System in which past customs and traditions are used to make economic decisions. This system is found in most remaining tribal communities and is often a subsistence economic system. Compare *mixed economic system, pure command economic system, pure market economic system*.

tragedy of the commons   Depletion or degradation of a resource to which people have free and unmanaged access. An example is the depletion of commercially desirable species of fish in the open ocean beyond areas controlled by coastal countries. See *common property resource*.

transpiration   Process by which water moves up through a living plant and is transferred to the atmosphere from exposed parts of the plant.

trawler fishing   Catching fish by dragging a funnel-shaped net along the ocean bottom. Compare *driftnet fishing, purse-seine fishing*.

tree farm   Site planted with one or only a few tree species in an even-aged stand. When the stand matures, it is usually harvested by clearcutting and replanted. Normally used to grow rapidly growing tree species for fuelwood, timber, or pulpwood.

tritium (T: hydrogen-3)   Isotope of hydrogen with a nucleus containing one proton and two neutrons, thus having a mass number of 3. Compare *deuterium*.

trophic level   All organisms that consume the same general types of food in a food chain or food web. For example, all producers belong to the first trophic level and all herbivores belong to the second trophic level in a food chain or a food web.

troposphere   Innermost layer of the atmosphere. It contains about 95% of the earth's air and extends about 11 miles above the earth's surface. Compare *stratosphere*.

true cost   Cost of a good when its internal costs and its short- and long-term external costs are included in its market price. Compare *external costs, internal cost*.

unconfined aquifer   Collection of groundwater above a layer of fairly impermeable rock or compacted clay. Compare *confined aquifer*.

undernutrition   Not taking in enough food to meet one's minimum daily energy requirement for a long enough time to cause harmful effects. Compare *malnutrition, overnutrition*.

undiscovered resources   Potential supplies of a particular mineral resource, believed to exist because of geologic knowledge and theory, though specific locations, quality, and amounts are unknown. Compare *resources, reserves*.

uneven-aged management   Method of forest management in which trees in a given stand are maintained at many ages and sizes to permit continuous natural regeneration. Compare *even-aged stand*.

uneven-aged stand   Stand of trees in which there are considerable differences in the ages of individual trees. Usually such stands have a variety of tree species. See *uneven-aged management*. Compare *even-aged stand*.

upwelling   Movement of nutrient-rich bottom water to the ocean's surface. This occurs along certain steep coastal areas where the surface layer of ocean water is pushed away from shore and replaced by cold, nutrient-rich bottom water.

urban area   Geographic area with a population of 2,500 or more people. The number of people used in this definition may vary in different countries.

urban growth Rate of growth of an urban population. Compare *degree of urbanization*.

urban heat island Buildup of heat in the atmosphere above an urban area. This heat is produced by the large concentration of cars, buildings, factories, and other heat-producing activities. See also *dust dome*.

urbanization See *degree of urbanization*.

wastewater lagoon Large pond 3 to 5 feet deep where air, sunlight, and microorganisms break down wastes, allow solids to settle out, and kill some disease-causing bacteria. Water typically remains in a lagoon for 30 days. Then it is treated with chlorine and pumped out for use by a city or spread over cropland.

wastewater pond See *wastewater lagoon*.

water consumption Water that has been withdrawn from a groundwater or a surface water source and is not available for reuse in the area from which it was withdrawn because of seepage, evaporation, or contamination. See *water withdrawal*.

water cycle See *hydrologic cycle*.

waterlogging Saturation of soil with irrigation water or excessive precipitation so that the water table rises close to the surface.

water pollution Any physical or chemical change in surface water or groundwater that can harm living organisms or make water unfit for certain uses.

watershed Land area that delivers run-off water, sediment, and dissolved substances to a major river and its tributaries.

water table Top of the water-saturated part of an unconfined aquifer.

water table aquifer See *unconfined aquifer*.

water withdrawal Removing water from a groundwater or surface water source and transporting it to a place of use. Compare *water consumption*.

watt Unit of power, or rate at which electrical work is done.

weather Short-term changes in the properties of the troposphere from place to place. Compare *climate*.

weathering Process in which rock is gradually broken down into small bits and pieces that make up most of the soil's inorganic material by being exposed to weather and chemicals and invaded by certain organisms.

wetland Land that stays flooded all or part of the year with fresh or salt water. See *coastal wetland, inland wetland*.

whole-tree harvesting Use of machines to cut trees off at ground level or to pull entire trees from the ground and then reduce the trunks and branches to small wood chips.

wilderness Area where the earth and its community of life have not been seriously disturbed by humans and where humans are only temporary visitors.

wilderness species Wild animal species that flourish only in undisturbed mature vegetational communities such as mature forest, tundra, grassland, and desert. Compare *early-successional species, late-successional species, midsuccessional species*.

wildlife All free, undomesticated species of plants, animals, and microorganisms.

wildlife conservation Activity of protecting, preserving, managing, and studying wildlife and wildlife resources.

wildlife education Education and training of wildlife scientists and managers in colleges and universities and providing the general public with information about wildlife.

wildlife habitat Place where an individual or population of a particular wild animal species naturally lives, grows, and reproduces.

wildlife management Manipulation of populations of wild species (especially game species) and their habitats for human benefit, the welfare of other species, and the preservation of threatened and endangered wildlife species.

wildlife resources Species of wildlife that have actual or potential economic value to people. See also *game species*.

wild species See *wildlife*.

windbreak Row of trees or hedges planted to partially block wind flow and reduce soil erosion on cultivated land.

wind farm Cluster of small to medium-sized wind turbines in a windy area to capture wind energy and convert it to electrical energy.

woodland See *open forest*.

work What happens when a force is used to move a sample of matter over some distance or to raise its temperature. Energy is defined as the capacity to do such work.

worldview How we think the world works and what we think our role is. See *sustainable-earth worldview, throwaway worldview*.

zero population growth (ZPG) State in which the birth rate (plus immigration) equals the death rate (plus emigration) so that population of a geographical area is no longer increasing.

zoning Regulating how various parcels of land can be used.

zooplankton Animal plankton. Small floating herbivores that feed on plant plankton (phytoplankton and nanoplankton). Compare *nanoplankton, phytoplankton*.

Index

How to Save Energy and Money

Transportation (50% of average personal energy use)

- Walk or ride a bike for short trips (100% savings).
- Use a car pool or mass transit as much as possible (50% or more).
- Use a bus or train for long trips (50% or 75%).
- Buy an energy-efficient car (30% to 70%).
- Consolidate trips to accomplish several purposes (up to 50%).
- Keep engine tuned and replace air filter regularly (20% to 50%).
- Obey speed limits (20% or more).
- Accelerate and brake gently and don't warm up the engine for more than a minute (15% to 20%).
- Use steel-belted radial tires and keep tire pressure at recommended level (2% to 5%).

Home Space Heating (25%)

- Build a superinsulated or highly energy-efficient house or retrofit an existing house (50% to 100% savings).
- Dress more warmly, humidify air, and use fans to distribute heat so that thermostat setting can be lowered without loss of comfort (saves 3% for each °F decrease).
- Install the most energy-efficient heating system available (15% to 50%).
- Install an electronic ignition system in furnace, have furnace cleaned and tuned once a year, and clean or replace intake filters every two weeks (15% to 35%).
- Install stack dampers in the furnace or boiler flue (variable).
- Insulate heating ducts that pass through unheated spaces (2% to 5%).
- Do not heat closets and unused rooms (variable savings).
- Insulate attic ceiling or floor, all outside walls, and floors over unheated spaces (20% to 50%).
- Caulk and weatherstrip cracks (10% to 30%).
- Use insulated steel or wood doors with magnetic weather stripping or install storm doors, storm windows, or insulated shutters, or, best, install modern superwindows (R-5 to R-12+) (5% to 25%).
- Extinguish furnace pilot lights during summer or, best of all, install an electronic ignition system (variable).
- Do not use electricity for space heating (30% to 50%).

Hot Water Heating (9%)

- Install the most energy-efficient system available, such as active solar, instant tankless, or high-efficiency-gas water heaters (15% to 60%).
- Turn down thermostat on water heater to 110°–120°F (5% to 25%).
- Insulate hot water pipes or use anti-connection valves or loops and insulate water heater (10% to 15%).

- Use less hot water by taking two- to five-minute showers instead of baths, washing dishes and clothes only with full loads, washing clothes with warm or cold water, repairing leaky faucets, installing aerators on faucets, using low-flow showerheads, and not letting water run while bathing, shaving, brushing teeth, or washing dishes (10% to 25%).
- Do not use an electric water heater.

Cooking, Refrigerating, and Other Appliances (9%)

- Buy only the most energy-efficient stove, refrigerator, and other appliances available—ideally powered by natural or LP gas, not electricity (25% to 60%).
- Use a gas stove instead of an electric stove.
- Install electronic ignition systems on all gas stoves and other appliances (10% to 30%).
- Use a chest freezer rather than an upright model to prevent unnecessary loss of cool air when door is opened, and keep it almost full (variable).
- Do not locate refrigerator or freezer near a stove or other source of heat and keep condenser coils on back clean (variable).
- Don't use oven for space heating (very expensive).

Cooling, Air Conditioning, and Lighting (7%)

- Buy the most energy-efficient air conditioning system available (30% to 50%+).
- Increase thermostat setting (3% to 5% for each °F).
- Close off and do not air condition closets and unused rooms (variable).
- Use small floor fans, ceiling fans, and whole-house window or attic fans to eliminate or reduce air conditioning needs (variable).
- Close windows and drapes on sunny days and open them on cool days and at night (variable).
- Close bathroom and laundry room doors and use an exhaust fan or open window to prevent transfer of heat and humid air to rest of house (variable).
- Try to schedule heat- and moisture-producing activities such as bathing, ironing, and washing during the coolest part of the day (variable).
- Cover pots while cooking (variable).
- Use compact fluorescent and other energy-saving bulbs wherever possible (50% to 75%).
- Use natural lighting whenever possible (variable).
- Turn off lights and appliances when not in use and reduce lighting levels by using dimmers and lower wattage (variable).
- Disconnect air conditioners at the circuit breaker during winter—otherwise a small heater in the compressor runs year-round.